W9-BIC-407

Fundamentals of Quality Control and Improvement

Fundamentals of Quality Control and Improvement

Amitava Mitra

Auburn University

Macmillan Publishing Company
New York

Maxwell Macmillan Canada
Toronto

Editor: Charles E. Stewart, Jr.
Production Supervisor: Publication Services, Inc.
Production Manager: Aliza Greenblatt
Text Designer: Publication Services, Inc.
Cover Designer: Proof Positive/Farrowlyne Associates
Cover Photograph: Comstock Inc./Comstock Inc
Illustrations: Publication Services, Inc.

This book was set in Sabon by Publication Services, Inc., and printed and bound by Rand McNally. The cover was printed by Lehigh Press.

Printed in the United States of America

Macmillan Publishing Company
866 Third Avenue, New York, New York, 10022

Macmillan Publishing Company is part of the Maxwell Communication Group of Companies.

Maxwell Macmillan Canada, Inc.
1200 Eglinton Avenue East
Suite 200
Don Mills, Ontario M3C 3N1

Library of Congress Cataloging-in-Publication Data

Mitra, Amitava.
Fundamentals of quality control and improvement / Amitava Mitra.
p. cm.
Includes bibliographical references and index.
ISBN 0-02-381791-7
1. Quality control—Statistical methods. I. Title.
TS156.M54 1993
658.5'62'015195—dc20 92-41164
CIP

Printing: 1 2 3 4 5 6 7 Year: 3 4 5 6 7 8 9

To my parents,
who instilled the importance of
an incessant inquiry for knowledge

PREFACE

This book covers the foundations of modern methods of quality control and improvement that may be applied to manufacturing and service industries. Quality is one of the key elements in surviving tough competition. Consequently, there is a need for technically competent people who are well-versed in the area of statistical quality control and improvement. This book should serve the needs of students in business, management, engineering, technology, and other related disciplines. It should also provide a valuable reference for professionals in the field.

The methods of this book may be applied to real-world situations but are based on statistical foundations. This book is an outgrowth of many years of teaching, research, and consulting in the field of quality assurance and statistical process control. Mathematical derivations and proofs have been kept to a minimum to allow a better flow of material. Although an introductory course in statistics would be useful to a reader of this text, the foundations of statistical tools and techniques are discussed in Chapter 3 in an effort to make the book as complete as possible.

A prominent feature of this book is the multitude of examples. For each major concept there is at least one example demonstrating its application. Furthermore, case studies are included at the end of almost every chapter. These case studies present realistic applications of quality control principles, and aid in the mastery of the material. The use of a particular quality control software package is also demonstrated in Chapter 15.

The book is divided into six parts. Part I, which deals with the philosophy and fundamentals of quality control, consists of two chapters. Chapter 1 is an introduction to quality control and the total quality system. In addition to introducing the reader to the nomenclature associated with quality control and improvement, it provides a framework for the systems approach to quality. Discussions of quality costs and their measurement as well as the management of the quality function are presented. Chapter 2 presents some philosophies of leading experts such as Deming, Crosby, and Juran and discusses their impact on quality. Deming's 14 points for management are analyzed, and the three philosophies are compared. The chapter also discusses the criteria for the Malcolm Baldrige National Quality Award in the United States and the International Standards Organization (ISO) 9000 standards used internationally.

Part II deals with the statistical foundations of quality control and consists of two chapters. Chapter 3 offers a detailed coverage of statistical concepts and techniques in quality control and improvement. It presents a thorough treatment of inferential statistics. Depending on the students' background, only selected sections of this chapter may need to be covered. Chapter 4 deals with graphical methods of data presentation and quality improvement. Modern tools such as cause-and-effect diagrams, box plots, quantile-quantile plots, and multivariable charts are covered in this chapter.

In general, the field of statistical quality control may be thought of as comprising two areas: statistical process control and acceptance sampling. Part III deals with statistical process control and consists of four chapters. Chapter 5 provides an overview of the principles and use of control charts. A variety of control charts for variables are discussed in detail in Chapter 6. In addition to charts for the mean and range, those for the mean and standard deviation, individual units, cumulative sum, moving average, geometric moving average, trends, and others are presented. Control charts for attributes are discussed in Chapter 7. Charts such as the p-chart, np-chart, c-chart, u-chart, and U-chart are presented. The topic of process capability analysis is discussed in Chapter 8. The ability of a process to meet customer specifications is a keen area of interest. Process capability analysis procedures and process capability indices are treated in depth. The chapter also discusses proper approaches to setting tolerances on assemblies and components. Part III should form a core of material to be covered in most courses.

Part IV deals with acceptance sampling procedures and consists of two chapters. Each chapter describes methods for acceptance of a product based on information from a sample. Chapter 9 presents acceptance sampling plans for attributes. In addition to lot-by-lot attribute sampling plans, those for continuous production are also included. Standardized plans such as *ANSI/ASQC Z1.4–1981* are covered as well. Chapter 10 discusses acceptance sampling plans for variables. Standardized plans such as *ANSI/ASQC Z1.9* are presented. With the emphasis on process control and improvement, sampling plans do not occupy the forefront. Nevertheless, they are included to make the discussion complete.

Part V deals with product and process design and consists of three chapters. With the understanding that quality improvement efforts are generally being moved further upstream, these chapters constitute the backbone of the available methodology. Chapter 11 deals with reliability and explores the effects of time on the proper functioning of a product. Design principles by which the reliability of a system may be improved are discussed. Chapter 12 provides the fundamentals of experimental design. Different designs, such as the completely randomized design, randomized block design, and Latin square design are presented. Estimation of treatment effects using factorial experiments is included. Chapter 13 provides a treatment of the Taguchi method for design and quality improvement; the philosophy and fundamentals of this method are discussed. Various sections of Part V could also be included in the core material for a quality control course.

Finally, Part VI deals with applications of quality control and improvement in the service sector and appropriate computer software. There are two chapters in this part. Chapter 14 describes applications of quality control and improvement methods to a variety of service industries such as banking, education, food, government, health care services, public utilities, and transportation. Chapter 15 discusses features of some available computer software in quality control. The application of one particular software package (*SAS/QC*) is demonstrated.

This book may serve as a text for an undergraduate or a graduate course for students in business, management, engineering, technology, and other related disciplines. For a one-semester or one-quarter course, Part I, selected portions of Part II (usually parts of Chapter 3 and all of Chapter 4), Part III, and selected portions of Part V and Part VI could be covered. For a two-semester or two-quarter course, all of Part V and Part VI, along with portions from Part IV could be covered as well.

Many individuals have contributed either directly or indirectly to the development of this book, and thanks are due to them. Modern trends in product/process quality through design and improvement, as well as discussions and questions from undergraduate and graduate classes over the years have shaped this book. Applications encountered in a consulting environment provided a scenario for examples and exercises. Constructive comments from the reviewers have been quite helpful. The manuscript preparation center of the College of Business at Auburn University under the able guidance of Bess Whitten did a remarkable job. Thanks are due to Bess and also to Loraine Hyde, Linda Mathis, and Margie Wright for their dexterity and proficiency. My editor, Charles E. Stewart, Jr., is to be commended for his patience and understanding. I have found that writing a book causes an enormous drain on one's time. For that reason, my wife, Sujata, and son, Arnab, were deprived of my time—my appreciation to them.

A. M.

BRIEF CONTENTS

CONTENTS

PART

I

Philosophy and Fundamentals

CHAPTER

1

Introduction to Quality Control and the Total Quality System

CHAPTER OUTLINE

1-1 INTRODUCTION

September 29, 1988; the countdown was in progress . . . Ten, nine, eight, seven, six, five, four, three, two, one, ignition, and liftoff. The United States Space Shuttle *Discovery* rose majestically from its launch pad and followed its calculated trajectory into the clear blue sky. Dense white fumes from the rocket engines completely covered the surroundings. Cheers from the spectators were belated rather than spontaneous. People were still nervous; memories of the ill-fated *Challenger*, which exploded in January 1986, haunted them. But soon thereafter the cloud of anxiety that seemed to engulf the spectators faded away, and at last the cheers of triumph, accomplishment, and applause drowned everything else. The shuttle was a little white speck in the sky and on its way to a successful mission. America was back as a leader in space programs, and nothing helped it regain this supremacy more than quality control. It was an example of quality from the total systems point of view—a scenario in which every unit contributing to the program had to develop a commitment to producing a quality product. And this goal had been accomplished. The myth of the staleness of the American management style and the resistance to accepting innovative ideas with an open mind had been destroyed. The United States was becoming, as in the past, a quality-conscious nation.

1-2 EVOLUTION OF QUALITY CONTROL

The quality of goods and services produced has been monitored, either directly or indirectly, since time immemorial. However, the use of a quantitative base involving statistical principles is quite modern compared to the time that the concept of quality has existed.

The ancient Egyptians demonstrated a commitment to quality through the construction of the pyramids. The Greeks set high standards in arts and crafts. The quality of Greek architecture of the fifth century B.C. was enviable to such an extent that it had a profound effect on subsequent architectural constructions of Rome. Structural designs created by the Romans for building cities, churches, bridges, roads, and so on left a lasting impression in the minds of the people and continue to inspire us even today.

During the Middle Ages and up to the 1800s, the production of goods and services was predominantly confined to a single individual or a small group of individuals. These small groups were often family-owned businesses, so the responsibility for controlling the quality of a product or service lay with that person or small group. The standard of quality was therefore determined by the individual who was in turn also responsible for producing the item that would conform to those standards. This phase, comprising the time period up to 1920, has been labeled by Feigenbaum (1983) as the *Operator Quality Control* period. The entire product was manufactured by one person or a very small group of persons. For this reason, the quality of the product could essentially be controlled by a person who was also the operator. The volume of production was limited. There was a sense of accomplishment on the part of the worker. This provided motivation and lifted the morale of the worker, which served as a stimulus. Controlling the quality of the product was embedded in the philosophy of the worker, for the worker's pride was associated with the product.

From the period starting in the early 1900s to about 1920, a second phase evolved called the *Foreman Quality Control* period (Feigenbaum, 1983). The Industrial Revolution brought about the concept of mass production. One result was the introduction of the principle of specialization of labor. An individual was responsible not for the production of the entire product but rather only a portion of it. One drawback of this approach was that there was a decrease in the sense of accomplishment and identitfication with the product by the worker. However, most tasks were still not very complicated, and workers became skilled at the particular operations that they performed. Foremen or supervisors were now responsible for controlling the quality of the product as they oversaw the different operations. Individuals who performed similar operations were grouped together. A supervisor who directed that operation now had the task of ensuring that quality was achieved. Foremen or supervisors were responsible for the operations in their span of control. As far as quality of the entire product was concerned, it was the combined responsibilities of those foremen, each having responsibilities on the quality of individual operations.

The period from about 1920 to 1940 saw the next phase in the evolution of quality control. Feigenbaum (1983) called this the *Inspection Quality Control* period. Products as well as processes became more complicated. Production volume saw an increase. As the number of workers reporting to a foreman increased, it became impossible for the foreman to keep close control on individual operations performed by each worker. Inspectors were therefore created whose task was to check the quality of a product after certain operations. A standard was provided, and inspectors compared the quality of the produced item with those standards. In the event of discrepancies between the value of the standard and that of the produced item, the items were set aside from those that did meet standards. The nonconforming items were either reworked, if feasible, or were discarded.

During this period, the foundations of statistical aspects dealing with quality control were being developed, even though they had not gained wide usage in U.S. industry. In 1924 Walter A. Shewhart of Bell Telephone Laboratories proposed the concept of using statistical charts for controlling the variables of a product. These came to be known as control charts (sometimes referred to as Shewhart control charts). They play a fundamental role in statistical process control. In the late 1920s, H. F. Dodge and H. G. Romig, also from Bell Telephone Laboratories, contributed to pioneering work in the areas of acceptance sampling plans. These plans were to become substitutes for 100 percent inspection.

The 1930s saw the application of acceptance sampling plans in industry, both domestic and abroad. Walter Shewhart continued his efforts to promote the fundamentals of statistical quality control to industry. In 1929 he was able to obtain the sponsorship of the American Society for Testing Materials (ASTM), the American Society of Mechanical Engineers (ASME), the American Statistical Association (ASA), and the Institute of Mathematical Statistics (IMS) in creating the Joint Committee for the Development of Statistical Applications in Engineering and Manufacturing. Interest in the field of quality control also started gaining acceptance in England at this time. The British Standards Institution Standard 600 dealt with applications of statistical methods to industrial standardization and quality control. In the United States, J. Scanlon introduced the *Scanlon Plan* that dealt with improvement of the overall quality of work life (Feigenbaum, 1983). Furthermore, the U.S. Food, Drug, and Cosmetic Act was instituted in 1938 and had jurisdiction over procedures and practices in the areas of processing, manufacturing, and packing.

The next phase in the evolution process was between 1940 and 1960 and was termed the *Statistical Quality Control* phase by Feigenbaum (1983). Production requirements escalated during World War II. Since 100 percent inspection was often infeasible, the principles of sampling plans gained acceptance. The American Society for Quality Control (ASQC) was formed in 1946. A set of sampling inspection plans for attributes called MIL–STD–105A was developed by the military in 1950. These plans underwent several modifications in the future, becoming MIL–STD–105B, MIL–STD–105C, MIL–STD–105D, and MIL–STD–105E. Furthermore, in 1957, a set of sampling plans for variables called MIL–STD–414 was also developed by the military.

Use of quality control procedures was, however, nowhere close to the level that it should have been. The fundamental principles had been developed in the United States, but the lackadaisical attitude of U.S. industry in adopting these principles caused its downfall in the next decade. No other country was in a better position to exploit the benefits of statistical quality control. Nonetheless, U.S. industry did not capitalize on this unique advantage, though other countries did. Japan, for instance, was totally destroyed during World War II, but when W. Edwards Deming visited Japan and lectured to Japanese engineers and top management in 1950, they were convinced of the importance of statistical quality control as a means of gaining a competitive edge in the world market. Subsequently, J. M. Juran, another pioneer in quality control, visited Japan in 1954 and impressed upon them the strategic role that management plays in the achievement of a quality program. The Japanese were quick to realize the profound effects that these principles would have in the future, and they made a commitment right away to undergo a massive program of training and education.

Meanwhile, in the United States, developments in the area of sampling plans were taking place. In 1958 the Department of Defense (DOD) developed the *Inspection and Quality Control Handbook H107,* which dealt with single-level continuous sampling procedures and tables for inspection by attributes. Subsequently, this book was revised in 1959 and became the *Inspection and Quality Control Handbook H108,* which also covered multilevel continuous sampling procedures, as well as topics in life testing and reliability.

The next phase was the *Total Quality Control* period during the 1960s, as described by Feigenbaum (1983). An important feature during this period was the beginning of the gradual involvement of several departments and management personnel in the quality control process. Previously, most of these activities were dealt with by either the people on the shop floor, the production foreman, or by people from the so-called inspection and quality control department. A misconception prior to this period was that quality control is the responsibility of the inspection department. Oddly enough, this concept was accepted by many, the idea of which led to quality being considered someone else's "stepchild." This created a lack of identification with quality on the part of many workers. The 1960s, however, saw some changes in attitude taking place. People began to realize that each department had an important role in the production of a quality item. The concept of *zero defects* (ZD), which centered around achieving productivity through worker involvement, emerged during this time. For critical products and assemblies—for example, missiles and rockets used in the space program by the National Aeronautics and Space Administration (NASA)—this concept proved to be very adequate. Along similar lines, the use of *quality control circles* was beginning to grow in Japan. The principle of quality control circles is based on the participative style of management. It assumes that productivity will improve through an uplift of morale and motivation, which are in turn achieved through consultation and discussion in informal subgroups.

The advent of the 1970s brought what Feigenbaum (1983) calls the *Total Quality Control Organizationwide* phase. This phase involved the participation of everyone in the company, from the operator to the first-line supervisor, manager, vice-president, and even the chief executive officer. Quality was associated with every individual. As this notion continued in the 1980s, it was termed by Feigenbaum (1983) the *Total Quality System,* which he defined as follows:

A quality system is the agreed on companywide and plantwide operating work structure, documented in effective, integrated technical and managerial procedures, for guiding the coordinated actions of the people, the machines, and the information of the company and plant in the best and most practical ways to assure customer quality satisfaction and economical costs of quality.

In Japan, the 1970s marked expanded use of a graphical tool known as the *cause-and-effect diagram.* This tool was originally introduced in 1943 by K. Ishikawa and is sometimes called an *Ishikawa diagram.* It has also been called a *fishbone diagram,* arising from the resemblance of the diagram to a fishbone. Such a graph aids in the identification of possible reasons for a process to go out of control as well as possible effects on the process. This diagram came to be an important tool in the use of control charts because it complemented the choice of actions to take in the event of a process being out of control. Also in this decade, G. Taguchi of Japan introduced the concept of quality improvement through statistically designed experiments. Expanded usage of this technique in the 1990s is foreseen as companies try to place more emphasis on the design phase.

In the 1980s, motivating slogans placed quality control in the limelight in the United States. Consumers were bombarded with advertisements relating to the high quality of the product, and frequent comparisons were made with those of the competitor. These promotional efforts tried to point out certain product characteristics that were superior to that of similar products. Within the industry itself, an awareness of the importance of quality was beginning to evolve at all levels. Top management saw the critical need for the marriage of the quality philosophy to the production of goods and services in all phases, starting with the determination of customer needs and product design and continuing on to product assurance and customer service.

Management provided more than lip service to the role of statistical quality control methods by adopting training programs in these areas. They realized that education and training for everyone, from hourly wage earners to top management personnel, is a fundamental condition for the successful adoption and implementation of a statistical quality control program. This lesson was learned the hard way, though. As management looked at the domestic and international market, they found that those corporations that produced quality products had a clear understanding of and background in statistical quality control. It was not a fluke that Japan dominated the world market. This decade saw the fruition of a commitment that Japanese industry had made almost 30 years ago. They had seen the importance of education and training in this area and had systematically developed a program such that all of the personnel in the company, down to the operator level, were provided with adequate instruction. The tools and techniques that Japanese industry adopted in the 1950s were not new to the United States. In fact, those methods had originated in the United States. But the miserable irony of the situation was that they were not accepted and used by U.S. industry. The success of Japanese industry served as an eye-opener; only then was the importance of training and implementation of statistical quality control recognized.

With the continued growth of computer use in industry during the 1980s, an abundance of quality control software programs emerged on the market. The notion of a total quality system created an increased emphasis on vendor quality control, product design assurance, product quality audit, and other related areas. Industrial giants such as the Ford Motor Company and General Motors Corporation adopted the quality philosophy and made strides in the implementation of statistical quality control methods. They in turn continued to influence other companies to use quality control techniques. For example, Ford demanded documentation of statistical process control from its vendors. Thus, smaller companies who had previously not used statistical quality control methods were forced to adopt these methods in order to maintain their contracts. This process of requiring evidence of using quality control procedures will likely continue down to the smallest contractor or vendor. The 1990s will see expanded use of quality control measures and increased attention to the customers' needs. There will be no escape from the reality that the customer is the determinant of the level of quality. Industry will have to adjust to meet the needs of the customer.

1-3 QUALITY

The notion of quality has been defined in different ways by various authors. Garvin (1984) divided the definition of quality into five categories, namely, transcendent, product-based, user-based, manufacturing-based, and value-based. Furthermore, he identified a framework of the following eight attributes that may be used for defining quality: performance, features, reliability, conformance, durability, serviceability, aesthetics, and perceived quality. One frequently used definition attributed to Crosby (1979) is as follows:

Quality is conformance to requirements or specifications.

A more general definition proposed by Juran (1974) is as follows:

Quality is fitness for use.

This text adopts the latter definition and clarifies it so that it may apply to both the manufacturing and service sectors. The service sector accounts for almost 70% of the present economy; it is a major constituent that is not to be neglected. It is projected that this proportion will expand even further in the future. Hence, quality may be defined as follows:

The quality of a product or service is the fitness of that product or service for meeting its intended use as required by the customer.

This definition makes an important point as to who is the driving force behind determining the level of quality that should be designed into the product or service: the customer. As the needs of customers change, so should the level of quality. If, for example, the customer prefers to have an automobile that would provide adequate service for 15 years, then that is precisely what the notion of a quality product should be. Quality, in this sense, is not something that has a constant universal level. Likewise, the term quality may imply different levels of expectations for different groups of consumers. For instance, to some, a quality restaurant may be one which provides good cuisine served on the finest china with an ambience of soft music. However, to another group of consumers, the characteristics which comprise quality may be different. Excellent food served buffet-style with moderate prices until the early morning hours may define an acceptable level of quality.

Quality Characteristics

The above example demonstrates that there may be one or more elements which define the intended quality level of a product or service. These elements are known as *quality characteristics*. Several groupings of these characteristics can be formed. *Structural characteristics* include such elements as the length of a part, the weight of a can, the strength of a beam, the viscosity of a fluid, and so on. *Sensory characteristics* include the taste of good food, the smell of a sweet fragrance, and the beauty of a model, among others. *Time-oriented characteristics* include such measures as a warranty, reliability, and maintainability, while *ethical characteristics* include honesty, courtesy, friendliness, and so on.

Variables and Attributes

Quality characteristics may be grouped into two broad classes, namely, *variables* and *attributes*. *Characteristics that are measurable and are expressed on a numerical scale are called variables.* The diameter of a bearing expressed in millimeters is a variable, as are the density of a liquid in grams per cubic centimeter and the resistance of a coil in ohms.

Nonconformity and Nonconforming Unit Prior to defining an attribute, the terms *nonconformity* and a *nonconforming unit* should be defined. *A nonconformity is a quality characteristic that does not meet its stipulated specifications requirement.*

For instance, the specifications of the thickness of steel washers could be 2 ± 0.1 millimeters (mm). If we have a washer with a thickness of 2.15 mm, then its thickness is a nonconformity. A *nonconforming unit is one that has one or more nonconformities such that the unit is unable to meet the intended standards and is unable to function as required.* An example of a nonconforming unit might be a cast iron pipe that has an internal diameter and a weight that both fail to satisfy specifications, thereby making the unit dysfunctional.

A quality characteristic is said to be an attribute if it can be classified as either conforming or nonconforming to a stipulated specifications requirement. Sometimes a quality characteristic is such that it cannot be measured on a numerical scale, and so it must inherently be expressed as an attribute. For example, the smell of a cologne is characterized as either acceptable or not; the color of a fabric is either acceptable or not. There are some characteristics, though, that are inherently variables, but due to their ease of measurement or the infeasibility of obtaining variables data, they are observed as attributes. Examples in this category are numerous. For instance, the diameter of a bearing to be used in an assembly is, in theory, a variable. However, if one measures the diameter using a go/no-go gage and classifies it as either conforming or nonconforming (with respect to some established specifications), then the characteristic is expressed as an attribute. The reasons for using a go/no-go gage, as opposed to a micrometer, could be economic feasibility. The time needed to obtain a measurement using a go/no-go gage may be much lower and consequently less expensive. Alternately, an inspector may not have enough time to obtain measurements on a numerical scale using a micrometer, so such an approach would not be feasible.

Defect

A defect is associated with a quality characteristic that does not meet certain standards. Furthermore, the severity of one or more defects in a product or service may cause it to be unacceptable (or defective). The modern term for a defect is nonconformity and the term for a defective is a nonconforming item.

The American National Standards Institute (ANSI) and the American Society for Quality Control (ASQC) provide the following definition of a defect as stated in ANSI/ASQC Standard A3 (1987):

A defect is a departure of a quality characteristic from its intended level or state that occurs with a severity sufficient to cause an associated product or service not to satisfy intended normal or reasonably foreseeable usage requirements.

Standard or Specification

Since the definition of quality involves meeting the requirements of the customer, these requirements need to be documented. *A standard, or a specification, refers to a precise statement that formalizes the requirements of the customer; it may relate to a product, a process, or a service.* For example, the specifications for an axle might be 2 ± 0.1 centimeters (cm) for the inside diameter, 4 ± 0.2 cm for the outside diameter, and 10 ± 0.5 cm for the length. This means that for an axle to be acceptable to the customer, each of the above dimensions must be within the specified values. A definition given by the U.S. National Bureau of Standards (1983) is as follows:

Specification: **a set of conditions and requirements, of specific and limited application, that provide a detailed description of the procedure, process, material, product, or service for use primarily in procurement and manufacturing. Standards may be referenced or included in a specification.**

Additionally, the U.S. National Bureau of Standards (1983) defines a standard as follows:

Standard: **a prescribed set of conditions and requirements, of general or broad application, established by authority or agreement, to be satisfied by a material, product, process, procedure, convention, test method; and/or the physical, functional, performance, or conformance characteristic thereof. A physical embodiment of a unit of measurement (for example, an object such as the standard kilogram or an apparatus such as the cesium beam clock).**

Acceptable bounds on individual quality characteristics (say, 2 ± 0.1 cm for the inside diameter) are usually known as *specification limits,* whereas the document which addresses the requirements of all the quality characteristics is labeled the *standard.*

Three aspects are usually associated with the definition of quality: *quality of design, quality of conformance,* and *quality of performance.*

Quality of Design

Quality of design deals with the stringent conditions that the product or service must minimally possess in order to satisfy the requirements of the customer. *It implies that the product or service must be designed to meet at least minimally the needs of the consumer.* Generally speaking, the design should be the simplest and least expensive while still meeting the customers' expectations. Quality of design is influenced by such factors as the type of product, cost, profit policy of the firm, demand for product, availability of parts and materials, and product safety. For example, suppose the quality level of the yield strength of steel cables desired by the customer is 100 kg/cm^2. When designing such a cable, the parameters of the cable that influence the yield strength would be selected so as to satisfy this requirement at least minimally. In practice, the product is typically overdesigned so that the desired conditions are exceeded. The choice of a safety factor (k) normally accomplishes this purpose. Thus, to design a product with a 25 percent stronger load characteristic over the specified weight, the value of k would equal 1.25, and the product will be designed for a yield strength of $100 \times 1.25 = 125$ kg/cm^2.

In most situations, the effect of an increase in the designed quality level is to increase the cost at an exponential rate. The value of the product, however, increases at a decreasing rate, with the rate of increase approaching zero beyond a certain designed quality level. Figure 1-1 shows the impact of the designed quality level on the cost and value of the product or service. Sometimes, it might be of interest to choose a design quality level b which maximizes the difference between value and cost, given that the minimal customer requirements a are met. This is done with the idea of maximizing the return on investment. It may be observed from Figure 1-1 that for a designed quality level c, the cost and value are equal. For any level above c (say, d) the cost exceeds the value. This information could help in the choice of a suitable design level.

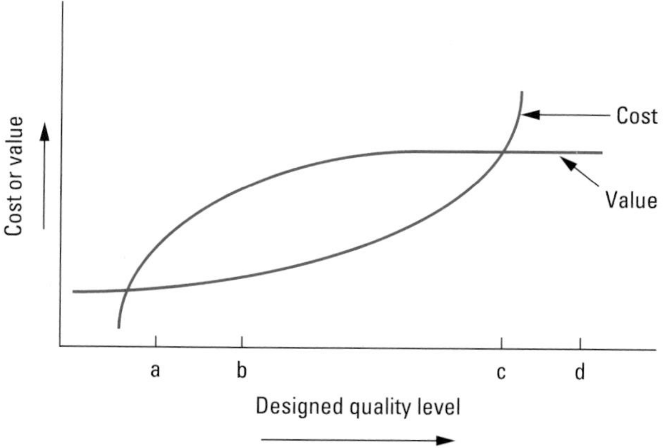

Figure 1-1 Cost and value as a function of designed quality.

Quality of Conformance

Quality of conformance implies that the manufactured product or the service rendered must meet the standards selected in the design phase. With respect to the manufacturing sector, this phase is concerned with the degree to which quality is controlled from the procurement of raw material to the shipment of finished goods. It consists of the three broad areas of defect prevention, defect finding, and defect analysis and rectification. As the name suggests, defect prevention deals with the means to deter the occurrence of defects and is usually achieved using statistical process control techniques. The finding of defects is conducted through inspection, test, and statistical analysis of data from the process. Finally, the causes behind the presence of defects are investigated, and corrective actions are taken.

Figure 1-2 shows how quality of design, quality of conformance, and quality of performance influence the quality of a product or service. The quality of design has an impact on the quality of conformance. Obviously, one must be able to produce what was designed. Thus, if the design specification for the length of iron pins is 20 ± 0.2 mm, the question to be addressed deals with the design of the tools, equipment, and operations such that a product can actually be manufactured to meet the design specifications. If such a system of production can be achieved, the conformance phase will be capable of meeting the stringent requirements of the design phase. On the other hand, if such a production system is not feasibly attained (for instance, if the process is capable of producing pins with a specification of 20 ± 0.36 mm), the design phase is affected. This feedback of information will suggest that consideration be given to redesigning the product, since

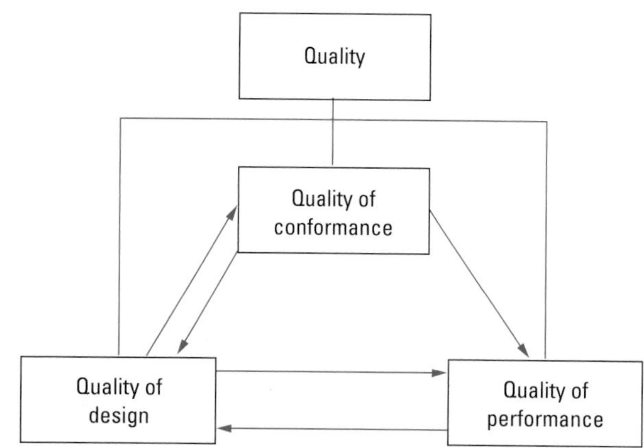

Figure 1-2 The three aspects of quality.

the current design cannot be produced using the existing capability. Therefore, there should be a constant exchange of information between the design and manufacturing phases to help create a feasible design that can actually be achieved.

Quality of Performance

Quality of performance is concerned with the operation of the product when actually put to use or the service when performed and measures the degree to which it satisfies the consumer. This is a function of both the quality of design and the quality of conformance. It must always be remembered that the final test of product or service acceptance lies with the customers. Meeting their expectations is the major goal. If a product does not function so as to meet these expectations, or if a service performed does not live up to customer standards, then adjustments need to be made in the design or conformance phase. This feedback from the performance to the design phase, as shown in Figure 1-2, may cause a change in the design, since the current design does not produce a product that performs adequately.

1-4 QUALITY CONTROL

Quality control may generally be defined as a system that is used to maintain a desired level of quality in a product or service. This task may be achieved through different measures such as planning, design, use of proper equipment and procedures, inspection, and taking corrective action in case a deviation is observed between the product, service, or process output and a specified standard (ASQC, 1983; Walsh et al., 1986). This general area may be divided into two main subareas, namely, *statistical process control* and *acceptance sampling plans.*

Statistical Process Control

Statistical process control involves the comparison of the output of a process or a service with a standard and the taking of remedial actions in case of a discrepancy between the two. It also involves the determination of the ability of a process to produce a product that meets desired specifications or requirements.

For example, to control the errors in an administrative framework involving paperwork, information might be gathered daily on the number of errors. If the observed number exceeds some specified standard, then on identification of possible causes, action should be taken to reduce the number of errors. This task may involve training of the administrative staff, simplifying operations if the error is of an arithmetic nature, redesigning the form, or other appropriate measures.

Statistical process control may be divided into two main categories, *on-line* and *off-line. On-line process control* means that information is gathered about the product, process, or service while it is functional, and in case of a difference between the output of the product or service from a determined norm, corrective action is taken in that operational phase. It is preferable to take corrective actions if necessary on a real-time basis for on-line quality control problems. This approach would attempt to bring the system to an acceptable state as soon as possible, thus minimizing the production of unacceptable items or the time over which undesirable service is rendered. Chapters 5, 6, 7, and 8 address the background and procedures of on-line statistical process control methods. *Off-line quality control* procedures, on the other hand, deal with measures to select and choose controllable product and process parameters in such a way that the deviation between the product or process output and the standard will be minimized when the operation of the process takes place. Much of this task is accomplished through product and process design. In other words, the goal is to come up with a design, within the constraints of resources and environmental parameters, such that when production of the component takes place, operation is at a desirable level. Thus, to the extent possible, the goal is to select the product and process parameter settings before production takes place, so that the deviation between the output and the goal will be minimized. Principles of experimental design discussed in Chapter 12 and the Taguchi method discussed in Chapter 13 provide information on off-line process control procedures.

One question that may come to mind is: Shouldn't all processes be controlled on an off-line basis? The answer is yes, to the extent possible. The prevailing theme of quality control is that quality has to be designed into the product or service; it cannot be inspected into it. However, in spite of taking off-line quality control measures, there may be a need for on-line quality control, because variation in the manufacturing stage of a product or the delivery stage of a service is inevitable. Therefore, some rectifying measures are needed in this phase. Ideally, a combination of off-line and on-line quality control measures may lead to a desirable level of operation.

Acceptance Sampling Plans

This branch of quality control deals with inspection of the product or service. When 100 percent inspection of all items is not feasible, a decision has to be made on the number of items to sample from a batch of items. The information obtained from this sample is used to make a decision on the entire batch, or lot—namely, to accept or reject it. A parameter that needs to be determined in the case of attributes is the acceptable number of nonconforming items in the sample, such that if the observed number of nonconforming items is less than or equal to this number, the batch is accepted. This acceptable number of nonconforming items in the sample is known as the acceptance number. In the case of variables, acceptance of the lot may be based on the proportion of items in the sample that are outside the specifications. This proportion would have to be less than or equal to a standard in order to allow acceptance of the lot. *A plan that determines the number of items to sample and the acceptance criteria of the lot, based on meeting certain stipulated conditions such as the risk of rejecting a good lot or accepting a bad lot, is known as an acceptance sampling plan.*

For instance, consider a case of attribute inspection where an item is classified as conforming or not conforming to a thickness specification of 12 ± 0.4 mm. Suppose the items come in batches of 500 units. If an acceptance sampling plan with a sample size of 50 and an acceptance number of 3 is specified, then the interpretation of the plan is as follows. Fifty items will be randomly selected by the inspector from the batch of 500 items. Each of the 50 selected items will then be inspected, as far as the length specification is concerned (say, with a go/no-go gage) and classified as conforming or not conforming. If the number of nonconforming items in the sample is 3 or less, the entire batch of 500 items is accepted. Alternately, if the number of nonconforming items is greater than 3, the batch is rejected. Upon rejection, as an alternative, the batch may have to go through screening; that is, each item will be inspected, and nonconforming items will be sorted from the rest.

Acceptance sampling plans for attributes are discussed in Chapter 9; those for variables are discussed in Chapter 10.

1-5 QUALITY ASSURANCE

The important message is that quality is not just the responsibility of one person in the organization. Everyone involved directly or indirectly in the production of a quality item or in the performance of a quality service has an important role. Unfortunately, something that is viewed as everyone's responsibility may fall apart in the implementation phase due to one person feeling that someone else will follow the appropriate procedures. This behavior may create an ineffective system where the assurances of producing a quality product exist only on paper. Thus, *what is needed is a system that will ensure that all procedures that have been designed and planned are being followed in implementation. This is precisely the role and purpose of the quality assurance function.*

The objective of the quality assurance function is to have a formal system that will continually survey the effectiveness of the quality philosophy of the company. In doing so, it should audit the various departments and assist them in meeting their responsibilities for producing a quality product. The ANSI/ASQC Standard A3 (1987) defines quality assurance as follows:

Quality assurance: **all those planned or systematic actions necessary to provide confidence that a product or service will satisfy given needs.**

Quality assurance may be conducted, for example, at the product design level by surveying the procedures followed by that department. An audit may be carried out to determine the type of information that is being received from the marketing department for subsequent use in designing the product. Is this information representative of the customer's requirements? If one of the customer's key needs in a food wrap is that it withstand a certain amount of force, is that information incorporated in the design? Do the collected data represent that information? How frequently is the data updated? Are the forms and procedures used to calculate the withstanding force adequate and proper? Are the measuring instruments calibrated and accurate? Does the design provide a safety margin? The answers to all of these questions would be sought by the quality assurance function. If any discrepancies are found, the quality assurance function would then advise the department in question of the changes that should be adopted. This function acts as a watchdog over the whole system.

1-6 QUALITY CIRCLES

A quality circle is typically an informal group of people, which may consist of operators, supervisors, managers, and so on, who get together to seek improved ways of making the product or delivering the service. The concept behind the formulation of quality circles is that, in most cases, the persons who are closest to an operation being performed are in a better position to contribute ideas that would lead to improvement in that operation. Thus, we need not expect improvement-seeking ideas only from managers but also from all other personnel who are involved in the particular activity. A quality circle tries to overcome barriers that may exist within the prevailing organizational structure so as to foster an open exchange of ideas.

A quality circle can become an effective productivity improvement tool through this informal gathering because it generates a collection of new ideas and implements them in practice. It makes use of the participative style of management. The group members feel a sense of involvement in the decision-making process and develop a positive attitude toward creating a better product or service. They identify themselves with it and no longer feel that they are outsiders or that only management may dictate how things are done. Of course, whatever suggestions that a quality circle comes up with will be considered by management to consider the feasibility of its adoption and implementation. Thus, members of the management team must be in a position to clearly understand the workings and advantages of the proposed action. Only then can they objectively evaluate its feasibility.

Quality circles have been in usage in Japan since the early 1960s. They were successful in generating a variety of ideas that led to improvements in product quality. Toyota, for example, has used this approach to identify critical problems and determine remedial measures. Brainstorming sessions are usually conducted under the guidance of a group leader. In the United States, quality circles were implemented in the early 1970s. Lately, the activity in this area has not seen much increase and is nowhere close to the level of activity in Japan. One possible reason for this difference is the lack of statistical training of the workers and the people in these quality circles. Another reason is the reluctance of managers to share power with employees. Identification of possible problems and suggestion of remedial actions may require a background in statistical foundations. Japan has undergone a phase encompassing almost two decades, starting in the 1950s, of conducting training programs in statistical methods for all of their personnel. This approach is lacking in the United States. Companies are now realizing the importance of understanding statistical concepts. However, what must lie ahead is a commitment to exposing all people, including operators and management, to these techniques so that they may have an adequate background to effectively contribute to productivity and quality improvement.

1-7 BENEFITS OF QUALITY CONTROL

The goal of most companies is to conduct business in such a manner that an acceptable rate of return is obtained by the shareholders. What must be considered in this setting is the short-term versus the long-term goal. If the goal is to show a certain rate of return this coming year, then this goal may not be appropriate, because the benefits of quality control may not be realized immediately. However, from a long-term perspective, the use of a quality control system may lead to achievement of the rate of return goal.

One of the drawbacks of the manner in which many U.S. companies operate is that the output of managers is measured in short time frames. It is difficult for a manager to show an increase of a five percent rate of return, say, in the quarter after implementing a quality system. Top management may then become doubtful of the benefits of quality control.

The advantages of a quality control system, however, become obvious in the long run. First and foremost among the benefits is the improvement in the quality of products and services. With the existence of a quality control system, a well-defined structure for achieving the production goal is present. Second, the system is continually evaluated and modified to meet the changing needs of the customer. Therefore, a mechanism exists to modify product or process design, manufacture, and service to meet customer requirements and allow the company to remain competitive. Third, a quality control system improves productivity, which is one of the goals of all organizations. It reduces the production of scrap and rework, thereby producing more usable products. Fourth, such a system reduces costs in the long run. The notion that improved productivity and cost reduction do not go hand in hand is a myth. On the contrary, a quality control system achieves precisely these two desirable features in the long run. With the production of fewer nonconforming items, total costs decrease, which may lead to a reduction in selling price. Fifth, with improved productivity, the lead time on the production of parts and subassemblies is reduced, which may result in an improvement in meeting customer due dates. Once again, keeping the customers satisfied is a fundamental goal. Meeting their needs on a timely basis will help sustain a good relationship for a long time. Last and not least, a quality control system maintains an environment of forever striving for the goal of continued improvement in quality and productivity. There is no end to the improvement process—there is always room for betterment. A company that adopts this philosophy and uses a quality control system to help in meeting this objective is one that will be competitive for a long time.

1-8 RESPONSIBILITY FOR QUALITY

During the industrial revolution of the late nineteenth and early twentieth centuries, the concept of specialization of labor was introduced. Prior to this time, the entire product was made by an individual, who was therefore solely responsible for its quality. Mass production methods were introduced during the era of industrial revolution, and jobs became more specialized as products became complicated. A supervisor was responsible for quality control, with the focus primarily on inspection. In 1924, when W. A. Shewhart developed the control chart for controlling the product's variables through process control, the emphasis changed from defect detection through inspection to defect prevention. Over the years, that concept of defect prevention has permeated different departments throughout organizations. Thus, no longer is one person or one department responsible for quality; it is everyone's responsibility. It starts with a commitment from top management and filters down to the operator level. The quality assurance system must evaluate and oversee each department's functional responsibility in producing a quality product or service. The following are some specific functional responsibilities associated with the various departments or units within an organization. Figure 1-3 depicts the responsibilities of the different departments for ensuring quality.

Marketing and Product Planning

The role of the marketing and product planning department is to determine the needs and requirements of the customer. Additionally, information on the price that the customer is willing to pay is also needed. The data obtained here will have an impact on the product quality design. Information may be obtained through such means as market surveys conducted via questionnaires, feedback from sales representatives, and customer complaints.

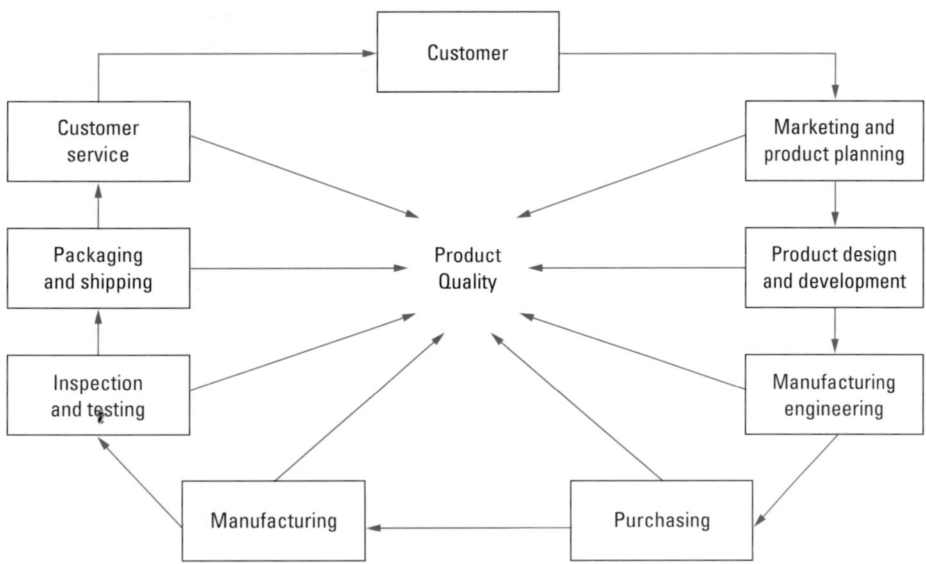

Figure 1-3 Responsibility for quality. (Dale H. Besterfield, *Quality Control,* 3rd ed., © 1990, pp. 4, 87–90. Adapted by permission of Prentice Hall, Englewood Cliffs, New Jersey.)

Product Design and Development

The responsibility of the product design and devolpment unit is to develop product specifications, determine the raw materials or components to be used, and decide upon the performance characteristics of the product. As input it uses the information on customer needs found by the marketing department. For example, the marketing department may have found that, for a particular fertilizer, the nitrogen content required by the consumer is 15 percent. Product design may have come up with tolerances for a nitrogen content of 15 ± 1 percent. Furthermore, the raw material to be used to produce the fertilizer with the above specification is identified. Remember that quality has to be designed into a product. Also, a good design is one that is feasible given the constraints under which the organization operates. Therefore, a representative from manufacturing should be involved in the design phase.

Manufacturing Engineering

The manufacturing engineering department is responsible for determining the details of the manufacturing process for use in production. It also develops the design of equipment, work methods and procedures, inspection tools, and sequence of operations. It conducts an analysis to determine whether the existing manufacturing facilities and resources are capable of producing the product with the quality specified in the design phase. Chapter 8 discusses some methods of analyzing process capability. If production is not feasible, this information must be conveyed to the product design department so that a modified design can be suggested.

Purchasing

The purchasing department is responsible for obtaining quality raw materials and components in order to produce a quality product. It has the job of selecting vendors whose products meet certain incoming quality requirements. If there is a lot of variation in the incoming quality of raw materials, an undesirable variability in the product quality characteristics might be observed in the outgoing product. *Vendor quality control* is under the jurisdiction of this department. In selecting vendors, quality, along with cost, should be a factor. Several companies, such as Ford, demand that their vendors demonstrate the use and results of statistical quality control procedures in order to maintain their contracts. Alternatively, vendor selection could be considered in the product design phase.

Another important concept in the selection of vendors involves developing a long-term relationship with a few of them. This, of course, assumes that the chosen vendors are able to supply the raw materials or components at the desired quality level. Such a practice has been followed in Japan and has several advantages for both parties. For instance, a company does not have to frequently go through the process of choosing vendors, which is good because evaluation of vendor ratings and history can be a time-consuming and costly affair. Furthermore, because of its establishment of a good relationship with the vendor, a company could depend upon the vendor in situations involving an uncertainty in the demand for the company's product; in peak periods of demand, the company may still obtain all of its materials from the same vendor without searching for additional ones. From the vendor's point of view, mutual trust is extremely desirable. In the case of an occasional poor shipment, the vendor knows that its contract will not be terminated right away. In order to achieve the company goals, it is easier to work with one source rather than many. Moreover, because of a long-lasting relationship, a vendor does not have to worry about seeking new contracts on a frequent basis. A stable environment exists at the vendor company level, which is also influential in maintaining a desirable quality level at the company in question.

Manufacturing

The manufacturing unit is responsible for producing a quality product. It must control the operations, process parameters, and operator performance to achieve the desired level of quality that was designed in the first place. Control charts, discussed in Chapters 5, 6, and 7, may be used for such purposes. Also, for the quality system to work, operators and management must have an adequate background in statistical foundations. Training sessions can help achieve this objective.

Inspection and Test

The inspection and test unit is responsible for appraising the quality of incoming raw materials and components as well as the quality of the manufactured product or service. It also has to specify the type of inspection devices to use and the procedures to follow in order to obtain measurements of the quality characteristics of interest. For instance, to measure the thickness of a component produced, is it better to use a micrometer, an optical sensing device, or a go/no-go gage? Is it to be done automatically or with manual intervention? Will it be conducted for all components or only for some? If only for some, with what frequency will the measurements be taken? How will the values be recorded, and what type of analysis will be conducted? These are some of the questions to be addressed. The functions of the inspection and test department may also be part of the manufacturing department. Say, for an automatic lathe machine, a thickness could be measured at the end of the operation; this task may be done by a member of the manufacturing team. If inspection is conducted manually, there may be a need for training the inspectors.

Despite the importance of inspection, it is important to note that quality cannot be inspected into a product or service. Inspection is an activity that measures the degree of conformance of a quality characteristic with a specified standard, in the case of variables. In the case of attribute inspection, the procedure merely separates the nonconforming from the conforming. Inspection does not show why nonconformities or nonconforming units are produced. It does not address the possible actions to take in the event of such nonconformities. Methods of statistical process control (Banks, 1989; Wadsworth, 1986), discussed in Chapters 5, 6, and 7, will take into account some of these issues.

Packaging and Shipping

The packing and shipping unit concerns itself with how the product is packaged and transported to the customer. This function must be carried out in order to protect the quality of the product during the process of storage and shipment. For instance, in the case of products that are brittle (such as glass mirrors), proper packing methods must be used so that no scratch marks are created during transportation and delivery to the customer. Furthermore, care should be taken during unloading and installation if necessary. Nothing can be more irritating to the customer than opening a box containing the ordered product and finding it not totally acceptable. Since the whole idea of a quality system evolves around satisfying the customer, this unit has an important role in the system.

Customer Service

The customer service department is responsible for installation, maintenance, and repair of products. Its purpose is to help the consumer in getting the most out of the product and to assist the customer when requested. The promptness and accuracy of servicing may differentiate between a satisfied and dissatisfied customer. On certain occasions, the customer needs to be trained and made aware of the different functions of a new piece of equipment, say, a drilling machine. This department would conduct training programs for the customer. Furthermore, this unit also deals with issues pertaining to product liability and warranty. A goal of this unit should be to continually obtain feedback from the customers on the degree of their satisfaction with the product or service. This information should be conveyed to the marketing and product planning department. Therefore, it is desirable that the customer service unit and the marketing and product planning unit work closely with each other.

1-9 QUALITY AND RELIABILITY

Reliability refers to the ability of a product to function effectively over a certain period of time when in use by the consumer. It therefore relates to the concept of quality of performance. Since the consumer ultimately determines the acceptability of a product or service, the better the performance over a given time frame, the higher the reliability and the greater the degree of satisfaction. Achievement of desirable standards of reliability is obtained by careful analysis in the product design phase. Reliability is built in through quality of design. The product is typically overdesigned to more than meet the performance requirements over a specified time frame. For example, consider the quality of a highway system where roads are expected to last some minimum time period under certain conditions of use. Conditions of use may include the rate at which the road system is used, the weight of vehicles, and such atmospheric conditions as the proportion of days that the temperature exceeds a certain value. Suppose the performance requirements are for the road system to last at least 20 years. In the design phase, in order to account for the variation in the uncontrollable parameters during use of the roads, they might be designed for 25 years. The design may be achieved through proper selection of new materials and the thickness of the layers of concrete and tar. Analysis of data, obtained on a timely basis during the performance phase of the product, helps to update the design and production parameters so that the product may perform in an acceptable manner.

1-10 TOTAL QUALITY SYSTEM

As previously stated, quality is everyone's responsibility. This means that, considering the company as a unit, comprehensive plans should be developed to show the precise responsibilities of the different units, procedures should be defined to check their conformance to the plans, and remedial measures should be suggested in the event of discrepancies between performance and standard. The quality assurance function, as defined earlier, will be helpful for monitoring such a system. The definition of a quality system as given by the American National Standards Institute (ANSI)/American Society for Quality Control (ASQC) Standard A3 (1987) is as follows:

Quality system: **The collective plans, activities, and events that are provided to ensure that a product, process, or service will satisfy given needs.**

The *systems approach* to quality integrates the various functions and responsibilities of the different units, and it provides a mechanism to ensure that the goal of the organization is being met through the coordination of the goals of the individual units.

ANSI and ASQC have developed some generic guidelines for quality systems. This standard, ANSI/ASQC Standard Z-1.15 (1979), defines the following elements of a total quality system.*

1. *Policy, planning, organization, and administration.* A quality policy is essential for developing consistency in the goals of the organization. Once a plan is developed, an organization to aid in the achievement of the plan must be established. Quality manuals may be created for this purpose. Furthermore, procedures for administering the plans in practice should be detailed, and costs should be identified.

2. *Product design assurance, specification development, and control.* With the customers' requirements in mind, a product design is formulated. Through prototype development and testing, this design may undergo modifications until it satisfactorily meets all requirements. Tolerances on the product's characteristics will be developed based on careful consideration of the manufacturing capabilities. During the production phase, procedures should be defined to check and control the product characteristics to conform to the standards of design.

3. *Control of purchased materials and component parts.* The production of a quality product is very much influenced by the quality of the raw materials and components used. Procedures must be developed to evaluate the capability and performance of the vendors. Some companies require the vendors to demonstrate an adequate use of statistical quality control methods before they can be considered as candidates for selection. Specifications should be set for incoming items and explained to the vendors. If incoming inspection is to be performed, then the vendors must be informed. Quality, cost, and ability to meet due dates should be considered in choosing vendors. A company should attempt to develop a harmonious long-term relationship with a vendor. Procedures for controlling purchased materials should address corrective actions to pursue if there is nonconformance and if some inspection is to be conducted. The American Society for Quality Control has developed a series of publications in this area, some of the titles being *Procurement Quality Control: A Handbook of Recommended Practices, How to Evaluate a Supplier's Product,* and *How to Conduct a Supplier Survey.*

4. *Production quality control.* This is a critical aspect of the whole framework for quality. It involves determining process specifications, selecting equipment, training personnel, designing forms and charts, selecting inspection points, collecting and analyzing process data to determine whether it is under control, determining process capability, conducting planned experimentation to determine process improvement methods, and performing final inspection. It should be emphasized that preventive maintenance and feed-forward structures, in addition to feedback control, should be used to aid in production and process control. Minimizing in-process inventory and using the just-in-time concept, where items are received just when they are needed, may be done to improve productivity. Proper application of the just-in-time principle is dependent, however, on the reliability of vendors for incoming parts as well as the reliability of the equipment and resources of the company. Developing accurate forecasts for demand may influence the success of a just-in-time system. Other items of concern are designing and developing product quality audits, which would attempt to detect departures of the product quality level from specified standards, even before mass production. Doing so will allow the manufacturer to correct problems before large amounts are produced. One objective in this area is the dissemination of quality information to key people throughout the organization.

5. *User contact and field performance.* A system must exist to collect information from the consumer

* ASQC (1979), ANSI/ASQC Standard Z–1.15–1979. Reprinted with the permission of ASQC.

and determine the level of performance of the product or service. Poor field performance may necessitate changes in design. How will the information be collected from consumers? Design of the data forms, the frequency with which data is to be collected, the types of analyses to conduct to determine the level of performance, advertising and promotion schemes to use, and installation plans and procedures are some of the items to be considered. Feedback on performance where product failure is concerned has implications on the type of warranties to be offered and should dictate the procedures for handling product liability issues. Developing policies for installation and servicing and determining guidelines for compliance with these policies are critical to providing customer satisfaction. Careful thought should be given to designing a system that will collect, analyze, and act upon information that is received as feedback from the consumer.

6. *Corrective action.* The key to creating and maintaining a quality system is to take corrective action when there is a difference between the observed product or process characteristic and a specified standard. Problems, therefore, need to be detected, categorized, and systematically documented. Remedial actions for the detected problems also need to be documented in order to be consistent in solving problems. Furthermore, an organization needs to be created to detect problems and take corrective actions, with well-defined procedures for implementation. Corrective action may apply to such different entities as the incoming materials and components, the vendors, the process and equipment, the operators, and the products. Procedures must be specified for taking action in each of those categories as well as for conducting a follow-up of the actions taken.

7. *Employee selection, training, and motivation.* The backbone behind the success of a total quality system is the employee, a fact that pertains to production as well as nonmanufacturing personnel. People in staff roles contribute significantly to the implementation of a quality system. Errors in administrative paperwork, which can lead to delays in ordering raw materials and components, are as critical as maladjustments made by the operator in the machine setting. Guidelines should be established to select people for particular jobs, a task which may involve a job analysis and identification of skills of the available pool of personnel. Manuals should be developed to train selected people for the job in question. In every situation, there must be a clear demonstration of management commitment to help select, train, and motivate employees to produce a better-quality product. Recognition of superior effort and the use of motivation programs help reassure the employee of the support of management. Some of the common motivational programs are the zero defects, quality circles, and participative quality control programs. The *zero defects program* originated in 1961–62, during which time the Martin Company of Orlando, Florida delivered a Pershing missile to Cape Canaveral with zero nonconformities. Since then, such a program has been used as a motivational tool to draw the support of operators and supervisors by challenging them to do their best all the time. It gives the authority to operators to make changes in the process when problems occur. However, in order for the program to work, they must first be trained in the process of detecting problems and taking appropriate actions.

8. *Legal requirements—product liability and user safety.* The failure of products within the warranty period or the hazardous effects of malfunction are of grave concern to manufacturers. Liability suits can be an enormous expense, and companies have to budget for warranty costs. Consumer tolerances also change with time. Minor blemishes or cosmetic defects that were once acceptable may not be so because of more stringent demands imposed by the consumer. Furthermore, the U.S. judicial system enforces the rule of *strict liability*, which creates the need to plan for field failures and their possible legal implications. Strict liability refers to the presumption of liability when a given event occurs. For example, if foreign matter is found in food products, strict liability assigns negligence to the manufacturer. Under the rule of strict liability, any enterprise—the manufacturer as well as the seller—must respond immediately to unsatisfactory quality. This response may take place through product service, repair, or replacement. The responsibility extends through the period of use of the product and also includes coverage of environmental effects (say, noise pollution) and safety aspects for use of the item. There must be clear directions of what safe usage means (for example, a precise description of conditions under which a product should not be used; a hair dryer should not be operated while resting in water). Second, all advertising statements must be supportable by certification data. Therefore, product durability, safety, and impact on the environment are principles that are to be integrated in the quality system.

9. *Sampling and other statistical techniques.* This segment of the total quality system is comprised of the analytical tools and techniques. Most of these procedures are described in the following chapters and constitute the main subject matter of this text. Chapter 3 covers the fundamentals of sta-

tistical concepts and techniques used in quality control. Chapter 4 presents some statistical techniques for quality analysis and improvement. The idea of process control through control charts, which is one of the primary quality control tools, is covered in Chapters 5–8. The fundamental principles of control charts are introduced in Chapter 5. Chapter 6 focuses on control charts for variables, while those for attributes are covered in Chapter 7. Statistical methods for determining whether a process is capable of producing items that conform to a standard are described in Chapter 8. These methods involve process capability analysis. The topic of acceptance sampling is covered in Chapters 9 and 10. Sampling plans for attributes are presented in Chapter 9, while those for variables are found in Chapter 10. Statistical methods dealing with life testing and reliability may be found in Chapter 11; these techniques concern the performance of a product over a period of time. The subject of designing experiments for use in systematically analyzing and guiding process parameter settings is covered in Chapter 12. Some fundamental concepts of the Taguchi method of off-line quality control are presented in Chapter 13. Taguchi methods may also be used for on-line quality control, a limited discussion of which is found in Chapter 13. Chapter 14 includes applications of quality control techniques in the service sector. Since more than 70% of the gross national product comes from the service sector, it warrants use of the techniques for monitoring quality that have primarily been used in the manufacturing sector. Finally, computers are playing a fundamental role in quality control and will see expanded use in the years to come. Chapter 15 reviews the computer software that is used for the different types of statistical techniques in quality control.

1-11 QUALITY IMPROVEMENT

Quality improvement is a neverending process, and efforts to reduce the variability of a process and reduce the production of nonconforming items should continue forever. Whereas process control deals with identification and elimination of special causes that force a system to go out of control (for example, tool wear, operator fatigue, poor raw materials), in order to bring the process to a state of statistical control, quality improvement relates to the detection and elimination of common causes. Common causes are those that are inherent to the system and are always present. Their impact on the output may be minor relative to special causes. An example of a common cause is the variability in a characteristic (say, a diameter) caused by the inherent capability of the particular equipment used (say, a milling machine). This means that, all other factors being held constant to the extent possible, the milling machine is not able to produce all parts with exactly the same diameter. In order to reduce the inherent variability of that machine, an alternative might be to get a better or more sophisticated machine. Whereas special causes are mainly controllable by the operator, common causes need the attention of management. Therefore, quality improvement can take place only through the joint effort of the operator and management, with the emphasis primarily on the latter. For instance, a decision to replace the milling machine from the above example must be made by management. The elimination of common causes will result in an improved process capability, as measured by less variation of the output.

Quality improvement should be the objective of all companies and individuals. It improves the rate of return or profitability by an improvement in productivity and reduction in costs. It is consistent with the philosophy that a company should continually seek to improve its competitive edge over others. It supports the principle that no deviation from a standard is acceptable, which is akin to the principle of the loss function developed in the Taguchi methods (Taguchi, 1986; Taguchi and Wu, 1979). So, even if the product is within the specification limits, an ongoing effort should be made to reduce its variability around the target value. The specifications for the weight of a product (say, packages of sugar) could be 5.00 ± 0.05 lb. If the output from the process reveals that all packages weigh between 4.95 and 5.05 lb, then the process is capable and all items will be acceptable. However, not all of the packages will weigh exactly 5.00 lb, the target value. There will be some variability in the weights of the packages. The Taguchi philosophy is based on the notion that any deviation from the target value of 5.00 lb is unacceptable, with the loss being proportional to the deviation. Quality improvement is a logical result of this philosophy.

Some methods for quality improvement are discussed in Chapter 4. These include such graphical techniques as Pareto analysis, histograms, and cause-and-effect or fishbone diagrams. Furthermore, additional techniques discussed in Chapter 8 deal with process capability analysis. Also, quality improvement through design may be achieved through experimental design techniques and the Taguchi

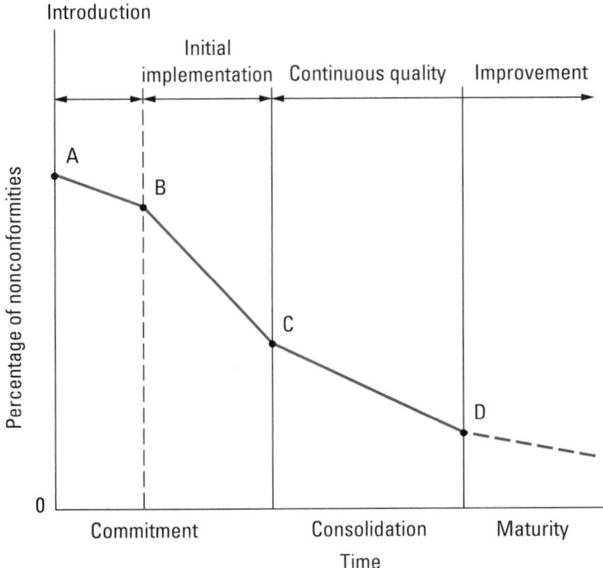

Figure 1-4 The three stages of quality improvement. (Gabriel A. Pall, *Quality Process Management,* © 1987, pp. 34, 46. Adapted by permission of Prentice Hall, Englewood Cliffs, New Jersey.)

method, which are subjects of discussion in Chapters 12 and 13.

Several authors have identified and categorized the different stages associated with quality improvement. Pall (1987) divides the process into three stages: commitment, consolidation, and maturity. Figure 1-4 shows these three stages of quality improvement.

Commitment Stage

In the commitment stage, management makes a commitment to the quality improvement program. A formal plan and policy are developed, and the organizational structure to implement the plan is put into place. This stage may be subdivided into two phases, introduction and initial implementation. The introduction phase may take anywhere from three to six months. Keep in mind that these are rough estimates; the actual time taken in practice will be influenced by many factors such as type of company, product, process, management perception, and resource availability. During the introduction phase, a policy statement might be developed, and plans for creating the infrastructure to implement quality improvement methods might be discussed. In the initial implementation phase, which may take between six months and a year, problems are identified, and causes associated with production of nonconformities are removed. This phase usually deals with the elimination of special causes, such as a poor incoming quality of raw materials, operator mistakes, or improper tools. The process is thereby brought to a state of statistical control. In Figure 1-4, point A represents the percentage of nonconformities produced by the system before this process is implemented. With the introduction of the plan, education and training of personnel, and adequate management support, the percentage drops to B. As special causes are detected and eliminated, the quality improves to point C.

Consolidation Stage

In the consolidation stage, the objectives are to produce an item that conforms to requirements (quality of conformance) and to start a continual improvement in the efficiency and productivity of the process. Although elimination of special causes helps in attaining the first objective, the removal or improvement of common causes is necessary to accomplish the second objective. The latter action improves process capability. A large investment is made in the prevention of defects, which may therefore reduce total costs by reducing the production of items that have to be scrapped or reworked. Education and training are an integral part of this stage. Managing both the intent and the outcome is key to the successful implementation of this phase. As seen in Figure 1-4, quality level improves from point C to D, but the rate of improvement is slower than in the initial implementation phase.

Maturity Stage

In the maturity stage, quality improvement and management are a way of life. The process parameters are adjusted to create optimum operating conditions. Very few defects or nonconformities are actually produced; efforts and costs are focused on defect prevention. Improvements in productivity and quality continue to take place. Every person in the organization believes in the quality philosophy. They are enthusiastic about seeking innovative ways to improve the process. They are convinced that quality management is an integral part of the system and are fully aware of its benefits. The rate of improvement, as can be seen from Figure 1-4, slows down. From point D, the goal is to asymptotically approach the ideal condition of zero nonconformities while continually improving the process performance.

1-12 QUALITY COSTS

A measure of performance of the total quality system is the total cost associated with it. Careful identification, measurement, and analysis of the total cost as a function of time aids in tracking the impact of an effective statistical quality control system. Remember that the benefits of a quality system, as measured by the total quality costs, may be realized in the long run rather than in the short run. The full impact of a particular change in the process is felt only after a certain time.

The American Society for Quality Control (1971) has defined four major categories for quality costs, each of which is discussed below.

Prevention Costs

Prevention costs are the costs incurred for planning, implementing, and maintaining a quality system. They include salaries and developmental costs for product design, process and equipment design, process control techniques (through means such as control charts), information systems design, and all other costs associated with making the product right the first time. Also, costs associated with education and training regarding quality control procedures for all involved personnel are included in this category. Other such costs include those associated with defect cause removal, process changes, and the cost of a quality audit. Figure 1-5 shows a typical breakdown of the quality costs as a function of time into four categories. As the figure shows, prevention costs increase with the introduction of a quality system and may be a significant proportion of the total quality costs. The rate of increase decreases with time. Even though prevention costs increase, they are more than justified by causing a decrease in total quality costs.

Appraisal Costs

Appraisal costs include the costs associated with measuring, evaluating, or auditing products, components, or purchased materials to determine their degree of conformance to the specified standards. Such costs include dealing with the inspection and test of incoming materials as well as product inspection and test at various phases of manufacturing and at final acceptance. Other costs in this category include the cost of calibrating and maintaining the measuring instruments and equipment and the cost of materials and products consumed in a destructive test or devalued by reliability tests. Appraisal costs typically occur during or after production but before the product is released to the customer. Hence, they are regarded as the costs associated with managing the outcome, whereas prevention costs are associ-

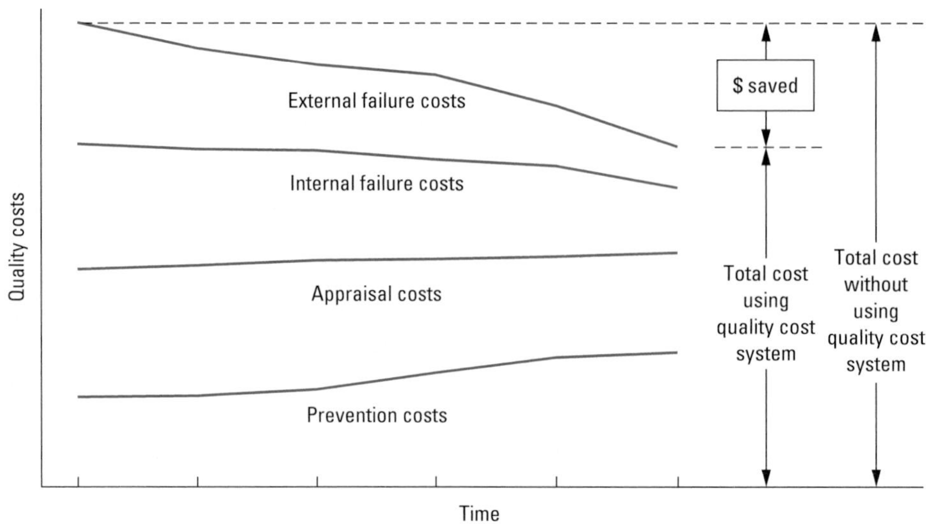

Figure 1-5 Quality cost trend prediction as a function of time. (Adapted from American Society for Quality Control (1971), *Quality Costs—What and How*, 2nd ed. Reprinted with the permission of ASQC.)

ated with managing the intent or goal. Figure 1-5 shows that appraisal costs normally decline with time as more nonconformities are prevented from occurring.

Internal Failure Costs

Internal failure costs are incurred when products, components, materials, and services fail to meet quality requirements prior to the transfer of ownership to the customer. These costs would disappear if there were no nonconformities in the product. Achieving a zero defects program is the appropriate course of action. Internal failure costs include scrap and rework costs that may include materials, labor, and overhead associated with production. The cost of correcting nonconforming units, as in rework, may include such additional manufacturing operations as regrinding the outside diameter of an oversized part. If the outside diameter were undersized, it may not be feasible for use in the finished product. Costs to determine the cause of product failure or the costs to reinspect or retest products that had to be reworked are other examples of costs in this category. The cost of lost production time due to nonconformities must also be considered (for example, poor quality of raw materials may require retooling of equipment). Furthermore, downgrading costs that include lost revenue from selling a flawed product at a lower price than normal are another component. As a total quality system is implemented and becomes effective with time, internal failure costs will decline, as shown in Figure 1-5. Less scrap and rework will result as problems are prevented. This is one of the reasons for the reduction in total quality costs over time following the implementation of a quality control system.

External Failure Costs

External failure costs are incurred when the product does not perform satisfactorily after ownership is transferred to the customer. If no nonconforming units were produced, this cost would vanish. Such costs include those due to customer complaints, which include the costs of investigation and adjustments, and those associated with receipt, handling, repair, or replacement of nonconforming products. Also, warranty charges related to failure of a product within the warranty time should be budgeted for. Product liability costs, which involve costs or awards as an outcome of product liability litigation, also fall under this category. As shown in Figure 1-5, a reduction in external failure costs takes place over time following the successful implementation of a quality control system. The major impact of a quality system is to cause a reduction in the internal and external failure costs, which in turn reduces the total quality costs.

Quality Costs Data Requirements

The measurement of quality costs should be clearly monitored by the quality system, and corresponding procedures should be identified. Since indirect costs are as important as such direct costs as raw material and labor, well-defined accounting procedures should be set up to determine realistic quality cost estimates. For example, consider the case where quality cost data may cross departmental lines. If a quality control supervisor in a staff position identifies the reason for the production of scrap or rework, and a lathe operator conducts an extra operation to rework those items, then quality costs cross departmental lines. Likewise, if the identification of rework or scrap inspires a change in the product design, then the proportion of the time spent by the design personnel in making the changes should be assigned to quality costs data. Therefore, special forms may be needed to report quality and figures. Figure 1-6 shows the quality costs data requirements at different management levels. Quality cost data may be collected for each product line or project and distributed to each level of management. The needs are somewhat different at each level. Top management may prefer a summary of the total quality costs, broken down into each of the four categories, at the division or plant level. On the other hand, line management or supervisors may want a summary of the direct costs, which include labor and material costs, as it relates to their area.

This means that if a change is made in product or process design, then it is possible for one or more quality cost categories to be affected. The time spent by the design engineer would be allocated, cost-wise, to prevention cost. On the other hand, if the new design calls for new inspection equipment, then that component of the cost would be allocated to appraisal cost.

Thus, for the different functions performed by management and operators, a cost-wise break-down into the four quality cost categories of prevention, appraisal, internal failure, and external failure could be accomplished.

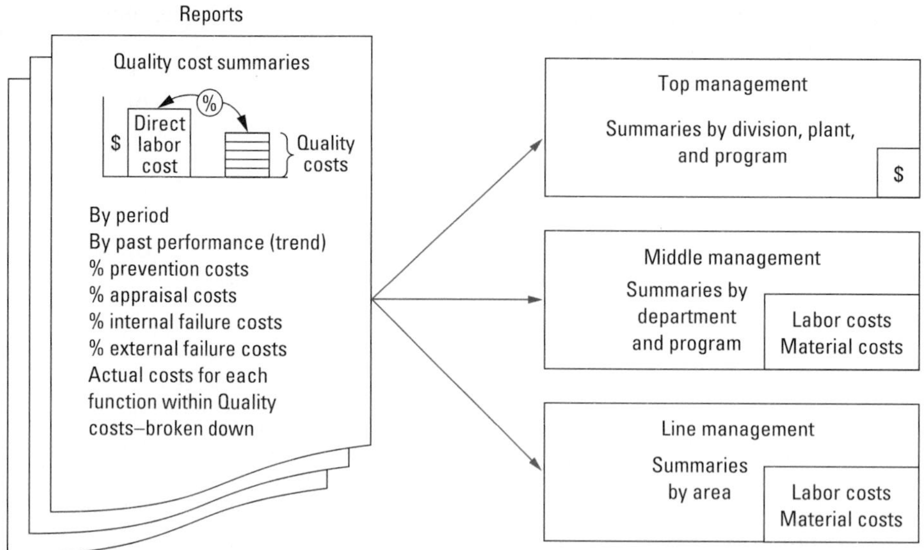

Figure 1-6 Quality costs data requirements at different management levels. (Adapted from American Society for Quality Control (1971), *Quality Costs—What and How*, 2nd ed. Reprinted with the permission of ASQC.)

1-13 MEASURING QUALITY COSTS

The actual magnitude in dollars of quality costs is important to management, as it provides input to the calculation of such overall indices as return on investment. However, for a comparison of quality costs over time, this magnitude may not be the measure to use because several conditions may change from one quarter to the next. The number of units produced may change, which would change the direct costs of labor and materials. So the total cost in dollars may not be comparable. To alleviate this situation, a measurement base accounting for labor hours, manufacturing costs, sales dollars, or units produced could be used to produce an index. These ideas are discussed below.

Labor base index. One index that is commonly used is the quality costs per direct labor hour. The information required to compute this index is readily available, since direct labor hour data is available from the accounting department. This index should be used over a short period of time, since it is possible that over an extended period the impact of automation on direct labor hours may be significant. Another index lists quality costs per direct labor dollar. This index eliminates the effect of inflation over time. For line and middle management, this index may be appealing.

Cost base index. This index is based on calculating the quality costs per dollar of manufacturing costs. Direct labor, material, and overhead costs make up manufacturing costs, and the relevant information is easily available from accounting. This index is more stable than the labor base index since it is not significantly affected by price fluctuations or changes in the level of automation. For middle management, this might be an index of importance.

Sales base index. For top management, quality costs per sales dollar may be an attractive index. It is not a good measure for short-term analysis, but top management should focus on long-term aspects and make strategic decisions. Sales lag behind production and are subject to seasonal variations (for example, increased sale of toys during Christmas). These variations have an impact in the short run. Furthermore, changes in selling price also affect this index.

Unit base index. This index calculates the quality costs per unit of production. If the output of different production lines are similar, then this index is valid. Otherwise, if a company produces a variety of products, then the product lines would have to be weighted, and a standardized product measure would need to be computed. For an organization producing, say, refrigerators, washers, dryers, and electric ranges, it may be difficult to calculate the weights based on a standard product. For example, if an electric range is assumed to be a standard product, is a refrigerator 1.5 standard units of a product or a washer 0.9 standard units? One should consider any of the other alternative indexes in such cases.

For all of the above indexes, a change in the denominator will cause the value of the index to change, even if the quality costs do not change. If the cost of direct labor decreases, which could happen as a result of productivity improvement, the labor base index could increase. This increase should be interpreted cautiously since it could be misinterpreted as an increase in quality costs.

1-14 MANAGEMENT OF QUALITY

Management of the total quality system is achieved through the functions of planning, organizing, staffing, directing, and controlling. Figure 1-7 shows the various functions of management. It also indicates the phases in the product development and the corresponding actions in each phase.

The major objectives of the management system are to integrate all the processes and functional units to meet the goals of the company. It is responsible for the prevention of nonconformities, and its goal is to design, manufacture, and maintain the product or the service at the least possible cost while still meeting all customer requirements. Presently, company officials are finding out that meeting customer requirements is not enough to remain competitive. One has to satisfy the customers to such a degree at the performance phase that they will be motivated to repurchase the product. This feat can be achieved only through an organized and thorough evaluation and analysis of performance data integrated into the design phase.

Planning for Quality

Planning for quality is one of the necessary requirements for the success of an organization. In the process of developing such a plan, one must consider the company's quality mission and objectives, the key qualities perceived by the consumer, the market commitments, the available human resources and production facilities, and the financial constraints. Planning for quality assurance takes place in a hierarchical manner. Strategic plans involving broad product quality decisions are made at the top management level. A mission statement must be clearly defined, which is often stated in terms of the key products that are made or the market share it is

Management functions	Product phase	Action to be taken
Plan	Proposal phase	Develop quality policy Plan for quality Set up guidelines for system administration Consider product liability/user safety
Organize	Design/planning phase	Develop an organization structure Design assurance Design change control Develop production quality planning
Staff	Pre-production phase	Select employee Train employee Motivate employee
Direct	Production phase	Monitor purchased materials quality Monitor process quality control Direct final inspection Direct handling/inspection
Control	Production and post-production phase	Obtain quality information Get data on field performance Take corrective action Conduct statistical quality control Manage quality costs

Figure 1-7 Functions of management in the quality system. (E. G. Schilling (1984), "The Role of Statistics in the Management of Quality," *Quality Progress*, Vol. 17, No. 8, p. 33.)

intended to capture. Missions should be realistic and achievable. A steel manufacturing company may have a mission of capturing 15 percent of the market share. Plans for new products or improving the quality of existing products should also be considered and developed in conjunction with resource requirements planning and facilities design.

Based on the company's mission, the different areas of the organization develop goals to support that mission. The rolling mill division of a steel company may set a goal of reduction of scrap to 0.5 percent. It is important that adequate data be gathered and analyzed, to describe customer demand, competition for the market, and resource constraints in order to determine feasible goals. The next step in the planning process is to develop specific objectives based on the formulated goals. An objective of the rolling mill division may be to produce 1000 tons of acceptable rolled sheets per day. The objectives set at one level in an organization provide boundaries for objectives at a lower level. The strategic plans developed by top management may be formulated into tactical plans at the middle management level. These plans include the design of quality assurance systems.

Next, the goals and objectives of middle management must be converted to operational plans to be implemented by all levels of management. This task requires the identification of standards in quantitative terms. A high technology firm making integrated circuits might specify a target or standard such as achieving sales of $20 million annually. Resources, including people, must be allocated in order to meet the strategic objectives. Furthermore, guidelines for the system of administration to support quality control have to be clearly set up. Quality planning may be categorized as administrative plans and product-oriented plans. Administrative plans deal with the operational and business aspects of the company. They begin with the development of an overall quality program and contain a multitude of other activities. First, they require the formation of a quality policy and procedures manual, which serve as guidelines for the entire quality activity. Second, plans must be designed for audits. Third, resource planning (such as personnel requirements for the coming year, new equipment needs, and space requirements) needs to be incorporated. Product-oriented plans, on the other hand, may cross functional lines such as marketing, product and process design, and production engineering. These would also include plans for vendor evaluation, receiving inspection if any, process control, and inspection and test. Planning answers the fundamental questions of what, when, and how it is to be done and who will do it.

Organizing for Quality

The reasons for creating an organizational structure are to establish lines of authority and responsibility, to improve communication, and to improve productivity. The major activities involved in organizing for quality consist of defining quality-related activities and the interrelationships between them, assigning responsibility for each of the tasks, and subdividing tasks down to the worker level.

The specific form of the organizational structure is influenced by a variety of factors. An organizational structure is created to suit the company, and what is best for it may not necessarily be the best for some other company. The size of the organization, the nature of the product (does it deal with general consumer goods, or does it work on special projects that are narrow in scope?), and the management culture (the informal channels of communication in the organization) are some factors that mold the formal organizational structure. Authority gives one the right to have access to the resources needed to carry out a task. Responsibility determines who is to be held accountable for decisions made. Thus, one principle that should be adhered to is that authority must be granted to match responsibility.

Formal organizational structure is represented through an organizational chart which shows the channels of authority and responsibility. Organizational structures may be categorized as either line, staff, or matrix structures. In a line organization structure, the channels are grouped on a functional basis. Each functional unit is responsible for quality in its own unit. Typical functional units in organizations are marketing, finance, design and development, and manufacturing. So, the vice-president of the marketing department would be responsible for quality functions in that department. These functions may include conducting analyses to determine key requirements of customers, designing data collection forms, and implementing a field survey or audit for obtaining information on customer needs. The heads of the other functional groups would have similar quality-related responsibilities in their respective areas. On paper, the organizational structure may seem unrelated to the quality function, since no individual unit or person would be shown as having the overall responsibility for quality. Figure 1-8 shows a segment of the line organizational structure. The levels of managers who would report to the vice-president of each function and the levels of supervisors who would report to their respective managers are not shown. The blocks with dotted

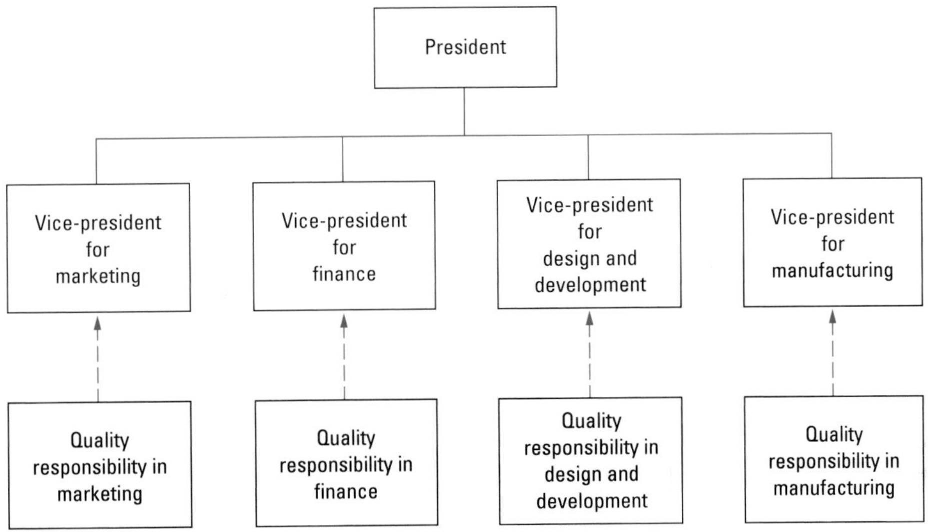

Figure 1-8 Line organizational structure.

arrows indicate the responsibility in the quality area for each vice-president.

In the structure of a layout where the responsibility for quality is formally dealt with by a staff, there may be a vice-president for quality assurance who reports to the president. In this case, the vice-president for quality assurance would have overall responsibility in the quality area and must be given the authority to make changes as appropriate in the respective functional areas in order to adhere to the formulated quality policy. Reporting to the vice-president for quality assurance may be the manager of quality assurance and quality improvement, the manager of quality control, and the manager of reliability and maintainability. Under each manager would be corresponding supervisors. Figure 1-9 illustrates an organizational structure where quality assurance is a staff function.

In general, the layers of management levels should be kept as small as possible to facilitate efficient flow of communication and flow of information. The span of supervision should be kept as broad as possible. For small organizations the span of control is usually broad. In such cases, quality assurance managers may have a diverse group of people reporting to them, such as receiving inspection, in-process inspection, final inspection, data collection, process control, shipping, and customer service. The levels of management are few. For large organizations the span of supervision is usually narrower. Tasks are more specialized. However, the number of levels of management are greater, so the efficiency of information flow is affected. The top person in the quality assurance area should be at a sufficiently high level in the organization, given the significance and importance of this area.

A matrix organizational structure usually exists in situations involving large and complex projects. The duration of these projects is long, and they may be varied in nature. For example, projects may deal with construction of a space shuttle or a nuclear submarine. Tasks are of a specialized nature. In such cases, there may be a quality assurance manager for each project. Figure 1-10 shows the truncated organizational structure for this situation. Reporting to the quality assurance manager of each project may be the respective supervisors of quality assurance and quality control for that project. It is possible for a person in a lower level of the organizational structure to report to more than one person. This will happen if the person is involved in more than one project. For jobs of a highly specialized nature, a person having the necessary skills may work on tasks that are related to multiple projects. Also, as projects are completed, a person may be assigned to other ongoing projects and thus report to different persons.

Staffing for Quality

The success of a company-wide quality program depends on all personnel being indoctrinated in the quality philosophy. Everyone must develop a sense of involvement in the production of a quality item. Selection of personnel in key positions with the appropriate training in statistical quality control tech-

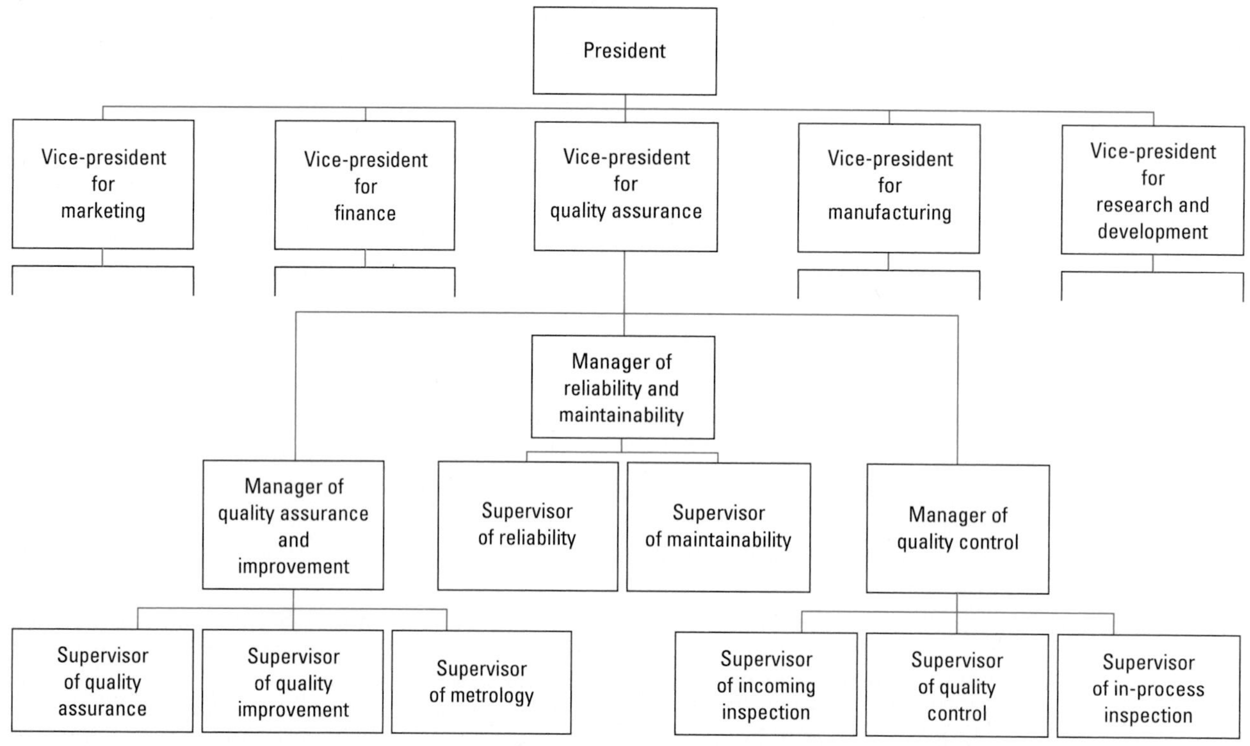

Figure 1-9 Quality assurance in a staff organizational structure.

niques makes the implementation of a quality program easier. In order to ensure the achievement of a certain level of knowledge regarding quality, certification programs are administered by the American Society for Quality Control. Examples of such certification programs are those for the Certified Quality Engineer (CQE) and the Certified Reliability Engineer (CRE). An organization should attempt to staff its managerial positions by those who are certified in the respective quality area. Additionally, a company

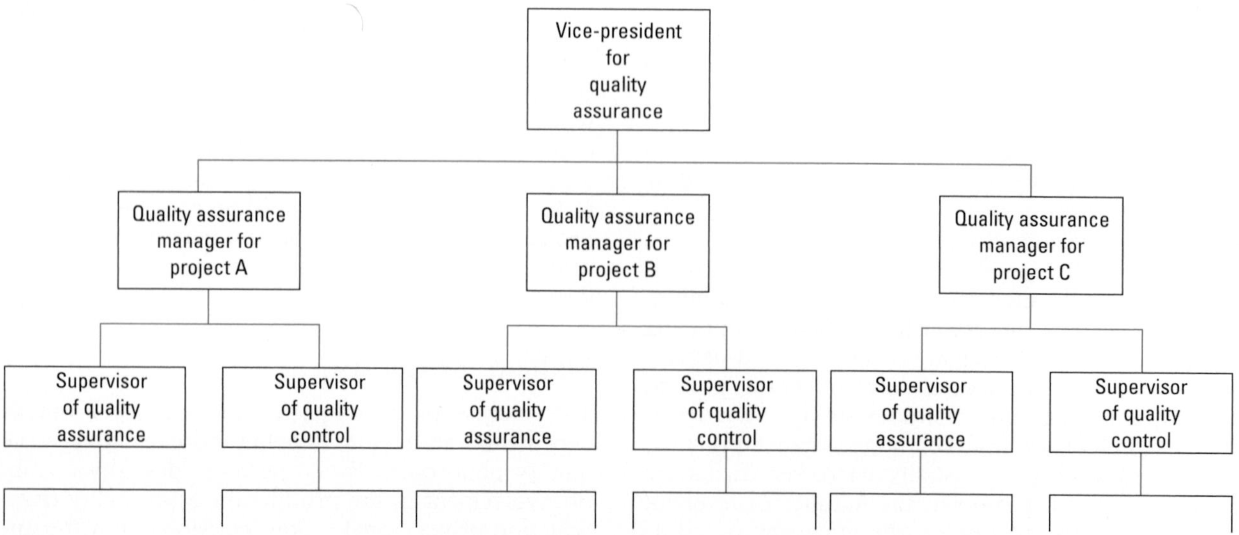

Figure 1-10 Quality assurance in a matrix organizational structure.

could send its personnel to workshops dealing with quality, and should provide them with an incentive to become certified (either through salary increases, promotion, or acknowledgment through awards). Motivating the employee to produce a quality item is critical to the success of the quality program. The employee must be made a contributing member with the opportunity to suggest changes that could lead to an improvement in quality. Deming's points for management (as discussed in Chapter 2) provide some specific guidelines for motivational enhancement.

Directing for Quality

Once quality has been incorporated into the design of the product, the production phase consists of measures to ensure that the item is produced so as to conform to the designed specifications. The quality of purchased raw materials and components is monitored through vendor quality control. Companies may require documentation of the use of statistical quality control procedures from vendors. Those vendors unable to produce such evidence may lose their orders. A company should strive to develop a long-term relationship with its vendors. Such relationships promote a more uniform and acceptable quality level of incoming goods. Each company has a need for monitoring process quality. This implies that the procedures for conducting process control, such as those involving control charts, must be in place. The appropriate data forms should be designed. The inspection points from where the data is to be collected should be decided upon along with the inspection frequency. Furthermore, if final inspection is to be conducted, such procedures must be finalized. Qualified inspectors for both intermediate and final inspection should be selected. Provisions must be made for the training and certification of inspectors. Rules for the acceptance or rejection of lots should be selected in the case of sampling inspection.

Controlling for Quality

The control aspects may occur during the production and postproduction phase. The objective is to determine out-of-control process conditions and product nonconformance as early in the production phase as possible. In order to achieve this end, procedures must be established to obtain relevant process information on a timely basis. The ability to process information in real time will expedite the identification of process problems. Possible sets of rectifying actions must be identified in case the process is found to be out of control. Such rectifying actions must be taken when appropriate. The concept of control through a feedforward (as opposed to feedback) approach should be investigated when information on the effect of the controllable process variables on the output characteristics of the product is known. For example, suppose we know the impact on tensile strength of the temperature of a furnace and the manganese content in the product. Thus, if we are limited to certain settings of the furnace temperature, we can predetermine and thereby control the manganese content such that the product will have a desired tensile strength. An important concern deals with control of the costs of quality. As mentioned previously, the four main categories of costs are prevention, appraisal, internal failure, and external failure. Actions should be taken to minimize the total cost of quality—which may be attained through sufficient reductions of internal and external failures.

1-15 QUALITY AND PRODUCTIVITY

A misconception that has existed among businesses (and is hopefully in the process of being brushed aside) is the notion that quality and productivity do not go hand in hand. On the contrary, the relationship between the two is just the opposite. Making a product right the first time leads to lower total costs and improvement in productivity. More time is available for the production of defect-free output rather than for reworking items that do not conform to requirements or producing extra items to replace those that had to be scrapped. In fact, adherence to the philosophy of doing it right the first time increases the available capacity of the production line. As waste is reduced, valuable resources such as people, equipment, material, time, and effort can be saved and utilized for added production of defect-free goods or services. The competitive position of the company is enhanced in the long run, and an improvement is observed in short-term profits.

Effect on Cost

As discussed previously, quality costs can be grouped into the categories of prevention, appraisal, internal failure, and external failure. Improved productivity may have a different effect on costs in each of the above categories. However, in the long run it will result in a lowering of the total cost of quality.

Prevention and Appraisal Costs With initial improvement in productivity, it is possible to see an increase in the costs of prevention and appraisal. As adequate process control procedures are installed, they contribute to prevention and appraisal costs. Furthermore, process improvement procedures may also cause an increase in costs in these two categories. These costs are labeled the costs of conformance to quality requirements. Continuous quality improvement should be subscribed to by all organizations because it yields a reduction in nonconformities and thereby reduces total costs and increases productivity. With time, a reduction in appraisal costs is usually observed. As process quality improves, it leads to efficient and simplified operations. This may yield further improvements in productivity.

Internal and External Failure Costs A major impact of an improvement in quality is reduction in the internal and external failure costs. The decrease of costs in these two categories offsets the increase of costs in the prevention and appraisal categories in the long run. The total cost of quality thus decreases. Moreover, as less scrap and rework is produced, more time becomes available for productive output. This causes an increase in the profitability of the company. As external failures are reduced, more satisfied customers are encountered. Not only does this emphasis on quality reduce the tangible costs in this category (such as product warranty costs and liability suits), but it also has a significant effect on the intangible costs due to customer dissatisfaction. Figure 1-11 shows how improved quality may lead to a reduction in costs, an improvement in productivity, and eventually increased profits. It should be noted that management must focus on long-term profits rather than those in the short run. One of the reasons frequently cited

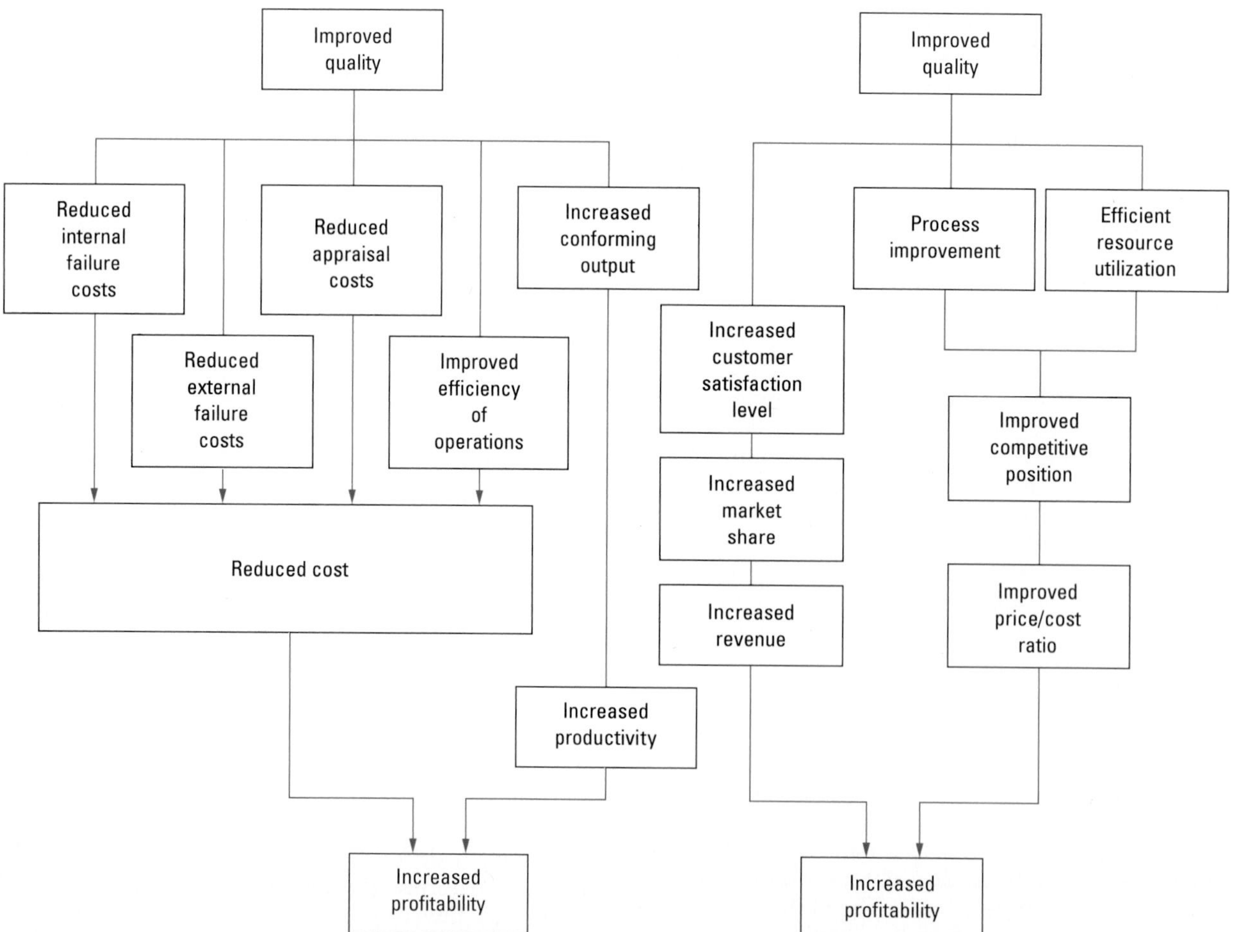

Figure 1-11 Effect of quality on productivity and profitability. (Gabriel A. Pall, *Quality Process Management*, © 1987, pp. 34, 46. Adapted by permission of Prentice Hall, Englewood Cliffs, New Jersey.)

for not adopting a total quality system is the undue emphasis by management on short-term profits. As is well known, short-term profits can be earned by postponing much-needed investment in process improvement equipment and methods, by reducing research and development, or by delaying preventive maintenance. All of these actions contribute nothing to the long-term goal of competitiveness and profitability.

Effect on Market

An improvement in quality can lead to increased market shares, improved competitive position, and increased profitability.

Market Share With a reduction in external failure costs and improved performance of the product in its functional phase, the company is in a position to raise the satisfaction level of its customers. Many of them return to buy the product again. Also, satisfied customers spread the word about good quality, which leads to additional customers. Market share goes up as the quality level goes up. Figure 1-11 demonstrates the effect of quality improvement on profitability via the market route.

Competitive Position The mission of any organization is to stay competitive and to constantly strive to improve its competitive position. Efforts to improve quality help in the attainment of that mission. Figure 1-11 shows that through process control and improvement and efficient resource utilization (reduced production of scrap and rework) a firm can keep its costs minimal. So, even if the selling price remains fixed, an improved price/cost ratio is achieved. Alternately, as quality improves, the firm can charge a higher price for its product. Customer satisfaction and expectations will eventually determine the price of the product. In any event, an improved competitive position paves the way for increased profitability.

1-16 SUMMARY

This chapter has provided the framework on which the concept of the total quality system is based. It has introduced some of the basic terminology and provided an overview of the design, production, and implementation phase of the quality concept. It traces the evolution of quality control and presents specifics on the benefits of quality control, who is responsible for it, and how it is to be adopted. The subject of quality costs is explored, and the tradeoffs among the cost categories that take place with the successful usage of a total quality system are discussed. A critical consideration in the whole scheme is the management of the quality function. Subfunctions within this area are outlined along with the role of management. An important outcome of improvement in quality is an increase in productivity and profitability. The relationship between quality and productivity has been demonstrated in this chapter.

1-17 CASE STUDY

TOTAL QUALITY AT CORNING GLASS WORKS*

Quality: The Competitive Advantage. I like that conference title. For me, as a businessman, it sums it up neatly, because very simply, quality is the competitive advantage.

It's easy to define: "Understand the customer's requirements, and meet them 100 percent of the time." You can quote all the statistics in the world. You can put all the numbers you like on all the pieces of paper you can find. The answer is going to be the same. If you offer quality products and services, you're going to win. It doesn't matter what those products or services are—cars, a banking service, garbage pickup, machine tools, or the defense budget. If they rigorously meet the requirements of their users, they're going to be used.

* Adapted from: J. R. Houghton (1988), Quality: The Competitive Advantage, *Quality Progress*, pp. 16–18.

Quality works! Total quality works totally! And, America, quality is a way out of the jam we're in. Quality can restore us to leadership in a shrinking world where every dog is quickly eating every other dog. Quality can give us back our pride. Quality can make us believe in ourselves again. We can do it. We know how to do it. We invented it.

The notion that quality is the competitive advantage isn't new, at least for me. The real question is, How do we get there from here? The answer is to start with a little faith in our fellow human beings. Why? Because quality, plain and simple, depends on people.

Quality is just a name. Quality is a name we give to people doing it better each and every time. Quality is a name for people trying to do it right. I think that's what America has been about from the start: people working together to do it better.

If we want to win, the first thing we must do is to remember where we started and what we have stood for as a people, as a nation, all these years. America is a country that tries to meet the requirements of its people. You can't achieve higher quality than that. But you can lose your way. You can forget that people matter. You can stop giving people what they want and need. You can start acting like you know it all, like people have to take what you're handing out. That is what we've been doing. We've been paying that sky-high price. That is the real cost of our quality.

But there is a better way to go. It starts with people, with what they can accomplish when they get the chance. At Corning, we've started saying "You're the one who's doing the job, so tell us what you need to do it better, to do it right." Our job, then, is to go out and get what they need. Our people are proud of what they do. They're proud of who they are. They want to do the best that they are able. They realize we're all in this together. They want to pitch in and help.

So we have people who are designing their own machines and teams of people completely redesigning processes, from the office to the factory floor. They are beginning to build quality right into the design. They're all kinds of people, too, because quality is a great equalizer. They're plant workers, managers, engineers, and secretaries. They are treating each other differently than they used to. There is a new air of respect and a new attitude that says "We'd better get on with it, 'cause time's a-wasting."

We are just beginning, of course, and it's not perfect—it probably won't ever be. But we're not talking about perfection. We're talking about working toward error-free work. Work that simply meets a customer's needs the first, and every succeeding, time. We're challenging anything that falls short of that. It has been a radical change for us, and while it's not perfection, I have to say it's awe-inspiring! It has a name, too: Total Quality.

In the four years since we introduced Total Quality, it's become the day-to-day operating philosophy at Corning Glass Works. We came to Total Quality as skeptics. There were a lot of people in our company who didn't really believe. We were typical of most companies, I'm afraid. People weren't sure if quality was going to be permanent or just the managerial flavor of the month. We've had to keep at it constantly.

We are achieving quality slowly. It took us a while to realize that we were up against a task of great magnitude but a philosophy of tremendous positive power. I'll give you an example. Of all the components in a TV set—and I admit to some bias here—the key component is the glass picture-tube bulb. It's the most precise element. The quality of the glass in a tube's panel is as high as that used to make prescription eyeglasses, yet the glass is many times thicker and many times larger. We were the inventors, the innovators. In fact, during the 1930s, Corning supplied the first glass to Alan Dumont, who invented the television in his garage in New Jersey.

We committed large amounts of capital to production during the forties and fifties in time to catch the twin booms for black and white and color television. However, using the technology we developed, the Japanese became a major force in this market. They began to beat us at our own game.

During the 1970s, the U.S. market began to slow. Imports of television sets and picture tubes slashed the sales of our top U.S. customers. Our TV glass business was reeling, but we made a basic decision. We weren't going to be driven out; Corning is in the TV business to stay. As we made that decision it dawned on us that our staying power is directly related to the quality of our products and services. Only with top-quality products would our customers be able to compete with foreign manufacturers. We started with manufacturing operations. We consolidated our operations into our plant in State College, Pennsylvania and began closely analyzing our process so we could significantly improve our performance.

It was the right thing to do. After a thorough application of statistical process control techniques and a commitment of millions of dollars, we tightened our product specifications by 40 percent and boosted output more than 20 percent—and as high as 40 percent on occasion.

Let me be even more specific. A customer can reject a panel—the front of the picture tube—if it has a blister or small bubble-like defect that's as big as twenty thousandths of an inch. In the past our defect rate for blisters was around 1 percent. We thought that was darned good! But our customers were talking in parts per million—and 1 percent is 10,000 parts per million. It wasn't nearly good enough. With the improved process, we've pushed our batting average to around 1,000 parts per million. That's an entire order of magnitude better.

That is Total Quality at work. You can see what it does to a process, but the story doesn't end there, not by a long shot. Our commitment to Total Quality has gone a lot further. Here's what it's meant to some of the people at the State College plant:

- The workers are visiting customer's plants to learn more about their processes and how we can meet their requirements exactly.
- We sent the plant's union president to Japan to study manufacturing techniques and the quality philosophy.
- We're training all our plant employees in basic statistics. We've found that training pays off so much that we've committed 10 percent of time worked to training.

- We now have more than 80 active quality circles and corrective action teams.
- We have leadership. Our plant manager has a Total Quality attitude. On one occasion, he wouldn't ship ware that was slightly out of specification, even though it had been cleared with the customer. Instead, he had it dumped. You don't have to do that too many times to convince everyone that when you say "Total Quality," you mean it.

Corning is simply not going to make or ship products that don't meet our customers' requirements if we can possibly help it. The amazing thing is that we can help it. In our television bulb plant, we are helping it. Here are the results:

- One domestic customer saves $1 million a year by using State College glass in their operations.
- Another reports that State College glass runs at one-third the process loss of glass from the competition.
- When we send our glass for qualification by the Japanese tube makers, they're telling us "We don't believe your numbers—they're too good." This has happened several times.
- Here's the best news of all. Demand for our products is growing so rapidly we've launched a major expansion of this plant. We're building a 175,000-square-foot addition. We're adding a new glass furnace and a new production line. We're hiring about 100 more people. It took time, and we've still only just started!

That, my friends, is the way Total Quality works. Our people did it entirely. That's why I think quality is the ultimate weapon in the battle for competitive advantage.

Now comes the hardest part. How do you get willing and able people to want to change their lives, to want to adopt quality as a philosophy of action? This is where we come in, every one of us. This is what this forum is all about. We've gathered here to share information on quality, but I suggest that we go beyond that. I'd like each and every one of us to start a new role. I'm asking each of us to take up the mantle, the responsibility of leadership. I'm asking each of us to bring quality back home to America—back to American business, back to American education, back to American government.

Fan the fires! Forge quality as the weapon we need to win our battle for survival! We are the keepers of the flame. We have the secret. The magic is in our hands.

Do our government leaders talk about quality? Do you read about it in the press? Why aren't they teaching it in school? Because they don't understand it. They don't understand it because we haven't told them what it is. We haven't made an issue of it. It's high time to change all this. And we are the people who have the obligation to do it.

Put it all together, and we have the power to do what needs to be done. This is what I have been doing. I've been talking to newspeople, telling them I think they're missing the biggest story around. I've been talking to government officials, saying they could be doing a lot more. I've been talking to folks in the education system. And I'm constantly talking to other business people. My message is always the same: Quality, quality, and more quality. Total Quality. We won't survive without it.

But I need your help. Help me spread that message to the farthest corners of this great nation. I suggest that you talk to everyone within reach: your local paper; television and radio stations; government officials, from the President to your congressman to your city councilwoman; educators, from the school board to your kids' principal; and everyone where you work.

Tell them all how you feel. Tell them quality gives you pride. Tell them if we're going to win, we have to have quality in everything we do. It's our competitive advantage. Tell them quality works. Tell them, "America, we can fix it with quality." Tell them it's a smaller world, a single world, and we're at the crossroads in it. We've got to turn toward quality. Tell them if we don't do it now, we'll be second-class citizens in the new global economy.

I, for one, am not going to stand by and let that happen. And I do not think you ought to either.

Questions for Discussion

1. What are some reasons for the negligence of a focused approach toward quality in the past? Why did many businesses in the United States not adopt a total quality system during the period of 1940 to 1970?
2. What factors do you feel made Corning Glass Works turn around in their approach to producing a quality product?
3. Describe specific actions taken by Corning to pursue the goal of quality control and improvement forever.
4. Select an industry of your choice. Discuss specific actions that a company should take to adopt and implement a total quality system.
5. Discuss how a total quality system at Corning helped reduce total cost and improve productivity.
6. Explain the role of an individual in creating a quality-conscious environment.

KEY TERMS

Acceptance sampling plans
Attributes
Cause-and-effect diagram
Causes
  Common or chance
  Special or assignable
Customer service
Defect
Fishbone diagram
Inspection
Ishikawa diagram
Liability
  Product
  Strict
Management of quality
  Planning for quality
  Organizing for quality
  Staffing for quality
  Directing for quality
  Controlling for quality
Manufacturing
Manufacturing engineering
Marketing
Nonconformity
Nonconforming unit
Packaging
Productivity
Product design
Product planning
Purchasing
Quality
  Quality of design
  Quality of conformance
  Quality of performance
  Responsibility for quality
Quality assurance
Quality circles
Quality control
  Benefits of quality control
  Responsibility for quality control
Quality cost mesurement
  Labor base index
  Cost base index
  Sales base index
  Unit base index
Quality costs
  Prevention costs
  Appraisal costs
  Internal failure costs
  External failure costs
Quality improvement
  Commitment stage
  Consolidation stage
  Maturity stage
Reliability
Sampling
Specification
Standard
Statistical process control
  On-line process control
  Off-line process control
Systems approach
Total quality control
Total quality system
Training
Variables
Zero defects program

EXERCISES

1-1 Define quality, and explain its role in the modern business environment.

1-2 What are the three major aspects of quality? Explain the relationship between them.

1-3 Distinguish the philosophical difference of the underlying concepts of statistical process control and acceptance sampling plans.

1-4 Explain the role of the quality assurance function.

1-5 What is a quality circle? Describe an application where it could be used.

1-6 What are the benefits of quality control?

1-7 Discuss the responsibilities of the different departments of an organization as far as the quality function is concerned.

1-8 Define a quality system.

1-9 Discuss the different elements of a total quality system. Give an example of the implementation of such a system with respect to a selected company.

1-10 Explain the difference between quality control and quality improvement.

1-11 Describe the stages of quality improvement. Also, discuss the costs incurred in each stage.

1-12 What are the major categories of quality costs? Explain each of them, and give examples.

1-13 Explain the various indices for measuring quality costs. Discuss the relative advantages of each.

1-14 Discuss the role of top management in the planning function associated with the management of quality.

1-15 What are the various forms of organizational structures? Discuss how the quality function is accomplished through such structures?

1-16 Select a company of your choice. Discuss the organizational structure that exists to achieve the quality commitment.

1-17 Explain how quality affects productivity. Discuss the implications on cost.

1-18 Select a company for which you have access to profit and cost data. Draw a graph of total quality costs over the past five years, and indicate the amount in each of the four cost categories. Compare this data with the profit for the same period. What inferences can you draw?

REFERENCES

American Society for Quality Control (1971). *Quality Costs—What and How,* 2nd edition. ASQC, Milwaukee, WI.

American Society for Quality Control (1979). *ANSI/ASQC Standard Z-1.5-1979, Generic Guidelines for Quality Systems,* ASQC, Milwaukee, WI.

American Society for Quality Control, Statistics Division (1983). *Glossary and Tables for Statistical Quality Control,* 2nd edition. SQC, Milwaukee, WI.

American Society for Quality Control (1987). *ANSI/ASQC Standard A3-1987, Quality Systems Terminology,* ASQC, Milwaukee, WI.

Banks, J. (1989). *Principles of Quality Control.* John Wiley & Sons, New York.

Crosby, P. B. (1979). *Quality Is Free.* McGraw-Hill, New York.

Evans, J. R., and Lindsay, W. M. (1989). *The Management and Control of Quality.* West, St. Paul, MN.

Feigenbaum, A. V. (1983). *Total Quality Control.* McGraw-Hill, New York.

Garvin, D. A. (1984). "What Does Product Quality Really Mean?" *Sloan Management Review,* 26(1), pp. 25–43.

Houghton, J. R. (1988). "Quality—The Competitive Advantage," *Quality Progress,* 21(2), pp. 16–18.

Juran, J. M., (Ed.) (1974). *Quality Control Handbook,* 3rd edition. McGraw-Hill, New York.

Pall, G. A. (1987). *Quality Process Management,* Prentice-Hall, Englewood Cliffs, NJ.

Schilling, E. G. (1984). "The Role of Statistics in the Management of Quality," *Quality Progress,* 17(8), p. 33.

Taguchi, G. (1986). *Introduction to Quality Engineering: Designing Quality into Products and Processes.* Asian Productivity Organization (available in North America, U.K., and Western Europe from the American Supplier Institute, Inc. and UNIPUB/Kraus International Publications, White Plains, New York).

Taguchi, G., and Wu, Yuin (1979). *Introduction to Off-Line Quality Control.* Central Japan Quality Control Association, Nagoya.

U.S. Department of Commerce, National Bureau of Standards (1983). *NBS Handbook 130, Model State Laws and Regulations,* Gaithersberg, MD.

Wadsworth, H. M., Stephens, K. S., and Godfrey, A. B. (1986). *Modern Methods for Quality Control and Improvement.* John Wiley & Sons, New York.

Walsh, L., Wursten, R., and Kimber, R. J., (Eds.) (1986). *Quality Management Handbook.* Marcel Dekker, New York.

CHAPTER

2

Some Philosophies and Their Impact on Quality

CHAPTER OUTLINE

2-1 INTRODUCTION

Several people have made significant contributions in the field of quality control. This chapter takes a look at the philosophical ideas of three persons, namely W. Edwards Deming, Ph.D., Philip B. Crosby, and Joseph M. Juran, Ph.D. These three pioneers have played a fundamental role in the adoption and integration of quality assurance and control in industry. Through their teachings, articles, books, and consultation, they have taught management the significance of quality control. Management commitment is the key to a successful program in quality. By convincing management of the need to use a quality program on a total company-wide basis, the three men have created a positive change in the attitude of management. Industries in the United States have been able to turn around and focus on finding ways to satisfy customers in the manufacturing and service sectors. A change has taken place in corporate culture. The attitude toward acceptance of an ongoing quality control and improvement program is a positive one. While all three men have influenced U.S. industry, Deming and Juran have also had an enormous impact on Japanese industry. Deming was instrumental in turning around the quality of Japanese products after World War II (a difficult task). But success came after years of following his philosophy. Of course, Deming now has received his due recognition in the United States.

This chapter emphasizes Deming's philosophy and his 14 points for management that are fundamental to the implementation of a quality program. These points should be thoroughly understood by management, since a change in the system can come only through their involvement. The 14 points provide a "road map" for management. Crosby's and Juran's philosophies are also discussed, and comparison is made of the three philosophies. All three have the same goal in mind of creating and adopting a world-class quality culture. Although the paths to achieving this goal may be slightly different, a company could benefit by combining the philosophies of these three quality experts.

2-2 W. EDWARDS DEMING AND HIS CONTRIBUTION

Historical Background

W. Edwards Deming is the renowned consultant credited with much of the high-quality work in the Japanese industrial world since World War II. His educational background is in mathematics and physics, and he received his Ph.D. from Yale University in 1928. He has a thorough knowledge of statistical quality control methods. In 1939 he joined the Bureau of the Census and continued to work for it and the War Department during World War II. After the war he served in many advisory capacities, including a position as the advisor on sampling techniques to the Supreme Command of the Allied Powers in 1947 and 1950.

In 1950 the Union of Japanese Scientists and Engineers (JUSE) invited Deming to address their leading industrialists. Up through that point in time, Japan had a poor reputation for quality. They were concerned about capturing foreign markets because their domestic economy was shattered at the end of the war. Deming was instrumental in instilling in them the ways in which they could improve the slipshod quality of their products. Many were skeptical initially. However, as they took Deming's advice and developed a total philosophical commitment to his methods, Japanese quality moved to the forefront in the world. What we see today is the outcome of adopting Deming's philosophy over the last four decades. Improvement in quality did not happen overnight, but Deming knew with certainty that it would happen. To this day, the Japanese continue to use the ideas of Deming and seek ways to constantly improve their processes and products. Deming was bestowed the prestigious Second Order Medal of the Sacred Treasure by Emperor Hirohito for his contributions to the Japanese economy. In 1951 the Union of Japanese Scientists and Engineers instituted the coveted Deming Award, an annual award given to the individual or firm contributing most to the advancement of industrial quality. Recipients of this award include companies like Toyota, Nissan, Nippon Steel, and Hitachi. The first U.S. company to win the Deming Award was Texas Instruments in 1985.

It is somewhat ironic that the biggest name in Japanese quality control is an American. Truth is stranger than fiction! At the end of World War II, complacent U.S. companies shunned Deming's advice. During that period, demand for U.S. goods was high, and quality was acceptable. Whatever was produced was devoured by the consumer. In the domestic market there was very little competition. Given this setting, major companies thought that it would be foolish to change their way of doing things. They failed to look at the long-term competition that would evolve. The plight of the U.S. industry in the seventies and eighties is now, of course, history. It seems that the message associated with Deming's philosophy is finally spreading in the United States. The big automobile companies such as Ford Motor Company and General Motors are adopting Deming's teachings. Other companies are following suit. Once the larger companies accept the new emphasis on quality, they will impose it on their suppliers and vendors. This trend is already happening today. The message of adopting a total company-wide quality philosophy is filtering down from the larger corporations to the medium and small companies. Eventually, everyone will be forced to adopt it. To many it will be a means to survival—there will be no other alternative.

Philosophy

Deming's philosophy places an emphasis on the role of management. Almost 85 percent of the problems in industry can be tackled by management alone. These tasks involve changing the system of operation and are not influenced by the workers. Workers *do* have the responsibility of communicating to management the information they possess regarding the system, for both must work in harmony. The management style that Deming preaches deals with a holistic approach that views the organization as an integrated entity. He says to plan for the long run and provide a course of action for the short run. In the past, many U.S. companies focused instead on short-term gains.

Deming believes in the adoption of a total quality program and emphasizes the neverending nature of quality control in the quality improvement process. Such a program leads to desired goals of improved quality, customer satisfaction, higher productivity, and lower total costs in the long run. One of his main philosophical ideas disproves the myth that an improvement in quality and increase in productivity cannot go hand in hand. On the contrary, he demonstrates that an improvement in quality will inevitably lead to an increase in available capacity and an improvement in productivity. Furthermore, improved quality will yield the production of less scrap and rework and thus a decrease in costs and an increase in profit. Additionally, improved quality produces a competitive edge in the market and aids in capturing an increased market share, which also improves profits. As experience demonstrates, these desirable changes occur over an extended period of time. Thus, Deming's philosophy does not offer a "quick fix" to problems but rather a plan of action for achievement of long-term goals. He stresses the need for firms to develop a corporate culture where one abandons such short-term goals as quarterly profits. Deming's philosophy is something that must be adopted, practiced, and used as a way of life in an organization. The principles should be relearned and refined based on experience in the particular organizational setting. At the heart of this philosophy is the need for management and workers to speak a common language. This is the language of statistics—statistical process control. Real benefits from the adoption of Deming's philosophy will occur only when everyone associated with the process understands the statistical foundations and principles for use in process control and improvement.

Therefore, the fundamental ideas in Deming's philosophy deal with the understanding and use of statistical tools and a change in management attitude. The 14 points that Deming provides for management identify a framework for action. They provide a path for management to follow in order to be competitive in the long run. Management must develop a commitment to these points in thought, word, and deed if the plan is to work. These points are discussed in detail later in this chapter.

2-3 EXTENDED PROCESS

The concept of an extended process as envisioned by Deming expands the traditional imaginary boundaries of an organization to include suppliers, customers, investors, employees, and the community. Figure 2-1 shows an extended process. An organization consists of people, machines, materials, methods, and money. The extended process includes a key entity, namely, the consumer. An organization is in business to satisfy the consumer. This should be its primary goal. Goals such as providing the investors an acceptable rate of return are secondary. Achievement of the primary goal of customer satisfaction will automatically cause other secondary goals to be realized. This primary goal is especially relevant to a provider of a service; here the customer is more directly involved with the performer of the service. Hence, it makes sense to include the customer as a vital component of the extended process.

An organization must continuously determine the needs of the customer by means of consumer research. Information obtained from such analysis must be integrated into the design of the product. Such a procedure enables the organization to maximize customer satisfaction. As the needs and desires of customers change with time, changes in the product design should reflect these changes if the company is to keep or expand its market share. Designing the process to produce a product as required by the customer will then be the next step for the company.

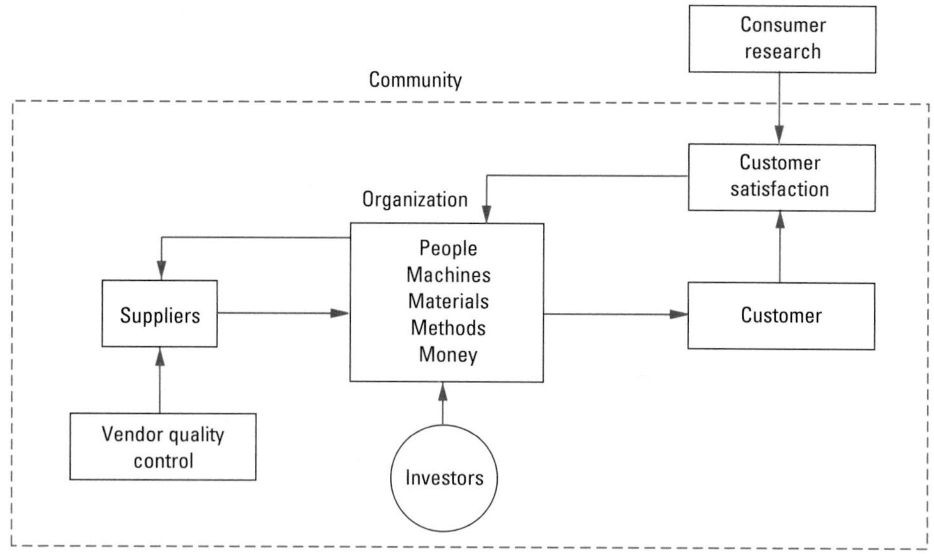

Figure 2-1 An extended process in Deming's philosophy.

In a broader sense, the community in which the organization operates is also part of this extended process. This community includes consumers, employees, and anyone else who is influenced by the operations of the company, directly or indirectly. It is well known that an acceptable and happy community that supports the activities of the organization will make it easier for the company to achieve a total quality program. Support from the community ensures one less obstacle in the resistance to the changes proposed by Deming.

Suppliers are another component of the extended process. The production of a quality item is influenced by the quality of the incoming raw materials, parts, and components. An effort must be made to ensure that suppliers or vendors are consistent in the quality of their product. Companies may demand evidence of quality control measures from the suppliers in order to accept the incoming material. Deming's philosophy promotes the development of a long-term relationship between the supplier and the organization. This promotes good quality, because the supplier knows that as long as it can provide acceptable quality, it will retain its business with the company. Furthermore, the supplier does not feel like an outsider. The supplier has the same degree of motivation as the organization to produce an acceptable product since it is part of the same team. If the organization's market share improves due to product or service acceptance by the customer, an increase in the input from the suppliers will result.

 2-4 DEMING'S 14 POINTS FOR MANAGEMENT

The focus of Deming's philosophy is on management. Since a major proportion of problems are those that can be solved by management, Deming points out that management cannot shun its responsibility and try to blame others. Although a minority of problems can be attributed to the suppliers or the workers, Deming sees the need for a fundamental change in the style of management and also in the corporate culture.

Under the Deming philosophy, management must create an environment of security for the workers where they feel a pride in workmanship and are rewarded accordingly. The two groups must work as a team along with the suppliers and investors. The corporate culture should remove fear from the system so that workers may feel comfortable in recommending changes to the product or process. Most importantly, management must be committed to the adoption and implementation of a total quality system. This involvement in an ongoing process improvement must be real, so that a sense of trust may develop between the employees and management. Deming's 14 points for management are guidelines that provide a sense of direction. Deming's methods incorporate the use of statistical tools. The adoption of these principles will sustain productivity and competitiveness of the company in the long run. A good discussion of these points may be found in books by Deming (1982, 1986). Scherkenbach (1986), Gitlow and Gitlow (1987), and Walton (1988, 1990) provide explanations and interpretations of each of the 14 points.

Point 1: *Create and publish to all employees a statement of the aims and purposes of the company or other organization. The management must demonstrate constantly their commitment to this statement.**

This principle stresses the need for the creation of strategic plans to steer the company in the right direction in the long run. Mission statements should be developed and clearly expressed such that everyone in the organization understands them. This includes top management, middle management, supervisors, workers, staff personnel, vendors, investors, and the community in which the business is located. Examples of mission statements are the continued improvement of quality and productivity, better competitive position, stable employment, ensuring a company's existence in the future by staying competitive, and reasonable return for the investors. Such statements need not give a numerical value for each of these goals. However, feasible means of making the mission statement a living document, such that the stated goals may be achieved, should exist. Management must take the lead in developing such strategic plans with input from all levels. The challenges of the future should be taken into account in the formulation phase. Management should further demonstrate a commitment to the plan by creating an atmosphere where everyone is convinced of its utility.

Product Improvement Cycle Providing a stated rate of return on investment to the investors should not be the strategic goal of a company. The customers are the most important element, and satisfying them through better-quality products or services should be the driving force in the creation of strategic plans. The old approach of designing a product, producing it, and marketing it to customers without determining their needs is no longer valid. Instead, the new approach is a four-step cycle that is customer-driven. Figure 2-2 shows this cycle, which includes designing the product (based on needs of the customer), making and testing it in the laboratory, selling it on the market, determining its performance in service, conducting market research to determine reactions from the consumer and reasons of dissatisfaction, and using this information to start the cycle again. This approach supports the integration of the phases of quality of design, conformance, and performance discussed in Chapter 1. Determination of customer needs in clearly understood terms is key to the improvement of product quality. For instance, saying that the customer prefers a better refrigerator that is less noisy and can produce ice quickly is not sufficient. What noise level (say, in decibels) is acceptable? Also, within how much time (say, in minutes) does the customer expect the ice to be produced? These attributes should be clarified in order to help achieve a better product design.

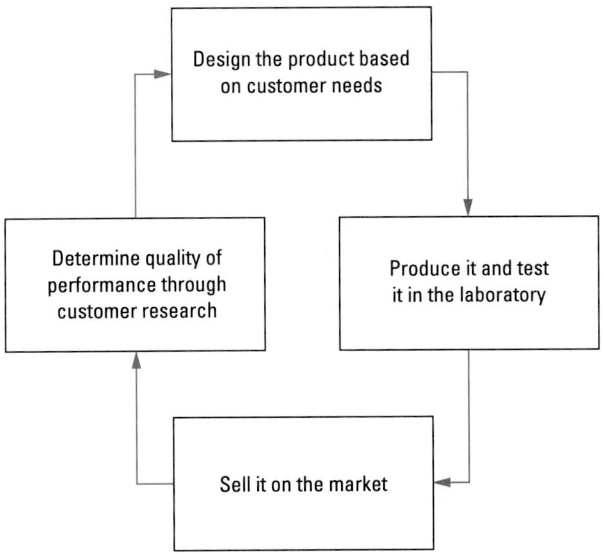

Figure 2-2 Product improvement cycle.

Constancy and Consistency of Purpose Management should have the foresight to establish a constancy of purpose for the long run. This implies setting a course for the mean or the average of the goal or performance measure (for example, all departments within the organization pursuing a common objective of quality improvement). Too often, attention on short-term results such as weekly production reports or quarterly profits deters management from concentrating on the more important strategic issues. Actions that would create a profit for the next quarter may not necessarily create a profit for the next 10 years. Management must be innovative. They

* Deming's 14 points (January 1990 revision) reprinted by permission of MIT and W. Edwards Deming from *Quality, Productivity, and Competitive Position* and *Out of the Crisis* by W. Edwards Deming. Published by MIT, Center for Advanced Engineering Study, Cambridge, MA 02139. Copyright 1986 by W. Edwards Deming.

must allocate resources for long-term planning including consumer research, training of personnel and supervisors, education of management and personnel in the new philosophies, cost of determining quality of performance, possible new methods of production or changes in equipment, and new materials. Research and education should take a priority along with a desire to constantly improve the design of the product or service.

U.S. industries need to reevaluate their time frames. They should strive to keep companies in a competitive position for years to come by taking appropriate actions today. Of course, blame for actions emphasizing the short term rests with management itself. Managers have often been fired for not yielding short-term profits. This behavior has to change, with the new corporate culture having a proper focus for long-term survival. Actions in support of this new philosophy will provide employment security for all and create a stable and happy environment leading to improved productivity.

In addition to constancy of purpose, there should be a consistency of purpose. This means that the variability or dispersion associated with the long-term objectives should be small. For example, are all units of the company working towards the company goal to improve quality synergistically? Or are they working for a departmental subgoal which may be to increase production? Figure 2-3 depicts the concepts of constancy and consistency of purpose. Deming clarifies this point further by stating, "Doing your best is not good enough. You have to know what to do. Then do your best." Management should also accept the fact that variability exists and will continue to exist in any operation. What they must try to do is determine ways in which this variation can be reduced. And this is a neverending process.

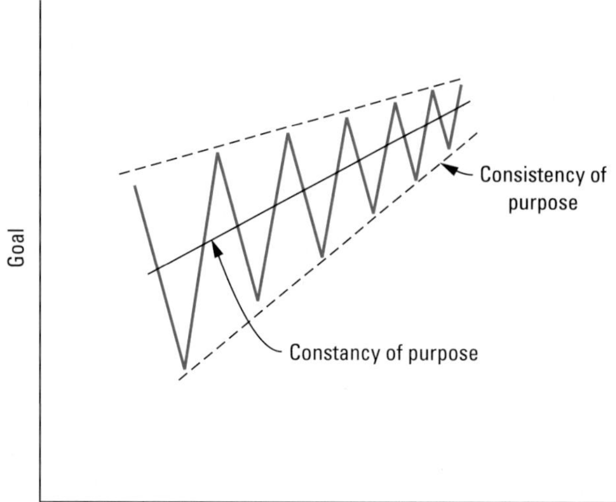

Figure 2-3 Constancy and consistency of purpose.

Point 2: *Learn the new philosophy, top management and everybody.*

This point deals with the adoption of the new attitude of quality consciousness. Previously acceptable levels of defects should be abandoned with the theme of pursuing the neverending process of improvement. Human beings are resistant to change. Managers who have been successful under the old system where certain levels of defects were acceptable may find it difficult to accept the new philosophy. Overcoming this resistance is a formidable task to be accomplished by management. Also, the focus has to change from limiting defects caused by not meeting certain specification limits to addressing customer requirements. Furthermore, even if specification limits are based on the needs of the customer, meeting specifications is not enough. Rather, one must try to continually reduce the variability of the products' characteristics.

One reason for U.S. industries losing their global market share in the eighties was that companies were too busy looking at each other. They ignored the importance of satisfying customer needs. By contrast, Japanese companies were looking at the needs of customers and they made improvements in processes and products that led to satisfied customers who came back for more. Just meeting the competition is not a long-term strategy. A change must take place in the company so as to focus on the customer and not the competition. In the case of a stable process, improvements in the system can be created by management alone.

We have to stop accepting poor-quality goods and services. Declaring any level of defect to be acceptable in a contract leads one to believe that defects are acceptable. For example, if a contract for the acceptance of incoming parts specifies that a defective rate of 4 units in 1000 is acceptable, this will support the philosophy that defects are tolerated. Adopting such a plan will also ensure that incoming parts will be 0.4% defective. It is necessary to change this philosophy and adopt a system where no defectives are tolerated. In the event that the supplier has difficulty in meeting this criterion, the company should work with the vendor in a cooperative manner to identify ways in which the vendor can improve its quality. After all, it is important to realize that the supplier and the organization are part of the same system known as the extended process. Improvement in quality will take place when both help each other.

Point 3: *Understand the purpose of inspection, for improvement of processes and reduction of cost.*

Quality has to be designed into the product; it cannot be inspected into it. Creating a "design for manufacturability" is important since making what is designed must be feasible. Inspection is merely a process of separating the acceptable from the unacceptable. It does not address the root cause of the problem, that is, what is causing the production of nonconformities and how to eliminate them. The emphasis has to be on defect prevention rather than on defect detection.

The production of unacceptable items (those not meeting specifications) is not free. Some proportion of these items can be reworked, but others may have to be scrapped. Moreover, resources are used to produce these items, and hence the manufacturer adjusts the unit price of the product based on the proportion of nonconforming items. Not only does this lead to an increased unit price and thereby lower market share, but the manufacturer's available capacity is effectively reduced. Thus, the elimination of nonconformities reduces the unit cost and increases available capacity.

Drawbacks of Mass Inspection Depending on mass inspection to separate the good from the bad does not provide the incentive to meticulously investigate the process in order to prevent the occurrence of defects. In fact, such a dependence ensures that defects will continue. Also, if more than one person is responsible for inspection, either at different stages of production or after the finished product, even 100 percent inspection may not eliminate all the defectives. The reason is that each inspector may not do an effective job if he or she assumes that the other inspectors will detect the presence of nonconformities. If every inspector has this belief, no one assumes responsibility, which results in defects that slip by. Additionally, with 100 percent inspection, inspector fatigue comes into play, which also interferes with the detection of all nonconformities.

Mass inspection stems from an attitude of mistrust and fails to yield improvement in the process. Reliance on it implies that defects are expected. Deming believes that "routine 100 percent inspection is the same thing as planning for defects, acknowledgement that the process cannot make the product correctly, or that specifications made no sense in the first place" (Deming, 1982). We should not tolerate the mentality that allows the production of defects. Instead, feedback from the customer and the process should be used to monitor and control the process.

Action based on feedback information should be done on a real-time basis. However, a word of caution is necessary regarding the time frame on which to take action based on feedback information. Adjustments to the process based on individual measurements rather than on statistical signals will cause more variability than when the process is left alone. This usually results in overcontrol and does not bring stability to the process in terms of reducing the fluctuation of the characteristic under consideration. For example, consider the outside diameter of a shaft being turned on a lathe. The nominal diameter might be 50 mm, with specifications of 50 ± 2 mm. Say an operator produces a shaft that has a diameter of 51 mm and adjusts his machine to a lower setting with the intention of reducing the diameter of the next part produced. If the operator makes similar subsequent adjustments (that is, if the part has a smaller diameter than the nominal value and he makes an upward adjustment on the machine based on each shaft produced), the end result will be increased variability in the diameter. On the other hand, if adjustments are made based on a statistical control chart for the average diameter—which states when to leave the process even if there is variation and when to take corrective action— the effect will be to cause an improvement in the process. Details on statistical control charts will be discussed in later chapters.

Deming's Recommendation If inspection must be performed for critical parts or assemblies, Deming advocates a plan that minimizes the total cost of incoming materials and the final product. The plan is an inspect-all-or-none rule. Such a plan is derived from a basis of statistical evidence of quality and may be applied to a stable process. This plan is known as the *kp rule* and is discussed in Chapter 9.

In order to go from defect detection to defect prevention, an organization must consider all of the elements of the extended process. Companies must help vendors improve their quality by communicating to them what the precise problems are with their product. Therefore, they should work together on ways to improve the vendor's process if incoming quality is a problem area. Working on process improvement through such mutual assistance will facilitate the implementation of this goal.

Point 4: *End the practice of awarding business on the basis of price tag alone.*

Many companies, as well as state and federal governments, award contracts to the lowest bidder as long as they minimally satisfy certain specifications defined in the call for bids. However, as these companies and agencies review the submitted proposals, they usually see no information regarding the use of statistical quality control in the vendor's plants. Such procedures for awarding contracts should cease. Companies should thoroughly review the system of total quality consciousness as it exists in each organization submitting a bid. What quality assurance procedures are used? What methods are used for the control and improvement of quality? What is the attitude of management towards quality? Answers to these questions should, along with price, be used to select a vendor. In the long run, such a judicious process of selection leads to a minimization of total cost.

Unless the quality aspect is considered, the effective price per unit that a company would pay a vendor would be understated and in some cases unknown. Knowledge of the fraction of nonconforming products and the stability of the process will provide a better estimate of the price per unit that the company ends up paying. For example, suppose there are three vendors A, B, and C submitting bids of \$15, \$16, and \$17 per unit, respectively. If the contract is awarded on the basis of price alone, vendor A will get the job.

Now consider the following information on the existing quality levels of the three vendors. Vendor B has started using techniques of statistical process control and has a rather stable defective rate of 8 percent. The vendor is constantly working on methods of process improvement. The effective price the company would pay vendor B for the acceptable items is $\$16/(1 - 0.08) = \$17.39$ per unit (assuming that defectives cannot be returned to the vendor for credit). Vendor C has adopted for some time the total quality philosophy of continual process improvement and has been successful in reducing the process defective rate to 2 percent. Therefore, the effective price the company would pay vendor C for the acceptable items is $\$17/(1-0.02) = \$17.35$ per unit. Suppose vendor A has no formal documentation on the stability of its process. It does not use any statistical procedures to determine when the process is out of control. The outgoing product goes through sampling inspection to determine which ones should be shipped to the company. In this case, the vendor has no information on whether the process is stable, what its capability is, or how to improve on the process. Thus, the effective price the company would pay vendor A for the acceptable items is unknown. This demonstrates the drawback of using price as the only basis for selection.

Principles of Vendor Selection In selecting a vendor, the total cost (which includes the purchase cost plus the cost to put the material into production) should be taken into account. A company using Deming's philosophy is buying not only a vendor's products but also its process. Purchasing agents have an important role to play in the extended process. They must understand the precise problems encountered with the purchased material as it moves through the extended process of manufacture, assembly, and eventual shipment to the consumer. The buyers must be familiar with statistical methods so as to assess the quality of the vendor's plant and to make rational decisions. They must be able to determine the degree of customer satisfaction with the products, tell what features are not liked, and convey all related information to the vendor. Such information will provide the vendor some guidelines regarding what to improve in its product and thereby what changes to incorporate in its process. Information on whether the product satisfies certain specifications is not enough. The new role of the purchasing agent will close the gap between vendor and buyer, allowing them to work as a team in choosing methods and materials to improve customer satisfaction with the product.

Management must change the process through which vendor selection is conducted. An area where a definite change is needed is the municipal transit authority in urban areas. These agencies are forced to select the lowest bidder in order to comply with the policy set by the Urban Transit Authority of the United States. The poor state of affairs caused by complying with this policy is visible in many urban areas around the country.

Another important principle concerns the reduction of the number of suppliers for any given item. The goal is to move toward having a single supplier for an item. Companies in the United States have had multiple vendors for several reasons, including a fear of price increases, a vendor's inability to meet projected increases in demand, and a vendor's lack of timeliness in meeting delivery schedules. There are several disadvantages to having multiple vendors for each item purchased. First, it promotes a feeling of mistrust toward the vendor and thereby creates a short-term, price-dependent relationship between the buyer and the vendor. Furthermore, the vendor has no motivation to change its process to meet the buyer's specifications. The vendor knows that the buyer is also working with other vendors and may select another vendor if its price is lower. There is no long-term commitment between the buyer and vendor in such a situation.

Other disadvantages exist in terms of cost. Increased paperwork leads to increased order preparation costs. Travel costs of the vendor to purchaser sites increase. A loss of volume discounts occurs, since bulk order sizes are reduced by having more than one vendor for the same part. Setup costs also go up because the buyer's process changes when the incoming supplier is changed. Machine settings may have to be changed along with tooling. In continuous process industries, such as chemical companies producing sulfuric acid, a change in the incoming raw materials may require changes in the proportion of the composition mix created by adding two or more input ingredients. Also, if the process is to be idle during the set-up period, the effective capacity of the process will be reduced. Also, the cost of training people who work with vendors is higher for multiple vendors. One major disadvantage is that there is an increased variability in the incoming quality, even if the individual vendor's process is stable. Figure 2-4 explains this concept. Suppose there are three vendors A, B, and C, each quite stable and having a small dispersion as far as the quality characteristic of interest are concerned (say, density of a red color pigment in producing a dye). However, the combined incoming product of three good suppliers may turn out to be mediocre. This happens because of the intervendor variability.

Many benefits are gained by moving to a single vendor for each item purchased. The disadvantages mentioned in the previous paragraphs can be eliminated. In addition, selecting a quality-conscious vendor for a long-term relationship promotes the improvement of quality. The vendor can afford to make changes in its process, based on the needs of the customer, as communicated by the purchaser. The vendor knows that there is no fear of losing the contract; there is a long-term commitment. Such a relationship permits open negotiation of the contract so that the buyer and the supplier may work together to meet the needs of the customer.

Point 5: *Improve constantly and forever the system of production and service.*

Deming's philosophy is to move from defect detection to defect prevention and continue with process improvement to meet and exceed customer requirements on a neverending basis. Defect prevention and process improvement are carried out by the use of statistical methods. Statistical training is therefore a necessity for everyone and should be implemented on a gradual basis.

Deming Cycle The continuous cycle of process improvement is based on the scientific method for addressing problems and was originally called the *Shewhart cycle* after its originator Walter A. Shewhart, who is also the discoverer of the technique of

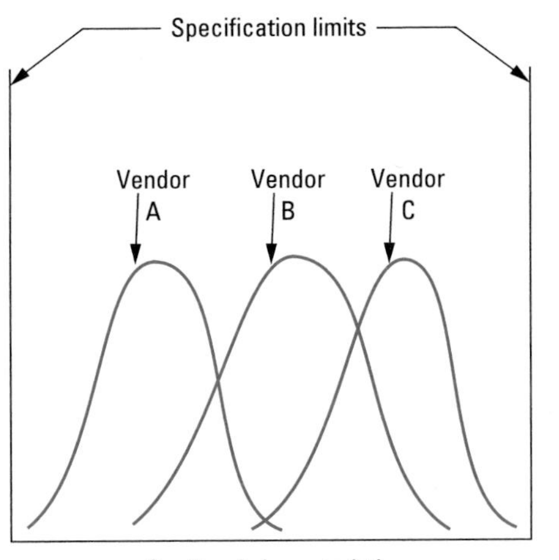

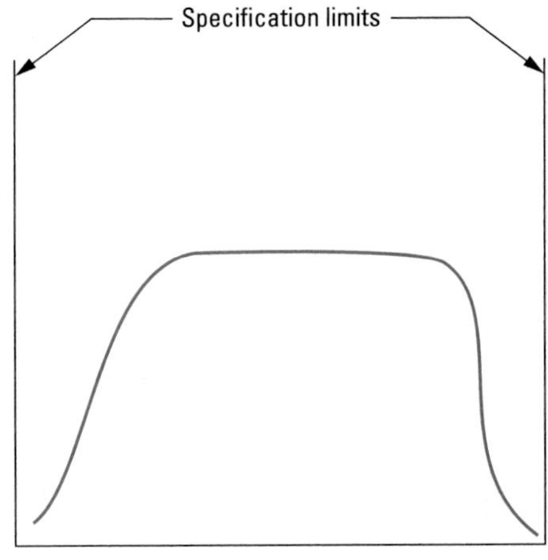

Figure 2-4 Mediocre incoming quality due to multiple vendors.

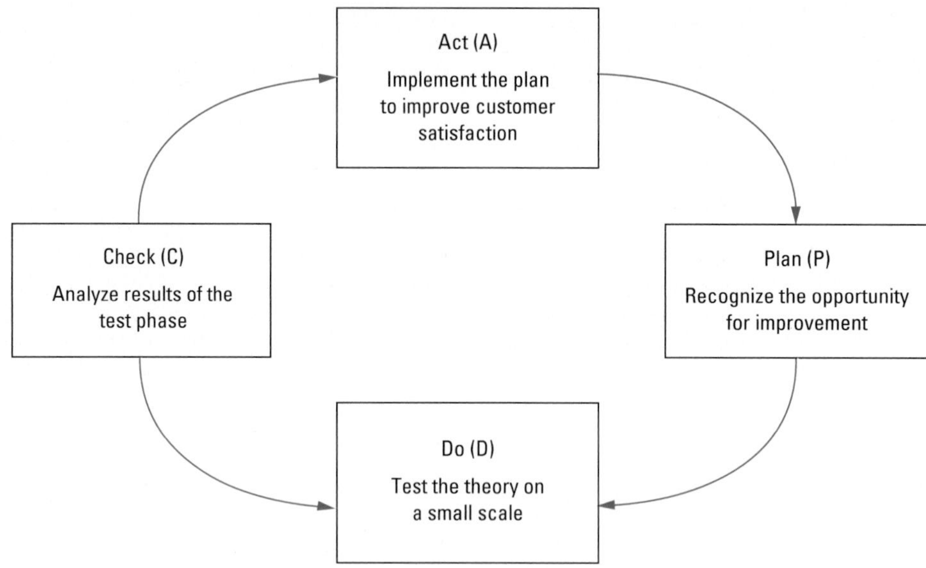

Figure 2-5 The Deming cycle.

control charts. In the 1950s the Japanese renamed it the *Deming cycle,* which consists of four basic stages—*plan, do, check,* and *act*—usually referred to as the PDCA cycle. The Deming cycle is shown in Figure 2-5, and the four stages of the cycle are discussed below.

Plan Stage. The plan stage consists of recognizing and operationally defining the opportunity for improvement. It also involves developing a framework to theorize as to the effect of the controllable process variables on process performance. Since customer satisfaction is the focal point, the degree of difference between customer needs (as obtained through market survey and consumer research) and process performance (obtained as feedback information) is analyzed. Figure 2-6 graphically depicts the opportunity for improvement. The goal is to reduce this difference between customer needs and process performance. One must hypothesize as to possible relationships between the variables in the process and their effect on producing a product that satisfies

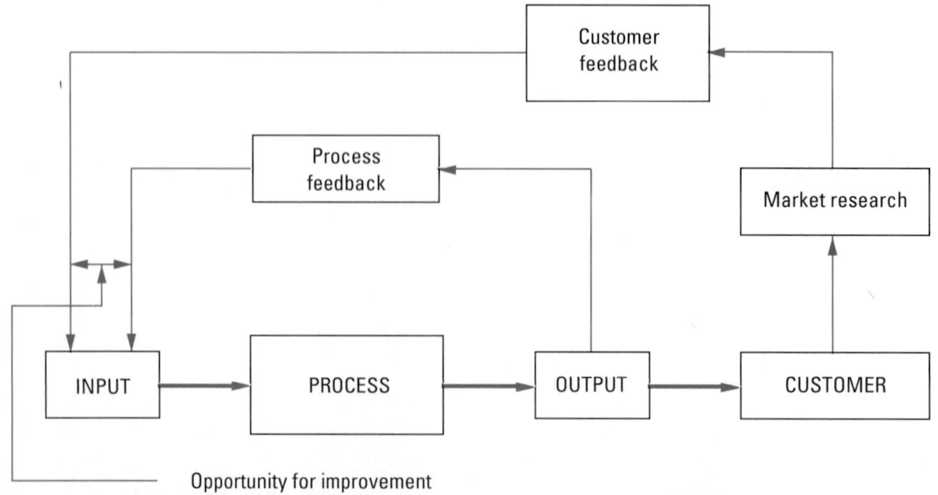

Figure 2-6 Plan stage of Deming cycle.

the customer. For instance, a company making paint may have found that one major concern of the customer is the drying time; the preferred time may be 1 minute. Information based on feedback from the output of the process says that the actual drying time is 1.5 minutes. Hence, at this planning stage, the opportunity for improvement, in operational terms, is to reduce the drying time by 0.5 minute.

The next task is to determine an approach to accomplish a reduction of drying time of 0.5 minute. This will require knowledge of the components used, process parameter settings, and interaction between them in order to hypothesize as to their precise effect on drying time. Thus quality of design and quality of conformance studies come into the picture. Suppose it is hypothesized that reducing a certain ingredient A by 5 percent in the initial mixing process will reduce the drying time by 0.5 minute. This hypothesis will be investigated in the following steps.

Do Stage. The theory and course of action developed in the plan stage is put into action in the do stage. Trial runs are conducted in a laboratory or prototype setting. Feedback information is obtained from the customer and the process. Continuing with the paint example, at this stage the paint company will test the proposed plan on a small scale. They will reduce the proportion of component A by 5 percent in the initial mixing process and obtain the product.

Check Stage. In the check stage, the results of conducting the plan on a small scale are investigated. Is the degree of difference between customer needs and process performance reduced by adopting the plan? Are there any potential drawbacks relating to other quality characteristics that are important to the customer? Answers to such questions are obtained at this stage. Statistical methods will be of assistance in analyzing the results. For example, with the objective of reducing the drying time by 0.5 minute, samples will be taken from the modified output. An analysis may be conducted to determine the mean drying time and a measure of variability associated with it. Suppose the analysis yields a mean drying time of 1.3 minutes with a standard deviation of 0.2 minute. Prior to the modification, the mean was 1.5 minutes with a standard deviation of 0.3 minute, say. The results show a positive improvement of the product which will reduce the degree of customer dissatisfaction.

Act Stage. In the act stage a decision is made to implement the plan to increase customer satisfaction. If the results of the analysis conducted in the previous stage are positive, then the proposed plan will be adopted. Feedback will be obtained from the process and the customer after full-scale implementation. Such information will provide a true measure of success of the plan. One should be aware that customers' needs are not constant. They change with time, competition, societal outlook, and other factors. Therefore, it should be determined if the proposed plan is keeping abreast of those changing customer needs. Doing so may require further changes in plans whereby the neverending process of improvement continues once again with the plan stage. If the results of the check stage show no significant improvement in meeting customer needs, alternate plans must be developed, and the cycle continues. In the paint example, a positive improvement in the process caused a reduction in the drying time. The suggested procedure of reducing the proportion of ingredient A by 5 percent is then implemented on a full-scale. The drying time of the paint produced by this new process is found. Is the mean drying time 1.3 minutes with a standard deviation of 0.2 minute, as for the previous phase? Or has full-scale implementation caused these statistics to change? If so, what are they? What can be done to further reduce the mean drying time and the standard deviation of drying time? Customer needs are determined once again. Do they still desire a drying time of 1 minute? Do they have other needs higher in priority now compared to the drying time? Answers to these questions guide us through this neverending Deming cycle.

Variability Reduction and Loss Function

Deming's philosophy calls for abandoning the idea that everything is fine if specifications are met. The idea behind this old attitude is that there is no loss associated with producing items that are off-target but within specifications. However, just the opposite is true, which is the reason for striving for continual process improvement. Reducing process variability is an ongoing objective which helps minimize loss. Following the course set by Deming, Genichi Taguchi of Japan formalized some loss functions in 1960. His approach is based on the belief that there is an economic loss associated with any deviation from the target value. Achievement of the target value yields high praise from the customer. Small deviations from the target value will yield small losses. However, the losses may increase in a nonlinear relationship (say, quadratic) with deviations from the target. Figure 2-7 demonstrates this

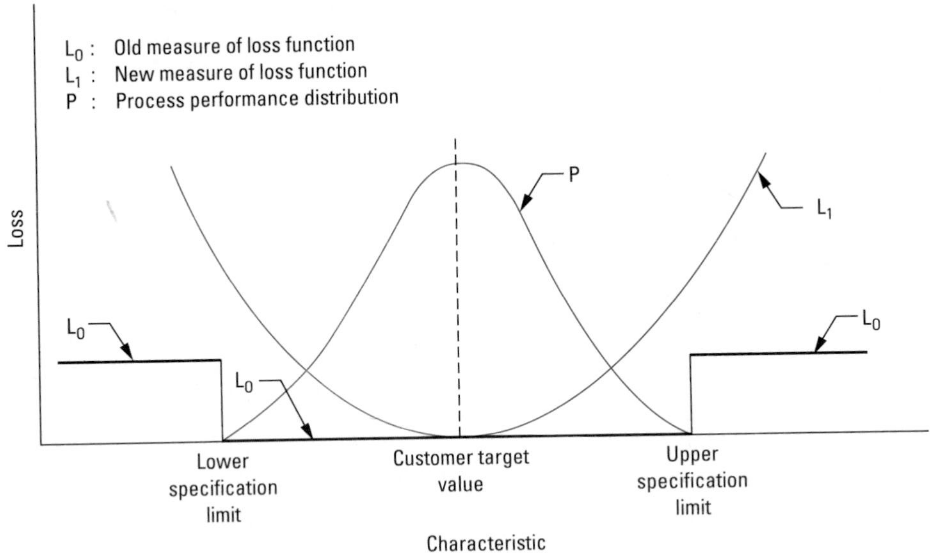

Figure 2-7 Comparison of old and new measures of the loss function.

new loss function along with the old viewpoint. The new loss function ties into the idea that companies must strive for continual variability reduction; only then will losses be reduced. Any deviation from the customer target will not allow the fullest possible satisfaction to the customer. These losses may arise because of such problems as lost opportunities, warranty costs, customer complaint costs, and other tangible and intangible costs. For instance, there is a loss associated with the customers not praising the product even though they are not unhappy with it. The customer is concerned about the total value of the product or service received. It is important to get people to praise the product or service.

Point 6: *Institute training.*

Training is integral to proper individual performance in the extended process setting. If individuals function in accordance with the goals of the company, an improvement in quality and productivity will result. This in turn will reduce costs and increase profits.

A fundamental asset of any company is its employees. When an employee is hired, he or she should be instructed in the goals of the company in clear and operational terms. Just saying that the company supports a total quality program is not sufficient. Instead, the employee should be enlightened as to the long-term objectives of the firm (for example, continually reducing the proportion of nonconforming items to a value of zero in about three years). An understanding of the goals of the company is essential to performing adequately. Otherwise, the employee may have an individual goal or objective which may not be compatible with the long-term company goals. For example, an employee goal of producing 50 items per day may not be consistent with the company goal of defect-free production. Through instruction, which may be one part of the full training process, the employee should be made aware of his or her responsibility for meeting customers' needs.

Within the context of the extended process, employee training must be presented in unambiguous operational terms. They must know exactly what is to be done and its importance in the entire process. Such an approach will not only improve their job understanding but will create an atmosphere in which workers develop pride in their work, feel more secure, have better morale, and improve their productivity. Even the employee who performs only one operation of the many that a product goes through must be instructed as to the needs of the customer and the role of the supplier in the extended process.

Training should be conducted on an ongoing basis. It should start when employees are hired and continue throughout their time with the company. It may be done in segments, and procedures may vary from company to company. Training may be done through such means as classroom instruction, handing out of instructional materials, discussion of experiential situations, or exposure to quality improvement procedures. It is imperative to remember that human beings are the most important asset of an organization.

Familiarity with statistical concepts and techniques is important in the Deming philosophy for continuing the neverending cycle of process improvement. Consequently, there are several statistical tools that deserve attention for training, including flow diagrams, histograms, control charts, cause and effect diagrams, pareto diagrams, scatter diagrams, and design of experiments. The technical aspects of these tools will be discussed later. Evaluation of a training program should be done on a statistical basis to determine if significant improvements have taken place. Furthermore, statistical methods should also be used to determine when to end the training program, since no statistically significant improvements arise from training beyond this period. If, after this phase of training, an employee is still unable to meet the requirements of the job, then he or she may have to be reassigned to a more appropriate job.

Some obstacles may reduce the benefits that can be achieved from a training program. Many of these obstacles stem from the attitudes of people in the organization. For instance, claiming that training is only useful for others, or that it applies only to those in manufacturing, is detrimental. Also, the idea that experience determines reliability is not appropriate. A person may not have been making the right decisions under the conditions that he or she had experienced. Hoping to gain solutions to complex problems in a short time frame is often unrealistic. Training will help in achieving a better solution.

Point 7: *Teach and institute leadership.*

A supervisor serves as a vital link between management and the workers. Since there usually is no direct contact between these two groups, the supervisor has the difficult job of maintaining communication channels between them. Thus, the supervisor must understand the problems of the workers and comprehend top management's goals at the same time. Communicating management's commitment to quality improvement to the workers is a function of the supervisor. In order to be an effective leader, the supervisor's attitude has to change from one of being punitive to one of helping the workers do a better job. This shift from a negative attitude to a positive one creates an atmosphere of self-respect and pride for the workers.

Supervisors need to be trained in statistical methods so that they are in a position to provide leadership and instruction in these areas to the workers. The Deming philosophy dictates that supervisors create an atmosphere in which workers can benefit from a supportive system. This will improve employee morale, promote teamwork by establishing communication links, and help in achieving the overall goal of quality improvement. Using modern methods of leadership helps the workers understand their place in the extended process, creates an atmosphere of trust and support, and helps in achieving the organization's goals.

It is important that supervisors identify common causes inherent to the system for which the workers should not be blamed. It is management's responsibility to minimize the effects of common causes. Special causes, such as poor quality of an incoming raw material, improper tooling, and poor operational definitions should be eliminated first. Identification of these special causes can be accomplished through the use of control charts, which will be discussed in later chapters. Training supervisors in the Deming philosophy should be a prerequisite to asking them to serve as role models or leaders. It is often found that supervisors end up managing things (equipment, for instance) and not people. Such an approach overlooks the fundamental asset of an organization—people.

Point 8: *Drive out fear. Create trust. Create a climate for innovation.*

One of the responsibilities of management is to eliminate fear from all members of the organization, including the workers, supervisory staff, management, suppliers and vendors, investors, and community. Functioning in an environment of fear is counterproductive, because employee actions are dictated by behavior patterns that will please supervisors rather than meet the long-term goals of the organization. The economic loss associated with fear in organizations is immense. Employees are hesitant to ask questions about their job, the methods involved in production, the process conditions and influence of process parameters, the operational definition of what is acceptable, and other such important issues. The wrong signal is given when a supervisor or manager gives the impression that asking these questions is a waste of time. What could be more important to the worker than to know exactly what his or her job entails? How can employees perform effectively if they cannot clarify questions about the process? If they think that their suggestions to management regarding process improvement are just a waste of time, how can they identify with the company and feel like a part of the team?

Deming suggests that as management starts to implement the 14 points, removing or reducing fear should be one of the foremost tasks to tackle, because an environment of fear will impede implementation of his other points.

There is wasteful action in a fear-filled organization. Consider an employee who produces a quota of 50 parts per day—without regard to whether they are all acceptable—just to satisfy the immediate supervisor. Many of these parts may have to be scrapped, leading to wasted resources and unproductive usage of capacity. Fear can cause physical or physiological disorders which lead to poor morale and productivity. A lack of job security is probably one of the main causes of fear. Assuring an employee of life-long employment with the company (as is the case in many Japanese companies) will lift a big burden off his or her shoulders and reduce fear. The process of eliminating fear should start at the top. The philosophy of managing by fear is totally unacceptable; it does not create trust among everyone, and it fails to remove barriers that exist between different levels of the organization.

Point 9: *Optimize toward the aims and purposes of the company the efforts of teams, groups, staff areas.*

Organizational Barriers Barriers are obstacles that impede the flow of information. They may exist within the organization as well as between the organization and components of the extended process. Figure 2-8 shows such barriers schematically. Internal to the organization, there may be barriers within the levels of hierarchy (for instance, between the supervisor and workers). Another form of internal barrier may be one that exists between departments. For example, there may be very little communication between engineering and production or between product design and marketing. The presence of any of these barriers impedes the flow of information, prevents a global perspective on the goals of the extended process to each entity within the

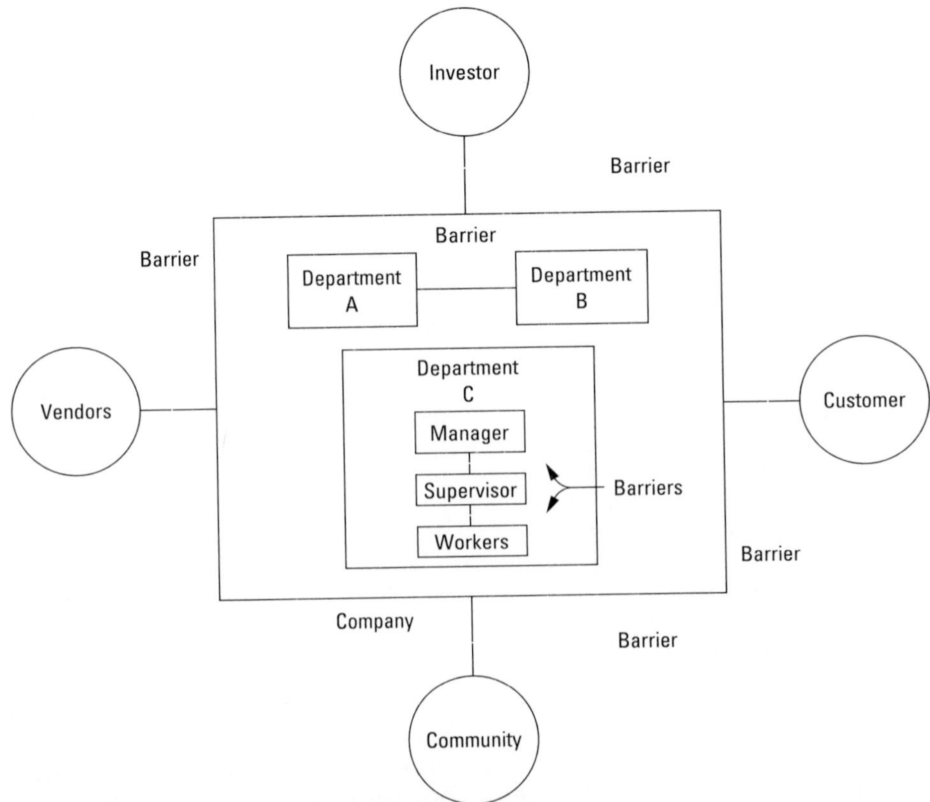

Figure 2-8 Examples of organizational barriers.

system, and fosters the pursuit of individual or departmental goals that are not necessarily consistent with the organizational goals.

External to the organization but within the extended process, examples of barriers are those between the vendors and the company, the company and the customer, the company and the community, and the company and its investors. The detrimental effects of any of these barriers is obvious. If the company does not have a clear and concise understanding of the needs of the consumer, how can it make use of that information to come up with acceptable product designs? Survival of the company may also become difficult if it does not incorporate the sentiments of the community in which it exists. A feeling of harmony must exist between the company, the customers, the vendors, and the community.

One of the main reasons for the existence of barriers is poor communication. This may arise from the failure of top management to motivate everyone to accept the systems approach in pursuit of the organization's overall goal. Also, management must create a fear-free atmosphere so that anyone may ask questions regarding the product, process, or relationships among the different units. The employees should feel that, by elimination of these barriers, they are part of the same team trying to achieve the overall mission of the company. Breaking down barriers usually takes time; it requires changing the attitudes of those who have worked in an environment where barriers existed. These people usually feel insecure when they are initially presented with this new framework of operation. Everyone must be convinced of the unified goal and the importance of a team effort in achieving it. At Ford Motor Company, for instance, implementation of this concept is found in their design approval process. This process incorporates input from all related units such as design, sales and marketing, advance product planning, vehicle engineering, body and assembly purchasing, body and assembly manufacturing, product planning, and others. Management should also emphasize open lines of communication at all levels and among different departments. The reward system used to facilitate this process should be based on teamwork rather than an individual person's production.

Point 10: *Eliminate exhortations for the work force.*

Such numerical goals as a 10 percent improvement in productivity set arbitrarily by management for the workers have a demoralizing effect. Rather than serving as a positive motivational tool, setting such standards without concern for feasibility or a basis for achievement has a negative impact on the morale and productivity of employees.

Consider, for example, a company producing the housing for a certain bearing. Based on customer needs, the specifications for the housing diameter are 20 ± 0.2 mm. The company keeps track daily of the proportion of housings that are nonconforming (that is, do not meet specifications). A plot of the proportion of nonconforming housings versus time is shown in Figure 2-9. The figure shows that the proportion of nonconforming items hovers around 6 percent. Suppose management now sets a goal of 4 percent for the maximum proportion of unacceptable housings. What are the implications of this? First, what was the rationale in choosing the goal of 4 percent? Second, did management specify ways in which the goal might be achieved? The lack of satisfactory answers to these two questions will create further frustration for the employees when this new goal is presented. If the process is stable, the employees will have no means of achieving the goal unless management makes a change in the process or product. Management has to come up with a feasible course of action so that the desired goal can be achieved. Failing to do so will have the drastic effect of lowering the morale and productivity of the workers, who will find the goal impossible to attain. By taking such an action, management is basically shirking its responsibility. Hence, goals should be set by management in a participative style, and procedures for accomplishment should be given.

Management should demonstrate its commitment to the neverending process of quality improvement. Rather than providing slogans, they should describe

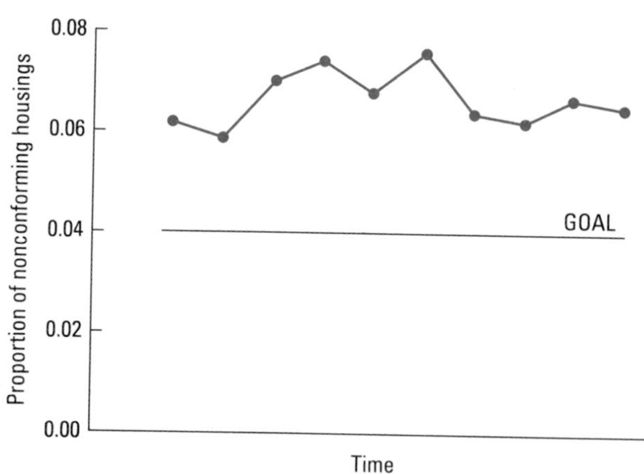

Figure 2-9 Arbitrarily established numerical goals.

to the employees precisely what they are doing to implement this long-term goal. Only then will employees sense management's devotion to the goal, which will lead the employees to make every effort to achieve it. Setting goals on the basis of intuition should be avoided. Instead, goals should be based on information from the basic worker level. A bottom-up financial planning approach is recommended, assuming that the process is in a state of statistical control. Being in a state of statistical control allows one to make projections as to what might be expected from the process. This information can then be used by management to set goals and allocate resources.

Point 11: *(a) Eliminate numerical quotas for production. Instead, learn and institute methods for improvement. (b) Eliminate M.B.O. [management by objectives]. Instead, learn the capabilities of processes, and how to improve them.*

Work standards are typically established by someone other than those who perform the particular job in question. They are determined based on quantity without regard to quality. According to Deming, setting such work standards guarantees inefficiency and increases costs. The numerical quota defined by a work standard may prohibit deployment of the neverending improvement cycle because it encourages people to meet the quota rather than producing acceptable goods. As such, a numerical quota actually promotes the production of nonconforming items.

Another drawback of the standards is that they give no information about the procedure that might be adopted to meet the quota. Is the numerical value a feasible one? Usually, when determining work standards, an allowance is made for the production of nonconforming items, but this may just end up ensuring that a certain proportion of defectives will be produced. It moves the company away from the desirable goal of continuous improvement. Quotas provide no game plan for the implementation of a quality system.

A third drawback of the quota system is that it fails to distinguish between chance causes and assignable causes when seeking to improve the process. Consequently, workers may be penalized for not meeting the quota when it is really not their fault. As discussed previously, changes in the process can be brought about only by management. Thus, one should not expect any improvement in process output unless a conscientious effort is made by management. If the quota is set too high, very few workers will meet the objectives. This will lead to the production of more defective units by workers, since they will try to meet the numerical goal without regard for quality. Furthermore, workers will experience a loss of pride in their work, and worker morale and motivation will drop significantly.

Work standards are typically established through union negotiation and have nothing to do with the capability of the process. Changes in process capability are not pursued, so the standards do not reflect the potential of the current system. Workers who surpass a standard that has been set too high may be producing several defectives, and they may know it. They may realize that they are being rewarded for producing nonconforming items—which is totally against Deming's philosophy. On the other hand, if quotas are set too low, productivity will be reduced. A worker may meet the quota with ease, but once the quota is achieved, he or she may have no motivation to exceed it; if management finds out that several people's output meets or exceeds the quota, the quota will likely be increased. This will impose an additional burden on the employee to meet the new quota, without the help of improved methods or procedures. All of these factors support the elimination of the numerical quota system.

Following the work standard system is inappropriate because it takes a short-term view for the company. On the other hand, using control charts over time to analyze and monitor a process to seek continual improvement offers a proper focus on long-term goals. Statistical methods are preferable over the arbitrary establishment of work standards; they help an organization in the extended process stay competitive.

Point 12: *Remove barriers that rob people of pride of workmanship.*

A total quality system in an organization will exist only when all employees unite to synergistically produce output that conforms to the goals of the company in the extended process. Quality will be achieved in all segments of the extended process if the employees are happy and motivated, understand their role in the context of the organization's goals, and take pride in their work. It is management's duty to eliminate all barriers that prevent the association between contentment and producing a quality product. A direct effect of pride in workmanship is an increased level of motivation and a greater impetus for employees to identify themselves as part of the same team, a team that is working for the goals of the company.

Factors That Cause a Loss of Pride There are several factors that may lead to a loss of worker pride. First, management may not treat the employees with proper dignity. They may show no personal attention to the workers or be insensitive to the workers' problems (which may include personal and family matters). A happy employee will usually be productive and vice versa. Such an employee does not need to be monitored often (in hourly terms, for example) to determine if the desired quota of production is being output. Second, management may not have fulfilled its task of communicating the company's mission to all levels. How can an employee contribute to achieving the companies' mission if he or she does not really understand in operational terms what that mission is? Third, management may inappropriately assign blame to the employees for not meeting certain company goals when the real fault is with management. If problems in product output are caused by drawbacks of the system (such as poor-quality raw materials, inadequate methods, or inappropriate equipment), then the employees should not be penalized, even though the best employee might be able to produce a quality product under these circumstances. Assigning blame to the employees further demoralizes them and affects quality. As Deming states, the problem is usually the system, not the people. The most wasted resource in industry is management. It is high time that industry wake up and utilize the talents of management for long-term gains.

A management focus on short-term goals compounds this problem. Consider the measurement tool of daily production reports. As different units meet their obligation of providing related numerical figures, it gives them the idea that top management is "micro-managing" and paying no attention to long-term goals. The pressure to constantly increase quantity on a daily basis does not promote the notion of quality. How many times have we heard of a department manager having to provide an explanation for why production dropped today, by say, 50 units compared to yesterday? Even more frustrating is the fact that such a drop may not even be statistically significant. Inferences should be based on sound statistical principles.

Performance Classification System Another obstacle that robs employees of their pride in workmanship is an inadequate performance evaluation system designed for the short run. It is common for many industries to categorize their employees as excellent, good, average, fair, or unacceptable. Annual increments in salary are then based on the category that the individual is placed in. The failing of such a system is that there are often no clear-cut operational definitions of the differences between categories. The lack of such definitions may lead to inconsistencies in the evaluation of individuals. A person may be identified as "good" by one manager and "average" by another because of such deficiencies.

A major drawback is that management does not have a statistical basis for saying that there are significant differences between the output of someone in the "good" category and someone in the "average" category. For instance, if a difference in output between two workers were statistically insignificant (that is, due to chance), then it would be unfair to place the two individuals in two different categories. Assume that Figure 2-10 shows such a classification system composed of five categories. The categories numbered 1 through 5 (unacceptable through excellent) have variabilities that are not due to a fundamental difference in the output of the individuals. In fact, the employees may not even have a chance to improve their output because of system deficiencies. Thus, two employees may be rated by their supervisors as 3 (average) and 4 (good), respectively, with the employee rated as 4 to be considered superior in performance to the other. However, both of these employees may be part of the same distribution, implying that there is no statistically significant difference between them. With this particular system, whatever aggregate measure of evaluation is being used to lump employees into categories, there are no statistically significant differences between the values for categories 1, 2, 3, 4, or 5. The only two groups that may be considered part of another system, whose output therefore varies significantly from those in categories 1–5, are categories 0 and 6. Those placed in group 0 may be classified as performing poorly (so low that they are considered part of a different system). Likewise, those placed in group 6 may be classified as performing exceptionally well.

Placing employees in categories has a demoralizing effect. What is worse is that even though we apply labels such as "average" or "good" to people, it may be statistically unsound to place them in these different groups in the first place. As people in the "average" group try to emulate the behavior of those in the "good" group in order to improve their rating for the next evaluation period, the results may be catastrophic. There is no assurance that an individual in the "average" group will in fact "move up" to a "good" rating, since the perceived differences are not really significant. Note that the above discussion is based on the assumption that the numerical measure of performance being used to categorize individuals into groups is normally distributed as in Figure 2-10. Only those significant deviations from the mean (say, three or more standard deviations on

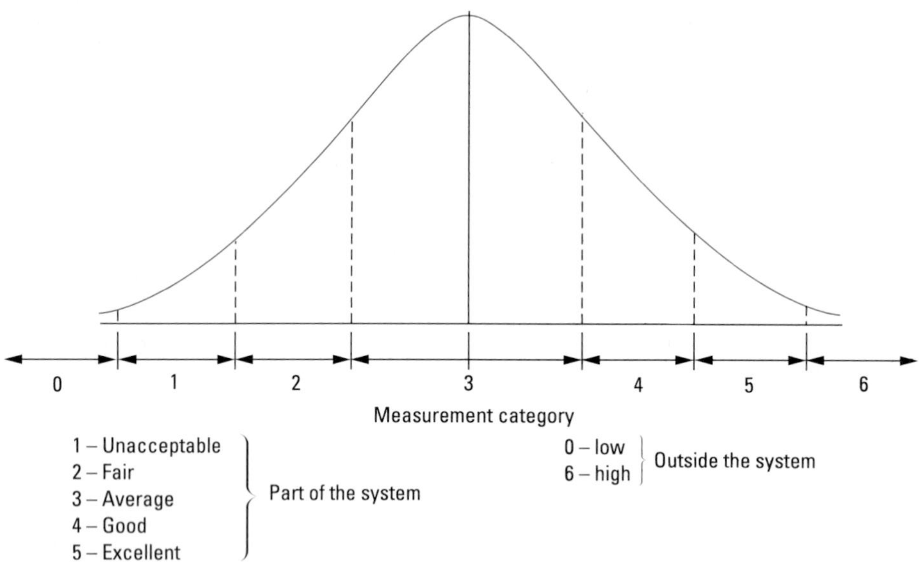

Figure 2-10 Improper classification system where categories are part of the same system.

either side) may be considered extraordinary, that is, not belonging to the same system that produces ratings of 1–5. Under these circumstances, category 0 (whose cutoff point is three standard deviations below the mean, say) and category 6 (whose cutoff point is three standard deviations above the mean, say) would be considered different from categories 1–5.

Thus, statistically speaking, the only categories should be the three groups corresponding to the original categories 0, 1–5, and 6. In Deming's approach, teamwork is considered extremely important. Consideration should be given to this point when conducting performance appraisal. The procedure should be designed so that promoting teamwork is a necessary criterion for placing someone in the highest category. Such individuals should be rewarded through merit raises. For those placed in categories 1–5, monies set aside for investment in the system should be evenly distributed.

Point 13: *Encourage education and self-improvement for everyone.*

Deming's philosophy is based on long-term, continuous process improvement. In order to meet the goals of the organization, its most important resource, people, has to be kept motivated and adequately trained. This is the only way that the company can guarantee its survival in the long run. Management must commit resources for education and retraining. Such expenditures represent a meaningful investment. Management must take a futuristic approach. They can safeguard improvements in quality and productivity as well as maintain a competitive position by investing in their employees.

Advantages of Education and Retraining Investments, such as education and retraining of workers and management at all levels, serve a multifold purpose. First, they create a feeling of security among the employees, who believe that if the company is willing to incur such expenditures for their benefit, it must be interested in their well-being. Such a belief fosters motivation to excel at work. Second, through the process of education, the company can explain to management and workers the goals of the organization. As stated previously, everyone should be thoroughly familiar with the company's goals so as to work in a synergistic manner. The content and duration of the educational process may vary among employees. Top management have to be instructed periodically about the missions of the company and its philosophy. All employees may have to undergo instruction on basic statistical methods and their relevance to improvement of quality. Technical personnel may need further training in advanced statistical techniques and applications. Third, education and retraining not only keeps the employees up-to-date in performing their job but also promotes teamwork, which is important in meeting the company's goals. As employees learn more about the product and process, they realize the significance of tasks different from their own. Changes in consumer needs may cause changes in product design, which in turn may require changes in the process. As processes and methods change, retraining might be necessary for certain workers. Fourth, as employees grow with the company and their job responsibilities change, retraining will provide a mechanism to ensure adequate performance in their new jobs. Such progressive action by the company will make it easier to adapt to the changing needs of the consumer.

Education should also include dissemination of the principles behind the 14 points of Deming. These principles will provide a road map to achieve quality at a lower total cost while meeting customer requirements. Also, education and retraining applies to people in nonmanufacturing or service areas as well. Thus, employees in accounting, purchasing, marketing, sales, or maintenance need this instruction to participate in the neverending process of improvement. Industry should work with academia to aid in this process of education and retraining. Management, of course, should be aware that the process of education and retraining is a lengthy one.

Point 14: *Take action to accomplish the transformation.*

Point 14 involves accepting the Deming philosophy and making a commitment to see that it is implemented by the organization in the extended process setting. A structure must be created and maintained for the dissemination of the concepts associated with the first 13 points. Responsibility for the creation of such a structure lies with top management. Prior to setting up such an environment, top management must be committed to it. Along with commitment, they must have the vision to recognize the impact of these principles in the long run, they must be knowledgeable, and they must have the mental strength to wholeheartedly accept the philosophy.

In order for the implementation to succeed, the structure must be strengthened with the help of people trained in statistics at all levels of the organization. A company requires statistical assistance for its top management, senior managers, middle-level managers, lower-level managers, supervisors, and hourly workers. Figure 2-11 shows the importance of statistical training for a successful implementation of Deming's philosophy. Numerous people trained in statistical methods are needed to maintain this structure. The underlying theme of this structure is the integration of statistical principles in a holistic manner such that the first 13 points are a way of life in the organization.

Successful companies have a free flow of information among their different levels. An information flow from the workers to the supervisors to lower management to middle management and eventually to top management creates the necessary base for determining the areas where improvement is needed. This upward flow of information assists in the development of plans for quality improvement. Consequently, the implementation of these plans will provide a flow of information in the downward direction. Statistical assistance must also be provided to the suppliers and the customers, since they are part of the extended process. This assistance may take the form of statistical aid to the vendor in developing and documenting a quality program of its own. Providing the customer with statistical information regarding the quality of the product (for example, mean life of the product) could be another necessary function.

2-5 PHILIP B. CROSBY'S PHILOSOPHY

Philip B. Crosby is a management consultant who founded Philip Crosby Associates in 1979 and is now its chairman. Prior to that, he spent 14 years as a corporate vice-president for ITT, where he was responsible for worldwide quality operations. Crosby has a thorough understanding of the various operations in industry because he started as a line inspector and worked his way up. About 25 years of firsthand experience in different positions in industry has provided him with the knowledge of what quality is, what the obstacles are, and what can be done to overcome them. Crosby has since trained and consulted with many people in manufacturing and service industries. He has written many books (Crosby, 1979, 1984, 1989) on the subject of quality management.

The Crosby approach begins with an evaluation of the existing quality system. His quality management grid (Crosby, 1979) provides a method of identifying where the existing quality operation lies and pinpointing operations which have potential for improvement. Figure 2-12 shows an example of a quality management grid. The grid is divided into five stages of maturity: uncertainty, awakening, enlightenment, wisdom, and certainty. There are six management categories which aid in the evaluation

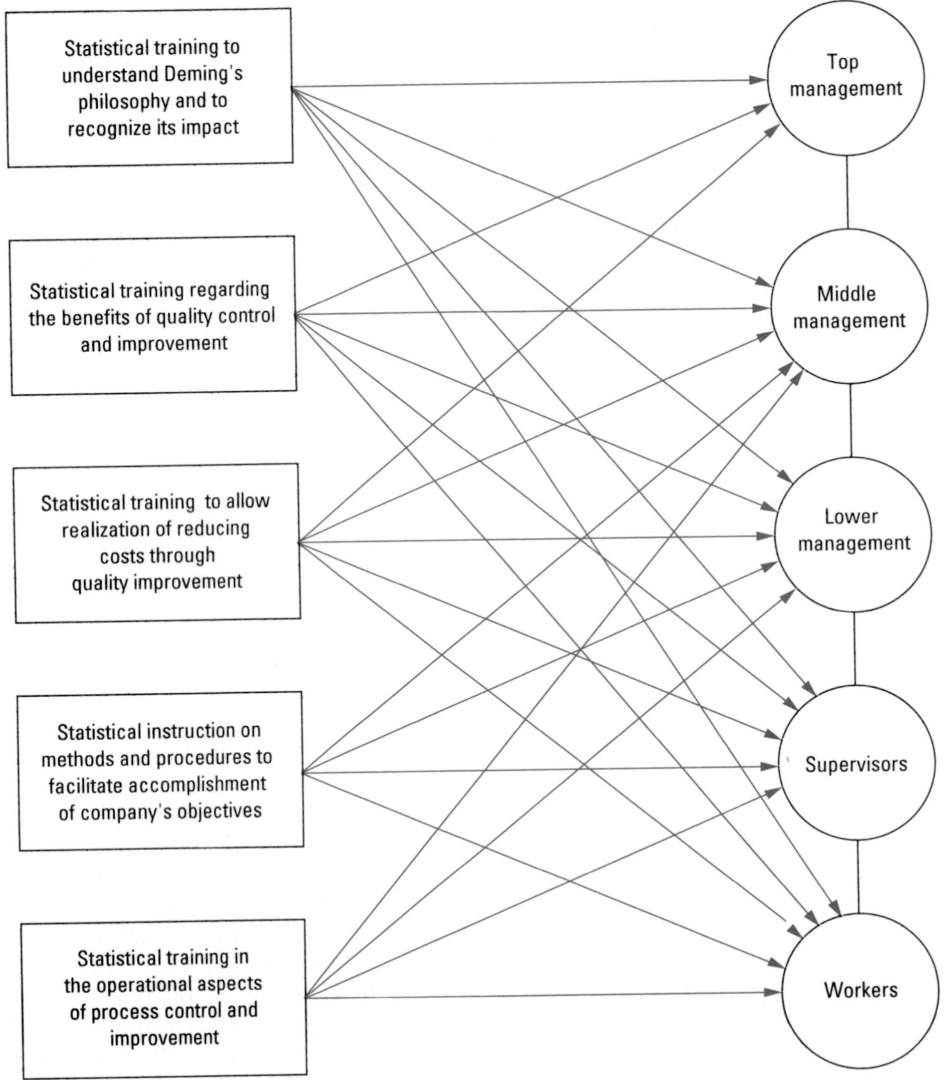

Figure 2-11 An organizational structure to promote Deming's philosophy.

process: management understanding and attitude, quality organization status, problem handling, cost of quality as a percentage of sales, quality improvement actions, and summary of company quality posture. Descriptions of each of the elements of this grid are found in Figure 2-12.

Four Absolutes of Quality Management

In order to understand the meaning of quality, Crosby (1979) has identified four absolutes of quality management.

- Definition of quality: Quality means conformance to requirements.
- System for achievement of quality: The rational approach is prevention of defects.
- Performance standard: The only performance standard is zero defects.
- Measurement: The performance measurement is the cost of quality. In fact, Crosby emphasizes the costs of unquality such as scrap, rework, service, inventory, inspection, and tests.

Measurement categories	Stage I: Uncertainty	Stage II: Awakening	Stage III: Enlightenment	Stage IV: Wisdom	Stage V: Certainty
Management understanding and attitude	No comprehension of quality as a management tool. Tend to blame quality department for "quality problems."	Recognizing that quality management may be of value but not willing to provide money or time to make it all happen.	While going through quality improvement program learn more about quality management. Recognize their personal role in continuing emphasis.	Participating. Understand absolutes of quality management. Recognize their personal role in continuing emphasis.	Consider quality management as essential part of company system.
Quality organization status	Quality is hidden in manufacturing or engineering departments. Inspection probably not part of organization. Emphasis on appraisal and sorting.	A stronger quality leader is appointed but main emphasis is still on appraisal and moving the product. Still part of manufacturing or other.	Quality department reports to top management, all appraisal is incorporated, and manager has role in management of company.	Quality manager is an officer of company, effective status reporting and preventive action. Involved with consumer affairs and special assignments.	Quality manager on board of directors. Prevention is main concern. Quality is a thought leader.
Problem handling	Problems are fought as they occur; no resolution; inadequate definition; lots of yelling and accusations.	Teams are set up to attack major problems. Long-range solutions are not solicited.	Corrective action communication established. Problems are faced openly and resolved in an orderly way.	Problems are identified early in their development. All functions are open to suggestion and improvement.	Except in the most unusual cases, problems are prevented.
Cost of quality as a percentage of sales	Reported: unknown Actual: 20%	Reported: 3% Actual: 18%	Reported: 8% Actual: 12%	Reported: 6.5% Actual: 8%	Reported: 2.5% Actual: 2.5%
Quality improvement actions	No organized activities. No understanding of such activities.	Trying obvious "motivational" short-range efforts.	Implementation of the 14-step program with thorough understanding and establishment of each step.	Continuing the 14-step program.	Quality improvement is a normal and continued activity.
Summary of company quality posture	"We don't know why we have problems with quality."	"Is it absolutely necessary to always have problems with quality?"	"Through management commitment and quality improvement we are identifying and resolving our problems."	"Defect prevention is a routine part of our operation."	"We know why we do not have problems with quality."

Figure 2-12 Crosby's quality management grid. (Philip B. Crosby. *Quality Is Free*, copyright 1979, McGraw-Hill, Inc. Reprinted with permission.)

Fourteen-Step Plan for Quality Improvement

Crosby has a 14-step plan, discussed briefly below, to help businesses in a quality improvement program.* The reader who is interested in a thorough discussion of these steps should consult the suggested references.

* Philip B. Crosby. *Quality Is Free*, copyright 1979, McGraw-Hill, Inc. Reprinted with permission.

1. *Management commitment.* For quality improvement to take place, commitment must start from the top. The emphasis on defect prevention has to be communicated, and a quality policy that states the individual performance requirements needed to match customer requirements must be developed.

2. *Quality improvement team.* Representatives from each department or division should be brought together to form a quality improvement team. These individuals will serve as spokespersons for each group they represent. They will be responsible for ensuring that any suggested operation is brought to action. Formation of such a team brings all the necessary tools together.

3. *Quality measurement.* Measurement is necessary to determine the status of quality for each activity. It helps identify the areas where corrective action is needed and where quality improvement efforts should be directed. The results of measurement should be placed in highly visible charts in order to establish a foundation for the quality improvement program. These principles apply to service operations as well, such as counting the number of billing or payroll errors in the finance department, the number of drafting errors in engineering, the number of contract or order description errors in marketing, and the number of orders shipped late.

4. *Cost of quality evaluation.* The cost of quality (or rather unquality) provides an indication of where corrective action and quality improvement will result in savings for the company. A study to determine these costs should be conducted through the comptroller's office, where precise definitions should be laid out to identify the categories that comprise quality costs. This study will establish a measure of management's performance.

5. *Quality awareness.* The results of the cost of nonquality should be shared with all employees including service and administrative people. Getting everybody involved with quality will facilitate changing the quality attitude in the organization.

6. *Corrective action.* Communication and discussion of problems create the groundwork for coming up with feasible solutions. Furthermore, such discussion also helps to expose other problems not identified previously and to thereby determine procedures to eliminate them. Thus, as problems arise, an attempt may be made to resolve them. For those problems that do not have an immediately identifiable remedy, discussion is postponed to subsequent meetings. The whole process creates a stimulating environment of problem identification and correction.

7. *Ad hoc committee for the zero defects program.* The concept of zero defects must be communicated clearly to all employees; everyone must understand that the achievement of such a goal is the company's objective. Setting up this committee will give credibility to the quality program and will demonstrate the commitment of top management.

8. *Supervisor training.* All levels of management must be made aware of the steps of the quality improvement program. Also, they must be trained so that they develop the ability to explain it to the employees who work for them. This will ensure the propagation of the quality concepts from the chief executive officers to the hourly worker.

9. *Zero defects (ZD) day.* The philosophy of zero defects (ZD) should be established companywide and should originate on one day. This will help in a uniform understanding of the concept by everyone. Management has the responsibility of explaining the program to the employees, and they should describe the day as signifying a "new attitude." Management must foster this type of quality culture in the organization.

10. *Goal setting.* Employees, in conjunction with their supervisors, should set specific measurable goals. These could be 30-, 60-, or 90-day goals. This process creates a favorable attitude for people to ultimately achieve their own goals.

11. *Error cause removal.* The employees are asked to identify reasons that prevent them from meeting the zero defects goal—not to make suggestions but to list the problems. It becomes the task of the appropriate functional group to come up with procedures for removing these problems. Reporting of such problems should be done quickly. Employees should learn to trust management so that both groups can work as a team to eliminate the problems.

12. *Recognition.* There should be award programs, based on recognition rather than money, to identify those employees who have either met or exceeded their goals or have excelled in other ways. Such programs will encourage the participation of everyone in the quality program.

13. *Quality councils.* Chairpersons, team leaders, and professionals associated with the quality program should meet on a regular basis to keep everyone up to date on progress. These meetings will also help create new ideas for further improvement of quality.

14. *Do it over again.* The whole process of quality improvement is continuous. It has to be repeated over and over again for the quality philosophy to be ingrained in the company.

2-6 JOSEPH M. JURAN'S PHILOSOPHY

Joseph M. Juran, Ph.D., is founder and chairman emeritus of the Juran Institute. The institute offers consulting and management training in quality. Since 1924, Juran has pursued a career in industry in a variety of positions as an engineer, labor arbitrator, and corporate director. He has also been a government administrator and a university professor. A holder of degrees in engineering and law, Juran has published many books on the subjects of quality planning, control, management, and improvement (Juran and Gryna, 1980; Juran, 1986, 1988a, 1988b, and 1989). At the invitation of the Japanese Federation of Economic Associations and the Japanese Union of Scientists and Engineers, he visited Japan in the early 1950s to conduct training courses in quality management. Subsequently, he repeated these seminars for over three decades in over 40 countries, on all continents. In the 1980s, an explosive demand arose for seminars on quality management, which Juran met by offerings through the Juran Institute. His books and videotapes have been translated into many languages (such as French, German, Hungarian, Italian, Japanese, Korean, Polish, Portuguese, Romanian, Russian, and Spanish), and he has trained thousands of managers and specialists.

Juran believes that management will have to adopt a unified approach to tackle the crisis in quality. Juran defines quality as fitness for use. Such a definition has its focus on the needs of the customer. There are certain nonuniformities in a company which deter the development of a unified process. One is the existence of multiple functions—such as marketing, product design and development, manufacture, and procurement—where each function believes itself to be unique and special. Second, the presence of hierarchical levels in the organizational structure creates groups of people who have different responsibilities. These groups vary in their background and may have different levels of exposure to the concepts of quality management. Third, a variety of product lines which differ in their markets and production processes may seemingly cause a lack of unity. Juran proposes a universal way of thinking about quality. This concept will fit all functions, levels of management, and product lines. He suggests the quality trilogy of quality planning, quality control, and quality improvement as the three basic quality-oriented processes for managing quality.

Quality Trilogy Process

The quality trilogy process starts with the quality planning done at various levels of the organization, each of which has a distinct goal. At the upper management level, planning is termed strategic quality management. Broad quality goals are established. A structured approach is selected in which management chooses a plan of action and allocates resources to achieve the goals. Planning at the middle management level is termed operational quality management. Departmental goals consistent with the strategic goals are established. At the workforce level, planning involves a clear assignment to each worker. Each worker must be informed of how his or her individual goal contributes toward meeting the departmental goals.

After the planning phase, quality control takes over. Here, the goal is to run the process effectively such that the plans are enacted. If there are deficiencies in the planning process, the process may operate at a high level of chronic waste. Quality control will try to prevent the waste from getting worse. If unusual symptoms are sporadically detected, quality control will attempt to identify the cause behind this abnormal variation. Upon identifying the cause, remedial action will be taken to bring the process back to control. Figure 2-13 shows the three phases of planning, control, and improvement and the cost trends associated with poor quality. The objectives of the control phase are to eliminate the causes associated with the sporadic spikes and to bring the process output within the zone of quality control.

The next phase of the trilogy process is quality improvement, which deals with the continuous improvement of the product and the process. This phase is also called the *quality breakthrough sequence* by Juran. Such improvements usually require an action on the part of upper and middle management. They deal with actions such as creating a new design, changing methods or procedures of manufacturing, and investing in new equipment. As can be seen from Figure 2-13, quality improvement will usually cause a reduction in the cost of poor quality. The chronic waste drops to a lower level due to quality improvement. Repeating the whole cycle lets the company strive for further improvements.

Short descriptions of each of these phases follow.* Readers should consult the listed references (Juran

* These descriptions are adapted, with permission, from J. M. Juran. "The Quality Trilogy," *Quality Progress*, August 1986, pp. 19–24.

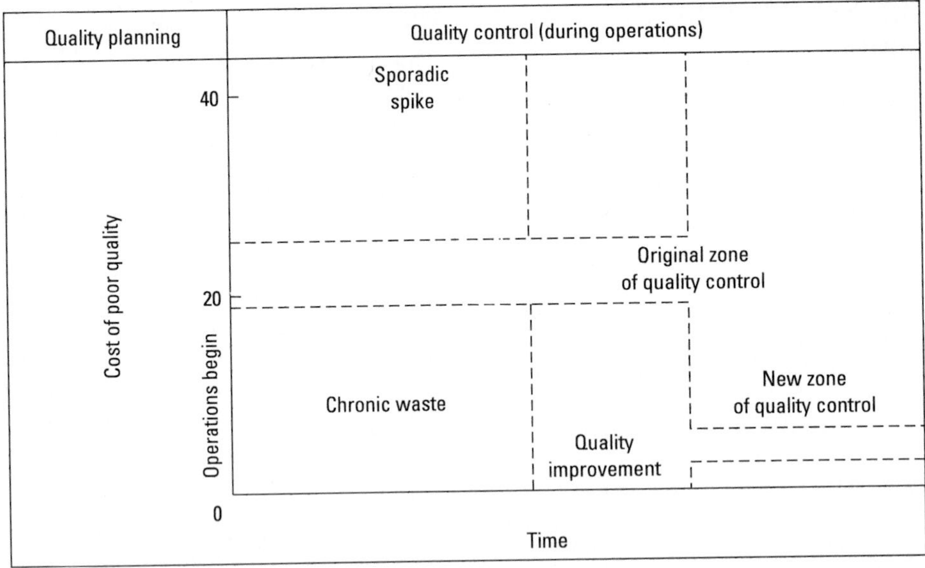

Figure 2-13 Juran's quality trilogy. (J. M. Juran. "The Quality Trilogy," *Quality Progress*, August 1986, pp. 19–24.)

1986, 1988a, 1988b, 1989) for an elaborate treatment of the details of each phase.

Quality Planning

1. *Identify the customer—both external and internal.* Juran has a similar concept of the extended process described previously in the section on the Deming philosophy. It is meant to include the vendors and customers. He places importance on identifying the customer. In cases where the output from one department flows to another, the customer is considered internal.

2. *Determine customer needs.* Survival of the company in the long run is contingent upon meeting the needs of the customer. Conducting analysis and research, surveying clients and nonclients, and studying customer needs are a few examples of activities in this category.

3. *Develop product features that respond to customer needs.* With customer satisfaction as the utmost objective, the product or service should be designed to meet the customer requirements. As customer needs change, the product should be redesigned to conform to these changes.

4. *Establish quality goals that meet the needs of customers and suppliers alike, and do so at a minimum combined cost.* This point embraces the concept of the extended process involving the vendors and customers as well as the organization. Pursuit of individual or departmental goals should be avoided. The total cost from an organizational point of view should be minimized, and corresponding goals should be determined.

5. *Develop a process that can produce the needed product features.* A product is designed based on a knowledge of customer needs. This step deals with the manufacturing process of that product. Methods must be developed, and adequate equipment must be available to make the product match its design specifications.

6. *Prove process capability.* The task here is to establish that the given process is adequate to make a product that will conform to the design specifications. This task may require analyzing output from a stable process and determining its level of operation. If the operating level meets the desirable goals, the process is labeled as capable.

Quality Control

1. *Choose control subjects.* Product characteristics that are to be controlled in order to make the product conform to the design requirements should be chosen. For instance, a wheel's control characteristics may be the hub diameter and the outside diameter. Selection is done by prioritizing the important characteristics which influence the operation or appearance of the product and hence impact the customer.

2. *Choose units of measurement.* Based on the quality characteristics that have been selected for control, appropriate units of measure should be selected. As an example, if the hub diameter is be-

ing controlled, the unit of measurement might be millimeters.

3. *Establish measurement.* Procedures must be defined for taking measurements. These procedures should take into account the equipment to be used, the way in which it is to be used, who should take the measurements, how the measurements should be taken (that is, what sampling plan if any is to be used), and other related issues. Care must be taken to ensure that all measuring instruments are properly calibrated and that persons taking measurements are adequately trained.

4. *Establish standards of performance.* These standards should be based on customer requirements. For instance, a standard of performance for the hub diameter could be 20 ± 0.2 mm. A hub having a diameter within this range would be compatible in final assembly and would also lead to making a product that will satisfy the customer.

5. *Measure actual performance.* This phase of quality control is concerned with the measurement of the actual process output. Measurements are taken on the previously selected control subjects (or quality characteristics). Such measurements will provide information on the operational level of the process.

6. *Interpret the difference (actual versus standard).* This involves a comparison of the performance of the process with the established standard. If the process is stable and capable, then there may not be any significant difference between the actual and the standard.

7. *Take action on the difference.* In the event that a discrepancy is found between the actual output of the process and the established standard, remedial action needs to be taken. In Figure 2-13, the sporadic spike shows a big difference between what is observed and the standard. It becomes management's responsibility to suggest a course of action that would reduce this spike.

Quality Improvement

1. *Prove the need for improvement.* Juran associates his breakthrough sequence with quality improvement. This sequence tackles the chronic problems which have existed through a change in the current process, a task requiring management involvement. First, however, one has to convince management of the need for this improvement. Problems such as rework and scrap could be converted to dollar figures to draw management's attention. It would also help to look at problems as cost savings opportunities.

2. *Identify specific projects for improvement.* Because of the limited availability of resources, not all problems can be addressed simultaneously. Therefore, problems that are more critical should be identified and chosen for study. A Pareto analysis (which will be discussed in a later chapter), for use in identifying the few vital problems is often used. Juran's quality improvement process works on a project-by-project basis. A problem area is identified as a project, and an effort is directed toward the eliminating the problem.

3. *Organize to guide the projects.* The organizational structure must be clearly established in order for the project to run smoothly. As mentioned previously, this requires the assignment of authority and responsibility at all levels of management. While top management may deal with strategic responsibilities, lower management will be involved in the operational aspects of the actions. Furthermore, the structure should precisely establish responsibility for the following levels: guidance of overall improvement program, guidance for each individual project, and diagnosis and analysis for each project.

4. *Organize for diagnosis—for discovery of causes.* Juran defines a diagnostic arm as a person or group of persons brought together to determine the causes (not remedies) of the problem. The organization needs to enlist the right people and ensure that the required tools and resources are available. This is accomplished through a steering arm. This investigation may require technical skills which managers may not possess. In such instances, use of professional specialists is appropriate.

5. *Find the causes.* This is often the most difficult step in the whole process. It involves data gathering and analysis to determine the cause of a problem. The diagnostic procedure may first consist of studying the symptoms surrounding the defects in order to develop a hypothesis for the causes. The investigator may then hypothesize as to the causes of the symptoms and finally conduct an analysis to establish the validity of the hypothesized causes.

6. *Provide remedies.* The diagnostic step identifies the cause-and-effect relationship. Here, remedial actions are developed to alleviate the chronic problems. Remedies may deal with problems that are controllable by management or those that are controllable by operators. Actions requiring a change in methods or equipment should be considered by management and will require a good deal of financial investment. Frequently, an analysis of the return on investment is conducted. Remedies may also involve a change in the standards. If tighter specifications have no real impact on the performance of the product, can the standards be relaxed? Errors con-

trollable by the operators may be inadvertent, due to lack of skill or knowledge, or willful.

7. *Prove that the remedies are effective under operating conditions.* This is the real test of the effectiveness of the remedies proposed in the previous step. Can the suggested actions be implemented, and do they have the beneficial effect that has been hypothesized? The breakthrough process requires overcoming resistance to change. Changes may be technological or social in nature. The proposed procedure may require new equipment, and operators may have to be trained. Management commitment is vital to the effective implementation of such a change. By the same token, social changes which deal with human habits, beliefs, and traditions will require patience, understanding, and the participation of everyone involved.

8. *Provide for control to hold the gains.* Once the remedial actions have been implemented and gains have been realized, there must be a control system to sustain this new level of achievement. In other words, if we have been able to reduce the proportion of nonconforming items to 2 percent, we must make sure that the process does not go back to the former nonconformance rate. A mechanism to provide this guidance is necessary. It may require performing audits in certain departments. Further, such control will provide a basis for further process improvement as the whole cycle is repeated.

2-7 COMPARISON OF THE THREE PHILOSOPHIES

The previous sections have introduced the quality philosophies of three experts—Deming, Crosby, and Juran. All three of them have the same goal of developing an integrated total quality system with a continual drive for improvement. There are many similarities in the plans proposed by these persons. However, some differences exist in the manner in which the quality goals may be achieved. A good discussion of these three philosophies may be found in the article by Lowe and Mazzeo (1986).*

Definition of Quality

It is interesting to observe how each expert defines quality. Deming's definition of quality deals with a predictable uniformity of the product. His emphasis on the use of statistical process control through control charts is reflected in this definition. Deming's concern about the quality of the product is reflected in the quality of the process, which is his focal point of attention. Thus, his definition of quality does not seem to put as much emphasis on the customer as that of the other two experts. It's not that he doesn't consider the customer important; after all, his concept of the extended process includes the customer. Crosby defines quality as conformance to requirements. Here, requirements are formulated based on customer needs. Crosby's performance standard of zero defects implies seeking to meet the set requirements every time. Juran's definition of quality—fitness of a product for its intended use—seems to incorporate the customer the most. Here, the definition explicitly relates to meeting the needs of the customer.

Management Commitment

All three experts stress the importance of top management commitment. Deming's first and second points (creating a constancy of purpose toward improvement and adopting the new philosophy) define the tasks of management. In fact, all of his 14 points are aimed at management, implying that management's undivided attention is necessary to create a total quality system. Point 1 in Crosby's 14-step process deals with management commitment. He stresses the importance of management communicating its understanding and commitment. Crosby's philosophy is most dedicated to the creation of a "quality culture," which can be attained through management commitment. Juran's quality planning, control, and improvement process seeks management support at all levels. He believes in quality improvement on a project basis. The project approach gets managers involved and assigns responsibilities to each. Thus, in all three philosophies, the support of top management is crucial.

Strategic Approach to a Quality System

Deming advocates a strategy for top management. Not only must they pursue the first 13 points, but they must also create a structure to continually promote the 13 points in a neverending cycle of improvement (creating such a structure is the fourteenth point). Crosby's approach to quality improvement is structured. His second step calls for the creation of quality improvement teams. Under Juran's philosophy, the formation of a quality council is recommended to guide the quality improvement process. Furthermore, his breakthrough sequence

* Ted A. Lowe and Joseph M. Mazzeo, "Three Preachers, One Religion," *Quality*, September 1986, pp. 22–25. Adapted with permission from *Quality*, a publication of Hitchcock Publishing, a Capital Cities/ABC Inc., company.

of quality improvement involves the creation of problem-solving steering arms and diagnostic arms. The function of a steering arm is to establish the direction of the problem-solving effort and organize priorities and resources. The diagnostic arm has the responsibility of analyzing problems and tracking down their root causes.

Measurement of Quality

All three experts believe in quality as a measurable entity to varying degrees. Often, top management has to be convinced of the effects of good quality in dollars and cents. Once they see it as a cost-reducing measure, offering the potential for a profit increase, it becomes easier to obtain their support. A fundamental aim of the quality strategy is to reduce and eliminate scrap and rework, which will reduce the cost of quality. A measurable framework for doing so is necessary. The total cost of quality may be divided into subcategories of prevention, appraisal, internal failure, and external failure. One of the difficulties faced in this setting is the determination of the cost of nonquality, such as customer nonsatisfaction. Notice that it is difficult to come up with dollar values for such concerns as customer dissatisfaction—which is one of Deming's concerns in deriving a dollar value for the total cost of quality. Crosby believes that quality is free; it is unquality that costs.

Neverending Process of Improvement

The philosophies of Deming, Crosby, and Juran share a belief in the neverending process of improvement. Deming calls for repeating his 14 steps over and over again to continuously improve quality. Crosby also recommends continuing the cycle of quality planning, control, and improvement, and Juran's breakthrough sequence shares this philosophy, too. Deming's PDCA cycle (plan-do-check-act) is a mechanism that sustains this neverending process, as does Juran's trilogy.

Education and Training

Fundamental to quality improvement is the availability of an adequate supply of people who are educated in the philosophy and technical aspects of quality. Deming specifically refers to this in his sixth point which talks about training all employees, and in his thirteenth point, which describes the need for retraining to keep pace with the changing needs of the customer through product and process changes. Deming focuses on education in statistical techniques. Education is certainly one of Crosby's concerns as well; his eighth step deals with quality education. However, his emphasis is more on developing a quality culture within the organization so that the right climate exists. Juran's steps do not explicitly call for education and training. However, they may be implicit, since in organizing for the diagnosis of defects and determining remedies thereafter, it is imperative that people be knowledgeable of the process and the cause-and-effect relationships.

Eliminating the Causes of Problems

Deming uses the phrases *special causes* and *common causes* to label problems that arise due to the occurrence of something unusual or that are inherent to the system, respectively. Examples of special causes would be problems due to poor quality from an unqualified vendor or use of an improper tool. With common causes, no special reason can be attributed. They can be eliminated, however, through a change in the system. Examples of common causes are inherent machine variability or worker capability. These problems are controllable by management. Both Deming and Juran claim that about 85 percent of the problems are management-controllable. Hence, action on the part of management can eliminate the problems, or management can provide the necessary authority and tools to the workers to aid in removal of them.

The heart of Deming's philosophy is the use of statistical techniques for identification of special causes and chance causes. Statistical process control through the use of control charts plays an important role in the Deming approach. Deming attributes variations outside the control limits to special causes. These variations are worker-controllable, and the workers can take action to eliminate the causes. On the other hand, variations within the control limits are viewed as the result of common causes. These variations are management-controllable and require an action on their part to be removed. Juran has an approach similar to that of Deming's. He says that special causes create sporadic problems and that common causes create chronic problems. Juran provides detailed guidelines for identifying sporadic problems. For example, he categorizes operator error as being inadvertent, willful, or due to inadequate training or improper technique. Thus, Juran provides specifics for achieving the performance standard of zero defects that Crosby promotes. Crosby, of course, suggests a course of action for error cause removal in his eleventh step.

Goal Setting

Deming is careful to point out that arbitrarily established numerical goals should be avoided. He asserts that such goals impede, rather than hasten, the implementation of a total quality system. Short-term goals based mainly on productivity levels without regard to quality are deemed unacceptable by Deming. By emphasizing the neverending quality improvement process, Deming does not see the need for short-term goals. On the other hand, both Crosby and Juran call for setting goals. Crosby's tenth point deals with goal setting, where employees (with guidance from their supervisors) are asked to set measurable goals for even short-term periods such as 30, 60, or 90 days. Juran recommends an annual quality improvement program with specified goals. He believes that such goals help in measuring the success of the quality projects undertaken in a given year. The goals should be set according to the requirements of the customer. In a way, Juran's approach probably fits the framework of management by objectives, where performance is measured by achievement of stipulated numerical goals.

Structural Plan

Deming's 14-point plan for quality improvement emphasizes using statistical tools at all levels. First bringing a process into a state of statistical control (using control charts) and then seeking improvements on it is essentially a bottom-up approach. The elimination of special causes in order to bring the process under control may take place at lower levels in the hierarchy of the organizational structure. As these causes are removed and the process assumes a state of statistical control, further improvements in the process require the attention of upper-level management.

Crosby, on the other hand, emphasizes a change in the management culture as one of the first steps in his plan. Once the new culture has been ingrained, he proposes a plan for managing the transition. Thus, Crosby's plan takes a top-down approach.

Finally, Juran emphasizes quality improvement through a project-by-project approach. His concept is most applicable to middle management.

To summarize, each company has its own culture. A company should look at all three approaches and select the approach (or combination of approaches) that is most suited to its own setting.

2-8 INTERNATIONAL STANDARDS ISO 9000–9004*

The quality philosophies have had a global impact. Development of total quality systems in manufacturing and service organizations is seen as a necessity. The emphasis on customer satisfaction and continuous quality improvement has led to the development of a quality system of standards and guidelines that complement relevant product or service requirements given in technical specifications. In order to create a benchmark for the large number of national and international standards in the field, the International Standards Organization (ISO) prepared a set of five standards, *ISO 9000-9004*. In order to be consistent with these international standards, the American National Standards Institute and the American Society for Quality Control developed the standards *ANSI/ASQC Q90–Q94,* in 1987. *The American standards are technically equivalent to the ISO 9000–9004 series,* the difference being that they incorporate American language usage and spelling. As the marketplace becomes international and the European Economic Community consolidates at the end of 1992, meeting international standards such as *ISO 9000–9004* may become a necessity.

The purpose of this section is to provide an overview of these standards. For the reader who is interested in additional details, the standards themselves should be consulted. Excerpts from the *ANSI/ASQC Q90–Q94* standards have been chosen, and a comparison of their features has been provided. Meeting and exceeding customer expectations is a central theme of these standards. The scope and application of these standards are briefly described below:

- *ISO 9000 or ANSI/ASQC Q90–1987—Quality Management and Quality Assurance Standards—Guidelines for Selection and Use.* These standards provide guidelines for the selection and use of the series of standards *ISO 9001–9004* or the equivalent *ANSI/ASQC Q91–Q94. ISO 9001–9003* and the equivalent *ANSI/ASQC Q91–Q93* provide quality system standards for external quality assurance purposes, whereas *ISO 9004* and the equivalent *ANSI/ASQC Q94* provide standards for internal quality management purposes.

* Adapted from ASQC (1987), ANSI/ASQC Q90–Q94. Reprinted with the permission of ASQC.

- *ISO 9001 or ANSI/ASQC Q91–1987—Quality Systems—Model for Quality Assurance in Design/Development, Production, Installation, and Servicing.* These standards are used when conformance to specified requirements needs to be assured by the supplier during several stages which may include design/development, production, installation, and servicing.
- *ISO 9002 or ANSI/ASQC Q92–1987—Quality Systems—Model for Quality Assurance in Production and Installation.* These standards are used when conformance to specified requirements needs to be assured by the supplier during production and installation. *ISO 9002* is a subset of *ISO 9001*.
- *ISO 9003 or ANSI/ASQC Q93–1987—Quality Systems—Model for Quality Assurance in Final Inspection and Test.* These standards are used when conformance to specified requirements needs to be assured by the supplier solely at final inspection and test.
- *ISO 9004 or ANSI/ASQC Q94–1987—Quality Management and Quality System Elements—Guidelines.* These standards describe a basic set of elements by which quality management systems can be developed and implemented for internal quality management purposes. The selection of appropriate elements contained in this standard and the extent to which these elements are adopted and applied by a company depend upon such factors as the market being served, the nature of the product, the production processes, and consumer needs.

ISO 9000 and ANSI/ASQC Q90–1987

ISO 9000 and *ANSI/ASQC Q90–1987* provide guidance for the selection and use of the following two groups of standards:

1. *ISO 9004* or *ANSI/ASQC Q94–1987,* which help give guidance to all organizations for quality management purposes. Activities aimed at providing confidence for management that the intended quality is being achieved are often referred to as *internal quality assurance.*

   These standards also provide guidance on the technical, administrative, and human factors affecting the quality of products or services at all stages of the quality loop, from detection of need to customer satisfaction. Throughout these standards emphasis is placed on customer satisfaction, the establishment of functional responsibilities, and the importance of assessing (as far as possible) the potential risks and benefits. All of these aspects should be considered in establishing and maintaining an effective quality system.
2. *ISO 9001–9003 or ANSI/ASQC Q91–Q93 (1987),* which are used for external quality assurance purposes in contractual situations. Activities aimed at providing confidence to the purchaser that the supplier's quality system will provide a product or service that will satisfy the purchaser's stated quality requirements are often referred to as *external quality assurance.*

Another objective of this standard is to clarify the distinctions and interrelationships among the following three principal quality objectives:

1. The organization should achieve and sustain the quality of the product or service so as to continually meet the purchaser's stated or implied needs.
2. The organization should provide confidence to its own management that the intended quality is being achieved and sustained.
3. The organization should provide confidence to the purchaser that the intended quality is being, or will be, achieved in the delivered product or service. When contractually required, this provision of confidence may involve agreeing upon demonstration requirements.

In this context, the standard defines quality policy, quality management, quality system, quality control, and quality assurance as follows:

- *Quality policy:* The overall quality intentions and direction of an organization concerning quality, as formally expressed by top management. The quality policy forms one element of the corporate policy and is authorized by top management.
- *Quality management:* That aspect of the overall management function that determines and implements the quality policy. The attainment of desired quality requires the commitment and participation of all members of the organization, whereas the responsibility for quality management belongs to top management. Quality management includes strategic planning, allocation of resources, and other systematic activities for quality, such as quality planning, operations, and evaluations.
- *Quality system:* The organizational structure, responsibilities, procedures, processes, and resources for implementing quality management. The quality system should be only as comprehensive as needed to meet the quality objectives. For contractual, mandatory, and assessment purposes, demonstration of the implementation of identified elements in the system may be required.

- *Quality control:* The operational techniques and activities used to fulfill requirements for quality. In order to avoid confusion, care should be taken to include a modifying term when referring to a subset of quality control such as "manufacturing quality control" or when referring to a broader concept such as "company-wide quality control." Quality control involves operational techniques and activities aimed both at monitoring a process and at eliminating causes of unsatisfactory performance at relevant stages of the quality loop in order to result in economic effectiveness.

- *Quality assurance:* All those planned and systematic actions necessary to provide adequate confidence that a product or service will satisfy given requirements for quality. Unless given requirements fully reflect the needs of the user, quality assurance will not be complete. To be effective, quality assurance usually requires a continuing evaluation of factors that affect the adequacy of the design or specification for intended applications as well as verifications and audits of production, installation, and inspection operations. Providing confidence may involve producing evidence. Within an organization, quality assurance serves as a management tool. In contractual situations, quality assurance also serves to provide confidence in the supplier.

The relationship of these various concepts is depicted in Figure 2-14. The figure should not, however, be interpreted as a rigid model. The elements that comprise a quality system are shown in Table 2-1. Table 2-1 provides an overall comparison of the four standards *ISO 9001–9003*, or the equivalent *ANSI/ASQC Q91–Q93*. The table is found in *ANSI/ASQC Q90* and does not form an integral part of the standard. It is given for information purposes only.

Table 2-1 shows that *Q92* is less stringent than *Q91*. This is as expected because *Q92*, which deals with quality assurance in production and installation, is a subset of standard *Q91*, which deals with quality assurance in design/development, production, installation, and servicing. Furthermore, *Q93*, which deals with quality assurance in final inspection and test, is less stringent than *Q92*. Table 2-1 shows the specific paragraphs or subsections dealing with the various topics of quality assurance that can be found in each of the standards *Q91–Q94*. It thus provides the user with guidelines as to where to look in the standards for a specific topic.

Q92 is less stringent then *Q91* (as a whole) since it is a subset of *Q91*. While *Q91* deals with quality assurance in design/development, production, installation, and servicing, *Q92* deals with quality assurance in production and installation. Thus, even though portions of *Q91* dealing with production and installation may be the same as in *Q92*, the overall standards of *Q91* would be more stringent since it has additional restrictions relating to design/development and servicing.

Among the standards for external quality assurance, *ISO 9001* and *Q91* are the most stringent, with *ISO 9002* and *Q92* less stringent than *ISO 9001* and *Q91*, and *ISO 9003* and *Q93* less strin-

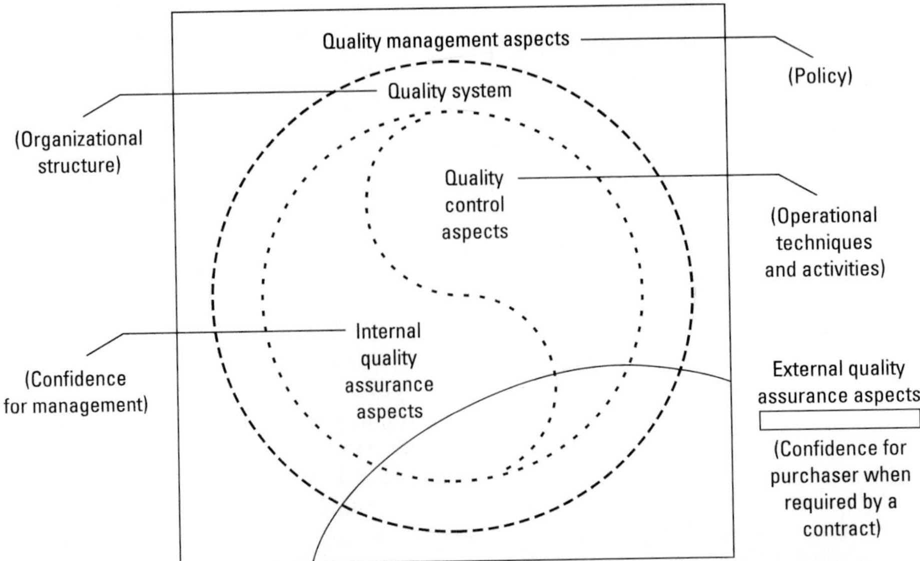

Figure 2-14 Relationship of quality concepts.

TABLE 2-1 Cross-reference list of quality system elements[a] (Adapted from ASQC (1987), ANSI/ASQC Q 90–94. Reprinted by permission of ASQC.

Paragraph (or subsection) no. in Q94	Title[b]	Corresponding paragraph (or subsection) nos. in		
		Q91	Q92	Q93
4	Management Responsibility	4.1 ●	4.1 ◐	4.1 ○
5	Quality System Principles	4.2 ●	4.2 ●	4.2 ◐
5.4	Auditing The Quality System (Internal)	4.17 ●	4.16 ◐	—
6	Economics—Quality-Related Cost Considerations	—	—	—
7	Quality In Marketing (Contract Review)	4.3 ●	4.3 ●	—
8	Quality In Specification and Design (Design Control)	4.4 ●	—	—
9	Quality In Procurement (Purchasing)	4.6 ●	4.5 ●	—
10	Quality in Production (Process Control)	4.9 ●	4.8 ●	—
11	Control Of Production	4.9 ●	4.8 ●	—
11.2	Material Control and Traceability (Product Identification and Traceability)	4.8 ●	4.7 ●	4.4 ◐
11.7	Control of Verification Status (Inspection and Test Status)	4.12 ●	4.11 ●	4.7 ◐
12	Product Verification (Inspection and Testing)	4.10 ●	4.9 ●	4.5 ◐
13	Control of Measuring and Test Equipment (Inspection, Measuring, and Test Equipment)	4.11 ●	4.10 ●	4.6 ◐
14	Nonconformity (Control of Nonconforming Product)	4.13 ●	4.12 ●	4.8 ◐
15	Corrective Action	4.14 ●	4.13 ●	—
16	Handling and Post-Production Functions (Handling, Storage, Packaging, and Delivery)	4.15 ●	4.14 ●	4.9 ◐
16.2	After-sales Servicing	4.19 ●	—	—
17	Quality Documentation and Records (Document Control)	4.5 ●	4.4 ●	4.3 ◐
17.3	Quality Records	4.16 ●	4.15 ●	4.10 ◐
18	Personnel (Training)	4.18 ●	4.17 ◐	4.11 ○
19	Product Safety and Liability	—	—	—
20	Use of Statistical Methods (Statistical Techniques)	4.20 ●	4.18 ●	4.12 ◐
—	Purchaser Supplied Product	4.7 ●	4.6 ●	—

Key: ● full requirement; ◐ less stringent than ANSI/ASQC Q91; ○ less stringent than ANSI/ASQC Q92; — element not present.

[a] Attention is drawn to the fact that the quality system element requirements in Q91, Q92, and Q93 are in many cases, but not in every case, identical.

[b] The paragraph (or subsection) titles quoted in the table above have been taken from Q94; the titles given in parentheses have been taken from the corresponding paragraphs and subsections in Q91, Q92, and Q93.

Source: Adapted from ASQC (1987), ANSI/ASQC Q90–94. Reprinted with the permission of ASQC.

gent than *ISO 9002* and *Q92*. *ISO 9004* and its equivalent *Q94* deal with internal quality assurance. Since there is a good bit of overlap among these standards, some features of one of these standards are presented next. *ISO 9001* and its equivalent *ANSI/ASQC Q91* are discussed, because they are the most stringent of the standards for external quality assurance.

ISO 9001 and ANSI/ASQC Q91–1987

ISO 9001 and the equivalent *ANSI/ASQC Q91* are part of a series of three standards (*ISO 9001-9003*, or *ANSI/ASQC Q91–Q93*) dealing with quality systems that can be used for external quality assurance models. The standard specifies quality system requirements for use when a contract between two parties requires the demonstration of a supplier's capability to design and supply the product or service. The specified requirements are aimed at *preventing nonconformity* at all stages from design to servicing (reinforcing the notion that quality assurance efforts should be directed toward defect prevention rather than defect detection). A variety of features of the standard are discussed below.

Management responsibility is described in all aspects of the quality system. The supplier's management should define a quality policy which documents its goals and objectives for attaining quality. In creating an organizational structure for a quality system, the responsibilities, distribution of authority, and interrelationship of all personnel who manage, perform, and verify work affecting quality must be defined. The supplier should provide adequate resources for such verification activities as inspection, test, monitoring of the design, production, installation, and servicing of the process and/or product. The personnel responsible for design reviews and audits of the quality system must be distinct from those having direct responsibility for the work performed. The supplier's management should conduct management reviews at appropriate intervals to ensure the effectiveness of the quality system.

Maintaining a documented *quality system* is essential to ensure product conformance to specified requirements. Documentation should keep track of the procedures for implementing the quality assurance system. Standards for the following are fundamental to the creation of a quality system: acceptability, measurement procedures and their capabilities, design compatibility, production processes, installation, inspection and test procedures, preparation of quality plans and a quality manual, and maintenance of quality records.

Quality in marketing is maintained through a *contract review*. It is expected that the supplier will review each contract to ensure that the requirements are adequately defined and documented. Also, the supplier should make sure that the capability exists for meeting the contractual requirements.

An important section of the standard deals with *design control*, for which the supplier is expected to establish and maintain procedures to control and verify the design in order to ensure that the specified requirements are met. In order to achieve this control, the supplier should draw up plans that identify the responsibility for each design and development activity. Review of design input requirements related to the product or service is necessary, along with a review of design output. The design output is expected to meet the design input requirements, conform to appropriate regulatory requirements, and identify those characteristics of the design that are crucial to the safe and proper functioning of the product. The above function is conducted through design verification.

The *document control* section of the standard ensures the availability of pertinent information from appropriate documents at all locations where such documents are essential for conducting operations. Obsolete documents should promptly be removed.

The *purchasing* section of the standard requires the supplier to ensure that the purchased product conforms to specified requirements. Selection of subcontractors should be based on an ability to meet specified subcontract requirements, as demonstrated through records of past performance. Purchasing documents should contain data describing the product ordered, the type (or other form of identification), the requirements for approval or qualification of product, the procedures, the process equipment, and the personnel. The purchaser or purchaser's representative should be given the right to verify the purchased product at the source or upon receipt of the product. Such verification, however, cannot be used by the supplier as evidence of effective quality control for the subcontract.

The supplier is expected to establish and maintain procedures for *identifying the product* from applicable drawings or other documents during all stages of production, delivery, and installation. If *traceability* is a specified requirement, an individual product or batch should have a unique identification.

Guidelines for *process control* are defined in the standard. They require the supplier to identify and plan production and installation processes and to operate them under controlled conditions. The control section requires documenting work instructions that define the manner of production and installation in addition to monitoring suitable product and process characteristics. Product and process control should be monitored continuously in order to ensure that specified requirements are met.

Product verification through inspection and testing could involve in-process as well as final inspection. The supplier should ensure that the incoming product conforms to specified requirements. The amount and nature of receiving inspection could be influenced by the control exercised at the source and by the documented evidence of quality conformance. In-process product conformance can be monitored by process monitoring and control methods. Nonconforming products should be identified. Final inspection and testing should be conducted according to the quality plan, and documented procedures and appropriate records should be maintained.

Control of measuring and test equipment through calibration and appropriate selection is the responsibility of the supplier. Inspection, measuring, and test equipment should be capable of achieving the required accuracy and precision. The environmental conditions under which calibrations, inspections, and measurements are carried out should be adequate. Furthermore, handling, preservation, and storage of such test equipment should be such that the accuracy and fitness for use are maintained.

The standard requires that the *inspection and test status* of products be identified to indicate conformance or nonconformance. Such identification must be maintained throughout production and installation to ensure the delivery of conforming products only. *Control of nonconforming products* should be established by the supplier through identification, documentation, evaluation, segregation (or disposal), and notification of the relevant departments. Review of nonconforming products may be conducted to determine whether they should be reworked, regraded for alternative applications, or rejected.

The maintenance of procedures for *corrective action* by the supplier is critical. Such procedures should investigate the cause of nonconforming products and the corrective action needed to prevent recurrence. Analysis of processes, work operations, quality records, service reports, and customer complaints to detect and eliminate potential causes of nonconforming products is fundamental to quality control and improvement. The supplier should implement and record changes in procedures resulting from corrective action.

The standard assigns responsibility to the supplier to establish, document, and maintain *procedures for handling and post-production functions* such as storage, packaging, and delivery. The supplier should provide means of handling that prevent damage or deterioration. The supplier should provide secure areas for storage with appropriate methods stipulated for authorizing receipt and dispatch. Packing and preservation processes should ensure conformance to specified requirements. The protection of quality, where contractually specified, should be extended to include delivery to destination.

An important feature of the standard makes the supplier responsible for establishing and maintaining procedures for identification, collection, indexing, filing, storage, maintenance, and disposition of *quality records*. These records should be maintained to demonstrate achievement of the required quality and the effective operation of the quality system. Pertinent subcontractor quality records should be included in this data. Retention times for quality records should be established and recorded. Where agreed upon contractually, quality records should be made available for evaluation by the purchaser or purchaser's representative for a specified period.

In order to verify whether quality activities comply with planned arrangements and to determine the effectiveness of the quality system, the supplier should carry out a comprehensive system of planned and documented *internal quality audits*. These audits should be scheduled based on the status and importance of the activity. The results of the audits should be documented and brought to the attention of the personnel having responsibility in the area audited. The management personnel with responsibility in the audited area should then take timely corrective action on the deficiencies found by the audit.

The supplier should be responsible for establishing and maintaining procedures for identifying the *training needs* and providing for the training of all personnel performing activities affecting quality. The assignment of personnel to specific tasks should be based on such qualifications as appropriate education, training, and experience, as required. Appropriate records of training should be maintained.

In the event that *servicing* is specified in the contract, the supplier should establish and maintain procedures for performing and verifying that servicing meets the specified requirements.

Finally, where appropriate, the supplier should establish procedures for identifying adequate *statistical techniques* required for verifying the acceptability of process capability and product characteristics.

The above are some of the areas addressed by *ISO 9001* and its equivalent *ANSI/ASQC Q91–1987*. The interested reader may consult the standard for a detailed discussion of each of these areas.

2-9 MALCOLM BALDRIGE NATIONAL QUALITY AWARD*

In the United States, the strategic importance of quality control and improvement has been formally recognized through the *Malcolm Baldrige National Quality Award,* which was created by *Public Law 100–107* and signed into effect on August 20, 1987. The findings of *Public Law 100—107* revealed that poor quality has cost companies as much as 20 percent of sales revenues nationally and that an improved quality of goods and services goes hand in hand with improved productivity, lower costs, and increased profitability. Furthermore, improved management understanding of the factory floor, worker involvement in quality, and greater emphasis on statistical process control can lead to dramatic improvements in the cost and quality of products and services. Quality improvement programs must

* Adapted from "*1992 Award Criteria—Malcolm Baldrige National Quality Award,*" U.S. Department of Commerce, Technology Administration, National Institute of Standards and Technology, Gaithersburg, MD 20899.

be management-led and customer-oriented. All of these findings are quite consistent with the quality philosophies discussed previously in this chapter.

The U.S. Government felt that a national quality award would stimulate American companies to improve quality and productivity for the pride of recognition, while at the same time promoting a competitive edge. Such recognition of achievements in quality would provide an example to others and would establish guidelines and criteria that can be used by business, industrial, governmental, and other organizations in evaluating their own quality improvement efforts. Furthermore, detailed information on the quality practices of the winning organizations would be made available to others so that they in turn could adopt the desirable features.

Award Eligibility Criteria and Categories

Responsibility for the award is assigned to the National Institute of Standards and Technology (NIST), an agency of the U.S. Department of Commerce. The American Society for Quality Control assists in administering the award program under contract to NIST. Awards are made annually to U.S. companies that excel in quality management and quality achievement; the first award was given in 1988.

Any for-profit business located in the United States or its territories is eligible to apply. Local, state, or national government agencies may not apply. There are four restrictions that apply. These *eligibility criteria* are described below:

1. A company or its subsidiary is eligible only if the quality practices of its major business functions are inspectable in the United States or its territories. One or both of the following conditions must apply:
   - More than 50 percent of the employees must be located in the United States or its territories.
   - More than 50 percent of the physical assets must be located in the United States or its territories.
2. At least 50 percent of a subsidiary's customer base (dollar volume for products and services) must be free of direct financial and line organization control by the parent company. For example, a subsidiary is not eligible if its parent company or another subsidiary of the parent company is the customer for more than one-half of its total products or services.
3. Individual units or partial aggregations of units of "chain" organizations (such as hotels, retail stores, banks, or restaurants) are not eligible.
4. Subsidiaries performing any of the business support functions of the company are not eligible. Examples of business support functions include sales/marketing/distribution, customer service, finance and accounting, human resources, purchasing, legal services, and research and development.

Multiple-application restrictions exist in that a subsidiary and its parent company may not both apply for awards in the same year. Furthermore, if a company receives an award, the company and all its subsidiaries are ineligible to apply for another award for a period of five years.

There are three *award eligibility categories:* manufacturing, service, and small business. Up to two awards may be given in each of the three categories. A brief description of each category is as follows:

1. *Manufacturing*—Companies or subsidiaries that produce and sell manufactured products or manufacturing processes or produce agricultural, mining, or construction products. For a complete list of manufacturing and products, the *Standard Industrial Classification (SIC)* codes may be consulted. Typical examples are agriculture (crops and livestock), forestry, building and heavy construction contractors, food and tobacco products, apparel, chemicals, petroleum refining, machinery/computer equipment, electrical/electronic equipment, and transportation equipment.
2. *Service*—Companies or subsidiaries that sell services. The list of SIC codes may be consulted for a complete listing of services. Some examples are agricultural services, transportation (air, railroad, buses, water, and so on), communications, utilities (electricity, gas, and so on), automobile dealers and service stations, banking and insurance, real estate, hotels and lodging places, personal and business services, health and legal services, and amusement and recreation centers.
3. *Small business*—Complete businesses with no more than 500 full-time employees. Business activities may include manufacturing and/or service. A small business must be able to document that it functions independently of any other businesses that are equity owners.

Criteria for Evaluation

Applying for the award is a two-step process. First, potential applicants must establish their eligibility in one of the three award categories previously described. Second, an application form and a report must be completed. These forms are reviewed in a four-stage process. In the first stage, a review is conducted by at least four members of a board of examiners. At the conclusion of the first stage, the panel determines which applications should be referred for consensus review. In the second stage, the application report is reviewed by at least four members of a board of examiners led by a senior examiner. After the second stage, the panel determines which applicants should receive site visits. The third stage involves an on-site verification of the application report. The site-visit review team develops a report for the panel of judges, leading to the fourth stage involving the judges' final review. The panel of judges develops a set of recommendations for the National Institute of Standards and Technology. Awards are traditionally presented by the President of the United States.

The award criteria are built upon the following core values:

Customer-driven quality

Leadership of senior management

Continuous improvement

Full participation of all personnel

Fast response through reduction of cycle time

Emphasis on problem prevention through design quality

Development of long-range strategies and plans

Management by fact based on data analysis

Partnership development between labor-management, suppliers, and customers.

Satisfaction of public responsibility, such as meeting public health and safety requirements

There are seven categories that incorporate the core values and concepts. These categories determine the criteria framework for evaluation. Each category has some subcategories. A brief description of each major category follows.

1. *Leadership*. The leadership category examines senior executives' *personal* leadership and involvement in creating and sustaining a customer focus and clear and visible quality values. The way in which these quality values are integrated into the company's management system and the way they are reflected in how the company addresses its public responsibilities are also examined.

2. *Information and analysis*. This category examines the scope, validity, analysis, management, and use of data and information to drive quality excellence and improve competitive performance. The adequacy of the company's data, information, and analysis system to support improvement of the company's customer focus, products, services, and internal operations is also examined.

3. *Strategic quality planning*. This category examines the company's planning process and how all key quality requirements are integrated into overall business planning. Also examined are the company's short-term and longer-term plans and how quality and performance requirements are deployed to all work units.

4. *Human resource development and management*. This category examines the key elements of how the company develops and realizes the full potential of its work force in pursuing the company's quality and performance objectives. The company's efforts to build and maintain an environment for quality excellence conducive to full participation and personal and organizational growth are also examined.

5. *Management of process quality*. This category examines the systematic processes the company uses to pursue ever-higher quality and company performance. The key elements of process management, including design, management of process quality for all work units and suppliers, systematic quality improvement, and quality assessment are examined.

6. *Quality and operational results*. This category examines the company's quality levels, improvement trends in quality, operational performance, and supplier quality. Also examined are current quality and performance levels relative to those of competitors.

7. *Customer focus and satisfaction*. This category examines the company's relationships with customers as well as its knowledge of customer requirements and quality factors that determine marketplace competitiveness. Also examined are the company's methods to determine customer satisfaction, current trends, and levels of satisfaction relative to competitors.

Table 2-2 shows the seven main categories used in the evaluation process, along with the subcategories of each. Also shown are the point values for each subcategory used in determining the overall score of an applicant. Note that the evaluation criteria embody the tenets of the quality philosophies discussed previously. For further details concerning each of the

TABLE 2-2 Examination categories for the 1992 Malcolm Baldrige Award

Examination category/Items		Point value
1.0 Leadership		90
1.1 Senior executive leadership	45	
1.2 Management for quality	25	
1.3 Public responsibility	20	
2.0 Information and analysis		80
2.1 Scope and management of quality and performance data and information	15	
2.2 Competitive comparisons and benchmarks	25	
2.3 Analysis and uses of company-level data	40	
3.0 Strategic quality planning		60
3.1 Strategic quality and company performance planning process	35	
3.2 Quality and performance plans	25	
4.0 Human resource development and management		150
4.1 Human resource management	20	
4.2 Employee involvement	40	
4.3 Employee education and training	40	
4.4 Employee performance and recognition	25	
4.5 Employee well-being and morale	25	
5.0 Management of process quality		140
5.1 Design and introduction of quality products and services	40	
5.2 Process management—product and service production and delivery processes	35	
5.3 Process management—business processes and support services	30	
5.4 Supplier quality	20	
5.5 Quality assessment	15	
6.0 Quality and operational results		180
6.1 Product and service quality results	75	
6.2 Company operational results	45	
6.3 Business process and support service results	25	
6.4 Supplier quality results	35	
7.0 Customer focus and satisfaction		300
7.1 Customer relationship management	65	
7.2 Commitment to customers	15	
7.3 Customer satisfaction determination	35	
7.4 Customer satisfaction results	75	
7.5 Customer satisfaction comparison	75	
7.6 Future requirements and expectations of customers	35	
TOTAL POINTS		1000

subcategories, the reader should consult the relevant reference, U.S. Department of Commerce (1992).

2-10 SUMMARY

This chapter discusses the quality philosophies of Deming, Crosby, and Juran, with the emphasis on Deming's 14 points for management. Each point is discussed, and its impact on the goal of creating a world-class quality system is presented. Many companies are adopting the Deming approach to quality and productivity. The quality philosophies of Crosby and Juran provide the reader with a broad framework of the various approaches that exist for management. All three approaches are compared and contrasted. They all have the same goal, with slightly different paths. Whereas Deming's approach emphasizes the importance of using statistical techniques as a basis for quality control and improvement, Crosby focuses on the creation of a new corporate culture dealing with the attitude of all employees toward quality. Juran advocates quality improvement through problem-solving techniques on a project-by-project basis. He emphasizes the need to correctly diagnose the root causes of a problem based on the observed symptoms. Once these causes have been identified, Juran focuses on finding remedies. Management, upon understanding all three philosophies, should select one or a combination of these approaches to best fit their own environment. These philosophies of quality have had a global impact. International standards on quality assurance practices have been developed. In particular, the standards *ISO 9000–9004* and their U.S. equivalents, *ANSI/ASQC Q90–Q94* are discussed in this chapter. Also, the criteria for the *Malcolm Baldrige National Quality Award* bestowed annually in the United States are presented.

2-11 CASE STUDY

GUIDELINES FOR IMPLEMENTING A TOTAL QUALITY SYSTEM*

When W. Edwards Deming describes an organization committed to quality, he provides a compelling picture of how things ought to be. But there are precious few instructions on how to begin such a transformation. However, there are some practical elements involved in becoming a quality organization. The approach must be based on the pragmatic realities of business life: that change is difficult; that resistance to change is often strong and persistent; that no matter how much a company might want to transform itself to some new order, it must continue doing business in the way it knows best for the time being. Transformation, therefore, involves a sort of adolescence—a period of inelegance when we shift from one way of being to a new way of being.

Guidelines for Quality

1. *Quality begins with delighting the customers.* A company should strive to delight customers, giving them even more than they imagined possible. Management may be ecstatic, the board of directors blissful, and the company may be considered a legend on Wall Street, but if your customers are not delighted, you have not begun to achieve quality.

2. *The quality organization must learn how to listen to customers and help customers identify and articulate their needs.* If quality is to be defined by the customer, the quality organization must remain close to the customer. Closeness means much more than surveys and interviews. It means knowing in detail the work the customer does, how the customer uses your products, and what concerns and problems the customer has. Be aware not only of problems resulting directly from defects in the product but also of related problems experienced by customers even when the product is functioning properly.

Those who are not yet your customers can also provide you invaluable feedback on your product or service. Why don't they use the product? What do they use, and what has been their experience with it?

3. *The quality organization leads customers into the future.* We depend today on photocopiers, personal computers, disposable diapers, and other products that we didn't even imagine possible in the past. A quality organization knows the consumers so well and explores technological possibilities so far that products and services not yet imagined are the inevitable result.

4. *Flawless, customer-pleasing products and services result from well-planned systems and processes that function flawlessly.* Inspection may be a way to avoid embarrassment, but it is not a way to achieve quality. A flawless system provides what the customer wants when the customer wants it, with efficiency, precision, and consistency—and without waste, defects, or rework. A quality system is continuously being improved.

5. *In a quality organization, the vision, values, systems, and processes must be consistent with, and complementary to, each other.* The vision answers the question, "What businesses are we in?" Values or operating policies describe how businesses are conducted. Systems and processes are the sequences of activities by which all work gets done. When these components work at cross purposes, the result is waste and frustration: engineers design a product that production can't make; purchasing buys materials that production can't use; sales makes promises that can't be kept. Each step of a process must be the perfect antecedent to the next step.

6. *Everyone in the quality organization—managers, supervisors, and operators—must work in concert.* A spirit of teamwork must pervade the organization. This spirit must be strong and pervasive enough to supersede the attachments that people normally form to bonds such as profession, function, or rank.

7. *Teamwork in a quality organization must be based on commitment to the customers and to constant improvement.* Teamwork is a term used two ways in a quality organization. First, it refers to a spirit of loyalty and collegiality throughout the organization. Second, it refers to the greater use of teams and participative

* Adapted from Peter R. Scholtes and Heero Hacquebord. "Beginning the Quality Transformation, Part I," *Quality Progress*, July 1988, pp. 28–33. Copyright © 1988 Joiner Associates, Inc. All rights reserved. Reprinted by Macmillan Publishing Co. with permission.

processes in the conduct of business. In neither case is teamwork a product of pep talks and exhortation. Nor is it blind loyalty. Nor merely feeling good. Teamwork results from a common understanding of the organization's vision and values, a dedication to delighting customers, an understanding of the organization's systems and processes, and a shared commitment to the ongoing improvement of those systems and processes.

8. *In a quality organization, everyone must know his or her job.* A job is not learned simply by reading a job description or operations manual. Employees must

- Understand where their work fits into the various larger systems and processes of which they are a part, what and who precedes and follows them in the sequence of activities, and how their work relates to the final product and ultimate user or consumer.
- Know what their internal customers want and don't want and what will delight these customers.
- Master the information and skills necessary to perform tasks related to their work and constantly renew and upgrade knowledge and skills.
- Understand the process or technology with which they work: how it functions, its capabilities, and what causes variation and break-down. They must constantly get to know it better and learn how to improve its performance.

This level of understanding requires both continuous education and regular feedback from each employee's external and internal customers.

9. *The quality organization uses data and a scientific approach to plan work, solve problems, make decisions, and pursue improvements.* Managers help everyone focus on the method by which the organization's work is accomplished. All types of initiatives and activities are monitored to see how well they are working and how they can be further improved.

10. *The quality organization develops a working partnership with suppliers.* The quality-minded company exercises great care over the materials and services it receives. The quality organization seeks a long-term collaborative relationship with a single source for each type of supply.

11. *The culture of the quality organization supports and nourishes the improvement efforts of every group and individual in the company.* The organization seeks to establish and maintain a spirit based on the following: being close to the customer, the importance of precision and data, internal teamwork and mutual respect, constant improvement, and pride of work (both processes and products).

The New Concept of the Organization

The old way to view an organization is known as the chain of command (see Figure 2-15). This view

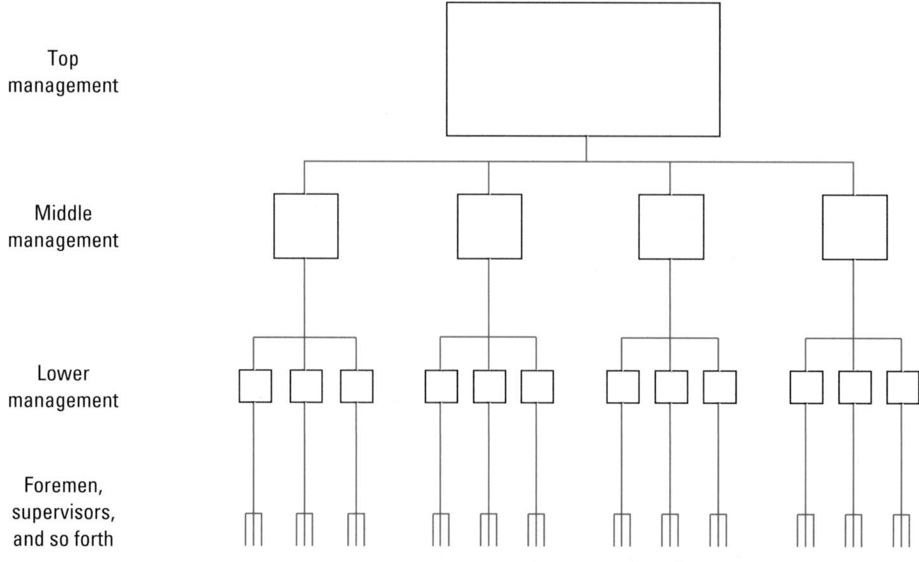

Figure 2-15 The old way to view an organization: The chain of command.

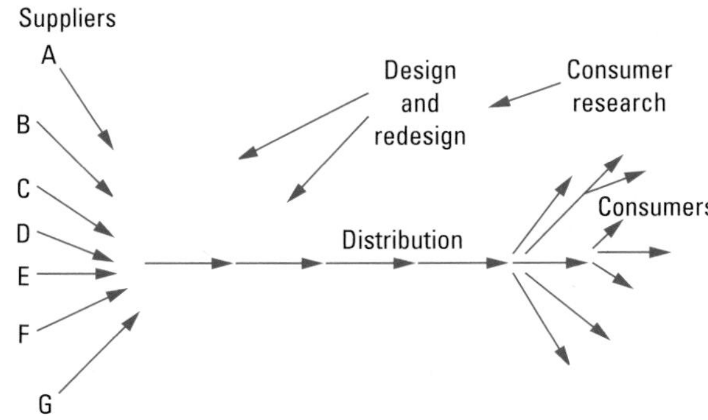

Figure 2-16 The new way to view an organization: The system.

of an organization was developed in the 1840s, when businesses needed for the first time to manage mass production, wide distribution, and geographically dispersed organizations. This view has some shortcomings. It doesn't portray the interdependence of functional areas. It doesn't describe the organization as a flow of processes. It tends to emphasize individual accountability rather than the group, the process, or the output of the group and process. There is no reference to products or customers in this view. Therefore, the purpose of the organization implied in this chart is accountability and control. All paths lead to or from the figure at the top.

The new way to view an organization is shown in Figure 2-16. This diagram was first used by W. Edwards Deming in Japan in 1950. It depicts

- The interdependency of organizational processes
- The primacy of the customer (consumer)
- The effect of customer feedback (consumer research)
- The need for continuous improvement based on customer feedback
- The importance of suppliers
- The network of internal supplier/customer relationships

Figures 2-15 and 2-16 symbolize different ways of thinking and a difference in priorities. If you ask someone, "In your work, who is it important for you to please?" and that person answers "My boss," then that person experiences the organization as a chain of command. If the answer is, "The people in the next step of the process, my internal customer, and our external customer," then that person has a systems perspective.

Figure 2-17 offers a different illustration of this new concept. Various functional units must work in concert with each other. The quality organization has no appetite for turf wars or intramural one-upmanship.

It is necessary to have a systems view of the organization to become a leader or member of a quality organization. A leader who views the organization as a chain of command and accountability will not be able to visualize the company as customer- and quality-oriented and thus impedes the pursuit of quality.

Guidelines for Transformation

Ordinarily, people in organizations will not simply convert from an old way to a new way, even when the new way is demonstrably better. Change takes more than an authoritarian edict: "Beginning next Monday we will practice quality management—or else!"

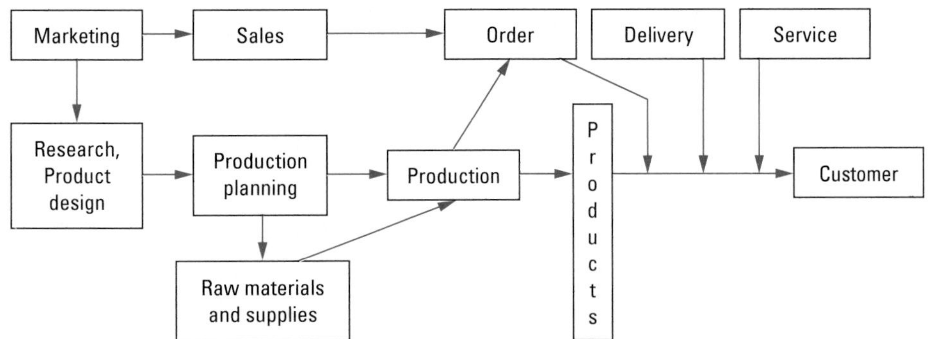

Figure 2-17 The new concept from the perspective of functional divisions and sections.

To some extent, this section and the following section were written with small- and medium-sized companies in mind. To a corporation with hundreds of thousands of employees scattered around the world, these initiatives will seem geared to a hopelessly small scale. However, two points are worth mentioning.

First, a huge corporation is in many respects a vast multiplicity of smaller organizations. The guidelines described here can be applied to the corporate headquarters as one organization and to each successive cluster of organizational units. With a steady, gradual process of transformation, it is easier to develop the corporation's human resources into a commonwealth of support for quality transformation. One should be leery of the impatience of some managers who try to force growth when it should be nourished.

Second, the goals of transformation must be consistent throughout the corporation. There should also be some consistency in the method and means used to achieve those goals. Can such consistency be achieved in a huge corporation without some kind of coercion? Probably not. But what is prescribed should be kept to a minimum. Moreover, the need for whatever is prescribed should be explained in some detail. Whenever possible, what is prescribed should be a process rather than the end result. Finally, when the leaders of an organization announce a change to which they expect everyone to conform, they themselves must undergo change. Their change must be a clear demonstration to everyone of the importance of this transformation.

Guidelines for Change

1. *Recognize the informal organization.* Think of a company as a small town or a large high school. Along with its official work system, the organization is also a social system—a loose network of small groups of people. These groups offer their members support and friendship. People in these groups can form a strong bond of loyalty to the company. These informal groups have leaders. Often, these groups have rules that can determine, for example, the pace of work, what kind of contact or communication with managers is okay, and so on. If the informal organization and the informal leaders accept whatever change is being proposed, that change will occur much more smoothly. If they oppose the change, it may be nearly impossible to implement. Therefore, it is important to identify the informal leaders, get to know them, and spend time wooing them.

2. *Seek the active support of a critical mass.* In the context of organizational change, a critical mass is a dynamic and somewhat elusive quantity. It is not simply a majority. What constitutes a critical mass at one stage of innovation may be inadequate in later stages. Critical mass is a sufficient number of influential people supporting a proposed change to give the impression of a growing, formidable movement, a sense of momentum, a groundswell of interest. Critical mass describes the constituency behind a proposed change and the ability of that constituency to attract more and more support as time goes by. Critical mass may be defined laterally in an organization (for example, a sufficient number of champions among division managers) or vertically (a sufficient number of committed people in division X). Because of a changeover of people and the ongoing nature of a change, an ultimate critical mass may be hard to achieve.

3. *People don't resist change, they resist being changed.* Transformation is a campaign for people's hearts as well as their minds. A change is successful because a critical mass has rallied around the proposed change. Creating such a loyal constituency is not ordinarily an undertaking permeated with logic. Nor can it be created through fear.

People need to feel included in the decision to change. At least they need to be presented with the rationale for change. Their needs, fears, desires, and concerns about the change deserve to be listened to, responded to, and accommodated whenever possible.

4. *When possible, organizational change should be planned and treated like a courtship—with a mixture of gradualism and surprise.* For example consider the following:

- When some facet of the change represents a very different way of behaving, allow people time to warm up to it and experiment with it. Give them time to be inelegant and make mistakes.
- Plan change in increments of gradually increased risk or adjustment. Help the organization stretch itself, but not too much at a time. A localized implementation of some innovation may be easier to undertake than a widespread implementation. Something approached as a temporary experiment may be more acceptable than a permanent change.
- Look for visible signs of the old order and replace them with symbols of the new order. A shift of symbols can help facilitate a shift of vision, policies, systems, and processes.
- Woo the undecided movers and shakers and the formal or informal leaders. Here, wooing means spending time listening to them. This is time spent not exhorting them to support the change, but rather listening to what concerns they have in general. Don't focus only on concerns related to the proposed change. Listen actively. Learn if any of their needs might be addressed by the proposed change or if the change might be adjusted to accommodate their concerns.

5. *Efforts to implement change should be "anchored."* Anchoring means that individuals or groups directly involved in innovative activities should be surrounded by a network of others involved in similar activities. There must also be services that offer support and guidance to the innovators. Without such anchoring, the innovators will more likely feel isolated, as if they are floundering or inadequate. For example, imagine a project team assigned to study and improve a process. Rather than allowing it to function in isolation, have it report to a team of managers who can support and advise the project team. This creates several levels of anchoring—that is, reinforcement. The connection here is not to a single manager, but to a team of managers, each reinforcing the other and all of them reinforcing—and being reinforced by—the project team. Thus, several people are engaged in growth, change, and improvement, and each supports the other in that effort.

The project team will need technical assistance, particularly in project planning, team management, and the scientific approach. Therefore, a technical adviser is assigned to coach the project team and the managers.

There are several advantages in having more than one task force or project team operating at a time. Project teams can learn from each other and share some training. Concurrent projects can also create challenge and mutual support. Each group is anchored to other groups through occasional contact and interaction.

With such a well-connected network of activity, those involved in implementing change will not feel as though they are isolated or floundering. They will feel part of a common effort of learning and change. Checks and assistance are available if a group should falter. Meanwhile, overall progress can be maintained.

6. *The more profound, comprehensive, and widespread the proposed change, the more absolute is the need for deep understanding and active leadership by the top managers.* Responsibility for leading the transformation cannot be delegated by the top manager. Without the active leadership of top managers, efforts at profound change may flourish for a while, but they will not last. Without the active leadership of top managers, many of those in the second echelon of leadership will wait for some indication of lasting direction. Thus the effort to change will have passive, shallow, tentative support. Such efforts will be displaced by other priorities and will be vulnerable to activities that contradict the goals of the proposed change.

Questions for Discussion

1. What are some considerations regarding quality that must be taken into account prior to implementing a total quality system?
2. What is the new way of viewing an organization? Comment on formal and informal organizational structure and their importance in the implementation of a total quality system.
3. Discuss some specific guidelines for adopting a quality system on an organization-wide basis.
4. How do the philosophies of Deming, Juran, and Crosby complement the suggested guidelines for a quality transformation?
5. Select a company of your choice. Describe its organizational structure, and comment on whether it is complementary to the adoption of a total quality system.
6. Describe the importance of the segments of the extended process on the development and acceptance of a total quality system.

KEY TERMS

ANSI/ASQC Q90–Q94
Causes
  Common
  Special
Chronic problems
Consistency of purpose
Constancy of purpose
Corporate culture
Crosby's 14-step plan for quality improvement
Crosby's philosophy
Deming cycle
Deming's 14 points for management
Diagnostic arm
Extended process
International standards
  ISO 9000–9004
  Internal quality assurance
  External quality assurance
Juran's philosophy
Leadership
Loss function
Malcolm Baldrige Award
  U.S. Public Law 100–107
  Eligibility criteria
  Eligibility categories
  Evaluation criteria
Organizational barriers
Performance classification

Process capability
Product improvement cycle
Productivity
Quality
Quality breakthrough sequence
Quality culture
Quality improvement
Quality management maturity grid
Quality trilogy
Sporadic problems
Standard Industrial Classification (SIC) codes
Total quality system
Training
Vendor selection
Work standards
Zero defects

EXERCISES

2-1 What is the fundamental theme in Deming's philosophy for quality improvement?

2-2 Briefly state and describe Deming's 14 points for management.

2-3 Explain the notion of the extended process.

2-4 Explain the Deming cycle and its role in quality improvement.

2-5 What is the difference between constancy and consistency of purpose?

2-6 What are the reasons for mass inspection not being a viable alternative for quality improvement?

2-7 Describe some characteristics for selecting vendors. Consider a company of your choice. Describe their selection process for vendors, and make recommendations.

2-8 Explain why there is a loss associated with product meeting specifications but deviating from the target value.

2-9 Describe the role of managers and supervisors in Deming's approach.

2-10 Explain the organizational barriers that prevent a company from adopting the total quality philosophy.

2-11 According to Deming, explain the drawbacks of setting up numerical goals.

2-12 What are the drawbacks of some traditional performance appraisal systems, and how may they be modified?

2-13 What is the theme behind Crosby's quality management philosophy?

2-14 Describe and explain the "four absolutes" of quality management prescribed by Crosby.

2-15 Explain the role and function of the quality management maturity grid. Select a company, and locate their position on the grid.

2-16 State and explain Crosby's 14-step plan for quality improvement.

2-17 Explain the meaning of the term "quality culture." What is the importance of management's role in this context?

2-18 Describe Juran's quality trilogy program and its significance.

2-19 What is the difference between quality control and quality improvement? Discuss the role of management in each of these settings.

2-20 Discuss the importance of the diagnostic process from symptom to cause in Juran's approach.

2-21 Compare and contrast the philosophies of Deming, Crosby, and Juran.

2-22 Select a company. Analyze and develop a quality philosophy for this company. How does your recommendation differ from the existing approach?

REFERENCES

ANSI/ASQC Q90–1987—American National Standard—Quality Management and Quality Assurance Standards—Guidelines for Selection and Use. (1987). American Society for Quality Control, Milwaukee, WI.

ANSI/ASQC Q91–1987—American National Standard—Quality Systems—Model for Quality Assurance in Design/Development, Production, Installation, and Servicing. (1987). American Society for Quality Control, Milwaukee, WI.

ANSI/ASQC Q92–1987—American National Standard—Quality Systems—Model for Quality Assurance in Production and Installation. (1987). American Society for Quality Control, Milwaukee, WI.

ANSI/ASQC Q93–1987—American National Standard—Quality Systems—Model for Quality Assurance in Final Inspection and Test. (1987). American Society for Quality Control, Milwaukee, WI.

ANSI/ASQC Q94–1987—American National Standard—Quality Management and Quality System Elements—Guidelines. (1987). American Society for Quality Control, Milwaukee, WI.

Crosby, Philip B. (1979). *Quality Is Free*. McGraw-Hill, New York.

Crosby, Philip B. (1984). *Quality Without Team—The Act of Hassle-Free Management*. McGraw-Hill, New York.

Crosby, Philip B. (1989). *Let's Talk Quality*. McGraw-Hill, New York.

Deming, W. Edwards (1982). *Quality, Productivity, and Competitive Position*. Center for Advanced Engineering Study, Massachusetts Institute of Technology, Cambridge, MA.

Deming, W. Edwards (1986). *Out of the Crisis*. Center for Advanced Engineering Study, Massachusetts Institute of Technology, Cambridge, MA.

Gitlow, Howard S., and Gitlow, Shelly J. (1987). *The Deming Guide to Quality and Competitive Position*. Prentice-Hall, Englewood Cliffs, NJ.

ISO 9000—Quality Management and Quality Assurance Standards—Guidelines for Selection and Use. (1987). Geneva, Switzerland.

ISO 9001—Quality Systems—Model for Quality Assurance in Design/Development, Production, Installation, and Servicing. (1987). Geneva, Switzerland.

ISO 9002—Quality Systems—Model for Quality Assurance in Production and Installation. (1987). Geneva, Switzerland.

ISO 9003—Quality Systems—Model for Quality Assurance in Final Inspection and Test. (1987). Geneva, Switzerland.

ISO 9004—Quality Management and Quality System Elements—Guidelines. (1987). Geneva, Switzerland.

Juran, J. M. (1988a). *Juran on Planning for Quality*. The Free Press, New York.

Juran, J. M. (1988b). *Juran's Quality Control Handbook*. McGraw-Hill, New York.

Juran, J. M. (1989). *Juran on Leadership for Quality—An Executive Handbook*. The Free Press, New York.

Juran, J. M. (August 1986) "The Quality Trilogy," *Quality Progress*, pp. 19–24.

Juran, J. M., and Gryna, Frank M., Jr. (1980). *Quality Planning and Analysis—From Product Development through Use*. McGraw-Hill, New York.

Lowe, Ted A., and Mazzeo, Joseph M., (September 1986). "Three Preachers, One Religion," *Quality*, pp. 22–25.

Scherkenbach, William W. (1986). *The Deming Route to Quality and Productivity*. Ceep Press, Washington, D.C.

Scholtes, P. R., and Hacquebord, H., (July 1988). "Beginning the Quality Transformation," *Quality Progress*, pp. 28–33.

U.S. Department of Commerce (1992). *1992 Award Criteria—Malcolm Baldrige National Quality Award*. National Institute of Standards and Technology, Gaithersberg, MD.

Walton, M. (1988). *The Deming Management Method*. G. P. Putnam, New York.

Walton, M. (1990). *Deming Management at Work*. G. P. Putnam, New York.

PART

II

Statistical Foundations and Methods of Quality Improvement

CHAPTER

3

Fundamentals of Statistical Concepts and Techniques in Quality Control and Improvement

CHAPTER OUTLINE

SYMBOLS

$P(A)$	Probability of event A
μ	Population mean of a quality characteristic
$\overline{X}$	Sample average
s	Sample standard deviation
n	Sample size
X_i	ith observation in a sample
N	Population size
$T(\alpha)$	α-percent trimmed mean
σ	Population standard deviation
s^2	Sample variance
σ^2	Population variance
R	Range
γ_1	Skewness coefficient
γ_2	Kurtosis coefficient
r	Correlation coefficient
M	Sample median
s_m	Standard deviation of the sample median
$p(x)$	Probability distribution (or mass function) for a discrete random variable
$f(x)$	Probability density function for a continuous random variable
$F(x)$	Cumulative distribution function
$E(X)$	Expected value or mean of a random variable X
Z	Standard normal random variable
p	Probability of success on a trial in a binomial experiment
λ	Mean of a Poisson random variable
λ	Failure rate for an exponential distribution
γ	Location parameter for a Weibull distribution
α	Scale parameter for a Weibull distribution
β	Shape parameter for a Weibull distribution
$\Gamma(u)$	Gamma function for the variable u
$(1-\alpha)$	Level of confidence for confidence intervals

3-1 INTRODUCTION

The purpose of this chapter is to provide a foundation for the statistical concepts and techniques used in quality control and improvement. Statistics plays an important role in this area—consequently, a clear understanding of the related principles provides a basis for a comprehensive assimilation of the different procedures. Knowledge of the statistical principles will help in the formulation of procedures to use in a given situation and will aid in interpreting the analyses. When considering the extended process, it is necessary to study the characteristics of a process to determine if some identifiable cause forced a deviation from the expected norm and if a remedial action needs to be taken. Furthermore, for a process operating at its "best" level, in the absence of any identifiable causes that may be detrimental to the process, improvement may be desired. In such instances one will have to identify certain procedures for the improvement of quality; exposure to statistical concepts will certainly be beneficial. The objective of this chapter is to provide a brief review of different statistical concepts and techniques. Thus, should one encounter a statistical concept in a later chapter that needs clarification, this chapter may be referred to. This chapter focuses on concepts as they apply to quality control and improvement.

3-2 POPULATION AND SAMPLE

A *population* is defined to be the set that includes the complete collection of all items that possess a certain characteristic of interest.

Example 3-1: Suppose the objective is to determine the average weight of cans of brand A soup processed by a company for the month of July. The population in this case is the set of all cans of brand A soup that are output in the month of July (say, 50,000). Even if the company processes various brands of soup in this case only brand A is of interest, so only brand A makes up the population.

A *sample* is a subset of a population. Realistically, in many manufacturing or service industries, it may not be feasible to obtain data on every element in the population. Measurement, storage, and retrieval of large volumes of data may be impractical, and the associated costs of obtaining such information may be high. In such situations, obtaining data from only a portion of the population may be the practical choice.

Example 3-2: Consider again the situation involving brand A soup. A sample may be a set of 500 cans of brand A soup, randomly selected from the output during the month of July.

 3-3 PARAMETER AND STATISTIC

A *parameter* is a characteristic of a population, something that describes it.

Example 3-3: For brand A cans of soup, a parameter could be the average weight of all 50,000 cans processed in the month of July.

A *statistic* is a characteristic of a sample. It is used to make inferences on the population parameters that are typically unknown.

Example 3-4: For brand A cans of soup, a statistic could be the average weight of a sample of 500 cans chosen from the output during the month of July. This value could be 12.11 ounces, which would then be an estimate of the average weight of all 50,000 cans. A statistic is sometimes called an estimator.

 3-4 PROBABILITY

This section provides an intentionally brief introduction to the concepts of probability. The *probability* of an event describes the chance of occurrence of that event. A probability function is bounded between 0 and 1, with 0 representing the definite nonoccurrence of the event and 1 representing the certain occurrence of the event.

The set of all outcomes of an experiment is known as the *sample space (S)*.

Relative Frequency Definition of Probability

If each of the events in the sample space is equally likely to happen, then the probability of an event A is given by

$$P(A) = \frac{n_A}{N} \tag{3.1}$$

where $P(A)$ = Probability of event A
n_A = Number of ways in which event A can happen
N = Number of points in the sample space

This definition is associated with the relative frequency concept of probability. It is applicable to situations where historical data on the outcome of interest is available. The probability associated with the sample space is 1 (that is, $P(S) = 1$).

Example 3-5: A company makes plastic storage bags for the food industry. Out of the hourly production of 2000 16-ounce bags, 40 were found to be nonconforming. If the inspector randomly chooses a bag from the hour's production, what is the probability of it being nonconforming?

Solution. We define the event A as getting a bag that is nonconforming. The sample space S consists of 2000 points (that is, $N = 2000$). The number of ways in which event A can happen (n_A) is 40. Thus, if the inspector is equally likely to choose any one of the 2000 bags,

$$P(A) = \frac{40}{2000} = 0.02$$

If it were necessary to make an inference on the chance of a new process (not yet operational) producing a nonconforming bag, one would have to resort to other methods.

Simple Events and Compound Events

Simple events are those that cannot be decomposed any further. They represent the most elementary form of the outcomes possible in an experiment.

Compound events are made up of two or more simple events.

Example 3-6: Consider a situation where an inspector is sampling transistors from an assembly line and identifying them as acceptable or not. Suppose the inspector chooses two transistors. What are the simple events? Give an example of a compound event. Find the probability of finding at least one acceptable transistor.

Solution. Consider the following outcomes:

A_1: Event that the first transistor is acceptable
N_1: Event that the first transistor is unacceptable
A_2: Event that the second transistor is acceptable
N_2: Event that the second transistor is unacceptable.

There are four simple events which make up the sample space S:

$$S = \{A_1A_2,\ A_1N_2,\ N_1A_2,\ N_1N_2\}$$

These events may be described as follows:

$E_1 = \{A_1A_2\}$: Event that the first and second transistors are acceptable

$E_2 = \{A_1N_2\}$: Event that the first transistor is acceptable and the second one is not

$E_3 = \{N_1A_2\}$: Event that the first transistor is unacceptable and the second one is acceptable

$E_4 = \{N_1N_2\}$: Event that both transistors are unacceptable.

A compound event B may be the event that at least one of the transistors is acceptable. In this case event B consists of the following three simple events: $B = \{E_1, E_2, E_3\}$. Assuming that each of the simple events is equally likely to

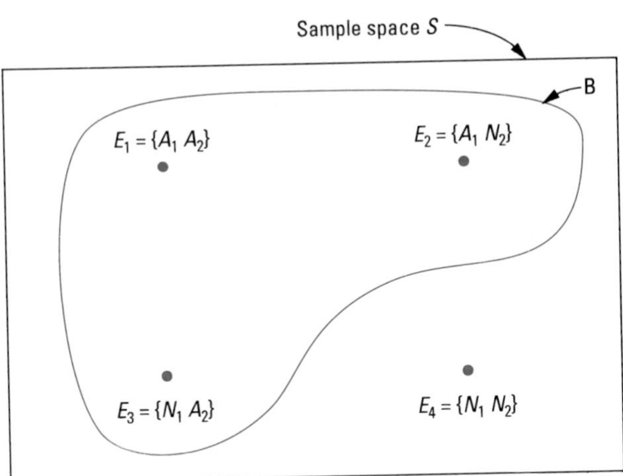

Figure 3-1 Venn diagram.

happen, $P(B) = P(E_1) + P(E_2) + P(E_3) = 1/4 + 1/4 + 1/4 = 3/4$. Figure 3-1 shows a Venn diagram, which is a graphical representation of the sample space and its associated events.

Complementary Events

The complement of an event A implies the occurrence of everything but A. If we define A^c to be the complement of A, then

$$P(A^c) = 1 - P(A) \tag{3.2}$$

Figure 3-2 shows the probability of the complement of an event by means of a Venn diagram. Continuing with the information from Example 3-6, suppose we want to find the probability of the event that both transistors are unacceptable. Note that this is the complement of event B, which was defined as at least one of the transistors being acceptable. So

$$P(B^c) = 1 - P(B) = 1 - 3/4 = 1/4$$

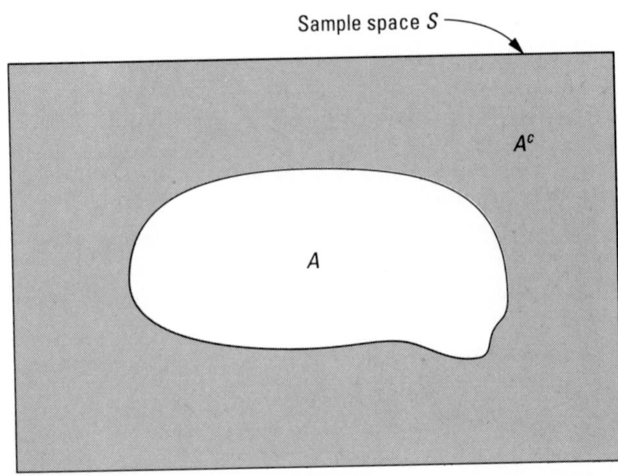

Note: The shaded area represents $P(A^c)$.

Figure 3-2 An event and its complement.

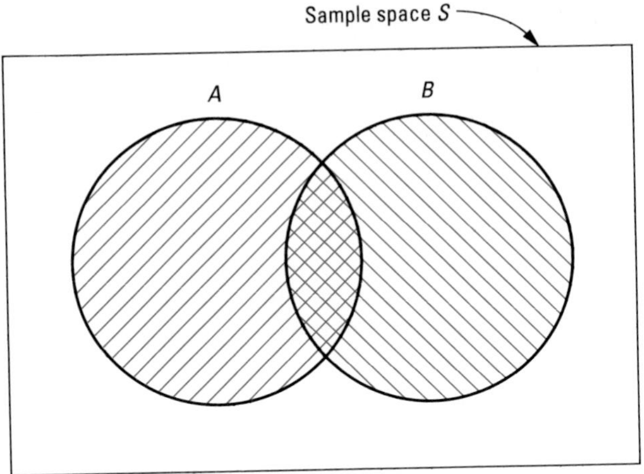

Figure 3-3 Union of two events.

Additive Law

The additive law of probability defines the probability of the union of two or more events happening. If we have two events A and B, then the union of these two implies that A happens or B happens or both happen. Figure 3-3 shows the union of two events, A and B by means of a Venn diagram. The proportion of shaded area in the sample space represents the probability of the union of the two events. The additive law is as follows:

$$\begin{aligned} P(A \cup B) &= P(A \text{ or } B \text{ or both}) \\ &= P(A) + P(B) - P(A \cap B) \end{aligned} \tag{3.3}$$

$P(A \cap B)$ represents the probability of the intersection of the events A and B, that is, the occurrence of both A and B. The logic behind the additive law can easily be seen from the Venn diagram in Figure 3-3. $P(A)$ represents the area within the boundary defining event A. Similarly $P(B)$ represents the area within the boundary defining event B. The common area or overlap between the areas defining A and B represents the probability of the intersection, $P(A \cap B)$. Upon adding $P(A)$ to $P(B)$, this intersection is included twice. Thus Equation 3.3 adds $P(A)$ to $P(B)$ and subtracts $P(A \cap B)$ once.

Multiplicative Law

The multiplicative law of probability defines the probability of the intersection of two or more events. Intersection of a group of events means that all of the events in that group occur. In general, for two events A and B,

$$P(A \cap B) = P(A \text{ and } B) = P(A)\, P(B \mid A) = P(B)\, P(A \mid B) \quad (3.4)$$

The term $P(B \mid A)$ represents the conditional probability of B given that event A has happened (that is, the probability that B will occur if A has). Likewise, $P(A \mid B)$ represents the conditional probability of A given that event B has happened. Of the two forms of the formula given by Equation 3.4, the problem information will dictate which version to use.

Independence and Mutually Exclusive Events

Two events A and B are said to be *independent* if the outcome of one has no influence on the outcome of the other. If A and B are independent, then $P(B \mid A) = P(B)$, that is, the conditional probability of B given that A has happened equals the unconditional probability of B. Similarly, $P(A \mid B) = P(A)$ if A and B are independent. From Equation 3.4, it can be seen that if A and B are independent, the general multiplicative law reduces to

$$P(A \cap B) = P(A \text{ and } B) = P(A)\, P(B) \quad \text{if } A \text{and } B \text{are independent} \quad (3.5)$$

Two events A and B are said to be *mutually exclusive* if they cannot happen simultaneously. The intersection of two mutually exclusive events is the null set, and the probability of their intersection is zero. Notationally, $P(A \cap B) = 0$ if A and B are mutually exclusive. Figure 3-4 shows a Venn diagram for two mutually exclusive events. Note that when

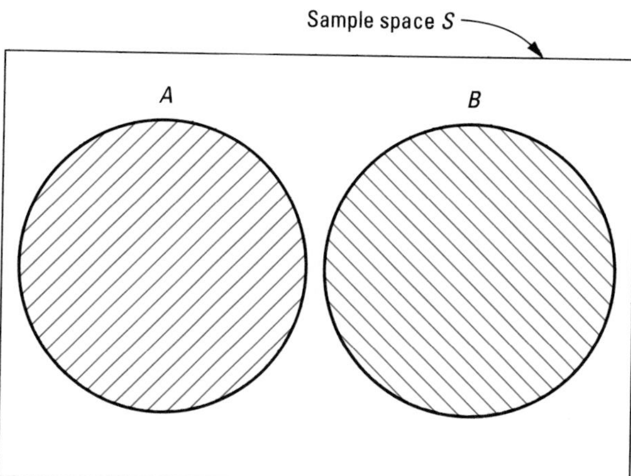

Figure 3-4 Mutually exclusive events.

A and B are mutually exclusive events, the probability of their union is just the sum of their individual probabilities. In other words, the additive law takes on the following special form:

$$P(A \cup B) = P(A) + P(B) \quad \text{if } A \text{ and } B \text{ are mutually exclusive}$$

Now, consider combining these two concepts of independence and mutual exclusiveness. If events A and B are mutually exclusive, what can we say about their dependence or independence? Obviously, if A happens, B cannot happen, and vice versa. Therefore, if A and B are mutually exclusive, they are dependent. If A and B are independent, the additive rule from Equation 3.3 becomes

$$P(A \text{ or } B \text{ or both}) = P(A) + P(B) - P(A)\, P(B) \quad (3.6)$$

Example 3-7:

a. In the production of metal plates that are needed in an assembly, it is known from past experience that 5 percent of the plates do not meet the length requirements. Also, from historical records, 3 percent of the plates do not meet the width requirements. Assume that there are no dependencies between the processes that make the length and those that trim the width. What is the probability of getting a plate that will meet both the length and the width requirements?

Solution. Let A be the outcome that the plate meets length requirements and B be the outcome that the plate meets width requirements. From the problem information, $P(A^c) = 0.05$ and $P(B^c) = 0.03$. Then

$$P(A) = 1 - P(A^c) = 1 - 0.05 = 0.95$$
$$P(B) = 1 - P(B^c) = 1 - 0.03 = 0.97$$

Using the special case of the multiplicative rule when events are independent, we have

P (meeting both length *and* width requirements)
$= P(A \cap B)$
$= P(A)\, P(B)$ (since A and B are independent events)
$= (0.95)(0.97) = 0.9215$

b. What proportion of the parts will not meet at least one of the requirements?

Solution. The required probability $= P(A^c \text{ or } B^c \text{ or both})$. Using the additive rule we get

$$P(A^c \text{ or } B^c \text{ or both}) = P(A^c) + P(B^c) - P(A^c \cap B^c) = 0.05 + 0.03 - (0.03)(0.05) = 0.0785$$

Therefore 7.85 percent of the parts will have at least one characteristic (length, width, or both) not meeting the requirements.

c. What proportion of parts will meet neither length nor width requirements?

Solution. We want to find $P(A^c \cap B^c)$, which has already been found.

$$P(A^c \cap B^c) = P(A^c)\,P(B^c) = (0.03)(0.05) = 0.0015.$$

Thus 0.15 percent of the parts will be deficient in meeting both the length and width requirements.

d. Suppose the operations that produce the length and the width are not independent. If the length does not satisfy the requirement, it causes an improper positioning of the part while trimming the width and thereby increases the chances of the width not meeting requirements. From experience, it is estimated that if the length does not conform to the requirements, the chance of the width not conforming to the requirements is 60 percent. Find the proportion of parts which will conform to neither the length nor the width requirements.

Solution. The probability of interest is $P(A^c \cap B^c)$. The problem information gives $P(B^c \mid A^c) = 0.60$. Using the general form of the multiplicative law,

$$\begin{aligned} P(A^c \cap B^c) &= P(A^c)\,P(B^c \mid A^c) \\ &= (0.05)(0.60) = 0.03 \end{aligned}$$

So 3 percent of the parts will meet neither the length nor width requirements. Notice that this value is quite different from the answer to part c, where the events were assumed to be independent.

e. In part a, are events A and B mutually exclusive?

Solution. We have found $P(A) = 0.95, P(B) = 0.97$, and $P(A \cap B) = 0.9215$. If A and B were mutually exclusive, $P(A \cap B)$ would have to be zero, that is, the probability of the plate meeting both the length and width requirements would be zero. However, this is not the case, since $P(A \cap B) = 0.9215$. So A and B are *not* mutually exclusive.

f. Describe two events in this example setting that are mutually exclusive.

Solution. A and A^c are mutually exclusive, to name one instance. $P(A \cap A^c) = 0$, since A and A^c cannot happen simultaneously. This means that it is not possible to get a part that both meets and does not meet the length requirements!

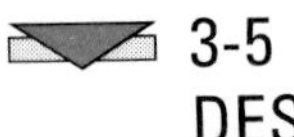

3-5 DESCRIPTIVE STATISTICS—DESCRIBING PRODUCT OR PROCESS CHARACTERISTICS

Statistics is the science that deals with the collection, classification, analysis, and making of inferences from data or information. Statistics may be subdivided into two categories—*descriptive statistics* and *inferential statistics*.

Descriptive statistics deals with describing the characteristics of a product or process based on information collected regarding it. For instance, suppose we have information on the time taken to serve a customer in a fast-food restaurant for 500 persons. This information, if plotted as a frequency histogram with the horizontal axis representing a range of time values needed to serve a customer and the vertical axis denoting the number of persons observed in each of the time ranges, would give some idea of the process condition. Likewise, if the average time to serve a customer were calculated for 500 customers, this value could also tell us something about the process. More details on procedures used in descriptive statistics are discussed in later sections.

Inferential statistics deals with drawing conclusions on unknown process parameters based on information contained in a sample. Assume that we want to test the validity of a claim that the average time to serve a customer in the above fast-food restaurant is no more than 3 minutes. We would follow a statistical procedure to test the above claim. Suppose the sample average time to serve a customer (based on a sample of 500 people) is 3.5 minutes. It is then important to determine whether this observed average of 3.5 minutes is significantly greater than the claimed mean of 3 minutes. Such procedures fall under the heading of inferential statistics. They help us draw conclusions about the conditions of a process. They also help us determine if certain improvements have taken place in a process by statistically comparing conditions before and after changes. For example, suppose the management of the fast-food restaurant is interested in reducing the average time to serve a customer. They decide to add two persons to their service staff. Once this change is implemented, they sample 500 customers and find that the average time to serve a customer is 2.8 minutes. The question then is to determine whether there has been a statistically significant decrease in the average time to serve a customer or whether the observed decrease in the average is due to random variation inherent to sampling. Procedures that address such problems are discussed later.

Data Collection

Information on the extended process is needed for process control and process improvement. The gathering of information can be done in several ways. One of the most common methods of data collection is through *direct observation*. Here, a measurement of the quality characteristic is taken by an observer (or automatically by an instrument). For instance, data taken on the depth of tread in automobile tires by an inspector is in this category. On the other hand, collecting data regarding the time period of satisfactory performance of a particular brand of hair dryer through questionnaires mailed to consumers is an example of *indirect observation*. In this case, data is reported by the consumers and is not necessarily observed by the experimenter. An incorrect interpretation of the question by the responder, an error in estimating the satisfactory performance period, or an inconsistent degree of precision among the different responders' answers may be sources of errors in such data.

Continuous Variable Data on quality characteristics may be categorized as *continuous* or *discrete*. A variable which can assume any value on a continuous scale within a range is said to be *continuous*. Examples of continuous variables are the hub length of lawnmower tires, the viscosity of a certain resin, the specific gravity of a toner used in photocopying machines, the thickness of a metal plate, and the time to admit a patient to a hospital. Such variables are measurable and may have a numerical value associated with them. The precision of the data is influenced by the precision of the measuring instrument. For example, the thickness of a metal plate may be 12.5 mm when measured by callipers; however, a micrometer may yield a value of 12.52 mm, while an optical sensor may give a measurement of 12.523 mm.

Discrete Variable Variables that can assume a finite or countably infinite number of values are said to be *discrete*. The number of defective rivets in an assembly is a discrete random variable. Other examples include the number of paint blemishes in an automobile, the number of operating capacitors in an electrical instrument, and the number of satisfied customers in an automobile repair shop. Note that count data falls in this category. Recording an observation usually costs less than a corresponding continuous variable since the variable is merely classified as being, say, unacceptable or not (which can be done through a go/no-go gage) rather than specify its exact measurement. Thus, the reduced cost of getting information may be offset by the lack of complete information offered by the data. Sometimes, characteristics that are really continuous may be viewed as discrete to allow easier measurement and reduced inspection costs. For example, the hub diameter in a tire is actually a continuous random variable; but rather than numerically measuring the hub diameter using, say, a micrometer, a go/no-go gage may be used to quickly identify the characteristic as either acceptable or not. Hence, the acceptability of the hub diameter is a discrete random variable. In this case, the goal is not to know the exact hub diameter but rather to know if it is within certain acceptable limits.

Accuracy and Precision The *accuracy* of a data set or a measuring instrument refers to the degree of uniformity of the observations around a desired value such that, on the average, the target value is realized. Assume that the target thickness of a metal plate is 5.25 mm. Figure 3-5*a* shows observations spread on either side of the target value in almost equal proportions; these observations are said to be accurate. Even though individual observations may be quite different from the target value, a data set is considered accurate if the average of a large number of observations is close to the target.

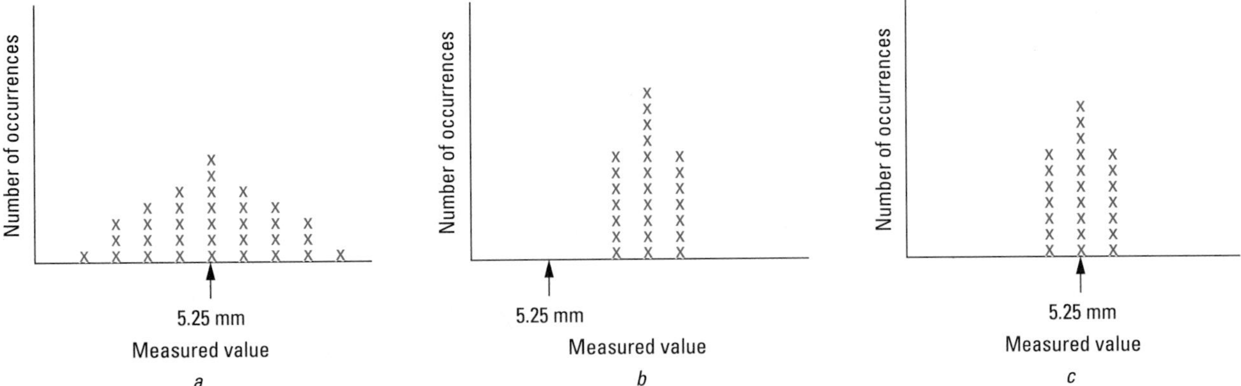

Figure 3-5 Accuracy and precision of observations: (*a*) accurate; (*b*) precise; (*c*) accurate and precise.

The *precision* of a data set or a measuring instrument refers to the degree of variability of the observations. Observations may be off the target value but still considered precise, as shown in Figure 3-5*b*. A sophisticated measuring instrument should show very little variation in output values if a constant value is used multiple times as input. Similarly, sophisticated equipment in a process should be able to produce an output characteristic with as low a variability as possible.

For measuring instruments, accuracy may be related to *calibration*. If a measuring device is properly calibrated, the average output value given by the device for a particular quality characteristic should, after repeated use, equal the true input value.

Both accuracy and precision are desirable. Figure 3-5*c* depicts a situation where not only do the values exhibit small variability but they are also centered around the desired target value. In equipment or measuring instruments, accuracy can usually be altered by changing the setting of a certain adjustment (such as an adjustment screw, pin, or lever). However, precision is an inherent function of the equipment itself and cannot be improved by changing a setting.

Measurement Scales

When obtaining data either directly or indirectly, four scales of measurement may be used to classify the type of information—the nominal, ordinal, interval, and ratio scales.

Nominal Scale If the data is such that it can be placed in one of several categories where a numerical value associated with the observation has no real meaning, then the scale of measurement used for such data is nominal. Items classified as conforming or nonconforming without a need to know the exact numerical value of the characteristic (for example, a diameter in millimeters) are categorized using a nominal scale of measurement. Likewise, categorizing defects as critical, major, or minor is another example of using a nominal scale.

Ordinal Scale For observations where the rank associated with a data point is meaningful and can be used to provide order, the ordinal scale of measurement is appropriate. Consider the situation where customers are asked to provide feedback on the quality of service in a retail garment store. The level of quality is divided into the following five groups: 1 (outstanding), 2 (good), 3 (average), 4 (fair), 5 (poor). The responder is asked to check one of these groups. Thus, we have data on the quality of service varying from 1 to 5. Note that a rating of 1 does not necessarily imply that the service is twice as good as service earning a rating of 2. But we can say that a rating of 1 is preferable to a rating of 2, and so forth.

Interval Scale The interval scale is appropriate when both the order of and the difference between numerical observations can be compared. For instance, suppose we are interested in the temperature of a furnace used in steel smelting. Five readings taken during a two-hour interval are 2050, 2070, 2100, 2150, and 2200°F. Obviously, these data values could be placed in, say, ascending order of temperature to indicate the coolest temperatures, the next coolest, and so on. Furthermore, the differences between the values can be compared. The difference between the data values 2050 and 2100 represents a 50°F increase in temperature. Similarly, the difference between the values of 2100 and 2150 represents the same increase (50°F) in temperature. However, note that a zero in a Fahrenheit scale is different from that of a Celsius scale.

Ratio Scale The ratio scale is suitable when both the order of and difference between observations can be compared and when there exists a natural zero for the measurement scale. Consider a situation where the weight of certain castings to be used in an assembly is of interest. Suppose the weights of four castings are 2.0, 2.1, 2.3, and 2.5 kg. The order of and difference in weights can be compared. Thus the increase in weight from 2 to 2.1 is 0.1 kg, which is the same as the increase from 2.3 to 2.4 kg. Also, when we compare the weights of 2.0 and 2.4 kg, we can say that the casting that weighs 2.4 kg is 20 percent heavier than that which weighs 2.0 kg. There is a natural zero for the scale—0 kg implies no weight.

Measures of Central Tendency

In statistical quality control, collected data needs to be described such that analysts can get a feel for the process or product characteristic. Such descriptions can be given through graphical methods or numerical measures. This section describes some of the commonly used numerical measures for deriving summary information from observed values. Measures of central tendency tell something about the locations of the observations and the value about which they are clustered. They help us decide whether it is necessary to change the settings of process variables.

Mean The mean is the simple average of the observations in a data set. In quality control, the mean is one of the most commonly used measures. It is easy to calculate and understand. The mean may be used to determine if, on the average, the process is operating around a desirable target value. The *sample mean*, or average, (denoted by $\overline{X}$), is found by adding all observations in a sample and dividing by the number of observations (n) in that sample. If the ith observation is denoted by X_i, then the sample mean is calculated as

$$\overline{X} = \frac{\sum_{i=1}^{n} X_i}{n} \tag{3.7}$$

The *population mean* (μ) is found by adding all of the data values in the population and dividing by the size of the population (N). It is calculated as

$$\mu = \frac{\sum_{i=1}^{N} X_i}{N} \tag{3.8}$$

The population mean is sometimes denoted as $E(X)$, the expected value of the random variable X. It is also called the mean of the probability distribution of X. Probability distributions are discussed later in this chapter.

Example 3-8: A random sample of five observations of the waiting time of customers in a bank is taken. The times (in minutes) are 3, 2, 4, 1, and 2. The sample average ($\overline{X}$), or mean waiting time, is calculated as

$$\overline{X} = \frac{3+2+4+1+2}{5} = \frac{12}{5} = 2.4 \text{ minutes}$$

This information can be used by a bank to determine if the customer satisfaction level needs to be improved by increasing the number of tellers.

Median The median is the value in the middle, when the observations are ranked. If there are an even number of observations, the simple average of the two middle numbers is chosen as the median. The median has the property that 50 percent of the values are less than or equal to it.

Example 3-9:

a. A random sample of 10 observations of piston ring diameters (in mm) yielded the following values: 52.3, 51.9, 52.6, 52.4, 52.4, 52.1, 52.3, 52.0, 52.5, and 52.5. We first rank the observations:

51.9, 52.0, 52.1, 52.3, 52.3,
52.4, 52.4, 52.5, 52.5, 52.6

The two observations in the middle are 52.3 and 52.4. The median is equal to (52.3 + 52.4)/2 = 52.35.

The median is less influenced by the extreme values in the data set. It is said to be more robust than the mean.

b. A department store is interested in expanding its facilities and wants to do a preliminary analysis of the number of customers that it serves. Five weeks are chosen at random, and the number of customers served during those weeks were as follows:

3000, 3500, 500, 3300, 3800

The median number of customers is 3300, while the mean is 2820. On further investigation of the week for which the number of customers was 500, it was found that a major university which has a significant impact on the number of customers was closed for spring break. Thus, in this case the median (3300) might be a better measure of central tendency than the mean (2820). It gives a better idea of the number of customers per week. In fact, even if the data value had been 100 instead of 500, the median would still be 3300, though the mean would further decrease. This demonstrates the robustness of the median compared to the mean.

If there are *outliers* (values that are very large or small compared to the majority of the data points), the mean is influenced by them and is pulled towards the outliers. Figure 3-6 demonstrates the effect of outliers on the mean.

Mode The mode is the value that occurs most frequently in the data set. It is used to denote a "typical" value from the process.

Example 3-10: A hardware store wants to determine the size of circular saws to stock. From past sales data, a random sample of 30 showed the following sizes (in mm):

80, 120, 100, 100, 150, 120, 80, 150, 120, 80,
120, 100, 120, 120, 150, 80, 120, 100, 120, 80,
100, 120, 120, 150, 120, 100, 120, 120, 100, 100

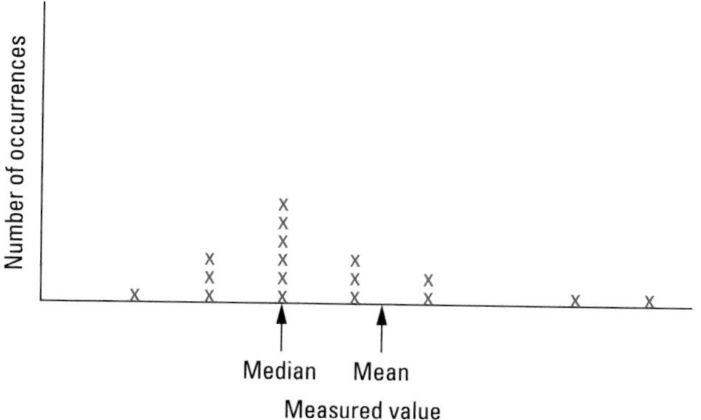

Figure 3-6 Effect of outliers on a mean.

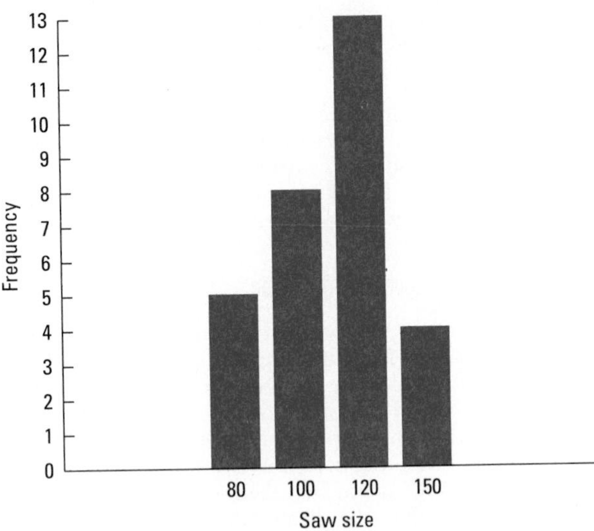

Figure 3-7 Frequency plot of saw size.

The mode is 120 because this value occurs most frequently (13 times). So, if the manager has to choose from among the sizes to stock, he or she may decide to stock those of size 120. A frequency plot of the number of saws of each size sold is shown in Figure 3-7. Note that the mode has the highest frequency. A data set can have more than one mode, in which case it is said to be multimodal.

Trimmed Mean The trimmed mean is a robust estimator of the central tendency of a set of observations. It is obtained by calculating the mean of the observations that are left after deleting a proportion of the high and low values. The α-percent trimmed mean, denoted by $T(\alpha)$, is the average of the observations that are left after trimming (or deleting) α-percent of the high observations and α-percent of the low observations. It is a suitable measure when there are outliers in the data set which are believed not to represent usual process characteristics. Sometimes, if there are extreme observations caused by a faulty measurement process, trimming may be used to delete those extreme observations. A better estimate of the population central tendency can then be obtained.

Example 3-11: The time taken to tune-up automobiles (in minutes) was observed for 20 randomly selected cars. The data values were as follows:

15, 10, 12, 20, 16, 18, 30, 14, 16, 15,
18, 40, 20, 19, 17, 15, 22, 20, 19, 22

To find the 5 percent trimmed mean [that is, $T(5)$], first rank the data in increasing order. The ranked data values are as follows:

10, 12, 14, 15, 15, 15, 16, 16, 17, 18,
18, 19, 19, 20, 20, 20, 22, 22, 30, 40

The number of observations to be deleted on each side (high and low) is $20(.05) = 1$. Delete the lowest observation (10) and the highest observation (40). The mean of the remaining 18 observations is found to be 18.222. The trimmed mean is obviously more robust than the mean. For example, if the largest observation of 40 had been 60, the 5 percent trimmed mean would still be 18.222. However, the mean of all 20 observations would be 19.9.

Measures of Dispersion

The numerical measures of location described above give an indication of the central tendency, or middle, of a data set. They do not tell much about the variability of the observations. Consequently, measures of dispersion that provide information on the variability, or scatter, of the observations around a given value (usually the mean) are fundamental to statistical quality control. One of the important functions of quality control and improvement is to analyze and reduce the variability of a process. Thus, means of measuring variability must be understood.

Range A widely used measure of dispersion in quality control is the range, which is the difference between the largest and smallest values in a data set. Notationally, the range R is defined as

$$R = X_L - X_S \tag{3.9}$$

where X_L is the largest observation and X_S is the smallest observation.

Example 3-12: The following 10 observations of the time to receive baggage after landing were randomly taken in an airport. The data values (in minutes) were as follows:

15, 12, 20, 13, 22, 18, 19, 21, 17, 20.

The range $R = 22 - 12 = 10$ min. This value of 10 gives some idea of the variability in the observations and may also suggest whether action should be taken to reduce the spread.

Variance The variance is a measure of the fluctuation of the observations around the mean. The larger the value, the greater the dispersion. The population variance σ^2 is given by

$$\sigma^2 = \frac{\sum_{i=1}^{N}(X_i - \mu)^2}{N} \tag{3.10}$$

where μ is the population mean and N represents the number of number of data points in the population. The sample variance s^2 is given by

$$s^2 = \frac{\sum_{i=1}^{n}(X_i - \overline{X})^2}{n - 1} \tag{3.11}$$

where $\overline{X}$ represents the sample mean and n is the number of observations in the sample. In most applications, the sample variance is calculated rather than the population variance because calculation of the latter is possible only by knowing every value in the population. A modified version of Equation 3.11 for calculating the sample variance is

$$s^2 = \frac{\sum_{i=1}^{n} X_i^2 - (\sum_{i=1}^{n} X_i)^2/n}{n-1} \qquad (3.12)$$

This version is sometimes easier to use. It involves accumulating the sum of the observations and the sum of squares of the observations as data values become available. On the other hand, to use Equation 3.11, one first has to calculate the sample mean $\overline{X}$ using all the observations and then go back to each data value to find the deviation from the sample mean. Thus, using Equation 3.11 requires two passes through the data, whereas using Equation 3.12 requires only one pass. Equations 3.11 and 3.12 are algebraically equivalent.

Observe that in calculating either the population variance or the sample variance, the deviation of each observation from the corresponding mean is obtained. Thereafter, the sum of squares of the deviations from the mean is obtained, which represents the numerator of Equations 3.10 and 3.11. If the sum of the deviations is obtained, it should equal zero because of the nature of the mean. Note that in calculating the sample variance the denominator is $(n-1)$, whereas for the population variance the denominator is N. Equation 3.10 can be interpreted as the average of the squared deviations of the observations from the mean. Equation 3.11 has a similar interpretation except for the difference in the denominator, where $(n-1)$ is used instead of n. An explanation for this difference is as follows. First, a population variance σ^2 is a parameter, whereas a sample variance s^2 is an estimator, or a statistic. The value of s^2 may therefore change from sample to sample, whereas σ^2 should be constant. One desirable property of s^2 would be that even though it may not be equal to σ^2 for every sample, its value on the average would equal σ^2. This is known as the property of unbiasedness, where the mean or expected value of the estimator equals the corresponding parameter. If a denominator of $(n-1)$ is used for calculating the sample variance, then it can be shown mathematically that the sample variance is an unbiased estimator of the population variance. On the other hand, if a denominator of n were used, then on the average the sample variance would underestimate the population variance.

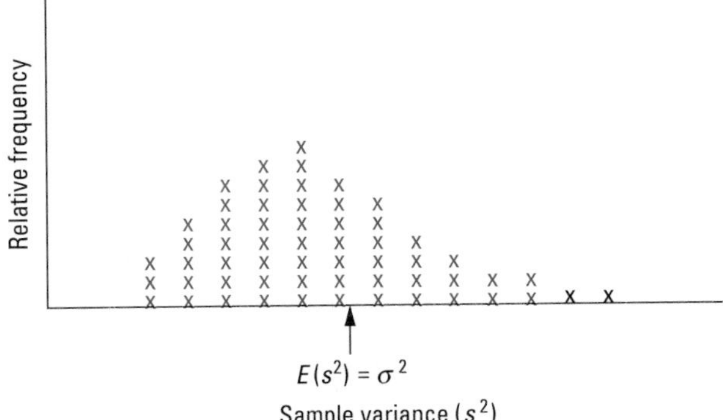

Figure 3-8 Sampling distribution of an unbiased sample variance.

Figure 3-8 denotes the sampling distribution (that is, the relative frequency) of s^2 calculated using Equation 3.11 or 3.12 over repeated samples. Suppose the value of σ^2 is as shown in the figure. If the average value of s^2 is calculated over repeated samples, that average will equal the population variance. Technically, the expected value of s^2 will equal σ^2 (that is, $E(s^2) = \sigma^2$). If a denominator of n were used in Equation 3.11 or 3.12, then $E(s^2)$ would be less than σ^2.

Unlike the range, which uses only the extreme values of the data set, the sample variance makes use of the information associated with each observation. Two data sets could have the same range, yet the degree of their variability could be different. As Figure 3-9 shows, data sets A and B have the same value for the range. However, the degree of variability of the data sets is indeed different. The sample variances would not be the same if calculated, indicating different degrees of fluctuation around the mean. The units of variance are the square of the units of measurement for the individual values. For example, if the observations are in millimeters, then the units of variance are mm^2.

Standard Deviation The standard deviation, like the variance, is a measure of the variability of the observations around the mean. It is equal to the positive square root of the variance. Thus, a standard deviation has the same units as the observations and is easier to interpret than the variance. It is probably the most widely used measure of dispersion in quality control. Using Equation 3.10, the population standard deviation is given by

$$\sigma = \sqrt{\frac{\sum_{i=1}^{N}(X_i - \mu)^2}{N}} \qquad (3.13)$$

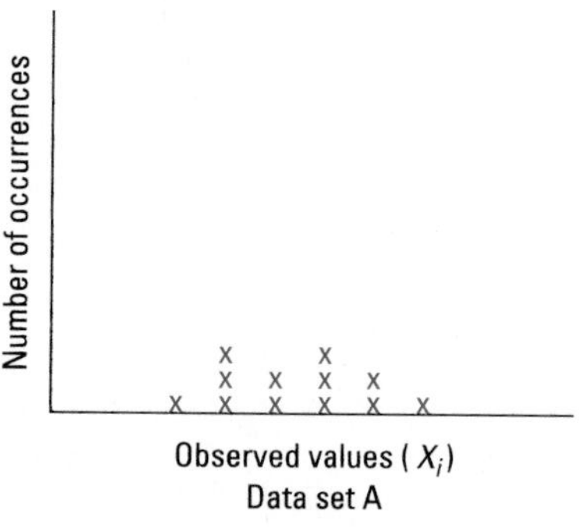

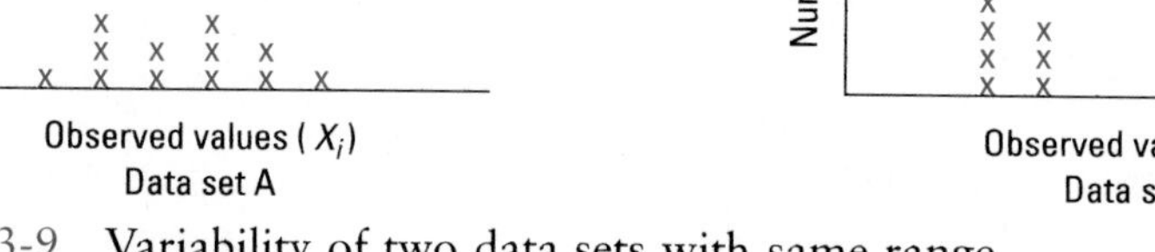

Figure 3-9 Variability of two data sets with same range.

Similarly, the sample standard deviation s is found using Equation 3.11 or 3.12 as

$$s = \sqrt{\frac{\sum_{i=1}^{n}(X_i - \overline{X})^2}{n - 1}} \quad (3.14)$$

$$= \sqrt{\frac{\sum_{i=1}^{n} X_i^2 - (\sum_{i=1}^{n} X_i)^2/n}{n - 1}} \quad (3.15)$$

As with the variance the data set with the largest standard deviation will be identified as having the most variability about its average. If the probability distribution of the random variable (a topic which is discussed later) is known—for instance, if it is a normal distribution—then information concerning the proportion of observations that are within a certain number of standard deviations of the mean can be obtained. The means of obtaining such information is discussed later in the section on probability distributions.

Example 3-13: A random sample of 10 observations of the output voltage of transformers was taken. The values obtained were as follows:

9.2, 8.9, 8.7, 9.5, 9.0, 9.3, 9.4, 9.5, 9.0, 9.1

Using Equation 3.11, the sample mean $\overline{X}$ is calculated.

$$\overline{X} = \frac{9.2+8.9+8.7+9.5+9.0+9.3+9.4+9.5+9.0+9.1}{10}$$

$$= 9.16 \text{ volts}$$

Table 3-1 shows the computations of the sum of the squared deviations of the observations around the sample mean. From Table 3-1, $\sum(X_i - \overline{X})^2 = 0.644$. The sample variance is given by

$$s^2 = \frac{\sum(X_i - \overline{X})^2}{n - 1} = \frac{0.644}{9} = 0.0715 \text{ volts}^2$$

The sample standard deviation given by Equation 3.14 is

$$s = \sqrt{0.0715} = 0.2675 \text{ volts}$$

TABLE 3-1 Tabulation for calculation of sample variance and standard deviation

Observation, X_i	Deviation from mean, $(X_i - \overline{X})$	Squared deviation, $(X_i - \overline{X})^2$
9.2	0.04	0.0016
8.9	−0.26	0.0676
8.7	−0.46	0.2116
9.5	0.34	0.1156
9.0	−0.16	0.0256
9.3	0.14	0.0196
9.4	0.24	0.0576
9.5	0.34	0.1156
9.0	−0.16	0.0256
9.1	−0.06	0.0036
	$\sum(X_i - \overline{X}) = 0$	$\sum(X_i - \overline{X})^2 = 0.644$

Next, using Equation 3.12, computations for the sample variance are shown in Table 3-2. The sample variance is given by

$$s^2 = \frac{\sum X_i^2 - (\sum X_i)^2/n}{n - 1}$$

$$= \frac{839.70 - (91.60)^2/10}{9}$$

$$= \frac{(839.70 - 839.056)}{9}$$

$$= \frac{0.644}{9}$$

$$= 0.0715 \text{ volts}^2$$

The sample standard deviation (s) is 0.2675 volts as before.

Interquartile Range The lower quartile Q_1 is the value such that one-fourth of the observations fall below it and three-fourths fall above it. The middle quartile is the median, such that half of the observations fall below it. The third quartile Q_3 is the

TABLE 3-2 Tabulation for calculation of sample variance from raw data

Observation, X_i	Squared observation, X_i^2
9.2	84.64
8.9	79.21
8.7	75.69
9.5	90.25
9.0	81.00
9.3	86.49
9.4	88.36
9.5	90.25
9.0	81.00
9.1	82.81
$\sum X_i = 91.60$	$\sum X_i^2 = 839.70$

value such that three-fourths of the observations are below it and one-fourth above it. A measure of dispersion is the interquartile range IQR, which is the difference between the third quartile and the first quantile. Thus

$$\text{IQR} = Q_3 - Q_1 \tag{3.16}$$

Observe that IQR contains 50 percent of the observations. Figure 3-10 shows graphically the interquartile range for a given distribution of values of a quality characteristic. The larger the value of IQR, the greater the spread of the data values. To find IQR, the data values are ranked in ascending order. The data point representing the first quartile (Q_1) has a rank of $0.25(n+1)$, where n is the number of data points in the sample. Likewise, the location of the third quartile (Q_3) is $0.75(n+1)$.

Example 3-14: A random sample of 20 observations on the welding time (in minutes) of an operation gave the following values:

2.2, 2.5, 1.8, 2.0, 2.1, 1.7, 1.9, 2.6, 1.8, 2.3,
2.0, 2.1, 2.6, 1.9, 2.0, 1.8, 1.7, 2.2, 2.4, 2.2

Ranking the data values yields the following order:

1.7, 1.7, 1.8, 1.8, 1.8, 1.9, 1.9, 2.0, 2.0, 2.0,
2.1, 2.1, 2.2, 2.2, 2.2, 2.3, 2.4, 2.5, 2.6, 2.6

The rank of the first quartile is $0.25(n+1) = 0.25(21) = 5.25$. The rank of the third quartile is $0.75(n+1) = 0.75(21) = 15.75$. From the ordered data set, the fifth value is 1.8, while the sixth value is 1.9. Linearly interpolating between these two values of 1.8 and 1.9, a rank of 5.25 corresponds to $Q_1 = 1.825$. Similarly, the fifteenth value is 2.2, and the sixteenth value is 2.3. Linear interpolation between these two values for a rank of 15.75 yields $Q_3 = 2.275$. The interquartile range is

$$\begin{aligned}\text{IQR} &= Q_3 - Q_1 \\ &= 2.275 - 1.825 = 0.45 \text{ min}\end{aligned}$$

Measures of Skewness and Kurtosis

In addition to the measures of central tendency and dispersion that are used to describe data sets, two other measures are used to describe other features of the data set: the skewness coefficient and the kurtosis coefficient.

Skewness Coefficient The skewness coefficient describes the asymmetry of the data set about the

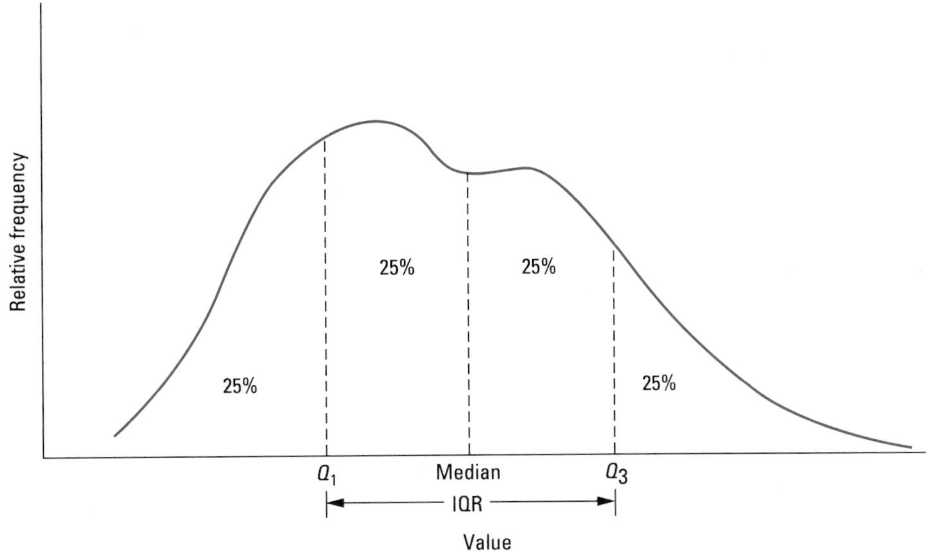

Figure 3-10 Interquartile range for a distribution.

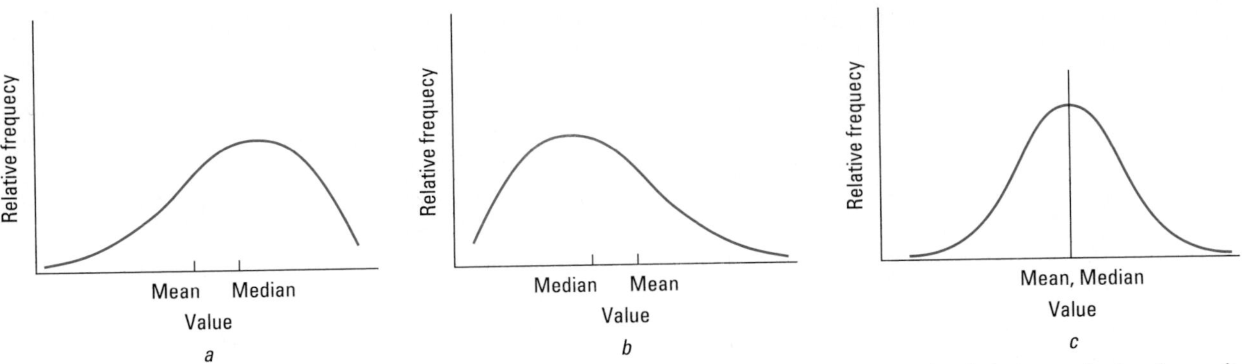

Figure 3-11 Symmetric and skewed distributions: (*a*) distribution skewed to the left (negatively skewed); (*b*) distribution skewed to the right (positively skewed); (*c*) distribution symmetric about mean.

mean. The skewness coefficient is calculated as follows:

$$\gamma_1 = \left\{ \frac{n[\sum_{i=1}^{n}(X_i - \overline{X})^3]^2}{[\sum_{i=1}^{n}(X_i - \overline{X})^2]^3} \right\}^{1/2} \tag{3.17}$$

Figure 3-11 shows a distribution that is negatively skewed (skewed to the left), another that is positively skewed (skewed to the right), and a third that is symmetric about the mean. The skewness coefficient should equal zero for a symmetric distribution, where the mean and the median are equal to each other. For a positively skewed distribution, the mean is greater than the median because of a few values that are large compared to the others, and the skewness coefficient is positive. If a distribution is negatively skewed, the mean is less than the median because of the outliers that are very small compared to the other values. The skewness coefficient in such a case is negative. The skewness coefficient gives an indication of the degree to which a distribution deviates from symmetry. It should be used for data sets that are unimodal and have a sample size of at least 100. The larger the magnitude of the skewness coefficient, the stronger the case for rejecting the notion that the distribution is symmetric.

Kurtosis Coefficient Kurtosis is a measure of the peakedness of the data set. It is also viewed as a measure of the heaviness of the tails of a distribution. The kurtosis coefficient is given by

$$\gamma_2 = \frac{n\sum_{i=1}^{n}(X_i - \overline{X})^4}{\{\sum_{i=1}^{n}(X_i - \overline{X})^2\}^2} \tag{3.18}$$

The value of the kurtosis coefficient is a relative measure. For a normal distribution (to be discussed in depth later), the kurtosis coefficient is 3. Figure 3-12 shows a normal distribution (identified as mesokurtic), a distribution that is more peaked than the normal (called a leptokurtic distribution), and one that is less peaked than the normal (known as a platykurtic distribution). For a leptokurtic distribution, the kurtosis coefficient is greater than 3. The more pro-

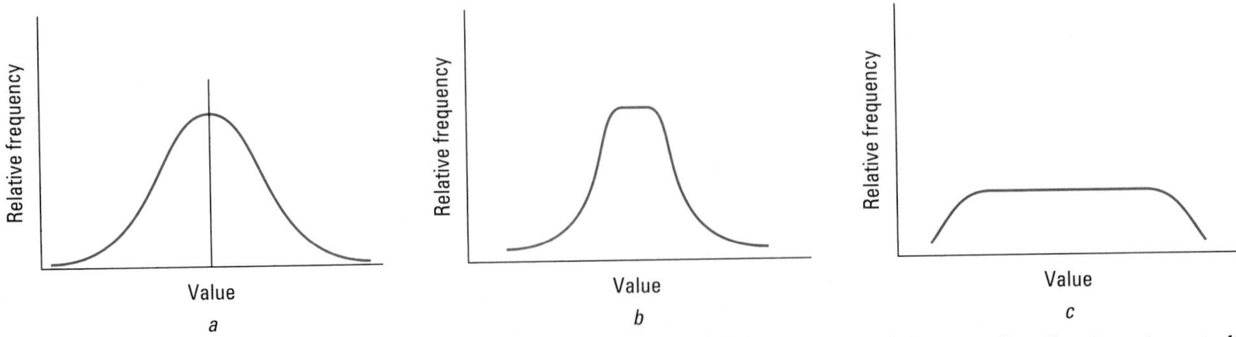

Figure 3-12 Distributions with different degrees of peakedness: (*a*) mesokurtic distribution (normal); (*b*) leptokurtic distribution; (*c*) platykurtic distribution.

nounced the peakedness, the larger the value of the kurtosis coefficient. The kurtosis coefficient should only be used to make inferences on a data set when the sample size is at least 100 and the distribution is unimodal.

Example 3-15: A random sample of 50 coils to be used in an electrical circuit was chosen, and the resistance of each was measured. The data is shown in Table 3-3. The sample mean $\overline{X}$ is found by adding all the observations and dividing by 50.

$$\overline{X} = \frac{1505.9}{50} = 30.118$$

The calculations for obtaining the skewness coefficient, γ_1 are also shown in Table 3-3. The square of the deviations of each observation from the mean as well as the cube of the deviations are shown. Table 3-3 gives

$$\sum(X_i - \overline{X})^2 = 727.907$$

$$\sum(X_i - \overline{X})^3 = 718.851$$

The skewness coefficient is

$$\gamma_1 = \sqrt{\frac{50(718.851)^2}{(727.907)^3}} = 0.259$$

The positive skewness coefficient indicates that the distribution of the data points is slightly skewed to the right.

Next, Table 3-3 gives

$$\sum(X_i - \overline{X})^4 = 26128.609$$

The kurtosis coefficient is found to be

$$\gamma_2 = \frac{50(26,128.609)}{(727.907)^2} = 2.466$$

These values imply that the given distribution is slightly less peaked than a normal distribution.

TABLE 3-3 Data and calculations for skewness and kurtosis coefficients for Example 3-15

Sample number	Resistance of coils, X_i	$(X_i - \overline{X})^2$	$(X_i - \overline{X})^3$	$(X_i - \overline{X})^4$	Sample number	Resistance of coils, X_i	$(X_i - \overline{X})^2$	$(X_i - \overline{X})^3$	$(X_i - \overline{X})^4$
1	35.1	24.820	123.655	616.048	26	27.5	6.854	−17.944	46.976
2	35.4	27.900	147.365	778.383	27	26.5	13.090	−47.359	171.346
3	36.3	38.217	236.258	1460.549	28	26.9	10.355	−33.324	107.237
4	38.8	75.377	654.424	5681.711	29	26.7	11.683	−39.932	136.486
5	39.0	78.890	700.700	6223.120	30	27.2	8.515	−24.846	72.500
6	22.5	58.034	−442.102	3367.936	31	31.8	2.829	4.759	8.004
7	23.7	41.191	−264.362	1696.676	32	32.1	3.928	7.786	15.432
8	25.0	26.194	−134.061	686.122	33	31.5	1.910	2.640	3.648
9	25.3	23.213	−111.841	538.849	34	31.2	1.171	1.267	1.361
10	25.0	26.194	−134.061	686.122	35	31.4	1.643	2.107	2.701
11	34.7	20.995	96.198	440.778	36	28.5	2.618	−4.236	6.854
12	34.2	16.663	68.017	277.646	37	28.4	2.951	−5.071	8.711
13	34.4	18.336	78.513	336.191	38	27.6	6.340	−15.965	40.200
14	34.7	20.995	96.198	440.778	39	27.6	6.340	−15.965	40.200
15	34.3	17.489	73.140	305.869	40	28.2	3.679	−7.056	13.533
16	26.4	13.824	−51.396	191.090	41	30.8	0.465	0.317	0.216
17	25.5	21.326	−98.483	454.795	42	30.6	0.232	0.112	0.054
18	25.8	18.645	−80.510	347.641	43	30.4	0.079	0.022	0.006
19	26.4	13.824	−51.396	191.090	44	30.5	0.146	0.056	0.021
20	25.6	20.412	−92.223	416.663	45	30.5	0.146	0.056	0.021
21	33.1	8.892	26.517	79.073	46	28.5	2.618	−4.236	6.854
22	33.6	12.124	42.217	146.999	47	30.2	0.007	0.001	0.000
23	32.3	4.761	10.389	22.668	48	30.1	0.000	−0.000	0.000
24	32.6	6.160	15.290	37.950	49	30.0	0.014	−0.002	0.000
25	32.2	4.335	9.025	18.790	50	28.9	1.483	−1.807	2.201
Sum		638.811	917.471	25444.037	Sum		89.096	−198.620	684.572

Measures of Association

Measures of association are used to indicate how two or more variables are related to each other. For instance, as one variable increases, how on the average does it influence another variable? Sometimes, two variables may not be related to each other, in which case the measure of association would be small, indicating a nonexistent or weak relationship.

Correlation Coefficient A correlation coefficient is a measure of the strength of the linear relationship between two variables. If two variables are denoted by X and Y, then the correlation coefficient r of a sample of observations is found from

$$r = \frac{\sum_{i=1}^{n}(X_i - \overline{X})(Y_i - \overline{Y})}{\sqrt{\sum_{i=1}^{n}(X_i - \overline{X})^2}\ \sqrt{\sum_{i=1}^{n}(Y_i - \overline{Y})^2}} \tag{3.19}$$

where (X_i, Y_i) denote the coordinates of the ith observation, $\overline{X}$ is the sample average of the X_i values, $\overline{Y}$ is the sample average of the Y_i values, and n is the sample size. An alternate version for calculating the sample correlation coefficient is

$$r = \frac{\sum X_iY_i - (\sum X_i)(\sum Y_i)/n}{\sqrt{(\sum X_i^2 - (\sum X_i)^2/n)(\sum Y_i^2 - (\sum Y_i)^2/n)}} \tag{3.20}$$

The sample correlation coefficient r is always between -1 and 1. An r-value of 1 denotes a perfect positive linear relationship between X and Y. This means that as X increases, Y increases linearly and that as X decreases, Y decreases linearly. Similarly, an r-value of -1 indicates a perfect negative linear relationship between X and Y. If the value of r is 0, the two variables X and Y are uncorrelated. This implies that if X increases, we cannot really say how Y would change. A value of r that is close to 0 indicates that the relationship between the variables is weak. Statistical tests exist for determining whether the strength of the linear relationship is significant.

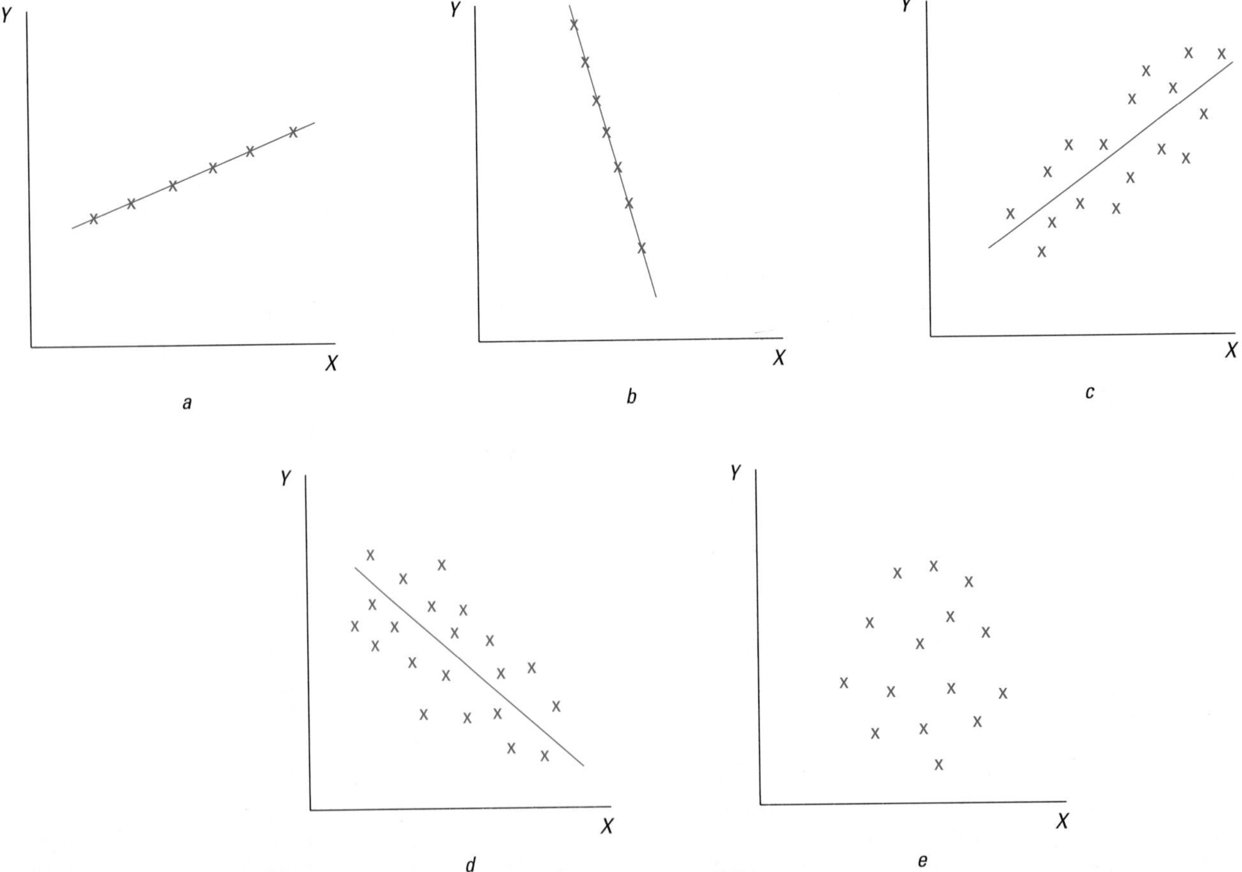

Figure 3-13 Scatterplots indicating different degrees of correlation: (*a*) perfect positive linear relationship, $r = 1$; (*b*) perfect negative linear relationship, $r = -1$; (*c*) X and Y positively correlated; (*d*) X and Y negatively correlated; (*e*) X and Y uncorrelated.

TABLE 3-4 Data and calculations for correlation coefficient in Example 3-16

Observation number	Depth of cut, X_i	Tool wear, Y_i	X_iY_i	X_i^2	Y_i^2	Observation number	Depth of cut, X_i	Tool wear, Y_i	X_iY_i	X_i^2	Y_i^2
1	2.1	0.035	0.0735	4.41	0.0012	21	5.6	0.073	0.4088	31.36	0.0053
2	4.2	0.041	0.1722	17.64	0.0017	22	4.7	0.064	0.3008	22.09	0.0041
3	1.5	0.031	0.0465	2.25	0.0010	23	1.9	0.030	0.0570	3.61	0.0009
4	1.8	0.027	0.0486	3.24	0.0007	24	2.4	0.029	0.0696	5.76	0.0008
5	2.3	0.033	0.0759	5.29	0.0011	25	3.2	0.039	0.1248	10.24	0.0015
6	3.8	0.045	0.1710	14.44	0.0020	26	3.4	0.038	0.1292	11.56	0.0014
7	2.6	0.038	0.0988	6.76	0.0014	27	3.8	0.040	0.1520	14.44	0.0016
8	4.3	0.047	0.2021	18.49	0.0022	28	2.2	0.031	0.0682	4.84	0.0010
9	3.4	0.040	0.1360	11.56	0.0016	29	2.0	0.033	0.0660	4.00	0.0011
10	4.5	0.058	0.2610	20.25	0.0034	30	2.9	0.035	0.1015	8.41	0.0012
11	2.6	0.039	0.1014	6.76	0.0015	31	3.0	0.032	0.0960	9.00	0.0010
12	5.2	0.056	0.2912	27.04	0.0031	32	3.6	0.038	0.1368	12.96	0.0014
13	4.1	0.048	0.1968	16.81	0.0023	33	1.9	0.032	0.0608	3.61	0.0010
14	3.0	0.037	0.1110	9.00	0.0014	34	5.1	0.052	0.2652	26.01	0.0027
15	2.2	0.028	0.0616	4.84	0.0008	35	4.7	0.050	0.2350	22.09	0.0025
16	4.6	0.057	0.2622	21.16	0.0032	36	5.2	0.058	0.3016	27.04	0.0034
17	4.8	0.060	0.2880	23.04	0.0036	37	4.1	0.048	0.1968	16.81	0.0023
18	5.3	0.068	0.3604	28.09	0.0046	38	4.3	0.049	0.2107	18.49	0.0024
19	3.9	0.048	0.1872	15.21	0.0023	39	3.8	0.042	0.1596	14.44	0.0018
20	3.5	0.036	0.1260	12.25	0.0013	40	3.6	0.045	0.1620	12.96	0.0020
						Sum	141.1	1.730	6.5738	548.25	0.0798

Figure 3-13 shows some plots of bivariate data with different degrees of strength of the linear relationship. Figure 3-13*a* shows a perfect positive linear relationship between X and Y. As X increases, Y very definitely increases linearly, and vice versa. Figure 3-13*c* depicts a situation where X and Y are positively correlated (say, with a correlation coefficient of 0.8) but not perfectly related. Here, on the whole, as X increases, Y tends to increase, and vice versa. Similar analogies can be drawn by comparing Figures 3-13*b* and 3-13*d*, where X and Y are negatively correlated. In Figure 3-13*e*, note that it is not evident what happens to Y as X increases or decreases. No general trend can be established from the plot. Here, X and Y may be uncorrelated or very weakly correlated. Statistical tests are available for testing the significance of the sample correlation coefficient and for determining if the population correlation coefficient is significantly different from zero (Neter, Wasserman, and Kutner, 1985).

Example 3-16: Consider the data shown in Table 3-4 on the depth of cut and tool wear in a milling operation. The strength of linear relationship between these two variables is given by the correlation coefficient. The results of using Equation 3.20 are shown in Table 3-4. The correlation coefficient is

$$r = \frac{6.5738 - [(141.1)(1.730)]/40}{[(548.25 - (141.1)^2/40)(0.0798 - (1.730)^2/40)]^{\frac{1}{2}}}$$

$$= 0.9397$$

This value indicates quite a strong positive linear relationship between depth of cut and tool wear. As the depth of cut increases, the tool wear increases.

3-6 PROBABILITY DISTRIBUTIONS

Data in a sample can be described by means of frequency histograms or variations thereof (such as relative frequency or cumulative frequency, which are discussed later). Data values in a population are described by a probability distribution. As previously described, random variables may be discrete or continuous. For discrete random variables, a probability distribution shows the values that the random variable can assume and the corresponding probabilities for those values. For continuous random variables, the number of values that the variable can take on is infinite, so the probability distribution is usually expressed as a mathematical function of the random variable. This function can be used to find the probability that the random variable will be between certain bounds. Almost all variables for which numerical measurements can be obtained are continuous in nature, for example, the length of a pin, the diameter of a bolt, the tensile strength of a cable, or the specific gravity of a liquid. Some examples of discrete random variables are the number of defects in an assembly, the number of customers served over a period of time, and the number of acceptable compressors.

For a discrete random variable X, which takes on the values x_1, x_2, and so on, a *probability distribution function* $p(x)$ has the following properties:

1. $p(x_i) \geq 0$ for all i, where $p(x_i) = P(X = x_i)$, $i = 1, 2, \ldots$
2. $\sum_{\text{all } i} p(x_i) = 1$

When X is a continuous random variable, the *probability density function* is represented by $f(x)$, which has the following properties:

1. $f(x) \geq 0$ for all x, where $P(a \leq x \leq b) = \int_a^b f(x)\,dx$
2. $\int_{-\infty}^{\infty} f(x)\,dx = 1$

Note the similarity of these two properties to those for discrete random variables.

Example 3-17: Let X denote a random variable that represents the number of defective transistors in an assembly. The probability distribution of the discrete random variable X may be given by

x	0	1	2	3
$p(x)$	0.3	0.4	0.2	0.1

This table gives the values taken on by the random variable and the corresponding probabilities. For instance, $P(X = 1) = 0.4$, that is, there is a 40 percent chance of finding 1 defective transistor. A graph of the probability distribution of this discrete random variable is shown in Figure 3-14.

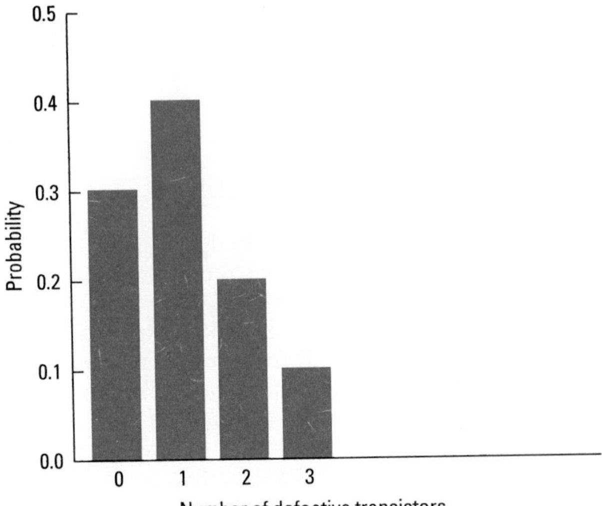

Figure 3-14 Probability distribution of a discrete random variable.

Example 3-18: Consider a continuous random variable X representing the time taken to assemble a part. The variable X is known to be between 0 and 2 minutes, and its probability density function (pdf), $f(x)$, is given by

$$f(x) = x/2, \qquad 0 < x \leq 2$$

The graph of this probability density function is shown in Figure 3-15. Note that

$$\int_0^2 f(x)\,dx = \int_0^2 \left(\frac{x}{2}\right)dx = 1$$

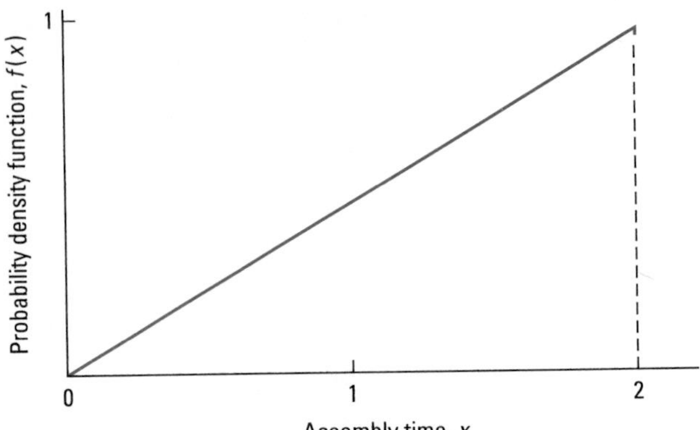

Figure 3-15 Probability density function, $f(x) = x/2$, $0 < x \leq 2$.

The probability that X is between 1 and 2 is

$$P(1 \leq X \leq 2) = \int_1^2 \frac{x}{2}\,dx = 3/4$$

Cumulative Distribution Function

The cumulative distribution function (cdf) is usually denoted by $F(x)$ and represents the probability of the random variable X taking on a value less than or equal to x, that is

$$F(x) = P(X \leq x)$$

For a discrete random variable,

$$F(x) = \sum_{\text{all } i} p(x_i) \qquad \text{for } x_i \leq x \tag{3.21}$$

If X is a continuous random variable,

$$F(x) = \int_{-\infty}^{x} f(t)\, dt \tag{3.22}$$

$F(x)$ is a nondecreasing function of x such that

$$\lim_{x\to\infty} F(x) = 1 \qquad \text{and} \qquad \lim_{x\to-\infty} F(x) = 0$$

Expected Value

The expected value or mean of a distribution is given as follows:

$$\mu = E(X) = \sum_{\text{all } i} x_i p(x_i) \qquad \text{if } X \text{ is discrete} \tag{3.23}$$

$$\mu = E(X) = \int_{-\infty}^{\infty} x f(x)\, dx \qquad \text{if } X \text{ is continuous} \tag{3.24}$$

The variance of a random variable X is given by

$$\begin{aligned} \text{Var}(X) &= E[(X - \mu)^2] \\ &= E(X^2) - [E(X)]^2 \end{aligned} \tag{3.25}$$

Example 3-19: For the probability distribution of Example 3-17, the mean μ or expected value $E(X)$ is given by

$$\begin{aligned} \mu = E(X) &= \sum_{\text{all } i} x_i p(x_i) \\ &= 0(0.3) + 1(0.4) + 2(0.2) + 3(0.1) \\ &= 1.1 \end{aligned}$$

The variance of X is

$$\sigma^2 = \text{Var}(X) = E(X^2) - [E(X)]^2$$

First, $E(X^2)$ is calculated as follows:

$$\begin{aligned} E(X^2) &= \sum_{\text{all } i} x_i^2 p(x_i) \\ &= (0)^2(0.3) + (1)^2(0.4) + (2)^2(0.2) + (3)^2(0.1) \\ &= 2.1 \end{aligned}$$

So

$$\text{Var}(X) = 2.1 - (1.1)^2 = 0.89$$

Hence, the standard deviation of X is $\sigma = \sqrt{0.89} = 0.943$.

Example 3-20: For the probability distribution function in Example 3-18, the mean (μ) or expected value $E(X)$, is given by

$$\begin{aligned} E(X) &= \int_{-\infty}^{\infty} x f(x)\, dx \\ &= \int_{0}^{2} x\left(\frac{x}{2}\right) dx \\ &= 1.333 \end{aligned}$$

This is the mean assembly time.

Discrete Distributions

The discrete class of probability distributions deals with those random variables that can take on a finite or countably infinite number of values. Several discrete distributions have applications in quality control, three of which are discussed in this section (Montgomery, 1991).

Hypergeometric Distribution A hypergeometric distribution is applicable to circumstances involving sampling from a finite lot (population) without replacement (that is, without placing the samples back into the population) when the items or outcomes can be categorized into one of two groups (usually called success and failure). If finding a nonconforming item is considered a success for, say, an inspection process, the probability distribution of the number of nonconforming items (x) in the sample is given by

$$p(x) = \frac{\binom{D}{x}\binom{N-D}{n-x}}{\binom{N}{n}}, \qquad x = 0, 1, 2, \ldots, \min(n, D) \tag{3.26}$$

where D = Number of nonconforming items in the population
N = Size of the population
n = Size of the sample
x = Number of nonconforming items in the sample
$\binom{D}{x}$ = Combination of D items taken x at a time, $= \frac{D!}{x!(D-x)!}$

The factorial of a positive integer x is written as $x! = x(x-1)(x-2)\ldots3\cdot2\cdot1$, and $0!$ is defined to be 1. The mean (or expected value) of a hypergeometric distribution is given by

$$\mu = E(X) = \frac{nD}{N} \tag{3.27}$$

The variance of a hypergeometric random variable is given by

$$\sigma^2 = \text{Var}(X) = \frac{nD}{N}\left(1 - \frac{D}{N}\right)\left(\frac{N-n}{N-1}\right) \qquad (3.28)$$

Example 3-21: A lot of 20 transistors contains 5 nonconforming ones. If an inspector randomly samples 4 items, find the probability of 3 nonconforming transistors.

Solution. In this problem, $N = 20$, $D = 5$, $n = 4$, and $x = 3$.

$$P(X = 3) = \frac{\binom{5}{3}\binom{15}{1}}{\binom{20}{4}} = 0.031$$

Binomial Distribution Consider a series of independent trials where each trial may result in one of two outcomes. These outcomes are labeled as either a success or a failure. The probability p of success on any trial is assumed to be constant. Let X denote the number of successes if n such trials are conducted. Then the probability of x successes is given by

$$p(x) = \binom{n}{x}p^x(1-p)^{n-x}, \qquad x = 0, 1, 2, \cdots, n \qquad (3.29)$$

and X is said to have a binomial distribution. The mean of the binomial random variable is given by

$$\mu = E(X) = np \qquad (3.30)$$

and the variance is expressed as

$$\sigma^2 = \text{Var}(X) = np(1-p) \qquad (3.31)$$

A binomial distribution is a distribution using the two parameters n and p. If the values of these parameters are known, then all information associated with the binomial distribution can be determined. Such a distribution is applicable to instances of sampling without replacement from a population (or lot) that is large compared to the sample, or to instances of sampling with replacement from a finite population. It is also used for situations in which items are selected from an ongoing process (implying that the population size is very large). The major differences between binomial and hypergeometric distributions are as follows: the trials are independent in a binomial distribution, whereas they are not in a hypergeometric one; the probability of success on any trial remains constant in a binomial distribution but not so in a hypergeometric one. A hypergeometric distribution approaches a binomial distribution as $N \to \infty$ and D/N remains constant. Tables of cumulative binomial probabilities are shown in Appendix A-1.

A variable that is frequently used in statistical quality control is the proportion of nonconforming items in a sample. This may be expressed as

$$\hat{p} = \frac{x}{n}$$

where X has a binomial distribution with parameters n and p, and x denotes an observed value of X. The probability distribution of $\hat{p}$ is obtained using

$$P(\hat{p} \le a) = P\left(\frac{x}{n} \le a\right) = P(x \le na)$$

$$= \sum_{x=0}^{[na]} \binom{n}{x} p^x(1-p)^{n-x} \qquad (3.32)$$

where $[na]$ is the largest integer less than or equal to na. It can be shown that the mean of $\hat{p}$ is p and that the variance of $\hat{p}$ is given by

$$\text{Var}(\hat{p}) = \frac{p(1-p)}{n}$$

Example 3-22: A manufacturing process is estimated to produce 5 percent nonconforming items. If a random sample of five items is chosen, find the probability of getting two nonconforming items.

Solution. Here, $n = 5$, $p = .05$ (if success is defined as getting a nonconforming item), and $x = 2$.

$$P(X = 2) = \binom{5}{2}(.05)^2(.95)^3 = 0.021$$

This probability may be checked using Table A.1 in the appendix.

$$\begin{aligned} P(X = 2) &= P(X \le 2) - P(X \le 1) \\ &= 0.999 - 0.977 \\ &= 0.022 \end{aligned}$$

The discrepancy between the two values is due to rounding to three decimal places the values of Table A-1. Using Table A-1, the complete probability distribution of X, the number of nonconforming items, may be obtained:

x	0	1	2	3	4	5
$p(x)$	0.774	0.203	0.022	0.001	0.000	0.000

Figure 3-16 is a graph of this probability distribution. The expected number of nonconforming items in the sample is

$$\mu = E(X) = 5(.05) = 0.25$$

while the variance is

$$\sigma^2 = 5(.05)(.95) = 0.2375$$

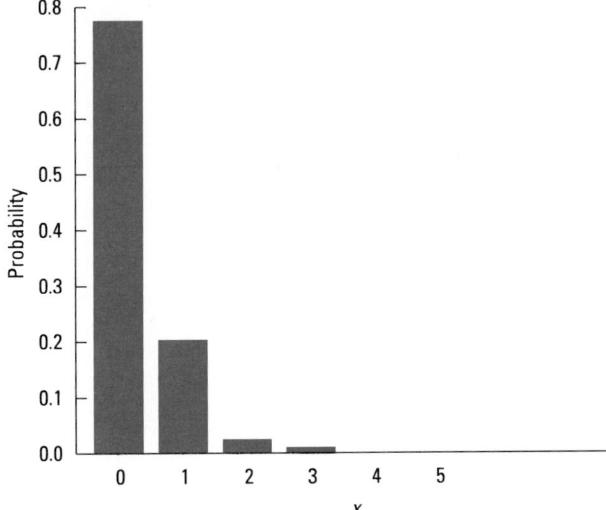

Figure 3-16 Binomial distribution with $n = 5, p = 0.05$.

Poisson Distribution A Poisson distribution is used to model the number of events that happen over a period of time, space, or volume. It is assumed that the events happen randomly and independently. Typical applications include estimating the number of defects or nonconformities per unit of a product. For example, the number of rivet defects in an airplane wing, the number of blemishes in 200 square-yards of a fabric, or the number of machine breakdowns per month could be represented by a Poisson random variable denoted by X. An observed value of X is represented by x. The probability distribution (or mass) function of the number of events (x) is given by

$$p(x) = \frac{e^{-\lambda}\lambda^x}{x!}, \qquad x = 0, 1, 2, \cdots \qquad (3.33)$$

where $\lambda =$ mean or average number of events that happen over the specified period of time, space, or volume

The symbol e represents the base of natural logarithms, which is equal to about 2.7183. The Poisson distribution has one parameter, λ. The mean and the variance of a Poisson distribution are equal and are given by

$$\mu = \sigma^2 = \lambda \qquad (3.34)$$

The Poisson distribution is sometimes used as an approximation to the binomial distribution when n is large ($n \to \infty$) and p is small ($p \to 0$), such that $np = \lambda$ is a constant. That is, a Poisson distribution may be used when all of the following hold:

1. The number of possible occurrences of defects or nonconformities per unit is large.
2. The probability or chance of a defect or nonconformity happening is small.
3. The average number of defects or nonconformities per unit is constant.

Table A-2 in the appendix lists cumulative Poisson probabilities for various value of λ.

Example 3-23: It is estimated that the average number of surface defects in 20 square meters of paper produced by a process is 3. What is the probability of finding no more than 2 defects in 40 square meters of paper through random selection?

Solution. Here, one unit is 40 square meters of paper. So, λ is found to equal 6 by determining the average number of surface defects per 40 square meters. The required probability is

$$\begin{aligned} P(X \leq 2) &= P(X = 0) + P(X = 1) + P(X = 2) \\ &= \frac{e^{-6}6^0}{0!} + \frac{e^{-6}6^1}{1!} + \frac{e^{-6}6^2}{2!} \\ &= 0.062 \end{aligned}$$

Table A-2 in the appendix gives this probability as

$$P(X \leq 2) = 0.062$$

The mean and variance of the distribution are both equal to 6. Using Table A-2, the probability distribution is as follows:

x	0	1	2	3	4	5	6	7	8
$p(x)$	0.002	0.015	0.045	0.089	0.134	0.161	0.160	0.138	0.103

x	9	10	11	12	13	14	15	16
$p(x)$	0.069	0.041	0.023	0.011	0.005	0.003	0.000	0.000

A graph of this probability distribution is shown in Figure 3-17.

Continuous Distributions

Continuous random variables may assume an infinite number of values over a finite or infinite range. The probability distribution of a continuous random variable X is often called the probability density function $f(x)$. The total area under the probability density function is 1. This section describes some common continuous distributions.

Normal Distribution The most widely used distribution in the theory of statistical quality control is the normal distribution. The probability den-

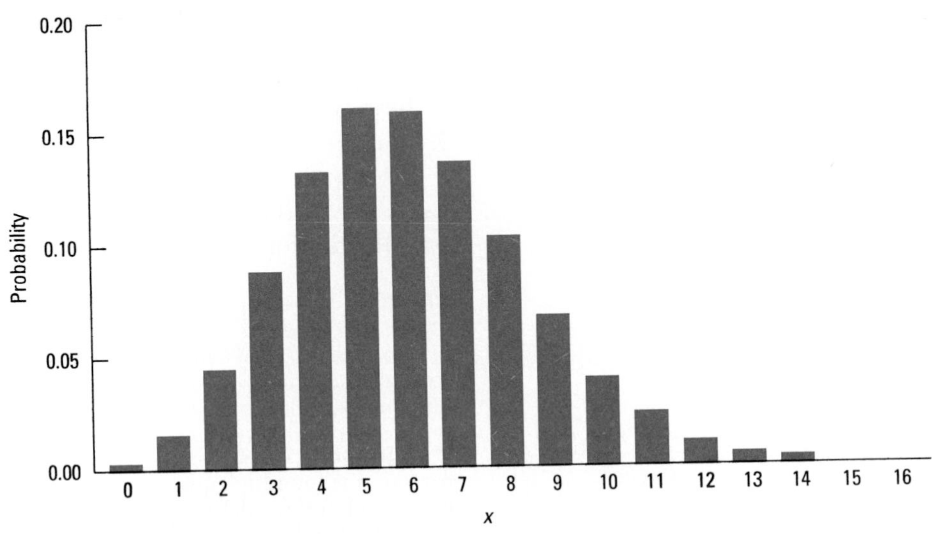

Figure 3-17 Poisson distribution with $\lambda = 6$.

sity function of a normal random variable is given by

$$f(x) = \frac{1}{\sqrt{2\pi}\sigma} \exp\left[\frac{-(x-\mu)^2}{2\sigma^2}\right] \qquad -\infty < x < \infty \tag{3.35}$$

where μ = Population mean
σ = Population standard deviation

The two parameters of a normal distribution are the mean and the variance (or standard deviation). Note that the variance (σ^2) is the square of the standard deviation. Figure 3-18 shows normal probability density function. The effect of the parameters μ and σ^2 on the shape of the probability density function is shown in Figure 3-19. A change in the mean causes a change in the location of the distribution. As the mean increases, the distribution shifts to the right, and as the mean decreases, the distribution shifts to the left. As the variance (or standard deviation) increases, the distribution becomes more spread about the mean. A normal distribution is symmetric about the mean. The mean, median, and mode are equal to each other. For a normal distribution, the standard deviation is very important. The proportion of the population values that fall in the range of $\mu \pm \sigma$ is 68.26 percent. Similarly, 95.44 percent of the total area is within $\mu \pm 2\sigma$, and 99.74 percent of the area is between $\mu \pm 3\sigma$. This relationship is shown in Figure 3-20.

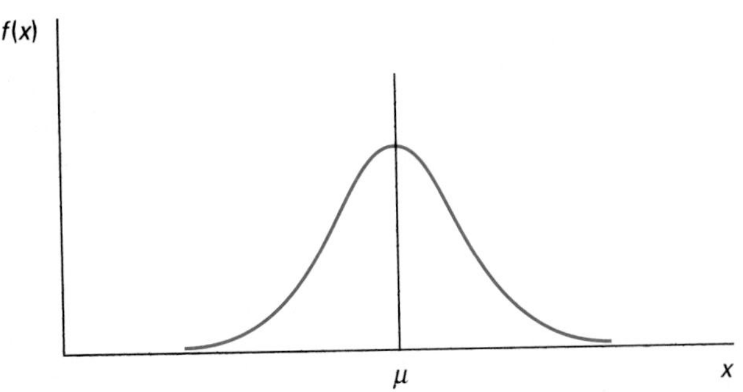

Figure 3-18 Normal distribution.

Finding the area under a normal curve would involve integrating Equation 3.35 within the prescribed limits of the random variable, a fairly involved task. Fortunately, tables are provided that enable us to find the area between any set of limits in a normal distribution. Note that because the shape of the density function changes with each possible combination of μ and σ^2, it is impossible to tabulate areas for each conceivable normal distribution. Nevertheless, an important property is that the area within certain limits for any normal distribution can be found by looking up tabulated areas for a *standard normal distribution.* The standardized normal random variable Z is given by

$$Z = \frac{X - \mu}{\sigma} \tag{3.36}$$

The z-value, or standardized value, represents the number of standard deviations a raw value x is from the mean. The z-value can be positive or negative. If the z-value is positive, the raw value is to the right of

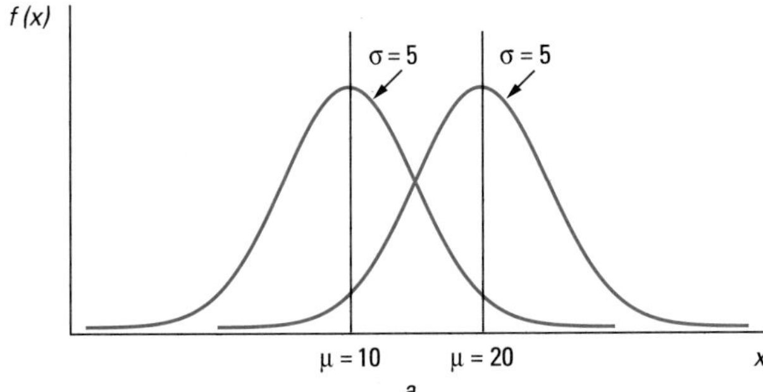

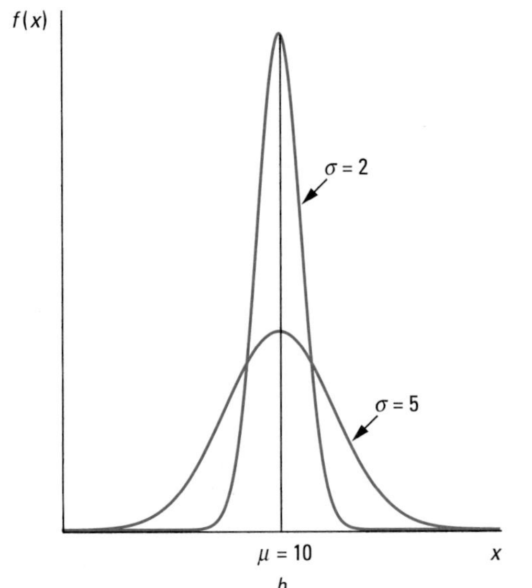

Figure 3-19 Effects of the parameters μ and σ^2 on the normal distribution: (*a*) effect of a change in the mean; (*b*) effect of a change in the standard deviation.

the mean, whereas negative z-values indicate points to the left of the mean. At the mean, the z-value is zero. The distribution of the standardized normal random variable has a mean of zero and a variance of one. It is represented as an $N(0, 1)$ variable, where the first parameter represents the mean and the second the variance, and its density function is given by

$$f(z) = \frac{1}{\sqrt{2\pi}} e^{-z^2/2}, \qquad -\infty < z < \infty \qquad (3.37)$$

The cumulative distribution function of Z is

$$\Phi(z) = F(z) = \int_{-\infty}^{z} f(t)\,dt \qquad (3.38)$$

Figure 3-21 shows the standard normal distribution and its relationship to the raw variable X.

Tables are available for the cumulative distribution function of Z and are shown in Appendix A-3. The normal distribution has the property that the area between certain limits a and b for a variable X is the same as the area between the standardized values for a and b under the standard normal distribution. Thus, we need only one set of tables—those for the standard normal distribution function—to calculate the area between certain limits for any normal distribution. Usage of the standard normal distribution is demonstrated through the following example.

Example 3-24: The length of a machined part is known to have a normal distribution with a mean of 100 mm and a standard deviation of 2 mm.

a. What proportion of the parts will be above 103.3 mm?

Solution. Let X denote the length of the part. The parameter values for the normal distribution are $\mu = 100$ and $\sigma = 2$. The required probability is shown in Figure 3-22*a*. The standardized value of 103.3 corresponds to

$$z_1 = \frac{x_1 - \mu}{\sigma} = \frac{103.3 - 100}{2} = 1.65$$

Thus, $P(X > 103.3) = P(Z > 1.65)$. From Table A-3 in the appendix, $P(Z \le 1.65) = 0.9505$, which also equals $P(X \le 103.3)$. So,

$$\begin{aligned} P(Z > 1.65) &= 1 - P(Z \le 1.65) \\ &= 1 - 0.9505 \\ &= 0.0495 \end{aligned}$$

The desired probability $P(X > 103.3)$ is 0.0495, or 4.95 percent.

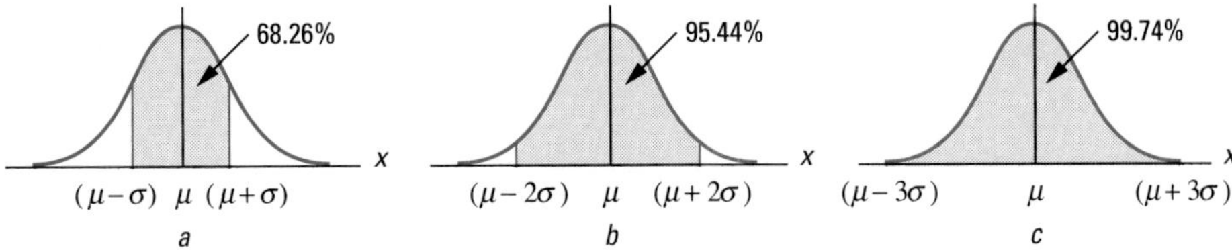

Figure 3-20 Areas under a normal distribution.

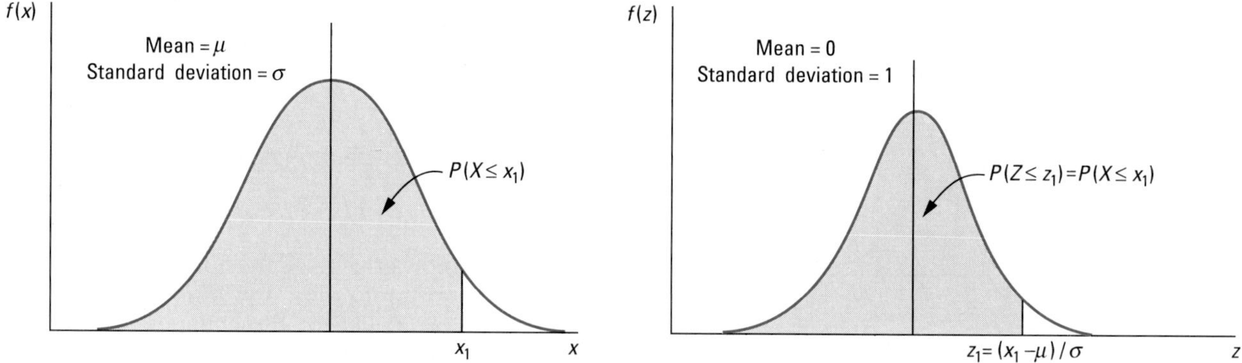

Figure 3-21 Normal distributions: (*a*) general form; (*b*) standardized.

b. What proportion of the output will be between 98.5 and 102.0 mm?

Solution. We wish to find $P(98.5 \leq X \leq 102.0)$, which is shown in Figure 3-22*b*. The standardized values are computed as

$$z_1 = \frac{102.0 - 100}{2} = 1.00$$

$$z_2 = \frac{98.5 - 100}{2} = -0.75$$

From Table A-3, we have $P(Z \leq 1.00) = 0.8413$ and $P(Z \leq -0.75) = 0.2266$. The required probability equals $0.8413 - 0.2266 = 0.6147$. Thus, 61.47 percent of the output is expected to be between 98.5 and 102.0 mm.

c. What proportion of the parts will be shorter than 96.5 mm?

Solution. We want $P(X < 96.5)$, which is equivalent to $P(X \leq 96.5)$, since for a continuous random variable the probability that the variable equals a particular value is zero. The standardized value is

$$z_1 = \frac{96.5 - 100}{2} = -1.75$$

The required proportion is shown in Figure 3-22*c*. Using Table A-3, $P(Z \leq -1.75) = 0.0401$. Thus 4.01 percent of the parts will have a length less than 96.5 mm.

d. It is important for the length of the part not to be very long compared to the desirable value. If a manager decides that no more than 5 percent of the parts should be oversized, what specification limit should be recommended?

Solution. Let the specification limit be A. From the problem information, $P(x \geq A) = .05$. We want to find A. We first find the standardized value at the point where the raw value is A. Here, the approach will be the reverse of what was done for the previous three parts of this example. That is, we are given an area, and we want to find the z-value. Here $P(X \leq A) = 1 - .05 = 0.95$. The next step is to look for an area of 0.95 in Appendix A-3 and find that the linearly interpolated z-value is 1.645. The final step is to unstandardize this value to determine the limit A.

$$1.645 = \frac{x_1 - 100}{2}$$

$$x_1 = 103.29 \text{ mm}$$

Thus the specification limit A should be set at 103.29 mm to achieve the desired stipulation.

Exponential Distribution The exponential distribution is used in reliability analysis to describe the time to the failure of a component or system. Its probability density function is given by

$$f(x) = \lambda e^{-\lambda x}, \qquad x \geq 0 \tag{3.39}$$

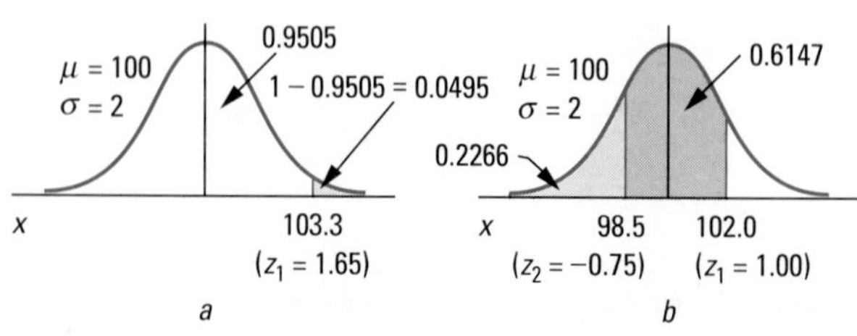

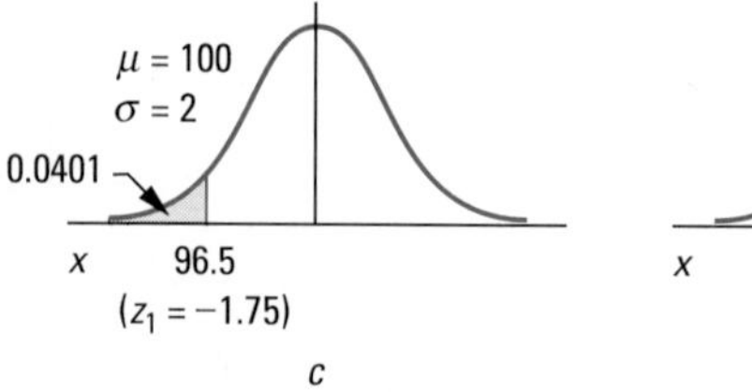

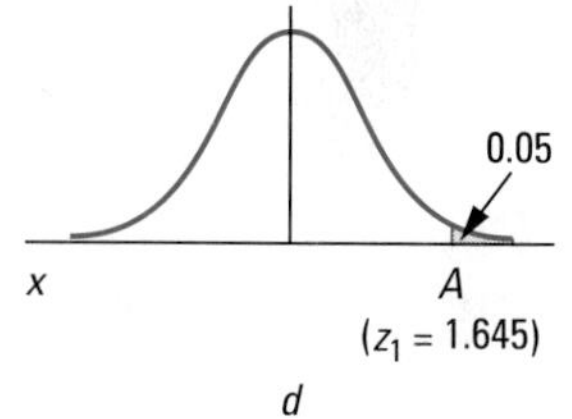

Figure 3-22 Calculation of normal probabilities: (*a*) $P(X > 103.3)$; (*b*) $P(98.5 \leq X \leq 102.0)$; (*c*) $P(X < 96.5)$; (*d*) $P(X \geq A) = .05$.

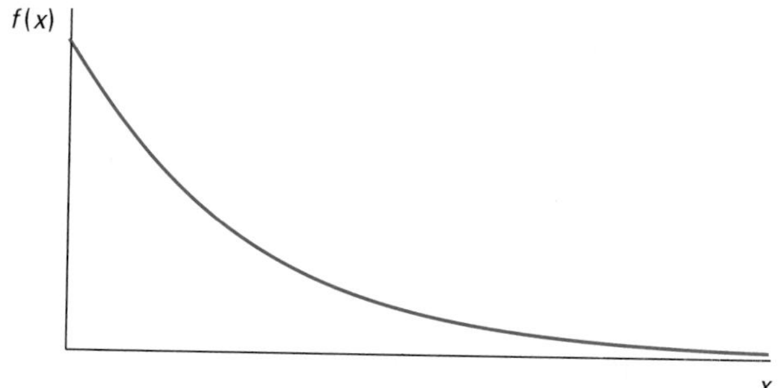

Figure 3-23 Exponential density function.

where λ denotes the failure rate. Figure 3-23 shows the density function. An exponential distribution represents a constant failure rate and is used to model failures that happen randomly and independently. If we consider the typical life cycle of a product, the useful life of the product occurs after the debugging phase and before the wearout phase. During the useful life, the failure rate is fairly constant, and failures happen randomly and independently. An exponential distribution, which has the above properties, is therefore appropriate for modeling failures in the useful phase of the product. The mean and the variance of an exponential random variable are given by

$$\mu = \frac{1}{\lambda}, \qquad \sigma^2 = \frac{1}{\lambda^2} \tag{3.40}$$

Thus, the mean and the standard deviation are equal for an exponential random variable.

The exponential cumulative distribution function is obtained as follows:

$$\begin{aligned} F(x) &= P(X \le x) \\ &= \int_0^x \lambda e^{-\lambda t}\, dt \\ &= 1 - e^{-\lambda x} \end{aligned} \tag{3.41}$$

This function is shown in Figure 3-24.

An exponential distribution has the property of being *memoryless*. This means that the probability of a component's life exceeding $(s + t)$ time units, given that it has lasted t time units, is the same as the probability of the life exceeding s time units. Mathematically, this property may be represented as

$$P(X > s + t \mid X > t) = P(X > s) \quad \text{for all } s \text{ and } t \ge 0 \tag{3.42}$$

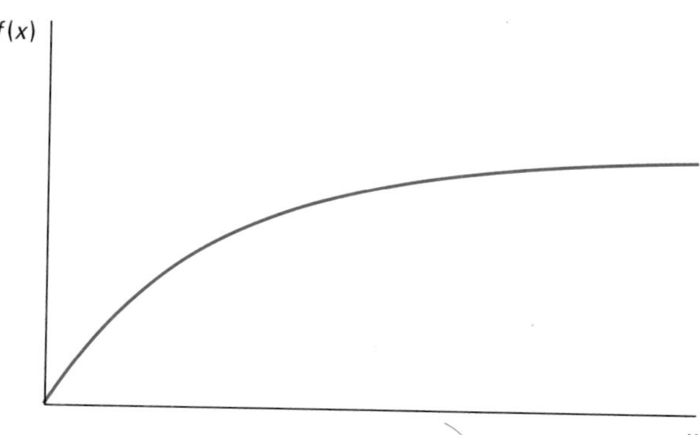

Figure 3-24 Exponential cumulative distribution function.

Example 3-25: It is known that a battery for a video game has an average life of 500 hours. The failures of batteries are known to be random and independent and may be described by an exponential distribution.

a. Find the probability that a battery will last at least 600 hours.

Solution. Since the average life of a battery, or the mean life, is given to be 500 hours, the failure rate is

$$\lambda = \frac{1}{500}$$

If the life of a battery is denoted by X, we wish to find $P(X > 600)$.

$$\begin{aligned} P(X > 600) &= 1 - P(X \le 600) \\ &= 1 - [1 - e^{-(1/500)600}] \\ &= e^{-1.2} = 0.301 \end{aligned}$$

b. Find the probability of a battery failing within 200 hours.

Solution.

$$\begin{aligned} P(X \le 200) &= 1 - e^{-(1/500)200} \\ &= 1 - e^{-0.04} = 0.330 \end{aligned}$$

c. Find the probability of a battery lasting between 300 and 600 hours.

Solution.

$$\begin{aligned} P(300 \le X \le 600) &= F(600) - F(300) \\ &= e^{-(1/500)300} - e^{-(1/500)600} \\ &= e^{-0.6} - e^{-1.2} = 0.248 \end{aligned}$$

d. Find the standard deviation of the life of a battery.

Solution.

$$\sigma = 1/\lambda = 500 \text{ hours}$$

e. If it is known that a battery has lasted 300 hours, what is the probability that it will last at least 500 hours?

Solution.

$$\begin{aligned} P(X > 500|X > 300) &= P(X > 200) = 1 - P(X \leq 200) \\ &= 1 - (1 - e^{-(1/500)200}) \\ &= e^{-0.4} = 0.670 \end{aligned}$$

Weibull Distribution A Weibull random variable is typically used in reliability analysis to describe the time to failure of mechanical and electrical components. It is a three-parameter distribution (Banks, 1989; Henley and Kumamoto, 1981). A Weibull probability density function is given by

$$f(x) = \frac{\beta}{\alpha}\left(\frac{x-\gamma}{\alpha}\right)^{\beta-1} \exp\left[-\left(\frac{x-\gamma}{\alpha}\right)^{\beta}\right], x \geq \gamma \tag{3.43}$$

The parameters are a location parameter γ ($-\infty < \gamma < \infty$), a scale parameter α ($\alpha > 0$), and a shape parameter β ($\beta > 0$). Figure 3-25 shows the probability density functions for $\gamma = 0$, $\alpha = 1$, and several values of β. This figure reveals the importance of a Weibull distribution as a general distribution that can be used to model a variety of situations. The shape can vary depending on the parameter values. For certain parameter combinations it may approach a normal distribution. If $\gamma = 0$ and $\beta = 1$, a Weibull distribution reduces to an exponential distribution. The mean and the variance of the Weibull distribution are

$$\mu = E(X) = \gamma + \alpha\Gamma\left(\frac{1}{\beta} + 1\right) \tag{3.44}$$

$$\sigma^2 = \text{Var}(X) = \alpha^2\left\{\Gamma\left(\frac{2}{\beta} + 1\right) - \left[\Gamma\left(\frac{1}{\beta} + 1\right)\right]^2\right\} \tag{3.45}$$

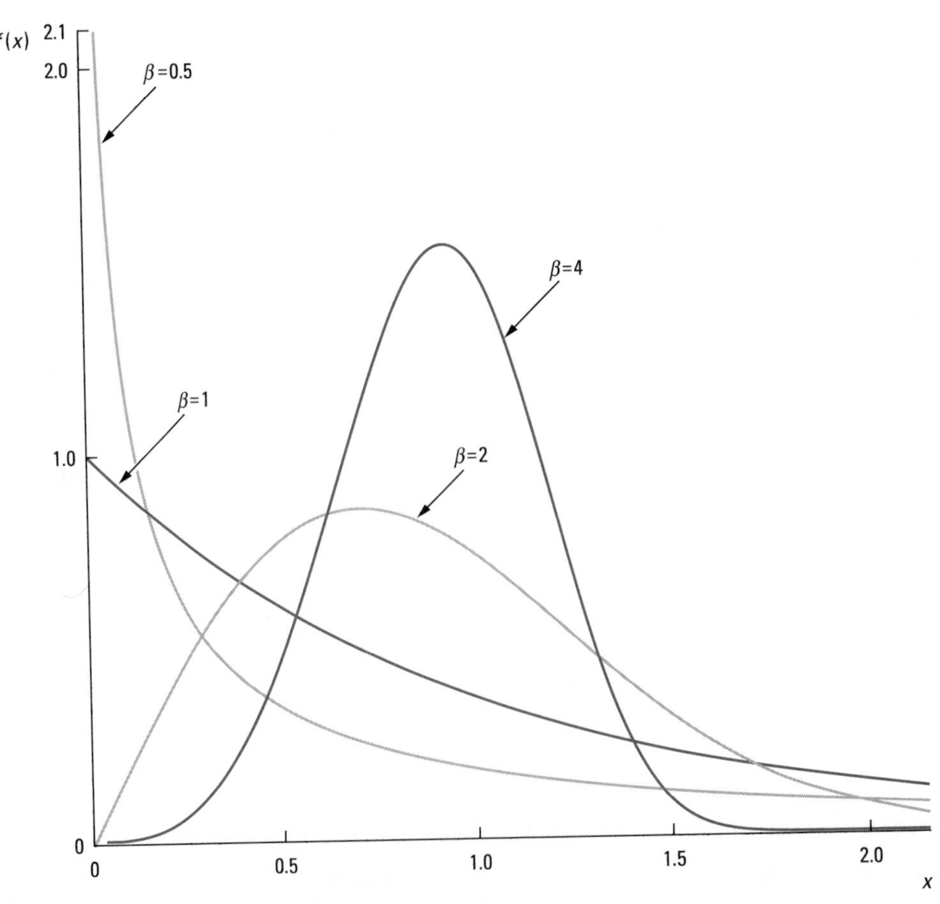

Figure 3-25 Weibull probability density functions ($\gamma = 0$, $\alpha = 1$, $\beta = 0.5, 1, 2, 4$).

where $\Gamma(t)$ represents the gamma function given by

$$\Gamma(t) = \int_0^\infty e^{-x} x^{t-1} dx$$

If u is an integer such that $u \geq 1$, then $\Gamma(u) = (u - 1)!$. Note that $u! = u(u-1)(u-2)\ldots 1$ and $0! = 1$.

The cumulative distribution function of a Weibull random variable is given by

$$F(x) = 1 - \exp[-\left(\frac{x-\gamma}{\alpha}\right)^\beta], \qquad x \geq \gamma \quad (3.46)$$

Example 3-26: The time to failure for a cathode ray tube can be modeled using a Weibull distribution with parameters $\gamma = 0$, $\beta = 1/3$, and $\alpha = 200$ hours.

a. Find the mean time to failure and its standard deviation.

Solution. The mean time to failure is given by

$$\begin{aligned}\mu &= E(X)\\ &= 0 + 200\ \Gamma(3+1)\\ &= 200\ \Gamma(4) = 1200 \text{ hours}\end{aligned}$$

The variance is given by

$$\begin{aligned}\sigma^2 &= (200)^2\{\Gamma(6+1) - [\Gamma(3+1)]^2\}\\ &= (200)^2\{\Gamma(7) - [\Gamma(4)]^2\} = 2736 \times 10^4\end{aligned}$$

The standard deviation is $\sigma = 5230.679$ hours.

b. What is the probability of a tube operating for at least 800 hours?

Solution.

$$\begin{aligned}P(X > 800) &= 1 - P(X \leq 800)\\ &= 1 - \{1 - \exp[-(800/200)^{1/3}]\}\\ &= \exp[-(4)^{1/3}] = \exp[-1.587]\\ &= 0.204\end{aligned}$$

3-7 INFERENTIAL STATISTICS—DRAWING CONCLUSIONS ON PRODUCT AND PROCESS QUALITY

This section describes statistical procedures that are used to make inferences about a population, which usually concerns a process or product characteristic, on the basis of information in a sample. As mentioned previously, one of the major uses of statistics is to help draw conclusions about a process based on limited information. The two main procedures of inferential statistics are estimation (point and interval) and hypothesis testing. Usually, the parameters of a process such as average furnace temperature, average component length and average component diameter are unknown. These values may need to be estimated, or claims as to these parameter values may need to be tested for verification. For a more thorough treatment of estimation and hypothesis testing, see Duncan (1986) or Mendenhall, Reinmuth, and Beaver (1989).

Sampling Distributions

An estimator, or statistic, (which is a characteristic of a sample) is used to make inferences on the corresponding parameter. For example, an estimator of sample average part diameter may be used to draw conclusions as to the population mean part diameter. Similarly, a sample variance is an estimator of the population variance. It is important to learn of the behavior of these estimators through repeated sampling in order to draw some conclusions about the corresponding parameters. The behavior of an estimator in repeated sampling is known as the *sampling distribution* of the estimator or expressed as the probability distribution of the statistic. Sampling distributions will be discussed in greater detail in the section on interval estimation.

The sample mean is one of the most widely used estimators in quality control because of the frequency with which the population mean is estimated. It is therefore of interest to know the sampling distribution of the sample mean. The Central Limit Theorem describes the sampling distribution of the mean. Suppose we have a population with mean μ and standard deviation σ. If random samples of size n are selected from this population, the following hold if the sample size is large:

1. The sampling distribution of the sample mean will be approximately normal.
2. The mean of the sampling distribution of the sample mean ($\mu_{\overline{X}}$) will be equal to the population mean μ.
3. The standard deviation of the sample mean is given by $\sigma_{\overline{X}} = \sigma/\sqrt{n}$.

The degree to which a sampling distribution of a sample mean approximates a normal distribution becomes greater as the sample size n becomes larger. Figure 3-26 shows a sampling distribution of a sample mean. A sample size should be 30 or more to allow a close approximation of a normal distribution. However, it has been shown that if a population distribution is symmetric and unimodal, then sample sizes as small as 4 or 5 yield

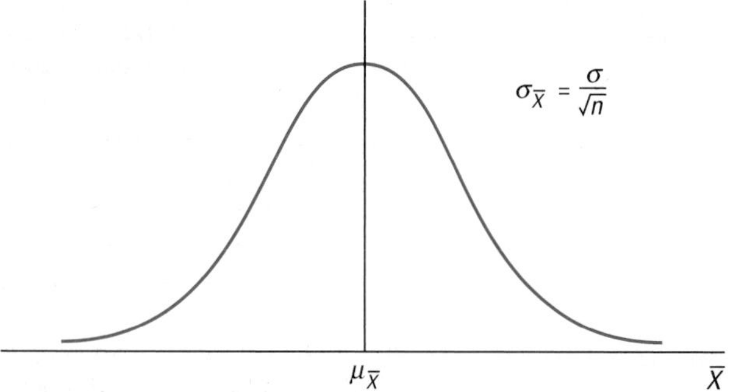

Figure 3-26 Sampling distribution of a sample mean.

sample means that are approximately normally distributed. In the case of a population distribution already being normal, then samples of any size (even $n = 1$) will lead to sample means that are normally distributed. Note that the variability of the sample means, as measured by the standard deviation, decreases as the sample size increases.

Example 3-27: The tuft bind strength of a synthetic material used to make carpets is known to have a mean of 100 lbs and a standard deviation of 20 lbs. If a sample of size 40 is randomly selected, what is the probability that the sample mean will be less than 105 lbs?

Solution. Using the Central Limit Theorem, the sampling distribution of the sample mean will be approximately normal with a mean $\mu_{\overline{X}}$ of 100 lb and a standard deviation of

$$\sigma_{\overline{X}} = \frac{20}{\sqrt{40}} = 3.162$$

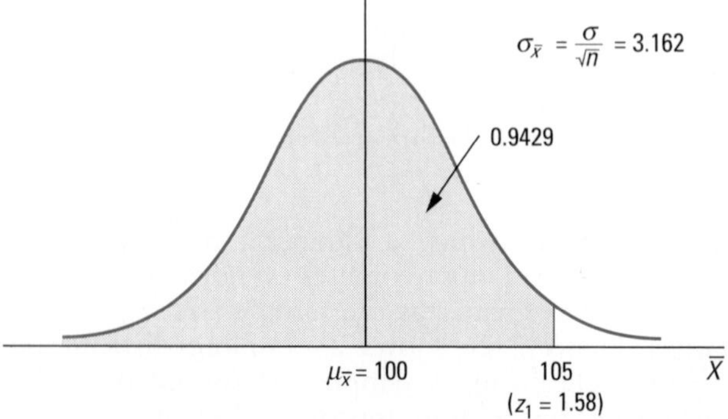

Figure 3-27 Determining probability of sample mean being less than 105.

We want $P(\overline{X} < 105)$ as depicted in Figure 3-27. We first find the standardized value as

$$z_1 = \frac{\overline{X} - \mu_{\overline{X}}}{\sigma_{\overline{X}}} = \frac{105 - 100}{3.162} = 1.58$$

Then $P(\overline{X} < 105) = P(Z < 1.58) = 0.9429$ using Appendix A-3.

Estimation of Product and Process Parameters

One branch of statistical inference deals with the estimation of unknown population parameters using data from a sample. Estimation can be subdivided into *point estimation* and *interval estimation.* In point estimation, a single numerical value is obtained as an estimate of the population parameter. In interval estimation, a range or interval is determined such that there is some desired level of probability that the true parameter value is contained within it. Interval estimates are also called confidence intervals.

Point Estimation A point estimate consists of a single numerical value that is used to make an inference about an unknown product or process parameter. For instance, suppose we wish to estimate the average diameter of all piston rings produced in a certain month. We randomly select 100 piston rings and compute the sample average diameter, which is 50 mm. The value of 50 mm is thus a point estimate of the mean diameter of all piston rings produced that month. A common convention for denoting an estimator is to put a ^ on top of the corresponding parameter. For example, an estimator of the population mean μ is $\hat{\mu}$, which is the sample mean $\overline{X}$. An estimator of the population variance σ^2 is $\hat{\sigma}^2$, which is usually the sample variance, s^2.

Desirable Properties of Estimators. Two desirable properties of estimators are worth noting here. A point estimator is said to be *unbiased* if the expected value, or mean, of its sampling distribution is equal to the parameter that is being estimated. A point estimator is said to have a *minimum variance* if its variance is smaller than that of any other point estimator for the parameter under consideration.

The point estimators $\overline{X}$ and s^2 are unbiased estimators of the parameters μ and σ^2, respectively. We know that $E(\overline{X}) = \mu$ and $E(s^2) = \sigma^2$. In fact, using a denominator of $(n - 1)$ in the computation of s^2 in Equations 3.11 or 3.12, makes s^2 unbiased. The Central Limit Theorem supports the idea that the sample mean is unbiased. Also note from the Central Limit Theorem that the variance of the sample mean $\overline{X}$ is inversely proportional to the square root of the sample size.

Interval Estimation Interval estimation consists of finding an interval defined by two end points L and U, say, such that the probability of the parameter θ being contained in the interval is some value $(1 - \alpha)$. That is,

$$P(L \leq \theta \leq U) = 1 - \alpha \tag{3.47}$$

The above expression represents a two-sided confidence interval, with L representing the lower confidence limit and U the upper confidence limit. If a large number of such confidence intervals were constructed, each found from independent samples, then $100(1 - \alpha)$ percent of these intervals would be expected to contain the true parameter value of θ. (The methods for using sample data to construct such intervals are discussed in the next subsections.) Suppose a 90 percent confidence interval for the mean piston ring diameter is desired. One sample may yield an interval of (48.5, 51.5)—that is, $L = 48.5$ and $U = 51.5$. Then, if 100 such intervals were constructed (one each from 100 samples), we would expect 90 of them to contain the population mean piston ring diameter. Figure 3-28 shows this concept. The quantity $(1 - \alpha)$ is called the level of confidence or the confidence coefficient.

Confidence intervals may be one-sided also. An interval of the type

$$L \leq \theta, \qquad \text{such that } P(L \leq \theta) = 1 - \alpha$$

is a one-sided lower $100(1 - \alpha)$ percent confidence interval for θ. On the other hand, an interval of the type

$$\theta \leq U, \qquad \text{such that } P(\theta \leq U) = 1 - \alpha$$

is an upper $100(1 - \alpha)$ percent confidence interval for θ. The context of a situation will influence the type of confidence interval to be selected. For example, when concerned with the breaking strength of steel cables, the customer may prefer a one-sided lower confidence interval. Since the exact expression for the determination of the confidence intervals is determined by the estimator that is used to make an inference on the parameter, the estimation of several types of parameters is discussed next.

Confidence Interval about the Mean.

1. *Variance known.* Suppose we want to estimate the mean μ of a product or process characteristic when the population variance σ^2 is known. A random sample of size n is chosen, and the sample average $\overline{X}$ is calculated. From the Central Limit Theorem we know that the sampling distribution of the point estimator $\overline{X}$ is approximately normal with mean μ and variance σ^2/n. A $100(1 - \alpha)$ percent two-sided confidence interval for μ is given by

$$\overline{X} - z_{\alpha/2}\frac{\sigma}{\sqrt{n}} \leq \mu \leq \overline{X} + z_{\alpha/2}\frac{\sigma}{\sqrt{n}} \tag{3.48}$$

The value of $z_{\alpha/2}$ is the standard normal variate, such that the tail area of the standardized normal distribution is $\alpha/2$. Figure 3-29 shows the location of $z_{\alpha/2}$. It can be found from the tables in Appendix A-3. Equation 3.48 represents an approximate $100(1 - \alpha)$ percent confidence interval for any distribution of a random variable X. However, if X is normally distributed, then Equation 3.48 becomes an exact $100(1 - \alpha)$ percent confidence interval.

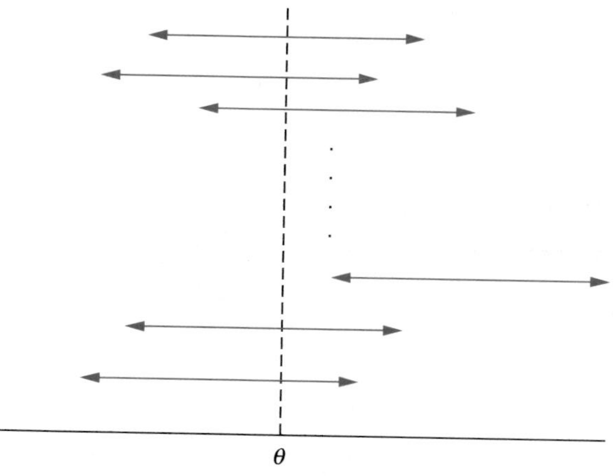

Figure 3-28 Interpreting confidence intervals.

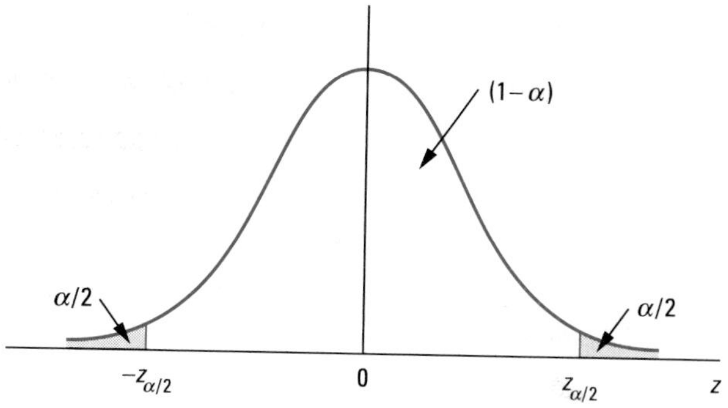

Figure 3-29 Finding $z_{\alpha/2}$ for confidence intervals.

Example 3-28: The output voltage of a power source is known to have a standard deviation of 10 volts. Fifty readings were randomly selected, yielding an average of 118 volts. Find a 95 percent confidence interval for the population mean voltage.

Solution. For this example, $n = 50$, $\sigma = 10$, $\overline{X} = 118$, and $1 - \alpha = 0.95$. From Appendix A-3, we have $z_{.025} = 1.96$. Hence, a 95 percent confidence interval for the population mean voltage μ is

$$118 - \frac{(1.96)(10)}{\sqrt{50}} \leq \mu \leq 118 + \frac{(1.96)(10)}{\sqrt{50}}$$

or

$$115.228 \leq \mu \leq 120.772$$

Hence, there is a 95 percent chance that the population mean voltage falls within this range.

2. *Variance unknown.* Suppose we have a random variable X that is normally distributed with unknown mean μ and unknown variance σ^2. A random sample of size n is selected, and the sample mean $\overline{X}$ and sample variance s^2 are computed. It is known that the sampling distribution of the quantity $(\overline{X} - \mu)/(s/\sqrt{n})$ is what is known as a t-distribution with $(n - 1)$ degrees of freedom, that is,

$$\frac{\overline{X} - \mu}{s/\sqrt{n}} \sim t_{n-1} \qquad (3.49)$$

where the symbol "~" stands for "is distributed as." The shape of a t-distribution is very similar to that of the standard normal distribution and is shown in Figure 3-30. As the sample size n increases, the t-distribution approaches the standard normal distribution. The number of degrees of freedom of t, in this case $(n - 1)$ is the same as denominator used to calculate s^2 in Equations 3.11 or 3.12. The number of degrees of freedom represents the fact that if we are given the sample mean $\overline{X}$ of n observations, then $(n - 1)$ of the observations are free to be any value. Once these $(n - 1)$ values are found, there is only one value for the nth observation that will yield a sample mean of $\overline{X}$. Hence, one observation is "fixed," and $(n - 1)$ are "free."

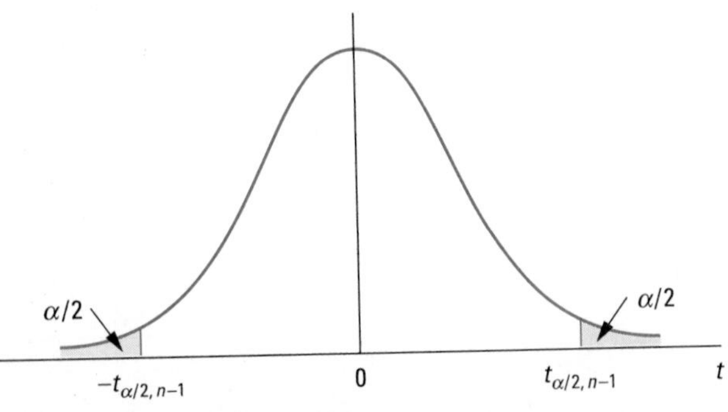

Figure 3-30 A t-distribution.

The values of t corresponding to particular right-hand tail areas and numbers of degrees of freedom are given in Appendix A-4. For a right tail area of 0.025 and 10 degrees of freedom, the t-value is 2.228. As the number of degrees of freedom, increases for a given right tail area, the t-value decreases. When the number of degrees of freedom is large (say, greater than 120), notice that the t-value given in Appendix A-4 is equal to the corresponding z-value given in Appendix A-3. A $100(1 - \alpha)$ percent two-sided confidence interval for the population mean μ is given by

$$\overline{X} - t_{\alpha/2,n-1}\frac{s}{\sqrt{n}} \leq \mu \leq \overline{X} + t_{\alpha/2,n-1}\frac{s}{\sqrt{n}} \qquad (3.50)$$

where $t_{\alpha/2,n-1}$ represents the axis point of the t-distribution where the right tail area is $\alpha/2$ and the number of degrees of freedom is $(n - 1)$.

Example 3-29: A new process has been developed that can transform ordinary iron into a kind of super-iron called metallic glass. This new product is stronger than steel alloys and is much more corrosion-resistant than steel. However, it has a tendency to become brittle at high temperatures. It is desired to estimate the mean temperature at which it becomes brittle. A random sample of 20 pieces of metallic glass was selected. The temperature at which brittleness was first noticed was recorded for each piece. The summary results gave a sample mean $\overline{X}$ of 600°F and a sample standard deviation s of 15°F. Find a 90 percent confidence interval for the mean temperature at which metallic glass becomes brittle.

Solution. We have $n = 20$, $\overline{X} = 600$, and $s = 15$. Using the t-distribution tables in Appendix A-4, $t_{.05,19} = 1.729$. A 90 percent confidence interval for μ is

$$600 - (1.729)\frac{15}{\sqrt{20}} \leq \mu \leq 600 + (1.729)\frac{15}{\sqrt{20}}$$

or

$$594.201 \leq \mu \leq 605.799$$

Confidence Interval for the Difference Between Two Means.

1. *Variances known.* Suppose we have a random variable X_1 from a first population with mean μ_1 and variance σ_1^2. X_2 represents a random variable from a second population with mean μ_2 and variance σ_2^2. Assume that μ_1 and μ_2 are unknown, and σ_1^2 and σ_2^2 are known. Suppose a sample of size n_1 is selected from the first population and a sample of size n_2 is selected from the second population.

Let the sample means be denoted by $\overline{X}_1$ and $\overline{X}_2$. A $100(1-\alpha)$ percent two-sided confidence interval for the difference between the two means is given by

$$(\overline{X}_1 - \overline{X}_2) - z_{\alpha/2}\sqrt{\frac{\sigma_1^2}{n_1} + \frac{\sigma_2^2}{n_2}} \leq \mu_1 - \mu_2 \leq (\overline{X}_1 - \overline{X}_2) + z_{\alpha/2}\sqrt{\frac{\sigma_1^2}{n_1} + \frac{\sigma_2^2}{n_2}} \qquad (3.51)$$

2. *Variances unknown.* Consider two cases under this category. The first is the situation where, the unknown variances are equal or are assumed to be equal, that is, $\sigma_1^2 = \sigma_2^2$. Suppose the random variable X_1 is from a normal distribution with mean μ_1 and variance σ_1^2, that is $X_1 \sim N(\mu_1, \sigma_1^2)$, and the random variable X_2 is from $N(\mu_2, \sigma_2^2)$. Using the same notation as before, a $100(1-\alpha)$ percent confidence interval for the difference in the population means $(\mu_1 - \mu_2)$ is

$$(\overline{X}_1 - \overline{X}_2) - t_{\alpha/2,n_1+n_2-2}s_p\sqrt{\frac{1}{n_1} + \frac{1}{n_2}} \leq \mu_1 - \mu_2 \leq (\overline{X}_1 - \overline{X}_2) + t_{\alpha/2,n_1+n_2-2}s_p\sqrt{\frac{1}{n_1} + \frac{1}{n_2}} \qquad (3.52)$$

where a pooled estimate of the common variance, obtained by combining the information on the two sample variances, is given by

$$s_p^2 = \frac{(n_1 - 1)s_1^2 + (n_2 - 1)s_2^2}{n_1 + n_2 - 2} \qquad (3.53)$$

The validity of assuming that the population variances are equal $(\sigma_1^2 = \sigma_2^2)$ can be tested using a statistical test which is discussed in the section on hypothesis testing of variances.

In the second case, the population variances are not equal, that is, $\sigma_1^2 \neq \sigma_2^2$ (a situation known as the Behrens-Fisher problem). A $100(1 - \alpha)$ percent two-sided confidence interval is

$$(\overline{X}_1 - \overline{X}_2) - t_{\alpha/2,\nu}\sqrt{\frac{s_1^2}{n_1} + \frac{s_2^2}{n_2}} \leq \mu_1 - \mu_2 \leq (\overline{X}_1 - \overline{X}_2) + t_{\alpha/2,\nu}\sqrt{\frac{s_1^2}{n_1} + \frac{s_2^2}{n_2}} \qquad (3.54)$$

where the number of degrees of freedom of t is denoted by ν, which is given by

$$\nu = \frac{\left(\frac{s_1^2}{n_1} + \frac{s_2^2}{n_2}\right)^2}{\frac{(s_1^2/n_1)^2}{(n_1-1)} + \frac{(s_2^2/n_2)^2}{(n_2-1)}} \qquad (3.55)$$

Example 3-30: Two operators perform the same machining operation. It is desired to estimate the difference in the mean machining times between the two operators. No assumption can be made as to whether the variabilities of machining time are the same for both operators. It can be assumed, however, that the distribution of machining times is normal for each operator. A random sample of 10 from the first operator gave an average machining time of 4.2 minutes with a standard deviation of 0.5 minutes. A random sample of 6 from the second operator yielded an average machining time of 5.1 minutes with a standard deviation of 0.8 minutes. Find a 95 percent confidence interval for the difference in the mean machining times between the two operators.

Solution. We have $n_1 = 10$, $\overline{X}_1 = 4.2$, $s_1 = 0.5$, and $n_2 = 6$, $\overline{X}_2 = 5.1$, $s_2 = 0.8$. Since the assumption of equal variances cannot be made, Equation 3.54 must be used. The number of degrees of freedom of t is (from Equation 3.55)

$$\nu = \frac{\left(\frac{0.25}{10} + \frac{0.64}{6}\right)^2}{\frac{\left(\frac{0.25}{10}\right)^2}{9} + \frac{\left(\frac{0.64}{6}\right)^2}{5}} = 7.393$$

As an approximation, using seven degrees of freedom rather than the calculated value of 7.393, Appendix A-4 gives $t_{.025,7} = 2.365$. A 95 percent confidence interval for the difference in the mean machining times is

$$(4.2 - 5.1) - 2.365\sqrt{\frac{.25}{10} + \frac{.64}{6}} \leq (\mu_1 - \mu_2) \leq (4.2 - 5.1) + 2.365\sqrt{\frac{.25}{10} + \frac{.64}{6}}$$

or

$$-1.758 \leq (\mu_1 - \mu_2) \leq -0.042$$

Confidence Interval for a Proportion. Consider the parameter p, the proportion of successes in a binomial distribution. In statistical quality control, this parameter may correspond to the proportion of nonconforming items in a process or in a large lot. A point estimator of p is $\hat{p}$, the sample proportion of nonconforming items, which is found from $\hat{p} = x/n$, where x denotes the number of nonconforming items and n the number of trials or items sampled. A $100(1-\alpha)$ percent two-sided confidence interval for p, when n is large is given by

$$\hat{p} - z_{\alpha/2}\sqrt{\frac{\hat{p}(1-\hat{p})}{n}} \leq p \leq \hat{p} + z_{\alpha/2}\sqrt{\frac{\hat{p}(1-\hat{p})}{n}} \qquad (3.56)$$

For small n, the binomial tables should be used to determine the confidence limits for p. When n is large and p is small $(np < 5)$, the Poisson approximation to the binomial may be used. If n is large and p is neither too small nor too large ($np \geq 5$, $n(1-p) \geq 5$), the normal distribution serves as a good approximation to the binomial.

Confidence Interval for the Difference between Two Binomial Proportions. Suppose a sample of size n_1 is selected from a binomial population with parameter p_1, while a sample of size n_2 is selected from another binomial population with parameter p_2. For large sample sizes of n_1 and n_2, a $100(1-\alpha)$-percent confidence interval for $(p_1 - p_2)$ is

$$(\hat{p}_1-\hat{p}_2)-z_{\alpha/2}\sqrt{\frac{\hat{p}_1(1-\hat{p}_1)}{n_1}+\frac{\hat{p}_2(1-\hat{p}_2)}{n_2}} \leq p_1-p_2 \leq (\hat{p}_1-\hat{p}_2)+z_{\alpha/2}\sqrt{\frac{\hat{p}_1(1-\hat{p}_1)}{n_1}+\frac{\hat{p}_2(1-\hat{p}_2)}{n_2}} \quad (3.57)$$

Example 3-31: Two operators perform the same operation of applying a plastic coating to plexiglass. Say we want to estimate the difference in the proportion of nonconforming parts produced by the two operators. A random sample of 100 parts from the first operator showed that 6 were nonconforming. A random sample of 200 parts from the second operator showed that 8 were nonconforming. Find a 90 percent confidence interval for the difference in the proportion of nonconforming parts produced by the two operators.

Solution. We have $n_1 = 100$, x_1 (number of nonconforming parts produced by the first operator) $= 6$, $n_2 = 200$, $x_2 = 8$, $(1-\alpha) = .90$. From the standard normal table in Appendix A-3, using linear interpolation, $z_{.05} = 1.645$ (for a right tail area of 0.05). So, $\hat{p}_1 = x_1/n_1 = 6/100 = 0.06$, and $\hat{p}_2 = x_2/n_2 = 8/200 = 0.04$. A 90 percent confidence interval for the difference in the proportion of nonconforming parts is

$$(0.06-0.04)-1.645\sqrt{\frac{(0.06)(0.94)}{100}+\frac{(0.04)(0.96)}{200}} \leq p_1-p_2 \leq (0.06-0.04) +1.645\sqrt{\frac{(0.06)(0.94)}{100}+\frac{(0.04)(0.96)}{200}}$$

or

$$-0.025 \leq p_1 - p_2 \leq 0.065$$

Confidence Interval for the Variance. Consider a random variable X which is from a normal distribution with mean μ and variance σ^2 (both unknown). An estimator of σ^2 is the sample variance s^2. It is known that the sampling distribution of $(n-1)s^2/\sigma^2$

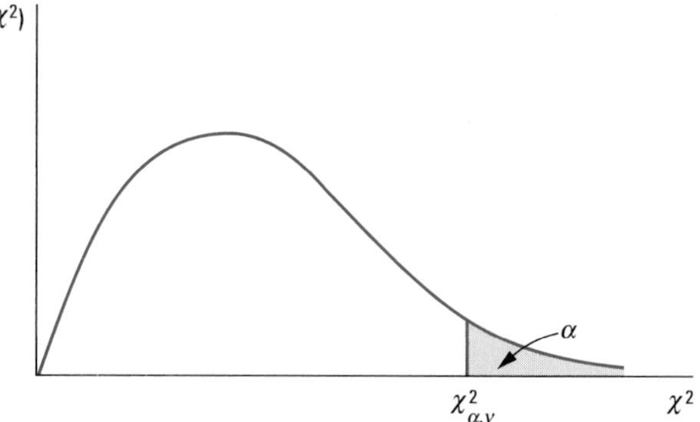

Figure 3-31 A chi-squared distribution.

is a chi-squared (χ^2) distribution with $(n-1)$ degrees of freedom. Notationally,

$$\frac{(n-1)s^2}{\sigma^2} \sim \chi^2_{n-1} \quad (3.58)$$

A chi-squared distribution is skewed to the right as shown in Figure 3-31. It is dependent on the number of degrees of freedom ν. The table in Appendix A-5 shows the values of χ^2 corresponding to the right tail area α for various numbers of degrees of freedom ν. A $100(1-\alpha)$ percent two-sided confidence interval for the population variance σ^2 is given by

$$\frac{(n-1)s^2}{\chi^2_{\alpha/2,n-1}} \leq \sigma^2 \leq \frac{(n-1)s^2}{\chi^2_{1-\alpha/2,n-1}} \quad (3.59)$$

where $\chi^2_{\alpha/2,n-1}$ denotes the axis point of the chi-squared distribution with $(n-1)$ degrees of freedom and a right tail area of $\alpha/2$.

Example 3-32: The time to process customer orders is known to be normally distributed. A random sample of 20 orders was selected. The average processing time $\overline{X}$ was found to be 3.5 days with a standard deviation s of 0.5 days. Find a 90 percent confidence interval for the variance σ^2 of the order processing times.

Solution. We have $n = 20, \overline{X} = 3.5$, and $s = 0.5$. From Appendix A-5, $\chi^2_{.05,19} = 30.14$ and $\chi^2_{.95,19} = 10.12$. A 90 percent confidence interval for σ^2 is

$$\frac{19(0.05)^2}{30.14} \leq \sigma^2 \leq \frac{19(0.5)^2}{10.12}$$

or

$$0.158 \leq \sigma^2 \leq 0.469$$

Confidence Interval for the Ratio of Two Variances. Suppose we have a random variable X_1, from a normal distribution with mean μ_1 and variance σ_1^2, and a random variable X_2, from a normal distribution with mean μ_2 and variance σ_2^2. A random sample of size n_1 is chosen from the first population, yielding a sample variance s_1^2, and a random sample of size n_2 selected from the second population yields a sample variance s_2^2. It is known that the statistic $(s_1^2/\sigma_1^2)/(s_2^2/\sigma_2^2)$ has what is known as an F-distribution with $(n_1 - 1)$ degrees of freedom in the numerator and $(n_2 - 1)$ in the denominator (Kendall and Stuart, 1967). This distribution can be represented as

$$\frac{s_1^2/\sigma_1^2}{s_2^2/\sigma_2^2} \sim F_{(n_1-1),(n_2-1)} \tag{3.60}$$

An F-distribution is skewed to the right as shown in Figure 3-32. It is dependent on the number of degrees of freedom of both the numerator and denominator. Appendix A-6 shows the axis points of the F-distribution corresponding to a specified right tail area α and various numbers of degrees of freedom of the numerator and denominator (ν_1 and ν_2), respectively). A $100(1 - \alpha)$ percent two-sided confidence interval for σ_1^2/σ_2^2 is given by

$$\frac{s_1^2}{s_2^2}\frac{1}{F_{\alpha/2,\nu_1,\nu_2}} \le \frac{\sigma_1^2}{\sigma_2^2} \le \frac{s_1^2}{s_2^2}\frac{1}{F_{1-\alpha/2,\nu_1,\nu_2}}$$

The lower tail F-value, $F_{1-\alpha/2,\nu_1,\nu_2}$, can be obtained from the upper tail F-value using the following relation:

$$F_{1-\alpha/2,\nu_1,\nu_2} = \frac{1}{F_{\alpha/2,\nu_2,\nu_1}} \tag{3.61}$$

Using Equation 3.61 yields a $100(1-\alpha)$ percent two-sided confidence for σ_1^2/σ_2^2 of

$$\frac{s_1^2}{s_2^2}\frac{1}{F_{\alpha/2,\nu_1,\nu_2}} \le \frac{\sigma_1^2}{\sigma_2^2} \le \frac{s_1^2}{s_2^2}F_{\alpha/2,\nu_2,\nu_1} \tag{3.62}$$

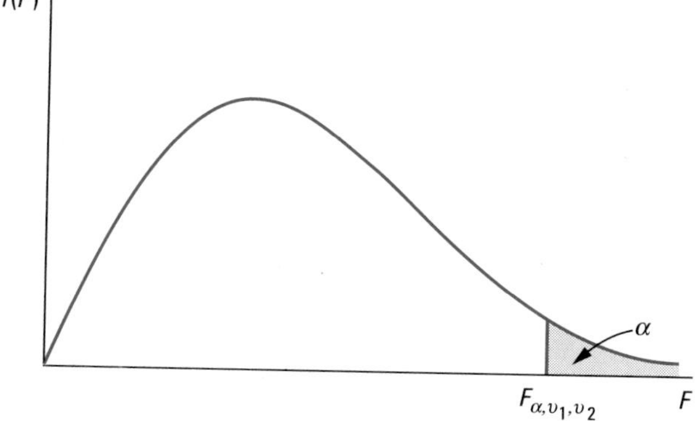

Figure 3-32 An F-distribution.

Example 3-33: The chassis assembly time for a certain model of television set is observed for two operators. A random sample of 10 assemblies from the first operator gave an average assembly time of 22 minutes with a standard deviation of 3.5 minutes. A random sample of 8 assemblies from the second operator gave an average assembly time of 20.4 minutes with a standard deviation of 2.2 minutes. Find a 95 percent confidence interval for the ratio of the variances of the assembly times for the two operators.

Solution. For this problem, $n_1 = 10$, $\overline{X}_1 = 22$, $s_1 = 3.5$, $n_2 = 8$, $\overline{X}_2 = 20.4$, and $s_2 = 2.2$. From Appendix A-6,

$$F_{.025,9,7} = 4.82, \qquad F_{.025,7,9} = 4.20$$

Hence, a 95 percent confidence interval for the ratio of the variances of the assembly times is

$$\frac{(3.5)^2}{(2.2)^2}\frac{1}{(4.82)} \le \frac{\sigma_1^2}{\sigma_2^2} \le \frac{(3.5)^2}{(2.2)^2}(4.20)$$

or

$$0.525 \le \frac{\sigma_1^2}{\sigma_2^2} \le 10.630$$

Note: Table 3-5 summarizes the formulas for the various confidence intervals and the assumptions required for each.

Hypothesis Testing

Concepts Testing claims on product or process parameters is the aim of hypothesis testing. Suppose the mean length of a part is expected to be 30 mm. A manager is interested in determining if, for the month of March, the mean length differs from 30 mm. Determining such information would be an example of hypothesis testing. In any hypothesis-testing problem, there are two hypotheses: the *null hypothesis* H_o and the *alternative hypothesis* H_a. The null hypothesis represents the status quo, the circumstance being tested (which is not rejected unless proven incorrect). The alternative hypothesis represents what we wish to prove or establish. It is formulated to contradict the null hypothesis. For the situation described above, the hypotheses are

$$H_o : \mu = 30$$
$$H_a : \mu \ne 30$$

where μ represents the mean length of the part. This is an example of a *two-tailed test,* where the alternative hypothesis is designed to detect departures of a parameter from a specified value in both directions. On the other hand, if we were interested in deter-

TABLE 3-5 Summary of formulas for confidence intervals

Parameter	Assumptions	Two-sided confidence interval	Equation number
μ	σ^2 known n large	$\bar{X} \pm z_{a/2}\dfrac{\sigma}{\sqrt{n}}$	(3.48)
μ	σ^2 unknown $X \sim N(\mu,\sigma^2)$	$\bar{X} \pm t_{\alpha/2,n-1}\dfrac{s}{\sqrt{n}}$	(3.50)
$\mu_1 - \mu_2$	σ_1^2,σ_2^2 known n_1,n_2 large	$(\bar{X}_1 - \bar{X}_2) \pm z_{\alpha/2}\sqrt{\sigma_1^2/n_1 + \sigma_2^2/n_2}$	(3.51)
$\mu_1 - \mu_2$	σ_1^2,σ_2^2 unknown $X_1 \sim N(\mu_1,\sigma_1^2)$ $X_2 \sim N(\mu_2,\sigma_2^2)$ $\sigma_1^2 = \sigma_2^2$	$(\bar{X}_1 - \bar{X}_2) \pm t_{\alpha/2,n_1+n_2-2}s_p\sqrt{1/n_1 + 1/n_2}$, where $s_p^2 = \dfrac{(n_1-1)s_1^2 + (n_2-1)s_2^2}{n_1+n_2-2}$	(3.52) (3.53)
$\mu_1 - \mu_2$	σ_1^2,σ_2^2 unknown $X_1 \sim N(\mu_1,\sigma_1^2)$ $X_2 \sim N(\mu_2,\sigma_2^2)$ $\sigma_1^2 \neq \sigma_2^2$	$(\bar{X}_1 - \bar{X}_2) \pm t_{\alpha/2,\nu}\sqrt{s_1^2/n_1 + s_2^2/n_2}$, where $\nu = \dfrac{(s_1^2/n_1 + s_2^2/n_2)^2}{\dfrac{(s_1^2/n_1)^2}{n_1-1} + \dfrac{(s_2^2/n_2)^2}{n_2-1}}$	(3.54) (3.55)
p	$X \sim$ Binomial(n,p) n large	$\hat{p} \pm z_{\alpha/2}\sqrt{\dfrac{\hat{p}(1-\hat{p})}{n}}$	(3.56)
$p_1 - p_2$	$X_1 \sim$ Binomial(n_1,p_1) $X_2 \sim$ Binomial(n_2,p_2) n_1,n_2 large	$(\hat{p}_1 - \hat{p}_2) \pm z_{\alpha/2}\sqrt{\dfrac{\hat{p}_1(1-\hat{p}_1)}{n_1} + \dfrac{\hat{p}_2(1-\hat{p}_2)}{n_2}}$	(3.57)
σ^2	$X \sim N(\mu,\sigma^2)$	$\left(\dfrac{(n-1)s^2}{\chi^2_{\alpha/2,n-1}}, \dfrac{(n-1)s^2}{\chi^2_{1-\alpha/2,n-1}}\right)$	(3.59)
σ_1^2/σ_2^2	$X_1 \sim N(\mu_1,\sigma_1^2)$ $X_2 \sim N(\mu_2,\sigma_2^2)$	$\left(\dfrac{s_1^2}{s_2^2 F_{\alpha/2,\nu_1,\nu_2}}, \dfrac{s_1^2 F_{\alpha/2,\nu_2,\nu_1}}{s_2^2}\right)$	(3.62)

mining whether the average length *exceeds* 30 mm, the hypotheses would be

$$H_o : \mu \leq 30$$
$$H_a : \mu > 30$$

This is an example of a *one-tailed test,* where the alternative hypothesis detects departures of a parameter from a specified value in only one direction. If the objective were to find whether the average part length is less than 30 mm, the two hypotheses would be

$$H_o : \mu \geq 30$$
$$H_a : \mu < 30$$

This is also an example of a one-tailed test.

In hypothesis testing the null hypothesis is assumed to be true unless proven otherwise. Hence, if we wish to establish the validity of a certain claim, that claim must be formulated as the alternative hypothesis. If there is statistically significant evidence contradictory to the null hypothesis, the null hypothesis will be rejected; otherwise, it will not be rejected. Defining what is statistically significant will of course depend on what the decision maker deems tolerable. For example, consider the following:

$$H_o : \mu \geq 30$$
$$H_a : \mu < 30$$

Say we wish to prove that the mean length is less than 30. Assume that the population standard deviation σ is 2 mm. Now, suppose we take a sample of size 36 and find the sample average length to be 25 mm. Is this difference statistically significant?

Hypothesis tests are conducted based on information contained in samples. A sample statistic that is used to test hypotheses is known as a *test statistic*. For example, in this case, the sample average length could be a test statistic. Usually, rather than using a point estimate (like the sample average which is an estimator of the population mean), a standardized quantity based on the point estimate is found and used as a test statistic. For instance, either the normalized or standardized value of the sample mean could be used as the test statistic, depending on whether or not the population standard deviation is known, respectively. If the population standard deviation is known, the normalized value of the sample mean is given by

$$z = \frac{\overline{x} - \mu}{\sigma/\sqrt{n}}$$

On the other hand, if the population standard deviation is unknown, the standardized value of the sample mean is the t-statistic given by

$$t = \frac{\overline{x} - \mu}{s/\sqrt{n}}$$

Detailed expressions for test statistics will be given later, in accordance with the parameters for which hypothesis tests are being performed. Figure 3-33 shows the sampling distribution of the sample mean $\overline{X}$ under the assumption that $\mu = 30$. According to the Central Limit Theorem, for large sample sizes, the distribution of $\overline{X}$ will be approximately normal. The important question for the above scenario is whether the sample average length of 25 mm is significantly less statistically than the specified value of 30 mm? Can we reject the null hypothesis?

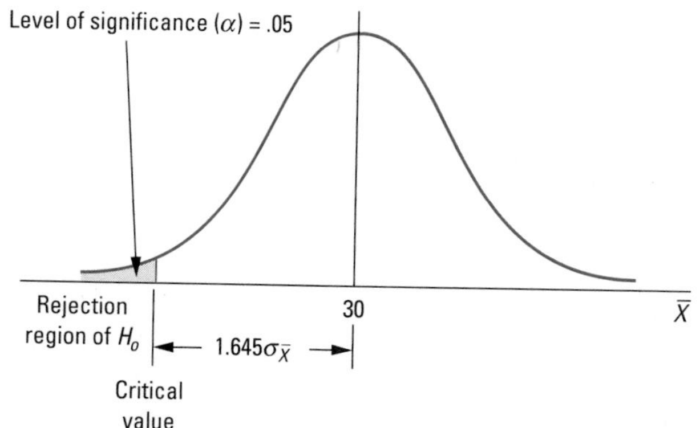

Figure 3-33 Sampling distribution of $\overline{X}$ assuming $\mu = 30$.

We must therefore determine a cutoff point past which the null hypothesis will be rejected. That is, how small must the sample mean be for us to conclude that the mean length is less than 30 mm? In this example suppose we decide to use the sample average as a test statistic. There is a critical value, in this case on the left tail, such that if the sample average (or test statistic) falls below it, we will reject the null hypothesis. This value defines the *rejection region* of the null hypothesis. If the test statistic does not fall in the rejection region, we do not have significant evidence to conclude that the population mean is less than 30, and so we will not reject the null hypothesis. But how is the precise location of the critical value—and hence the rejection region—selected? How small a value of the sample mean is considered significantly less than 30?

The answer to this question is influenced by the choice of the *level of significance* of the test. The rejection region is chosen such that if the null hypothesis is true, the probability of the test statistic falling in that region is small (say, .01 or .05); this probability is known as the level of significance and is denoted by α. Hence, the choice of α will dictate the rejection region. Suppose that for a suitable choice of α (say, 0.05), the *critical value* is found to be $1.645\sigma_{\overline{X}}$ below the population mean of 30. (Details as to how to arrive at an expression for the critical value are given later.) The rejection region is then the portion where the sample mean is at a distance more than $1.645\sigma_{\overline{X}}$ below the population mean, as shown in Figure 3-33. For the above scenario, $\sigma_{\overline{X}} = \sigma/\sqrt{n} = 2/\sqrt{36} = 0.333$. So the critical value is 0.548 [1.645(0.333)] units below 30. The rejection region then is $\overline{X} < 29.452$. If a smaller value of α were chosen, the rejection region would shift further to the left.

For a given α, once the rejection region is selected, a framework for *decision making* in hypothesis testing is defined. Only if the test statistic falls in the rejection region will the null hypothesis be rejected. In the above example, the rejection region was found to be $\overline{X} < 29.452$, which is equivalent to $Z < 1.645$. The observed sample average was 25 mm. The appropriate decision then is to reject the null hypothesis.

Errors in Hypothesis Testing There are two types of errors in hypothesis testing: Type I and Type II. A *Type I error* refers to rejecting a null hypothesis when the null hypothesis is actually true. The probability of a Type I error is indicated by α, the level of significance of the test. Thus, $\alpha = P$ (Type I error)

= P (rejecting H_o | H_o is true). For example, in testing ($H_o : \mu \geq 30$) against ($H_a : \mu < 30$), suppose a random sample of 36 parts yields a sample average length of 28 mm when the true mean length of all parts is really 30 mm. If the rejection region is selected to be $\overline{X} < 29.452$, then the decision would be to reject the null hypothesis. The magnitude of such an error can be controlled by selecting an acceptable level of α.

A *Type II error* occurs when a decision is made not to reject the null hypothesis even though the null hypothesis is false. The probability of a Type II error is denoted by β. Thus, $\beta = P$(Type II error) $= P$(Not rejecting $H_o | H_o$ is false). For example, consider testing ($H_o : \mu \geq 30$) versus ($H_a : \mu < 30$) with a rejection region of $\overline{X} < 29.452$. Now, suppose the true population mean length of all parts is 28 mm and a sample of 36 parts yields a sample average of 29.8 mm. In this case, the decision is not to reject the null hypothesis (because 29.8 does not lie in the region $\overline{X} < 29.452$). This is an example of a Type II error. Calculating the probability of a Type II error requires information about the population parameter (or at least an assumption about it). In such instances one predicts the probability of a Type II error based on the actual or assumed parameter value; this prediction serves as a measure of the goodness of the testing procedure and the acceptability of the chosen rejection region. The values of α and β may be shown to be inversely related. If all other problem parameters remain the same, β will decrease as α increases, and vice versa. Increasing the sample size can reduce both α and β.

The *power* of a test is the complement of β and is defined as

$$\text{power} = 1 - \beta = P(\text{rejecting } H_o | H_o \text{ is false}).$$

The power is the probability of correctly rejecting a null hypothesis that is false. It is desirable for a test to have a high power.

Steps in Hypothesis Testing In hypothesis testing the associated formulas for the test statistic are different depending on which parameter is being tested (such as the population mean or difference between two population means). For each situation, the appropriate test statistic is based on an estimator of the population parameter, and the rejection region is found accordingly. The following four steps summarize the hypothesis testing procedure:

1. Formulate the null and alternative hypotheses.
2. Determine the test statistic.
3. Determine the rejection region of the null hypothesis based on a chosen level of significance α.
4. Make the decision. If the test statistic lies in the rejection region, reject the null hypothesis. Otherwise, do not reject the null hypothesis.

In an alternative procedure, the rejection region is not specifically found, though a chosen level of significance α is given. Upon determining the test statistic, the probability of obtaining that value (or an even more extreme value) for the test statistic, assuming that the null hypothesis is true, is computed. This is known as the probability value or the *p-value* associated with the test statistic. This p-value, also known as the observed level of significance, is then compared to α, the chosen level of significance. If the p-value is smaller than α, the null hypothesis is rejected. Consider again the mean part length scenario and refer back to Figure 3-33. Suppose the observed sample average ($\overline{X}$) was 25, for a sample of size 36. The standard deviation of the sample mean ($\sigma_{\overline{X}}$) is $2/\sqrt{36} = 0.333$ (assuming a population standard deviation of 2). The observed average of 25 is 5 less than the population mean of 30, which corresponds to being $(25 - 30)/0.333 = -15.015$ standard deviations away from the population mean. The probability of observing a sample mean of 25 or less represents the p-value and may be found using the standard normal table:

$$\begin{aligned}\text{p-value} &= P(\overline{X} \leq 25)\\ &= P(Z \leq -15.015) \simeq 0.0000\end{aligned}$$

Therefore, if the chosen level of significance α is 0.05, the p-value is essentially zero (which is less than α), so we reject H_o. This means that if the null hypothesis is true, the chances of observing an average of 25 or something even more extreme is highly unlikely. Therefore, since we observed a sample mean of 25, we would be inclined to conclude that the null hypothesis must not be true, and we would therefore reject it.

Hypothesis Testing of the Mean

1. *Variance known.* Assume here that the sample size is large (allowing the Central Limit Theorem to hold) or that the population distribution is normal. The appropriate test statistics and rejection regions are given below. The steps to be followed in testing the hypothesis are the same four steps as described above. Let α denote the chosen level of significance and z_α denote the axis point of the standard normal distribution such that the right tail area is α.

HYPOTHESES	REJECTION REGION	TEST STATISTIC
H_o: $\mu = \mu_o$ H_a: $\mu \neq \mu_o$	$\|z_o\| > z_{\alpha/2}$	$z_o = \dfrac{\overline{X} - \mu_o}{\sigma/\sqrt{n}}$
H_o: $\mu \leq \mu_o$ H_a: $\mu > \mu_o$	$z_o > z_\alpha$	$z_o = \dfrac{\overline{X} - \mu_o}{\sigma/\sqrt{n}}$
H_o: $\mu \geq \mu_o$ H_a: $\mu < \mu_o$	$z_o < -z_\alpha$	$z_o = \dfrac{\overline{X} - \mu_o}{\sigma/\sqrt{n}}$

(3.63)

2. *Variance unknown.* Assume here that the population distribution is normal. If the sample size is large ($n \geq 30$), slight departures from normality do not strongly influence the test. The notation refers to t-distributions as described in the section on interval estimation.

HYPOTHESES	REJECTION REGION	TEST STATISTIC
H_o: $\mu = \mu_o$ H_a: $\mu \neq \mu_o$	$\|t_o\| > t_{\alpha/2,n-1}$	$t_o = \dfrac{\overline{X} - \mu_o}{s/\sqrt{n}}$
H_o: $\mu \leq \mu_o$ H_a: $\mu > \mu_o$	$t_o > t_{\alpha,n-1}$	$t_o = \dfrac{\overline{X} - \mu_o}{s/\sqrt{n}}$
H_o: $\mu \geq \mu_o$ H_a: $\mu < \mu_o$	$t_o < -t_{\alpha,n-1}$	$t_o = \dfrac{\overline{X} - \mu_o}{s/\sqrt{n}}$

(3.64)

Example 3-34: In Example 3-29, the mean temperature at which metallic glass became brittle was of interest. Suppose we would like to determine whether this mean temperature exceeds 595°F. A random sample of 20 was taken, yielding a sample mean $\overline{X}$ of 600°F and a sample standard deviation s of 15°F. Use a level of significance α of 0.05.

Solution. The hypotheses are

$$H_o : \mu \leq 595$$
$$H_a : \mu > 595$$

The test statistic is

$$t_o = \frac{(600 - 595)}{15/\sqrt{20}} = 1.491$$

From Appendix A-4, $t_{.05,19} = 1.729$. The rejection region is therefore $t_o > 1.729$. Since the test statistic t_o does not lie in the rejection region, we do not reject the null hypothesis. Thus even though the sample mean is 600°F, the 5-percent level of significance does not allow us to conclude that there is statistically significant evidence that the mean temperature exceeds 595°F.

Hypothesis Testing for the Difference Between Two Means

1. *Variances known.* Assume here that the sample sizes are large enough for the Central Limit Theorem to hold. However, if the population distribution is normal, then the test statistic as shown will be valid for any sample size.

HYPOTHESES	REJECTION REGION	TEST STATISTIC
H_o: $\mu_1 - \mu_2 = \mu_o$ H_a: $\mu_1 - \mu_2 \neq \mu_o$	$\|z_o\| > z_{\alpha/2}$	$z_o = \dfrac{(\overline{X}_1 - \overline{X}_2) - \mu_o}{\sqrt{\sigma_1^2/n_1 + \sigma_2^2/n_2}}$
H_o: $\mu_1 - \mu_2 \leq \mu_o$ H_a: $\mu_1 - \mu_2 > \mu_o$	$z_o > z_\alpha$	$z_o = \dfrac{(\overline{X}_1 - \overline{X}_2) - \mu_o}{\sqrt{\sigma_1^2/n_1 + \sigma_2^2/n_2}}$
H_o: $\mu_1 - \mu_2 \geq \mu_o$ H_a: $\mu_1 - \mu_2 < \mu_o$	$z_o < -z_\alpha$	$z_o = \dfrac{(\overline{X}_1 - \overline{X}_2) - \mu_o}{\sqrt{\sigma_1^2/n_1 + \sigma_2^2/n_2}}$

(3.65)

Example 3-35: In the lumber industry, the average unloading time of logs from a shipment is of interest. Two different methods are used for unloading. A random sample of size 40 for the first method gave an average unloading time $\overline{X}_1$ of 20.5 minutes. A random sample of size 50 for the second method yielded an average unloading time $\overline{X}_2$ of 17.6 minutes. It is known that the variance of the unloading times using the first method is 3, while that for the second method is 4. At a significance level α of 0.05, can we conclude that there is a difference in the mean unloading times for the two methods?

Solution. The hypotheses are

$$H_o : \mu_1 - \mu_2 = 0$$
$$H_a : \mu_1 - \mu_2 \neq 0$$

The test statistic is

$$z_o = \frac{(20.5 - 17.6) - 0}{\sqrt{\frac{3}{40} + \frac{4}{50}}} = 7.366$$

From Appendix A-3, $z_{.025} = 1.96$. The critical values are ± 1.96, and the rejection region is $|z_o| > 1.96$. Since the test statistic z_o lies in the rejection region, we reject the null hypothesis and conclude that there is a difference in the mean unloading times for the two methods.

2. *Variances unknown.* Assume here that each of the populations is normally distributed. If we assume that the population variances, though unknown, are equal (that is, $\sigma_1^2 = \sigma_2^2$), then we get the following:

HYPOTHESES	REJECTION REGION	TEST STATISTIC
H_o: $\mu_1 - \mu_2 = \mu_o$ H_a: $\mu_1 - \mu_2 \neq \mu_o$	$\lvert t_o \rvert > t_{\alpha/2, n_1+n_2-2}$	$t_o = \dfrac{(\overline{X}_1 - \overline{X}_2) - \mu_o}{s_p\sqrt{(1/n_1) + (1/n_2)}}$ [s_p is given by (3.53)]
H_o: $\mu_1 - \mu_2 \leq \mu_o$ H_a: $\mu_1 - \mu_2 > \mu_o$	$t_o > t_{\alpha, n_1+n_2-2}$	$t_o = \dfrac{(\overline{X}_1 - \overline{X}_2) - \mu_o}{s_p\sqrt{(1/n_1) + (1/n_2)}}$ [s_p is given by (3.53)]
H_o: $\mu_1 - \mu_2 \geq \mu_o$ H_a: $\mu_1 - \mu_2 < \mu_o$	$t_o < -t_{\alpha, n_1+n_2-2}$	$t_o = \dfrac{(\overline{X}_1 - \overline{X}_2) - \mu_o}{s_p\sqrt{(1/n_1) + (1/n_2)}}$ [s_p is given by (3.53)]

(3.66)

If the population variances cannot be assumed to be equal ($\sigma_1^2 \neq \sigma_2^2$), we have the following:

HYPOTHESES	REJECTION REGION	TEST STATISTIC
H_o: $\mu_1 - \mu_2 = \mu_o$ H_a: $\mu_1 - \mu_2 \neq \mu_o$	$\lvert t_o \rvert > t_{\alpha/2, \nu}$ (ν from Equation 3.55)	$t_o = \dfrac{(\overline{X}_1 - \overline{X}_2) - \mu_o}{\sqrt{s_1^2/n_1 + s_2^2/n_2}}$
H_o: $\mu_1 - \mu_2 \leq \mu_o$ H_a: $\mu_1 - \mu_2 > \mu_o$	$t_o > t_{\alpha, \nu}$ (ν from Equation 3.55)	$t_o = \dfrac{(\overline{X}_1 - \overline{X}_2) - \mu_o}{\sqrt{s_1^2/n_1 + s_2^2/n_2}}$
H_o: $\mu_1 - \mu_2 \geq \mu_o$ H_a: $\mu_1 - \mu_2 < \mu_o$	$t_o < -t_{\alpha, \nu}$ (ν from Equation 3.55)	$t_o = \dfrac{(\overline{X}_1 - \overline{X}_2) - \mu_o}{\sqrt{s_1^2/n_1 + s_2^2/n_2}}$

(3.67)

Example 3-36: A large corporation is interested in determining if the average number of days of sick leave taken annually is more for night shift employees than for day shift employees. It is assumed that the distribution of the days of sick leave is normal for both shifts and that the variances of sick leave taken are equal for both shifts. A random sample of 12 employees from the night shift yielded an average sick leave $\overline{X}_1$ of 16.4 days with a standard deviation s_1 of 2.2 days. A random sample of 15 employees from the day shift yielded an average sick leave $\overline{X}_2$ of 12.3 days with a standard deviation s_2 of 3.5 days. At a level of significance α of 0.05, can we conclude that the average sick leave for those in the night shift exceeds that for those in the day shift?

Solution. The hypotheses are

$$H_o : \mu_1 - \mu_2 \leq 0$$
$$H_a : \mu_1 - \mu_2 > 0$$

The pooled estimate of the variance, s_p^2, from Equation 3.53 is

$$s_p^2 = \frac{11(2.2)^2 + 14(3.5)^2}{25} = 8.990$$

So, $s_p = \sqrt{8.990} = 2.998$. The test statistic is

$$t_o = \frac{(16.4 - 12.3) - 0}{2.998\sqrt{\frac{1}{12} + \frac{1}{15}}} = 3.531$$

From Appendix A-4, $t_{.05,25} = 1.708$. Since the test statistic t_o exceeds 1.708 and falls in the rejection region, we reject the null hypothesis and conclude that the average sick leave for those in the night shift exceeds that for those in the day shift.

Hypothesis Testing for a Proportion Assume here that the number of trials n in a binomial experiment is large, that $np \geq 5$, and that $n(1-p) \geq 5$, thus allowing the distribution of the sample proportion of successes ($\hat{p}$) to approximate a normal distribution.

HYPOTHESES	REJECTION REGION	TEST STATISTIC
H_o: $p = p_o$ H_a: $p \neq p_o$	$\lvert z_o \rvert > z_{\alpha/2}$	$z_o = \dfrac{\hat{p} - p_o}{\sqrt{p_o(1-p_o)/n}}$
H_o: $p \leq p_o$ H_a: $p > p_o$	$z_o > z_\alpha$	$z_o = \dfrac{\hat{p} - p_o}{\sqrt{p_o(1-p_o)/n}}$
H_o: $p \geq p_o$ H_a: $p < p_o$	$z_o < -z_\alpha$	$z_o = \dfrac{\hat{p} - p_o}{\sqrt{p_o(1-p_o)/n}}$

(3.68)

Example 3-37: The timeliness with which due dates are met is an important factor in maintaining customer satisfaction. A medium-sized organization wants to test if the proportion of times that it does not meet due dates is less than 6 percent. Based on a random sample of 100 customer orders, they found that they missed the due date 5 times. What is your conclusion? Test at a level of significance α of 0.05.

Solution. The hypotheses are

$$H_o : p \geq 0.06$$
$$H_a : p < 0.06$$

The test statistic is

$$z_o = \frac{0.05 - 0.06}{\sqrt{\frac{(0.06)(0.94)}{100}}} = -0.421$$

From Appendix A-3, $z_{.05} = 1.645$. Since the test statistic z_o is not less than -1.645, it does not lie in the rejection region. Hence, we do not reject the null hypothesis. At the five-percent level of significance, we cannot conclude that the proportion of due dates missed is less than 6 percent.

Hypothesis Testing for the Difference Between Two Binomial Proportions Assume here that the sample sizes are large enough to allow a normal distribution for the difference between the sample proportions. Also, we consider the case, where in the null hypothesis, the difference between the two proportions is zero. For a treatment of other cases, such as the hypothesized difference between two proportions being 3 percent, say where the null hypothesis is given by $H_0 : p_1 - p_2 = 0.03$, consult Mendenhall, Reinmuth, and Beaver (1989) and Duncan (1986).

HYPOTHESES	REJECTION REGION	TEST STATISTIC
H_o: $p_1 - p_2 = 0$ H_a: $p_1 - p_2 \neq 0$	$\lvert z_o \rvert > z_{\alpha/2}$	$z_o = \frac{\hat{p}_1 - \hat{p}_2}{\sqrt{\hat{p}(1-\hat{p})(1/n_1 + 1/n_2)}}$, where $\hat{p} = \frac{n_1\hat{p}_1 + n_2\hat{p}_2}{n_1 + n_2}$ is the pooled estimate of the proportion of nonconforming items
H_o: $p_1 - p_2 \leq 0$ H_a: $p_1 - p_2 > 0$	$z_o > z_\alpha$	$z_o = \frac{\hat{p}_1 - \hat{p}_2}{\sqrt{\hat{p}(1-\hat{p})(1/n_1 + 1/n_2)}}$, where $\hat{p} = \frac{n_1\hat{p}_1 + n_2\hat{p}_2}{n_1 + n_2}$ is the pooled estimate of the proportion of nonconforming items
H_o: $p_1 - p_2 \geq 0$ H_a: $p_1 - p_2 < 0$	$z_o < -z_\alpha$	$z_o = \frac{\hat{p}_1 - \hat{p}_2}{\sqrt{\hat{p}(1-\hat{p})(1/n_1 + 1/n_2)}}$, where $\hat{p} = \frac{n_1\hat{p}_1 + n_2\hat{p}_2}{n_1 + n_2}$ is the pooled estimate of the proportion of nonconforming items

(3.69)

Example 3-38: A company is interested in determining if the proportion of nonconforming items (that is, fallout) is different for two of its vendors. A random sample of 100 items from the first vendor revealed 4 nonconforming items. A random sample of 200 items from the second vendor showed 10 nonconforming items. What is your conclusion? Test at a level of significance α of 0.05.

Solution. The hypotheses are

$$H_o : p_1 - p_2 = 0$$
$$H_a : p_1 - p_2 \neq 0$$

The pooled estimate of the proportion of nonconforming items is

$$\hat{p} = \frac{100(.04) + 200(.05)}{300} = 0.047$$

The test statistic is

$$z_o = \frac{0.04 - 0.05}{\sqrt{(0.047)(0.953)(\frac{1}{100} + \frac{1}{200})}} = -0.386$$

From Appendix A-3, $z_{.025} = 1.96$. Since the test statistic z_o does not lie in the rejection region, we do not reject the null hypothesis. We cannot conclude that there is a difference in the proportion of nonconforming items between the two vendors.

Hypothesis Testing for the Variance Assume here that the population distribution is normal.

HYPOTHESES	REJECTION REGION	TEST STATISTIC
H_o: $\sigma^2 = \sigma_o^2$ H_a: $\sigma^2 \neq \sigma_o^2$	$\chi_o^2 > \chi^2_{\alpha/2,n-1}$ or $\chi_o^2 < \chi^2_{1-\alpha/2,n-1}$	$\chi_o^2 = \frac{(n-1)s^2}{\sigma_o^2}$
H_o: $\sigma^2 \leq \sigma_o^2$ H_a: $\sigma^2 > \sigma_o^2$	$\chi_o^2 > \chi^2_{\alpha,n-1}$	$\chi_o^2 = \frac{(n-1)s^2}{\sigma_o^2}$
H_o: $\sigma^2 \geq \sigma_o^2$ H_a: $\sigma^2 < \sigma_o^2$	$\chi_o^2 < \chi^2_{1-\alpha,n-1}$	$\chi_o^2 = \frac{(n-1)s^2}{\sigma_o^2}$

(3.70)

Example 3-39: The variability of the downtime of equipment in a job shop is of concern. A random sample of 15 machines that had to be repaired showed an average downtime $\bar{X}$ of 2.2 hours with a standard deviation s of 0.2 hours. Can we conclude that the variance of downtimes is less than 0.06? Use a level of significance α of 0.01.

Solution. The hypotheses are

$$H_o : \sigma^2 \geq 0.06$$
$$H_a : \sigma^2 < 0.06$$

The test statistic is

$$\chi_o^2 = \frac{(14)(0.2)^2}{0.06} = 9.333$$

From Appendix A-5, $\chi^2_{.99,14} = 4.66$. The test statistic value of 9.333 is not less than 4.66 and so does not lie in the rejection region. Hence, we do not reject the null hypothesis. At the one percent level of significance we cannot conclude that the variance of downtimes is less than 0.06.

Hypothesis Testing for the Ratio of Two Variances Assume here that both populations are normally distributed.

HYPOTHESES	REJECTION REGION	TEST STATISTIC
$H_o: \sigma_1^2 = \sigma_2^2$ $H_a: \sigma_1^2 \neq \sigma_2^2$	$F_o > F_{\alpha/2,\nu_1,\nu_2}$ or $F_o < F_{1-\alpha/2,\nu_1,\nu_2}$	$F_o = \frac{s_1^2}{s_2^2}$
$H_o: \sigma_1^2 \leq \sigma_2^2$ $H_a: \sigma_1^2 > \sigma_2^2$	$F_o > F_{\alpha,\nu_1,\nu_2}$	$F_o = \frac{s_1^2}{s_2^2}$
$H_o: \sigma_1^2 \geq \sigma_2^2$ $H_a: \sigma_1^2 < \sigma_2^2$	$F_o < F_{1-\alpha,\nu_1,\nu_2}$	$F_o = \frac{s_1^2}{s_2^2}$

(3.71)

Example 3-40: The variabilities of the service times of two bank tellers are of interest. It is desired to determine if the variance of service time for the first teller is greater than that of the second. A random sample of 8 observations from the first teller yielded a sample average $\overline{X}_1$ of 3.4 minutes with a standard deviation s_1 of 1.8 minutes. A random sample of 10 observations from the second teller yielded a sample average $\overline{X}_2$ of 2.5 minutes with a standard deviation of 0.9 minutes. Can we conclude that the variance of the service time is greater for the first teller than for the second? Use a level of significance α of 0.05.

The hypotheses are

$$H_o: \sigma_1^2 \leq \sigma_2^2$$
$$H_a: \sigma_1^2 > \sigma_2^2$$

The test statistic is

$$F = \frac{s_1^2}{s_2^2} = \frac{(1.8)^2}{(0.9)^2} = 4.00$$

From Appendix A-6, $F_{.05,7,9} = 3.29$. The test statistic lies in the rejection region, and so we reject the null hypothesis.

3-8 CONCEPTS IN SAMPLING

Introduction

In quality control, it is often not feasible to obtain data regarding a certain quality characteristic for each item in a population due to a lack of time and resources. Furthermore, sample data may provide adequate information about a product or process characteristic at a fraction of the cost of obtaining data from each item. It is therefore important to have an idea of the different ways in which samples may be selected and the desirable properties of sampling procedures.

A *sampling design* is a description of the procedure by which the observations in a sample are to be chosen. It does not necessarily deal with the measuring instrument to be used. For example, a sampling design might specify choosing every tenth item produced.

In the context of sampling, an *element* is an object (or group of objects) for which data or information is gathered. A *sampling unit* is an individual element or a collection of nonoverlapping elements from the population. A *sampling frame* is a list of all sampling units. For example, if our interest is confined to a set of parts produced in the month of July, the sampling unit could be an individual part, while the sampling frame would be a list of the part numbers of all of the items produced.

Sampling Designs and Schemes

One of the major objectives of any sampling design or scheme is that the sample should be selected in such a way as to accurately portray the population from which it is drawn. After all, a sample is supposed to be representative of the population.

Sampling in general has certain advantages. If in the process of obtaining a measurement from an item the object is destroyed (destructive testing), then we cannot afford to obtain data from each item. Also, the heavy workload associated with obtaining information for each item in situations involving manual methods and high production rates may actually result in fatigue, which may yield data that is inaccurate.

Errors in Sampling There are three sources of errors in sample surveys. The first is that due to *random variation*. The inherent nature of sampling variability will sometimes cause such errors to occur. The more sophisticated the measuring instrument, the lower the random variation.

Misspecification of the population is a second source of error. This type of error may occur in public opinion polling, in obtaining responses regarding consumer satisfaction with the product, in listing a sampling frame incorrectly, and so on.

The third source of error deals with *nonresponses* (usually in sample surveys). This category also includes situations where a measurement is not feasible due to an inoperative measuring instrument, a shortage of people responsible for taking the measurement, or other such reasons.

Simple Random Sample One of the most widely used sampling designs in quality control is that of a simple random sample. Suppose we have a finite population of N items from which a sample of n items is to be selected. If samples are chosen such that each possible sample of size n has an equal chance of being selected, the sampling process is said to be random, and the sample obtained is known as a simple random sample.

Random number tables (or those generated by a computer) could be used to draw a simple random sample. For example, if there are 1000 elements in the population, the three-digit numbers 000–999 may be used to identify each element. A random number may be selected. The selected element corresponds to the chosen number. This procedure may be repeated until the desired sample of size n is chosen. If a number shows up that has already been selected, it is ignored, and another random number is chosen.

Stratified Random Sample Sometimes the population from which samples are to be selected is heterogeneous. For instance, consider the output from two operators who are known to differ greatly in their performance. Rather then randomly selecting a sample from the combined output that is a mixture of the output of the two operators, a random sample would be selected from the output of each operator. That way, we would be able to represent both operators and be in a position to determine if there are significant differences between them. Thus, a stratified random sample is obtained by separating the elements of the population into nonoverlapping distinct groups (called strata) and then selecting a simple random sample from each stratum.

Cluster Sample In the event that a sampling frame is not available, or if obtaining samples from all segments of the population is not feasible for geographic reasons, a cluster sample may be chosen. Here, the population is first divided into groups of elements, or clusters. Clusters are randomly selected, upon which a census of data is obtained (that is, all of the elements within the chosen clusters are examined). A company may have six plants throughout the southeastern U.S. If it is not feasible to sample from each plant, clusters may be defined (say, one for each plant). Some of the clusters are then randomly chosen (say, three of the five clusters). For each selected cluster, a census of data is obtained.

Sample Size Determination

The size of a sample has a direct impact on the information given by the data. The larger the sample size, the more valuable the information. It is usually of interest to know the minimum sample size that one must select in order to estimate an unknown product or process parameter.

Estimating Population Mean Suppose the mean of a product or process characteristic is of interest (for example, the average width of a component used in an assembly). There is a $(1 - \alpha)$ probability that the difference between the estimated value and actual value will be no greater than some number B. Figure 3-34 shows the principle behind the selection of an appropriate sample size for estimating the population mean. The quantity B is sometimes referred to as the tolerable error bound and is given by

$$B = z_{\alpha/2}\sigma_{\overline{X}} = z_{\alpha/2}\frac{\sigma}{\sqrt{n}} \tag{3.72}$$

or

$$n = \frac{z^2_{\alpha/2}\sigma^2}{B^2} \tag{3.73}$$

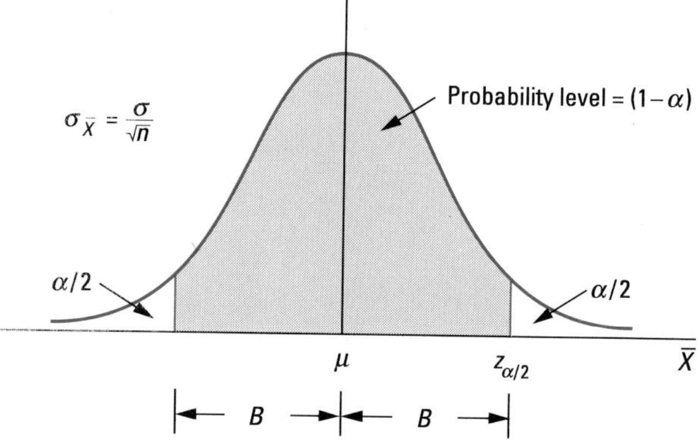

Figure 3-34 Sample size determination for estimating population mean μ.

Example 3-41: An analyst wishes to estimate the average bore size of a large casting. Based on historical data, it is estimated that the standard deviation of the bore sizes is 4.2 mm. If it is desired to estimate with a probability of 0.95 the average bore size to within 0.8 mm, find the number of items that should be selected.

Solution. We have

$$\sigma = 4.2, \quad B = 0.8, \quad z_{.025} = 1.96$$

$$\text{Sample size } n = \frac{(1.96)^2(4.2)^2}{(0.8)^2} = 105.88 \simeq 106$$

Estimating Population Proportion Consider a binomial population where the objective is to estimate the proportion of "successes" (p). Examples might include estimating the proportion of nonconforming stamped parts in a press shop or the proportion of unsatisfied customers in a restaurant. Here again, it is necessary to select a tolerable error bound B such that that estimate will have a probability of $(1 - \alpha)$ of being within B units of the parameter value. Figure 3-35 shows the sampling distribution of the sample proportion of successes ($\hat{p}$), which is approximately normal for large sample sizes. The equation for determining the sample size n is given by

$$B = z_{\alpha/2}\sigma_{\hat{p}} = z_{\alpha/2}\sqrt{\frac{p(1-p)}{n}} \tag{3.74}$$

or

$$n = \frac{z^2_{\alpha/2}\,p(1-p)}{B^2} \tag{3.75}$$

Since the true parameter value p is not known, there are a couple of ways in which Equation 3.75 may be modified for use in practice. First, if a historical estimate of p is available (say, $\hat{p}$), it may be used in place of p in Equation 3.75. Second, if no prior information is available, a conservative estimate of n may be calculated from Equation 3.75 by using $p = 0.5$. Using $p = 0.5$ maximizes the value of $p(1 - p)$ and hence produces a conservative estimate.

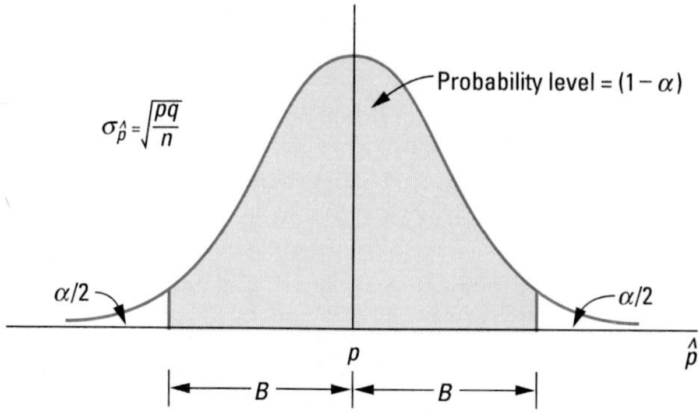

Figure 3-35 Sampling distribution of $\hat{p}$.

Example 3-42: For producing rubber tubes, the tube stock has to be first cut into a piece of a specified length. This piece is then formed into a circular shape and joined using pressure and the right temperature. The operator training and such process parameters as temperature, pressure, and die size influence the production of conforming tubes. It is desired to estimate with a probability of .90 the proportion of nonconforming tubes to within four percent. How large a sample should be chosen if no prior information is available on the process?

Solution. Using the above notation, $B = 0.04$. From Appendix A-3, $z_{.05} = 1.645$. Since no information on p, the proportion of nonconforming tubes, is available, use $p = 0.5$. Hence

$$n = \frac{(1.645)^2(.05)(0.5)}{(0.04)^2} = 422.8 \simeq 423$$

If a prior estimate of p had been available, it would have reduced the required sample size.

3-9 SUMMARY

This chapter has presented the statistical foundations necessary for quality control and improvement. The procedures for summarizing data that describe product or process characteristics have been discussed. A review of common discrete and continuous probability distributions with applications in quality control has been included. The chapter has also presented inferential statistics which can be used for drawing conclusions as to product and process quality. In particular, the topics of estimation and hypothesis testing have been emphasized. Finally, some fundamental concepts of sampling designs have been presented. The variety of statistical procedures presented in this chapter are meant to serve as an overview. Technical details have been purposely limited. For further discussion of any of the topics, the reader should consult corresponding references on the subject matter of interest.

APPENDIX: APPROXIMATIONS TO SOME PROBABILITY DISTRIBUTIONS

In some situations, if tables for the needed probability distributions are not available for the parameter values in question or if the calculations using the formula become tedious and prone to error due to roundoffs, approximations for the probability distribution under consideration may be considered.

Binomial Approximation of the Hypergeometric

When the ratio of sample size to population size is small, that is, n/N is small (≤ 0.1, as a rule of thumb), the binomial distribution serves as a good approximation to the hypergeometric distribution. The parameter values to be used for the binomial distribution would be the same value of n as in the hypergeometric distribution, and $p = D/N$.

Example A-1: Consider a lot of 100 parts, of which 6 are nonconforming. If a sample of 4 parts is selected, what is the probability of obtaining 2 nonconforming items? If a binomial approximation is used, what is the required probability?

Solution. Using the hypergeometric distribution, $N = 100$, $D = 6$, $n = 4$, and $x = 2$. We have

$$P(X = 2) = \frac{\binom{6}{2}\binom{94}{2}}{\binom{100}{4}} = 0.017$$

Note that $n/N = 0.04$, which is less than 0.1. Using the binomial distribution as an approximation to the hypergeometric, with $p = 6/100 = 0.06$, yields

$$P(X = 2) = \binom{4}{2}(.06)^2(.94)^2 = 0.019$$

Poisson Approximation to the Binomial

In a binomial distribution, if n is large and p is small ($p < 0.1$) such that np is constant, the Poisson distribution serves as a good approximation to the binomial. The parameter λ in the Poisson distribution is used as np. The larger the value of n and smaller the value of p, the better the approximation. As a rule of thumb, when $np < 5$, the approximation is acceptable.

Example A-2: A process is known to have a nonconformance rate of 0.02. If a random sample of 100 items is selected, what is the probability of finding 3 nonconforming items?

Solution. Using the binomial distribution, $n = 100$, $p = .02$, and $x = 3$. We have

$$P(X = 3) = \binom{100}{3}(.02)^3(.98)^{97} = 0.182$$

Next, use the Poisson distribution as an approximation to the binomial. Using $\lambda = (100)(.02) = 2$ yields

$$P(X = 3) = \frac{e^{-2}2^3}{3!} = 0.180$$

Normal Approximation to the Binomial

In a binomial distribution, if n is large and p is close to 0.5, the normal distribution may be used to approximate the binomial. Usually, if p is neither too large nor too small ($0.1 \leq p \leq 0.9$), the normal approximation is acceptable when $np \geq 5$. A continuity correction factor is used, by finding an appropriate z-value because the binomial is discrete, whereas the normal is continuous.

Example A-3: A process is known to produce about 6 percent nonconforming items. If a random sample of 200 items is chosen, what is the probability of finding between 6 and 8 nonconforming items?

Solution. If we decide to use the binomial distribution with $n = 200$, $p = 0.06$, we have

$$\begin{aligned} P(6 \leq X \leq 8) &= P(X = 6) + P(X = 7) + P(X = 8) \\ &= \binom{200}{6}(0.06)^6(0.94)^{194} \\ &\quad + \binom{200}{7}(0.06)^7(0.94)^{193} \\ &\quad + \binom{200}{8}(0.06)^8(0.94)^{192} \\ &= 0.0235 + 0.0416 + 0.0641 \\ &= 0.1292 \end{aligned}$$

Using the normal distribution to approximate a binomial probability, the mean is given by $np = 200(0.06) = 12$, and the variance is given by $np(1 - p) = 200(0.06)(1 - 0.06) = 11.28$. The required probability is

$$P(6 \leq X \leq 8) \simeq P(5.5 \leq X \leq 8.5)$$

The 0.5 adjustment is often known as the continuity correction factor. The binomial random variable is discrete. When using a continuous random variable such as the normal to approximate it, this adjustment makes the approximation better. In other words $P(X \leq 8)$ is written as $P(X \leq 8.5)$, while $P(X \geq 6)$ is written as $P(X \geq 5.5)$.

$$\begin{aligned} \text{Required probability} &= P\left(\frac{5.5 - 12}{\sqrt{11.28}} \leq z \leq \frac{8.5 - 12}{\sqrt{11.28}}\right) \\ &= P(-1.94 \leq z \leq -1.04) \\ &= .1492 - .0262 = 0.1230 \end{aligned}$$

Normal Approximation to the Poisson

If the mean λ of a Poisson distribution is large ($\lambda \geq 10$), a normal distribution may be used to approximate it. The parameters of this normal distribution are the mean μ, which is set equal to λ and the variance σ^2, which is also set equal to λ. As in Example A-3, the continuity correction factor of 0.5 may be used since a discrete random variable is approximated by a continuous one.

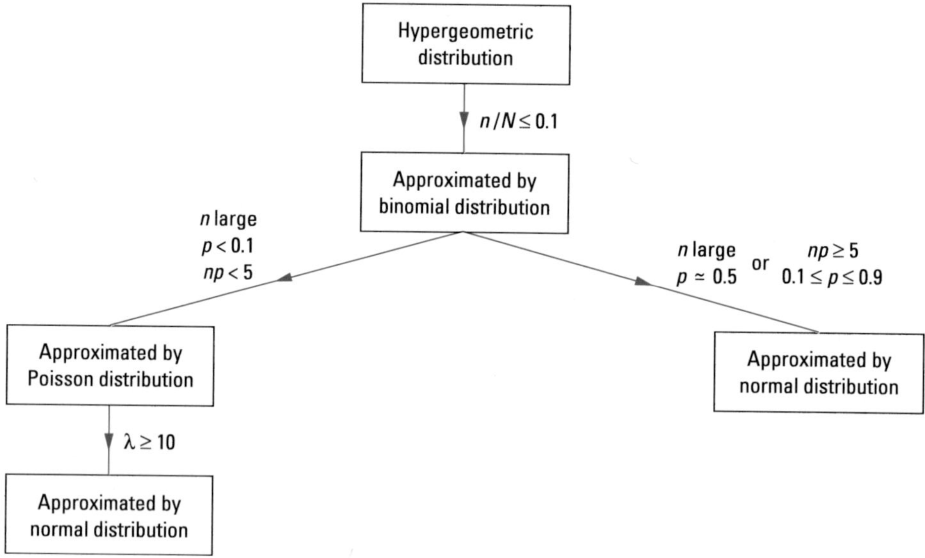

Figure 3A-1 Necessary conditions for using approximations to distributions.

Example A-4: The number of small businesses that fail each year is known to have a Poisson distribution with a mean of 16. Find the probability that in a given year there will be no more than 18 small business failures.

Solution. Using the Poisson distribution ($\lambda = 16$), the required probability is $P(X \leq 18)$. From the table in Appendix A-2, this probability is 0.742. When using the normal distribution as an approximation, the mean and variance are set equal to λ. The 0.5 continuity correction factor is used in a similar manner as in Example A-3.

$$\begin{aligned} P(X \leq 18) &\simeq P(X \leq 18.5) \\ &= P\left(z \leq \frac{18.5 - 16}{\sqrt{16}}\right) \\ &= P(z \leq 0.625) \\ &= 0.7340 \text{ (using linear interpolation)} \end{aligned}$$

Figure 3A-1 summarizes the conditions under which the different approximations to these common distributions may be used.

 KEY TERMS

Accuracy
Additive law
Alternative hypothesis
Association, measures of
Binomial distribution
Calibration
Central tendency, measures of
Central Limit Theorem
Chi-squared distribution
Combinations
Confidence interval
Continuous variable
Correlation coefficient
Critical value
Cumulative distribution function
Data collection
Degrees of freedom
Descriptive statistics
Discrete variable
Dispersion, measures of
Distributions
- Continuous
- Discrete

Estimation
- Point
- Interval

Events
- Complementary
- Compound
- Independent
- Mutually exclusive
- Simple

Expected value
Exponential distribution
F-distribution

Gamma function
Hypergeometric distribution
Hypothesis testing
    One-tailed
    Two-tailed
    Power
Inferential statistics
Interquartile range
Interval estimation
Kurtosis coefficient
Level of significance
Mean
Measurement scales
    Interval
    Nominal
    Ordinal
    Ratio
Median
Misspecification
Mode
Multiplicative law
Nonresponse
Normal distribution
    Standard normal
Null hypothesis
Outlier
p-value
Parameter
Poisson distribution
Population
Power
Precision
Probability
Probability density
Probability distribution
Random variable
Random variation
Range
Rejection region
Sample
    Cluster
    Simple random
    Stratified
Sample size, determination of
Sample space
Sampling
    Design
    Element
    Errors in
    Frame
    Unit
Sampling distribution
Skewness coefficient
Standard deviation
Statistic
t-distribution
Test statistic
Trimmed mean
Type I error
Type II error
Unbiased
Variance
Weibull distribution

EXERCISES

Discussion Questions

3-1 Explain the difference between a parameter and a statistic. Give examples of each.

3-2 Explain the concept of independence of events. How does this relate to events being mutually exclusive.

3-3 Find an expression for the probability of the union of three events that are mutually independent of each other.

3-4 Are complementary events independent? Are they mutually exclusive?

3-5 How do procedures in descriptive statistics help in obtaining information about a product or a process?

3-6 Explain the importance of inferential statistics in decision making regarding a product or a process.

3-7 Explain the difference between accuracy and precision of measurements.

3-8 Explain the different types of measurement scales, and give examples of each type.

3-9 Distinguish between the usage of the mean, median, and mode in quality control applications. When would you prefer to use the trimmed mean?

3-10 What are the advantages of the standard deviation over the range as a measure of dispersion? Explain and interpret the interquartile deviation.

3-11 Why are measures of central tendency insufficient to describe the characteristics of a product or process?

3-12 Explain the skewness and kurtosis coefficients. How does information about these two quantities aid in quality control and improvement?

3-13 What does the correlation coefficient measure? How may this information contribute to quality improvement?

3-14 Describe the properties that must be satisfied by the probability distribution function of a discrete random variable.

3-15 Distinguish between a hypergeometric and binomial random variable.

3-16 State and explain the Central limit theorem. Explain its role in quality control.

3-17 What are the desirable properties of estimators?

3-18 A 95 percent confidence interval for the mean thickness of a part in millimeters is (10.2, 12.9). Interpret this interval.

3-19 Distinguish between a stratified sample and a cluster sample. Give some examples of where these two might be used.

3-20 What guidelines must be selected before a sample size required for the purpose of estimation can be chosen?

3-21 Explain the difference between a null and alternative hypothesis.

3-22 Discuss a Type I error and Type II error in hypothesis testing. Explain these in the context of a quality control setting.

Problems

3-23 In order to satisfy certain environmental standards set by the EPA, a utility company conducts some tests of its own. One sample is chosen from each of the company's six plants. It is suspected that two of the plants are in violation of the standards. If an inspector randomly chooses samples for inspection, answer the following:

a. What is the probability that at least one of the suspected companies will be represented in the selected sample?
b. What is the probability that none of the suspected companies are represented for inspection?

3-24 The use of warranties as a means of assuring the customer of the quality of the product is quite common. Doing so may lead to an increased market share of the product and thus become profitable. Based on historical data, it is estimated that 12 percent of the new products will have a profitable market share. Furthermore, if two products are newly introduced in the same year, there is only a 5 percent chance of both products becoming profitable. A company is planning to market two new products, 1 and 2, this coming year. What is the probability of

a. only product 1 becoming profitable?
b. only product 2 becoming profitable?
c. at least one of the products becoming profitable?
d. neither product becoming profitable?
e. either product 1 or product 2 (but not both) becoming profitable?
f. product 2 becoming profitable, if product 1 is found to be profitable?

3-25 Two types of defects are observed in the production of integrated circuit boards. It is estimated that 6 percent of the boards have solder defects while 3 percent of them have some surface finish defects. The occurrence of the two types of defects are assumed to be independent of each other. If a circuit board is randomly selected from the output, find the probabilities for the following situations:

a. Either a solder defect or a surface finish defect or both is found.
b. Only a solder defect is found.
c. Both types of defects are found.
d. The board is free of defects.
e. If a surface finish defect is found, what are the chances of also finding a solder defect?

3-26 The settling of unwanted material in a mold is causing some defects in the output. Based on recent data it is estimated that 5 percent of the output has one or more defects. In spot checking some parts, an inspector randomly selects 2 parts. Find the following probabilities:

a. The first part is defect-free.
b. The second part is defect-free.
c. Both parts are defect free.
d. One of the parts is acceptable.
e. At least one part is acceptable.

3-27 The time (in minutes) to process hot-rolled steel was observed for a random sample of size 10 and is shown below:

5.4	6.2	7.9	4.8	7.5
6.2	5.5	4.5	7.2	6.2

a. Find the mean, median, and mode of the processing times. Interpret the differences between them.

b. Compute the range, variance, and standard deviation of the processing times, and interpret them.

3-28 A random sample of 50 observations on the mileage per gallon of a particular brand of gasoline is shown below:

33.2	29.4	36.5	38.1	30.0
29.1	32.2	29.5	36.0	31.5
34.5	33.6	27.4	30.4	28.4
32.6	30.4	31.8	29.8	34.6
30.7	31.9	32.3	28.2	27.5
34.9	32.8	27.7	28.4	28.8
30.2	26.8	27.8	30.5	28.5
31.8	29.2	28.6	27.5	28.5
30.8	31.8	29.1	26.9	34.2
33.5	27.4	28.5	34.8	30.5

a. Find the mean, median, and standard deviation, and interpret them.

b. Find the interquartile range, skewness, and kurtosis coefficient, and interpret their values.

3-29 An insurance company is interested in determining if the amount of life insurance coverage is influenced by the amount of disposable income. A randomly chosen sample of size 20 produced the data shown in the accompanying table. Calculate the correlation coefficient between disposable income and the amount of life insurance coverage, and interpret it. How can a company use this information for decision making?

Disposable income (in \$1000)	Life insurance coverage (in \$1000)	Disposable income (in \$1000)	Life insurance coverage (in \$1000)
45	60	65	80
40	58	60	90
65	100	45	50
50	50	40	50
70	120	55	70
80	100	55	60
70	80	60	80
40	50	75	100
50	70	45	50
45	60	65	70

3-30 A distribution company has ordered 12 computers. Unknown to the company, three of the computers have some defects. If the purchasing division of the company selects four computers from the shipment, what is the probability that none of them will have any defects? What is the probability that no more than two will have any defects?

3-31 A sampling plan currently in use in a software company producing diskettes involves selecting 5 items from a lot of 35 diskettes. If no more than 1 nonconforming diskette is found, the lot is accepted. If a lot actually has 3 nonconforming diskettes, what is the probability of accepting such a lot under this plan?

3-32 A pharmaceutical company making antibiotics has to abide by certain standards set by the Food and Drug Administration. The company performs some testing on the strength of the antibiotic. In a case of 25 bottles, 4 bottles are selected for testing. If a case actually contains 5 bottles that are of understrength, what is the probability that the chosen sample will contain no understrength bottles? Exactly 1 bottle that is of understrength? How many understrength bottles would be expected in the sample? What is the standard deviation of the number of bottles that are of understrength in the sample?

3-33 A company involved in making solar panels estimates that 3 percent of its product are nonconforming. If a random sample of 5 items is selected from the production output, what is the probability that none are nonconforming? that 2 are nonconforming? The cost of rectifying a nonconforming panel is estimated to be $5. For a shipment of 1000 panels, what is the expected cost of rectification?

3-34 A university has purchased a service contract for its computers and pays $20 annually for each computer. Maintenance records show that 8 percent of the computers require some sort of servicing during a year. Furthermore, it is estimated that the average expenses for each repair, had the university not been covered by the service contract, would be about $200. If the university currently has 20 computers, would you advise buying the service contract. Based on expected costs, for what annual premium per computer will the university be indifferent to the buying of the service contract? What is the probability of the university spending no more than $500 annually on repairs if it does not buy the service contract?

3-35 The probability of an electronic sensor malfunctioning is known to be 0.10. A random sample of 12 sensors is chosen. Find the probability that

a. at least 3 will malfunction,
b. no more than 5 will malfunction,
c. at least 1 but no more than 5 will malfunction
d. What is the expected number of sensors that will malfunction?
e. What is the standard deviation of the number of sensors that will malfunction?

3-36 A process is known to produce 5 percent nonconforming items. A sample of 40 items is selected from the process.

a. What is the distribution of the number of nonconforming items in the sample?
b. Find the probability of obtaining no more than 3 nonconforming items in the sample.
c. Using the Poisson distribution as an approximation to the binomial, calculate the probability of the event in part b.
d. Compare the answers to parts b and c. What are your observations?

3-37 The guidance system of a satellite is designed for reliability by placing several components in parallel. The system will function as long as at least one of the components is operational. In a particular satellite, four such components are placed in parallel. If the probability of a component operating successfully is 0.9, what is the probability of the system functioning? What is the probability of the system failing? Assume that the components operate independently of each other.

3-38 In a lot of 200 electrical fuses, 20 are known to be nonconforming. A sample of 10 fuses is selected.

a. What is the probability distribution of the number of nonconforming fuses in the sample? What are its mean and standard deviation?
b. Using the binomial distribution as an approximation to the hypergeometric, find the probability of getting 2 nonconforming fuses. What is the probability of getting at most 2 nonconforming fuses?

3-39 A local hospital estimates that the number of patients admitted daily to the emergency room has a Poisson probability distribution with a mean of 4.0. What is the probability that on a given day

a. only 2 patients will admitted?
b. at most six patients will be admitted?
c. no one will be admitted?
d. What is the standard deviation of the number of patients admitted?
e. For each patient admitted, the expected daily operational expenses to the hospital is $800. If the hospital wants to be 94.9 percent sure of meeting the daily expenses, how much money should it keep for operational expenses daily?

3-40 In the painting of automobiles, it is known that the average number of paint blemishes per car is 3. If two cars are randomly chosen for inspection, what is the probability that

a. the first car has no more than 2 blemishes?
b. each of the cars has no more than 2 blemishes?
c. the total number of blemishes in both of the cars combined is no more than 2?

3-41 The number of bank failures per year among those insured by the Federal Deposit Insurance Company has a mean of 7.0. The failures occur independently. What is the probability that

a. there will be at least 4 failures in the coming year?
b. there will be between 2 and 8 failures,inclusive, in the coming year?
c. during the next two years there will be at most 8 failures?

3-42 A legal consulting firm is examining the prospects of expansion. Based on information over the last five years, it has found that the average number of suits filed in the local county court is 4.0 per month. The suits are independent of each other. Find the probability that

a. no more than 6 suits will be filed in a given month
b. at least 5 suits will be filed in a given month
c. at least 6 suits will be filed in a span of two months

3-43 The outside diameter of a part used in a gear assembly is known to be normally distributed with a mean of 40 mm and a standard deviation of 2.5 mm. The specifications on the diameter are (36, 45), which means that part diameters between 36 mm and 45 mm are considered acceptable. The unit cost of rework is \$0.20, while the unit cost of scrap is \$0.50. If the daily production rate is 2000, what is the total daily cost of rework and scrap?

3-44 The breaking strength of a cable is known to be normally distributed with a mean of 4000 kg and a standard deviation of 25 kg. The manufacturer prefers that at least 95 percent of his product meet a strength requirement of 4050 kg. Is this requirement being met? If not, by changing the process parameter, what should the process mean target value be?

3-45 The specifications for the thickness of nonferrous washers are 1.0 ± 0.04 mm. From process data, the distribution of the washer thickness is estimated to be normal with a mean of 0.98 and a standard deviation of 0.02 mm. The unit cost of rework is \$0.10, and the unit cost of scrap is \$0.15. For a daily production of 10,000 items:

a. What proportion of the washers are conforming? What is the total daily cost of rework and scrap?
b. In its study of constant improvement, the manufacturer changes the mean setting of the machine to 1.0 mm. If the standard deviation is the same as before, what is the total daily cost of rework and scrap?
c. The manufacturer is trying to further improve on the process and reduces its standard deviation to 0.015 mm. If the process mean is maintained at 1.0 mm, what is the percent decrease in the total daily cost of rework and scrap compared to that of part a?

3-46 A company has been able to restrict the use of electrical power through energy conservation measures. The monthly use is known to be normal with a mean of 60,000 kWh and a standard deviation of 400 kWh.

a. What is the probability that the monthly consumption will be less than 59,100 kWh?
b. What is the probability that the monthly consumption will be between 59,000 and 60,300 kWh?
c. The capacity of the utility that supplies this company is 61,000 kWh. What is the probability that demand will not exceed supply by more than 100 kWh?

3-47 A component is known to have an exponential time-to-failure distribution with a mean life of 10,000 hours.

a. What is the probability of the component lasting at least 8000 hours?
b. If the component is in operation at 9000 hours, what is the probability that it will last another 6000 hours?
c. Two such components are put in parallel, so that the system will be in operation if at least one of the components is operational. What is the probability of the system being operational for 12,000 hours? Assume that the components operate independently.

3-48 The time to repair an equipment is known to be exponentially distributed with a mean of 45 minutes.

a. What is the probability of the machine being repaired within half an hour?
b. If the machine breaks down at 3 p.m. and a repairman is available immediately, what is the probability of the machine being available for production by the start of the next day? Assume that the repairman is available until 5 p.m.
c. What is the standard deviation of the repair time?

3-49 A limousine service catering to a large metropolitan area has found that the time for a trip (from dispatch to return) is exponentially distributed with a mean of 30 minutes.

a. What is the probability that a trip will take more than an hour?
b. If a limousine has already been gone for 45 minutes, what is the probability that it will return within the next 20 minutes?
c. If two limousines have just been dispatched, what is the probability that both will not return within the next 45 minutes? Assume that the trips are independent of each other.

3-50 The time to failure of an electronic component can be described by a Weibull distribution with $\gamma = 0$, $\beta = 0.25$, and $\alpha = 800$ hours.

a. Find the mean time to failure.
b. Find the standard deviation of the time to failure.
c. What is the probability of the component lasting at least 1500 hours?

3-51 The time to failure of a mechanical component under friction may be modeled by a Weibull distribution with $\gamma = 20$ days, $\beta = 0.2$, and $\alpha = 35$ days.

a. What proportion of these components will fail within 30 days?
b. What is the expected life of the component?
c. What is the probability of a component lasting between 40 and 50 days?

3-52 The diameter of bearings is known to have a mean of 35 mm with a standard deviation of 0.5 mm. A random sample of 36 bearings is selected. What is the probability that the average diameter of these selected bearings will be between 34.95 and 35.18 mm?

3-53 Refer to Exercise 3-52. Suppose the machine is considered to be out of statistical control if the average diameter of a sample of 36 bearings is less than 34.75 mm or greater than 35.25 mm.

a. If the true mean diameter of all bearings produced is 35 mm, what is the probability of the test indicating that the machine is out of control?
b. Suppose the setting of the machine is accidentally changed such that the mean diameter of all bearings produced is 35.05 mm. What is the probability of the test indicating that the machine is in statistical control?

3-54 Vendor quality control is an integral part of a total quality system. A soft drink bottling company requires its vendors to produce bottles with an internal pressure strength of at least 300 kg/cm^2. A vendor claims that its bottles have a mean strength of 310 kg/cm^2 with a standard deviation of 5 kg/cm^2. As part of a vendor surveillance program, the bottling company samples 50 bottles from the production and finds the average strength to be 308.6 kg/cm^2.

a. What are the chances of getting that sample average that was observed, or even less, if the assertion by the vendor is correct?
b. If the standard deviation of the strength of the vendor's bottles is 8 kg/cm^2, with the mean (as claimed) of 310 kg/cm^2, what are the chances of seeing what the bottling company observed (or an even smaller sample average)?

3-55 The average time to assemble a product as found from a sample of size 40 is 10.4 minutes. The standard deviation of the assembly times is known to be 1.2 minutes.

a. Find a two-sided 90 percent confidence interval for the mean assembly time, and interpret it.
b. Find a two-sided 99 percent confidence interval for the mean assembly time, and interpret it.
c. What assumptions are needed to answer parts a and b?
d. The manager in charge of the assembly line believes that the mean assembly time is less than 10.8 minutes. Can he make this conclusion at a significance level α of 0.05?

3-56 A company that dumps its industrial waste into a river has to meet certain restrictions. One particular constraint involves the minimum amount of dissolved oxygen [in parts per million (ppm)] that is needed to support aquatic life. A random sample of 10 specimens taken from a given location gave the following results of dissolved oxygen (in ppm):

9, 8.6, 9.2, 8.4, 8.1,
9.5, 9.3, 8.5, 9.0, 9.4

a. Find a two-sided 95 percent confidence interval for the mean dissolved oxygen, and interpret it.
b. What assumptions do you need to make to answer part a?
c. Suppose the environmental standards stipulate a minimum of 9.5 ppm of average dissolved oxygen. Is the company violating the standard? Test at a level of significance α of 0.05.

3-57 An automobile company is working on changes in a fuel injection system to improve gasoline mileage. A random sample of 15 test runs gave the following mileage (in mpg):

38, 42, 40, 39, 44, 37, 39, 45,
40, 42, 38, 39, 44, 41, 42

a. Find a two-sided 90 percent confidence interval for the mean gasoline mileage. State the assumptions necessary to find the confidence interval.
b. The average miles-per-gallon rating when using the previous fuel injection system

was 35. Can we conclude that the new system has improved gasoline mileage? Use a level of significance of 0.01.

3-58 A beverage bottling company fills bottles that are labeled as 12 ounces. The variability of the machine that dispenses the beverage has a standard deviation of 0.10 ounces. A random sample of size 60 yielded an average content weight of 12.05 ounces.

a. Find a 98 percent confidence interval for the mean beverage content weight.
b. Can we conclude that the mean beverage content weight exceeds the advertised weight? Use a level of significance of 0.05.

3-59 The Occupational Safety and Health Administration (OSHA) mandates certain regulations that have to be adopted by corporations. Prior to the implementation of the OSHA program, a company found that for a sample of 40 randomly selected months, the average employee time lost due to job related accidents was 45 hours. After the implementation of the OSHA program, for a random sample of 45 months, the average employee time lost due to job-related accidents was 39 hours. If it can be assumed that the variability of time lost due to accidents is about the same before and after implementation of the OSHA program (with a standard deviation being 3.5 hours):

a. Find a 90 percent confidence interval for the difference in the mean time lost due to accidents.
b. Test the hypothesis that implementation of the OSHA program has reduced the average employee lost time. Use a level of significance of 0.10.

3-60 Refer to Exercise 3-59. Suppose the standard deviations of the values of lost time due to accidents before and after usage of the OSHA program are unknown but assumed to be equal. The first sample of size 40 gave a mean of 45 hours with a standard deviation of 3.8 hours. Similarly, the second sample of size 45, taken after the implementation of the OSHA program, yielded a mean of 39 hours with a standard deviation of 3.5 hours.

a. Find a 95 percent confidence interval for the difference in the mean time lost due to job-related accidents.
b. What assumptions are needed to answer part a?
c. Can you conclude that the average employee time lost due to accidents has decreased due to the OSHA program? Use a level of significance of 0.05.
d. How would you test the assumption of equality of the standard deviations of time lost due to job related accidents before and after implementation of the OSHA program? Use a level of significance of 0.05.

3-61 A company is experimenting with synthetic fibers as a substitute for natural fibers. The quality characteristic of interest is the breaking strength. A random sample of 8 natural fibers yielded an average breaking strength of 540 kg with a standard deviation of 55 kg. A random sample of 10 synthetic fibers gave an average breaking strength of 610 kg with a standard deviation of 22 kg.

a. Can you conclude that the variances of the breaking strengths of natural and synthetic fibers are different? Use a level of significance α of 0.05. What assumptions are necessary to perform this test?
b. Based on the conclusions in part a, test to determine if the mean breaking strength for synthetic fibers exceeds that for natural fibers. Use a significance level α of 0.10.
c. Find a two-sided 95 percent confidence interval for the ratio of the variances of the breaking strengths of natural and synthetic fiber.
d. Find a two-sided 90 percent confidence interval for the difference in the mean breaking strength for synthetic and natural fiber.

3-62 Consider the data in Exercise 3-27 on the time (in minutes) to process hot-rolled steel for a sample of size 10.

a. Find a 98 percent confidence interval for the mean time to process hot-rolled steel. What assumptions do you have to make to solve this problem?
b. Find a 95 percent confidence interval for the variance.
c. Test the hypothesis that the process variability, as measured by the variance, exceeds 0.80. Use $\alpha = 0.05$.

3-63 The machine shop in an aircraft manufacturing company deals with a variety of jobs. It is desirable to estimate the proportion of nonconforming parts that are output from this shop since that value has a major impact on the cost of the product. A random sample of 200 parts showed that 6 were nonconforming.
   a. Find a 90-percent confidence interval for the true proportion of nonconforming parts.
   b. Can we conclude that the percent nonconforming of all parts output from the shop is less than 4 percent? Use a level of significance of 0.05.

3-64 Price deregulation in the airline industry has promoted competition and a variety of fare structures. Prior to deciding on a price change, a particular airline is interested in obtaining an estimate of the proportion of the market that it presently captures for a certain city. A random sample of 300 passengers indicated that 80 used that airline.
   a. Find a point estimate of the proportion that use the particular airline.
   b. Find a 95 percent confidence limit for the proportion that use the airline in question.
   c. Can the airline conclude that its market share is more than 25 percent? Use a level of significance of 0.01.

3-65 An advertising agency is judged by the increase in the proportion of people that buy a particular product after the advertising campaign is conducted. In a random sample of 200 people prior to the campaign, 40 said that they prefer the product in question. After the advertising campaign, out of a random sample of 300, 80 said that they preferred the product.
   a. Find a 90 percent confidence interval for the difference in the proportion of people who prefer the stipulated product before and after the advertising campaign.
   b. Can you conclude that the advertising campaign has been successful in increasing the proportion of people who prefer the product? Use a level of significance of 0.10.

3-66 A state university is seeking to increase its enrollment by providing more financial assistance, by making tuition competitive, and by improving the academic rigor. Prior to the institution of these measures, the university found that out of a random sample of 100 prospective students, 30 were interested in attending. After implementation of the proposed measures, a random sample of 200 showed that 90 were interested in attending.
   a. Find a 90 percent confidence interval for the difference in the proportion of students that are interested in attending the university before and after the proposed measures.
   b. Were the proposed measures effective in increasing the interest of students to attend the university? Use a significance level of 0.05.

3-67 Two similar machines used in performing the same operation are to be compared. A random sample of 80 parts from the first machine yielded 6 nonconforming ones. A random sample of 120 parts from the second machine showed 14 nonconforming ones.
   a. Can we conclude that there is a difference in the output of the machines? Use a level of significance of 0.10.
   b. Find a 95 percent confidence interval for the difference in the proportion nonconforming between the two machines.

3-68 Budget deficits have reduced the funding of several federal programs. A random sample of 100 people showed that 20 received either full or partial federal aid that they had applied for.
   a. Find a 98 percent confidence interval for the proportion of people who apply for and receive some federal aid.
   b. Can we conclude that the proportion of people receiving federal aid has dropped below 22 percent? Use a level of significance of 0.10.

3-69 The precision of equipment and instruments is measured by the variability of their operation under repeated conditions. The output from an automatic lathe producing the diameter (in mm) of a part gave the following readings for a random sample of size 10:

10.3, 9.7, 9.6, 9.9, 9.5,
10.2, 9.8, 10.1, 9.8, 10.2

   a. Find a 90 percent confidence interval for the variance of the diameters.
   b. Find a 90 percent confidence interval for the standard deviation of the diameters.

c. Test the null hypothesis that variance of the diameters does not exceed 0.05. Use a significance level of 0.10.

d. Does the mean setting for the machine need adjustment? Is it significantly different from 9.5 mm? Test at a significance level of 0.10.

3-70 A company is investigating two potential vendors on the timeliness of their deliveries. A random sample of size 10 from the first vendor produced an average delay time of 4.5 days with a standard deviation of 2.3 days. A random sample of size 12 from the second vendor yielded an average delay time of 3.4 days with a standard deviation of 6.2 days.

a. Find a 90 percent confidence interval for the ratio of the variances of the delay times for the two vendors.

b. What assumptions are needed to solve part a?

c. Can we conclude that the first vendor has a smaller variability regarding delay times than the second? Use a significance level of 0.05.

d. Which vendor would you select and why?

3-71 It is of interest in a plant making alloy to estimate with a probability of 0.90 the copper content in a mixture to within 4 percent. How many samples must be selected if no prior information is available on the proportion of copper in the mixture?

3-72 The temperature of the oven in a steel smelting process is an important process parameter. We would like to estimate with a probability of 0.95 the average oven temperature to within 40°C. Based on previous information, the standard deviation of the oven temperature is estimated to be 150°C. How many samples must be selected?

3-73 The production of nonconforming items is of critical concern. It increases costs and reduces productivity. Identifying the causes behind the production of unacceptable items and taking remedial action are a step in the right direction. It is desired to estimate the proportion of nonconforming items in a process to within 3 percent with a probability of 0.98.

a. Previous information suggests that the percentage nonconforming is approximately 4 percent. How large a sample must be chosen?

b. If no prior information is available on the proportion nonconforming, how large a sample must be chosen?

3-74 At the check-in counter of an airline, management is exploring the possibility of adding more agents in order to reduce the waiting time of customers. Based on available information, the standard deviation of the waiting times is approximately 5.2 minutes. If it is desired to estimate the mean waiting time to within 2 minutes, with a probability of 0.95, how many samples must be selected?

REFERENCES

Banks, J. (1989). *Principles of Quality Control.* Wiley, New York.

Duncan, Acheson J. (1986). *Quality Control and Industrial Statistics,* 5th edtion, Richard D. Irwin, Homewood, IL.

Henley, E. J., and Kumamoto, H. (1981). *Reliability Engineering and Risk Assessment.* Prentice Hall, Englewood Cliffs, NJ.

Kendall, M. G., and Stuart, A. (1967). *The Advanced Theory of Statistics,* 2nd edition, Vol. 1. Hafner, New York.

Mendenhall, W., Reinmuth, J. E., and Beaver, R. (1989). *Statistics for Management and Economics,* 6th edition. PWS-Kent, Boston.

Montgomery, D. C. (1991). *Introduction to Statistical Quality Control,* 2nd edition. Wiley, New York.

Neter, J., Wasserman, W., and Kutner, M. H. (1985). *Applied Linear Statistical Models,* 2nd edition. Richard D. Irwin, Homewood, IL.

CHAPTER

4

Graphical Methods of Data Presentation and Quality Improvement

CHAPTER OUTLINE

SYMBOLS

$\overline{X}$	Sample average
s	Sample standard deviation
n	Sample size
X_i	ith observation in a sample
s_m	Standard deviation of the sample median
$F(x)$	Cumulative distribution function
M	Median
Q_1	First quartile
Q_3	Third quartile
IQR	Interquartile range

4-1 INTRODUCTION

This chapter presents methods for describing data sets graphically. These methods help us learn about the characteristics of a process, its operating state of affairs, and the kind of output that we may expect from it. Some of these methods may be used for quality improvement. As discussed in previous sections, quality control involves taking action to remove the identifiable factors that cause the output of a process to be unstable or off-target. Once the process is in a state of statistical control, if the output does not meet desirable norms, then fundamental changes are needed in the process, the product, or both. Such changes are the focus of quality improvement. Because they are easy to understand and are able to provide comprehensive information, graphical methods are a viable tool for the analysis of product and process data. They provide information on existing product or process characteristics and help us determine whether these characteristics are close to the desired norm. Some of the graphical techniques described here may help identify where to focus quality improvement efforts. Given the emphasis on never ending quality improvement, such tools are beneficial to any company, regardless of its current level of quality achievement.

4-2 FREQUENCY DISTRIBUTIONS AND HISTOGRAMS

Seldom is one able to get an idea of process characteristics by just looking at the individual data values gathered from the process. Such data is sometimes voluminous. Frequency distributions and histograms summarize such information and present it in a format that allows conclusions to be drawn regarding the process condition.

A *frequency distribution* is a rearrangement of raw data in ascending or descending order of magnitude, such that the quality characteristic is subdivided into classes and the number of occurrences in each class is presented.

Table 4-1 shows the inside diameter (in millimeters) of metal sleeves produced in a machine shop for 100 randomly selected parts. Twenty samples, each of size 5, were taken. Simply looking at the data in Table 4-1 provides very little insight about the process. Even though we realize that there is variability in the sleeve diameters, we can hardly identify a pattern in the data (for example, what is the degree of variability?) or comment about the central tendency of the process (for example, about which value are most of the parts concentrated?). Using the data in Table 4-1, a frequency distribution may be constructed as shown in Table 4-2. Here, the diameters are categorized into classes (49.89 to 49.91, 49.91 to 49.93, and so on), and the number, or frequency, in each group is reported. Care must be taken to set the class, or cell, boundaries such that there is no overlap between them. Double counting of observations should be avoided. Classes are usually of equal width. However, when there are outliers (values that are too large or too small compared to the majority of the observations), the two end classes may be kept open-ended.

TABLE 4-1 Inside diameter of metal sleeves in millimeters

Sample number	Observations X (five per sample)				
1	50.04	50.03	50.02	50.00	49.94
2	49.96	49.99	50.03	50.01	49.98
3	50.01	50.01	50.01	50.00	49.92
4	49.95	49.97	50.02	50.10	50.02
5	50.00	50.01	50.00	50.00	50.09
6	50.02	50.05	49.97	50.02	50.09
7	50.01	49.99	49.96	49.99	50.00
8	50.02	50.00	50.04	50.02	50.00
9	50.06	49.93	49.99	49.99	49.95
10	49.96	49.93	50.08	49.92	50.03
11	50.01	49.96	49.98	50.00	50.02
12	50.04	49.94	50.00	50.03	49.92
13	49.97	49.90	49.98	50.01	49.95
14	50.00	50.01	49.95	49.97	49.94
15	49.97	49.98	50.03	50.08	49.96
16	49.98	50.00	49.97	49.96	49.97
17	50.03	50.04	50.03	50.01	50.01
18	49.98	49.98	49.99	50.05	50.00
19	50.07	50.00	50.02	49.99	49.93
20	49.99	50.06	49.95	49.99	50.02

TABLE 4-2 Frequency distribution of metal sleeves

Classes for sleeve diameter X (in mm)	Tally	Frequency	Relative frequency	Cumulative frequency	Cumulative relative frequency
$49.89 \leq X < 49.91$	|	1	0.01	1	0.01
$49.91 \leq X < 49.93$	|||	3	0.03	4	0.04
$49.93 \leq X < 49.95$	~~||||~~ |	6	0.06	10	0.10
$49.95 \leq X < 49.97$	~~||||~~ ~~||||~~ |	11	0.11	21	0.21
$49.97 \leq X < 49.99$	~~||||~~ ~~||||~~ ||||	14	0.14	35	0.35
$49.99 \leq X < 50.01$	~~||||~~ ~~||||~~ ~~||||~~ ~~||||~~ |||	23	0.23	58	0.58
$50.01 \leq X < 50.03$	~~||||~~ ~~||||~~ ~~||||~~ ~~||||~~ |	21	0.21	79	0.79
$50.03 \leq X < 50.05$	~~||||~~ ~~||||~~ |	11	0.11	90	0.90
$50.05 \leq X < 50.07$	||||	4	0.04	94	0.94
$50.07 \leq X < 50.09$	|||	3	0.03	97	0.97
$50.09 \leq X < 50.11$	|||	3	0.03	100	1.00
	Total	100	1.00		

Table 4-2 shows the frequency in each class (for example, 1 observation between 49.89 and 49.91, 3 observations between 49.91 and 49.93, and so on). It also depicts the *relative frequency* in each cell, which is found by dividing the frequency in each cell by the total number of observations. For example, the cell given by $49.93 \leq X < 49.95$, contains six percent of all observations. Table 4-2 also shows the *cumulative frequency* for each cell. The cumulative frequency for a given class is the number of observations in that class and in all classes preceding it. Note that the cumulative frequency for the cell given by $49.93 \leq X < 49.95$ is 10, which means that of the 100 parts, 10 have inside diameters that are less than 49.95 mm. The *cumulative relative frequency* of a class is simply the cumulative frequency for that class divided by the total number of observations. For the class given by $49.93 \leq X < 49.95$, the cumulative frequency is 0.10, meaning that 10 percent of the parts have a diameter less than 49.95 mm.

A *histogram* is a graphical display of data such that the characteristic is subdivided into classes, or cells. In a frequency histogram, the vertical axis represents the number of observations in each class. The following steps are used to construct a frequency histogram (refer to the data shown in Table 4-1):

Step 1: Find the range of the observations—the difference between the largest and the smallest value.

Step 2: Choose the number of classes, or cells. Usually, 5 to 20 classes should be selected. If too few classes are chosen, specific details of the data are lost. On the other hand, if too many classes are selected, a summary of how the data is distributed (which is the objective of a histogram) will not be achieved. As a rule of thumb, if n represents the number of data points, the number of classes should be approximately $\sqrt{n}$.

Step 3: Determine the width of the classes. Usually, all classes are of equal width except for the first or last class. If outliers are present, the first or the last class may be kept open-ended to include them. The class width is found by dividing the range by the number of classes.

Step 4: Determine the class boundaries. Find the number of observations in each class. Make sure that the classes are not overlapping.

Step 5: Draw the frequency histogram. Construct rectangles above the classes such that the heights of the rectangles correspond to the frequencies.

Example 4-1: For the data in Table 4-1, the range is $50.10 - 49.90 = 0.2$. The number of data points is 100, corresponding to $\sqrt{100} = 10$ classes. The class width is $0.2/10 = 0.02$. Note that if the midpoint of the first class is 49.90, we actually end up with 11 classes in order to account for the value 50.10, but this is acceptable. There is no rigid rule saying that the number of classes must be exactly 10. If an initially calculated class width does not turn out to be a round number, it may be modified. The actual number of classes may not end up being exactly what is originally calculated.

The classes should be designated such that an observation will fall in one class only. The midpoint of our first class is chosen as 49.90. Thus, the first class includes values from 49.89 to 49.91. The upper boundary of each class will be noninclusive; if we have a data point with a

TABLE 4-3 Class boundaries, midpoints, and frequencies for Example 4-1

Class boundaries	Midpoint	Frequency	Cumulative frequency
$49.89 \leq X < 49.91$	49.90	1	1
$49.91 \leq X < 49.93$	49.92	3	4
$49.93 \leq X < 49.95$	49.94	6	10
$49.95 \leq X < 49.97$	49.96	11	21
$49.97 \leq X < 49.99$	49.98	14	35
$49.99 \leq X < 50.01$	50.00	23	58
$50.01 \leq X < 50.03$	50.02	21	79
$50.03 \leq X < 50.05$	50.04	11	90
$50.05 \leq X < 50.07$	50.06	4	94
$50.07 \leq X < 50.09$	50.08	3	97
$50.09 \leq X < 50.11$	50.10	3	100

value of 49.91, it will be included in the second class. Such explicit labeling avoids ambiguity as to where to place observations, and it avoids double-counting. The class boundaries, their midpoints, and the frequencies of the classes are shown in Table 4-3.

Using the class boundaries and midpoints shown in Table 4-3, a frequency histogram may be constructed as shown in Figure 4-1. Note that this figure gives some idea of the general characteristics of the data set. It provides a sense of where the clustering of the observations takes place and the degree of variability of the observations. Such histograms also tell us if some observations are far removed from the others and provide information regarding the uniformity of a process. Furthermore, they enable us to determine the conformance of a process with respect to established specification limits. Using the same classes as in the frequency histogram, a cumulative frequency histogram is shown in Figure 4-2.

4-3 RUN CHARTS

A run chart is a plot of a quality characteristic as a function of time. Such a chart usually plots data point-by-point in the order in which it is obtained. Though this does not summarize any information, it does provide some idea of the general trend, and degree of variability present in the process.

Example 4-2: In a chemical process, the acidity of a compound used to dye fabrics is of interest. Twenty random samples were selected from the process, and their pH values were measured. The data values are shown in Table 4-4. A run chart is shown in Figure 4-3. From the

TABLE 4-4 Samples of pH values

Sample number	pH value	Sample number	pH value
1	6.5	11	5.8
2	3.8	12	6.7
3	5.9	13	6.6
4	5.5	14	6.8
5	7.3	15	7.0
6	6.1	16	6.6
7	6.5	17	5.5
8	5.2	18	5.2
9	5.8	19	5.2
10	6.0	20	4.8

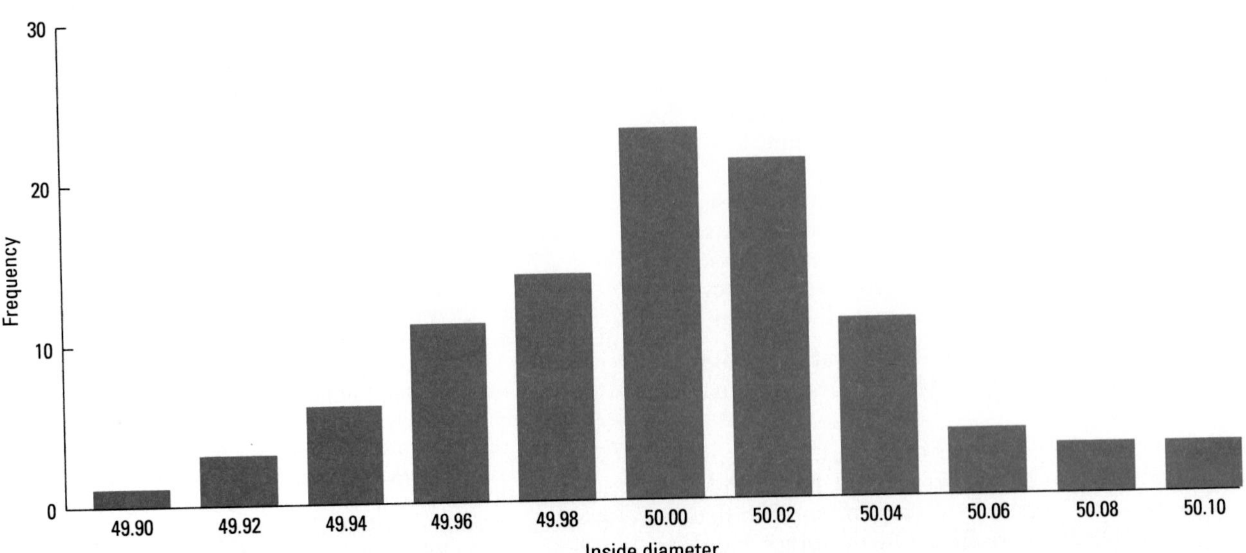

Figure 4-1 Frequency histogram of sleeve diameters.

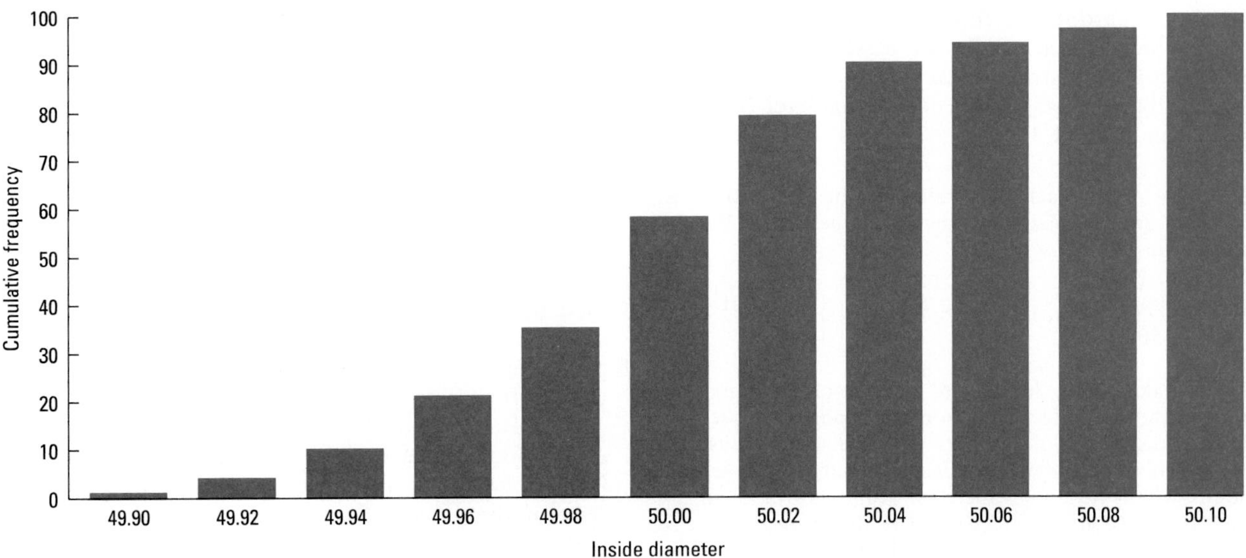

Figure 4-2 Cumulative frequency histogram of sleeve diameters.

data in Table 4-4, not much of an opinion can be formed concerning the process. The run chart, on the other hand, portrays graphically the sequence of values obtained from the process. It helps us derive some notion as to the operating conditions of the process. The run chart shows an increasing trend in the pH value between sample number 8 through sample number 15. Furthermore, a decreasing trend in pH value is observed between sample number 15 and sample number 20. Such information can provide some insight into the process.

 4-4 STEM-AND-LEAF PLOTS

Stem-and-leaf plots are another graphical approach to plotting observations and obtaining an interpretation of process characteristics. With frequency histograms, the identities of the individual observations are lost in the process of plotting. In the stem-and-leaf plot, however, the actual numerical values are retained. In plotting a histogram, a decision has to

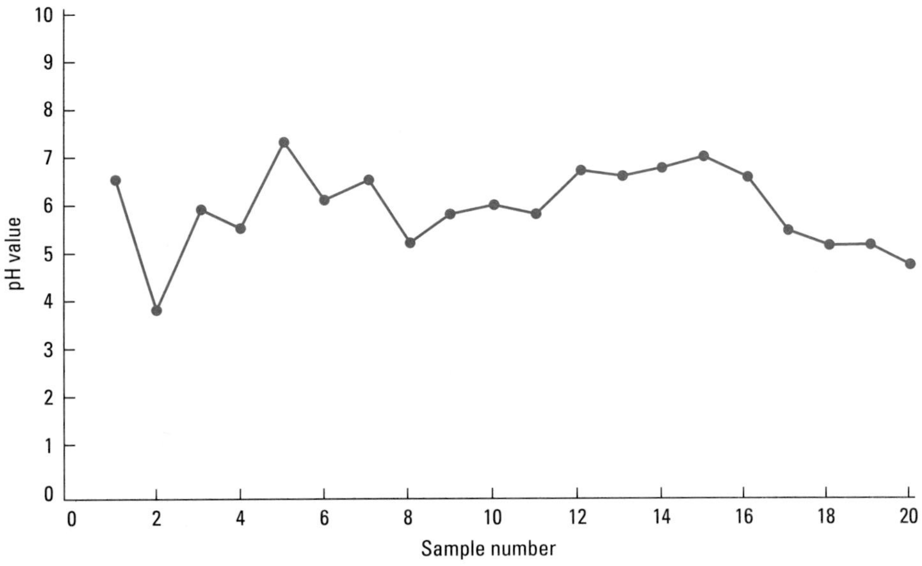

Figure 4-3 Run chart for acidity.

be made regarding the classes and class width, something which is not required in a stem-and-leaf plot. Consider the construction of a stem-and-leaf plot using the data values for the inside diameter of metal sleeves in Table 4-1.

Example 4-3: Each data value is split into two parts, the stem and the leaf. Consider the value 50.04. We can display this as follows:

Data value	Stem	Leaf
50.04	500	4

A decimal point is implicit to the left of the rightmost digit in the stem. The digit in the leaf portion represents hundredths. The choice of the stem and leaf positions may be influenced by the magnitude and variability of the data points. Upon observing the data points, all of them are found to have either 499 or 500 in the stem portion, so the following modification is used: In the stem portion, use an asterisk (*) for leaves 0 and 1, a "t" for leaves 2 and 3 (first letter of *t*wo and *t*hree), an "f" for leaves 4 and 5 (*f*our and *f*ive), an "s" for leaves 6 and 7 (*s*ix and *s*even), and a dot (·) for leaves 8 and 9. Thus, in this modified scheme the data value 50.04 is represented as follows:

Data value	Stem	Leaf
50.04	500f	4

This procedure may be repeated for the other data values. The complete stem-and-leaf plot is shown in Figure 4-4.

```
499* | 1
499t | 2 2 2 3 3 3
499f | 4 4 4 5 5 5 5 5
499s | 6 6 6 6 6 6 7 7 7 7 7 7 7
499· | 8 8 8 8 8 8 8 9 9 9 9 9 9 9 9 9
500* | 0 0 0 0 0 0 0 0 0 0 0 0 0 0 1 1 1 1 1 1 1 1 1 1
500t | 2 2 2 2 2 2 2 2 2 2 3 3 3 3 3 3 3
500f | 4 4 4 4 5 5
500s | 6 6 7
500· | 8 8 9 9
501* | 0
```

Figure 4-4 Stem-and-leaf plot for inside diameter of sleeves.

4-5 PARETO DIAGRAMS

Pareto diagrams are important tools in the quality improvement process. Named after the Italian economist Alfredo Pareto, Pareto diagrams were first applied to the area of quality control by Joseph Juran. Like Pareto, who found that the distribution of wealth was concentrated in a few people, Juran realized that a similar principle holds in other fields. For instance, in manufacturing or service, most problems are created by a few causes, even though there are many causes that may influence the occurrence of these problems. These categories of problems were identified as the *vital few* and the *trivial many*, respectively.

The Pareto principle lends support to the 80/20 rule, which states that 80 percent of the problems (nonconformities or defects) are created by 20 percent of the causes. Pareto diagrams help management quickly identify the critical areas (those causing most of the problems) which deserve immediate attention. They identify the important problems, the resolution of which will lead to substantial improvements in quality. They provide guidance in the allocation of limited resources to problem-solving activities. Through the use of Pareto diagrams, problems may be arranged in order of importance. "Importance" may refer to the financial impact of a problem (which is usually most appropriate) or the relative number of occurrences of the problem.

The steps for constructing a Pareto diagram are as follows:

Step 1: Decide on the means of classifying the data—say, by problem causes, type of nonconformity (critical, major, minor), or whatever else seems appropriate.

Step 2: Determine how relative importance is to be judged, that is, whether it should be based on associated dollar values or the frequency of occurrence.

Step 3: Rank the categories from most important to least important.

Step 4: Compute the cumulative frequency of the data categories in their chosen order.

Step 5: Plot a bar graph, showing the relative importance of each problem area in descending order. Identify the vital few that deserve immediate attention.

Example 4-4: Data was gathered regarding the causes of problems in a textile mill. Table 4-5 shows the causes of nonconformance along with the percentage of occurrence of each and the associated annual dollar values. The data in Table 4-5 shows that the four most significant problem causes are a subpar quality of cotton, an improper ten-

TABLE 4-5 Types of nonconformities in a textile mill

Code letter of problem cause	Problem cause	Percentage of occurrence	Dollar value (in $1000)	Cumulative percentage of occurrence
A	Subpar quality of cotton	40	20	40
B	Improper tension setting	20	6	60
C	Inadequate operator training	14	3	74
D	Bale storage problems	10	2	84
E	Drop in hydraulic pressure in presses	8	2	92
F	Cutter not sharp	5	1.5	97
G	Dye for use in color not adequate	3	1.8	100

sion setting, inadequate operator training, and bale storage problems. It was decided to focus attention on a minimal number of causes that represent an occurence rate of at least 80 percent. These four areas comprise 84 percent of the problems. Dollar-wise, their combined impact is $31,000. Thus, looking critically into these four areas and making corresponding improvements could potentially result in a savings of $31,000. Table 4-5 also shows the cumulative percentages of occurrence for the different causes. From a cost-savings viewpoint, the four problem areas that deserve attention are the ones mentioned. A Pareto diagram is shown in Figure 4-5.

Management should definitely address the issue of subpar quality of cotton first. Eliminating this problem may result in a savings of about $20,000, more than for any other cause listed. If the next three problem causes are also analyzed, then 84 percent of the problems will be addressed. The problems should be addressed in order of importance as resources permit, with a particular emphasis given to the four most significant problems.

Another use of Pareto diagrams is to compare process conditions (in terms of the problem causes or nonconformities) before and after action is taken to improve the process. For instance, after a thorough investigation of the problem areas of Example 4-4, remedial actions would be taken. It may be of interest to determine whether a reduction of problems in those areas has actually taken place. Furthermore, one may also wish to determine the critical areas and their impact on the process after the improvements have been implemented. Pareto diagrams from before and after the changes can be compared to determine the impact of the actions taken for process improvement.

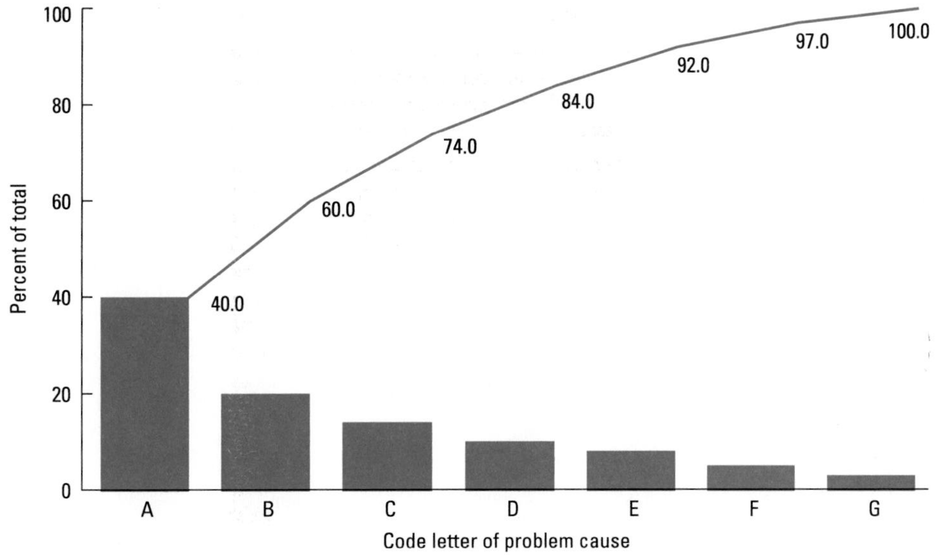

Figure 4-5 Pareto diagram for problem causes in textile mill.

4-6 CAUSE-AND-EFFECT (FISHBONE OR ISHIKAWA) DIAGRAMS

Cause-and-effect diagrams were developed by Kaoru Ishikawa, Ph.D. in 1943 and are often called Ishikawa diagrams. Because of their appearance (in the plotted form), they are also known as fishbone diagrams. Basically, they are used to identify and systematically list the different causes that can be attributed to a problem (or an effect) (Ishikawa, 1976). By first listing the various causes, such diagrams can help in determining which of several causes have the greatest effect. A cause-and-effect diagram can aid in identifying reasons which cause a process to go out of control. Alternatively, if a process is stable, such a diagram can provide guidance on causes to be investigated for process improvement. There are three main applications of cause-and-effect diagrams: cause enumeration, dispersion analysis, and process analysis.

Cause Enumeration

Cause enumeration is one of the most widely used graphical techniques for quality control and improvement. It usually develops through a brainstorming session in which all possible types of causes (however remote they may be) are listed to show their influence on the problem (or effect) in question. The procedure consists of first defining the problem or quality characteristic selected for study so that everyone knows what is being tackled. Next, the major causes which influence the characteristic are noted. For example, in a manufacturing process, the major causes in producing a nonconforming part (say, a length not meeting specifications) could be equipment, operator, methods, environment, and so forth. After this step, subcauses within each of the major causes are listed. Before evaluating each of the listed causes, more thought should be given to clearly defining and identifying them and also to evaluating present methods of keeping tabs on them. Next, possible causes which influence the characteristic in question should be singled out and analyzed. This may be done systematically by first selecting the cause which is thought to be the predominant one, followed by the next one in that sequence, and so on.

An advantage of using cause-and-effect diagrams is that the process of their construction creates a better understanding of the interrelationships that exist in the process and thereby imparts a better understanding of the process itself.

Example 4-5: In tire manufacturing, one of the quality characteristics of interest is the bore size, which should be within certain specifications. The final bore size is the effect. Some of the main causes which influence the bore size are the incoming material, mixing process, tubing operation, splicing, press operation, operator, and measuring equipment. For each of the main causes, subcauses should be identified and listed. For the raw material category, the incoming quality is affected by such subcauses as the type of vendor (for instance, is the vendor certified?), the content of scrap tire in the raw material, the density, and the ash content. A similar process is undertaken for the other main causes. Figure 4-6 shows a cause-and-effect diagram for this example.

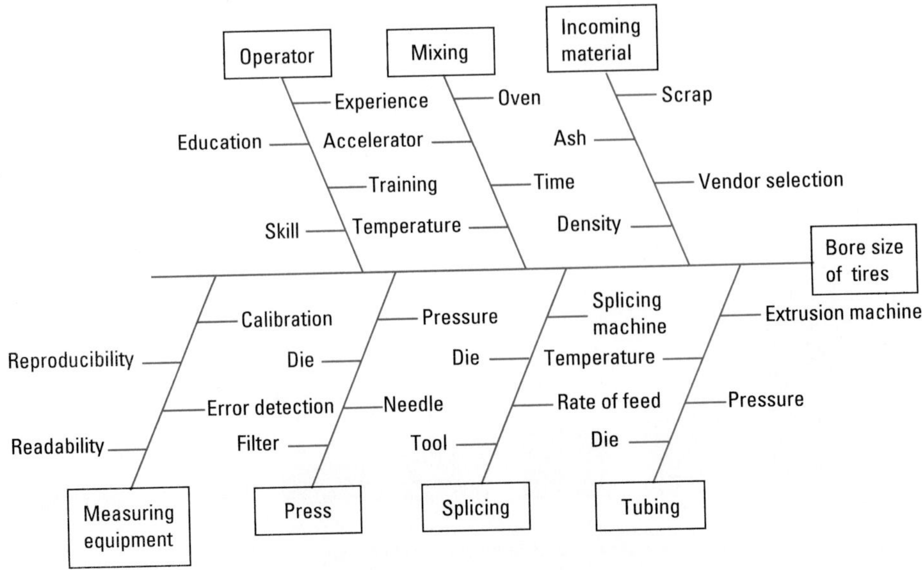

Figure 4-6 Cause-and-effect diagram for bore size of tires.

Dispersion Analysis

In dispersion analysis, each major cause is thoroughly analyzed by investigating the subcauses and their impact on the quality characteristic (or effect) in question. This process is repeated for each major cause in a preferred sequential order. The purpose of using a cause-and-effect diagram is to analyze the reasons for the variability, or dispersion. Even though this approach is similar to cause enumeration, there are some differences. Here, causes are grouped under similar headings, such as methods, materials, environment, and so on. In the cause enumeration approach, smaller causes which are perceived to be insignificant are listed, since that method tries to list all causes. However, some causes which do not fit the selected categories may not be listed in the dispersion analysis approach. Hence, there is a possibility of not identifying the root cause in dispersion analysis. The cause enumeration approach should facilitate the identification of root causes because all conceivable causes are listed.

Example 4-6: In the production of plastic reels for computer tapes, the width of the reel (the effect) is an important dimension. The main causes may be grouped into the following categories: materials, methods, machines, measurements, and people. Each of these is analyzed individually in sequence after the current main cause has been investigated thoroughly.

Figure 4-7 shows a partially completed cause-and-effect diagram. Here, one of the main causes, material, has been broken down into subcauses to be investigated. The subcauses include composition of the material, availability of materials, the choice of vendor, and the type of incoming tests performed on the material. These subcauses are further explored. For instance, under composition, we could consider the chemical properties of the compound. These properties may influence the flow of the compound in the molding process, which in turn influences the width of the reel. The uniformity of the raw material mixture (that is, its degree of consistency within a given shipment) will have a major influence on the quality of the plastic produced. This again may have an impact on the reel width. Another primary cause could be the storage conditions of the raw material and the storage time necessary before processing can occur. If environmental conditions such as temperature or humidity are not adequate, the result could be an adverse effect on the quality of the raw materials. The other subcauses could similarly be subdivided and further analyzed. The eventual structure of the cause-and-effect diagram would be similar to one found using cause enumeration.

Process Analysis

In using cause-and-effect diagrams for process analysis, the emphasis is on writing down the causes in the sequence in which the operations are actually conducted when making the product or performing the service. This process is similar to creating a flow diagram except that a cause-and-effect diagram should list in detail the causes that influence the quality characteristic of interest at each step of the production process.

Example 4-7: Consider aluminum casings produced for gear boxes. An increase in the production of unacceptable casings has warranted an analysis of the causes responsible.

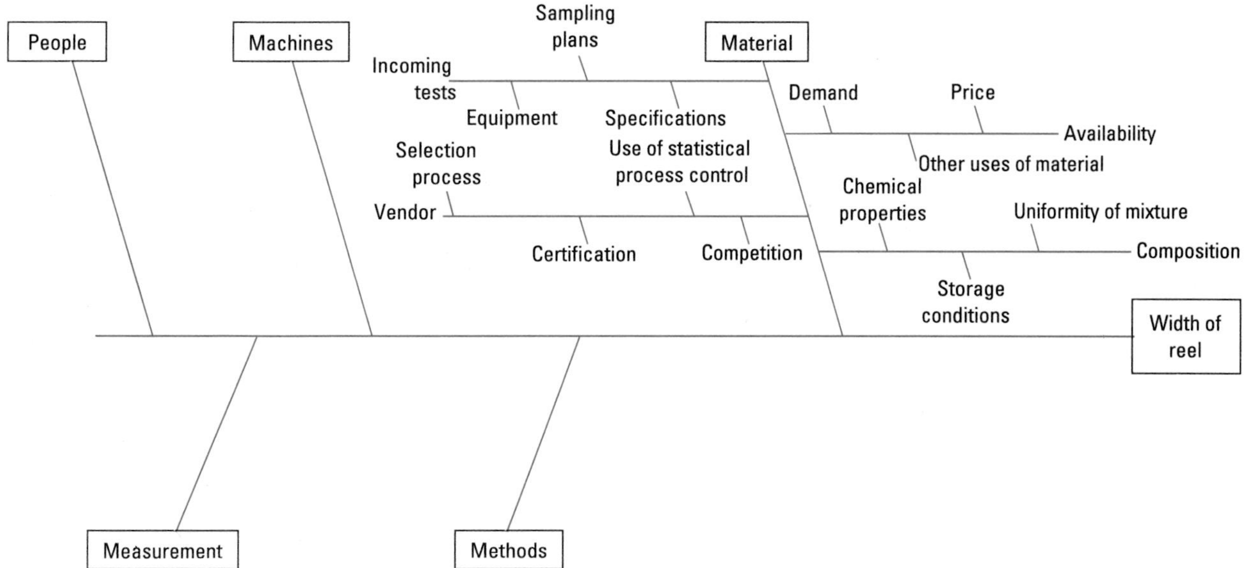

Figure 4-7 Dispersion analysis using cause-and-effect diagram.

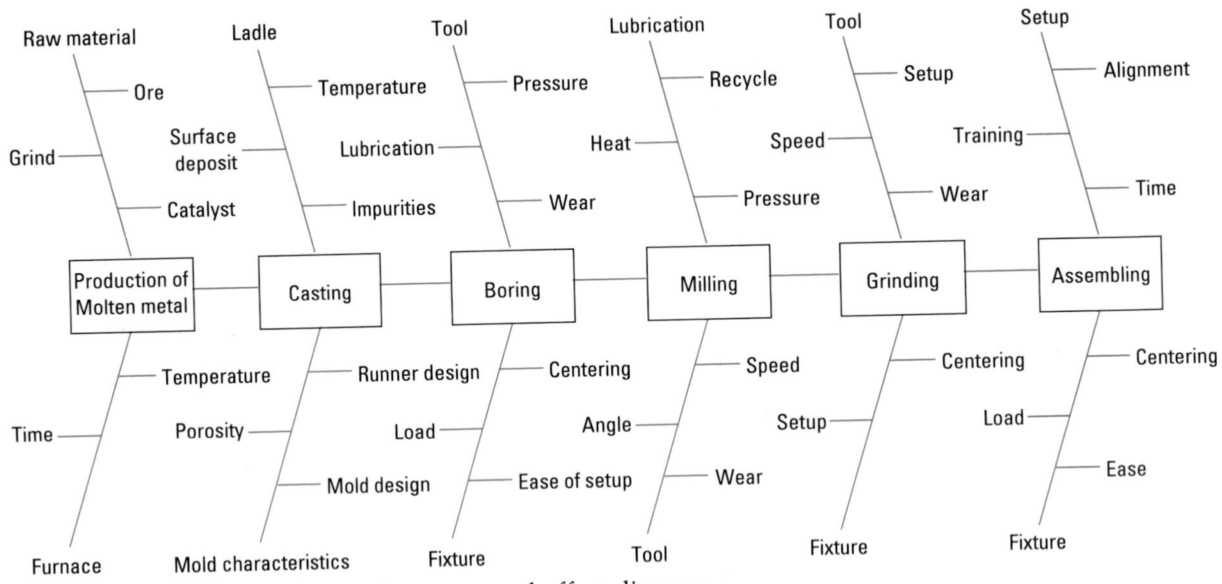

Figure 4-8 Process analysis using cause-and-effect diagram.

The process is analyzed, and the causes at each sequential step in the operation are listed.

Figure 4-8 shows an example of process analysis through a cause-and-effect diagram. The steps in the production process are shown as the major causes. Each of the production steps is then broken down into subcauses, and a similar decomposition continues until the root level of causes is reached. The main operations are the production of molten metal, casting, boring, milling, grinding, and assembly. Figure 4-8 gives details as to the breakdown of each of these operations. Such a diagram tracks the product from one step to the next in a sequential manner. It is easy to construct. However, a given cause may be repeated several times in the diagram if similar concerns exist in two or more operations. For example, in Figure 4-8, "tool" appears three times. Similarly, "fixture" is also found three times. The advantage of conducting process analysis through cause-and-effect diagrams is that it shows a systematic sequential development of causes—analysis of which will lead to remedies.

4-7 BOX PLOTS

Box plots are an alternative method of graphically depicting data while displaying some summary measures (Chambers, 1977; Chambers et al., 1983). A box plot shows the central tendency and dispersion of a data set and also provides an indication of the skewness (deviation from symmetry) and kurtosis (measure of tail length). From the plot, one may also determine if there are extreme observations (outliers). The construction of a box plot is described below.

Step 1: Determine the first quartile Q_1 (the twenty-fifth percentile). This value determines the lower edge of the box.

Step 2: Determine the third quartile Q_3 (the seventy-fifth percentile). This value determines the upper edge of the box. The length of the box is the difference between Q_3 and Q_1. This is known as the inter-quartile range (IQR).

Step 3: Find the median of the data set. A line is drawn at the median that divides the box.

Step 4: Two lines, known as whiskers, are drawn outward from the box. One line extends from the top edge of the box at Q_3 to either the maximum data value or $Q_3 + 1.5(\text{IQR})$, whichever is lower. Similarly, a line from the bottom edge of the box at Q_1 extends downward to a value that is either the minimum data value or $Q_1 - 1.5(\text{IQR})$, whichever is greater. The end points of the whiskers are known as the upper and lower adjacent values, respectively.

Step 5: Values that fall outside the adjacent values are candidates for consideration as outliers. They are each plotted as an asterisk (*).

Example 4-8: The Rockwell hardness values of metal fasteners were found for a randomly chosen sample of 20 parts. The observed values were as follows:

31.5	36.2	30.1	44.6	35.8
30.2	34.3	34.5	49.2	35.4
37.2	38.2	34.6	33.0	36.1
34.8	36.4	34.8	30.1	37.0

To construct a box plot, the data is first ranked:

30.1	30.1	30.2	31.5	33.0
34.3	34.5	34.6	34.8	34.8
35.4	35.8	36.1	36.2	36.4
37.0	37.2	38.2	44.6	49.2

The first quartile Q_1, is found to be 33.0. Next, from the ranked data, the third quartile Q_3 is found to be 37.0. The median is found to be 34.8. The interquartile range is $Q_3 - Q_1 = 4.0$, so $1.5(\text{IQR}) = 6.0$. Further calculations yield $Q_3 + 1.5(\text{IQR}) = 43.0$ and $Q_1 - 1.5(\text{IQR}) = 27.0$. The length of the top whisker is the lesser of 49.2 and 43.0, while the length of the bottom whisker is the greater of 30.1 and 27.0. The box plot is shown in Figure 4-9. Observe that there are two data values, 44.6 and 49.2, that are beyond the top whisker and are plotted as asterisks.

Several insights can be gained about the data from the box plot. The box itself, extending from 33 to 37, contains 50 percent of the observations. The relative location of the median, which has a value of 34.8, indicates the degree of skewness or asymmetry in the distribution of the data. Half of the values are less than or equal to the median, which is closer to the bottom edge of the box Q_1. If the distribution were symmetric, the median would be located midway between the edges of the box, that is, at a value of $(Q_1 + Q_3)/2$. Therefore, since the median is closer to Q_1, the data is positively skewed. Conversely, if the median had been closer to Q_3, the distribution would be negatively skewed. An idea of the tail lengths can be formed by observing the lengths of the whiskers. Note that the top whisker is much longer than the bottom one. The distribution, thus, has a longer right tail. Furthermore, two values (plotted as asterisks) are beyond the top whisker, and there are no values below the bottom whisker. These two possible outliers should be further investigated to determine why their values are so large compared to the other data points. Doing so may provide management with some possible course of action.

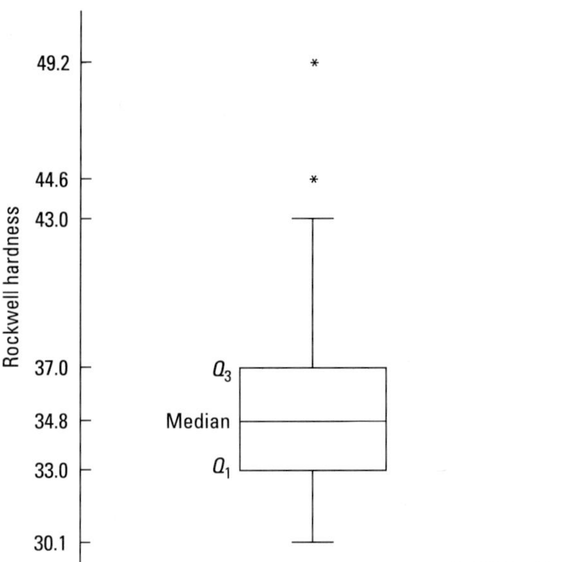

Figure 4-9 Box plot of hardness data.

Variations of the Basic Box Plot

One variation of the basic form of the box plot is the *notched box plot.* A notch, the width of which corresponds to the length of the confidence interval for the median, is constructed on the box around the median. Assuming the data values are normally distributed, the standard deviation of the median is given by Kendall and Stuart (1967) as

$$s_m = 1.25(\text{IQR})/(1.35\sqrt{n}) \tag{4.1}$$

The notch around the median M should start at values of

$$M \pm Cs_m \tag{4.2}$$

where C is a constant representing the level of confidence. For a level of confidence of 95 percent, a value of $C = 1.96$ may be used. Further details may be found by consulting McGill, Tukey, and Larsen (1978).

Example 4–9: Refer to the data on the Rockwell hardness of metal fasteners from Example 4-8. The sample size n is 20. The sample median M was found to be 34.8, with an interquartile range of 4.0. Using Equation 4.1, the standard deviation of the median is found to be

$$s_m = (1.25)(4.0)/(1.35\sqrt{20}) = 0.828$$

A 95 percent confidence interval for the median, found using Equation 4.2, is

$$\begin{aligned} 34.8 \pm (1.96)(0.828) &= 34.8 \pm 1.623 \\ &= (33.177,\ 36.423) \end{aligned}$$

Figure 4-10 shows this notched box plot. The notches are plotted around the median on the plot.

One use for a notched box plot is to compare the median of the quality characteristic for more than one plot and determine if there are significant differences. If there is no overlap between the notches of two box plots, it may be concluded that there is a significant difference between the medians of the two plots. This may indicate that the actions that were taken were significant in changing the process parameter conditions.

Another variation of the basic box plot is the *variable-width box plot.* If we are comparing two or more data sets which may have different sample sizes, then the widths of the boxes are set such that they are proportional to the sample sizes.

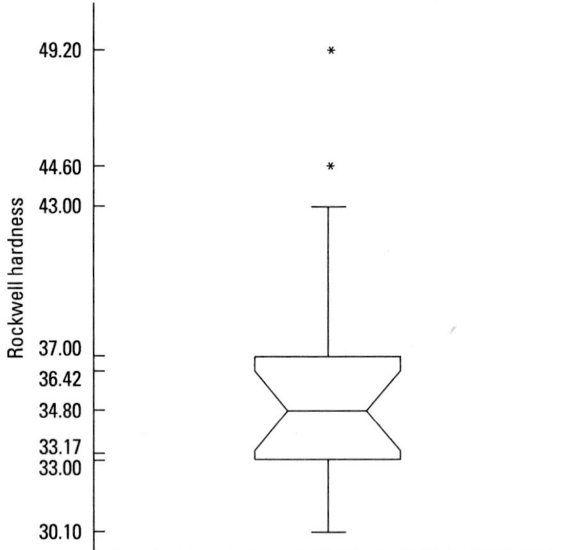

Figure 4-10 Notched box plot of hardness data.

Specifically, the width of the box is selected to be proportional to the natural logarithm of the sample size.

Example 4-10: After some process changes for the situation described in Example 4-8, a sample of 50 observations of the Rockwell hardness was taken. For these 50 observations the sample mean $\overline{X}$ is 34.2, the sample standard deviation s is 3.550, the sample median is 34.0, the first quartile Q_1 is 31.6, and the third quartile Q_3 is 36.3. The observations range from 27.5 to 43.0.

The interquartile range is $Q_3 - Q_1 = 4.7$, so $1.5(\text{IQR}) = 7.05$. Next, $Q_1 - 1.5(\text{IQR}) = 24.55$, and $Q_3 + 1.5(\text{IQR}) = 43.35$. Hence, the length of the top whisker is the lesser of 43.35 and 43.0. The length of the bottom whisker is the greater of 24.55 and 27.5.

Using a 95 percent level of confidence, the confidence interval for the median (using Equations 4.1 and 4.2) is

$$\begin{aligned} 34.0 \pm 1.96[1.25(4.7)/(1.35\sqrt{50})] &= 34.0 \pm 1.206 \\ &= (32.794,\ 35.206) \end{aligned}$$

The width of this boxplot should be proportional to $\ln(n) = \ln(50) = 3.912$. The width of the previous box plot (where the sample size was 20) should be proportional to $\ln(20) = 2.996$. Figure 4-11 shows the variable-width box plots before and after the process changes. Note that since there is some overlap in the notches of the two plots, we can conclude that at a 95 percent level of confidence there is no significant difference between the medians.

4-8 NORMAL PROBABILITY PLOTS

In many statistical techniques, the population from which the data is selected is assumed to be normally distributed. Moreover, if the distribution of the population is normal, then certain inferences can be made about the quality characteristic. Chapter 8 will show instances of three situations where the goal is to determine the proportion of a product below

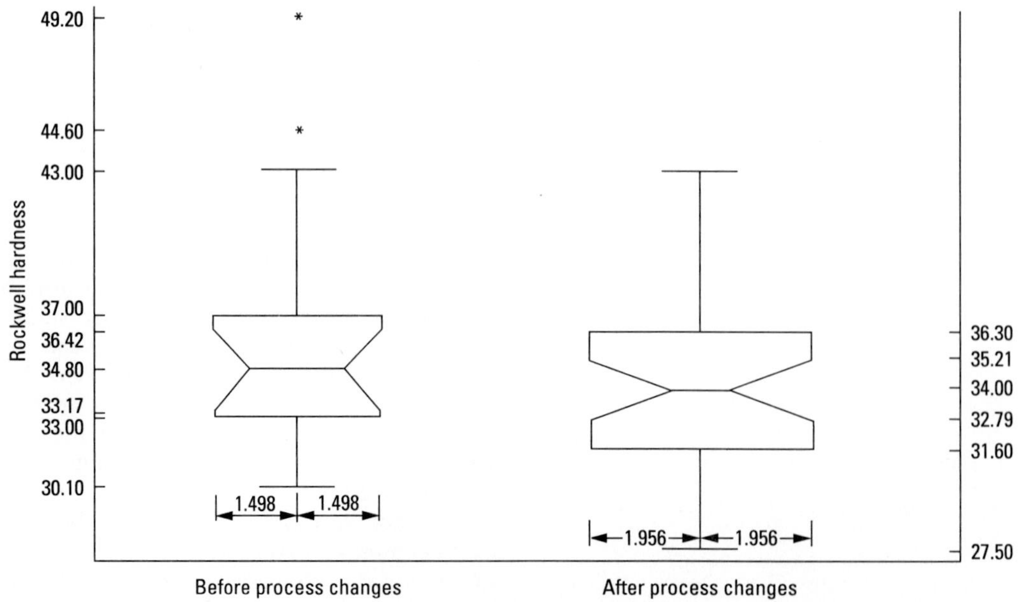

Figure 4-11 Variable-width box plots before and after process changes.

or above certain values known as specification limits. If the assumption of normality holds, then this proportion can readily be found.

Plotting is often done on normal probability paper. The ordinate represents the theoretical percentile (assuming the data is from a normal distribution), while the abscissa represents the ordered sample values. Basically, the vertical scale of normal probability paper is designed so that if the data is from a normal distribution, the observations will plot as a straight line. Deviations of the plotted points from a straight line indicate departures from normality. An analyst may have to use subjective judgement to define what a "significant deviation" from a straight line is. Statistical methods including goodness-of-fit tests (such as chi-squared tests; see Duncan 1986) or Kolmogorov-Smirnov tests (see Massey, 1951) could also be used, but they are not discussed here. Further discussion of probability plotting may be found in Michael (1983). Several software packages are available for normal probability plots (SAS, 1990).

The following steps are taken to construct a normal probability plot:

Step 1: Rank the observations in ascending order from smallest to largest. Assign a rank to each data value. The rank of the observations may be denoted by i such that $i = 1, 2, \ldots n$, where n is the number of data points in the sample.

Step 2: The probability plotting position of the observation with rank i is calculated from

$$F_i = \frac{(i - 0.5)}{n} \tag{4.3}$$

Step 3: On normal probability paper, plot the value of each observation (along the horizontal axis) versus its probability percentage ($100F_i$) along the ordinate.

Step 4: Estimate a straight line through the plotted points. A best-fit straight line through the points will estimate its cumulative probability distribution function.

Step 5: Based on step 4, make a decision as to whether the data is from a normal distribution. Consider the closeness of the values to a straight-line fit as well as any systematic deviations from the line.

Example 4-11: A random sample of 50 coils to be used in an electrical circuit was chosen, and their resistances were measured. The data values are shown in Table 4-6. First, rank the observations in ascending order. The probability plotting position (F_i) of each is calculated using Equation 4.3. Table 4-7 shows the ranked data and the

TABLE 4-6 Resistance of coils

Sample number	Coil resistance	Sample number	Coil resistance
1	35.1	26	27.5
2	35.4	27	26.5
3	36.3	28	26.9
4	38.8	29	26.7
5	39.0	30	27.2
6	22.5	31	31.8
7	23.7	32	32.1
8	25.0	33	31.5
9	25.3	34	31.2
10	25.0	35	31.4
11	34.7	36	28.5
12	34.2	37	28.4
13	34.4	38	27.6
14	34.7	39	27.6
15	34.3	40	28.2
16	26.4	41	30.8
17	25.5	42	30.6
18	25.8	43	30.4
19	26.4	44	30.5
20	25.6	45	30.5
21	33.1	46	28.5
22	33.6	47	30.2
23	32.3	48	30.1
24	32.6	49	30.0
25	32.2	50	28.9

computed plotting positions. A normal probability plot may be constructed as shown in Figure 4-12. A straight line is fitted through the plotted points. Observe that a majority of the plotted points are in close proximity of the straight line. A few points on the extremes deviate from the line. Overall, we can conclude that the observations seem to have come from a normal distribution.

If the assumption of normality is accepted, then several inferences can be made from the normal probability plot. First, an estimate of the population mean can be obtained by reading the value of the fiftieth percentile off the fitted straight line. From Figure 4-12, the population mean may be estimated as approximately 30.0. Second, the population standard deviation can be estimated as the difference between the eighty-fourth and fiftieth percentile data values. This is because the eighty-fourth percentile of a normal distribution is approximately one standard deviation away from the mean (the fiftieth percentile). From Figure 4-12, the population standard deviation may be estimated to be $33.625 - 30.0 = 3.625$. Third, a normal probability plot can be used to estimate the proportion of a process output that does not meet certain specification limits. For example, if the lower specification limit of the resistance of cables is 25, from the normal probability plot we may estimate that approximately 8 percent of the output is less than the specification limit.

The pattern of a normal probability plot gives some idea of the process from which the data comes. Nelson

TABLE 4-7 Resistance of coils in order of rank and the corresponding plotting positions

Resistance	Rank, i	Probability plotting position, F_i	Resistance	Rank, i	Probability plotting position, F_i
22.5	1	0.01	30.4	26	0.51
23.7	2	0.03	30.5	27	0.53
25.0	3	0.05	30.5	28	0.55
25.0	4	0.07	30.6	29	0.57
25.3	5	0.09	30.8	30	0.59
25.5	6	0.11	31.2	31	0.61
25.6	7	0.13	31.4	32	0.63
25.8	8	0.15	31.5	33	0.65
26.4	9	0.17	31.8	34	0.67
26.5	10	0.19	32.1	35	0.69
26.7	11	0.21	32.2	36	0.71
26.8	12	0.23	32.3	37	0.73
26.9	13	0.25	32.6	38	0.75
27.2	14	0.27	33.1	39	0.77
27.5	15	0.29	33.6	40	0.79
27.6	16	0.31	34.2	41	0.81
27.6	17	0.33	34.3	42	0.83
28.2	18	0.35	34.4	43	0.85
28.4	19	0.37	34.7	44	0.87
28.5	20	0.39	34.7	45	0.89
28.5	21	0.41	35.1	46	0.91
28.9	22	0.43	35.4	47	0.93
30.0	23	0.45	36.3	48	0.95
30.1	24	0.47	38.8	49	0.97
30.2	25	0.49	39.0	50	0.99

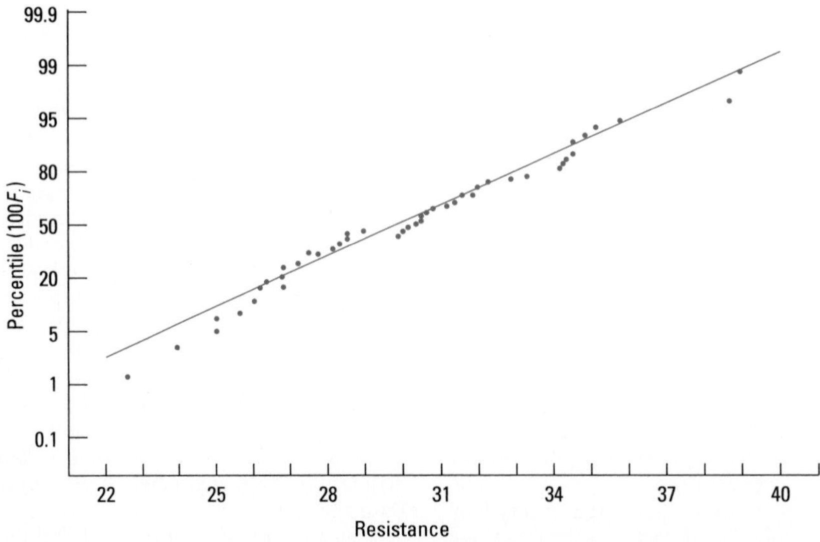

Figure 4-12 Normal probability plot of resistance of coils.

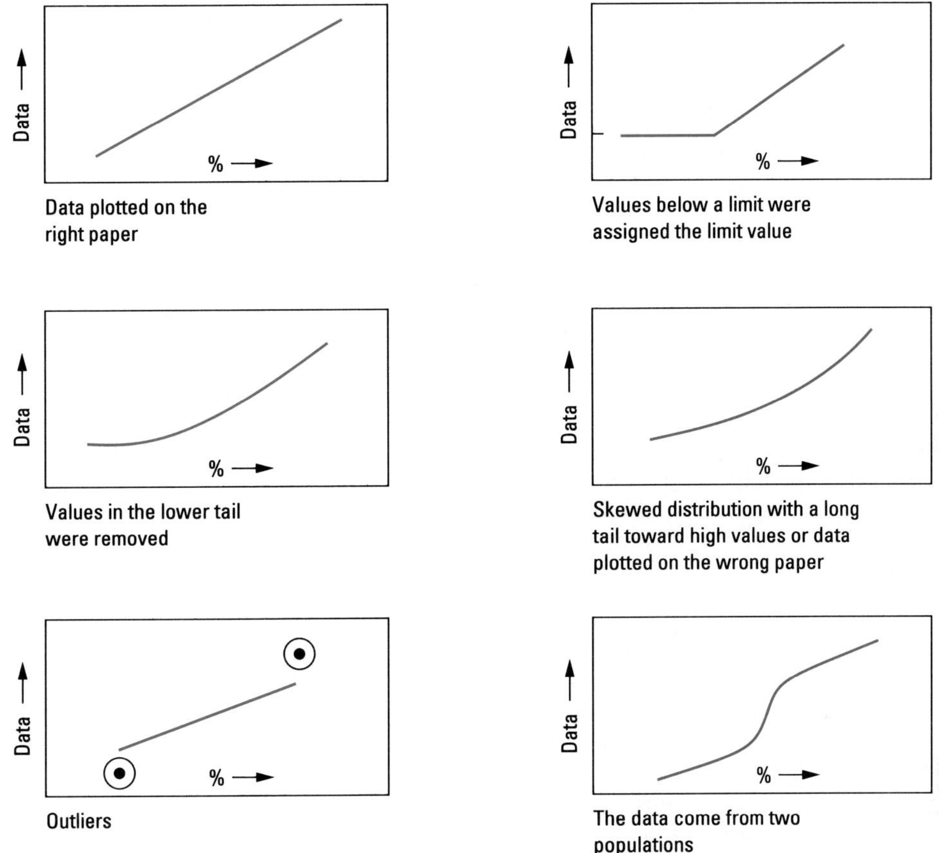

Figure 4-13 Normal probability plot patterns. (W. Nelson (1979), *How to Analyze Data with Simple Plots*. Reprinted with the permission of ASQC.)

(1979) describes the interpretation of different types of patterns encountered in normal probability plots. Figure 4-13 illustrates these patterns and their possible interpretations. In all instances, one must be aware of the subjectivity involved in forming interpretations. Experience and good judgment are essential to accurately determining whether a set of points deviates significantly from linearity. The use of probability plots in conjunction with statistical goodness-of-fit tests should provide a reliable means of making inferences regarding normality.

4-9 EMPIRICAL QUANTILE-QUANTILE PLOTS

A comparison of the distributions of two data sets can be made through the use of empirical quantile-quantile plots. The notion of a quantile is similar to that of a percentile. The quantile of a data set are just the ordered data values themselves. The pth quantile, $Q(p)$, is the data value such that the proportion of data values that are less than or equal to it is p. Thus the median is $Q(0.5)$. For example, consider a company that has two mixers for making a compound. The amount of polypropylene is measured from random samples taken from each of the two processes. We would like to know if the distribution of polypropylene content is the same for the two mixers. Constructing a quantile-quantile plot will enable us to determine if changes need to be made to the process. Or, if such plots are constructed using data obtained before and after changes have been made to the process, we can find out how the changes have influenced the process characteristic. Thus, the effects of actions can be investigated.

A quantile-quantile plot is simple to construct. Consider first the case in which the sample sizes of two data sets are equal to n. The values in the first data set should be ranked in ascending order. The values in this ordered data set are denoted by X_i for $i = 1, 2, \ldots, n$. Next, the values in the second data set are also ranked in ascending order. The ordered values are denoted by Y_i for $i = 1, 2, \ldots, n$. So, X_i is the $(i - 0.5)/n$ quantile of the first data set, and Y_i is the same quantile of the second data set. Bivariate points are created by grouping the pairs (X_i, Y_i). These points are plotted, and the resulting graph is known as an empirical quantile-quantile plot. If the plotted points lie on or close to a straight line, then the samples are assumed to be from the same distribution.

In case the number of observations from the two data sets are unequal, a minor modification is necessary. All of the ordered observations from the smaller data set are used. The empirical quantiles are found for these observations. Next, the larger data set is ranked in ascending order. From this data set, a corresponding set of quantiles based on the smaller data set is found through interpolation. The chosen points are then plotted to give the quantile-quantile plot. Thus, not all of the observations of the larger data set will be plotted. For example, suppose the first data set has 10 observations, the ordered values of which are denoted by $X_i, i = 1, 2, \ldots, 10$. Suppose the second data set has 20 observations; the ordered values of which are denoted by $Y_j, j = 1, 2, \ldots, 20$. The smallest observation in the first data set is X_1, which is the $(1 - 0.5)/10$, or 0.05 quantile. Observe that for the second data set Y_1 is the $(1 - 0.5)/20$, or 0.025 quantile and that Y_2 is the $(2 - 0.5)/20$, or 0.075 quantile. So for the value X_1, to determine the corresponding plotting value from the second data set, one would linearly interpolate between Y_1 and Y_2 to obtain the 0.05 quantile. Since Y_1 is the 0.025 quantile and Y_2 is the 0.075 quantile, the 0.05 quantile from the second data set would be interpolated as $(Y_1 + Y_2)/2$. Thus, a plotted point will be $(X_1, (Y_1 + Y_2)/2)$. This procedure is used to determine the other bivariate points for obtaining the plot.

TABLE 4-8 Polypropylene content in samples from two mixers

Data for mixer A—polypropylene content, X				
48.6	49.6	48.3	48.9	48.9
49.5	49.3	49.4	49.4	49.2
54.5	54.6	54.9	52.9	53.2
55.5	53.5	53.3	54.1	53.7
49.8	51.5	52.8	52.1	49.9
50.9	51.4	50.2	50.4	49.8
Data for mixer B—polypropylene content, Y				
49.8	47.9	47.6	48.5	48.9
47.7	49.6	49.5	48.3	48.2
52.4	52.0	50.2	50.5	53.2
52.7	50.9	51.9	51.6	51.2
47.4	47.0	47.6	45.8	45.4
46.2	45.9	46.4	46.8	47.2

Example 4-12: Samples of size 30 were collected from each of two mixers A and B in a production facility. The polypropylene content was measured for each sample. Table 4-8 shows the data from the two mixers. It is of interest to determine if the distribution of polypropylene content is the same for the two mixers.

Solution. Each of the two samples is ranked in ascending order. The two ranked samples are then merged to create a bivariate observation. Table 4-9 shows the or-

TABLE 4-9 Ordered bivariate data on polypropylene content from two mixers

Observation number, i	X_i	Y_i	Observation number, i	X_i	Y_i
1	48.3	45.4	16	50.9	48.5
2	48.6	45.8	17	51.4	48.9
3	48.9	45.9	18	51.5	49.5
4	48.9	46.2	19	52.1	49.6
5	49.2	46.4	20	52.8	49.8
6	49.3	46.8	21	52.9	50.2
7	49.4	47.0	22	53.2	50.5
8	49.4	47.2	23	53.3	50.9
9	49.5	47.4	24	53.5	51.2
10	49.6	47.6	25	53.7	51.6
11	49.8	47.6	26	54.1	51.9
12	49.8	47.7	27	54.5	52.0
13	49.9	47.9	28	54.6	52.4
14	50.2	48.2	29	54.9	52.7
15	50.4	48.3	30	55.5	53.2

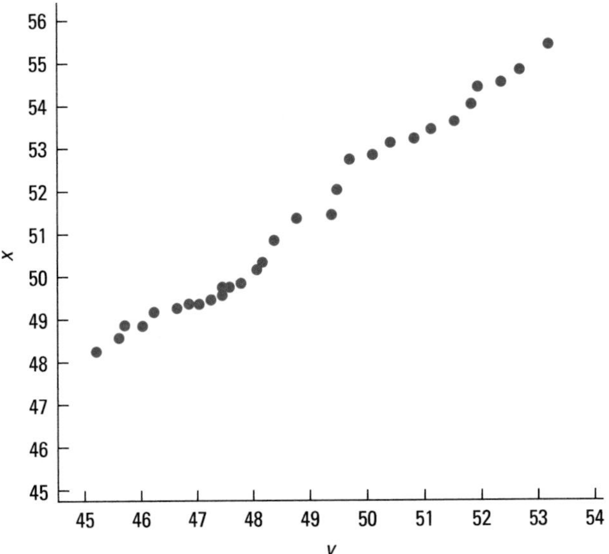

Figure 4-14 Quantile-quantile (empirical) plot of data from mixers.

dered samples and the 30 bivariate points. These points may be plotted as in Figure 4-14 to yield an empirical quantile-quantile plot. The plot shows that a straight line can be drawn to approximate the plotted observations. Most of the points lie close to the straight line. We may infer that distributions of polypropylene content from the two mixers are the same. There is some subjectivity in making this decision since determining the "closeness" of plotted points to a straight-line is subjective. However, the accuracy in making these decisions should improve with added experience in using these plots. Their ease of construction makes them an attractive tool for studying process characteristics.

4-10 SCATTER DIAGRAMS

The simplest form of a scatter diagram consists of plotting bivariate data. Here, the relationship between two variables is depicted. Frequently, in analyzing processes, the relationship between a controllable variable and a desired quality characteristic is of importance. Knowing this relationship may help an analyst decide how to set a controllable variable in order to achieve a desired level for the output characteristic.

Example 4-13: Suppose we are interested in determining the relationship between the depth of cut in a milling operation and the amount of tool wear. Forty observations are taken from the process such that the depth of cut (in millimeters) is varied over a range of values and the corresponding amount of tool wear (also in millimeters) over 40 operation cycles are noted. The data values are shown in Table 4-10. A scatterplot of the data is shown in Figure 4-15. This plot gives an idea of the type of relationship that may exist between the depth of cut and the amount of tool wear. In this case, it seems that the relationship is generally nonlinear. For depth-of-cut values less than 3.0 mm, the rate of tool wear seems to be constant whereas with increases in the depth of cut, the tool wear starts increasing at an increasing rate. For depth-of-cut values above 4.5 mm, the tool wear seems to drastically increase. This information may be useful in determining the depth of cut to use in the milling operation so that the downtime due to tool changes is minimized.

4-11 MULTIVARIABLE CHARTS

In many manufacturing or service operations there are usually several variables or attributes for which it is useful to determine their effects on product or service quality. The types of plots discussed up to this point have dealt with no more than two variables on a graph. Since realistic problems are likely to deal with more than two variables, multivariable charts are useful means of displaying collective information.

Several types of multivariable charts are available (Blazek et al., 1987; Kleiner and Hartigan, 1981). One of these is known as a radial plot, or star, for which the different variables of interest correspond to different rays emanating from a star. The length of each ray represents the magnitude of the variable.

Example 4-14: Suppose the controllable variables in a process are temperature, pressure, manganese content, and silicon content. Figure 4-16 shows radial plots, or stars, for two samples of size 10, taken an hour apart. For each sample, the averages of the 10 observed values for the respective variables are calculated. These averages are then represented by the length of the rays. A relative measure of quality performance may be used to locate the center of a star vertically, while the horizontal axis might represent time. In this example, a measure of quality could be the percentage of the product that is nonconforming.

From Figure 4-16 several process characteristics can be observed. First, from time 1 to time 2, an improvement in the performance of the process is seen, as indicated by a decline in the percentage nonconforming. Next, we can examine what changes in the controllable variables led to this improvement. We find that a decrease in temperature, an increase in both pressure and manganese content, and a basically constant level of silicon caused this reduction in the percentage nonconforming.

TABLE 4-10 Data on depth of cut and tool wear

Observation number	Depth of cut (mm)	Tool wear (mm)	Observation number	Depth of cut (mm)	Tool wear (mm)
1	2.1	0.035	21	5.6	0.073
2	4.2	0.041	22	4.7	0.064
3	1.5	0.031	23	1.9	0.030
4	1.8	0.027	24	2.4	0.029
5	2.3	0.033	25	3.2	0.039
6	3.8	0.045	26	3.4	0.038
7	2.6	0.038	27	2.8	0.040
8	4.3	0.047	28	2.2	0.031
9	3.4	0.040	29	2.0	0.033
10	4.5	0.058	30	2.9	0.035
11	2.6	0.039	31	3.0	0.032
12	5.2	0.056	32	3.6	0.038
13	4.1	0.048	33	1.9	0.032
14	3.0	0.037	34	5.1	0.052
15	2.2	0.028	35	4.7	0.050
16	4.6	0.057	36	5.2	0.058
17	4.8	0.060	37	4.1	0.048
18	5.3	0.068	38	4.3	0.049
19	3.9	0.048	39	3.8	0.042
20	3.5	0.036	40	3.6	0.045

Other forms of multivariable plots (such as standardized stars, glyphs, trees, faces, and weathervanes), are conceptually similar to radial plots. For details on these forms, refer to Friedman et al. (1972), Gnanadesikan (1977), Chernoff (1973), and Bruntz et al. (1974).

4-12 SUMMARY

This chapter presents a number of graphical methods that are useful for analyzing the existing status of characteristics associated with products and processes. Since the variability of relevant characteris-

Figure 4-15 Scatterplot of tool wear versus depth of cut.

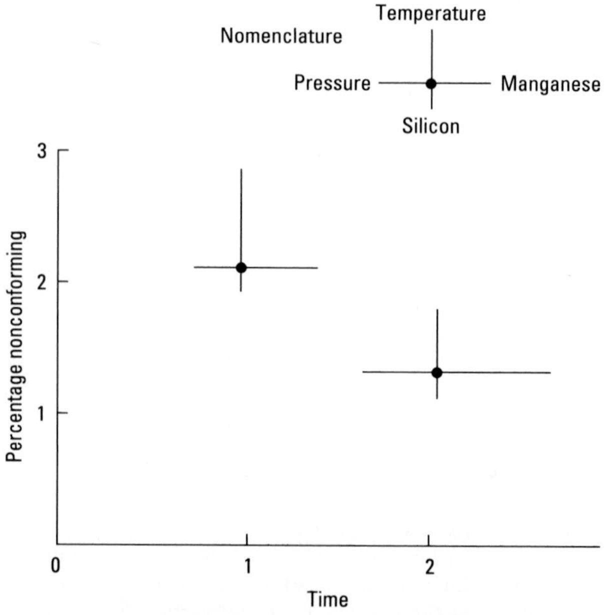

Figure 4-16 Radial plot of multiple variables.

tics is always a matter of concern, the techniques presented herein provide an idea of the degree of variability. Methods such as frequency histograms, stem-and-leaf plots, box plots, and normal probability plots are useful for interpreting measures of both central tendency and dispersion. They may be used to compare product and process performance before and after certain changes are made in the process. In addition to methods of data presentation, the chapter discusses several graphical methods that are useful in the analysis of quality improvement. Neverending improvements in products and their corresponding processes are a necessity. Thus, after achieving control in a process, management must seek means for further improvement in order to remain competitive. The methods discussed in this chapter provide guidelines for determining possible areas where such changes should be investigated. Pareto diagrams identify major causes for concern. Cause-and-effect diagrams go a step further by analyzing the various subcauses associated with each major cause. A graphical display of the effect of a certain variable on an output characteristic is obtained through a scatterplot, while a comparison of the output of two different process conditions is achieved by using an empirical quantile-quantile plot. Since realistic problems may involve more than one variable, multivariable charts are useful for displaying the relative impacts of such variables on an output characteristic. All of these methods are easy to understand and apply.

4-13 CASE STUDY

ACCELERATING IMPROVEMENT*

The need to improve quality has captured the attention of American industry. The need to accelerate the improvement process, however, is just now being realized, and ways to accelerate it are just beginning to be explored. The Seven-Step Method and the Project Team Review Process are related techniques that, in the proper management setting, can accelerate process improvement.

The Seven-Step Method is a structured approach to problem solving and process improvement. It leads a team through a logical sequence of steps that force a thorough analysis of the problem, its potential causes, and possible solutions. The structure imposed by the Seven-Step Method helps a team focus on the correct issues rather than diffuse its energy on tangential or even counterproductive undertakings.

The Seven-Step Method is most successful when accompanied by regular project reviews performed by managers with a vested interest in the project's outcome. In many organizations, project teams are not reviewed until a solution or recommendation is to be presented—the notion of a status review is foreign. However, there is a formal review process in which peers and superiors guide, support, and monitor project teams while they are working on problems. This Project Team Review Process structures a session so that it becomes a productive meeting with positive consequences, thereby providing teams with support and focus.

*Adapted from: M. Gaudard, R. Coates, and L. Freeman (1991), "Accelerating Improvement," *Quality Progress,* Vol. 24, No. 10, pp. 81–88.

The Seven-Step Method

The value of the Seven-Step Method lies in the discipline and logic that it imposes. The seven steps are now briefly described.

Step 1: Define the Project

1. Define the problem in terms of a gap between what is and what should be. (For example, "Customers report an excessive number of errors. The team's objective is to reduce the number of errors.")
2. Document why it is important to be working on this particular problem:
   - Explain how you know it is a problem, providing any data you might have that supports this.
   - List the customer's key quality characteristics. State how closing the gap will benefit the customer in terms of these characteristics.
3. Determine what data you will use to measure progress:
   - Decide what data you will use to provide a baseline against which improvement can be measured.
   - Develop an operational definition you will need to collect the data.

Step 2: Study the Current Situation

1. Collect the baseline data and plot them. (Sometimes historical data can be used for this purpose.) A run chart or control chart is usually used to exhibit baseline data. Decide how you will exhibit these data on the run chart. Decide how you will label your axes.
2. Develop flowcharts of the processes.
3. Provide any helpful sketches or visual aids.
4. Identify any variables that might have a bearing on the problem. Consider the variables of what, where, to what extent, and who. Data will be gathered on these variables to localize the problem.
5. Design data collection instruments.
6. Collect the data and summarize what you have learned about the variables' effects on the problem.
7. Determine what additional information would be helpful at this time. Repeat substeps 2 through 7 until there is no additional information that would be helpful at this time.

Step 3: Analyze the Potential Causes

1. Determine potential causes of the current conditions:
   - Use the data collected in step 2 and the experience of the people who work in the process to identify conditions that might lead to the problem.
   - Construct cause-and-effect diagrams for these conditions of interest.
   - Decide on the most likely causes by checking against the data from step 2 and the experience of the people working in the process.
2. Determine whether more data are needed. If so, repeat substeps 2 through 7 of step 2.
3. If possible, verify the causes through observation or by directly controlling variables.

Step 4: Implement a Solution

1. Develop a list of solutions to be considered. Be creative.
2. Decide which solutions should be tried:
   - Carefully assess the feasibility of each solution, the likelihood of success, and potential adverse consequences.
   - Clearly indicate why you are choosing a particular solution.
3. Determine how the preferred solution will be implemented. Will there be a pilot project? Who will be responsible for the implementation? Who will train those involved?
4. Implement the preferred solution.

Step 5: Check the Results

1. Determine whether the actions in step 4 were effective:
   - Collect more data on the baseline measure from step 1.
   - Collect any other data related to the conditions at the start that might be relevant.
   - Analyze the results. Determine whether the solution tested was effective. Repeat prior steps as necessary.
2. Describe any deviations from the plan and what was learned.

Step 6: Standardize the Improvement

1. Institutionalize the improvement
   - Develop a strategy for institutionalizing the improvement, and assign responsibilities.
   - Determine whether the improvement should be applied elsewhere, and plan for its implementation.

Step 7: Establish Future Plans

1. Determine your plans for the future:
   - Decide whether the gap should be narrowed further and, if so, how another project should be approached and who should be involved.
   - Identify related problems that should be addressed.
2. Summarize what you learned about the project team experience, and make recommendations for future project teams.

Application

A restaurant caters to business travelers and has a self-service breakfast buffet. Interested in customer satisfaction, the manager constructs a survey, distributes it to customers over a three-month period, and summarizes the results in a Pareto chart (see Figure 4-17). The Pareto chart indicates that the restaurant's major problem is that customers have to wait too long to be seated. A team of employees is formed to work on this problem.

Step 1: Define the project. With the survey as the background, the team undertakes the first step. The problem is that customers wait too long to be seated. They should not have to wait at all. The problem is important because customers have complained, and this

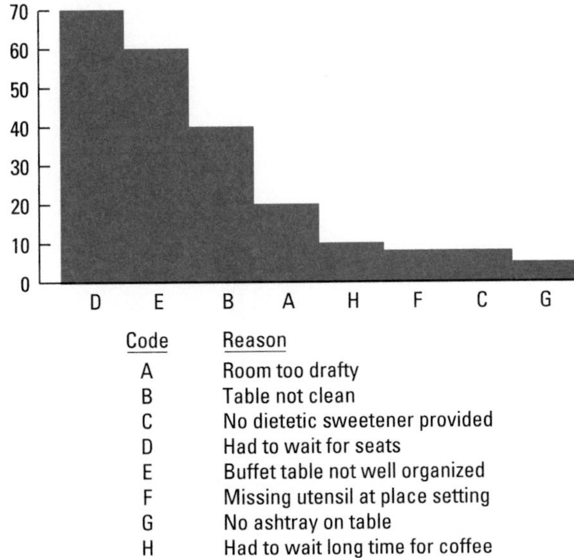

Figure 4-17 Pareto chart of complaints.

is supported by the Pareto chart constructed from the survey data. Most of the customers are business travelers who want either a speedy breakfast or a chance to conduct business during breakfast. Decreasing the wait to be seated will increase the restaurant's ability to respond to these key quality characteristics. Progress can be measured by the percent of customers each day who have to wait in excess of, say, one minute to be seated. The team develops an operational definition of "waiting to be seated" to answer such questions as: When does the wait start? When does it end? How is it measured?

Step 2: Study the current situation. The team collects baseline data and plots it (see Figure 4-18). At the same time, the team develops a flowchart of seating a party. The team members feel that a floor diagram might be helpful, so they produce one (see Figure 4-19). The variables they identify as potentially affecting the problem are day of the week, size of the party, reason for waiting, and time of the morning. Data relating to these variables are collected.

From the baseline data, the team learns that the percent of people served who have to wait is higher early in the week and decreases during the week, with only a small percent waiting on weekends. This is reasonable, since the restaurant's clientele primarily consists of business travelers. The size of the party does not appear to be a factor, because parties of all sizes wait in approximately the same proportions. A histogram of the number of people waiting by the time of the morning reveals nothing surprising: more people wait during the busy hours than during the slow hours (see Figure 4-20) The reason for waiting, however, is interesting. Most people wait because a table is not available or because they have a seating preference (as opposed to the hostess not being around to seat customers or customers waiting for friends to join them).

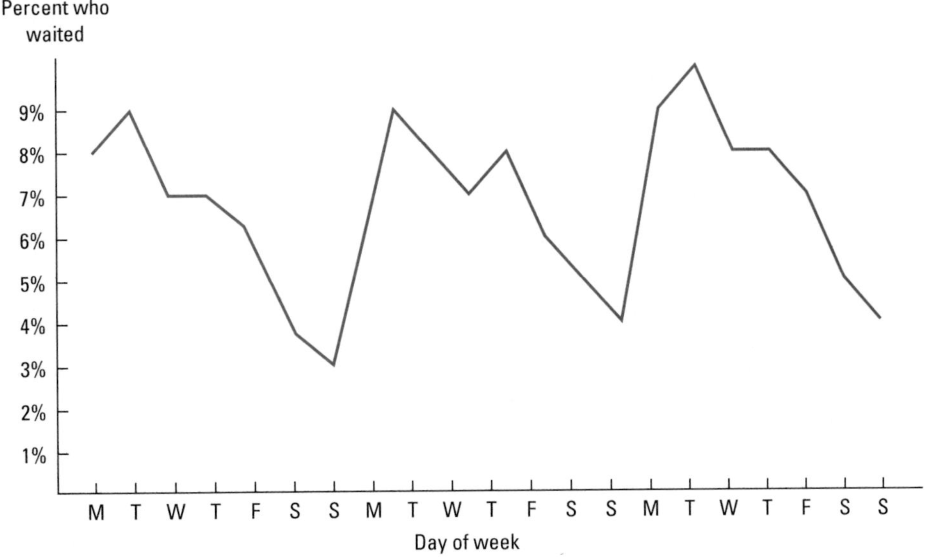

Figure 4-18 Run chart of percent of customers waiting more than one minute to be seated.

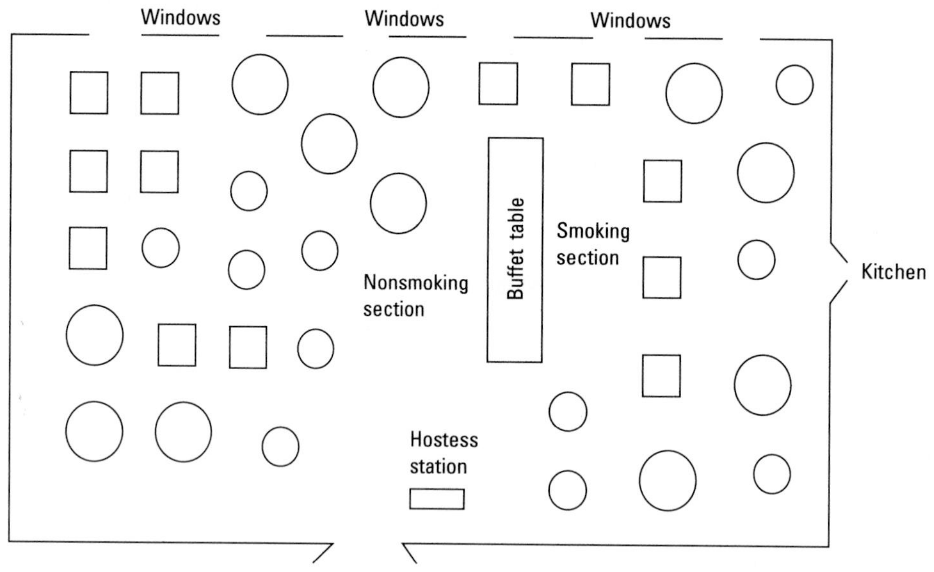

Figure 4-19 Restaurant floor plan.

At this point, it would be easy for the team to jump to the solution of putting more staff on early in the week and during busy hours in the morning—but analyzing causes is not done until the next step.

The team decides additional information is needed on why tables are not available and how seating preferences affect waiting. After data are collected, it learns that tables are generally unavailable because they are not cleared (as opposed to being occupied) and that most of the people who have a seating preference wait for a table in the nonsmoking area.

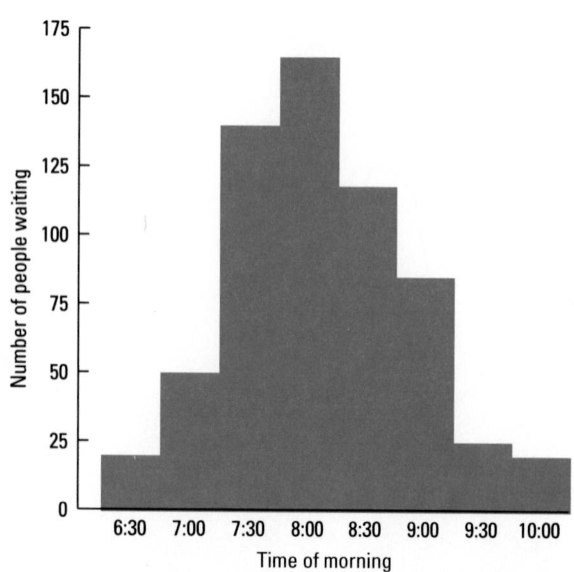

Figure 4-20 Histogram of the number of customers waiting more than one minute for particular times of morning.

Step 3: Analyze the potential causes. A cause-and-effect diagram is constructed showing why tables are not cleared quickly, with particular emphasis on identifying root causes (see Figure 4-21). This diagram, together with the rest of the data the team has gathered, leads the team to conclude that the most likely cause is the distance from the tables to the kitchen, particularly in the nonsmoking area.

Step 4: Implement a solution. The team develops a list of possible solutions. Since the team has not been able to verify the cause by controlling the variables, it chooses a solution that can be easily tested: set up temporary workstations in the nonsmoking area. No other changes are made. The team continues to collect data on the percent of people waiting longer than one minute to be seated.

Step 5: Check the results. After a month, the team analyzes the data collected in step four. As Figure 4-22 shows, the improvement is dramatic.

Step 6: Standardize the improvement. The temporary workstations are replaced with permanent ones.

Step 7: Establish future plans. The team decides that the next highest bar in the Pareto chart of customer complaints—the buffet table being not well organized—should be addressed.

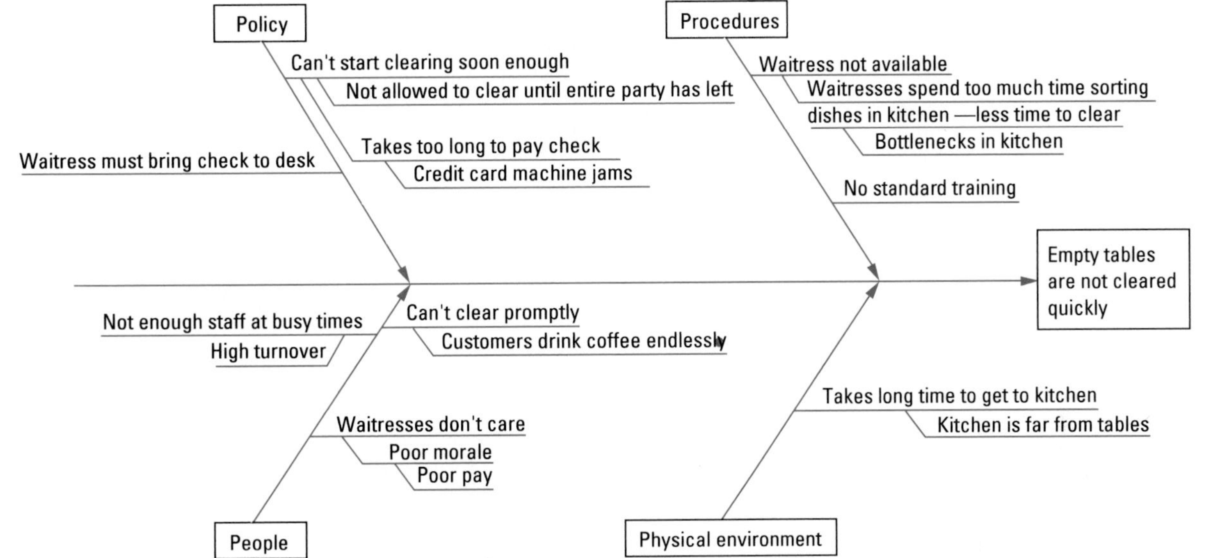

Figure 4-21 Cause-and-effect diagram describes why tables are not cleared quickly.

The Purpose of the Seven Steps

The overall purpose of the Seven-Step Method is to facilitate process improvement.

Since the plan-do-check-act (PDCA) process, alternatively known as the Deming cycle, also has process improvement as its goal, it seems natural to ask how it and the Seven-Step Method are related. The *plan* step consists of planning a change or test aimed at improvement; the *do* step consists of carrying out the change or test, preferably on a small scale; the *check* step involves studying the results to understand what has

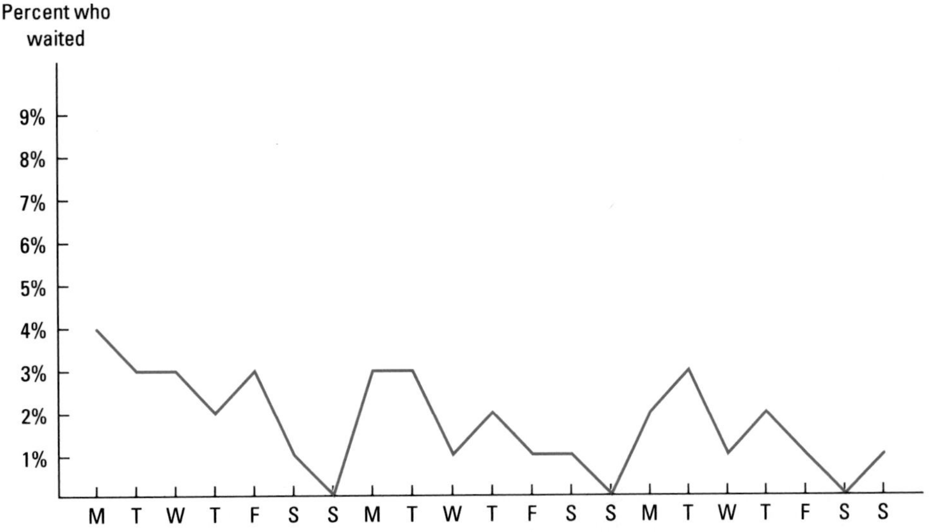

Figure 4-22 Run chart of percent of customers waiting more than one minute to be seated after implementation of solution.

been learned; and the *act* step consists of adopting the change, abandoning it, or repeating the cycle.

It seems clear that much of the PDCA thinking is present in the Seven-Step Method. The PDCA cycle, however, is a broad paradigm for process improvement that applies to situations where the Seven-Step Method does not. The Seven-Step Method is appropriate when a deep understanding of the problem is needed to determine and plan an effective solution. A team acquires this understanding through the data-based localization and cause analysis in steps 2 and 3. In these steps, the team is continually restrained from jumping to solutions. Only in step 4 does the team formulate and implement a solution. This step is similar to the plan and do steps in the PDCA cycle. In step 5, which is comparable to the PDCA cycle's check step, the team checks its results. After checking, the team either standardizes its findings (step 6) or returns to a prior step to obtain an even deeper understanding of the problem or possible solutions—a process much like the act step of the PDCA cycle. In addition to reflecting on its experience in terms of tasks, group processes, and organizational issues, in step 7 the team identifies future needs. Identification of these needs continues the PDCA cycle, and if appropriate, those needs are addressed using the Seven-Step Method.

The Seven-Step Method is directed at analytic rather than enumerative studies. In an enumerative study, an existing population is studied; an analytic study focuses on prediction. In analytic situations, the key is to learn about the cause systems that underlie the processes of interest to understand the effects of various conditions. Since organizations are usually interested in learning about the future, almost all problems in industry—and certainly the most important ones—are of an analytic nature. The Seven-Step Method helps solve analytic problems efficiently because it focuses on understanding causal relationships, as evidenced in steps 2 through 5.

The Method's Value

After management had been using the Seven-Step Method in their project teams for about three months, we asked them at a training session to brainstorm regarding what they had learned as a result of the method. The managers overwhelmingly found the method's focus and restraint to be difficult but valuable. They also valued the way the method provides organization, logic, and thoroughness. They were impressed by the use of data instead of opinions. A number of people commented on how they were listening to each other more carefully and respecting each other's ideas more and on how, perhaps because of the focus on data, there had been a lowering of territorial fences and a promotion of cooperation and trust. The manager's perceptions concerning the method were also shaped by the group process skills they had been practicing and the project reviews they had undertaken.

Difficult Issues

The three project teams found several concepts in the first two steps extremely difficult. The first was arriving at a problem statement. The initial tendency was to frame a solution as a problem. The analog of this in the restaurant case study would be to state the problem as "There aren't enough tables" or "The waitresses and waiters need to work harder" instead of "The customers wait too long." Once this hurdle was crossed, there were others. One team needed to agree on several operational definitions before it could even begin to formulate a problem statement. Another team kept revisiting its problem statement during the first four months before settling on one that was consistent with what the team was doing. The third team arrived at a problem statement relatively easily by comparison, but even they struggled.

Localization—the process of focusing on smaller and smaller vital pieces of the problem—is another task that the teams found difficult. Localization is usually achieved by stratifying data using Pareto charts with categorical data and run charts with continuous data. Localization is what makes a problem tractable. Although team members could see the value of localization in solving sample problems, they found it hard to internalize this in solving their own problems. Realizing that their own problems were not overwhelming but instead tractable through localization was an important achievement for the project teams.

There were other issues that proved difficult. It was much easier for the teams to justify the importance of the problem in terms of internal considerations rather than in terms of the customer's key quality characteristics. We sensed that this occurred because the team members had not yet internalized the idea that improvement should be driven by customer requirements, not internal indicators. Some team members could not see the benefits of collecting data accurately and consistently, so they resisted devising ways to accomplish this. The teams had trouble understanding how baseline data would be used to validate a solution. Causes of the problem often crept into discussions where they did not belong. The teams had difficulty keeping an open mind about potential causes. For example, they resisted investigating the effects of variables that they felt were not causes. The teams needed a significant amount of coaching in how to obtain information in a nonthreatening way (through interviews or surveys) from the people who work in the system. The teams also faced several organizational challenges, such as finding the time to work on their projects, arranging meetings, and getting support from workers who were to collect the data.

Questions for Discussion

1. Discuss the Seven-Step Method used for problem solving and process improvement.
2. Discuss the similarities between the Seven-Step Method and Deming's plan-do-check-act (PDCA) cycle.
3. In addition to the waiting time of customers, if you had one or more characteristics that you decided to examine, what method would you have used?
4. Develop a cause-and-effect diagram to conduct dispersion analysis for one of the main causes identified in the case study.
5. What are some of the difficulties faced in applying the Seven-Step Method along with a Project Team Review?

KEY TERMS

Box plot
  Notched
  Variable-width
  Whisker
Cause-and-effect diagram
Cause enumeration
Causes
  Vital few
  Trivial many
Cumulative distribution function
Dispersion analysis
Fishbone diagram
Frequency distribution
  Histogram
Interquartile range
Ishikawa diagram
Kurtosis
Mean
Measure
  Central tendency
  Dispersion
Median
Multivariable chart
Nonconformities
Normal probability plot
Normal distribution
Outlier
Pareto diagram
Percentile
Process analysis
Quantile–quantile plot
Quartile
Radial plot
Range
Run chart
Sample
Scatter diagram
Skewness
Standard deviation
Stem-and-leaf plot
Tail length

EXERCISES

Discussion Questions

4-1 What is the advantage of stem-and-leaf plots over frequency histograms?

4-2 Explain the importance of cause-and-effect diagrams in process improvement. Select a problem of your choice, and draw a cause-and-effect diagram.

4-3 Describe the importance of Pareto diagrams in process improvement.

4-4 What is a box plot used for? How does it help in the assimilation of product or process information?

4-5 Explain the importance of normal probability plots in quality control and improvement.

4-6 Compare and contrast quantile-quantile plots and scatter plots. Explain their roles in product or process improvement.

4-7 What are the advantages of multivariable charts over scatter diagrams in quality improvement?

Problems

4-8 A random sample of 50 observations of the mileage per gallon of a particular brand of gasoline is shown below:

33.2	29.4	36.5	38.1	30.0
29.1	32.2	29.5	36.0	31.5
34.5	33.6	27.4	30.4	28.4
32.6	30.4	31.8	29.8	34.6
30.7	31.9	32.3	28.2	27.5
34.9	32.8	27.7	28.4	28.8
30.2	26.8	27.8	30.5	28.5
31.8	29.2	28.6	27.5	28.5
30.8	31.8	29.1	26.9	34.2
33.5	27.4	28.5	34.8	30.5

a. Construct a frequency histogram.
b. Construct a relative frequency histogram and a cumulative frequency histogram.

c. What conclusions can you draw regarding the product?
d. If the company has a goal of a gas mileage of 31 miles per gallon, is it achieving its objective?

4-9 For the data shown in Exercise 4-8, construct a stem-and-leaf plot. What inferences can you make from the plot?

4-10 For the data in Exercise 4-8, construct a normal probability plot. What inferences can you make from the plot?

4-11 For the data in Exercise 4-8, construct a box plot. What insights do you get from this plot?

4-12 For the data in Exercise 4-8, construct a notched box plot using a 95 percent level of confidence.

4-13 The waiting time (in minutes) before being served in a local post office was observed for 50 randomly chosen customers and is shown below:

2.1	0.5	3.6	1.4	2.0
0.8	0.4	4.2	3.5	2.5
4.8	2.8	1.9	1.2	3.2
1.6	2.5	2.4	1.9	2.0
3.5	5.2	3.1	1.6	1.5
1.9	2.4	2.7	2.1	1.8
4.6	3.8	1.5	4.5	3.9
5.5	2.5	3.8	5.0	4.6
2.1	2.8	1.6	3.8	4.2
3.5	5.2	4.8	3.9	2.6

a. Construct a frequency histogram and a relative frequency histogram.
b. What conclusions can you draw?
c. If the post office's goal is to have a waiting time of less than 4.0 minutes, has this goal been achieved? Comment.

4-14 For the data in Exercise 4-13, construct a stem-and-leaf plot. What inferences can you make?

4-15 For the data in Exercise 4-13, construct a normal probability plot, and comment on the conclusions that you draw from this plot.

4-16 For the data in Exercise 4-13, construct a box plot. What do you conclude from the plot?

4-17 For the data in Exercise 4-13, construct a notched box plot using a 95 percent level of confidence.

4-18 Consider again the situation of problem 4-8. The company, on further experimentation with product development, has come up with a new brand of gasoline. A random sample of 30 observations yielded the following values of mileage per gallon:

32.9	31.5	34.3	36.8	35.0
29.4	33.2	37.8	35.0	32.7
28.5	30.4	32.6	31.5	30.6
35.8	36.4	34.2	35.0	33.5
31.8	32.5	28.4	33.8	35.1
30.2	33.0	34.6	32.4	32.0

a. Construct a relative frequency histogram
b. Has an improvement taken place in the product?
c. Is the company meeting its goal of a gas mileage of 31 miles per gallon?

4-19 Using the data in Exercises 4-8 and 4-18, construct a quantile-quantile plot. What can you conclude from this plot?

4-20 Construct notched box plots using a 95 percent level of confidence of appropriate widths for the data in Exercise 4-8 and 4-18. Can you draw any conclusions on product improvement?

4-21 An analysis of defects of the output from a job shop produced the results listed in the accompanying table.

Type of defect	Frequency	Dollar value (in $1000)
Nonconforming diameter	40	3
Rough surface	80	7
Warped flange	50	2
Nonconforming length	20	1
Nonconforming ream	60	2.5

a. Construct a Pareto diagram and discuss the results.
b. If management has an allocation of $10,000, which problem areas should they tackle?

4-22 The pH values of a dye were found for 30 samples taken consecutively over time. They are listed row-wise as follows:

20.3	15.5	18.2	18.0	20.5	22.8
21.6	21.0	22.5	23.8	23.9	24.2
23.6	24.9	27.4	25.5	20.9	25.8
24.6	25.5	27.3	26.4	26.8	27.5
26.4	26.8	27.2	27.1	27.4	27.8

Construct a run chart. What conclusions can you draw?

4-23 An insurance company is interested in determining if the amount of life insurance coverage is influenced by the amount of disposable income. A randomly chosen sample of size 20 produced the data in the accompanying table. Construct a scatter plot. What conclusions can you draw?

Disposable income (in $1000)	Life insurance coverage (in $1000)	Disposable income (in $1000)	Life insurance coverage (in $1000)
45	60	65	80
40	58	60	90
65	100	45	50
50	50	40	50
70	120	55	70
80	100	55	60
70	80	60	80
40	50	75	100
50	70	45	50
45	60	65	70

4-24 In a chemical process, the parameters of temperature, pressure, proportion of catalyst, and pH value of the mixture are important in influencing the acceptability of the batch. The data in the accompanying table lists the process parameter values and the proportion of nonconforming output based on a sample of 10 values. Draw a multivariable chart. What inferences can you make regarding the desirable values of the process parameters?

Sample number	Temperature (°C)	Pressure (kg/cm^2)	Proportion of catalyst	Acidity (pH value)	Proportion nonconforming
1	300	100	0.03	10	0.080
2	350	90	0.04	20	0.070
3	400	80	0.05	15	0.040
4	500	70	0.06	25	0.060
5	550	60	0.04	10	0.070
6	500	50	0.06	15	0.050
7	450	40	0.05	15	0.055
8	450	30	0.04	20	0.060
9	350	40	0.04	15	0.054
10	400	40	0.04	15	0.052

REFERENCES

Blazek, L. W., Novic, B., and Scott, D. M. (1987). "Displaying Multivariate Data Using Polyplots," *Journal of Quality Technology*, 19(2) pp. 69–74.

Bruntz, S. M., Cleveland, W. S., Kleiner, B., and Warner, S. L. (1974). "The Dependence of Ambient Ozone on Solar Radiation, Wind, Temperature, and Mixing a height," *Proceedings of the Symposium of Atmospheric Diffusion of Air Pollution*. American Meteorological Society, pp. 125–128.

Chambers, John M. (1977). *Computational Methods for Data Analysis*. Wiley, New York.

Chambers, John M., Cleveland, William S., Kleiner, Beat, and Tukey, Paul A. (1983). *Graphical Methods for Data Analysis*. Wadsworth International Group, Belmont, CA.

Chernoff, H. (1973), "The Use of Faces to Represent Points in *K*-Dimensional Space Graphically," *Journal of the American Statistical Association*, 68, pp. 361–368.

Duncan, Acheson J. (1986). *Quality Control and Industrial Statistics*, 5th edition. Richard D. Irwin, Homewood, IL.

Friedman, H. P., Farrell, E. S., Goldwyn, R. M., Miller, M., and Siegel, S. H. (1972). "A Graphic Way of Describing Changing Multivariate Patterns," *Proceedings of the Sixth Interface Symposium on Computer Science and Statistics*. University of California, Berkeley, CA, pp. 56–59.

Gnanadesikan, R. (1977). *Methods of Statistical Data Analysis of Multivariate Observations*. Wiley, New York.

Gaudard, M., Coates, R., and Freeman, L. (1991). "Accelerating Improvement," *Quality Progress*, 24 (10), pp. 81–88.

Ishikawa, Kaoru (1976). *Guide to Quality Control*. Asian Productivity Organization, Nordica International Limited, Hong Kong. (Available in the United States from UNIPUB, New York.)

Kendall, M. G., and Stuart, A. (1967). *The Advanced Theory of Statistics*, 2nd edition, Vol. 1. Hafner, New York.

Kleiner, B., and Hartigan, J. A. (1981). "Representing Points in Many Dimensions by Trees and Castles," *Journal of the American Statistical Association*, 76, pp. 260–276.

McGill, R., Tukey, J. W., and Larsen, W. A. (1978). "Variations of Box Plots," *The American Statistician*, 32(1), pp. 12–16.

Massey, Frank J., Jr. (1951). "The Kolmogorov-Smirnov Test of Goodness of Fit," *Journal of the American Statistical Association*, 46, pp. 68–78.

Michael, J. R. (1983). "The Stabilized Probability Plot," *Biometrika*, 70(1), pp. 11-17.

Nelson, W. (1979). *How to Analyze Data With Simple Plots*. American Society for Quality Control, Milwaukee, WI.

SAS Institute Inc. (1990). *SAS/STAT User's Guide: Volumes 1 and 2*, Version 6, 4th edition. Cary, NC.

PART III

Statistical Process Control

CHAPTER

5

Statistical Process Control Using Control Charts

CHAPTER OUTLINE

SYMBOLS

θ	Parameter
$\hat{\theta}$	Estimator
α	Probability of a Type I error
β	Probability of a Type II error
$\sigma_{\bar{X}}$	Standard deviation of sample mean
σ	Process standard deviation
n	Subgroup or sample size

5-1 INTRODUCTION

The importance of satisfying the customer with a product or service has already been discussed. An acceptable and attractive product or service can be achieved by having an adequate process capable of meeting or exceeding customer requirements. Part III of this book deals with the topic of process control and improvement. It provides the necessary background for understanding statistical process control using control charts. This chapter provides the foundations for using control charts. Chapter 6 gives details on control charts for variables, and Chapter 7 discusses control charts for attributes. Process capability analysis is covered in Chapter 8.

A *control chart* is a graphical tool for monitoring the activity of an ongoing process. Control charts are sometimes referred to as *Shewhart control charts,* because Walter A. Shewhart first proposed their general theory. The value of the quality characteristic to be monitored is plotted along the vertical axis, while the horizontal axis represents the samples, or subgroups (in order of time), from which the quality characteristic is found. Figure 5-1 shows a typical control chart. Some examples of quality characteristics are average length, average diameter, average tensile strength, average resistance, and average service time. All of these characteristics are called variables, and numerical values can be obtained for each. The term attribute applies to such quality characteristics as the proportion of nonconforming items, the number of nonconformities in a unit, and the number of demerits per unit. Samples of a certain size (say, 4 or 5 items) are selected, and the quality characteristic (say, average length) is calculated based on the number of items in the sample. These characteristics are then plotted in the order in which the samples were taken.

Three lines are indicated on the control chart. The *center line,* which typically represents the average value of the characteristic that is being plotted, is an indication of where the process is centered. Two limits, the *upper control limit* and the *lower control limit,* are used to make decisions regarding the process. If the points plot within the control limits and do not exhibit any identifiable pattern, the process is said to be in *statistical control.* If a point plots outside the control limits or if an identifiable nonrandom pattern exists (such as 12 out of 14 successive points plotting above the center line), the process is said to be out of statistical control. Details will be given later as to specific rules regarding out-of-control conditions.

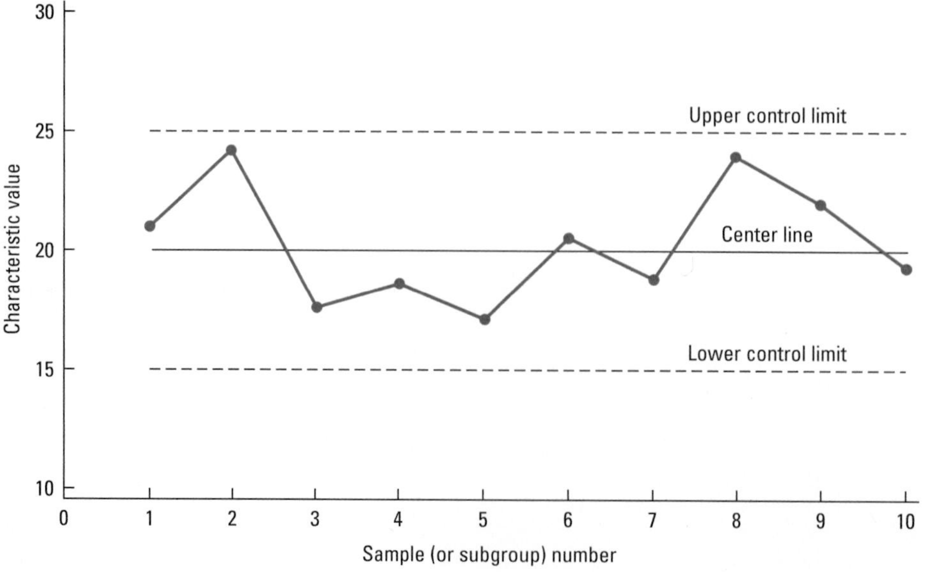

Figure 5-1 Typical control chart.

Several benefits can be realized by using control charts. Such charts indicate the following:

1. *When to take corrective action.* A control chart serves as a guide to indicate when something is possibly wrong with a process such that corrective action is needed.
2. *Type of remedial action necessary.* The pattern of the plot on a control chart may provide diagnostic information about possible causes and hence possible types of remedial actions that may be taken.
3. *When to leave a process alone.* Variation is a part of any process. A control chart can be used to determine when an exhibited variability is normal and inherent such that no corrective action is necessary. As explained in Chapter 2, inappropriate overcontrol of a process through frequent adjustments will only increase the variability of that process.
4. *Process capability.* If the control chart shows a process to be in statistical control, one can estimate the capability of the process and hence its ability to meet customer requirements. This will also help product and process design.
5. *Possible means of quality improvement.* In addition to assisting in the control of a process, the control chart may be used as a base for instituting and measuring quality improvement. Control charts can provide useful information regarding actions to take for quality improvement.
6. *How to set product specifications.* Since the information from control charts may be used to determine the capability of a process, this information (when coupled with customer requirements) may help in determining realistic product specifications. Furthermore, if information from a control chart tells us that a process is not capable of producing a product that satisfies customer requirements, we would focus on quality improvement and changes in the existing process to meet the desirable standards.

5-2 CAUSES OF VARIATION

Variability is a part of any process, no matter how sophisticated, so management and operators must understand it. Several factors over which we have some control, such as methods, equipment, people, materials, and policies, exert an influence on variability. Environmental factors may also contribute. The causes of variation may be subdivided into two groups—chance causes and assignable causes.

Chance Causes

Variability due to chance causes is something inherent to a process. It always exists, and it is referred to as the natural variation in a process. This variation is the effect of many small causes and cannot be totally eliminated. When this variation is small, we have what is known as a stable system of chance causes. A process that is operating under a stable system of chance causes is said to be in *statistical control.* Deming refers to such causes as common causes of variation. Examples include inherent variation in incoming raw material from a qualified vendor, a lack of adequate supervision skills, the vibration of machines, and fluctuations in working conditions. Management—not workers—should be held responsible for such problems with the system. Deming believes that about 85 percent of all problems are due to common causes and hence can be solved only by action on the part of management. In a control chart, if quality characteristic values are within the control limits and no nonrandom pattern is visible, it is assumed that a system of chance causes exists and that the process is in a state of statistical control.

Assignable Causes

Variability caused by assignable cause is something for which an identifiable reason can be determined. The magnitude of variation in this circumstance is greater than that due to chance causes. Examples of such causes may be use of a wrong tool, an improper raw material, and an operator error. Deming refers to these as special causes. With control charts, if an observation falls outside the control limits or if a nonrandom pattern is exhibited, assignable causes are assumed to exist, and the process is said to be out of control. One objective of a control chart is to detect the presence of assignable causes as soon as possible to allow appropriate corrective action. Once the assignable causes are eliminated through remedial actions, the process is again brought to a state of statistical control. Deming believes that 15 percent of all problems are due to special causes. Actions on the part of management as well as the workers will reduce the occurrence of such causes. Control of a process is achieved through the elimination of assignable causes. Improvement of a process is accomplished through the reduction of chance causes.

5-3 STATISTICAL BASIS FOR CONTROL CHARTS

Basic Principles

Normal distributions play an important role in the use of control charts (Duncan, 1986). A control chart has a center line and lower and upper control limits. The center line is usually found in accordance with the data in the samples. It is an indication of the location (or mean) of a process and is usually found by taking the average of the values in the sample. Sometimes, however, the center line may be a desirable target or standard value.

The values of the statistic plotted on a control chart (for example, average diameter) are assumed to have an approximately normal distribution. For large sample sizes or for small sample sizes with population distribution that is close to symmetric and unimodal, the Central Limit Theorem states that if the plotted statistic is a sample average, it will tend to have a normal distribution. Thus, even if the parent population is not normally distributed, control charts for averages and other related statistics are based on normal distributions.

The control limits are two lines, one above and one below the center line, that aid in the decision-making process when using a control chart. These limits are chosen so that the probability of the sample points falling between them is almost one (usually about 99.7 percent for 3σ limits) if the process is in statistical control. As discussed previously, if a system is operating under a stable system of chance causes, it is assumed to be in statistical control. Typical control limits are placed at three standard deviations away from the mean of the statistic being plotted. Normal distribution theory states that a sample statistic will fall within the limits 99.74 percent of the time if the process is in control. If a point falls outside the control limits, there is a reason to believe that an assignable cause exists in the system. One must then try to identify the assignable cause and take corrective action to bring the process back to control.

The most common basis for deciding whether a process is out of control is the presence of a sample statistic outside the control limits. Other rules exist for determining out-of-control process conditions and will be discussed in detail later. These other rules focus on nonrandom or systematic behavior of a process as evidenced by a nonrandom plot pattern. For example, if seven successive points plot above the center line but within the upper control limit, there is a reason to believe that something might be wrong with the process. If the process were in control, the chances of this happening would be extremely small. Such a pattern might suggest that the process mean has shifted upward. Hence, appropriate actions would need to be identified in order to lower the process mean.

A control chart is a means of *on-line* process control. Data values are collected for a process, and the appropriate sample statistics (such as sample mean, sample range, or sample standard deviation) based on the quality characteristic of interest (such as diameter, length, or strength) are obtained. These sample statistics are then plotted on a control chart. If they fall within the control limits and do not exhibit any systematic or nonrandom pattern, the process may be judged to be in statistical control. If the control limits are calculated from current data, the chart tells us whether the process is presently in control. If the control limits were calculated from previous data based on a process that was in control, the chart can be used to determine if the process has drifted out of control.

Control charts can serve as management control tools. If management has in mind some target value of the process mean (say, average part strength), a control chart can be constructed with that target value as the center line. Sample statistics obtained from the process, when plotted on the control chart, will show how close the actual process output comes to the desirable standard. If the deviation is unsatisfactory to management, they will have to come up with remedial actions. Control charts can also help management set realistic goals. For example, suppose the output of a process shows that the average part strength is 3000 kg, with a standard deviation of 100 kg. If management has a target average strength of at least 3500 kg, the control chart will indicate that such a goal is unrealistic and may not be feasible for the existing process. Major changes in the system and process, possible only through action on the part of management, will be needed to create a process that will meet the desirable goal.

If a process is in statistical control, then control chart information may be used to estimate such process parameters as the process mean, process standard deviation, and the proportion of nonconforming items (also known as fallout). These estimates can then be used to determine the capability of the process. Capability refers to the ability of the process to produce within desirable specifications (ASQC, 1987; Montgomery, 1991). Conclusions drawn from studies of process capability have a tremendous influence on major management decisions such as whether to make or subcontract, how to direct capital expenditures for machinery, how to select and control vendors, and how to implement process improvements to reduce variability. Process capability is discussed in Chapter 8.

For variables, the value of a quality characteristic is measurable on a numerical scale. Control charts for variables are constructed to show measures of central tendency as well as dispersion. Variable control charts display such information as sample mean, sample range, sample standard deviation, cumulative sum, individual values, and moving average. Control charts for variables are described in Chapter 6. Attributes, on the other hand, indicate the presence or absence of a condition. Typical attribute charts deal with the fraction of nonconforming items, the number of nonconforming items, the total number of nonconformities, the number of nonconformities per unit, or the number of demerits per unit. Control charts for attributes are described in Chapter 7.

There are several issues pertinent to the construction of a control chart: the number of items that are in a sample or subgroup, the frequency with which subgroups are to be selected, the means of minimizing possible errors in making inferences from control charts, the analysis and interpretation of the plot patterns, and rules for determining out-of-control conditions. These are discussed in the following sections.

Making inferences from a control chart is analogous to conducting a test of a hypothesis. For instance, suppose we are interested in testing the null hypothesis that the average diameter θ of a part from a particular process is 25 mm. This situation is represented by the null hypothesis H_o: $\theta = 25$ versus the alternative hypothesis H_a: $\theta \neq 25$. The rejection region of the null hypothesis is thus two-tailed. The control limits serve as the critical points that separate the rejection and acceptance regions. If a sample value (sample average diameter, in this case) falls above the upper control limit or below the lower control limit, we will reject the null hypothesis. In such a case we will conclude that the process mean differs from 25 mm and that the process is therefore out of control.

Selection of Control Limits

Let θ represent a quality characteristic of interest and $\hat{\theta}$ represent an estimate of θ. For example, θ could be the mean diameter of parts produced by a process and $\hat{\theta}$ would be the sample average diameter of a set of parts chosen from the process. Let $E(\hat{\theta})$ represent the mean, or expected value, and let $SD(\hat{\theta})$ be the standard deviation of the estimator $\hat{\theta}$.

The center line and control limits for this arrangement are given by

$$\begin{aligned} CL &= E(\hat{\theta}) \\ UCL &= E(\hat{\theta}) + k\ SD(\hat{\theta}) \\ LCL &= E(\hat{\theta}) - k\ SD(\hat{\theta}) \end{aligned} \tag{5.1}$$

where k represents the number of standard deviations of the sample statistic that the control limits are to be placed from the center line. Typically, the value of k is chosen to be 3 (hence the name 3σ limits).

If the sample statistic can be assumed to have an approximately normal distribution, a value of $k = 3$ implies that there is a probability of only 0.0026 of a sample statistic falling outside the control limits if the process is in control.

Sometimes, the value of k in Equation 5.1 may be selected based on a desired probability of the sample statistic falling outside the control limits when the process is in control. Such limits are known as *probability limits*. For example, if we desire the probability of the sample statistic falling outside the control limits to be 0.002, then Appendix A-3 gives $k = 3.09$ (assuming the sample statistic is normally distributed). The probabilities of the sample statistic falling above the upper control limit and below the lower control limit are each equal to 0.001. Using this principle, the value of k and hence the control limits may be found for any desired probability.

The choice of k is influenced by error considerations also. As is discussed later, there are two types of errors (Type I and Type II) that can be made in drawing conclusions from control charts. The choice of a value k is influenced by how significant we consider the impact of such errors to be.

Example 5-1: A semiautomatic turret lathe machines the thickness of a part that is subsequently used in an assembly. The process mean is known to be 30 mm with a standard deviation of 1.5 mm. Construct a control chart for the average thickness using 3σ limits if samples of size 5 are randomly selected from the process. Table 5-1 shows the average thickness of 15 samples selected from the process. Plot these on a control chart, and make inferences.

Solution. The center line is

$$CL = 30 \text{ mm}$$

The standard deviation of the sample mean $\overline{X}$ is given by

$$\sigma_{\overline{X}} = \frac{\sigma}{\sqrt{n}} = \frac{1.5}{\sqrt{5}} = 0.671$$

TABLE 5-1 Average part thickness values

Sample number	Average part thickness $\overline{X}$, mm
1	31.56
2	29.50
3	30.50
4	30.72
5	28.92
6	31.45
7	29.70
8	31.48
9	29.52
10	28.30
11	30.20
12	29.10
13	30.85
14	31.55
15	29.43

Assuming a normal distribution of the sample mean diameters, the value of k in Equation 5.1 is selected as 3. The control limits are calculated as follows:

$$UCL = 30 + 3(0.671) = 32.013$$
$$LCL = 30 - 3(0.671) = 27.987$$

The center line and control limits of the control chart for the average thickness are shown in Figure 5-2. The sample means for the 15 samples shown in Table 5-1 are plotted on this control chart. Figure 5-2 shows that all of the sample means are within the control limits. Also, the pattern of the plot does not exhibit any nonrandom behavior. Thus we conclude that the process is in control.

Errors in Making Inferences from Control Charts

There are two types of errors—Type I and Type II—that can be made when making inferences from control charts.

Type I Errors Type I errors result from inferring that a process is out of control when it is actually in control. The probability of a Type I error is denoted by α. Suppose a process is in control such that only a system of chance causes is present. If a point on the control chart falls outside the control limits, we will assume that the process is out of control. However, since the control limits are a finite distance (usually three standard deviations) away from the mean, there is a small chance (about 0.0026) of a sample statistic falling outside the control limits. In such instances, inferring that the process is out-of-control is a wrong conclusion. Figure 5-3 shows the probability of a Type I error in making inferences from control charts. It is the sum of the two tail areas outside the control limits.

Type II Errors Type II errors result from inferring that a process is in control when it is really out

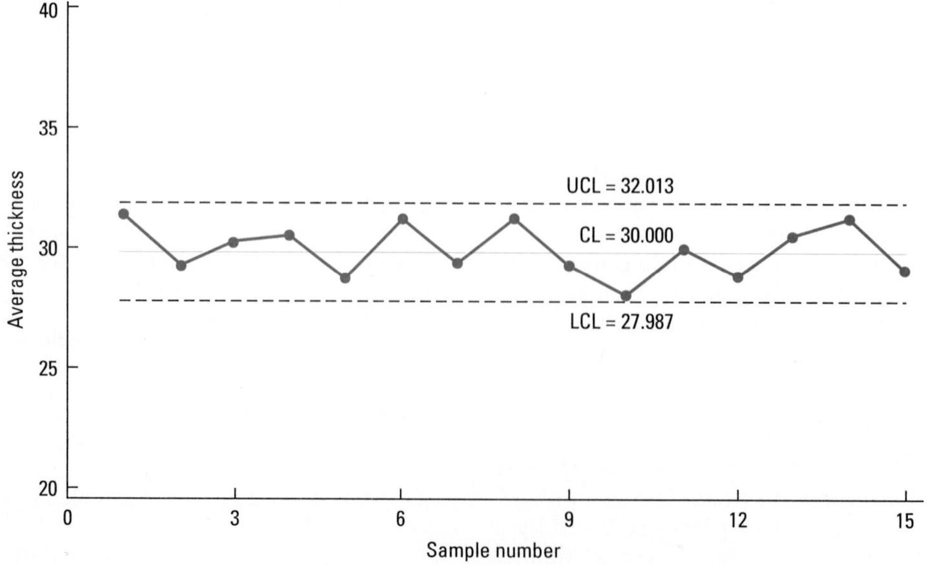

Figure 5-2 Control chart for average thickness.

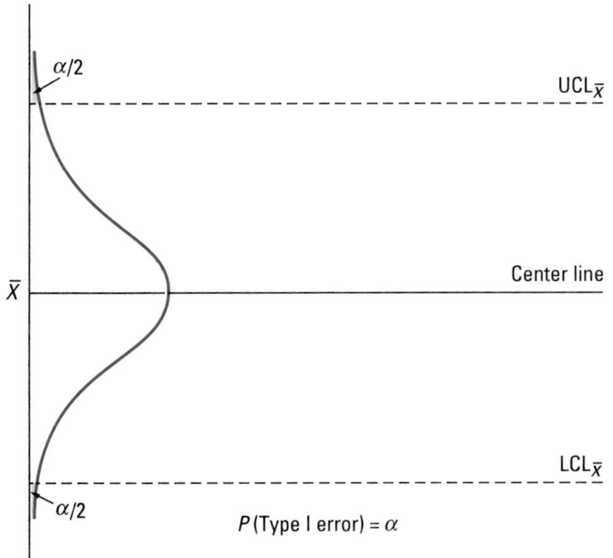

Figure 5-3 Type I error in control charts.

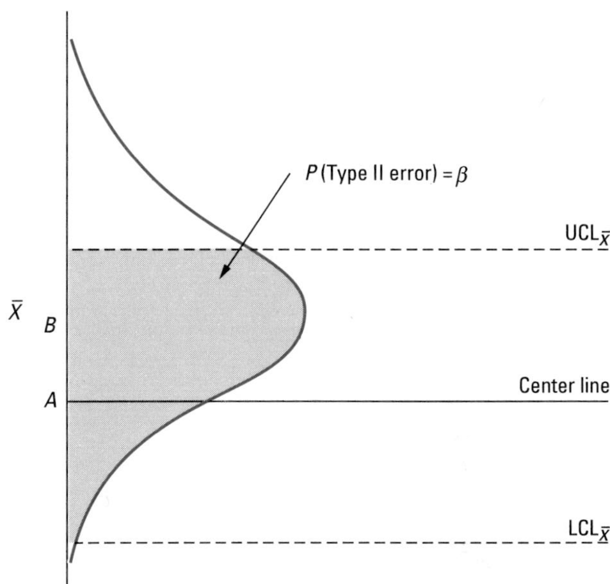

Figure 5-4 Type II error in control charts.

of control. If no observations fall outside the control limits, only chance or common causes are assumed, and we conclude that the process is in control. Suppose, however, that a process is actually out of control. This may happen because of a change in the process mean (say, due to an operator inadvertently changing a depth of cut or a change in the quality level of raw materials from a new vendor). Or, the process could go out of control because of a change in the process variability (say, due to the presence of a new operator). Under such circumstances, it is still probable that a sample statistic would fall within the control limits, but concluding that the process is in control is a Type II error.

Consider Figure 5-4, which depicts a process going out of control due to a change in the process mean from A to B. For this situation, the correct conclusion is that the process is out of control. However, there is a strong possibility of the sample statistic falling within the control limits (as indicated by the shaded area in Figure 5-4), in which case we would conclude that the process is in control.

Example 5-2: A control chart is to be constructed for the average breaking strength of nylon fibers. Samples of size 5 are randomly chosen from the process. The process mean and standard deviation are estimated to be 120 kg and 8 kg, respectively.

a. If the control limits are placed three standard deviations away from the process mean, what is the probability of a Type I error?

Solution. From the problem information, $\hat{\mu} = 120$ and $\hat{\sigma} = 8$. The center line for the control chart is at 120 kg. The control limits are

$$\text{UCL}_{\bar{X}} = 120 + 3\left(\frac{8}{\sqrt{5}}\right) = 130.733$$

$$\text{LCL}_{\bar{X}} = 120 - 3\left(\frac{8}{\sqrt{5}}\right) = 109.267$$

These limits are shown in Figure 5-5a.

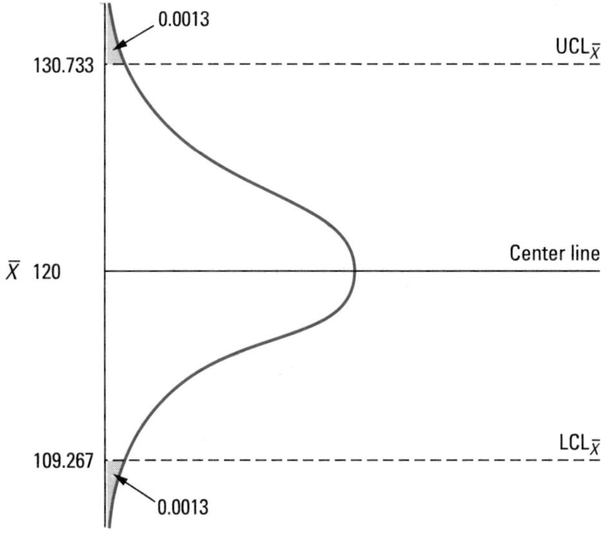

Figure 5-5 (*a*) Probability of a Type I error.

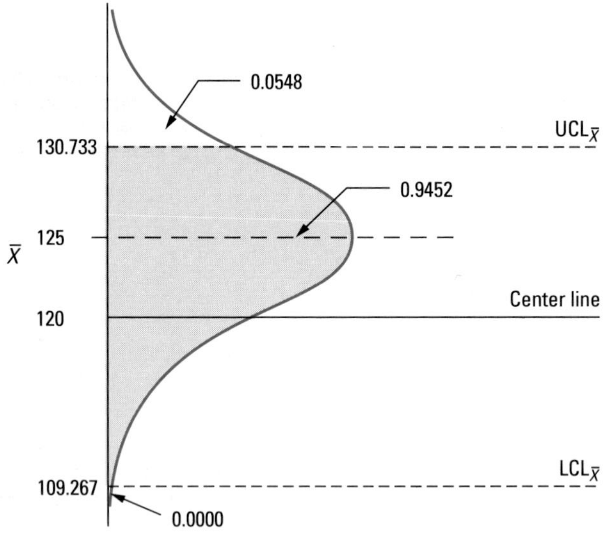

Figure 5-5 *(Continued)* (*b*) Probability of a Type II error.

Since the control limits are placed three standard deviations away, the standardized normal value at the upper control limit is

$$Z = \frac{\overline{X} - \mu}{\sigma_{\overline{X}}} = \frac{130.733 - 120}{8/\sqrt{5}} = 3.00$$

Similarly, the Z-value at the lower control limit is -3.00. For these Z-values in the standard normal table in Appendix A-3, each tail area is found to be 0.0013. The probability of a Type I error, as shown by the shaded tail areas in Figure 5-5*a*, is therefore 0.0026.

b. If the process mean shifts to 125 kg, what is the probability of concluding that the process is in control and hence making a Type II error on the first subgroup plotted after the shift?

Solution. The process mean shifts to 125 kg. Assuming that the process standard deviation is the same as before, the distribution of the sample means is shown in Figure 5-5*b*. The probability of concluding that the process is in control is equivalent to finding the area between the control limits under the distribution shown in Figure 5-5*b*. We find the standardized normal value at the upper control limit as

$$Z_1 = \frac{130.733 - 125}{8/\sqrt{5}} = 1.60$$

From the standard normal table in Appendix A-3, the tail area above the upper control limit is 0.0548. The standardized normal value at the lower control limit is

$$Z_2 = \frac{109.267 - 125}{8/\sqrt{5}} = -4.40$$

From Appendix A-3, the tail area below the lower control limit is 0.0000. The area between the control limits is $1 - (0.0548 + 0.0000) = 0.9452$. Hence, the probability of concluding that the process is in control and making a Type II error is 0.9452 or 94.52%. This implies that for a shift of this magnitude, there is a pretty good chance of not detecting it on the first subgroup drawn after the shift.

c. What is the probability of detecting the shift by the second subgroup plotted after the shift if the subgroups are chosen independently?

Solution. The probability of detecting the shift *by* the second subgroup point plotted after the shift is P (detecting shift on first subgroup) + P (not detecting shift on first subgroup and detecting shift on second subgroup). This first probability was found in part b to be 0.0548. The second probability, using Equations 3.2 and 3.5, is found to be $(1 - 0.0548)(0.0548) = 0.0518$, assuming independence of the two subgroups. The total probability is $0.0548 + 0.0518 = 0.1066$. Thus, there is a 10.66 percent chance of detecting the shift in the process by the second subgroup plotted after the shift.

Operating Characteristic (OC) Curve An operating characteristic (OC) curve is a measure of goodness of a control chart's ability to detect changes in process parameters. Specifically, it is a plot of the probability of the Type II error versus the shifting value of a process parameter from its value while in control. OC curves enable us to determine the chances of not detecting a shift of a certain magnitude in a process parameter by means of a control chart.

A typical OC curve is shown in Figure 5-6. The shape of an OC curve is similar to an inverted S.

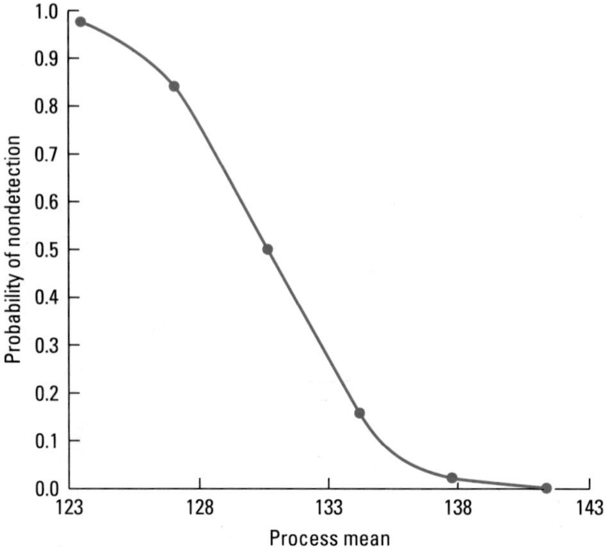

Figure 5-6 Operating characteristic curve for a control chart.

For small shifts in the process parameter, the probability of nondetection is high. As the change in the process parameter increases, the probability of nondetection decreases. For large changes, the probability of nondetection is very close to zero. The discriminatory power of a control chart to quickly detect changes in process parameter values is indicated by the steepness of the OC curve and the quickness with which the probability of nondetection approaches zero. Calculations for constructing an operating characteristic curve are identical to those for finding the probability of a Type II error.

Example 5-3: Refer to the data in Example 5-2 involving the control chart for the average breaking strength of nylon fibers. Samples of size 5 are randomly chosen from a process whose mean and standard deviation are estimated to be 120 kg and 8 kg, respectively. Construct the operating characteristic curve for increases in the process mean from 120 kg.

Solution. A sample calculation for the probability of the shift not being detected when the process mean increases to 125 kg, was given in Example 5-2. This same procedure is used to calculate the probabilities of nondetection for several values of the process mean. Table 5-2 displays some sample calculations. The vertical axis of the operating characteristic curve in Figure 5-6 represents the values for probability of nondetection given in Table 5-2 (these values are also the probabilities of a Type II error). The graph shows that for changes in the process mean exceeding 15 kg, the probability of nondetection is fairly small (less than 10 percent), while shifts of 5 kg have a high probability (over 85 percent) of nondetection.

Effect of Control Limits on Errors in Inference Making

The choice of the control limits influences the likelihood of occurrence of Type I and Type II errors. As the control limits are placed further apart, the probability of a Type I error decreases (refer back to Figure 5-3). For control limits placed three standard deviations away from the center line, the probability of a Type I error is about 0.0026. If the control limits are placed at 2.5 standard deviations from the center line, Appendix A-3 gives the probability of a Type I error as 0.0124. On the other hand, if the control limits are placed at 4 standard deviations from the mean, the probability of a Type I error is negligible. If a process is in control, the chance of a sample statistic falling outside the control limits decreases as the control limits expand. Hence, the probability of making a Type I error decreases, too. The control limits could be placed sufficiently far apart, say 4 or 5 standard deviations on each side of the center line, to reduce the probability of a Type I error, but doing so would have an effect on the probability of making a Type II error. Movement of the control limits has the opposite effect on the probability of a Type II error as compared to the probability of a Type I error. As the control limits are placed further apart, the probability of a Type II error increases (refer back to Figure 5-4). Ideally, to reduce the probability of a Type II error, we would tend to have the control limits placed closer to each other. But this, of course, has the detrimental effect of increasing the probability of a Type I error. Thus, the two types of errors are inversely related to each other as the control limits change. As the probability of a Type I error decreases, the probability of a Type II error increases.

If all other process parameters are held fixed, a decrease in the probability of a Type II error will occur with an increase in sample size. As n increases, the standard deviation of the sampling distribution of the sample mean decreases. Thus the control limits will be drawn closer, and the probability of a Type II error will be reduced. Figure 5-7 demonstrates this effect. The new sample size is larger than the old sample size. The sampling distribution of the new sample mean has a reduced variance, so the new control limits are closer to each other. As can be seen from the figure, the probability of a Type II error is smaller than what it was for the smaller sample size.

Because of the inverse relationship between Type I and Type II errors as a function of the control limits, a judicious choice of the control limits is desirable.

TABLE 5-2 Computation of probabilities for OC curve

Process mean	Z-value at UCL, Z_1	Area above UCL	Z-value at LCL, Z_2	Area below LCL	Probability of nondetection
123.578	2.00	0.0228	−4.00	0.0000	0.9772
127.156	1.00	0.1587	−5.00	0.0000	0.8422
130.733	0.00	0.5000	−6.00	0.0000	0.5000
134.311	−1.00	0.8413	−7.00	0.0000	0.1587
137.888	−2.00	0.9772	−8.00	0.0000	0.0228
141.466	−3.00	0.9987	−9.00	0.0000	0.0013

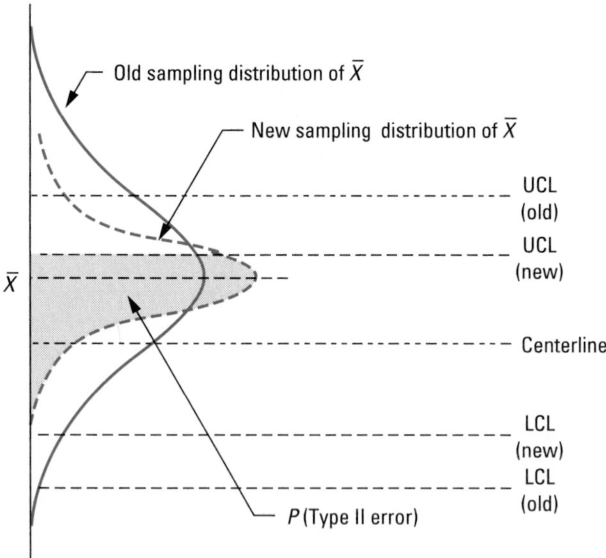

Figure 5-7 Effect of an increase in sample size on the probability of a Type II error.

In the majority of uses of control charts, the control limits are placed at three standard deviations from the center line, thereby restricting the probability of a Type I error to 0.0026. The reasoning behind this choice of limits is that the chart user does not want to often look unnecessarily for assignable causes in a process when there are none. By placing the control limits at three standard deviations, the probability of a false alarm is small, and minimal resources will be spent on locating nonexistent problems with the process. However, the probability of a Type II error may be large for small shifts in the process average. Thus, if it is more important to a company to detect small changes in the process than to avoid spending time looking for nonexistent problems, it may be desirable to place the control limits closer to each other (at, say, 2 or 2.5 standard deviations from the mean). For sophisticated processes it may be crucial to detect small changes as soon as possible, since if they are not detected right away, the impact on the downstream activities is enormous. In this case, management would prefer to have tighter control limits, even if it means incurring some costs for unnecessary investigation of problems when the process is in control.

Warning Limits

Warning limits are two horizontal lines, usually placed at two standard deviations on each side of the center line. If a sample statistic falls outside the warning limits but within the control limits, the process is not considered to be out of control, but it serves as a warning to the user. It may imply an increased likelihood of the process going out of control. If the sample statistic is normally distributed, Appendix A-3 gives the probability of it falling in the band between the warning limit and the control limit to be 0.043 (that is, there is about a 4.3 percent chance of it happening). So if it does happen, there is reason to be wary of the process going out of control. If two successive sample statistics fall within the band between the warning and control limits, there may be sufficient reason to believe that the process is indeed out of control, because the chance of this happening if the process is in control is very small (0.0018, obtained from 0.043 × 0.043).

Effect of Sample Size on Control Limits

The sample size usually has an influence on the standard deviation of the sample statistic being plotted on the control chart. For example, consider a control chart for the sample mean $\overline{X}$. The standard deviation of $\overline{X}$ is given by

$$\sigma_{\overline{X}} = \frac{\sigma}{\sqrt{n}}$$

where σ represents the process standard deviation and n is the subgroup size. We see that the standard deviation of $\overline{X}$ is inversely related to the square root of the subgroup size. Since the control limits are placed a certain number of standard deviations (say, three) from the center line, an increase in the subgroup size causes the control limits to be drawn closer. Similarly, decreasing the subgroup size causes the limits to expand. Increasing the sample size provides more information, intuitively speaking, and causes the sample statistics to have less variability. A lower variability reduces the frequency with which errors occur in making inferences.

5-4 SELECTION OF RATIONAL SUBGROUPS

Walter A. Shewhart described the fundamental criteria for the selection of rational subgroups. The premise is that a *rational subgroup* is chosen in such a manner that the variation within it is considered to be due only to chance causes. So, subgroups are selected such that if assignable causes are present, the differences between subgroups will be maximized, and differences within subgroups will be minimized.

In most cases, time order is a basis for the choice of rational subgroups. For example, consider a job shop with several machines. Samples or subgroups could be collected at random times from each machine. Control charts for the average value of the characteristic for each machine would be plotted separately. If there are two operators producing output, subgroups would be formed from the output of each operator. A separate control chart would be plotted for each operator. If there is a difference in the output between two shifts, then when selecting rational subgroups, the two outputs should not be mixed together. Rather, subgroups should first be selected from the first shift only. A control chart should be constructed to determine the stability of that shift's output. Next, rational subgroups should be selected from the second shift, and a control chart should monitor the output from this process.

In terms of how to select individual units in a subgroup, two approaches may be used (Besterfield, 1990). In the first approach, known as the *instant-of-time method,* individual observations are selected from those produced at approximately the same time for the population under consideration. This method provides a time frame to be associated with each subgroup. An advantage of this method is the ease with which any problems with the process are identified. If the goal is to identify shifts in process parameters, the instant-of-time method will create an environment for the detection of such shifts. It affords minimum variability within a subgroup and maximum variability between subgroups if assignable causes are present.

The second approach is known as the *period-of-time method.* Here, observations are selected randomly from the process output such that they are representative of those that were produced since the time when the previous sample was drawn. If the objective is to decide whether all of the products produced since the previous sample was drawn are acceptable, this method might be appropriate. If the process goes out of control at periodic intervals, subgroups selected using the instant-of-time method will not indicate such changes unless the subgroups happen to be chosen during those periods. With the period-of-time method, information about the subgroups may represent composite information about the overall process conditions, both in and out of control.

Subgroup Size

Selecting subgroup size—the number of items in each subgroup—is a necessity in using control charts. The degree of shift in the process parameter that is expected to take place will influence the choice of subgroup size. As seen in the discussion of operating characteristic curves, large shifts in a process parameter (say, the process mean) may be detected by samples of smaller size than those needed to detect smaller shifts. Having an idea of the degree of shift in the process parameter that we wish to detect enables us to select an appropriate sample size. If we can tolerate smaller changes in the process parameters, then a small sample size might suffice. Alternatively, if it is important to detect slight changes in process parameters, a larger sample size will be needed.

Frequency of Sampling

In addition to sample size, the frequency of sampling is also a factor that must be decided upon prior to the construction of control charts. Ideally, the sampling scheme that will provide the most information for the detection of changes in process parameters is to choose large samples very frequently. However, this may not be feasible at times due to resource constraints. The available options are usually to either choose small sample sizes at frequent intervals or choose large sample sizes at infrequent intervals. In practice, the former is usually adopted. There are some other factors which influence the frequency of sampling and the sample size. The type of inspection needed to obtain the measurement, that is, destructive or nondestructive, could be a factor. The current state of the process, (in control or out of control) influences the choice of both the sample size and frequency of sampling. If the process is quite stable and in control, we could get by with samples chosen at infrequent intervals. However, for processes that indicate greater variability, one would need to choose samples more frequently. The cost of sampling and inspection per unit is another area of concern. An intangible cost is the loss due to the process being out of control and the customer dissatisfaction that results, which is sometimes difficult to identify and quantify. The choice of sample size is influenced by the loss incurred due to a nonconforming item being passed on to the consumer. Note that larger sample sizes will detect shifts in process parameters sooner than smaller sample sizes.

5-5 ANALYSIS OF PATTERNS IN CONTROL CHARTS

One of the main objectives of using a control chart is to determine when a process is out of control so that necessary actions may be taken. The position of the control limits affects decision making because of its impact on the risks of Type I and Type II errors. As mentioned before, the plot pattern may indicate whether the process is in control or not; a systematic or nonrandom pattern suggests an out-of-control process. Control charts offer the ability to determine when to leave a process alone and when to make changes. There are a few other criteria in addition to the presence of a plotted point falling outside the control limits that are used to determine whether a process is out of control. These are described in the next subsection. Later, some typical control chart patterns and the reasons for their occurrence are discussed. Analyzing the patterns on a control chart is more difficult than plotting the chart. Identifying the associated causes of nonrandom patterns requires a knowledge of the process, equipment, and operating conditions as well as their impact on the characteristic of interest.

Some Rules for Identifying an Out-of-Control Process

Rule 1 A process is assumed to be out of control if a single point plots outside the control limits.

This rule is the most commonly used one. If the control limits are placed at three standard deviations away from the mean of the quality characteristic being plotted (assuming a normal distribution), the probability of a point falling outside these limits if the process is in control is very small (about 0.0026). Figure 5-8*a* depicts this situation.

Rule 2 A process is assumed to be out of control if two out of three consecutive points fall outside the 2σ warning limits on the same side of the center line.

Warning limits at two standard deviations of the quality characteristic from the center line can be constructed. These are known as 2σ limits. If the process is in control, the chance of two of the three points falling outside the warning limits is small. In Figure 5-8*b*, observe that sample numbers 7 and 9 fall above the upper 2σ limit. We can infer that this process has gone out of control, so assignable causes should be investigated.

Rule 3 A process is assumed to be out of control if four out of five consecutive points fall beyond the 1σ limit on the same side of the center line.

If the control limits are first determined, then the standard deviation can be calculated. Note that the distance between the center line and the upper con-

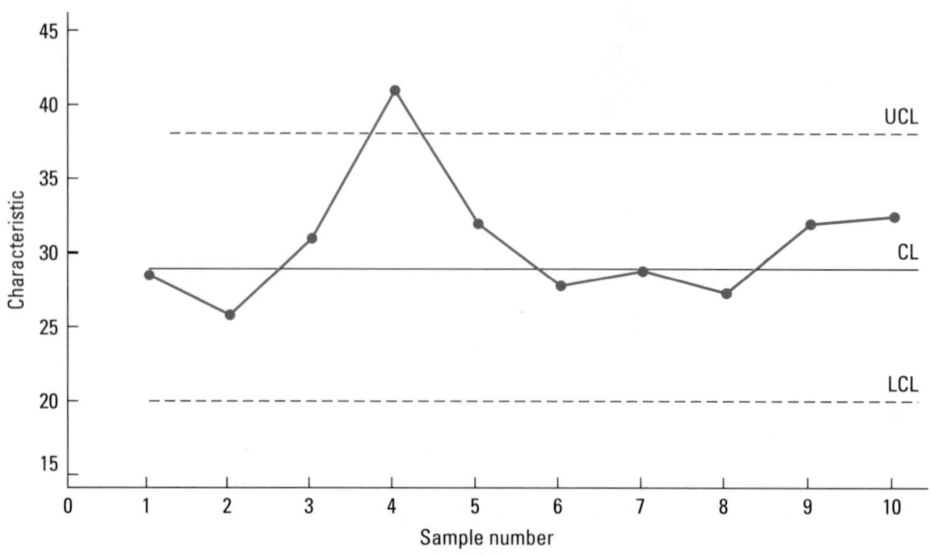

Figure 5-8 Out of control patterns (*a*) Rule 1.

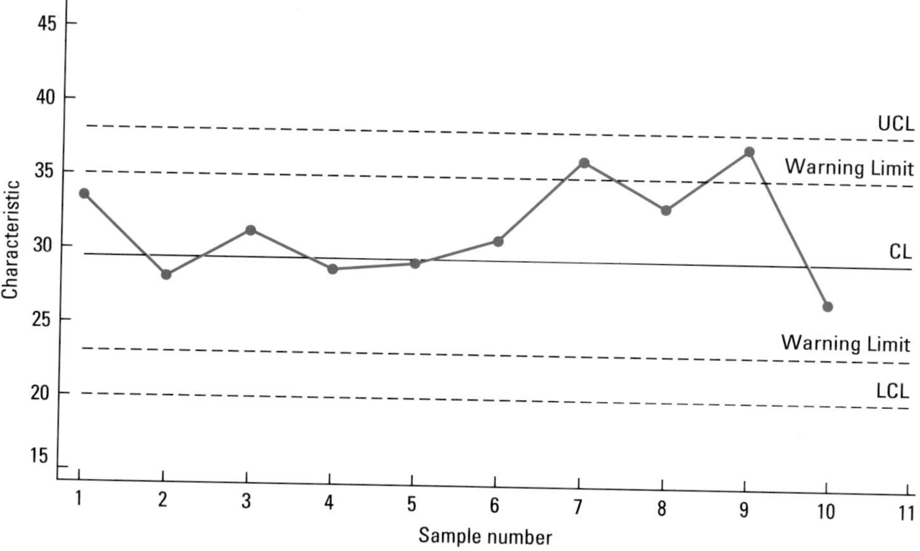

Figure 5-8 *(Continued)* (*b*) Rule 2.

trol limit is three standard deviations (assuming 3σ limits). Dividing this distance by three gives the standard deviation of the characteristic being plotted. Adding and subtracting this standard deviation from the center line value gives the 1σ limits. Consider Figure 5-8*c,* for which sample numbers 4, 5, 6, and 8 plot below the lower 1σ limit. Based on Rule 3, this process would be considered out of control.

Rule 4 A process is assumed to be out of control if eight or more consecutive points fall to one side of the center line.

For a process in control, a roughly equal number of points should be above or below the center line, with no systematic pattern visible. The condition stated in Rule 4 is highly unlikely if a process is in control. For instance, if eight or more consecu-

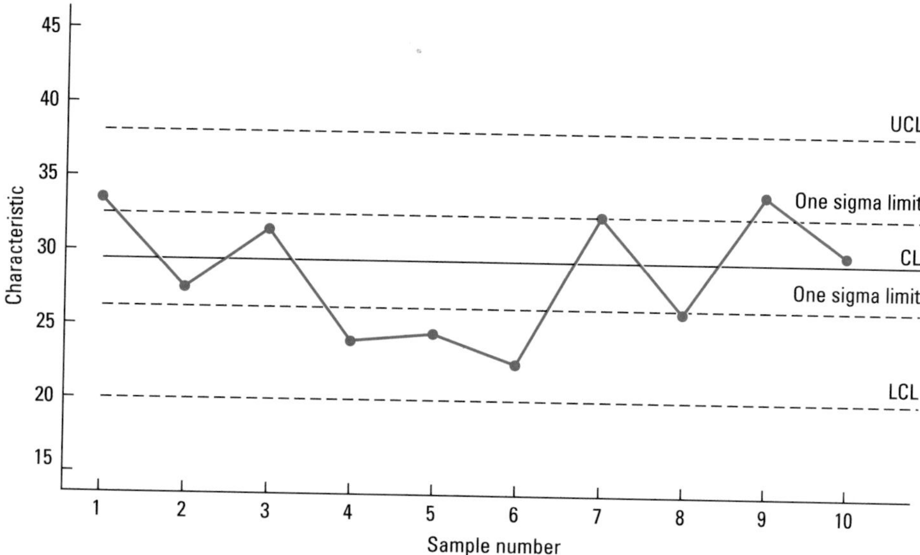

Figure 5-8 *(Continued)* (*c*) Rule 3.

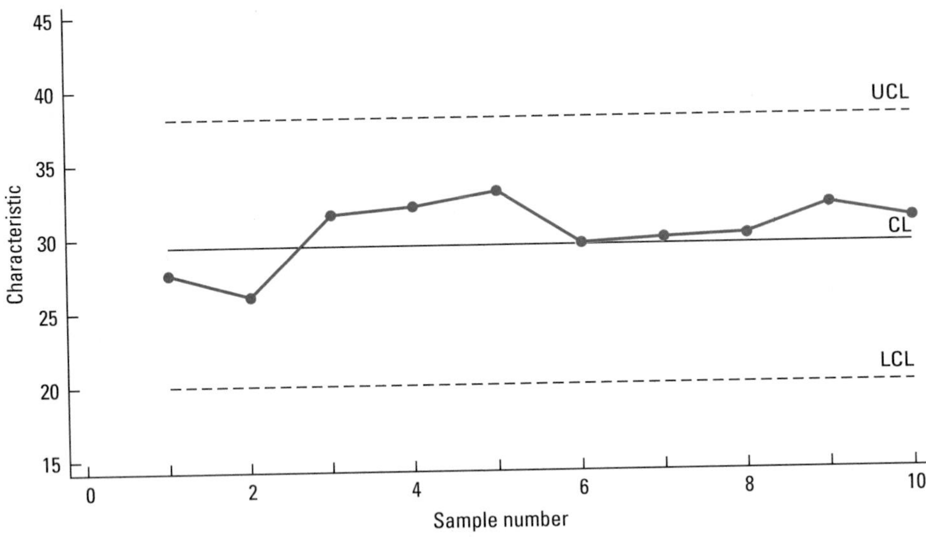

Figure 5-8 *(Continued)* (*d*) Rule 4.

tive points plot above the center line on an $\overline{X}$-chart, an upward shift in the process average may have occurred. In Figure 5-8*d*, sample numbers 3, 4, 5, 6, 7, 8, 9, and 10 plot above the center line. The process is assumed to be out of control.

Rule 5 A process is assumed to be out of control if there is a run of eight or more consecutive points—up, down, above, or below the center line, or above or below the median.

A run is a sequence of like observations. For example, if three successive points increase in magnitude, we would have a run up of three points. If five successive points lie below the center line, it would be a run of five below the center line. Consider Figure 5-8*e*. Observe that sample numbers 2 through 10 show a continual increase. This is a run up of 8 consecutive points, so this process would be deemed out of control.

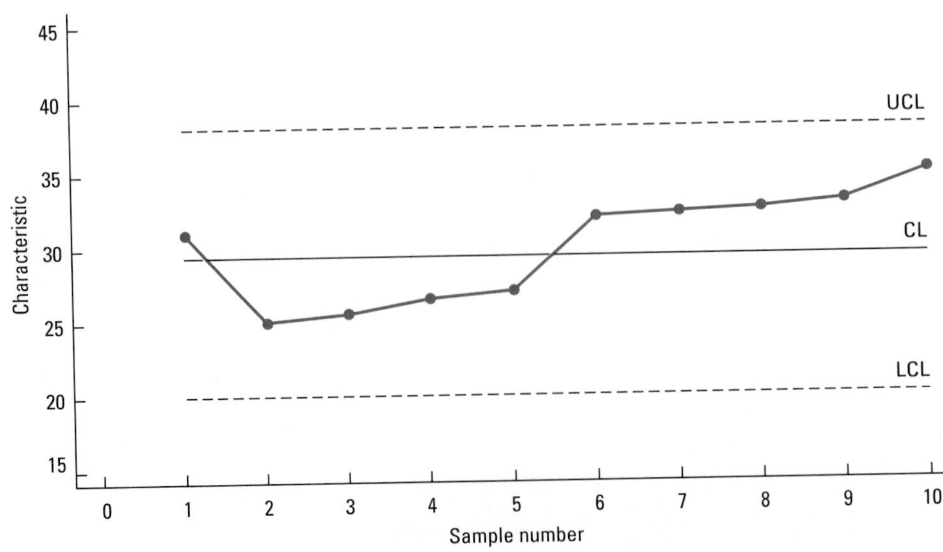

Figure 5-8 *(Continued)* (*e*) Rule 5.

Interpretation of Plots

The five rules for determining out-of-control conditions are not usually used simultaneously. Rule 1 is routinely used along with a couple of the other rules (say, Rule 2 and Rule 3). The reason for not using all the rules simultaneously is that doing so increases the chance of a Type I error. In other words, the probability of a false alarm increases as more rules are used to determine an out-of-control state. Even though the probability of the stated condition occurring is rather small for any one rule if the process is in control, the *overall Type I error,* based on the number of rules that are used, may not be small.

Suppose the number of independent rules used for out of control criteria is k. Let α_i be the probability of a Type I error of rule i. Then, the overall probability of a Type I error is

$$\alpha = 1 - \prod_{i=1}^{k}(1 - \alpha_i) \tag{5.2}$$

Suppose four independent rules are being used to determine whether a process is out of control. Let the probability of a Type I error for each of the rules be given by $\alpha_1 = 0.005, \alpha_2 = 0.02, \alpha_3 = 0.03$, and $\alpha_4 = 0.05$, respectively. The overall false alarm rate, or the probability of a Type I error, would be

$$\alpha = 1 - (0.995)(0.98)(0.97)(0.95) = 0.101$$

If several more rules were to be used simultaneously, it is quite possible that the probability of Type I error would become too large to be acceptable. Note that the relationship in Equation 5.2 is derived under the assumption that the rules are independent. In actuality, they may not be, in which case Equation 5.2 should be treated as an approximation to the probability of a Type I error. Furthermore, using many rules for determining out-of-control conditions might make the decision process complicated, which would defy the purpose of using control limits. One of the major advantages of using control charts is that they are easy to construct, interpret, and use.

In addition to the rules for identifying out-of-control conditions, there are many other nonrandom patterns that a control chart user has to judiciously interpret. It is possible for none of the five rules mentioned above to be applicable but for the process to still be out of control. This is where the experience, judgment, and interpretive skills of the user come into the picture. Consider, for example, Figure 5-9, where none of the five rules for out-of-control conditions are satisfied. However, the pattern displayed is clearly nonrandom. Notice the systematic nature of the plot, showing somewhat cyclic behavior. Based on this pattern, one would conclude that assignable causes are present and assume the process to be out of control. The user should always keep an eye out for nonrandom patterns when considering any plot on a control chart.

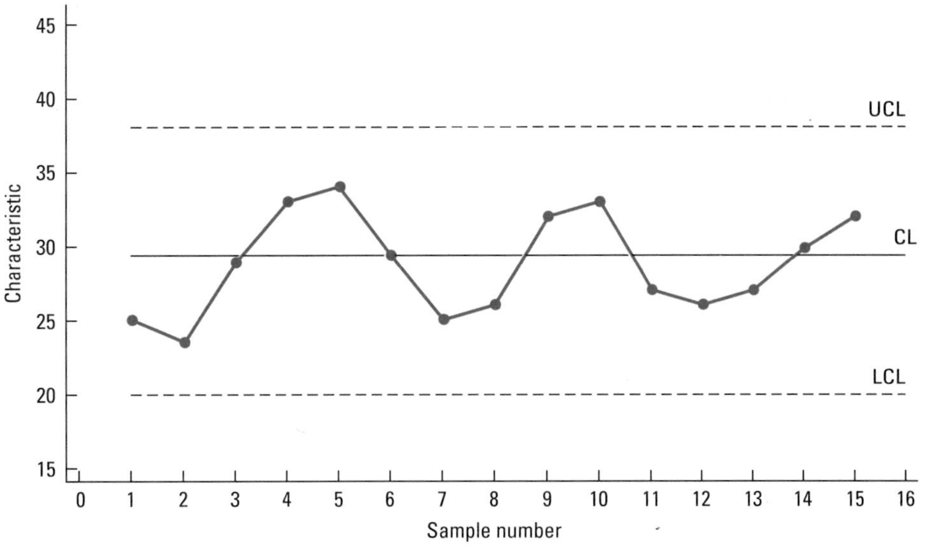

Figure 5-9 A nonrandom pattern in a control chart.

Determination of Causes Associated with Out-of-Control Points*

The task of the control chart user does not end with the identification of any out-of-control points. In fact, the difficult part of the whole process starts after out-of-control points have been determined. It is then that the causes associated with these points must be pinpointed, a task which is sometimes not trivial. It requires a thorough knowledge of the process and the sensitivity of the output quality characteristic to the process parameters. The cause determination phase may be conducted with the collective effort of several people including representatives from product design, process design, tooling, production, purchasing and vendor control, and so on. A cause-and-effect chart can be an appropriate tool in such circumstances. Once assignable causes have been identified, appropriate remedial actions to eliminate the assignable causes need to be proposed. The following paragraphs describe some typical patterns that may be seen when a process is out of control and some possible causes for those conditions. It must be emphasized that each control chart pattern must be analyzed in the context of its respective process and that causes specific to that process may in some cases be unique. Thus, the patterns and associated causes illustrated below are not applicable to all situations. These patterns include:

1. *Change in the level of the plotted pattern (a jump).* Figure 5-10 depicts the situation where a distinctive change in the level of the plot is observed. The first four samples seem to be around a certain level, but the remainder of the samples starting with number 5 are at a higher level compared to the first four. Some possible assignable causes for such a pattern may include the following:

1. Change in the incoming quality of raw material and parts due to a change of vendor
2. Inadvertent or intentional change in the process setting
3. Change of operator
4. Error in calibration of the measuring instrument
5. Failure of a component in the equipment
6. Chipping of a tool

2. *Trend in the plotted pattern.* Sometimes the pattern in a control chart may represent a gradual increase or decrease. Figure 5-11 indicates such a pattern. The following assignable causes may be responsible:

1. Tool wear
2. Gradual change in pressure or temperature

* Some of the material in this section is adapted from Dale H. Besterfield, *Quality Control*, 2e, © 1986, pp. 87–90, with permission of Prentice Hall, Englewood Cliffs, New Jersey.

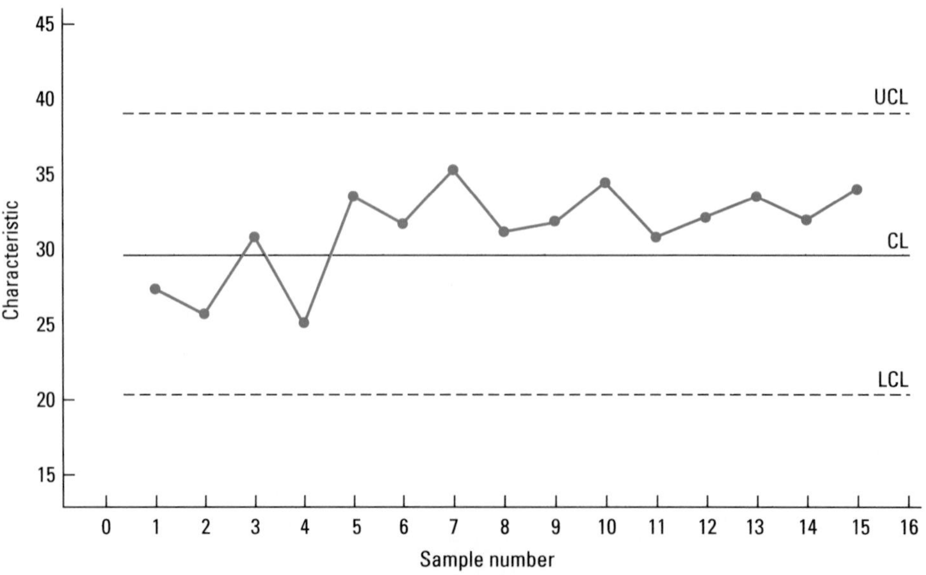

Figure 5-10 Change in the level of the plotted pattern.

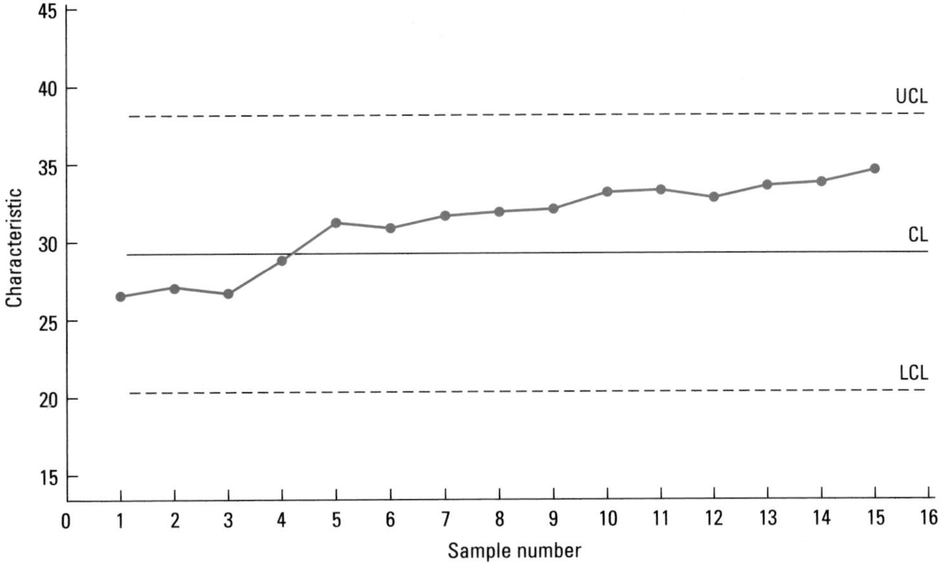

Figure 5-11 Trend in the plotted pattern.

3. Operator having to learn on the job
4. Gradual deterioration of machinery
5. Accumulation of unwanted matter in jigs and fixtures

3. *Cyclic behavior in the plotted pattern.* When changes in the quality characteristic take place on a periodic basis, one looks for assignable causes and process parameters which also change in a cyclic manner. Figure 5-12 shows an example of such be-

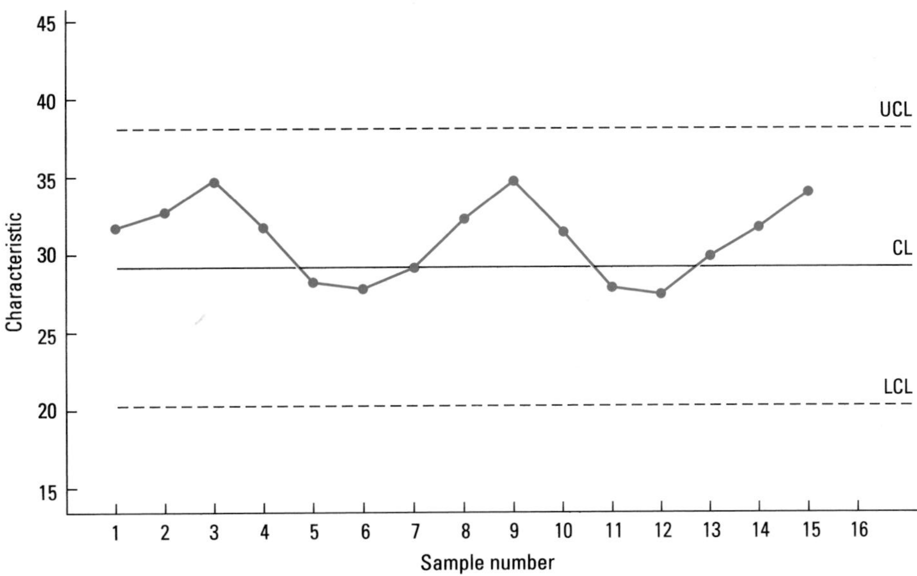

Figure 5-12 Cyclic behavior in the plotted pattern.

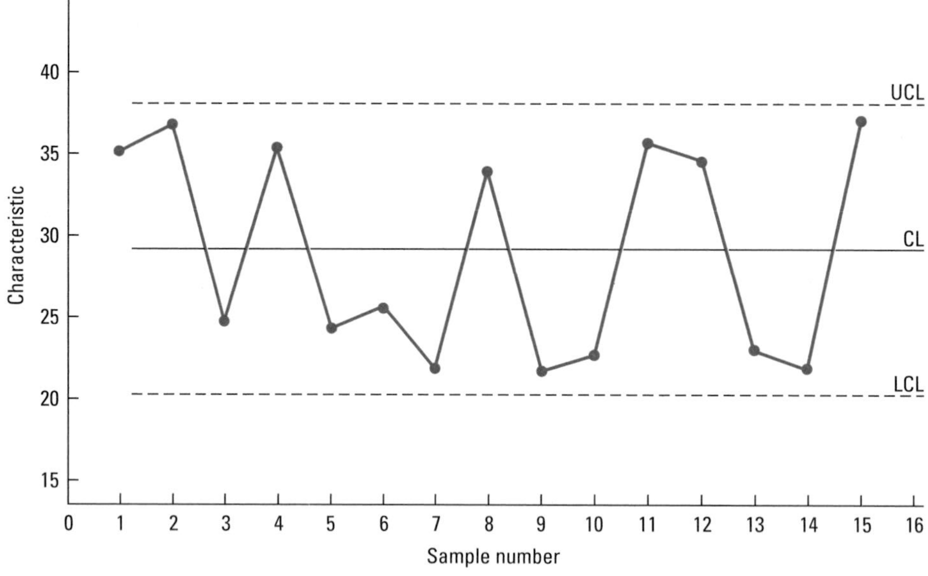

Figure 5-13 Out-of-control pattern due to mixture of populations.

havior. Some possible assignable causes are as follows:

1. Buildup or loss of pressure or temperature associated with the starting and stopping of machines
2. Seasonal effects of quality of incoming material and components from vendors
3. Periodicity in the performance of machines due to periodic preventive maintenance
4. Operator fatigue and subsequent reenergization from periodic breaks
5. Periodicity in the mechanical or chemical properties of the material

4. *Concentration of points near the control limits.* If subgroups are not properly selected, the result may be sample statistics that plot near the control limits. For example, if the outputs from two operators who perform differently are plotted on the same chart, it is possible that the plotted points will fall near or outside each of the control limits. Figure 5-13 demonstrates such a pattern, where the existence of a mixture of populations is prevalent. A few reasons that may cause such patterns are as follows:

1. Two or more operators plotted on the same chart
2. Two or more machines plotted on the same chart
3. Drastic difference between incoming quality of two vendors plotted on the same chart
4. Differences in two or more pieces of testing or measuring equipment
5. Differences in production methods of two or more lines

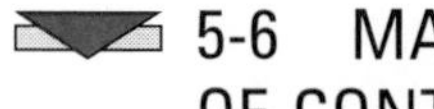

5-6 MAINTENANCE OF CONTROL CHARTS

Although the construction of control charts is an important step in statistical process control, it should be emphasized that quality control and improvement are part of an ongoing process. Therefore, the implementation and maintenance of control charts also represent a vital link in the context of a total quality system. If observations plotted on control charts are found to be out of control, then the center line and control limits need to be revised. If assignable causes are identified for the out-of-control points and appropriate remedial actions are taken, then in the process of revising the control limits, those out-of-control points will be eliminated. There are some exceptions to the elimination of out-of-control points, however, especially for points below the lower control limit. These will be discussed in Chapters 6 and 7. Once the computation of the revised center line and control limits is completed, these lines are drawn on charts where future observations are to be plotted. The process of revising the center line and control limits is an ongoing one.

Proper placement of the control charts on the shop floor is important. Each person who is associated with the making or rendering of the particular quality characteristic should have easy access to the chart. When a statistical process control system is first implemented, the chart is usually placed in a conspicuous place where operators can look at it. The involvement of everyone, from the operator to the manager to the chief executive officer, is essential to the success of the program. The control charts should draw the attention and curiosity of everyone involved. Proper maintenance of these charts on a regular ongoing basis will ensure the prominence of the quality systems approach. If a particular quality characteristic becomes insignificant, its control chart may be replaced by others that are relevant. Products, processes, vendors, and equipment change with time. Similarly, the different control charts that are kept should be chosen to reflect the important characteristics.

5-7 SUMMARY

This chapter has introduced the basic concepts behind the use of control charts for statistical process control. The benefits that can be derived from using control charts have been discussed. This chapter explains the statistical background for the use of control charts, the selection of the control limits, and the manner in which inferences can be drawn from the charts. It provides a discussion of the two types of errors that may be encountered in making inferences from control charts. Guidelines for the proper selection of subgroup size and rules for determining out-of-control conditions have been explored. Some control chart patterns have been studied with a focus on identifying possible assignable causes. Since this chapter is intended solely to explain the fundamentals of control charts, such technical details as formulas for various types of control charts have intentionally been omitted here. They are discussed in Chapters 6 and 7 and may also be found in Banks (1989), Montgomery (1991), and Wadsworth, Stephens, and Godfrey (1986).

5-8 CASE STUDY

SPC: WHAT DATA SHOULD I COLLECT? WHAT CHARTS SHOULD I USE?*

Statistical process control (SPC) can help companies cut costs, improve quality, and pursue continuous improvement. However, those people unfamiliar with statistics who try to implement SPC usually have two questions: "What data should I collect?" and "What control chart can I use under some specific circumstances?" Employees in Boeing's Fabrication Division were confronted with these two questions and were able to answer them using two straightforward tools: the data definition process and the control chart decision tree.

What Data Should I Collect? In one of Boeing's foundries, a team was formed to ensure that the shop would meet its goals of continuous improvement and producing the highest-quality castings using the most cost-effective methods. The team initially developed a process flow diagram (see Figure 5-14) to analyze and measure plan development.

* Adapted from: J. Munoz and C. Nielson (1991), "SPC: What Data Should I Collect? What Charts Should I Use?" *Quality Progress*, Vol. 24, No. 1, pp. 50–52.

Realizing that decisions are only as good as the data collected for analysis, the measurement plan started with the data definition process. The work sheet shown in Table 5-3 helped the team with this task.

The problem statement was: "The defect rate in the foundry casting process results in unwanted scrap and rework." The foundry team used this statement to identify the quality characteristics that needed to be measured to improve the process: casting defect rate, scrap, and rework.

Then the team used the data definition model to define the data requirements. The model provides a plan to identify and collect the data required to ensure proper analysis and achieve optimum process improvement. The model focuses on four important aspects of data collection:

1. *Scope of study.* The scope defines the boundary and population of the process to be measured.
2. *Parameters to measure.* The parameters define the types of attributes and variables to be measured and identify where in the process they will be measured.
3. *Data analysis requirements.* The requirements define the methods and tools needed to analyze the data.

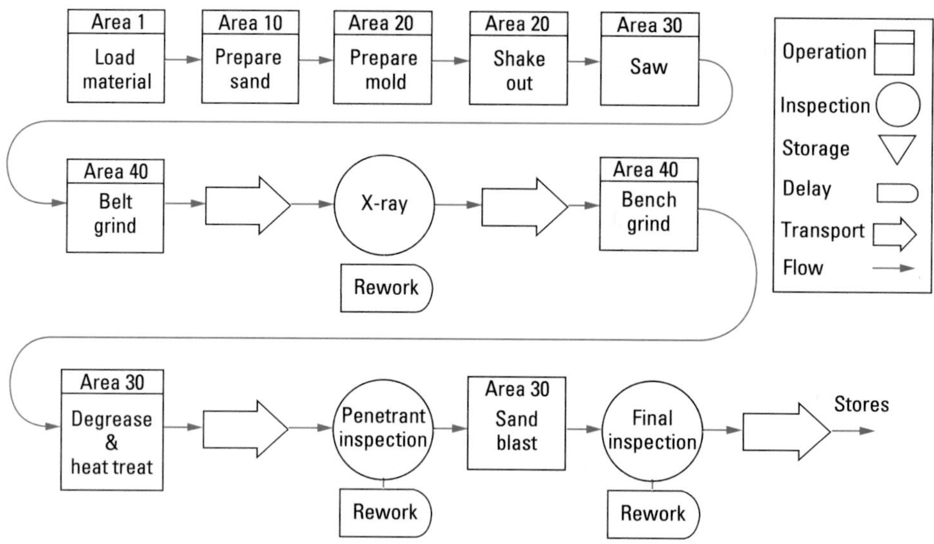

Figure 5-14 Simplified process flow diagram.

TABLE 5-3 Data definition work sheet

Problem statement: The defect rate in foundry casting process results in unwanted scrap and rework.

Quality characteristic(s): Defect rate, scrap, and rework.

Scope of study	Data definition	Parameters to measure
Boundaries? Starts: Shop load Ends: Final shop	Attribute(s): In-process: Defects/part (identify defect type)	Where: Saw, belt grind, bench grind
Population? All part orders processed on all shifts	Q.C.: Same as above	
Time period? Three months to determine current status. Continuously monitor performance	Variable(s): n/a	Where: n/a
Charts/graphs? Run chart, *u* control chart, and Pareto chart	Who? In-process: Operators and shop leaders (recorded during shift and collected at end)	
Charting frequency? Monthly (quality characteristics) Daily (attribute)	How? Two automatic data collectors In-house developed software	
Type of comparisons? Part types, shift to shift	Sampling? Only at QC Inspections	
Means of summarizing? Quality char.: Monthly average and totals Attribute: Weekly defect totals and types		
Statistics to calculate? Process average, totals, control limits, percentages	Cost? Data collectors plus .5 labor hours/day	
Data analysis requirements	DATA COLLECTION RESOURCES	

4. *Data collection resources.* The resources required to collect the data are defined.

Using the process flow diagram, the team defined each section of the model.

Scope of Study

Boundaries: The casting process beginning with shop load and ending with the final inspection of the part (see Figure 5-14).

Population: Includes all part orders processed on all shifts.

Time period: Data will be collected for three months to determine which attribute has the greatest effect on the defect rate, scrap, and rework. Data collection will continue in order to monitor improvements and determine the next attribute to be eliminated.

Parameters to Measure

Attributes: Casting defects will be tracked at each foundry operation previously identified. Defects will be measured by defect types and defects per part. The same defect data will also be collected at three inspection points (X-ray, penetrant, and final).

Variables: No variable measures were needed.

Data Analysis Requirements

Charts/graphs: Charts will include the run (trend) chart to display the monthly defect rate, scrap, and rework; the Pareto chart to display occurrence of defects; and the *u*-chart to monitor the number of defects per unit.

Charting frequency: The run chart will be compiled and reviewed monthly. Pareto charts will be produced weekly and monthly. The *u*-chart will be compiled daily.

Types of comparisons: Defect rates and types will be compared between part types. Shift-to-shift variations will also be compared.

Means of summarization: Data for the quality characteristics will be summarized as monthly averages and totals. Attribute data will be summarized weekly by total defects and types.

Statistics to calculate: Process average (defects per unit), defect totals (occurrence and type), control limits, and Pareto analysis.

Data Collection Resources

Who: In-process data will be recorded by operators at defined data collection points. Shop leaders will collect data at shift end. QC data will be provided by QC personnel.

How: Automated data collectors will gather in-process and QC data; software developed in-house will chart and analyze the data.

Sampling: Sampling will be used only at QC inspection points. *Cost:* Data collection costs include the expense of two automated units and 0.5 labor hours per day.

Having completed the data definition process, the foundry team had a documented plan to collect data for measuring and improving the foundry casting process. All that was left was to get the resources and begin collecting data.

What Control Chart Should I Use? During the data definition process, the foundry team struggled in deciding what type of statistical control chart it should use to monitor the variation in the process. The team was then introduced to the decision tree process (see Figure 5-15). In using the decision tree, the first item that must be identified is the type of data being collected: variable (measurable quality characteristics) or attribute (nonmeasurable but countable quality characteristics).

If variable data are used, two control charts are required: one to monitor the process average and one to monitor process variation. The control chart used to monitor the process average is the $\overline{X}$-chart. The chart used to monitor process variation is determined by the sample size n. When n is small, the R-chart (range) is generally preferred over the s-chart (sample standard deviation) because there is little difference in efficiency between the two charts and the R-chart is much simpler to use. As n increases, the efficiency of the R-chart

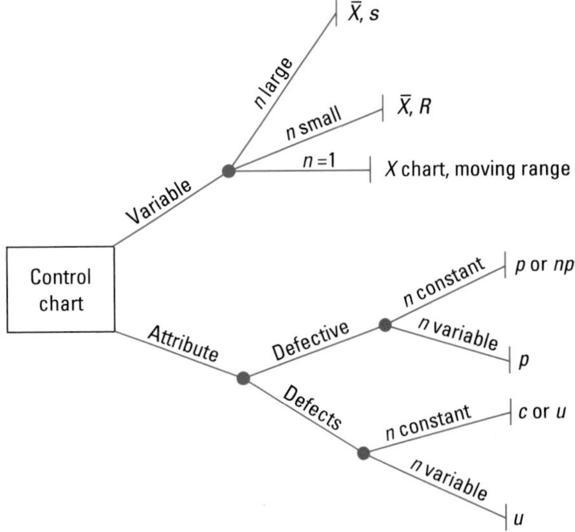

Figure 5-15 Control chart decision tree.

as compared to that of the s-chart decreases. So, if n is large, the s-chart should be used instead of the R-chart.

Thus, n determines which variable control charts to use. If n is large (10 or more observations per sample), $\overline{X}$ and s-charts are desirable. If n is small (fewer than 10 observations per sample), $\overline{X}$ and R-charts are preferred. If only one observation per sample is possible, then the X-chart (control chart for individuals) and the moving range chart are appropriate.

If attribute data are collected, just one control chart is required in most cases. It must be decided whether defective units or number of defects are being counted. If the process is being monitored through the collection of data on nonconforming (defective) parts, the question is whether the sample size is constant. If it is constant, then a p-chart (fraction defective) or an np-chart (number-of-defective-units) would work. But if the sample size varies, only the p-chart can be used, and the control limits will vary with sample size.

If the attribute is monitored through the collection of data on the number of defects (nonconformances or discrepancies), the condition of the sample size will again determine the type of chart. If n is constant, c-charts (number of defects per sample) or u-charts (number of defects per unit) can be used, but if n is variable, only the u-chart is acceptable.

The foundry team used this simple decision tree, making its search to find the most appropriate control chart (the u-chart) chart a lot easier.

QUESTIONS FOR DISCUSSION

1. Describe how information from the Pareto chart could influence the control chart to monitor the number of defects per unit.
2. What is the purpose of constructing a run chart and a chart for defects per unit?
3. Describe some characteristics, in this setting, for which a variables chart for the mean and range would be used.
4. Describe some attributes, in this setting, for which a control chart for the proportion nonconforming would be appropriate.

KEY TERMS

Assignable cause
Center line
Chance cause
Control chart
Control chart maintenance
Control limits
  Upper control limit
  Lower control limit
Instant-of-time method
On-line control
Operating characteristic curve
Out-of-control rules
Period-of-time method
Probability limits
Process capability
Rational subgroups
Remedial actions
Sample size
Sampling frequency
Shewhart control charts
Statistical control
Standard error
Subgroup size
Type I error
  Overall rate
Type II error
Warning limits

EXERCISES

Discussion Questions

5-1 What are the benefits of using control charts?

5-2 Explain the difference between chance causes and assignable causes. Give examples of each.

5-3 Explain the rationale behind placing the control limits at three standard deviations from the mean.

5-4 Define and explain a Type I and Type II error in the context of control charts. Are they related? How does the choice of control limits influence these two errors?

5-5 What are warning limits, and what purpose do they serve?

5-6 What is the utility of the operating characteristic curve? How can the discriminatory power of the curve be improved?

5-7 How are rational subgroups selected? Explain the importance of this in the total quality systems approach.

5-8 State and explain each rule for determining out-of-control points.

5-9 What are some reasons for a process to go out of control due to a sudden shift in the level?

5-10 Explain some causes that would make the control chart pattern follow a gradually increasing trend.

Problems

5-11 What is meant by an overall Type I error rate? If Rules 1, 2, and 3 of this chapter are simultaneously used, what is the probability of an overall Type I error if 3σ control limits are used?

5-12 The diameter of cotter pins produced by an automatic machine is a characteristic of interest. Based on historical data, the process average diameter is 15 mm with a process standard deviation of 0.8 mm. If samples of size 4 are randomly selected from the process:

a. Find the 1σ and 2σ control limits.
b. Find the 3σ control limits for the average diameter.
c. What is the probability of a false alarm?
d. If the process mean shifts to 14.5 mm, what is the probability of not detecting this shift on the first subgroup plotted after the shift?
e. What is the probability of failing to detect the shift by the second subgroup plotted after the shift?
f. Construct the operating characteristic curve for this control chart.

5-13 The length of industrial filters is a quality characteristic of interest. Thirty samples, each of size 5, were chosen from the process. The data yielded an average length of 110 mm, with the process standard deviation estimated to be 4 mm.

a. Find the warning limits for a control chart for the average length.
b. Find the 3σ control limits. What is the probability of a Type I error?
c. If the process mean shifts to 112 mm, what are the chances of detecting this shift by the third sample drawn after the shift?
d. What is the chance of detecting the shift for the first time on the second subgroup point drawn after the shift?

5-14 The tensile strength of nonferrous pipes is of importance. Samples of size 5 are selected from the process output, and their tensile strength values are found. After 30 such samples, the process mean strength is estimated to be 3000 kg with a standard deviation of 50 kg.

a. Find the 1σ and 2σ control limits. For the 1σ limits, what is the probability of concluding that the process is out of control when it is really in control?
b. Find the 3σ limits.
c. If Rule 1 and Rule 2 are simultaneously used to detect out of control conditions, what is the overall probability of a Type I error if 3σ control limits are used?

5-15 Suppose 3σ control limits are constructed for the average temperature in a furnace. Samples of size 4 were selected with the average temperature being 5000°C and a standard deviation of 50°C.

a. Find the 3σ control charts.
b. Suppose Rule 2 and Rule 3 are used simultaneously used to determine out-of-control conditions. What is the overall probability of a Type I error?
c. Approximately how many samples, on the average, will be analyzed before detecting a change when Rules 2 and 3 are simultaneously used?
d. If the process average temperature drops to 4960°C, what is the probability of failing to detect this change by the third subgroup point drawn after the change?
e. What is the probability of the shift being detected within the first two subgroups?

5-16 A manager is contemplating using Rules 1 and 4 for determining out-of-control conditions. Suppose the manager constructs 3σ limits.

a. What is the overall Type I error probability?
b. On the average, how many samples will be analyzed before detecting a change in the process mean? Assume that the process mean is now at 110 mm (having moved from 105 mm) and that the process standard deviation is 6 mm. Samples of size 4 are selected from the process.

REFERENCES

American Society for Quality Control, ANSI/ASQC A1-1987. *Definitions, Symbols, Formulas, and Tables for Control Charts.* Milwaukee, WI.

Banks, J. (1989). *Principles of Quality Control,* Wiley, New York.

Besterfield, Dale H. (1990). *Quality Control,* 3rd edition, Prentice Hall, Englewood Cliffs, NJ.

Duncan, A. J. (1986). *Quality Control and Industrial Statistics,* 5th edition, Irwin, Homewood, IL.

Montgomery, Douglas C. (1991). *Introduction to Statistical Quality Control.* 2nd edition, Wiley, New York.

Munoz, J., and Nielsen, J. (1991). "SPC: What Data Should I Collect? What Charts Should I Use?," *Quality Progress,* 24 (1), pp. 50–52.

Wadsworth, Harrison M., Stephens, Kenneth S., and Godfrey, A. Blanton (1986). *Modern Methods for Quality Control and Improvement.* Wiley, New York.

CHAPTER

6

Control Charts for Variables

CHAPTER OUTLINE

SYMBOLS

μ	Process (or population) mean	σ_0	Target or standard value of process standard deviation
σ	Process (or population) standard deviation	$\sigma_{\overline{X}}$	Standard deviation of the sample mean
$\hat{\sigma}$	Estimate of process standard deviation	S_m	Cumulative sum at sample number m
$\overline{X}$	Sample average	w	Span, or width, in calculation of moving average
R	Sample range	$\overline{\overline{X}}$	Mean of sample means
s	Sample standard deviation	$\overline{R}$	Mean of sample ranges
n	Sample or subgroup size	G_t	Geometric moving average at time t
X_i	ith observation	M_t	Arithmetic moving average at time t
W	Relative range	T^2	Hotelling's T^2 multivariate statistic
g	Number of samples or subgroups		
X_0	Target or standard value of process mean		

6-1 INTRODUCTION

Chapter 5 introduced the fundamentals of control charts. This chapter provides details on control charts for variables—quality characteristics that are measurable on a numerical scale. Examples of variables are length, thickness, diameter, breaking strength, temperature, acidity, and viscosity. It is important to be able to control the mean value of a quality characteristic as well as its variability; both provide meaningful information about a process. The mean gives an indication of the central tendency of a process, and the variability provides an idea of the process dispersion. Therefore, information about both of these statistics is needed to keep a process in control.

Consider Figure 6-1. A change in the process average of a quality characteristic (say, length of a part) is shown in Figure 6-1*a*, where the mean shifts from μ_0 to μ_1. It is important that this change in the lo-

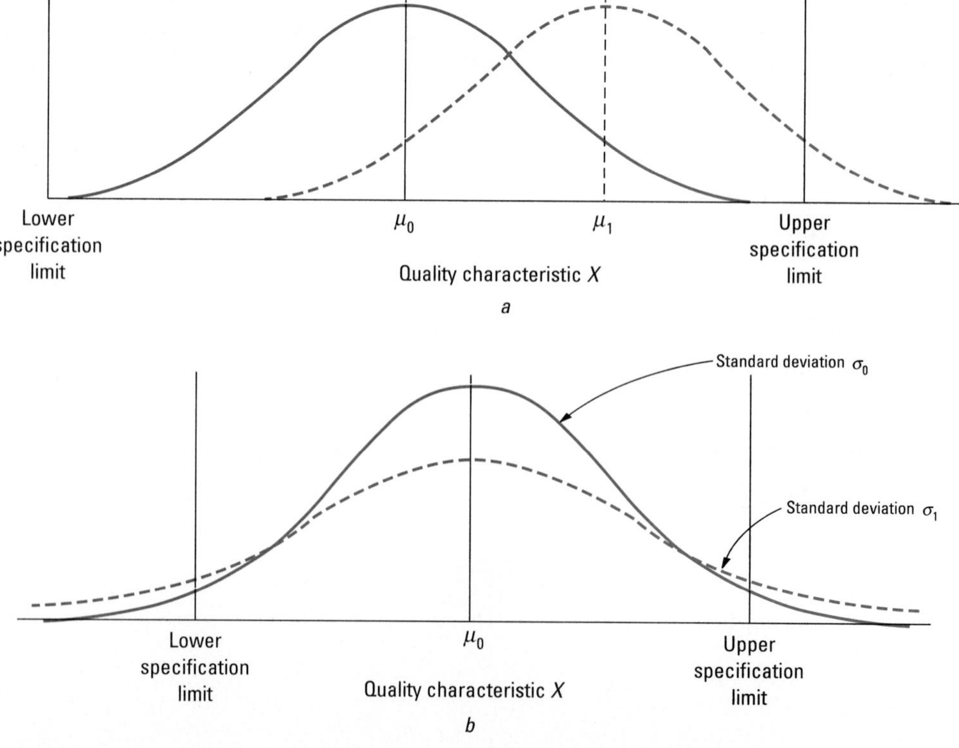

Figure 6-1 Changes in the location and dispersion of a process.

cation of the process be detected. For instance, if the specification limits are as shown in Figure 6-1*a*, a change in the process average would change the proportion of parts that do not meet specifications. Figure 6-1*b* shows a change in the dispersion of the process; the process standard deviation has changed from σ_0 to σ_1, with the process mean remaining stationary at μ_0. Note that the proportion of the output that does not meet specifications has increased. Control charts aid in determining such changes in process parameters.

Variables provide more information than attributes. Attributes usually deal with qualitative information such as whether an item is nonconforming or what the number of nonconformities in an item is. Thus, attributes do not show the degree to which a quality characteristic is nonconforming. For instance, the specifications on the length of a part may be 40 ± 0.5 mm. If a part has a length of 40.6 mm, attribute information would indicate as nonconforming both that part and a part that has a length of 42 mm. The degree to which these two lengths deviate from the specifications is lost in attribute information. This is not so with variables, however, for which the numerical value of the quality characteristic (length, in this case) is retained and may be used in the construction of control charts. The cost of obtaining data through inspection is usually higher for variables than for attributes because attribute inspection may be performed by go/no-go gages, for example, which are easier to use since numerical values of the characteristics are not obtained. The total cost of inspection may be considered as the sum of two components: a fixed cost and a variable cost. Fixed costs might include the investment cost in buying the equipment; variable costs may include the cost of inspecting units. The more units are inspected, the more will be the total variable cost, whereas the total investment cost (fixed cost) remains the same. As the use of automated devices for measuring quality characteristic values becomes more prevalent, the difference in the variable unit cost portion of the total unit cost of inspection between variables and attributes may not be much. However, the fixed costs, such as investment costs, may increase.

At the plant level, where information is in an aggregate form representing the output of several operators or machines, a variables chart might not be able to identify differences among the operators or machines. For example, the average length of parts calculated from the output of several operators will not provide information to distinguish between their performance. An attribute chart for the proportion nonconforming at the plant level might represent a measure of the operational level of the plant. As problems are narrowed down, variable charts are used at a more specific level.

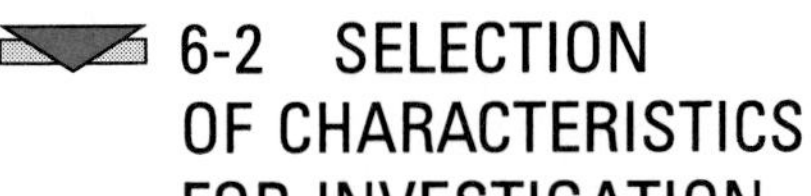

6-2 SELECTION OF CHARACTERISTICS FOR INVESTIGATION

Even in small organizations, for which the number of products may be few, there can be many possible quality characteristics. A single component can have several quality characteristics such as length, width, height, surface finish, and elasticity. When considering a product made up of several different components, you can see that the number of quality characteristics can be quite large. As the number of products increases, the total number of characteristics may quickly increase to some unmanageable value. It is frequently not feasible to maintain a control chart for each possible variable. With each increase in the number of control charts, the decision-making process becomes more complicated, and the primary advantage of using the control charts—ease of use—diminishes. Operators will find it difficult to look at 10 or 15 control charts simultaneously to make decisions based on the collective information. Only a manageable number of control charts should be maintained at a given time, so that a total quality systems approach remains feasible. Accomplishing this task involves selecting a few vital quality characteristics from the many candidates.

Proper selection of the quality characteristics for which to keep control charts requires giving higher priority to those which are more critical in terms of causing more nonconforming items and increasing costs. The goal is to select the "vital few" from among the "trivial many." In most manufacturing or service industries, there is an innumerable number of variables, and one variable control chart is needed for each variable. This is where *Pareto analysis* can be used to select the "important" quality characteristics—those which most influence the total cost and for which the number of nonconformities or nonconforming items is the greatest.

If nonconformities occur due to different types of defects, a tally can be kept of the frequency with which each type of nonconformity occurs. Table 6-1 shows frequencies of occurrence for various defects for an assembly. As an alternative to frequency, the cost of producing the nonconformity may also be used. Table 6-1 shows that the three most important

TABLE 6-1 Pareto analysis of frequency of defects

Defect code number	Type of defect	Frequency	Percentage
1	Outside diameter of hub	30	8.82
2	Depth of keyway	20	5.88
3	Hub length	60	17.65
4	Inside diameter of hub	90	26.47
5	Width of keyway	30	8.82
6	Thickness of flange	40	11.77
7	Depth of slot	50	14.71
8	Hardness (measured by Brinell hardness number)	20	5.88
		340	100.00

quality characteristics are the inside hub diameter, the hub length, and the slot depth. Table 6-1 also shows the percent of occurrence for each type of defect.

The types of defects given in Table 6-1 may be plotted on a graph in decreasing order of importance. Figure 6-2 shows such a plot, which is known as a Pareto diagram. The percentage of each type of defect is plotted in a nonincreasing order. From the figure it can be seen that if there are only enough resources to support the construction of three variable charts, the defect types chosen would be inside hub diameter (code 4), hub length (code 3), and slot depth (code 7). Variable control charts would then be constructed for those three variables.

6-3 CONSIDERATIONS PRIOR TO CONSTRUCTION OF CONTROL CHARTS

Before constructing control charts, certain related issues must be addressed. Some of these have been discussed in detail in Chapter 5. These issues are briefly summarized in this section.

Selection of Rational Subgroups

The manner in which subgroups are to be selected from the process deserves attention. The primary consideration is that the chance for differences among subgroups should be maximized while the chance for differences within subgroups should be minimized. Lots from which subgroups are chosen should be homogeneous. This means that separate control charts may have to be kept for different operators, machines, or vendors. As mentioned in Chapter 5, if one of the main objectives is to determine shifts in process parameters, then subgroups should be made up of items produced at nearly the same time. Such a method of selection provides a time reference for the items and may be helpful if it becomes necessary to determine assignable causes. Alternatively, if one is interested in making decisions regarding the acceptance of items produced since the previous subgroup was selected, then subgroup items should be chosen from among all those produced since that time.

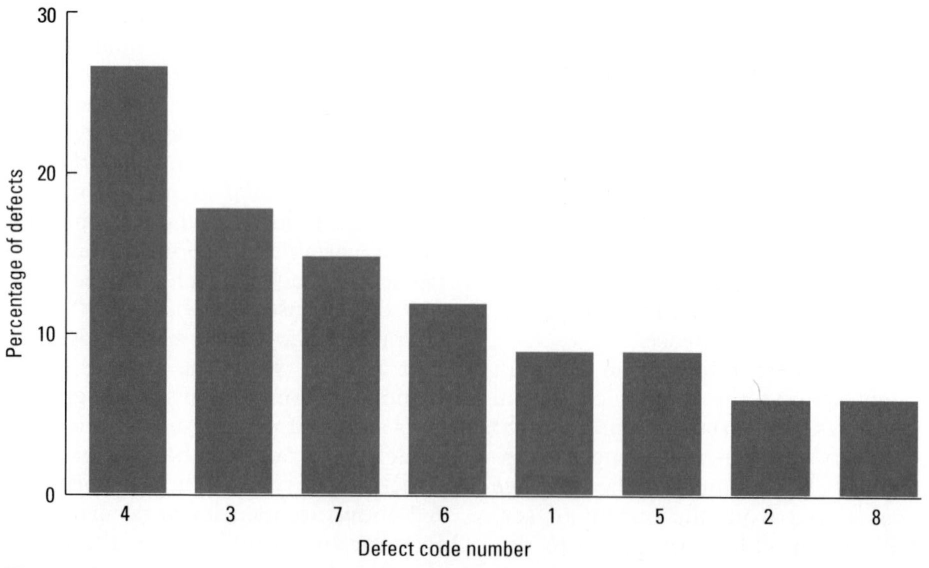

Figure 6-2 Pareto diagram for assembly data.

Subgroup Size

Subgroup sizes are normally between 4 and 10. It is quite common in industry to have subgroup sizes of 4 or 5. The larger the subgroup or sample size, the better the chance of detecting small shifts. Other factors such as cost of inspection or cost of shipping a nonconforming item to the customer can influence the choice of subgroup size.

Frequency of Subgroup Selection

Deciding upon the frequency with which to select subgroups may be based on the cost of obtaining information compared to the cost of not detecting a nonconforming item. As processes are brought into control, the frequency of sampling may diminish.

Types of Measuring Instruments to Be Used

The accuracy of the measuring instrument directly influences the values of process characteristics being measured. Measuring instruments should be calibrated and tested for repeatability under controlled conditions. Otherwise, the measured value will be of dubious worth and may lead to erroneous conclusions. The characteristic being controlled and the desired degree of measurement precision both have an impact on the choice of measuring instrument or equipment. In measuring dimensions such as length, height, or thickness, a set of calipers or a micrometer may be acceptable for certain components. On the other hand, for measuring the thickness of silicon wafers, optical sensory equipment may be necessary. Other quality characteristics such as specific gravity, viscosity, pressure, temperature, strength, and so on require different equipment.

Design of Recording Forms for Data

The chart for recording the data should be designed in accordance with the type of control chart that is to be constructed. Some common features of all control charts include the subgroup number, the date and time when the subgroup was chosen, and the raw values of the observations. A column for comments about the process while selecting the observations should be incorporated into the recording data form. A typical recording form for a chart showing the mean $\overline{X}$ and range R is shown in Figure 6-3. Note that the top portion of the form contains information about part name, lot number, operation, operator, machine, gage used, unit of measurement, and specifications. The next segment of the chart contains information about the date and time the subgroup is taken, the raw observations, and such summary information such as the sum, average, and range for each subgroup, as well as space for comments. Below this segment is space for drawing the control chart for the average and range.

6-4 CONTROL CHARTS FOR THE MEAN AND RANGE

After preliminary decisions related to the construction of control charts have been made, the following steps may be used as guidelines for their development.

Development of the Charts

Step 1: Using a preselected sampling scheme and sample size, measurements of the selected quality characteristic are recorded on appropriate forms.

Step 2: For each subgroup, the sample average and range are calculated using the following formulas:

$$\overline{X} = \frac{\sum_{i=1}^{n} X_i}{n} \tag{6.1}$$

$$R = X_{\max} - X_{\min} \tag{6.2}$$

where X_i represents the ith observation, n is the sample or subgroup size, $X_{\max}$ is the largest observation, and $X_{\min}$ is the smallest observation.

Step 3: The center line and the trial control limits are obtained for each of the charts. For the $\overline{X}$ chart, the center line $\overline{\overline{X}}$ is given by

$$\overline{\overline{X}} = \frac{\sum_{i=1}^{g} X_i}{g} \tag{6.3}$$

where g represents the number of subgroups or samples chosen. For the R-chart, the center line $\overline{R}$ is found from

$$\overline{R} = \frac{\sum_{i=1}^{g} R_i}{g} \tag{6.4}$$

Conceptually, the 3σ control limits for the $\overline{X}$-chart are

$$\overline{\overline{X}} \pm 3\sigma_{\overline{X}} \tag{6.5}$$

Rather than computing $\sigma_{\overline{X}}$ from the raw data, one can make use of the relation between the process standard deviation σ

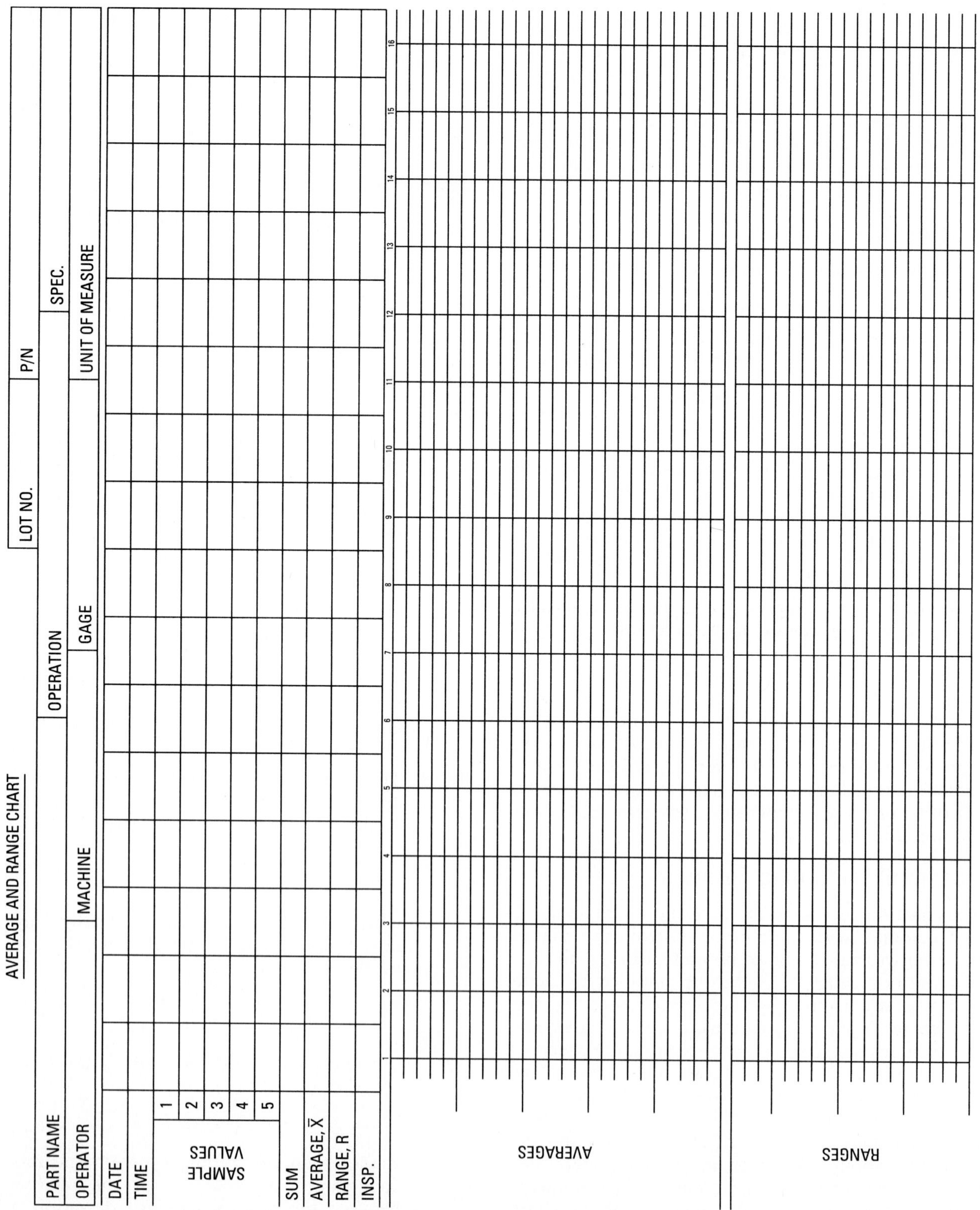

Figure 6-3 Sample data recording form for $\overline{X}$ and R chart.

(or the standard deviation of the individual items) and the mean of the ranges ($\overline{R}$). Multiplying factors used to calculate the center line and control limits are given in Appendix A-7. It is known that, when sampling from a population that is normally distributed, the distribution of the statistic $W = R/\sigma$, known as the relative range, is dependent on the sample size n. The mean of W is represented by d_2 and is tabulated in Appendix A-7. Thus, an estimate of the process standard deviation is

$$\hat{\sigma} = \frac{\overline{R}}{d_2} \tag{6.6}$$

The control limits for an $\overline{X}$-chart are therefore

$$(\text{UCL}_{\overline{X}}, \text{LCL}_{\overline{X}}) = \overline{\overline{X}} \pm \frac{3\hat{\sigma}}{\sqrt{n}}$$

$$= \overline{\overline{X}} \pm \frac{3\overline{R}}{\sqrt{n}d_2}$$

$$(\text{UCL}_{\overline{X}}, \text{LCL}_{\overline{X}}) = \overline{\overline{X}} \pm A_2\overline{R} \tag{6.7}$$

where $A_2 = 3/\sqrt{n}d_2$ and is tabulated in Appendix A-7. Equation 6.7 is the working equation for determining the $\overline{X}$-chart control limits, given $\overline{R}$.

The control limits for the range chart are conceptually given by

$$(\text{UCL}_R, \text{LCL}_R) = \overline{R} \pm 3\sigma_R \tag{6.8}$$

Since $R = \sigma W$, we have $\sigma_R = \sigma\sigma_w$. In Appendix A-7, σ_w is tabulated as d_3. Using Equation 6.6, we get

$$\hat{\sigma}_R = \left(\frac{\overline{R}}{d_2}\right)d_3$$

The control limits for the R-chart are written as

$$\begin{aligned} \text{UCL}_R &= \overline{R} + 3d_3\left(\frac{\overline{R}}{d_2}\right) = D_4\overline{R} \\ \text{LCL}_R &= \overline{R} - 3d_3\left(\frac{\overline{R}}{d_2}\right) = D_3\overline{R} \end{aligned} \tag{6.9}$$

where

$$D_4 = 1 + \frac{3d_3}{d_2} \text{ and } D_3 = 1 - \frac{3d_3}{d_2}$$

Equation 6.9 is the working equation for the calculation of the control limits. Values of D_4 and D_3 are tabulated in Appendix A-7.

Step 4: Plot the values of the range on the respective control chart, with the center line and the control limits drawn. Determine if all of the points are in statistical control. If not, investigate the assignable causes associated with the out-of-control points, and take appropriate remedial action.

The rules for out-of-control conditions described in Chapter 5 may be used to determine if a process is out of control. Typically, only some of the rules are used simultaneously. The most commonly used criterion for determining an out-of-control situation is the presence of a point outside the control limits. Other rules are given in Chapter 5.

If some points are found to be out of control, the reasons behind this must be investigated. Remedial actions that will eliminate those assignable causes should be proposed in order to bring the process to control. An R-chart is usually analyzed before an $\overline{X}$-chart to determine out-of-control situations. An R-chart reflects process variability, which should be brought to control first. As shown by Equation 6.7, the control limits for an $\overline{X}$-chart involve the process variability and hence $\overline{R}$. Therefore, if an R-chart shows an out-of-control situation, the limits on the $\overline{X}$-chart may not be meaningful. Consider Figure 6-4, for example. On the R-chart, sample number 12 plots above the upper control limit and so is out of control. The $\overline{X}$-chart, however, does not show the process to be out of control. Suppose the assignable cause is identified as a problem with a new vendor supplying raw materials and components. The task is to eliminate the cause perhaps by choosing a new vendor or requiring evidence of statistical process control at the vendor's plant.

Step 5: Determine the revised center line and control limits for the $\overline{X}$- and R-charts. Once remedial actions have been taken to remove the assignable causes, the out-of-control points should be deleted. The center lines and control limits on both the R-chart and the $\overline{X}$-chart may change. For the R-chart of Figure 6-4, subgroup 12, which is out of control, should be deleted. The revised center line and control limits on the R-chart should then be found. Next, using the remaining subgroups, the center line and control limits on the $\overline{X}$-chart should be

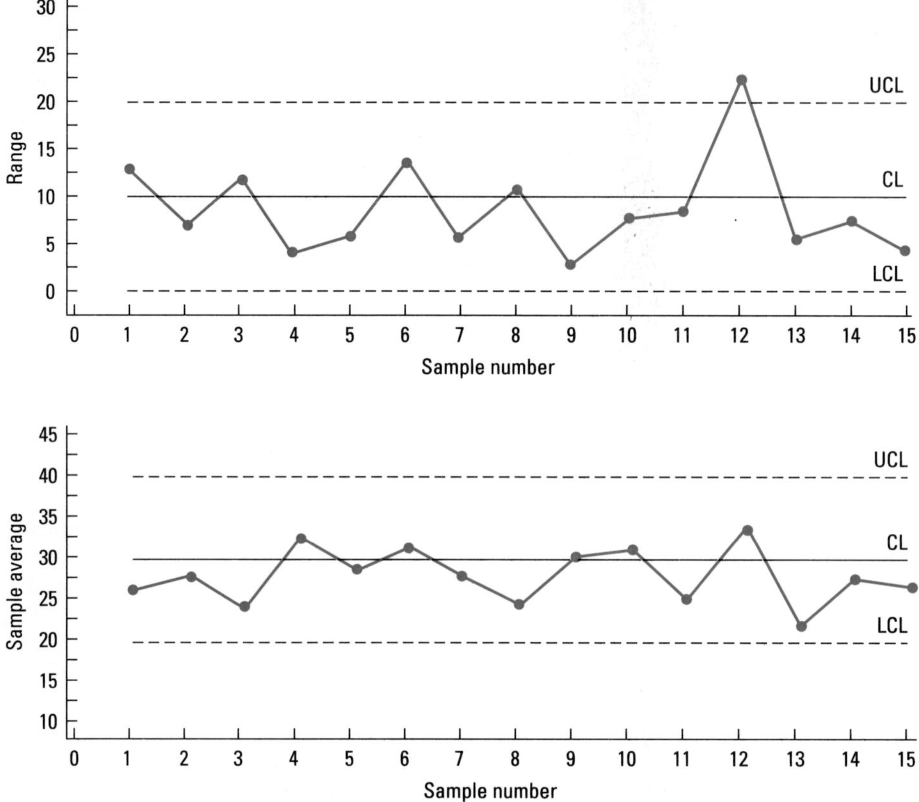

Figure 6-4 Plot of sample values on an $\overline{X}$ and R chart.

found. These limits are known as the revised control limits. The cycle of obtaining information, determining the trial limits, finding out-of-control points, identifying and correcting assignable causes, and determining revised control limits continues. The revised control limits will serve as trial control limits for the immediate future until the limits are revised again. This ongoing process is a critical component of continuous improvement.

A point of interest regarding the revision of control charts for the range concerns observations that plot below the lower control limit on the range chart when the lower control limit is greater than zero. Such points that fall below LCL_R are, statistically speaking, out of control; however, they are quite desirable. These points indicate unusually small variability within a sample or subgroup, which is, after all, one of the main objectives. Such small variability is most likely due to assignable causes. The control chart user should make sure that there were no measurement or recording errors associated with the particular observation. If the user is convinced that the small variability does indeed represent the operating state of the process during that period of time, an effort should be made to identify the causes behind the small variability. Upon determining these causes, the goal should be to create such conditions consistently in order to reduce the process variability. Therefore, accurate observations that fall below LCL_R should not be deleted during the revision process. If assignable causes for their occurrence are found, the process should be set to match those favorable conditions, and the observations should be retained for calculating the revised center line and the revised control limits for the R-chart.

Step 6: Implement the control charts. The $\overline{X}$ and R control charts should be implemented for future observations, using the revised center line and control limits. The charts should be displayed in a conspicuous place where they will be visible to operators, supervisors, and managers. Statistical process control will be effective only if everyone is committed to it—from the operator to the chief executive officer.

Example 6-1: Consider a process by which coils are manufactured. Samples of size 5 are randomly selected from the process, and the resistance values (in ohms) of the coils are measured. The data values are given in Table 6-2. From the raw data, summary measures such as the sample mean $\overline{X}$ and the range R are computed for each sample and shown in Table 6-2. First, the sum of the ranges is found, and then the center line $\overline{R}$ is plotted on the range chart. We have

$$\overline{R} = \frac{\sum_{i=1}^{g} R_i}{g} = \frac{92}{25} = 3.68$$

For a sample of size 5, Appendix A-7 gives $D_4 = 2.114$ and $D_3 = 0$. The trial control limits for the R-chart are calculated as follows:

$$\text{UCL}_R = D_4\overline{R} = (2.114)(3.68) = 7.780$$
$$\text{LCL}_R = D_3\overline{R} = (0)(3.68) = 0$$

The sample ranges are plotted on a control chart showing the center line, UCL_R, and LCL_R. Figure 6-5 shows this R-chart. Sample number 3 plots above UCL_R and so is considered to be out of control. The cause of this should be investigated to allow appropriate action to be taken. The large value of R could possibly be due to raw materials and components purchased from a new vendor. Suppose management decides that the new vendor should provide documentation showing that adequate control measures have been implemented at the vendor's plant and that the delivered raw materials and components conform to certain specified standards. If this action is taken, the limits for the R-chart may be revised by deleting sample number 3. The revised center line is

$$\overline{R} = \frac{84}{24} = 3.50$$

TABLE 6-2 Data values for resistance of coils

Sample number	Observations	$\overline{X}$	R	Comments
1	20, 22, 21, 23, 22	21.60	3	
2	19, 18, 22, 20, 20	19.80	4	
3	25, 18, 20, 17, 22	20.40	8	New vendor
4	20, 21, 22, 21, 21	21.00	2	
5	19, 24, 23, 22, 20	21.60	5	
6	22, 20, 18, 18, 19	19.40	4	
7	18, 20, 19, 18, 20	19.00	2	
8	20, 18, 23, 20, 21	20.40	5	
9	21, 20, 24, 23, 22	22.00	4	
10	21, 19, 20, 20, 20	20.00	2	
11	20, 20, 23, 22, 20	21.00	3	
12	22, 21, 20, 22, 23	21.60	3	
13	19, 22, 19, 18, 19	19.40	4	
14	20, 21, 22, 21, 22	21.20	2	
15	20, 24, 24, 23, 23	22.80	4	
16	21, 20, 24, 20, 21	21.20	4	
17	20, 18, 18, 20, 20	19.20	2	
18	20, 24, 22, 23, 23	22.40	4	
19	20, 19, 23, 20, 19	20.20	4	
20	22, 21, 21, 24, 22	22.00	3	
21	23, 22, 22, 20, 22	21.80	3	
22	21, 18, 18, 17, 19	18.60	4	High temperature
23	21, 24, 24, 23, 23	23.00	3	Wrong die
24	20, 22, 21, 21, 20	20.80	2	
25	19, 20, 21, 21, 22	20.60	3	
		Sum = 521.00	Sum = 92	

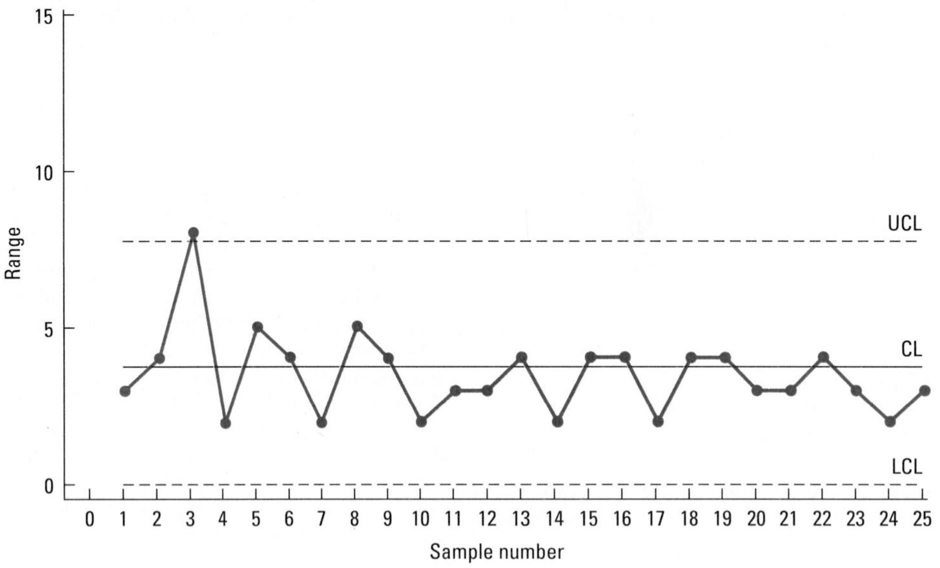

Figure 6-5 R chart for data on resistance of coils.

The revised control limits are

$$UCL_R = D_4\overline{R} = (2.114)(3.50) = 7.399$$
$$LCL_R = D_3\overline{R} = (0)(3.50) = 0$$

All of the remaining points are now found to be in control on the R-chart.

The center line for the chart showing the mean $\overline{X}$ is

$$\overline{\overline{X}} = \frac{\sum_{i=1}^{g}\overline{X}_i}{g} = \frac{500.6}{24} = 20.858$$

Appendix A-7, for $n = 5$, gives $A_2 = 0.577$. Hence, the control limits on the $\overline{X}$-chart are

$$UCL_{\overline{X}} = \overline{\overline{X}} + A_2\overline{R} = 20.858 + (0.577)(3.50) = 22.878$$
$$LCL_{\overline{X}} = \overline{\overline{X}} - A_2\overline{R} = 20.858 - (0.577)(3.50) = 18.838$$

Figure 6-6 shows this $\overline{X}$-chart with the plotted values of the sample averages. It can be seen that sample numbers 22 and 23 are out of control. Upon investigation of possible assignable causes for these two observations, it is discovered that the oven temperature was too high for sample number 22 and that the wrong die was used for sample number 23. Remedial actions were taken to rectify these situations. The center line and control limits for the $\overline{X}$-chart may be revised by deleting these two observations.

The revised center line is

$$\overline{\overline{X}} = \frac{459}{22} = 20.864$$

The revised center line on the range chart is

$$\overline{R} = \frac{77}{22} = 3.50$$

The revised control limits on the $\overline{X}$-chart are

$$UCL_{\overline{X}} = \overline{\overline{X}} + A_2\overline{R} = 20.864 + (0.577)(3.50) = 22.884$$
$$LCL_{\overline{X}} = \overline{\overline{X}} - A_2\overline{R} = 20.864 - (0.577)(3.50) = 18.844$$

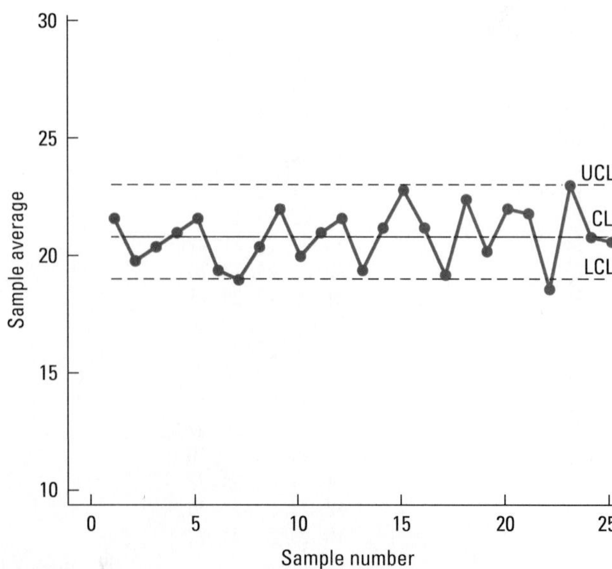

Figure 6-6 $\overline{X}$-chart for data on resistance of coils.

All of the sample averages are now in control. The revised R-chart limits are

$$UCL_R = D_4\overline{R} = (2.114)(3.50) = 7.399$$

$$LCL_R = D_3\overline{R} = (0)(3.50) = 0$$

These limits should be used for future observations until they are revised.

Variable Subgroup Size

Up to now the subgroup size has been assumed to be constant. A change in the subgroup size has an impact on the control limits for the $\overline{X}$- and R-charts. From Equations 6.7 and 6.9, it can be seen that an increase in the sample size n reduces the width of the control limits. For an $\overline{X}$-chart, the width of the control limits from the center line is inversely proportional to the square root of the sample size. Appendix A-7 shows the pattern in which the values of the control chart factors A_2, D_4, and D_3 decrease with an increase in sample size.

Control Limits for a Given Target or Standard

Sometimes management may want to specify values for the process mean and standard deviation. These values may represent goals or desirable standard or target values. Control charts that are constructed based on these target values may help in determining whether the existing process is capable of meeting the desirable standards. Furthermore, they may also help management set realistic goals for the existing process.

Let $\overline{X}_0$ and σ_0 represent the target values of the process mean and standard deviation, respectively. The center line and control limits based on these standard values for the $\overline{X}$-chart are given by

$$CL_{\overline{X}} = \overline{X}_0$$

$$UCL_{\overline{X}} = \overline{X}_0 + 3\frac{\sigma_0}{\sqrt{n}} \qquad (6.10)$$

$$LCL_{\overline{X}} = \overline{X}_0 - 3\frac{\sigma_0}{\sqrt{n}}$$

Let $A = 3/\sqrt{n}$. Values for A are tabulated in Appendix A-7. Equations 6.10 may be rewritten as

$$CL_{\overline{X}} = \overline{X}_0$$

$$UCL_{\overline{X}} = \overline{X}_0 + A\sigma_0 \qquad (6.11)$$

$$LCL_{\overline{X}} = \overline{X}_0 - A\sigma_0$$

For the range chart, the center line is found as follows. Since $\hat{\sigma} = \overline{R}/d_2$, we have

$$CL_R = d_2\sigma_0 \qquad (6.12)$$

where d_2 is tabulated in Appendix A-7. The control limits for the R-chart are obtained as follows:

$$UCL_R = \overline{R} + 3\sigma_R = d_2\sigma_0 + 3d_3\sigma_0$$
$$= (d_2 + 3d_3)\sigma_0 = D_2\sigma_0 \qquad (6.13)$$

where $D_2 = d_2 + 3d_3$ (as tabulated in Appendix A-7) and $\sigma_R = d_3\sigma$.

Similarly,

$$LCL_R = \overline{R} - 3\sigma_R = d_2\sigma_0 - 3d_3\sigma_0$$
$$= (d_2 - 3d_3)\sigma_0 = D_1\sigma_0 \qquad (6.14)$$

where $D_1 = d_2 - 3d_3$, as tabulated in Appendix A-7.

One must be cautious in interpreting control charts based on target or standard values. It is quite possible that the sample observations will fall outside the control limits even though no assignable causes are present in the process. This is because the desirable standards upon which the control limits are based may not be consistent with the process conditions. Thus, one could unnecessarily waste time and resources looking for assignable causes. On an $\overline{X}$-chart, plotted points could fall outside the control limits because of a target process mean that is specified as too high or too low compared to the existing process mean. Usually, it is easier to meet a desirable target value for the process mean than for the process variability. For example, adjusting the average diameter or length of a part can be accomplished by changing some controllable process parameters. However, correcting for R-chart points that plot above the upper control limit generally is much more difficult. An R-chart may indicate that the process variability exceeds the desirable standard, but this can happen even without any assignable causes present in the system. Therefore, reducing the process variability to meet the target value σ_0 may involve drastic change in the process, equipment, methods, and so on. The implication of such an R-chart may be that the existing process, in the absence of assignable causes, is not capable of meeting the desired standard. Such information may help management in setting realistic goals.

Example 6-2: Refer to the data for the resistance of coils in Example 6-1. Suppose the given target values for the average resistance and standard deviation are 21.0 and 1.0 ohms, respectively. The sample size is 5. The center line and the control limits for the $\overline{X}$-chart are as follows:

$$CL_{\overline{X}} = \overline{X}_0 = 21.0$$

$$\mathrm{UCL}_{\overline{X}} = \overline{X}_0 + A\sigma_0 = 21.0 + (1.342)(1.0) = 22.342$$

$$\mathrm{LCL}_{\overline{X}} = \overline{X}_0 - A\sigma_0 = 21.0 - (1.342)(1.0) = 19.658$$

The center line and control limits for the R-chart are

$$\mathrm{CL}_R = d_2\sigma_0 = (2.326)(1.0) = 2.326$$

$$\mathrm{UCL}_R = D_2\sigma_0 = (4.918)(1.0) = 4.918$$

$$\mathrm{LCL}_R = D_1\sigma_0 = (0)(1.0) = 0$$

Figure 6-7 shows the control chart for the range based on the standard value. Since the control charts were revised for the data in Example 6-1, we plot the 22 samples that were in control by excluding sample numbers 3, 22, and 23. Normally, we would have plotted all of the samples on the control chart. However, since we know in this case that three samples were out of control for which assignable causes had been identified, we assume that the remedial actions taken have eliminated those causes. By using this reduced data, we can see how close the process, which is in control, comes to meeting the stipulated target values.

Figure 6-7 shows that the process seems to be out of control with respect to the given standard. Sample numbers 5 and 8 are above the upper control limit, and a majority of the points lie above the center line. Only six of the plotted values are below the center line. In Example 6-1, eliminating sample numbers 3, 22, and 23 allowed the process to be in control. Figure 6-7 reveals that the process is not capable of meeting the stipulated guidelines. The target standard deviation σ_0 is 1.0. The estimated process standard deviation from Example 6-1 (calculated after the process was brought to control) is

$$\hat{\sigma} = \frac{\overline{R}}{d_2} = \frac{3.50}{2.326} = 1.505$$

This estimate exceeds the target value of 1.0. Management must look for a means of reducing the process variability if the standard is to be met. This may require major changes in the methods of operation, the incoming material, or the equipment. Process control will not be sufficient to achieve the desired target.

The $\overline{X}$ control chart based on the standard value is depicted in Figure 6-8. Several points fall outside the control limits. Four points are below the lower control limit, and two points are above the upper control limit. From Example 6-1, the revised center line for the $\overline{X}$-chart was found to be 20.864. The target center line is 21.0. An adjustment in controllable process parameters could possible shift the average level up to 21.0. However, the fact that there are points outside both the upper and lower control limits signifies that the process variability must be reduced in order for all points to be within the control limits. This task must be achieved through process improvement rather than process control. This information might also indicate to management that the target standard deviation of 1.0 may not be realistic for the current process. Unless management decides to make major changes in the process to bring about improvement, the target value may not be feasible. Actions on the part of the operators alone are unlikely to cause the necessary reduction in process variability.

Interpretation of the Charts

As discussed in Chapter 5, there are several guidelines for determining out-of-control conditions. The presence of a point falling outside the 3σ limits is the most widely used criterion. Other guidelines are based on identifiable patterns in the plot. Useful diagnostic information can be obtained from such patterns. Knowledge of the process may provide clues as to possible remedial actions for situations involving a process that is out of control. On the

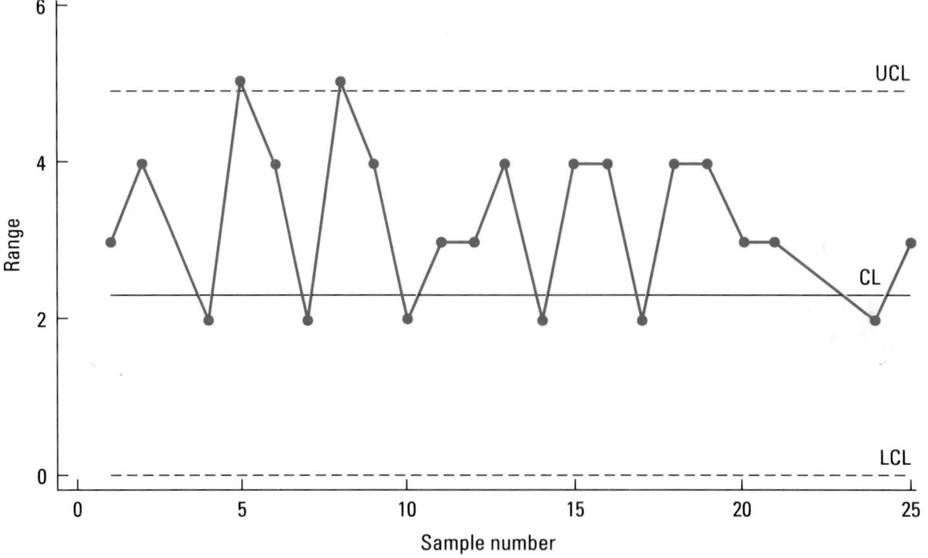

Figure 6-7 R control chart based on a standard value.

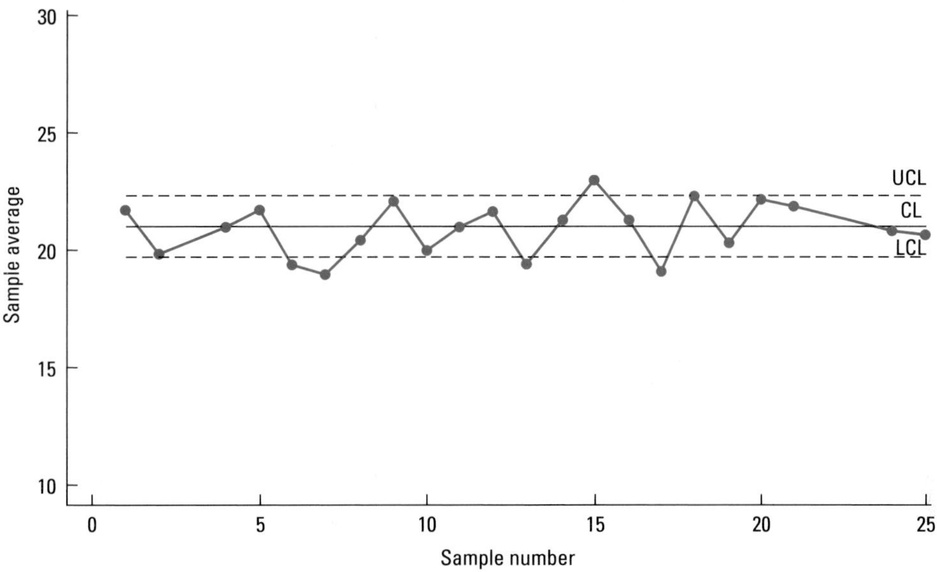

Figure 6-8 $\overline{X}$ control chart based on a standard value.

whole, the difficult parts of the analysis are the determination and interpretation of the assignable causes that force the process to go out of control and the selection of actions to be taken. For an effective operational system of control charts, the user should be familiar with not only the statistical foundations of control charts but also the process itself. He or she should have a thorough understanding of how the different controllable parameters influence the dependent variable of interest. The quality assurance manager or analyst should work closely with the product design engineer and the process designer or analyst to come up with optimal policies.

For many situations, if the R-chart is brought to control, many assignable causes for the $\overline{X}$-chart will be eliminated as well. The $\overline{X}$-chart monitors the centering of the process. An abrupt jump on the $\overline{X}$-chart implies that the process average has jumped. Similarly, an increasing or decreasing trend on the $\overline{X}$-chart indicates that the process center is gradually increasing or decreasing. Process centering usually takes place through machine setting, while other process adjustments take place through controllable parameters such as proper tool, proper depth of cut, or proper feed. On the other hand, reducing process variability in order to allow an R-chart to exhibit control is a difficult task that is accomplished through quality improvement.

Once a process is in statistical control, an estimate of its capability as measured by the process standard deviation can be obtained. This measure can then be used to determine how the process performs with respect to some stated specification limits. The proportion of nonconforming items can be estimated. Depending on the characteristic being considered, some of the output may be reworked, while some may become scrap. Given the unit cost of rework and scrap, an estimate of the total cost of rework and scrap can be obtained. A more detailed discussion of process capability measures is given in Chapter 8. From an R-chart that exhibits control, the process standard deviation can be estimated as

$$\hat{\sigma} = \frac{\overline{R}}{d_2}$$

where $\overline{R}$ is the center line and d_2 is a factor that is tabulated in Appendix A-7. If the distribution of the quality characteristic can be assumed to be normal, then given some specification limits, the standard normal table can be used to determine the proportion of output that is nonconforming.

Example 6-3: Refer to the data for the resistance of coils in Example 6-1. Suppose the specifications are 21 ± 3 ohms.

a. Determine the proportion of the output that is nonconforming, assuming that the resistance of coils is normally distributed.

Solution. From the revised R-chart, we found the center line to be $\overline{R} = 3.50$. The estimated process standard deviation is

$$\hat{\sigma} = \frac{\overline{R}}{d_2} = \frac{3.50}{2.236} = 1.505$$

The revised center line on the $\overline{X}$-chart is $\overline{\overline{X}} = 20.864$, which we use as an estimate of the process mean. Fig-

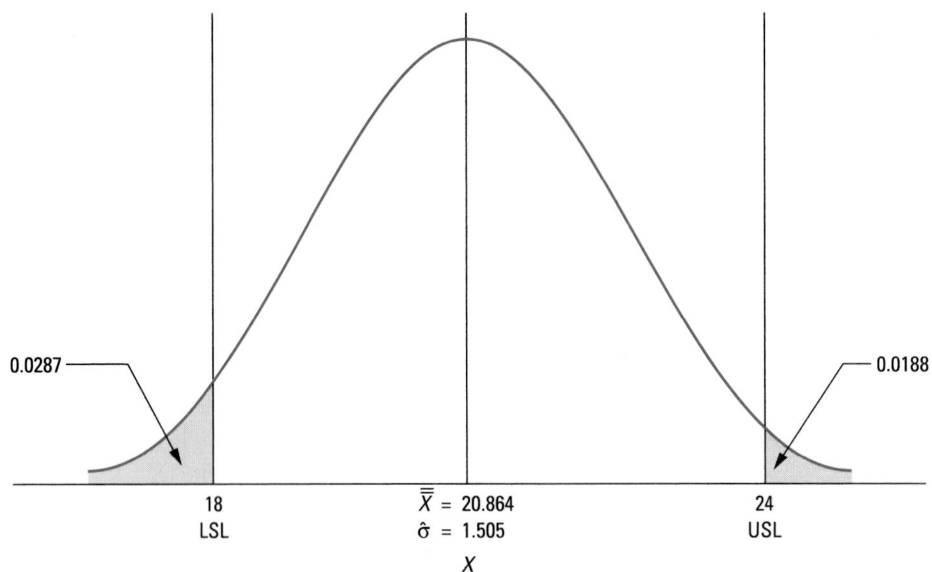

Figure 6-9 Proportion of nonconforming output.

ure 6-9 shows the proportion of the output that is nonconforming. The standardized normal value at the lower specification limit (LSL) is found as

$$z_1 = \frac{(18 - 20.864)}{1.505} = -1.90$$

The standardized normal value at the upper specification limit (USL) is

$$z_2 = \frac{(24 - 20.864)}{1.505} = 2.08$$

Looking up these standard normal values in Appendix A-3, we find that the proportion of the product that is below the LSL is 0.0287, and the proportion above the USL is 0.0188. Thus, the total proportion of the output that is nonconforming is 0.0475.

b. If the daily production rate is 10,000 coils and if coils that have a resistance less than the LSL cannot be used for the desired purpose, what is the loss to the manufacturer if the unit cost of scrap is 50 cents?

Solution. The daily cost of scrap is

$$(10,000)(0.0287)(0.50) = \$143.50$$

Control Chart Patterns and Corrective Actions

A nonrandom identifiable pattern in the plot of a control chart might provide sufficient reason to look for assignable, or special, causes in the system. Chance, or common, causes of variation are inherent to a system; a system operating under only chance causes is said to be in a state of statistical control. Assignable causes, however, could be due to periodic and persistent disturbances that affect the process intermittently. The objective is to identify the assignable causes and take appropriate remedial action.

Western Electric Company engineers have identified 15 characteristic patterns found in control charts. The ability to recognize these patterns may be useful in determining when action needs to be taken as well as the possible type of action to take (AT&T, 1984). Some of the general pattern categories include more than one characteristic pattern. For example, multi-universe patterns include stable mixtures, associated with systematic variables and stratification, and unstable mixtures, associated with freaks and bunches, or groups. The major pattern categories are discussed below.

Natural Patterns A natural pattern is one for which there is no identifiable arrangement of the plotted points. Furthermore, no points fall outside the control limits, the majority of the points are near the centerline, and few points are close to the control limits (Gitlow et al., 1989). Natural patterns are indicative of a process that is in control. They demonstrate the presence of a stable system of chance causes, an example of which is shown in Figure 6-10.

Sudden Shifts in the Level Many causes can bring about a sudden change in the level of the plotted pattern on an $\overline{X}$- or R-chart. A remedial action will therefore depend on the pertinent assignable cause. Figure 6-11 shows an example of a sudden shift on an $\overline{X}$-chart. Such shifts may occur because of changes—intentional or otherwise—in such pro-

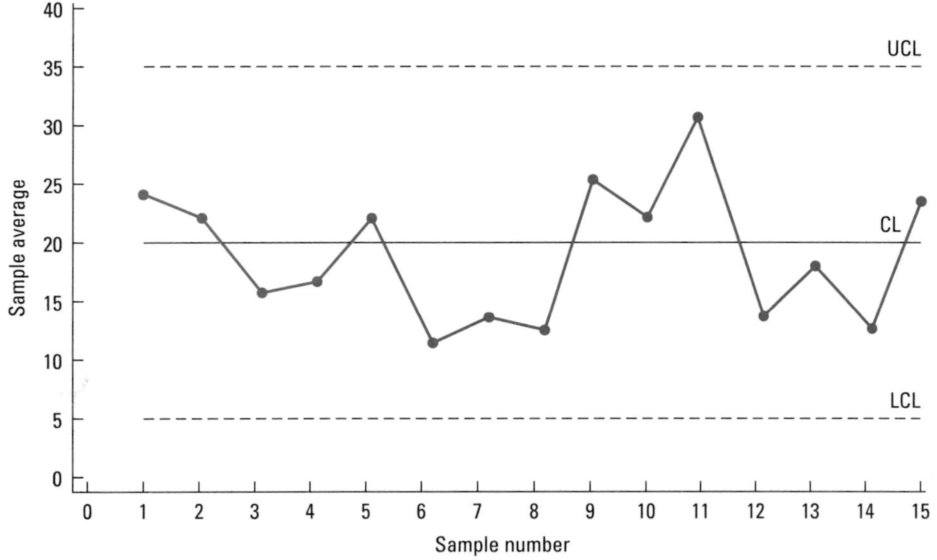

Figure 6-10 Control chart pattern for a system of chance causes.

cess settings as temperature, pressure, or depth of cut. An example of a sudden change in the average level of a service would be a change in customer waiting time at a bank resulting from a change in the number of servers or tellers. New operators, new equipment, new measuring instruments, new vendors, and new methods of processing are some other reasons for the occurrence of sudden shifts on $\overline{X}$- and R-charts.

Gradual Shifts in the Level Gradual shifts in the level of the plotted pattern may occur for situations in which the effect of changing a process parameter takes place over a period of time after which the process stabilizes. An $\overline{X}$-chart might exhibit such a shift because of a change in the incoming quality of raw materials or components over time, a change in the maintenance program, or a change in the style of supervision. An R-chart might exhibit such a shift because of a new operator, a decrease in worker skill due to fatigue or monotony, or a gradual improvement in the incoming quality of raw materials because a vendor has implemented a

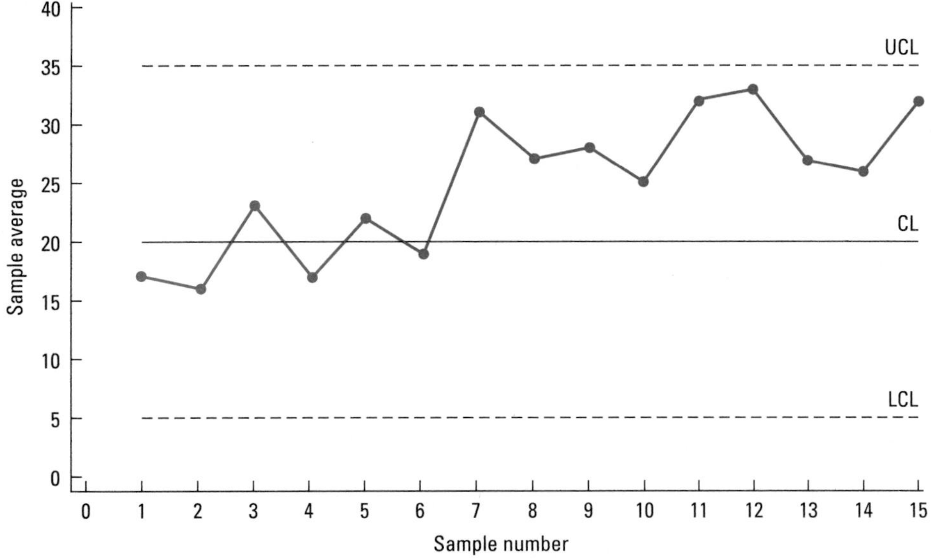

Figure 6-11 Sudden shift in the level of the plotted pattern.

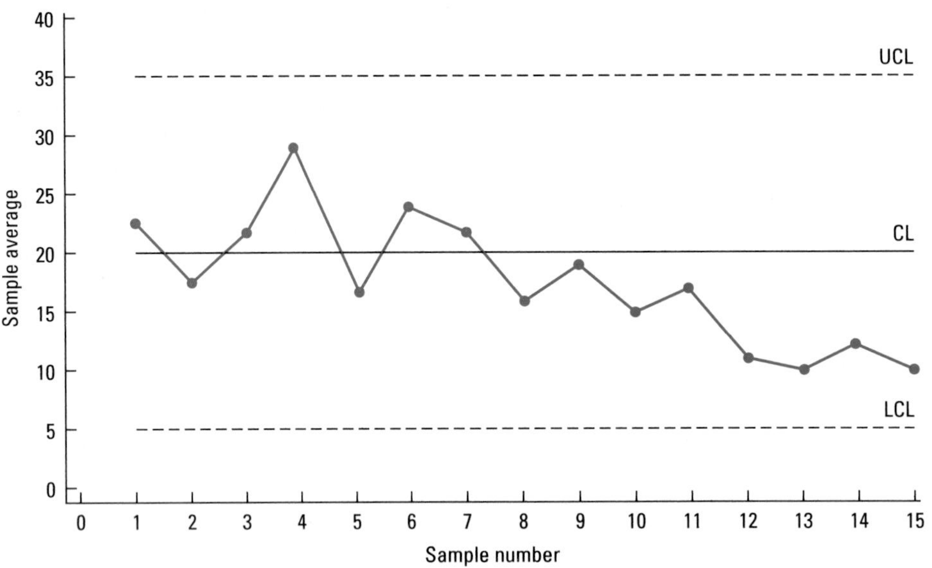

Figure 6-12 Gradual shift in the level of the plotted pattern.

statistical process control system. Figure 6-12 shows an $\overline{X}$-chart exhibiting a gradual shift in the level.

Trends in the Pattern of Plotted Points Trends differ from gradual shifts in the level in that trends do not stabilize or settle down. Trends represent changes that steadily increase or decrease. An $\overline{X}$-chart may exhibit a trend because of tool wear, die wear, gradual deterioration of equipment, buildup of debris in jigs and fixtures, gradual change in temperature, and so on. An *R*- chart may exhibit a trend because of a gradual improvement in operator skill resulting from on-the-job training, a decrease in operator skill due to fatigue, and so on. Figure 6-13 depicts a pattern indicating a trend on an $\overline{X}$-chart.

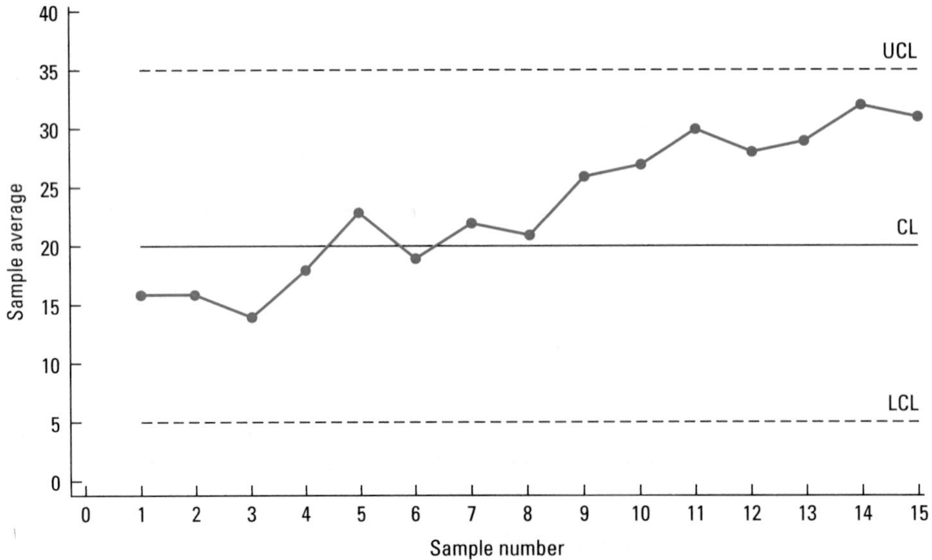

Figure 6-13 Pattern indicating a trend on an $\overline{X}$ chart.

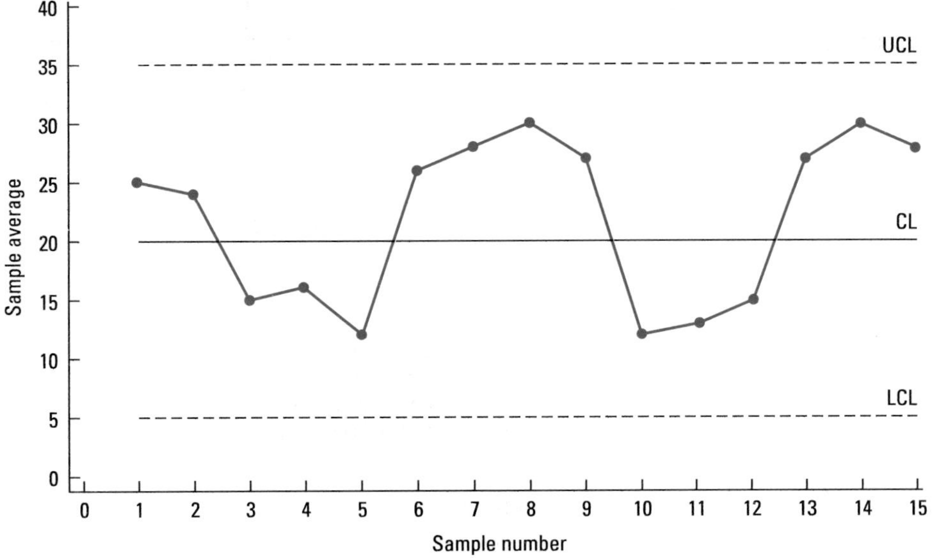

Figure 6-14 Cyclic pattern on a control chart.

Cyclic Patterns Cyclic patterns are characterized by a repetition of periodic behavior in the system as shown by cycles of low and high points on a control chart. An $\overline{X}$-chart may exhibit cyclic behavior because of a rotation of operators, periodic changes in temperature and humidity (such as a cold morning startup), or seasonal variation of incoming components. An R-chart may exhibit cyclic patterns because of operator fatigue and subsequent energization following breaks, a difference between shifts, or periodic maintenance of equipment. Figure 6-14 shows a cyclic pattern for an $\overline{X}$-chart. If samples are taken too infrequently, it is possible that only the high or the low points will be represented and the graph will not exhibit a cyclic pattern. If a control chart user suspects cyclic behavior, then he or she should take samples frequently enough to investigate the possibility of a cyclic pattern.

Wild Patterns Wild patterns may be divided into two categories—freaks and bunches (or groups). Control chart points exhibiting either of these two properties are, statistically speaking, significantly different from the other points. Assignable causes are generally associated with these points.

Freaks are caused by external disturbances that influence one or more subgroups. They are plotted points too small or too large with respect to the control limits. Such points usually fall outside the control limits and are easily distinguishable from the other points on the chart. It is often not difficult to identify assignable causes. One should make sure, however, that there is no measurement or recording error associated with the freak point. Some assignable causes of freaks include sudden, very short-lived power failures, the use of a new tool for a brief test period, the failure of a component, and so on. Figure 6-15 shows an example of a control chart exhibiting a freak pattern.

Bunches, or *groups,* are clusters of a few observations that are close together and are decidedly different from the other points on the plot. Figure 6-16 shows an example of a control chart pattern exhibiting bunching behavior. Possible assignable causes of such behavior could be the use of a new vendor for a short period of time, use of a different machine for a brief time period, a new operator used for a short period, and so on.

Mixture Patterns (or the Effect of Two or More Populations) A mixture pattern is caused by the presence of two or more population distributions of the quality characteristic and is characterized by points that fall near the control limits, with an absence of points near the center line. A mixture pattern could occur when one set of values is too high and another set too low because of differences in the incoming quality of material from two vendors. A remedial action would be to have a separate

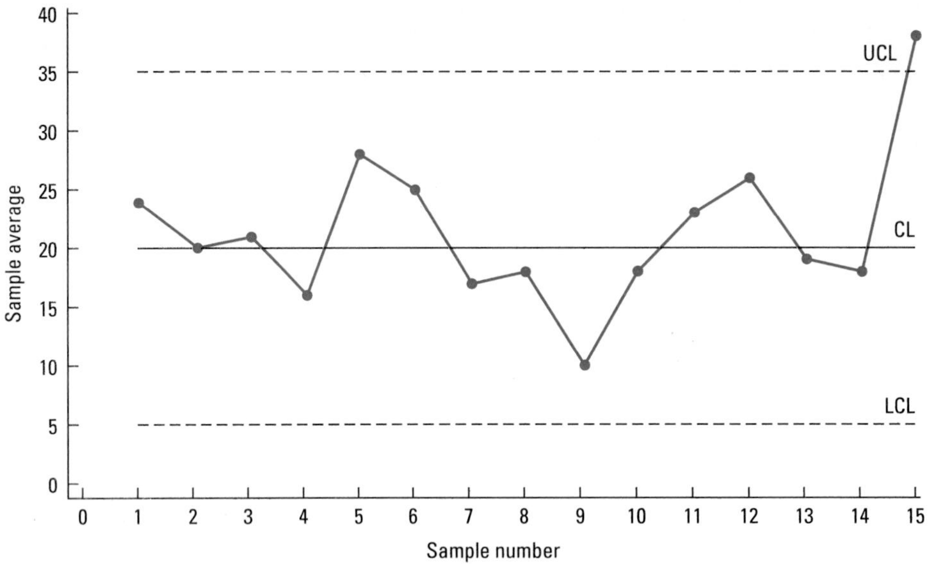

Figure 6-15 Freak pattern on a control chart.

control chart for each vendor. Figure 6-17 shows an example of a mixture pattern. On an $\overline{X}$-chart, it is possible for a mixture pattern to result from overcontrol. If an operator looks at the last plotted point and finds that it is near the upper control limit, he or she may adjust the machine or process to reduce the value of the quality characteristic, which may result in the next point plotting near the lower control limit. The operator may then adjust the process again to increase the value of the quality characteristic. Such overcontrol will cause a pattern of large swings. Mixture patterns can also occur on both $\overline{X}$- and R-charts because of two or more machines being represented on the same control chart.

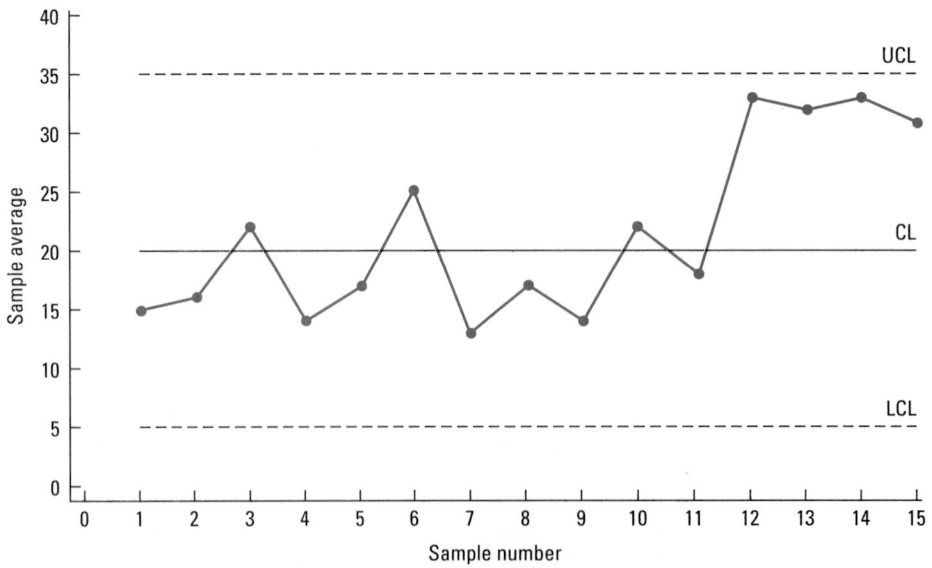

Figure 6-16 Bunching pattern in a control chart.

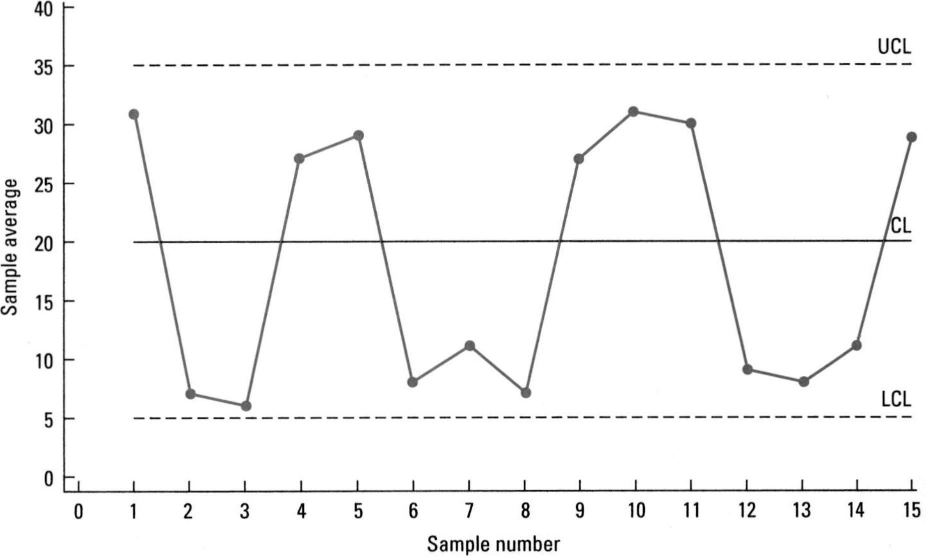

Figure 6-17 Mixture pattern on a control chart.

Stratification Patterns A stratification pattern is another possible result of the presence of two or more population distributions of the quality characteristic. However, in this case the output is combined, or mixed, and samples are chosen from the mixed output. This may result in a pattern where the majority of the points are very close to the center line, with very few points near the control limits. Thus the plot may be misinterpreted as indicating unusually good control. An example of a plot with stratification is shown in Figure 6-18. Such a plot could have resulted from plotting data for samples composed of the combined output of two shifts, each different in its performance. It is possible for

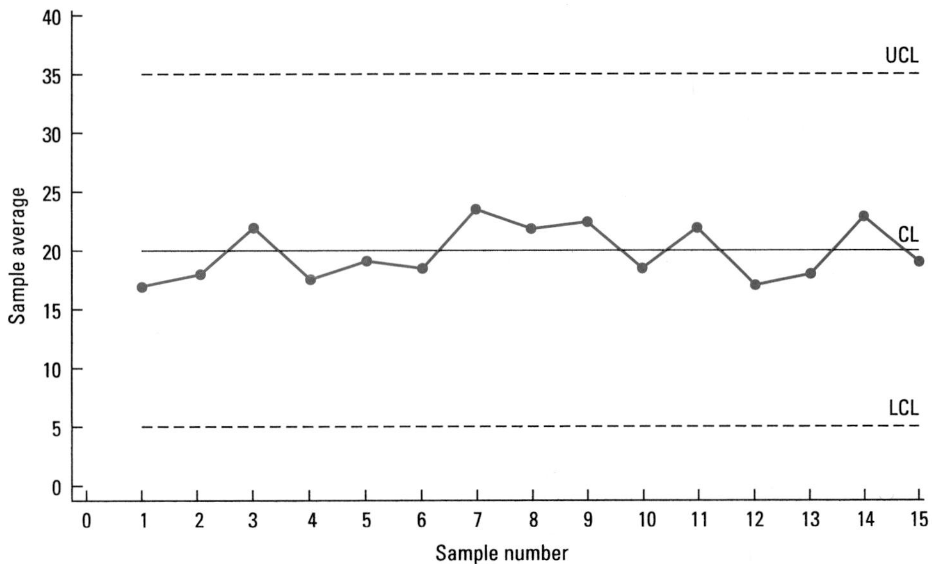

Figure 6-18 Stratification pattern on a control chart.

the sample average (which is really the average of parts chosen from both shifts) to fluctuate very little, resulting in a stratification pattern in the plot. Remedial measures in such situations involve having separate control charts for each shift. The method of choosing rational subgroups should be carefully analyzed so that component distributions are not mixed when subgroups are chosen.

Interaction Patterns An interaction pattern occurs when the level of one variable affects the behavior of other variables associated with the quality characteristic of interest. Furthermore, the combined effect of two or more variables on the output quality characteristic may be different from the individual effect of each variable. An interaction pattern can be detected by changing the scheme for rational subgrouping of the observations. Suppose that in a chemical process the temperature and pressure are two important controllable variables which affect the output quality characteristic of interest. A low level of pressure and a high level of temperature may produce a very desirable effect on the output characteristic, whereas a low level of pressure by itself may not have that effect. An effective method of subgrouping would involve controlling the temperature at several high values and then determining the effect of pressure on the output characteristic for each of these controlled values of temperature. Subgroups composed of random combinations of temperature and pressure may fail to identify the interactive effect of those variables on the output characteristic. Figure 6-19 demonstrates an example of interaction between variables. The first plot is constructed from observations for which the temperature was maintained at level A, whereas for the second plot, the temperature was held at level B. Note that there is a change in the average level and variability of the output characteristic for the two temperature levels. Also note that if the R-chart shows the sample ranges to be small, then information regarding the interaction that produced those small values could be used to help establish guidelines for desirable process parameter settings.

Control Charts for Other Variables The various control chart patterns described in this section may also occur in other types of control charts besides $\overline{X}$-and R-charts. Therefore, the patterns will not be discussed separately for the other control charts. The causes associated with the patterns found on other types of charts may be different from those discussed in this section, but similar reasoning can still be used to determine the assignable causes and to decide upon remedial actions. Furthermore, both the preliminary considerations and the steps for the construction of control charts described in this section apply to other control charts as well. For this reason, these steps will not be repeated in the discussion of the other types of control charts.

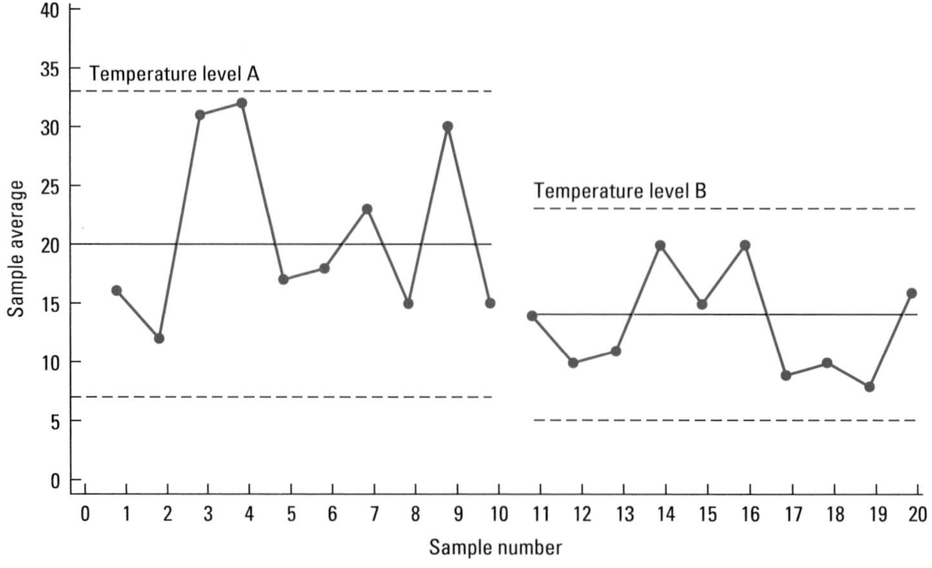

Figure 6-19 Pattern showing interaction among variables.

6-5 CONTROL CHARTS FOR THE MEAN AND STANDARD DEVIATION

Although a chart for the range is easy to construct and use, a chart for the standard deviation is preferable for larger sample sizes (greater than 10, usually). As mentioned in Chapter 2, the range accounts for only the maximum and minimum values of a sample and consequently is less effective for large sample sizes. The sample standard deviation serves as a better measure of process variability in these circumstances. The sample standard deviation is given by

$$s = \sqrt{\frac{\sum_{i=1}^{n}(X_i - \overline{X})^2}{n-1}} \tag{6.15}$$

$$= \sqrt{\frac{\sum_{i=1}^{n} X_i^2 - (\sum_{i=1}^{n} X_i)^2/n}{n-1}} \tag{6.16}$$

If the population distribution of a quality characteristic is normal with a population standard deviation denoted by σ, the mean and standard deviation of the sample standard deviation are given by

$$E(s) = c_4\sigma \tag{6.17}$$

$$\sigma_s = \sigma\sqrt{1 - c_4^2} \tag{6.18}$$

respectively, where c_4 is a factor that depends on the subgroup size and is given by (Montgomery, 1991; Wadsworth et al., 1986)

$$c_4 = \left[\frac{2}{(n-1)}\right]^{1/2} \frac{[(n-2)/2]!}{[(n-3)/2]!} \tag{6.19}$$

Values of c_4 are tabulated in Appendix A-7.

No Given Standards

The center line of a standard deviation chart is

$$CL_s = \bar{s} = \frac{\sum_{i=1}^{g} s_i}{g} \tag{6.20}$$

where g is the number of samples and s_i is the standard deviation of the ith sample. The upper control limit is

$$UCL_s = \bar{s} + 3\sigma_s = \bar{s} + 3\sigma\sqrt{1 - c_4^2}$$

In accordance with Equation 6.17, an estimate of the population standard deviation σ is

$$\hat{\sigma} = \frac{\bar{s}}{c_4} \tag{6.21}$$

Substituting this estimate of σ in the above expression yields

$$UCL_s = \bar{s} + \frac{3\bar{s}\sqrt{(1 - c_4^2)}}{c_4} = B_4\bar{s}$$

where $B_4 = 1 + 3\frac{\sqrt{(1-c_4^2)}}{c_4}$ and is tabulated in Appendix A-7. Similarly,

$$LCL_s = \bar{s} - \frac{3\bar{s}\sqrt{(1 - c_4^2)}}{c_4} = B_3\bar{s}$$

where $B_3 = 1 - 3\frac{\sqrt{(1-c_4^2)}}{c_4}$ and is also tabulated in Appendix A-7. Thus, the 3σ control limits are

$$\begin{aligned} UCL_s &= B_4\bar{s} \\ LCL_s &= B_3\bar{s} \end{aligned} \tag{6.22}$$

The center line of the chart for the mean $\overline{X}$ is given by

$$CL_{\overline{X}} = \overline{\overline{X}} = \frac{\sum_{i=1}^{g} \overline{X}_i}{g} \tag{6.23}$$

The control limits on an $\overline{X}$-chart are

$$\overline{\overline{X}} \pm 3\sigma_{\overline{X}} = \overline{\overline{X}} \pm 3\sigma/\sqrt{n}$$

By using Equation 6.21 to obtain an estimate of σ, we can find the control limits to be

$$\begin{aligned} UCL_{\overline{X}} &= \overline{\overline{X}} + 3\bar{s}/(c_4\sqrt{n}) = \overline{\overline{X}} + A_3\bar{s} \\ LCL_{\overline{X}} &= \overline{\overline{X}} - 3\bar{s}/(c_4\sqrt{n}) = \overline{\overline{X}} - A_3\bar{s} \end{aligned} \tag{6.24}$$

where $A_3 = 3/(c_4\sqrt{n})$, and is tabulated in Appendix A-7.

The process of constructing trial control limits, determining assignable causes associated with out-of-control points, taking remedial actions, and finding the revised control limits is similar to that explained in the section on $\overline{X}$- and R-charts. The s-chart should be constructed first. Only if it is in control should the $\overline{X}$-chart be developed, because the standard deviation of $\overline{X}$ is dependent on $\bar{s}$. If the s-chart is not in control, any estimate of the standard deviation of $\overline{X}$ will be unreliable, which will in turn create unreliable control limits for $\overline{X}$.

Given Standard

If a target standard deviation is specified as σ_0, the center line of the s-chart is found by using Equation 6.17 to be

$$CL_s = c_4\sigma_0 \tag{6.25}$$

The upper control limit for the s-chart is found by using Equation 6.18 to be

$$\begin{aligned} UCL_s &= c_4\sigma_0 + 3\sigma_s = c_4\sigma_0 + 3\sigma_0\sqrt{1 - c_4^2} \\ &= (c_4 + 3\sqrt{1 - c_4^2})\sigma_0 = B_6\sigma_0 \end{aligned}$$

where $B_6 = c_4 + 3\sqrt{1 - c_4^2}$ and is tabulated in Appendix A-7. Similarly, the lower control limit for the s-chart is

$$LCL_s = (c_4 - 3\sqrt{1 - c_4^2})\sigma_0 = B_5\sigma_0$$

where $B_5 = c_4 - 3\sqrt{1 - c_4^2}$ and is tabulated in Appendix A-7. Thus, the control limits for the s-chart are

$$\begin{aligned} UCL_s &= B_6\sigma_0 \\ LCL_s &= B_5\sigma_0 \end{aligned} \qquad (6.26)$$

If a target value for the mean is specified as $\overline{X}_0$, then the center line is given by

$$CL_{\overline{X}} = \overline{X}_0 \qquad (6.27)$$

Equations for the control limits will be the same as those given by Equations 6.11 in the section on $\overline{X}$ and R-charts:

$$\begin{aligned} UCL_{\overline{X}} &= \overline{X}_0 + A\sigma_0 \\ LCL_{\overline{X}} &= \overline{X}_0 - A\sigma_0 \end{aligned} \qquad (6.28)$$

where $A = 3/\sqrt{n}$ and is tabulated in Appendix A-7.

Example 6-4: The thickness of the magnetic coating on audio tapes is an important characteristic. Random samples of size four were selected and the thicknesses were measured using an optical instrument. Table 6-3 shows the mean $\overline{X}$ and standard deviation s for 20 samples. The specifications are 38 ± 4.5. If a coating thickness is less than the specifications call for, that tape can be used for a different purpose by running it through another coating operation.

TABLE 6-3 Data values for thickness of magnetic coating

Sample number	Sample mean, $\overline{X}$	Sample standard deviation, s
1	36.4	4.6
2	35.8	3.7
3	37.3	5.2
4	33.9	4.3
5	37.8	4.4
6	36.1	3.9
7	38.6	5.0
8	39.4	6.1
9	34.4	4.1
10	39.5	5.8
11	36.7	5.3
12	35.2	3.5
13	38.8	4.7
14	39.0	5.6
15	35.5	5.0
16	37.1	4.1
17	38.3	5.6
18	39.2	4.8
19	36.8	4.7
20	37.7	5.4

a. Find the trial control limits for an $\overline{X}$- and s-chart.

Solution. The standard deviation chart must first be constructed. The center line of the s-chart is

$$CL_s = \bar{s} = \frac{\sum_{i=1}^{20} s_i}{20} = \frac{95.80}{20} = 4.790$$

The control limits for the s-chart are

$$\begin{aligned} UCL_s &= B_4\bar{s} = (2.266)(4.790) = 10.854 \\ LCL_s &= B_3\bar{s} = (0)(4.790) = 0 \end{aligned}$$

Figure 6-20 shows this standard deviation control chart. None of the points fall outside the control limits, and the process seems to be in a state of control, so the $\overline{X}$ control chart is constructed next. The center line of the $\overline{X}$-chart is

$$CL_{\overline{X}} = \overline{\overline{X}} = \frac{\sum_{i=1}^{20} \overline{X}_i}{20} = \frac{741.5}{20} = 37.075$$

The control limits for the $\overline{X}$-chart are

$$UCL_{\overline{X}} = \overline{\overline{X}} + A_3\bar{s} = 37.075 + (1.628)(4.790) = 44.873$$

$$LCL_{\overline{X}} = \overline{\overline{X}} - A_3\bar{s} = 37.075 - (1.628)(4.790) = 29.277$$

Figure 6-21 depicts the $\overline{X}$ control chart. All the points are within the control limits, and no unusual nonrandom pattern is visible on the plot.

b. Assuming assignable causes for the out-of-control points, determine the revised control limits.

Solution. In this case the revised control limits will be the same as the trial control limits since it is believed that no assignable causes are present in the system.

c. Assuming the thickness of the coating to be normally distributed, what proportion of the product will not meet specifications?

Solution. The process standard deviation may be estimated as

$$\hat{\sigma} = \frac{\bar{s}}{c_4} = \frac{4.790}{0.9213} = 5.199$$

Figure 6-22 shows a normal distribution for the coating thickness, with a process mean of 37.075 and an estimated process standard deviation $\hat{\sigma}$ of 5.199. The specification limits are also visible in Figure 6-22. To find the propor-

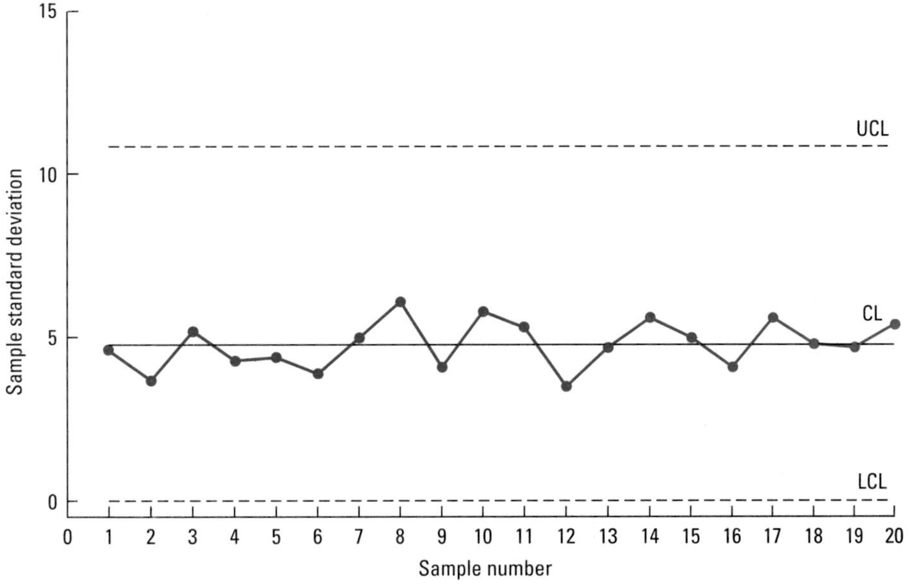

Figure 6-20 Control chart for standard deviation.

tion of the output that does not meet specifications, the standard normal values at the upper and lower specification limits must be found. At the lower specification limit we get

$$z_1 = \frac{33.5 - 37.075}{5.199} = -0.69$$

The area below the LSL, found by using the standard normal table in Appendix A-3, is 0.2451. Similarly, the standard normal value at the upper specification limit is

$$z_2 = \frac{42.5 - 37.075}{5.199} = 1.04$$

From Appendix A-3, the area above the USL is 0.1492. Hence, the proportion of product not meeting specifications is 0.2451 + 0.1492 = 0.3943.

d. Comment on the ability of the process to produce items that meet specifications.

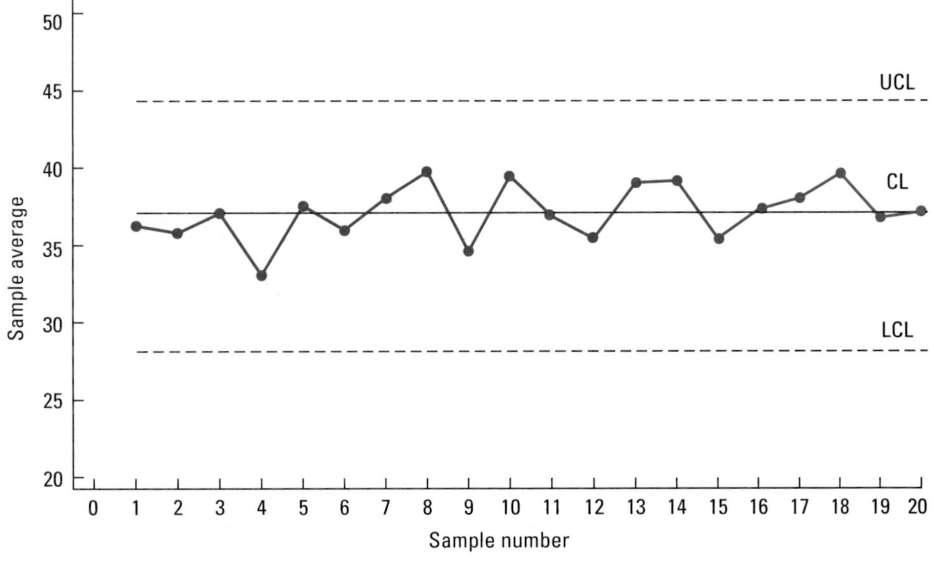

Figure 6-21 Control chart for $\overline{X}$.

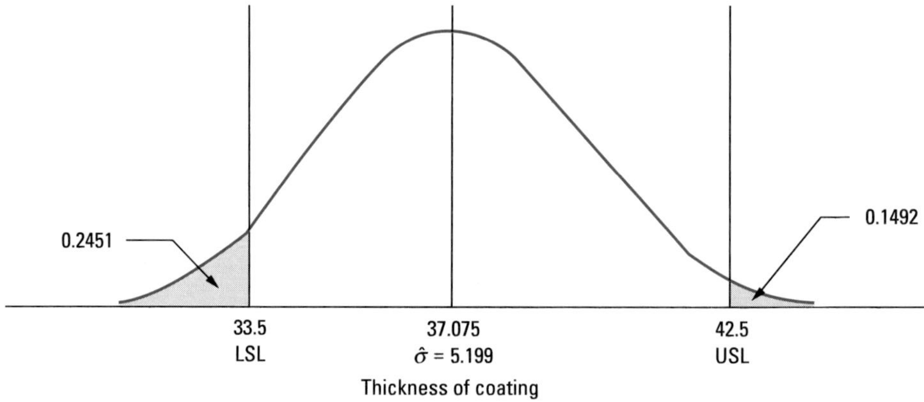

Figure 6-22 Distribution of coating thickness.

Solution. A value of 39.43 percent of product not meeting specifications is quite high. On the other hand, we found the process to be in control. This example teaches an important lesson. It is possible for a process to be in control and still not produce conforming items. In such cases, management must look for the prevailing common causes and come up with ideas for process improvement. The existing process is not capable of meeting the stated specifications.

e. If the process average shifts to 37.8, what proportion of the product will be acceptable?

Solution. If the process average shifts to 37.8, the standard normal values must be recalculated. At the LSL,

$$z_1 = \frac{33.5 - 37.8}{5.199} = -0.83$$

From the standard normal table in Appendix A-3, the area below the LSL is 0.2033. The standard normal value at the USL is

$$z_2 = \frac{42.5 - 37.8}{5.199} = 0.90$$

The area above the USL is 0.1841. So, the proportion nonconforming is 0.2033 + 0.1841 = 0.3874. Although this change in the process average does reduce the proportion nonconforming, 38.74 percent nonconforming is still quite significant.

If output that falls below the LSL can be salvaged at a lower expense than that for output above the USL, the manufacturer could consider adjusting the process mean in the downward direction in order to reduce the proportion above the USL. Being aware of the unit costs associated with salvaging output that is either below the LSL or above the USL will enable a manufacturer to choose a target value for the process mean. Keep in mind, though, that this approach does not solve the basic problem. The underlying problem concerns the process variability. In order to make the process more capable, we must find ways of reducing the process standard deviation. This cannot come through process control, because the process is currently in a state of statistical control. It must come through process improvement, some analytical tools of which are discussed at length in Chapter 4.

6-6 CONTROL CHARTS FOR INDIVIDUAL UNITS

For some situations in which the rate of production is low, it is not feasible for a sample size to be greater than one. Additionally, if the testing process is destructive and the cost of the item is expensive, the sample size might be chosen to be one. Furthermore, if every manufactured unit from a process is inspected, the sample size is essentially one.

In a control chart for individual units—for which the value of the quality characteristic is represented by X—the variability of the process is estimated from the *moving range* found from two successive observations. The moving range of two observations is simply the result of subtracting the lesser value. The moving ranges are correlated because they use common rather than independent values in their calculations. For example, the moving range of the first and second observation is correlated with the moving range of the second and third observation. Since the moving ranges are correlated, care must be taken to properly interpret the pattern of the moving range chart so as to determine out-of-control points. It is important to note that there is no guarantee that individual X-values will be normally distributed. So normal theory may not hold as far as establishment of the control chart limits is concerned. In order to get an idea of how the individual values are distributed, an initial analysis using frequency histograms might be conducted. Such an analysis would identify the shape of the distribution, its skewness, and its kurtosis. This information would give an idea of the validity of assuming a normal distribution when establishing the control limits.

No Given Standards

An estimate of the process standard deviation is given by

$$\hat{\sigma} = \frac{\overline{R}}{d_2}$$

where $\overline{R}$ is the average of the moving ranges of successive observations. Note that if we have a total of g individual, observations, there will be $(g - 1)$ moving ranges. The center line and control limits of the moving range chart are

$$\begin{aligned} CL_R &= \overline{R} \\ UCL_R &= D_4\overline{R} \\ LCL_R &= D_3\overline{R} \end{aligned} \tag{6.29}$$

For $n = 2$, $D_4 = 3.267$, and $D_3 = 0$, the control limits become

$$\begin{aligned} UCL_R &= 3.267\overline{R} \\ LCL_R &= 0 \end{aligned}$$

The center line of the X-chart is

$$CL_X = \overline{X} \tag{6.30}$$

The control limits of the X-chart are

$$\begin{aligned} UCL_X &= \overline{X} + 3\frac{\overline{R}}{d_2} \\ LCL_X &= \overline{X} - 3\frac{\overline{R}}{d_2} \end{aligned} \tag{6.31}$$

where (for $n = 2$) Appendix A-7 gives $d_2 = 1.128$.

Given Standard

The above derivation is based on the assumption that no standard values are given for either the mean or the process standard deviation. If standard values are specified as $\overline{X}_0$ and σ_0, respectively, the center line and control limits of the X-chart are

$$\begin{aligned} CL_X &= \overline{X}_0 \\ UCL_X &= \overline{X}_0 + 3\sigma_0 \\ LCL_X &= \overline{X}_0 - 3\sigma_0 \end{aligned} \tag{6.32}$$

Assuming $n = 2$, the moving range chart for standard values has the following center line and control limits:

$$\begin{aligned} CL_R &= d_2\sigma_0 = (1.128)\sigma_0 \\ UCL_R &= D_4 d_2\sigma_0 = (3.267)(1.128)\sigma_0 = (3.685)\sigma_0 \\ LCL_R &= D_3 d_2\sigma_0 = 0 \end{aligned} \tag{6.33}$$

An advantage of an X-chart is the ease with which it can be understood. However, it has several *disadvantages* compared to an $\overline{X}$-chart. An X-chart is not as sensitive to changes in the process parameters. It typically requires more subgroups to detect parametric changes of the same magnitude. The main disadvantage of an X-chart, though, is that the control limits may become distorted if the individual items don't fit a normal distribution.

Example 6-5: Table 6-4 shows the Brinell hardness numbers of 20 individual steel fasteners. The testing process dents the parts so that they cannot be used for their intended purpose. Construct the X-chart and the moving range chart based on two successive observations (Table 6-4 gives these moving range values).

Solution. Note that there are 19 moving range values for 20 observations. The average of the moving ranges is

$$\overline{R} = \frac{\sum R_i}{19} = \frac{96}{19} = 5.053$$

TABLE 6-4 Brinell hardness data for individual fasteners

Sample number	Brinell hardness	Moving range
1	36.3	—
2	28.6	7.7
3	32.5	3.9
4	38.7	6.2
5	35.4	3.3
6	27.3	8.1
7	37.2	9.9
8	36.4	0.8
9	38.3	1.9
10	30.5	7.8
11	29.4	1.1
12	35.2	5.8
13	37.7	2.5
14	27.5	10.2
15	28.4	0.9
16	33.6	5.2
17	28.5	5.1
18	36.2	7.7
19	30.0	3.5
20	28.3	4.4

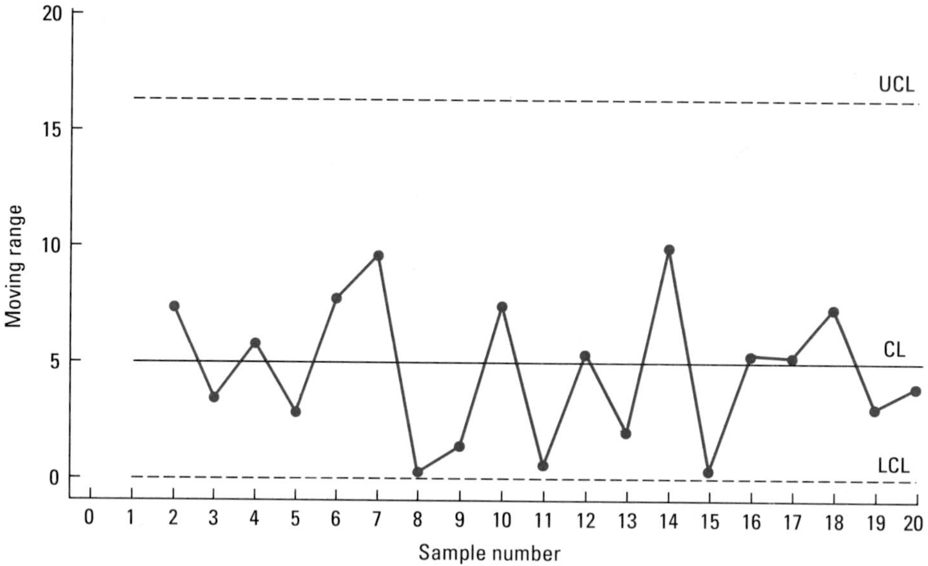

Figure 6-23 Moving range control chart for hardness data.

which is also the center line of the R-chart. The control limits for the R-chart are

$$UCL_R = D_4\overline{R} = (3.267)5.053 = 16.508$$

$$LCL_R = D_3\overline{R} = (0)5.053 = 0$$

This R-chart is shown in Figure 6-23. No points are observed to be out of control. Since the R-chart exhibits control, we can construct the X-chart for individual hardness data values. The center line of the X-chart is

$$\overline{X} = \frac{\sum X_i}{20} = \frac{656}{20} = 32.8$$

The control limits for the X-chart are given by

$$UCL_X = \overline{X} + \frac{3\overline{R}}{d_2} = 32.8 + 3\frac{(5.053)}{1.128} = 46.239$$

$$LCL_X = \overline{X} - \frac{3\overline{R}}{d_2} = 32.8 - \frac{3(5.053)}{1.128} = 19.361$$

The control chart for X is shown in Figure 6-24. No out-of-control points are visible.

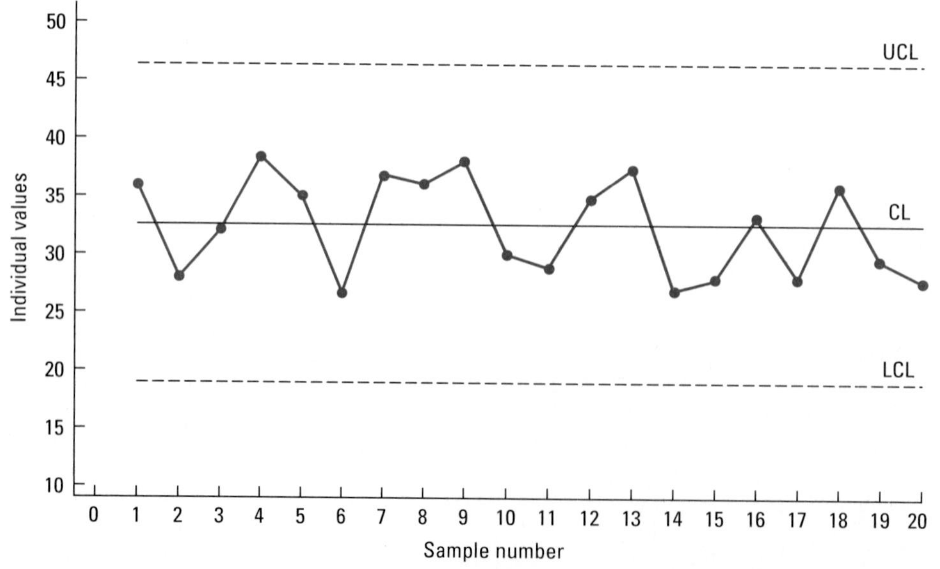

Figure 6-24 Control chart for individual values of hardness data.

6-7 OTHER CONTROL CHARTS

The previous sections have described some control charts commonly used in practice. This section discusses a few other types of control charts. Each of these charts is suited to certain specific situations as described below. The different procedures for constructing $\overline{X}$ and R-charts and interpreting their patterns have already been discussed. Since many of these steps apply to the other types of charts, they are not repeated here. Only conceptual differences are pointed out.

Cumulative Sum Control Chart for the Process Mean

In the Shewhart control charts, such as the $\overline{X}$ and R-charts, a plotted point represents information corresponding to that observation only. It does not use information from previous observations. On the other hand, a cumulative sum chart, usually called a cusum chart, uses information from all of the prior samples by displaying the cumulative sum of the deviation of the sample values (for instance, the sample mean) from a specified target value.

The cumulative sum at sample number m is given by

$$S_m = \sum_{i=1}^{m}(\overline{X}_i - \mu_0) \tag{6.34}$$

where $\overline{X}_i$ is the sample mean for sample number i and μ_0 is the target mean of the process.

An important advantage of a cumulative sum chart over the Shewhart control charts is that a cusum chart is more effective in detecting relatively small shifts in the process mean (of magnitude $0.5\sigma_{\overline{X}}$ to about $2\sigma_{\overline{X}}$). Since a cumulative sum chart uses information from previous samples, the effect of a small shift is more pronounced. For situations in which the sample size n is 1 (say, when each part is automatically measured by a machine), the cusum chart is better suited to determining shifts in the process mean than a Shewhart control chart. Because of the magnified effect of a small change in the process mean for a cumulative sum, the point for which the process mean changes is determined readily by finding the point where the slope of the plotted cusum pattern changes.

There are some disadvantages to using a cusum chart, however. First, if the cusum chart is designed to detect small changes in the process mean, it may be slow to detect large changes in the process parameters. This is true because, if a decision criterion is formed to do well under a specific situation, it may not perform equally well under different situations. Details on modification of the decision process to detect large shifts may be found in Lucas (1976). Second, the cusum chart is not an effective tool in analyzing the historical performance of a process to see if it is in control or to bring it in control. Recall that for Shewhart control charts, the individual points are assumed to be uncorrelated to each other. Cumulative values, however, are not unrelated. That is, S_{i-1} and S_i are related because $S_i = S_{i-1}+(\overline{X}_i-\mu_0)$. It is therefore possible for a cusum chart to exhibit runs or other patterns as a result of this relationship. The rules for describing out-of-control conditions based on the plot patterns of Shewhart charts may not be applicable to cusum charts. Finally, the cost of training workers to use and maintain cusum charts may be more than that for Shewhart charts.

Cumulative sum charts can be used to model the proportion of nonconforming items, the number of nonconformities, the sample range, the sample standard deviation, or the process mean. This section focuses on their application to detecting shifts in the process mean. Suppose the target value of a process mean when the process is in control is denoted by μ_0. If the process mean shifts upward to a higher value μ_1, an upward drift will be observed in the value of the cusum S_m given by Equation 6.34 because the old lower value μ_0 will still be used in the equation despite the fact that the X-values will generally be higher. Similarly, if the process mean shifts downward to a lower value μ_2, a downward trend will be observed in S_m. The task is to determine whether the trend in S_m, either upward or downward, is significant enough to allow us to conclude that a change has taken place in the process mean. A template known as a V-mask, proposed by Barnard (1959), is used in practice to make this determination.

Figure 6-25 shows a V-mask used for determining shifts in the process mean on a cusum chart. There are two parameters of a V-mask, the lead distance d and the angle θ of each decision line with respect to the horizontal. A V-mask is positioned such that the point P coincides with the last plotted value of the cumulative sum and the line OP is parallel to the horizontal axis. If all of the previous plotted values of the cumulative sum are within the two arms of the V-mask, that is, between the upper decision line and the lower decision line, the process is judged to be in control. If any value of the cusum lies outside the arms of the V-mask, the process is considered to be out of control. In Figure 6-25, notice that strong upward shift in the process mean is visible for sample number 5. This shift makes sense given the fact that the cusum value for sample number 1 is below

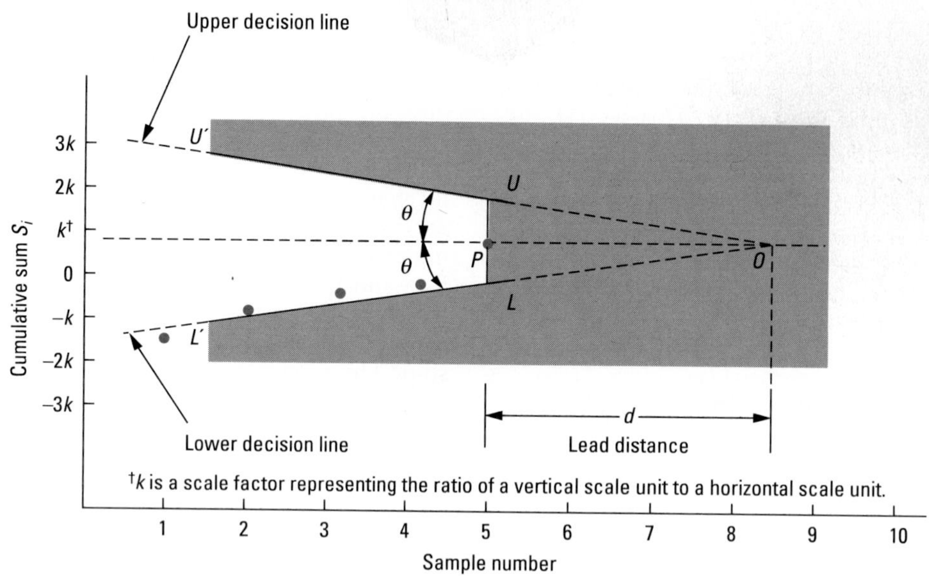

Figure 6-25 V-mask for use in making decisions about cumulative sum charts.

the lower decision line, indicating an out-of-control situation. Likewise, the presence of a plotted value above the upper decision line would indicate a downward drift in the process mean.

Determination of V-Mask Parameters The two parameters of a V-mask, d and θ, are determined based on the levels of risk that the decision maker is willing to tolerate. These risks are the Type I and Type II errors described previously. The probability of a Type I error, α, is the risk of concluding that a process is out of control when it is really in control. The probability of a Type II error, β, is the risk of failing to detect a change in the process parameter and concluding that the process is in control when it is really out of control. Let $\Delta\overline{X}$ denote the amount of shift in the process mean that we want to be able to detect, and let $\sigma_{\overline{X}}$ denote the standard deviation of $\overline{X}$. Next, consider the following equation:

$$\delta = \frac{\Delta\overline{X}}{\sigma_{\overline{X}}} \tag{6.35}$$

where δ represents the degree of shift in the process mean, relative to the standard deviation of the mean, that we wish to detect. Then, the lead distance for the V-mask is given by

$$d = \frac{2}{\delta^2}\ln\left(\frac{1-\beta}{\alpha}\right) \tag{6.36}$$

If the probability of a Type II error, β, is selected to be small, then Equation 6.36 reduces to

$$d = -\frac{2}{\delta^2}\ln(\alpha) \tag{6.37}$$

The angle of the arm with respect to the horizontal is obtained from

$$\theta = \tan^{-1}\left(\frac{\Delta\overline{X}}{2k}\right) \tag{6.38}$$

where k is a scale factor representing the ratio of a vertical scale unit to a horizontal scale unit on the plot. It is recommended that the value of k be between $\sigma_{\overline{X}}$ and $2\sigma_{\overline{X}}$. A preferred value of k is $2\sigma_{\overline{X}}$.

One measure of a control chart's performance is the average run length (ARL). This value represents the average number of points that must be plotted before an out-of-control condition is indicated. For a Shewhart control chart, if p represents the probability that a single point will fall outside the control limits, then the average run length is given by

$$\text{ARL} = \frac{1}{p} \tag{6.39}$$

For 3σ limits on a Shewhart $\overline{X}$-chart, the value of p is about 0.0026 when the process is in control. Hence, the ARL for an $\overline{X}$-chart exhibiting control is

$$\text{ARL} = \frac{1}{0.0026} = 385$$

The implication of this is that on the average, if the process is in control, every 385th sample statistic will indicate an out-of-control state. The ARL is usually larger for a cumulative sum chart than for a Shewhart chart. For example, for a cusum chart with comparable risks, the ARL is around 500. This means that, if the process is in control, on the average every 500th sample statistic will indicate an out-of-control situation, so there will be fewer false alarms.

Example 6-6: In the preparation of a drug, the percentage of calcium is a characteristic that is to be controlled. Five random samples are chosen from a batch, and the average percentage of calcium is found. The data values from 15 such subgroups are shown in Table 6-5. From past data, the standard deviation of the percentage of calcium may be estimated as 0.2. The target value for the average percentage of calcium content is 26.5. It is desired to notice shifts in the average percentage of calcium content of 0.1. Assume an acceptable Type I error level of 0.05.

Solution. We must first find the deviation of each sample mean $\overline{X}_i$ from the target mean $\mu_0 = 26.5$ and then find the cumulative sum S_i. These values are shown in Table 6-6. From the information given, $\sigma = 0.2$, so $\sigma_{\overline{X}} = \sigma/\sqrt{n} = 0.2/\sqrt{5} = 0.089$. Next,

$$\delta = \frac{\Delta \overline{X}}{\sigma_{\overline{X}}} = \frac{0.1}{0.089} = 1.124$$

The lead distance for the V-mask is

$$d = -\frac{2}{\delta_2} \ln \alpha = -\frac{2}{(1.124)^2} \ln(0.05) = 4.742$$

TABLE 6-5 Average percentage of calcium

Sample number	Average percentage of calcium, $\overline{X}$
1	25.5
2	26.0
3	26.6
4	26.8
5	27.5
6	25.9
7	27.0
8	25.4
9	26.4
10	26.3
11	26.9
12	27.8
13	26.2
14	26.8
15	26.6

TABLE 6-6 Cumulative sum of data for calcium content

Sample number, i	Deviation of sample mean from target, $(\overline{X}_i - \mu_0)$	Cumulative sum, S_i
1	−1.0	−1.0
2	−0.5	−1.5
3	0.1	−1.4
4	0.3	−1.1
5	1.0	−0.1
6	−0.6	−0.7
7	0.5	−0.2
8	−1.1	−1.3
9	−0.1	−1.4
10	−0.2	−1.6
11	0.4	−1.2
12	1.3	0.1
13	−0.3	−0.2
14	0.3	0.1
15	0.1	0.2

The units for d are the same as those for the horizontal scale. The angle of the V-mask for $k = 0.125$ is

$$\theta = \tan^{-1}\left(\frac{\Delta \overline{X}}{2k}\right) = \tan^{-1}\left[\frac{0.1}{2(0.125)}\right] = \tan^{-1}(0.40) = 21.80^\circ$$

This cumulative sum plot is shown in Figure 6-26. Using a V-mask with $d = 4.742$ and $\theta = 21.80°$, a downward shift in the process mean is detected rather quickly by the second sample. When the V-mask is positioned on the cumulative sum point for sample number 2, the cusum for sample number 1 is found to lie above the upper decision line of the V-mask, indicating that the process mean has shifted downward.

Designing a Cumulative Sum Chart Based on a Specified ARL for a Given Degree of Shift The average run length (ARL) can be used as a design criteria for control charts. If a process is in control, the ARL should be long, whereas if the process is out of control, the ARL should be short. Recall that δ is the degree of shift in the process mean, relative to the standard deviation of the sample mean, that we are interested in detecting; that is, $\delta = \Delta\overline{X}/\sigma_{\overline{X}}$. Let $L(\delta)$ denote the desired ARL when a shift in the process mean is on the order of δ. An ARL curve is a plot of δ versus its corresponding average run length, $L(\delta)$. For a process in control, when $\delta = 0$, a large

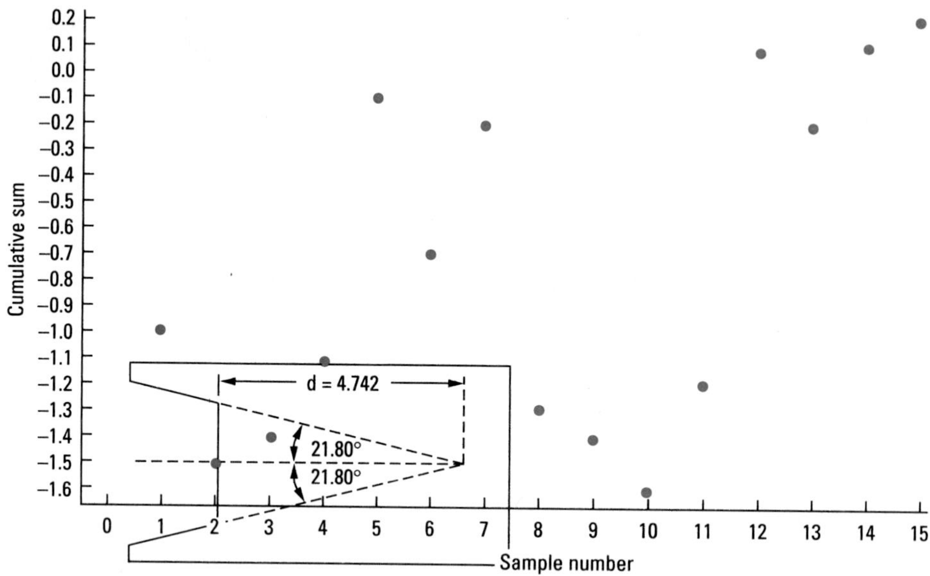

Figure 6-26 Cumulative sum plot for average percentage of calcium content.

value of $L(0)$ is desirable. For a specified value of δ, we may have a desirable value of $L(\delta)$. Thus, two points on the ARL curve, $[0, L(0)]$ and $[\delta, L(\delta)]$, are specified. The goal is to find the cusum chart parameters d and θ that will satisfy these desirable goals.

Bowker and Lieberman (1972) provide a table (see Table 6-7) for selecting the V-mask parameters d and θ when the objective is to minimize $L(\delta)$ for a given δ. It is assumed that the decision maker has a specified value of $L(0)$ in mind. Table 6-7 gives values for $(k/\sigma_{\overline{X}}) \tan\theta$ and d, and the minimum value of $L(\delta)$ for a specified δ. Example 6-7 shows how to use this table.

Example 6-7: Suppose that for a process in control, we desire the ARL to be 400. It is also of interest to detect shifts in the process mean of magnitude $1.5\sigma_{\overline{X}}$, that is, $\Delta\overline{X} = 1.5\sigma_{\overline{X}}$, which means that $\delta = 1.5$. Find the parameters of a V-mask for this process.

Solution. From Table 6-7, for $L(0) = 400$ and $\delta = 1.5$, we have

$$(k/\sigma_{\overline{X}}) \tan\theta = 0.75$$
$$d = 4.5$$
$$L(1.5) = 5.2$$

If k, the ratio of the vertical scale to the horizontal scale, is selected to be $2\sigma_{\overline{X}}$, we have

$$2\tan\theta = 0.75 \quad \text{or} \quad \tan\theta = 0.375$$

The angle of the V-mask is

$$\theta = \tan^{-1}(0.375) = 20.556°$$

If we feel that 5.2 is too large a value of $L(1.5)$, we then need to reduce the average number of plotted points it takes to first detect a shift in the process mean of magnitude 1.5 $\sigma_{\overline{X}}$. Currently, it will take about 5.2 plotted points, on the average, to detect a shift of this magnitude. Assume that we prefer $L(1.5)$ to be less than 5.0. From Table 6-7, for $\delta = 1.5$ and $L(1.5) < 5.0$, we could choose $L(1.5) = 4.6$, which corresponds to $(k/\sigma_{\overline{X}}) \tan\theta = 0.75$, and $d = 3.9$. If k is chosen to be $2\sigma_{\overline{X}}$, we get

$$\tan\theta = 0.75/2 = 0.375$$

Hence, $\theta = 20.556°$ (the same value as before), and $d = 3.9$ (a reduced value). For $L(1.5) = 4.6$, which is less than 5.0, we have increased the sensitivity of the cusum chart to detect changes of magnitude 1.5 $\sigma_{\overline{X}}$, but by doing so we have reduced the ARL for $\delta = 0$ (that is, L(0)) to 200 from the previous value of 400. So now every 200th observation, on the average, will be plotted as an out-of-control point when the process is actually in control.

Moving-Average Control Chart

As mentioned previously, standard Shewhart control charts are quite insensitive to small shifts. Using a cumulative sum chart, as discussed in the previous section, is one way to alleviate this problem. A control chart using the moving average method is another. Such charts are effective for detecting shifts of

TABLE 6-7 Selection of cumulative sum control charts based on specified ARL

δ = Deviation from target value (in standard deviations)		L(0) = Expected run length when process is in control					
		50	100	200	300	400	500
0.25	$(k/\sigma_{\overline{X}})\tan\theta$	0.125			0.195		0.248
	d	47.6			46.2		37.4
	$L(0.25)$	28.3			74.0		94.0
0.50	$(k/\sigma_{\overline{X}})\tan\theta$	0.25	0.28	0.29	0.28	0.28	0.27
	d	17.5	18.2	21.4	24.7	27.3	29.6
	$L(0.5)$	15.8	19.0	24.0	26.7	29.0	30.0
0.75	$(k/\sigma_{\overline{X}})\tan\theta$	0.375	0.375	0.375	0.375	0.375	0.375
	d	9.2	11.3	13.8	15.0	16.2	16.8
	$L(0.75)$	8.9	11.0	13.4	14.5	15.7	16.5
1.0	$(k/\sigma_{\overline{X}})\tan\theta$	0.50	0.50	0.50	0.50	0.50	0.50
	d	5.7	6.9	8.2	9.0	9.6	10.0
	$L(1.0)$	6.1	7.4	8.7	9.4	10.0	10.5
1.5	$(k/\sigma_{\overline{X}})\tan\theta$	0.75	0.75	0.75	0.75	0.75	0.75
	d	2.7	3.3	3.9	4.3	4.5	4.7
	$L(1.5)$	3.4	4.0	4.6	5.0	5.2	5.4
2.0	$(k/\sigma_{\overline{X}})\tan\theta$	1.0	1.0	1.0	1.0	1.0	1.0
	d	1.5	1.9	2.2	2.4	2.5	2.7
	$L(2.0)$	2.26	2.63	2.96	3.15	3.3	3.4

Source: Albert H. Bowker and Gerald J. Lieberman, *Engineering Statistics*, 2e, © 1972, p. 498. Reprinted by permission of Prentice Hall, Englewood Cliffs, New Jersey.

small magnitude in the process mean. Moving average control charts can also be used in situations for which the sample size is one, such as when product characteristics are measured automatically or when the time to produce a unit is long. It should be noted that, by their very nature, moving average values are correlated to each other.

Suppose samples of size n are collected from the process. Let the first t sample means be denoted by $\overline{X}_1, \overline{X}_2, \overline{X}_3, \ldots, \overline{X}_t$. (One sample is taken for each time step.) The moving average of width w (that is, of w samples) at time step t is given by

$$M_t = \frac{\overline{X}_t + \overline{X}_{t-1} + \cdots + \overline{X}_{t-w+1}}{w} \tag{6.40}$$

At any time step t, the moving average is updated by dropping the oldest mean and adding the newest mean. The variance of each of the sample means is

$$\mathrm{Var}(\overline{X}_t) = \frac{\sigma^2}{n}$$

where σ^2 is the population variance of the individual values. The variance of M_t is

$$\begin{aligned}\mathrm{Var}(M_t) &= \frac{1}{w^2}\sum_{i=t-w+1}^{t}\mathrm{Var}(\overline{X}_i)\\ &= \frac{1}{w^2}\sum_{i=t-w+1}^{t}\frac{\sigma^2}{n}\\ &= \frac{\sigma^2}{nw}\end{aligned} \tag{6.41}$$

The center line and control limits for the moving average chart are given by

$$\begin{aligned}\mathrm{CL} &= \overline{\overline{X}}\\ \mathrm{UCL} &= \overline{\overline{X}} + 3\frac{\sigma}{\sqrt{nw}}\\ \mathrm{LCL} &= \overline{\overline{X}} - 3\frac{\sigma}{\sqrt{nw}}\end{aligned} \tag{6.42}$$

From Equation 6.42 we can see that as w increases, the width of the control limits decreases. So, in order to detect shifts of smaller magnitudes, larger values of w should be chosen. For the startup period (when $t < w$) the moving average is given by

$$M_t = \frac{\sum_{i=1}^{t} \bar{X}_i}{t}, \qquad t = 1, 2, \ldots, w - 1 \qquad (6.43)$$

The control limits for this startup period are

$$\text{UCL} = \bar{\bar{X}} + \frac{3\sigma}{\sqrt{nt}}, \qquad t = 1, 2, \ldots, w - 1$$

$$\text{LCL} = \bar{\bar{X}} - \frac{3\sigma}{\sqrt{nt}}, \qquad t = 1, 2, \ldots, w - 1$$

$$(6.44)$$

Since these control limits change at each sample point during this startup period, an alternative procedure would be to use the ordinary $\bar{X}$-chart for $t < w$; and use the moving average chart for $t \geq w$.

Example 6-8: The amount of a coloring pigment used in the production of polypropylene plastic, produced in batches, is a variable of interest. For 20 random samples of size five, the average amount of pigment used is shown in Table 6-8, Construct a moving average control chart of width 6. The process has up to this point been in control with an average range $\bar{R}$ of 0.40 kg.

Solution. Table 6-8 shows the computed values of the moving average M_t based on a width w of 6. For values of $t < 6$, the moving average is calculated using Equation 6.43. For $t \geq 6$, M_t is calculated using Equation 6.40. Also shown in Table 6-8 are the calculated lower and upper control limits for the moving average chart. To find these limits, Equation 6.44 is used for $t < 6$, and Equation 6.42 is used for $t \geq 6$. The mean of the sample averages is

$$\bar{\bar{X}} = \frac{\sum_{t=1}^{20} \bar{X}_t}{20} = \frac{503}{20} = 25.15$$

Since $\bar{R} = 0.40$, an estimate of the process standard deviation is

$$\hat{\sigma} = \frac{\bar{R}}{d_2} = \frac{0.40}{2.326} = 0.172$$

To calculate the control limits, consider sample number 3:

$$\text{UCL} = \bar{\bar{X}} + 3\frac{\sigma}{\sqrt{nt}} = 25.15 + 3\frac{(0.172)}{\sqrt{(5)(3)}} = 25.283$$

$$\text{LCL} = \bar{\bar{X}} - 3\frac{\sigma}{\sqrt{nt}} = 25.15 - 3\frac{(0.172)}{\sqrt{(5)(3)}} = 25.017$$

TABLE 6-8 Data and results for a moving average control chart

Sample number	Sample average, $\bar{X}_t$	Moving average, M_t	Control limits for M_t: LCL	Control limits for M_t: UCL
1	25.0	25.0	24.919	25.381
2	25.4	25.2	24.987	25.313
3	25.2	25.2	25.017	25.283
4	25.0	25.15	25.035	25.265
5	25.2	25.16	25.047	25.253
6	24.9	25.12	25.056	25.244
7	25.0	25.12	25.056	25.244
8	25.4	25.12	25.056	25.244
9	24.9	25.07	25.056	25.244
10	25.2	25.10	25.056	25.244
11	25.0	25.07	25.056	25.244
12	25.7	25.20	25.056	25.244
13	25.0	25.20	25.056	25.244
14	25.1	25.15	25.056	25.244
15	25.0	25.17	25.056	25.244
16	24.9	25.12	25.056	25.244
17	25.0	25.12	25.056	25.244
18	25.1	25.02	25.056	25.244
19	25.4	25.08	25.056	25.244
20	25.8	25.20	25.056	25.244

For sample numbers 6 through 20, the control limits stay the same; the LCL is 25.056, and the UCL is 25.244. Figure 6-27 shows a plot of the moving averages and control limits. The moving average for subgroup 18 plots below the lower control limit, indicating that the process mean has drifted downward. Assignable causes should be investigated for this out-of-control condition, and appropriate corrective action should be taken.

Geometric Moving Average Control Chart

The previous subsection showed that a moving average chart could be used as an alternative to an ordinary $\bar{X}$-chart in detecting small changes in process parameters. The moving average method is basically a weighted-average schematic. For sample number t, the sample means $\bar{X}_t, \bar{X}_{t-1}, \ldots, \bar{X}_{t-w+1}$ are each weighted by $1/w$ (see Equation 6.40), while the sample means for time steps less than $(t - w + 1)$ are weighted by 0. Along similar lines, a chart can be constructed based on varying weights for the prior observations. More weight can be assigned to the most recent observation, with the weights decreasing for less recent observations. A geometric moving average control chart is based on this premise. One

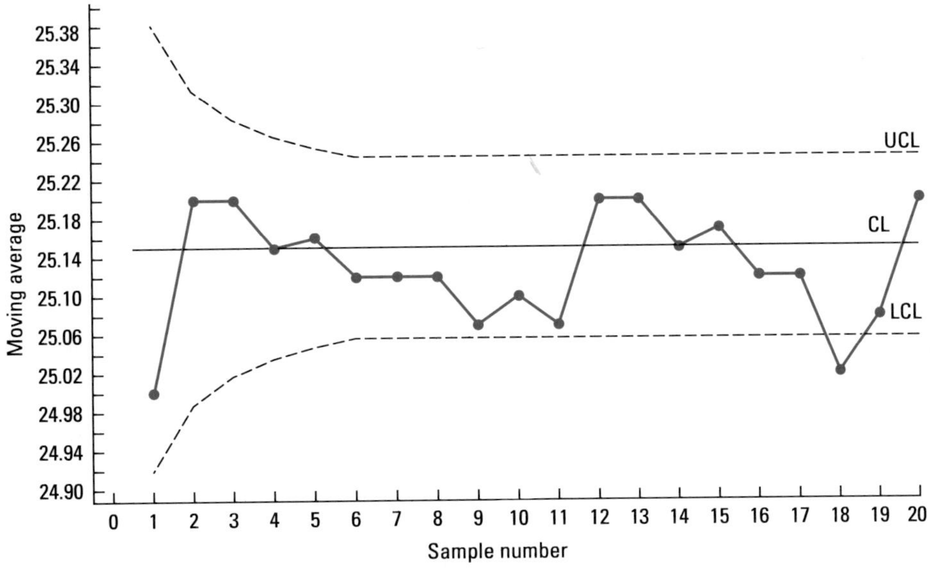

Figure 6-27 Moving average control chart.

of the advantages of a geometric moving average chart over a moving average chart is that the former is more effective in detecting small changes in process parameters. The geometric moving average at time step t is given by

$$G_t = r\overline{X}_t + (1 - r)G_{t-1}, \qquad (6.45)$$

where r is a weighting constant $(0 < r \le 1)$ and G_0 is $\overline{\overline{X}}$. By using Equation 6.45 repeatedly we get

$$\begin{aligned} G_t &= r\overline{X}_t + r(1 - r)\overline{X}_{t-1} + r(1 - r)^2 G_{t-2} \\ &= r\overline{X}_t + r(1 - r)\overline{X}_{t-1} + r(1 - r)^2\overline{X}_{t-2} \\ &\quad + \cdots + (1 - r)^t G_0 \end{aligned} \qquad (6.46)$$

Equation 6.46 shows that the weight associated with the ith mean from $t(\overline{X}_{t-i})$ is $r(1 - r)^i$. The weights decrease geometrically as the sample mean becomes less recent. The sum of all the weights is 1. Consider, for example, the case for which $r = 0.3$. This implies that in calculating G_t, the most recent sample mean $(\overline{X}_t)$ has a weight of 0.3, the next most recent observation $(\overline{X}_{t-1})$ has a weight of $(0.3)(1 - 0.3) = 0.21$, the next observation $(\overline{X}_{t-2})$ has a weight of $0.3(1 - 0.3)^2 = 0.147$, and so on. Here, G_0 has a weight of $(1 - 0.3)^t$. Since these weights appear to decrease exponentially, Equation 6.46 describes what is known as the exponentially weighted moving average model.

If the sample means $\overline{X}_1, \overline{X}_2, \overline{X}_3, \ldots, \overline{X}_{t-1}$ are assumed to be independent of each other and if the population standard deviation is σ, then the variance of G_t is given by

$$\mathrm{Var}(G_t) = \left(\frac{\sigma^2}{n}\right)\left(\frac{r}{2 - r}\right)[1 - (1 - r)^{2t}] \qquad (6.47)$$

For large values of t, the standard deviation of G_t is

$$\sigma_G = \sqrt{\mathrm{Var}(G_t)} = \sqrt{\frac{\sigma^2}{n}\left(\frac{r}{2 - r}\right)}$$

The upper and lower control limits are

$$\begin{aligned} \mathrm{UCL} &= \overline{\overline{X}} + 3\sigma\sqrt{\frac{r}{(2 - r)n}} \\ \mathrm{LCL} &= \overline{\overline{X}} - 3\sigma\sqrt{\frac{r}{(2 - r)n}} \end{aligned} \qquad (6.48)$$

For small values of t, the control limits are found by using Equation 6.47 to be

$$\begin{aligned} \mathrm{UCL} &= \overline{\overline{X}} + 3\sigma\sqrt{\frac{r}{n(2 - r)}[1 - (1 - r)^{2t}]} \\ \mathrm{LCL} &= \overline{\overline{X}} - 3\sigma\sqrt{\frac{r}{n(2 - r)}[1 - (1 - r)^{2t}]} \end{aligned} \qquad (6.49)$$

A geometric moving average control chart is based on a concept similar to that of a moving average control chart. By choosing an adequate set of weights, however, for which recent sample means are given more weight, the ability to detect small changes in process parameters is increased. If the weighting factor r is selected as

$$r = \frac{2}{w+1} \tag{6.50}$$

where w is the moving average span, then the moving average method and the geometric moving average method are equivalent to each other. There are some guidelines for choosing the value of r. If the goal is to detect small shifts in the process parameters as soon as possible, a small value of r (say, 0.1) should be used. If the value of r is chosen to be 1, the geometric moving average chart reduces to the standard Shewhart chart for the mean.

Example 6-9: Refer to Example 6-8 regarding the amount of a coloring pigment used in the production of polypropylene plastic. Table 6-8 gives the sample averages for 20 samples of size five. Construct a geometric moving average control chart. Choose a weighting factor r of 0.2.

TABLE 6-9 Data and results for a geometric moving average control chart

Sample number	Sample average, $\bar{X}_t$	Geometric moving average, G_t	Control limits for geometric average	
			LCL	UCL
1	25.0	25.120	25.104	25.196
2	25.4	25.176	25.091	25.209
3	25.2	25.181	25.084	25.216
4	25.0	25.145	25.080	25.220
5	25.2	25.156	25.077	25.223
6	24.9	25.105	25.076	25.224
7	25.0	25.084	25.075	25.225
8	25.4	25.147	25.074	25.226
9	24.9	25.098	25.074	25.226
10	25.2	25.118	25.074	25.226
11	25.0	25.094	25.073	25.227
12	25.7	25.215	25.073	25.227
13	25.0	25.172	25.073	25.227
14	25.1	25.158	25.073	25.227
15	25.0	25.126	25.073	25.227
16	24.9	25.081	25.073	25.227
17	25.0	25.065	25.073	25.227
18	25.1	25.072	25.073	25.227
19	25.4	25.138	25.073	25.227
20	25.8	25.270	25.073	25.227

Solution. For the data in Table 6-8, the mean of the sample averages was found to be

$$\bar{\bar{X}} = \frac{503}{20} = 25.150$$

Since $\bar{R}$ was given as 0.40 in Example 6-8, the estimated process standard deviation was

$$\hat{\sigma} = \frac{\bar{R}}{d_2} = \frac{0.40}{2.326} = 0.172$$

The geometric moving average for sample number 1 is (for $G_0 = \bar{\bar{X}}$)

$$\begin{aligned} G_1 &= r\bar{X}_1 + (1-r)G_0 \\ &= (0.2)25.0 + (1-0.2)25.15 = 25.12 \end{aligned}$$

The other geometric moving averages may be calculated similarly by using Equation 6.45. These values are shown in Table 6-9. The control limits for sample number 1 may be calculated using Equation 6.49:

$$\begin{aligned} \text{LCL} &= 25.150 - 3(0.172)\sqrt{\frac{0.2}{5(2-0.2)}[1-(1-0.2)^2]} \\ &= 25.104 \end{aligned}$$

$$\begin{aligned} \text{UCL} &= 25.150 + 3(0.172)\sqrt{\frac{0.2}{5(2-0.2)}[1-(1-0.2)^2]} \\ &= 25.196 \end{aligned}$$

Similar computations can be performed for the other samples. For large values of t (say, $t = 15$), the control limits may be found by using Equation 6.48:

$$\begin{aligned} \text{LCL} &= 25.150 - 3(0.172)\sqrt{\frac{0.2}{(2-0.2)5}} \\ &= 25.073 \end{aligned}$$

$$\begin{aligned} \text{UCL} &= 25.150 + 3(0.172)\sqrt{\frac{0.2}{(2-0.2)5}} \\ &= 25.227 \end{aligned}$$

Figure 6-28 shows a plot of this geometric moving average control chart. Notice that sample numbers 17 and 18 are below the lower control limit and that sample number 20 plots above the upper control limit. The assignable causes for these points should be investigated in order to take corrective action. Note that in the moving average chart, sample number 18 had plotted below the lower control limit, but sample numbers 17 and 20 were within the control limits. The geometric moving average chart, which is a little more sensitive to small shifts in the process parameters than the moving average chart, identified these additional points as being out of control.

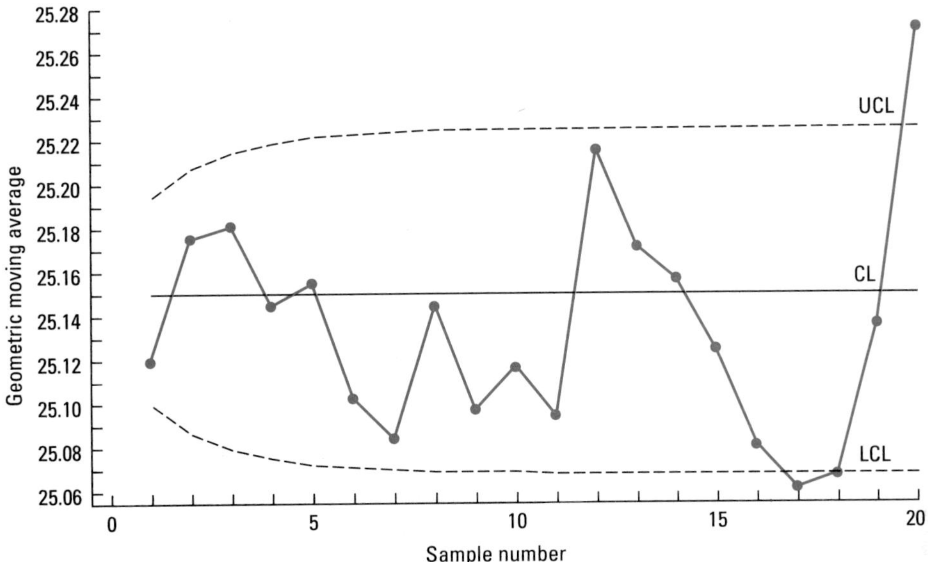

Figure 6-28 Geometric moving average control chart.

Trend Chart (Regression Control Chart)

In certain circumstances—such as those involving tool wear or die wear—the characteristic of interest (say, the average outside diameter of a part) is expected to gradually increase or decrease, as the case may be. Hence, the center line, rather than being horizontal, will slope upward or downward. The control limits for the sample average will be parallel to the center line. Under such conditions, the allowable initial and final values of the process mean will be determined by the specification limits. Furthermore, it is assumed that the range of the specification limits is wider than the range of the inherent process variability. This implies that the process can be allowed, for a certain period of time, to drift upward or downward as long as the output from the process remains within the set specifications.

The ordinate-intercept and slope of the center line are influenced by the pattern of the plot. If the principle of least squares, which minimizes the sum of the squared deviations of the observed values from the fitted values, is used to find the best-fitting straight line through the plotted points, then the equation of this fitted center line is of the form

$$C = a + bi \tag{6.51}$$

where C = Fitted value of the sample average for sample number i

a = Intersection point of the fitted center line with the vertical axis

b = Slope of the fitted center line

i = Subgroup, or sample number

Estimates for the parameters of the fitted center line are given by

$$\begin{aligned} a &= \frac{(\sum \overline{X})(\sum i^2) - (\sum \overline{X}i)(\sum i)}{g\sum i^2 - (\sum i)^2} \\ b &= \frac{g(\sum \overline{X}i) - (\sum \overline{X})(\sum i)}{g\sum i^2 - (\sum i)^2} \end{aligned} \tag{6.52}$$

where $\overline{X}$ = Subgroup or sample average for sample number i

g = Number of subgroups

The upper and the lower control limits are drawn parallel to the fitted center line and have slope b. Using the same principle discussed in the section about typical $\overline{X}$- and R-charts, the control limits should be placed at a distance of $3\sigma_{\overline{X}}$ from the center line. If the control chart multiplying factors from Appendix A-7 are being used, then the control limits are $A_2\overline{R}$ away from the center line. In other words, the control limits are

$$\begin{aligned} \text{UCL} &= (a + A_2\overline{R}) + bi \\ \text{LCL} &= (a - A_2\overline{R}) + bi \end{aligned} \tag{6.53}$$

Careful attention should be given to setting the equipment so that virtually all of the parts produced will conform to specifications. This consideration will determine when to take remedial action for the drift (by changing the tool, for instance) and when the control chart will have to start a new cycle. Typically, the initial and final positions of the center line are set three times the process standard deviation (that is, 3σ) away from the appropriate specification limits. Consider a situation where the outside diameter of a part is increasing due to the wear of a cutting tool. When a new tool replaces the old one, the center line will initially be set at a distance of 3σ above the lower specification limit. As the tool wears out, the tool would be replaced when the center line is a distance of 3σ below the upper specification limit. This recommendation is based on the assumption that the distribution of the quality characteristic is normal. If the distribution is indeed normal, only about 0.13 percent of the output will fall outside the given specification limit for this center line arrangement. Figure 6-29 is an example of a trend chart.

Example 6-10: Over the course of machining the diameter of steel hubs, tool wear takes place on a gradual basis. Samples of size 4 were randomly selected, and the mean and range of the hub diameters were found. Table 6-10 shows the sample mean $\overline{X}$ and the range R for 25 such samples. Find the center line and control limits of a trend chart for the sample average. If the specification limits state that the hub diameter must be from 34 mm to 78 mm, when should the tool be changed?

TABLE 6-10 Sample mean and range for tool wear data

Sample number	Average $\overline{X}$	Range, R
1	36.2	8.0
2	42.4	11.8
3	38.6	6.2
4	45.5	14.3
5	53.1	16.2
6	46.7	9.5
7	55.4	10.2
8	42.8	12.0
9	57.3	13.9
10	52.6	7.8
11	50.4	11.3
12	59.5	15.1
13	60.5	11.7
14	53.8	8.8
15	54.5	12.8
16	61.2	14.5
17	60.4	12.0
18	63.8	10.4
19	64.2	13.5
20	61.4	9.4
21	66.7	16.6
22	63.2	12.2
23	62.1	10.5
24	64.5	12.6
25	69.6	14.7

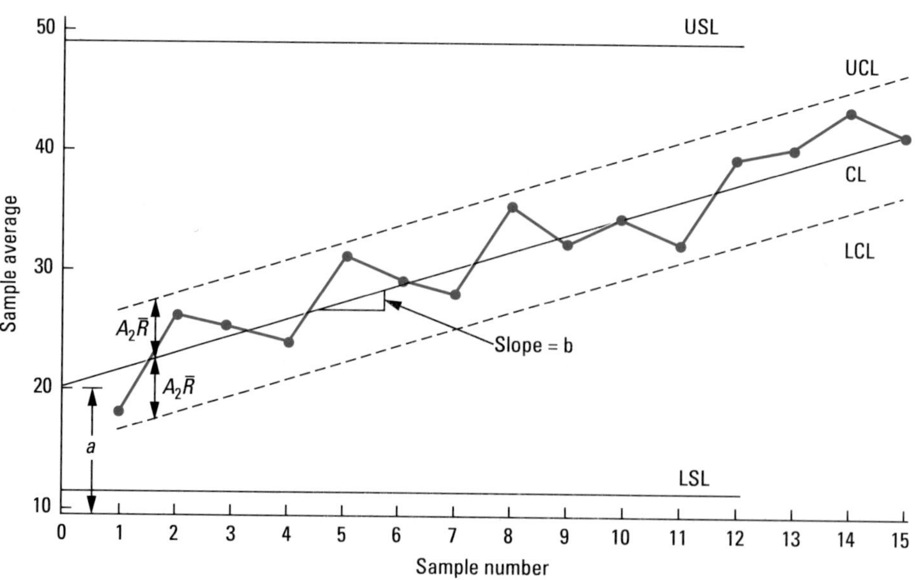

Figure 6-29 A trend chart.

TABLE 6-11 Calculations for determining trend chart

	Sample number, i	Average, $\overline{X}$	$\overline{X}i$	i^2	R
	1	36.2	36.2	1	8.0
	2	42.4	84.8	4	11.8
	3	38.6	115.8	9	6.2
	4	45.5	182.0	16	14.3
	5	53.1	265.5	25	16.2
	6	46.7	280.2	36	9.5
	7	55.4	387.8	49	10.2
	8	42.8	342.4	64	12.0
	9	57.3	515.7	81	13.9
	10	52.6	526.0	100	7.8
	11	50.4	554.4	121	11.3
	12	59.5	714.0	144	15.1
	13	60.5	786.5	169	11.7
	14	53.8	753.2	196	8.8
	15	54.5	817.5	225	12.8
	16	61.2	979.2	256	14.5
	17	60.4	1026.8	289	12.0
	18	63.8	1148.4	324	10.4
	19	64.2	1219.8	361	13.5
	20	61.4	1228.0	400	9.4
	21	66.7	1400.7	441	16.6
	22	63.2	1390.4	484	12.2
	23	62.1	1428.3	529	10.5
	24	64.5	1548.0	576	12.6
	25	69.6	1740.0	625	14.7
Sum	$\sum i = 325$	$\sum \overline{X} = 1386.4$	$\sum \overline{X}i = 19{,}471.6$	$\sum i^2 = 5525$	$\sum R = 296$

Solution. The calculations necessary for determining the vertical axis intercept and slope of the center line are shown in Table 6-11. By using Equation 6.52, we get

$$a = \frac{(1386.4)(5525) - (19{,}471.6)(325)}{25(5525) - (325)^2} = 40.972$$

$$b = \frac{25(1947.6) - (1386.4)(325)}{25(5525) - (325)^2} = 1.114$$

The center line is therefore given by $C = 40.972 + 1.114i$.

From the data, $\overline{R} = 11.84$. From Appendix A-7, $A_2 = 0.729$. The control limits are

$$\begin{aligned} \text{UCL} &= (a + A_2\overline{R}) + bi \\ &= [40.972 + 0.729(11.84)] + 1.114i \\ &= 49.6035 + 1.114i \end{aligned}$$

$$\begin{aligned} \text{LCL} &= (a - A_2\overline{R}) + bi \\ &= [(40.972 - 0.729(11.84)] + 1.114i \\ &= 32.341 + 1.114i \end{aligned}$$

Figure 6-30 shows the trend chart, the center line, and control limits along with the plotted values of the sample average $\overline{X}$.

The tool should be changed when the center line reaches a value that is 3σ below the upper specification limit. An estimate of the process standard deviation σ is given by $\overline{R}/d_2 = 11.84/2.059 = 5.750$. Thus, the maximum value that the center line should be allowed to reach is $78.0 - 3(5.750) = 60.75$ mm. Once the center line reaches this limit, the tool should be changed. Alternatively, if the rate of tool wear per unit of production were given, we could estimate the number of units that would be produced between tool changes.

Modified Control Chart

In the discussions of the previous types of control charts, except for the trend chart, it has been assumed that the process spread (6σ) is close to and hopefully less than the difference between the specification limits. That is, we hope that $6\sigma < (\text{USL} - \text{LSL})$. This section assumes that the natural process spread of 6σ is significantly less than the difference

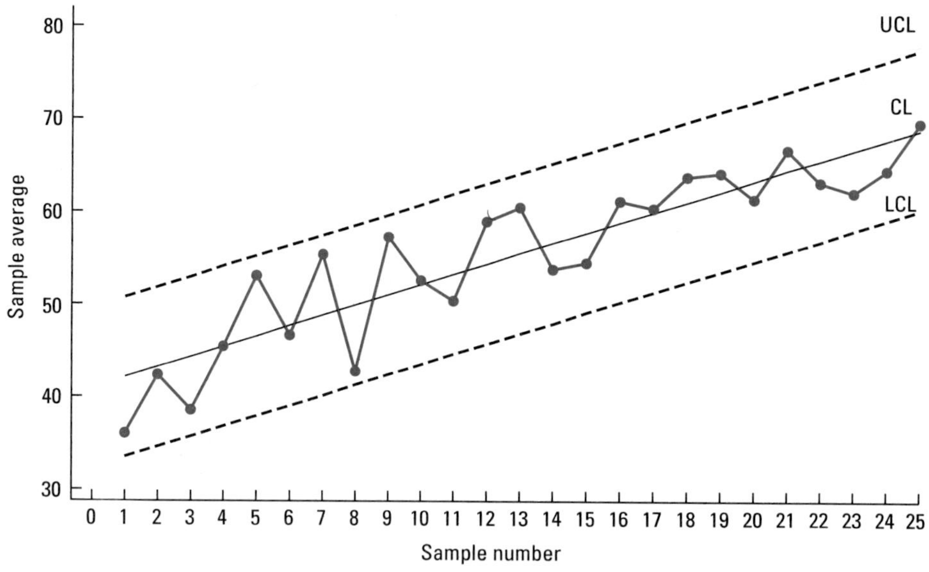

Figure 6-30 Trend chart for Example 6-10.

between the specification limits, that is, the process capability ratio (PCR) = (USL − LSL)/(6σ) $\gg$ 1. Figure 6-31 depicts such a situation.

Up to this point, the specification limits have not been placed on $\overline{X}$-charts. One reason for this is that the specification limits correspond to the conformance of individual items. If the distribution of the individual items is plotted, it makes sense to show the specification limits on that distribution, but a control chart for the mean $\overline{X}$ deals with the distribution of the averages, not the individual values. Therefore, it is not appropriate to plot the specification limits on a regular $\overline{X}$-chart.

For a modified control chart, however, the specification limits are integrated into the constructed chart. The objective is to determine bounds on the process mean such that the proportion of nonconforming items does not exceed a desirable value δ. The focus is not on detecting the statistical state of control, because a process can drift out of control and still produce parts that conform to specifications. An assumption here is that the process variability is in a state of statistical control. An estimate of the process standard deviation σ can be obtained from the mean of the range chart $\overline{R}$ or the mean of the standard deviation chart ($\overline{s}$). Furthermore, it is assumed that the distribution of the individual values is normal and that a change in the process mean can be accomplished without much difficulty.

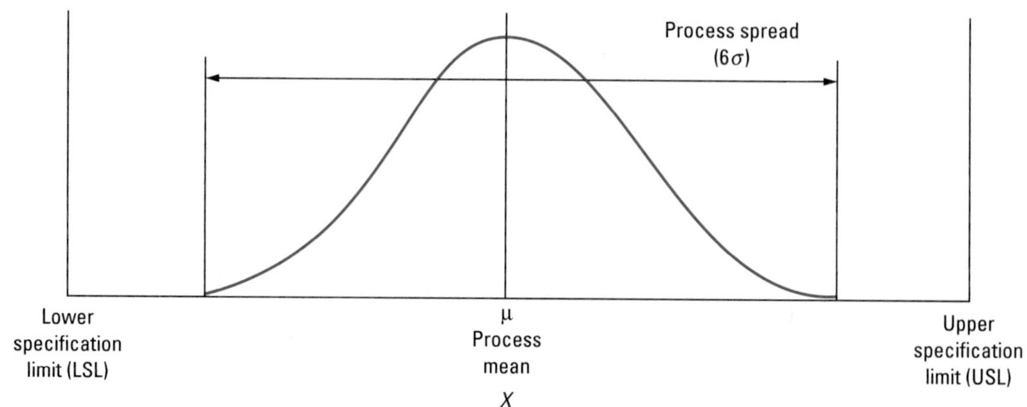

Figure 6-31 A process with a capability ratio much greater than one.

The aim of constructing a modified control chart is to determine if the process mean μ is within certain acceptable limits such that the proportion of nonconforming items does not exceed the chosen value δ. Consider Figure 6-32*a*, which shows a distribution of individual values at two different means—one the lowest allowable mean (μ_L) and the other the highest allowable mean (μ_U). Suppose the process standard deviation is σ. If the distribution of individual values is normal, let z_δ denote the standard normal value corresponding to a tail area of δ. By the definition of a standard normal value, z_δ represents the number of standard deviations that LSL is from μ_L, or that USL is from μ_U. So the distance between LSL and μ_L is $z_\delta\sigma$, which is also the same as the distance between USL and μ_U. The bounds within which the process mean should be contained so that the fraction nonconforming does not exceed δ are $\mu_L \le \mu \le \mu_U$. From Figure 6-32*a*,

$$\begin{aligned} \mu_L &= \text{LSL} + z_\delta\sigma \\ \mu_U &= \text{USL} - z_\delta\sigma \end{aligned} \tag{6.54}$$

Suppose a Type I error probability of α is chosen. The control limits are placed such that the probability of a Type I error is α, as shown in Figure 6-32*b*. The control limits are placed one at each end to incorporate the situation that the sampling distribution of the sample mean can vary over the entire range. Figure 6-32*b* shows the distribution of the sample means. Given the sampling distribution of $\overline{X}$, with standard deviation $\sigma_{\overline{X}} = \sigma/\sqrt{n}$, the upper and lower control limits as shown in Figure 6-32*b* are

$$\begin{aligned} \text{LCL} &= \mu_L - \frac{z_{\alpha/2}\sigma}{\sqrt{n}} \\ \text{UCL} &= \mu_U + \frac{z_{\alpha/2}\sigma}{\sqrt{n}} \end{aligned} \tag{6.55}$$

By substituting for μ_L and μ_U the following equations are obtained:

$$\begin{aligned} \text{LCL} &= \text{LSL} + \left(z_\delta - \frac{z_{\alpha/2}}{\sqrt{n}}\right)\sigma \\ \text{UCL} &= \text{USL} - \left(z_\delta - \frac{z_{\alpha/2}}{\sqrt{n}}\right)\sigma \end{aligned} \tag{6.56}$$

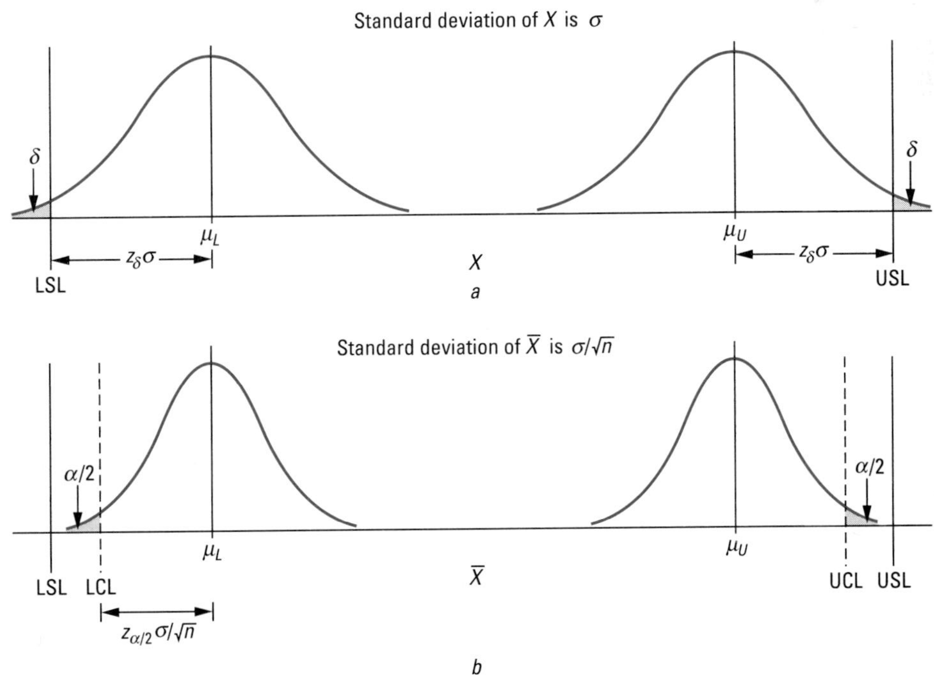

Figure 6-32 Distribution of (*a*) individual values X from the process; (*b*) sample averages $\overline{X}$ from the process.

If the process standard deviation σ is to be estimated from an $\overline{R}$-chart, then $\overline{R}/d_2$ may be substituted for σ in Equation 6.56. Alternatively, if σ is to be estimated from an s-chart, then $\overline{s}/c_4$ may be used in place of σ in Equation 6.56.

Example 6-11: The nitrogen content of a certain fertilizer mix is a characteristic of interest. Random samples of size five were chosen, and the percentage of nitrogen content was found for each. The sample mean $\overline{X}$ and range R are shown for 20 such samples in Table 6-12. The specification limits allow values from 12 percent to 33 percent. A process nonconformance rate of more than 1 percent is unacceptable. It is desired to construct 3σ modified control limits, that is, limits with a Type I error rate α of 0.0026.

Solution. First, determine if the variability of the process is in control. Using the data in Table 6-12,

$$\overline{R} = \frac{39.8}{20} = 1.99$$

The center line of the R-chart is 1.99. The control limits for the R-chart are

$$\text{UCL}_R = D_4\overline{R} = 2.114(1.99) = 4.207$$

$$\text{LCL}_R = D_3\overline{R} = 0(1.99) = 0$$

By checking the range values we find that the variability is in control. Next, calculate the modified control limits.

TABLE 6-12 Sample average and range values for the percentage of nitrogen content

Sample number	Sample average, $\overline{X}$	Range, R
1	14.8	2.2
2	15.2	1.6
3	16.7	1.8
4	15.5	2.0
5	18.4	1.8
6	17.6	1.9
7	21.4	2.2
8	20.5	2.3
9	22.8	2.5
10	16.9	1.8
11	25.0	2.1
12	16.4	1.8
13	18.6	1.5
14	23.9	2.3
15	17.2	2.1
16	16.8	1.6
17	21.1	2.0
18	19.5	2.2
19	18.3	1.8
20	20.2	2.3

For $\alpha = 0.0026$, the standard normal tables show that $z_{\alpha/2}$ is approximately 3.00. For $\delta = 0.01$, we find that $z_\delta = 2.33$. An estimate of the process standard deviation σ is

$$\hat{\sigma} = \overline{R}/d_2 = 1.99/2.326 = 0.855$$

The modified control limits are

$$\text{LCL} = \text{LSL} + \left(z_\delta - \frac{z_{\alpha/2}}{\sqrt{n}}\right)\sigma$$

$$= 12 + \left(2.33 - \frac{3.00}{\sqrt{5}}\right)0.855 = 12.845$$

$$\text{UCL} = \text{USL} - \left(z_\delta - \frac{z_{\alpha/2}}{\sqrt{n}}\right)\sigma$$

$$= 33 - \left(2.33 - \frac{3.00}{\sqrt{5}}\right)0.855 = 32.155$$

All of the sample average values shown in Table 6-12, are within the control limits. All of the values are well below the upper control limit and are closer to the lower control limit. The closest value to the lower control limit is 14.8.

Acceptance Control Chart

The previous subsection outlined a procedure for obtaining the modified control limits given the sample size (n), the proportion nonconforming (δ), and the acceptable level of probability of a Type I error (α). This section discusses a procedure to calculate the control chart limits when the sample size is known and when we have a specified level of proportion nonconforming (γ) that we desire to detect with a probability of $(1-\beta)$. Such a control chart is known as an acceptance control chart. The same assumptions are made here as for modified control charts. First, assume that the inherent process spread (6σ) is much less than the difference between the specification limits. Second, assume that the process variability is in control. Third, assume that the distribution of the individual values is normal.

Figure 6-33*a* shows the distribution of the individual values and the borderline locations of the process mean so that the proportion nonconforming does not exceed the desirable level of γ. From Figure 6-33*a* we have

$$\begin{aligned}\mu_U &= \text{USL} - z_\gamma\sigma \\ \mu_L &= \text{LSL} + z_\gamma\sigma\end{aligned} \tag{6.57}$$

Figure 6-33*b* shows the distribution of the sample mean and the bounds within which the process mean

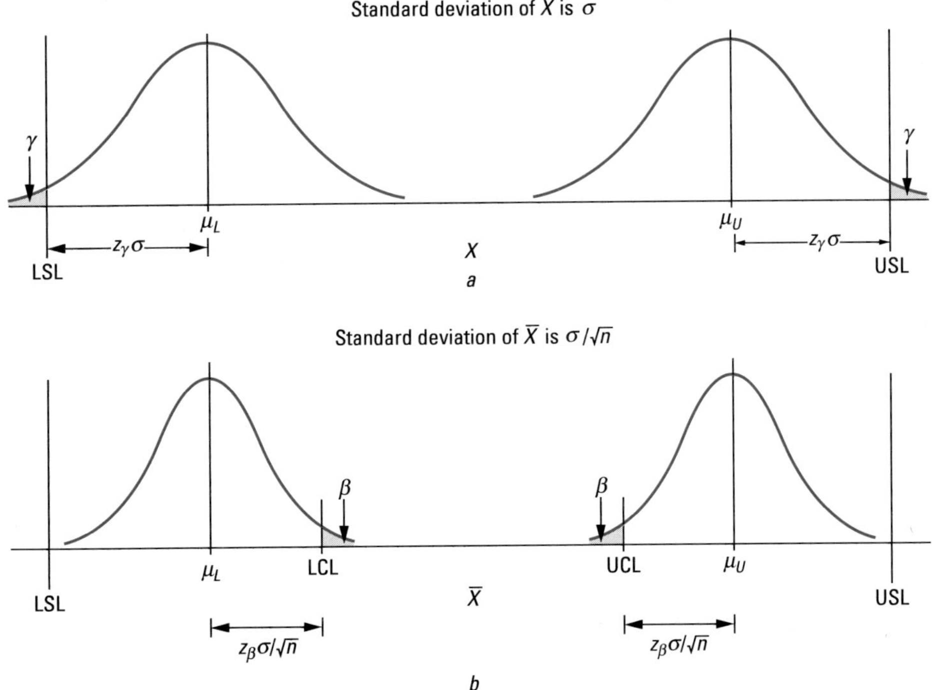

Figure 6-33 Determination of acceptance control chart limits (a) distribution of X; (b) distribution of $\overline{X}$.

should lie such that the probability of detecting a nonconformance proportion of γ is $(1-\beta)$. From Figure 6-33b we have

$$\begin{aligned} \text{UCL} &= \mu_U - z_\beta \frac{\sigma}{\sqrt{n}} \\ \text{LCL} &= \mu_L + z_\beta \frac{\sigma}{\sqrt{n}} \end{aligned} \tag{6.58}$$

Substituting from Equation 6.57, we get

$$\begin{aligned} \text{UCL} &= \text{USL} - \left(z_\gamma + \frac{z_\beta}{\sqrt{n}}\right)\sigma \\ \text{LCL} &= \text{LSL} + \left(z_\gamma + \frac{z_\beta}{\sqrt{n}}\right)\sigma \end{aligned} \tag{6.59}$$

If an R-chart is used to control the process variability, σ may be estimated by $\overline{R}/d_2$. If an s-chart is used, σ may be estimated by $\overline{s}/c_4$. These estimates may then be used in Equation 6.59.

Example 6-12: Refer to Example 6-11 and the data for the percent nitrogen content. Suppose that if the proportion of nonconforming product is 3 percent, it is desired to detect an out-of-control condition with a probability of 0.95. Find the acceptance control chart limits.

Solution. For this problem, $\gamma = .03$, $1-\beta = 0.95$, LSL = 12 percent, USL = 33 percent. From the standard normal tables, $z_{.03} \simeq 1.88$ and $z_{.05} = 1.645$. From Example 6-11, $\overline{R} = 1.99$ and $n = 5$. We have

$$\hat{\sigma} = \overline{R}/d_2 = 1.99/2.326 = 0.855$$

The acceptance control chart limits are

$$\begin{aligned} \text{LCL} &= \text{LSL} + \left[z_\gamma + \frac{z_\beta}{\sqrt{n}}\right]\sigma \\ &= 12 + \left[1.88 + \frac{1.645}{\sqrt{5}}\right](0.855) = 14.616 \\ \text{UCL} &= \text{USL} - \left[z_\gamma + \frac{z_\beta}{\sqrt{n}}\right]\sigma \\ &= 33 - \left[1.88 + \frac{1.645}{\sqrt{5}}\right](0.855) = 30.384 \end{aligned}$$

None of the sample averages are outside these control limits.

The principles of modified control charts and acceptance control charts can be combined to determine an acceptable sample size n for chosen levels of δ, α, γ, and β. By equating the expressions for the UCL in Equations 6.56 and 6.59, we have

$$\text{USL} - \left(z_\delta - \frac{z_{\alpha/2}}{\sqrt{n}}\right)\sigma = \text{USL} - \left(z_\gamma + \frac{z_\beta}{\sqrt{n}}\right)\sigma$$

which yields

$$n = \left[\frac{z_{\alpha/2} + z_\beta}{z_\delta - z_\gamma}\right]^2 \tag{6.60}$$

6-8 MULTIVARIATE CONTROL CHARTS

All of the control charts mentioned thus far have dealt with controlling one characteristic at a time on any given control chart. However, in many practical situations we may have to deal with two or more variables simultaneously in order to keep the process in control. For instance, we may want to simultaneously control both the length and inside diameter of a pipe to be used for assembly. In other words, both the length and inside diameter must be acceptable for the pipe to be usable. Controlling both characteristics separately may not yield a product such that both of the quality characteristics will be acceptable.

Controlling Several Related Quality Characteristics

Suppose we have two quality characteristics that must both be in control for the process to be in control. If control charts for the averages of these two characteristics are kept independently, the result is a rectangular control region on a two-dimensional plot. Figure 6-34 shows such a control region depicted by ABCD. The boundaries of this region are basically the upper and lower control limits of the two quality characteristics and may be calculated using Equation 6.5. If for a sample, the bivariate observation of sample means $(\overline{X}_1, \overline{X}_2)$ plots within the region ABCD, the process would seem to be in control.

Such rectangular boundaries, however, can often be incorrect. As shown below, an actual control region for two characteristics is elliptic in nature. The equation of a statistic that incorporates two characteristics is that of an ellipse, as shown later in Equation 6.62. If the two characteristics are independent of each other, the major and minor axes

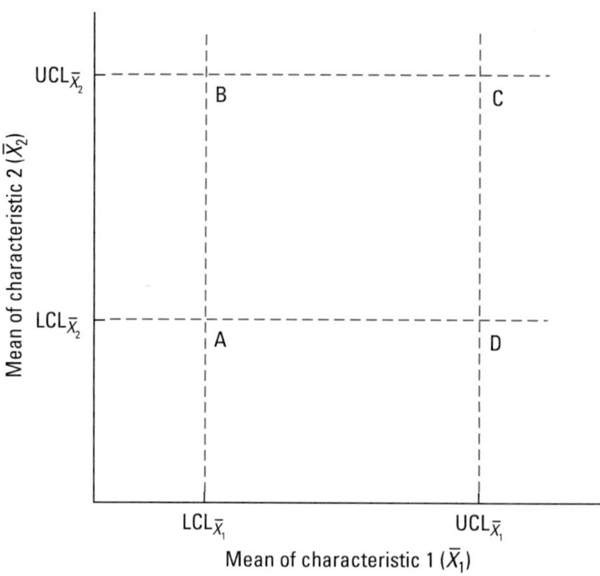

Figure 6-34 Rectangular control region when control charts are constructed independently.

of the ellipse are parallel to the respective plot axes (see ellipse A in Figure 6-35). If the pair of sample means $(\overline{X}_1, \overline{X}_2)$ falls within the boundary of the ellipse, the process is said to be in control. If there is a negative correlation between the two characteristics, the shape of the control ellipse will be similar to that of ellipse B. On the other hand, if the two

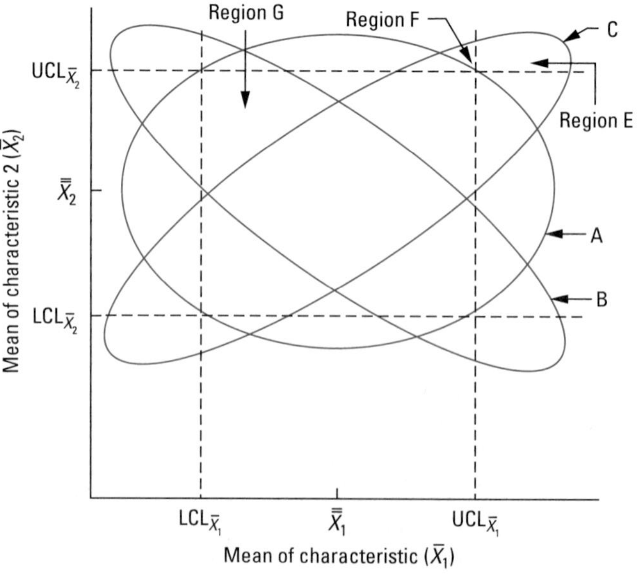

Figure 6-35 Elliptical control region.

variables are positively correlated, the control ellipse will be similar to that of ellipse C. Note from Figure 6-35 that if the variables are positively correlated and one erroneously uses the rectangular region as the control region, various incorrect conclusions could be drawn. For instance, if $(\overline{X}_1, \overline{X}_2)$ falls in Region E, the process is in control even though the point falls outside the rectangular region. A point in Region G, on the other hand, is within the rectangular region, but the process is nonetheless out of control.

The degree of correlation between the variables influences the magnitude of the errors encountered in making inferences. If a separate $\overline{X}$-chart is constructed for each characteristic based on a Type I error probability of α and if a rectangular control region is used, then for independent variables the true probability of a Type I error for the joint control procedure is

$$\alpha' = 1 - (1 - \alpha)^p \tag{6.61}$$

where p represents the number of jointly controlled variables. The probability of all p sample means plotting within the rectangular region is $(1 - \alpha)^p$. Moderate or large values of p have a major impact on the errors associated with inference making. Suppose individual control chart limits are constructed using a Type I error probability of 0.0026. If we have four independent characteristics (that is, $p = 4$), the overall Type I error probability (α') for the joint control procedure is

$$\alpha' = 1 - (0.9974)^4 = 0.0104$$

If the variables are not independent, the magnitude of the Type I error will be difficult to obtain. In actuality, a control ellipse should be chosen so that the probability of the sample means being plotted within the elliptical region when the process is in control is $(1 - \alpha)$, where α is the desired overall probability of a Type I error.

Hotelling's T^2 Control Chart and Its Variations

Suppose we have two quality characteristics, X_1 and X_2, jointly distributed according to a bivariate normal distribution. Assume that the nominal, or target, mean values of the characteristics are represented by $\overline{\overline{X}}_1$ and $\overline{\overline{X}}_2$, respectively. Let the sample means be $\overline{X}_1$ and $\overline{X}_2$, with sample variances s_1^2 and s_2^2, and the covariance between the two variables represented by s_{12} for a sample of size n. Under these conditions, the statistic

$$T^2 = \frac{n}{(s_1^2 s_2^2 - s_{12}^2)}[s_2^2(\overline{X}_1 - \overline{\overline{X}}_1)^2 + s_1^2(\overline{X}_2 - \overline{\overline{X}}_2)^2 - 2s_{12}(\overline{X}_1 - \overline{\overline{X}}_1)(\overline{X}_2 - \overline{\overline{X}}_2)] \tag{6.62}$$

is distributed according to Hotelling's T^2 distribution with 2 and $(n - 1)$ degrees of freedom (Hotelling, 1947). The 2 in this case comes from the two characteristics being considered, and the $(n - 1)$ is the degrees of freedom associated with the sample variance. If the calculated value of T^2, given by Equation 6.62 exceeds $T^2_{\alpha,2,n-1}$—the point on the T^2 distribution such that the proportion to the right is α—then at least one of the characteristics is out of control.

This procedure may be shown graphically. Equation 6.62 represents the equation for the control ellipses shown in Figure 6-35. If the variables are independent, then the covariance between them is zero (that is, $s_{12} = 0$), the control ellipse is A, and the joint control region is represented by the area within the control ellipse A. If a plot of the bivariate means $(\overline{X}_1, \overline{X}_2)$ falls within this control region, a state of statistical control may be assumed. If the two variables are positively correlated, then $s_{12} > 0$, and the control ellipse is similar to ellipse C in Figure 6-35. If the variables are negatively correlated, $s_{12} < 0$, and the control ellipse will be similar to B in Figure 6-35.

Hotelling's control ellipse procedure has a couple of disadvantages. First, the time sequence of the plotted points $(\overline{X}_1, \overline{X}_2)$ is lost. This implies that we cannot check for runs in the plotted pattern as with control charts. Second, the construction of the control ellipse becomes quite difficult for more than two characteristics. In order to overcome these disadvantages, the values of T^2 given by Equation 6.62 may be plotted on a control chart on a subgroup-by-subgroup basis to preserve the time order in which the data values were obtained. Such a control chart has an upper control limit of $T^2_{\alpha,p,(n-1)}$, where p represents the number of characteristics. Patterns of nonrandom runs can be investigated in such plots. Values of Hotelling's T^2 percentile points may be obtained from the percentile points of the F-distribution given in Appendix A-6 by using the following relation:

$$T^2_{\alpha,p,(n-1)} = p\frac{(n-1)}{(n-p)}F_{\alpha,p,n-p} \tag{6.63}$$

where $F_{\alpha,p,n-p}$ represents the point on the F-distribution such that the proportion to the right is α, with p degrees of freedom in the numerator and $(n - p)$ degrees of freedom in the denominator. If more than two characteristics are being considered jointly, the value of T^2 give by Equation 6.62 for a given sample may be generalized as

$$T^2 = n(\overline{\mathbf{X}} - \overline{\overline{\mathbf{X}}})'\mathbf{S}^{-1}(\overline{\mathbf{X}} - \overline{\overline{\mathbf{X}}}) \qquad (6.64)$$

where $\overline{\mathbf{X}}$ represents the vector of sample means of p characteristics for a sample of size n, $\overline{\overline{\mathbf{X}}}$ represents the vector of nominal values for each characteristic, and $\mathbf{S}$ denotes the variance–covariance matrix of the p quality characteristics. In practice, $\overline{\overline{\mathbf{X}}}$ and $\mathbf{S}$ are usually estimated from sample information when the process is in control. Under such conditions, the upper control limit of the T^2 chart given by Equation 6.63 may be modified to take the following form (Alt, 1982):

$$\text{UCL} = \left(\frac{mnp - mp - np + p}{mn - m - p + 1}\right)F_{\alpha,p,(mn-m-p+1)} \qquad (6.65)$$

where m represents the number of subgroups, each of size n, used to estimate $\overline{\overline{\mathbf{X}}}$ and $\mathbf{S}$. The value of T^2 for each of the m subgroups is calculated by using Equation 6.64 and is compared to the UCL given by Equation 6.65. If the value of T^2 for the jth subgroup (that is, T_j^2) is above the UCL, it should be treated as an out-of-control point, and investigative action should be started.

In order to calculate T_j^2, the vector of the sample means is given by

$$\overline{\mathbf{X}}_j = \begin{bmatrix} \overline{X}_{1j} \\ \overline{X}_{2j} \\ \vdots \\ \overline{X}_{pj} \end{bmatrix}, \qquad j = 1, 2, \ldots, m$$

where $\overline{X}_{ij}$ represents the sample mean of the ith characteristic for the jth sample and is found from

$$\overline{X}_{ij} = \frac{\sum_{k=1}^{n} X_{ijk}}{n}, \qquad \begin{cases} i = 1, 2, \ldots, p \\ j = 1, 2, \ldots, m \end{cases} \qquad (6.66)$$

where X_{ijk} represents the value of the kth observation of the ith characteristic in the jth sample. The sample variances for the ith characteristic in the jth sample are given by

$$s_{ij}^2 = \frac{1}{(n-1)}\sum_{k=1}^{n}(X_{ijk} - \overline{X}_{ij})^2, \qquad \begin{cases} i = 1, 2, \ldots, p \\ j = 1, 2, \ldots, m \end{cases} \qquad (6.67)$$

The covariance between characteristic i and characteristic h in the jth sample is calculated from

$$s_{ihj} = \frac{1}{(n-1)}\sum_{k=1}^{n}(X_{ijk} - \overline{X}_{ij})(X_{hjk} - \overline{X}_{hj}), \qquad \begin{cases} j = 1, 2, \ldots, m \\ i \neq h \end{cases} \qquad (6.68)$$

The vector of nominal means of each characteristic for m samples is estimated as

$$\overline{\overline{X}}_i = \frac{\sum_{j=1}^{m} \overline{X}_{ij}}{m}, \qquad i = 1, 2, \ldots, p \qquad (6.69)$$

The elements of the variance–covariance matrix $\mathbf{S}$ in Equation 6.64 are estimated from the following averages for m samples:

$$s_i^2 = \frac{\sum_{j=1}^{m} s_{ij}^2}{m}, \qquad i = 1, 2, \ldots, p \qquad (6.70)$$

and

$$s_{ih} = \frac{\sum_{j=1}^{m} s_{ihj}}{m}, \qquad i \neq h \qquad (6.71)$$

Finally, the vector $\overline{\overline{\mathbf{X}}}$ may be estimated using the elements $\{\overline{\overline{X}}_i\}$, and the matrix $\mathbf{S}$ may be estimated as follows (only the upper diagonal part is shown because the matrix is symmetric):

$$\mathbf{S} = \begin{bmatrix} s_1^2 & s_{12} & s_{13} & \cdots & s_{1p} \\ & s_2^2 & s_{23} & \cdots & s_{2p} \\ & & & & \vdots \\ & & & & s_p^2 \end{bmatrix} \qquad (6.72)$$

The use of Equation 6.64 requires inverting this matrix.

Figure 6-36 shows a Hotelling's control chart constructed by using the upper control limit given by Equation 6.65 and the plotted values of T^2 for each subgroup given by Equation 6.64, where the vector $\overline{\overline{\mathbf{X}}}$ and the matrix $\mathbf{S}$ are found by using the procedure discussed above. Notice that for sample number 4, the value of T^2 is above the upper control limit, indicating an out-of-control situation. This sample should be investigated to determine the reason for going out of control. In particular, it might be of interest to determine which of the quality characteristics caused the out-of-control state.

Even if only two characteristics are being considered jointly ($p = 2$), the situation can still be complex. If the two quality characteristics are highly positively correlated, we expect the averages for each

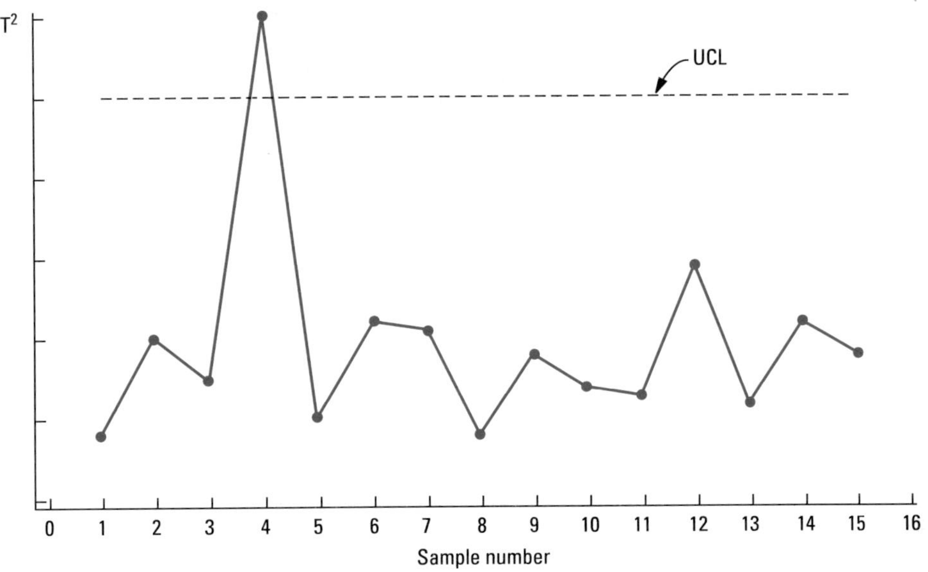

Figure 6-36 Example of a Hotelling's T^2 control chart.

characteristic in a subgroup to maintain the same type of relationship as to their location relative to the process average $\overline{\overline{X}}$. For example, in the jth sample, if $\overline{X}_{1j} > \overline{\overline{X}}_1$, then we could expect $\overline{X}_{2j} > \overline{\overline{X}}_2$. Likewise, if $\overline{X}_{1j} < \overline{\overline{X}}_1$, then we would expect $\overline{X}_{2j} < \overline{\overline{X}}_2$, which would confirm that the sample averages for each characteristic move in the same direction relative to their means. If the two characteristics are highly positively correlated and $\overline{X}_{1j} > \overline{\overline{X}}_1$, we would not expect $\overline{X}_{2j} < \overline{\overline{X}}_2$. However, if this does happen, then it is possible that this situation will show up as an out-of-control point in Hotelling's T^2 procedure, thereby indicating that the bivariate process is out of control. This same inference may be made based on individual 3σ control limit charts constructed for each characteristic if $\overline{X}_{1j}$ exceeds $\overline{\overline{X}}_1 + 3\sigma_{\overline{X}_1}$ or $\overline{X}_{2j}$ exceeds $\overline{\overline{X}}_2 + 3\sigma_{\overline{X}_2}$. However, it is possible for individual quality characteristic means to plot within the control limits on separate control charts even though the joint control statistic T^2 plots above the UCL on the joint control chart. This indicates the advantage of using joint control charts to detect out-of-control conditions for characteristics that need to be considered simultaneously.

However, it is also possible that an individual chart for a quality characteristic may indicate an out-of-control condition when all of the points on a joint control chart fall below the UCL. In general, larger sample sizes are needed to detect process changes when there is positive correlation between the characteristics than when there is a negative correlation. Furthermore, for large positive correlations between the characteristics, larger sample sizes are needed to detect large positive shifts in the process means than to detect small positive shifts.

Generally speaking, if an out-of-control condition is detected by means of a Hotelling's control chart, for joint control of quality characteristics, then individual control intervals are calculated for each characteristic for that subgroup. If the probability of a Type I error for a joint control procedure is α, then for subgroup j, the individual control interval for the ith quality characteristic is

$$\overline{\overline{X}}_i \pm t_{\alpha/2p,m(n-1)}\, s_i \sqrt{\frac{m-1}{mn}}, \qquad i = 1, 2, \ldots, p \tag{6.73}$$

where $\overline{\overline{X}}_i$ and s_i^2 are given by Equations 6.69 and 6.70, respectively. If $\overline{X}_{ij}$ falls outside of this interval, then the corresponding characteristic should be investigated for a lack of control. If assignable causes are detected, the subgroup of information relating to all of the characteristics should be deleted when recomputing the upper control limit for the joint control procedure.

Example 6-13: The single-strand break factor (a measure of the breaking strength) and weight of textile fibers are both of interest in keeping a fabric-production process in control. Twenty samples of size four are selected randomly from the process, and data values for the two characteristics are shown in Table 6-13. For instance, the bivariate observations for sample number 1 are as follows: (80,19), (82,22), (78,20), and (85,20).

Consider the construction of the Hotelling's T^2 control chart for this arrangement. The number of characteristics (p) is 2, the sample size (n) is 4, and the number of samples (m) is 20. The sample means of each characteristic for each sample are found by using Equation 6.66 and are shown in Table 6-14. For example, for sample number 1, the mean of the break factor readings is

$$\overline{X}_{11} = (80 + 82 + 78 + 85)/4 = 81.25$$

Similarly, the mean fiber weight for sample number 1 is 20.25. This procedure is repeated for each sample and for each characteristic, yielding the results shown in Table 6-14. Next, the sample variance of each characteristic for each sample is found by using Equation 6.67 and is recorded. For the single-strand break factor, which is the first characteristic ($i = 1$), the sample variance of the first sample is found to be

$$s_{11}^2 = \frac{1}{3}[(80 - 81.25)^2 + (82 - 81.25)^2 + (78 - 81.25)^2 + (85 - 81.25)^2] = 8.92$$

The covariance values between the two characteristics are calculated for each sample by using Equation 6.68 and

TABLE 6-13 Data for the bivariate process characteristics of single-strand break factor and weight of textile fibers

Sample number	Single strand break factor, $i = 1$				Weight of textile fibers, $i = 2$			
1	80	82	78	85	19	22	20	20
2	75	78	84	81	24	21	18	21
3	83	86	84	87	19	24	21	22
4	79	84	80	83	18	20	17	16
5	82	81	78	86	23	21	18	22
6	86	84	85	87	21	20	23	21
7	84	88	82	85	19	23	19	22
8	76	84	78	82	22	17	19	18
9	85	88	85	87	18	16	20	16
10	80	78	81	83	18	19	20	18
11	86	84	85	86	23	20	24	22
12	81	81	83	82	22	21	23	21
13	81	86	82	79	16	18	20	19
14	75	78	82	80	22	21	23	22
15	77	84	78	85	22	19	21	18
16	86	82	84	84	19	23	18	22
17	84	85	78	79	17	22	18	19
18	82	86	79	83	20	19	23	21
19	79	88	85	83	21	23	20	18
20	80	84	82	85	18	22	19	20

TABLE 6-14 Data for construction of Hotelling's T^2 chart

Sample number, j	Sample means: Break factor, $\overline{X}_{1j}$	Weight, $\overline{X}_{2j}$	Sample variances: s_{1j}^2	s_{2j}^2	Sample covariance s_{12j}	Hotelling's T^2
1	81.25	20.25	8.92	1.58	0.92	0.78
2	79.50	21.00	15.00	6.00	−9.00	5.25
3	85.00	21.50	3.33	4.33	3.00	5.98
4	81.50	17.75	5.67	2.92	1.17	7.95
5	81.75	21.00	10.92	4.67	5.33	1.03
6	85.50	21.25	1.67	1.58	0.17	6.72
7	84.75	20.75	6.25	4.25	4.58	3.36
8	80.00	19.00	13.33	4.67	−7.33	5.27
9	86.25	17.50	2.25	3.67	−2.50	15.25
10	80.50	18.75	4.33	0.92	−0.50	4.86
11	85.25	22.25	0.92	2.92	0.92	10.08
12	81.75	21.75	0.92	0.92	0.58	3.17
13	82.00	18.25	8.67	2.92	−0.33	4.74
14	78.75	22.00	8.92	0.67	1.33	10.66
15	81.00	20.00	16.67	3.33	−7.33	1.21
16	84.00	20.50	2.67	5.67	−2.67	1.45
17	81.50	19.00	12.33	4.67	3.00	2.31
18	82.50	20.75	8.33	2.92	−4.50	0.41
19	83.75	20.50	14.25	4.33	3.17	1.06
20	82.75	19.75	4.92	2.92	2.92	0.25
Means	$\overline{\overline{X}}_1 = 82.46$	$\overline{\overline{X}}_2 = 20.17$	$\overline{s}_1^2 = 7.51$	$\overline{s}_2^2 = 3.29$	$\overline{s}_{12} = -0.35$	

are also shown in Table 6-14. For the first sample, the calculation proceeds as follows:

$$\begin{aligned} s_{121} &= \frac{1}{3}[(80 - 81.25)(19 - 20.25) \\ &\quad + (82 - 81.25)(22 - 20.25) \\ &\quad + (78 - 81.25)(20 - 20.25) \\ &\quad + (85 - 81.25)(20 - 25)] \\ &= 0.917 \end{aligned}$$

Next, estimates of the nominal mean of each characteristic are found by using Equation 6.69. Estimates of the elements of the variance–covariance matrix $\boldsymbol{S}$ as averaged over the 20 samples in accordance with Equations 6.70 and 6.71 are found and shown in Table 6-14. The values of T^2 given by Equation 6.62 are also shown in Table 6-14 for each sample.

The upper control limit for the T^2 chart for an overall Type I error probability of 0.0054 is found by using Equation 6.65 to be

$$\begin{aligned} &\text{UCL} \\ &= \left[\frac{(20)(4)(2) - (20)(2) - (4)(2) + 2}{(20)(4) - 20 - 2 + 1}\right] F_{0.0054,2,[(20)(4)-20-2+1]} \\ &= 1.932 F_{.0054,2,59} = (1.932)(6.406) = 12.376 \end{aligned}$$

The value of $F_{.0054,2,59}$ may be approximated from the F-tables in Appendix A-6 by using linear interpolation.

The multivariate T^2 control chart for these two characteristics is shown in Figure 6-37. Sample number 9 is out of control. For this sample, $T^2 = 15.25$, which exceeds the upper control limit of 12.376. The next step is to investigate which of the two characteristics is the cause of this out-of-control condition.

The mean of the ranges ($\overline{R}$) of the single-strand break factors for the 20 samples is 5.75, while that for the weight of the fibers is 3.95. If individual 3σ limits were constructed ($\alpha/2p = .0054/4 = .0013$, which yields a z-value of 3.00), the control limits would be found as follows. For the single-strand break factor, the upper control limit would be

$$\begin{aligned} \text{UCL} &= \overline{\overline{X}}_1 + A_2\overline{R} \\ &= 82.46 + (0.729)(5.75) \\ &= 86.652 \end{aligned}$$

For the fiber weight, the upper control limit would be

$$\begin{aligned} \text{UCL} &= \overline{\overline{X}}_2 + A_2\overline{R} \\ &= 20.17 + (0.729)(3.95) \\ &= 23.050 \end{aligned}$$

Note that for sample number 9, the single-strand break factor does not exceed the UCL of a separate control chart for this characteristic. The sample mean of fiber weight for sample number 9 is also less than the UCL of its own control chart. Hence, in this case the joint control chart indicates an out-of-control condition which individual control charts would not have detected.

The next step should be to determine what caused the single-strand break factor or fiber weight to go out of control. Once the necessary corrective action has been taken, the Hotelling T^2 control limits should be revised by deleting sample number 9 for both characteristics.

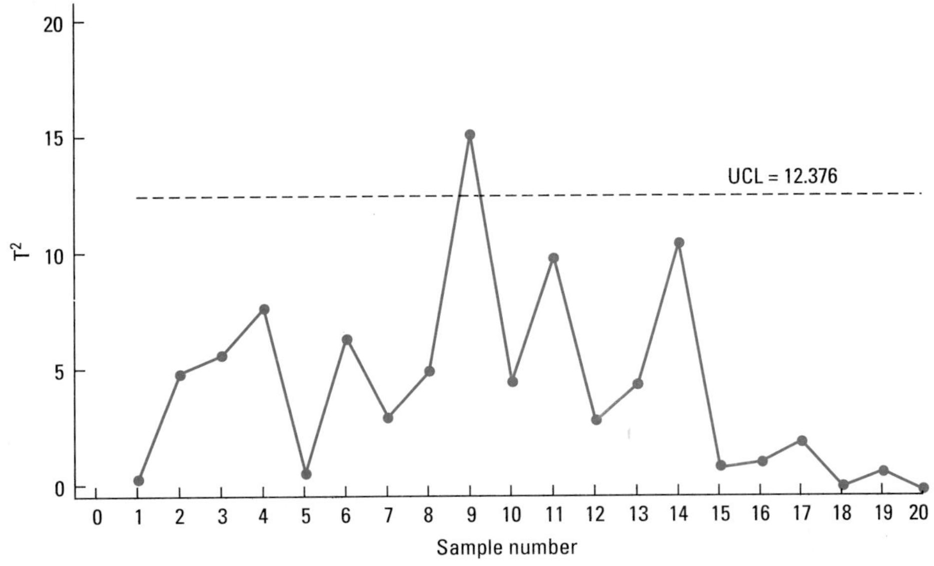

Figure 6-37 T^2 control chart for bivariate fabric-production data.

If we had decided to use the individual control limits for a joint control procedure as given by Equation 6.73, the limits would have been as follows. For the single-strand break factor,

$$\begin{aligned}\overline{\overline{X}}_1 \pm t_{.0054/(2)(2),20(3)} s_1 \sqrt{\frac{19}{(20)(4)}} &= 82.46 \pm t_{.0013,60}(2.740)\sqrt{0.2375} \\ &= 82.46 \pm (3.189)(1.3353) \\ &= (78.202, 86.718)\end{aligned}$$

The sample mean of sample number 9 for this characteristic does not exceed the upper control limit of 86.718 and so would not be considered out of control. The control limits for the fiber weight are found in a similar manner:

$$\begin{aligned}\overline{\overline{X}}_2 \pm t_{.0013,60} s_2 \sqrt{\frac{19}{(20)(4)}} &= 20.17 \pm (3.189)(\sqrt{3.29})(0.4873) \\ &= (17.351, 22.989)\end{aligned}$$

For sample number 9, the mean fiber weight is within these calculated limits and so would also be considered in control.

Thus, based on the joint control procedure, this process has been identified as out of control. Remedial actions based on the assignable causes for sample number 9 should be identified and implemented. The control limits for Hotelling's T^2 chart should be revised by deleting the observations for this sample. This example illustrates the fact that it is possible for the value of T^2 for a joint control procedure to exceed the UCL given by Equation 6.65 even though the individual characteristic sample means may be within the control limits of their individual charts. This example shows that it is imperative to jointly control the quality characteristics, even though individual characteristics may be within certain prescribed limits of their own. On the other hand, when the value of T^2 for the joint control procedure exceeds the UCL given by Equation 6.65, it is possible for one or more of the individual characteristic means to fall outside the control limits of an individual chart. Such an occurrence provides a clue as to which characteristics to closely monitor.

6-9 SUMMARY

This chapter has introduced different types of control charts for use when the quality characteristic is a variable (in other words, is measurable on a numerical scale). Details as to the construction, analysis, and interpretation of each chart have been presented. Guidelines are provided for the appropriate settings in which each control chart may be used. The rationale behind each type of control chart has been discussed. A set of general considerations that deserve attention prior to the construction of a control chart is given. Statistical process control by means of control charts for variables is the backbone of many processes. This chapter discusses at length the procedures to construct and maintain these control charts.

6-10 CASE STUDY

THE ROLE OF STATISTICAL PROCESS CONTROL (SPC) IN POLYMER PROCESSING*

The Approach—What Is SPC, and How Should It Be Used?

What is Statistical Process Control? SPC is a system of process control where most of the system consists of the engineering and technological aspects—the statistical component is small but vital (see Figure 6-38).

*Adapted from: S. H. Coulson and J. A. Cousans (1989), "The Role of Statistical Process Control in Polymer Processing," *Quality Assurance,* Vol. 15, No. 2, pp. 45–51. The Institute of Quality Assurance, 10 Grosvener Gardens, London, SW1WODQ, United Kingdom.

The historical performance of the process is defined in simple statistical terms by the *mean,* the central tendency or average, and by the *standard deviation,* a measure of the random inherent variability or spread of the process. These values are used to construct control charts, where the limits define the normal historic working range of the process. If the process runs within the limits, no actions are taken; if the results move out of the limits, then actions are taken immediately to return the process to its normal operating mode.

Ideally, the control parameters should be *process* variables, for example, cycle time, injection pressure, or extruder die head temperature. Often, the control parameters are *product* properties such as melt flow, shot weight, compound viscosity, or hardness. However, someone has to know how to adjust the *process* to give the correct *product* properties.

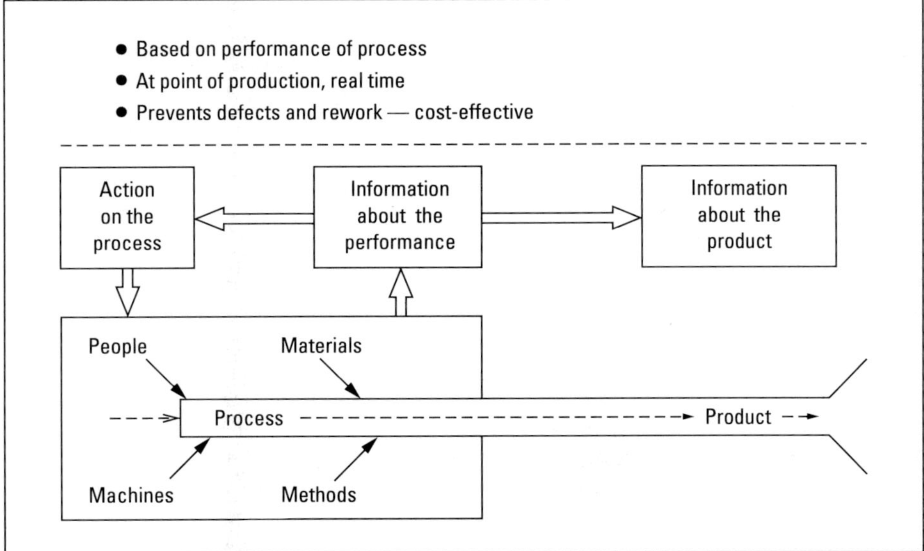

Figure 6-38 Statistical process control (SPC).

What Are the "Seven Tools" of SPC? The "seven tools" of SPC are the simple methods of graphical problem solving (see Figure 6-39). The *flow chart* is essential for the precise definition of the process, *any* process. Flow charts are used in Exxon Chemical for defining accounting procedures; their use is not limited to the manufacturing operation. *Check sheets* are the first stage in data collection. Eventually, data collection will be one function of the processing equipment; we see this trend in injection moulding machines for plastics and in "computerized mixing" in the rubber industry. The *Pareto analysis* is so simple that it does not seem to be obvious! It is the simplest possible ranking technique and is used to focus attention on the "critical few" rather than the "trivial many" problems. *Cause-and-effect analysis* is the method for the determination of the root cause of problems so that corrective actions can be taken. *Histograms, control charts,* and *scatter plots* are all ways of giving a picture of the data; this is important with computerized analysis systems, too.

SPC and the Total Quality Management System In the Exxon Chemical total quality system model (see Figure 6-40), SPC is just one interactive element of a complete quality system. There is a significant interaction between the quality assurance element and the SPC element—both are needed.

What is the Purpose of a Total Quality Management System? The most important aspect of the total quality management system (see Figure 6-41) is its use as the basis for quality and productivity improvement. Improvements in quality and productivity are a most effective way of improving profitability. It is possible to improve quality and productivity without total quality management, but improvement is much easier if there is the foundation of a total quality system.

To summarize: the application of SPC alone will not ensure improvements in quality and productivity, but, in a total quality system, SPC is an important tool for improvement.

Problem 1: What Do You Do with Control Charts? If something is worth measuring, the measurements should be recorded in a proper manner; once the measurements have been recorded, they should be analyzed; as a result of the analysis, actions should be taken. This is why control charts are used: to measure the performance of the process and to indicate when corrective actions have to be taken. The most important stage is *take [corrective] action,* and for both manual and automatic systems the actions to be taken have to be understood, quantified, and defined. In addition, the analysis and action steps should be recorded for further progress. What is the most frequent corrective action? What can be done to correct the cause so one prevention step will eliminate the need for any other actions? What happens when control charts are correctly used?

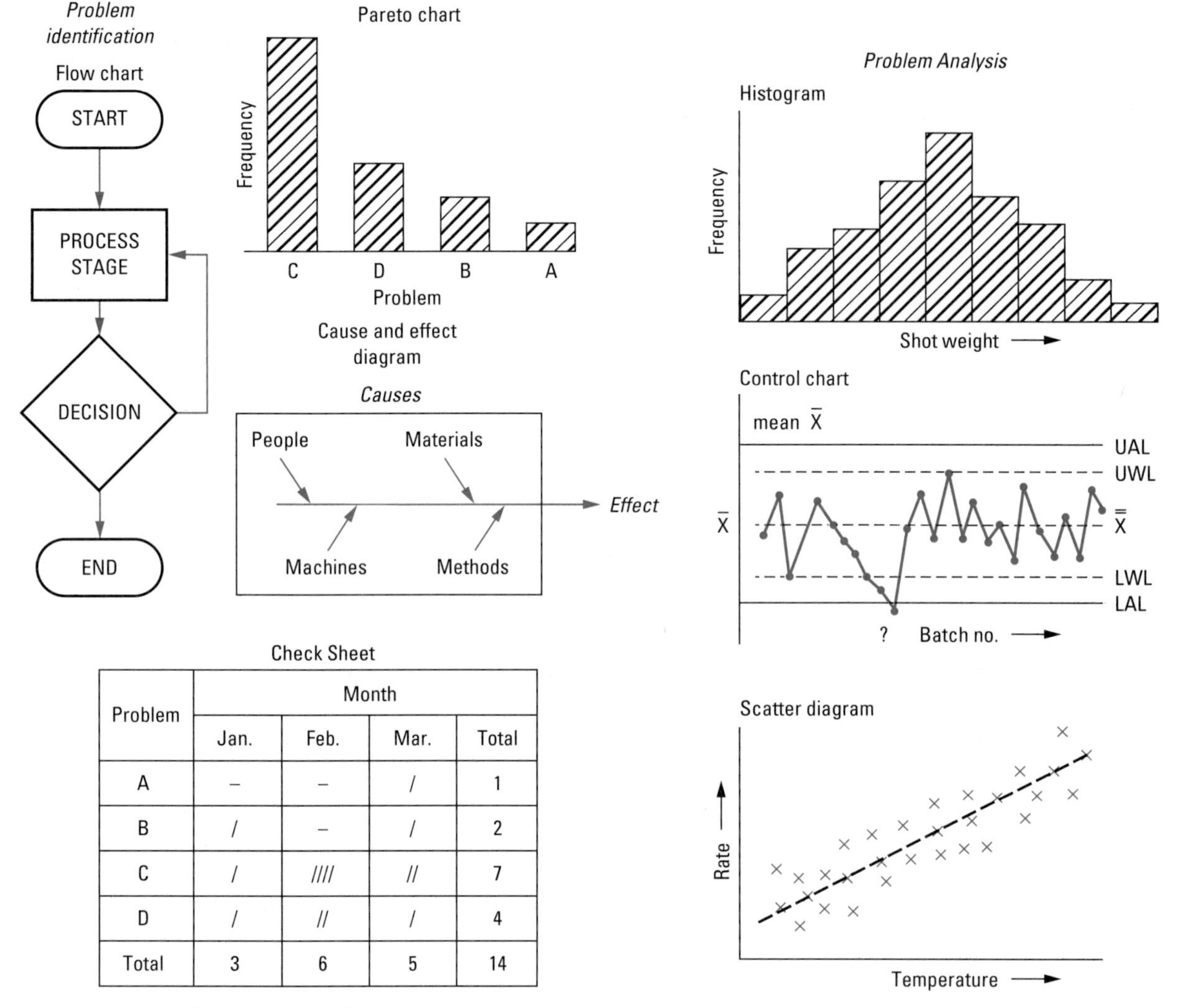

Problem	Month			
	Jan.	Feb.	Mar.	Total
A	–	–	/	1
B	/	–	/	2
C	/	////	//	7
D	/	//	/	4
Total	3	6	5	14

Figure 6-39 The "seven tools" of SPC.

The first stage is that the process is centered, that is, the process is controlled so that it centers on a target value, with random variation around the target value. The second stage is that the causes of out-of-control or abnormal results are determined and corrective actions are taken to prevent their recurrence. The third stage is the attainment of a statistical state of control such that the process results are now predictable, run to run, year to year, with no surprises.

This could be a dangerous state in that the level of variability or level of defects is accepted as the norm and the process becomes in control but fossilized.

Problem 2: Why Improve? (Beyond Control Charts) Every manufacturing and service business needs to improve because of a number of challenges from outside. We see the challenge from the Far East all around us, where the Japanese manufacturing industry has taken over world market dominance in many product areas. Japanese industry has adopted Deming's concept of making higher-quality products at lower costs through the total quality route.

Our customers are also challenging us as suppliers to improve. One way to reduce variability is to reduce the number of suppliers. Ford has halved their number of suppliers and has not finished yet. The move is towards cost-effective, high-quality suppliers who can and do demonstrate their level of performance for quality of product, service, and information.

There is another market challenge—1992 and an open Europe. This can be seen as a threat or a challenge—the perception depends on the management

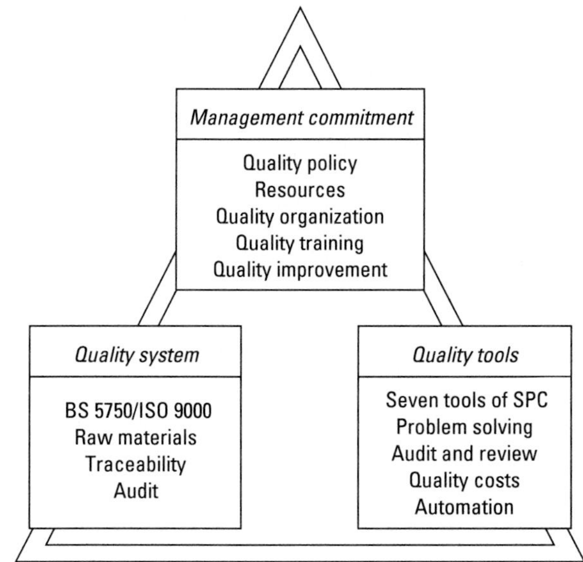

Figure 6-40 The total quality triangle.

approach of each company. Already in Europe, market leaders are exploiting their quality and their benefits from quality management.

Three major customers of the polymer processing industry, namely Ford, Jaguar, and Nissan, now expect continuous improvements in quality and productivity. Since improvements in quality via the total quality management route must reduce costs, price reductions may be anticipated. Ford's total quality excellence program is based on improvement. Some of the key suppliers to the rubber and plastics processing industry are practicing total quality management. In fact, we at Exxon Chemical (Polymers) have a number of programs in hand where we are helping our customers improve the quality of their processes and products.

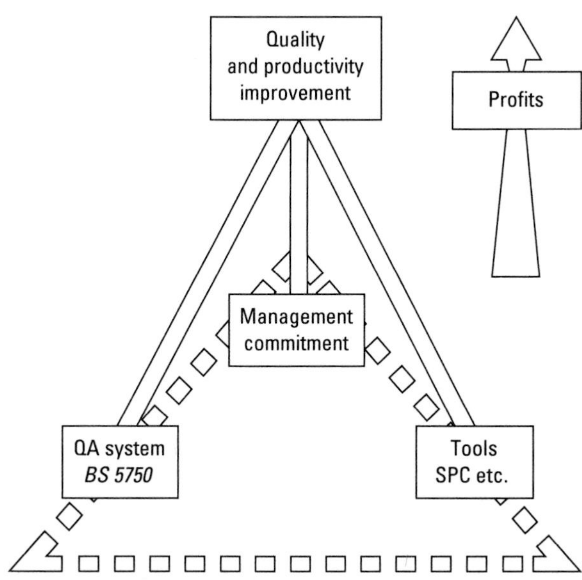

Figure 6-41 The total quality pyramid.

Problem 3: How to Improve? The basis of an ideal model for the improvement of the process should be the following:

1. Management commitment
2. Quality management system
3. Tools of SPC

Then it is relatively simple to implement improvement programs.

The most serious limitations in achieving this ideal are time and resources. It takes a great deal of time and effort to achieve accreditation, to train everyone in SPC techniques, and to implement SPC. Often there just is not enough time to respond in the short term to the challenges from the marketplace, so what can be done? A short cut is possible, but only if there is real management commitment—that is, to initiate a quality improvement program via quality improvement teams.

Management should select a major problem to tackle, perhaps from cost-of-quality studies, a major customer problem or a major process problem. It may be better to select a process problem which is a source of trouble to production, since resolution of this sort of problem would give better acceptance of continuing improvement. This improvement team is appointed by, resourced by, stewarded by, and driven by management. The techniques used are the basic seven tools of SPC—the quality improvement team (QIT) can be a training process for the team members if someone in the team has the necessary skills. The team works by tapping the knowledge of people involved in the problem, such as operators, maintenance, laboratory, quality, purchasing, dispatch, and sales. Once actions for improvement have been recommended, implemented, and confirmed, the team is disbanded, and the next problem is tackled by a different team.

Let us look closer at the team. The subject for improvement is—in Pareto terms—one of the "vital few" rather than the "trivial many." This is not an "Any volunteers?" group but a team carefully selected and appointed by management. Team members have to reflect any possible involvement, ideally day-to-day, with the problem. For this short-cut route, someone must have the necessary statistical skills. The involvement of a supplier or customer may add a resource, perhaps for training, data analysis, etc. This is where Ford's Supplier Program or Exxon Chemical/Customer Quality Improvement Programs are of real benefit. The team *must* be supported by management. If a recommendation is made it must be followed up, or the whole team, and perhaps other staff, may be completely demotivated regarding quality improvement.

Problem 4: What to Improve? The real aim is to eliminate waste and the cost of doing things more than once, which in the polymer industry translates into an aim to eliminate scrap and rework. Rework is the bane of thermoplastics processing; many factories lose, say, 15 percent productivity because of rework or recycle operations. Scrap and rework are caused by variability—thus the causes of variability need to be found and then eliminated.

The *whole process* must be examined (see Figure 6-42).

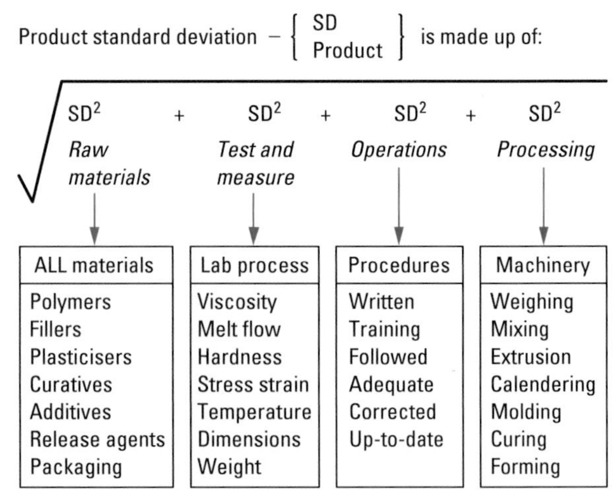

Figure 6-42 Equation for the sum of the variances.

Because this equation is a sum of squares of standard deviations (SD), just one higher cause of variability will dominate. *All* materials must be considered, not just the expensive polymer, which may well have the lowest variability anyway! Measurement error must be considered, too; polymer and compound viscosity and melt flow are very difficult to measure accurately. The introduction of SPC into Exxon Chemical Polymers started with laboratory SPC and improvement. The effect on the Mooney viscosity test was to improve the process capability by 33 per cent before even starting on the process.

Everybody believes it is the material coming into them which is variable, not their particular *process.* In fact, process variability can be the key factor. In the rubber industry, the weighing out of compounding ingredients often is the main cause of variability; mixing is another. These are well-known factors, but the variability from downstream operations is often not even considered. *Every* conversion operation has some variability. This variability must be measured and known.

Once the major causes of variability are established, then effective corrective actions can be taken. But do not rely on opinion, for example, "We *know* the compound coming in is variable; that's why we have to keep adjusting our extruder or injection moulding machine." Make decisions based on *facts,* not *opinions.*

This equation can be expanded to cover one topic. For example, consider viscosity and break down all the causes of viscosity variation.

Ishikawa's cause-and-effect diagram acts as a "street map" (see Figure 6-43) to help find your way through this complex area.

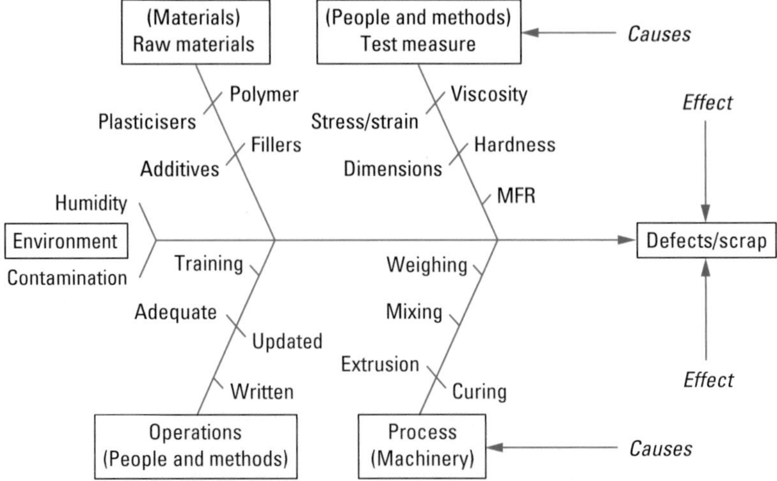

Figure 6-43 Cause-and-effect diagram for the whole process.

This is the focus for the brainstorming activities of the quality improvement team. It can be made to match the equation of variance in its main branches, and the detailed subbranches will be filled in by the team. Like the equation of variance, it can be made wide-ranging or restricted to examining a small area in depth. Once the cause-and-effect diagram has been constructed, then the quality improvement team can do a Pareto analysis and rank each item for the contribution to variation. Ideally, the ranking should be based on facts rather than opinions. If hard facts are not available then they *must* be obtained; they are the highest priority.

Problem 5: What to Improve? What Process Stage? If the chief chemist is asked "What to improve?" the usual response is that factory problems are related to the polymer. Often the problem is perceived as being caused by variation in polymer molecular weight: Mooney viscosity or melt flow rate. It is clearly the supplier's problem, and the specification should be narrowed. If the production manager for the extrusion of molding shop is asked "What to improve?" a common response is that processing problems and scrap arise because the incoming compounds or blends are variable (see Figure 6-44). Therefore, extruder or molding press conditions have to be "adjusted" to compensate for this variability. The cause of variability is either raw material inconsistency and mixing or blending variation—in the user's opinion.

In one of the Exxon Chemical/Customer Quality Improvement studies we had the above response, but the customer's top management were persuaded to extend the scope of the study to the *whole process*. Once data had been collected and analyzed, the true picture emerged (see Figure 6-45). So much of the variability, or "noise," was due to the extrusion line operation and extruder hardware control that effects of raw materials could *not* be seen. The findings were quite a surprise, since this company had been focusing its attention on the polymers and the mixing operation.

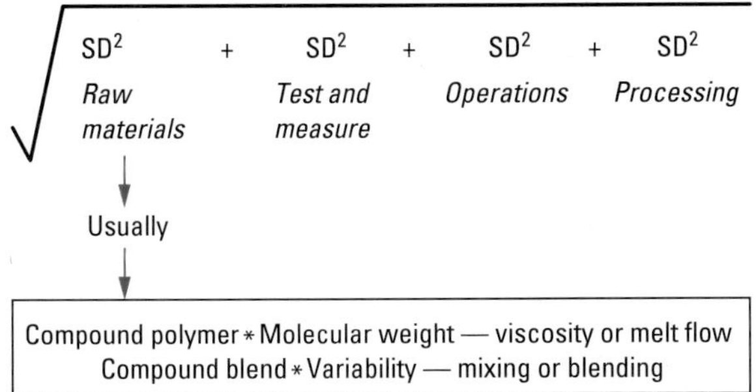

Figure 6-44 Assumptions for cause of defects.

The recommendations for improvement were to update and redefine the extrusion line operating procedures, to retrain the operators, and to make simple improvements to the extruder temperature control systems. The lessons to be learned from this study are:

1. Make decisions based on facts, not opinions.
2. Consider the whole process.
3. Improvements in the variability of the polymer would have no effect on variability or scrap from this process.

Problem 6: Machines with "Built-In SPC" Now there are many pieces of polymer processing equipment available with "built-in SPC" facilities. These machines represent a major step forward, if the SPC features can be used effectively. It is still necessary to *understand* the process so that the correct control parameters can be selected and used. This means that the equations of variance and cause-and-effect relationships between machine control parameters and processing behavior and product properties must be established—for *all materials* and for *all products*. Only then will it be possible to capitalize on the benefits from investment in advanced processing equipment. If the correct control parameters can be determined and used, then SPC charting should not be necessary.

The Role of SPC in the Future SPC alone is not the answer to quality problems; SPC is one important interactive element in total quality management. As process quality improvement progresses, SPC will be used less and less for routine quality control, more and more as a tool for quality improvement.

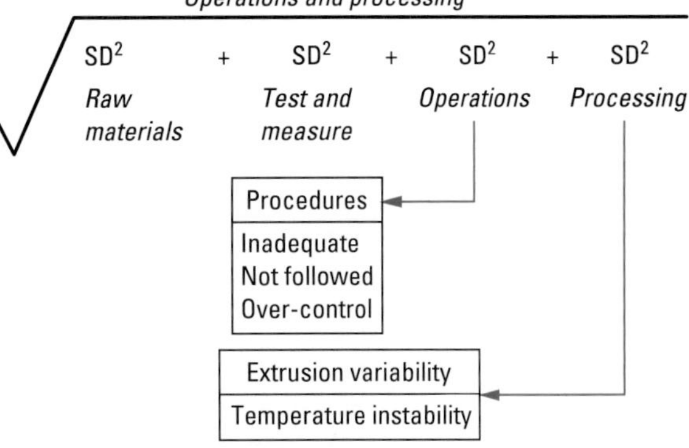

Figure 6-45 Determination of true cause of defects.

The seven tools of SPC must be understood and used by everyone, everywhere, in any successful business. SPC and the seven tools of SPC are key tools for the improvement of quality and productivity.

Improvements in quality and productivity are the means of survival, profit, and growth in today's hugely competitive global marketplace.

Questions for Discussion

1. What is the importance of the seven tools of SPC?
2. Describe the fundamental conditions which must exist in a company for SPC to be effective.
3. Discuss some difficulties in the implementation of SPC.
4. Describe the approach that led to the identification of the problem areas.
5. Discuss how meeting certain accreditation standards (for example, *ISO 9000*) may facilitate statistical process control and improvement.

KEY TERMS

Attribute
Average run length (ARL)
Causes
  Chance
  Assignable
Center line
Control chart
  $\overline{X}$-chart
  R-chart
  s-chart
  X-chart
  Cumulative sum chart
  Moving average chart
  Geometric moving average chart
  Trend chart
  Regression chart
  Modified control chart
  Acceptance control chart
  Hotelling's T^2 control chart
Control chart patterns
  Natural pattern
  Sudden shift in level
  Gradual shift in level
  Trend
  Cyclic
  Wild patterns
  Freaks
  Bunches/Groups
  Mixture of two or more populations
  Stratification
  Interaction
Control limits
  Lower
  Upper
  Trial limits
  Revised limits
Corrective actions
Correlation
Covariance
F-distribution
Geometric moving average
  Exponentially-weighted moving average
  Weighting factor
Hotelling's T^2
Mean
  Population
  Sample
Moving average
  Span
Multivariate control charts
  Control region
Normal distribution
Out of Control
  Rules
Pareto analysis
Principle of least squares
Process
  Mean
  Standard deviation
  Shift in mean
Process capability
Proportion nonconforming
Range
Regression
Specification limits
Standard deviation
  Population
  Sample
  Sample mean
Standardized normal value
Statistical control
Subgroup
  Rational
  Selection of

Frequency of
Size
Variable size
Target value
3σ limits
Type I error
Overall rate
Type II error
V-mask
Lead distance
Angle of decision line
Variable
Variance
Population
Sample
Sample mean

EXERCISES

Discussion Questions

6-1 What are the advantages and disadvantages of using variables rather than attributes in control charts?

6-2 Describe the Pareto concept. Discuss its significance in practical applications.

6-3 Discuss some of the general considerations prior to the construction of control charts. What concepts should be followed when selecting rational subgroups?

6-4 Explain the difference in interpretation between an observation falling below the lower control limit on an $\overline{X}$-chart and one falling below the lower control limit on an R chart. Discuss the impact of each on the revision of control charts.

6-5 What are some considerations in the interpretation of control charts based on standard values? Is it possible for a process to be in control when its control chart is based on standard values but to be out of control when its control chart is based on observations from the process? Explain.

6-6 Discuss some of the rules for out-of-control conditions. Select a company that uses control charts. Investigate what rules they use for determining out-of-control conditions.

6-7 Explain the concept of process capability. When should it be estimated? Discuss its impact on the production of scrap and/or rework.

6-8 Discuss some typical control chart patterns and their likely remedial actions.

6-9 Is it easier to bring about a change in the process mean or a decrease in the process variability? Discuss the practical implications.

6-10 Under what situations would control charts be set up for individual values? What precautions should be taken in these situations?

6-11 What are the advantages and disadvantages of cumulative sum charts compared to Shewhart control charts?

6-12 What are the conditions under which a moving average control chart is preferable? Compare the moving average chart with the geometric moving average chart.

6-13 Discuss the appropriate settings for using a regression control chart.

6-14 Discuss the appropriate setting for using a modified control chart and an acceptance control chart. Compare and contrast the two charts.

6-15 What is the motivation behind constructing multivariate control charts? How do they better serve us than control charts for individual characteristics?

Problems

6-16 Random samples of size 5 of the length of a connector pin are selected. For each sample, the sample mean and range in millimeters are calculated and shown in Table 6-15. The length specifications are 50 ± 3.5 mm. The daily production rate is 2000. The unit cost of scrap is \$1.00, and the unit cost of rework is \$0.25.

a. Find the trial control limits for an $\overline{X}$- and R-chart.
b. Assuming assignable causes for out-of-control points, find the revised control limits.
c. Find the total daily cost of scrap and rework.
d. If the process average changes to 52 mm, what is the probability of detecting it on the next sample drawn after the change?

6-17 A major automobile company is interested in reducing the time that customers have to wait while having their car serviced with one of the dealers. They select four customers randomly each day and find the total time that

TABLE 6-15 Data for length of connector pins

Sample number	Average Length, $\overline{X}$	Range, R
1	50.3	4
2	48.4	2
3	48.5	5
4	49.1	4
5	52.6	3
6	46.2	4
7	50.8	3
8	52.2	4
9	49.5	5
10	51.7	4
11	52.5	5
12	47.8	3
13	49.6	5
14	50.8	9
15	48.5	4
16	49.3	6
17	53.3	3
18	52.1	4
19	50.2	5
20	51.9	4
21	52.1	2
22	49.5	3
23	50.7	4
24	52.6	5
25	52.3	6
26	48.6	5
27	51.0	4
28	52.3	3
29	50.6	2
30	51.5	4

each of those customers has to wait (in minutes) while having their car serviced. From these four observations, the sample average and range are found. This process is repeated for 25 days. The summary data for these observations are

$$\sum_{i=1}^{25} \overline{X}_i = 1000, \qquad \sum_{i=1}^{25} R_i = 250$$

a. Find the $\overline{X}$- and R-chart control limits.
b. Assuming the process is in control and the distribution of waiting time is normal, find the percentage of customers who will not have to wait more than 50 minutes.
c. Find the 2σ control limits.
d. The service manager is developing a promotional program and is interested in reducing the average waiting time to 30 minutes by employing more mechanics. If the plan is successful, what proportion of the customers will have to wait more than 40 minutes? More than 50 minutes?

6-18 In a textile company, it is important that the acidity of the solution used to dye fabric be within certain acceptable values. Data values were gathered for a control chart by randomly taking four observations from the solution and determining the average pH value and range. After 25 such subgroups, the following summary information was obtained:

$$\sum_{i=1}^{25} \overline{X}_i = 195, \qquad \sum_{i=1}^{25} R_i = 10$$

The specifications for the pH value are 7.5 ± 0.5.

a. Find the $\overline{X}$- and R-chart control limits.
b. Find the 1σ and 2σ $\overline{X}$-chart limits.
c. What fraction of the output is nonconforming (assuming a normal distribution of pH values)?

6-19 The bore size on a component to be used in assembly is a critical dimension. Subgroups of size four have been collected, and the sample average diameter and range have been calculated. After 25 subgroups, we have

$$\sum_{i=1}^{25} \overline{X}_i = 107.5, \qquad \sum_{i=1}^{25} R_i = 12.5$$

The specifications on the bore size are 4.4 ± 0.2 mm. The unit costs of scrap and rework are \$2.40 and \$0.75, respectively. The daily production rate is 1200.

a. Find the $\overline{X}$- and R-chart control limits.
b. Assuming the process is in control, estimate its standard deviation.
c. Find the proportion of scrap and rework.
d. Find the total daily cost of scrap and rework.
e. If the process average shifts to 4.5 mm, what is the impact on the proportion of scrap and rework produced?

6-20 The time to be seated at a popular restaurant is of importance. Subgroups of five randomly selected customers are chosen, and their average and range (in minutes) are calculated. After 30 such subgroups the summary data values are

$$\sum_{i=1}^{30} \overline{X}_i = 306, \qquad \sum_{i=1}^{30} R_i = 24$$

a. Find the $\overline{X}$- and R-chart control limits.
b. Find the 1σ and 2σ $\overline{X}$-chart limits.
c. The manager has found that customers usually leave if they are informed of an estimated waiting time of over 10.5 minutes. What fraction of customers will this restaurant lose? Assume a normal distribution of waiting times.

6-21 Control charts for $\overline{X}$ and R are kept on the tensile strength (in kg/cm^2) of steel beams. The subgroup or sample size is five. After 30 subgroups, the summary information is

$$\sum_{i=1}^{30} \overline{X}_i = 7518, \qquad \sum_{i=1}^{30} R_i = 375$$

The specifications are 250 ± 10 kg/cm^2.

a. Find the $\overline{X}$- and R-chart control limits.
b. Assuming the process to be in control, estimate the process standard deviation.
c. What proportion of the output is now unacceptable?
d. If the company wants to make sure that the output tensile strength of the product is not less than 265 kg/cm^2, what proportion of the output will not meet this criterion?

6-22 The thickness of sheet metal in millimeters used for making automobile bodies is a characteristic of interest. Random samples of size four are taken. The average and standard deviation are calculated for each subgroup and are shown in Table 6-16 for 20 subgroups. The specification limits are 9.95 ± 0.3 mm.

a. Find the control limits for an $\overline{X}$- and s-chart. If there are out-of-control points, assume assignable causes, and revise the limits.
b. Estimate the process mean and the process standard deviation.
c. If the thickness of sheet metal exceeds the upper specification limit, it can be reworked. However, if the thickness is less than the lower specification limit, it cannot be used for its intended purpose and must be scrapped for other uses. The cost of rework is \$0.25 per linear foot, and the cost of scrap is \$0.75 per linear foot. The rolling mills are 100 ft. in length. The manufacturer has four such mills and runs 80 batches on each mill daily. What is the daily cost of rework? What is the daily cost of scrap?

TABLE 6-16 Sample average and standard deviation for thickness of sheet metal

Sample number	Sample average, $\overline{X}$	Sample standard deviation, s
1	10.19	0.15
2	9.80	0.12
3	10.12	0.18
4	10.54	0.19
5	9.86	0.14
6	9.45	0.09
7	10.06	0.16
8	10.13	0.18
9	9.82	0.14
10	10.17	0.13
11	10.18	0.16
12	9.85	0.15
13	9.82	0.06
14	10.18	0.34
15	9.96	0.11
16	9.57	0.09
17	10.14	0.12
18	10.08	0.15
19	9.82	0.09
20	10.15	0.12

d. If the manufacturer has the flexibility to change the process mean, should it be moved to 10.00?
e. What alternative courses of action should be considered if the product is nonconforming?

6-23 Light bulbs are tested for their luminance, with the intensity of brightness desired to be within a certain range. Random samples of five bulbs are chosen from the output, and the luminance is measured. The sample mean $\overline{X}$ and standard deviation s are found. After 30 samples, the following summary information is obtained:

$$\sum_{i=1}^{30} \overline{X}_i = 2550, \qquad \sum_{i=1}^{30} s_i = 195$$

The specifications are 90 ± 15.

a. Find the control limits for an $\overline{X}$- and s-chart.
b. Assuming that the process is in control, estimate the process mean and process standard deviation.
c. Comment on the ability of the process to meet specifications. What proportion of the output is nonconforming?
d. If the process mean is moved to 90, what is the proportion of output that will be

nonconforming? What suggestions would you make to improve the performance of the process?

6-24 The advertised weight of frozen food packages is 16 ounces, and the specifications are 16 ± 0.3 ounces. Random samples of size eight are selected from the output and weighed. The sample mean and standard deviation are calculated. Information on 25 such samples yields the following:

$$\sum_{i=1}^{25} \overline{X}_i = 398, \qquad \sum_{i=1}^{25} s_i = 3.00$$

a. Determine the center lines and control limits for an $\overline{X}$- and s-chart.
b. Estimate the process mean and standard deviation, assuming that the process is in control.
c. Find the 1σ and 2σ control limits for each chart.
d. What proportion of the output is nonconforming? Is the process capable?
e. What proportion of the output weighs less than the advertised weight?
f. If the manufacturer is interested in reducing potential complaints and lawsuits from customers who feel they have been cheated by packages weighing less than what is advertised, what action should the manufacturer take?

6-25 The baking time of painted corrugated sheet metal is of interest. Too much time will cause the paint to flake, and too little time will result in an unacceptable finish. The specifications on baking time are 10 ± 0.2 minutes. Random samples of size six were selected from the process, and their baking times were noted. The sample means and standard deviations were calculated. Summary results from 20 samples gave the following:

$$\sum_{i=1}^{20} \overline{X}_i = 199.8, \qquad \sum_{i=1}^{20} s_i = 1.40$$

a. Calculate the center line and control limits for an $\overline{X}$- and s-chart.
b. Estimate the process mean and standard deviation, assuming the process to be in control.
c. Is the process capable? What proportion of the output is nonconforming?
d. If the mean of the process can be shifted to 10 minutes, would you recommend such a change?
e. If the process mean changes to 10.2 minutes, what is the probability of detecting this change on the first subgroup taken after the shift? Assume that the process variability has not changed.

6-26 In a gasoline blending plant the quality of the output as indicated by its octane rating is measured for a sample taken from each batch. The observations from 20 such samples are shown in Table 6-17. Construct a chart for the moving range of two successive observations and a chart for individuals.

6-27 In a chemical plant involved in making paint for household use, the viscosity of the liquid has to be maintained. Table 6-18 shows the viscosity values of 26 samples. Construct a moving range chart based on two successive observations. Also, construct a chart for individuals.

TABLE 6-17 Octane ratings of gasoline

Sample number	Octane rating	Sample number	Octane rating
1	89.2	11	85.4
2	86.5	12	91.6
3	88.4	13	87.7
4	91.8	14	85.0
5	90.3	15	91.5
6	87.5	16	90.3
7	92.6	17	85.6
8	87.0	18	90.9
9	89.8	19	82.1
10	92.2	20	85.8

TABLE 6-18 Data for viscosity of liquid

Sample number	Viscosity of liquid	Sample number	Viscosity of liquid
1	16.2	14	16.7
2	13.8	15	15.9
3	17.0	16	14.6
4	15.8	17	16.5
5	13.5	18	18.4
6	14.7	19	15.2
7	14.0	20	14.6
8	14.8	21	17.2
9	13.2	22	16.1
10	16.8	23	14.4
11	14.9	24	17.0
12	13.0	25	13.8
13	12.5	26	15.5

TABLE 6-19 Average weights of packages of all-purpose flour

Sample number	Average weight, $\overline{X}$
1	80.2
2	80.0
3	79.6
4	80.3
5	80.1
6	80.4
7	79.5
8	79.4
9	79.7
10	79.5
11	80.3
12	80.5
13	79.8
14	80.4
15	80.2

6-28 Automatic machines that fill packages of all-purpose flour to a desired standard weight need to be closely monitored. A random sample of 4 packages is selected and weighed. The average weight is then computed. Observations from 15 such samples are shown in Table 6-19. The desired weight of packages is 80 ounces. Past information on the automatic machine reveals that the standard deviation of the weights of individual packages is 0.2 ounces. Assume an acceptable Type I error rate of 0.05. Also assume that it is desired to detect shifts in the process mean of 0.15 ounces.

a. Construct a cumulative sum chart and determine whether the machine needs to be adjusted to meet the target weight.
b. Determine the parameters of an appropriate V-mask. Specify the scale factor you use in your cusum plot.

6-29 To a manufacturer of fiberglass fishing rods, the bending strength of the poles is a consideration. Samples are chosen from the process, and the average bending strength of four samples is found. The target mean bending strength is 30 lb., with a process standard deviation of 0.8 lb. Suppose that it is desired to detect a shift of $\pm 0.75\sigma_{\overline{X}}$ from the target value. It is also desirable, if the process mean is not significantly different from the target value, for the average run length to be 300. Find the parameters of an appropriate V-mask. If the manufacturer desires that the average run length not exceed 13 so as to detect shifts of the magnitude indicated, what will be the parameters of a V-mask if there is some flexibility in the allowable ARL when the process is in control?

TABLE 6-20 Average waiting times of customers

Sample number	Average waiting time, $\overline{X}$	Sample number	Average waiting time, $\overline{X}$
1	8.4	11	8.8
2	6.5	12	10.0
3	10.8	13	9.5
4	9.7	14	9.6
5	9.0	15	8.3
6	9.4	16	9.9
7	10.2	17	10.2
8	8.1	18	8.3
9	7.4	19	8.6
10	9.6	20	9.9

6-30 The average time that a customer has to wait (in minutes) for the arrival of a cab after calling the company has been observed for random samples of size four. The data for 20 such samples are shown in Table 6-20. Previous analysis gave the upper and lower control limits for an $\overline{X}$-chart, when the process was in control as 10.5 and 7.7, respectively. What is your estimate of the standard deviation of the waiting time for a customer? Construct a moving average control chart using a span of 3. What conclusions can you draw from the chart?

6-31 Consider Example 6-8 regarding the amount of pigment used in the production of plastic. Using the data for sample averages shown in Table 6-8, construct a moving average chart for $w = 8$. What conclusions can you draw?

6-32 Consider Exercise 6-30, which deals with the average waiting time for the arrival of a cab. Using the data in Table 6-20, construct a geometric moving average control chart. Use a weighting factor of 0.10. What conclusions can you draw from the chart? How is it different from the moving average control chart constructed in Exercise 6-30?

6-33 Consider Example 6-9. Using the given information, construct a geometric moving average chart. Use a weighting factor of 0.15.

6-34 In an injection molding process, the die wears out gradually. In order to account for this wear, it is suggested that a trend chart be constructed for the outside diameter of the com-

TABLE 6-21 Sample average and range values for injection molding process

Sample number	Sample average, $\overline{X}$	Sample range, R
1	107.6	3.1
2	104.3	2.6
3	103.5	2.8
4	105.7	2.4
5	104.8	3.2
6	108.5	2.5
7	109.7	2.8
8	105.3	1.7
9	112.6	2.4
10	110.5	2.0
11	111.6	2.3
12	113.3	2.5
13	109.8	2.4
14	110.3	2.1
15	108.6	2.6
16	112.7	1.8
17	114.2	2.8
18	115.5	3.0
19	112.8	2.7
20	116.2	2.2

TABLE 6-22 Sample mean and range values of percentage of potassium content

Sample number	Sample average, $\overline{X}$	Sample range, R
1	23	1.9
2	20	2.3
3	24	2.2
4	19.6	1.6
5	20.5	1.8
6	22.8	2.4
7	19.3	2.3
8	21.6	2.0
9	20.3	2.1
10	19.6	1.7
11	24.2	2.3
12	21.9	1.8
13	20.6	1.8
14	23.6	2.0
15	20.8	1.6
16	20.2	2.1
17	19.5	2.3
18	22.7	2.5
19	21.2	1.9
20	22.9	2.2
21	20.6	2.1
22	23.5	2.4
23	21.6	1.8
24	22.6	2.3
25	20.5	2.2

ponent produced. Samples of size five are selected and the sample average $\overline{X}$ and range R are found. The results of 20 such samples are shown in Table 6-21. Construct the center line and control limits of a trend chart for the sample average. Is the process in control? If the process is out of control, assume assignable causes, and revise the limits. Suppose the specification limits are 110 ± 8 mm. At what point should the die be changed?

6-35 The percentage of potassium in a compound is expected to be within the specification limits of 18 percent to 35 percent. Samples of size four are taken from the process, and the mean and range of 25 such samples are shown in Table 6-22. It is desirable for the process nonconformance to be within 1.5 percent. If the acceptable level of Type I error is 0.05, find the modified control limits for the process mean.

6-36 Refer to Example 6-11 and the data for the nitrogen content in a certain fertilizer mix. If it is desired that the proportion nonconforming be within 0.5 percent and the level of Type I error be limited to 0.025, find the modified control limits for the process mean.

6-37 Refer to Exercise 6-35 and the data for the percentage of potassium content in a compound. Suppose we wish to detect an out-of-control condition with a probability of 0.90 if the process is producing at a nonconformance rate of 4 percent. Determine the acceptance control chart limits.

6-38 Refer to Example 6-12. If the nonconformance production rate is 2 percent and we wish to detect this with a probability of 0.98, what should be the acceptance control chart limits?

6-39 A component to be used in the assembly of a transmission mechanism is manufactured in a process for which the two quality characteristics of tensile strength (X_1) and diameter (X_2) are of importance. Twenty samples, each of size five, were obtained from the process. For each component, measurements on the tensile strength and diameter were taken and are shown in Table 6-23. Find a multivariate Hotelling's T^2 control chart using an overall Type I error probability of 0.01.

TABLE 6-23 Data on the bivariate process characteristics of tensile strength and diameter

Sample number	Tensile strength				Diameter			
1	66	70	68	72	16	18	15	20
2	75	60	70	75	17	22	18	19
3	65	70	70	65	20	18	15	18
4	72	70	75	65	19	20	15	17
5	73	74	72	70	21	21	23	19
6	72	74	73	74	21	19	20	18
7	63	62	65	66	22	20	24	22
8	75	84	75	66	22	20	20	22
9	65	69	77	71	18	16	18	18
10	70	68	67	67	18	17	19	18
11	80	75	70	69	24	18	20	22
12	68	65	80	50	20	21	20	22
13	74	80	76	74	19	17	20	21
14	76	74	75	73	20	17	18	18
15	71	70	74	73	18	16	17	18
16	68	67	70	69	18	16	19	20
17	72	76	75	77	22	19	23	20
18	76	74	75	77	19	23	20	21
19	72	74	73	75	20	18	20	19
20	72	68	74	70	21	19	18	20

REFERENCES

Alt, F. B. (1982). "Multivariate Quality Control: State of the Art," *American Society for Quality Control Annual Quality Congress Transactions,* pp. 886–893.

AT&T. (1984). *Statistical Quality Control Handbook,* 10th printing.

Banks, J. (1989). *Principles of Quality Control.* Wiley, New York.

Barnard, G. A. (1959). "Control Charts and Stochastic Processes," *Journal of the Royal Statistical Society,* Series B, Volume 21, pp. 239–257.

Bowker, A. H., and Lieberman, G. J. (1972). *Engineering Statistics,* 2nd edition. Prentice-Hall, Englewood Cliffs, NJ.

Coulson, S. H., and Cousans, J. A. (1989). "The Role of Statistical Process Control in Polymer Processing," *Quality Assurance,* 15(2), pp. 45–51.

Gitlow, H., Gitlow, S., Oppenheim, A., and Oppenheim, R. (1989). *Tools and Methods for the Improvement of Quality.* R.D. Irwin, Homewood, IL.

Hotelling, H. (1947). "Multivariate Quality Control," in C. Eisenhart, M. W. Hastny, and W. A. Wallis, Eds., *Techniques of Statistical Analysis.* McGraw Hill, New York.

Lucas, J. M. (1976). "The Design and Use of V-Mask Control Schemes," *Journal of Quality Technology,* 8(1), pp. 1–12.

Montgomery, D. C. (1991). *Statistical Quality Control,* 2nd edition Wiley, New York.

Wadsworth, H. M., Jr., Stephens, K. S., and Godfrey, A. B. (1986). *Methods for Quality Control and Improvement.* Wiley, New York.

CHAPTER

7

Control Charts for Attributes

CHAPTER OUTLINE

SYMBOLS

n	Constant sample or subgroup size	$\bar{c}$	Sample average number of nonconformities
n_i	Sample or subgroup size of ith sample	c_0	Specified goal or standard for the number of nonconformities
g	Number of samples or subgroups	u	Population average number of conformities per unit
p	Population fraction nonconforming	$\bar{u}$	Sample average number of conformities per unit
$\hat{p}$	Sample fraction nonconforming	D	Number of demerits for a sample
$\sigma_{\hat{p}}$	Standard deviation of $\hat{p}$	U	Demerits per unit for a sample
$\bar{p}$	Sample average fraction nonconforming	σ_U	Standard deviation of U
p_0	Specified goal or standard for fraction nonconforming	β	Probability of a Type II error
$\bar{p}_r$	Revised process average fraction nonconforming		
c	Population average number of nonconformities		

7-1 INTRODUCTION

Chapter 6 discussed statistical process control by means of control charts for variables. This chapter discusses control charts for attributes. In quality control, an attribute is a quality characteristic for which a numerical value is not specified. Rather, an attribute is a type of characteristic that either meets or does not meet certain guidelines. Alternatively, the characteristic may be categorized without a specific numerical value being reported. For instance, the taste of a certain dish may be labeled as acceptable or unacceptable. The taste may alternatively be divided into such categories as exceptional, good, fair, and poor.

A quality characteristic that does not meet certain prescribed standards (or specifications) is said to be a *nonconformity* (or defect). For example, if the length of steel bars is expected to be 50 ± 1.0 cm, a length of 51.5 cm will not be acceptable. A product with one or more nonconformities that render it nonfunctional, is a *nonconforming item* (or defective). It is possible for a product to have several nonconformities without being classified as a nonconforming item.

The different types of control charts considered in this chapter may be grouped into several categories. One category includes control charts that deal with the proportion of nonconforming items (p-chart) or the number of nonconforming items (np-chart); these charts are based on binomial distributions. A second category deals with charts for nonconformities. The chart for the total number of nonconformities (c-chart) is based on the Poisson distribution. Another type of chart which deals with nonconformities per unit (a u-chart) is applicable to situations in which the size of the sample unit may vary from sample to sample. For example, consider the number of nonconformities in pieces of fabric. The size of the piece of fabric selected for the first sample may be 50 m^2, whereas for the second sample it might be 30 m^2. To allow comparisons to be made in such circumstances, one could count the number of nonconformities per square meter rather than the total number. Another category of control charts deals with combining nonconformities on a weighted basis, such that the weights are influenced by the severity of each nonconformity. This type of chart is known as a demerits-per-unit chart (a U-chart).

7-2 ADVANTAGES AND DISADVANTAGES OF ATTRIBUTE CHARTS COMPARED TO VARIABLE CHARTS

Advantages

Certain quality characteristics can be observed only as attributes. For instance, the taste of a food item may be specified as acceptable or not. There are circumstances in which a quality characteristic can be measured as a variable but is measured as an attribute because of limitations regarding time, money, worker availability, or other resources. Consider the inside diameter of a hole. This characteristic could be measured with an inside micrometer, but it may be more convenient and cost-effective to use a go/no-go gage to determine whether the diameter conforms to specifications. Of course, the assumption is that attribute information will suffice.

In most manufacturing and service operations there are numerous quality characteristics that can be analyzed. If a variable chart (such as an $\overline{X}$- or R-chart), is selected, then one variable chart is needed for each characteristic. The total number of control charts being constructed and maintained might become overwhelming in terms of cost and difficulty. A control chart for attributes can provide overall quality information at a fraction of the cost. Consider, for example, a simple component as shown in Figure 7-1, for which the three quality characteristics of length L, width W, and height H are important. If variable charts were to be constructed, three such charts would be needed. However, it is possible to get by with one attribute chart for the proportion of nonconforming items if an item is classified as nonconforming when either the length, width, or height does not conform to specifications. The chart for the proportion of nonconforming items would then summarize the information for all three of these characteristics. Likewise, an attribute chart may be used to summarize information about several components that make up a product.

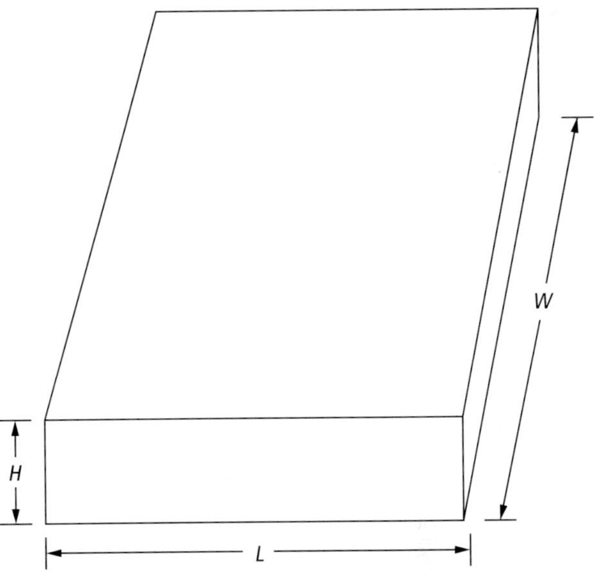

Figure 7-1 Quality characteristics for a simple component.

Attributes can be encountered at all levels of an organization—the company, plant, department, work center, and machine (or operator) level. Variable charts are typically used at the lowest level, namely the machine level. Figure 7-2 illustrates the levels at which attribute charts may be used. When one does not have an idea of the cause of a problem, it is sensible to start at a general level and become more specific. For example, if a high proportion of nonconforming items is detected at the company level, an attribute chart could be kept at the plant level to determine which plants are responsible for these items. Upon identification of these plants, the

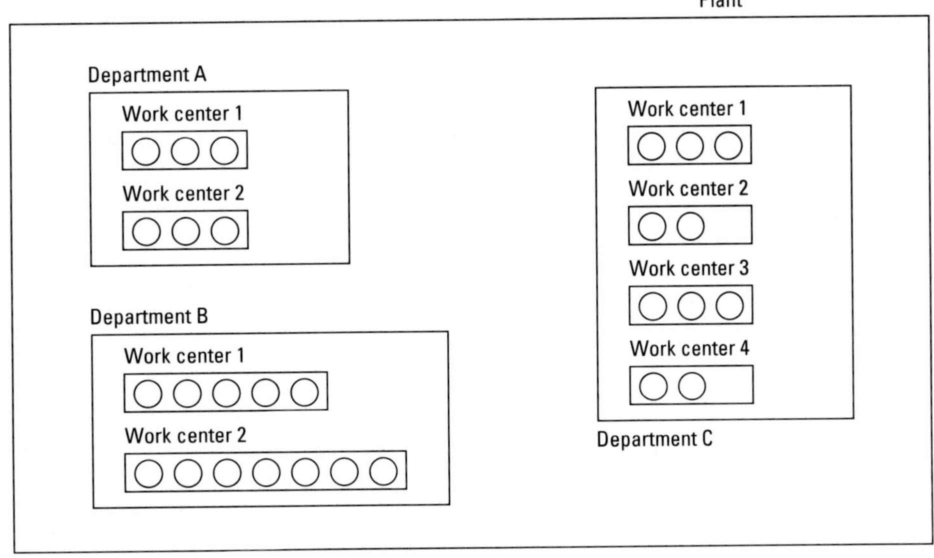

Figure 7-2 Levels at which attribute charts may be used.

next step might be to use an attribute chart for the output at the department level to pinpoint the problem areas. When the particular work center thought to be responsible for the increase in the production of nonconforming items is identified, one could then focus on the machine or operator level and try to further pinpoint the source of the problem. Thus, attribute charts can help to identify the root of a problem at a the general level or a narrower and more focused level. Once the lowest problem level has been identified, a variable chart is commonly used to determine specific reasons for an out-of-control situation.

Disadvantages

Attribute information indicates whether a certain quality characteristic is within specification limits. It does not state the degree to which specifications are not met. For example, the specification limits for the diameter of a part could be 20 ± 0.1 mm. Each of two parts, one having a diameter of 20.2 mm and the other a diameter of 22.3 mm, would be classified as nonconforming, but the relative closeness of each to the specifications would not be obtained through attribute information.

Variable information, on the other hand, would provide an indication of the level of the characteristic values. Variable control charts usually provide more information on the performance of a process than attribute charts. Specific information about the process mean and variability can be obtained. Furthermore, for out-of-control situations, variable plots generally provide more information as to the potential causes and hence make identification of remedial actions easier (Banks, 1989; Montgomery, 1991).

If it is reasonable to assume that the process is very much capable in that its inherent variability is much less than the spread between the specification limits, then it is possible for variable charts to provide forewarning of when the process is about to go out of control and thereby allow for corrective action to be taken before any nonconforming items are produced. In other words, a variable chart can indicate an upcoming out-of-control condition and allow assignable causes to be found and remedial action to be taken even though the items are not necessarily nonconforming.

Figure 7-3 depicts this situation. Suppose the nominal value of the process mean is at *A* and the process is in control, initially. If the process mean shifts to *B*, a variable chart may indicate an out-of-control condition. This will prompt a search for assignable causes and a course of action to restore the process back to its nominal mean *A*. Note that because of the wide spread of the specification limits, no nonconforming items would be produced when the process mean is at *B*, even though the process is out of control. An attribute chart, on the other hand, such as a chart for the proportion of nonconforming items, would not detect a lack of control until there is a sufficient change in the process parameters such that some nonconforming items are produced. If the process mean shifts to point *C*, an attribute chart for nonconforming items might detect an out-of-control situation because some nonconforming units are produced. However, for changes of the process mean to point B, it is unlikely for the attribute chart to indicate an

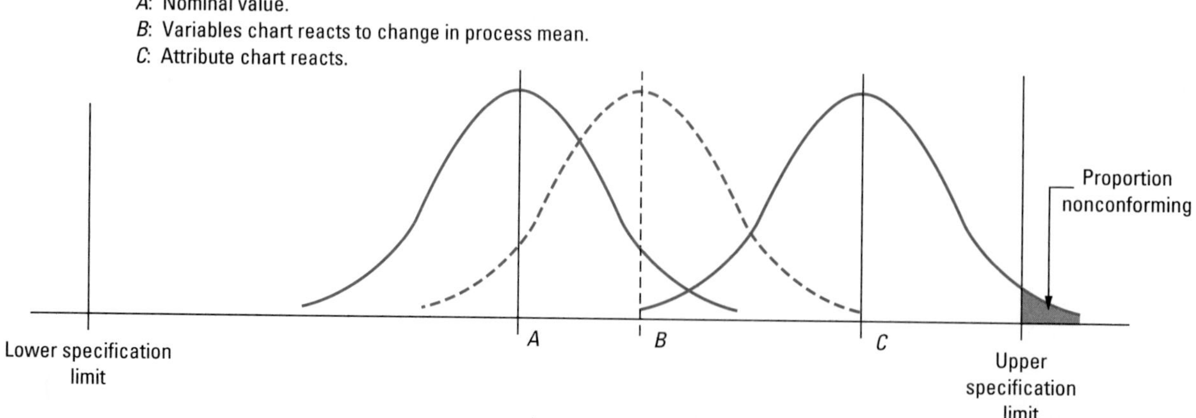

Figure 7-3 Forewarning of a lack of control in a process as indicated by a variable chart.

out-of-control situation. Note, however, that if the specifications are equal to or tighter than the inherent variability of the process, then attribute charts will of course indicate undesirable changes in process parameters.

Another disadvantage of attribute charts is that the sample size needed to ensure adequate protection against a certain level of process changes is larger than that required for a variable chart. Such larger sample sizes can be problematic if the measurements are expensive to obtain or the testing is destructive.

7-3 PRELIMINARY CONSIDERATIONS FOR ATTRIBUTE CHARTS

If no historical information regarding the sources of problems leading to the production of nonconforming items is available, attribute control charts are generally used at first. As problem areas are identified, the attribute charts may be replaced by variable charts to allow more specific information to be found.

The appropriate choice of sample size for attribute charts is important. It should be large enough to allow nonconformities or nonconforming items to be observed in the sample. For example, if a process has a nonconformance rate of 2.5 percent, a sample size of 25 would not be sufficient. The opportunity for the occurrence of nonconforming items, on the average, would be only 0.625 per sample. Thus, misleading inferences might be made, since no nonconforming items would be observed for many. One might erroneously attribute a better nonconformance rate to the process than that which actually exists. A sample size of 100 in this example might be sufficient, so that the average number of nonconforming items per sample would be 2.5.

For situations in which summary measures are required for the product and process, attribute charts are preferred. Information about the output at the plant level might be described best by a fraction-nonconforming chart or a chart for the number of nonconformities. When one is providing information to upper management, these charts might prove to be more effective. On the other hand, for technical problems at the operator or supervisor level, variable charts are more meaningful because they might provide specific clues for remedial actions.

Care should be given to properly defining what constitutes a nonconformity. This definition will depend on the product, its functional use, and customer needs. For example, a scratch mark in a machine vise might not be considered a nonconformity, whereas the same scratch on a television cabinet would.

7-4 CHART FOR FRACTION NONCONFORMING (p-CHART)

A chart for the fraction of nonconforming items is based on a binomial distribution. For a given sample, the fraction nonconforming is defined as

$$\hat{p} = \frac{x}{n} \tag{7.1}$$

where x is the number of nonconforming items in the sample and n represents the sample size.

For the use of a binomial distribution to be strictly valid, the probability of obtaining a nonconforming item must remain constant from item to item. The samples must be identical and are assumed to be independent. In certain situations these assumptions may not strictly hold. Consider a chemical process which makes a certain rubber mix compound. If something goes wrong with the oven temperature setting, the whole batch produced at that point in time will have a higher probability of being nonconforming. If one part is found to be nonconforming, there is a good chance that the other parts in that same batch will also be nonconforming. Thus, if for the purposes of this discussion the event of finding a nonconformity is considered a success, the probability of achieving success does not remain constant from item to item in a strict sense, and the trials are not independent.

Recall from Chapter 3 that the distribution of the number of nonconforming items in a sample, as given by a binomial distribution, is

$$P[X = x] = \frac{n!}{(n-x)!x!}p^x(1-p)^{n-x}, \quad x = 0, 1, 2, \ldots, n \tag{7.2}$$

where p represents the probability of getting a nonconforming item on each trial or unit selected. Given the mean and standard deviation of X, the mean of the sample proportion nonconforming is

$$E(\hat{p}) = p \tag{7.3}$$

and the variance of $\hat{p}$ is

$$\text{Var}(\hat{p}) = \frac{p(1-p)}{n} \tag{7.4}$$

These measures are used to determine the center line and control limits for fraction nonconforming charts.

A p-chart is one of the most versatile control charts. It may be used to control the acceptability of a single quality characteristic (say, the width of a part), a group of quality characteristics of the same type or on the same part (say, the length, width, or height of a component) or an entire product. Furthermore, a p-chart can be used to measure the quality of an operator or machine, a work center, a department, or an entire plant.

There are several objectives for the construction of p-charts. First, a p-chart may provide a fair indication of the general state of the process by depicting the average quality level of the proportion nonconforming.

It is a good tool for relating information about the average quality level to top management. For that matter, a p-chart may be used as a measure of the performance of top management. For instance, the performance of the chief executive officer of a company can be evaluated by considering the proportion of nonconforming items produced at the company level. Comparison of this information with values obtained from the near past would indicate whether an improvement has taken place for which the CEO could take credit. Values of the proportion nonconforming may also provide a benchmark against which to compare future output.

A p-chart can provide a source of information for *improving* product quality. It can be used to develop new concepts and ideas. Current values of the proportion nonconforming give an indication of whether a particular idea has been successful in reducing the proportion nonconforming resulting from past methods.

Use of a p-chart may, as a secondary objective, help to identify the circumstances for which an $\overline{X}$- and R-chart should be used. Variable charts are more sensitive to variations and are useful in diagnosing causes; a p-chart is most useful in locating the source of the difficulty.

Construction and Interpretation

The general procedures from Chapters 5 and 6 for the construction and interpretation of control charts apply to control charts for attributes as well. They are summarized below.

Step 1: *Select the objective.* A decision must be made regarding the level at which the fraction-nonconforming chart will be used, that is, the plant level, the department level, or the operator level. Furthermore, a decision must be made to control either a single quality characteristic, multiple characteristics, a single product, or a number of products. The choice will be influenced by the possible number of quality characteristics to consider, the number of products produced (as well the number nonconforming), the cost and time required for inspection, and other similar reasons.

Step 2: *Determine the subgroup size and the sampling interval.* An appropriate subgroup size is related to the existing quality level of the process. It must be large enough to allow the opportunity for some nonconforming items to be present on average. The sampling interval, that is, the time between successive samples, is a function of the production rate and the cost of sampling, among other factors.

Step 3: *Obtain the data, and record on an appropriate form.* The measuring instruments used to conclude whether an item is nonconforming should be decided upon in advance. A typical data sheet for a p-chart is shown in Figure 7-4. The date and time at which the sample is taken, along with the number of items inspected and the number of nonconforming items, are recorded. The fraction nonconforming is found by dividing the number of nonconforming items by the sample size. Usually 25 to 30 samples should be taken prior to performing an analysis.

Step 4: *Calculate the center line and the trial control limits.* Once they have been determined, the center line and control limits are drawn on the p-chart. The values of the fraction nonconforming (p) for each sample are plotted on the chart. This plot should then be examined to determine whether the process is in control. The rules for determining out-of-control conditions are the same as those discussed in Chapters 5 and 6 and are not repeated in this chapter. As usual, the most common criterion for an out-of-control condition is the presence of a plotted point outside the control limits. The means of calculating the center line and control limits are discussed below.

Sample number	Date	Time	Number inspected, n	Number of nonconforming items, x	Fraction nonconforming, $\hat{p}$	Comments
1	10/15	9:00 am	400	12	0.030	
2	10/15	9:30 am	400	10	0.025	
3	10/15	10:00 am	400	14	0.035	New supplier
.	.	.	.	.	.	.
.	.	.	.	.	.	.
.	.	.	.	.	.	.

Figure 7-4 Sample data sheet for a p-chart.

No standard specified. When no standard or target value of the fraction nonconforming is specified, it must be estimated from the sample information. Recall that for each sample, the sample fraction nonconforming ($\hat{p}$) given by Equation 7.1 is

$$\hat{p} = \frac{x}{n}$$

The average of these individual sample fractions nonconforming is used as the center line (CL_p). That is,

$$CL_p = \bar{p} = \frac{\sum_{i=1}^{g} \hat{p}_i}{g} = \frac{\sum_{i=1}^{g} x_i}{ng} \tag{7.5}$$

where g represents the number of samples. The variance of $\hat{p}$ is given by Equation 7.4. Since the true value of p is not known, the value of $\bar{p}$ given by Equation 7.5 is used as an estimate. In accordance with the concept of 3σ limits discussed in the previous chapters, the control limits are given by

$$\begin{aligned} UCL_p &= \bar{p} + 3\sqrt{\frac{\bar{p}(1-\bar{p})}{n}} \\ LCL_p &= \bar{p} - 3\sqrt{\frac{\bar{p}(1-\bar{p})}{n}} \end{aligned} \tag{7.6}$$

Standard specified. If the target value of the proportion of nonconforming items is known or specified, the center line is selected as that target value. In other words, the center line is given by

$$CL_p = p_0 \tag{7.7}$$

where p_0 represents the target or standard value. The control limits in this case are also based on the standard value. Thus,

$$\begin{aligned} UCL_p &= p_0 + 3\sqrt{\frac{p_0(1-p_0)}{n}} \\ LCL_p &= p_0 - 3\sqrt{\frac{p_0(1-p_0)}{n}} \end{aligned} \tag{7.8}$$

If the lower control limit for p turns out to be negative for Equations 7.6 or 7.8, the lower control limit is simply counted as zero, since the smallest possible value of the fraction nonconforming is zero.

Step 5: *Calculate the revised control limits.* The plotted values of p and the pattern of the plot should be analyzed for out-of-control conditions. All of the rules discussed in Chapters 5 and 6 should be considered. Typically, one or a few of them are used concurrently. Upon detection of an out-of-control condition, the assignable cause should be identified, and remedial actions should be proposed. The out-of-control point or points for which remedial actions have been taken may be deleted, and the revised process average $\bar{p}_r$ should be calculated from the remaining number of samples. It is important that the investigation of assignable causes be conducted in an objective manner. If an assignable cause cannot be identified nor a remedial action implemented for a particular sample point that is out-of-control, that sample should not be deleted in the calculation of the new process average nonconforming.

A word of caution is appropriate regarding points that fall below the lower control limit when the limit is positive. Such observations imply an unusually good process condition. Therefore, these points should be retained in the construction of the revised center line. In fact, the process should incorporate the conditions which led to this desirable situation.

The revised center line and control limits are given by

$$\begin{aligned} \text{CL}_p &= \bar{p}_r \\ \text{UCL}_p &= \bar{p}_r + 3\sqrt{\frac{\bar{p}_r(1-\bar{p}_r)}{n}} \\ \text{LCL}_p &= \bar{p}_r - 3\sqrt{\frac{\bar{p}_r(1-\bar{p}_r)}{n}} \end{aligned} \tag{7.9}$$

For fraction-nonconforming charts based on a specified standard p_0, the revised limits do not change from those given by Equation 7.8.

Step 6: *Implement the chart.* The revised center line and control limits of a p-chart should be used for future observations as they become available. Periodic revisions of the chart should take place based on guidelines similar to those discussed for variable charts. There are, however, a few unique features associated with a fraction-nonconforming chart. First, if a p-chart continually indicates an increase in the value of the average fraction nonconforming, management should investigate the reasons behind this increase rather than constantly revising the center line and control limits upward. If such an upward movement of the center line is allowed to persist, it will become more difficult in the future to bring down the level of nonconformance to the previously desirable values. Only if one is sure that the process cannot be maintained at the present average level of nonconformance given the resource constraints should the thought of moving the control limits upward be allowed. Some possible reasons for an increase in the level of nonconforming items include a lower incoming quality from suppliers or a tightening of specification limits. An increase in the observed level of nonconformance may also happen because of an increased enforcement of existing limits even though the basic quality level of the process remains unchanged.

Since the goal of any company should be to continuously seek quality improvement, a sustained downward trend in the fraction nonconforming is desirable. Management should revise the average fraction nonconforming level downward when it is convinced that actions have been taken to keep the fraction nonconforming at the better level. Revising these limits provides the incentive not only to maintain this better level but also to seek further improvements.

Example 7-1: Twenty-five samples, each of size 50, were chosen from a plastic-injection molding machine producing small containers. The number of nonconforming containers for each sample is shown in Table 7-1. The fraction nonconforming for each sample, found by using Equation 7.1, is also shown in Table 7-1. The average fraction nonconforming, found by using Equation 7.5, is

$$\bar{p} = \frac{90}{1250} = 0.072$$

This is the center line of a fraction nonconforming chart. Next, the trial control limits are found by using Equation 7.6:

$$\begin{aligned} \text{CL}_p &= 0.072 \\ \text{UCL}_p &= 0.072 + 3\sqrt{\frac{(0.072)(1-0.072)}{50}} = 0.182 \\ \text{LCL}_p &= 0.072 - 3\sqrt{\frac{(0.072)(1-0.072)}{50}} = -0.038 \rightarrow 0 \end{aligned}$$

Since the calculated value of the lower control limit is negative, it is converted to zero. This control chart for the fraction nonconforming is shown in Figure 7-5. Note that the process is in control with the exception of sample number 18, which has a fraction nonconforming of 0.20—above the upper control limit. Assume that, upon investigation of the assignable causes for sample number 18, the cause is found to be a drop in pressure inside the mold cavity, as indicated in the column for comments in Table 7-1. A proposed remedial action is taken to eliminate this assignable cause. The revised center line and control limits may be found after deleting sample number 18:

$$\begin{aligned} \text{CL}_p &= (90-10)/1200 = 0.067 \\ \text{UCL}_p &= 0.067 + 3\sqrt{\frac{(0.067)(1-0.067)}{50}} = 0.173 \\ \text{LCL}_p &= 0.067 - 3\sqrt{\frac{(0.067)(1-0.067)}{50}} = -0.039 \rightarrow 0 \end{aligned}$$

All of the samples are now in control.

TABLE 7-1 Data for nonconforming containers

Sample number	Date	Time	Number inspected, n	Number of nonconforming items, x	Fraction nonconforming, $\hat{p}$	Comments
1	10/6	8:30	50	4	0.08	
2	10/6	9:30	50	2	0.04	
3	10/6	10:00	50	5	0.10	
4	10/6	10:20	50	3	0.06	
5	10/7	8:40	50	2	0.04	
6	10/7	9:50	50	1	0.02	
7	10/7	10:10	50	3	0.06	
8	10/7	10:50	50	2	0.04	
9	10/8	9:10	50	5	0.10	
10	10/8	9:40	50	4	0.08	
11	10/8	10:40	50	3	0.06	
12	10/8	11:20	50	5	0.10	
13	10/9	8:20	50	5	0.10	
14	10/9	9:10	50	2	0.04	
15	10/9	9:50	50	3	0.06	
16	10/9	10:20	50	2	0.04	
17	10/10	8:40	50	4	0.08	
18	10/10	9:30	50	10	0.20	Drop in pressure
19	10/10	10:10	50	4	0.08	
20	10/10	11:30	50	3	0.06	
21	10/11	8:20	50	2	0.04	
22	10/11	9:10	50	5	0.10	
23	10/11	9:50	50	4	0.08	
24	10/11	10:20	50	3	0.06	
25	10/11	11:30	50	4	0.08	
		Total	1250	90		

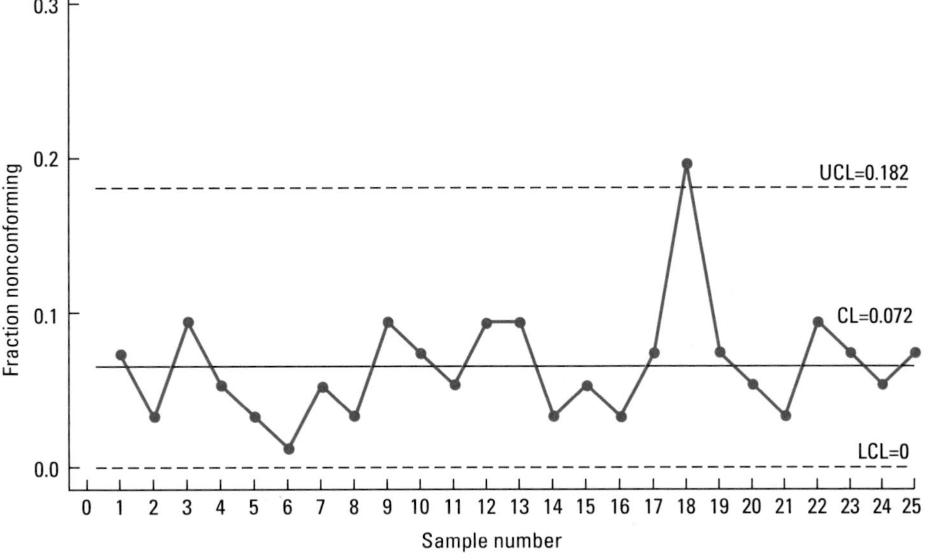

Figure 7-5 Fraction-nonconforming chart for containers.

Example 7-2: Management has decided to set a standard of 3 percent for the proportion of nonconforming test tubes produced in a plant. Data collected from 20 samples, each of size 100, is shown in Table 7-2. The proportion of nonconforming test tubes for each sample, is also shown in Table 7-2. The center line and control limits, based on the specified standard, are found to be

$$\mathrm{CL}_p = p_0 = 0.030$$

$$\mathrm{UCL}_p = 0.030 + 3\sqrt{\frac{(0.03)(1-0.03)}{100}} = 0.081$$

$$\mathrm{LCL}_p = 0.030 - 3\sqrt{\frac{(0.03)(1-0.03)}{100}} = -0.021 \rightarrow 0$$

A fraction-nonconforming chart using these limits is shown in Figure 7-6, where the sample fraction nonconforming values are plotted. From the figure, the process is seen to be out of control; sample numbers 8 and 11 plot above the upper control limit. The assignable cause for sample number 8 was found to be improper alignment of the die, for which a remedial action was taken. For sample number 11, no assignable cause could be identified. Hence, the process is viewed to be out of control with respect to the specified standard. From Figure 7-6, observe that the general level of the fraction nonconforming does not seem to match the specified standard value of 3 percent. The actual fraction nonconforming seems to be higher than the standard. Using the data from Table 7-2, the process average fraction nonconforming is

$$\bar{p} = \frac{84}{2000} = 0.042$$

This value exceeds the desired standard of 3 percent. From Figure 7-6, only three points are below the standard of 3 percent. This confirms the suspicion that the process mean is greater than the desired standard value. If sample number 8 is eliminated following removal of its assignable cause, the revised process average is

$$\bar{p} = (84 - 9)/1900 = 0.039$$

If the control limits are calculated based on this revised average, we have

$$\mathrm{CL}_p = 0.039$$

$$\mathrm{UCL}_p = 0.039 + 3\sqrt{\frac{(0.039)(1-0.039)}{100}} = 0.097$$

$$\mathrm{LCL}_p = 0.039 - 3\sqrt{\frac{(0.039)(1-0.039)}{100}} = -0.019 \rightarrow 0$$

If a control chart were constructed using these values, all of the observations (including sample number 11)

TABLE 7-2 Data for nonconforming test tubes

Sample number	Date	Time	Number inspected, n	Number of nonconforming items, x	Fraction nonconforming, $\hat{p}$	Comments
1	9/8	8:20	100	4	0.04	
2	9/8	8:45	100	2	0.02	
3	9/8	9:10	100	5	0.05	
4	9/8	9:30	100	3	0.03	
5	9/9	9:00	100	6	0.06	
6	9/9	9:20	100	4	0.04	
7	9/9	9:50	100	3	0.03	
8	9/9	10:20	100	9	0.09	Die not aligned
9	9/10	9:10	100	5	0.05	
10	9/10	9:40	100	6	0.06	
11	9/10	10:20	100	9	0.09	
12	9/10	10:45	100	3	0.03	
13	9/11	8:30	100	3	0.03	
14	9/11	8:50	100	4	0.04	
15	9/11	9:40	100	2	0.02	
16	9/11	10:30	100	5	0.05	
17	9/12	8:40	100	3	0.03	
18	9/12	9:30	100	1	0.01	
19	9/12	9:50	100	4	0.04	
20	9/12	10:40	100	3	0.03	
		Total	2000	84		

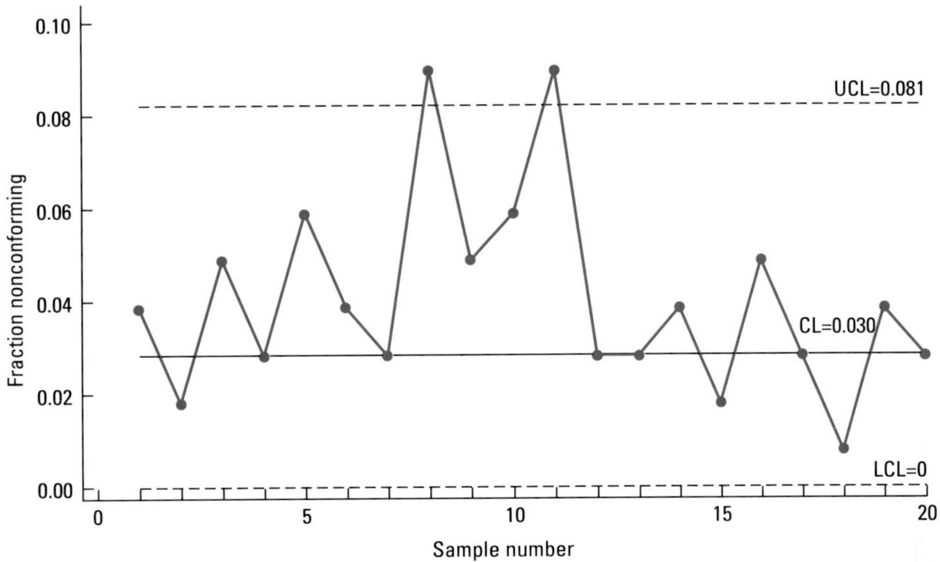

Figure 7-6 Fraction-nonconforming chart for test tubes (center line and control limits based on a standard).

would be in control. Furthermore, the pattern of the plot would hover around 0.039, the calculated average.

Keeping in mind the set standard of 3 percent, we must conclude that the process is currently out of control. We have no indication of the assignable causes for the point (sample number 11) that is out of control. Apparently, given the inherent variability of the process, this point would plot within control limits that are based on the process data. Thus, it is unclear what actions should be taken in order to bring the process to control. Furthermore, a reduction of the process average nonconforming would have to take place in order to bring it to the desired value of 3 percent. Actions to accomplish this task must originate from management and would require major changes in the product, process, or incoming material quality. Operator-assisted measures would not be sufficient to bring the process to control.

Another way of viewing this situation is that the present process is not capable of meeting the desired standard of a 3 percent nonconformance rate. Some basic changes which would require management input are needed to improve quality. If management is not committed to allocating resources to implement favorable changes in the process, then a goal of a three-percent nonconformance rate is probably not feasible. Management may have to increase this value to allow a more realistic standard. Otherwise, the control chart may always indicate a lack of control, and unnecessary blame may be assigned to operators.

Variable Subgroup Size

There are many reasons why the subgroup size might change from one sample to another. In processes for which 100-percent inspection is conducted to estimate the proportion nonconforming, a change in the rate of production may cause the subgroup size to change. A lack of available inspection personnel or a change in the unit cost of inspection are other factors which may influence the subgroup size.

A change in the subgroup size causes the control limits to change, though the center line remains fixed. As the subgroup size increases, the control limits become narrower. As stated before, the subgroup size is also influenced by the existing average process quality level. For a given process fraction nonconforming, the sample size should be carefully chosen so that there is ample opportunity for nonconforming items to be represented. Thus, changes in the quality level of the process may require a change in the subgroup size. The following subsections discuss the different ways of determining control limits when the subgroup size varies as well as guidelines as to when the different limits are appropriate.

Control Limits for Individual Subgroups Control limits can be constructed for each subgroup. If no standard is given and the sample average fraction nonconforming is $\bar{p}$, the control limits for subgroup i with subgroup size n_i, are

$$\text{UCL} = \bar{p} + 3\sqrt{\frac{\bar{p}(1-\bar{p})}{n_i}}$$
$$\text{LCL} = \bar{p} - 3\sqrt{\frac{\bar{p}(1-\bar{p})}{n_i}} \tag{7.10}$$

Control Limits Based on Average Subgroup Size A set of control limits can also be constructed based on the average sample size. The average subgroup size is

$$\bar{n} = \frac{\sum_{i=1}^{g} n_i}{g} \tag{7.11}$$

where g represents the number of subgroups. Control limits are then given by

$$\text{UCL} = \bar{p} + 3\sqrt{\frac{\bar{p}(1-\bar{p})}{\bar{n}}}$$
$$\text{LCL} = \bar{p} - 3\sqrt{\frac{\bar{p}(1-\bar{p})}{\bar{n}}} \tag{7.12}$$

Control Limits for Several Representative Subgroup Sizes A third approach to dealing with the issue of varying subgroup size is to construct control limits for some representative subgroup sizes. These representative subgroup sizes should span the range of variation of the subgroup sizes and should be determined for those sizes which occur more frequently. For example, suppose that the subgroup sizes range from 200 to 1000, with many subgroup sizes around 500 and 800. Representative subgroup sizes, for constructing control limits could be 200, 500, 800, and 1000. For instances in which the actual subgroup size varies significantly from the representative values, refer to the guidelines discussed in the next sub-section.

Guidelines for the Use of Control Limits Based on Average Subgroup Size There are some precautions to be observed while making inferences from a control chart whose limits are given by Equation 7.12. In some instances, the actual individual control limits may have to be determined to allow a proper decision to be made regarding the particular subgroup. The following four cases may arise.

Case 1: $\text{LCL} < \hat{p}_i < \text{UCL}; \quad n_i < \bar{n}$

In this case, the observed fraction nonconforming for the ith sample ($\hat{p}_i$) falls within the control limits, and the subgroup size is less than the average subgroup size. The actual control limits will be wider than those based on the average subgroup size. Thus, it is still reasonable to assume that the process is in control, and so there is no need to construct the actual control limits.

Case 2: $\text{LCL} < \hat{p}_i < \text{UCL}; \quad n_i > \bar{n}$

In this case, even though the sample proportion nonconforming is within the control limits, one cannot be sure of whether the plotted points indicate control. Since $n_i > \bar{n}$, the actual control limits are tighter than those found using $\bar{n}$. So, it is possible for a plotted point to fall outside the actual control limits, even though it remains within the limits for the average sample size. Thus, if any plotted points are close to the control limits based on the average subgroup size, it may be necessary to calculate the actual control limits.

Case 3: $\hat{p}_i < \text{LCL}$ or $\hat{p}_i > \text{UCL}, \quad n_i > \bar{n}$

In this case, the point falls outside the control limits based on $\bar{n}$ and the actual subgroup size exceeds the average subgroup size. The actual control limits will be tighter than those found by using $\bar{n}$, so an out-of-control situation would be indicated by either set of limits. Therefore, there is no need to obtain the actual control limits in this situation.

Case 4: $\hat{p}_i < \text{LCL}$ or $\hat{p}_i > \text{UCL}; \quad n_i < \bar{n}$

In this case, a plotted point lies outside the control limits based on $\bar{n}$. Since the actual subgroup size is less than the average subgroup size, the actual control limits will be outside those based on $\bar{n}$. It is therefore possible for the observation to lie within the actual control limits, which would mean we could consider the process to be in control. So, if a plotted point lies just outside the control limits based on $\bar{n}$, it is necessary to calculate the actual control limits to determine whether the process is actually out of control.

Example 7-3: Twenty random samples were selected from the output of a process which makes vinyl tiles. The number chosen in each sample as well as the number of

TABLE 7-3 Data for number inspected and number of nonconforming tiles

Sample number	Number inspected, n_i	Number of nonconforming tiles	Sample fraction nonconforming, $\hat{p}_i$	Upper control limit based on n_i	Lower control limit based on n_i
1	200	14	0.070	0.128	0.017
2	180	10	0.055	0.131	0.015
3	200	17	0.085	0.128	0.017
4	120	8	0.067	0.144	0.001
5	300	20	0.067	0.118	0.028
6	250	18	0.072	0.122	0.023
7	400	25	0.062	0.111	0.034
8	180	20	0.111	0.131	0.015
9	210	27	0.129	0.126	0.019
10	380	30	0.079	0.112	0.033
11	190	15	0.079	0.129	0.016
12	380	26	0.068	0.112	0.033
13	200	10	0.050	0.128	0.017
14	210	14	0.067	0.126	0.019
15	390	24	0.061	0.112	0.033
16	120	15	0.125	0.144	0.001
17	190	18	0.095	0.129	0.016
18	380	19	0.050	0.112	0.033
19	200	11	0.055	0.128	0.017
20	180	12	0.067	0.131	0.015
Total	4860	353			

nonconforming tiles are shown in Table 7-3. First, construct the actual control limits for each subgroup in a fraction nonconforming chart. The average fraction nonconforming is

$$\text{CL} = \bar{p} = \frac{353}{4860} = 0.0726$$

The upper control limit for each subgroup given by Equation 7.10 is

$$\text{UCL} = 0.0726 + 3\sqrt{\frac{(0.0726)(0.9274)}{n_i}}$$

$$= 0.0726 + \frac{0.7784}{\sqrt{n_i}}$$

Similarly,

$$\text{LCL} = 0.0726 - \frac{0.7784}{\sqrt{n_i}}$$

Table 7-3 shows the sample fraction nonconforming and the control limits for each subgroup. For instance, the calculations for sample number 1 are as follows:

$$\hat{p}_1 = 14/200 = 0.070$$

$$\text{UCL} = 0.0726 + 0.7784/\sqrt{200} = 0.128$$

$$\text{LCL} = 0.0726 - 0.7784/\sqrt{200} = 0.017$$

The fraction-nonconforming chart with the individual control limits plotted is shown in Figure 7-7. From this figure it can be see that sample number 9 is out of control. The fraction-nonconforming value of 0.129 plots above the upper control limit of 0.126 for that sample. Assignable causes should be investigated for this sample, and remedial actions should be taken. When the center line and control limits are revised, this sample should be deleted if remedial actions have been taken.

Example 7-4: For the data on vinyl tiles shown in Table 7-3, suppose it is desired to construct control limits based on the average subgroup size. The average subgroup size, given by Equation 7.11 is

$$\bar{n} = \frac{4860}{20} = 243 \simeq 240$$

A round number of 240 is used as an approximation to the average sample size because control limits are not very sensitive to small changes in the sample size. The control limits based on $\bar{n}$, found by using Equation 7.12, are

$$\text{UCL} = .0726 + 3\sqrt{\frac{(0.0726)\ (0.9274)}{240}} = 0.123$$

$$\text{LCL} = 0.0726 - 3\sqrt{\frac{(0.0726)\ (0.9274)}{240}} = 0.022$$

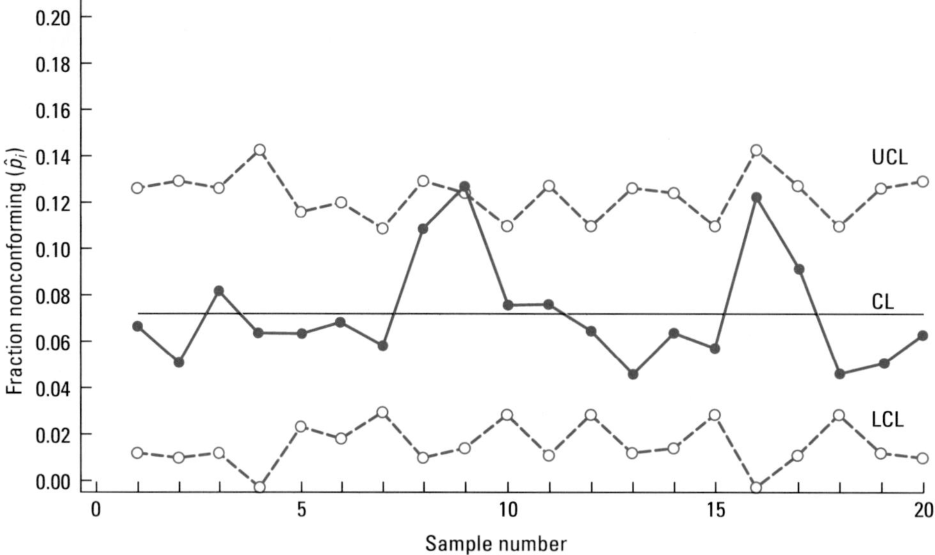

Figure 7-7 Fraction-nonconforming chart for variable subgroup sizes.

Figure 7-8 shows the control chart with control limits that have been calculated for the average subgroup size. When a plotted value of $\hat{p}_i$ is near the control limits, caution must be exercised in making inferences. Note that sample numbers 8, 9, and 16 plot near the upper control limit. For sample number 8, the fraction nonconforming is 0.111, which is below the UCL based on $\overline{n}$. The actual subgroup size is 180, which is less than the average subgroup size of 240 used to construct these limits. Hence, the actual control limits would be wider than those calculated for $\overline{n}$, so the value for sample number 8 will still fall within those limits. There is no need to calculate the actual control limits for sample number 8. This corresponds to Case 1 discussed above.

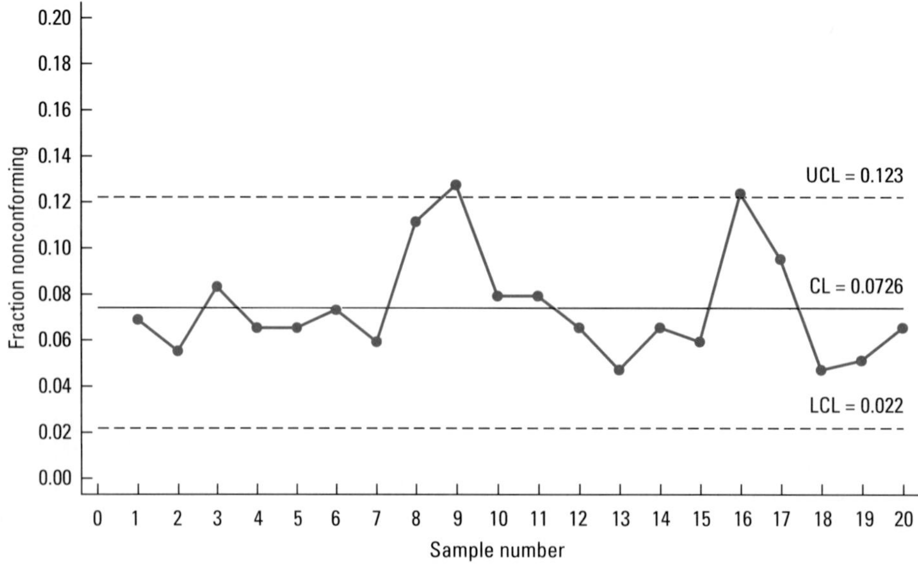

Figure 7-8 Fraction-non conforming chart with control limits based on average subgroup size.

Next, consider sample number 9. The fraction nonconforming is 0.129, which plots outside the UCL of 0.123 based on $\bar{n}$. The actual sample size is 210, which is less than the value of $\bar{n}$, so, the actual control limits would be wider than those based on the average subgroup size. The actual limits will need to be calculated to determine whether the plotted value lies outside the actual control limits. This situation corresponds to Case 4 discussed above. As it turns out, the actual upper control limit is 0.126 (as calculated in the previous example). The sample fraction nonconforming (0.129) is outside the actual upper control limit, so it is appropriate to conclude that the process is out of control.

For sample number 16, the sample fraction nonconforming (0.125) plots outside the UCL of 0.123 based on $\bar{n}$. The actual sample size is 120, which is less than $\bar{n}$. Therefore, the actual control limits will be wider than those based on $\bar{n}$. This situation also corresponds to Case 4 as discussed above. Calculating the actual control limits yields UCL= 0.144, as shown in the previous example. Since the value of $\hat{p}_i$ falls below the actual UCL, it is appropriate to conclude that the process is in control. In this case, if the actual control limits had not been calculated, sample number 16 would have been erroneously interpreted as indicating an out-of-control process.

This example demonstrates that the tedious calculation of control limits for each subgroup size may be avoided. However, in order to draw proper conclusions, close attention must be paid to points near the control limits as well as to the difference between the actual subgroup size and the average subgroup size used in calculating the control limits.

Example 7-5: For the data on vinyl tiles shown in Table 7-3, calculate the control limits for a few representative subgroup sizes.

Solution. Note that the subgroup size varies from 120 to 400. Several of the subgroup sizes are around 200. Likewise, there are several subgroup sizes around 400. Suppose the representative subgroup sizes selected for calculation of the control limits are 100, 200, and 400. The average fraction nonconforming is 0.0726.

For $n = 100$, the control limits are

$$\text{UCL} = 0.0726 + 3\sqrt{\frac{(0.0726)(0.9274)}{100}} = 0.150$$

$$\text{LCL} = 0.0726 - 3\sqrt{\frac{(0.0726)(0.9274)}{100}} = -0.005 \rightarrow 0$$

Similarly, for $n = 200$, the control limits are

$$\text{UCL} = 0.128, \qquad \text{LCL} = 0.017$$

and for $n = 400$, the control limits are

$$\text{UCL} = 0.111, \qquad \text{LCL} = 0.034$$

Figure 7-9 shows the p-chart with the control limits for these representative subgroup sizes. Note that the fraction-nonconforming values for sample numbers 8, 9 and 16 are close to the upper control limits for their respective sample sizes. For sample number 8 (which has a sample size of 180), the $\hat{p}_i$ value of 0.111 is below the UCL of 0.128 for $n = 200$. This point will indicate control even if actual control limits are drawn for $n = 180$. For sample number

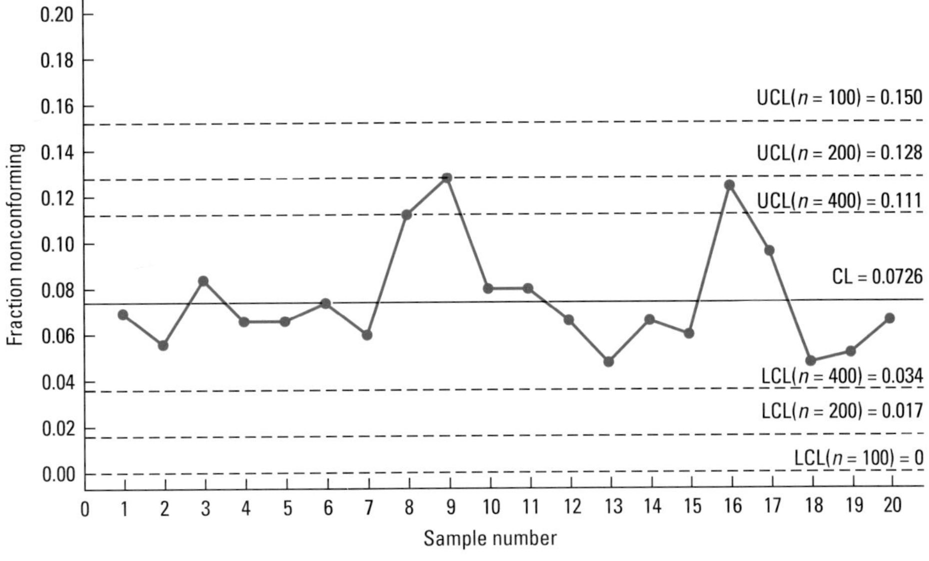

Figure 7-9 A p-chart with control limits for several representative subgroup sizes.

9 (which has a sample size of 210), the $\hat{p}_i$ value of 0.129 is outside the UCL for ($n = 200$). This point would also be outside the UCL for $n = 210$. The sample is therefore judged to be out of control. For sample number 16 (which has a sample size of 120), the $\hat{p}_i$-value of 0.125 is below the UCL for $n = 100$ of 0.150 and also below the UCL for $n = 200$. If the UCL were to be constructed for $n = 120$, the fraction-nonconforming value would be below it, indicating that the sample is in control. Thus, for most situations, a decision can be made without necessarily constructing the actual control limits, thereby allowing time and resources to be saved in addition to keeping the charts simple for operating personnel to follow.

Standardized Control Chart Another approach to dealing with the issue of varying subgroup size is to construct a chart of "normalized" or standardized values of the fraction nonconforming. The value of the proportion nonconforming for a sample is expressed as the sample's deviation from the average proportion nonconforming in units of standard deviations. Chapter 3 discussed the sampling distribution of a sample proportion nonconforming ($\hat{p}$). It showed that the mean and standard deviation of $\hat{p}$ are given by

$$E(\hat{p}) = p \tag{7.13}$$

$$\sigma_{\hat{p}} = \sqrt{\frac{p(1-p)}{n}} \tag{7.14}$$

respectively, where p represents the true process nonconformance rate and n is the subgroup size. In practice, p is usually estimated by $\bar{p}$, the sample average fraction nonconforming. So, in the working versions of Equations 7.13 and 7.14, p is replaced by $\bar{p}$.

The standardized value of the fraction nonconforming for the ith sample may be expressed as

$$Z = \frac{\hat{p}_i - \bar{p}}{\sqrt{\frac{\bar{p}(1-\bar{p})}{n_i}}} \tag{7.15}$$

where n_i is the size of ith subgroup. One of the advantages of a standardized control chart for the fraction nonconforming is that only one set of control limits needs to be constructed. These limits are placed ± 3 standard deviation units away from the center line. Additionally, tests for runs and pattern recognition are both difficult to apply to circumstances in which individual control limits change with each subgroup. They can, however, be applied in the same manner as with other variable charts when a standardized p-chart is constructed. The center line on a standardized p-chart is at 0, the UCL is at 3, and the LCL is at -3.

Example 7-6: Consider the data shown in Table 7-3 concerning the number of nonconforming tiles. Construct a standardized p-chart.

Solution. The standard deviation of the sample fraction nonconforming ($\hat{p}_i$) for the ith subgroup is

$$\sigma_{\hat{p}_i} = \sqrt{\frac{\bar{p}(1-\bar{p})}{n_i}} = \sqrt{\frac{(0.0726)(0.9274)}{n_i}} = \frac{0.2595}{\sqrt{n_i}}$$

For this value of $\sigma_{\hat{p}_i}$, the standardized value of $\hat{p}_i$ is calculated by using Equation 7.15 with $\bar{p} = 0.0726$. Table 7-4 shows the standardized Z-value of the fraction nonconforming. The standardized p-chart is shown in Figure 7-10. The control limits are at ± 3, and the center line is at zero. From Figure 7-10, observe that sample number 9 is above the upper control limit, indicating an out-of-control situation. This is in agreement with the conclusions based on control limits that were calculated for each subgroup.

Special Considerations for the Construction of and Inference Making from p-charts

Some issues that deserve attention in the construction and interpretation of fraction-nonconforming charts have already been mentioned. Some of those issues are presented in a comprehensive manner in this section.

Necessary Assumptions Recall that the occurrence of the number of nonconforming items is based on a binomial distribution. Some key assumptions associated with such a distribution are that the probability of occurrence of nonconforming items is constant for each item and that the items are independent of each other with respect to meeting any specifications. This assumption may not be valid if products are manufactured in groups. For instance, suppose that for a steel manufacturing process, a batch produced in a cupola did not have the correct proportion of an additive. If a sample steel ingot chosen from that batch were found to be nonconforming, it is quite possible that other samples chosen from that same batch would also be nonconforming, so the samples would not be independent of each other. Furthermore, the likelihood of a sample chosen from the bad batch being nonconforming will probably be different from that of a sample chosen from a good batch.

Observations Below the Lower Control Limit The presence of sample fraction nonconforming points that plot below the lower control limit, even though they indicate an out-of-control situation,

TABLE 7-4 Calculations for the standardized p-chart

Sample number	Number inspected, n_i	Number of nonconforming tiles	Fraction nonconforming, $\hat{p}_i$	Standard deviation, $\sigma_{\hat{p}_i}$	Standardized $\hat{p}_i$ z-value
1	200	14	0.070	0.0183	−0.142
2	180	10	0.055	0.0193	−0.912
3	200	17	0.085	0.0183	0.678
4	120	8	0.067	0.0237	−0.236
5	300	20	0.067	0.0150	−0.373
6	250	18	0.072	0.0164	−0.037
7	400	25	0.062	0.0130	−0.815
8	180	20	0.111	0.0193	1.990
9	210	27	0.129	0.0179	3.151
10	380	30	0.079	0.0133	0.481
11	190	15	0.079	0.0188	0.340
12	380	26	0.068	0.0133	−0.346
13	200	10	0.050	0.0183	−1.235
14	210	14	0.067	0.0179	−0.313
15	390	24	0.061	0.0131	−0.885
16	120	15	0.125	0.0237	2.211
17	190	18	0.095	0.0188	1.191
18	380	19	0.050	0.0133	−1.699
19	200	11	0.055	0.0183	−0.962
20	180	12	0.067	0.0193	−0.290

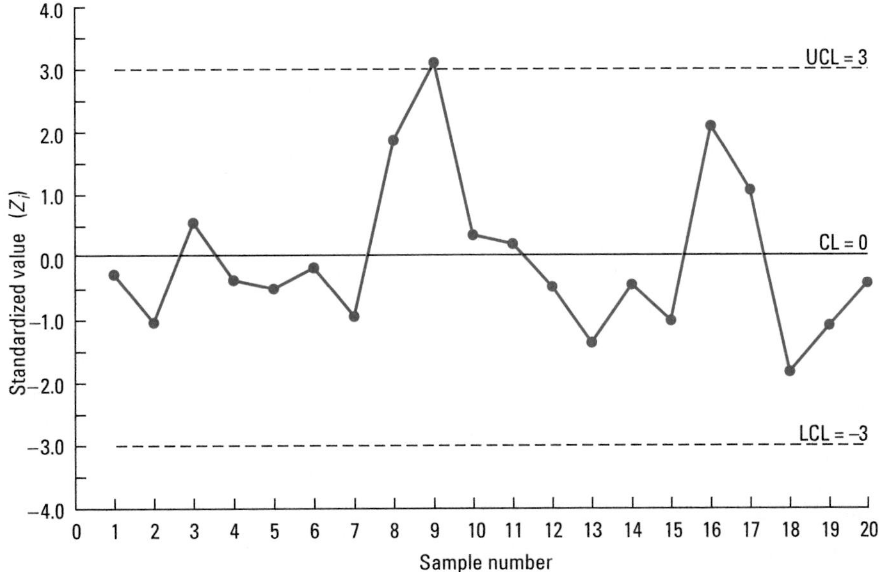

Figure 7-10 Standardized p-chart.

are desirable. Once the assignable causes for such points have been identified, the points should not be deleted. In fact, the process should be set to the conditions which led to these points in the first place. One must be certain, however, that there were no errors in measurement or recording that yielded such low values.

Comparison With a Specified Standard Sometimes, management might have a desirable goal or standard value for the fraction nonconforming (p_0). When control limits are based on a specified standard, care must be exercised in drawing inferences about the process. If the process yields points that fall above the upper control limit, assignable causes should be sought. Once they have been found and appropriate actions have been taken, the process performance may again be compared to the desirable standard. If the process is still out-of-control even though no further assignable cases may be located, one should question whether the existing process is capable of meeting the desired standards. Manufacturing personnel should not be held responsible for something that is beyond their control. Only through major changes in the process initiated by management can any process improvement be made. If resource limitations prevent management from being able to implement process improvement, it may not be advisable to compare the process to the desirable standards. Only if the standards are conceivably attainable should the control limits be based on them.

Impact of Design Specifications Since the definition of a nonconforming product is based on quality characteristics not meeting certain specifications, it is possible for the average fraction nonconforming to be too high even though the process is stable and in control. A fundamental change in the design of the product or in the specifications might reduce the proportion nonconforming. Tolerances may be loosened only if there is no substantial deviation in meeting customer requirements. There must be constant feedback between marketing, product/process design, and manufacturing in order to coordinate the determination of customer needs and the design and manufacture of a product to meet those needs.

Information About Overall Quality Level A fraction-nonconforming chart is ideal for summarizing information at the aggregate level. For a plant with many product lines, departments, and work centers, a p-chart can combine information and provide a measure of the overall product nonconformance rate. It may be used to evaluate the effectiveness of managers and even the chief executive officer.

7-5 CHART FOR NUMBER OF NONCONFORMING ITEMS (np-CHART)

As an alternative to calculating the fraction nonconforming, the number of nonconforming items that are directly observed when choosing samples can be the basis for constructing a control chart. Operating personnel sometimes find it easier to relate to the number nonconforming rather than the fraction nonconforming. The assumptions made for the construction of a fraction-nonconforming chart apply to number-nonconforming charts as well. The number of nonconforming items in a sample is assumed to be given by a binomial distribution. Since the properties of binomial distributions, as they relate to the fraction nonconforming were discussed in the previous section, they will not be repeated here. The same principles apply to number-nonconforming charts also. There is one drawback to this type of chart: If the sample size changes, the center line and control limits change as well. Making inferences in such circumstances is difficult. So, it is not recommended that an np-chart be used when the sample size varies. Since the steps to be followed for constructing an np-chart are similar to those for a p-chart, they are not repeated here. Instead, only the formulas for the center line and control limits are given.

No Standard Given

The center line for an np-chart is given by

$$\text{CL}_{np} = \frac{\sum_{i=1}^{g} x_i}{g} = n\bar{p} \tag{7.16}$$

where x_i represents the number nonconforming for the ith sample, g is the number of samples, n is the sample size, and $\bar{p}$ is the sample average proportion nonconforming. Since the number of nonconforming items is n times the fraction nonconforming, the average and standard deviation of the number nonconforming are n times the corresponding value for the fraction nonconforming. Thus, the standard deviation of the number nonconforming is

$$\sigma_{np} = \sqrt{n\bar{p}(1-\bar{p})} \tag{7.17}$$

The control limits for an np-chart are

$$\mathrm{UCL}_{np} = n\bar{p} + 3\sqrt{n\bar{p}(1-\bar{p})} \qquad (7.18)$$
$$\mathrm{LCL}_{np} = n\bar{p} - 3\sqrt{n\bar{p}(1-\bar{p})}$$

If the lower control limit calculation yields a negative value, it should be converted to zero.

Standard Given

Suppose that a specified standard for the number of nonconforming items is np_0. The center line and control limits are given by

$$\mathrm{CL}_{np} = np_0$$
$$\mathrm{UCL}_{np} = np_0 + 3\sqrt{np_0(1-p_0)} \qquad (7.19)$$
$$\mathrm{LCL}_{np} = np_0 - 3\sqrt{np_0(1-p_0)}$$

Example 7-7: Data for the number of dissatisfied customers in a department store observed for 25 samples of size 300 are shown in Table 7-5. Construct an np-chart for the number of dissatisfied customers.

Solution. The center line for the np-chart is

$$\mathrm{CL}_{np} = 184/20 = 9.2$$

The control limits are found by using Equation 7.18:

$$\mathrm{UCL}_{np} = 9.2 + 3\sqrt{9.2(1 - 9.2/300)} = 18.159$$
$$\mathrm{LCL}_{np} = 9.2 - 3\sqrt{9.2(1 - 9.2/300)} = 0.241$$

Figure 7-11 shows this np-chart for the number of dissatisfied customers. Note that for sample number 12, the number nonconforming is above the upper control limit and so indicates an out-of-control state. Assignable causes should be investigated for the sample. Assuming that they have been identified and that remedial actions have been taken, limits may be revised

TABLE 7-5 Number of dissatisfied customers

Sample number	Number inspected	Number of dissatisfied customers
1	300	10
2	300	12
3	300	8
4	300	9
5	300	6
6	300	11
7	300	13
8	300	10
9	300	8
10	300	9
11	300	6
12	300	19
13	300	10
14	300	7
15	300	8
16	300	4
17	300	11
18	300	10
19	300	6
20	300	7
	Total =	184

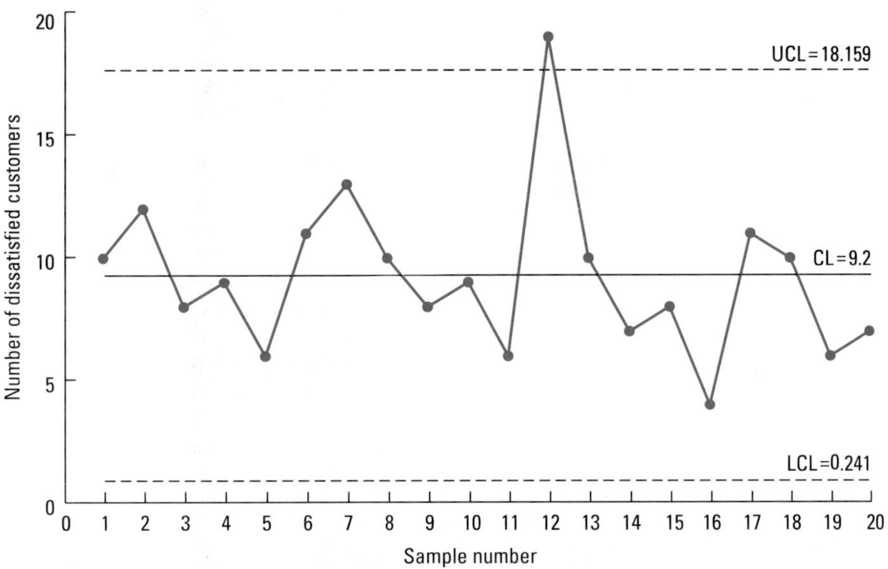

Figure 7-11 Number-nonconforming chart for dissatisfied customers.

by deleting sample number 12. Thus, the revised center line and control limits are

$$\begin{aligned} CL_{np} &= (184 - 19)/19 = 8.684 \\ UCL_{np} &= 8.684 + 3\sqrt{8.684(1 - 8.684/300)} = 17.396 \\ LCL_{np} &= 8.684 - 3\sqrt{8.684(1 - 8.684/300)} \\ &= -0.028 \rightarrow 0 \end{aligned}$$

These limits should be used for future observations.

7-6 CHART FOR THE NUMBER OF NONCONFORMITIES (c-CHART)

A nonconformity is defined as a quality characteristic that does not meet some set specifications. A nonconforming item has one or more nonconformities which make it nonfunctional. It is possible for a product to have one or more nonconformities and still be able to conform to standards. The p-chart and the np-chart deal with nonconforming items. A c-chart is used to track the total number of nonconformities in samples of constant size. For a sample size that varies, a u-chart is used to track the number of nonconformities per unit sample size.

Within the context of constructing control charts, the size of the sample is also referred to as the area of opportunity. The area of opportunity may be single or multiple units of a product (for example, one television set or a collection of 10 television sets). For items produced on a continuous basis, the area of opportunity could be, say, 100 m^2 of fabric or 50 m^2 of paper. As with p-charts, one must be careful about the choice of the area of opportunity. When both the average number of nonconformities per unit and the area of opportunity are small, most observations will show zero nonconformities, with one nonconformity showing up occasionally and two or more nonconformities even less frequently. Such information might be misleading as to the actual process conditions, so it is beneficial to choose a large enough area of opportunity to make it reasonable to expect some nonconformities to occur. If the average number of nonconformities per television set is really small (say, about 0.08), then it would make sense to choose 50 sets per sample rather than 10.

The occurrence of nonconformities is assumed to be given by a Poisson distribution. Such a distribution is well-suited to modeling the number of events that happen over a specified amount of time, space, or volume. Certain assumptions must hold to allow a Poisson distribution to be used. First, the opportunity for the occurrence of nonconformities must be large, and the average number of nonconformities per unit must be small. An example might be the number of flaws in 100 m^2 of fabric. Theoretically, this number could be quite large, but the average number of flaws in 100 m^2 of fabric is not necessarily a large value. The second assumption is that the occurrences of nonconformities must be independent of each other. Suppose that 100 m^2 of fabric is selected as the sample size. A nonconformity in a certain segment of the fabric must in no way influence the occurrence of other nonconformities. Third, each sample should have an equal likelihood of the occurrence of nonconformities; the prevailing conditions should be consistent from sample to sample. For instance, if different rivet guns were used to install the rivets in a ship, the opportunity for defects might be different for different guns, so the Poisson distribution would not be strictly applicable.

Since the steps involved in the construction and interpretation of c-charts are similar to those for p-charts, they are not repeated here. Instead, only the differences in the formulas are pointed out. If x represents the number of nonconformities in the sample unit and c is the mean, then the Poisson distribution yields (Duncan, 1986; Grant and Leavenworth, 1988)

$$p(x) = \frac{e^{-c}c^x}{x!} \tag{7.20}$$

where $p(x)$ represents the probability of observing x nonconformities. Recall that a property of the Poisson distribution is that the mean and the variance are equal.

No Standard Given

The average number of nonconformities per sample unit is found from the sample observations and is denoted by $\bar{c}$. The center line and control limits are

$$\begin{aligned} CL_c &= \bar{c} \\ UCL_c &= \bar{c} + 3\sqrt{\bar{c}} \\ LCL_c &= \bar{c} - 3\sqrt{\bar{c}} \end{aligned} \tag{7.21}$$

Standard Given

Let the specified goal for the number of nonconformities per sample unit be c_0. The center line and control limits are then calculated from

$$\begin{aligned} CL_c &= c_0 \\ UCL_c &= c_0 + 3\sqrt{c_0} \\ LCL_c &= c_0 - 3\sqrt{c_0} \end{aligned} \tag{7.22}$$

If the lower control limit is found to be less than zero, it is converted to zero. Many of the special considerations discussed for p-charts, such as observations below the lower control limit, comparison with a specified standard, impact of design specifications, and information about overall quality level, apply to c-charts as well.

Example 7-8: Samples of fabric from a textile mill, each 100 square meters in size, were selected, and the number of occurrences of foreign matter were recorded. The data values are shown in Table 7-6 for 25 samples. Construct a chart for the number of nonconformities.

Solution. The average number of nonconformities based on the sample information is found as follows: The center line is given by

$$\bar{c} = 189/25 = 7.560$$

The control limits are given by

$$UCL_c = 7.560 + 3\sqrt{7.560} = 15.809$$

$$LCL_c = 7.560 - 3\sqrt{7.560} = -0.689 \to 0$$

Figure 7-12 shows the control chart for the number of nonconformities. For sample number 9, the number of nonconformities is 16, which exceeds the upper control limit of 15.809. Assuming remedial action has been taken for the relevant assignable causes, the center line and control limits are revised as follows (note that sample number 9 has been deleted):

$$\bar{c} = (189 - 16)/24 = 7.208$$

$$UCL_c = 7.208 + 3\sqrt{7.208} = 15.262$$

$$LCL_c = 7.208 - 3\sqrt{7.208} = -0.846 \to 0$$

After this revision, all of the sample points are found to be in control.

TABLE 7-6 Number of occurrences of foreign matter in fabric

Sample number	Number of nonconformities	Sample number	Number of nonconformities
1	5	14	11
2	4	15	9
3	7	16	5
4	6	17	7
5	8	18	6
6	5	19	10
7	6	20	8
8	5	21	9
9	16	22	9
10	10	23	7
11	9	24	5
12	7	25	7
13	8		

7-7 CHART FOR NUMBER OF NONCONFORMITIES PER UNIT (u-CHART)

A c-chart is applicable to circumstances for which the sample size is constant. If the area of opportunity changes from one sample to another, the center line and control limits of a c-chart change as well. For situations in which the subgroup size varies, a u-chart is an alternative to a c-chart. For companies who inspect all items produced or services rendered for the presence of nonconformities, the output may

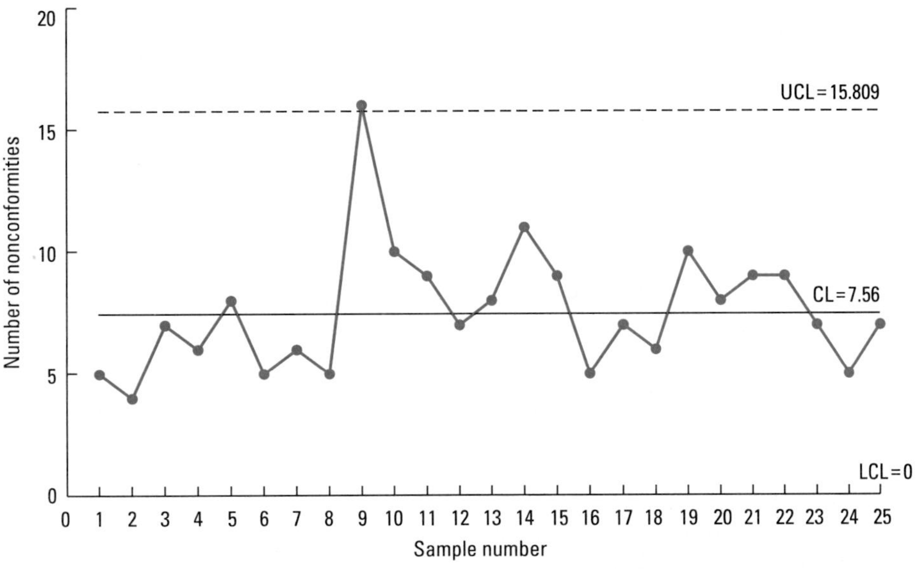

Figure 7-12 Control chart for the number of nonconformities.

vary as a result of fluctuations in the availability of labor, machinery, and raw material; consequently, the number inspected changes. This influences the sample size. A u-chart could be constructed to monitor the number of nonconformities per unit. Even though the control limits still change as the sample size varies, the center line of a u-chart remains constant, which permits meaningful comparisons to be made between subgroups of different sizes.

Constant Subgroup Size and No Specified Standard

For a given sample number i, the number of nonconformities per unit (u_i) is given by

$$u_i = \frac{c_i}{n} \tag{7.23}$$

where c_i represents the number of nonconformities in the ith sample and n is the sample size. The average number of nonconformities per unit ($\overline{u}$), which is also the center line, is obtained from

$$\overline{u} = \frac{\sum_{i=1}^{g} c_i}{ng} \tag{7.24}$$

where g is the number of samples, each of size n. Alternatively, since $c_i = u_i n$, Equation 7.24 can be rewritten as $\overline{u} = \overline{c}/n$. Note that $\overline{u}$ is a Poisson random variable since it is a linear combination of independent and identically distributed Poisson random variables (Duncan, 1986). Thus, the control limits for a u-chart are

$$\begin{aligned} \text{UCL}_u &= \overline{u} + 3\sqrt{\frac{\overline{u}}{n}} \\ \text{LCL}_u &= \overline{u} - 3\sqrt{\frac{\overline{u}}{n}} \end{aligned} \tag{7.25}$$

The process of revising these limits adheres to the same general principles as that for c-charts.

Variable Subgroup Size and No Specified Standard

If the subgroup size varies, the number of nonconformities per unit for the ith sample is given by

$$u_i = \frac{c_i}{n_i} \tag{7.26}$$

where n_i is the size of the ith sample. Note that the sample size n_i need not always be an integer. For instance, suppose the number of weaving nonconformities are being counted from finished pieces of cloth such that 100 m^2 represent one unit. If three samples of 250, 100, and 350 m^2, respectively, are chosen for inspection, the corresponding values of the sample size would be 2.5, 1, and 3.5, respectively.

The average number of nonconformities per unit ($\overline{u}$), which is also the center line of a u-chart, is given by

$$\overline{u} = \frac{\sum_{i=1}^{g} c_i}{\sum_{i=1}^{g} n_i} \tag{7.27}$$

The control limits are given by

$$\begin{aligned} \text{UCL}_u &= \overline{u} + 3\sqrt{\frac{\overline{u}}{n_i}} \\ \text{LCL}_u &= \overline{u} - 3\sqrt{\frac{\overline{u}}{n_i}} \end{aligned} \tag{7.28}$$

It can been seen from Equation 7.28 that the control limits draw closer as the sample size increases. The same behavior is observed for p-charts for variable subgroup sizes. Thus, the different options discussed previously for p-charts in circumstances involving variable subgroup size may be applied to u-charts as well. Equation 7.28 provides control limits that vary based on each subgroup size. Alternatively, control limits can be calculated based on the average subgroup size $\overline{n}$, where

$$\overline{n} = \frac{\sum_{i=1}^{g} n_i}{g}$$

as discussed in the section on p-charts. For points that plot close to the control limit based on $\overline{n}$, it is important to determine whether the actual control limits based on n_i are needed to confirm any decisions made regarding an out-of-control point.

Example 7-9: The number of nonconformities in carpets was determined for 20 samples. The number of square meters inspected for each sample is not constant. Results of the inspection are shown in Table 7-7. Construct a control chart for the number of nonconformities per 100 m^2.

Solution. With 100 m^2 as a unit, the sample sizes may be computed for each subgroup. Table 7-8 shows the sample sizes and the number of nonconformities per unit for each sample. Equation 7.26 is used to calculate u_i. For example, for the first subgroup, $u_1 = 5/2 = 2.5$. The center line $\overline{u}$ is found by using Equation 7.27. It is the ratio of the total number of nonconformities to the total number of units inspected. That is,

$$\overline{u} = \frac{192}{41} = 4.683$$

TABLE 7-7 Number of nonconformities in carpets

Sample number	Amount inspected, in m^2	Number of nonconformities	Sample number	Amount inspected, in m^2	Number of nonconformities
1	200	5	11	300	9
2	300	14	12	250	16
3	250	8	13	200	12
4	150	8	14	250	10
5	250	12	15	100	6
6	100	6	16	200	8
7	200	20	17	200	5
8	150	10	18	100	5
9	150	6	19	300	14
10	250	10	20	200	8

The control limits are found by using Equation 7.28. Table 7-8 shows the control limits for each sample. For instance, for the first sample, the control limits are found as follows:

$$\text{UCL} = 4.683 + 3\sqrt{\frac{4.683}{2}} = 9.274$$

$$\text{LCL} = 4.683 - 3\sqrt{\frac{4.683}{2}} = 0.092$$

TABLE 7-8 Control limits for the number of nonconformities per unit

Sample number	Sample size, n_i	Number of nonconformities per 100 m^2 u_i	Upper control limit, UCL	Lower control limit, LCL
1	2	2.500	9.274	0.092
2	3	4.667	8.431	0.935
3	2.5	3.200	8.789	0.577
4	1.5	5.333	9.984	0
5	2.5	4.800	8.789	0.577
6	1	6.000	11.175	0
7	2	10.000	9.274	0.092
8	1.5	6.667	9.984	0
9	1.5	4.000	9.984	0
10	2.5	4.000	8.789	0.577
11	3	3.000	8.431	0.935
12	2.5	6.400	0.577	0.577
13	2	6.000	9.274	0.092
14	2.5	4.000	8.789	0.577
15	1	6.000	11.175	0
16	2	4.000	9.274	0.092
17	2	2.500	9.274	0.092
18	1	5.000	11.175	0
19	3	4.667	8.431	0.935
20	2	4.000	9.274	0.092
Total	41			

The control limits for the other samples are calculated in the same manner. If a lower control limit calculation turns out to be negative, the limit is converted to zero.

Figure 7-13 shows this control chart for the number of nonconformities per unit. It is observed that sample number 7 plots above the upper control limit. Assuming that the assignable cause has been identified and appropriate corrective action taken, the revised center line is found by deleting sample number 7. It is calculated as

$$\bar{u} = (192 - 20)/39 = 4.410$$

The revised control limits are found by using this revised value of $\bar{u}$ in Equation 7.28. All of the remaining samples are found to be within these revised control limits.

Example 7-10: For the situation described in Example 7-9, find the control limits if only one set of limits is calculated based on the average sample size. Discuss any inferences that can be made regarding the process.

Solution. The average subgroup size is

$$\bar{n} = \frac{41}{20} = 2.05$$

The control limits based on this average subgroup size are

$$\text{UCL}_u = 4.683 + 3\sqrt{\frac{4.683}{2.05}} = 9.217$$

$$\text{LCL}_u = 4.683 - 3\sqrt{\frac{4.683}{2.05}} = 0.149$$

Figure 7-14 shows the chart for the number of nonconformities per unit based on this average subgroup size. Note that sample number 7 is the only point that is near the control limit, and it lies above the upper control limit. The sample size for sample number 7 is 2, which is less

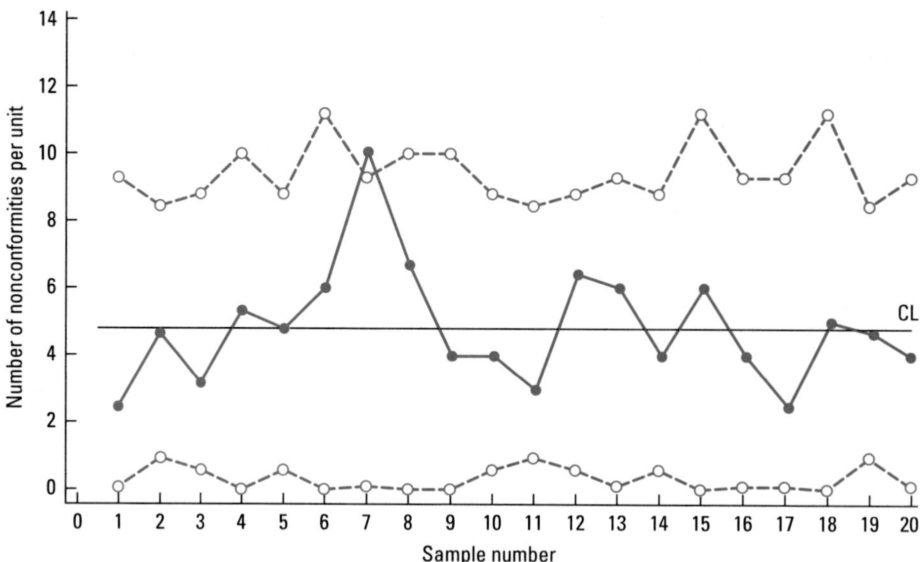

Figure 7-13 Control chart for the number of nonconformities per unit.

than the average subgroup size of 2.05. Thus, the actual control limits for sample number 7 would be wider than those based on $\bar{n}$. From Example 7-9, the actual control limits are (9.274, 0.092). This confirms that the number of nonconformities per unit for sample number 7 is above the upper control limit, indicating an out-of-control condition. Accordingly, assignable causes should be investigated to determine corrective action for the process.

If a specified standard for the number of nonconformities per unit (u_0) were given for this example, the procedure would be similar to that described previously for p-charts, with $\bar{u}$ replaced by u_0.

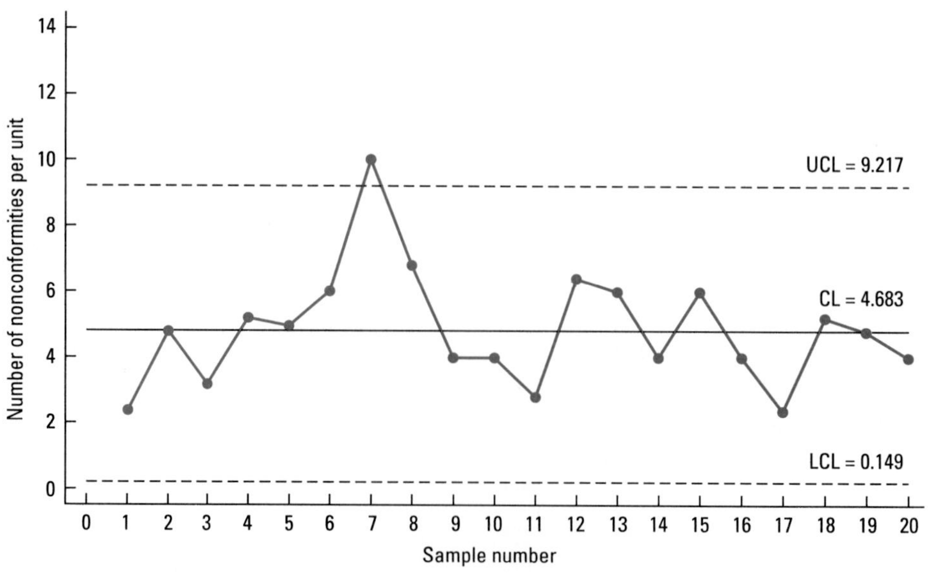

Figure 7-14 A u-chart with control limits based on the average sample size.

7-8 CHART FOR DEMERITS PER UNIT (U-CHART)

With control charts for the number of nonconformities (c-charts) or the number of nonconformities per unit (u-charts), all types of nonconformities are treated equally, regardless of their degree of severity. For instance, if one computer has trouble in retaining a consistent color in its monitor, whereas a second computer has five scratch marks on its surface, then the relative importance of the second computer's defects, in terms of the number of nonconformities, would be five times as great as that of the first computer. However, the single defect associated with the first computer is much more serious than the five defects associated with the second. Therefore, it seems rational to assign weights to nonconformities according to their relative degree of severity (Besterfield, 1990). A quality rating system which incorporates such a weighting scheme would overcome the deficiency of simply accumulating the total number of nonconformities. This is precisely what a chart for the demerits per unit (a U-chart) does.

Classification of Nonconformities

There are several systems which classify nonconformities according to their degree of seriousness. One such system is given by the *ANSI/ASQC Standard A3* (1978), which classifies nonconformities into the following four categories:*

1. *Class 1 Defects—Very Serious.* These are nonconformities which lead directly to severe injury or to catastrophic economic loss.
2. *Class 2 Defects—Serious.* These defects lead to significant injury or to significant economic loss.
3. *Class 3 Defects—Major.* These defects are related to major problems that may occur with normal use of a product or service rendered.
4. *Class 4 Defects—Minor.* These nonconformities are related to minor problems that may occur with normal use of a product or a service rendered.

Once such a classification of defects has been established, demerits per unit may be assigned to each class of defect. Control charts may then be constructed for demerits per unit rather than defects per unit. One should realize that the definitions of the classes are not rigid; they can be selected at the discretion of the user. The above-mentioned classification system is but one example. The number of severity categories and the definitions of each are flexible and are dependent on the user and the problem environment. For instance, one particular organization may have only three categories of nonconformities—critical, major, and minor—each with their own definitions. Another organization may define nonconformities as either serious or not serious. The weight assigned to a defect from each category is user-dependent. For the ANSI/ASQC standard discussed above, a weight system of 100, 50, 10 and 1, for example, may be chosen for the categories of very serious, serious, major, and minor, respectively.

*ASQC (1978), ANSI/ASQC Standard A3–1978: *Quality Systems Terminology*. Reprinted with the permission of ASQC.

Construction of a U-chart

Suppose we have four categories of nonconformities. In general, the procedure described in this section can be applied to any given number of categories. Let the sample size be n, and let c_1, c_2, c_3, and c_4 denote the total number of defects of each of the four types for a sample. Let w_1, w_2, w_3, and w_4 denote the weights associated with a defect for each respective category. Assume that defects in any one category are independent of defects in any other category. Furthermore assume that the occurrence of defects in any category is represented by a Poisson distribution. The applicability of a Poisson distribution to such circumstances is discussed in the section on u-charts.

For a given sample of size n, the total number of demerits is given by

$$D = w_1c_1 + w_2c_2 + w_3c_3 + w_4c_4 \tag{7.29}$$

The demerits per unit for a given sample are given by

$$U = \frac{D}{n} = \frac{w_1c_1 + w_2c_2 + w_3c_3 + w_4c_4}{n} \tag{7.30}$$

The quantity U is a linear combination of independent Poisson random variables. The center line of a U-chart is given by

$$\overline{U} = w_1\overline{u}_1 + w_2\overline{u}_2 + w_3\overline{u}_3 + w_4\overline{u}_4 \tag{7.31}$$

where $\overline{u}_1$, $\overline{u}_2$, $\overline{u}_3$, and $\overline{u}_4$ represent the average number of nonconformities per unit in their respective classes. Computation of $\overline{u}_1$, $\overline{u}_2$, $\overline{u}_3$, and $\overline{u}_4$ is similar to the calculation of $\overline{u}$ discussed in the section on u-charts. If the control limits are to be based on standard values, then those values (say u_{10}, u_{20}, u_{30}, and u_{40}) should be substituted in place of the average number of nonconformities per unit in each category.

The estimated standard deviation of U is given by

$$\sigma_U = \sqrt{\frac{w_1^2\bar{u}_1 + w_2^2\bar{u}_2 + w_3^2\bar{u}_3 + w_4^2\bar{u}_4}{n}} \quad (7.32)$$

The control limits of a U-chart are given by

$$\begin{aligned} \text{UCL} &= \overline{U} + 3\sigma_U \\ \text{LCL} &= \overline{U} - 3\sigma_U \end{aligned} \quad (7.33)$$

Example 7-11: A department store obtains feedback on customer satisfaction regarding a certain product. Twenty random samples, each involving 10 customers, were taken, and customers were asked about the number of serious, major, and minor nonconformities that they had experienced. Clear definitions of each category were provided. The results of the samples are shown in Table 7-9. The weights assigned to a serious, major, and minor nonconformity were 50, 10, and 1, respectively. Construct a control chart for the number of demerits per unit.

Solution. For each sample, the total number of demerits given by Equation 7.29 is shown in Table 7-9. The table also shows the number of demerits per unit (U), given by Equation 7.30. To find the center line $\overline{U}$, the average number of nonconformities per unit for each of the defect categories must be calculated. For serious nonconformities

$$\bar{u}_1 = \frac{9}{20(10)} = 0.045$$

Similarly,

$$\bar{u}_2 = \frac{74}{200} = 0.37$$

$$\bar{u}_3 = \frac{114}{200} = 0.57$$

The center line of the U-chart is found by using Equation 7.31 to be

$$\overline{U} = 50(0.045) + 10(0.37) + 1(0.57) = 6.52$$

The estimated standard deviation of U, found by using Equation 7.32, is

$$\sigma_U = \sqrt{\frac{(50)^2(.045) + (10)^2(0.37) + (1)^2(0.57)}{10}} = 3.807$$

Hence, the control limits are

$$\begin{aligned} \text{UCL} &= 6.52 + 3(3.807) = 17.941 \\ \text{LCL} &= 6.52 - 3(3.807) = -4.901 \rightarrow 0 \end{aligned}$$

Figure 7-15 shows this control chart for the demerits per unit. Note that sample number 15 plots above the upper

TABLE 7-9 Number of serious, major, and minor nonconformities

Sample number	Number of serious nonconformities, c_1	Number of major nonconformities, c_2	Number of minor nonconformities, c_3	Total number of demerits, D	Number of demerits per unit, U
1	1	4	2	92	9.2
2	0	3	8	38	3.8
3	0	5	10	60	6.0
4	1	2	5	75	7.5
5	0	6	2	62	6.2
6	0	0	8	8	0.8
7	0	7	5	75	7.5
8	1	1	1	61	6.1
9	1	3	2	82	8.2
10	0	4	12	52	5.2
11	1	5	3	103	10.3
12	2	0	2	102	10.2
13	0	0	9	9	0.9
14	0	6	8	68	6.8
15	1	12	10	180	18.0
16	0	5	7	57	5.7
17	0	1	1	11	1.1
18	1	2	5	75	7.5
19	0	5	6	56	5.6
20	0	3	8	38	3.8
Total	9	74	114		

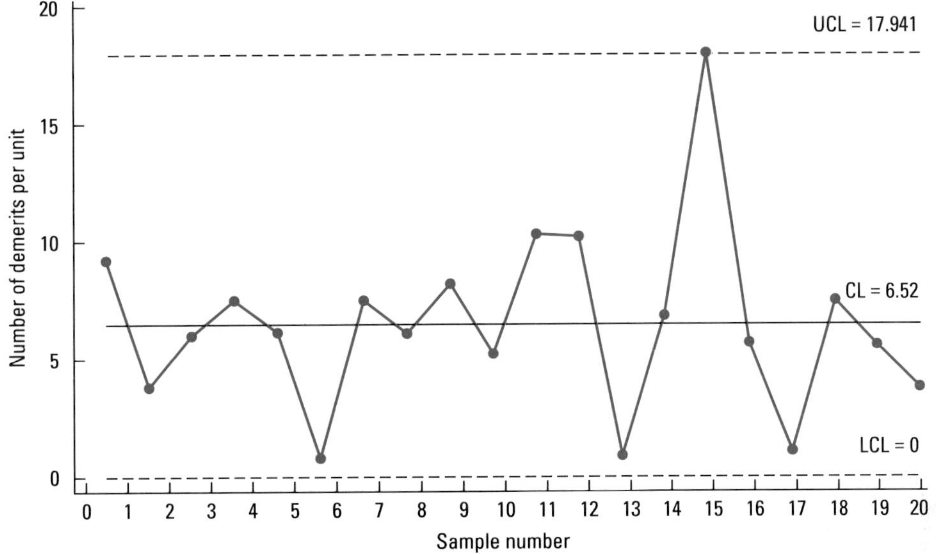

Figure 7-15 Control chart for demerits per unit.

control limit and so is considered to be out of control. Assuming that assignable causes have been remedied, the center line of the U-chart is revised as follows:

$$\begin{aligned}\bar{u}_1 &= 8/190 = 0.042\\ \bar{u}_2 &= 62/190 = 0.326\\ \bar{u}_3 &= 104/190 = 0.547\\ \bar{U} &= 50(.042) + 10(.326) + 1(0.547)\\ &= 5.907\end{aligned}$$

The standard deviation of U is

$$\sigma_U = \sqrt{\frac{(50)^2(.042) + (10)^2(0.326) + (1)^2(0.547)}{10}}$$
$$= 3.717$$

The revised control limits are

$$\begin{aligned}\text{UCL} &= 5.907 + 3(3.717) = 17.058\\ \text{LCL} &= 5.907 - 3(3.717) = -5.244 \to 0\end{aligned}$$

All of the points are observed to lie within the revised control limits.

7-9 OPERATING CHARACTERISTIC CURVES FOR ATTRIBUTE CONTROL CHARTS

An operating characteristic (OC) curve is basically a plot of the probability of incorrectly concluding that a process is in control as a function of a process parameter. In other words, it is a graph of the probability of a Type II error (denoted by β) versus the value of a process parameter.

The choice of process parameter depends on the type of attribute chart under consideration. For a fraction-nonconforming chart, the parameter of interest is usually the true process fraction nonconforming (p). An OC curve represents a measure of goodness of a control chart. It can be used to gauge the ability of a chart to detect changes in the process parameter values (Wadsworth, Stephens, and Godfrey, 1986). The probability of a change in a process parameter not being detected is related to the probability of a plotted point falling within the control limits. An OC curve is a measure of the sensitivity of a control chart in detecting small changes in process parameters.

For a p-chart, if the process fraction nonconforming is at some value p, the probability of a Type II error is

$$\begin{aligned}\beta &= P(\hat{p} < \text{UCL}_p \mid p) - P(\hat{p} \le \text{LCL}_p \mid p)\\ &= P(X < n\text{UCL} \mid p) - P(X \le n\text{LCL} \mid p) \quad (7.34)\end{aligned}$$

where n is the sample size, $\hat{p}$ is the sample proportion nonconforming, and X represents the number of nonconforming items. Recall that X is a binomial random variable with parameters n and p. The probability values needed for Equation 7.34 may be found from the binomial tables in Appendix A-1. Since X has to be an integer, and neither nUCL nor

nLCL are necessarily integers, an adjustment must be made. Let r_1 and r_2 be defined as follows:

$$\begin{aligned} r_1 &= \lceil n\text{UCL} \rceil \\ r_2 &= \lfloor n\text{LCL} \rfloor \end{aligned} \tag{7.35}$$

where $\lceil n\text{UCL} \rceil$ denotes the largest integer less than or equal to nUCL and $\lfloor n\text{LCL} \rfloor$ denotes the smallest integer greater than or equal to nLCL. The probability of a Type II error may then be expressed as

$$\beta = P(X \leq r_1) - P(X \leq r_2) \tag{7.36}$$

Example 7-12: Consider Example 7-1, which deals with the number of nonconforming containers produced by a plastic injection molding process. The revised control limits for the p-chart are $\text{UCL}_p = 0.173$, and $\text{LCL}_p = 0$, with the revised center line at 0.067. The sample size is 50. Construct an operating characteristic curve as a function of the process average fraction nonconforming.

Solution. The calculations correspond to a true process fraction nonconforming of .10. The probability of a Type II error found by using a binomial distribution is

$$\begin{aligned} \beta &= P[X < 50(0.173) \mid p = .10] - P[X \leq 50(0) \mid p = .10] \\ &= P[X < 8.65 \mid p = .10] - P[X \leq 0 \mid p = .10] \\ &= P(X \leq 8 \mid p = .10) - P(X \leq 0 \mid p = .10) \\ &= \sum_{i=1}^{8} \binom{50}{i} (0.10)^i (0.90)^{50-i} = 0.937 \end{aligned}$$

TABLE 7-10 Calculations for constructing OC curve

Process fraction noncomforming, p	$P(X \leq 8 \mid p)$	$P(X \leq 0 \mid p)$	P(Type II error), β
0.08	0.979	0.018	0.961
0.09	0.960	0.011	0.949
0.10	0.932	0.007	0.925
0.15	0.662	0.001	0.661
0.20	0.333	0.000	0.333
0.28	0.062	0.000	0.062
0.40	0.002	0.000	0.002

If a Poisson approximation to the binomial is used when n is large and p is small (such that np is less than or equal to 5), we have $np = 50(.10) = 5$. Next, by using the Poisson cumulative probability tables in Appendix A-2, we get

$$\begin{aligned} \beta &= P(X \leq 8 \mid np = 5) - P(X \leq 0 \mid np = 5) \\ &= 0.932 - 0.007 = 0.925 \end{aligned}$$

This approach can be repeated for other values of p to obtain P(Type II error) for each case. Table 7-10 shows the probability of a Type II error for several values of p. The Poisson cumulative probability tables in Appendix A-2 are used to obtain the value of β.

Figure 7-16 shows the OC curve for this p-chart. This figure gives an indication of the effectiveness of a p-chart in detecting changes in the process fraction nonconforming. For instance, if the process fraction nonconforming

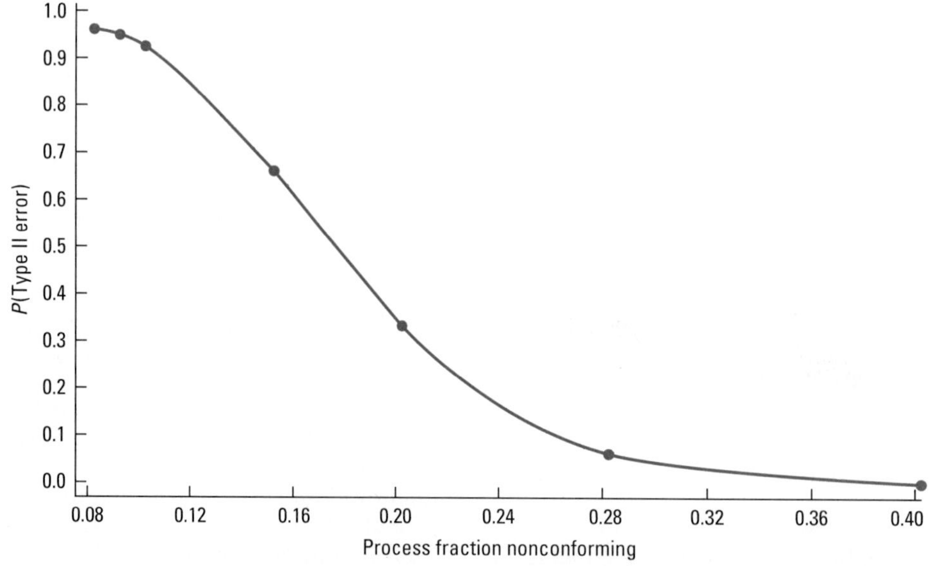

Figure 7-16 Operating characteristic curve for p-chart.

changes from the current value of 0.067 to 0.08, there is only a 3.9 percent probability of detecting this change by the first sample taken after the change. Therefore, this control chart is not very sensitive to such small changes in p. On the other hand, if the value of p changes to 0.15, this control chart has a 33.9 percent chance of detecting this change in the value of p by the first sample. As the value of p deviates further from its current state, the probability of detection improves. If the value of p changes to 0.28, there is a 93.8 percent chance of detecting this by the first subgroup after the change takes place. This example demonstrates the construction of one segment of the OC curve—the region for which the value of p increases. The same procedure can be used to calculate the OC curve corresponding to the region for which the value of p decreases from its present level.

Operating characteristic curves for the other attribute charts may be constructed in accordance with similar guidelines. Consider a chart for the number of nonconformities. If the process average number of nonconformities is c, then the probability of a Type II error is

$$\beta = P(X < \text{UCL}_c \mid c) - P(X \le \text{LCL}_c \mid c) \qquad (7.37)$$

where X represents the number of nonconformities for a process average of c. Incidentally, X is distributed according to a Poisson random variable with mean c. Since the value of X must be an integer and UCL_c and LCL_c need not be integers, we have

$$\beta = P(X \le \lceil \text{UCL} \rceil \mid c) - P(X \le \lfloor \text{LCL} \rfloor \mid c) \qquad (7.38)$$

where $\lceil \text{UCL} \rceil$ represents the largest integer less than or equal to the UCL, and $\lfloor \text{LCL} \rfloor$ represent the smallest integer greater than or equal to the LCL.

TABLE 7-11 Calculations for the OC curve for a c-chart

c	$P(X \le 15 \mid c)$	$P(X \le 0 \mid c)$	P(Type II error), β
0.5	1.000	0.607	0.393
1	1.000	0.368	0.632
3	1.000	0.050	0.950
5	1.000	0.007	0.993
7	0.998	0.001	0.997
9	0.978	0.000	0.978
10	0.951	0.000	0.951
12	0.844	0.000	0.844
14	0.669	0.000	0.669
18	0.287	0.000	0.237
20	0.157	0.000	0.157

Example 7-13: Consider Example 7-8, which deals with the number of occurrences of foreign matter in fabric samples. The revised center line of the c-chart is 7.208, and the revised control limits are $\text{UCL}_c = 15.262$, $\text{LCL}_c = 0$. Construct an OC curve for this c-chart.

Solution. Table 7-11 gives the relevant probabilities for various values of c. Equation 7.38 gives

$$\begin{aligned}\beta &= P(X < 15.262 \mid c) - P(X \le 0 \mid c)\\ &= P(X \le 15 \mid c) - P(X \le 0 \mid c)\end{aligned}$$

Making use of the cumulative Poisson tables in Appendix A-2, the above probabilities are found and are shown in Table 7-11. Figure 7-17 shows the OC curve for this

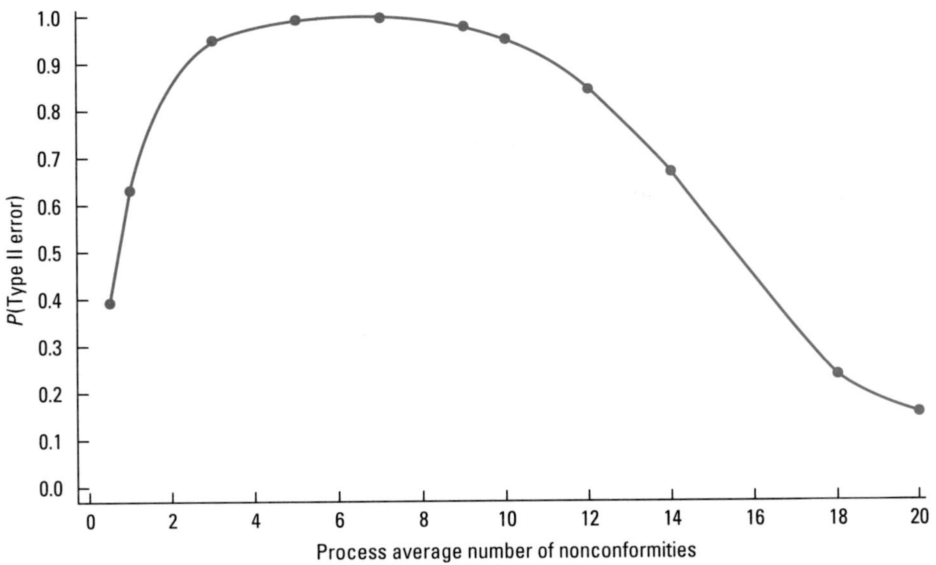

Figure 7-17 Operating characteristic curve for c-chart.

c-chart. The same line of reasoning, used to interpret an OC curve for a *p*-chart can be used to make inferences from this OC curve.

7-10 SUMMARY

This chapter has introduced a variety of control charts for attributes. Although attribute charts may not provide as much information as variable charts for the same sample size, they do have some advantages. They are a good tool for summarizing information and for providing data on the overall level of quality at an aggregate level. Attribute charts are useful when starting a quality control program. They may provide guidance as to where variable charts may eventually be used. Three main categories of attribute charts have been discussed in this chapter. The first deals with products or services that are nonconforming. The *p*-chart for the fraction nonconforming and the *np*-chart for the number nonconforming are in this category. The second category involves the number of nonconformities, or defects. The *c*-chart for the number of nonconformities and the *u*-chart for the number of nonconformities per unit are included in this group. The third category involves a classification of the nonconformities into groups based on their severity, with appropriate weights assigned to defects in each group. The *U*-chart for demerits per unit is discussed in this section. When making inferences from any control chart, there is always the risk of incorrectly declaring a process to be out of control, (a Type I error) or incorrectly declaring a process to be in control (a Type II error). A measure of goodness of a control chart's performance is its operating characteristic (OC) curve, which shows the probability of a Type II error as a function of the value of a process parameter such as the process fraction nonconforming or the process average number of nonconformities.

7-11 CASE STUDY

LOSSES CUT 76 PERCENT WITH CONTROL CHART SYSTEM*

The Ingersoll-Rand (IR) Energair plant at Davidson, North Carolina, is a small plant with a big success story. This plant reports success in dramatically reducing manufacturing losses—a 76-percent reduction over 10 months. These results were achieved through the use of statistical process control (SPC). Figure 7-18 shows the monthly trend of rejections at final test.

The IR plant is strictly an assembly and test operation for small air compressors used to operate air tools. The compressors are used in the highly competitive do-it-yourself consumer market, with sales in the construction and trade markets as well.

All manufactured parts for the compressors are shipped to the plant. A close relationship is therefore maintained between the plant and its suppliers. Packaging and distribution of the compressors are also handled from this facility.

ASME–1 coded air receivers are grit-blasted, painted, baked, and sent to the assembly process. There are two basic assembly lines: the "tilt piston" line and the "portable/vertical" package line. The tilt piston line assembles a $\frac{3}{4}$ HP tankless compressor and motor subassemblies. Other typical subassemblies at Energair are manifolds and pressure switches.

The portable/vertical line assembles tank-mounted compressors, which range from $\frac{3}{4}$ to 5 HP. After assembly, every compressor from both lines is tested on a computerized test stand to verify performance and ensure quality conformance. Specific criteria are used for testing performance. These include motor electrical standards, pump requirements, and the mechanical integrity of the compressor assembly.

Demos Control Chart System

The success achieved in reducing manufacturing losses at final test resulted from the company's commitment to continually improve product quality. To meet this objective, management decided to implement a continuous SPC program. This program was designed to catch defects at the point they occurred in the process and identify immediate corrective action. IR chose the Demos control chart system.

This system organizes all attribute and variable quality data into an integrated, plantwide SPC system. The system identifies and concentrates on the few major continuing problems and eliminates the wide proliferation of charts on minor or trivial problems. It summarizes all information into management control charts so that the program can be specifically directed by the management team.

*Adapted from: P. J. Cooper and N. Demos (1991), "Losses Cut 76 Percent with Control Chart System." Reprinted with permission from *Quality*, a publication of Hitchcock Publishing, a Capital Cities/ABC, Inc., Company.

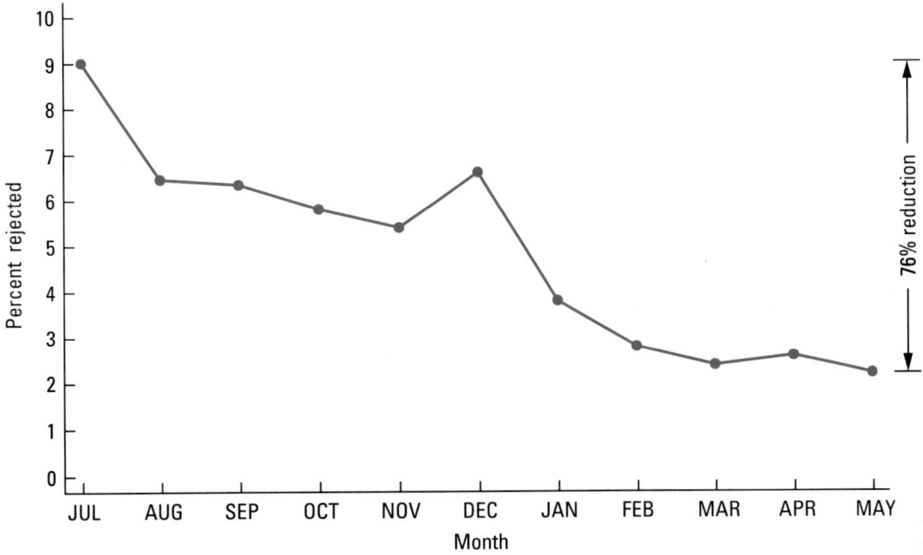

Figure 7-18 Monthly trend of rejections at final test.

Using a pyramid technique, inspection, scrap, and rework data are integrated and organized into a series of control charts. The entire system can include over 1000 items—defect types, operators, machine operations, and part types.

With pinpoint accuracy, the system points out each out-of-control item as well as each item that has improved in performance. Also, the system routinely and automatically directs major effort and corrective action by the entire organization toward those areas that have the poorest quality.

Using this system, plant managers set as their objective a rejection rate that is lower every month than the previous month until 0.1 percent is reached. If at any time the rejection percent were higher than the previous month, it would indicate that the program had lost momentum and that a strong effort would be needed to reestablish it, until the current month's percent again is the lowest point. For example, Figure 7-18 shows that upward trends occurred in December and April.

The trend in December resulted from changes in assembly workers during holiday vacations, coupled with increased production requirements at that time. This trend reversed after cross-training the assembly workers and maintaining continuity in assembly methods.

The upward trend in April resulted from a problem with small motor wiring fixtures. IR took up the problem with the motor manufacturer, resulting in improved methods and fixture controls at the supplier's site. Figure 7-18 shows that after corrective action the downward trend was reestablished the following month.

Implementing the System

At the introduction of the Demos control chart system at the plant, managers gathered data at final test stations on each assembly line. These data were put on control charts to identify out-of-control conditions and to evaluate corrective action taken on their causes. Table 7-12 shows the data for six days in the plant's daily overall production lines at final test.

The process averages ($\overline{p}$ in percent) appear in the left-hand column of Table 7-12. Overall plant performance is 6.5 percent. The portable and tilt piston lines have process averages of 8 and 4.8 percent, respectively. Daily performance for each line is shown progressively in the columns. For each day, the values in Table 7-12 show the number of rejections, the number of items produced, and the percentage of rejections, respectively.

On January 6, plant performance is 9.1 percent—the portable and tilt piston lines are 11.9 and 4.0 percent, respectively. The chart indicates that specific data and results since January have continued to show dramatic improvement.

When an entry exceeds the upper control limit for its process average, it is boxed; if it is below the lower limit, it is circled. The overall performance of the plant is out-of-control on the high side on January 6 and is worse on January 7. Performance is brought back into control on January 11, and on January 12 performance is better than the lower control limit. The boxes and circles show that the portable line is responsible. Therefore, the investigation is now focused on the portable

TABLE 7-12 Data for six days in the IR plant's daily overall production lines at final test

Process average ($\bar{p}$ in percent)	Production line	January 4	5	6	7	11	12
8.0	Portable/vertical						
	Number of rejections	12	16	69	16	28	19
	Number produced	247	367	578	120	453	531
	Percent rejections	4.9	(4.4)	[11.9]	[13.3]	6.2	(3.6)
4.8	Tilt Piston						
	Number of rejections	14	4	13	—	3	8
	Number produced	151	301	327	—	216	346
	Percent rejections	9.3	(1.3)	4.0	—	1.4	2.3
6.5	Total rejects	26	20	82	16	31	27
	Total production	398	668	905	120	669	877
	Percent defects	6.5	(3.0)	[9.1]	[13.3]	4.6	(3.1)

line. Details on the different types of rejections that occur on the portable line are investigated.

Table 7-13 shows the data on the portable line for the same time period. The daily totals on the different types of defects are shown along with the total production for the day. The average percentage of defects in each category is also shown. The portable line total percentage is out-of-control on the high side on January 6 and 7. It is in control on January 11 and is exceptionally good on January 12. The boxes show that leaks and pressure switches caused the high out-of-control condition on January 6. The pressure switch problem had been solved the next day but not the leak problem. On January 11, both the leak and pressure problems had been solved. Even though the pressure switch problem reoccurred on January 12, the performance for leaks is so superior that the overall performance for the portable line is exceptional and plots below its lower statistical limit.

Attention was now focused on the leaks on the portable line. Table 7-14 shows the number of defects of each type within this category for the same time period.

Table 7-14 shows that the out-of-control condition was caused by leaks from the manifold and the discharge tube. Although pressure switch leaks caused a problem one day, all leak problems were solved by January 12. Exceptional leak performance results are shown on January 12, and this performance is the main reason for the superior overall performance on this date.

Corrective Action

Once the problems were identified on the charts, corrective actions could be immediately taken. The main

TABLE 7-13 Data for the number of rejections on the portable line

Process average ($\bar{p}$ in %)	Defect	January 4	5	6	7	11	12
3.0	Leaks	4	6	[30]	[8]	17	(3)
2.6	Motors	4	3	15	6	9	8
0.4	Pumps		1	3	1	1	1
0.1	Sheaves					1	
0.3	Pressure switch	2	3	[14]			[5]
0.2	Cosmetic			2	1		
1.0	Miscellaneous	2	2	3			
0.4	Bad check valve		1	2			2
8.0	Total defects	12	16	69	16	28	19
	Total production	247	367	578	120	453	531
	Percent defects	4.9	(4.4)	[11.9]	[13.3]	6.2	(3.6)

TABLE 7-14 Data for leaks on the portable line

Process average ($\bar{p}$ in %)	Defect	January					
		4	5	6	7	11	12
0.5	Tank weld	1	1	5		1	1
0.1	Inspection plugs						
0.7	Manifold	1	3	12	4	3	1
	Pressure switch				1	10	
0.5	Check valve				1		1
0.1	Discharge elbow			1			
0.1	Nylon tube						
0.7	Discharge tube	1	2	11		1	
0.1	Drain valve	1		1			
0.3	Other				2	2	
3.0	Total defects	4	6	30	8	17	3
	Total production	247	367	578	120	453	531
	Percent defects	1.6	1.6	5.1	6.7	3.7	0.5

forum for corrective action at the plant is the daily action meeting. Each morning at 8:00 a.m. the operations manager meets with manufacturing and quality assurance supervisors and appropriate specialists. They review daily control charts, define current problems, review progress, and agree on corrective actions.

The greatest overall improvement was in reducing air leaks in the portable line. An 83-percent reduction was achieved by reducing the initial percentage of leaks from 6.5 to the latest value of 1.1 percent, as shown in Table 7-15.

IR identified several corrective actions needed to reduce leaks in the portable line. Training began immediately to achieve better discipline in the process. Upgrading of the tooling improved efficiency. Experiments were designed and monitored to qualify the methods, tools, and process. Also, rearranging the assembly lines produced better control of material flow and balanced assembly operations.

Another significant result came out of a supplier-oriented quality problem with motors. IR requested a resident quality engineer from the motor supplier. He and the IR plant workers monitored all defect characteristics and identified the root causes. After mutual agreement as to what the problems were, they took corrective actions. Some were taken in Energair's plant, others in the supplier's plant.

Engineers monitored these corrective actions on the portable line and data-FAXed control charts on the supplier's motor assembly facility. These charts clearly pointed out the problems requiring correction at the supplier plant and tracked them as they were addressed. Root cause identification and corrective action on the product lines initiated minor design changes and overall product improvement.

On the tilt piston line, the system identified specific failure modes and, as with the portable line, called for

TABLE 7-15 Improvement on the tilt piston line and portable line

Tilt piston line			
Defect mode	Initial percentage	Final percentage	Percent improvement
High amps	2.5	0.2	92
Pressure	1.9	0.1	95
Knock	1.5	0.0	100
Miscellaneous	0.8	0.2	75
No start	0.6	0.3	50
Hi pot	0.5	0.8	−60
Total	7.8	1.5	81

Portable line			
Defect mode	Initial percentage	Final percentage	Percent improvement
Leaks	6.5	1.1	83
Motors	2.4	1.0	58
Pumps	0.7	0.2	71
Miscellaneous	0.5	0.1	80
Pressure switch	0.2	0.1	50
Cosmetic	0.2	0.0	100
Sheaves	0.1	0.1	0
Check valve	0.0	0.3	$-\infty$
Total	10.4	2.9	72

extensive involvement with the motor manufacturer for corrective steps.

They agreed upon design changes and addressed assembly criteria at both the small compressor plant and the manufacturer's facility. The SPC charts monitored these changes at the small compressor plant, and feedback was data-FAXed daily to the supplier. Batch lots were identified to maintain control as each batch was monitored.

IR management believes that the benefits achieved by the continuous quality improvement program are many. The actions that reduced rejections at final test automatically and simultaneously improved product quality. Also, the benefits of reducing rejections significantly reduced quality costs. For example, a reduction in the rejection rate:

- Generated savings in scrap and rework costs
- Reduced failure costs
- Reduced in-process inventories
- Improved delivery performance
- Increased productivity

Therefore, rather than costing the company money, this quality improvement program made money. By reducing the rejection rate, quality improvement was free.

Another benefit was the increased visibility of problems. Through the visibility achieved with the Demos system, problems are defined—whether within the process or at the supplier's site. This information becomes a valuable tool when dealing with a supplier-oriented quality problem and permits an unemotional and objective discussion of the problem. Thus, the continuous quality program used at the Davidson plant has become an external program for constant quality improvement by some of its major suppliers.

Questions for Discussion

1. Describe the conceptual process through which the company was able to pinpoint problem areas.
2. Could a similar approach as used by the company be implemented for variable charts? Discuss the relative advantages and disadvantages.
3. Discuss the goal-setting process by the managers. How may this process be improved?
4. Discuss the implementation process and possible difficulties encountered.
5. What were some of the major corrective actions? What were the benefits of using SPC?
6. If the company were to focus on the portable line, what problem area would it next tackle?

KEY TERMS

Attribute
Average subgroup size
Binomial distribution
Causes
  Assignable
  Chance
Control chart
  Attributes
  Demerits per unit (U-chart)
  Number of nonconformities (c-chart)
  Number of nonconformities per unit (u-chart)
  Number of nonconforming units (np-chart)
  Proportion nonconforming (p-chart)
  Standardized p-chart
  Variables
Control limits
  Revised
  Trial
Defect classification
  Major
  Minor
  Serious
  Very Serious
Defective
Demerits
Nonconforming unit
Nonconformity
Operating characteristic (OC) curve
Poisson distribution
Standard or goal
Subgroup size
  Average
  Variable
Weights for defects
Type I error
Type II error

EXERCISES

Discussion Questions

7-1 Distinguish between a nonconformity and a nonconforming unit. Give examples of each.

7-2 What are the advantages and disadvantages of control charts for attributes over those for variables?

7-3 Discuss the significance of the choice of an appropriate sample size for a fraction-nonconforming chart.

7-4 The CEO of a company has been charged with reducing the fraction nonconforming of the product output. Discuss what type of control charts would be used and where they would be placed.

7-5 What is the effect of a change in the subgroup size on the center line and the control limits of a fraction-nonconforming chart?

7-6 Explain the different approaches that might be taken to deal with the problem of varying subgroup sizes for a p-chart.

7-7 Suppose that control limits are constructed for a p-chart based on the average subgroup size. The subgroup size is not constant for all subgroups. Under what conditions would it be necessary to calculate the actual control limits for a particular subgroup in order to make the right decision?

7-8 What are the advantages and disadvantages of the standardized p-chart over the regular fraction-nonconforming chart?

7-9 Discuss the assumptions that must be satisfied to justify using a p-chart. How are they different from the assumptions for using a c-chart?

7-10 Is it possible for a process to be in control and still not meet some desirable standards for the fraction nonconforming? How would one detect such a condition, and what remedial actions would one take?

7-11 Discuss the role of the customer in influencing the fraction nonconforming chart. How would the customer be integrated into a total quality systems approach?

7-12 Explain the conditions under which a u-chart would have to be used rather than a c-chart.

7-13 Explain the setting under which a demerits-per-unit chart would be used. How does the chart incorporate the user's perception of the relative degree of severity of the different categories of defects?

7-14 Determine which type of chart (p, np, c, u, or U) would be most appropriate to control the following situations:

a. The number of potholes in highways.
b. The proportion of customers that are satisfied with the operation of the local housing authority.
c. The satisfaction of customers at a restaurant where customers consider the quality of food and attitude of the server to be more important than the decor.
d. The number of errors in account transactions at a bank where the number of accounts vary from month to month.
e. The number of automobile accident claims filed per month at the insurance dealer, assuming a stable number of insured persons.
f. The responsiveness to customer needs of a local library where customers value the longer hours over short lines to check out books.
g. The number of thefts in a city over a period of time.
h. The proportion of people that favor the construction of condominiums in a certain neighborhood.
i. The number of weld defects in the construction of aircraft.
j. The number of seeds that germinate from a large pack of seeds sold by a nursery, when the actual number of seeds in a packet may vary.
k. The performance of the braking mechanism of a certain model of automobile. The car is expected to stop within a certain distance.
l. The number of firemen to have on duty during the first shift in order to provide an acceptable level of service. Each fire usually calls for having four firemen. The department has data on the number of calls that they receive during the specified period of time.
m. The performance of keypunch operators. If one or more punching errors are made, the card is rendered useless, and a new card has to be punched.
n. The supervisor of a stenographic pool is interested in controlling the number of typographical errors per page. Data is randomly chosen and obtained daily on the number of errors in 30 pages.
o. The manager of a plant wants to control the wiring and transistor defects in an electronic component. Wiring defects are considered more serious.

Problems

7-15 The number of nonconforming cables was found for 20 samples of size 100 and is

TABLE 7-16 Data for nonconforming cables

Sample number	Number of nonconforming cables	Sample number	Number of nonconforming cables
1	2	11	5
2	5	12	4
3	4	13	2
4	3	14	5
5	4	15	3
6	2	16	12
7	3	17	3
8	2	18	2
9	4	19	5
10	11	20	2

shown in Table 7-16. Construct a control chart for the proportion of nonconforming cables. Revise the control limits, assuming assignable causes for points outside the control limits.

7-16 Refer to the information from Exercise 7-15 on nonconforming cables. The desired standard for the nonconformance rate is set by management at 3 percent, so establish control limits based on this standard. Comment on the ability of the process to meet this standard. If management were to be stringent and set the standard at 2 percent, comment on the capability of the existing process to meet this goal. What actions would you recommend?

7-17 A company manufactures $3\frac{1}{2}$-inch diskettes for computers. Random samples, each of size 200, are chosen, and the number of nonconforming diskettes is recorded. Table 7-17 shows the relevant information for 25 such samples. Construct a control chart for the proportion of nonconforming diskettes. Revise the control limits, assuming assignable causes for points outside the control limits.

7-18 Refer to Exercise 7-17 on the nonconforming diskettes. If the goal of the manufacturer is a nonconformance rate of 1 percent, set up control limits, and comment on the ability of the process to meet these standards.

7-19 Observations were taken from the output of a company making semiconductors. Table 7-18 shows the subgroup size and the number of nonconforming semiconductors for each subgroup. Construct a fraction-nonconforming chart by setting up the exact control limits for each subgroup. Are there any samples out of control? If so, assuming assignable causes, revise the center line and control limits.

7-20 Refer to Exercise 7-19. Construct control limits for the fraction-nonconforming chart

TABLE 7-17 Data for nonconforming diskettes

Sample number	Number of nonconforming diskettes	Sample number	Number of nonconforming diskettes
1	3	14	4
2	4	15	3
3	2	16	7
4	6	17	4
5	5	18	12
6	6	19	5
7	6	20	3
8	5	21	6
9	6	22	5
10	3	23	3
11	4	24	5
12	2	25	4
13	5		

TABLE 7-18 Data for the inspection of semiconductors

Sample number	Number inspected	Number nonconforming
1	80	3
2	120	6
3	60	4
4	150	5
5	140	8
6	150	10
7	160	7
8	90	6
9	100	5
10	160	12
11	110	8
12	100	5
13	200	14
14	90	4
15	160	5
16	230	3
17	200	12
18	150	8
19	210	6
20	190	4
21	160	9
22	100	8
23	100	12
24	90	7
25	160	10

based on an average subgroup size. Is it necessary to construct the actual control limits for any of the subgroups? If so, explain.

7-21 Using the data from Exercise 7-19 on the nonconforming semiconductors, set up a p-chart with representative control limits based on sample sizes of 100, 150, and 200. What conclusions can you draw from this chart?

7-22 The numbers of nonconforming microchips obtained from 20 random samples are shown in Table 7-19. The corresponding subgroup size is also indicated. Construct a p-chart with control limits based on the average subgroup size. What inferences do you draw from this chart? Is it necessary to calculate the actual control limits for any of the subgroups? If so, calculate them, and make a decision about the process.

7-23 Refer to the information from Exercise 7-22 on the nonconforming microchips. Construct a control chart for the fraction nonconforming by using some representative subgroup sizes. Can you draw inferences using this control chart? Do you need to calculate the actual control limits for any subgroup?

7-24 Refer to Exercise 7-22. Construct a fraction-nonconforming chart, and set up control limits for each subgroup. What is your inference?

7-25 Refer to the information from Exercise 7-19 on the nonconforming semiconductors. The data values are shown in Table 7-18. Construct a standardized fraction-nonconforming chart, and discuss your conclusions.

7-26 Refer to the information from Exercise 7-22 on the nonconforming microchips. The data values are shown in Table 7-19. Construct a standardized p-chart and discuss your inferences.

7-27 The numbers of nonconforming door hinges found for samples of size 300 are shown in Table 7-20. Data values were collected for 30 samples. Construct a chart for the number of nonconforming hinges. What control limits would you use for the next period, assuming

TABLE 7-19 Data for nonconforming microchips

Sample number	Number inspected	Number of nonconforming microchips
1	50	4
2	90	6
3	100	8
4	90	7
5	80	8
6	40	4
7	50	6
8	50	5
9	110	8
10	70	6
11	80	6
12	120	8
13	100	20
14	80	5
15	110	8
16	40	6
17	40	4
18	50	7
19	120	5
20	50	4

TABLE 7-20 Number of nonconforming door hinges

Sample number	Number inspected	Number of nonconforming hinges
1	300	10
2	300	14
3	300	12
4	300	6
5	300	11
6	300	14
7	300	8
8	300	9
9	300	7
10	300	15
11	300	10
12	300	6
13	300	12
14	300	7
15	300	20
16	300	8
17	300	10
18	300	7
19	300	12
20	300	13
21	300	9
22	300	7
23	300	12
24	300	6
25	300	8
26	300	6
27	300	9
28	300	10
29	300	7
30	300	12

that assignable causes for the out-of-control points are identified?

7-28 Refer to the information from Exercise 7-15 on the number of nonconforming cables. The data values are shown in Table 7-16. Construct a control chart for the number of nonconforming cables. Revise the chart, assuming assignable causes for points outside the control limits.

7-29 The number of paint blemishes on automobile bodies are observed for 30 samples. Each sample consists of randomly selecting five automobiles of a certain make and style. Table 7-21 shows the data for the paint blemishes. Construct a chart for the number of paint blemishes. Assuming assignable causes for the out-of-control points, revise these limits accordingly.

7-30 The number of scratch marks for a particular piece of furniture is recorded for samples of size 10. The results are shown in Table 7-22 for 25 samples. Construct a chart for the number of scratch marks. Revise the control limits, assuming assignable causes for the out-of-control points.

7-31 Refer to the information from Exercise 7-29 on the paint blemishes on automobiles. Suppose the goal is to not exceed an average of five blemishes per five automobiles. Set up an appropriate control chart based on this goal, and discuss the capability of the process to meet this standard.

TABLE 7-21 Number of paint blemishes in automobiles

Sample number	Number of paint blemishes	Sample number	Number of paint blemishes
1	4	16	4
2	5	17	14
3	3	18	8
4	8	19	3
5	6	20	15
6	7	21	7
7	5	22	4
8	7	23	6
9	9	24	4
10	4	25	5
11	5	26	9
12	6	27	6
13	3	28	3
14	2	29	8
15	5	30	7

TABLE 7-22 Number of scratch marks on furniture pieces

Sample number	Number of scratch marks	Sample number	Number of scratch marks
1	6	14	9
2	3	15	11
3	12	16	6
4	8	17	7
5	9	18	5
6	7	19	8
7	17	20	4
8	5	21	9
9	6	22	8
10	4	23	4
11	8	24	7
12	7	25	6
13	18		

7-32 Refer to the information from Exercise 7-30 on the number of scratch marks on a particular piece of furniture. Suppose that management sets a goal of 4 scratch marks on average per 10 pieces. Set up an appropriate control chart, and discuss whether the process is capable of meeting this standard.

7-33 A building contractor subcontracts a job involving painting and putting on wallpaper to a local merchant. In order to have an idea of the quality level of the wallpapering work, the contractor randomly selects 300 ft^2 and counts the number of blemishes. The total number of blemishes for 30 samples is 80. Construct the center line and control limits for an appropriate chart. Is it reasonable for the contractor to set a goal of an average of 0.5 blemishes per 100 ft^2?

7-34 The number of typographical errors were counted over a certain number of pages for each sample. The data are shown in Table 7-23 for 25 samples. The number of pages used for each sample was not fixed. Construct a control chart for the number of typographical errors per page. Revise the limits, assuming assignable causes for points that are out of control.

7-35 Refer to the information from Exercise 7-34 on controlling the number of typographical errors per page. Construct control limits based on the average sample size. Comment on whether calculations are necessary for the exact control limits for any of the samples.

TABLE 7-23 Number of typographical errors

Sample number	Number of pages inspected	Number of typographical errors
1	10	4
2	5	3
3	8	8
4	6	4
5	12	14
6	10	8
7	8	4
8	10	5
9	6	2
10	8	12
11	10	7
12	12	5
13	6	15
14	4	3
15	8	2
16	8	4
17	12	6
18	10	8
19	12	10
20	8	5
21	6	8
22	10	4
23	10	5
24	8	4
25	12	5

TABLE 7-24 Number of imperfections in bond paper

Sample number	Area inspected, m^2	Number of imperfections
1	150	6
2	100	8
3	200	5
4	150	4
5	250	10
6	100	11
7	150	3
8	200	5
9	300	10
10	250	10
11	100	5
12	200	4
13	250	12
14	300	8
15	300	12
16	200	6
17	150	4
18	200	7
19	150	14
20	100	4
21	100	8
22	200	9
23	300	12
24	250	7
25	200	5

7-36 The number of imperfections in bond paper produced by a paper mill was observed over a period of several days. Table 7-24 shows the area inspected and the number of imperfections for each of 25 samples. Construct a control chart for the number of imperfections per square meter. Review the limits if necessary, assuming assignable causes for the out-of-control points.

7-37 Refer to the information from Exercise 7-36 on the number of imperfections in bond paper. If it is desired to control the number of imperfections per 100 m^2, how would the control chart be affected? What would the control limits be? In terms of decision making, would there be a difference between this problem and Exercise 7-36, depending upon which chart is constructed? What conclusions can you draw from this?

7-38 Refer to the information from Exercise 7-36 on the number of imperfections in bond paper. Construct a control chart for the number of imperfections per square meter. The control limits should be based on the average sample size.

7-39 Nonconformities in automobiles are classified into three categories—serious, major, and minor. Samples, each consisting of five automobiles, were chosen, and the total number of nonconformities in each category were reported. Table 7-25 shows the results from 25 samples. Assuming a weighting system of 50, 10, and 1 for serious, major, and minor nonconformities, respectively, construct a demerits-per-unit control chart. Revise the control limits if necessary, assuming assignable causes for points that are out-of-control.

7-40 Refer to the information from Exercise 7-39 on the number of nonconformities in automobiles. If the weighting system were different, namely 10, 5, and 1, how would the center line and the control limits change for a demerits-per-unit chart? Discuss changes, if any, on inferences made about the process.

7-41 Refer to the information from Exercise 7-15 on the proportion of nonconforming cables.

TABLE 7-25 Critical, major, and minor nonconformities in automobiles

Sample number	Number of serious defects	Number of major defects	Number of minor defects
1	0	5	8
2	0	3	2
3	1	0	6
4	1	2	1
5	0	6	8
6	0	3	3
7	0	1	10
8	1	2	5
9	0	4	9
10	2	6	6
11	1	3	2
12	0	5	8
13	0	0	9
14	0	7	12
15	0	2	8
16	0	4	3
17	1	0	5
18	0	3	2
19	0	5	8
20	0	2	6
21	1	1	4
22	0	3	10
23	0	2	12
24	0	4	7
25	0	2	4

Construct an OC curve for the p-chart. If the process proportion of nonconforming cables were to go up to 7 percent, what is the probability of not detecting this shift on the first sample drawn after the change has taken place? What is the probability of detecting the shift by the third sample?

7-42 Refer to the information from Exercise 7-16 on the proportion of nonconforming diskettes. Construct an OC curve for the p-chart. What would be the control limits if 2σ limits were constructed? What is the probability of making a Type I error under this setting? What impact does it have on the OC curve?

7-43 Refer to the information from Exercise 7-29 on the number of paint blemishes on automobile bodies. Construct an OC curve for the c-chart. If the process average number of nonconformities increases to two per automobile, what is the probability of detecting this on the first sample drawn after the change?

7-44 Refer to Exercise 7-43. Set up 2σ control limits. What is the probability of detecting a change in the process average number of nonconformities to two per automobile on the first sample drawn after the change? Explain under what conditions you would prefer to have these 2σ control limits over the traditional 3σ limits.

REFERENCES

American Society for Quality Control (1978). *ANSI/ASQC Standard A3-1978-Quality Systems Terminology.* Milwaukee, WI.

Banks, Jerry (1989). *Principles of Quality Control.* Wiley, New York.

Besterfied, Dale H. (1990). *Quality Control.* 3rd ed. Prentice Hall, Englewood Cliffs, NJ.

Cooper, P. J., and Demos, N. (1991). "Losses Cut 76 Percent with Control Chart System," *Quality,* April, pp. 22–24, Hitchcock Publishing, Carol Stream, IL.

Duncan, A. J. (1986). *Quality Control and Industrial Statistics,* 5th edition. Irwin, Homewood, IL.

Grant, E. L. and Leavenworth, R. S. (1988). *Statistical Quality Control,* 6th ed. McGraw-Hill, New York.

Montgomery, Douglas C. (1991). *Introduction to Statistical Quality Control* 2nd edition. Wiley, New York.

Wadsworth, H. M., Stephens, K. S., and Godfrey, A. B. (1986). *Modern Methods for Quality Control and Improvement.* Wiley, New York.

CHAPTER

8

Process Capability Analysis

CHAPTER OUTLINE

SYMBOLS

μ	Process mean	$\overline{R}$	Average of sample ranges
σ	Process standard deviation	$\overline{s}$	Average of sample standard deviations
$\sigma_{\overline{X}}$	Standard deviation of sample mean	g	Number of subgroups
$\overline{X}$	Sample mean	$\overline{\overline{X}}$	Average of sample averages
R	Sample range	σ_Y	Standard deviation of characteristic Y
s	Sample standard deviation	μ_Y	Mean of characteristic Y
m	Target value of characteristic	γ	Probability level associated with a statistical tolerance interval
k	Scaled distance of process mean from target value	$1-\alpha$	Proportion of the population distribution contained within the statistical tolerance interval
Z	Standard normal value		
X_i	Individual (ith) observation		
n	Sample size		
F_i	Probability plotting position of ith ranked observation		

8-1 INTRODUCTION

Chapters 5, 6, and 7 discussed various methods of keeping a process in control using control charts. Although there was some discussion of whether a product or service met the specifications required by the customer, this chapter analyzes the issue in detail. This chapter also defines measures that indicate the ability of the process to meet specifications; these are, in some sense, measures of process performance. This chapter also deals with the means of determining tolerances on assemblies when those of individual components are known, and vice versa. It is important to remember that process capability analysis should be conducted only when the process is in a state of statistical control.

8-2 SPECIFICATION LIMITS AND CONTROL LIMITS

Specification limits and *tolerance limits* are often used interchangeably and are defined by the *ANSI/ASQC Standard A1* (1987) as follows:

> Limits that define the conformance boundaries for an individual unit of a manufacturing or service operation.*

The standard suggests that tolerance limits are generally preferred in evaluating the manufacturing or service requirements, whereas specification limits are more appropriate for categorizing materials, products, or services in terms of their stated requirements.

For example, one specification for a building crane could be a hoist load of 5000 ± 300 kg. To satisfy this criterion, the diameter of the steel cable may have to be 4 ± 0.2 cm. This manufacturing requirement for the cable diameter may also be viewed as a tolerance. In general, tolerances are a subset of specifications. Usually, tolerances pertain to physical requirements (such as length, diameter, thickness, etc.), whereas specifications pertain to all requirements.

Tolerance limits may be two-sided (with upper and lower limits) or one-sided with either upper or lower limits. A *lower tolerance limit* defines the lower conformance boundary for an individual unit of a manufacturing or service operation; an *upper tolerance limit* applies to the upper conformance boundary. For example, a hub diameter requirement of 4 ± 0.1 mm is a two-sided tolerance limit. A cable tensile strength requirement of $(500 - 20)$ kg is a one-sided limit for which the lower tolerance limit is 480 kg.

Specification limits are determined by the needs of the customer. What the customer wants in the product or service is analyzed by means of market research and is incorporated through product or service design. These limits are placed on a product characteristic by designers and engineers for an individual unit in order to ensure adequate functioning of the product. This text uses the terms *specification limits* and *tolerance limits* interchangeably because the *ANSI/ASQC Standard A1* (1987) makes no distinction between them.

* ASQC (1987), ANSI/ASQC Standard A1: *Definitions, Symbols, Formulas, Tables for Control Charts.* Reprinted with the permission of ASQC.

Control limits, on the other hand, as discussed in previous chapters, help identify the variation that exists between subgroups, or samples, of measurements. They do not apply to individual units except in the case of control charts for individual measurements. Control limits reflect the variability of the process and may have no relationship to specification limits, which are chosen to meet customer needs for the product or service.

To further clarify the difference between specification limits and control limits, consider a situation in which the process is in control but the product does not meet specifications, as well as a situation in which a process is out of control but the product still meets specifications. Assume that the distribution of the quality characteristic X is normal. Consider a chart for the mean $\overline{X}$ and range R, from which the process is found to be in control. Figure 8-1*a* shows the $\overline{X}$-chart control limits, which are three standard deviations of the sample mean ($3\sigma_{\overline{X}}$) from the process average. From the Central Limit Theorem, we know that the standard deviation of the individual items, σ, is related to the standard deviation of the sample mean by $\sigma_{\overline{X}} = \sigma/\sqrt{n}$, where n is the sample size. Thus, $\sigma = \sqrt{n}\,\sigma_{\overline{X}}$; Figure 8-1*b* shows the distribution of X, assuming a normal distribution of individual items. This figure indicates the expected degree of variation in the quality characteristic of the individual items if the process is in control. The process spread (that is, the deviation expected between the maximum and minimum values of the characteristic, assuming normality) is 6σ. The normality assumption implies that about 99.74 percent of the distribution of the individual items will lie in a range of $\pm 3\sigma$ about the mean, a value which we assume to constitute practically all items produced by the process. If we superimpose the upper and lower specification limits (USL and LSL) on Figure 8-1*b*, we may see that some of the individual items lie outside the specifications. The control limits influence the process spread but are unrelated to the specification limits. This is an example of a situation in which the process is in control but some of the product does not meet specifications.

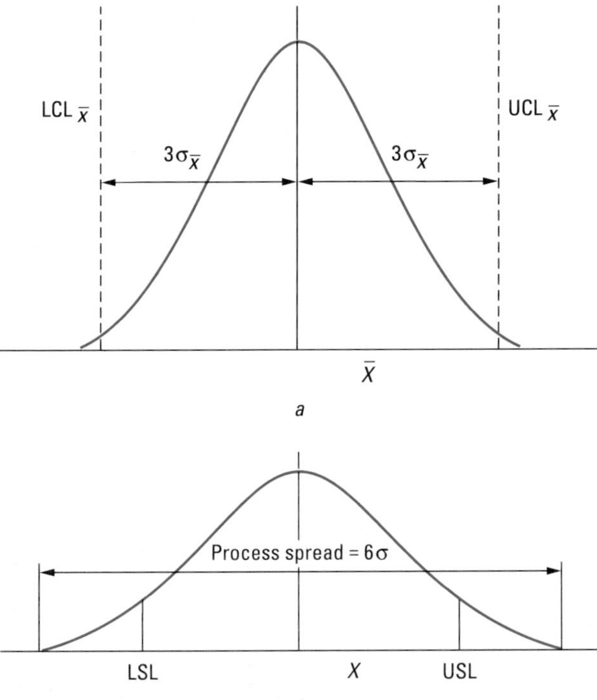

Figure 8-1 Distinction between (*a*) control limits, and (*b*) specification limits.

In keeping with this conceptual difference between control limits and specification limits, the latter should not be superimposed on control charts for the average $\overline{X}$. Remember that the control limits on an $\overline{X}$-chart are a measure of variability of the sample means. Specification limits represent the desired bound of variability for individual items.

It is now easy to envision a situation in which a process is out of control but still produces items that are within specifications. Refer again to Figure 8-1, and suppose that some points on the $\overline{X}$-chart are out of control. Recall that $\sigma = \sqrt{n}\,\sigma_{\overline{X}}$, so if $\sigma_{\overline{X}}$ increases relative to when the process was in control, σ will increase as well. Thus, the variability of the distribution of the individual items (Figure 8-1b) will also increase, meaning that the process spread will increase. Suppose, however, that the customer needs become less stringent, implying a relaxation of the specification limits. If the modified specification limits are outside the bounds indicating the process spread, the items produced will still be acceptable.

8-3 PROCESS CAPABILITY ANALYSIS

The determination of the capability of a process should begin only after the process has been brought to a state of statistical control. A process is said to be in statistical control when the only source of variation in the system is a result of chance causes. Details as to how this state may be achieved are discussed in Chapters 5, 6, and 7. Identification of assignable causes is a first step toward achievement of this objective. Taking corrective action to eliminate the assignable causes is the next step.

Process Capability

Process capability represents the performance of a process which is in a state of statistical control. Process capability is determined by the total variability that exists as a result of all chance causes present in the system. Note that chance causes are inherent to a system—they always exist. Thus, process capability can also be viewed as the variation in the product quality characteristic that can be attained upon removal of all assignable causes once a process is in statistical control. The product's performance is predictable because the assignable causes have been eliminated. This allows us to make projections as to the ability of the product to meet customer expectations.

Process capability is in some sense a measure of the uniformity of a process that makes a product whose quality characteristic of interest varies over a small range. Thus, it reflects an index of the uniformity of the output. A common measure of process capability is given by 6σ, which is also called the process spread. It is assumed that the distance of 6σ will encompass virtually all of the values of the output quality characteristic. If a normal distribution for the output quality characteristic can be assumed, 99.74 percent of the distribution will lie within the bounds of $\pm 3\sigma$ on either side of the mean. Thus, 6σ represents a reasonable value of the difference between the maximum and minimum sample values of the characteristic that one might observe.

Process Capability Analysis Process capability analysis represents a procedure to estimate the process capability. It may involve estimating the process mean and standard deviation of the quality characteristic. Additionally, the form of the relative frequency distribution of the characteristic of interest may be estimated. If specification limits are known, a process capability analysis might involve estimating the proportion of nonconforming product.

Frequently, a process capability study involves observing a quality characteristic of the product itself. For example, the mean and standard deviation of the bore size of a component may be found to be 12 cm and 0.1 cm, respectively. Since this information usually pertains to the product rather than the process, this analysis should strictly speaking be called a *product analysis* study. A true process capability study in this context would involve collecting and analyzing data that relates to process parameters. These process parameters could be, say, the depth of cut, the type of tool used, the tool material, the type of jigs or fixtures, the rate of feed of the tool, and so on. The objective is to know the relationship between the process parameters (or process settings) and the product characteristics. Any problems with product characteristics can then be related to process parameters, and remedial actions can be identified on a timely basis.

Benefits of Process Capability Analysis An ongoing quality improvement program requires continual estimation of the process parameters. Monitoring these parameters will ensure the best performance that the process is capable of achieving. If the process is not inherently capable (that is, not all of the individual units produced meet specifications), then actions should be taken to rectify the situation. These may include centering the process average on the nominal value, determining the feasibility of reducing the process spread by buying new equipment, or procuring higher-quality raw materials. Analyzing the flexibility of changing the specifications by identifying customer needs is also a possibility. Some of the benefits of process capability analysis are discussed below.

1. It creates uniformity of output. By conducting process capability studies and making necessary adjustments in the process parameters, the variability is closely controlled. Any undesirable shape in the distribution of the quality characteristic should be evaluated, and any feasible changes in the process parameters should be made.

2. The level of quality is maintained or improved. This is consistent with the goal of quality improvement in an ongoing cycle. Process capability analysis indicates whether new equipment is necessary. As these changes are added to the system, the new capability can be determined.

3. It facilitates product and process design. Information obtained from process capability analysis provides vital feedback from manufacturing to design. This is essential for a realistic design because product designers must be aware of the kind of variation that is inherent in the system. Designing tolerances in the product that the process is not capable of achieving will create a longer lead time in coming up with an efficient and achievable design.

4. It assists in vendor selection and control. Companies can require their suppliers to report process capability information, which will provide some guidance in choosing vendors. Moreover, for those vendors who have already been selected, regular reporting of process capability information serves as a means of controlling and improving quality at the vendor's premises.

5. It reduces the total cost by lowering the internal and external failure costs. By constantly keeping an eye on the process parameters, fewer nonconforming items are produced.

8-4 NATURAL TOLERANCE LIMITS

Natural tolerance limits are also known as *process capability limits* and are established or influenced by the process itself. They represent the inherent variation in the quality characteristic of the individual items output by a process in control. They are estimated based on the population of values or, more typically, from large representative samples.

The *upper natural tolerance limit* (UNTL), or the *upper process capability limit* (UPCL), assuming a normal distribution of the quality characteristic X, is three standard deviations above the process mean; the *lower natural tolerance limit* (LNTL), or the *lower process capability limit* (LPCL), is three standard deviations below the process mean. Thus, we have

$$\begin{aligned} \text{UNTL} &= \mu + 3\sigma \\ \text{LNTL} &= \mu - 3\sigma \end{aligned} \tag{8.1}$$

where μ represents the process mean and σ represents the process standard deviation, which is the standard deviation of the individual items.

Figure 8-2 shows the upper and lower natural tolerance limits, or process capability limits. The assumption of a normal distribution of the characteristic X implies that nearly all (approximately 99.74 percent) of the items produced will have a value of the characteristic that is within the bounds of the natural tolerance limits. Thus, for all practical purposes, these limits indicate the degree of inherent variation that exists in the process. If the distribution were non-normal, one would first determine whether it conforms to any well-known distribution. Chapter 3 discusses some common distributions. Using the theory of the type of distribution that models the characteristic, the natural tolerance limits would be found such that nearly the entire distribution is contained within those limits. The population values for the process mean μ and standard deviation σ as needed in Equation 8.1 are usually estimated from samples. Hence, the sample mean $\bar{X}$ and the sample standard deviation s are often used in obtaining the natural tolerance limits.

Example 8-1: The diameter of a part has to fit an assembly. The specifications for the diameter are 5 ± 0.015 cm. Information from samples taken from the process in control yielded a sample mean $\bar{X}$ of 4.99 cm and a sample standard deviation s of 0.004 cm. Find the natural tolerance limits of the process. Would you consider adjusting the process center?

Solution. The upper and lower natural tolerance limits based on the sample estimates are found using Equation 8.1:

$$\begin{aligned} \text{UNTL} &= 4.99 + 3(0.004) = 5.002 \\ \text{LNTL} &= 4.99 - 3(0.004) = 4.978 \end{aligned}$$

Assuming a normal distribution of diameters, Figure 8-3 shows these natural tolerance limits. Note that the process spread is $6(0.004) = 0.024$, which is the difference between the natural tolerance limits. For the current process we would expect the diameters to lie between 5.002 and 4.978 cm. The specification limits are also visible in

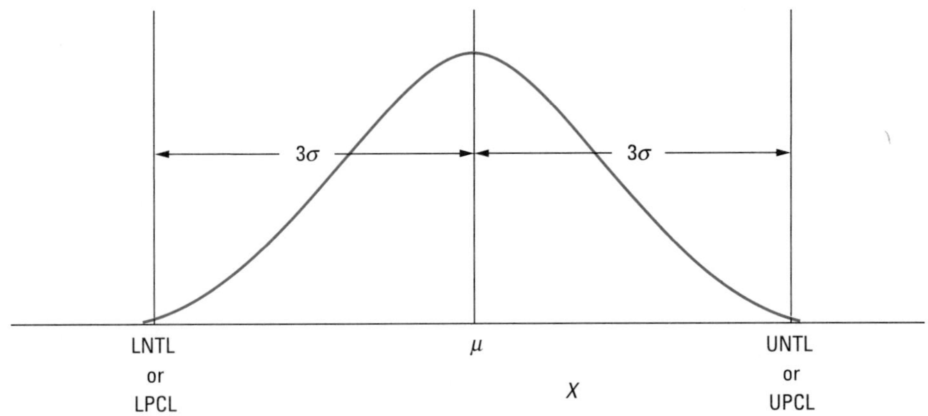

Figure 8-2 Natural tolerance limits.

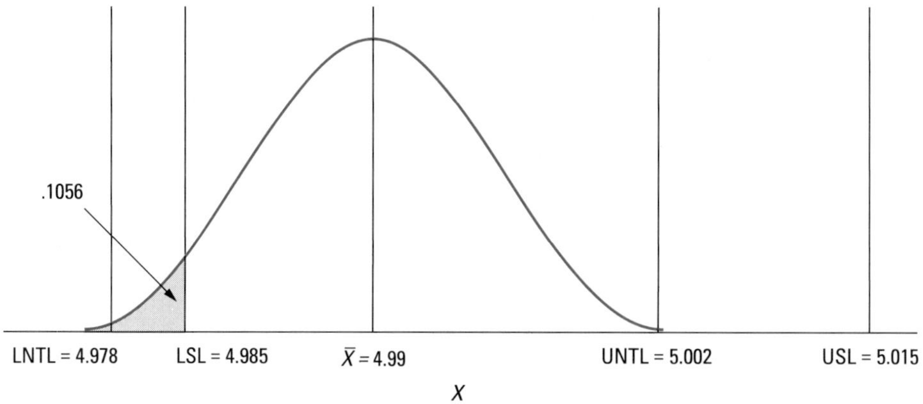

Figure 8-3 Natural tolerance limits and specification limits for part diameter.

Figure 8-3. The difference between the specification limits is 0.03 cm. If the process were left in its original state, some proportion of the parts would fall below the lower specification limit of 4.985. To calculate this proportion, the standardized normal value at the LSL must first be found as follows:

$$Z = (\text{LSL} - \overline{X})/s = (4.985 - 4.99)/0.004 = -1.25$$

This Z-value may be found in Appendix A-3, the cumulative standard normal distribution; the proportion below the LSL is 0.1056. Thus, it would be desirable to adjust the process center to the nominal value of 5 cm. If this is done, since the process spread is 0.024 cm and the difference between the specification limits is 0.03 cm, virtually all of the parts would fall between the specification limits, and we would have a capable process.

Statistical Tolerance Limits

Statistical tolerance limits as defined in *ANSI/ASQC Standard A1* (1987) are the limits of an interval for which it can be stated (with a given level of confidence γ) that the interval contains at least a specified proportion $(1 - \alpha)$ of the population.

These limits are found based on information from a sample. Sample estimates are used to infer population parameters; the limits are influenced by the sample size. As the sample size becomes large, the statistical tolerance limits approach the values found by using the population parameters.

An example of statistical tolerance limits could be as follows. With a probability (or level of confidence) of 0.98, we conclude that 95 percent of the parts have a part length between 30 and 35 mm, based on samples of size 10 used to obtain the sample mean and standard deviation. Estimation of statistical tolerance limits will be disussed further in Section 8-9. Estimation of these limits will be based on a normal distribution as well as on some nonparametric methods.

 8-5 RELATIONSHIP BETWEEN SPECIFICATIONS AND PROCESS CAPABILITY

Technically, there might not be any mathematical relationship between the process capability limits (or the natural tolerance limits) and the specification limits. The former are determined by the condition of the process and its inherent variability; the latter are influenced by the needs of the customer. There is, however, a desired relationship between these two sets of limits. The specification limits are preferably outside the natural tolerance limits, in which case most of the units produced will be acceptable. There are three cases that may arise regarding the relationship between specification limits and the process capability (or natural tolerance) limits. These are discussed below, assuming a normal distribution of the characteristic.

Case I—Process Spread Less Than the Difference Between Specification Limits

If the process spread is less than the difference between the specification limits, the process is quite capable. The spread between the specifications (USL−LSL) exceeds the spread between the natural tolerance limits (UNTL−LNTL). This case, shown in Figure 8-4*a*, represents the preferred situation. If the process mean μ is at the nominal value, assumed to be midway between the specification limits, all items produced are well within specifications. In fact, there is some flexibility for the process to go out of control and still produce items that are within specifications. For instance, the process mean could shift to μ_1 (see Figure 8-4*b*), or the process standard deviation could increase to σ_1 (see Figure 8-4*c*), but the items

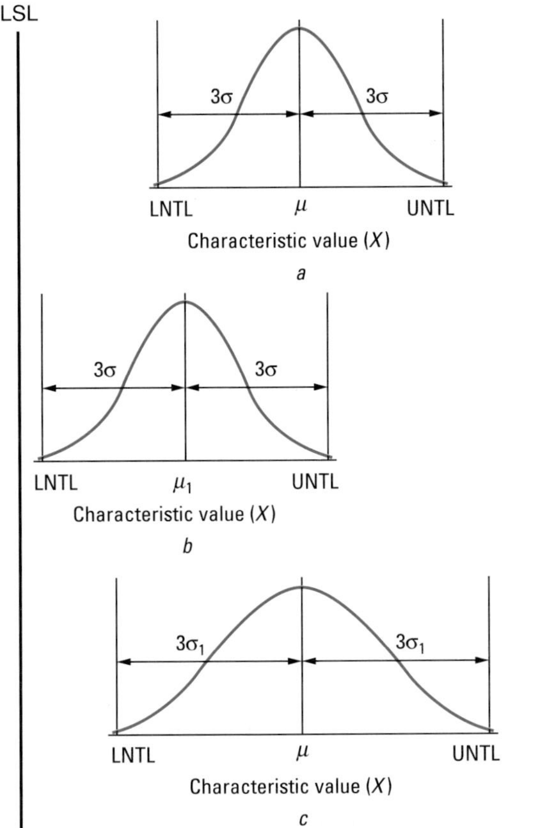

Figure 8-4 Process spread less than the difference between specification limits. (*a*) Process mean and standard deviation at nominal value; (*b*) Process mean shifted to μ_1 (process is still within specifications); (*c*) Process standard deviation shifted to σ_1 (process is still within specifications).

produced would still meet specifications. Of course, if a control chart is being kept, then any time an out-of-control signal is observed, action should be taken to bring the process back to control.

Case II—Process Spread Equal to the Difference Between Specification Limits

If the process spread is the same as the difference between the specification limits, the natural tolerance limits coincide with the specification limits. If the distribution of the characteristic can be assumed to be normal and the process is in control, virtually all (99.74 percent) of the items produced will be within specifications. Figure 8-5a shows this situation. If such a process goes out of control (for example, the process mean shifts from μ to μ_1), then a proportion of the product will be nonconforming (below the LSL). An increase in the standard deviation could result in a proportion of the product being nonconforming.

Case III—Process Spread Greater than the Difference Between Specification Limits

An undesirable situation exists when the process spread is greater than the difference between the specification limits. The inherent variability in the process exceeds the difference between the specification limits even though the process is in control. Figure 8-6 depicts this situation, for which some proportion of the items produced will not meet specifications. If there is a shift in the mean or an increase in the standard deviation, an increasing proportion of the product will not meet specifications. Such a process is not capable. There are several corrective approaches.

First, the possibility of increasing the specification limits may be explored. Careful consideration must be given to meeting the needs of the customer, for these needs are what determines the specification limits. Second, measures to reduce the process spread can be investigated. Investing in new equipment, better raw material, or experienced operators are some means of achieving this reduction. The

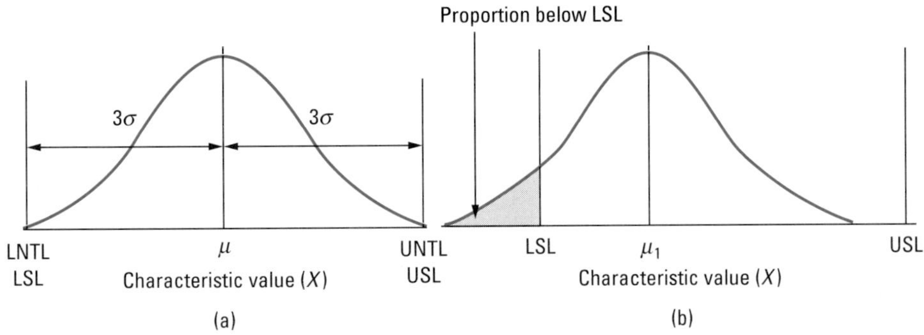

Figure 8-5 Process spread equal to the difference between specification limits.

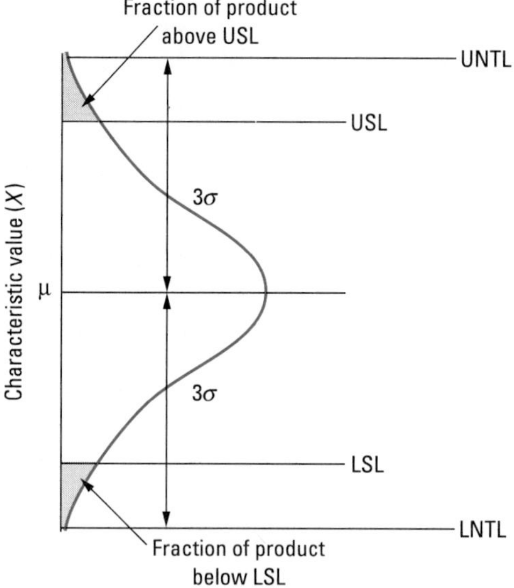

Figure 8-6 Process spread greater than the difference between specification limits.

financial aspects of the investment decision are usually dealt with prior to implementing these measures. Third, if it is not economically feasible to reduce the process variability through large capital investments, an alternative may be to shift the process average to achieve a desirable balance in the proportion of scrap and rework. The cost of scrap per unit is usually more than that of rework; producing less scrap and more rework is thus a feasible short-term plan. Of course, in the long run a company must strive for no scrap or rework. A fourth solution is to leave the process unchanged and perform 100-percent inspection to eliminate the nonconforming parts. This is not an ideal solution, since 100-percent inspection may not get rid of all nonconforming items. Furthermore, 100-percent inspection is merely a sorting mechanism. It does not get to the root of the problem; it cannot be used to analyze causes or determine corrective measures. The best approach is to do things right the first time and reduce reliance on inspection. The process must be monitored to yield acceptable product.

8-6 PROCESS CAPABILITY INDICES

It is sensible to estimate the ability of a process to meet specification limits only when it is in a state of statistical control. In that state, the process has no assignable causes, so the exhibited process variability is a reflection of what the process can achieve. A process should first be analyzed to verify that it is in control before its capability is estimated. An assumption made in this section is that the process output (that is, the distribution of the quality characteristic under consideration) is normal. This will enable us to estimate the proportion of nonconforming product. The assumption of normality can be validated by means of empirical plots of histograms, normal probability plots, or statistical tests for goodness of fit, such as chi-squared tests or the Kolmogorov–Smirnov test (Cochran, 1952; Duncan, 1986; Mage, 1982; Massey, 1951; Nelson, 1979; Shapiro, 1980).

One of the advantages of the process capability index is that it provides an easily understood aggregate measure of the goodness of the process performance. The ability to meet specifications is the criterion used for measuring the attractiveness of the process. The capability indices described below are nondimensional, which makes them more versatile and appealing because they do not depend on the specific process parameter units (Kane, 1986). The indices incorporate the location and/or the variation of the process.

Process Capability Ratio or the C_p Index

One of the common measures of describing the potential of a process to meet specifications is the process capability ratio (PCR), or the C_p index. It relates the process spread (the difference between the natural tolerance limits) to the spread between the specification limits, assuming two-sided specification limits. It is given by

$$\text{PCR or } C_p = \frac{\text{USL} - \text{LSL}}{6\sigma} \tag{8.2}$$

where USL and LSL represent the upper and lower specification limits, respectively, and σ represents the process standard deviation. When σ is unknown, it is replaced by its estimate, $\hat{\sigma}$. The sample standard deviation s is one estimate of σ. Another estimate of σ may be obtained from the control chart information for the range chart when the process is in control. It is given by $\hat{\sigma} = \overline{R}/d_2$, where $\overline{R}$ is the mean of the ranges and d_2 is a factor for constructing the control chart (obtained from Appendix A-7). If a chart for the standard deviation s is constructed, $\hat{\sigma}$ may be obtained as $\hat{\sigma} = \bar{s}/c_4$, where $\bar{s}$ is the mean of the sample standard deviations and c_4 is a factor for constructing control charts (tabulated in Appendix A-7).

A process that is centered between the specifications limits will produce a minimum proportion of items that fall outside those limits. Figure 8-7 shows the case of a centered process that is quite capable ($C_p > 1$) of meeting specifications, assuming nor-

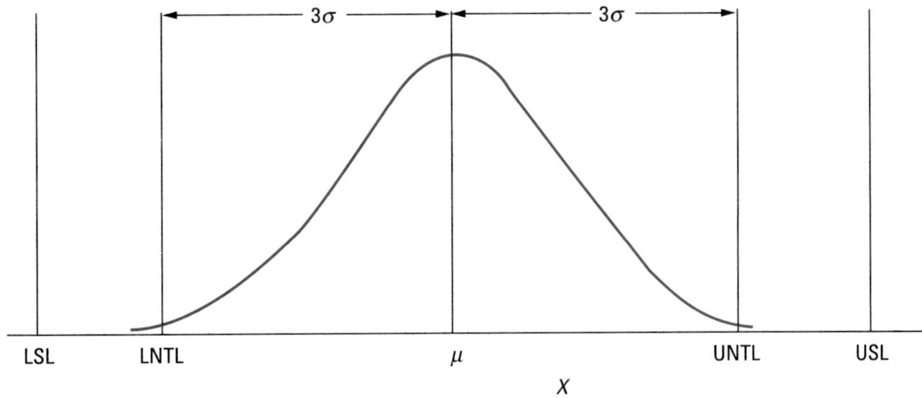

Figure 8-7 A capable process with $C_p > 1$.

mality. Note that it is desirable to have $C_p \geq 1$. When $C_p = 1$, the process spread equals the spread between the specifications, and the process is said to be barely capable. If the process is centered, then—assuming the characteristic is normally distributed—only 0.26 percent of the parts will fall outside the specification limits. Such a case was demonstrated in Case II of the previous section. Figure 8-5 shows that when $C_p = 1$, the natural tolerance limits coincide with the specification limits. The C_p value is an index that represents the process potential. If the process is not centered, it is possible that even for a process with $C_p > 1$, some proportion of the product will be nonconforming. If $C_p < 1$, it implies that the inherent variability in the process, as measured by the process spread 6σ, is greater than the difference between the specification limits. For this situation, it is possible for a process to be in control and still not meet specifications, as described in Case III of the previous section and shown in Figure 8-6. However, if $C_p > 1$, as shown in Figure 8-7, there is some flexibility in that the process could go out of control but the product might still be conforming. Equation 8.2 shows that C_p is the ratio of the allowable process spread to the actual process spread. If the allowable process spread exceeds the actual, the value of C_p is greater than 1.

Upper and Lower Capability Index

Suppose only a single specification limit is given. Indices may be derived that measure shifts in the process mean μ relative to the process spread. Note that the index C_p does not incorporate the location of the process mean μ. For a given upper specification limit, the upper capability index (CPU, or C_p upper) is given by

$$\text{CPU} = \frac{\text{USL} - \mu}{3\sigma} \tag{8.3}$$

It is desirable to have CPU $\geq$ 1. Observe that the denominator of Equation 8.3 is half the process spread. Because nonconformance occurs only if the quality characteristic value exceeds the USL, the more the USL is above the process mean μ, the less the chance for any nonconforming product. Figure 8-8 shows the case for which CPU $>$ 1. Assuming normality, if

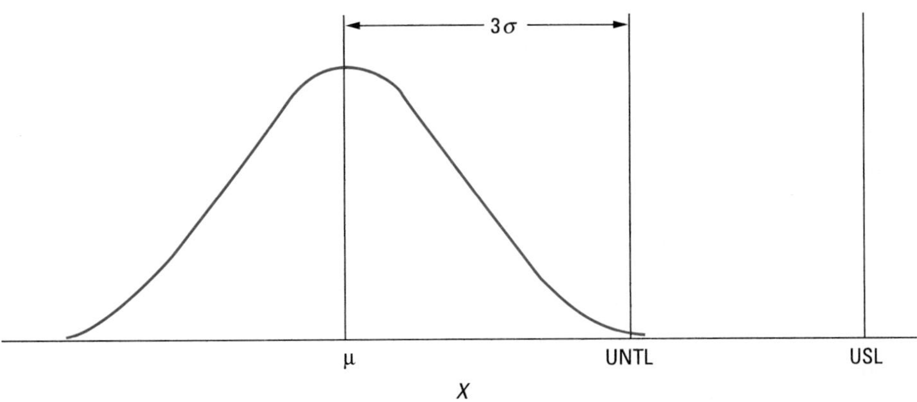

Figure 8-8 A capable process with CPU $>$ 1.

CPU = 1, only 0.13 percent of the product will be above the USL and thus nonconforming.

Similarly, if only the lower specification limit is given, the lower capability index (CPL, or C_p lower) is given by

$$\text{CPL} = \frac{\mu - \text{LSL}}{3\sigma} \tag{8.4}$$

Along the same lines, it is desirable to have CPL $\geq$ 1. For Equations 8.3 and 8.4, if the process parameters μ and σ are unknown, the sample mean $\overline{X}$ and the sample standard deviation s, respectively, are used as estimates. CPU is the ratio of the allowable upper spread to the actual upper spread (3σ), and CPL is the ratio of the allowable lower spread to the actual lower spread.

The indices C_p, CPU, and CPL are useful in evaluating the process performance relative to the specification limits. They also aid in determining process parameter settings (such as the process mean μ) or process parameter requirements (such as the process standard deviation σ). Some recommended guidelines for values of the process capability ratio for one-sided and two-sided specifications are shown in Table 8-1. The implication of having a C_p of at least 1.33 for an existing process with two-sided specifications is that the process standard deviation σ will be no more than one-eighth of the difference between the specification limits. Many companies prefer $C_p \geq 1.33$. This ensures an extremely low (0.007 percent) nonconformance rate. Furthermore, a C_p value of at least 1.67 implies a process standard deviation of no more than one-tenth of the spread between the specification limits.

Example 8-2: The relative humidity in a greenhouse is expected to be between 65 and 85 percent. Random samples taken over a span of one week yielded the following values: 60, 78, 70, 84, 81, 80, 85, 60, 88, 75. Find and interpret the process capability ratio.

Solution. The specification limits are LSL = 65 percent and USL = 85 percent. Assume that the process is in control. Using the sample of observations, the sample standard deviation s is

$$s = \sqrt{\frac{\sum(X_i - \overline{X})^2}{n-1}}.$$

The sample mean $\overline{X}$ is first found as

$$\begin{aligned}\overline{X} = \frac{\sum X_i}{n} &= (60 + 78 + 70 + 84 + 81 \\ &\quad + 80 + 85 + 60 + 88 + 75)/10 \\ &= 76.1\end{aligned}$$

The sample standard deviation s is

$$\begin{aligned}s &= [\{(60 - 76.1)^2 + (78 - 76.1)^2 + (70 - 76.1)^2 \\ &\quad + (84 - 76.1)^2 + (81 - 76.1)^2 + (80 - 76.1)^2 \\ &\quad + (85 - 76.1)^2 + (60 - 76.1)^2 \\ &\quad + (88 - 76.1)^2 + (75 - 76.1)^2\}/9]^{1/2} \\ &= 9.905\end{aligned}$$

The process capability ratio, or the C_p index, is

$$C_p = \frac{\text{USL} - \text{LSL}}{6s} = \frac{85 - 65}{6(9.905)} = 0.337$$

This value of C_p, which is less than 1, indicates that the process is not capable of meeting the specifications. The inherent variability in the process as measured by the process spread exceeds the difference between the specification limits. Actions that will reduce the process variability must be identified.

Suppose that the only required specification is the lower specification limit of 65 percent. Let us find the lower capability index. Using Equation 8.4 and replacing μ and σ by their estimates $\overline{X}$ and s, respectively, gives

$$\text{CPL} = \frac{\overline{X} - \text{LSL}}{3s} = \frac{76.1 - 65}{3(9.905)} = 0.374$$

The calculated value of CPL, which is less than 1, indicates an undesirable value. However, in this case, if the process variability cannot be reduced, another option would be to increase the process mean such that it is sufficiently above the LSL. This implies increasing the average humidity level significantly above the LSL of 65 percent.

To increase the value of CPL to 1, assuming that the process standard deviation cannot be reduced, the target value of the process mean should be

$$\mu = \text{LSL} + 3s = 6.5 + 3(9.905) = 94.715\%$$

TABLE 8-1 Recommended minimum values of the process capability ratio

Process	Two-sided specifications	One-sided specification
Existing process	1.33	1.25
New process	1.50	1.45
Safety, strength, or critical parameter—existing process	1.50	1.45
Safety, strength, or critical parameter—new process	1.67	1.60

Adapted from: D.C. Montgomery (1985), *Introduction to Statistical Quality Control*. Reprinted by permission of John Wiley & Sons, Inc.

The C_{pk} Index

We observed that one measure of process capability, the C_p index, does not incorporate the process location when calculating the ability of the process to meet specifications. It is quite evident that the process variability is not the only parameter that influences the ability of the process to produce a product that is conforming. The location of the process mean influences the degree to which the product is conforming (Gunter, 1989). A measure that accounts for this location is appropriate when the process mean is not at the nominal value, which is assumed to be halfway between the specification limits. The C_{pk} index is given by

$$C_{pk} = \min\left\{\frac{\text{USL} - \mu}{3\sigma}, \frac{\mu - \text{LSL}}{3\sigma}\right\}$$
$$= \min\{\text{CPK, CPL}\} \quad (8.5)$$

It can be seen from Equation 8.5 that C_{pk} represents the scaled distance, relative to three standard deviations (that is, half the process spread), between the process mean and the closest specification limit. Desirable values are $C_{pk} \geq 1$. Whereas the C_p index represents the process potential, the C_{pk} value represents the actual capability of the process with the existing parameter values.

Figure 8-9 shows the distribution of the quality characteristic X for a process that is not capable ($C_{pk} < 1$). Note that the process spread (6σ) is much less than the spread between the specifications. The value of C_p will be greater than 1, indicating that the process has a good chance of meeting specifications. However, the process mean μ is shifted to the right and is closer to the USL. The distance between USL and μ is less than 3σ, which is half of the process spread. Hence, some proportion of the product will lie above the USL. A corrective measure in this case could be to adjust the process mean downward to be near the midpoint m of the specification limits. Virtually all of the product will then be conforming.

If management assigns equal significance to a part being above the USL or below the LSL, the optimal setting for the process mean is midway between the specification limits. A measure of the deviation of the process mean from this target value m is given by the *scaled distance:*

$$k = \frac{|m - \mu|}{(\text{USL} - \text{LSL})/2} \quad (8.6)$$

where $m = (\text{USL} + \text{LSL})/2$. Note that the denominator of Equation 8.6 is half the allowable process spread. An estimate of k is obtained by using the sample mean $\overline{X}$ as an estimate of the process mean μ in Equation 8.6. The relationship between C_p and C_{pk} is given by

$$C_{pk} = C_p(1 - k) \quad (8.7)$$

If $\text{LSL} \leq \mu \leq \text{USL}$, we observe that $0 \leq k \leq 1$. If the process mean is at the nominal value m, then $k = 0$ and $C_{pk} = C_p$. If the process mean is at the USL or LSL, then $k = 1$ and $C_{pk} = 0$.

Let us compare the process capability indices C_p and C_{pk}. The C_p value is a measure of the process potential; it does not change as the process mean changes. It is desirable to have $C_p \geq 1$. A value of $C_p < 1$ indicates that the process is not capable. The C_{pk} value incorporates both the process mean and the standard deviation to form an index of actual process performance. It is desirable to have $C_{pk} \geq 1$. If the process is centered (that is, the process mean is equal to the nominal value), $C_{pk} = C_p$. A standard for benchmarking processes is a value of $C_{pk} = 1$, in which case practically all of the product is conforming. The value of C_{pk} is always less than or

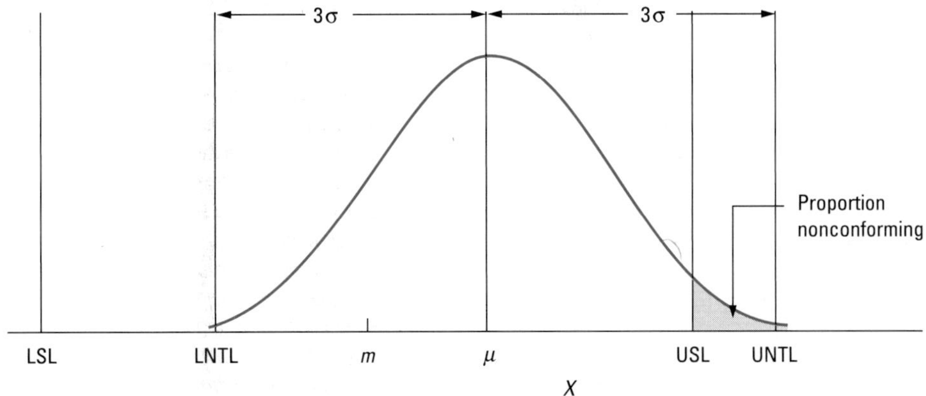

Figure 8-9 A process that is not capable ($C_{pk} < 1$).

equal to the value of C_p. When the process mean is outside the specifications, it results in a negative value of C_{pk}.

Example 8-3: In an electrical circuit, the capacitance of a component should be between 25 and 40 units. A sample of 25 components yielded a mean of 30 and a standard deviation of 3. Calculate the process capability index C_{pk}, and comment on the process performance. If the process is not capable, what is the proportion of nonconforming product, assuming a normal distribution of the characteristic?

Solution. The process capability index C_{pk} is

$$\begin{aligned} C_{pk} &= \min\left\{\frac{USL - \mu}{3\sigma}, \frac{\mu - LSL}{3\sigma}\right\} \\ &\simeq \min\left\{\frac{USL - \overline{X}}{3s}, \frac{\overline{X} - LSL}{3s}\right\} \\ &= \min\left\{\frac{40 - 30}{3(3)}, \frac{30 - 25}{3(3)}\right\} \\ &= \min\{1.111, 0.555\} = 0.555. \end{aligned}$$

The value of C_{pk} is less than one, so the process is not able to produce only conforming product at its current setting. Corrective actions would be to move the process mean toward the nominal value of 32.5 or, if feasible, to reduce the process variability.

Figure 8-10 shows the distribution of the characteristic relative to the specification limits. The standardized normal value (Z-value) at the LSL is

$$Z_A = (25 - 30)/3 = -5/3 = -1.67$$

The standardized value at the USL is

$$Z_B = (40 - 30)/3 = 3.33$$

After checking the standardized normal distribution from Appendix A-3, we find the area below the LSL to be 0.0475 and that above the USL to be $1 - 0.9995 = 0.0005$ (which is negligible). Thus, 4.75 percent of the product will lie below the LSL.

The process performance can be improved if the process mean is shifted to the nominal value of 32.5. In that case, the Z-value at the LSL would be $Z_A = (25 - 32.5)/3 = -2.50$, and that at the USL would be $Z_B = 2.50$. According to Appendix A-3, the proportion of the product below the LSL would be 0.0062, with the same proportion above the USL. The total proportion nonconforming would be 0.0124, or 1.24 percent.

8-7 PROCESS CAPABILITY ANALYSIS PROCEDURES

As explained previously in this chapter, process capability analysis may involve estimating process parameters as the mean and standard deviation, the form of the distribution of the characteristic, or the fraction of the product that is nonconforming when specifications are known. Several approaches exist for estimating the process standard deviation, some of which are described below.

Estimating Process Mean and Standard Deviation

The process mean provides a measure of the location of the process; the process standard deviation is a reflection of the variability of the process. An idea of the distribution of the quality characteristic can be obtained by constructing a frequency distribution. This empirical distribution can be used as

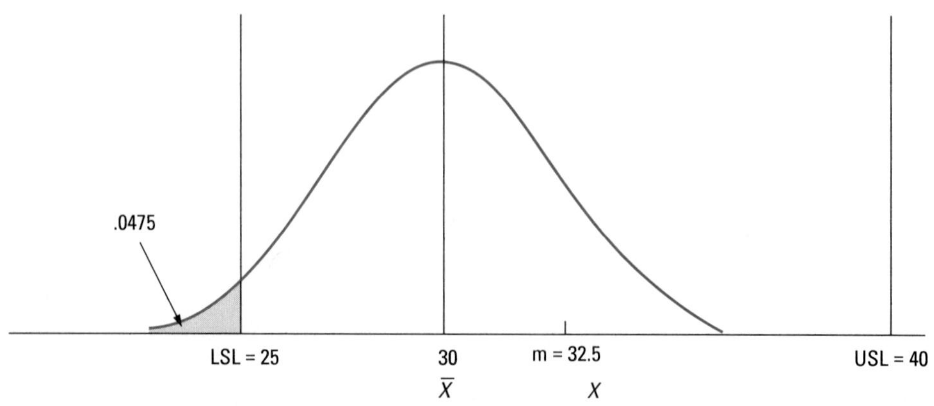

Figure 8-10 Calculation of C_{pk} and fraction nonconforming.

a basis for validating claims regarding the hypothesized distribution of the characteristic. First, process capability analysis using information from individual observations is discussed. The use of information from control chart analysis is then considered.

Using Individual Observations Before starting process capability analysis using individual observations, a minimum number of such measurements (usually, at least 50) must be taken. The process mean μ is estimated by the sample mean $\overline{X}$ as

$$\overline{X} = \frac{\sum_{i=1}^{n} X_i}{n} \tag{8.8}$$

where n represents the number of observations in the sample. The process standard deviation σ can be estimated by the sample standard deviation s using either of the following formulas:

$$s = \sqrt{\frac{\sum_{i=1}^{n}(X_i - \overline{X})^2}{n-1}}, \tag{8.9}$$

or

$$s = \sqrt{\frac{\sum_{i=1}^{n} X_i^2 - (\sum_{i=1}^{n} X_i)^2/n}{n-1}} \tag{8.10}$$

Next, a frequency or relative frequency histogram should be constructed for the quality characteristic. This will tell something more about the behavior of the characteristic. Procedures for the construction of histograms were discussed in Chapter 4. In many cases, the assumption of a normal distribution of the characteristic is made when calculating the proportion of nonconforming product; histograms can be used to determine the validity of this assumption. There are procedures for testing a hypothesis regarding a specified population distribution form (normal, for instance). These are known as goodness-of-fit tests and can be found in most books on statistics (Duncan, 1986). Prior to conducting statistical tests, a visual check for normality can be made. Calculating the skewness and kurtosis coefficients, as discussed in Chapter 3, and comparing the values with those of a normal distribution will establish the validity of the normality assumption.

If the distribution is close to normal, the process spread PS assuming normality is

$$\text{PS} = 6s \tag{8.11}$$

An estimate of the process capability limits, or the natural tolerance limits, is given by

$$\overline{X} \pm 3s \tag{8.12}$$

If the process is centered, a measure of the ability of the process can be obtained through the process capability ratio, or the C_p value, as discussed previously, where

$$C_p = \frac{(\text{USL} - \text{LSL})}{6s}$$

If the process is not centered, a better measure of the process capability index would be the C_{pk} ratio. Finally, if the distribution of the quality characteristic is assumed to be normal, it can be used to estimate the fraction nonconforming. If the assumption of normality cannot be supported, the frequency histogram can be used as a basis for choosing another distributional form.

Example 8-4: Consider the data for the inside diameter of metal sleeves, shown in Table 8-2. Figure 8-11 shows the frequency histogram of the sleeve diameters for a chosen set of class midpoints. Note that its appearance reasonably approximates a normal distribution. Statistical tests for determining normality could be used to substantiate this assumption.

The sample mean is

$$\begin{aligned}\overline{X} &= (50.04 + 50.03 + \cdots + 49.99 + 50.02)/100 \\ &= 49.998 \text{ mm}\end{aligned}$$

TABLE 8-2 Inside diameter of metal sleeves (in mm)

Sample number	Observations, X				
1	50.04	50.03	50.02	50.00	49.94
2	49.96	49.99	50.03	50.01	49.98
3	50.01	50.01	50.01	50.00	49.92
4	49.95	49.97	50.02	50.10	50.02
5	50.00	50.01	50.00	50.00	50.09
6	50.02	50.05	49.97	50.02	50.09
7	50.01	49.99	49.96	49.99	50.00
8	50.02	50.00	50.04	50.02	50.00
9	50.06	49.93	49.99	49.99	49.95
10	49.96	49.93	50.08	49.92	50.03
11	50.01	49.96	49.98	50.00	50.02
12	50.04	49.94	50.00	50.03	49.92
13	49.97	49.90	49.98	50.01	49.95
14	50.00	50.01	49.95	49.97	49.94
15	49.97	49.98	50.03	50.08	49.96
16	49.98	50.00	49.97	49.96	49.97
17	50.03	50.04	50.03	50.01	50.01
18	49.98	49.98	49.99	50.05	50.00
19	50.07	50.00	50.02	49.99	49.93
20	49.99	50.06	49.95	49.99	50.02

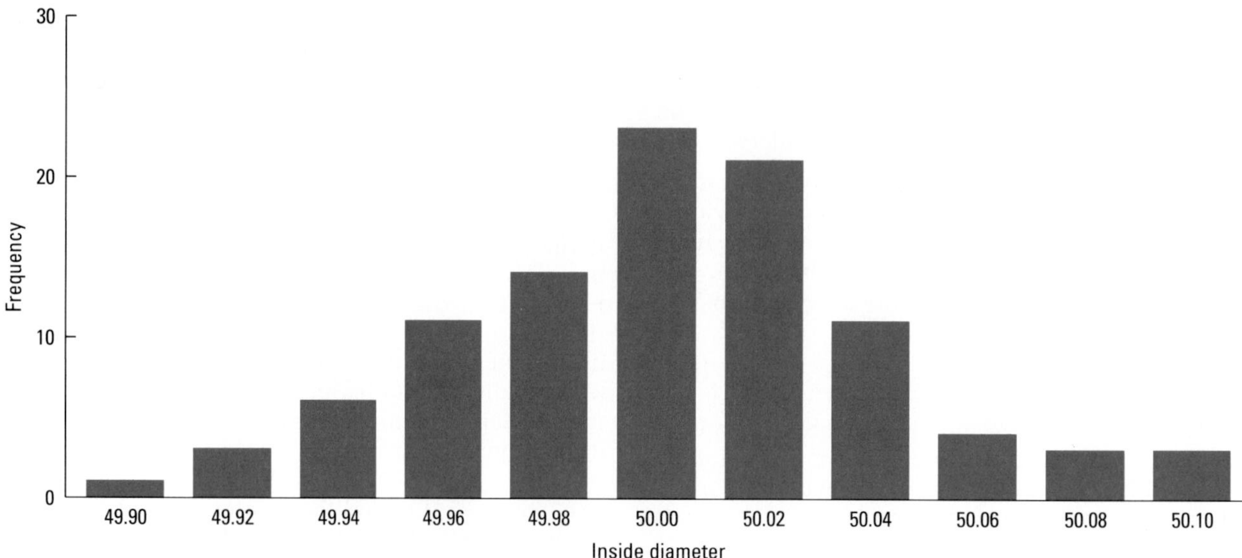

Figure 8-11 Frequency histogram of sleeve diameters.

The sample variance s^2 is

$$\begin{aligned} s^2 &= \{[(50.04)^2 + (50.03)^2 + \cdots \\ &\quad + (49.99)^2 + (50.02)^2] \\ &\quad - (50.04 + 50.03 + \cdots \\ &\quad + 50.02)^2/100\}/99 \\ &= 0.0016 \end{aligned}$$

The sample standard deviation is $s = \sqrt{0.0016} = 0.040$ mm, the process spread is $6s = 6(0.040) = 0.240$ mm, and the natural tolerance limits, or the process capability limits, are

$$\begin{aligned} \overline{X} \pm 3s &= 49.998 \pm 3(0.040) \\ &= 49.998 \pm 0.120 \\ &= (49.878, 50.118) \end{aligned}$$

Suppose that the specification limits for the inside diameter are 50.00 ± 0.5 mm. The process capability ratio, representing the process potential, is given by

$$C_p = \frac{\text{USL} - \text{LSL}}{6s} = \frac{50.5 - 49.5}{6(0.040)} = 4.167$$

This value indicates the process to be quite capable. The process capability index C_{pk}, which incorporates the location and spread of the process, is

$$\begin{aligned} C_{pk} &= \min\left\{\frac{50.5 - 49.998}{3(0.040)}, \frac{49.998 - 49.5}{3(0.040)}\right\} \\ &= \frac{0.498}{0.120} = 4.150 \end{aligned}$$

This value of C_{pk} is much greater than 1, indicating that virtually all of the product will be conforming.

Another method of estimating the distribution of the quality characteristic is to use *probability plotting*. The probability plotting method (in particular, normal probability plotting) was discussed in Chapter 4. The procedure for constructing probability plots in general is the same as that for normal probability plots. The basic idea is that the vertical scale, which represents the cumulative distribution function, is transformed such that a straight line is plotted for the chosen form of distribution. The horizontal axis represents the ordered values of the characteristic. Thus, in constructing normal probability plots on normal probability paper, the vertical axis has been transformed such that a normal distribution will plot as a straight line. Further discussion of probability plotting may be found in Michael (1983).

The procedure for probability plotting begins by ranking the observations in ascending order. Suppose the rank of the observations is denoted by $i = 1, 2, \ldots, n$, where n is the number of observations in the sample. The probability plotting position of the observation with rank i is then calculated as

$$F_i = \frac{(i - 0.5)}{n} \tag{8.13}$$

Next, on probability paper, each observation is plotted versus its probability plotting percentage ($100F_i$) along the ordinate. If the assumed distribution of the characteristic is appropriate, the points should plot along a straight line (Shapiro, 1980). The decision to reject some hypothesized distribution of the characteristic is of course subjective. However, the use of probability plots in conjunction with statistical goodness-of-fit tests should provide a reliable measure for making inferences regarding distributions.

In the area of quality control, many characteristics tend to be normally distributed, and the theory of some control charts is based on normality, so the normal probability plot is frequently constructed. Using the procedure described above, the plotting is done on normal probability paper (on which the vertical axis is scaled such that the plotted points fall along a straight line if the distribution is normal). Using normal theory, estimates of the process mean and the process standard deviation can be obtained.

The process mean is estimated by reading the value of the fiftieth percentile from the normal probability plot. In addition, a normal distribution has the property that the eighty-fourth percentile is one standard deviation away from the mean. Thus, an estimate of the process standard deviation is the difference between the eighty-fourth percentile and the fiftieth percentile. After obtaining estimates of the process mean and standard deviation, the process spread, process capability limits, and process capability indices (such as C_p and C_{pk}) may be found.

Example 8-5: Consider the example concerning the resistance of coils (Example 4-11) for a sample of size 50. The data are shown again in Table 8-3. We would like to test for normality and eventually find the process capability limits.

TABLE 8-3 Resistance of coils

Sample number	Resistance of coils	Sample number	Resistance of coils
1	35.1	26	27.5
2	35.4	27	26.5
3	36.3	28	26.9
4	38.8	29	26.7
5	39.0	30	27.2
6	22.5	31	31.8
7	23.7	32	32.1
8	25.0	33	31.5
9	25.3	34	31.2
10	25.0	35	31.4
11	34.7	36	28.5
12	34.2	37	28.4
13	34.4	38	27.6
14	34.7	39	27.6
15	34.3	40	28.2
16	26.4	41	30.8
17	25.5	42	30.6
18	25.8	43	30.4
19	26.4	44	30.5
20	25.6	45	30.5
21	33.1	46	28.5
22	33.6	47	30.2
23	32.3	48	30.1
24	32.6	49	30.0
25	32.2	50	28.9

Solution. After ranking the observations in ascending order, the probability plotting positions F_i are calculated using Equation 8.13. The ranked data and computed plotting positions are shown in Table 8-4. The normal probability plot is shown in Figure 8-12. The majority of the points are close to the fitted straight line shown in the figure. A few points on the extremes deviate from the line, but overall we may conclude that the observations seem to have come from a normal distribution.

After the assumption of normality is validated, the process mean may be estimated. The value of the fiftieth percentile from the fitted straight line in Figure 8-12 is approximately 30.0. The process standard deviation is estimated by taking the difference between the eighty-fourth and fiftieth percentiles. Using Figure 8-12, we may estimate the process standard deviation as

$$\hat{\sigma} = 33.625 - 30.0 = 3.625$$

The process spread is then estimated as

$$6\hat{\sigma} = 6(3.625) = 21.75$$

The natural tolerance limits, or the process capability limits, are

$$30.0 \pm 3(3.625) = 30.0 \pm 10.875 = (19.125, 40.875)$$

Suppose the specification limits for the resistance are 28 ± 10. The process capability index C_{pk} is given by

$$C_{pk} = \min\left\{\frac{38 - 30.0}{3(3.625)}, \frac{30.0 - 18}{3(3.625)}\right\}$$

$$= \frac{8}{10.875} = 0.736$$

The calculated value of C_{pk} is less than 1, which implies that some proportion of the product will not meet specifications. Assuming normality, let us now calculate the proportion of the product that will be nonconforming. Figure 8-13 shows the distribution of resistances. The standardized normal values at the specification limits are

$$Z_A = (38 - 30.0)/3.625 = 2.207 \simeq 2.21$$

$$Z_B = (18 - 30.0)/3.625 = -3.310 \simeq -3.31$$

According to the standard normal table in Appendix A-3, the area above the upper specification limit is $1-0.9864 = 0.0136$. The area below the lower specification limit is 0.0005. Thus, the total proportion nonconforming is 0.0141, or 1.41 percent.

Using Control Chart Information It has been emphasized that process capability analysis should be conducted only when the process is in a state

TABLE 8-4 Resistance of coils in rank order and corresponding plotting positions

Resistance	Rank, i	Probability plotting position, F_i	Resistance	Rank, i	Probability plotting position, F_i
22.5	1	0.01	30.4	26	0.51
23.7	2	0.03	30.5	27	0.53
25.0	3	0.05	30.5	28	0.55
25.0	4	0.07	30.6	29	0.57
25.3	5	0.09	30.8	30	0.59
25.5	6	0.11	31.2	31	0.61
25.6	7	0.13	31.4	32	0.63
25.8	8	0.15	31.5	33	0.65
26.4	9	0.17	31.8	34	0.67
26.5	10	0.19	32.1	35	0.69
26.7	11	0.21	32.2	36	0.71
26.8	12	0.23	32.3	37	0.73
26.9	13	0.25	32.6	38	0.75
27.2	14	0.27	33.1	39	0.77
27.5	15	0.29	33.6	40	0.79
27.6	16	0.31	34.2	41	0.81
27.6	17	0.33	34.3	42	0.83
28.2	18	0.35	34.4	43	0.85
28.4	19	0.37	34.7	44	0.87
28.5	20	0.39	34.7	45	0.89
28.5	21	0.41	35.1	46	0.91
28.9	22	0.43	35.4	47	0.93
30.0	23	0.45	36.3	48	0.95
30.1	24	0.47	38.8	49	0.97
30.2	25	0.49	39.0	50	0.99

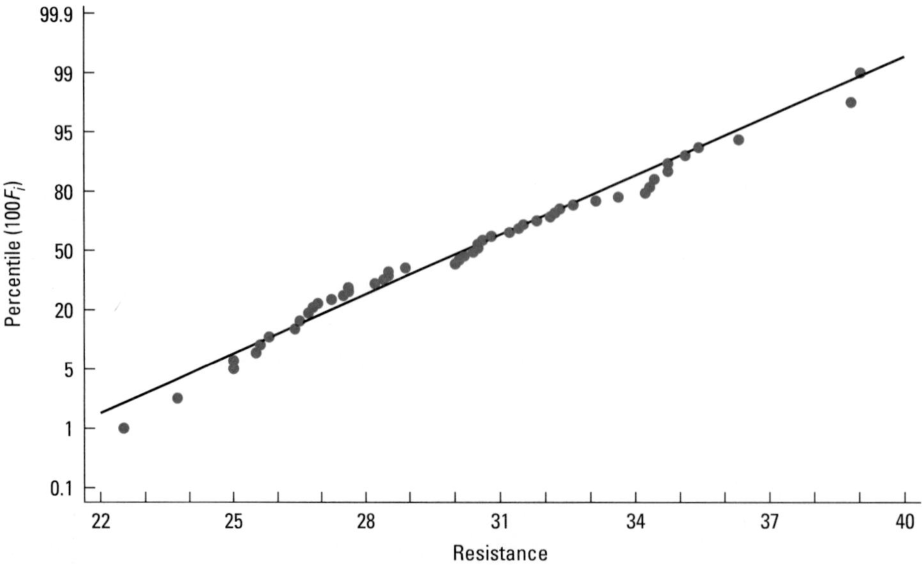

Figure 8-12 Normal probability plot of resistance of coils.

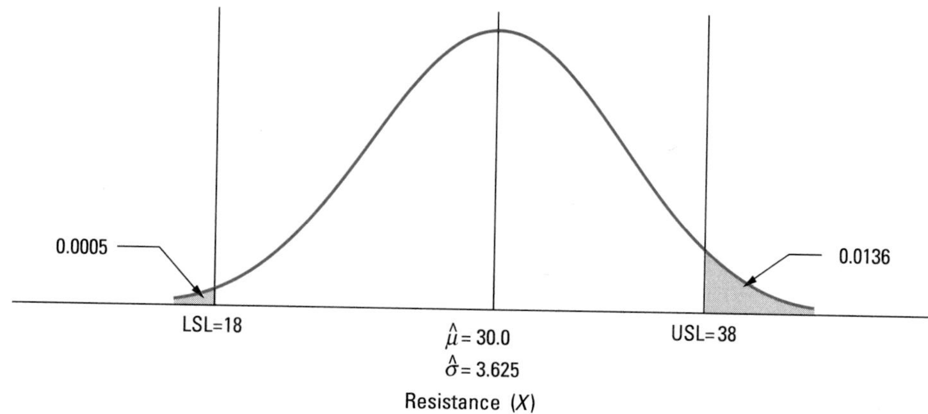

Figure 8-13 Proportion of coils that are nonconforming.

of statistical control. Control charts are the major tools for analyzing an existing process and bringing it to control, so it makes sense to use information from control charts in studying process control. An advantage that control charts have over individual observations is that individual observations do not tell us whether the process is in control. Analysis of a control chart will indicate whether assignable causes exist in the process, in which case we are not yet in a position to estimate the process capability.

Using Variable Charts Variable charts usually provide more information than attribute charts, so it is preferable to use them to estimate process capability whenever possible. If charts for the mean $\overline{X}$ and range R are used for a certain quality characteristic, once the process is in control, the process mean and standard deviation can be estimated as

$$\hat{\mu} = \overline{\overline{X}} \tag{8.14}$$

$$\hat{\sigma} = \frac{\overline{R}}{d_2} \tag{8.15}$$

where d_2 is a control chart factor tabulated in Appendix A-7, $\overline{\overline{X}}$ is the center line on the $\overline{X}$-chart, and $\overline{R}$ is the center line on the R-chart.

If control charts for the mean $\overline{X}$ and standard deviation s are used, then, for a process in control, the mean and standard deviation can be estimated from

$$\hat{\mu} = \overline{\overline{X}} \tag{8.16}$$

$$\hat{\sigma} = \frac{\overline{s}}{c_4} \tag{8.17}$$

where c_4 is a control chart factor tabulated in Appendix A-7, $\overline{\overline{X}}$ is the center line on the $\overline{X}$-chart, and $\overline{s}$ is the center line on the s-chart.

If control charts for individual values X and the moving range of two consecutive observations are used, once the process is in a state of statistical control, its mean and standard deviation can be estimated from

$$\hat{\mu} = \overline{X} \tag{8.18}$$

$$\hat{\sigma} = \frac{\overline{R}}{d_2} \tag{8.19}$$

where d_2 is a control chart factor tabulated in Appendix A-7 and is found using a subgroup size of 2, $\overline{X}$ is the center line on the X-chart, and $\overline{R}$ is the average of the moving ranges found from pairs of consecutive observations.

Using Attribute Charts Attribute charts are constructed based on some selected specifications. If the acceptable bounds for quality characteristics are known, the chart for the fraction nonconforming (p-chart) can be constructed to classify the product as conforming or not. The same holds true for the chart for the number nonconforming (np-chart). Similarly, the control chart for the number of nonconformities (c-chart) can be developed if the definition of a nonconformity (that is, a quality characteristic that does not meet certain specifications is known). The same also applies to a chart for the number of nonconformities per unit (u-chart) or the number of demerits per unit (U-chart).

For a p-chart, a measure of process capability is the center line $\overline{p}$, which represents the average fraction of nonconforming items produced by the process. Likewise, for an np-chart, a measure of process capability is the center line $n\overline{p}$, the average number of nonconforming items. A capability measure from the c-chart is $\overline{c}$, the average number of nonconformities, from the u-chart is $\overline{u}$, the average number of nonconformities per unit, and from the U-chart is $\overline{U}$, the average number of demerits per unit. All of these measures are estimates of the overall process capability. The upper control limits on each of these charts represent, to some extent, an upper bound on the nonconforming items or nonconformities, as the case may be. This is a measure of the "worst quality" that can be expected from the process.

Although the center lines of the attribute charts provide an aggregate measure of process capability, the information from attribute charts does not indicate the degree of nonconformance of the items. In other words, were the products barely outside the specifications, or were they far outside? Was the process mean off the target value of the quality characteristic, leading to nonconformities, or was the process variability too high? This information, which would help formulate actions to reduce nonconformities, is not available from attribute charts. This is one of the drawbacks of attribute charts. Variable charts, on the other hand, can provide measures of the process mean and standard deviation related to the quality characteristics in question and also present some possible reasons for the product nonconformance, which would lead to the identification of possible corrective actions.

Example 8-6: Consider Example 6-1 dealing with the resistance of coils. Samples of size 5 were randomly selected. The original data for 25 samples is shown in Table 8-5. Suppose the specifications for the resistance are 20 ± 4 ohms. Calculate the process capability index C_{pk}, and comment on its value. Assuming a normal distribution of the resistance of coils, will any proportion of the product be nonconforming?

Solution. The first part of this example is basically the same as in Example 6-1. It involves calculating the trial control limits for the mean $\overline{X}$ and range R, identifying out-of-control points, determining assignable causes associated with the out-of-control points, taking corrective actions, and calculating the revised control limits. The process should be in a state of statistical control before process capability is determined.

The center line $\overline{R}$ on the range chart is

$$\overline{R} = \frac{\sum R_i}{25} = \frac{92}{25} = 3.68$$

TABLE 8-5 Data on resistance of coils

Sample number	Observations	$\overline{X}$	R	Comments
1	20, 22, 21, 23, 22	21.60	3	
2	19, 18, 22, 20, 20	19.80	4	
3	25, 18, 20, 17, 22	20.40	8	New vendor
4	20, 21, 22, 21, 21	21.00	2	
5	19, 24, 23, 22, 20	21.60	5	
6	22, 20, 18, 18, 19	19.40	4	
7	18, 20, 19, 18, 20	19.00	2	
8	20, 18, 23, 20, 21	20.40	5	
9	21, 20, 24, 23, 22	22.00	4	
10	21, 19, 20, 20, 20	20.00	2	
11	20, 20, 23, 22, 20	21.00	3	
12	22, 21, 20, 22, 23	21.60	3	
13	19, 22, 19, 18, 19	19.40	4	
14	20, 21, 22, 21, 22	21.20	2	
15	20, 24, 24, 23, 23	22.80	4	
16	21, 20, 24, 20, 21	21.20	4	
17	20, 18, 18, 20, 20	19.20	2	
18	20, 24, 22, 23, 23	22.40	4	
19	20, 19, 23, 20, 19	20.20	4	
20	22, 21, 21, 24, 22	22.00	3	
21	23, 22, 22, 20, 22	21.80	3	
22	21, 18, 18, 17, 19	18.60	4	High temperature
23	21, 24, 24, 23, 23	23.00	3	Wrong die
24	20, 22, 21, 21, 20	20.80	2	
25	19, 20, 21, 21, 22	20.60	3	
		Sum = 521.00	Sum = 92	

The trial control limits on the R-chart are

$$UCL_R = D_4\bar{R} = (2.114)(3.68) = 7.780$$

$$LCL_R = D_3\bar{R} = (0)(3.68) = 0$$

A chart for the range is shown in Figure 8-14. Sample number 3, with a range of 8, plots above the UCL_R and is considered to be out of control. The assignable cause was the variability of the product of a new vendor. After adequate corrective measures are taken, the revised center line for the range, after deleting sample 3, becomes

$$\bar{R} = \frac{84}{24} = 3.50$$

The revised control limits on the R-chart are

$$UCL_R = D_4\bar{R} = (2.114)(3.50) = 7.399$$

$$LCL_R = D_3\bar{R} = (0)(3.50) = 0$$

All of the remaining points are found to be in control on the R-chart.

To construct the chart for the mean $\bar{X}$, the center line is

$$\bar{\bar{X}} = \frac{\sum X_i}{g} = \frac{500.6}{24} = 20.858$$

The control limits on the $\bar{X}$-chart are

$$\begin{aligned} UCL_{\bar{X}} &= \bar{\bar{X}} + A_2\bar{R} \\ &= 20.858 + (0.577)(3.50) = 22.878 \end{aligned}$$

$$\begin{aligned} LCL_{\bar{X}} &= \bar{\bar{X}} - A_2\bar{R} \\ &= 20.858 - (0.577)(3.50) = 18.838 \end{aligned}$$

The sample averages are plotted on a control chart with the above center line and control limits in Figure 8-15. Sample numbers 22 and 23 are out of control. The assignable cause for sample number 22 was found to be the high oven temperature; for sample number 23, it was the use of a wrong die. After taking remedial actions and deleting these two observations, the revised center line on the $\bar{X}$-chart is

$$\bar{\bar{X}} = \frac{459}{22} = 20.864$$

The revised center line on the range chart is

$$\bar{R} = \frac{77}{22} = 3.500$$

The revised control limits on the $\bar{X}$-chart are

$$\begin{aligned} UCL_{\bar{X}} &= \bar{\bar{X}} + A_2\bar{R} \\ &= 20.864 + (0.577)(3.500) = 22.884 \end{aligned}$$

$$\begin{aligned} LCL_{\bar{X}} &= \bar{\bar{X}} - A_2\bar{R} \\ &= 20.864 - (0.577)(3.500) = 18.844 \end{aligned}$$

The revised R-chart limits are

$$UCL_R = D_4\bar{R} = (2.114)(3.500) = 7.399$$

$$LCL_R = D_3\bar{R} = (0)(3.500) = 0$$

All of the remaining points are found to be in control. Now that the process is in control, the process mean and standard deviation may be estimated:

$$\hat{\mu} = \bar{\bar{X}} = 20.864$$

$$\hat{\sigma} = \frac{\bar{R}}{d_2} = \frac{3.500}{2.326} = 1.505$$

The process capability index C_{pk} is

$$\begin{aligned} C_{pk} &= \min\left\{\frac{24 - 20.864}{3(1.505)}, \frac{20.864 - 16}{3(1.505)}\right\} \\ &= \frac{3.136}{4.515} = 0.695 \end{aligned}$$

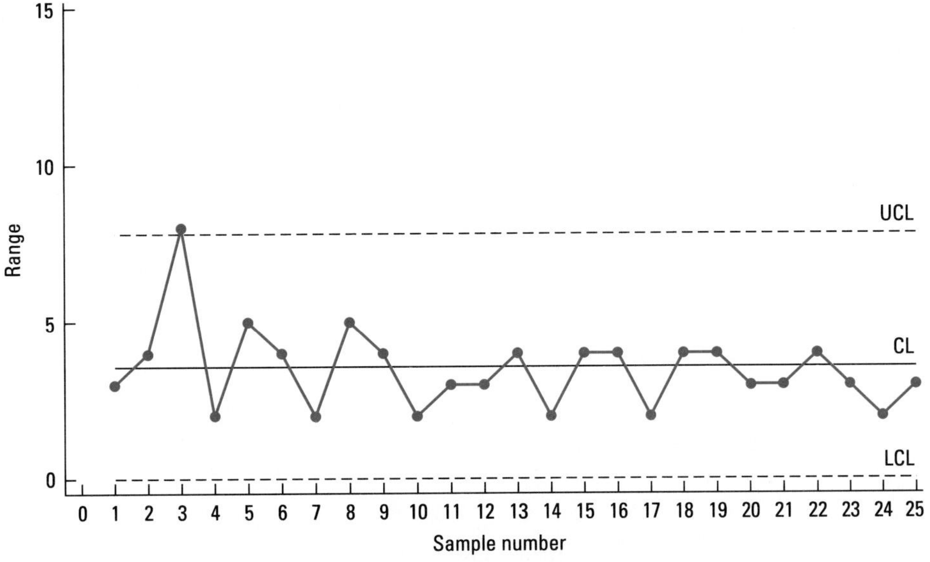

Figure 8-14 R-chart for data on resistance of coils.

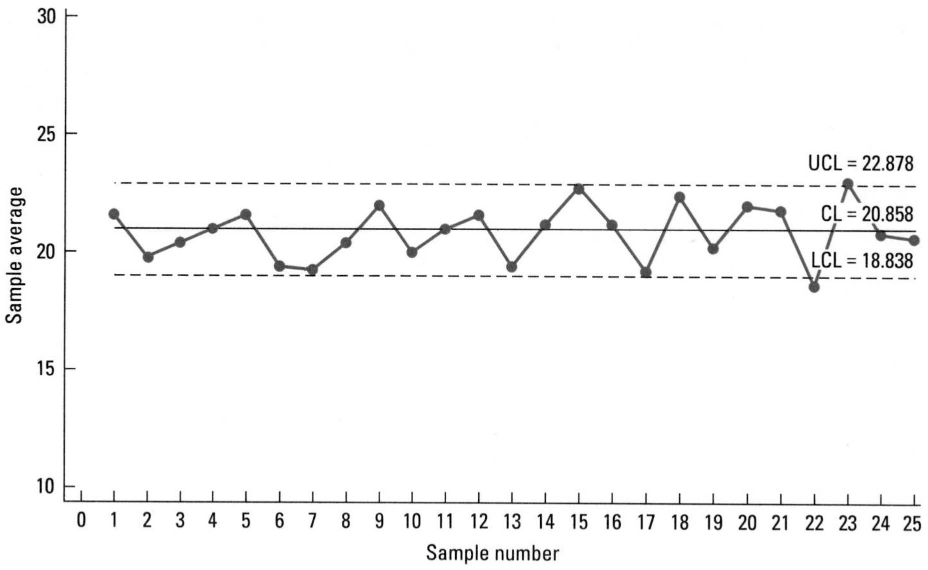

Figure 8-15 $\overline{X}$-chart for data on resistance of coils.

The value of C_{pk} is less than 1, indicating an undesirable situation. Some proportion of the product will be nonconforming. Let us now estimate the fraction nonconforming. From Figure 8-16, the standardized normal values for the USL and LSL may be found. We have

$$Z_A = \frac{24 - 20.864}{1.505} = 2.08$$

$$Z_B = \frac{16 - 20.864}{1.505} = -3.23$$

From the standard normal distribution tables in Appendix A-3, the proportion of the coils that will be above the USL is $(1 - 0.9812) = 0.0188$, or 1.88 percent; the proportion of coils below the LSL is 0.0006, or 0.06 percent. The total fraction nonconforming is 0.0194, or 1.94 percent.

On observing Figure 8-16, we find that a reduction in the fraction nonconforming could occur by adjusting the process to the nominal value of 20 ohms. Let us adjust the process mean downward to 20 and recalculate the fraction nonconforming. The standard normal values at the specification limits would be

$$Z_A = \frac{24 - 20}{1.505} = 2.66$$

$$Z_B = \frac{16 - 20}{1.505} = -2.66$$

From the standard normal tables in Appendix A-3, the proportion of coils above the USL is 0.0039, and the proportion below the LSL is also 0.0039. The total fraction nonconforming is 0.0078, or 0.78 percent. Thus, changing the setting for the process mean will reduce the fraction nonconforming from 1.94 percent to 0.78 percent. To further reduce the proportion of nonconforming product, we would have to consider ways of reducing the process variability. Management would need to come up with actions to bring about process improvement.

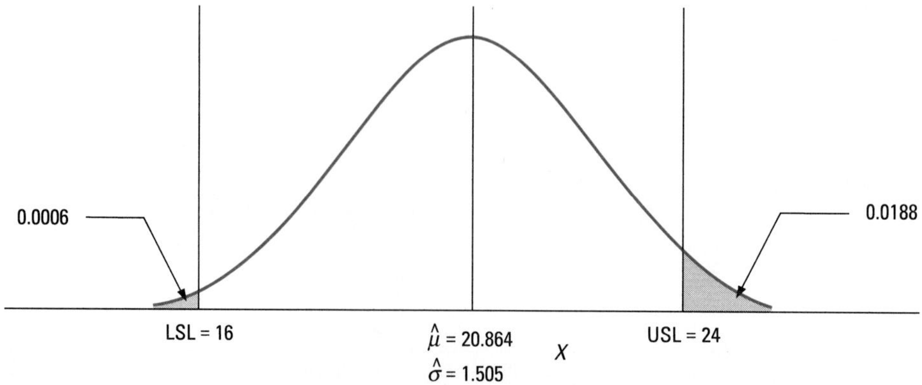

Figure 8-16 Fraction of nonconforming coils.

8-8 SETTING TOLERANCES ON ASSEMBLIES AND COMPONENTS

Frequently, it is of interest to determine the tolerance limits that should be set on assemblies or subassemblies, given the tolerances of the individual components. The assumption in this section regarding components and assemblies is that the processes making the assemblies or components are barely capable. This means that the spread between the tolerances are assumed to be the same as the process spread (that is, six times the process standard deviation). Implicitly, this means that the process potential as measured by the C_p index is 1, so that virtually all of the product will be within the specification limits.

Tolerances on Assemblies and Subassemblies

Assemblies and subassemblies are formed by combining two or more components. The dimension of interest in an assembly may be the sum or difference of the individual components. Consider an assembly made up of four components as shown in Figure 8-17. Suppose the components are welded together and that the weld thickness is negligible. The quality characteristic of interest is the length of the assembly, Y. Denoting the length of the components A, B, C, and D as X_1, X_2, X_3, and X_4, respectively, the length of the assembly is expressed as

$$Y = X_1 + X_2 + X_3 + X_4 \tag{8.20}$$

Consider another assembly of two components A and B, as shown in Figure 8-18. Here, the dimension of interest is the exposed length of the longer part, which is given by

$$Y = X_1 - X_2 \tag{8.21}$$

In general, the dimension of interest could be expressed as a linear combination of some individual component dimensions, for example,

$$\begin{aligned} Y &= a_1X_1 + a_2X_2 + \cdots + a_kX_k \qquad (8.22) \\ &= \sum_{i=1}^{k} a_iX_i \end{aligned}$$

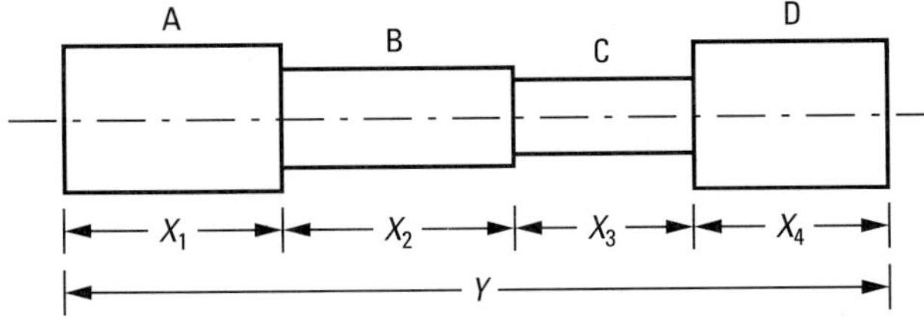

Figure 8-17 An assembly of four components.

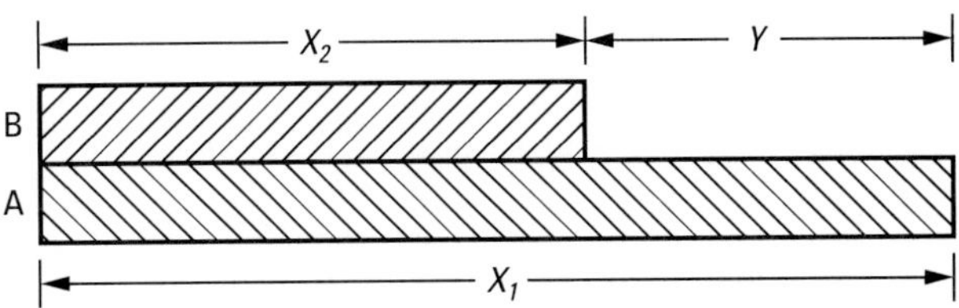

Figure 8-18 An assembly of two components.

where k represents the number of different individual dimensions. Note that the component dimensions X_i and hence the assembly dimensions Y are random variables. Suppose the component dimensions X_i are random variables with mean μ_i and standard deviation σ_i.

Two important properties of the characteristic Y are its mean and variance. If the component dimensions are independent of each other, the mean of Y is given by

$$\mu_Y = \sum_{i=1}^{k} a_i\mu_i \tag{8.23}$$

where μ_i is the mean of the variable X_i and the values of a_i are constants. For instance, in Figure 8-17, $k = 4$, $a_1 = 1$, $a_2 = 1$, $a_3 = 1$, and $a_4 = 1$. The mean of Y is

$$\mu_Y = \mu_1 + \mu_2 + \mu_3 + \mu_4$$

For the assembly in Figure 8-18,

$$\mu_Y = \mu_1 - \mu_2$$

In general, the variance of the dimension Y is given by

$$\text{Var}(Y) = \sigma_Y^2 = \sum_{i=1}^{k} a_i^2\text{Var}(X_i) = \sum_{i=1}^{k} a_i^2\sigma_i^2 \tag{8.24}$$

Equation 8.24 states that the variance of the dimension of interest (Y) is the sum of the weighted variances of the individual dimensions; the weights are the square of the coefficients of the linear combination. The assumption is that the individual dimensions are independent of each other.

Using Equation 8.24, we get the following for the assembly in Figure 8-17:

$$\begin{aligned} Y &= X_1 + X_2 + X_3 + X_4 \\ \text{Var}(Y) &= \sigma_Y^2 \\ &= \text{Var}(X_1) + \text{Var}(X_2) \\ &\quad + \text{Var}(X_3) + \text{Var}(X_4) \\ &= \sigma_1^2 + \sigma_2^2 + \sigma_3^2 + \sigma_4^2 \end{aligned}$$

For the assembly in Figure 8-18,

$$\begin{aligned} Y &= X_1 - X_2 \\ \text{Var}(Y) &= \sigma_Y^2 \\ &= \text{Var}(X_1) + \text{Var}(X_2) \\ &= \sigma_1^2 + \sigma_2^2 \end{aligned}$$

If we can make an assumption regarding the distribution of the component dimension, it is possible to derive the distribution for the dimension of the assembly characteristic. In particular, if each X_i is normally distributed with mean μ_i and standard deviation σ_i and is independent of all other X_i, the distribution of Y will also be normal, with mean given by Equation 8.23 and variance given by Equation 8.24. This property can be used to find the proportion of assemblies whose dimension of interest lies between certain bounds.

Assuming a normal distribution of Y, the natural tolerance limits are

$$\mu_Y \pm 3\sigma_Y \qquad (8.25)$$

where σ_Y represents the standard deviation of the dimension Y.

Example 8-7: Consider the assembly of four components shown in Figure 8-17. Suppose the mean lengths of the four components and their respective tolerances are as shown in the accompanying table.

Component	Mean length (cm)	Tolerances (cm)
A	2	2 ± 0.3
B	5	5 ± 0.2
C	6	6 ± 0.2
D	7	7 ± 0.1

Assume that the individual component dimensions are normally distributed. Find the natural tolerance limits for the length of the assembly. Suppose the design specifications for the length of the assembly are 20 ± 0.3 cm. What fraction of the assemblies will be nonconforming? Comment on the ability to make assemblies that meet the design specifications.

Solution. Assume that the tolerances on the individual components have been set such that they are at the natural capability limits. The standard deviation of the component dimensions are estimated assuming that the spread between the tolerances is equal to six standard deviations. We have the following results:

$$\begin{aligned} \text{Component A: } \sigma_1 &= (2.3 - 1.7)/6 = 0.100 \text{ cm} \\ \text{Component B: } \sigma_2 &= (5.2 - 4.8)/6 = 0.067 \text{ cm} \\ \text{Component C: } \sigma_3 &= (6.2 - 5.8)/6 = 0.067 \text{ cm} \\ \text{Component D: } \sigma_4 &= (7.1 - 6.9)/6 = 0.033 \text{ cm} \end{aligned}$$

The length of the assembly is given by

$$Y = X_1 + X_2 + X_3 + X_4$$

The mean length of the assembly is found using Equation 8.23:

$$\begin{aligned} \mu_Y &= \mu_1 + \mu_2 + \mu_3 + \mu_4 \\ &= 2 + 5 + 6 + 7 = 20 \text{ cm} \end{aligned}$$

The variance of the length of the assembly is found using Equation 8.24:

$$\begin{aligned} \sigma_Y^2 &= \sigma_1^2 + \sigma_2^2 + \sigma_3^2 + \sigma_4^2 \\ &= (0.1)^2 + (0.067)^2 + (0.067)^2 + (0.033)^2 \\ &= 0.020 \end{aligned}$$

The standard deviation of the length of the assembly is

$$\sigma_Y = \sqrt{0.020} = 0.142 \text{ cm}$$

From Equation 8.25, the natural tolerance limits for the assembly length are

$$\begin{aligned} \mu_Y \pm 3\sigma_Y &= 20 \pm 3(0.142) = 20 \pm 0.426 \\ &= (19.574, 20.426) \text{ cm} \end{aligned}$$

Since the individual component lengths are normally distributed, the assembly lengths will also be normally distributed with a mean of 20 cm and a standard deviation of 0.142 cm. Furthermore, virtually all (99.74 percent) of the assemblies will have a length between 19.574 and 20.426 cm.

The design specifications for the length of the assembly are 20 ± 0.3 cm. The proportion of nonconforming assemblies is shown in Figure 8-19. The standardized normal values at the USL and LSL are

$$\begin{aligned} Z_A &= \frac{20.3 - 20}{0.142} = 2.11 \\ Z_B &= \frac{19.7 - 20}{0.142} = -2.11 \end{aligned}$$

From the standard normal tables in Appendix A-3, the proportion above the USL is 0.0174, and that below the LSL is also 0.0174. The total proportion of nonconforming assemblies is 0.0348, or 3.48 percent.

The above illustrates that if the natural tolerance limits of the component lengths are as shown, the process is not capable of always making assemblies that conform to the design specifications. This suggests that when deciding on specifications to set for the assembly, we should first look at the consumer needs and functional use of the assembly. Based on these considerations, we should question whether tolerances that are tighter than the process capability of ±0.426 cm ($\pm 3\sigma_Y$) are needed. Re-

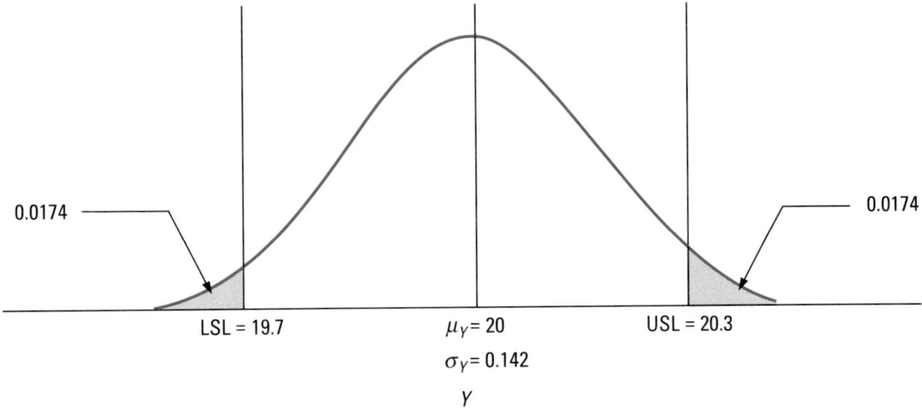

Figure 8-19 Proportion of nonconforming assemblies for Example 8-7.

call that ±0.426 cm represents the natural tolerances for the length of the assembly. If the specifications can be set to a value greater than ±0.426 from the nominal, we can produce the assembly length within the specifications practically all of the time. On the other hand, suppose that functional and consumer demands require the specifications to be less than ±0.426 from the nominal value. Under such circumstances we would be unable to consistently produce assemblies that meet the specification limits even if the process were in control.

Tolerance Limits on Individual Components

The specification limits on an assembly are often determined based on product function and customer needs. It is the task of the designer to determine the tolerances on individual components that will give the assembly the specified tolerances. It has been mentioned previously that, although product design should incorporate customer preferences, it must also be realistic and achievable. If the process that creates the assembly is not capable of meeting specifications, this must be corrected in the product/process design phase. Using the theory of assembly tolerances from the previous subsection, this subsection discusses the determination of tolerances of components that make up an assembly, assuming a desirable tolerance level of the assembly. The following example demonstrates this concept.

Example 8-8: Consider the assembly of four components shown in Figure 8-17. Suppose the lengths of the components are normally and independently distributed with the following means:

Component	Mean length (cm)
A	2
B	5
C	6
D	7

Suppose the specifications for the length of the assembly are 20 ± 0.3 cm. What should the tolerances on the individual components be? Assume that the tolerances for the components are equal to each other. Further assume that the specifications are barely equal to the natural tolerance limits, implying a capability ratio of 1.

Solution. The length of the assembly, Y, is the sum of the individual component lengths, that is $Y = X_1 + X_2 + X_3 + X_4$. Y will be normally distributed because the X-values are normally distributed. Under the assumption that the specification limits for the length of the assembly equal its natural tolerance limits, the standard deviation of the length of the assembly, σ_Y, is estimated as

$$\sigma_Y = (20.3 - 19.7)/6 = 0.100 \text{ cm}$$

Now, using Equation 8.24, we have

$$\sigma_Y^2 = \sigma_1^2 + \sigma_2^2 + \sigma_3^2 + \sigma_4^2$$

where σ_i^2 represents the variance of the dimension X_i (for $i = 1, 2, 3, 4$). Under the assumption that $\sigma_1^2 = \sigma_2^2 = \sigma_3^2 = \sigma_4^2$, we get,

$$\sigma_Y^2 = 4\sigma_1^2$$

or

$$\sigma_1^2 = \sigma_Y^2/4 = (0.100)^2/4 = 0.0025$$

The standard deviation of X_1 is $\sigma_1 = \sqrt{0.0025} = 0.05$ cm. Therefore, $\sigma_2 = \sigma_3 = \sigma_4 = \sigma_1 = 0.05$ cm.

The tolerances on the individual component dimensions are as follows:

Component	Tolerances (cm)
A	$2 \pm 3(0.05) = (1.85, 2.15)$
B	$5 \pm 3(0.05) = (4.85, 5.15)$
C	$6 \pm 3(0.05) = (5.85, 6.15)$
D	$7 \pm 3(0.05) = (6.85, 7.15)$

In the manufacture of these components, the process capability should be determined and compared to these natural tolerances. Doing so will help evaluate whether the process is capable of making components that meet these desired tolerances.

Tolerances on Mating Parts

The previous subsections discussed tolerances on assemblies and components. Mating parts (for example, a shaft and a bearing, a pin and a sleeve, a piston and a cylinder) represent a special form of assembly. In such assemblies, the type of fit between the mating parts may be classified into three categories.

Clearance Fit For a clearance fit, the size of the hole prior to assembly is always larger than the size of the shaft. In the assembly, there is always some room for play between the shaft and the hole. The natural tolerance limits for the hole are outside the tolerance limits for the shaft; in no instance will a shaft be larger than the hole. Figure 8-20 shows an example in which the shaft diameter X_s is smaller than the hole diameter X_h. The clearance between the two is also shown. Normality is assumed for the distribution of both the shaft and hole diameters; Figure 8-21 indicates their relative positioning. The mean shaft diameter is indicated by μ_s, and the mean hole diameter is denoted by μ_h. Given the natural tolerance limits for each, the shafts will all be smaller than the smallest hole, which will therefore provide a clearance fit. In an automobile engine, the assembly of a piston within a cylinder is an example of such a fit.

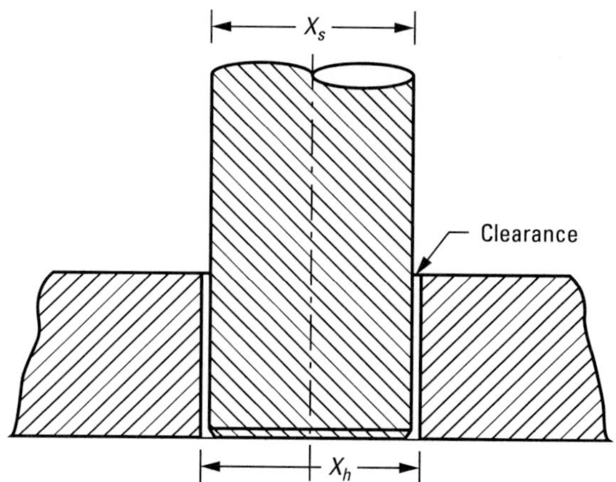

Figure 8-20 Clearance fit in an assembly.

Interference Fit For an interference fit, the size of the hole before assembly is always smaller than the size of the shaft. The shaft therefore has to be forced into the hole. The range of the natural tolerance limits for the hole is below that for the shaft, and all of the hole diameters will be smaller than the smallest shaft. An example of such a fit may be a pin that is forced into a sleeve to stay in place. Such a condition may be illustrated by switching the hole and shaft diameter distributions in Figure 8-21.

Transition Fit For a transition fit, there may be either a clearance or an interference in the assembly. Thus, in some instances the hole diameter will be larger than the shaft diameter, providing a clearance; in others, the shaft diameter may be greater than the hole diameter, in which case an interference fit will result. The natural tolerance ranges of the hole and shaft may overlap. Depending on the relative location of the mean values and the degree of variability of the hole and shaft diameters, an assembly will

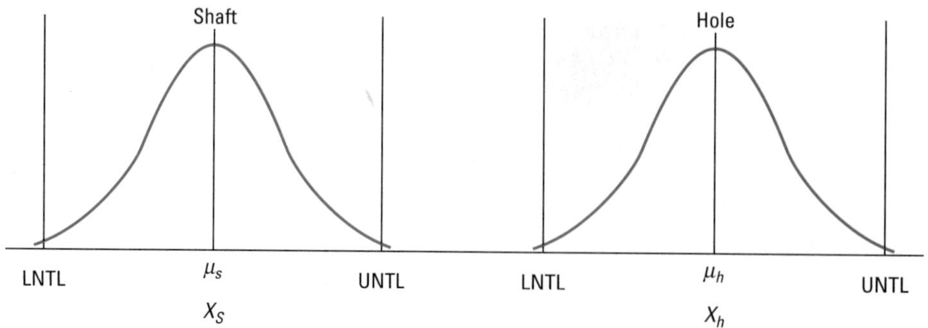

Figure 8-21 Distribution of shaft and hole diameters in a clearance fit.

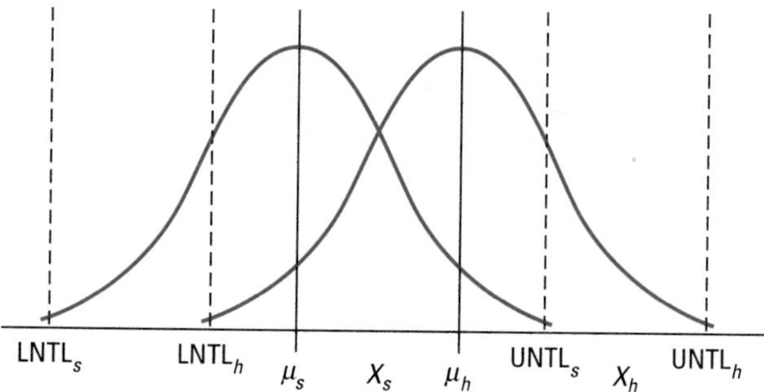

Figure 8-22 Distribution of shaft and hole diameters in a transition fit.

be either a clearance or interference fit. Figure 8-22 shows the distributions of the shaft and the hole diameters, indicated by X_s and X_h, respectively. Note that there is some overlap between the natural tolerance limits of the shaft (LNTL_s, UNTL_s) and the hole (LNTL_h, UNTL_h). If the shaft diameter is less than the hole diameter, the result is a clearance fit; if the shaft diameter exceeds the hole diameter, the result is an interference fit.

Example 8-9: The specifications for the outside diameter of a shaft are 9.0 ± 0.10 cm, and those for the inside diameter of a bearing are 9.1 ± 0.13 cm. Assume that it is possible to make each of the components such that the natural tolerance limits equal the specifications (implying a process capability ratio of 1). Also assume that the parts are produced independently and that the diameters are each normally distributed with their means at the respective nominal values. If a clearance fit is desired between the shaft and the bearing, what proportion of the assemblies will be unacceptable?

Solution. Let X_s denote the shaft outside diameter and X_b the bearing inside diameter. Let d represent the difference between the bearing inside diameter and the shaft outside diameter (that is, $d = X_b - X_s$). The mean of the shaft diameter, given by μ_s, is 9.0 cm; the mean of the bearing diameter, μ_b, is 9.1 cm. The mean of the difference between the bearing and the shaft diameter is

$$\mu_d = \mu_b - \mu_s = 9.1 - 9.0 = 0.1 \text{ cm}$$

The standard deviation of the shaft outside diameter is found from the relation

$$6\sigma_s = 9.1 - 8.9 = 0.2$$
$$\sigma_s = 0.2/6 = 0.033 \text{ cm}$$

The standard deviation of the bearing inside diameter is found from

$$6\sigma_b = 9.23 - 8.97 = 0.26$$
$$\sigma_b = 0.26/6 = 0.043 \text{ cm}$$

Since $d = X_b - X_s$, the variance of the difference between the bearing and shaft diameters is found using Equation 8.24 as follows:

$$\begin{aligned} \text{Var}(d) &= \sigma_b{}^2 + \sigma_s{}^2 \\ &= (0.043)^2 + (0.033)^2 = 0.00294 \end{aligned}$$

The standard deviation of d is

$$\sigma_d = \sqrt{0.00294} = 0.054 \text{ cm}$$

Since the bearing and shaft diameters are each independently normally distributed, the distribution of the difference d between the bearing and shaft diameters is also normally distributed with mean $\mu_d = 0.1$ cm and standard deviation $\sigma_d = 0.054$ cm.

Figure 8-23 shows the distribution of the statistic d. Since a clearance fit is desired, unacceptable assemblies are those for which $d < 0$. To find the proportion of unacceptable assemblies, the standard normal value is found at $d = 0$:

$$\begin{aligned} Z &= \frac{0 - \mu_d}{\sigma_d} \\ &= (0 - 0.10)/0.054 = -1.85 \end{aligned}$$

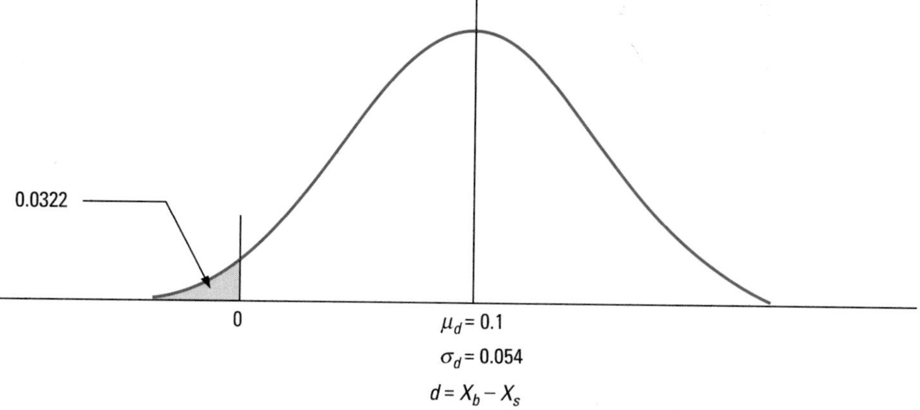

Figure 8-23 Proportion of unacceptable assemblies for Example 8-9.

Based on the standard normal tables in Appendix A-3, the proportion of nonconforming assemblies is 0.0322. In 3.22 percent of the assemblies, the shaft outside diameter will exceed the bearing inside diameter and therefore be unacceptable.

8-9 ESTIMATING NATURAL TOLERANCE LIMITS OF A PROCESS

The natural tolerance limits define the inherent capability of a process. Consequently, it is of interest to estimate these limits once a process is in statistical control. If control charts are used to bring a process to control, information from these charts may be used to determine the natural tolerance limits of the process. This approach has been described previously. An assumption made in this approach is that reliable estimates based on elaborate historical data are available for the process mean and process standard deviation. If, however, data from a small sample are used to generate estimates of the process mean and standard deviation, then statistical tolerance limits should be found. These limits are estimates of the natural tolerance limits, and, as the sample size increases, the statistical tolerance limits approach the natural tolerance limits.

Setting Specification Limits

Suppose a process has been brought to a state of statistical control through the use of control charts. Let the estimate of the process mean be denoted by $\hat{\mu} = \overline{\overline{X}}$, the revised center line of a chart for the mean of the quality characteristic of interest. Assume that an estimate of the process standard deviation ($\hat{\sigma}$) has been obtained. In previous sections, we saw how σ can be estimated from control chart information, depending on the charts that are constructed. For instance, from a range chart, it can be obtained as $\hat{\sigma} = \overline{R}/d_2$.

Depending on the desired process capability ratio, specification limits can be set up for the characteristic. Table 8-1 shows some recommended process capability ratio values depending on the type of process and whether one- or two-sided specifications are constructed. This table provides recommended guidelines for values of the process capability ratios, but customer requirements must still be the dominating criteria in setting specifications. Suppose a desired level of the process capability ratio (assuming two-sided specification limits) is 1.33. As discussed previously, for this condition to be met, the actual process spread must be three-fourths of the spread between the specification limits. In other words, the specification limits must be 4 standard deviations away from the process mean, whereas the natural tolerance limits are 3 standard deviations from the process mean. Figure 8-24 demonstrates the relationship that must exist between the natural tolerance limits and the specification limits if the process capability ratio C_p is to equal 1.33. The specification limits in this case are

$$\hat{\mu} \pm 4\hat{\sigma}$$

If a different value of the process capability ratio is selected, the multiplying factor associated with $\hat{\sigma}$ will change accordingly, assuming that the characteristic is normally distributed.

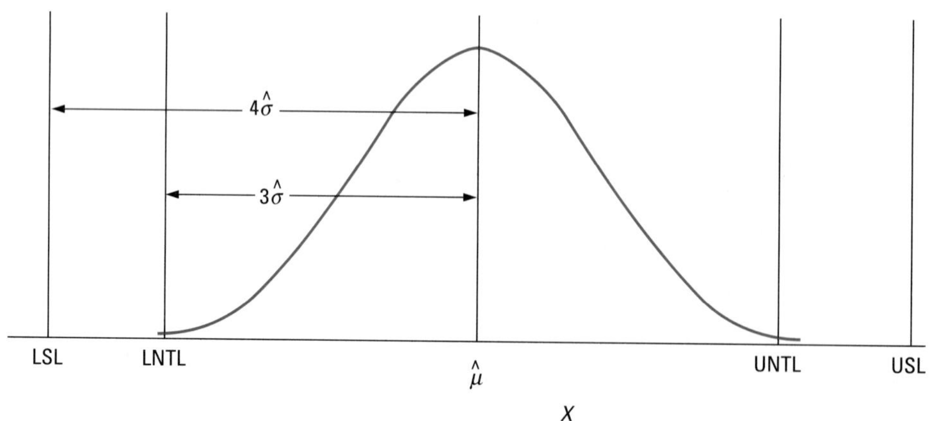

Figure 8-24 Relationship between natural tolerance limits and specification limits for a process with a capability ratio of 1.33.

Statistical Tolerance Limits Based on Normal Distribution

Suppose the quality characteristic X is normally distributed with mean μ and standard deviation σ. Tolerance limits that encompass $100(1-\alpha)$ percent of the product can be constructed as

$$\mu \pm Z_{\alpha/2}\sigma$$

In practice, however, the process mean and standard deviation are usually unknown. They are estimated from sample estimates. Suppose that for a sample of size n, the sample mean is $\overline{X}$ and the sample standard deviation is s. Since $\overline{X}$ and s are estimates of μ and σ, it is not necessarily true that $\overline{X} \pm Z_{\alpha/2}s$ will include $100(1-\alpha)$ percent of the distribution. Note that $\overline{X}$ and s are random variables, whereas μ and σ are constants. Different samples will lead to different values of $\overline{X}$ and s, which will in turn lead to different estimates of the limits. Some of these intervals may be very different from $\mu \pm Z_{\alpha/2}\sigma$ and may not include $100(1-\alpha)$ percent of the product.

Values of a constant k are tabulated such that in a large proportion (γ) of these intervals $\overline{X} \pm ks$, at least $100(1-\alpha)$ percent of the distribution will be included. This constant k depends on the sample size n, the level of confidence γ, and the percentage of the distribution, $100(1-\alpha)$ percent, that is to be minimally included in the interval. Appendix A-8 lists tables for determining the value of k. Two tables are given, based on whether one-sided or two-sided statistical tolerance limits are desired. Two-sided statistical tolerance limits are calculated from

$$\overline{X} \pm ks \tag{8.26}$$

where k is found from Table 1 of Appendix A-8.

If one-sided statistical tolerance limits are desired, the value of k is read from Table 2 of Appendix A-8. A one-sided upper tolerance limit is

$$\overline{X} + ks \tag{8.27}$$

and a one-sided lower tolerance limit is

$$\overline{X} - ks \tag{8.28}$$

Note that there is a fundamental difference between confidence limits and statistical tolerance limits. Confidence intervals are found for a parameter of the process. A 95-percent confidence interval for the process mean may be interpreted as follows: If a large number of such confidence intervals are constructed, 95 percent of those intervals will enclose the process mean. Statistical tolerance limits, on the other hand, are designed to contain at least a specified proportion, $100(1-\alpha)$ percent, of the population, with a certain probability γ. As the sample size becomes large, the width of the confidence interval diminishes. In the limiting case, as the sample size n approaches infinity, the width of the confidence interval approaches zero. The statistical tolerance limits, in this case for which n approaches infinity, approach the corresponding limits for the population. We find (from Table 1 in Appendix A-8, for $1-\alpha = 0.95$ and a two-sided interval) that the value of k approaches 1.96 as n becomes large. The value of 1.96 is the standardized normal value (Z value) for $1-\alpha = 0.95$.

Example 8-10: The breaking strength of yarn was obtained for a sample of size 20. The sample mean and sample standard deviation were 250 and 20 g, respectively. Find a two-sided 95-percent statistical tolerance interval such that at least 99 percent of the population is contained within it. Assume a normal distribution of breaking strengths.

Solution. We have $\overline{X} = 250$, $s = 20$, $\gamma = 0.95$, $1-\alpha = 0.99$, and $n = 20$. Using Table 1 of Appendix A-8, the coefficient $k = 3.62$. The two-sided statistical tolerance limits are given by

$$\begin{aligned} 250 \pm 3.62(20) &= 250 \pm 72.4 \\ &= (177.6, 322.4) \text{ g} \end{aligned}$$

Thus, we are 95 percent confident that 99 percent of the yarns have a breaking strength between 177.6 and 322.4 g.

Nonparametric Statistical Tolerance Limits

Nonparametric statistical tolerance limits do not depend on the distribution of the quality characteristic. These limits are valid for any continuous probability distribution. They are based on the largest and smallest observations in the sample.

For two-sided tolerance intervals, the number of observations n required so that there is a probability γ that at least $100(1-\alpha)$ percent of the distribution will lie between the smallest and largest sample observations is found approximately as

$$n \simeq 0.5 + \left(\frac{2-\alpha}{\alpha}\right)\frac{\chi^2_{1-\gamma,4}}{4} \tag{8.29}$$

where $\chi^2_{1-\gamma,4}$ is the upper $100(1-\gamma)$ percentile point of the chi-squared distribution with four degrees of freedom and is tabulated in Appendix A-5.

If a one-sided nonparametric lower statistical tolerance limit is desired such that there is a probability γ that at least $100(1-\alpha)$ percent of the population is greater than the smallest sample value, the sample size is given by

$$n = \frac{\ln(1-\gamma)}{\ln(1-\alpha)} \tag{8.30}$$

Equation 8.30 is also used to determine the sample size required to construct a one-sided nonparametric upper statistical tolerance limit. There is then a probability γ that at least $100(1-\alpha)$ percent of the population will be less than the largest value.

Nonparametric tolerance intervals usually require large sample sizes when both the desired probability level and the desired percentage of the population to be included in the constructed interval are high. Any available information on the quality characteristic should be used to estimate the form of the distribution. Given a distributional form, the sample size needed to achieve a comparable degree of confidence and proportion of population inclusion within the interval is usually less than that for a nonparametric tolerance interval.

Example 8-11: Compute the sample size for a two-sided nonparametric tolerance interval. It should contain 95 percent of the population with a probability of 0.99. The quality characteristic is the concentration of potassium in a chemical in parts per million.

Solution. We have $1-\alpha = 0.95$ and $\gamma = 0.99$. From the chi-squared tables in Appendix A-5, we have $\chi^2_{0.01,4} = 13.28$. The required sample size is

$$n = 0.5 + \left(\frac{2-0.05}{0.05}\right)\left(\frac{13.28}{4}\right) = 129.98 \simeq 130$$

Suppose a sample of size 130 is chosen. After ranking the sample values in ascending order, the minimum and maximum values are 28 and 49. The nonparametric tolerance interval is (28, 49). We are confident with a probability level of 0.99, that 95 percent of the population will be contained within this interval.

Example 8-12: Compute the sample size for a one-sided upper nonparametric tolerance limit. It should contain 98 percent of the distribution with a probability of 0.95. The quality characteristic is the number of grams of fat in 10 kg of processed poultry.

Solution. We have $1-\alpha = 0.98$ and $\gamma = 0.95$. Using Equation 8.30, the required sample size is

$$n = \frac{\ln(1-\gamma)}{\ln(1-\alpha)} = \frac{\ln(0.05)}{\ln(0.98)} = 148.28 \simeq 149$$

Suppose a sample of size 149 is chosen. The values in the sample are ranked; the maximum value is 36 g. We are confident with a probability level of 0.95 that 98 percent of the population will have a fat content of less than 36 g per 10 kg.

8-10 SUMMARY

This chapter has dealt with an important aspect that concerns all processes: the determination of the inherent capability of the process. This allows us to infer whether the process will be able to produce items that conform to desired specifications. For two-sided limits, the process spread must be less than the spread between the specification limits for the process to be considered capable. The process must be centered at the most desirable location in order to minimize the production of nonconforming items. For one-sided specification limits, the process mean and spread should be such that virtually all items will meet the specifications. Changing the process mean, which requires an adjustment of certain process parameters, is usually an easier task than reducing the process variability. The process spread may be reduced through fundamental changes in the process initiated by management.

Various measures of process capability involving the process mean, process standard deviation, and specification limits have been developed in this chapter. For processes that have been found not to be capable, procedures have been described for determining the proportion of nonconforming product. Procedures for determining process capability have been discussed. This chapter also has described the determination of tolerances for assemblies and subassemblies and the setting of tolerances for components depending on specifications of assemblies. Methods for determining statistical tolerance limits have also been elaborated.

The procedures described in this chapter may form a basis for deciding whether an existing process is capable or needs to be changed. Continual process improvement is a goal that should be adopted by every company.

8-11 CASE STUDY

MOTOROLA'S SECRET TO TOTAL QUALITY CONTROL*

The Galvin Manufacturing Corporation, later renamed Motorola, Inc., began operations on September 25, 1928, in a small section of a rented building at 847 Harrison Street in Chicago; the company had five employees. Now in its sixty-second year, Motorola is ranked among America's 150 largest industrial corporations with close to 98,000 employees worldwide and sales approaching $8 billion.

In 1988, Motorola received one of the first Malcolm Baldrige National Quality Awards. No single article can address all the elements in Motorola's corporate quality system or explain in detail how to set up a quality system that will win the Baldrige Award. Instead, I will examine some of the elements of quality control of manufacturing operations within the semiconductor products sector. The secret to Motorola's success in quality control is a focused effort in three major areas: material control, in-process control, and containment. Within each major area are several key items that must be addressed to achieve success.

Material Control

Motorola stresses to all suppliers that percent AQL (acceptable quality losses) is unacceptable and that their defective units are measured in parts per million. Moreover, Motorola's goal is to reduce the number of its suppliers by an average of about 50 percent each year; only those suppliers that meet its expectations for superior quality will be retained or added to its supplier base. Motorola has substantially improved as its suppliers have continually improved their quality. Each supplier must indicate its C_{pk} performance (process capability index, which accounts for noncentered process averages). Suppliers should have an acceptable C_{pk} and a program to achieve a C_{pk} of 2.

The supplier rating system measures suppliers on the quality of product delivered and the timeliness of those deliveries. Suppliers with higher ratings get more business; poor suppliers are dropped. Most suppliers now receive a monthly or quarterly rating of their performance.

Special programs are provided to individual suppliers as needed, including training for service suppliers. For example, a seminar for a travel industry supplier demonstrated how the principles of Six Sigma Quality (See Box 8-1) could be applied to that business.

Certifying Suppliers

The best way to address material control is through a supplier certification program. Motorola's program consists of five phases:

1. Agree on key parameter measurements, and then work on having supplies correlate with these measurements.

* Adapted from E. Peña (1990), "Motorola's Secret to Total Quality Control," *Quality Progress*, 23, pp. 43–55.

> When Motorola was awarded the Malcolm Baldrige National Quality Award in 1988, a summary of its quality achievements was distributed as part of an informational packet. That summary contained the following description of Six Sigma Quality:
>
> "To accomplish its quality and total customer satisfaction goals, Motorola concentrates on several key operational initiatives. At the top of the list is Six Sigma Quality, a statistical measure of variation from a desired result. In concrete terms, Six Sigma translates into a target of no more than 3.4 defects per million products, customer services included. At the manufacturing end, this requires designs that accommodate reasonable variation in component parts but production processes that yield consistently uniform final products. Motorola employees record the defects found in every function of the business, and statistical technologies are increasingly made part of each and every employee's job."

Box 8-1 Six Sigma Quality.

2. Demonstrate consistency on key parameters. Once products correlate with measurements, Motorola will continue to inspect incoming products and review measurements for correlation for an indefinite period of time, depending on volume and how long it takes to have confidence in the quality of incoming products.
3. Institute statistical process control (SPC) on critical processes to achieve preliminary certification. In this phase, agree to certain critical processes on which SPC is to be implemented. When review of SPC shows that the critical processes are under control, preliminary certification can be granted.
4. Develop and approve a neverending improvement plan, and grant full certification. In this phase, the supplier is expected to develop and share its plan for ongoing process cost and yield improvements. Once this plan is approved, the supplier is granted full certification.
5. Maintain an ongoing partnership. Review common goals on a quarterly basis. Long-term contracts and preferred supplier status are granted in this phase.

Also integral to the ongoing evolution of each supplier is a yearly audit of the following areas:

- Quality management
- Quality control
- Procurement
- Material control
- Record keeping
- Methods documentation
- Calibration

Process Control

Motorola uses two tools to establish in-process controls: SPC and process audits. During the last four years, more than $170 million has been invested in training people and improving their skills. Virtually all U.S. personnel are being trained in quality. For example, from 1986 to 1988, more then 10,000 technical personnel were trained in SPC and design for manufacturing techniques. More than 50,000 people are being trained in the concepts of Six Sigma (such as the use of SPC in all work, including nonmanufacturing tasks).

Motorola defines three phases of SPC implementation:

Phase I. Avoidance: Characterize the process and establish control limits.

Phase II. Path to Six Sigma: Identify and quantify critical circuit/device parameters that need tighter distributions to satisfy Six Sigma requirements.

Phase III. Neverending improvement: Continue to tighten distributions and establish new control limits.

Once the final phase is reached, ongoing improvement continues. Work is under way to computerize control techniques.

Motorola uses two types of audits for process control: engineering and monitor. The former is conducted by a QA engineer and entails an intense review of all process steps including equipment parameters, handling techniques, and SPC. Box 8-2 shows the audit checklist.

The monitor audit is conducted by a certified auditor; it reviews a broad range of issues such as whether specifications and revisions are correct, whether logs are filled and maintained properly, etc. The system is set up so that any discrepancy—critical, major, or minor—is documented, and corrective action is required in writing. Critical defects must be corrected immediately; major and minor problems must be remedied within five working days. The proof of success is that results from customer audits for the past two years have been excellent.

Containment

Containment means inspecting out defects until permanent corrective actions can be implemented. Statistical sampling plans are used to inspect each lot as it finishes each operation. The sampling plans are based on two items. The historical process capability in parts per million is determined and used with a sampling plan that has a high confidence level of rejecting lots that do not meet requirements. Each operator then decides either to scrap or to screen the product in question before sending it to the next operation. Screening means that 100-percent inspection is performed, and all product that does not meet requirements is scrapped. Rework is not allowed. The result is that each operation receives only product that is known to be good and can therefore concentrate on process control and avoiding defects. No sampling plan or even 100-percent inspection can guarantee that all defects will be eliminated, but the combination of these techniques makes near perfection possible.

The result of the focus on material control, in-process control, and containment is a total quality system that aims for neverending improvement in product quality and that eventually will lead to the ultimate goal of Six Sigma products.

1. Is the specification accessible to production staff?
2. Is the current revision on file?
3. Is the copy on file in good condition with all pages accounted for?
4. If referenced documents are posted on equipment, do they match the specification?
5. If the log sheet is referenced in specifications, is a sample included in the specification?
6. Is the operator completing the log sheet according to specification?
7. Are lots with out-of-specification readings authorized and taken care of in writing by the engineering department or the proper supervisor?
8. Are corrections to paperwork made according to specification?
9. Are equipment time settings according to specification?
10. Are equipment temperature settings according to specifications?
11. Is the calibration sticker on equipment current?
12. Do chemicals or gases listed in the specification match usage on line?
13. Do quantities listed in the specification match the line setup?
14. Are changes of chemicals or gases made according to specification?
15. Is the production operator certified? If not, is this person authorized by the supervisor?
16. Is the production operating procedure according to specification?
17. Is the operator performing the written cleaning procedure according to specification?
18. If safety requirements are listed in the specification, are they being followed?
19. If process control procedures are written in the specification, are the actions performed by process control verifiable?
20. If equipment maintenance procedures are written in the specification, are the actions performed verifiable?

Box 8-2 Audit checklist.

Questions for Discussion

1. What major efforts led to Motorola's selection as the recipient of the Malcolm Baldrige National Quality Award?
2. Prepare a sample form to rate suppliers based on characteristics that you consider to be important. Suggest a scheme to select suppliers.
3. Describe the role of auditing in maintaining an SPC system.
4. Discuss specific auditing tasks in operator and process control that could be beneficial to companies.
5. Describe how the philosophy of neverending improvement is incorporated in the company.

KEY TERMS

Assemblies
Causes
  Assignable
  Chance
Clearance fit
Components
Control limits
Cumulative distribution function
Fraction nonconforming
Frequency histogram
Interference fit
Mating parts
Natural tolerance limits
Nonparametric tolerance limits

Normal probability plot
Probability plot
Process capability
Process capability analysis
Process capability indices
  C_p
  C_{pk}
  Upper capability index (CPU)
  Lower capability index (CPL)
Process capability limits
Process capability ratio (PCR)
Process mean
Process spread
Process standard deviation
Sample mean
Sample standard deviation
Specification limits
Statistical tolerance limits
  Based on normality assumption
  Nonparametric approach
Tolerance limits
  Lower tolerance limit
  Upper tolerance limit
Transition fit

EXERCISES

Discussion Questions

8-1 Explain the difference between specification limits and control limits. Is there a desired relationship between the two?

8-2 Explain the difference between natural tolerance limits and specification limits. How does a process capability index incorporate both of them? What assumption is made implicitly in constructing the natural tolerance limits?

8-3 What is process capability analysis, and when should it be conducted? What are some of its benefits?

8-4 What are statistical tolerance limits? Explain how they differ from natural tolerance limits.

8-5 Is it possible for a process to be in control and still produce output that is nonconforming? Explain. What are some corrective measures under these circumstances?

8-6 What are the advantages of having a process spread that is less than the difference between the specification limits? What should the value of C_p be in this situation?

8-7 Compare and contrast the process capability indices C_p, CPU, CPL, and C_{pk}.

8-8 Under what conditions would the process capability indices C_p and C_{pk} both be equal to 1? Explain the relationship between these two indices, and discuss which index should normally be chosen to measure the performance of an existing process.

8-9 Discuss the methods available for estimating the distribution of a quality characteristic. State their relative advantages and disadvantages.

8-10 What is a fundamental condition that must exist prior to calculating the process capability? Discuss how process capability may be estimated through the use of various control charts.

8-11 Suppose the dimension of an assembly is a linear combination of several independent component dimensions. Determine the mean and standard deviation of the assembly dimension. If the individual dimensions are not independent, what effect will it have on the mean and standard deviation of the assembly dimension?

8-12 Suppose that the dimension of an assembly has to be within some specified tolerances. If the difference between two component dimensions makes up this assembly dimension, discuss how tolerances could be set for the components. Assume that the inherent variability of each component is equal.

8-13 Explain the difference between clearance, interference, and transition fits in an assembly. What relationship must exist between the shaft diameter and the hole diameter for the assembly to have an interference fit?

8-14 What are the relative advantages and disadvantages of parametric tolerance intervals based on a normal distribution and nonparametric tolerance intervals?

Problems

8-15 In a pharmaceutical company producing vitamin capsules, the proportion of calcium should be between 40 and 55 parts per million (ppm). A random sample of 20 capsules chosen from the output yielded a sample mean calcium content of 44 ppm with a standard deviation of 3 ppm. Find the natural tolerance limits of the process. If the process is in control at the present values of its parameters, what proportion of the output will be nonconforming, assuming a normal distribution of the characteristic?

8-16 For Exercise 8-15, find the C_p index, or the process capability ratio. Comment on the ability of the process to meet specifications. If it is easier to change the process mean rather than its variability, to what value should the process mean be set in order to minimize the proportion of nonconforming product?

8-17 The emergency service unit in a hospital has a goal of 3.5 minutes for the average waiting time of patients before being treated. A random sample of 20 patients was chosen from those who had reported there. The sample average waiting time was 2.3 minutes with a sample standard deviation of 0.5 minute. Find an appropriate process capability index. Comment on the ability of the emergency service unit to meet the desirable goal. What are some possible actions to consider?

8-18 Refer to Exercise 8-15. Find the process capability index C_{pk}, and comment on process performance. If the process center is shifted to the midpoint between the specification limits, what is the proportion of the product that will be nonconforming? Has it improved relative to the present setting of the process mean?

8-19 The diameter of a forged part has specifications of 120 ± 5 mm. A sample of 25 parts chosen from the process gave a sample mean of 122 mm with a sample standard deviation of 2 mm. Find the capability index C_{pk} for the process, and comment on its value. What is the fraction of nonconforming parts? If the process mean were to be set at the nominal value, how much of a reduction would occur in the fraction nonconforming? Suppose that parts with a diameter below the lower specification limit will cost \$1.00/part to be used in another assembly; those having a diameter above the upper specification limit will cost \$0.50/part for rework. If the daily production rate is 1500 parts, what is the daily total cost of nonconformance if the process is maintained at its current setting? If the process mean is set at the nominal value, what is the daily total cost of nonconformance?

TABLE 8-6 Miles per gallon of a brand of gasoline

Miles per gallon				
33.2	29.4	36.5	38.1	30.0
29.1	32.2	29.5	36.0	31.5
34.5	33.6	27.4	30.4	28.4
32.6	30.4	31.8	29.8	34.6
30.7	31.9	32.3	28.2	27.5
34.9	32.8	27.7	28.4	28.8
30.2	26.8	27.8	30.5	28.5
31.8	29.2	28.6	27.5	28.5
30.8	31.8	29.1	26.9	34.2
33.5	27.4	28.5	34.8	30.5

8-20 The miles-per-gallon rating of a particular brand of gasoline was observed for a random sample of 50 observations. Table 8-6 shows the data.

1. Construct a frequency distribution, and comment on the distribution of gasoline mileage.
2. Estimate the mean and standard deviation of gasoline mileage for the particular brand of gasoline.
3. Suppose the lower specification limit for gasoline mileage is 28 mpg. Compute the capability indices CPL and C_{pk}, and comment on the values. What proportion of the product will be unacceptable, if any, assuming normality?

8-21 Consider Exercise 8-20 concerning the miles per gallon of a particular brand of gasoline. Construct a normal plot, and discuss the inferences that you can draw from it. Using the normal probability plot, estimate the mean and standard deviation of gasoline mileage. If the lower specification limit is 28 mpg, calculate the capability indices CPL and C_{pk}. Assuming normality, what proportion of the product will be unacceptable?

8-22 The waiting time in minutes before being served in a local post office was observed for 50 randomly chosen customers. The values are shown in Table 8-7.

1. Construct a frequency histogram. What inferences can you draw from it?
2. Estimate the mean and standard deviation of the waiting times.
3. If the goal of the post office is for the waiting time not to exceed 4 minutes, find the capability indices CPU and C_{pk}, and com-

TABLE 8-7 Waiting time (in minutes) for customers in a post office

Waiting time for customers				
2.1	0.5	3.6	1.4	2.0
0.8	0.4	4.2	3.5	2.5
4.8	2.8	1.9	1.2	3.2
1.6	2.5	2.4	1.9	2.0
3.5	5.2	3.1	1.6	1.5
1.9	2.4	2.7	2.1	1.8
4.6	3.8	1.5	4.5	3.9
5.5	2.5	3.8	5.0	4.6
2.1	2.8	1.6	3.8	4.2
3.5	5.2	4.8	3.9	2.6

ment on these values. Assuming normality, what proportion of the customers will have to wait for more than 4 minutes, if any?

8-23 Refer to Exercise 8-22 concerning the waiting time of customers in a post office. Construct a normal probability plot, and comment on the inferences you can draw from it. Using the plot, estimate the mean and standard deviation of the waiting time of customers. Is the post office capable of meeting the goal of the upper bound on the waiting time being 4 minutes?

8-24 Random samples of size 5 were selected on the length of a connector pin. For each sample, the sample mean and range (in mm) were calculated and are shown in Table 8-8. The length specifications are 50 ± 3.5 mm. The daily production rate is 2000. The unit cost of scrap is \$1.00, and the unit cost of rework is \$0.25.

1. Find the trial control limits for an $\overline{X}$- and an R-chart.
2. Assuming assignable causes for out-of-control points, find the revised control limits.
3. Find the process capability index C_{pk}, and comment on its value.
4. Find the daily cost of scrap and rework.

8-25 A major automobile company is interested in reducing the time that customers have to wait while having their car serviced with one of the dealers. They selected four customers randomly each day and found the total time that each of those customers had to wait (in minutes) while having their car serviced. Next, from these four observations, the sample average and range were found. This process was repeated for 25 days. The summary data after these observations were obtained are

$$\sum_{i=1}^{25} \overline{X}_i = 1000 \qquad \sum_{i=1}^{25} R_i = 250$$

1. Find the $\overline{X}$- and R-chart control limits.
2. Assuming that the process is in control and that a desirable value on the upper bound of the waiting time is 50 minutes, calculate a process capability index, and comment on its value.

TABLE 8-8 Data on length of connector pins

Sample number	Average length, $\overline{X}$	Range, R	Sample number	Average length, $\overline{X}$	Range, R
1	50.3	4	16	49.3	6
2	48.4	2	17	53.3	3
3	48.5	5	18	52.1	4
4	49.1	4	19	50.2	5
5	52.6	3	20	51.9	4
6	46.2	4	21	52.1	2
7	50.8	3	22	49.5	3
8	52.2	4	23	50.7	4
9	49.5	5	24	52.6	5
10	51.7	4	25	52.3	6
11	52.5	5	26	48.6	5
12	47.8	3	27	51.0	4
13	49.6	5	28	52.3	3
14	50.8	9	29	50.6	2
15	48.5	4	30	51.5	4

3. Assuming a normal distribution of waiting times, find the proportion of customers that will have to wait more than 50 minutes.
4. The service manager is interested in reducing the waiting time of customers and hires some additional mechanics, which reduces the average waiting time to 35 minutes. What proportion of the customers will still have to wait more than 50 minutes if the variability in service times is the same as before?

8-26 Light bulbs were tested for their luminance, with the intensity of brightness desired to be within a certain range. Random samples of 5 bulbs were chosen from the output and their luminance values measured. The sample mean $\bar{X}$ and standard deviation s were found. After 30 samples, the following summary information was obtained:

$$\sum_{i=1}^{30} \bar{X}_i = 2550 \qquad \sum_{i=1}^{30} s_i = 195$$

The specifications are 90 ± 15.

1. Find the control limits for an $\bar{X}$- and an s-chart.
2. Assuming that the process is in control, estimate the process mean and process standard deviation.
3. Find the process capability ratios C_p and C_{pk}, and comment on their values.
4. What proportion of the output is nonconforming, assuming a normal distribution of the quality characteristic?
5. If the process mean is moved to 88, what proportion of the output is nonconforming? What are your proposals to improve process performance?

8-27 The advertised weight of frozen food packages is 16 ounces, and the specifications are 16 ± 0.3 ounces. Random samples of size 8 were selected from the output and weighed. The sample mean and standard deviation were subsequently calculated. Information on 25 such samples yielded the following:

$$\sum_{i=1}^{25} \bar{X}_i = 398 \qquad \sum_{i=1}^{25} s_i = 3.00$$

1. Determine the center lines and control limits for an $\bar{X}$- and an s-chart.
2. Estimate the process mean and standard deviation, assuming that the process is in control.
3. Find the process capability indices C_p and C_{pk}, and discuss their values.
4. Assuming a normal distribution of package weights, what proportion of the output is nonconforming?

8-28 Consider an assembly of three components as shown in Figure 8-25. The tolerances for these three components are given in the accompanying table.

Component	Mean length (cm)	Tolerances (cm)
A	10	10 ± 0.5
B	4	4 ± 0.2
C	5	5 ± 0.1

Assume that the tolerances on the components are independent of each other and that the lengths of the components are normally distributed. What is the tolerance of the gap? Assuming normality, if specifications for the gap are 0.9 ± 0.201, what fraction of the assemblies will not meet specifications? How could the fraction of nonconforming assemblies be reduced?

8-29 In Exercise 8-28, suppose the specifications for the gap are 1.05 ± 0.15. An assembly with a gap exceeding the upper specification limit is scrapped, whereas that with a gap less than the lower specification limit can be reworked to increase the gap dimension. The unit cost of rework is $0.15, and that for scrap is $0.40. If the daily production rate is 2000, calculate the daily total cost of scrap and rework. How can this cost be reduced?

8-30 Refer to Exercise 8-28. Suppose the desirable specifications on the gap are 2 ± 0.02. Assume the mean lengths of A, B, and C to be

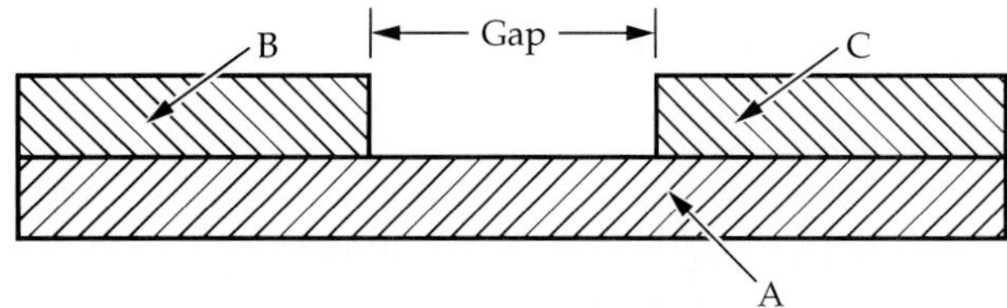

Figure 8-25 An assembly of three components.

11.1, 4.2, and 5.3 cm, respectively. Also assume the natural tolerances to be ±0.5, ±0.2, and ±0.1 for A, B, and C, respectively. Find the proportion of assemblies that will not be acceptable. How can the nonconforming proportion be reduced?

8-31 Refer to the assembly of four components shown in Figure 8-17. Assume that the length of each component is normally and independently distributed with the means as shown in the accompanying table.

Component	Mean length (cm)
A	3
B	8
C	10
D	14

The specifications for the length of the assembly are 35 ± 0.5 cm. Assuming that the natural tolerances (or process spread) for all the components are equal to each other and that the specifications barely match the natural tolerance limits, find the tolerances on the individual components.

8-32 Refer to Exercise 8-31 concerning the four-component assembly. Suppose the specifications for the length of assembly are 35 ± 0.3 cm. Assume that the tolerances of A and C are equal, and that those for B and D are each twice as large as that for A. In addition, assume that the specifications are barely equal to the natural tolerance limits. Find the specifications for each component.

8-33 Consider the assembly of two components shown in Figure 8-18. Suppose the specifications for the dimension X_2 are 5 ± 0.05 cm and those for X_1 are 12 ± 0.15 cm. Find the specifications for the dimension Y. Assume that the specification limits equal the natural tolerance limits. For what proportion of the assemblies will the dimension Y exceed the value 7.10 cm? Assume that the component dimensions X_1 and X_2 are normally distributed.

8-34 Consider the assembly of two components shown in Figure 8-18. Suppose the mean lengths are given as $\mu_1 = 14$ cm and $\mu_2 = 8$ cm. Assuming that the specifications for Y are 6 ± 0.2 cm, what are the specification limits for X_1 and X_2? Assume that the variance of X_1 is three times as large as that of X_2.

8-35 Four metal plates, each of thickness of 3 cm, are welded together to form a subassembly. The specifications for the thickness of each plate are 3 ± 0.2 cm. Assuming the weld thickness to be negligible, determine the tolerances for the thickness of the assembly.

8-36 Consider Figure 8-20, which shows the assembly of a shaft in a bearing. The specifications for the shaft diameter are 6 ± 0.06 cm, and those for the hole diameter are 6.2 ± 0.03 cm.

1. Find the probability of the assembly having a clearance fit.
2. What is the probability of the assembly having an interference fit?

8-37 The specifications for a shaft diameter in an assembly are 5 ± 0.03 cm, and those for the hole are 5.25 ± 0.08 cm. If the assembly is to have a clearance of 0.18 ± 0.05 cm, what proportion of the assemblies will be acceptable?

8-38 Refer to Exercise 8-37. If there is too much clearance between the hole and the shaft, a wobble will result. Clearances above 0.05 cm are not desirable and cause a wobble. Find the probability of a wobble.

8-39 In a piston assembly, the specifications for the piston diameter are 12 ± 0.5 cm, and those for the cylinder diameter are 12.10 ± 0.4 cm. Assume that the natural tolerance limits coincide with the specifications. A clearance fit is required for the assembly. What proportion of the assemblies will be nonconforming, assuming a normal distribution of the piston and cylinder diameters? Clearances more than 0.8 cm are undesirable. What proportion of the assemblies will not meet this stipulation?

8-40 The dyeing operation of fabric requires pigments of different colors which are to be mixed in certain proportions to produce a desired color. A random sample of 25 showed the sample mean and standard deviation of red pigment in a batch to be 520 and 22 g, respectively. Find a two-sided 99-percent tolerance interval such that at least 90 percent of the population is contained within it. Assume normality of the distribution of the amount of red pigment in a batch.

8-41 One of the critical dimensions in the manufacture of plastic reels for computer tapes is the flange diameter. From a random sample of 30 reels, the sample mean and standard deviation of the diameter were 50 and 0.8 mm, respectively. Find a two-sided 95-percent tolerance interval such that at least 99 percent of the population is contained within it. Assume a normal distribution of flange diameters.

8-42 Find the sample size required for a two-sided nonparametric tolerance interval for the viscosity of a grease used as a lubricant. It should contain 99 percent of the population with a probability of 0.95. How will the interval be found?

8-43 Refer to Exercise 8-42 concerning the viscosity of a grease. Find the sample size needed to construct a one-sided lower nonparametric tolerance limit. It should contain 90 percent of the population with a probability of 0.975. How will the limit be found?

8-44 The weight of plastic pellets for an injection molding process is a characteristic of interest. A random sample of 15 pellets was selected and gave the following weights (in g):

20, 19, 22, 20, 21, 17, 22, 21,
18, 20, 17, 19, 18, 20, 21

Assuming the distribution of the weight of pellets to be normal, find a two-sided 95-percent statistical tolerance interval such that at least 90 percent of the population is contained within it. If a one-sided 95-percent upper tolerance limit is desired that is greater than at least 90 percent of the population, find its value. Interpret the difference between the two answers.

8-45 In Exercise 8-44 concerning the weight of plastic pellets, suppose the distribution of the weights is unknown. For a two-sided nonparametric tolerance interval, find the required sample size. Assume that we desire to contain 95 percent of the population with a probability of 0.90.

REFERENCES

ANSI/ASQC A1-1987 (1987). *American National Standard—Definitions, Symbols, Formulas, and Tables for Control Charts.* American Society for Quality Control, Milwaukee, WI.

Cochran, W. G. (1952). "The χ^2 Test of Goodness of Fit," *Annals of Mathematical Statistics,* Vol. 23, pp. 315–345.

Duncan, Acheson J. (1986). *Quality Control and Industrial Statistics,* 5th edition. Richard D. Irwin, Homewood, IL.

Gunter, B. H. (1989). "The Use and Abuse of C_{pk}," *Quality Progress,* Vol. 22, No. 1, pp. 72–73.

Kane, V. E. (1986). "Process Capability Indices," *Journal of Quality Technology,* Vol. 18, No. 1, pp. 41–52.

Mage, D. T. (1982). "An Objective Graphical Method for Testing Normal Distributional Assumptions Using Probability Plots," *The American Statistician,* Vol. 36, No. 2, pp. 116–120.

Massey, Frank J., Jr. (1951). "The Kolmogorov–Smirnov Test of Goodness of Fit," *Journal of the American Statistical Association,* Vol. 46, pp. 68–78.

Michael, J. R. (1983). "The Stabilized Probability Plot," *Biometrika,* Vol. 70, No. 1, pp. 11–17.

Montgomery, D. C. (1991). *Introduction to Statistical Quality Control.* 2nd edition. Wiley, New York.

Nelson, W. (1979). *How to Analyze Data with Simple Plots.* American Society for Quality Control, Milwaukee, WI.

Peña, E. (1990). "Motorola's Secret to Total Quality Control," *Quality Progress,* Vol. 23, No. 10, pp. 43–45.

Shapiro, S. S. (1980). *How to Test for Normality and Other Distributional Assumptions.* American Society for Quality Control, Milwaukee, WI.

PART IV

Acceptance Sampling

CHAPTER

9

Acceptance Sampling Plans by Attributes

CHAPTER OUTLINE

SYMBOLS

p	Fraction nonconforming, or lot quality
N	Lot size
n	Sample size for a single sampling plan
c	Accepance number for a single sampling plan
P_a	Probability of accepting a lot
c_1	Acceptance number for the first sample of a double sampling plan
c_2	Acceptance number for the second sample of a double sampling plan
r_1	Rejection number for the first sample of a double sampling plan
r_2	Rejection number for the second sample of a double sampling plan
n_1	Size of the first sample in a double sampling plan
n_2	Size of the second sample in a double sampling plan
AOQ	Average outgoing quality
AOQL	Average outgoing quality limit
ATI	Average total inspection
ASN	Average sample number
AQL	Acceptable quality level
LQL	Limiting quality level

9-1 INTRODUCTION

Part III deals with methods and procedures to bring a process to control and thereby evaluate its capability, a major aspect of statistical process control. Part IV introduces the concept of acceptance sampling and presents procedures for product acceptance or rejection based on selecting a sample of items. From the inspection results of the chosen sample, the observed number of nonconforming items or nonconformities, as the case may be, is compared to a standard. Thereafter, if the observed number of nonconforming items or nonconformities is less than or equal to the standard, the lot is accepted without further inspection; if it is greater, the lot is rejected.

Chapter 9 deals with acceptance sampling plans for which inspection is by attributes. This implies that a product item is classified as conforming or not without specifying the degree to which the item is conforming. In certain standardized sampling plans, the terms *defect* and *defective* are used interchangeably with *nonconformity* and *nonconforming*. Here again, it is assumed that the specifications that define a quality characteristic to be a nonconformity are known prior to conducting acceptance sampling.

Chapter 10 contains some acceptance plans for which inspection is by variables. In these plans, the quality characteristic is expressed as a numerical value. Certain summary measures such as the sample mean and sample standard deviation are computed based on inspection of the sample units. Thereupon, depending on the guidelines of the sampling plan, certain statistics are computed using the sample information and are compared with standard values. Specified rules are then used to decide whether to accept or reject the batch.

Acceptance sampling can be performed during inspection of incoming raw materials, components, and assemblies; in various phases of in-process operations; or during final product inspection. It can be used as a form of product inspection between companies and their suppliers and vendors, between manufacturers and their customers, or between departments or divisions within the same company.

It must be emphasized that acceptance sampling does not control or improve the quality level of the process. It merely serves as a method for determining the disposition of the lot. As stressed previously, quality cannot be inspected in a product or service; it must be designed and built into it. Because of the very nature of sampling, it is possible that acceptance sampling procedures will accept some lots and reject others, even if they are of the same quality. Therefore, methods of process control and improvement are essential. Such methods alone will get to the heart of making a quality product. Acceptance sampling should be viewed as an auditing tool. Product acceptance based on some chosen standards is accomplished through the use of these plans.

9-2 ADVANTAGES AND DISADVANTAGES OF SAMPLING

Keeping in mind that acceptance sampling plans are auditing procedures, let us outline some of their advantages and disadvantages compared to 100 percent inspection (sometimes referred to as screening). Some advantages are as follows:

1. If inspection is destructive, 100 percent inspection is not feasible.
2. It is more economical and may cause less damage due to handling. If unit cost of inspection is

high or if unit time for inspection is long, the limited availability of resources may make sampling preferable.

3. It may reduce inspection error. In voluminous, repetitive inspection, such as 100 percent inspection, inspector fatigue may prevent the identification of all nonconformities or nonconforming units.
4. It provides a stronger motivation to improve quality because an entire batch or lot may be rejected.

Some disadvantages of acceptance sampling plans are as follows:

1. There is a risk of rejecting "good" lots or accepting "poor" lots, identified as the producer's risk and consumer's risk, respectively.
2. There is less information about the product, compared to that obtained from 100 percent inspection.
3. The selection and adoption of a sampling plan require more time and effort in planning and documentation.

9-3 PRODUCER'S RISK AND CONSUMER'S RISK

In acceptance sampling, units are randomly chosen from the batch, lot, or process. There are two types of risk inherent in any sampling plan for which a decision regarding the lot or batch is based on information from a sample. Some related definitions are given below.*

Producer's Risk: **This is the risk associated with rejecting (or not accepting) a lot of "good" quality. It is generally desired to frequently accept lots of this quality level (acceptable quality level), for which a numerical value is prescribed.**

Acceptable Quality Level (AQL): **This is the numerical definition of a good lot, associated with the producer's risk.** ***ANSI/ASQC Standard A2*** **(1987) describes AQL as "the maximum percentage or proportion of nonconforming items or number of nonconformities in a lot or batch that can be considered satisfactory as a process average." The AQL value refers to the process average, which, if kept stable at this value, would result in accepting a majority of the lots.**

Consumer's Risk: **This is the risk of accepting a "poor" lot. It is seldom desired to accept lots having this poor level of quality. A numerical value of this poor quality level (limiting quality level) is prescribed.**

Limiting Quality Level (LQL): **This is the numerical definition of a poor lot, associated with a consumer's risk. The** ***ANSI/ASQC Standard A2*****-(1987) describes LQL as "the percentage or proportion of nonconforming items or number of nonconformities in a lot or batch for which the consumer wishes the probability of acceptance to be a specified low value." LQL is sometimes referred to as the** ***rejectable quality level (RQL), unacceptable quality level (UQL), or limiting quality (LQ).*** **When LQL is expressed as a percentage of nonconforming items, it may be referred to as the** ***lot tolerance percent defective (LTPD).***

Thus, when we state a producer's risk of a sampling plan, we must correspondingly state a desirable level of good quality that we prefer to accept. For example, if we state that the producer's risk is 5 percent for an AQL of 0.02, it means that we consider batches that are 2 percent nonconforming to be good and would prefer to reject such batches no more than 5 percent of the time. Likewise, suppose the consumer's risk is 10 percent for an LQL of 0.08. This implies that batches that are 8 percent nonconforming are poor and we prefer to accept these batches no more than 10 percent of the time.

9-4 OPERATING CHARACTERISTIC CURVE

The operating characteristic (OC) curve is a measure of performance of a sampling plan. It is a plot of the probability of accepting the lot versus the fraction nonconforming of the lot. It shows the discriminatory power of the sampling plan. For all sampling plans, it is desirable to accept lots with a low fraction nonconforming a large proportion of the time and to accept batches with a high fraction nonconforming a small proportion of the time. The degree to which this objective is achieved is indicated by the operating characteristic curve.

Let us describe the ideal OC curve. Suppose a fraction-nonconforming level p_0 has been chosen such that if a lot has a fraction nonconforming less than or equal to this value it is considered to be a good lot and should be accepted. On the other hand, if the proportion nonconforming of the lot

* ASQC (1987), ANSI/ASQC AZ–1987: *American National Standard—Terms, Symbols, and Definitions for Acceptance Sampling.* Reprinted with the permission of ASQC.

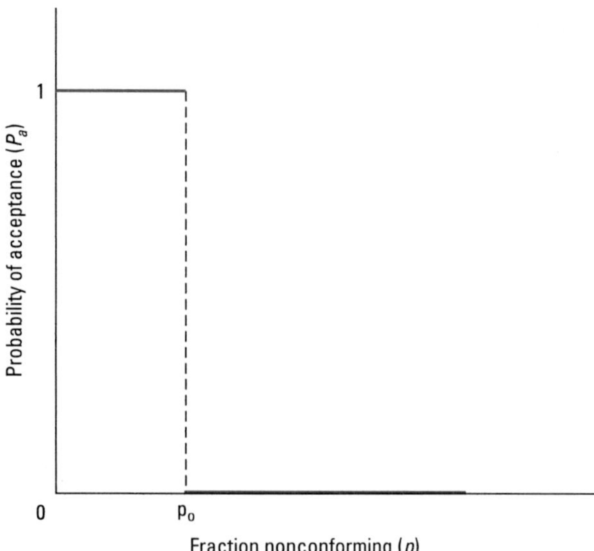

Figure 9-1 Ideal operating characteristic curve.

exceeds this value, the lot is considered to be poor and should be rejected. Under these circumstances, the ideal OC curve is shown in Figure 9-1. The probability of acceptance of the lot, P_a, is 1 for values of the fraction nonconforming $p \leq p_0$, and the value of P_a is 0 for $p > p_0$. This assumes that the user has selected a quality level p_0 that reflects the demarcation between acceptable and unacceptable lots. Furthermore, acceptable lots ($p \leq p_0$) must always be accepted by the sampling plan, and unacceptable lots ($p > p_0$) must always be rejected by the sampling plan. A sampling plan having such an OC curve is totally discriminatory in nature.

In practice, however, the shape of the OC curve for a sampling plan is not ideal. To construct the OC curve for a single sampling plan, let N denote the lot size, n the sample size, and c, the acceptance number. A random sample of size n is chosen from the lot of size N. If the observed number of nonconforming items or nonconformities is less than or equal to c, the lot is accepted. Otherwise, the lot is rejected.

An OC curve of type A is constructed assuming that the sample is chosen from an isolated lot of finite size. The probability of accepting the lot is calculated based on a hypergeometric distribution. The probability of finding x nonconforming items in the sample is given by

$$P(x) = \frac{\binom{D}{x}\binom{N-D}{n-x}}{\binom{N}{n}} \qquad (9.1)$$

where D represents the number of nonconforming items in the lot. Since the lot will be accepted if c or fewer nonconforming items are found, the probability of lot acceptance is

$$P_a = P(x \leq c) = \sum_{x=0}^{c} P(x) \qquad (9.2)$$

where $P(x)$ is given by Equation 9.1.

An OC curve of type B is constructed assuming that a stream of lots is produced by the process and that the lot size is large (at least ten times) compared to the sample size. As discussed in Chapter 3, a binomial distribution may be used to find the probability of observing x nonconforming items in a sample of size n. Assuming the lot proportion nonconforming to be p, this probability is given by

$$P(x) = \binom{n}{x} p^x (1-p)^{n-x} \qquad (9.3)$$

The lot acceptance probability is then

$$P_a = P(x \leq c) = \sum_{x=0}^{c} P(x) \qquad (9.4)$$

where $P(x)$ is given by Equation 9.3. Alternatively, cumulative binomial probability tables given in Appendix A-1 may be used if the appropriate parameter values n and p are tabulated.

If the lot size is large and the probability of a nonconforming unit is small, as explained in Chapter 3, a Poisson distribution may be used as an approximation to the binomial distribution. The probability of x nonconforming units in the sample is found from

$$P(x) = \frac{\lambda^x e^{-\lambda}}{x!} \qquad (9.5)$$

where $\lambda = np$ represents the average number of nonconforming items in the sample. The probability of lot acceptance, P_a, can then be found from

$$P_a = P(x \leq c) = \sum_{x=0}^{c} P(x) \qquad (9.6)$$

where $P(x)$ is given by Equation 9.5. The cumulative Poisson probability distribution tabulated in Appendix A-2 may be used for appropriate values of the parameter λ. In this chapter the Poisson distribution will be used to find probabilities associated with lot acceptance from sampling plans whenever appropriate. Because the lot size is usually large compared to the sample size and the values of the fraction nonconforming p in which we are interested are small, the Poisson distribution provides a reasonable approximation.

Example 9-1: Consider a single sampling plan for which the lot size is 2000, the sample size is 50, and the acceptance number is 2. Construct the operating characteristic curve for the plan.

Solution. We are given $N = 2000$, $n = 50$, and $c = 2$. The probability of lot acceptance is equivalent to the probability of obtaining 2 or fewer nonconforming items in the sample. The Poisson probability distribution in Appendix A-2 is used to obtain the lot acceptance probability for different values of the fraction nonconforming p. As an illustration, suppose p is 0.02 (that is, the batch is 2 percent nonconforming). Since $np = 50(.02) = 1.0$, the probability P_a of accepting the lot (using the tables in Appendix A-2) is 0.920. Table 9-1 shows values of P_a for various values of p. In some instances, the probability values are linearly interpolated from the table values. A plot of these values is shown in Figure 9-2. This is the operating characteristic curve of this sampling plan.

The discriminating power of the sampling plan $N = 2000$, $n = 50$, $c = 2$ is observed from its OC curve in Figure 9-2. If a series of batches, each of which is 1 percent nonconforming, comes in for inspection, then (using the above sampling plan) the probability of lot acceptance of such batches is 0.986. It means that, on average, about 986 out of 1000 such batches will be accepted by the sampling plan. On the other hand, if batches are 5 percent nonconforming, then only about 544 out of 1000 batches will be accepted. As the lot quality becomes poorer, the probability of lot acceptance decreases, as it should. The steeper the drop in the probability of lot acceptance as lot quality worsens, the higher is the discriminatory power of the sampling plan.

TABLE 9-1 Calculation of probability of lot acceptance for different values of fraction nonconforming for the plan $N = 2000$, $n = 50$, $c = 2$

Fraction nonconforming, p	np	Probability of lot acceptance, P_a
0.0	0.0	1.000
0.005	0.25	0.997
0.01	0.50	0.986
0.02	1.00	0.920
0.03	1.50	0.809
0.04	2.00	0.677
0.05	2.50	0.544
0.06	3.00	0.423
0.07	3.50	0.321
0.08	4.00	0.238
0.09	4.50	0.174
0.10	5.00	0.125
0.11	5.50	0.088
0.12	6.00	0.062
0.13	6.50	0.043
0.14	7.00	0.030
0.15	7.50	0.020

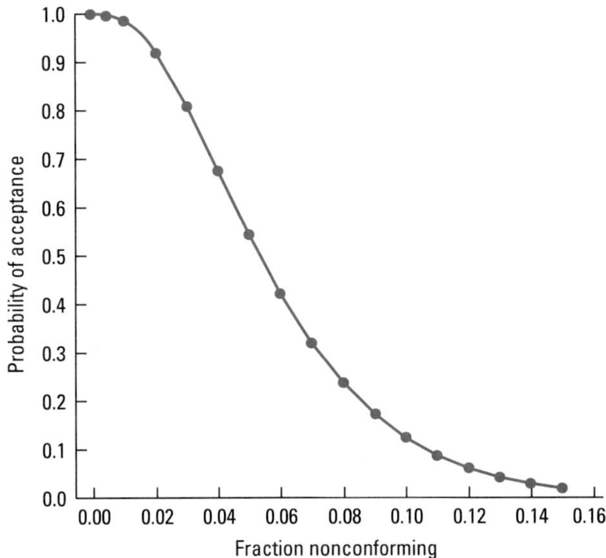

Figure 9-2 OC curve for the sampling plan $N = 2000$, $n = 50$, $c = 2$.

The notions of producer's risk and consumer's risk can also be demonstrated through the OC curve. Suppose the numerical definition of good quality, indicated by the acceptable quality level (AQL), is 0.01 and that, of poor quality, indicated by the limiting quality level (LQL), is 0.11. From the OC curve in Figure 9-2, the producer's risk α is $1 - 0.986 = 0.014$. We consider batches that are 1 percent nonconforming to be good. If the above sampling plan is used, such batches will be rejected about 1.4 percent of the time. Batches that are 11 percent nonconforming, on the other hand, will be accepted 8.8 percent of the time. The consumer's risk is therefore 8.8 percent. It is worth mentioning that even though the AQL is 0.01, the company should still pursue continued quality improvement. In fact, even if no nonconforming items are produced, the quality improvement goal still exists and should be practiced on an ongoing basis.

Effect of the Sample Size and the Acceptance Number

The parameters n and c of the sampling plan have an effect on the shape of its OC curve. As long as the lot size N is significantly large compared to the sample size n, the lot size does not have an appreciable impact on the shape of the OC curve. For fixed values of N and c, as the sample size becomes larger, the slope of the OC curve becomes steeper, implying a greater discriminatory power. Figure 9-3 shows the OC curves for the sampling plans $N = 2000$, $n = 50$, $c = 2$; $N = 2000$, $n = 100$, $c = 2$; and $N = 2000$, $n = 200$, $c = 2$. Note that for

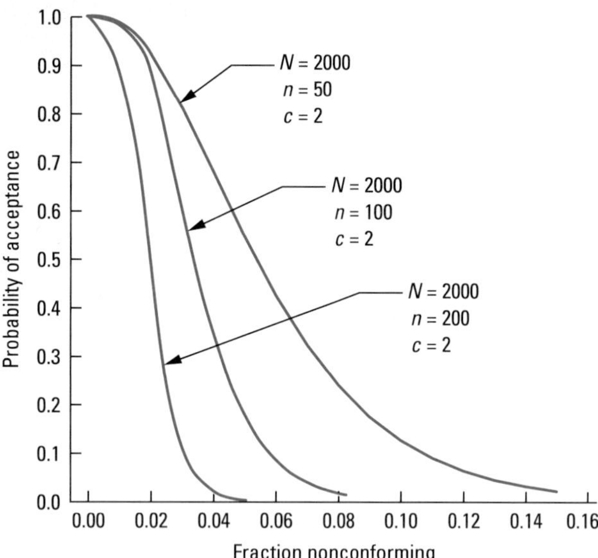

Figure 9-3 Effect of the sample size on the shape of the OC curve.

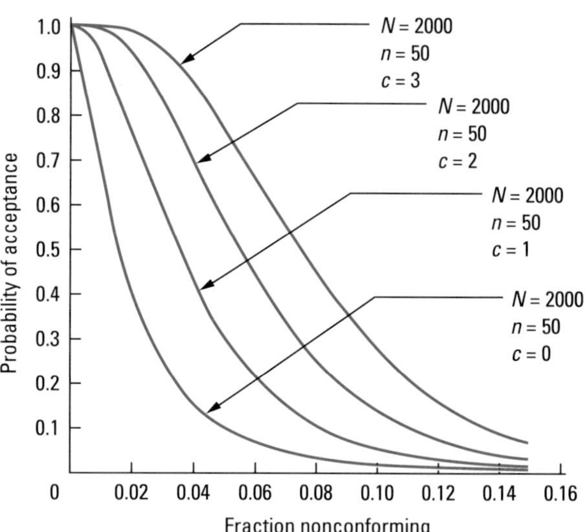

Figure 9-4 Effect of the acceptance number on the shape of the OC curve.

lots that are 2 percent nonconforming, the sampling plan $N = 2000$, $n = 50$, $c = 2$ will accept such lots about 92 percent of the time. However, for the same lots, the sampling plan $N = 2000$, $n = 200$, $c = 2$ will accept them only 23.8 percent of the time. Changing the sample size from 50 to 200 causes a drop in the acceptance probability of 68.2 percent.

For fixed values of the lot size N and the sample size n, as the acceptance number decreases, the slope of the OC curve becomes steeper. Figure 9-4 shows the OC curves for the sampling plans $N = 2000$, $n = 50$, $c = 3$; $N = 2000$, $n = 50$, $c = 2$; $N = 2000$, $n = 50$, $c = 1$; and $N = 2000$, $n = 50$, $c = 0$. Note that the probability of acceptance decreases for a given lot quality as the acceptance number decreases. For lots that are 2 percent nonconforming, the probability of acceptance using the sampling plan $N = 2000$, $n = 50$, $c = 3$ is 0.981. For lots of the same quality, the sampling plan $N = 2000$, $n = 50$, $c = 0$ will accept them only 36.8 percent of the time. This is quite a decrease in the acceptance probability. Thus, smaller acceptance numbers will provide better protection against the acceptance of lots that are of poor quality. One comment needs to be made regarding the case for which the acceptance number is 0. The OC curve starts dropping drastically even as the fraction nonconforming deviates slightly from zero. This may not be desirable from a producer's point of view. For example, if lots that are 0.5 percent nonconforming are considered acceptable, the sampling plan $N = 2000$, $n = 50$, $c = 0$ will reject such lots about 22 percent of the time, implying a high value of the producer's risk. Sampling plans with $c = 0$ do not have the desirable inverted-S shape of the ideal OC curve. They are, however, stringent and serve a need when such a degree of severity is desirable.

The chosen values of n and c should be such that they match the goals of the user. Given some desirable producer's risk and the associated quality level of a good lot (AQL) and/or a desirable consumer's risk and an associated quality level of a poor lot (LQL), the combination of n and c that produces an OC curve that matches these goals will provide an acceptable sampling plan. The OC curves of several sampling plans for a variety of combinations of n and c are often available on a single graph. Users can examine these graphs and pick the one that comes closest to satisfying their goals.

9-5 TYPES OF SAMPLING PLANS: SINGLE, DOUBLE, MULTIPLE

There are, generally speaking, three types of attribute sampling plans in addition to some special acceptance sampling procedures: the single, double, and multiple sampling plans. These plans are described below.

In a *single sampling plan* the information obtained from one sample is used to make a decision whether to accept or reject the lot. There are two parameters of this sampling plan: the sample size n and the acceptance number c. The plan operates as follows. A random sample of size n is selected from the batch. The number of nonconforming items or nonconformities in the sample is found and compared to the acceptance number c. If the observed number is less than or equal to the acceptance number, the lot is accepted. If more than c nonconforming items or nonconformities are found in the sample, the lot is rejected. Consider, for instance, the single sampling plan $N = 4000$, $n = 100$, $c = 2$. This implies that a random sample of size 100 is to be selected from a lot of size 4000. If 2 or fewer nonconforming items or nonconformities are found, the lot is accepted. Otherwise, the lot is rejected.

A *double sampling plan* involves making a decision to accept the lot, reject the lot, or take a second sample. If the inference from the first sample is that the lot quality is quite good, the lot is accepted. An inference of poor lot quality will lead to rejection of the lot. An inference of neither good nor poor quality based on the first sample will require a second sample. Thereafter, based on the combined number of nonconforming items or nonconformities in both samples, a decision is made to accept or reject the lot. The parameters of a double sampling plan are as follows:

n_1: Size of the first sample

c_1: Acceptance number for the first sample

r_1: Rejection number for the first sample

n_2: Size of the second sample

c_2: Acceptance number for the second sample

r_2: Rejection number for the second sample.

Consider the following double sampling plan where attribute inspection is conducted to find the number of nonconforming units: $N = 5000$, $n_1 = 40$, $c_1 = 1$, $r_1 = 4$, $n_2 = 60$, $c_2 = 5$, $r_2 = 6$. The working procedure for this plan is to initially select a random sample of 40 units from the lot of size 5000. If 1 or fewer nonconforming items are found, the lot is accepted, but if 4 or more nonconforming items are found, the lot is rejected. If the observed number of nonconforming items is 2 or 3, a second sample of size 60 is selected from the lot. If the combined number of nonconforming items in both samples is less than or equal to 5, the lot is accepted, whereas if it is 6 or more the lot is rejected. Although double sampling plans are more complicated than those for single sampling, they usually require fewer units to be sampled, on average, to make a decision regarding the lot. This is because a demonstration of extremely good or extremely poor batch quality in the first sample will cause acceptance or rejection of the lot without the need for a second sample.

Multiple sampling plans are an extension of double sampling plans. Three, four, five, or as many samples as desired may be needed to make a decision regarding the lot. The sampling plan may be terminated at any stage once the acceptance or rejection criteria have been met. The sample sizes in a multiple sampling plan are usually less than those for an equivalent double sampling plan, which in turn are usually less than that for an equivalent single sampling plan. The term *equivalence* means that the sampling plans have the same probability of acceptance for a specified lot quality. The ultimate extension of the multiple sampling plan is the sequential sampling plan, which is an item-by-item inspection plan. After each item is inspected, a decision is made to accept the lot, reject the lot, or choose another item for inspection, depending on whether the observed cumulative number of nonconforming items is less than or equal to the acceptance number, greater than or equal to the rejection number, or in between the two, respectively.

Consider the following example of a multiple sampling plan: $N = 4000, n_1 = 20, c_1 = 0, r_1 = 3, n_2 = 20, c_2 = 1, r_2 = 4, n_3 = 20, c_3 = 4, r_3 = 5$. The workings of this plan are as follows. A random sample of 20 items is selected from a lot of size 4000. If no nonconforming items are observed in the first sample, the lot is accepted; if 3 or more nonconforming items are found, the lot is rejected. If 1 or 2 nonconforming items are found, a second sample of size 20 is chosen. If the combined number of nonconforming items is 1 or fewer, the lot is accepted; if it is 4 or more, the lot is rejected. If the combined number of nonconforming units from the first two samples is 2 or 3, a third sample of size 20 is selected. If the combined number of nonconforming units in the three samples is 4 or fewer, the lot is accepted; if it is 5 or more, the lot is rejected.

Advantages and Disadvantages of Each

It is possible to design single, double, or multiple sampling plans that are equivalent to each other in the sense that they have the same probability of lot acceptance for batches of a given quality. Therefore, the criteria for selecting the type of sampling plan are based on other factors as well.

As far as simplicity is concerned, the single sampling plan is the best, followed by double and then multiple sampling plans. Administrative costs for record keeping, training, and inspection are the least for single, followed by double and multiple sampling plans.

On average, for equivalent plans, the number of units inspected to make a decision regarding the lot is usually more for a single sampling plan. This is because double and multiple sampling plans use fewer items in their samples, so if lots submitted for inspection are of very good or poor quality, a decision to accept or reject them is made as soon as possible. Inspection costs will therefore be the most for single, followed by double and then multiple sampling plans.

The information content of the samples is a function of the sample size, because the more samples we inspect, the more information we have about the product and consequently the process. Single sampling plans provide the most information, followed by double and then multiple sampling plans.

The psychological impact of the choice of plan could be another criterion for consideration. With a single sampling plan there is no second chance. With a double sampling plan, if the first sample is a borderline case, a second chance may be provided by the next sample. Similarly, for multiple sampling plans, there is a possibility of several second chances. Some producers prefer to have a second chance because even for a quality product there is the possibility of occasional nonconforming items. Under these circumstances, the preference order might be multiple, double, and single sampling plans.

9-6 MEASURES TO EVALUATE SAMPLING PLANS

The operating characteristic curve, discussed previously, is one measure of performance of a sampling plan. There are other measures that may also be used to evaluate the goodness of a sampling plan. These involve the average quality level of batches leaving the inspection station, the average number of items inspected before making a decision on the lot, and the average amount of inspection per lot if a rejected lot goes through 100 percent inspection. For the purpose of illustration, the following discussion centers around single sampling plans. The concepts, however, are applicable to all three types of plans.

Average Outgoing Quality

First, consider the concept of *rectifying inspection* as it applies to lots that are rejected through sampling plans. Usually, such lots go through 100-percent inspection, known as *screening,* where nonconforming items are replaced with conforming ones. Such a procedure is known as rectification inspection because it affects the quality of the product that leaves the inspection station. Nonconforming items found in the sample are also replaced.

The *average outgoing quality (AOQ)* is the average quality level of a series of batches that leave the inspection station, assuming rectifying inspection, after coming in for inspection at a certain quality level p. AOQ is not the quality level of a single batch that leaves the inspection station. For instance, a batch with incoming quality level p will leave the inspection station with about the same quality level if accepted by the sampling plan. The assumption is that a sample is a small enough proportion of the lot that if any nonconforming items are found in the sample and replaced with conforming ones, the quality level of the lot is not significantly affected. On the other hand, another batch with the same incoming quality p that is rejected by the sampling plan will be screened and so will leave the inspection station with no nonconforming units. (This assumes that screening detects all nonconforming units.) AOQ measures the average quality level of a large number of such batches of incoming quality p, assuming rectification.

Taking N as the lot size, n as the sample size, p as the incoming lot quality, and P_a as the probability of accepting the lot using the given sampling plan, the average outgoing quality is given by

$$\text{AOQ} = \frac{P_a p(N - n)}{N} \tag{9.7}$$

To understand this equation, note that n items in the sample will have no nonconforming units after they have been inspected. If the lot is rejected by the sampling plan, then the $(N - n)$ items left in the lot go through screening so that no nonconforming items are in the outgoing product. Only if the lot is accepted by the sampling plan will the $(N - n)$ items left in the lot leave the inspection station with $p(N - n)$ nonconforming units. However, the probability that the lot will be accepted by the sampling plan is P_a. So, $P_a p(N - n)$ is the number of nonconforming items per lot expected to leave the inspection station. The average proportion nonconforming is given by Equation 9.7.

The value of AOQ depends on the incoming quality level p of the batches. Thus, an AOQ curve that evaluates the effectiveness of the sampling plan for various levels of incoming quality is usually constructed. As an illustration, consider the single sampling plan $N = 2000$, $n = 50$, $c = 2$. Suppose the incoming quality of batches is 2 percent nonconforming. From the Poisson cumulative distribution tables in Appendix A-2, the probability P_a of accepting the lot using the sampling plan is 0.920. The average outgoing quality is

$$\text{AOQ} = \frac{(0.920)(0.02)(2000 - 50)}{2000} = 0.0179$$

Thus, if batches come in as 2 percent nonconforming, the average outgoing quality is 1.79 percent.

Example 9-2: Construct the AOQ curve for the sampling plan $N = 2000$, $n = 50$, $c = 2$.

Solution. The probability of lot acceptance for various values of the incoming lot quality p is listed in Table 9-1. Using these values of P_a and p, the values of AOQ are given in Table 9-2 for different values of p.

Figure 9-5 shows the AOQ curve for the sampling plan $N = 2000$, $n = 50$, $c = 2$. Figure 9-5 shows that when the incoming quality is very good, the average outgoing quality is also very good. When the incoming quality is very poor, the average outgoing quality is good because most of the lots are rejected by the sampling plan and go through screening. In between these extremes, the AOQ curve reaches a maximum.

TABLE 9-2 AOQ values for the sampling plan $N = 2000$, $n = 50$, $c = 2$

Incoming lot quality, p	Probability of lot acceptance, P_a	Average outgoing quality, AOQ
0.01	0.986	0.0096
0.02	0.920	0.0179
0.03	0.809	0.0237
0.04	0.677	0.0264
0.05	0.544	0.0265
0.06	0.423	0.0247
0.07	0.321	0.0219
0.08	0.238	0.0186
0.09	0.174	0.0153
0.10	0.125	0.0122
0.11	0.088	0.0094
0.12	0.062	0.0073
0.13	0.043	0.0055
0.14	0.030	0.0041
0.15	0.020	0.0029

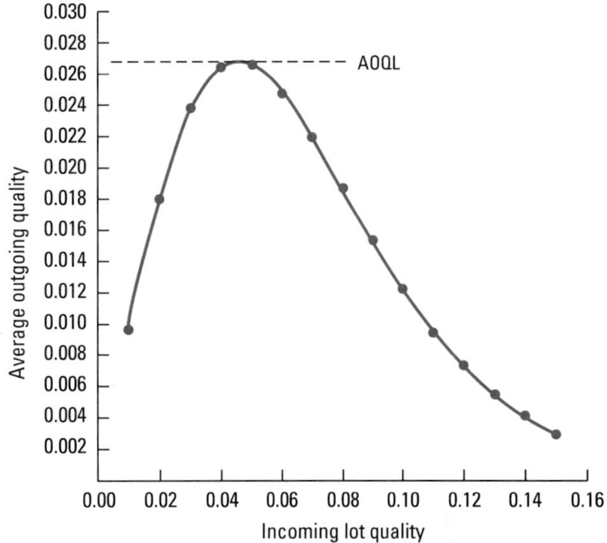

Figure 9-5 AOQ curve for the sampling plan $N = 2000$, $n = 50$, $c = 2$.

Average Outgoing Quality Limit The *average outgoing quality limit (AOQL)* is the maximum value, or peak, of the AOQ curve. It represents the worst average quality that would leave the inspection station, assuming rectification, regardless of the incoming lot quality.

The AOQL value is also a measure of goodness of a sampling plan. Note that the protection offered by the sampling plan, in terms of the AOQL value, does not apply to individual lots. It holds for the average quality of a series of batches.

Consider Example 9-2 and the AOQ curve in Figure 9-5. The AOQL based on the values shown in Table 9-2 is approximately 0.0265, or 2.65 percent. This means that, for the above sampling plan $N = 2000$, $n = 50$, $c = 2$, we have some protection against the worst quality for a series of batches that leave the inspection program. The average quality level will not be poorer than 2.65 percent nonconforming. However, it is possible for an individual lot to have an outgoing quality level of more than 2.65 percent nonconforming. The AOQL value and the shape of the AOQ curve depend on the particular sampling plan. Sampling plans may be designed such that their AOQL does not exceed a certain specified value.

Average Total Inspection

If rectifying inspection is conducted for lots rejected by the sampling plan, another measure for evaluation is the *average total inspection (ATI)*. ATI represents the average number of items inspected per lot. If a lot has no nonconforming items, it will obviously be accepted by the chosen sampling plan, and only n items (the sample size) will be inspected for a lot. At the other extreme, if the lot has 100 percent nonconforming items, the number inspected per lot will be N (the lot size) assuming that rejected lots are screened. For a lot quality between these extremes, the average amount inspected per lot will vary between these two values. For single sampling plans, the average total inspection per lot for lots with an incoming quality level p is given by

$$\text{ATI} = n + (1 - P_a)(N - n) \tag{9.8}$$

Here, P_a represents the probability of accepting a lot that has an incoming quality level of p. A plot of the average total inspection versus p is an ATI curve. Note that, for an individual lot, the amount inspected is either n or N.

For a double sampling plan, the ATI is given by

$$\text{ATI} = n_1(P_{a1}) + (n_1 + n_2)P_{a2} + N(1 - P_{a1} - P_{a2}) \tag{9.9}$$

where P_{a1} represents the probability of accepting the lot on the first sample, and P_{a2} represents the probability of lot acceptance on the second sample. The computations of P_{a1} and P_{a2} will be discussed further in the section on double sampling.

Example 9-3: Consider the sampling plan $N = 2000$, $n = 50$, $c = 2$. Construct the ATI curve for this sampling plan.

Solution. Consider the calculations for a given value of the lot quality p of 0.02. As shown in Table 9-2, the probability of accepting such a lot using the sampling plan is $P_a = 0.920$. The ATI for this value of p is

$$\text{ATI} = 50 + (1 - 0.920)(2000 - 50) = 206$$

For other values of p, the ATI is found in the same manner, and the results are shown in Table 9-3. The ATI curve is plotted in Figure 9-6. Given the unit cost of inspection, the ATI curve may be used to estimate the average inspection cost if the quality level of incoming batches is known.

TABLE 9-3 ATI values for the sampling plan $N = 2000$, $n = 50$, $c = 2$

Incoming lot quality, p	Probability of lot acceptance, P_a	Average total inspection, ATI
0.01	0.986	77.30
0.02	0.920	206.00
0.03	0.809	422.45
0.04	0.677	679.85
0.05	0.544	939.20
0.06	0.423	1175.15
0.07	0.321	1374.05
0.08	0.238	1535.90
0.09	0.174	1660.70
0.10	0.125	1756.25
0.11	0.088	1828.40
0.12	0.062	1879.10
0.13	0.043	1916.15
0.14	0.030	1941.50
0.15	0.020	1961.00

Average Sample Number

The average number of items inspected for a series of lots with a given incoming lot quality in order to make a decision is known as the *average sample number* (*ASN*). Assume that inspection is not curtailed for a single sampling plan when making a decision. For example, if 3 nonconforming items are found by the twentieth unit when using a single sampling plan $N = 800$, $n = 60$, $c = 2$, even though a decision can be made after the twentieth unit to reject the lot, inspection continues for all 60 items in the sample. Under this assumption, the average sample number for a single sampling plan is equal to the sample size n.

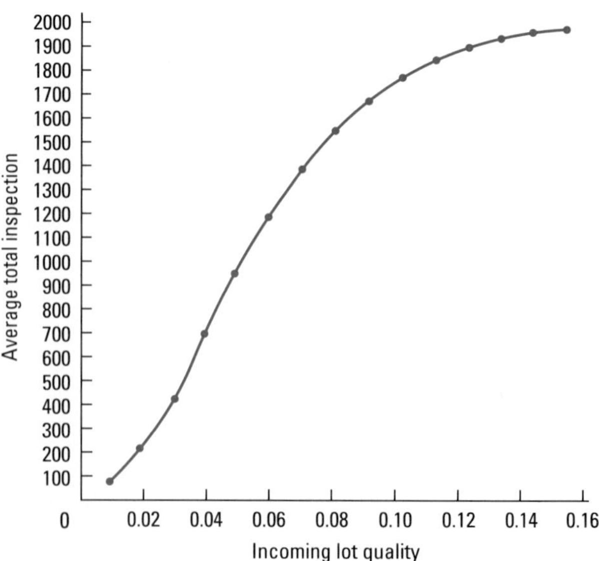

Figure 9-6 ATI curve for the sampling plan $N = 2000$, $n = 50$, $c = 2$.

For a double sampling plan, the ASN is given by

$$\begin{aligned} \text{ASN} &= n_1P_1 + (n_1 + n_2)(1 - P_1) \\ &= n_1 + n_2(1 - P_1) \end{aligned} \tag{9.10}$$

where P_1 is the probability of making a decision on the first sample. Again it is assumed that there is no curtailment on the first or second sample when making a decision.

There is a valid reason for not curtailing inspection in a single sampling plan or on the first sample of a double sampling plan. The estimate of the lot proportion nonconforming is biased if inspection is curtailed. Consider the situation for which the inspection of the first 3 items in a single sampling plan yields all nonconforming units. If the rejection number is 3 and inspection is curtailed on the third unit, an estimate of the lot fraction nonconforming would be 1.00 (or 100 percent), which is quite misleading. Sometimes, for a double sampling plan, inspection is curtailed on the second sample. This leads to a lowering of the average sample number. In cases where inspection costs per unit are high and batches are of neither very good nor very poor quality, curtailing inspection on the second sample will lower the costs associated with decision making.

Note that, for a given sample, the number of items inspected before making a decision is either n_1 or $(n_1 + n_2)$. There is a probability P_1 that a decision will be made after inspecting n_1 items; the probability of inspecting $(n_1 + n_2)$ items prior to making a decision is $(1 - P_1)$. This is the rationale behind the form of Equation 9.10. The probability P_1 can be expressed as

$$\begin{aligned} P_1 &= P(\text{lot accepted on first sample}) \\ &\quad + P(\text{lot rejected on first sample}) \\ &= P(x \le c_1) + P(x \ge r_1) \end{aligned}$$

where x represents the number of nonconforming items or nonconformities, c_1 is the acceptance number of the first sample, and r_1 is the rejection number of the first sample.

For a multiple sampling plan, the same concept used for the derivation of the ASN of a double sampling plan can be used. We have

$$\begin{aligned} \text{ASN} &= n_1P_1 + (n_1 + n_2)P_2 + \cdots \\ &\quad + (n_1 + n_2 + \cdots + n_k)P_k \end{aligned} \tag{9.11}$$

where k represents the number of levels of samples, n_i is the sample size at the ith level, and P_i represents the probability of making a decision at the ith level.

A plot of ASN values as a function of the lot fraction nonconforming p is known as the *ASN curve.*

Example 9-4: For the double sampling plan $N = 3000$, $n_1 = 40$, $c_1 = 1$, $r_1 = 4$, $n_2 = 80$, $c_2 = 3$, $r_2 = 4$, find the average sample number for batches with a fraction nonconforming of 0.02, assuming no curtailment.

Solution. First, calculate P_1, the probability of making a decision after the first sample:

$$P_1 = P(x \le 1) + P(x \ge 4)$$

where x represents the observed number of nonconforming items. From the cumulative Poisson tables in Appendix A-2, we get

$$\begin{aligned} P_1 &= P[x \le 1 \mid n_1p = 40(0.02)] \\ &\quad + P[x \ge 4 \mid n_1p = 40(0.02)] \\ &= P[x \le 1 \mid n_1p = 0.8] + P[x \ge 4 \mid n_1p = 0.8] \\ &= 0.809 + (1 - 0.991) \\ &= 0.818 \end{aligned}$$

The average sample number for batches with a fraction nonconforming of 0.02 is

$$\begin{aligned} ASN &= n_1 + n_2(1 - P_1) \\ &= 40 + 80(1 - 0.818) \\ &= 54.56 \end{aligned}$$

This value represents the average number of units inspected prior to making a decision. It suggests that because of the low value of p, most of the batches will be accepted on the first sample. On the basis of the first sample, lots will be accepted about 80.9 percent of the time, and lots will be rejected about 0.9 percent of the time.

The ASN values are calculated for several values of the fraction nonconforming p in order to construct the ASN curve (see Table 9-4). Figure 9-7 shows the ASN curve for this sampling plan. Observe that as the fraction nonconforming p increases from 0, the ASN rises until it reaches a peak and then starts falling. For very small and very large values of p, the value of ASN approaches the first sample size n_1, because a decision is made for these lots on the first sample. For lots of intermediate quality, the ASN value is higher because a second sample must be taken more frequently to make a decision.

For single sampling plans, ASN is constant and is represented by a horizontal line. Typically, for equivalent plans, the ASN for a double sampling plan is below that for a single sampling plan. It sometimes happens that the middle segment of the ASN curve for a double sampling plan is above the ASN for a single sampling plan. Management must then use historical information to obtain an idea of the process quality. If the quality level p happens to fall in the segment where the ASN is greater for a double than for a single sampling plan, the choice of a single sampling plan may be justified to cut down on inspection

TABLE 9-4 ASN values for the sampling plan $N = 3000$, $n_1 = 40$, $c_1 = 1$, $r_1 = 4$, $n_2 = 80$, $c_2 = 3$, $r_2 = 4$

Fraction conconforming, p	Probability of decision on first sample, P_1	Average sample number, ASN
0.005	0.982	41.44
0.01	0.939	44.88
0.02	0.818	54.56
0.03	0.697	64.24
0.04	0.604	71.68
0.05	0.549	76.08
0.06	0.529	77.68
0.07	0.539	76.88
0.0875	0.599	72.08
0.10	0.659	67.28
0.1125	0.719	62.48
0.125	0.775	58.00
0.150	0.866	50.72
0.175	0.925	46.00
0.20	0.961	43.12

time and costs. On the other hand, estimates of very high or low levels of process quality may justify the use of a double sampling plan that will yield smaller values of ASN. If curtailed inspection is used on the second sample of a double sampling plan, the ASN curve will be further lowered and will become even more attractive than a single sampling plan.

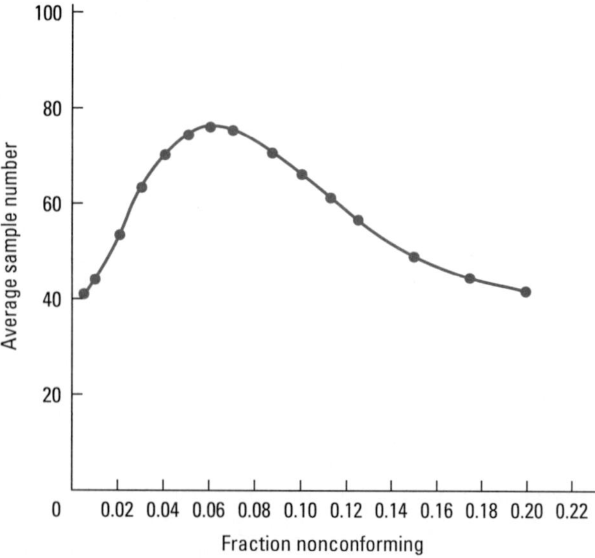

Figure 9-7 ASN curve for the sampling plan $N = 3000, n_1 = 40, c_1 = 1, r_1 = 4, n_2 = 80, c_2 = 3, r_2 = 4$.

9-7 LOT-BY-LOT ATTRIBUTE SAMPLING PLANS

Consider attribute sampling plans that are designed to make a decision regarding items that are submitted for inspection in batches. Batch production is typical of many industries in which inspection is conducted in lots. The objective is to find suitable sample sizes and acceptance numbers of sampling plans that meet certain levels of stipulated risks (such as the producer's risk, consumer's risk, or both). Furthermore, some other criteria, such as meeting the consumer's risk and minimizing average total inspection, or meeting a desirable level of the average outgoing quality limit and minimizing average total inspection, are considered in this section.

Single Sampling Plans

Single sampling plans deal with making a decision regarding a lot of size N based on information contained in one sample of size n. The acceptance number c of the sampling plan represents the number of nonconforming items or nonconformities, depending on the circumstances, that cannot be exceeded in the sample in order for the lot to be accepted.

Operating Characteristic Curve The OC curve of a single sampling plan has already been described in detail. It represents the probability of accepting the lot, P_a, as a function of the lot quality, which is simply the fraction nonconforming p if units are classified only as conforming or not. The effects of the parameters n and c on the shape of the OC curve have also been discussed. A study of these effects enables us to choose appropriate values of n and c, given desirable levels of protection against the producer's and consumer's risks.

Suppose that both the acceptable quality level (AQL), which is the measure of a good lot and is associated with the producer's risk α, and the limiting quality level (LQL), which is the measure of a poor lot and is associated with the consumer's risk, β, are specified. The OC curve in Figure 9-8 shows the relationship between these parameters. For a sampling plan specified by n and c, lots with a fraction-nonconforming level of AQL that come in for inspection should be accepted $100(1-\alpha)$ percent of the time. Suppose AQL is 0.03 and α is 0.05. Batches that are 3 percent nonconforming should then be accepted 95 percent of the time by the given sampling plan. Similarly, if the fraction nonconforming of lots coming in for inspection is LQL, they should be accepted 100β percent of the time.

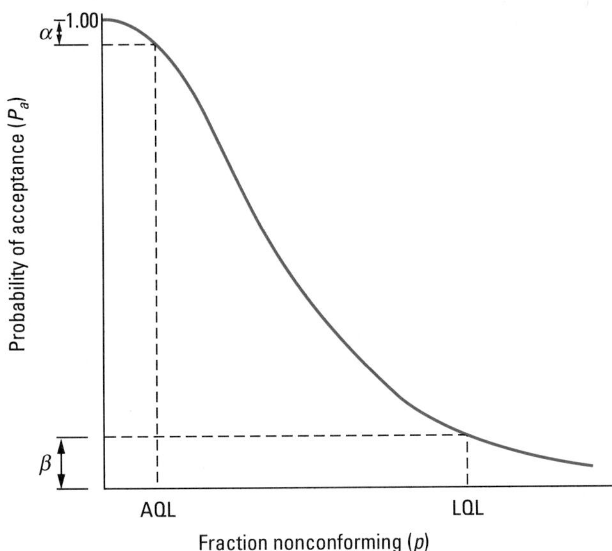

Figure 9-8 OC curve showing (AQL, $1 - \alpha$) and (LQL, β) for a sampling plan.

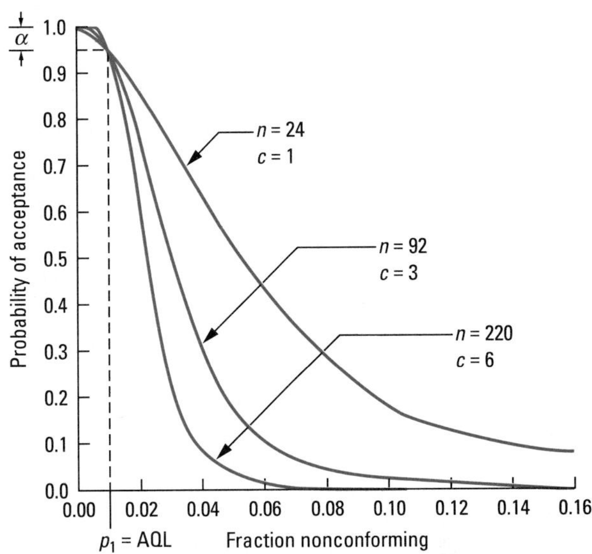

Figure 9-9 OC curves of single sampling plans for stipulated producer's risk and AQL.

For instance, suppose the LQL is 0.09 and β is 0.10. This implies that batches that are 9 percent nonconforming should be accepted only 10 percent of the time. The purpose of making a suitable choice of n and c is to ensure that good lots will be accepted a large percentage of the time and that bad lots will be accepted infrequently.

Design of Single Sampling Plans Several approaches for designing single sampling plans are discussed below. Basically, these approaches involve determining the sample size n and acceptance number c of the plan. The criteria selected will influence the parameter values of the plan. Sometimes, more than one plan may exist that will satisfy the stipulated criteria. What follows is a series of procedures for determining the parameters of a single sampling plan based on the specified criteria.

Stipulated Producer's Risk. Suppose the producer's risk α and its associated quality level p_1, which is the acceptable quality level (AQL), are specified. We desire single sampling plans that will accept lots of quality level p_1, $100(1-\alpha)$ percent of the time. Figure 9-9 shows the OC curves of sampling plans that meet this stipulated criteria. Observe that there are several plans that may satisfy this criteria. What is desired is a sampling plan whose OC curve passes through the single point (AQL, $1 - \alpha$). This criterion is not very restrictive; the OC curves of a variety of plans could pass through this point.

To find the appropriate sampling plan, first select a value of the acceptance number c. As discussed previously in this chapter, the Poisson distribution will be used to approximate the hypergeometric distribution when determining the lot acceptance probability. This is reasonable when the sample size is a small fraction of the lot size and the lot fraction nonconforming p is small. The mean number of nonconforming items in the sample is given by $\lambda = np$. Hence, for a probability of lot acceptance P_a equal to $1-\alpha$ at $p = p_1$, the value of λ is found from the Poisson probability tables in Appendix A-2. Because $\lambda = np_1 = n(\text{AQL})$, the sample size n may be found by dividing the value of $n(\text{AQL})$ by AQL. Fractional computed values of the sample size are always rounded up to be conservative.

For a producer's risk α of 0.05, Table 9-5 lists the values of np_1 for an acceptance probability P_a = 0.95 and various values of c.

Example 9-5: Find a single sampling plan that will satisfy a producer's risk of 5 percent for batches that are 1.5 percent nonconforming.

Solution. We are given $\alpha = 0.05$ and p_1 = AQL = 0.015. Suppose the acceptance number is chosen to be 1. For $c = 1$, Table 9-5, gives $np_1 = 0.355$. The sample size is

$$n = \frac{0.355}{p_1} = \frac{0.355}{0.015} = 23.67 \simeq 24$$

If the selected acceptance number is 3, we have $np_1 = 1.366$. The sample size is

$$n = \frac{1.366}{0.015} = 91.07 \simeq 92$$

TABLE 9-5 Values of np for a producer's risk of 0.05 and a consumer's risk of 0.10

Acceptance number, c	$P_a = 0.95$ np_1	$P_a = 0.10$ np_2	$(np_2)/(np_1)$
0	0.051	2.303	44.84
1	0.355	3.890	10.96
2	0.818	5.322	6.51
3	1.366	6.681	4.89
4	1.970	7.994	4.06
5	2.613	9.274	3.55
6	3.286	10.532	3.21
7	3.981	11.771	2.96
8	4.695	12.995	2.77
9	5.426	14.206	2.62
10	6.169	15.407	2.50
11	6.924	16.598	2.40
12	7.690	17.782	2.31
13	8.464	18.958	2.24
14	9.246	20.128	2.18
15	10.035	21.292	2.21

Source: F. E. Grubbs (1949), "On Designing Single Sampling Plans," *Annals of Mathematical Statistics*, XX, 256. Reprinted by permission of the Institute of Mathematical Statistics.

If the acceptance number is chosen to be 6, we have $np_1 = 3.286$, and the sample size is

$$n = \frac{3.286}{0.015} = 219.07 \simeq 220$$

Figure 9-9 shows the OC curves for these three sampling plans. The figure demonstrates that all three plans satisfy the producer's risk of 5 percent at the AQL value of 1.5 percent. However, they have varying degrees of protection against acceptance of poor quality lots, which would be of interest to the consumer. Of the three plans shown, $n = 220$, $c = 6$ would provide the best protection to the consumer by having the lowest probability of acceptance for poor quality lots. However, it is important to consider the increased inspection costs that would result from selecting this plan, because the sample size for $c = 6$ is the largest of the three. This example considers the values of c of 1, 3, and 6 for demonstration purposes. Other values of c could be selected as well.

Stipulated Consumer's Risk. Suppose the consumer's risk β and its associated quality level p_2, which is the limiting quality level (LQL), are given. It is desired to find sampling plans that will accept lots of quality level p_2, 100β percent of the time. Here again, a number of sampling plans could satisfy this criteria. Figure 9-10 shows the OC curves for some sampling plans that meet the specified criterion.

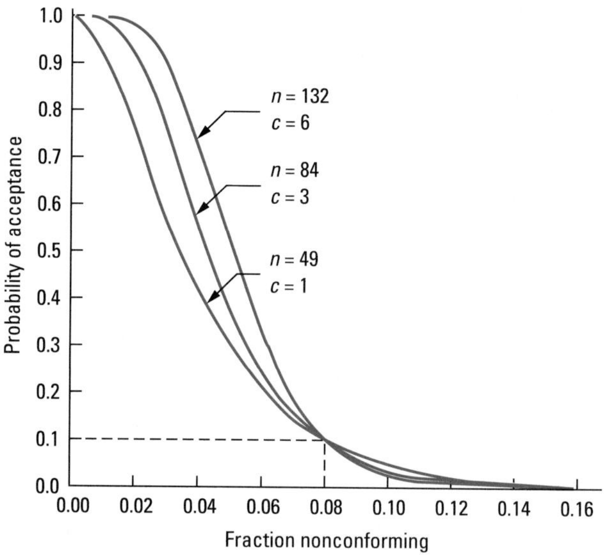

Figure 9-10 OC curves of single sampling plans for stipulated consumer's risk and LQL.

The procedure is similar to that used for a stipulated producer's risk. A value of the acceptance number c is chosen. Based on the probability of acceptance of β, for lots of quality $p_2 = \text{LQL}$, the value of $\lambda = np_2$ is found from the Poisson distribution tables in Appendix A-2. If the value of β is 0.10, Table 9-5 may be used to obtain the value of np_2. The sample size is calculated by dividing the value of np_2 by p_2.

Example 9-6: Find a single sampling plan that will satisfy a consumer's risk of 10 percent for batches that are 8 percent nonconforming.

Solution. We are given $\beta = 0.10$ and $p_2 = \text{LQL} = 0.08$. Suppose the acceptance number is selected as 1. For $c = 1$, Table 9-5 gives $np_2 = 3.890$. The sample size is

$$n = \frac{3.890}{p_2} = \frac{3.890}{0.08} = 48.62 \simeq 49$$

If the acceptance number is selected as 3, we have, $np_2 = 6.681$. The sample size is

$$n = \frac{6.681}{0.08} = 83.51 \simeq 84$$

If the acceptance number is chosen to be 6, we have, $np_2 = 10.532$. The sample size is

$$n = \frac{10.532}{0.08} = 131.65 \simeq 132$$

Figure 9-10 shows the OC curves for these three sampling plans. All three pass through the point (p_2, β), satisfying the consumer's stipulation. The degree of protection for extremely good batches, as far as the producer is concerned, is different. The plan $n = 132$, $c = 6$ will reject good batches (say, 1 percent nonconforming) the most infrequently of the three plans. Of course, it has the largest sample size, which may cause the inspection cost to be high. Other values of the acceptance number could be selected as well.

Stipulated Producer's and Consumer's Risk. We desire sampling plans that satisfy a producer's risk α, given an associated quality level p_1 = AQL, as well as a consumer's risk β, given an associated quality level p_2 = LQL. Good lots, with quality level given by AQL, are to be rejected no more than 100α percent of the time. Poor lots, with quality level specified by LQL, are to be accepted no more than 100β percent of the time.

Because the criteria are more stringent than for circumstances in which only the producer's or the consumer's stipulation must be satisfied, there may not be much flexibility in choosing the acceptance number and the associated sampling plans. It may be difficult to always find a sampling plan that exactly satisfies both the producer's and consumer's stipulation. Consider the approach shown in Figure 9-11. Two plans meet the producer's stipulation exactly and come close to meeting the consumer's stipulation. Two other plans meet the consumer's stipulation exactly and come close to meeting the producer's stipulation. Of these four plans, one must be selected based on additional criteria of concern to the user. It may be of interest to choose the plan with the smallest sample size in order to minimize inspection costs, or the one with the largest sample size in order to provide the most protection. Alternatively, a preference to satisfy either the producer's or consumer's risk could be incorporated in the decision-making framework. For example, a user may desire the producer's stipulation to be satisfied exactly, with the consumer's stipulation satisfied as closely as possible. Another user may be interested in a plan that satisfies the consumer's stipulation exactly and meets the producer's stipulation as closely as possible. Such criteria would aid in selecting the appropriate sampling plan. The following example demonstrates the calculation of the sampling plan parameters.

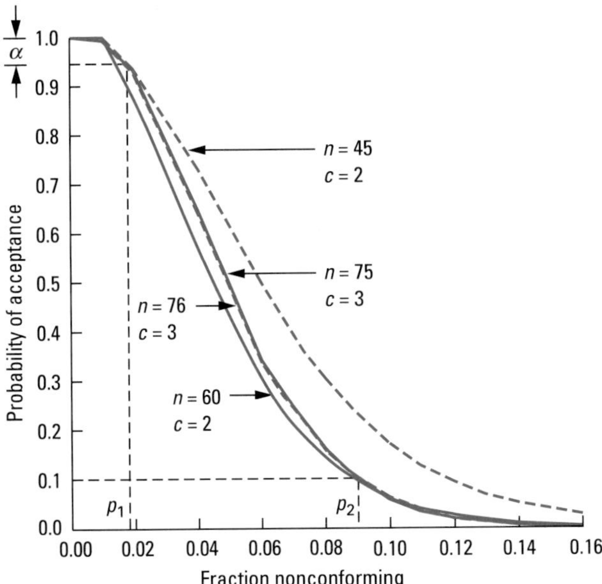

Figure 9-11 OC curves of sampling plans for stipulated producer's and consumer's risks.

Example 9-7: Find a single sampling plan that will satisfy a producer's risk of 5 percent for batches that are 1.8 percent nonconforming, and a consumer's risk of 10 percent for batches that are 9 percent nonconforming.

Solution. We have $\alpha = 0.05$, p_1 = AQL = 0.018, $\beta = 0.10$, and p_2 = LQL = 0.09. First, we compute the ratio of $(np_2)/(np_1)$, which is the ratio of p_2/p_1 because the n cancels out:

$$\frac{p_2}{p_1} = \frac{\text{LQL}}{\text{AQL}} = \frac{0.09}{0.018} = 5.00$$

For values of $\alpha = 0.05$ and $\beta = 0.10$, we can use Table 9-5. We may use the last column in Table 9-5 to determine the possible values of the acceptance number. We find that the ratio 5.00 falls between 6.51 and 4.89, corresponding to acceptance numbers of 2 and 3, respectively.

Two plans (one for $c = 2$ and one for $c = 3$) satisfy the producer's stipulation exactly.

For $c = 2$, $np_1 = 0.818$, and the sample size is

$$n = \frac{np_1}{p_1} = \frac{0.818}{0.018} = 45.44 \simeq 45$$

For $c = 3$, $np_1 = 1.366$, and the sample size is

$$n = \frac{np_1}{p_1} = \frac{1.366}{0.018} = 75.88 \simeq 76$$

So, the plans $n = 45$, $c = 2$ and $n = 76$, $c = 3$ both satisfy the producer's stipulation exactly.

Next, we find that two plans satisfy the consumer's stipulation exactly, one each for $c = 2$ and $c = 3$.

For $c = 2$, $np_2 = 5.322$, and the sample size is

$$n = \frac{np_2}{p_2} = \frac{5.322}{0.09} = 59.13 \simeq 60$$

For $c = 3$, $np_2 = 6.681$, and the sample size is

$$n = \frac{np_2}{p_2} = \frac{6.681}{0.09} = 74.23 \simeq 75$$

The plans $n = 60$, $c = 2$ and $n = 75$, $c = 3$ both satisfy the consumer's stipulation exactly.

The four candidate sampling plans are as follows:

1. $n = 45$, $c = 2$
2. $n = 76$, $c = 3$
3. $n = 60$, $c = 2$
4. $n = 75$, $c = 3$

Let us find how close plans 1 and 2, which satisfy the producer's stipulation, come to satisfying the consumer's stipulation. For a target value of the consumer's risk β of 0.10, let us find the proportion nonconforming p_2 of batches that would be accepted 100β percent of the time.

For $n = 45$ and $c = 2$, if $\beta = 0.10$, then $np_2 = 5.322$. Thus,

$$p_2 = \frac{np_2}{n} = \frac{5.322}{45} = 0.1183$$

For $n = 76$ and $c = 3$, if $\beta = 0.10$, then $np_2 = 6.681$. So,

$$p_2 = \frac{np_2}{n} = \frac{6.681}{76} = 0.0879$$

The sampling plan $n = 45$, $c = 2$ will accept batches that are 11.83 percent nonconforming 10 percent of the time. On the other hand, the sampling plan $n = 76$, $c = 3$ will accept batches that are only 8.79 percent nonconforming 10 percent of the time. Our goal is to find a plan that will accept batches that are 9 percent nonconforming 10 percent of the time.

Given that the target value of p_2 (the specified LQL) is 0.09, we find that for plan 2, the value of $p_2 = 0.0879$ is closer to the target value than the value of 0.1183 for plan 1. If the selection criterion calls for choosing a plan that meets the producer's stipulation exactly and comes closest to meeting the consumer's stipulation, we would choose the plan $n = 76$, $c = 3$. Note that this selected plan is a little more stringent and therefore more conservative than the goal we had in mind. We wanted to find a plan that accepts poor batches (lot quality 9 percent nonconforming) 10 percent of the time. The chosen sampling plan accepts batches that are 8.79 percent nonconforming 10 percent of the time. Thus, the plan $n = 76$, $c = 3$ will accept lots that have a quality level of 9 percent nonconforming less than 10 percent of the time.

Consider determining a plan that satisfies the consumer's stipulation exactly and comes as close as possible to satisfying the producer's stipulation. We consider plans 3 and 4. For a target value of the producer's risk α of 0.05, the proportion nonconforming level p_1 of batches that would be accepted 95 percent of the time may be determined.

For $n = 60$ and $c = 2$, if $\alpha = 0.05$, then $np_1 = 0.818$. So,

$$p_1 = \frac{np_1}{n} = \frac{0.818}{60} = 0.0136$$

For $n = 75$ and $c = 3$, if $\alpha = 0.05$, then $np_1 = 1.366$. So,

$$p_1 = \frac{np_1}{n} = \frac{1.366}{75} = 0.0182$$

The plan $n = 60$, $c = 2$ will reject batches that are 1.36 percent nonconforming 5 percent of the time. On the other hand, the plan $n = 75$, $c = 3$ will reject batches that are 1.82 percent nonconforming 5 percent of the time. Since the value of $p_1 = 0.0182$ is closer to the target value of $p_1 = 0.0180$, the selected plan based on this criterion is $n = 75$, $c = 3$. Note that this chosen plan will be more stringent than the specified goal. Since batches of quality level 1.82 percent will be rejected 5 percent of the time by the plan $n = 75$, $c = 3$, obviously batches that are 1.80 percent nonconforming will be rejected less frequently.

Another criterion that could be used to select a sampling plan is to choose the one with the smallest sample size in order to minimize inspection costs. Of the four candidate plans, the one selected would be $n = 45$, $c = 2$. This plan satisfies the producer's stipulation exactly.

An alternative criterion could be to select a plan with the largest sample size, which provides the most information. Using this criterion, the chosen plan would be $n = 76$, $c = 3$. As previously discussed, this plan satisfies the producer's stipulation exactly and comes as close as possible to the consumer's stipulation.

Stipulated Consumer's Risk and Minimized Average Total Inspection. Assume that items are submitted in lots of size N for inspection. If a lot is rejected by the sampling plan, we assume that it goes through 100 percent inspection. There are two objectives. First, for poor lots of quality level p_2 (the limiting quality level), we desire batches to be accepted with a probability as specified by the consumer's risk β. This is the consumer's stipulation. Second, we desire to minimize average total inspection for a certain quality level of incoming batches, denoted by p_0, say. This incoming quality level may be estimated from the process average fraction nonconforming. It represents the level of quality that we feel will generally be represented by the batches coming in for inspection. It should be pointed out that a sampling plan that minimizes ATI based on a certain value of incoming quality level p_0, may not do the same for other quality levels. Minimizing ATI is based on reducing the average total inspection cost per lot, when the quality level of the incoming lots is known.

The procedure for designing a plan proceeds as follows. First, an acceptance number is chosen. Based on satisfying a given level of consumer's risk

β, the value of np_2 is found from the Poisson tables (or from Table 9-5 if β is equal to 0.10). Since p_2 is given, the sample size n can be computed. For the chosen plan, the ATI is calculated using Equation 8.8, assuming the incoming quality level of batches to be p_0. This procedure is repeated through a trial-and-error scheme to determine the plan that minimizes ATI. The following example illustrates the procedure.

Example 9-8: Find a sampling plan that will satisfy a consumer's risk of 0.10 for lots of quality level 12 percent nonconforming and will minimize the average total inspection for incoming lots that are 3 percent nonconforming. The lot size is 1200.

Solution. Suppose the acceptance number is 1. Since $\beta = 0.10$, using Table 9-5, we get $np_2 = 3.890$. For $p_2 = 0.12$, the sample size is found to be

$$n = \frac{np_2}{p_2} = \frac{3.890}{0.12} = 32.42 \simeq 33$$

For the sampling plan $n = 33$, $c = 1$ and an incoming quality level of $p_0 = 0.03$, the probability of lot acceptance, P_a, is found from the Poisson tables in Appendix A-2. We have $np_0 = 33(.03) = 0.99 = \lambda$; we want to find $P(x \leq 1)$. By interpolating linearly between the table values of 0.772 and 0.736, we get $P_a = P(x \leq 1) = 0.7396$. Using Equation 9.8, the average total inspection is computed as follows:

$$\begin{aligned}\text{ATI} &= n + (1 - P_a)(N - n)\\ &= 33 + (1 - 0.7396)(1200 - 33) = 336.89\end{aligned}$$

In an effort to minimize ATI, let us now select an acceptance number of 3 and repeat the above procedure. For $c = 3$, $\beta = 0.10$ and $np_2 = 6.681$, the sample size is

$$n = \frac{np_2}{p_2} = \frac{6.681}{0.12} = 55.68 \simeq 56$$

For the plan $n = 56$, $c = 3$, with $p_0 = 0.03$, we have $np_0 = 1.68$. From the Poisson tables, $P_a = P(x \leq 3) = 0.9098$. The ATI is calculated as

$$\text{ATI} = 56 + (1 - 0.9098)(1200 - 56) = 159.19$$

Because a decrease is observed in the value of ATI, the next step could be to try $c = 5$. Repeating similar calculations, the sample size is calculated to be 78. For the plan $n = 78$, $c = 5$, with $p_0 = 0.03$, the ATI is 114.69. We now select $c = 7$ and obtain a sample size of 99. For $n = 99$, $c = 7$ and $p_0 = 0.03$, the ATI is 111.55. Since ATI is still decreasing, let us select $c = 9$. The sample size is found to be 119. For the plan $n = 119$, $c = 9$, and $p_0 = 0.03$, we obtain ATI = 123.00. Observe that the value of ATI has increased relative to its value for the plan $n = 99$, $c = 7$. Hence, we select $c = 8$ to check for the minimizing value of ATI. For $c = 8$, the sample size is found to be 109. For $n = 109$, $c = 8$, and $p_0 = 0.03$, ATI is 116.90. We now need to check the ATI value for an acceptance number of 6. For $c = 6$, the sample size is 88. For $n = 88$, $c = 6$, and $p_0 = 0.03$, ATI= 108.46. This is found to be the minimum value of ATI. Thus, the minimizing value of ATI is obtained for the plan $n = 88$, $c = 6$. This plan satisfies both of the stipulated criteria.

TABLE 9-6 ATI values of sampling plans that satisfy a consumer's stipulation ($\beta = 0.10, p_2 = 0.12$)

Acceptance number, c	Sample size, n	Average total inspection
1	33	336.89
3	56	159.19
5	78	114.69
6	88	108.46
7	99	111.55
8	109	116.90
9	119	123.00

Table 9-6 shows the sampling plans with their corresponding ATI values. Each of the plans satisfies the consumer's stipulation of accepting lots that are 12 percent nonconforming 10 percent of the time. Based on the additional objective of minimizing ATI for lots with an incoming quality level of 3 percent nonconforming, the plan selected is $n = 88$, $c = 6$.

Stipulated Average Outgoing Quality Limit and Minimized Average Total Inspection. Suppose that two criteria are to be satisfied. First, a specified value of the average outgoing quality limit (AOQL) is to be satisfied (that is, the worst average quality that would pass inspection should not exceed this value). Second, for a given quality level p_0 of the incoming lots, the average total inspection is to be minimized, ensuring minimum inspection costs. As in the previous section, this specified incoming quality level may be estimated from the recent history of the process average nonconforming. Assume that lots that are rejected by the sampling plan go through screening.

The average outgoing quality for an incoming fraction nonconforming level of p was given in Equation 9.7 as

$$\text{AOQ} = \frac{P_a p(N - n)}{N}$$

Note that for a given lot size N and sample size n, AOQ is a function of $P_a p$. Since AOQL represents the maximum value of AOQ, suppose AOQ is maximized at an incoming proportion nonconforming level of p_m, for which $P_a p$ is maximized. We have

$$\begin{aligned}\text{AOQL} &= \frac{P_a p_m(N - n)}{N}\\ &= \frac{P_a(np_m)(N - n)}{nN} \qquad (9.12)\end{aligned}$$

TABLE 9-7 Maximum values of $P_a(np)$

Acceptance number, c	Maximum $P_a(np)$	Acceptance number, c	Maximum $P_a(np)$
0	0.3679	21	14.66
1	0.8408	22	15.42
2	1.372	23	16.18
3	1.946	24	16.97
4	2.544	25	17.73
5	3.172	26	18.54
6	3.810	27	19.30
7	4.465	28	20.11
8	5.150	29	20.91
9	5.836	30	21.75
10	6.535	31	22.54
11	7.234	32	23.40
12	7.948	33	24.22
13	8.677	34	25.08
14	9.404	35	25.94
15	10.12	36	26.83
16	10.87	37	27.68
17	11.63	38	28.62
18	12.38	39	29.50
19	13.14	40	30.44
20	13.88		

Source: H. F. Dodge and H. G. Romig. *Sampling Inspection Tables—Single and Double Sampling*, 2nd ed. Copyright © 1959. Reprinted by permission of John Wiley & Sons, Inc.

By solving for the sample size n from Equation 9.12, we get

$$n = \frac{P_a(np_m)N}{(\text{AOQL})N + P_a(np_m)} \tag{9.13}$$

Values of $P_a(np_m)$, which represent the maximizing value of $P_a(np)$, are shown in Table 9-7 for different values of the acceptance number c.

The procedure for determining the sampling plan is a trial-and-error approach. First an acceptance number c is chosen. Using Table 9-7 for that chosen value of c, the maximum value of $P_a(np)$, which is $P_a(np_m)$, is found. The sample size is then found using Equation 9.13. For the computed sampling plan, the ATI is found using Equation 9.8. A different value of c is selected in an attempt to minimize the value of ATI, and the procedure is repeated. The optimal plan is one that minimizes the value of ATI and meets the selected value of AOQL. The following example illustrates the procedure.

Example 9-9: Find a sampling plan that will have an average outgoing quality limit of 4 percent and will minimize the average total inspection for incoming batches that are 1.5 percent nonconforming. The lot size is 1500.

Solution. We have $N = 1500$, AOQL$= 0.04$; ATI is to be minimized for a nonconformance level p_0 of 0.015. Suppose the acceptance number is selected to be 1. From Table 9-7, $P_a(np_m)$ is 0.8408. From Equation 9.13, the sample size is found to be

$$n = \frac{(0.8408)1500}{(0.04)1500 + 0.8408} = 20.73 \simeq 21$$

For the plan $n = 21$, $c = 1$ and a fraction nonconforming level p_0 of 0.015, the ATI is calculated from Equation 9.8. For $np_0 = 21(0.015) = 9.315$, the Poisson distribution tables in Appendix A-2 give $P_a = 0.9592$. The average total inspection is

$$\text{ATI} = 21 + (1 - 0.9592)(1500 - 21) = 81.34$$

Let us now determine whether ATI decreases with an increase in the acceptance number. We select an acceptance number c of 3. From Table 9-7, $P_a(np_m) = 1.946$. From Equation 9.13, $n = 48$. We have $np_0 = 0.72$, $P_a = 0.9934$, and ATI$= 57.58$. Since the ATI is less than that calculated for the plan $c = 1$, $n = 21$, we now select a value of c of 5. For $c = 5$ we have $P_a(np_m) = 3.172$ and $n = 76$. So, $np_0 = 1.14$, $P_a = 0.9986$, and ATI$=$ 77.99. Since the value of ATI has increased, we now select an acceptance number of $c = 4$. For $c = 4$, we have $P_a(np_m) = 2.544$ and $n = 62$. For $np_0 = 0.93$ we have $P_a = 0.9974$ and ATI$= 65.74$. This means that we have to check the plan with an acceptance number of 2 to see if it yields a smaller value of ATI than that for $c = 3$, $n = 48$. For $c = 2$ we have $P_a(np_m) = 1.372$ and $n = 34$. We have, $np_0 = 0.51$, $P_a = 0.9851$, and ATI$=$ 55.84. This is the minimum value of ATI for $p_0 = 0.015$. Table 9-8 shows the summary of these computations. It shows the sampling plans and the corresponding value of ATI for $p_0 = 0.015$. All of these plans satisfy the specified AOQL criteria. Thus, the optimal plan is $n = 34$, $c = 2$.

Double Sampling Plans

The parameters of a double sampling plan, as explained previously, are as follows:

n_1: Size of the first sample

c_1: Acceptance number for the first sample

TABLE 9-8 ATI values of sampling plans that satisfy a given AOQL (AOQL $= 0.04$)

Acceptance number, c	Sample size, n	Average total inspection for $p_0 = 0.015$ ATI
1	21	81.34
2	34	55.84
3	48	57.58
4	62	65.74
5	76	77.99

r_1: Rejection number for the first sample
n_2: Size of the second sample
c_2: Acceptance number for the second sample
r_2: Rejection number for the second sample

The advantages and disadvantages of a double sampling plan have been discussed previously. For the same degree of protection (that is, the same probability of accepting lots of a given quality), double sampling plans may have a smaller average sample number (ASN) than a corresponding single sampling plan. The size of the first sample, n_1, is always smaller than the sample size (n) of an equivalent single sampling plan. So, if a decision can usually be made on the first sample, the ASN will be lower for a double sampling plan. Or, if inspection can be curtailed during the second sample, the average sample number will be reduced (most likely, less than that for a single sampling plan). Double sampling plans also offer marginal lots a second chance, which can improve morale. Note, however, that double sampling plans are more costly than single sampling plans with regard to administrative costs.

Example 9-10: A double sampling plan is given as follows: $n_1 = 60$, $c_1 = 1$, $r_1 = 5$, $n_2 = 100$, $c_2 = 5$, $r_2 = 6$. Explain the workings of the plan.

Solution. A random sample of 60 units is selected from the lot. If the number of nonconforming units is 1 or less, the lot is accepted. If the number of nonconforming units is 5 or more, the lot is rejected. In both cases, no second sample is taken. If the number of nonconforming items is either 2, 3, or 4, a second sample of size 100 is randomly selected from the lot. If the combined number of nonconforming items in both of the samples is 5 or less, the lot is accepted. If the combined number of nonconforming items is 6 or more, the lot is rejected.

The OC Curve A measure of performance of a double sampling plan is its operating characteristic curve, which is a plot of the probability of accepting a lot versus the fraction nonconforming. Calculations for the construction of an OC curve for a single sampling plan have already been demonstrated. For a double sampling plan, the calculations are more involved. Note that acceptance of the lot can be based on information contained in the first sample, if the observed number of nonconforming units is less than or equal to the acceptance number of the first sample (c_1). Alternatively, the lot can be accepted on the second sample if the number of nonconforming units from the first sample is less than its rejection number r_1 and the combined number of nonconforming units is less than or equal to the acceptance number of the second sample (c_2). Let P_{a1} denote the probability of accepting the lot on the first sample and P_{a2} the probability of lot acceptance on the second sample. The combined probability of acceptance is given by $P_a = P_{a1} + P_{a2}$. Let x_1 and x_2 denote the observed number of nonconforming items on the first and second samples, respectively. We have

$$\begin{aligned} P_{a1} &= P(x_1 \leq c_1) \\ P_{a2} &= P(x_1 = c_1 + 1)P(x_2 \leq c_2 - x_1) \\ &\quad + P(x_1 = c_1 + 2)P(x_2 \leq c_2 - x_1) + \cdots \\ &\quad + P(x_1 = r_1 - 1)P(x_2 \leq c_2 - x_1) \\ P_a &= P_{a1} + P_{a2} \end{aligned} \tag{9.14}$$

The following example demonstrates the calculation of the probability of lot acceptance for a given fraction nonconforming of lots. The Poisson approximation to the hypergeometric distribution will be used for the calculation of the probabilities. This procedure can be used to construct the OC curve.

Example 9-11: Consider a double sampling plan with a lot size of 3000 given by the following parameters: $n_1 = 40$, $c_1 = 1$, $r_1 = 5$, $n_2 = 80$, $c_2 = 5$, $r_2 = 6$. For a lot fraction-nonconforming value of $p = 0.03$, find the probability of accepting such lots.

Solution. To find the probability of acceptance on the first sample (P_{a1}), we have $n_1 p = 40(0.03) = 1.2$. The Poisson cumulative probability distribution tables in Appendix A-2, give

$$P_{a1} = P(x_1 \leq 1) = 0.663$$

We calculate P_{a2} as follows:

$$P_{a2} = P(x_1 = 2)P(x_2 \leq 3) + P(x_1 = 3)P(x_2 \leq 2) + P(x_1 = 4)P(x_2 \leq 1)$$

Note that when calculating $P(x_2 \leq 3)$ and other probabilities dealing with x_2, the value of $n_2 p = 80(0.03) = 2.4$. So

$$P_{a2} = (0.216)(0.779) + (0.087)(0.570) + (0.026)(0.308) = 0.2259$$

The combined probability of acceptance is

$$P_a = P_{a1} + P_{a2} = 0.663 + 0.2259 = 0.8889$$

Thus, about 66.3 percent of lots which came in for inspection with a fraction nonconforming at 0.03 will be accepted on the first sample; for these lots a second sample will not be taken. For 22.59 percent of the lots, a second sample will be taken, and the lot will be accepted based on the evidence in both of the samples. Overall, 88.89 percent of the lots will be accepted by the sampling plan.

Repeating the above computation for several different values of the fraction nonconforming p will lead to the construction of the OC curve of the double sampling plan.

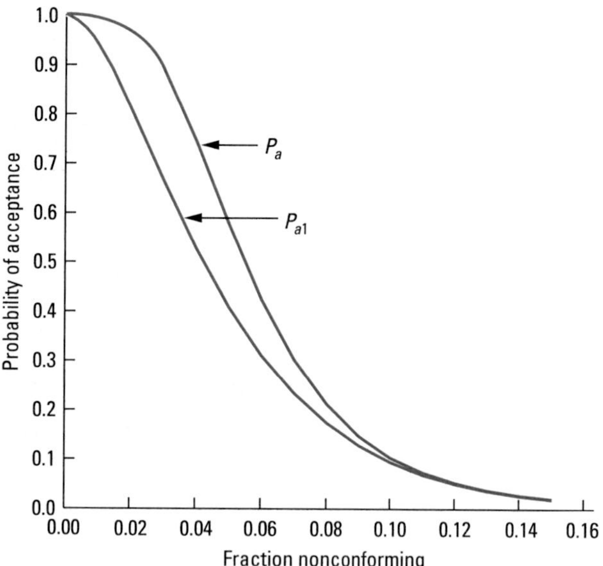

Figure 9-12 OC curve for the double sampling plan $N = 3000$, $n_1 = 40$, $c_1 = 1$, $r_1 = 5$, $n_2 = 80$, $c_2 = 5$, $r_2 = 6$.

Figure 9-12 shows the OC curve for the double sampling plan $N = 3000$, $n_1 = 40$, $c_1 = 1$, $r_1 = 5$, $n_2 = 80$, $c_2 = 5$, $r_2 = 6$. Both P_{a1}, the probability of acceptance on the first sample, and P_a, the combined probability of acceptance based on both samples, are shown. The difference between the ordinate values of the graphs for P_a and P_{a1}, for a given value of p, indicates the probability of lot acceptance on the second sample. For very small values of p, the graphs of P_a and P_{a1} are close because a majority of the lots are accepted on the first sample. Likewise, for very large values of p, the plots of P_a and P_{a1} are in close proximity because most of the lots are rejected on the first sample. In between these extremes, the increasing difference between the curves represents the increase in the probability of lot acceptance due to the second sample. When judging the overall performance of the double sampling plan, the combined probability of acceptance P_a should be considered. The effectiveness of the sampling plan will be determined by its discriminatory power. Lots whose quality level is acceptable or better should be rejected infrequently, preferably with a probability no more than the producer's risk α. Lots of limiting quality level or poorer should be accepted infrequently, preferably with a probability no more than the consumer's risk β.

The Average Sample Number and the Average Total Inspection Curves The average sample number has been explained previously. It represents the average number of items inspected per lot, for a series of lots with a given fraction nonconforming p, that are needed to make a decision. For a double sampling plan without curtailed inspection, the average sample number was given in Equation 9.10 as

$$\begin{aligned} \text{ASN} &= n_1 P_1 + (n_1 + n_2)(1 - P_1) \\ &= n_1 + n_2(1 - P_1) \end{aligned} \tag{9.15}$$

where P_1 is the probability of making a decision on the first sample.

A plot of ASN values for different values of p is known as an ASN curve (see Figure 9-7). One of the reasons for selecting a double over a single sampling plan is that a double sampling plan's ASN is expected to be less. If the relevant range of the fraction nonconforming p is known, then it is of interest if the ASN for a double sampling plan is less than that for an equivalent single sampling plan, at least for that range of p. Note that the ASN for a single sampling plan is equal to the sample size n. As shown in Figure 9-7, the ASN curve rises with an increase in p, attains a peak, and then declines. The reason is that for extremely good or extremely poor lots, a decision is made on the first sample, thus making a second sample unnecessary. This keeps the value of ASN small and closer to the size of the first sample. It is possible for the ASN curves for an equivalent double and single sampling plan to plot as shown in Figure 9-13. Assuming that there is no curtailment of inspection for either the single or double sampling plan, it may be that for values of the fraction nonconforming p between p_a and p_b, the single sampling plan will have a smaller ASN. It is then im-

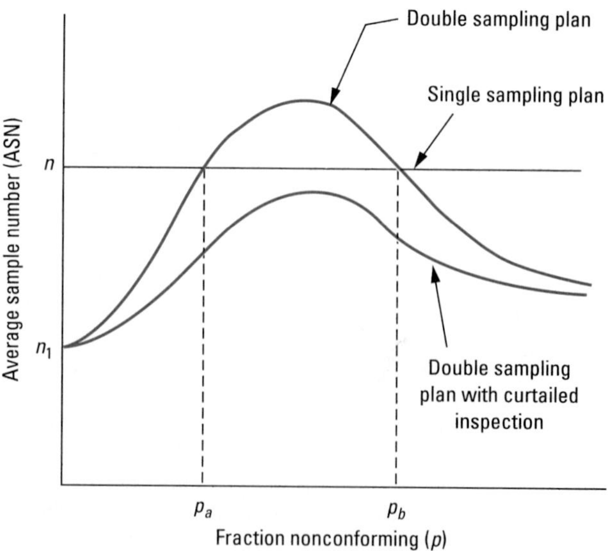

Figure 9-13 ASN curves of equivalent double and single sampling plans.

portant to have an idea of the average quality of the incoming batches. Such information will be helpful in determining the usefulness of a double sampling plan. If the average fraction nonconforming is less than p_a or greater than p_b, a double sampling plan may be chosen.

Curtailing inspection during the second sample of a double sampling plan reduces the average sample number. Thus, the ASN curve for a double sampling plan with curtailed inspection, as shown in Figure 9-13, may be below that for a single sampling plan over the entire range of the fraction-nonconforming values. In such a case, if reduction of inspection costs were a criterion, the double sampling plan would be preferred over the equivalent single sampling plan.

Another measure of performance, in conjunction with rectification inspection, is the average total inspection, which is the average number of items inspected per lot for a series of lots with a given fraction nonconforming level p, assuming that rejected lots go through screening. For a double sampling plan, the ATI is given by Equation 9.9 as

$$\text{ATI} = (n_1)P_{a1} + (n_1 + n_2)P_{a2} + N(1 - P_{a1} - P_{a2}) \tag{9.16}$$

where P_{a1} and P_{a2} represent the probability of accepting the lot on the first and second samples, respectively. The significance and computation of the ATI curve for a single sampling plan have already been explained. The ATI curve is a nondecreasing function of the fraction nonconforming p. When p is close to zero, ATI approaches n_1; for extremely large values of p, ATI approaches the lot size N. Given the quality level of the incoming product, minimizing the ATI serves to reduce total costs of inspection and rectification. A plot of the ATI values as a function of the fraction nonconforming p of the incoming lots is known as an ATI curve.

Example 9-12: Consider a double sampling plan with a lot size of 3000 given by the following parameters: $n_1 = 40$, $c_1 = 1$, $r_1 = 5$, $n_2 = 80$, $c_2 = 5$, $r_2 = 6$. Find the average total inspection for lots with an incoming fraction nonconforming of 0.03.

Solution. First, calculate P_{a1} and P_{a2}. These values were found in Example 9-11 for the same double sampling plan [note that $n_1 p = 40(0.03) = 1.2$ and $n_2 p = 80(0.03) = 2.4$]. The results were

$$P_{a1} = P(x_1 \leq 1) = 0.663$$

$$\begin{aligned} P_{a2} &= P(x_1 = 2)P(x_2 \leq 3) + P(x_1 = 3)P(x_2 \leq 2) \\ &\quad + P(x_1 = 4)P(x_2 \leq 1) \\ &= (0.216)(0.779) + (0.087)(0.570) + (0.026)(0.308) \\ &= 0.2259 \end{aligned}$$

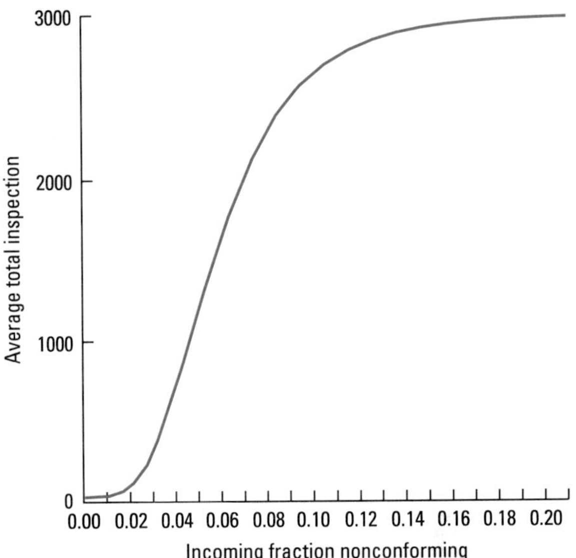

Figure 9-14 ATI curve for the double sampling plan $N = 3000$, $n_1 = 40$, $c_1 = 1$, $r_1 = 5$, $n_2 = 80$, $c_2 = 5$, $r_2 = 6$.

The average total inspection for incoming lots that are 3 percent nonconforming is

$$\begin{aligned} \text{ATI} &= 40(0.663) + (40 + 80)(0.2259) \\ &\quad + 3000(1 - 0.663 - 0.2259) = 386.93 \end{aligned}$$

So, the average total inspection per lot will be about 387 units if batches are 3-percent nonconforming. Recall that for a single lot, the total inspection will be either 40 or 120, respectively, if the lot is accepted on the first or second sample. If the lot is rejected on either sample, then the assumption of screening implies that all 3000 items in the lot will be inspected. An ATI curve for the selected sampling plan is shown in Figure 9-14.

Design of Double Sampling Plans One criterion for designing double sampling plans involves satisfying a specified level of the producer's risk α at an associated quality level p_1 = AQL as well as meeting a consumer's risk β at a quality level p_2 = LQL. This implies that we prefer to find a plan for which the OC curve passes through the two points (AQL, $1 - \alpha$) and (LQL, β). Another constraint may be imposed to help us find double sampling plans using a simple procedure. Assume the sample sizes to be given by either $n_2 = n_1$, or $n_2 = 2n_1$. Consider a pair of tables known as Grubbs' tables (Tables 9-9 and 9-10), named after their originator, Frank E. Grubbs, who proposed their use in the construction of single sampling plans. Table 9-9 is used when $n_1 = n_2$, and Table 9-10 is used when $n_2 = 2n_1$.

TABLE 9-9 Values for constructing double sampling plans for which $n_1 = n_2$ ($\alpha = 0.05, \beta = 0.10$)

Plan number	$R = p_2/p_1$	Acceptance numbers c_1	c_2	Approximate values of n_1p: $P_a = 0.95$	$P_a = 0.50$	$P_a = 0.10$	Approximate ASN/n_1 for $P_a = 0.95$ point
1	11.90	0	1	0.21	1.00	2.50	1.170
2	7.54	1	2	0.52	1.82	3.92	1.081
3	6.79	0	2	0.43	1.42	2.96	1.340
4	5.39	1	3	0.76	2.11	4.11	1.169
5	4.65	2	4	1.16	2.90	5.39	1.105
6	4.25	1	4	1.04	2.50	4.42	1.274
7	3.88	2	5	1.43	3.20	5.55	1.170
8	3.63	3	6	1.87	3.98	6.78	1.117
9	3.38	2	6	1.72	3.56	5.82	1.248
10	3.21	3	7	2.15	4.27	6.91	1.173
11	3.09	4	8	2.62	5.02	8.10	1.124
12	2.85	4	9	2.90	5.33	8.26	1.167
13	2.60	5	11	3.68	6.40	9.56	1.166
14	2.44	5	12	4.00	6.73	9.77	1.215
15	2.32	5	13	4.35	7.06	10.08	1.271
16	2.22	5	14	4.70	7.52	10.45	1.331
17	2.12	5	16	5.39	8.40	11.41	1.452

Source: Adapted from Chemical Corps Engineering Agency (1953).

TABLE 9-10 Values for constructing double sampling plans for which $n_2 = 2n_1$ ($\alpha = 0.05, \beta = 0.10$)

Plan number	$R = p_2/p_1$	Acceptance numbers c_1	c_2	Approximate values of n_1p: $P_a = 0.95$	$P_a = 0.50$	$P_a = 0.10$	Approximate ASN/n_1 for $P_a = 0.95$ point
1	14.50	0	1	0.16	0.84	2.32	1.273
2	8.07	0	2	0.30	1.07	2.42	1.511
3	6.48	1	3	0.60	1.80	3.89	1.238
4	5.39	0	3	0.49	1.35	2.64	1.771
5	5.09	1	4	0.77	1.97	3.92	1.359
6	4.31	0	4	0.68	1.64	2.93	1.985
7	4.19	1	5	0.96	2.18	4.02	1.498
8	3.60	1	6	1.16	2.44	4.17	1.646
9	3.26	2	8	1.68	3.28	5.47	1.476
10	2.96	3	10	2.27	4.13	6.72	1.388
11	2.77	3	11	2.46	4.36	6.82	1.468
12	2.62	4	13	3.07	5.21	8.05	1.394
13	2.46	4	14	3.29	5.40	8.11	1.472
14	2.21	3	15	3.41	5.40	7.55	1.888
15	1.97	4	20	4.75	7.02	9.35	2.029
16	1.74	6	30	7.45	10.31	12.96	2.230

Source: Adapted from Chemical Corps Engineering Agency, *Manual No. 2: Master Sampling Plans for Single, Duplicate, Double, and Multiple Sampling* (Edgewood Arsenal, MD: Army Chemical Center, 1953)

Both of the tables are based on a producer's risk α of 0.05 and a consumer's risk β of 0.10.

The use of these tables in the construction of double sampling plans is as follows. First, the ratio R of LQL to AQL (or p_2/p_1) is found. Using either Table 9-9 or 9-10, depending on the circumstances, the table value that is closest to the calculated value of R is found. Next, the value of n_1p is read from the table, depending on the criterion that is to be satisfied exactly (that is, the producer's or consumer's stipulation). Dividing n_1p by the value of p (which is either p_1 or p_2) will yield the size of the first sample (n_1). The complete sampling plan, involving the acceptance number for the two samples, is read from Table 9-9 or Table 9-10.

Example 9-13: Find a double sampling plan for a lot size of 2500 where it is desired to reject batches that are 1.2 percent nonconforming no more than 5 percent of the time, while batches that are 7.5 percent nonconforming should be accepted about 10 percent of the time. Assume that the sample sizes are equal and that it is preferred to satisfy the producer's stipulation exactly.

Solution. We have $N = 2500$, $\alpha = 0.05$, $p_1 = \text{AQL} = 0.012$, $\beta = 0.10$, $p_2 = \text{LQL} = 0.075$, and $n_1 = n_2$. Computing the ratio of p_2/p_1 we have:

$$R = \frac{p_2}{p_1} = \frac{\text{LQL}}{\text{AQL}} = \frac{0.075}{0.012} = 6.25$$

From Table 9-9, using the calculated value of R of 6.25, the closest value in the table is $R = 6.79$ for plan 3. For plan 3, the acceptance numbers are $c_1 = 0$ and $c_2 = 2$. If the producer's risk ($\alpha = 0.05$) is to be satisfied exactly, $P_a = 1 - 0.05 = 0.95$ for $p_1 = 0.012$. From Table 9-9, using the appropriate column of $P_a = 0.95$, the value of n_1p is 0.43. The size of the first sample is

$$n_1 = \frac{0.43}{0.012} = 35.83 \simeq 36$$

Because the sample sizes are assumed to be equal, $n_2 = n_1 = 36$. Thus, the double sampling plan is $n_1 = 36$, $c_1 = 0$, $n_2 = 36$, $c_2 = 2$. The values of r_1 and r_2 are each assumed to be 3.

The value of the average sample number (ASN) corresponding to the fraction-nonconforming value for which $P_a = 0.95$ can be found using Table 9-9. For $P_a = 0.95$, we have $p = p_1 = \text{AQL} = 0.012$. From Table 9-9, for plan 3, $\text{ASN}/n_1 = 1.340$. So, $\text{ASN} = (1.340)36 = 48.24$. For other values of p, the general formula for the ASN of a double sampling plan (Equation 9.15) would have to be used.

Example 9-14: Find a double sampling plan for a lot size of 3000 where it is desired to reject batches that are 2 percent nonconforming no more than 5 percent of the time, and to accept batches that are 11.5 percent nonconforming no more than 10 percent of the time. Assume that the size of the second sample is twice that of the first sample and that the consumer's stipulation is to be satisfied exactly.

Solution. We have $N = 3000$, $\alpha = 0.05$, $p_1 = \text{AQL} = 0.020$, $\beta = 0.10$, $p_2 = \text{LQL} = 0.115$, and $n_2 = 2n_1$. The ratio of p_2/p_1 is

$$R = \frac{p_2}{p_1} = \frac{0.115}{0.020} = 5.75$$

From Table 9-10, the closest value of R to this calculated value is $R = 5.39$ for plan 4. The acceptance numbers are $c_1 = 0$, $c_2 = 3$. Because the consumer's risk is to be satisfied exactly, the corresponding proportion nonconforming value for $P_a = \beta = 0.10$ is $p_2 = 0.115$. From Table 9-10, the value of n_1p for $P_a = 0.10$ is 2.64. The size of the first sample is

$$n_1 = \frac{2.64}{0.115} = 22.96 \simeq 23$$

The size of the second sample is $n_2 = 2n_1 = 2(23) = 46$. Hence, the sampling plan is $n_1 = 23$, $c_1 = 0$, $n_2 = 46$, $c_2 = 3$. The values of r_1 and r_2 are each assumed to be 4.

Multiple Sampling Plans

A multiple sampling plan is an extension of a double sampling plan. The decision making procedure is similar to that of a double sampling plan in that it is possible to require two or more samples prior to deciding the fate of the lot.

At each phase a sample size, acceptance number, and rejection number are specified. As an example, consider the multiple sampling plan in the accompanying table. A first sample of size 20 is chosen from the lot. If no nonconforming units are found, the lot is accepted. If 2 or more nonconforming units are found, the lot is rejected. If 1 nonconforming unit is found, a second sample of size 20 is chosen. If the combined number of nonconforming units is 1 or less, the lot is accepted. If the combined number of nonconforming items is 3 or more, the lot is rejected. If the combined number of nonconforming items is 2, a third sample of size 20 is selected. This process might continue similarly until a fourth sample of size 20 is chosen and the lot is either accepted or rejected at this final stage.

Sample level	Cumulative sample size	Acceptance number	Rejection number
1	20	0	2
2	40	1	3
3	60	2	4
4	80	3	4

The major advantage of multiple sampling plans is that the average number of units inspected prior to making a decision regarding a lot may be less than that for a corresponding single or a double sampling plan. In other words, the average sample number is usually less for a multiple sampling plan than for an equivalent single or double sampling plan. If lots are exceptionally good or poor, a decision will usually be made at an earlier stage of the multiple sampling plan. This will let us inspect fewer items, on average, to determine the disposition of the lot. The expression for the ASN for a multiple sampling was given previously by Equation 9.11 as

$$\text{ASN} = n_1P_1 + (n_1 + n_2)P_2 + \cdots + (n_1 + n_2 + \cdots + n_k)P_k \tag{9.17}$$

where k represents the number of levels of samples, n_i is the sample size at the ith level, and P_i represents the probability of making a decision at the ith level.

For the example just described, the number of levels (k) is 4. The sample sizes are $n_1 = 20$, $n_2 = 20$, $n_3 = 20$, $n_4 = 20$. P_1 is the probability of making a decision at the first level, which is

$$P_1 = P(x_1 = 0) + P(x_1 \geq 2)$$

where x_1 represents the number of nonconforming units observed for the first sample. Similarly, the probability of making a decision on the second sample is

$$P_2 = P(x_1 = 1)P(x_2 = 0) + P(x_1 = 1)P(x_2 \geq 2)$$

where x_2 represents the number of nonconforming units found for the second sample.

Along the same lines, the probability of making a decision on the third sample is given by

$$P_3 = P(x_1 = 1)P(x_2 = 1)P(x_3 = 0) + P(x_1 = 1)P(x_2 = 1)P(x_3 \geq 2)$$

where x_3 represents the number of nonconforming units found for the third sample. Lastly, the probability of making a decision on the fourth sample is

$$P_4 = P(x_1 = 1)P(x_2 = 1)P(x_3 = 1)P(x_4 = 0) + P(x_1 = 1)P(x_2 = 1)P(x_3 = 1)P(x_4 \geq 1)$$

where x_4 represents the number of nonconforming units found for the fourth sample. Now that P_1, P_2, P_3, and P_4 can be evaluated using the above expressions, the ASN may be calculated using Equation 9.17.

The disadvantage of multiple sampling plans compared to equivalent single or double sampling plans is their higher administrative cost. A single sampling plan is the easiest to administer, followed by the double sampling plan. Because multiple sampling plans are more complex, the administrative costs are higher.

Standard Sampling Plans

In the preceding sections, several methods for determining a sampling plan based on some stipulated criteria were discussed. Many organizations prefer to use plans that are already in existence (known as standardized sampling plans), rather than compute a sampling plan of their own. The organization may select a set of criteria and determine the standardized plans that are best suited. Standardized plans are based on some defined criteria. In most cases the company has the flexibility to adjust their criteria in order to be close to a specified value of the criteria in the standardized plan. The advantage of using a standardized plan is that a plan can be selected with very little effort. Moreover, characteristics and performance measures of the plans have already been calculated and tabulated.

This section presents two of the most common lot-by-lot attribute sampling plans. The first is a plan developed by the American National Standards Institute and the American Society for Quality Control. It is entitled *ANSI/ASQC Z1.4–1981—American National Standard—Sampling Procedures and Tables for Inspection by Attributes*. This standard is the outgrowth of sampling plans developed during World War II. In 1950, *Military Standard 105A* was developed and subsequently went through four modifications. *Military Standard 105D (MIL–STD–105D)* evolved through the collaboration of American, British, and Canadian groups and was issued in 1963. It was further revised in 1989 to become *MIL–STD–105E*. The military version was adopted as an American national standard and was labeled by ANSI as *ANSI/ASQC Z1.4* in 1971. A revision in 1981 created the present version, *ANSI/ASQC Z1.4–1981*. The revisions emphasize the system aspect of the sampling procedure through the operating characteristic curves in the scheme framework. All of the tables and procedures of *MIL–STD–105D* were retained. The International Standards Organization accepted the *ANSI/ASQC Z1.4* plans with some minor modifications in 1974 and created the standard *ISO 2859*. There are very few major differences between *ANSI/ASQC Z1.4–1981*, *MIL–STD–105E*, and *ISO 2859*.

ANSI/ASQC Z1.4 is used as an acceptable quality level system. This means that there is a notion of the quality level of good lots which should be rejected infrequently. If the process average fraction nonconforming is less than the AQL, the sampling plans in *ANSI/ASQC Z1.4* are designed to accept the majority of the lots. However, the protection to the consumer in terms of not accepting poor lots, whose quality level is indicated by the limiting quality level, was not a key criterion in *ANSI/ASQC Z1.4* plans.

The Dodge–Romig system, developed by H. F. Dodge and H. G. Romig (1959), is designed to minimize the average total inspection while satisfying a consumer's risk β for batches with a given quality level specified by the limiting quality level. Other Dodge–Romig plans are based on satisfying a given average outgoing quality limit while minimizing the average total inspection. Thus, Dodge–Romig plans are indexed by either the LQL or AOQL; *ANSI/ASQC Z1.4* plans are indexed by AQL. The Dodge–Romig system is based on a rectifying sampling scheme for which rejected lots go through 100 percent inspection, with nonconforming items being replaced with acceptable ones.

Note that *MIL–STD–105E* is a sampling plan, whereas *ANSI/ASQC Z1.4* is a sampling system. A *sampling plan* specifies a procedure for determining the fate of a lot based on a certain sample size and acceptance criteria. For example, consider the previously described single sampling plans that satisfy a producer's risk α at a certain quality level p_1 = AQL.

A *sampling scheme* is a set of sampling plans with rules provided for switching among them. A scheme is indexed by lot size and either AQL, LQL, or AOQL. A set of rules specifies the type of inspection to be used.

A *sampling system* is a collection of sampling schemes. It provides rules for the selection of an appropriate sampling plan.

More details will be provided later on the exact rules for switching between inspection levels and how a sampling scheme is chosen.

ANSI/ASQC Z1.4–1981 and MIL–STD–105E There are three major differences between MIL–STD–105E and its civilian counterpart ANSI/ASQC Z1.4. First, the term *nonconforming* is substituted for *defect* in *ANSI/ASQC Z1.4*. Second, an optional procedure for switching from normal inspection to reduced inspection without satisfying the limit number criterion is included in *ANSI/ASQC Z1.4*. Third, the scheme aspect of sampling is emphasized in *ANSI/ASQC Z1.4*. Five additional tables for scheme performance are included. These include tables for the average outgoing quality limit for schemes, the limiting quality for schemes with probabilities of acceptance of 10 percent and 5 percent, the average sample size for schemes, and the operating characteristic curves for scheme performance.

Three types of sampling plans (single, double, and multiple) are provided in the standard. The sampling plans can be applied to a variety of situations, such as end items, raw materials and components, operations, materials in process, maintenance operations, administrative procedures, and so on.

Measure of Nonconformance. Product nonconformance is expressed either in terms of the percentage of nonconforming units or in terms of the number of nonconformities per 100 units. The percent nonconforming is given by

$$\text{Percent nonconforming} = \frac{\text{Number nonconforming}}{\text{Number of units inspected}} \times 100$$

The number of nonconformities per 100 units is given by

$$\text{Nonconformities per hundred units} = \frac{\text{Number of conformities}}{\text{Number of units inspected}} \times 100$$

Acceptable Quality Level. The acceptable quality level is the most important part of the standard. As defined previously, AQL is the maximum percent nonconforming (or the maximum number of nonconformities per 100 units) that, for the purposes of sampling inspection, can be considered satisfactory as a process average. When a specific value of AQL is designated, it is implicit that the selected sampling plan will accept a great majority of the lots, provided the process average does not exceed the value of AQL. Note, however, that the AQL is a parameter of the sampling scheme, whereas the process average is a representation of the actual operating level of the process. Furthermore, the specification of an AQL does not provide protection for individual lots. Rather, if a series of lots with a quality level specified by AQL are submitted for inspection, then about $100(1 - \alpha)$ percent of those lots will be accepted, where α denotes the level of the producer's risk. In the process of setting up the standard, the desirable value of the producer's risk was 5 percent. In actuality, the value of α varies from 1 percent to 10 percent in the standard.

The value of AQL is designated in the contract by the responsible authority. It is possible to designate the value of AQL for groups of nonconformities considered collectively or for individual nonconformities. The degree of severity of the nonconformities or nonconforming units could influence the value of AQL that is to be selected. For example, critical, major, and minor nonconformities may have different AQLs. The AQL values should be the smallest for critical nonconformities, followed by the AQLs of major and minor nonconformities, respectively. As a guide, AQL values could be 0.10 percent or less for critical, 1.0 percent for major, and 2–4 percent for minor nonconformities.

The values of AQL in the standard are known as the preferred AQLs. If the selected AQL does not match any of the ones shown in the standard, the user will have to be flexible to ensure a match. When the standard is used with the percent nonconforming as the measure of nonconformance, the AQL values range from 0.010 percent to 10.0 percent. On the other hand, when nonconformities per hundred units is used as the measure of nonconformance, the AQL values range from 0.010 to 1000 nonconformities per 100 units. The AQL values are arranged in a geometric progression, each approximately 1.585 times the preceding one.

A point to be remembered is that the AQL is only a reference point in the OC curve of the sampling plan. It does not mean that any level of percent nonconforming or nonconformities per 100 units is tolerable. Thus, the notion of striving for no nonconformance and for continual process and product improvement should always be kept in mind.

General Inspection Levels. There are three general inspection levels provided in the standard: levels I, II, and III. The different inspection levels provide about the same degree of protection to the producer by rejecting on average about 100α percent of the lots that have a level of nonconformance given by the AQL. However, the general inspection levels provide differing degrees of protection to the consumer as far as acceptance of poor-quality batches is concerned. Inspection level II is the norm, with level I being less discriminating and requiring about half the amount of inspection as level II. Level III, on the other hand, is the most discriminating of the three general levels and requires about twice the amount of inspection as level II. Level III has the steepest OC curve and provides the most protection for the consumer against the acceptance of poor lots.

Figure 9-15 shows the difference in the OC curves for sampling plans that use different levels of general inspection. As shown in the figure, inspection level III is the most discriminating. Thus, depending on the user preference for the desired level of protection against poor lots, the general inspection level may be selected. Of course, the sample size and hence the cost of inspection also increase as the inspection level changes from I to III. The method of inspection and the type of product also influence the general inspection level. If testing is destructive, inspection level I or II may be chosen. When items are costly, inspection level III may be selected as well.

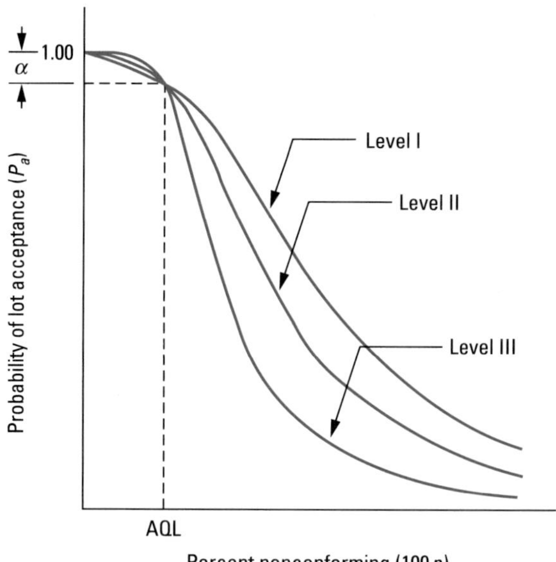

Figure 9-15 Effect of the general inspection level on the OC curve.

In addition to the three general inspection levels, four special levels of inspection (denoted by S–1, S–2, S–3, and S–4) are provided by the standard. These special inspection levels may be used when relatively small sample sizes are necessary and large sampling risks can or must be tolerated.

Types of Inspection and Rules for Switching. The standard provides sampling schemes for single, double, and multiple sampling. For each of these, three types of inspection are possible: normal, tightened, and reduced. Normal inspection is used at the start of inspection unless otherwise directed by the responsible authority. As long as the product quality level is at AQL or better, normal inspection continues. Tightened inspection is used when the recent quality history of the producer shows a deterioration. This will force vendors to submit products at a quality level that is at least equal to the AQL. Similarly, reduced inspection is used when the producer's recent quality history has been outstanding. Reduced inspection uses a smaller sample size and cuts the inspection costs.

It should be mentioned that whereas the general inspection level is selected prior to the implementation of the sampling plan, the specific levels of normal, tightened, and reduced inspection are dictated by the outcomes of the inspection process. The recent quality history of the disposition of the lots influences the type of inspection that must be followed according to the standard. Figure 9-16 shows the effect of the type of inspection (normal, tightened, and reduced) on the OC curve. Of the three, tightened inspection has the most stringent requirements and the most discriminatory power.

Although normal inspection is used at the start of the procedure, changes to tightened or reduced inspection are a function of the quality encountered. The standard provides a procedure for switching between the levels of normal, tightened, and reduced inspection when there is an indication of possible changes in the quality of the product. The rules for switching are shown in Figure 9-17 and are also given below.

- *Normal to tightened.* When normal inspection is in effect, tightened inspection is instituted when two out of five consecutive lots have been rejected upon original inspection (ignoring resubmitted lots for this procedure).
- *Tightened to normal.* When tightened inspection is in effect, normal inspection is instituted when five consecutive lots are accepted upon original inspection.

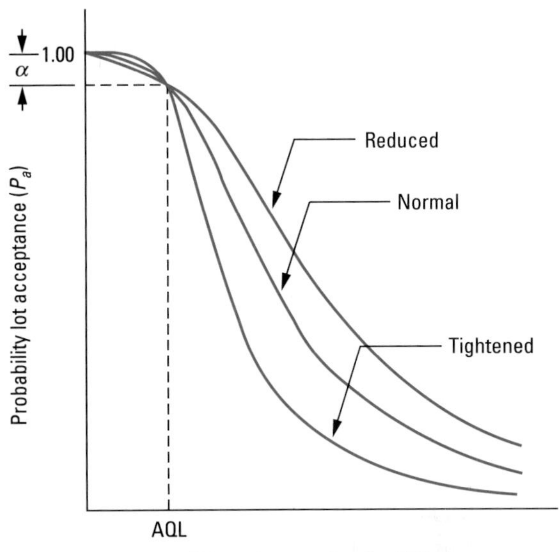

Figure 9-16 Effect of the type of inspection (normal, tightened, and reduced) on the OC curve.

- *Normal to reduced.* When normal inspection is in effect, reduced inspection is instituted if all of the following conditions are satisfied:

1. The preceding 10 lots have been on normal inspection and have all been accepted upon original inspection.

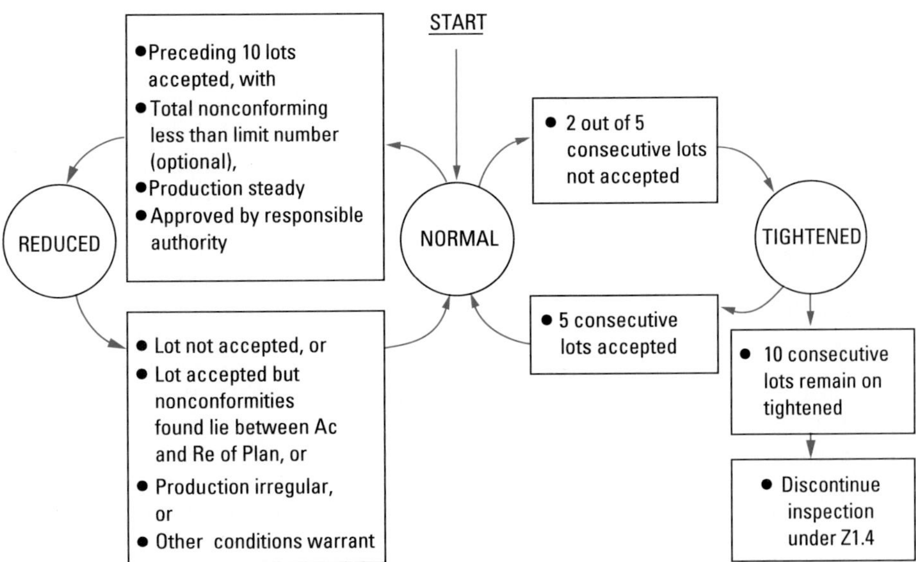

Figure 9-17 Switching rules for normal, tightened, and reduced inspection. (ASQC (1981), ANSI/ASQC Z1.4–1981: *American National Standard—Sampling Procedures and Tables for Inspection by Attributes*. Reprinted with the permission of ASQC.)

2. The total number of nonconforming units (or nonconformities per 100 units) in the samples from the preceding 10 lots is equal to or less than the applicable limit number (given in Table 9-21 on page 374). If double or multiple sampling is in use, all samples inspected should be included, not the first samples only. This condition may be dropped if both the supplier and the customer agree.
3. Production is at a steady rate.
4. Reduced inspection is considered desirable by the responsible authority.

- *Reduced to normal.* When reduced inspection is in effect, normal inspection shall be instituted if any of the following occur upon original inspection:
  1. A lot is rejected.
  2. A lot is accepted under reduced inspection, even though the number of nonconforming units (or number of nonconformities per 100 units) is greater than the acceptance number but less than the rejection number.
  3. Production is irregular or delayed.
  4. Other conditions warrant that normal inspection be instituted.
- *Discontinuance of inspection.* In the event that 10 consecutive lots remain on tightened inspection, inspection should be discontinued pending action to improve the quality of submitted material.

Selection of Sample Size. The sample size is determined by first selecting a sample size code letter based on the lot size and the general inspection level (I, II, or III). Knowing the type of sampling plan (single, double, or multiple) and the type of inspection level (normal, tightened, or reduced), the appropriate table is chosen. Given the sample size code, the sample size may be identified from the table.

Implementation of ANSI/ASQC Z1.4

The sequence of steps for using the plan given in *ANSI/ASQC Z1.4* is as follows:

1. Determine the AQL.
2. Select the general inspection level (level II usually is selected; change as needed).
3. Determine the lot size.
4. The sample size code letter is found from the appropriate table.
5. Determine the type of sampling plan (single, double, or multiple).
6. Identify the sampling plan from an appropriate table.
7. For initial inspection, start with normal inspection and change to tightened or reduced inspection based on the described switching rules.

TABLE 9-11 Sample size code letters

	Special inspection levels				General inspection levels		
Lot or Batch Size	S–1	S–2	S–3	S–4	I	II	III
2 to 8	A	A	A	A	A	A	B
9 to 15	A	A	A	A	A	B	C
16 to 25	A	A	B	B	B	C	D
26 to 50	A	B	B	C	C	D	E
51 to 90	B	B	C	C	C	E	F
91 to 150	B	B	C	D	D	F	G
151 to 280	B	C	D	E	E	G	H
281 to 500	B	C	D	E	F	H	J
501 to 1,200	C	C	E	F	G	J	K
1,201 to 3,200	C	D	E	G	H	K	L
3,201 to 10,000	C	D	F	G	J	L	M
10,001 to 35,000	C	D	F	H	K	M	N
35,001 to 150,000	D	E	G	J	L	N	P
150,001 to 500,000	D	E	G	J	M	P	Q
500,001 and over	D	E	H	K	N	Q	R

Source: ASQC (1981), ANSI/ASQC Z1.4–1981: *American National Standard—Sampling Procedures and Tables for Inspection by Attributes.* Reprinted with permission of ASQC.

The procedure is illustrated below through examples. Some tables from *ANSI/ASQC Z1.4* are reprinted with permission from the American Society for Quality Control. Table 9-11 shows the sample size codes. Given the lot size and the general inspection level, the sample size code may be found. Thereupon, given the type of the sampling plan (single, double, or multiple) and the type of inspection (normal, tightened, or reduced), the sampling plan is found from the appropriate table. Tables 9-12, 9-13, and 9-14 give the plans for single sampling based on normal, tightened, and reduced inspection, respectively. Master tables for double sampling plans for normal, tightened, and reduced inspection are given in Tables 9-15, 9-16, and 9-17, respectively. Tables 9-18, 9-19, and 9-20 provide multiple sampling plans for normal, tightened, and reduced inspection, respectively. Table 9-21 provides limit numbers for switching from normal to reduced inspection. This is an optional criteria to be selected upon agreement of both the supplier and the customer. The total number of nonconforming units (or the number of nonconformities per 100 units) for the last 10 lots must be less than or equal to the limit number.

TABLE 9-12 Single sampling plans for normal inspection (master table)

Sample Size Code Letter	Sample Size	0.010 Ac Re	0.015 Ac Re	0.025 Ac Re	0.040 Ac Re	0.065 Ac Re	0.10 Ac Re	0.15 Ac Re	0.25 Ac Re	0.40 Ac Re	0.65 Ac Re	1.0 Ac Re	1.5 Ac Re	2.5 Ac Re	4.0 Ac Re	6.5 Ac Re	10 Ac Re	15 Ac Re	25 Ac Re	40 Ac Re	65 Ac Re	100 Ac Re	150 Ac Re	250 Ac Re	400 Ac Re	650 Ac Re	1000 Ac Re
A	2	↓	↓	↓	↓	↓	↓	↓	↓	↓	↓	↓	↓	↓	↓	0 1	↓	↓	1 2	2 3	3 4	5 6	7 8	10 11	14 15	21 22	30 31
B	3	↓	↓	↓	↓	↓	↓	↓	↓	↓	↓	↓	↓	↓	0 1	↑	↓	1 2	2 3	3 4	5 6	7 8	10 11	14 15	21 22	30 31	44 45
C	5	↓	↓	↓	↓	↓	↓	↓	↓	↓	↓	↓	↓	0 1	↑	↓	1 2	2 3	3 4	5 6	7 8	10 11	14 15	21 22	30 31	44 45	↑
D	8	↓	↓	↓	↓	↓	↓	↓	↓	↓	↓	↓	0 1	↑	↓	1 2	2 3	3 4	5 6	7 8	10 11	14 15	21 22	30 31	44 45	↑	↑
E	13	↓	↓	↓	↓	↓	↓	↓	↓	↓	↓	0 1	↑	↓	1 2	2 3	3 4	5 6	7 8	10 11	14 15	21 22	30 31	44 45	↑	↑	↑
F	20	↓	↓	↓	↓	↓	↓	↓	↓	↓	0 1	↑	↓	1 2	2 3	3 4	5 6	7 8	10 11	14 15	21 22	↑	↑	↑	↑	↑	↑
G	32	↓	↓	↓	↓	↓	↓	↓	↓	0 1	↑	↓	1 2	2 3	3 4	5 6	7 8	10 11	14 15	21 22	↑	↑	↑	↑	↑	↑	↑
H	50	↓	↓	↓	↓	↓	↓	↓	0 1	↑	↓	1 2	2 3	3 4	5 6	7 8	10 11	14 15	21 22	↑	↑	↑	↑	↑	↑	↑	↑
J	80	↓	↓	↓	↓	↓	↓	0 1	↑	↓	1 2	2 3	3 4	5 6	7 8	10 11	14 15	21 22	↑	↑	↑	↑	↑	↑	↑	↑	↑
K	125	↓	↓	↓	↓	↓	0 1	↑	↓	1 2	2 3	3 4	5 6	7 8	10 11	14 15	21 22	↑	↑	↑	↑	↑	↑	↑	↑	↑	↑
L	200	↓	↓	↓	↓	0 1	↑	↓	1 2	2 3	3 4	5 6	7 8	10 11	14 15	21 22	↑	↑	↑	↑	↑	↑	↑	↑	↑	↑	↑
M	315	↓	↓	↓	0 1	↑	↓	1 2	2 3	3 4	5 6	7 8	10 11	14 15	21 22	↑	↑	↑	↑	↑	↑	↑	↑	↑	↑	↑	↑
N	500	↓	↓	0 1	↑	↓	1 2	2 3	3 4	5 6	7 8	10 11	14 15	21 22	↑	↑	↑	↑	↑	↑	↑	↑	↑	↑	↑	↑	↑
P	800	↓	0 1	↑	↓	1 2	2 3	3 4	5 6	7 8	10 11	14 15	21 22	↑	↑	↑	↑	↑	↑	↑	↑	↑	↑	↑	↑	↑	↑
Q	1250	0 1	↑	↓	1 2	2 3	3 4	5 6	7 8	10 11	14 15	21 22	↑	↑	↑	↑	↑	↑	↑	↑	↑	↑	↑	↑	↑	↑	↑
R	2000	↑	↑	1 2	2 3	3 4	5 6	7 8	10 11	14 15	21 22	↑	↑	↑	↑	↑	↑	↑	↑	↑	↑	↑	↑	↑	↑	↑	↑

Acceptable Quality Levels (Normal Inspection)

↓ = Use first sampling plan below arrow. If sample size equals, or exceeds, lot or batch size, do 100 percent inspection.

↑ = Use first sampling plan above arrow.

Ac = Acceptance number.

Re = Rejection number.

Source: ASQC (1981), ANSI/ASQC Z1.4–1981: *American National Standard—Sampling Procedures and Tables for Inspection by Attributes.* Reprinted with the permission of ASQC.

TABLE 9-13 Single sampling plans for tightened inspection (master table)

Sample Size Code Letter	Sample Size	Acceptable Quality Levels (tightened inspection)																									
		0.010	0.015	0.025	0.040	0.065	0.10	0.15	0.25	0.40	0.65	1.0	1.5	2.5	4.0	6.5	10	15	25	40	65	100	150	250	400	650	1000
		Ac Re	Ac Re	Ac Re	Ac Re	Ac Re	Ac Re	Ac Re	Ac Re	Ac Re	Ac Re	Ac Re	Ac Re	Ac Re	Ac Re	Ac Re	Ac Re	Ac Re	Ac Re	Ac Re	Ac Re	Ac Re	Ac Re	Ac Re	Ac Re	Ac Re	Ac Re
A	2	↓	↓	↓	↓	↓	↓	↓	↓	↓	↓	↓	↓	↓	↓	↓	↓	↓	↓	1 2	2 3	3 4	5 6	8 9	12 13	18 19	27 28
B	3	↓	↓	↓	↓	↓	↓	↓	↓	↓	↓	↓	↓	↓	↓	0 1	↓	↓	1 2	2 3	3 4	5 6	8 9	12 13	18 19	27 28	41 42
C	5	↓	↓	↓	↓	↓	↓	↓	↓	↓	↓	↓	↓	↓	0 1	↓	↓	1 2	2 3	3 4	5 6	8 9	12 13	18 19	27 28	41 42	↑
D	8	↓	↓	↓	↓	↓	↓	↓	↓	↓	↓	↓	↓	0 1	↓	↓	1 2	2 3	3 4	5 6	8 9	12 13	18 19	27 28	41 42	↑	↑
E	13	↓	↓	↓	↓	↓	↓	↓	↓	↓	↓	↓	0 1	↓	↓	1 2	2 3	3 4	5 6	8 9	12 13	18 19	27 28	41 42	↑	↑	↑
F	20	↓	↓	↓	↓	↓	↓	↓	↓	↓	↓	0 1	↓	↓	1 2	2 3	3 4	5 6	8 9	12 13	18 19	↑	↑	↑	↑	↑	↑
G	32	↓	↓	↓	↓	↓	↓	↓	↓	↓	0 1	↓	↓	1 2	2 3	3 4	5 6	8 9	12 13	18 19	↑	↑	↑	↑	↑	↑	↑
H	50	↓	↓	↓	↓	↓	↓	↓	↓	0 1	↓	↓	1 2	2 3	3 4	5 6	8 9	12 13	18 19	↑	↑	↑	↑	↑	↑	↑	↑
J	80	↓	↓	↓	↓	↓	↓	↓	0 1	↓	↓	1 2	2 3	3 4	5 6	8 9	12 13	18 19	↑	↑	↑	↑	↑	↑	↑	↑	↑
K	125	↓	↓	↓	↓	↓	↓	0 1	↓	↓	1 2	2 3	3 4	5 6	8 9	12 13	18 19	↑	↑	↑	↑	↑	↑	↑	↑	↑	↑
L	200	↓	↓	↓	↓	↓	0 1	↓	↓	1 2	2 3	3 4	5 6	8 9	12 13	18 19	↑	↑	↑	↑	↑	↑	↑	↑	↑	↑	↑
M	315	↓	↓	↓	↓	0 1	↓	↓	1 2	2 3	3 4	5 6	8 9	12 13	18 19	↑	↑	↑	↑	↑	↑	↑	↑	↑	↑	↑	↑
N	500	↓	↓	↓	0 1	↓	↓	1 2	2 3	3 4	5 6	8 9	12 13	18 19	↑	↑	↑	↑	↑	↑	↑	↑	↑	↑	↑	↑	↑
P	800	↓	↓	0 1	↓	↓	1 2	2 3	3 4	5 6	8 9	12 13	18 19	↑	↑	↑	↑	↑	↑	↑	↑	↑	↑	↑	↑	↑	↑
Q	1250	↓	0 1	↓	↓	1 2	2 3	3 4	5 6	8 9	12 13	18 19	↑	↑	↑	↑	↑	↑	↑	↑	↑	↑	↑	↑	↑	↑	↑
R	2000	0 1	↑	↓	1 2	2 3	3 4	5 6	8 9	12 13	18 19	↑	↑	↑	↑	↑	↑	↑	↑	↑	↑	↑	↑	↑	↑	↑	↑
S	3150		↑	1 2								↑	↑	↑	↑	↑	↑	↑	↑	↑	↑	↑	↑	↑	↑	↑	↑

↓ = Use first sampling plan below arrow. If sample size equals, or exceeds, lot or batch size, do 100 percent inspection.

↑ = Use first sampling plan above arrow.

Ac = Acceptance number.

Re = Rejection number.

Source: ASQC (1981), ANSI/ASQC Z1.4–1981: *American National Standard—Sampling Procedures and Tables for Inspection by Attributes*. Reprinted with the permission of ASQC.

TABLE 9-14 Single sampling plans for reduced inspection (master table)

Sample Size Code Letter	Sample Size	Acceptable Quality Levels (Reduced Inspection)†																									
		0.010	0.015	0.025	0.040	0.065	0.10	0.15	0.25	0.40	0.65	1.0	1.5	2.5	4.0	6.5	10	15	25	40	65	100	150	250	400	650	1000
		Ac Re	Ac Re	Ac Re	Ac Re	Ac Re	Ac Re	Ac Re	Ac Re	Ac Re	Ac Re	Ac Re	Ac Re	Ac Re	Ac Re	Ac Re	Ac Re	Ac Re	Ac Re	Ac Re	Ac Re	Ac Re	Ac Re	Ac Re	Ac Re	Ac Re	Ac Re
A	2	↓	↓	↓	↓	↓	↓	↓	↓	↓	↓	↓	↓	↓	↓	0 1	↓	↓	1 2	2 3	3 4	5 6	7 8	10 11	14 15	21 22	30 31
B	2	↓	↓	↓	↓	↓	↓	↓	↓	↓	↓	↓	↓	↓	0 1	↑	↓	0 2	1 3	2 4	3 5	5 6	7 8	10 11	14 15	21 22	30 31
C	2	↓	↓	↓	↓	↓	↓	↓	↓	↓	↓	↓	↓	0 1	↑	↓	0 2	1 3	1 4	2 5	3 6	5 8	7 10	10 13	14 17	21 24	↑
D	3	↓	↓	↓	↓	↓	↓	↓	↓	↓	↓	↓	0 1	↑	↓	0 2	1 3	1 4	2 5	3 6	5 8	7 10	10 13	14 17	21 24	↑	↑
E	5	↓	↓	↓	↓	↓	↓	↓	↓	↓	↓	0 1	↑	↓	0 2	1 3	1 4	2 5	3 6	5 8	7 10	10 13	14 17	21 24	↑	↑	↑
F	8	↓	↓	↓	↓	↓	↓	↓	↓	↓	0 1	↑	↓	0 2	1 3	1 4	2 5	3 6	5 8	7 10	10 13	↑	↑	↑	↑	↑	↑
G	13	↓	↓	↓	↓	↓	↓	↓	↓	0 1	↑	↓	0 2	1 3	1 4	2 5	3 6	5 8	7 10	10 13	↑	↑	↑	↑	↑	↑	↑
H	20	↓	↓	↓	↓	↓	↓	↓	0 1	↑	↓	0 2	1 3	1 4	2 5	3 6	5 8	7 10	10 13	↑	↑	↑	↑	↑	↑	↑	↑
J	32	↓	↓	↓	↓	↓	↓	0 1	↑	↓	0 2	1 3	1 4	2 5	3 6	5 8	7 10	10 13	↑	↑	↑	↑	↑	↑	↑	↑	↑
K	50	↓	↓	↓	↓	↓	0 1	↑	↓	0 2	1 3	1 4	2 5	3 6	5 8	7 10	10 13	↑	↑	↑	↑	↑	↑	↑	↑	↑	↑
L	80	↓	↓	↓	↓	0 1	↑	↓	0 2	1 3	1 4	2 5	3 6	5 8	7 10	10 13	↑	↑	↑	↑	↑	↑	↑	↑	↑	↑	↑
M	125	↓	↓	↓	0 1	↑	↓	0 2	1 3	1 4	2 5	3 6	5 8	7 10	10 13	↑	↑	↑	↑	↑	↑	↑	↑	↑	↑	↑	↑
N	200	↓	↓	0 1	↑	↓	0 2	1 3	1 4	2 5	3 6	5 8	7 10	10 13	↑	↑	↑	↑	↑	↑	↑	↑	↑	↑	↑	↑	↑
P	315	↓	0 1	↑	↓	0 2	1 3	1 4	2 5	3 6	5 8	7 10	10 13	↑	↑	↑	↑	↑	↑	↑	↑	↑	↑	↑	↑	↑	↑
Q	500	0 1	↑	↓	0 2	1 3	1 4	2 5	3 6	5 8	7 10	10 13	↑	↑	↑	↑	↑	↑	↑	↑	↑	↑	↑	↑	↑	↑	↑
R	800	↑	↑	0 2	1 3	1 4	2 5	3 6	5 8	7 10	10 13	↑	↑	↑	↑	↑	↑	↑	↑	↑	↑	↑	↑	↑	↑	↑	↑

↓ = Use first sampling plan below arrow. If sample size equals, or exceeds, lot or batch size, do 100 percent inspection.
↑ = Use first sampling plan above arrow.
Ac = Acceptance number.
Re = Rejection number.
† = If the acceptance number has been exceeded, but the rejection number has not been reached, accept the lot, but reinstate normal inspection.

Source: ASQC (1981), ANSI/ASQC Z1.4–1981: *American National Standard—Sampling Procedures and Tables for Inspection by Attributes.* Reprinted with the permission of ASQC.

TABLE 9-15 Double sampling plans for normal inspection (master table)

Sample Size Code Letter	Sample	Sample Size	Cumulative Sample Size	Acceptable Quality Levels (Normal Inspection) 0.010	0.015	0.025	0.040	0.065	0.10	0.15	0.25	0.40	0.65	1.0	1.5	2.5	4.0	6.5	10	15	25	40	65	100	150	250	400	650	1000
				Ac Re	Ac Re	Ac Re	Ac Re	Ac Re	Ac Re	Ac Re	Ac Re	Ac Re	Ac Re	Ac Re	Ac Re	Ac Re	Ac Re	Ac Re	Ac Re	Ac Re	Ac Re	Ac Re	Ac Re	Ac Re	Ac Re	Ac Re	Ac Re	Ac Re	Ac Re
A				↓	↓	↓	↓	↓	↓	↓	↓	↓	↓	↓	↓	↓	↓	*	↓	↓	*	*	*	*	*	*	*	*	*
B	First	2	2	↓	↓	↓	↓	↓	↓	↓	↓	↓	↓	↓	↓	↓	*	↑	↓	0 2	0 3	1 4	2 5	3 7	5 9	7 11	11 16	17 22	25 31
	Second	2	4																	1 2	3 4	4 5	6 7	8 9	12 13	18 19	26 27	37 38	56 57
C	First	3	3	↓	↓	↓	↓	↓	↓	↓	↓	↓	↓	↓	↓	*	↑	↓	0 2	0 3	1 4	2 5	3 7	5 9	7 11	11 16	17 22	25 31	↑
	Second	3	6																1 2	3 4	4 5	6 7	8 9	12 13	18 19	26 27	37 38	56 57	
D	First	5	5	↓	↓	↓	↓	↓	↓	↓	↓	↓	↓	↓	*	↑	↓	0 2	0 3	1 4	2 5	3 7	5 9	7 11	11 16	17 22	25 31	↑	↑
	Second	5	10															1 2	3 4	4 5	6 7	8 9	12 13	18 19	26 27	37 38	56 57		
E	First	8	8	↓	↓	↓	↓	↓	↓	↓	↓	↓	↓	*	↑	↓	0 2	0 3	1 4	2 5	3 7	5 9	7 11	11 16	17 22	25 31	↑	↑	↑
	Second	8	16														1 2	3 4	4 5	6 7	8 9	12 13	18 19	26 27	37 38	56 57			
F	First	13	13	↓	↓	↓	↓	↓	↓	↓	↓	↓	*	↑	↓	0 2	0 3	1 4	2 5	3 7	5 9	7 11	11 16	↑	↑	↑	↑	↑	↑
	Second	13	26													1 2	3 4	4 5	6 7	8 9	12 13	18 19	26 27						
G	First	20	20	↓	↓	↓	↓	↓	↓	↓	↓	*	↑	↓	0 2	0 3	1 4	2 5	3 7	5 9	7 11	11 16	↑	↑	↑	↑	↑	↑	↑
	Second	20	40												1 2	3 4	4 5	6 7	8 9	12 13	18 19	26 27							
H	First	32	32	↓	↓	↓	↓	↓	↓	↓	*	↑	↓	0 2	0 3	1 4	2 5	3 7	5 9	7 11	11 16	↑	↑	↑	↑	↑	↑	↑	↑
	Second	32	64											1 2	3 4	4 5	6 7	8 9	12 13	18 19	26 27								
J	First	50	50	↓	↓	↓	↓	↓	↓	*	↑	↓	0 2	0 3	1 4	2 5	3 7	5 9	7 11	11 16	↑	↑	↑	↑	↑	↑	↑	↑	↑
	Second	50	100										1 2	3 4	4 5	6 7	8 9	12 13	18 19	26 27									
K	First	80	80	↓	↓	↓	↓	↓	*	↑	↓	0 2	0 3	1 4	2 5	3 7	5 9	7 11	11 16	↑	↑	↑	↑	↑	↑	↑	↑	↑	↑
	Second	80	160									1 2	3 4	4 5	6 7	8 9	12 13	18 19	26 27										
L	First	125	125	↓	↓	↓	↓	*	↑	↓	0 2	0 3	1 4	2 5	3 7	5 9	7 11	11 16	↑	↑	↑	↑	↑	↑	↑	↑	↑	↑	↑
	Second	125	250								1 2	3 4	4 5	6 7	8 9	12 13	18 19	26 27											
M	First	200	200	↓	↓	↓	*	↑	↓	0 2	0 3	1 4	2 5	3 7	5 9	7 11	11 16	↑	↑	↑	↑	↑	↑	↑	↑	↑	↑	↑	↑
	Second	200	400							1 2	3 4	4 5	6 7	8 9	12 13	18 19	26 27												
N	First	315	315	↓	↓	*	↑	↓	0 2	0 3	1 4	2 5	3 7	5 9	7 11	11 16	↑	↑	↑	↑	↑	↑	↑	↑	↑	↑	↑	↑	↑
	Second	315	630						1 2	3 4	4 5	6 7	8 9	12 13	18 19	26 27													
P	First	500	500	↓	*	↑	↓	0 2	0 3	1 4	2 5	3 7	5 9	7 11	11 16	↑	↑	↑	↑	↑	↑	↑	↑	↑	↑	↑	↑	↑	↑
	Second	500	1000					1 2	3 4	4 5	6 7	8 9	12 13	18 19	26 27														
Q	First	800	800	*	↑	↓	0 2	0 3	1 4	2 5	3 7	5 9	7 11	11 16	↑	↑	↑	↑	↑	↑	↑	↑	↑	↑	↑	↑	↑	↑	↑
	Second	800	1600				1 2	3 4	4 5	6 7	8 9	12 13	18 19	26 27															
R	First	1250	1250	↑	↑	0 2	0 3	1 4	2 5	3 7	5 9	7 11	11 16	↑	↑	↑	↑	↑	↑	↑	↑	↑	↑	↑	↑	↑	↑	↑	↑
	Second	1250	2500			1 2	3 4	4 5	6 7	8 9	12 13	18 19	26 27																

↓ = Use first sampling plan below arrow. If sample size equals or exceeds lot or batch size, do 100 percent inspection.
↑ = Use first sampling plan above arrow.
Ac = Acceptance number
Re = Rejection number
* = Use corresponding single sampling plan (or alternatively, use double sampling plan below, where available).

Source: ASQC (1981), ANSI/ASQC Z1.4–1981: *American National Standard—Sampling Procedures and Tables for Inspection by Attributes.* Reprinted with the permission of ASQC.

TABLE 9-16 Double sampling plans for tightened inspection (master table)

Sample Size Code Letter	Sample	Sample Size	Cumulative Sample Size	Acceptable Quality Levels (Tightened Inspection)																									
				0.010	0.015	0.025	0.040	0.065	0.10	0.15	0.25	0.40	0.65	1.0	1.5	2.5	4.0	6.5	10	15	25	40	65	100	150	250	400	650	1000
				Ac Re	Ac Re	Ac Re	Ac Re	Ac Re	Ac Re	Ac Re	Ac Re	Ac Re	Ac Re	Ac Re	Ac Re	Ac Re	Ac Re	Ac Re	Ac Re	Ac Re	Ac Re	Ac Re	Ac Re	Ac Re	Ac Re	Ac Re	Ac Re	Ac Re	Ac Re
A				↓	↓	↓	↓	↓	↓	↓	↓	↓	↓	↓	↓	↓	↓	↓	↓	↓	↓	*	*	*	*	*	*	*	*
B	First	2	2	↓	↓	↓	↓	↓	↓	↓	↓	↓	↓	↓	↓	↓	↓	*	↓	↓	0 2	0 3	1 4	2 5	3 7	6 10	9 14	15 20	23 29
	Second	2	4																		1 2	3 4	4 5	6 7	11 12	15 16	23 24	34 35	52 53
C	First	3	3	↓	↓	↓	↓	↓	↓	↓	↓	↓	↓	↓	↓	↓	*	↓	↓	0 2	0 3	1 4	2 5	3 7	6 10	9 14	15 20	23 29	↑
	Second	3	6																	1 2	3 4	4 5	6 7	11 12	15 16	23 24	34 35	52 53	
D	First	5	5	↓	↓	↓	↓	↓	↓	↓	↓	↓	↓	↓	↓	*	↓	↓	0 2	0 3	1 4	2 5	3 7	6 10	9 14	15 20	23 29	↑	↑
	Second	5	10																1 2	3 4	4 5	6 7	11 12	15 16	23 24	34 35	52 53		
E	First	8	8	↓	↓	↓	↓	↓	↓	↓	↓	↓	↓	↓	*	↓	↓	0 2	0 3	1 4	2 5	3 7	6 10	9 14	15 20	23 29	↑	↑	↑
	Second	8	16															1 2	3 4	4 5	6 7	11 12	15 16	23 24	34 35	52 53			
F	First	13	13	↓	↓	↓	↓	↓	↓	↓	↓	↓	↓	*	↓	↓	0 2	0 3	1 4	2 5	3 7	6 10	9 14	↑	↑	↑	↑	↑	↑
	Second	13	26														1 2	3 4	4 5	6 7	11 12	15 16	23 24						
G	First	20	20	↓	↓	↓	↓	↓	↓	↓	↓	↓	*	↓	↓	0 2	0 3	1 4	2 5	3 7	6 10	9 14	↑	↑	↑	↑	↑	↑	↑
	Second	20	40													1 2	3 4	4 5	6 7	11 12	15 16	23 24							
H	First	32	32	↓	↓	↓	↓	↓	↓	↓	↓	*	↓	↓	0 2	0 3	1 4	2 5	3 7	6 10	9 14	↑	↑	↑	↑	↑	↑	↑	↑
	Second	32	64												1 2	3 4	4 5	6 7	11 12	15 16	23 34								
J	First	50	50	↓	↓	↓	↓	↓	↓	↓	*	↓	↓	0 2	0 3	1 4	2 5	3 7	6 10	9 14	↑	↑	↑	↑	↑	↑	↑	↑	↑
	Second	50	100											1 2	3 4	4 5	6 7	11 12	15 16	23 24									
K	First	80	80	↓	↓	↓	↓	↓	↓	*	↓	↓	0 2	0 3	1 4	2 5	3 7	6 10	9 14	↑	↑	↑	↑	↑	↑	↑	↑	↑	↑
	Second	80	160										1 2	3 4	4 5	6 7	11 12	15 16	23 24										
L	First	125	125	↓	↓	↓	↓	↓	*	↓	↓	0 2	0 3	1 4	2 5	3 7	6 10	9 14	↑	↑	↑	↑	↑	↑	↑	↑	↑	↑	↑
	Second	125	250									1 2	3 4	4 5	6 7	11 12	15 16	23 24											
M	First	200	200	↓	↓	↓	↓	*	↓	↓	0 2	0 3	1 4	2 5	3 7	6 10	9 14	↑	↑	↑	↑	↑	↑	↑	↑	↑	↑	↑	↑
	Second	200	400								1 2	3 4	4 5	6 7	11 12	15 16	23 24												
N	First	315	315	↓	↓	↓	*	↓	↓	0 2	0 3	1 4	2 5	3 7	6 10	9 14	↑	↑	↑	↑	↑	↑	↑	↑	↑	↑	↑	↑	↑
	Second	315	630							1 2	3 4	4 5	6 7	11 12	15 16	23 24													
P	First	500	500	↓	↓	*	↓	↓	0 2	0 3	1 4	2 5	3 7	6 10	9 14	↑	↑	↑	↑	↑	↑	↑	↑	↑	↑	↑	↑	↑	↑
	Second	500	1000						1 2	3 4	4 5	6 7	11 12	15 16	23 24														
Q	First	800	800	↓	*	↓	↓	0 2	0 3	1 4	2 5	3 7	6 10	9 14	↑	↑	↑	↑	↑	↑	↑	↑	↑	↑	↑	↑	↑	↑	↑
	Second	800	1600					1 2	3 4	4 5	6 7	11 12	15 16	23 24															
R	First	1250	1250	*	↑	↓	0 2	0 3	1 4	2 5	3 7	6 10	9 14	↑	↑	↑	↑	↑	↑	↑	↑	↑	↑	↑	↑	↑	↑	↑	↑
	Second	1250	2500				1 2	3 4	4 5	6 7	11 12	15 16	23 24																
S	First	2000	2000			0 2									↑	↑	↑	↑	↑	↑	↑	↑	↑	↑	↑	↑	↑	↑	↑
	Second	2000	4000			1 2																							

↓ = Use first sampling plan below arrow. If sample size equals or exceeds lot or batch size, do 100 percent inspection.

↑ = Use first sampling plan above arrow.

Ac = Acceptance number

Re = Rejection number

* = Use corresponding single sampling plan (or alternatively, use double sampling plan below, where available).

Source: ASQC (1981), ANSI/ASQC Z1.4–1981: *American National Standard—Sampling Procedures and Tables for Inspection by Attributes*. Reprinted with the permission of ASQC.

TABLE 9-17 **Double sampling plans for reduced inspection (master table)**

Sample Size Code Letter	Sample	Sample Size	Cumulative Sample Size	Acceptable Quality Levels (Reduced Inspection)†																									
				0.010	0.015	0.025	0.040	0.065	0.10	0.15	0.25	0.40	0.65	1.0	1.5	2.5	4.0	6.5	10	15	25	40	65	100	150	250	400	650	1000
				Ac Re	Ac Re	Ac Re	Ac Re	Ac Re	Ac Re	Ac Re	Ac Re	Ac Re	Ac Re	Ac Re	Ac Re	Ac Re	Ac Re	Ac Re	Ac Re	Ac Re	Ac Re	Ac Re	Ac Re	Ac Re	Ac Re	Ac Re	Ac Re	Ac Re	Ac Re
A				↓	↓	↓	↓	↓	↓	↓	↓	↓	↓	↓	↓	↓	↓	*	↓	↓	*	*	*	*	*	*	*	*	*
B				↓	↓	↓	↓	↓	↓	↓	↓	↓	↓	↓	↓	↓	*	↓	↓	*	*	*	*	*	*	*	*	*	*
C				↓	↓	↓	↓	↓	↓	↓	↓	↓	↓	↓	↓	*	↑	↑	*	*	*	*	*	*	*	*	*	*	↑
D	First	2	2	↓	↓	↓	↓	↓	↓	↓	↓	↓	↓	↓	*	↑	↓	0 2	0 3	0 4	0 4	1 5	2 7	3 8	5 10	7 12	11 17	↑	↑
	Second	2	4	↓	↓	↓	↓	↓	↓	↓	↓	↓	↓	↓		↑	↓	0 2	0 4	1 5	3 6	4 7	6 9	8 12	12 16	18 22	26 30	↑	↑
E	First	3	3	↓	↓	↓	↓	↓	↓	↓	↓	↓	↓	*	↑	↓	0 2	0 3	0 4	0 4	1 5	2 7	3 8	5 10	7 12	11 17	↑	↑	↑
	Second	3	6	↓	↓	↓	↓	↓	↓	↓	↓	↓	↓		↑	↓	0 2	0 4	1 5	3 6	4 7	6 9	8 12	12 16	18 22	26 30	↑	↑	↑
F	First	5	5	↓	↓	↓	↓	↓	↓	↓	↓	↓	*	↑	↓	0 2	0 3	0 4	0 4	1 5	2 7	3 8	5 10	↑	↑	↑	↑	↑	↑
	Second	5	10	↓	↓	↓	↓	↓	↓	↓	↓	↓		↑	↓	0 2	0 4	1 5	3 6	4 7	6 9	8 12	12 16	↑	↑	↑	↑	↑	↑
G	First	8	8	↓	↓	↓	↓	↓	↓	↓	↓	*	↑	↓	0 2	0 3	0 4	0 4	1 5	2 7	3 8	5 10	↑	↑	↑	↑	↑	↑	↑
	Second	8	16	↓	↓	↓	↓	↓	↓	↓	↓		↑	↓	0 2	0 4	1 5	3 6	4 7	6 9	8 12	12 16	↑	↑	↑	↑	↑	↑	↑
H	First	13	13	↓	↓	↓	↓	↓	↓	↓	*	↑	↓	0 2	0 3	0 4	0 4	1 5	2 7	3 8	5 10	↑	↑	↑	↑	↑	↑	↑	↑
	Second	13	26	↓	↓	↓	↓	↓	↓	↓		↑	↓	0 2	0 4	1 5	3 6	4 7	6 9	8 12	12 16	↑	↑	↑	↑	↑	↑	↑	↑
J	First	20	20	↓	↓	↓	↓	↓	↓	*	↑	↓	0 2	0 3	0 4	0 4	1 5	2 7	3 8	5 10	↑	↑	↑	↑	↑	↑	↑	↑	↑
	Second	20	40	↓	↓	↓	↓	↓	↓		↑	↓	0 2	0 4	1 5	3 6	4 7	6 9	8 12	12 16	↑	↑	↑	↑	↑	↑	↑	↑	↑
K	First	32	32	↓	↓	↓	↓	↓	*	↑	↓	0 2	0 3	0 4	0 4	1 5	2 7	3 8	5 10	↑	↑	↑	↑	↑	↑	↑	↑	↑	↑
	Second	32	64	↓	↓	↓	↓	↓		↑	↓	0 2	0 4	1 5	3 6	4 7	6 9	8 12	12 16	↑	↑	↑	↑	↑	↑	↑	↑	↑	↑
L	First	50	50	↓	↓	↓	↓	*	↑	↓	0 2	0 3	0 4	0 4	1 5	2 7	3 8	5 10	↑	↑	↑	↑	↑	↑	↑	↑	↑	↑	↑
	Second	50	100	↓	↓	↓	↓		↑	↓	0 2	0 4	1 5	3 6	4 7	6 9	8 12	12 16	↑	↑	↑	↑	↑	↑	↑	↑	↑	↑	↑
M	First	80	80	↓	↓	↓	*	↑	↓	0 2	0 3	0 4	0 4	1 5	2 7	3 8	5 10	↑	↑	↑	↑	↑	↑	↑	↑	↑	↑	↑	↑
	Second	80	160	↓	↓	↓		↑	↓	0 2	0 4	1 5	3 6	4 7	6 9	8 12	12 16	↑	↑	↑	↑	↑	↑	↑	↑	↑	↑	↑	↑
N	First	125	125	↓	↓	*	↑	↓	0 2	0 3	0 4	0 4	1 5	2 7	3 8	5 10	↑	↑	↑	↑	↑	↑	↑	↑	↑	↑	↑	↑	↑
	Second	125	250	↓	↓		↑	↓	0 2	0 4	1 5	3 6	4 7	6 9	8 12	12 16	↑	↑	↑	↑	↑	↑	↑	↑	↑	↑	↑	↑	↑
P	First	200	200	↓	*	↑	↓	0 2	0 3	0 4	0 4	1 5	2 7	3 8	5 10	↑	↑	↑	↑	↑	↑	↑	↑	↑	↑	↑	↑	↑	↑
	Second	200	400	↓		↑	↓	0 2	0 4	1 5	3 6	4 7	6 9	8 12	12 16	↑	↑	↑	↑	↑	↑	↑	↑	↑	↑	↑	↑	↑	↑
Q	First	315	315	*	↑	↓	0 2	0 3	0 4	0 4	1 5	2 7	3 8	5 10	↑	↑	↑	↑	↑	↑	↑	↑	↑	↑	↑	↑	↑	↑	↑
	Second	315	630		↑	↓	0 2	0 4	1 5	3 6	4 7	6 9	8 12	12 16	↑	↑	↑	↑	↑	↑	↑	↑	↑	↑	↑	↑	↑	↑	↑
R	First	500	500	↑	↑	0 2	0 3	0 4	0 4	1 5	2 7	3 8	5 10	↑	↑	↑	↑	↑	↑	↑	↑	↑	↑	↑	↑	↑	↑	↑	↑
	Second	500	1000	↑	↑	0 2	0 4	1 5	3 6	4 7	6 9	8 12	12 16	↑	↑	↑	↑	↑	↑	↑	↑	↑	↑	↑	↑	↑	↑	↑	↑

↓ = Use first sampling plan below arrow. If sample size equals or exceeds lot or batch size, do 100 percent inspection.
↑ = Use first sampling plan above arrow.
Ac = Acceptance number.
Re = Rejection number.
* = Use corresponding single sampling plan (or alternatively, use double sampling plan below, when available.)
† = If, after the second sample, the acceptance number has been exceeded, but the rejection number has not been reached, accept the lot, but reinstate normal inspection.

Source: ASQC (1981), ANSI/ASQC Z1.4–1981: *American National Standard—Sampling Procedures and Tables for Inspection by Attributes*. Reprinted with the permission of ASQC.

TABLE 9-18 Multiple sampling plans for normal inspection (master table)

Sample Size Code Letter	Sample	Sample Size	Cumulative Sample Size	Acceptable Quality Levels (Normal Inspection) 0.010	0.015	0.025	0.040	0.065	0.10	0.15	0.25	0.40	0.65	1.0	1.5	2.5	4.0	6.5	10	15	25	40	65	100	150	250	400	650	1000
				Ac Re	Ac Re	Ac Re	Ac Re	Ac Re	Ac Re	Ac Re	Ac Re	Ac Re	Ac Re	Ac Re	Ac Re	Ac Re	Ac Re	Ac Re	Ac Re	Ac Re	Ac Re	Ac Re	Ac Re	Ac Re	Ac Re	Ac Re	Ac Re	Ac Re	Ac Re
A																	↓	*		↓	*	*	*	*	*	*	*	*	*
B																↓	*	↑	↓	++	++	++	++	++	++	++	++	++	++
C															↓	*	↑	↓	++	++	++	++	++	++	++	++	++	++	↑
D	First	2	2												*	↑		# 2	# 2	# 3	# 4	0 4	0 5	1 7	2 9	4 12	6 16	↑	
	Second	2	4															# 2	0 3	0 3	1 5	1 6	3 8	4 10	7 14	11 19	17 27		
	Third	2	6															0 2	0 3	1 4	2 6	3 8	6 10	8 13	13 19	19 27	29 39		
	Fourth	2	8															0 3	1 4	2 5	3 7	5 10	8 13	12 17	19 25	27 34	40 49		
	Fifth	2	10															1 3	2 4	3 6	5 8	7 11	11 15	17 20	25 29	36 40	53 58		
	Sixth	2	12															1 3	3 5	4 6	7 9	10 12	14 17	21 23	31 33	45 47	65 68		
	Seventh	2	14											↓			↓	2 3	4 5	6 7	9 10	13 14	18 19	25 26	37 38	53 54	77 78		
E	First	3	3											*	↑		# 2	# 2	# 3	# 4	0 4	0 5	1 7	2 9	4 12	6 16	↑		
	Second	3	6														# 2	0 3	0 3	1 5	1 6	3 8	4 10	7 14	11 19	17 27			
	Third	3	9														0 2	0 3	1 4	2 6	3 8	6 10	8 13	13 19	19 27	29 39			
	Fourth	3	12														0 3	1 4	2 5	3 7	5 10	8 13	12 17	19 25	27 34	40 49			
	Fifth	3	15														1 3	2 4	3 6	5 8	7 11	11 15	17 20	25 29	36 40	53 58			
	Sixth	3	18														1 3	3 5	4 6	7 9	10 12	14 17	21 23	31 33	45 47	65 68			
	Seventh	3	21									↓			↓		2 3	4 5	6 7	9 10	13 14	18 19	25 26	37 38	53 54	77 78			
F	First	5	5										*	↑		# 2	# 2	# 3	# 4	0 4	0 5	1 7	2 9	↑	↑	↑			
	Second	5	10													# 2	0 3	0 3	1 5	1 6	3 8	4 10	7 14						
	Third	5	15													0 2	0 3	1 4	2 6	3 8	6 10	8 13	13 19						
	Fourth	5	20													0 3	1 4	2 5	3 7	5 10	8 13	12 17	19 25						
	Fifth	5	25													1 3	2 4	3 6	5 8	7 11	11 15	17 20	25 29						
	Sixth	5	30													1 3	3 5	4 6	7 9	10 12	14 17	21 23	31 33						
	Seventh	5	35								↓			↓		2 3	4 5	6 7	9 10	13 14	18 19	25 26	37 38						
G	First	8	8									*	↑		# 2	# 2	# 3	# 4	0 4	0 5	1 7	2 9	↑						
	Second	8	16												# 2	0 3	0 3	1 5	1 6	3 8	4 10	7 14							
	Third	8	24												0 2	0 3	1 4	2 6	3 8	6 10	8 13	13 19							
	Fourth	8	32												0 3	1 4	2 5	3 7	5 10	8 13	12 17	19 25							
	Fifth	8	40												1 3	2 4	3 6	5 8	7 11	11 15	17 20	25 29							
	Sixth	8	48												1 3	3 5	4 6	7 9	10 12	14 17	21 23	31 33							
	Seventh	8	56	↓	↓	↓	↓	↓	↓	↓	↓			↓	2 3	4 5	6 7	9 10	13 14	18 19	25 26	37 38							

↓ = Use first sampling plan below arrow (refer to continuation of table on following page, when necessary). If sample size equals or exceeds lot or batch size, do 100 percent inspection.

↑ = Use first sampling plan above arrow.

Ac = Acceptance number.

Re = Rejection number.

* = Use corresponding single sampling plan (or alternatively, use multiple sampling plan below, where available).

++ = Use corresponding double sampling plan (or alternatively, use multiple sampling plan below, where available).

\# = Acceptance not permitted at this sample size.

Source: ASQC (1981), ANSI/ASQC Z1.4–1981: *American National Standard—Sampling Procedures and Tables for Inspection by Attributes*. Reprinted with the permission of ASQC.

TABLE 9-18 *(Continued)*

Sample Size Code Letter	Sample	Sample Size	Cumulative Sample Size	Acceptable Quality Levels (Normal Inspection)																									
				0.010	0.015	0.025	0.040	0.065	0.10	0.15	0.25	0.40	0.65	1.0	1.5	2.5	4.0	6.5	10	15	25	40	65	100	150	250	400	650	1000
				Ac Re	Ac Re	Ac Re	Ac Re	Ac Re	Ac Re	Ac Re	Ac Re	Ac Re	Ac Re	Ac Re	Ac Re	Ac Re	Ac Re	Ac Re	Ac Re	Ac Re	Ac Re	Ac Re	Ac Re	Ac Re	Ac Re	Ac Re	Ac Re	Ac Re	Ac Re
H	First	13	13	↓	↓	↓	↓	↓	↓	↓	*	↑	↓	# 2	# 2	# 3	# 4	0 4	0 5	1 7	2 9	↑	↑	↑	↑	↑	↑	↑	↑
	Second	13	26											# 2	0 3	0 3	1 5	1 6	3 8	4 10	7 14								
	Third	13	39											0 2	0 3	1 4	2 6	3 8	6 10	8 13	13 19								
	Fourth	13	52											0 3	1 4	2 5	3 7	5 10	8 13	12 17	19 25								
	Fifth	13	65											1 3	2 4	3 6	5 8	7 11	11 15	17 20	25 29								
	Sixth	13	78											1 3	3 5	4 6	7 9	10 12	14 17	21 23	31 33								
	Seventh	13	91											2 3	4 5	6 7	9 10	13 14	18 19	25 26	37 38								
J	First	20	20	↓	↓	↓	↓	↓	↓	*	↑	↓	# 2	# 2	# 3	# 4	0 4	0 5	1 7	2 9	↑	↑	↑	↑	↑	↑	↑	↑	↑
	Second	20	40										# 2	0 3	0 3	1 5	1 6	3 8	4 10	7 14									
	Third	20	60										0 2	0 3	1 4	2 6	3 8	6 10	8 13	13 19									
	Fourth	20	80										0 3	1 4	2 5	3 7	5 10	8 13	12 17	19 25									
	Fifth	20	100										1 3	2 4	3 6	5 8	7 11	11 15	17 20	25 29									
	Sixth	20	120										1 3	3 5	4 6	7 9	10 12	14 17	21 23	31 33									
	Seventh	20	140										2 3	4 5	6 7	9 10	13 14	18 19	25 26	37 38									
K	First	32	32	↓	↓	↓	↓	↓	*	↑	↓	# 2	# 2	# 3	# 4	0 4	0 5	1 7	2 9	↑	↑	↑	↑	↑	↑	↑	↑	↑	↑
	Second	32	64									# 2	0 3	0 3	1 5	1 6	3 8	4 10	7 14										
	Third	32	96									0 2	0 3	1 4	2 6	3 8	6 10	8 13	13 19										
	Fourth	32	128									0 3	1 4	2 5	3 7	5 10	8 13	12 17	19 25										
	Fifth	32	160									1 3	2 4	3 6	5 8	7 11	11 15	17 20	25 29										
	Sixth	32	192									1 3	3 5	4 6	7 9	10 12	14 17	21 23	31 33										
	Seventh	32	224									2 3	4 5	6 7	9 10	13 14	18 19	25 26	37 38										
L	First	50	50	↓	↓	↓	↓	*	↑	↓	# 2	# 2	# 3	# 4	0 4	0 5	1 7	2 9	↑	↑	↑	↑	↑	↑	↑	↑	↑	↑	↑
	Second	50	100								# 2	0 3	0 3	1 5	1 6	3 8	4 10	7 14											
	Third	50	150								0 2	0 3	1 4	2 6	3 8	6 10	8 13	13 19											
	Fourth	50	200								0 3	1 4	2 5	3 7	5 10	8 13	12 17	19 25											
	Fifth	50	250								1 3	2 4	3 6	5 8	7 11	11 15	17 20	25 29											
	Sixth	50	300								1 3	3 5	4 6	7 9	10 12	14 17	21 23	31 33											
	Seventh	50	350								2 3	4 5	6 7	9 10	13 14	18 19	25 26	37 38											
M	First	80	80	↓	↓	↓	*	↑	↓	# 2	# 2	# 3	# 4	0 4	0 5	1 7	2 9	↑	↑	↑	↑	↑	↑	↑	↑	↑	↑	↑	↑
	Second	80	160							# 2	0 3	0 3	1 5	1 6	3 8	4 10	7 14												
	Third	80	240							0 2	0 3	1 4	2 6	3 8	6 10	8 13	13 19												
	Fourth	80	320							0 3	1 4	2 5	3 7	5 10	8 13	12 17	19 25												
	Fifth	80	400							1 3	2 4	3 6	5 8	7 11	11 15	17 20	25 29												
	Sixth	80	480							1 3	3 5	4 6	7 9	10 12	14 17	21 23	31 33												
	Seventh	80	560							2 3	4 5	6 7	9 10	13 14	18 19	25 26	37 38												

TABLE 9-18 *(Continued)*

Sample Size Code Letter	Sample	Sample Size	Cumulative Sample Size	0.010	0.015	0.025	0.040	0.065	0.10	0.15	0.25	0.40	0.65	1.0	1.5	2.5
				Ac Re	Ac Re	Ac Re	Ac Re	Ac Re	Ac Re	Ac Re	Ac Re	Ac Re	Ac Re	Ac Re	Ac Re	Ac Re
N	First	125	125	↓	↓	*	↑	↓	# 2	# 2	# 3	# 4	0 4	0 5	1 7	2 9
	Second	125	250						# 2	0 3	0 3	1 5	1 6	3 8	4 10	7 11
	Third	125	375						0 2	0 3	1 4	2 6	3 8	6 10	8 13	13 19
	Fourth	125	500						0 3	1 4	2 5	3 7	5 10	8 13	12 17	19 25
	Fifth	125	625						1 3	2 4	3 6	5 8	7 11	11 15	17 20	25 29
	Sixth	125	750						1 3	3 5	4 6	7 9	10 12	14 17	21 23	31 33
	Seventh	125	875						2 3	4 5	6 7	9 10	13 14	18 19	25 26	37 38
P	First	200	200	↓	*	↑	↓	# 2	# 2	# 3	# 4	0 4	0 5	1 7	2 9	↑
	Second	200	400					# 2	0 3	0 3	1 5	1 6	3 8	4 10	7 14	
	Third	200	600					0 2	0 3	1 4	2 6	3 8	6 10	8 13	13 19	
	Fourth	200	800					0 3	1 4	2 5	3 7	5 10	8 13	12 17	19 25	
	Fifth	200	1000					1 3	2 4	3 6	5 8	7 11	11 15	17 20	25 29	
	Sixth	200	1200					1 3	3 5	4 6	7 9	10 12	14 17	21 23	31 33	
	Seventh	200	1400					2 3	4 5	6 7	9 10	13 14	18 19	25 26	37 38	
Q	First	315	315	*	↑	↓	# 2	# 2	# 3	# 4	0 4	0 5	1 7	2 9	↑	
	Second	315	630				# 2	0 3	0 3	1 5	1 6	3 8	4 10	7 14		
	Third	315	945				0 2	0 3	1 4	2 6	3 8	6 10	8 13	13 19		
	Fourth	315	1260				0 3	1 4	2 5	3 7	5 10	8 13	12 17	19 25		
	Fifth	315	1575				1 3	2 4	3 6	5 8	7 11	11 15	17 20	25 29		
	Sixth	315	1890				1 3	3 5	4 6	7 9	10 12	14 17	21 23	31 33		
	Seventh	315	2205				2 3	4 5	6 7	9 10	13 14	18 19	25 26	37 38		
R	First	500	500	↑		# 2	# 2	# 3	# 4	0 4	0 5	1 7	2 9	↑		
	Second	500	1000			# 2	0 3	0 3	1 5	1 6	3 8	4 10	7 14			
	Third	500	1500			0 2	0 3	1 4	2 6	3 8	6 10	8 13	13 19			
	Fourth	500	2000			0 3	1 4	2 5	3 7	5 10	8 13	12 17	19 25			
	Fifth	500	2500			1 3	2 4	3 6	5 8	7 11	11 15	17 20	25 29			
	Sixth	500	3000			1 3	3 5	4 6	7 9	10 12	14 17	21 23	31 33			
	Seventh	500	3500			2 3	4 5	6 7	9 10	13 14	18 19	25 26	37 38			

Sample Size Code Letter	4.0	6.5	10	15	25	40	65	100	150	250	400	650	1000
	Ac Re	Ac Re	Ac Re	Ac Re	Ac Re	Ac Re	Ac Re	Ac Re	Ac Re	Ac Re	Ac Re	Ac Re	Ac Re
N	↑												
P													
Q													
R													

Acceptable Quality Levels (Normal Inspection)

↓ = Use first sampling plan below arrow. If sample size equals or exceeds lot or batch size, do 100 percent inspection.

↑ = Use first sampling plan above arrow (refer to preceding page, when necessary).

Ac = Acceptance number.

Re = Rejection number.

* = Use corresponding single sampling plan (or alternatively, use multiple plan below, where available).

\# = Acceptance not permitted at this sample size.

TABLE 9-19 Multiple sampling plans for tightened inspection (master table)

Sample Size Code Letter	Sample	Sample Size	Cumulative Sample Size	Acceptable Quality Levels (Tightened Inspection)																									
				0.010	0.015	0.025	0.040	0.065	0.10	0.15	0.25	0.40	0.65	1.0	1.5	2.5	4.0	6.5	10	15	25	40	65	100	150	250	400	650	1000
				Ac Re	Ac Re	Ac Re	Ac Re	Ac Re	Ac Re	Ac Re	Ac Re	Ac Re	Ac Re	Ac Re	Ac Re	Ac Re	Ac Re	Ac Re	Ac Re	Ac Re	Ac Re	Ac Re	Ac Re	Ac Re	Ac Re	Ac Re	Ac Re	Ac Re	Ac Re
A				↓	↓	↓	↓	↓	↓	↓	↓	↓	↓	↓	↓	↓	↓	↓	↓	↓	↓	*	*	*	*	*	*	*	*
B				↓	↓	↓	↓	↓	↓	↓	↓	↓	↓	↓	↓	↓	↓	*	↓	↓	‡	‡	‡	‡	‡	‡	‡	‡	‡
C				↓	↓	↓	↓	↓	↓	↓	↓	↓	↓	↓	↓	↓	*	↓	↓	‡	‡	‡	‡	‡	‡	‡	‡	‡	↑
D	First	2	2	↓	↓	↓	↓	↓	↓	↓	↓	↓	↓	↓	↓	*	↓	↓	# 2	# 2	# 3	# 4	0 4	0 6	1 8	3 10	6 15	↑	↑
	Second	2	4	↓	↓	↓	↓	↓	↓	↓	↓	↓	↓	↓	↓		↓	↓	# 2	0 3	0 3	1 5	2 7	3 9	6 12	10 17	16 25	↑	↑
	Third	2	6	↓	↓	↓	↓	↓	↓	↓	↓	↓	↓	↓	↓		↓	↓	0 2	0 3	1 4	2 6	4 9	7 12	11 17	17 24	26 36	↑	↑
	Fourth	2	8	↓	↓	↓	↓	↓	↓	↓	↓	↓	↓	↓	↓		↓	↓	0 3	1 4	2 5	3 7	6 11	10 15	16 22	24 31	37 46	↑	↑
	Fifth	2	10	↓	↓	↓	↓	↓	↓	↓	↓	↓	↓	↓	↓		↓	↓	1 3	2 4	3 6	5 8	9 12	14 17	22 25	32 37	49 55	↑	↑
	Sixth	2	12	↓	↓	↓	↓	↓	↓	↓	↓	↓	↓	↓	↓		↓	↓	1 3	3 5	4 6	7 9	12 14	18 20	27 29	40 43	61 64	↑	↑
	Seventh	2	14	↓	↓	↓	↓	↓	↓	↓	↓	↓	↓	↓	↓		↓	↓	2 3	4 5	6 7	9 10	14 15	21 22	32 33	48 49	72 73	↑	↑
E	First	3	3	↓	↓	↓	↓	↓	↓	↓	↓	↓	↓	↓	*	↓	↓	# 2	# 2	# 3	# 4	0 4	0 6	1 8	3 10	6 15	↑	↑	↑
	Second	3	6	↓	↓	↓	↓	↓	↓	↓	↓	↓	↓	↓		↓	↓	# 2	0 3	0 3	1 5	2 7	3 9	6 12	10 17	16 25	↑	↑	↑
	Third	3	9	↓	↓	↓	↓	↓	↓	↓	↓	↓	↓	↓		↓	↓	0 2	0 3	1 4	2 6	4 9	7 12	11 17	17 24	26 36	↑	↑	↑
	Fourth	3	12	↓	↓	↓	↓	↓	↓	↓	↓	↓	↓	↓		↓	↓	0 3	1 4	2 5	3 7	6 11	10 15	16 22	24 31	37 46	↑	↑	↑
	Fifth	3	15	↓	↓	↓	↓	↓	↓	↓	↓	↓	↓	↓		↓	↓	1 3	2 4	3 6	5 8	9 12	14 17	22 25	32 37	49 55	↑	↑	↑
	Sixth	3	18	↓	↓	↓	↓	↓	↓	↓	↓	↓	↓	↓		↓	↓	1 3	3 5	4 6	7 9	12 14	18 20	27 29	40 43	61 64	↑	↑	↑
	Seventh	3	21	↓	↓	↓	↓	↓	↓	↓	↓	↓	↓	↓		↓	↓	2 3	4 5	6 7	9 10	14 15	21 22	32 33	48 49	72 73	↑	↑	↑
F	First	5	5	↓	↓	↓	↓	↓	↓	↓	↓	↓	↓	*	↓	↓	# 2	# 2	# 3	# 4	0 4	0 6	1 8	↑	↑	↑	↑	↑	↑	↑	↑
	Second	5	10	↓	↓	↓	↓	↓	↓	↓	↓	↓	↓		↓	↓	# 2	0 3	0 3	1 5	2 7	3 9	6 12	↑	↑	↑	↑	↑	↑	↑	↑
	Third	5	15	↓	↓	↓	↓	↓	↓	↓	↓	↓	↓		↓	↓	0 2	0 3	1 4	2 6	4 9	7 12	11 17	↑	↑	↑	↑	↑	↑	↑	↑
	Fourth	5	20	↓	↓	↓	↓	↓	↓	↓	↓	↓	↓		↓	↓	0 3	1 4	2 5	3 7	6 11	10 15	16 22	↑	↑	↑	↑	↑	↑	↑	↑
	Fifth	5	25	↓	↓	↓	↓	↓	↓	↓	↓	↓	↓		↓	↓	1 3	2 4	3 6	5 8	9 12	14 17	22 25	↑	↑	↑	↑	↑	↑	↑	↑
	Sixth	5	30	↓	↓	↓	↓	↓	↓	↓	↓	↓	↓		↓	↓	1 3	3 5	4 6	7 9	12 14	18 20	27 29	↑	↑	↑	↑	↑	↑	↑	↑
	Seventh	5	35	↓	↓	↓	↓	↓	↓	↓	↓	↓	↓		↓	↓	2 3	4 5	6 7	9 10	14 15	21 22	32 33	↑	↑	↑	↑	↑	↑	↑	↑
G	First	8	8	↓	↓	↓	↓	↓	↓	↓	↓	↓	*	↓	↓	# 2	# 2	# 3	# 4	0 4	0 6	1 8	↑	↑	↑	↑	↑	↑	↑	↑	↑
	Second	8	16	↓	↓	↓	↓	↓	↓	↓	↓	↓		↓	↓	# 2	0 3	0 3	1 5	2 7	3 9	6 12	↑	↑	↑	↑	↑	↑	↑	↑	↑
	Third	8	24	↓	↓	↓	↓	↓	↓	↓	↓	↓		↓	↓	0 2	0 3	1 4	2 6	4 9	7 12	11 17	↑	↑	↑	↑	↑	↑	↑	↑	↑
	Fourth	8	32	↓	↓	↓	↓	↓	↓	↓	↓	↓		↓	↓	0 3	1 4	2 5	3 7	6 11	10 15	16 22	↑	↑	↑	↑	↑	↑	↑	↑	↑
	Fifth	8	40	↓	↓	↓	↓	↓	↓	↓	↓	↓		↓	↓	1 3	2 4	3 6	5 8	9 12	14 17	22 25	↑	↑	↑	↑	↑	↑	↑	↑	↑
	Sixth	8	48	↓	↓	↓	↓	↓	↓	↓	↓	↓		↓	↓	1 3	3 5	4 6	7 9	12 14	18 20	27 29	↑	↑	↑	↑	↑	↑	↑	↑	↑
	Seventh	8	56	↓	↓	↓	↓	↓	↓	↓	↓	↓		↓	↓	2 3	4 5	6 7	9 10	14 15	21 22	32 33	↑	↑	↑	↑	↑	↑	↑	↑	↑

Source: ASQC (1981), ANSI/ASQC Z1.4–1981: *American National Standard—Sampling Procedures and Tables for Inspection by Attributes.* Reprinted with the permission of ASQC.

TABLE 9-19 *(Continued)*

Sample Size Code Letter	Sample	Sample Size	Cumulative Sample Size	Acceptable Quality Levels (Tightened Inspection)																									
				0.010	0.015	0.025	0.040	0.065	0.10	0.15	0.25	0.40	0.65	1.0	1.5	2.5	4.0	6.5	10	15	25	40	65	100	150	250	400	650	1000
				Ac Re	Ac Re	Ac Re	Ac Re	Ac Re	Ac Re	Ac Re	Ac Re	Ac Re	Ac Re	Ac Re	Ac Re	Ac Re	Ac Re	Ac Re	Ac Re	Ac Re	Ac Re	Ac Re	Ac Re	Ac Re	Ac Re	Ac Re	Ac Re	Ac Re	Ac Re
H	First	13	13	↓	↓	↓	↓	↓	↓	↓	↓	*	↓	↓	# 2	# 2	# 3	# 4	0 4	0 6	1 8	↑	↑	↑	↑	↑	↑	↑	↑
	Second	13	26												# 2	0 3	0 3	1 5	2 7	3 9	6 12								
	Third	13	39												0 2	0 3	1 4	2 6	4 9	7 12	11 17								
	Fourth	13	52												0 3	1 4	2 5	3 7	6 11	10 15	16 22								
	Fifth	13	65												1 3	2 4	3 6	5 8	9 12	14 17	22 25								
	Sixth	13	78												1 3	3 5	4 6	7 9	12 14	18 20	27 29								
	Seventh	13	91												2 3	4 5	6 7	9 10	14 15	21 22	32 33								
J	First	20	20	↓	↓	↓	↓	↓	↓	↓	*	↓	↓	# 2	# 2	# 3	# 4	0 4	0 6	1 8	↑	↑	↑	↑	↑	↑	↑	↑	↑
	Second	20	40											# 2	0 3	0 3	1 5	2 7	3 9	6 12									
	Third	20	60											0 2	0 3	1 4	2 6	4 9	7 12	11 17									
	Fourth	20	80											0 3	1 4	2 5	3 7	6 11	10 15	16 22									
	Fifth	20	100											1 3	2 4	3 6	5 8	9 12	14 17	22 25									
	Sixth	20	120											1 3	3 5	4 6	7 9	12 14	18 20	27 29									
	Seventh	20	140											2 3	4 5	6 7	9 10	14 15	21 22	32 33									
K	First	32	32	↓	↓	↓	↓	↓	↓	*	↓	↓	# 2	# 2	# 3	# 4	0 4	0 6	1 8	↑	↑	↑	↑	↑	↑	↑	↑	↑	↑
	Second	32	64										# 2	0 3	0 3	1 5	2 7	3 9	6 12										
	Third	32	96										0 2	0 3	1 4	2 6	4 9	7 12	11 17										
	Fourth	32	128										0 3	1 4	2 5	3 7	6 11	10 15	16 22										
	Fifth	32	160										1 3	2 4	3 6	5 8	9 12	14 17	22 25										
	Sixth	32	192										1 3	3 5	4 6	7 9	12 14	18 20	27 29										
	Seventh	32	224										2 3	4 5	6 7	9 10	14 15	21 22	32 33										
L	First	50	50	↓	↓	↓	↓	↓	*	↓	↓	# 2	# 2	# 3	# 4	0 4	0 6	1 8	↑	↑	↑	↑	↑	↑	↑	↑	↑	↑	↑
	Second	50	100									# 2	0 3	0 3	1 5	2 7	3 9	6 12											
	Third	50	150									0 2	0 3	1 4	2 6	4 9	7 12	11 17											
	Fourth	50	200									0 3	1 4	2 5	3 7	6 11	10 15	16 22											
	Fifth	50	250									1 3	2 4	3 6	5 8	9 12	14 17	22 25											
	Sixth	50	300									1 3	3 5	4 6	7 9	12 14	18 20	27 29											
	Seventh	50	350									2 3	4 5	6 7	9 10	14 15	21 22	32 33											
M	First	80	80	↓	↓	↓	↓	*	↓	↓	# 2	# 2	# 3	# 4	0 4	0 6	1 8	↑	↑	↑	↑	↑	↑	↑	↑	↑	↑	↑	↑
	Second	80	160								# 2	0 3	0 3	1 5	2 7	3 9	6 12												
	Third	80	240								0 2	0 3	1 4	2 6	4 9	7 12	11 17												
	Fourth	80	320								0 3	1 4	2 5	3 7	6 11	10 15	16 22												
	Fifth	80	400								1 3	2 4	3 6	5 8	9 12	14 17	22 25												
	Sixth	80	480								1 3	3 5	4 6	7 9	12 14	18 20	27 29												
	Seventh	80	560								2 3	4 5	6 7	9 10	14 15	21 22	32 33												

↓ = Use first sampling plan below arrow (refer to continuation of table on following page, when necessary). If sample size equals or exceeds lot or batch size, do 100 percent inspection.

↑ = Use first sampling above arrow.

Ac = Acceptance number.

Re = Rejection number.

* = Use corresponding single sampling plan (or alternatively, use multiple sampling plan below, where available).

++ = Use corresponding double sampling plan (or alternatively, use multiple sampling plan below, where available).

= Acceptance not permitted at this sample size.

TABLE 9-19 (Continued)

Sample Size Code Letter	Sample	Sample Size	Cumulative Sample Size	0.010	0.015	0.025	0.040	0.065	0.10	0.15	0.25	0.40	0.65	1.0	1.5	2.5	4.0	6.5	10	15	25	40	65	100	150	250	400	650	1000
				Acceptable Quality Levels (Tightened Inspection)																									
				Ac Re	Ac Re	Ac Re	Ac Re	Ac Re	Ac Re	Ac Re	Ac Re	Ac Re	Ac Re	Ac Re	Ac Re	Ac Re	Ac Re	Ac Re	Ac Re	Ac Re	Ac Re	Ac Re	Ac Re	Ac Re	Ac Re	Ac Re	Ac Re	Ac Re	Ac Re
N	First	125	125	↓	↓	↓	*	↓	↓	# 2	# 2	# 3	# 4	0 4	0 6	1 8	↑												
	Second	125	250							# 2	0 3	0 3	1 5	2 7	3 9	6 12													
	Third	125	375							0 2	0 3	1 4	2 6	4 9	7 12	11 17													
	Fourth	125	500							0 3	1 4	2 5	3 7	6 11	10 15	16 22													
	Fifth	125	625							1 3	2 4	3 6	5 8	9 12	14 17	22 25													
	Sixth	125	750							1 3	3 5	4 6	7 9	12 14	18 20	27 29													
	Seventh	125	875							2 3	4 5	6 7	9 10	14 15	21 22	32 33													
P	First	200	200			*	↓		# 2	# 2	# 3	# 4	0 4	0 6	1 8	↑													
	Second	200	400						# 2	0 3	0 3	1 5	2 7	3 9	6 12														
	Third	200	600						0 2	0 3	1 4	2 6	4 9	7 12	11 17														
	Fourth	200	800						0 3	1 4	2 5	3 7	6 11	10 15	16 22														
	Fifth	200	1000						1 3	2 4	3 6	5 8	9 12	14 17	22 25														
	Sixth	200	1200						1 3	3 5	4 6	7 9	12 14	18 20	27 29														
	Seventh	200	1400						2 3	4 5	6 7	9 10	14 15	21 22	32 33														
Q	First	315	315		*	↓		# 2	# 2	# 3	# 4	0 4	0 6	1 8	↑														
	Second	315	630					# 2	0 3	0 3	1 5	2 7	3 9	6 12															
	Third	315	945					0 2	0 3	1 4	2 6	4 9	7 12	11 17															
	Fourth	315	1260					0 3	1 4	2 5	3 7	6 11	10 15	16 22															
	Fifth	315	1575					1 3	2 4	3 6	5 8	9 12	14 17	22 25															
	Sixth	315	1890					1 3	3 5	4 6	7 9	12 14	18 20	27 29															
	Seventh	315	2205					2 3	4 5	6 7	9 10	14 15	21 22	32 33															
R	First	500	500	*	↑		# 2	# 2	# 3	# 4	0 4	0 6	1 8	↑															
	Second	500	1000				# 2	0 3	0 3	1 5	2 7	3 9	6 12																
	Third	500	1500				0 2	0 3	1 4	2 6	4 9	7 12	11 17																
	Fourth	500	2000				0 3	1 4	2 5	3 7	6 11	10 15	16 22																
	Fifth	500	2500				1 3	2 4	3 6	5 8	9 12	14 17	22 25																
	Sixth	500	3000				1 3	3 5	4 6	7 9	12 14	18 20	27 29																
	Seventh	500	3500				2 3	4 5	6 7	9 10	14 15	21 22	32 33																
S	First	800	800			# 2																							
	Second	800	1600			# 2																							
	Third	800	2400			0 2																							
	Fourth	800	3200			0 3																							
	Fifth	800	4000			1 3																							
	Sixth	800	4800			1 3																							
	Seventh	800	5600			2 3																							

↓ = Use first sampling plan below arrow. If sample size equals or exceeds lot or batch size, do 100 percent inspection.

↑ = Use first sampling above arrow (refer to preceding page, when necessary).

Ac = Acceptance number.

Re = Rejection number.

* = Use corresponding single sampling plan (or alternatively, use multiple sampling plan below, where available).

= Acceptance not permitted at this sample size.

TABLE 9-20 Multiple sampling plans for reduced inspection (master table)

Sample Size Code Letter	Sample	Sample Size	Cumulative Sample Size	*Acceptable Quality Levels (Reduced Inspection)*†																									
				0.010	0.015	0.025	0.040	0.065	0.10	0.15	0.25	0.40	0.65	1.0	1.5	2.5	4.0	6.5	10	15	25	40	65	100	150	250	400	650	1000
				Ac Re	Ac Re	Ac Re	Ac Re	Ac Re	Ac Re	Ac Re	Ac Re	Ac Re	Ac Re	Ac Re	Ac Re	Ac Re	Ac Re	Ac Re	Ac Re	Ac Re	Ac Re	Ac Re	Ac Re	Ac Re	Ac Re	Ac Re	Ac Re	Ac Re	Ac Re
A				↓	↓	↓	↓	↓	↓	↓	↓	↓	↓	↓	↓	↓	↓	*	↓	↓	*	*	*	*	*	*	*	*	*
B				↓	↓	↓	↓	↓	↓	↓	↓	↓	↓	↓	↓	↓	*	↑	↓	*	*	*	*	*	*	*	*	*	*
C				↓	↓	↓	↓	↓	↓	↓	↓	↓	↓	↓	↓	*	↑	↓	*	*	*	*	*	*	*	*	*	*	↑
D				↓	↓	↓	↓	↓	↓	↓	↓	↓	↓	↓	*	↑	↓	++	++	++	++	++	++	++	++	++	++	↑	↑
E				↓	↓	↓	↓	↓	↓	↓	↓	↓	↓	*	↑	↓	++	++	++	++	++	++	++	++	++	++	↑	↑	↑
F	First	2	2	↓	↓	↓	↓	↓	↓	↓	↓	↓	*	↑	↓	# 2	# 2	# 3	# 3	# 4	# 4	0 5	0 6	↑	↑	↑	↑	↑	↑
	Second	2	4	↓	↓	↓	↓	↓	↓	↓	↓	↓		↑	↓	# 2	# 3	# 3	0 4	0 5	1 6	1 7	3 9	↑	↑	↑	↑	↑	↑
	Third	2	6	↓	↓	↓	↓	↓	↓	↓	↓	↓		↑	↓	0 2	0 3	0 4	0 5	1 6	2 8	3 9	6 12	↑	↑	↑	↑	↑	↑
	Fourth	2	8	↓	↓	↓	↓	↓	↓	↓	↓	↓		↑	↓	0 3	0 4	0 5	1 6	2 7	3 10	5 12	8 15	↑	↑	↑	↑	↑	↑
	Fifth	2	10	↓	↓	↓	↓	↓	↓	↓	↓	↓		↑	↓	0 3	0 4	1 6	2 7	3 8	5 11	7 13	11 17	↑	↑	↑	↑	↑	↑
	Sixth	2	12	↓	↓	↓	↓	↓	↓	↓	↓	↓		↑	↓	0 3	1 5	1 6	3 7	4 9	7 12	10 15	14 20	↑	↑	↑	↑	↑	↑
	Seventh	2	14	↓	↓	↓	↓	↓	↓	↓	↓	↓		↑	↓	1 3	1 5	2 7	4 8	6 10	9 14	13 17	18 22	↑	↑	↑	↑	↑	↑
G	First	3	3	↓	↓	↓	↓	↓	↓	↓	↓	*	↑	↓	# 2	# 2	# 3	# 3	# 4	# 4	0 5	0 6	↑	↑	↑	↑	↑	↑	↑
	Second	3	6	↓	↓	↓	↓	↓	↓	↓	↓		↑	↓	# 2	# 3	# 3	0 4	0 5	1 6	1 7	3 9	↑	↑	↑	↑	↑	↑	↑
	Third	3	9	↓	↓	↓	↓	↓	↓	↓	↓		↑	↓	0 2	0 3	0 4	0 5	1 6	2 8	3 9	6 12	↑	↑	↑	↑	↑	↑	↑
	Fourth	3	12	↓	↓	↓	↓	↓	↓	↓	↓		↑	↓	0 3	0 4	0 5	1 6	2 7	3 10	5 12	8 15	↑	↑	↑	↑	↑	↑	↑
	Fifth	3	15	↓	↓	↓	↓	↓	↓	↓	↓		↑	↓	0 3	0 4	1 6	2 7	3 8	5 11	7 13	11 17	↑	↑	↑	↑	↑	↑	↑
	Sixth	3	18	↓	↓	↓	↓	↓	↓	↓	↓		↑	↓	0 3	1 5	1 6	3 7	4 9	7 12	10 15	14 20	↑	↑	↑	↑	↑	↑	↑
	Seventh	3	21	↓	↓	↓	↓	↓	↓	↓	↓		↑	↓	1 3	1 5	2 7	4 8	6 10	9 14	13 17	18 22	↑	↑	↑	↑	↑	↑	↑
H	First	5	5	↓	↓	↓	↓	↓	↓	↓	*	↑	↓	# 2	# 2	# 3	# 3	# 4	# 4	0 5	0 6	↑	↑	↑	↑	↑	↑	↑	↑
	Second	5	10	↓	↓	↓	↓	↓	↓	↓		↑	↓	# 2	# 3	# 3	0 4	0 5	1 6	1 7	3 9	↑	↑	↑	↑	↑	↑	↑	↑
	Third	5	15	↓	↓	↓	↓	↓	↓	↓		↑	↓	0 2	0 3	0 4	0 5	1 6	2 8	3 9	6 12	↑	↑	↑	↑	↑	↑	↑	↑
	Fourth	5	20	↓	↓	↓	↓	↓	↓	↓		↑	↓	0 3	0 4	0 5	1 6	2 7	3 10	5 12	8 15	↑	↑	↑	↑	↑	↑	↑	↑
	Fifth	5	25	↓	↓	↓	↓	↓	↓	↓		↑	↓	0 3	0 4	1 6	2 7	3 8	5 11	7 13	11 17	↑	↑	↑	↑	↑	↑	↑	↑
	Sixth	5	30	↓	↓	↓	↓	↓	↓	↓		↑	↓	0 3	1 5	1 6	3 7	4 9	7 12	10 15	14 20	↑	↑	↑	↑	↑	↑	↑	↑
	Seventh	5	35	↓	↓	↓	↓	↓	↓	↓		↑	↓	1 3	1 5	2 7	4 8	6 10	9 14	13 17	18 22	↑	↑	↑	↑	↑	↑	↑	↑
J	First	8	8	↓	↓	↓	↓	↓	↓	*	↑	↓	# 2	# 2	# 3	# 3	# 4	# 4	0 5	0 6	↑	↑	↑	↑	↑	↑	↑	↑	↑
	Second	8	16	↓	↓	↓	↓	↓	↓		↑	↓	# 2	# 3	# 3	0 4	0 5	1 6	1 7	3 9	↑	↑	↑	↑	↑	↑	↑	↑	↑
	Third	8	24	↓	↓	↓	↓	↓	↓		↑	↓	0 2	0 3	0 4	0 5	1 6	2 8	3 9	6 12	↑	↑	↑	↑	↑	↑	↑	↑	↑
	Fourth	8	32	↓	↓	↓	↓	↓	↓		↑	↓	0 3	0 4	0 5	1 6	2 7	3 10	5 12	8 15	↑	↑	↑	↑	↑	↑	↑	↑	↑
	Fifth	8	40	↓	↓	↓	↓	↓	↓		↑	↓	0 3	0 4	1 6	2 7	3 8	5 11	7 13	11 17	↑	↑	↑	↑	↑	↑	↑	↑	↑
	Sixth	8	48	↓	↓	↓	↓	↓	↓		↑	↓	0 3	1 5	1 6	3 7	4 9	7 12	10 15	14 20	↑	↑	↑	↑	↑	↑	↑	↑	↑
	Seventh	8	56	↓	↓	↓	↓	↓	↓		↑	↓	1 3	1 5	2 7	4 8	6 10	9 14	13 17	18 22	↑	↑	↑	↑	↑	↑	↑	↑	↑

↓ = Use first sampling plan below arrow (refer to continuation of table on following page, when necessary). If sample size equals or exceeds lot or batch size, do 100 percent inspection.

↑ = Use first sampling plan above arrow.

Ac = Acceptance number.

Re = Rejection number.

* = Use corresponding single sampling plan (or alternatively, use multiple sampling plan below, where available).

++ = Use corresponding double sampling plan (or alternatively, use multiple sampling plan below, where available).

= Acceptance not permitted at this sample size.

† = If, after the final sample, the acceptance number has been exceeded, but the rejection number has not been reached, accept the lot but reinstate normal inspection.

Source: ASQC (1981), ANSI/ASQC Z1.4–1981: *American National Standard—Sampling Procedures and Tables for Inspection by Attributes.* Reprinted with the permission of ASQC.

TABLE 9-20 *(Continued)*

Sample Size Code Letter	Sample	Sample Size	Cumulative Sample Size	Acceptable Quality Levels (Reduced Inspection)†																									
				0.010	0.015	0.025	0.040	0.065	0.10	0.15	0.25	0.40	0.65	1.0	1.5	2.5	4.0	6.5	10	15	25	40	65	100	150	250	400	650	1000
				Ac Re	Ac Re	Ac Re	Ac Re	Ac Re	Ac Re	Ac Re	Ac Re	Ac Re	Ac Re	Ac Re	Ac Re	Ac Re	Ac Re	Ac Re	Ac Re	Ac Re	Ac Re	Ac Re	Ac Re	Ac Re	Ac Re	Ac Re	Ac Re	Ac Re	Ac Re
K	First	13	13	↓	↓	↓	↓	↓	*	↑	↓	# 2	# 2	# 3	# 3	# 4	# 4	0 5	0 6	↑	↑	↑	↑	↑	↑	↑	↑	↑	↑
	Second	13	26									# 2	# 3	# 3	0 4	0 5	1 6	1 7	3 9										
	Third	13	39									0 2	0 3	0 4	0 5	1 6	2 8	3 9	6 12										
	Fourth	13	52									0 3	0 4	0 5	1 6	2 7	3 10	5 12	8 15										
	Fifth	13	65									0 3	0 4	1 6	2 7	3 8	5 11	7 13	11 17										
	Sixth	13	78									0 3	1 5	1 6	3 7	4 9	7 12	10 15	14 20										
	Seventh	13	91									1 3	1 5	2 7	4 8	6 10	9 14	13 17	18 22										
L	First	20	20	↓	↓	↓	↓	*	↑	↑	# 2	# 2	# 3	# 3	# 4	# 4	0 5	0 6	↑	↑	↑	↑	↑	↑	↑	↑	↑	↑	↑
	Second	20	40								# 2	# 3	# 3	0 4	0 5	1 6	1 7	3 9											
	Third	20	60								0 2	0 3	0 4	0 5	1 6	2 8	3 9	6 12											
	Fourth	20	80								0 3	0 4	0 5	1 6	2 7	3 10	5 12	8 15											
	Fifth	20	100								0 3	0 4	1 6	2 7	3 8	5 11	7 13	11 17											
	Sixth	20	120								0 3	1 5	1 6	3 7	4 9	7 12	10 15	14 20											
	Seventh	20	140								1 3	1 5	2 7	4 8	6 10	9 14	13 17	18 22											
M	First	32	32				*	↑	↓	# 2	# 2	# 3	# 3	# 4	# 4	0 5	0 6	↑	↑	↑	↑	↑	↑	↑	↑	↑	↑	↑	↑
	Second	32	64							# 2	# 3	# 3	0 4	0 5	1 6	1 7	3 9												
	Third	32	96							0 2	0 3	0 4	0 5	1 6	2 8	3 9	6 12												
	Fourth	32	128							0 3	0 4	0 5	1 6	2 7	3 10	5 12	8 15												
	Fifth	32	160							0 3	0 4	1 6	2 7	3 8	5 11	7 13	11 17												
	Sixth	32	192							0 3	1 5	1 6	3 7	4 9	7 12	10 15	14 20												
	Seventh	32	224							1 3	1 5	2 7	4 8	6 10	9 14	13 17	18 22												
N	First	50	50			*	↑	↓	# 2	# 2	# 3	# 3	# 4	# 4	0 5	0 6	↑	↑	↑	↑	↑	↑	↑	↑	↑	↑	↑	↑	↑
	Second	50	100						# 2	# 3	# 3	0 4	0 5	1 6	1 7	3 9													
	Third	50	150						0 2	0 3	0 4	0 5	1 6	2 8	3 9	6 12													
	Fourth	50	200						0 3	0 4	0 5	1 6	2 7	3 10	5 12	8 15													
	Fifth	50	250						0 3	0 4	1 6	2 7	3 8	5 11	7 13	11 17													
	Sixth	50	300						0 3	1 5	1 6	3 7	4 9	7 12	10 15	14 20													
	Seventh	50	350	↓	↓				1 3	1 5	2 7	4 8	6 10	9 14	13 17	18 22													

TABLE 9-20 (Continued)

Sample Size Code Letter	Sample	Sample Size	Cumulative Sample Size	Acceptable Quality Levels (Reduced Inspection)†																									
				0.010	0.015	0.025	0.040	0.065	0.10	0.15	0.25	0.40	0.65	1.0	1.5	2.5	4.0	6.5	10	15	25	40	65	100	150	250	400	650	1000
				Ac Re	Ac Re	Ac Re	Ac Re	Ac Re	Ac Re	Ac Re	Ac Re	Ac Re	Ac Re	Ac Re	Ac Re	Ac Re	Ac Re	Ac Re	Ac Re	Ac Re	Ac Re	Ac Re	Ac Re	Ac Re	Ac Re	Ac Re	Ac Re	Ac Re	Ac Re
P	First	80	80	↓	*	↑	↓	# 2	# 2	# 3	# 3	# 4	# 4	0 5	0 6	↑													
	Second	80	160					# 2	# 3	# 3	0 4	0 5	1 6	1 7	3 9														
	Third	80	240					0 2	0 3	0 4	0 5	1 6	2 8	3 9	6 12														
	Fourth	80	320					0 3	0 4	0 5	1 6	2 7	3 10	5 12	8 15														
	Fifth	80	400					0 3	0 4	1 6	2 7	3 8	5 11	7 13	11 17														
	Sixth	80	480					0 3	1 5	1 6	3 7	4 9	7 12	10 15	14 20														
	Seventh	80	560					1 3	1 5	2 7	4 8	6 10	9 14	13 17	18 22														
Q	First	125	125	*	↑	↓	# 2	# 2	# 3	# 3	# 4	# 4	0 5	0 6	↑														
	Second	125	250				# 2	# 3	# 3	0 4	0 5	1 6	1 7	3 9															
	Third	125	375				0 2	0 3	0 4	0 5	1 6	2 8	3 9	6 12															
	Fourth	125	500				0 3	0 4	0 5	1 6	2 7	3 10	5 12	8 15															
	Fifth	125	625				0 3	0 4	1 6	2 7	3 8	5 11	7 13	11 17															
	Sixth	125	750				0 3	1 5	1 6	3 7	4 9	7 12	10 15	14 20															
	Seventh	125	875				1 3	1 5	2 7	4 8	6 10	9 14	13 17	18 22															
R	First	200	200	↑		# 2	# 2	# 3	# 3	# 4	# 4	0 5	0 6	↑															
	Second	200	400			# 2	# 3	# 3	0 4	0 5	1 6	1 7	3 9																
	Third	200	600			0 2	0 3	0 4	0 5	1 6	2 8	3 9	6 12																
	Fourth	200	800			0 3	0 4	0 5	1 6	2 7	3 10	5 12	8 15																
	Fifth	200	1000			0 3	0 4	1 6	2 7	3 8	5 11	7 13	11 17																
	Sixth	200	1200			0 3	1 5	1 6	3 7	4 9	7 12	10 15	14 20																
	Seventh	200	1400			1 3	1 5	2 7	4 8	6 10	9 14	13 17	18 22																

↓ = Use first sampling plan below arrow. If sample size equals, or exceeds, lot or batch size, do 100 percent inspection.

↑ = Use first sampling above arrow (refer to preceding page when necessary).

Ac = Acceptance number.

* = Use corresponding single sampling plan (or alternatively, use multiple sampling plan below, where available).

Re = Rejection number.

\# = Acceptance not permitted at this sample size.

† = If, after the final sample, the acceptance number has been exceeded, but the rejection number has not been reached, accept the lot, but reinstate normal inspection.

TABLE 9-21 Limit numbers for reduced insp

Number of Sample Units from Last 10 Lots or Batches	Acceptable Quality Level																								
	0.010	*0.015*	*0.025*	*0.040*	*0.065*	*0.10*	*0.15*	*0.25*	*0.40*	*0.65*	*1.0*	*1.5*	*2.5*	*4.0*	*6.5*	*10*	*15*	*25*	*40*	*65*	*100*	*150*	*250*	*400*	*650*	*1000*
20–29	*	*	*	*	*	*	*	*	*	*	*	*	*	*	*	0	0	2	4	8	14	22	40	68	115	181
30–49	*	*	*	*	*	*	*	*	*	*	*	*	*	*	0	0	1	3	7	13	22	36	63	105	178	277
50–79	*	*	*	*	*	*	*	*	*	*	*	*	*	0	0	2	3	7	14	25	40	63	110	181	301	
80–129	*	*	*	*	*	*	*	*	*	*	*	*	0	0	2	4	7	14	24	42	68	105	181	297		
130–199	*	*	*	*	*	*	*	*	*	*	*	0	0	2	4	7	13	25	42	72	115	177	301	490		
200–319	*	*	*	*	*	*	*	*	*	*	0	0	2	4	8	14	22	40	68	115	181	277	471			
320–499	*	*	*	*	*	*	*	*	*	0	0	1	4	8	14	24	39	68	113	189						
500–799	*	*	*	*	*	*	*	*	0	0	2	3	7	14	25	40	63	110	181							
800–1249	*	*	*	*	*	*	*	0	0	2	4	7	14	24	42	68	105	181								
1,250–1,999	*	*	*	*	*	*	0	0	2	4	7	13	24	40	69	110	169									
2,000–3,149	*	*	*	*	*	0	0	2	4	8	14	22	40	68	115	181										
3,150–4,999	*	*	*	*	0	0	1	4	8	14	24	38	67	111	186											
5,000–7,999	*	*	*	0	0	2	3	7	14	25	40	63	110	181												
8,000–12,499	*	*	0	0	2	4	7	14	24	42	68	105	181													
12,500–19,999	*	0	0	2	4	7	13	24	40	69	110	169														
20,000–31,499	0	0	2	4	8	14	22	40	68	115	181															
31,500–49,999	0	1	4	8	14	24	38	67	111	186																
50,000 & Over	2	3	7	14	25	40	63	110	181	301																

*Denotes that the number of sample units from the last 10 lots or batches is not sufficient for reduced inspection for this AQL. In this instance more than 10 lots or batches may be used for the calculation, provided that the lots or batches used are the most recent ones in sequence, that they have been on normal inspection, and that none has been rejected while on original inspection.

Source: ASQC (1981), ANSI/ASQC Z1.4–1981: *American National Standard—Sampling Procedures and Tables for Inspection by Attributes.* Reprinted with the permission of ASQC.

Example 9-15: Lots of size 2000 are submitted for inspection. The acceptable quality level is agreed to be 0.65 percent nonconforming. If the general inspection level is chosen to be level II, find the single sampling plan for normal inspection using *ANSI/ASQC Z1.4*.

Solution. From Table 9-11, for a lot size of 2000 and general inspection level II, the sample size code letter is K. We use Table 9-12 for single sampling plans for normal inspection. Indexing the sample size code letter of K and the AQL of 0.65 percent, the following plan is obtained: sample size $n = 125$, acceptance number $c = 2$, rejection number $r = 3$.

Instead of the AQL value of 0.65 percent, suppose it had been chosen to be 0.065 percent. Let us now find the single sampling plan under normal inspection, using the same lot size N of 2000 and general inspection level II. The sample size code letter is still K. Using Table 9-12 for a sample size code letter of K and AQL = 0.065 percent, we find that the sample size code letter changes to L. The sampling plan obtained is $n = 200$, $c = 0$, $r = 1$.

Example 9-16: Products are submitted for inspection in batches of size 1000. The AQL is chosen to be 15 nonconformities per 100 units. If the general inspection level is chosen to be III, find a double sampling plan under reduced inspection using *ANSI/ASQC Z1.4*.

Solution. The sample size code letter from Table 9-11 for a lot size of 1000 and general inspection level III is K. From Table 9-17, indexing the sample size code letter of K and AQL = 15, the sample size code letter changes to J. The double sampling plan is $n_1 = 10$, $c_1 = 5$, $r_1 = 10$, $n_2 = 20$, $c_2 = 12$, $r_2 = 16$. Notice that the value of r_2 is greater than $(c_2 + 1)$. The decision-making rule for the combined results of both samples is as follows. If the combined number of nonconformities in both samples is less than or equal to 12, the lot is accepted. If it is 16 or more, the lot is rejected. If the combined number of nonconformities is 13, 14, or 15, the lot is accepted, but inspection changes from reduced to normal inspection on the next lot.

Example 9-17: Items are submitted for inspection in lots of size 80. The AQL is 2.5 percent nonconforming. If the general inspection level is level II, find a multiple sampling plan under tightened inspection using *ANSI/ASQC Z1.4*.

Solution. From Table 9-11, for a lot size of 80 and general inspection level II, the sample size code letter is E. Using Table 9-19, a sample size code letter of E, and AQL = 2.5 percent, we find that the sample size code letter changes to G. The multiple sampling plan under tightened inspection is given as follows: $n_1 = 8$, $c_1 = \#$, $r_1 = 2$, $n_2 = 8$, $c_2 = \#$, $r_2 = 2$, $n_3 = 8$, $c_3 = 0$, $r_3 = 2$, $n_4 = 8$, $c_4 = 0$, $r_4 = 3$, $n_5 = 8$, $c_5 = 1$, $r_5 = 3$, $n_6 = 8$, $c_6 = 1$, $r_6 = 3$, $n_7 = 8$, $c_7 = 2$, $r_7 = 3$. For the first two samples, the symbol # associated with the acceptance numbers implies that acceptance is not permitted upon those two samples.

Example 9-18: Items are submitted for inspection in lots of size 400 using *ANSI/ASQC Z1.4*. The acceptable quality level is established to be 1.0 percent nonconforming. General inspection level II and a single sampling plan are used. Normal inspection is initiated at the start of the inspection of lot number 1. The inspection results for 10 consecutive lots are shown in the accompanying table.

Lot number	Number nonconforming	Lot number	Number nonconforming
1	1	6	1
2	0	7	0
3	2	8	1
4	3	9	1
5	1	10	2

What type of inspection is used for lot 5? What type of inspection is used for lot 9 and lot 10? What will be the type of inspection for lot 11?

Solution. First, we determine the corresponding single sampling plan under normal inspection. For a lot size of 400 and general inspection level II, the sample size code letter from Table 9-11 is H. Using Table 9-12, the single sampling plan under normal inspection is $n = 50$, $c = 1$, $r = 2$. For this sampling plan, lot number 1 is accepted, lot number 2 is accepted, lot number 3 is rejected, and lot number 4 is rejected. Based on the rules of switching, since 2 out of 5 consecutive lots are rejected, we have to switch from normal inspection to tightened inspection at the end of lot number 4. Thus, for lot number 5, a single sampling plan with tightened inspection is used. From Table 9-13 this sampling plan is $n = 80$, $c = 1$, $r = 2$. Using this sampling plan, the decision is to accept lot numbers 5, 6, 7, 8, and 9. Since 5 consecutive lots are accepted, the switching rules state that we can now switch from tightened inspection to normal inspection at the end of lot number 9. For lot number 10, normal inspection using a single sampling plan is used. Thus, the sampling plan to be used for lot number 10 becomes $n = 50$, $c = 1$, $r = 2$. Lot number 10 is rejected using this plan. For lot number 11, single sampling under normal inspection will continue to be used.

OC Curve for Individual Plans. *ANSI/ASQC Z1.4* is basically an AQL system. This means that emphasis was placed on the producer's segment of the OC curve (small values of the fraction nonconforming or number of nonconformities per 100 units) during the design of the plans. As mentioned previously, for a given value of AQL, the target value of the producer's risk α is 0.05. So, in order to control the discriminatory power of the plan, the appropriate inspection level must be chosen. Figure 9-18 shows the OC curves for individual single sampling plans for sample size code J. Table 9-22 shows the tabulated values for OC curves for individual single sampling plans for sample size code letter J. Note that if the AQL is 1.5 percent nonconforming, then for a single sampling plan under normal inspection

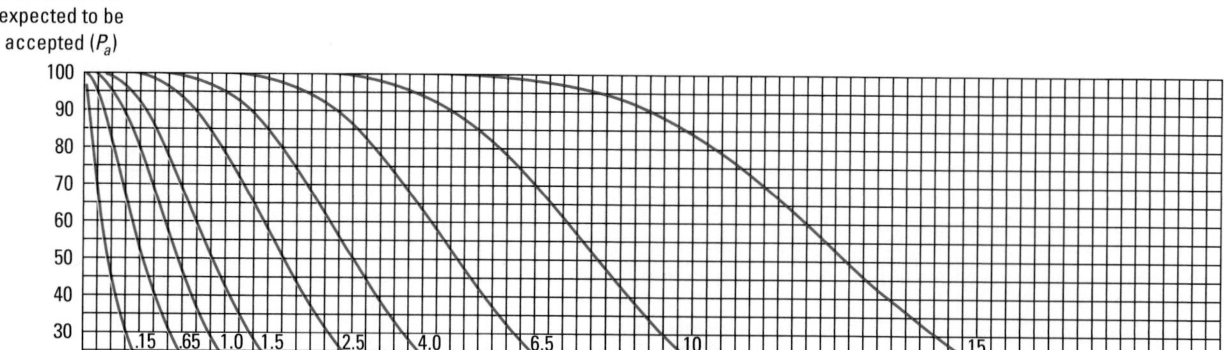

Figure 9-18 OC curves for individual single sampling plans for sample size code letter J (curves for double and multiple sampling are matched as closely as practicable). (ASQC (1981), ANSI/ASQC Z1.4–1981: *American National Standard—Sampling Procedures and Tables for Inspection by Attributes*. Reprinted with the permission of ASQC.)

and a sample size code of J, there is a probability of 0.90 of accepting batches that are 2.20 percent non-conforming.

Scheme Performance of *ANSI/ASQC Z1.4*. It has been pointed out that one of the major differences between *MIL–STD–105E* and *ANSI/ASQC Z1.4* is the focus on the scheme performance. Switching between normal, tightened, and reduced inspection takes place based on the rules described previously. The operating characteristic curves for the scheme performance (which is based on the fact that such switching takes place) is shown in Figure 9-19

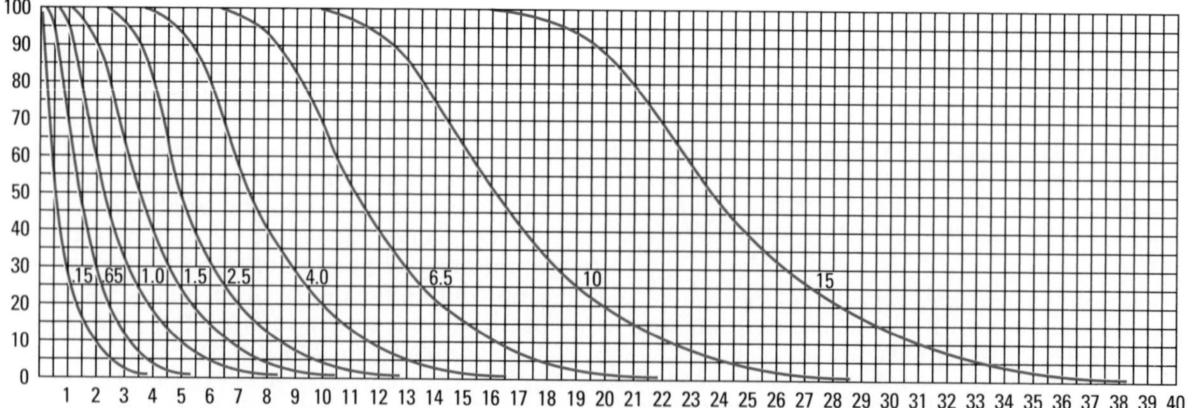

Figure 9-19 OC curves for ANSI/ASQC Z1.4 scheme performance for single sampling plans with code letter J (curves for double and multiple sampling are matched as closely as practicable). (ASQC (1981), ANSI/ASQC Z1.4–1981: *American National Standard—Sampling Procedures and Tables for Inspection by Attributes*. Reprinted with the permission of ASQC.)

TABLE 9-22 Tabulated values for OC curves for individual single sampling plans for sample size code letter J

P_a	Acceptable Quality Levels (normal inspection)																					
	0.15	0.65	1.0	1.5	2.5	4.0	X	6.5	X	10	0.15	0.65	1.0	1.5	2.5	4.0	X	6.5	X	10	X	15
	p (in percent nonconforming)										p (in nonconformities per hundred units)											
99.0	0.013	0.188	0.550	1.05	2.30	3.72	4.50	6.13	7.88	9.75	0.013	0.186	0.545	1.03	2.23	3.63	4.38	5.96	7.62	9.35	12.9	15.7
95.0	0.064	0.444	1.03	1.73	3.32	5.06	5.98	7.91	9.89	11.9	0.064	0.444	1.02	1.71	3.27	4.98	5.87	7.71	9.61	11.6	15.6	18.6
90.0	0.132	0.666	1.38	2.20	3.98	5.91	6.91	8.95	11.0	13.2	0.131	0.665	1.38	2.18	3.94	5.82	6.79	8.78	10.8	12.9	17.1	20.3
75.0	0.359	1.202	2.16	3.18	5.30	7.50	8.62	10.9	13.2	15.5	0.360	1.20	2.16	3.17	5.27	7.45	8.55	10.8	13.0	15.3	19.9	23.4
50.0	0.863	2.09	3.33	4.57	7.06	9.55	10.8	13.3	15.8	18.3	0.866	2.10	3.34	4.59	7.09	9.59	10.8	13.3	15.8	18.3	23.3	27.1
25.0	1.72	3.33	4.84	6.31	9.14	11.9	13.3	16.0	18.6	21.3	1.73	3.37	4.90	6.39	9.28	12.1	13.5	16.3	19.0	21.8	27.2	31.2
10.0	2.84	4.78	6.52	8.16	11.3	14.2	15.7	18.6	21.4	24.2	2.88	4.86	6.65	8.35	11.6	14.7	16.2	19.3	22.2	25.2	30.9	35.2
5.0	3.68	5.80	7.66	9.39	12.7	15.8	17.3	20.3	23.2	26.0	3.75	5.93	7.87	9.69	13.1	16.4	18.0	21.2	24.3	27.4	33.4	37.8
1.0	5.59	8.00	10.1	12.0	15.6	18.9	20.5	23.6	26.5	29.5	5.76	8.30	10.5	12.6	16.4	20.0	21.8	25.2	28.5	31.8	38.2	42.9
	0.25	1.0	1.5	2.5	4.0	X	6.5	X	10	X	0.25	1.0	1.5	2.5	4.0	X	6.5	X	10	X	15	X
	Acceptable Quality Levels (tightened inspection)																					

Note: Binomial distribution used for percent nonconforming computations; Poisson for nonconformities per hundred units.

Source: ASQC (1981), ANSI/ASQC Z1.4–1981: *American National Standard—Sampling Procedures and Tables for Inspection by Attributes*. Reprinted with the permission of ASQC.

TABLE 9-23 Tabulated values for OC curves for *ANSI/ASQC Z1.4* scheme performance for single sampling plans with code letter J

P_a	Acceptable quality levels (normal inspection)																
	.15	.65	1.0	1.5	2.5	4.0	6.5	10	.15	.65	1.0	1.5	2.5	4.0	6.5	10	15
	p (in percent nonconforming)								*p* (in nonconformities per hundred units)								
99.0	0.0260	0.240	0.715	1.16	2.39	3.88	6.49	10.2	0.0260	0.239	0.710	1.15	2.35	3.80	6.35	9.87	15.9
95.0	0.0896	0.458	1.01	1.68	3.12	4.89	7.74	11.8	0.0897	0.457	1.00	1.66	3.08	4.80	7.56	11.4	18.4
90.0	0.144	0.617	1.21	2.01	3.49	5.43	8.48	12.7	0.144	0.615	1.20	2.00	3.46	5.35	8.32	12.4	19.6
75.0	0.282	0.928	1.59	2.59	4.06	6.23	9.58	14.2	0.282	0.928	1.59	2.58	4.04	6.19	9.50	14.0	21.4
50.0	0.571	1.39	2.20	3.44	4.85	7.31	11.0	16.0	0.573	1.39	2.21	3.45	4.86	7.34	11.1	16.1	23.7
25.0	1.10	2.14	3.34	4.85	6.32	9.15	13.3	18.6	1.11	2.16	3.37	4.90	6.40	9.29	13.5	19.0	27.2
10.0	1.83	3.08	4.77	6.52	8.16	11.3	15.7	21.4	1.84	3.11	4.86	6.65	8.35	11.6	16.2	22.2	30.9
5.0	2.37	3.74	5.79	7.66	9.41	12.7	17.3	23.2	2.40	3.79	5.93	7.87	9.69	13.1	18.0	24.3	33.4
1.0	3.62	5.19	8.01	10.1	12.0	15.6	20.5	26.6	3.69	5.31	8.30	10.5	12.6	16.4	21.8	28.5	38.2

Source: ASQC (1981), ANSI/ASQC Z1.4–1981: *American National Standard—Sampling Procedures and Tables for Inspection by Attributes*. Reprinted with the permission of ASQC.

for single sampling plans with sample size code J. Table 9-23 shows the tabulated values for OC curves for *ANSI/ASQC Z1.4* scheme performance for single sampling plans with code letter J.

Note from Table 9-23 that if the AQL is 1.5 percent nonconforming at the normal inspection level, assuming that switching takes place based on the prescribed rules, there is a probability of 0.90 of accepting batches that are 2.01 percent nonconforming. Note that the scheme performance is more discriminating than that of an individual plan. For a single sampling plan under normal inspection with the same AQL, batches that are 2.20 percent nonconforming would be accepted with a probability of 0.90 (from Table 9-22). As the probability of acceptance decreases, this discriminatory power increases. For instance, at the scheme level, with AQL = 1.5 percent nonconforming at the normal inspection level and sample size code J, there is a probability of 5.0 percent of accepting batches that are 7.66 percent nonconforming (from Table 9-23). Alternatively, at the plan level, there is a probability of 5.0 percent of accepting batches that are 9.39 percent nonconforming (from Table 9-22).

For a scheme performance point of view, *ANSI/ASQC Z1.4* also provides values of the average outgoing quality limit. Table 9-24 shows the AOQL factors (in percentage) for *ANSI/ASQC Z1.4* scheme performance using a single sampling plan. Consider a situation for which the lot size is 250, the general inspection level is level II, AQL is 1.5 percent nonconforming, and we are starting out with normal inspection. From Table 9-11, the sample size code is G. From Table 9-12, the sample size is 32. Assuming that switching takes place between normal, tightened, and reduced inspection levels based on the prescribed rules, the AOQL (in percentage) for the scheme performance is found using Table 9-24 to be

$$\text{AOQL} = 1.8(1 - 32/250) = 1.5696 \text{ percent}$$

Thus, on the average, the worst outgoing quality based on the scheme performance will not exceed 1.5696 percent.

ANSI/ASQC Z1.4 also provides the limiting quality level for which the probability of lot acceptance from a scheme performance point of view is 5 or 10 percent. Table 9-25 shows the limiting quality for *ANSI/ASQC Z1.4* scheme performance for which the probability of lot acceptance is 10 percent. These values indicate a measure of the degree of protection that is provided for the consumer (against the acceptance of poor quality batches) at the scheme level. Consider the example for which the lot size is 400, the general inspection level is level II, AQL is 1.0 percent nonconforming, and a single sampling plan starting out with normal inspection is used. From Table 9-11, the sample size code letter is H. From Table 9-25, the limiting quality level for the scheme performance (assuming that switching between normal, tightened, and reduced inspection takes place according to the prescribed rules) is 4.77 percent. This means that, at the scheme level, batches that are 4.77 percent nonconforming will be accepted 10 percent of the time. It is a measure of protection for the consumer, who prefers to accept poor lots a small proportion of the time.

Dodge–Romig Plans Dodge and Romig (1959) designed a set of plans that were based on achieving a certain overall level of quality for products that are sent to the consumer. Although *ANSI/ASQC Z1.4* is a system based on AQL, it has little impact on the overall quality level because the sample sizes are quite small compared to the lot sizes and only the nonconforming items in the sample are detected. Dodge–Romig plans, however, are based on rectifying inspection. It assumes that lots that are rejected by the sampling plans go through 100 percent inspection and that nonconforming units are replaced by acceptable ones. This rectification process has an impact on the overall quality level of the product that is sent to the consumer.

Dodge–Romig plans can be single or double sampling plans. There are two sets of plans. One of these is based on satisfying a given limiting quality level based on a consumer's risk β, the target value of which is 0.10. The other set is based on meeting a certain value of the average outgoing quality limit. For both of these sets of plans, the objective used to formulate the plans is to minimize the average total inspection. It has already been described in detail how plans can be derived that meet an LQL or AOQL criteria and also minimize ATI for a given quality level of incoming product. The Dodge–Romig plans are essentially standardized versions of those plans. If the parameter values of the plan under consideration—for example, lot size and process average—are within certain ranges, the Dodge–Romig tables allow us to determine feasible plans very readily. Methods used to determine these plans from basic principles would take much more time. The trade-off is that the Dodge–Romig tables provide a sampling plan for a range of values of lot size and process average. Thus, the plans listed may not be unique in minimizing ATI. Also, the plans may minimize ATI only approximately because in listing a given plan, ranges are used for the lot size and process average. The two types of Dodge–Romig plans are discussed below.

TABLE 9-24 AOQL factors for *ANSI/ASQC Z1.4* scheme performance (in nonconformities per hundred units. Also applicable to percent nonconforming for AQL less than 15, with specific values for percent nonconforming shown in parentheses)

Code letter	Acceptable quality level																									
	0.010	0.015	0.025	0.040	0.065	0.10	0.15	0.25	0.40	0.65	1.0	1.5	2.5	4.0	6.5	10	15	25	40	65	100	150	250	400	650	1000
A															(11) 13			30	48	78	130	200	310	450	710	1100
B														(6.8) 7.5			19	32	52	84	130	210	300	480	710	1100
C													(4.4) 4.7			(12) 12	20	31	51	78	130	180	290	430	660	
D												(2.8) 2.9			(7.0) 7.0	(13) 12	20	32	49	76	120	180	270	410		
E											(1.9) 1.9			(4.5) 4.5	(7.5) 7.4	(13) 12	20	30	47	69	110	170	260			
F										(1.2) 1.2			(2.9) 2.9	(4.9) 4.8	(7.9) 7.8	(14) 13	20	31	45	71						
G									(.74) .75			(1.8) 1.8	(3.0) 3.0	(4.9) 4.9	(8.1) 7.9	(13) 13	19	28	45							
H								(.47) .47			(1.2) 1.2	(2.0) 2.0	(3.2) 3.1	(5.1) 5.1	(8.0) 7.8	(13) 13	18	29								
J							(.30) .30			(.72) .72	(1.2) 1.2	(2.0) 2.0	(3.2) 3.2	(5.0) 4.9	(7.7) 7.6	(12) 12	18									
K						.19			.46	.77	1.3	2.1	3.2	4.9	7.2	12										
L					.12			.29	.48	.78	1.3	2.0	3.1	4.5	7.1											
M				.075			.18	.31	.50	.80	1.3	2.0	2.9	4.5												
N			.047			.12	.20	.31	.51	.78	1.3	1.8	2.9													
P		.030			.072	.12	.20	.32	.49	.76	1.2	1.8														
Q	.019			.046	.077	.13	.21	.32	.49	.72	1.2															
R			.029	.048	.078	.13	.20	.31	.45	.71																

Source: ASQC (1981), ANSI/ASQC Z1.4–1981: *American National Standard—Sampling Procedures and Tables for Inspection by Attributes*. Reprinted with the permission of ASQC.

Note: For a better approximation to the AOQL, the above values must be multiplied by $\left(1 - \dfrac{\text{Normal plan sample size}}{\text{Lot or batch size}}\right)$

TABLE 9-25 Limiting quality for *ANSI/ASQC Z1.4* scheme performance for which $P_a = 10\%$ (in nonconformities per hundred units. Also applicable to percent nonconforming for AQL less than 15, with specific values for percent nonconforming shown in parentheses)

Code letter	Acceptable quality level																									
	0.010	0.015	0.025	0.040	0.065	0.10	0.15	0.25	0.40	0.65	1.0	1.5	2.5	4.0	6.5	10	15	25	40	65	100	150	250	400	650	1000
A															(53.6) 76.7			130	194	266	334	464	650	889	1240	1750
B														(36.9) 46.0			77.8	130	177	223	309	433	593	825	1170	1680
C													(25.0) 28.8			(40.6) 48.6	77.8	106	134	185	260	356	495	699	1010	
D												(16.2) 17.7			(26.8) 29.9	(40.6) 48.6	66.5	83.5	116	162	222	309	437	631		
E											(10.9) 11.5			(18.1) 19.4	(26.8) 29.9	(36.0) 40.9	51.4	71.3	100	137	190	269	388			
F										(6.94) 7.19			(11.6) 12.2	(18.1) 19.4	(24.5) 26.6	(30.4) 33.4	46.4	65.0	88.9	124						
G									(4.50) 4.60			(7.56) 7.78	(11.6) 12.2	(15.8) 16.6	(19.7) 20.9	(27.1) 29.0	40.6	55.6	77.4							
H								(2.84) 2.88			(4.77) 4.86	(7.56) 7.78	(10.3) 10.6	(12.9) 13.4	(17.8) 18.5	(24.7) 26.0	35.6	49.5								
J							(1.83) 1.84			(3.08) 3.11	(4.77) 4.86	(6.52) 6.65	(8.16) 8.35	(11.3) 11.6	(15.7) 16.2	(21.4) 22.2	30.9									
K						1.15			1.94	3.11	4.26	5.34	7.42	10.4	14.2	19.8										
L					.731			1.23	1.94	2.66	3.34	4.64	6.50	8.89	12.4											
M				.460			.778	1.23	1.69	2.12	2.94	4.13	5.64	7.86												
N			.288			.486	.778	1.06	1.34	1.85	2.60	3.56	4.95													
P		.184			.311	.486	.665	.835	1.16	1.62	2.22	3.09														
Q	.115			.194	.311	.426	.534	.742	1.04	1.42	1.98															
R			.123	.194	.266	.334	.464	.650	.889	1.24																

Source: ASQC (1981), ANSI/ASQC Z1.4–1981: *American National Standard—Sampling Procedures and Tables for Inspection by Attributes*. Reprinted with the permission of ASQC.

Plans Based on Limiting Quality Level. Plans based on limiting quality level are used when protection is desired for the acceptance of individual lots of a certain quality level. The Dodge–Romig LQL-based plans are based on the premise that lots with a quality level given by the LQL will be accepted 100β percent of the time (a β of 0.10 was used in developing these plans). The plans were developed for LQL values of 0.5, 1.0, 2.0, 3.0, 4.0, 5.0, 7.0, and 10.0 percent nonconforming. Both single and double sampling plans are listed. The choice between these two types is influenced by such factors as the inspection cost per unit and administrative costs of operating the plan. In order to use the Dodge–Romig tables, an estimate of the process average nonconforming $\overline{p}$ is necessary. Recent data from the process can be used to develop this estimate. If no data are available for the process, the largest value of the process average nonconforming found in the table may be used as a conservative estimate. As more information on the process becomes available, the value of the process average nonconforming rate should be updated; consequently, a new sampling plan may be found.

For the purpose of illustration, the Dodge–Romig table for a single sampling plan with an LQL of 5 percent is shown in Table 9-26, and that for a double sampling plan with an LQL of 3 percent is shown in Table 9-27. Note that the process average in Table 9-26 is listed up to a value of 2.5 percent. For values of the process average over 2.5 percent (which is half the LQL), sampling plans may not be preferable as 100 percent inspection becomes more economical. The table also provides a value of the AOQL (in percentage) for a given sampling plan.

Note from Tables 9-26 and 9-27 that the plans are indexed by lot size. A range of lot sizes is provided, as well as a range of the process average nonconforming. As the lot size increases, the sample size also increases, but the relative sample size (as a function of lot size) decreases. Thus, total inspection costs become more economical for large lot sizes. Furthermore, as the process average increases, the average amount inspected also increases. Reducing the process average will help to lower inspection costs.

Example 9-19: Find a Dodge–Romig plan when the lot size is 700, the limiting quality level is 5 percent, and the process average is 1.30 percent nonconforming. A single sampling plan is desired.

Solution. From Table 9-26, indexing the lot size of 700 and process average of 1.30 percent nonconforming, the single sampling plan is found to be $n = 130$, $c = 3$. For this chosen sampling plan, the AOQL is 1.2 percent. This means that the worst average outgoing quality, regardless of the incoming quality, will not exceed 1.2 percent. If the process average were not known, the maximum listed value of the process average would be used (in this case, the range 2.01–2.5 percent), and the plan would be $n = 200$, $c = 6$.

Example 9-20: Find a Dodge–Romig double sampling plan when the lot size is 800, the limiting quality level 3.0 percent, and the process average is 0.5 percent nonconforming.

Solution. From Table 9-27, indexing the lot size of 800 and the process average of 0.5 percent nonconforming, the double sampling plan is found to be $n_1 = 90$, $c_1 = 0$, $n_2 = 135$, $c_2 = 3$. The value of r_1 is implied to be $c_2 + 1$, which is 4. Furthermore, for this chosen plan, the AOQL is 0.70 percent.

Plans Based on Average Outgoing Quality Limit. When it is desired to choose plans that provide a level of protection for the average quality level of a stream of batches, a plan based on the average outgoing quality limit might be appropriate. A specified value of AOQL is selected. Plans are desired such that the worst average outgoing quality for a stream of lots, regardless of the incoming quality, will not exceed this chosen value. Dodge–Romig plans have been designed to meet this AOQL criterion and also minimize the average total inspection. The values of AOQL for which the plans are tabulated are 0.10, 0.25, 0.50, 0.75, 1.00, 1.50, 2.00, 2.50, 3.00, 4.00, 5.00, 7.00, and 10.00 percent, respectively. For each of these AOQL values, both single and double sampling plans are available. As in the previous set of plans, the lot size and process average must be known in order to use the tables. The tables also provide the limiting quality level values for a consumer's risk β of 0.10.

For the purpose of illustration, the Dodge–Romig table for a single sampling plan with an AOQL of 3.0 percent is shown in Table 9-28, and that for a double sampling plan with an AOQL of 3.0 percent is shown in Table 9-29. Note that the process average is listed up to a value of 3.0 percent (equal to the AOQL value of 3.0 percent). For process averages exceeding this value, 100 percent inspection becomes economical.

Example 9-21: Find a Dodge–Romig single sampling plan when the lot size is 1200, the average outgoing quality limit is 3 percent, and the process average is 1.4 percent nonconforming.

Solution. From Table 9-28, indexing the lot size of 1200 and process average of 1.4 percent nonconforming, the single sampling plan is found to be $n = 65$, $c = 3$. For

TABLE 9-26 **Dodge–Romig single sampling table for limiting quality level of 5.0%**

	Process Average																	
	0–0.05%			*0.06–0.50%*			*0.51–1.00%*			*1.01–1.50%*			*1.51–2.00%*			*2.01–2.50%*		
Lot Size	*n*	*c*	*AOQL* %	*n*	*c*	*AOQL* %	*n*	*c*	*AOQL* %	*n*	*c*	*AOQL* %	*n*	*c*	*AOQL* %	*n*	*c*	*AOQL* %
1–30	All	0	0	All	0	0	All	0		All	0	0	All	0	0	All	0	0
31–50	30	0	0.49	30	0	0.49	30	0	0.49	30	0	0.49	30	0	0.49	30	0	0.49
51–100	37	0	0.63	37	0	0.63	37	0	0.63	37	0	0.63	37	0	0.63	37	0	0.63
101–200	40	0	0.74	40	0	0.74	40	0	0.74	40	0	0.74	40	0	0.74	40	0	0.74
201–300	43	0	0.74	43	0	0.74	70	1	0.92	70	1	0.92	95	2	0.99	95	2	0.99
301–400	44	0	0.74	44	0	0.74	70	1	0.99	100	2	1.0	120	3	1.1	145	4	1.1
401–500	45	0	0.75	75	1	0.95	100	2	1.1	100	2	1.1	125	3	1.2	150	4	1.2
501–600	45	0	0.76	75	1	0.98	100	2	1.1	125	3	1.2	150	4	1.3	175	5	1.3
601–800	45	0	0.77	75	1	1.0	100	2	1.2	130	3	1.2	175	5	1.4	200	6	1.4
801–1000	45	0	0.78	75	1	1.0	105	2	1.2	155	4	1.4	180	5	1.4	225	7	1.5
1001–2000	45	0	0.80	75	1	1.0	130	3	1.4	180	5	1.6	230	7	1.7	280	9	1.8
2001–3000	75	1	1.1	105	2	1.3	135	3	1.4	210	6	1.7	280	9	1.9	370	13	2.1
3001–4000	75	1	1.1	105	2	1.3	160	4	1.5	210	6	1.7	305	10	2.0	420	15	2.2
4001–5000	75	1	1.1	105	2	1.3	160	4	1.5	235	7	1.8	330	11	2.0	440	16	2.2
5001–7000	75	1	1.1	105	2	1.3	185	5	1.7	260	8	1.9	350	12	2.2	490	18	2.4
7001–10,000	75	1	1.1	105	2	1.3	185	5	1.7	260	8	1.9	380	13	2.2	535	20	2.5
10,001–20,000	75	1	1.1	135	3	1.4	210	6	1.8	285	9	2.0	425	15	2.3	610	23	2.6
20,001–50,000	75	1	1.1	135	3	1.4	235	7	1.9	305	10	2.1	470	17	2.4	700	2*i*	2.7
50,001–100,000	75	1	1.1	160	4	1.6	235	7	1.9	355	12	2.2	515	19	2.5	770	30	2.8

Source: H. F. Dodge and H. G. Romig, *Sampling Inspection Tables—Single and Double Sampling,* 2nd ed. Copyright © 1959. Reprinted by permission of John Wiley & Sons, Inc.

TABLE 9-27 Dodge–Romig double sampling table for limiting quality level of 3%

Lot Size	Process Average 0 to 0.03%						Process Average 0.04 to 0.30%						Process Average 0.31 to 0.60%					
	Trial 1		Trial 2			AOQL	Trial 1		Trial 2			AOQL	Trial 1		Trial 2			AOQL
	n_1	c_1	n_2	n_1+n_2	c_2	in %	n_1	c_1	n_2	n_1+n_2	c_2	in %	n_1	c_1	n_2	n_1+n_2	c_2	in %
1–40	All	0	—	—	—	0	All	0	—	—	—	0	All	0	—	—	—	0
41–55	40	0	—	—	—	0.18	40	0	—	—	—	0.18	40	0	—	—	—	0.18
56–100	55	0	—	—	—	0.30	55	0	—	—	—	0.30	55	0	—	—	—	0.30
101–150	70	0	30	100	1	0.37	70	0	30	100	1	0.37	70	0	30	100	1	0.37
151–200	75	0	40	115	1	0.45	75	0	40	115	1	0.45	75	0	40	115	1	0.45
201–300	75	0	40	115	1	0.50	75	0	40	115	1	0.50	75	0	40	115	1	0.50
301–400	80	0	45	125	1	0.52	80	0	45	125	1	0.52	80	0	85	165	2	0.57
401–500	85	0	50	135	1	0.53	85	0	50	135	1	0.53	85	0	90	175	2	0.60
501–600	85	0	50	135	1	0.54	85	0	50	135	1	0.54	85	0	95	180	2	0.62
601–800	90	0	50	140	1	0.55	90	0	95	185	2	0.64	90	0	135	225	3	0.70
801–1000	90	0	55	145	1	0.56	90	0	100	190	2	0.66	90	0	140	230	3	0.72
1001–2000	90	0	60	150	1	0.58	90	0	105	195	2	0.70	90	0	190	280	4	0.84
2001–3000	90	0	60	150	1	0.59	90	0	155	245	3	0.80	90	0	200	290	4	0.86
3001–4000	95	0	105	200	2	0.72	95	0	150	245	3	0.80	95	0	235	330	5	0.92
4001–5000	95	0	105	200	2	0.73	95	0	155	250		0.81	150	1	230	380	6	0.98
5001–7000	95	0	105	200	2	0.73	95	0	155	250	3	0.81	150	1	230	380	6	1.0
7001–10,000	95	0	105	200	2	0.73	95	0	155	250	3	0.81	150	1	275	425	7	1.0
10,001–20,000	95	0	105	200	2	0.74	95	0	200	295	4	0.92	150	1	320	470	8	1.1
20,001–50,000	95	0	105	200	2	0.74	95	0	200	295	4	0.93	150	1	365	515	9	1.2
50,001–100,000	95	0	105	200	2	0.75	95	0	245	340	5	1.0	150	1	405	555	10	1.2

Source: H. F. Dodge and H. G. Romig, *Sampling Inspection Tables—Single and Double Sampling*, 2nd ed. Copyright © 1959. Reprinted by permission of John Wiley & Sons, Inc.

TABLE 9-27 *(Continued)*

	Process Average 0.61 to 0.90%						Process Average 0.91 to 0.20%						Process Average 1.21 to 1.50%					
	Trial 1		Trial 2			AOQL	Trial 1		Trial 2			AOQL	Trial 1		Trial 2			AOQL
Lot Size	n_1	c_1	n_2	n_1+n_2	c_2	in %	n_1	c_1	n_2	n_1+n_2	c_2	in %	n_1	c_1	n_2	n_1+n_2	c_2	in %
1–40	All	0	—	—	—	0	All	0	—	—	—	0	All	0	—	—	—	0
41–55	40	0	—	—	—	0.18	40	0	—	—	—	0.18	40	0	—	—	—	0.18
56–100	55	0	—	—	—	0.30	55	0	—	—	—	0.30	55	0	—	—	—	0.30
101–150	70	0	30	100	1	0.37	70	0	30	100	1	0.37	70	0	30	100	1	0.37
151–200	75	0	40	115	1	0.45	75	0	65	140	2	0.47	75	0	65	140	2	0.47
201–300	75	0	80	155	2	0.54	75	0	80	155	2	0.54	75	0	80	155	2	0.54
301–400	80	0	85	165	2	0.57	80	0	120	200	3	0.62	80	0	120	200	3	0.62
401–500	85	0	125	210	3	0.64	85	0	125	210	3	0.64	85	0	160	245	4	0.69
501–600	85	0	130	215	3	0.67	85	0	170	255	4	0.72	135	1	185	320	6	0.76
601–800	90	0	170	260	4	0.74	140	1	195	335	6	0.79	140	1	210	350	7	0.81
801–1000	90	0	180	270	4	0.77	145	1	235	380	7	0.85	145	1	270	415	8	0.86
1001–2000	150	1	210	360	6	0.90	150	1	325	475	9	1.0	195	2	350	545	11	1.1
2001–3000	150	1	300	450	8	1.0	200	2	365	565	11	1.1	290	4	470	760	16	1.2
3001–4000	150	1	350	500	9	1.1	245	3	405	650	13	1.2	330	5	545	875	19	1.2
4001–5000	200	2	340	540	10	1.2	250	3	445	695	14	1.2	380	6	620	1000	22	1.3
5001–7000	200	2	385	585	11	1.2	250	3	530	780	16	1.3	380	6	700	1080	24	1.4
7001–10,000	200	2	425	625	12	1.2	250	3	575	825	17	1.3	425	7	785	1210	27	1.5
10,001–20,000	200	2	475	675	13	1.3	295	4	655	950	20	1.4	470	8	900	1370	31	1.6
20,001–50,000	200	2	515	715	14	1.3	295	4	755	1050	23	1.5	515	9	1165	1680	39	1.7
50,001–100,000	200	2	555	755	15	1.3	340	5	840	1180	26	1.6	515	9	1315	1830	43	1.8

Trial 1: n_1 = first sample size; x_1 = acceptance number for first sample
"All" indicates that each piece in the lot is to be inspected
Trial 2: n_2 = *second sample size;* c_2 = acceptance number for first and second samples combined
AOQL = Average Outgoing Quality Limit

TABLE 9-28 Dodge–Romig single sampling table for AOQL of 3.0%

	PROCESS AVERAGE (%)																	
	0–0.06			0.07–0.60			0.61–1.20			1.21–1.80			1.81–2.40			2.41–3.00		
LOT SIZE	*n*	*c*	LQL (%)	*n*	*c*	LQL (%)	*n*	*c*	LQL (%)	*n*	*c*	LQL (%)	*n*	*c*	LQL (%)	*n*	*c*	LQL (%)
1–10	All	0	—	All	0	—	All	0	—	All	0	—	All	0	—	All	0	—
11–50	10	0	19.0	10	0	19.0	10	0	19.0	10	0	19.0	10	0	19.0	10	0	19.0
51–100	11	0	18.0	11	0	18.0	11	0	18.0	11	0	18.0	11	0	18.0	22	1	16.4
101–200	12	0	17.0	12	0	17.0	12	0	17.0	25	1	15.1	25	1	15.1	25	1	15.1
201–300	12	0	17.0	12	0	17.0	26	1	14.6	26	1	14.6	26	1	14.6	40	2	12.8
301–400	12	0	17.1	12	0	17.1	26	1	14.7	26	1	14.7	41	2	12.7	41	2	12.7
401–500	12	0	17.2	27	1	14.1	27	1	14.1	42	2	12.4	42	2	12.4	42	2	12.4
501–600	12	0	17.3	27	1	14.2	27	1	14.2	42	2	12.4	42	2	12.4	60	3	10.8
601–800	12	0	17.3	27	1	14.2	27	1	14.2	43	2	12.1	60	3	10.9	60	3	10.9
801–1,000	12	0	17.4	27	1	14.2	44	2	11.8	44	2	11.8	60	3	11.0	80	4	9.8
1,001–2,000	12	0	17.5	28	1	13.8	45	2	11.7	65	3	10.2	80	4	9.8	100	5	9.1
2,001–3,000	12	0	17.5	28	1	13.8	45	2	11.7	65	3	10.2	100	5	9.1	140	7	8.2
3,001–4,000	12	0	17.5	28	1	13.8	65	3	10.3	85	4	9.5	125	6	8.4	165	8	7.8
4,001–5,000	28	1	13.8	28	1	13.8	65	3	10.3	85	4	9.5	125	6	8.4	210	10	7.4
5,001–7,000	28	1	13.8	45	2	11.8	65	3	10.3	105	5	8.8	145	7	8.1	235	11	7.1
7,001–10,000	28	1	13.9	46	2	11.6	65	3	10.3	105	5	8.8	170	8	7.6	280	13	6.8
10,001–20,000	28	1	13.9	46	2	11.7	85	4	9.5	125	6	8.4	215	10	7.2	380	17	6.2
20,001–50,000	28	1	13.9	65	3	10.3	105	5	8.8	170	8	7.6	310	14	6.5	560	24	5.7
50,001–100,000	28	1	13.9	65	3	10.3	125	6	8.4	215	10	7.2	385	17	6.2	690	29	5.4

[a] *n*, size of sample; entry of "All" indicates that each piece in lot is to be inspected. *c*, acceptance number for sample. LQL, limiting quality level corresponding to a consumer's risk (β) = 0.10.

Source: H. F. Dodge and H. G. Romig, *Sampling Inspection Tables—Single and Double Sampling*, 2nd ed. Copyright © 1959. Reprinted by permission of John Wiley & Sons, Inc.

TABLE 9-29 Dodge–Romig double sampling table for AOQL of 3.0%

	PROCESS AVERAGE (%)																	
	0–0.06						0.07–0.60						0.61–1.20					
	TRIAL 1		TRIAL 2			LQL	TRIAL 1		TRIAL 2			LQL	TRIAL 1		TRIAL 2			LQL
LOT SIZE	n_1	c_1	n_2	$n_1 + n_2$	c_2	(%)	n_1	c_1	n_2	$n_1 + n_2$	c_2	(%)	n_1	c_1	n_2	$n_1 + n_2$	c_2	(%)
1–10	All	0	—	—	—	—	All	0	—	—	—	—	All	0	—	—	—	—
11–50	10	0	—	—	—	19.0	10	0	—	—	—	19.0	10	0	—	—	—	19.0
51–100	16	0	9	25	1	16.4	16	0	9	25	1	16.4	16	0	9	25	1	16.4
101–200	17	0	9	26	1	16.0	17	0	9	26	1	16.0	17	0	9	26	1	16.0
201–300	18	0	10	28	1	15.5	18	0	10	28	1	15.5	21	0	23	44	2	13.3
301–400	18	0	11	29	1	15.2	21	0	24	45	2	13.2	23	0	37	60	3	12.0
401–500	18	0	11	29	1	15.2	21	0	25	46	2	13.0	24	0	36	60	3	11.7
501–600	18	0	12	30	1	15.0	21	0	25	46	2	13.0	24	0	41	65	3	11.5
601–800	21	0	25	46	2	13.0	21	0	25	46	2	13.0	24	0	41	65	3	11.5
801–1,000	21	0	26	47	2	12.8	21	0	26	47	2	12.8	25	0	40	65	3	11.4
1,001–2,000	22	0	26	48	2	12.6	22	0	26	48	2	12.6	27	0	58	85	4	10.3
2,001–3,000	22	0	26	48	2	12.6	25	0	40	65	3	11.4	28	0	62	90	4	10.0
3,001–4,000	23	0	26	49	2	12.4	25	0	45	70	3	11.0	29	0	76	105	5	9.6
4,001–5,000	23	0	26	49	2	12.4	26	0	44	70	3	11.0	30	0	75	105	5	9.5
5,001–7,000	23	0	27	50	2	12.2	26	0	44	70	3	11.0	30	0	80	110	5	9.4
7,001–10,000	23	0	27	50	2	12.2	27	0	43	70	3	11.0	30	0	80	110	5	9.4
10,001–20,000	23	0	27	50	2	12.2	27	0	43	70	3	11.0	31	0	94	125	6	9.2
20,001–50,000	23	0	27	50	2	12.2	28	0	67	95	4	9.7	55	1	120	175	8	8.0
50,001–100,000	23	0	27	50	2	12.2	31	0	84	115	5	9.0	60	1	140	200	9	7.6

[a] n_1, size of sample; n_2, size of second sample; entry of "All" indicates that each piece in lot is to be inspected. c_1, acceptance number for sample; c_2, acceptance number for first and second samples combined. LQL, limiting quality level corresponding to a consumer's risk $(\beta) = 0.10$.

Source: H. F. Dodge and H. G. Romig, *Sampling Inspection Tables—Single and Double Sampling*, 2nd ed. Copyright © 1959. Reprinted by permission of John Wiley & Sons, Inc.

TABLE 9-29 *(Continued)*

	PROCESS AVERAGE (%)																	
	1.21–1.80						1.81–2.40						2.41–3.00					
	TRIAL 1		TRIAL 2			LQL	TRIAL 1		TRIAL 2			LQL	TRIAL 1		TRIAL 2			LQL
LOT SIZE	n_1	c_1	n_2	$n_1 + n_2$	c_2	(%)	n_1	c_1	n_2	$n_1 + n_2$	c_2	(%)	n_1	c_1	n_2	$n_1 + n_2$	c_2	(%)
1–10	All	0	—	—	—	—	All	0	—	—	—	—	All	0	—	—	—	—
11–50	10	0	—	—	—	19.0	10	0	—	—	—	19.0	10	0	—	—	—	19.0
51–100	17	0	17	34	2	15.8	17	0	17	34	2	15.8	17	0	17	34	2	15.8
101–200	20	0	21	41	2	13.7	22	0	33	55	3	12.4	22	0	33	55	3	12.4
201–300	23	0	37	60	3	12.0	23	0	37	60	3	12.0	24	0	51	75	4	11.1
301–400	23	0	37	60	3	12.0	25	0	55	80	4	10.8	42	1	63	105	6	10.4
401–500	24	0	36	60	3	11.7	25	0	55	80	4	10.8	46	1	79	125	7	9.7
501–600	26	0	54	80	4	10.7	46	1	69	115	6	9.7	48	1	97	145	8	9.2
601–800	26	0	54	80	4	10.7	49	1	81	130	7	9.4	50	1	115	165	9	8.9
801–1,000	27	0	58	85	4	10.3	49	1	86	135	7	9.2	70	2	120	190	10	8.4
1,001–2,000	49	1	76	125	6	9.1	50	1	150	200	10	8.0	100	3	180	280	14	7.5
2,001–3,000	50	1	95	145	7	8.7	80	2	165	245	12	7.6	130	4	260	390	19	6.9
3,001–4,000	55	1	110	165	8	8.5	105	3	200	305	14	7.0	155	5	330	485	23	6.5
4,001–5,000	60	1	135	195	9	7.8	110	3	225	335	15	6.7	215	7	390	605	27	6.0
5,001–7,000	60	1	165	225	10	7.3	110	3	250	360	16	6.6	270	9	505	775	34	5.7
7,001–10,000	85	2	160	245	11	7.2	115	3	290	405	18	6.5	285	9	680	965	41	5.4
10,001–20,000	85	2	180	265	12	7.2	140	4	315	455	20	6.3	315	10	805	1,120	47	5.3
20,001–50,000	85	2	205	290	13	7.0	170	5	420	590	26	6.0	390	13	940	1,330	56	5.2
50,001–100,000	90	2	245	335	15	6.8	200	6	505	705	30	5.7	445	15	1,105	1,550	65	5.1

[a] n_1, size of sample; n_2, size of second sample; entry of "All" indicates that each piece in lot is to be inspected. c_1, acceptance number for sample; c_2, acceptance number for first and second samples combined. LQL, limiting quality level corresponding to a consumer's risk (β) = 0.10.

this chosen plan, the limiting quality level is 10.2 percent. This means that for individual lots with a nonconformance rate of 10.2 percent, the probability of accepting such lots would be 10 percent, the consumer's risk.

9-8 OTHER ACCEPTANCE SAMPLING PLANS

The acceptance sampling plans described in the previous sections are, in a sense, general-purpose. The design of single and double sampling plans based on certain stipulated criteria were discussed. Additionally, some standardized sampling plans such as *ANZI/ASQC Z1.4* and the Dodge–Romig plans were outlined. This section considers some sampling plans that apply to special situations in order to reduce inspection time and effort, achieve simplification, or provide better protection under special conditions. The chain sampling plan, sequential sampling plan, and skip-lot sampling plan are discussed.

Chain Sampling Plan

The chain sampling plan (ChSP-1) was proposed by Dodge (1955). It is used for tests that are costly or destructive. In these situations, the sampling plans have a small sample size by necessity. Sampling plans with small sample sizes usually have an acceptance number c that is zero.

However, the operating characteristic curve for single sampling plans with $c = 0$ has an undesirable shape. The entire OC curve is convex; consequently, even for extremely good lots with a low fraction nonconforming, the probability of lot acceptance P_a decreases rapidly from 1.00. So, from a producer's point of view, there is a chance of good lots being rejected more frequently than they should. Figure 9-20 shows the shape of the OC curve for single sampling plans with an acceptance number c of 0. It also shows the shape of OC curves for plans with an acceptance number of 1 or 2, which have the desirable feature of having high values of P_a for small values of p.

The chain sampling plan was devised to achieve this desirable shape of the OC curve for an acceptance number of zero when the value of p is small. There are two parameters of the plan. The sample size n is the number of units to be selected at random from each lot. The second parameter, i, represents the number of preceding samples, the inspection results of which must be considered when deciding the fate of the current lot. The plan works as follows. A random sample of n items is chosen from the lot. If no nonconforming units are found in the sample,

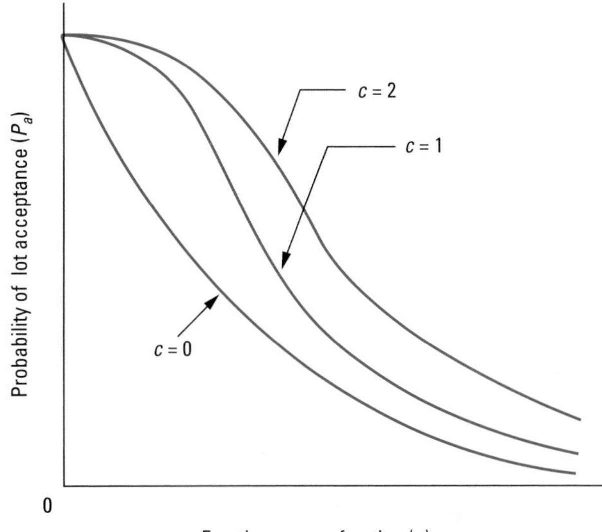

Figure 9-20 Shape of OC curve for $c = 0$ and $c > 0$.

the lot is accepted. If the number of nonconforming units is 2 or more, the lot is rejected. If the sample has 1 nonconforming unit, the lot is accepted if the previous i samples each had 0 nonconforming units. Using such a scheme for the chain sampling plan, the OC curve has a shape that is preferable to that for a single sampling plan with $c = 0$. Figure 9-21

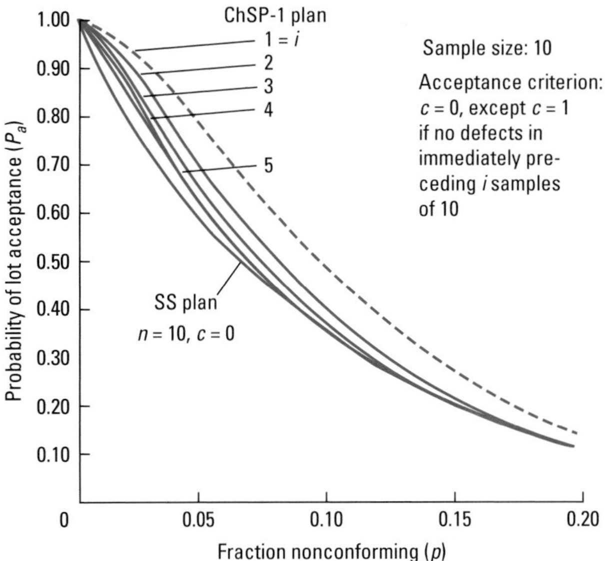

Figure 9-21 OC curves for ChSP-1 plans. (H. F. Dodge (1955), "Chain Sampling Plans," *Industrial Quality Control*, Vol. 11, No. 4, pp. 10–13.)

(Banks, 1989) shows the OC curves for chain sampling plans for which the sample size is 10 and i is varied from 1 to 5. It also shows the OC curve for a single sampling plan with $n = 10$ and $c = 0$. The chain sampling plan for $i = 1$ is shown as a dotted curve, as it is not preferred. It deviates quite a bit from the OC curve for $n = 10$, $c = 0$ over the entire range of p.

Note that the OC curves for a chain sampling plan are influenced by the cumulative results of more than one sample. It is assumed that the quality level of the lot, as given by p, remains fixed over the accumulation period of the results. In contrast, for ordinary lot-by-lot attribute inspection, decisions are based on information from each lot and are independent of the outcomes of previous lots.

The probability of lot acceptance P_a is calculated using the binomial distribution as an approximation to the hypergeometric distribution. It is given by

$$P_a = P(0, n) + P(1, n)[P(0, n)]^i \tag{9.18}$$

where $P(0, n)$ and $P(1, n)$ represent the probabilities of obtaining 0 and 1 nonconforming units, respectively, from a sample of size n. The lot fraction nonconforming is assumed to be p.

For example, consider the chain sampling plan given by $n = 10$, $i = 4$. The workings of the plan are as follows. If no nonconforming units are obtained in the current sample of size 10, the lot is accepted. If 2 or more nonconforming units are found in the current sample, the lot is rejected. If 1 nonconforming unit is found in the current sample, the lot could be accepted if each of the previous 4 samples had no nonconforming units.

Criteria that should be met for chain sampling to be appropriate are as follows.

1. The lot should be one of a continuing series of product that is sampled, preferably in the order of production.
2. The lots should be of essentially the same quality.
3. The consumer is confident that the producer will not send an unacceptable lot when it would have a good chance of acceptance.

Example 9-22 A chain sampling plan is used with a sample size of 10 and a value of i of 3. If lots have a fraction-nonconforming value of 0.04, find the probability of accepting such lots.

Solution. We have $n = 10$, $i = 3$, and $p = 0.04$. The probability of lot acceptance is given by

$$P_a = P(0, 10) + P(1, 10)[P(0, 10)]^3$$

Using the binomial distribution,

$$P(0, 10) = \frac{10!}{0!10!}(0.04)^0(0.96)^{10} = 0.6648$$

$$P(1, 10) = \frac{10!}{1!9!}(0.04)^1(0.96)^9 = 0.2770$$

Hence,

$$P_a = 0.6648 + (0.2770)(0.6648)^3 = 0.7462$$

There is a 74.62 percent probability of accepting such a lot, assuming it has a fraction nonconforming level of 0.04, using this chain sampling plan. If a single sampling plan with $n = 10$, and $c = 0$ had been used, the probability would have been only 66.48 percent.

Sequential Sampling Plan

A sequential sampling plan is similar to a multiple sampling plan in that the number of units that are required to be sampled is influenced by the results of the sampling process itself. At each phase, based on the cumulative inspection results, a decision can be made to either accept the lot, reject the lot, or continue sampling. Theoretically, the sampling process can continue indefinitely. However, if the number inspected is equal to approximately three times the number that would be inspected by an equivalent single sampling plan, a decision is made to terminate the plan and notify the supplier of the need to demonstrate that the product is at an improved level, before any further product can be accepted.

Sequential sampling is usually an item-by-item inspection process, even though it is possible to have groups of items at any given phase. It is used when it is desirable to arrive at a decision to either accept or reject the lot as soon as possible (that is, when testing is expensive or destructive). The plan is based on the concept of a sequential probability ratio test developed by Wald (1947). Figure 9-22 shows the concept on which the item-by-item sequential sampling plan is based. There are two lines on the chart, an acceptance line and a rejection line. They determine the acceptance region, rejection region, and the continue sampling region. The equations of the acceptance line and rejection line are influenced by the producer's risk α and its associated quality level p_1, and by the consumer's risk β and its associated quality level p_2. The cumulative number of nonconforming units, d, is plotted versus the number of units inspected, n. If the plot of the cumulative number of nonconforming units touches the acceptance line or is below it, the lot is accepted. If it touches the rejection line or is above it, the lot is rejected. If

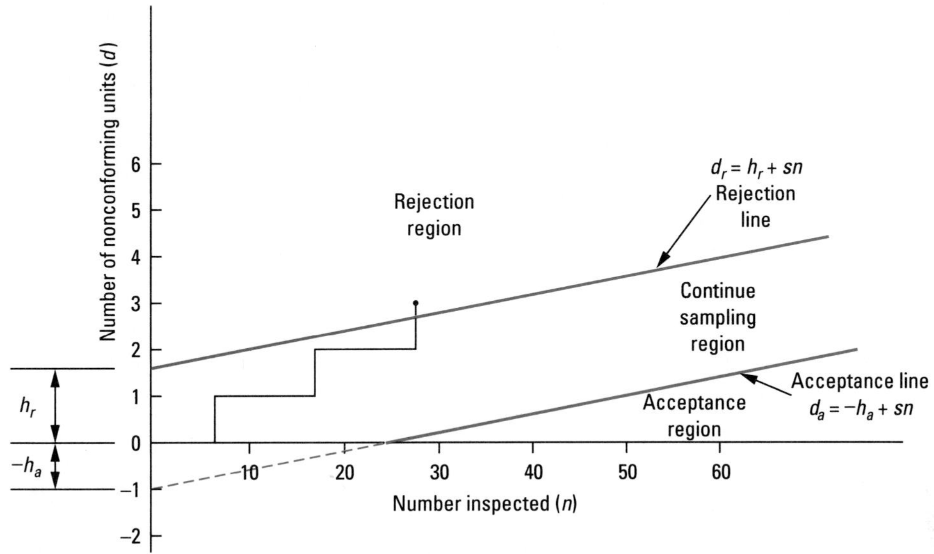

Figure 9-22 Sequential sampling plan.

the cumulative number of nonconforming items is within the region defined by the acceptance and rejection line, sampling is continued, and one more unit is inspected.

The equation of the acceptance line (in slope-intercept form) is given by

$$d_a = -h_a + sn \tag{9.19}$$

where $-h_a$ represents the intercept on the vertical axis and s represents the slope. The equation of the rejection line is given by

$$d_r = h_r + sn \tag{9.20}$$

where h_r represents the intercept on the vertical axis and s represents the slope. These equations are based on satisfying a given level of producer's risk at an associated quality level p_1 (the acceptable quality level) and also satisfying a given level of consumer's risk at an associated quality level by p_2 (the limiting quality level). The expressions for the parameters of the acceptance line, h_a and s, and those for the rejection line, h_r and s, are as follows:

$$h_a = \ln\left(\frac{1-\alpha}{\beta}\right)/k \tag{9.21}$$

$$h_r = \ln\left(\frac{1-\beta}{\alpha}\right)/k \tag{9.22}$$

$$s = \ln[(1-p_1)/(1-p_2)]/k \tag{9.23}$$

where

$$k = \ln\{[p_2(1-p_1)]/[p_1(1-p_2)]\} \tag{9.24}$$

The following example demonstrates the calculations for constructing a sequential sampling plan.

Example 9-23: Calculate the acceptance and rejection lines for a sequential sampling plan with the following parameters: producer's risk $\alpha = 0.05$, associated quality level $p_1 = 0.005$, consumer's risk $\beta = 0.10$, associated quality level $p_2 = 0.07$ nonconforming.

Solution. Given the values of $\alpha = 0.05$, $p_1 = 0.005$, $\beta = 0.10$, and $p_2 = 0.07$, we have

$$k = \ln\left[\frac{0.07(1-0.005)}{0.005(1-0.07)}\right] = 2.7066$$

$$h_a = \ln\left(\frac{1-0.05}{0.10}\right)/2.7066 = 0.832$$

$$h_r = \ln\left(\frac{1-0.10}{0.05}\right)/2.7066 = 1.068$$

$$s = \ln\frac{(1-0.005)}{(1-0.07)}/2.7066 = 0.025$$

The acceptance line is

$$d_a = -0.832 + (0.025)n$$

The rejection line is:

$$d_r = 1.068 + (0.025)n$$

After these two lines are graphed, a decision regarding the lot may be made by plotting the cumulative number of nonconforming items, as sampled on an item-by-item basis.

An alternative to the graphical procedure consists of setting up a table showing the acceptance number and rejection number, based on the number of items inspected. If the cumulative number of nonconforming items at that stage is less than or equal to the acceptance number, the lot is accepted. If the cumulative number of nonconforming items is equal to or greater than the rejection number, the lot is rejected. If the cumulative number of nonconforming items is strictly in between the acceptance number and rejection number, another sample unit is selected, and the procedure continues.

For example, the calculations for sample number 30 are

$$d_a = -0.832 + (0.025)n$$
$$= -0.832 + (0.025)(30) = -0.082$$
$$d_r = 1.068 + (0.025)n = 1.068 + (0.025)(30) = 1.818$$

Because the cumulative number of nonconforming units is a whole number, the rejection number is the smallest integer that is greater than or equal to the calculated value of d_r, and the acceptance number is the greatest integer that is less than or equal to the calculated value of d_a. So, for $n = 30$, the rejection number d_r is 2, and acceptance is not permitted because the calculated value of d_a is negative. Table 9-30 shows the acceptance and rejection numbers for the sequential sampling plan considered in Example 9-23, up to the 44th item. This table can be used to make a decision about the lot without plotting the acceptance and rejection lines and cumulative number of nonconforming items.

Skip-Lot Sampling Plan

Skip-lot sampling was first devised by Dodge (1955) as an extension to sampling plans for continuous production. The concepts of continuous sampling plans are used in the context of lots rather than individual product units. The purpose in designing these plans was to minimize inspection costs. The plan devised by Dodge is known as SkSP–1. The plan is applicable to situations where extensive and costly tests are conducted on characteristics of a series of

TABLE 9-30 Item-by-item sequential sampling plan for $\alpha = 0.05, p_1 = 0.005, \beta = 0.10, p_2 = 0.07$

Number of items inspected, n	Acceptance number	Rejection number	Number of items inspected, n	Acceptance number	Rejection number
1	a	b	23	a	2
2	a	2	24	a	2
3	a	2	25	a	2
4	a	2	26	a	2
5	a	2	27	a	2
6	a	2	28	a	2
7	a	2	29	a	2
8	a	2	30	a	2
9	a	2	31	a	2
10	a	2	32	a	2
11	a	2	33	a	2
12	a	2	34	0	2
13	a	2	35	0	2
14	a	2	36	0	2
15	a	2	37	0	2
16	a	2	38	0	3
17	a	2	39	0	3
18	a	2	40	0	3
19	a	2	41	0	3
20	a	2	42	0	3
21	a	2	43	0	3
22	a	2	44	0	3

a—Acceptance not permitted
b—Rejection not permitted

lots for which the level of quality is generally high. It may be used for testing batches from reliable suppliers or lots passed from one department to another within an organization.

The skip-lot sampling plan SkSP–1 is based on the average outgoing quality limit (AOQL). However, AOQL refers to lots rather than individual units. For instance, an AOQL of 2 percent in this setting would mean that, on average, the worst outgoing quality will be such that no more than 2 percent of the lots are nonconforming. There are two parameters of the SkSP–1 plan: the clearance number i and the sampling fraction f.

The procedure starts with inspecting each lot consecutively. If i lots in succession are found to be conforming, lots may be selected on a sampling basis. The frequency of sampling of the lots is f. Each sampled lot is tested for the relevant quality characteristics. If a sampled lot is found to be nonconforming, the procedure reverts to testing each lot, and the sequence starts all over again.

The values of the sampling fraction f and the clearance number i are shown in Table 9-31 for chosen values of AOQL. This is essentially the same table that is used for a continuous sampling plan (CSP–1). SkSP–1 is generally used for large values of f ($\frac{1}{2}$ to $\frac{1}{5}$), correspondingly small values of i, and large values of AOQL (1 percent or higher). Note that when using Table 9-31 for SkSP–1 plans, AOQL is to be interpreted in the context of lots rather than individual units.

Example 9-24: Consider a skip-lot sampling plan for which the desired AOQL is 1.90 percent for lots. It is desired to keep the sampling frequency as high as possible. Find the SkSP–1 sampling plan, and describe its operation.

Solution. Using Table 9-31, for lots with an AOQL of 1.90 percent, choosing the highest sampling frequency f of $\frac{1}{2}$ yields a clearance number i of 15. The operation of the plan is as follows. Each lot is inspected until 15 consecutive lots are found to be conforming. Thereafter, a sampling procedure is used in which one out of every two lots, chosen randomly, is inspected. If the sampled lot is conforming, sampling of the lots continues at the specified frequency. However, once a sampled lot is found to be nonconforming, each subsequent lot has to be inspected, and the above procedure must be repeated.

9-9 SAMPLING PLANS FOR CONTINUOUS PRODUCTION

Most of the sampling plans discussed previously have dealt with the acceptance of a product on a lot-by-lot basis. It is feasible to use such plans when the identification of the product into lots follows naturally. Sometimes the formation of lots is not feasible. For instance, items produced on a continuous basis (such as those on a conveyor belt, where successive operations are conducted on the unit) are difficult to form into lots. Doing so may force some operations to be temporarily stopped while the items are grouped into lots. Furthermore, to be compatible with the just-in-time concept (where the goal is to reduce inventory and to eventually approach zero-inventory levels), formation of units into lots may not support this goal. Sampling plans for continuous production might be feasible in such instances. These plans involve nondestructive, attribute-type inspection that is simple and quick so as not to create a bottleneck in the process.

The first sampling plan for continuous production was devised by Dodge (1943). Subsequently, modifications and alternatives have been proposed. The United States Department of Defense has compiled continuous sampling plans in a standard *MIL-STD-1235C* (1988) entitled "Single and Multi-Level Continuous Sampling Procedures and Tables for Inspection by Attributes." Continuous sampling plans are based on achieving a certain level of the average outgoing quality limit for a series of items in the long run. It is therefore based on a concept similar to that of a Dodge–Romig plan. These plans alternate between 100 percent inspection and sampling inspection, based on how the inspection results satisfy certain criteria. Line personnel typically perform the 100 percent inspection, whereas inspectors may perform sampling inspection. There are two principal parameters of these sampling plans: the clearance number i and the sampling frequency f. The clearance number i represents the number of consecutive units that must be conforming in order to allow a switch from 100 percent inspection to sampling inspection. The sampling frequency f defines the proportion of units to be selected for sampling. For example, $f = \frac{1}{2}$ implies that, on average, one out of every two units produced will be randomly chosen for inspection. The various continuous sampling plans found in *MIL-STD-1235C* are discussed below.

Military Standard *MIL-STD-1235C*

The standard includes five types of continuous sampling plans by attributes:

1. CSP–1: A single-level continuous sampling procedure that provides for alternating between se-

TABLE 9-31 Values of the clearance number (i) for CSP–1 and SkSP–1 plans

Samp. Freq. Code Ltr.	f	AQL (percent)[a]															
		0.010	0.015	0.025	0.040	0.065	0.10	0.15	0.25	0.40	0.65	1.0	1.5	2.5	4.0	6.5	10.0
A	1/2	1540	840	600	375	245	194	140	84	53	36	23	15	10	6	5	3
B	1/3	2550	1390	1000	620	405	321	232	140	87	59	38	25	16	10	7	5
C	1/4	3340	1820	1310	810	530	420	303	182	113	76	49	32	21	13	9	6
D	1/5	3960	2160	1550	965	630	498	360	217	135	91	58	38	25	15	11	7
E	1/7	4950	2700	1940	1205	790	623	450	270	168	113	73	47	31	18	13	8
F	1/10	6050	3300	2370	1470	965	762	550	335	207	138	89	57	38	22	16	10
G	1/15	7390	4030	2890	1800	1180	930	672	410	255	170	108	70	46	27	19	12
H	1/25	9110	4970	3570	2215	1450	1147	828	500	315	210	134	86	57	33	23	14
I	1/50	11730	6400	4590	2855	1870	1477	1067	640	400	270	175	110	72	42	29	18
J	1/100	14320	7810	5600	3485	2305	1820	1302	790	500	330	215	135	89	52	36	22
K	1/200	17420	9500	6810	4235	2760	2178	1583	950	590	400	255	165	106	62	43	26
		.018	.033	.046	.074	.113	.143	.198	0.33	0.53	0.79	1.22	1.90	2.90	4.94	7.12	11.46
		AOQL (percent)															

[a]AQLs are provided as indices to simplify use of this table, but have no other meaning relative to the plans

Source: H. F. Dodge and H. G. Romig, *Sampling Inspection Tables—Single and Double Sampling,* 2nd ed. Copyright © 1959. Reprinted by permission of John Wiley & Sons, Inc.

quences of 100 percent inspection and sampling inspection

2. CSP–F: A variation of the CSP–1 plan in that CSP–F plans are applied to a relatively short run of product, thereby permitting smaller clearance numbers to be used
3. CSP–2: A modification of the CSP–1 plan in that 100 percent inspection resumes only when a second nonconforming item is found in the next i or fewer sampled units
4. CSP–T: A multilevel continuous sampling procedure that provides for reducing the sampling frequency upon demonstration of superior product quality
5. CSP–V: A single-level continuous sampling procedure that is an alternative to CSP–T plans in that these plans provide for reducing the clearance number in good-quality situations, where reduction of sampling frequency has no economic merit

Each of these plans is described below. The sampling frequency is designated by a code letter. Table 9-32 shows the range of permissible sampling frequency code letters based on the number of units manufactured in the production interval, typically considered to be an eight-hour shift.

CSP–1 Plans A CSP–1 plan starts out with 100 percent inspection. If i consecutive units are found to be conforming, a switch to sampling inspection may take place. The units are sampled at a frequency f. Any time a nonconforming item is found, 100 percent inspection is reinstated. The values of the clearance number i and the sampling frequency f are found from Table 9-31 based on a selected value of the average outgoing quality limit.

TABLE 9-32 Sampling frequency code letters

Number of units in production interval	Permissible code letters
2 – 8	A,B
9 – 25	A through C
26 – 90	A through D
91 – 500	A through E
501 – 1200	A through F
1201 – 3200	A through G
3201 – 10,000	A through H
10,000 – 35,000	A through I
35,001 – 150,000	A through J
150,001 – up	A through K

One can observe from Table 9-31 that for a given AOQL, as f decreases, the value of i increases. The choice of f is influenced by practical considerations (such as the production rate, the workload, and available time of the sampling inspector).

For long periods of screening (or 100 percent inspection), when a nonconforming unit is found prior to obtaining i consecutive conforming units, there is a rule for notifying the supplier and possibly stopping inspection. If the number of units screened is greater than or equal to the appropriate value of S shown in Table 9-33, the supplier may be notified, and an effort should be made to improve the production process. The consumer may wish to suspend acceptance until the supplier corrects the high rate of nonconformity.

Example 9-25: Consider a continuous sampling plan for which the desired AOQL is 1.22 percent. The sampling inspector has some available time, and it is desired to choose a value of the sampling frequency (up to $\frac{1}{5}$). Find and explain the workings of an appropriate CSP–1 plan.

Solution. Because a large value of the sampling frequency f (up to $\frac{1}{5}$) is desired, the clearance number i from Table 9-31 for $f = \frac{1}{5}$ and an AOQL of 1.22 percent is 58. This means that the inspection procedure starts with 100 percent inspection. If 58 consecutive conforming units are found, sampling inspection can be started. A random sample of 1 out of every 5 units produced is chosen. If a nonconforming unit is obtained during this sampling process, 100 percent inspection is reinstated, and the procedure starts all over again. From Table 9-33, $S = 165$ for AOQL $= 1.22$ percent and $f = 1.5$. So, if a nonconforming unit is found during 100 percent inspection and the number of units screened is 165 or more, the consumer notifies the supplier of this poor level of quality. The supplier must then take action to improve the process condition. The consumer has the option of suspending inspection at any time after 165 units are screened unless the supplier improves the incoming quality. If corrective action is taken by the supplier, 100 percent inspection is reinitiated.

CSP–F Plans CSP–F is a single-level continuous sampling procedure that provides for alternating sequences of 100 percent inspection (screening) and sampling inspection. Its operating procedure is the same as that of the CSP–1 plan, with the exception that the plans are indexed by the AOQL and the number of units manufactured (N) in a given production interval. This allows a smaller clearance number to be used, thus making CSP–F plans feasible for situations involving short production runs. Twelve values of AOQL are considered, so there are

TABLE 9-33 Values of S for CSP–1 plans

Sample frequency code letter	f	AQL* (%)															
		.010	.015	.025	.040	.065	0.10	0.15	0.25	0.40	0.65	1.0	1.5	2.5	4.0	6.5	10.0
A	1/2	1850	925	721	451	295	273	197	119	75	55	36	22	17	11	10	6
B	1/3	4080	1950	1600	993	649	579	442	268	166	120	78	52	36	24	19	16
C	1/4	6010	2915	2360	1460	1010	926	699	421	262	177	115	79	57	36	28	20
D	1/5	8320	3890	3100	1930	1390	1150	975	589	367	258	165	109	76	45	40	27
E	1/7	11400	5670	4660	2895	1980	1750	1355	813	507	376	244	154	109	63	54	34
F	1/10	16900	7590	6640	4120	2800	2595	1985	1245	624	543	352	221	164	90	82	51
G	1/15	24400	11300	9250	5760	4020	3820	2960	1810	922	856	524	327	241	141	138	75
H	1/25	35500	16900	13900	8640	5950	5740	4560	2760	1390	1350	839	524	390	212	189	105
I	1/50	59800	26900	23000	14300	10300	10100	8440	5070	3170	2445	1590	913	733	368	334	212
J	1/100	96000	39800	36400	23300	16900	16500	14300	8710	6020	3980	2600	1640	1360	642	601	352
K	1/200	148100	63700	58000	36000	29000	28500	25400	15200	9470	8030	4365	2835	2150	1080	1025	636
		.018	.033	.046	.074	.113	.143	.198	0.33	0.53	0.79	1.22	1.90	2.90	4.94	7.12	11.46
		AOQL (%)															

*AQLs are provided as indices to simplify use of this table, but have no other meaning relative to the plans.

TABLE 9-34 Values of i for CSP–F plans (AOQL = 0.198%)

	Sample frequency code letter							
	A	B	C	D	E	F	G	H
N \ f	1/2	1/3	1/4	1/5	1/7	1/10	1/15	1/25
1–500	103	138	155	164	174	182	187	192
501–1,000	119	173	201	219	239	254	266	275
1,001–2,000	130	199	242	271	306	335	358	377
2,001–3,000	133	209	260	295	342	382	415	443
3,001–4,000	135	215	270	310	364	413	455	492
4,001–5,000	136	219	276	319	379	434	485	530
5,001–6,000	137	221	281	326	390	451	508	561
6,001–7,000	138	223	284	331	398	463	526	586
7,001–8,000	138	224	287	334	404	473	541	607
8,001–9,000	139	226	289	337	409	481	553	625
9,001–10,000	139	226	290	340	413	487	563	640
10,001–11,000	139	227	291	342	417	493	572	654
11,001–12,000	139	228	293	343	420	498	579	666
12,001–15,000	140	229	295	347	426	508	597	694
15,001–20,000	140	230	298	351	433	520	615	725
20,001–30,000	140	232	300	355	440	531	635	760
30,001 and over	140	232	303	360	450	550	672	828

12 tables, each of which gives values of i and f for a given AOQL. Table 9-34 shows values of the clearance number i for CSP–F plans for an AOQL of 0.198 percent.

Finally, as in CSP–1 plans, there is a cutoff value S for long periods of screening. If the number of units screened is greater than or equal to the appropriate value of S, the consumer may choose to suspend acceptance until the supplier corrects the high rate of nonconformance. The value of S for CSP–F plans is the same as that for CSP–1 plans and is shown in Table 9-33.

Example 9-26: Consider a CSP–F continuous sampling plan for which the production rate is 1200 in a given interval and the desired AOQL is 0.198 percent. Find the sampling plan, and explain its workings.

Solution. Given that AOQL = 0.198 percent and $N = 1200$, Table 9-32 shows the sampling frequency to be between A and F. Suppose the sampling inspector is often available for inspection, indicating a large value of f. For $f = \frac{1}{5}$, the clearance number i is 271. Also, from Table 9-33, for AOQL = 0.198 percent and $f = \frac{1}{5}$, we have $S = 975$.

The procedure starts with 100 percent inspection. If 271 or more consecutive items are conforming, inspection switches to a sampling plan. Here, 1 out of every 5 items is randomly selected. If a nonconforming item is found, 100 percent inspection is reinstated. If 975 consecutive items are inspected such that the criterion for reinstating the sampling plan is not met, the consumer would have the option of not accepting any of the products.

CSP–2 Plans CSP–2 is a modification of the CSP–1 plan. In the CSP–1 plan we found that whenever a nonconforming unit is found, a return to 100 percent inspection is mandated. CSP–2 modifies this in that a return to 100 percent inspection is required if a second nonconforming unit is found within the next i sampled units. Figure 9-23 shows the flowchart for the CSP–2 plan. Such a plan provides some protection for the occurrence of an isolated nonconforming unit, which would trigger a return to 100 percent inspection if CSP–1 plan were being used. As with all other continuous sampling plans, CSP–2 plans are based on a specified level of the average outgoing quality. Table 9-35 shows values of the clearance number i for selected values of AOQL and the sampling frequency f. For long periods of screening for which a nonconforming unit is found prior to i consecutive conforming

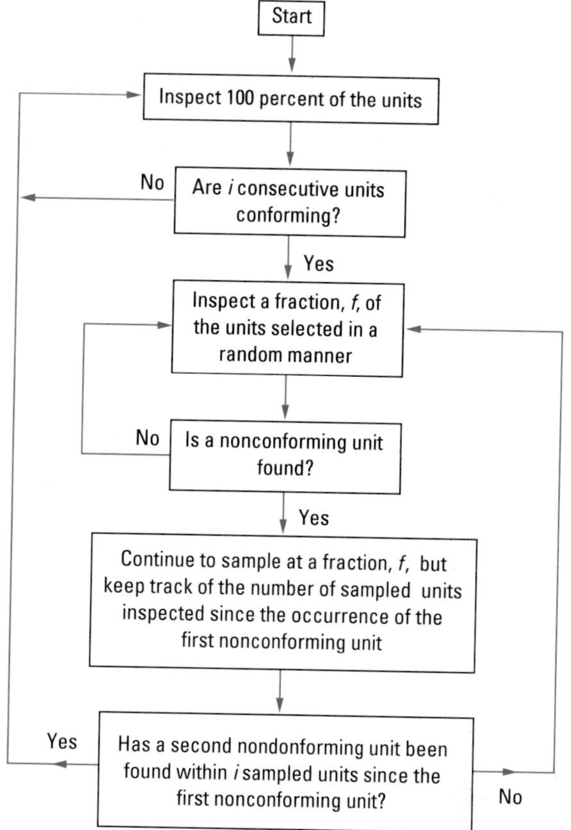

Figure 9-23 Flowchart for CSP-2 plans.

TABLE 9–35 Values of i for CSP–2 plans

Sample frequency code letter	f	AQL* (%)							
		0.40	0.65	1.0	1.5	2.5	4.0	6.5	10.0
A	1/2	80	54	35	23	15	9	7	4
B	1/3	128	86	55	36	24	14	10	7
C	1/4	162	109	70	45	30	18	12	8
D	1/5	190	127	81	52	35	20	14	9
E	1/7	230	155	99	64	42	25	17	11
F	1/10	275	185	118	76	50	29	20	13
G	1/15	330	220	140	90	59	35	24	15
H	1/25	395	265	170	109	71	42	29	18
I, J, K	1/50	490	330	210	134	88	52	36	22
		0.53	0.79	1.22	1.90	2.90	4.94	7.12	11.46
		AOQL (%)							

*AQLs are provided as indices to simplify use of this table, but have no other meaning relative to the plans.

ones, acceptance can be suspended at the discretion of the consumer if the number of units screened is greater than or equal to the value of S given in Table 9-36. After corrective action has been taken by the supplier to improve the nonconformance rate, 100 percent inspection may be reinstated.

Example 9-27: Find a CSP–2 plan if the desired AOQL is 1.22 percent and the unit inspection costs are low enough to mandate the highest sampling frequency possible. The sampling inspector has enough time to conduct the inspection.

TABLE 9–36 Values of S for CSP–2 plans

Sample frequency code letter	f	AQL* (%)							
		0.40	0.65	1.0	1.5	2.5	4.0	6.5	10.0
A	1/2	145	105	68	45	32	20	19	11
B	1/3	322	235	151	100	70	42	33	27
C	1/4	473	352	288	138	106	63	46	34
D	1/5	746	461	296	181	141	76	62	42
E	1/7	902	687	431	274	199	115	91	62
F	1/10	1380	987	608	386	292	154	132	91
G	1/15	1990	1480	946	566	440	243	200	127
H	1/25	3090	2265	1455	905	652	368	334	212
I, J, K	1/50	5400	3980	2540	1625	1165	642	601	352
		0.53	0.79	1.22	1.90	2.90	4.94	7.12	11.46
		AOQL (%)							

*AQLs are provided as indices to simplify use of this table, but have no other meaning relative to the plans.

Solution. Using Table 9-35, we select the highest sampling frequency f possible, which is $f = \frac{1}{2}$. For AOQL = 1.22 percent and $f = \frac{1}{2}$, the clearance number i is found to be 35. For protection against long periods of screening, the value of S from Table 9-36 is 68.

CSP–T Plans The CSP–T plan is a multilevel continuous sampling procedure that provides for alternate sequences of 100 percent inspection and sampling inspection. This plan provides for a reduced sampling frequency upon demonstration of superior product quality. A return to 100 percent inspection is required upon finding a nonconforming unit. Figure 9-24 shows the flowchart for CSP–T plans. The plan starts with 100 percent inspection. If i consecutive units are conforming, sampling inspec-

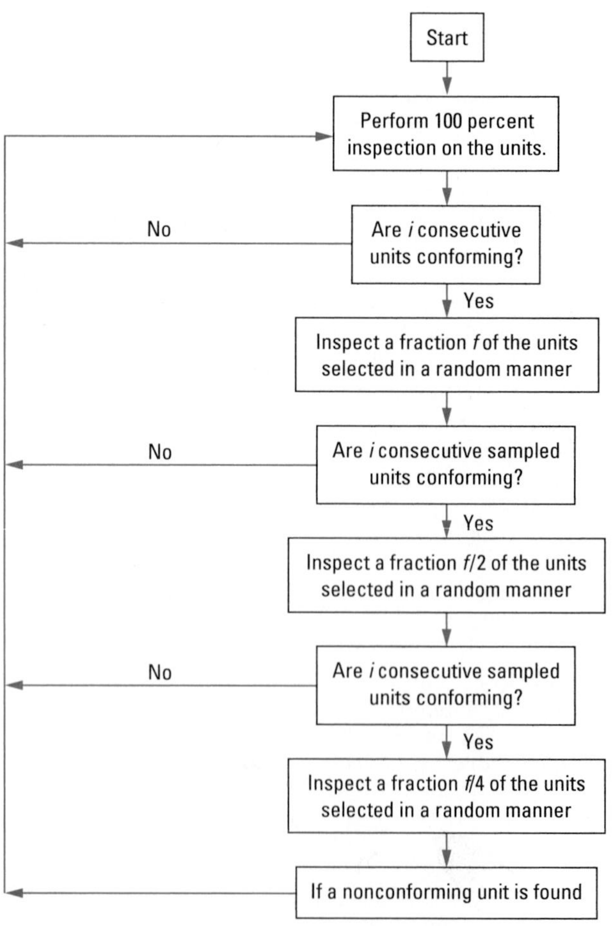

Figure 9-24 Flowchart for CSP-T plans.

tion can be initiated at a frequency f. During this sampling mode, if i consecutive units are conforming, the plan calls for a reduction in the sampling frequency to $f/2$, which is half the original sampling frequency. While sampling at a frequency of $f/2$, if i consecutive units are conforming, sampling can be reduced further to a frequency of $f/4$. If no nonconforming units are found, inspection continues at this sampling frequency. Any time a nonconforming unit is found, a return to 100 percent inspection is required. The CSP–T plan provides motivation to demonstrate superior product quality. A reduction in the sampling frequency will reduce inspection costs. Table 9-37 shows values of the clearance number i for CSP–T plans based on values of AOQL and sampling frequency f. As with the other continuous sampling plans, for protection against long periods of screening, if the number of units screened is greater than or equal to the value of S, (given in Table 9-38), the consumer may choose to discontinue acceptance of the product. Upon demonstration of improvement in process conditions and hence product quality, the consumer may reinitiate 100 percent inspection.

Example 9–28: Find a CSP–T plan if the desired AOQL is 2.90 percent. Assume that the inspector is free to sample at a frequency of at most $\frac{1}{4}$. Explain the workings of the plan.

Solution. For AOQL= 2.90 percent and $f = \frac{1}{4}$, Table 9-37 gives the clearance number i as 26. From Table 9-38, the value of S is 78. The plan starts with 100 percent inspection. If 26 consecutive units are conforming, sampling inspection can be initiated at a frequency of $\frac{1}{4}$. One out of every four units is randomly sampled; if 26 consecutive sampled units are conforming, the sampling frequency is reduced to $\frac{1}{8}$. Now, one out of every eight units is randomly sampled; if 26 consecutive sampled units are conforming, the sampling frequency is reduced further to $\frac{1}{16}$. Sampling inspection continues at this frequency of $\frac{1}{16}$ until a nonconforming unit is found. At any phase during this procedure, if a nonconfomring unit is found, 100 percent inspection is reinitiated. If 100 percent inspection (or screening) continues for 78 or more consecutive units, the consumer has the option of discontinuing product acceptance.

TABLE 9–37 Values of i for CSP–T plans

Sample frequency code letter	f	AQL* (%) 0.40	0.65	1.0	1.5	2.5	4.0	6.5	10.0
A	1/2	87	58	38	25	16	10	7	5
B	1/3	116	78	51	33	22	13	9	6
C	1/4	139	93	61	39	26	15	11	7
D	1/5	158	106	69	44	29	17	12	8
E	1/7	189	127	82	53	35	21	14	9
F	1/10	224	150	97	63	41	24	17	11
G	1/15	266	179	116	74	49	29	20	13
H	1/25	324	217	141	90	59	35	24	15
I	1/50	409	274	177	114	75	44	30	19
J, K	1/100	499	335	217	139	91	53	37	23
	AOQL (%)	0.53	0.79	1.22	1.90	2.90	4.94	7.12	11.46

*AQLs are provided as indices to simplify use of this table, but have no other meaning relative to the plans.

TABLE 9–38 Values of S for CSP–T plans

Sample frequency code letter	f	AQL* (%) 0.40	0.65	1.0	1.5	2.5	4.0	6.5	10.0
A	1/2	159	117	77	52	34	22	13	12
B	1/3	256	197	128	80	59	35	25	18
C	1/4	379	253	167	103	78	43	38	24
D	1/5	444	320	210	130	93	54	43	30
E	1/7	725	460	289	188	137	81	59	34
F	1/10	857	619	398	261	189	104	88	58
G	1/15	1254	900	584	368	376	152	126	84
H	1/25	1885	1396	923	545	421	235	198	122
I	1/50	3283	2477	1604	1013	764	408	374	223
J, K	1/100	5753	4541	2948	1754	1341	708	653	391
	AOQL (%)	0.53	0.79	1.22	1.90	2.90	4.94	7.12	11.46

*AQLs are provided as indices to simplify use of this table, but have no other meaning relative to the plans.

CSP–V Plans CSP–V is a single-level continuous sampling plan. A return to 100 percent inspection is required whenever a nonconforming unit is discovered within the first i sampled units when sampling inspection at a frequency f is in effect. However, once the initial i sampled units have passed successfully, if a nonconforming unit is found thereafter, a return to 100 percent inspection is mandated, but the clearance number is reduced by $\frac{2}{3}$. The new clearance number x in this situation is $(1/3)i$, where i is the original clearance number. If x consecutive units are conforming, the original sampling inspection with clearance number i is reinstated. Figure 9-25 shows the flowchart for CSP–V plans. Such plans are applicable to situations for which there is no motivation to reduce the sampling frequency when product

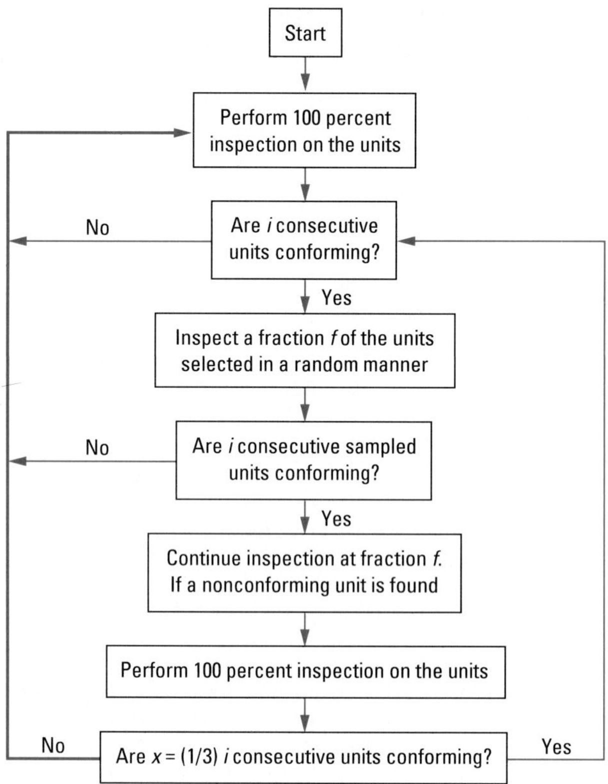

Figure 9-25 Flowchart for CSP-V plans.

of good quality is submitted (for instance, a reduced sampling frequency would merely give the inspector more idle time). Values of the clearance number i for CSP–V plans based on AOQL and sampling frequency f are shown in Table 9-39. This plan provides a means of protection against long periods of screening: if a nonconforming unit is found before i consecutive conforming units and if the number of units screened is greater than or equal to the value of S (given in Table 9-40), the consumer may opt to discontinue acceptance of product. Once an improvement in the process condition is demonstrated, the consumer may reinitiate 100 percent inspection.

Example 9-29: Find a CSP–V plan for an AOQL of 2.90 percent and a sampling frequency of $\frac{1}{4}$. Describe the working procedure of the plan.

Solution. From Table 9-39, for AOQL = 2.90 percent and $f = \frac{1}{4}$, the clearance number i is 24. Also, from Table 9-40, the value of S, which represents the optional cutoff value for the number of units inspected when screening, is 66. The plan starts with 100 percent inspection. If 24 consecutive units are conforming, sampling inspection is initiated at a frequency of $\frac{1}{4}$, where 1 out of 4 units is randomly selected. The occurrence of a nonconforming unit prior to obtaining 24 consecutive conforming units would reinitiate 100 percent inspection with a clearance number of 24. During sampling inspection, if 24 consecutive sampled units are conforming, the sampling phase continues. If a nonconforming unit is found, a switch to 100 percent inspection takes place,

TABLE 9-39 Values of i for CSP–V plans

Sample frequency code letter	f	AQL* (%) 0.40	0.65	1.0	1.5	2.5	4.0	6.5	10.0
A	1/2	60	39	27	18	12	9	6	3
B	1/3	96	63	42	27	18	12	9	6
C	1/4	120	81	54	36	24	15	12	6
D	1/5	144	96	63	42	27	18	12	9
E	1/7	177	120	78	51	33	21	15	9
F	1/10	213	144	93	60	39	24	18	12
G	1/15	258	174	114	72	48	30	21	12
H	1/25	318	213	138	90	60	36	24	15
I	1/50	405	273	177	114	75	45	30	21
J	1/100	498	333	216	138	90	54	39	24
K	1/200	594	399	258	165	108	63	45	27
	AOQL (%)	0.53	0.79	1.22	1.90	2.90	4.94	7.12	11.46

*AQLs are provided as indices to simplify use of this table, but have no other meaning relative to the plans.

TABLE 9-40 Values of S for CSP–V plans

Sample frequency code letter	f	AQL* (%) 0.40	0.65	1.0	1.5	2.5	4.0	6.5	10.0
A	1/2	98	65	46	28	22	18	13	5
B	1/3	192	127	85	55	38	28	25	19
C	1/4	267	214	141	98	66	53	44	19
D	1/5	390	261	172	119	80	58	44	39
E	1/7	533	409	260	176	121	82	65	39
F	1/10	772	579	377	237	167	102	97	71
G	1/15	1165	857	563	357	249	158	139	71
H	1/25	1754	1327	848	537	427	254	198	120
I	1/50	3251	2467	1604	944	762	415	373	301
J	1/100	5491	4508	2826	1741	1279	746	731	433
K	1/200	8931	7208	4670	2828	2516	1210	1192	659
	AOQL (%)	0.53	0.79	1.22	1.90	2.90	4.94	7.12	11.46

*AQLs are provided as indices to simplify use of this table, but have no other meaning relative to the plans.

but the clearance number is reduced to 8. Thus, during this 100 percent inspection, if 8 consecutive units are conforming, the procedure reverts to the original sampling phase with a sampling frequency of $\frac{1}{4}$ and a clearance number of 24.

9-10 DEMING'S *kp* RULE

Deming's *kp* rule is based on minimizing the average total cost of inspection of incoming materials and final product for processes that are stable. It calls for 0 percent or 100 percent inspection. The motivation behind Deming's kp rule is that it can be shown that, if a process is stable, the distribution of the number of nonconforming units in a sample is independent of the distribution of the number of nonconforming units in the remainder of the lot. In this case it is assumed that items are submitted in lots and that a random sample is drawn from that lot to make a decision regarding the entire lot.

The assumptions made for the use of the kp rule are as follows. First, the inspection process is assumed to be completely reliable. This means that a nonconforming item, if inspected, will be labeled as such by the inspection process. Second, all items are inspected prior to moving forward to the next customer in the process. The next customer can be another department within the organization or a different company. The implication is that all nonconforming units will be detected prior to shipment to the succeeding customer. Third, the vendor provides the buyer with an extra supply of items in order to replace any nonconforming units that are found. The cost of providing these additional units is included by the supplier and may be considered as an overhead cost, which would thus be present regardless of the type of inspection plan used. Therefore, this cost is not included in the average cost function that is being minimized.

The following notation is necessary. Let

p = Average fraction of nonconforming items in the lots

k_1 = Cost of initial inspection of a unit

k_2 = Cost of repair or reassembly due to the usage of a nonconforming unit

k = Average cost to find a conforming unit from the additional supply to replace a detected nonconforming unit

$= k_1/(1-p)$

x_i = 1 if item i is nonconforming;

x_i = 0 otherwise

If unit i is randomly selected from the lot, there is an initial inspection cost of k_1. If the unit is found to be nonconforming, the cost to replace it with a conforming one is k. Thus, the unit cost of initial inspection and replacement if nonconforming is given by

$$C_1 = \begin{cases} k_1 + kx_i & \text{if unit } i \text{ is inspected} \\ 0 & \text{if unit } i \text{ is not inspected} \end{cases} \tag{9.25}$$

Similarly, the cost to repair and replace a nonconforming unit is given by

$$C_2 = \begin{cases} (k_2 + k)x_i & \text{if unit } i \text{ is not initially inspected} \\ 0 & \text{if unit } i \text{ is initially inspected} \end{cases} \tag{9.26}$$

Under the assumptions considered, C_1 and C_2 are mutually exclusive. If one is nonzero, the other is zero, and the total cost is given by $C = C_1 + C_2$. Thus, if unit i is inspected, the total cost is $(k_1 + kx_i)$; if it is not inspected, the total cost is $(k_2+k)x_i$. This concept may be extended to the average total cost per part for the entire lot. The parameter p represents the lot proportion nonconforming. So, the average total cost per part if items are inspected is $(k_1 + kp)$; if items are not inspected it is $(k_2 + k)p$. The break-even value of p is obtained by equating the average total cost for inspection to that for no inspection. In other words,

$$k_1 + kp = (k_2 + k)p$$

or

$$p = k_1/k_2 \tag{9.27}$$

The kp rule is as follows:

1. If k_1/k_2 is greater than p, conduct no inspection. This situation occurs if the fraction nonconforming of incoming product is low, the unit cost of an incoming inspection is high, and the cost of repairing a nonconforming unit is low. Basically, this implies that there is very little risk associated with nonconforming items if the incoming quality is quite good.
2. If k_1/k_2 is less than p, conduct 100 percent inspection. This condition happens when the incoming fraction nonconforming is high, the unit cost of incoming inspection is low, and the cost of repairing a nonconforming unit is high. In this situation, it is quite expensive for a nonconforming unit to be allowed into production.

3. If k_1/k_2 equals p, then either no inspection or 100 percent inspection may be conducted. Usually, if the estimated value of p is not very reliable, 100 percent inspection will be conducted.

It should be mentioned that conducting no inspection does not imply no information. Small samples should be drawn from lots, even when the rule suggests no inspection, in order to obtain information regarding the process. If 100 percent inspection is in operation, every effort must be made to upgrade the process quality level through process improvement procedures upon the initiative of management.

Example 9-30: In the manufacture of television sets, the cost to inspect a printed circuit board is \$0.15. If a nonconforming circuit board is allowed in the assembly, the cost to subsequently disassemble it and replace the unit is \$100. It is estimated that the proportion nonconforming of incoming circuit boards is 0.4 percent. What should the inspection policy be using Deming's kp rule?

Solution. We have $k_1 = 0.15$, $k_2 = 100$, and $p = 0.004$. The ratio $k_1/k_2 = 0.15/100 = 0.0015$. Since $k_1/k_2 < p$, the policy calls for 100 percent inspection of all incoming printed circuit boards.

9-11 SUMMARY

This chapter has discussed a variety of acceptance sampling plans for attribute inspection. From the items that are selected for inspection, a count of the number of nonconformities or the number of nonconforming units, depending on the case at hand, is made. This count, if less than or equal to a standard value (based on certain criteria that are to be satisfied by the sampling plan), determines acceptance of the lot. Alternatively, if the count exceeds the standard value of the acceptance number, the lot is rejected. The above represents the simplest form of decision making associated with single sampling plans; this chapter has introduced double and multiple sampling plans, too. Much of the chapter is devoted to lot-by-lot attribute sampling plans, for which items are submitted for inspection in lots, or batches. Single sampling plans are designed based on such criteria as producer's risk, consumer's risk, average outgoing quality limit, and minimization of average total inspection. Double sampling plans are also derived based on stipulated producer's risk and consumer's risk. This chapter has also presented some standardized sampling plans that provide the user with a host of sampling plans based on certain specified criteria. *ANSI/ASQC Z1.4* plans based on AQL and Dodge–Romig plans based on LQL or AOQL are discussed. In addition to lot-by-lot attribute inspection plans, some special plans such as chain sampling, sequential sampling, and skip-lot sampling have also been discussed. This chapter has presented some sampling plans for continuous production such as the standard, *MIL-STD-1235C*. Finally, a discussion of Deming's kp rule for sampling, which provides a prescription for either 0 percent or 100 percent inspection, has been included.

9-12 CASE STUDY

SUPPLIER TEAM ADDS VALUE FOR CUSTOMER*

The buyer-seller relationship has long been a primary focus for quality improvement efforts. The goal of these programs is not simply to reduce nonconformance rates in incoming products—although that, of course, is important. The goal is to form a partnership that will address quality from the broadest management perspective. Issues like cost, efficiency, and productivity are crucial.

A good example of the value of these partnerships comes from Tara Tape (formerly RJM Manufacturing, Inc.), a producer of reinforced industrial packaging tapes. Tara Tape has worked closely with its key suppliers—including its tape core supplier, Sonoco Products Company—to improve its production quality and manufacturing efficiency.

Established 15 years ago, Tara Tape produces a full line of reinforced tapes used primarily to seal, bundle, and palletize cartons and other packages. The company also manufactures a variety of tear tapes used for overnight delivery packages, corrugated containers, and other products.

In September 1987, Tara Tape was the subject of a leveraged buyout by Tom Dodd and Jack Saylor, formerly with the American Tape Company. This management change ushered in a new philosophy about suppliers: They are to be business partners. Tara Tape's goal is to work with suppliers, helping them realize their important role in better meeting the final customer's needs.

Tara Tape's tape core supplier, Sonoco, responded to this new approach by forming a value team. The team brings top Tara Tape management and key Sonoco per-

* J. A. Liberatore (1990), "Supplier Team Adds Value for Customer," *Quality Progress*, Vol. 23, No. 2, p. 43.

sonnel together to discuss methods of improving products and services. The principal team members meet monthly to discuss different issues, ranging from tape core specifications to packaging to deliveries. They discuss any problems or concerns and then work to resolve them. The value team also discusses the buyer-supplier relationship; both the buyer and supplier analyze all areas of the relationship and present recommendations for improvement.

Value Team Trims Costs

Previously, Tara Tape trimmed tape cores to specification in-house and maintained a small supplemental supply of purchased precut tape cores. During value team meetings, the two companies developed a system for Sonoco to provide precut cores in widths ranging from $\frac{3}{8}$ to 9 inches. This move eliminated Tara Tape's own core-trimming operations.

Sonoco delivers tape cores several times a week, providing Tara Tape with adequate inventory levels and eliminating scheduling problems. More important, Tara Tape isn't dividing its time, assets, and efforts between cutting cores and producing tapes. Now, it concentrates solely on manufacturing tapes.

Eliminating the in-house core-cutting function enabled Tara Tape to trim some extra operating costs. For example, the company redirected the labor that formerly trimmed the cores to work directly in the production of finished tape products. In addition, the company reduced the number of warehoused cores, saving expensive inventory costs.

Using the precut tapes cores also significantly reduced the presence of scrap rings—the odd-dimensional cores that remain after trimming a parent-length tape core to specification. Scrap rings often become mixed with trimmed cores. Since scrap ring dimensions vary from the specified core width, they can easily jam the core chutes on the slitting equipment. These chutes feed trimmed cores onto a mandrel, which then winds slit tape onto the core to produce a finished tape package. Jammed scrap rings prevent cores from reaching the mandrel, resulting in costly production downtime. The scrap rings can also slip into the mandrel, allowing the tape to be incorrectly wound on the mandrel and the incomplete core. Problems with scrap rings are largely a thing of the past.

Another improvement involved the cartons in which tape cores were delivered. The value team found that Tara Tape personnel often had difficulty handling and emptying the delivery cartons into the winding equipment hoppers. Consequently, an operator would shut down the slitting equipment to assist the loaders, reducing productivity and labor efficiency. In response, Sonoco modified the package size so the loaders can easily dump cores into the hopper, allowing operators to keep equipment running.

Both Tara Tape and Sonoco are pleased with the new customer–supplier relationship. With the value team, Sonoco doesn't just send Tara Tape a commodity and an invoice—Tara Tape has a supplier committed to its business.

Questions for Discussion

1. Discuss the benefits of developing and maintaining preferred suppliers.
2. Describe the implications of including the supplier as a team member in meeting the long-term goals of quality improvement.

KEY TERMS

Acceptable quality level (AQL)
Acceptance number
Attribute sampling plans
Average outgoing quality (AOQ)
Average outgoing quality limit (AOQL)
Average sample number (ASN)
Average total inspection (ATI)
Chain sampling plans
Consumer's risk
Deming's kp rule
Double sampling plan
Limiting quality level (LQL)
Lot size
Lot tolerance percent defective (LTPD)
Multiple sampling plan
Operating characteristic (OC) curve
  Type A OC curve
  Type B OC curve
Plans for continuous production
  CSP–1 plan
  CSP–2 plan
  CPS–F plan
  CSP–T plan
  CPS–V plan
  MIL–STD-1235C
Producer's risk
Rectifying inspection

Rejectable quality level (RQL)
Sample size
Sampling plans
  Design
Sampling scheme
Sampling system
Screening
Sequential sampling plan
Single sampling plan
Skip-lot sampling plan
Standardized plans
  MIL–STD–105E
  ANSI/ASQC Z1.4
  Dodge–Romig plans based on LQL
  Dodge–Romig plans based on AOQL
  ISO 2859
Unacceptable quality level (UQL)

EXERCISES

Discussion Questions

9-1 Discuss the advantages and disadvantages of sampling.

9-2 Distinguish between producer's risk and consumer's risk. In this context, explain the terms *acceptable quality level* and *limiting quality level*. Discuss instances for which one of the types of risks might be more important than the other.

9-3 What is the importance of the OC curve in the selection of sampling plans? Describe the impact of the sample size and the acceptance number on the OC curve. What is the disadvantage of having an acceptance number of zero?

9-4 Discuss the relative advantages and disadvantages of single, double, and multiple sampling plans.

9-5 Distinguish between average outgoing quality and acceptable quality level. Explain clearly the meaning and importance of the average outgoing quality limit.

9-6 If you were interested in protection for acceptance of a single lot from a vendor with whom you do not expect to conduct much business, what criteria would you select and why?

9-7 Explain the difference between average sample number and average total inspection. State any assumptions made.

9-8 If rectification inspection is used, discuss possible criteria to use in choosing sampling plans.

9-9 Discuss the context in which minimizing the average sample number would be a feasible criterion. Which type of sampling plan (single, double, or multiple) would be preferable, and what factors would influence your choice?

9-10 Discuss the basis on which *ANSI/ASQC Z1.4* plans are formulated. How does this differ from the basis of Dodge–Romig plans?

9-11 Compare and contrast chain sampling and sequential sampling plans. When are they used?

9-12 Compare and contrast skip-lot sampling and CSP–1 plans.

9-13 Distinguish between single level and multilevel sampling plans for continuous production. Give examples of each.

9-14 Distinguish between a CSP–T and a CSP–V plan for continuous production. Explain the conditions under which each would be used.

9-15 Discuss the assumptions made in Deming's kp rule.

Problems

9-16 Consider a single sampling plan with a lot size of 1500, sample size of 150, and acceptance number of 3. Construct the OC curve. If the acceptable quality level is 0.05 percent nonconforming and the limiting quality level is 6 percent nonconforming, describe the protection offered by the plan at these quality levels.

9-17 Consider Exercise 9-16. Answer the same questions for the sampling plan $N = 1500$, $n = 200$, $c = 3$. Discuss the degree of protection of this plan compared to that in Exercise 9-16.

9-18 Suppose the desirable producer's risk is 3 percent and consumer's risk is 6 percent. Which of the plans described in Exercises 9-16 and 9-17 are preferable? Discuss your choice.

9-19 For the sampling plan $N = 1500$, $n = 150$, $c = 3$, construct the average outgoing quality curve. What is the AOQL? Interpret it.

9-20 For the sampling plan $N = 1000$, $n = 100$, $c = 2$, construct the AOQ curve. Find and interpret the AOQL.

9-21 Construct the ATI curve for the sampling plan $N = 1200$, $n = 50$, $c = 1$. Suppose the process average nonconforming rate is 3 percent. Explain the value of ATI for that level of nonconformance.

9-22 Construct the ATI curve for the plan $N = 3000$, $n = 80$, $c = 2$.

9-23 For the double sampling plan $N = 2000$, $n_1 = 80$, $c_1 = 1$, $r_1 = 3$, $n_2 = 100$, $c_2 = 2$, $r_2 = 3$, construct and interpret the ASN curve. Suppose the process average nonconforming rate is 1.5 percent. Would you prefer the above double sampling plan or a single sampling plan with $n = 100$, $c = 2$ to minimize ASN?

9-24 For the double sampling plan $N = 2200$, $n_1 = 60$, $c_1 = 1$, $r_1 = 5$, $n_2 = 120$, $c_2 = 4$, $r_2 = 5$, construct the ASN curve. Within what range of fraction-nonconforming values would you prefer the above double sampling plan over a single sampling plan with $n = 85$, $c = 2$ in order to minimize ASN?

9-25 Determine the single sampling plans that will reject lots that are 1.3 percent nonconforming 8 percent of the time. Use acceptance numbers of 1, 3, and 5. From a consumer's point of view, which of these three plans would you choose?

9-26 Determine the single sampling plans that will accept lots that are 6 percent nonconforming 12 percent of the time. Use acceptance numbers of 1, 2, and 4. From a producer's point of view, which of these plans would you choose?

9-27 Determine single sampling plans that will accept lots that are 0.8 percent nonconforming with a probability of 0.96. Use acceptance numbers of 1, 3, and 4. If we desire batches that are 5 percent nonconforming to be accepted with a probability of no more than 0.04, which of the above plans would be preferable? Will the plan meet these criterion?

9-28 A sampling plan is desired to have a producer's risk of 0.05 at AQL= 0.9 percent and a consumer's risk of 0.10 at LQL = 6.5 percent nonconforming. Find the single sampling plan that meets the consumer's stipulation and comes as close as possible to meeting the producer's stipulation.

9-29 A sampling plan is desired to have a producer's risk of 0.05 at AQL= 1.3 percent nonconforming and a consumer's risk of 0.10 at LQL= 7.1 percent nonconforming. Find the single sampling plan that meets the producer's stipulation and comes as close as possible to meeting the consumer's stipulation.

9-30 For the data given in Exercise 9-28, find the single sampling plan that meets the producer's stipulation and comes as close as possible to meeting the consumer's stipulation.

9-31 For the data given in Exercise 9-29, find the single sampling plan that meets the consumer's stipulation and comes as close as possible to meeting the producer's stipulation.

9-32 A sampling plan is desired to have a producer's risk of 5 percent at AQL= 2.0 percent nonconforming and a consumer's risk of 0.10 at LQL= 7 percent nonconforming. Find the single sampling plan with the largest sample size. Find the single sampling plan with the smallest sample size.

9-33 For the data given in Exercise 9-32, find the single sampling plan that meets the producer's stipulation exactly and comes as close as possible to the consumer's stipulation.

9-34 Find a single sampling plan that will satisfy a consumer's risk of 10 percent at LQL= 8.5 percent nonconforming and will also minimize average total inspection for incoming lots that are 4 percent nonconforming. The lot size is 1600. If the AQL is 0.008, what is the producer's risk?

9-35 It is desired to meet a consumer's risk of 0.08 at LQL = 9.2 percent nonconforming and also minimize average total inspection for incoming lots that are 3 percent nonconforming. Find a single sampling plan if the lot size is 1400. What is the producer's risk for the plan if AQL= 1.1 percent nonconforming?

9-36 A single sampling plan is desired that will have an AOQL of 3.2 percent nonconforming and also minimize the average total inspection for incoming batches that are 1.9 percent nonconforming. If the lot size is 900, find the sampling plan. If AQL= 0.7 percent nonconforming, what is the producer's risk for this plan?

9-37 Find a single sampling plan that will have an AOQL of 4.6 percent nonconforming and also minimize average total inspection for incoming lots that are 2.0 percent nonconforming. If LQL= 6.4 percent nonconforming, what is the consumer's risk for this plan?

9-38 Consider a double sampling plan given by the following parameters: $N = 1200$, $n_1 = 50$, $c_1 = 1$, $r_1 = 4$, $n_2 = 110$, $c_2 = 5$, $r_2 = 6$. Find the probability of accepting lots that are 4 percent nonconforming. What is the probability of rejecting a lot on the first sample?

9-39 Consider a double sampling plan given by the following parameters: $N = 2200$, $n_1 = 60$, $c_1 = 0$, $r_1 = 5$, $n_2 = 100$, $c_2 = 6$, $r_2 = 7$. Find the probability of accepting lots that are 3 percent nonconforming. What is the probability of accepting a lot on the first sample? What is the probability of making a decision on the first sample?

9-40 Refer to Exercise 9-38. What is the average sample number of incoming lots that are 2 percent nonconforming? What is the average total inspection for this quality level of 2 percent nonconforming?

9-41 Refer to Exercise 9-39. Find the average sample number for incoming lots that are 4 percent nonconforming. Also, find the average total inspection at this 4 percent level of nonconformance.

9-42 A double sampling plan is desired that has a producer's risk of 5 percent at AQL= 1.8 percent nonconforming and a consumer's risk of 10 percent at LQL= 8.5 percent nonconforming. The lot size is 1500, and the sample sizes are assumed to be equal. Find the sampling plan if the producer's stipulation is to be satisfied exactly. Find the average sample number for batches that are 1.8 percent nonconforming.

9-43 It is desired to accept lots that are 9.5 percent nonconforming with a probability of 0.10 and to accept lots that are 2.3 percent nonconforming with a probability of 0.95. Find a double sampling plan for a lot size of 2000 if the second sample is to be twice as large as the first sample and the consumer's stipulation is to be satisfied exactly. Find the average sample number for batches that are 2.3 percent nonconforming.

9-44 Refer to Exercise 9-42. Find the double sampling plan if the second sample is to be twice as large as the first sample and the consumer's stipulation is to be satisfied exactly.

9-45 Refer to Exercise 9-43. Find the double sampling plan if the sample sizes for the first and the second samples are to be equal and the producer's stipulation is to be satisfied exactly.

9-46 Refer to Exercise 9-42. Find the sampling plan if it is desired to accept batches that are 5 percent nonconforming with a probability of 0.5.

9-47 Items are submitted for inspection using the *ANSI/ASQC Z1.4* standard. Find the single sampling plans for the following conditions:

Problem number	Lot size	General inspection level	Inspection	AQL
a	1600	I	Normal	0.5 percent nonconforming
b	800	III	Reduced	40 nonconformities per 100 units
c	2500	II	Tightened	0.25 percent nonconforming
d	1000	I	Normal	25 nonconformities per 100 units
e	400	II	Reduced	1.0 percent nonconforming

9-48 Items are submitted for inspection using the *ANSI/ASQC Z1.4* standard. Find the double sampling plans for the following conditions:

Problem number	Lot size	General inspection level	Inspection	AQL
a	900	II	Normal	0.4 percent nonconforming
b	1500	I	Tightened	0.5 percent nonconforming
c	2000	III	Reduced	15 nonconformities per 100 units
d	700	II	Normal	0.10 percent nonconforming

9-49 Items are submitted for inspection using the *ANSI/ASQC Z1.4* standard. Find the multiple sampling plans for the following conditions:

Problem number	Lot size	General inspection level	Inspection	AQL
a	700	I	Tightened	4.0 percent nonconforming
b	1500	I	Normal	0.65 percent nonconforming
c	1400	III	Reduced	10 nonconformities per 100 units
d	400	I	Tightened	15 nonconformities per 100 units

9-50 Items are submitted for inspection in lots of size 600 using the *ANSI/ASQC Z1.4* standard. The general inspection level is level I, and AQL is 0.65 percent nonconforming for single sampling plans. Normal inspection is initiated at the start of lot number 1. The inspection results for 10 consecutive lots are shown below:

Lot number	Number nonconforming	Lot number	Number nonconforming
1	0	6	1
2	2	7	0
3	0	8	0
4	1	9	0
5	0	10	1

What type of inspection is used for lot 3? For lot 5, lot 9, and lot 11?

9-51 Double sampling inspection using the *ANSI/ASQC Z1.4* standard is adopted for items submitted in lots of 800. The general inspection level is level I, and AQL is 1.0 percent nonconforming. Normal inspection is used for lot number 1. The inspection results for 13 consecutive lots are as follows:

Lot Number	Number inspected	Number nonconforming
1	32	0
2	32	1
3	32	1
4	64	2
5	64	1
6	32	2
7	50	1
8	50	0
9	100	1
10	50	1
11	100	1
12	64	2
13	32	2

What type of inspection is used for lot 4? For lot 6, lot 7, lot 10, and lot 14?

9-52 Items are submitted for inspection using the *ANSI/ASQC Z1.4* in lots of 400. Single sampling plans using general inspection level III are to be used. For normal inspection, the AQL is 2.5 percent nonconforming. At the scheme performance level, what is the quality level of batches that will be rejected 5 percent of the time? What is the quality level of batches that will be accepted 25 percent of the time?

9-53 Consider Exercise 9-52. Find the AOQL at the scheme performance level for the sampling plan selected.

9-54 Consider Exercise 9-52. Find the limiting quality at the scheme performance level for which the probability of lot acceptance is 10 percent.

9-55 Find a Dodge–Romig single sampling plan if the lot size is 900, LQL= 5 percent nonconforming, and the process average is 0.8 percent nonconforming. What is the AOQL for the plan? Interpret it.

9-56 Find a Dodge–Romig single sampling plan if the lot size is 2200 and LQL= 5.0 percent. Determine and interpret the AOQL for the plan.

9-57 Find a Dodge-Romig double sampling plan for a lot size of 1800, LQL= 3 percent nonconforming, and a process average of 0.75 percent nonconforming. Determine the AOQL for the plan.

9-58 Find a Dodge–Romig single sampling plan if the lot size is 600, the process average is 1.4 percent nonconforming, and AOQL= 3 percent. Determine and interpret the LQL for the plan.

9-59 Find a Dodge–Romig double sampling plan if the lot size is 800 and AOQL= 3.0 percent. What is the LQL? Interpret it.

9-60 Find a Dodge–Romig double sampling plan if the lot size is 2400 and AOQL= 3.0 percent. Interpret the value of the LQL for the plan.

9-61 A chain sampling plan is used with a sample size of 5 and a parameter i of 3. If lots have a function nonconforming of 0.06, find the probability of accepting such lots.

9-62 A chain sampling plan is used in a costly destructive testing procedure. The sample size is 6, and the parameter i is 2. Find the probability of accepting incoming lots that have a fraction-nonconforming value of 0.04.

9-63 An item-by-item sequential sampling plan is desired with a producer's risk of 0.03 at AQL= 0.012 and a consumer's risk for 0.08 at LQL= 0.063. Find the equations of the acceptance and rejection lines. Explain the operation of the plan. Set up a table showing the acceptance and rejection numbers for the first 50 items inspected.

9-64 The equations for the acceptance and rejection lines for a sequential sampling plan are given as follows:

$$d_a = -0.95 + 0.06n$$
$$d_r = 1.22 + 0.06n$$

What is the first opportunity to reject? What is the first opportunity to accept? Set up a table showing the acceptance and rejection numbers for the first 30 items inspected.

9-65 A sequential sampling plan is to be used. It is desirable to have a producer's risk of 0.05 at AQL= 0.008 and a consumer's risk of 0.07 at LQL= 0.082. Determine the equations for the acceptance and rejection lines. What is the first opportunity to reject? What is the first opportunity to accept?

9-66 Consider a skip-lot sampling plan for a desired AOQL of 0.79 percent. Determine the plans for sampling frequencies f of $\frac{1}{2}$, $\frac{1}{5}$, and $\frac{1}{10}$. Explain the workings of the plan.

9-67 For an AOQL= 0.53 percent, determine the skip-lot sampling plan for $f = \frac{1}{3}, \frac{1}{7}$, and $\frac{1}{15}$.

9-68 A contractor used the *MIL–STD–1235C* plan for continuous production. Find a CSP-1 plan if the desired AOQL is 0.79 percent and the inspector has the time to conduct sampling at a frequency of $\frac{1}{4}$. What is the value of the maximum number of consecutive units that may be screened? Explain the workings of the plan.

9-69 In a continuous production facility, *MIL–STD–1235C* is used. The number of units produced in an eight-hour shift is 2200, and the desired AOQL is 0.198 percent. Find a CSP–F plan if the inspector is available for sampling at a frequency of no more than $\frac{1}{5}$. Explain the workings of the plan.

9-70 Using *MIL–STD–1235C*, a CSP–2 plan is desired. If the AOQL is not to exceed 1.22 percent, and a sampling frequency of $\frac{1}{3}$ is acceptable, find the plan. What is the value of the maximum number of consecutive units that may be screened? Explain the workings of the plan.

9-71 *MIL–STD–1235C* is being used in an organization using a CSP–1 plan. If the AOQL is 2.5 percent, find the plan and explain how it works if $f = \frac{1}{3}$.

9-72 For a vendor using *MIL–STD–1235C*, find a CSP–2 plan if the desired AOQL is 0.53 percent, and a sampling frequency of $\frac{1}{5}$ is suitable. What is the maximum number of consecutive units that may be screened?

9-73 Using *MIL-STD-1235C*, find a CSP–T plan if the desired AOQL is 4.94 percent and the inspector is free to perform sampling inspection at a frequency not to exceed $\frac{1}{5}$. Explain the workings of the plan.

9-74 For a company using *MIL–STD–1235C*, find a CSP–V plan for an AOQL of 1.90 percent and a sampling frequency of $\frac{1}{5}$. Explain the workings of the plan.

9-75 The initial inspection of transmission systems in automobiles is estimated to cost \$0.50 per unit. If a nonconforming transmission is allowed in the assembly, the unit cost to eventually disassemble and replace it is \$225. The estimated fraction nonconforming of the transmission systems is 0.003. Using Deming's kp rule, what inspection policy should be used?

9-76 In Exercise 9-75, if the initial inspection costs of the transmission systems is $1.00 per unit, what inspection policy should be followed using Deming's kp rule?

9-77 Refer to Exercise 9-75. Suppose the monthly production is 3000 units. What is the average savings in total inspection costs per month when using the policy found from Deming's kp rule as opposed to 100 percent inspection?

9-78 Refer to Exercise 9-76. If the monthly production is 2000 units, what is the average savings in total inspection costs when using Deming's kp rule as opposed to no inspection?

9-79 In the construction industry, the initial inspection of tie beams is estimated to cost $0.20 per unit. If, however, a nonconforming beam is allowed for construction purposes, the unit cost of rectifying and replacing it is $50. What inspection policy should be followed, using Deming's kp rule, if the nonconformance rate of beams is 0.5 percent? What is the average savings in total inspection costs if 100 percent inspection is used as opposed to no inspection?

REFERENCES

American Society for Quality Control (1981). *American National Standard-Sampling Procedures and Tables for Inspection by Attributes, ANSI/ASQC Z1.4–1981*. Milwaukee, WI.

American Society for Quality Control (1987). *American National Standard-Terms, Symbols, and Definitions for Acceptance Sampling, ANSI/ASQC A2–1987*. Milwaukee, WI.

Banks, J. (1989). Principles of Quality Control. Wiley, New York.

Chemical Corps Engineering Agency (1953). *Manual No. 2: Master Sampling Plan for Single, Duplicate, Double, and Multiple Sampling*. Edgewood Arsenal, Army Chemical Center, MD.

Dodge, H. F. (1943). "A Sampling Inspection-Plan for Continuous Production," *Annals of Mathematical Statistics,* Volume 14, pp. 264–269.

Dodge, H. F. (1955). "Chain Sampling Inspection Plans," *Industrial Quality Control,* 11 (4), pp. 10–13.

Dodge, H. F. (1955). "Skip-lot Sampling Plans," *Industrial Quality Control,* 11 (5), pp. 3–5.

Dodge, H. F., and Romig, H. G. (1959). *Sampling Inspection Tables—Single and Double Sampling,* 2nd edition Wiley, New York.

Grubbs, F. E. (1949). "On Designing Single Sampling Inspection Plans," *Annals of Mathematical Statistics,* Volume XX, p. 256.

Liberatore, J. A. (1990). "Supplier Team Adds Value for Customer," *Quality Progress,* 23 (2), p. 43.

United States Department of Defense (1988). *Single and Multi-Level Continuous Sampling Procedures and Tables for Inspection by Attributes, MIL–STD–1235C*. Washington, DC.

Wald, A. (1947). *Sequential Analysis*. Wiley, New York.

CHAPTER

10

Acceptance Sampling Plans by Variables

CHAPTER OUTLINE

SYMBOLS

$\overline{X}_a$	Acceptance limit	Z	Standard normal value
n	Sample size	L	Lower specification limit
α	Producer's risk	U	Upper specification limit
β	Consumer's risk	X	Quality characteristic
AQL	Acceptable quality level	Q_L, Q_U	Quality index
μ	Process mean	M	Maximum allowable percent nonconforming
σ	Process standard deviation		
$\overline{X}$	Sample mean	k	Acceptability constant
s	Sample standard deviation	$\hat{p}$	Estimated lot percent nonconforming

10-1 INTRODUCTION

This chapter presents sampling plans for variables. A variable is a quality characteristic that is measured on a numerical scale, such as weight, pressure, temperature, viscosity, tensile strength, elasticity, resistance, and so on. The characteristic is often inherently a variable. Treating it as an attribute will not allow the precision of information offered by variables to be retained. If testing is destructive or costly, smaller sample sizes may be necessary. Acceptance sampling plans for variables are more suitable in these instances because they require smaller sample sizes than corresponding attribute sampling plans for the same degree of protection.

There are two basic types of variable sampling plans. The first deals with controlling a process parameter such as the mean or standard deviation. The desirable settings of the parameters are such that certain conditions regarding the mean lot quality and the corresponding probability of lot acceptance are satisfied. Plans can be designed for single or double specification limits and a process standard deviation that is known or unknown. Some plans in this category involve acceptance control charts, sequential sampling plans for variables, and hypothesis testing on process parameters (which is not treated in this chapter). This chapter deals with acceptance control charts. Sequential sampling plans for variables are used when the quality characteristic is normally distributed and the process standard deviation is known. The procedure is similar to that for the sequential plans for attributes discussed in Chapter 9; in such plans the ordinate is the cumulative sum of the characteristic ($\sum X$), which is plotted as a function of the number of units inspected.

The second type of plan deals with controlling the proportion of the product that is nonconforming (that is, does not satisfy specifications). Here as well, single or double specification limits and a process variability that is known or unknown can be used in determining sampling plans. This chapter focuses on single sampling for both of these types of plans, though single, double, or multiple sampling plans may be designed. Standardized sampling plans for variables, such as *ANSI/ASQC Z1.9* and its military equivalent *MIL–STD–414,* are discussed in the context of plans of the second type. The international version of the standardized plan is *ISO 3951,* which is similar to *ANSI/ASQC Z1.9.*

10-2 ADVANTAGES AND DISADVANTAGES OF VARIABLE PLANS

Some advantages of variable sampling plans compared to those for attributes are as follows:

1. For a comparable level of protection as specified by the producer's risk α, the acceptable quality level (AQL), the consumer's risk β, and the limiting quality level (LQL), the sample sizes are smaller for a variable plan than for an attribute plan.
2. Variable sampling plans provide more information than attribute plans. Since a numerical value for the characteristic is specified, the extent to which the item is conforming or not is obtained. An attribute plan, on the other hand, specifies the item as simply conforming or not.
3. Variable sampling plans provide insight into the areas that deserve attention for quality improvement. The information from a variable plan may provide clues for specific actions that could be explored for improving process quality. Continual process improvement should be the goal of every organization; variable plans can help achieve it.

Some of the disadvantages of variable sampling plans are as follows.

1. Each quality characteristic requires a separate sampling plan. Because the number of quality characteristics is usually large, this implies that several sampling plans must be monitored. With attribute sampling plans, several variables may be combined to form a single attribute plan.
2. The administrative and unit inspection costs are usually higher for variable plans than for attribute plans. The measuring instruments are more expensive because an exact measurement value is taken.
3. In order to make inferences from the variable sampling plans, one must know or estimate the distribution of the quality characteristic for the process under consideration.

10-3 VARIABLE SAMPLING PLANS FOR A PROCESS PARAMETER

Variable sampling plans for a process parameter are used when either the average quality of the product or process or the variability of the quality is of concern. These plans may be used for items that are submitted in bulk (for example, in bags, boxes, drums, or bins). There are plans for situations in which the process standard deviation is known or unknown. All of the sampling plans in this section require that the distribution of the quality characteristic be normal. However, minor departures from normality may not significantly affect the tests.

Variable Sampling Plans to Estimate Process Average—Single Specification Limit and Known Process Standard Deviation

Consider a single sampling plan to estimate the process average; a single specification limit is given, and the process standard deviation is known. The two parameters of the sampling plan are the sample size n and the acceptance limit $\overline{X}_a$. For example, suppose the lower specification limit for the density of a chemical is specified. A variable sampling plan may call for selecting a random sample of size n from the lot. The sample's average density is found. If the sample average is less than the acceptance limit $\overline{X}_a$, the lot is rejected. Otherwise, the lot is accepted. Alternatively, if an upper specification limit for a characteristic were specified, the lot would be rejected if the sample average were greater than the corresponding acceptance limit. The process standard deviation σ is assumed to be known.

Consider the derivation of a variable sampling plan under the following conditions. Suppose it is desired to accept batches of good average quality, as denoted by $\overline{X}_1$, with a probability of $1 - \alpha$ and to accept batches of poor average quality, as denoted by $\overline{X}_2$, with a probability of β. Thus, we desire a sampling plan whose OC curve should pass through the two points $(1 - \alpha, \overline{X}_1)$ and $(\beta, \overline{X}_2)$. The sample size is denoted by n and the acceptance limit by $\overline{X}_a$. Suppose the quality characteristic is to meet a minimum specification limit.

Figure 10-1 shows the relationship of $\overline{X}_1$ and $\overline{X}_2$ to $\overline{X}_a$ when considering the sampling distribution of the sample mean $\overline{X}$. Let Z_α denote the standard normal value corresponding to the tail area of α, and let Z_β denote the standard normal value corresponding to the tail area of β. We have

$$Z_\alpha = \frac{\overline{X}_a - \overline{X}_1}{\sigma/\sqrt{n}} \tag{10.1}$$

and

$$Z_\beta = \frac{\overline{X}_a - \overline{X}_2}{\sigma/\sqrt{n}} \tag{10.2}$$

Note that for the case shown in Figure 10-1, Z_α will be negative and Z_β will be positive. Equations (10.1) and (10.2) involve two unknowns, $\overline{X}_a$ and n. By solving the two equations simultaneously, we get the sample size as

$$n = \left[\frac{(Z_\beta - Z_\alpha)\sigma}{\overline{X}_1 - \overline{X}_2}\right]^2 \tag{10.3}$$

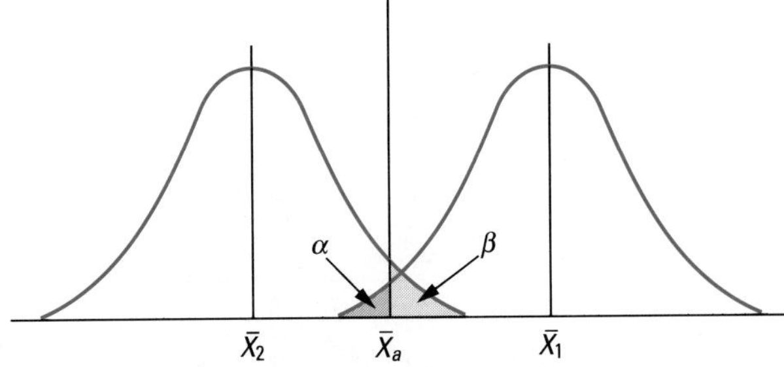

Figure 10-1 Relationship of $\overline{X}_1$ and $\overline{X}_2$ to $\overline{X}_a$ in the sampling distribution of $\overline{X}$.

Using the form of n in Equation 10.3, Equation 10.2 gives the acceptance limit as

$$\overline{X}_a = \frac{Z_\beta \overline{X}_1 - Z_\alpha \overline{X}_2}{Z_\beta - Z_\alpha} \tag{10.4}$$

Example 10-1: Ammonium nitrate is shipped in 500-kg bags; the lower specification for the concentration of nitrogen is 13 percent. The distribution of the concentration of nitrogen is known to be normal, with a standard deviation of 1.5 percent. Find a variable sampling plan that satisfies the following conditions:

1. Batches with a mean that is 2.5 standard deviations above the lower specification limit should be accepted with a probability of 0.95.
2. Batches with a mean that is 1.5 standard deviations above the lower specification limit should be accepted with a probability of 0.10.

Solution. First, we calculate the process average quality levels associated with the two conditions that are to be satisfied. Denoting the lower specification limit by LSL, we have

$$\begin{aligned}\overline{X}_1 &= \text{LSL} + 2.5(\sigma)\\ &= 0.13 + (2.5)(0.015) = 0.1675\\ \overline{X}_2 &= \text{LSL} + 1.5(\sigma)\\ &= 0.13 + 1.5(0.015) = 0.1525\end{aligned}$$

Thus, we wish to accept lots that have a mean quality level of 16.75 percent with a probability of 0.95. Additionally, we wish to accept lots that have a mean quality level of 15.25 percent with a probability of 0.10. Figure 10-2 shows the relationship of these conditions with respect to the acceptance limit $\overline{X}_a$. We have $1 - \alpha = 0.95$, $\overline{X}_1 = 0.1675$, $\beta = 0.10$, $\overline{X}_2 = 0.1525$. From the standard normal distribution tables in Appendix A-3, we have $Z_\alpha = Z_{0.05} = -1.645$ and $Z_\beta = Z_{0.10} = 1.282$. From Equation 10.3, the sample size is

$$\begin{aligned}n &= \left\{\frac{[1.282 - (-1.645)]0.015}{(0.1675 - 0.1525)}\right\}^2\\ &= 8.57 \simeq 9\end{aligned}$$

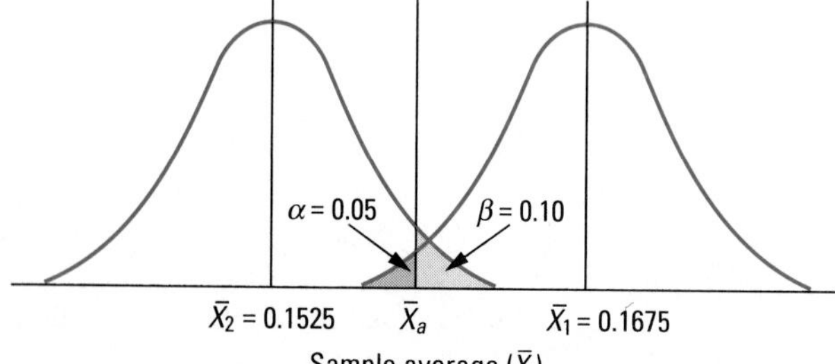

Figure 10-2 Process means $\overline{X}_1$ and $\overline{X}_2$ and their relationship to $\overline{X}_a$.

From Equation 10.4, the acceptance limit is

$$\overline{X}_a = \frac{1.282(0.1675) - (-1.645)(0.1525)}{[1.282 - (-1.645)]} = 0.1591$$

The sampling plan works as follows. A random sample of size 9 is chosen from the lot, and the sample average concentration of nitrogen is found. If the sample average is less than 0.1591, the lot is rejected; otherwise, it is accepted.

Variable Sampling Plans to Estimate Process Average—Double Specification Limits and Known Process Standard Deviation

In certain instances, it is desirable for the quality characteristic to be within a range of values, which necessitates the existence of double specification limits. For example, the diameter of an acceptable bearing should lie between upper and lower specification limits. Thus, the levels of poor quality for the process average are given by two values, $\overline{X}_{2L}$ and $\overline{X}_{2U}$, and the associated consumer's risk is denoted by β. As in the previous section, the level of good quality of the process average, denoted by $\overline{X}_1$, is such that the producer's risk is given by α. Thus, the OC curve of the sampling plan should pass through the points $(1-\alpha, \overline{X}_1)$, $(\beta, \overline{X}_{2L})$, and $(\beta, \overline{X}_{2U})$. Accordingly, there will be two acceptance limits, $\overline{X}_{La}$ and $\overline{X}_{Ua}$, the lower and upper acceptance limits, respectively. The process standard deviation is assumed to be known and represented by σ; the sample size is denoted by n.

Figure 10-3 shows the relationship between the various parameters of the sampling plan. It is assumed in this section that $\overline{X}_1$ is at the midpoint of $\overline{X}_{2L}$ and $\overline{X}_{2U}$. Assuming a normal distribution of the sample means, the following equations are obtained:

$$Z_{\alpha/2} = \frac{\overline{X}_{Ua} - \overline{X}_1}{\sigma/\sqrt{n}} \tag{10.5}$$

$$-Z_{\alpha/2} = \frac{\overline{X}_{La} - \overline{X}_1}{\sigma/\sqrt{n}} \tag{10.6}$$

$$Z_\beta = \frac{\overline{X}_{La} - \overline{X}_{2L}}{\sigma/\sqrt{n}} \tag{10.7}$$

$$-Z_\beta = \frac{\overline{X}_{Ua} - \overline{X}_{2U}}{\sigma/\sqrt{n}} \tag{10.8}$$

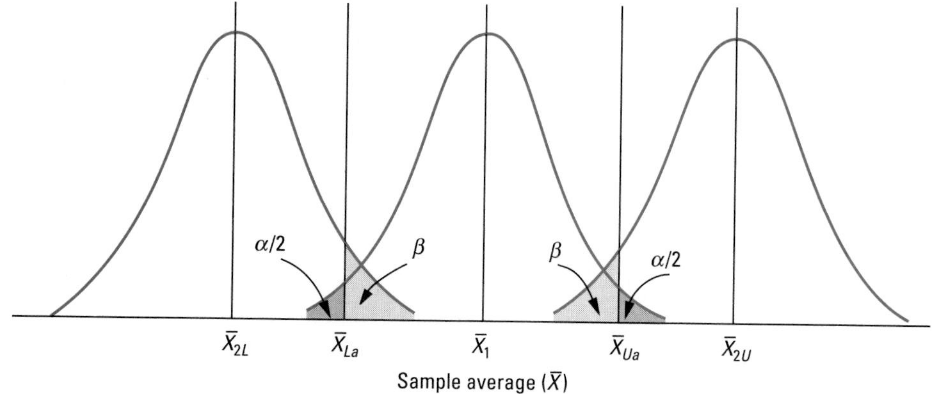

Figure 10-3 Relationship between the various parameters for a plan using double specification limits.

where $Z_{\alpha/2}$ and Z_β are the standard normal variate values when the right tail areas are $\alpha/2$ and β, respectively. Note that there are three unknowns: $\overline{X}_{La}$, $\overline{X}_{Ua}$, and n. One of the above four equations can be eliminated as being redundant, and the unknown parameters of the sampling plan can be solved.

Example 10-2: The diameter of an axle must lie within a desirable upper and lower bound. Consequently, if the process average diameter is below 45 mm or above 47 mm, the desired probability of lot acceptance is 0.10. Let the producer's risk be 0.05 and the process standard deviation of the axle diameters be 0.6 mm. Find the variable acceptance sampling plan.

Solution. We have $\overline{X}_{2L} = 45$, $\overline{X}_{2U} = 47$, $\beta = 0.10$, $\alpha = 0.05$, and $\sigma = 0.6$. The value of $\overline{X}_1$ (midway between 45 and 47) is 46. Figure 10-4 shows the relationship between the various parameters, where $\overline{X}_{La}$ and $\overline{X}_{Ua}$ denote the lower and upper acceptance limits, respectively. After finding the standard normal variates and using Equations 10.5–10.8, we get

$$1.96 = \frac{\overline{X}_{Ua} - 46}{\sigma/\sqrt{n}} \tag{10.9}$$

$$-1.96 = \frac{\overline{X}_{La} - 46}{\sigma/\sqrt{n}} \tag{10.10}$$

$$1.282 = \frac{\overline{X}_{La} - 45}{\sigma/\sqrt{n}} \tag{10.11}$$

$$-1.282 = \frac{\overline{X}_{Ua} - 47}{\sigma/\sqrt{n}} \tag{10.12}$$

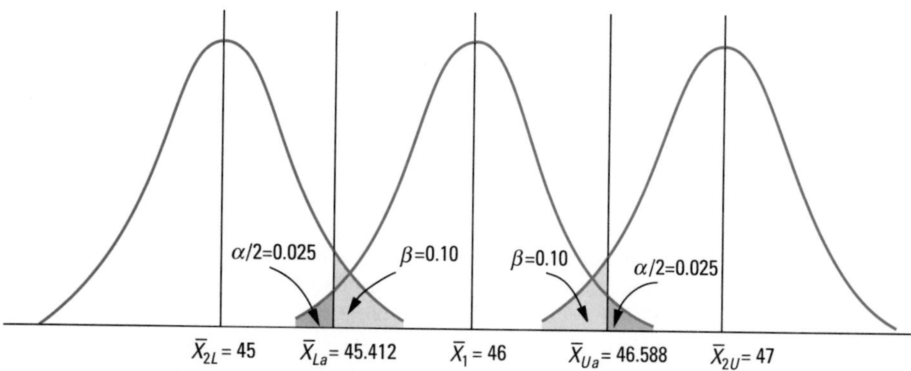

Figure 10-4 Relationship between various parameters for a plan with double specification limits for Example 10-2.

From Equations 10.11 and 10.12 we get

$$\overline{X}_{La} + \overline{X}_{Ua} = 92$$

From Equations 10.10 and 10.11 we have

$$\sqrt{n} = \frac{(1.282 + 1.96)\sigma}{(46 - 45)} = (1.282 + 1.96)(0.6) = 1.945$$

The sample size is computed as $n = (1.945)^2 = 3.784 \simeq 4$. For this computed value of n, Equation 10.10 gives

$$\overline{X}_{La} = 46 - (1.96)\frac{(0.6)}{\sqrt{4}} = 45.412$$

Therefore, $\overline{X}_{Ua} = 46.588$. The sampling plan operates as follows. A random sample of size 4 is chosen from the lot, and the average diameter of the axles is computed. If the sample average is less than 45.412 mm or greater than 46.588 mm, the lot is rejected. Otherwise, the lot is accepted.

Variable Sampling Plans to Estimate Process Average—Single Specification Limit and Unknown Process Standard Deviation

In most cases, the process standard deviation of the quality characteristic is not known, and estimates of it are obtained on the basis of a sample. Assume that the distribution of the quality characteristic is normal. The sample variance s^2, for a sample of size n (as given previously) is

$$s^2 = \frac{\sum X_i^2 - (\sum X_i)^2/n}{n - 1} \tag{10.13}$$

where X_i represents the value of the quality characteristic for the ith unit in the sample. As before, suppose that the good quality level of the process is denoted by $\overline{X}_1$, such that the probability of accepting batches with this mean is $(1 - \alpha)$, where α denotes the producer's risk. For batches with a poor quality level, whose average is denoted by $\overline{X}_2$, the probability of acceptance is low and is given by β, the consumer's risk.

The sampling distribution of $(\overline{X} - \overline{X}_1)/(s/\sqrt{n})$ is approximately a t-distribution with $(n - 1)$ degrees of freedom. The t-distribution is discussed in Chapter 3, and the t-tables are shown in Appendix A-4. The problem here is that because the sample size is not known, the t-statistic cannot be computed. One way to circumvent this is to estimate the process standard deviation, as denoted by $\hat{\sigma}$. After additional information is obtained, this estimate may be updated. Neyman and Tobarska (1936) constructed OC curves for sampling plans with single specification limits based on the

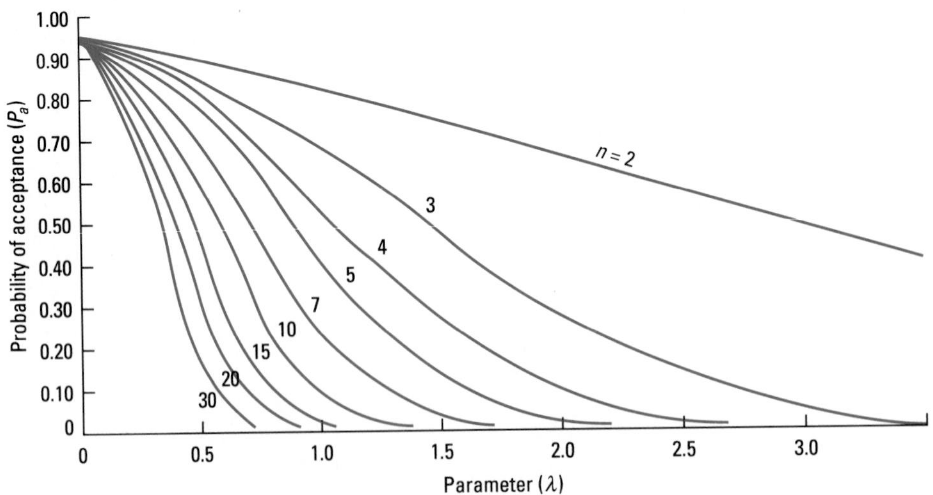

Figure 10-5 OC curves for sampling plans with a single specification limit when the process standard deviation is unknown for $\alpha = 0.05$. (J. Neyman and B. Tobarska (1936), "Errors of the Second Kind in Testing Student's Hypothesis," *Journal of the American Statistical Association*, 31, pp. 318–326. Reprinted with permission from the *Journal of the American Statistical Association*. Copyright © 1936 by the American Statistical Association. All rights reserved.)

t-statistic for a producer's risk α of 0.05. Figure 10-5 shows these OC curves for different values of n. The abscissa represents the parameter λ, which is given by

$$\lambda = \frac{|\overline{X}_1 - \overline{X}_2|}{\hat{\sigma}} \tag{10.14}$$

If the probability of lot acceptance P_a is set equal to β, the sample size can be found from Figure 10-5. Once the sample size is determined, the decision-making process is as follows. A random sample of size n is chosen, and the t-statistic, as given below, is computed:

$$t = \frac{\overline{X} - \overline{X}_1}{(s/\sqrt{n})} \tag{10.15}$$

where $\overline{X}$ and s represent the sample average and sample standard deviation, respectively. If a lower specification limit is given, the lot is rejected if the calculated value of $t < t_{\alpha,n-1}$, where $t_{\alpha,n-1}$ is the 100α percentile point of the t-distribution with $(n-1)$ degrees of freedom. Appendix A-4 may be used to obtain the percentile points of the t-distribution. If an upper specification limit is given, the lot is rejected if $t > t_{1-\alpha,n-1}$, where $t_{1-\alpha,n-1}$ is the $100(1-\alpha)$ percentile point of the t-distribution with $(n-1)$ degrees of freedom.

Example 10-3: A soft drink bottling company has a lower specification limit of 3.00 liters. Bottles with an average content of 3.08 liters or more are accepted 95 percent of the time. Bottles with an average content of 2.97 liters or less are to be accepted 10 percent of the time. The standard deviation of the bottle contents is unknown. However, management feels that a reasonable estimate is 0.2 liters. Find a variable sampling plan.

Solution. We have $\overline{X}_1 = 3.08$, $\alpha = 0.05$, $\overline{X}_2 = 2.97$, $\beta = 0.10$, $\hat{\sigma} = 0.2$. The parameter λ given by Equation 10.14 is calculated as

$$\lambda = \frac{|3.08 - 2.97|}{0.2} = 0.55$$

From Figure 10-5, for $\alpha = 0.05$, $\lambda = 0.55$, and a probability of acceptance of 0.10, the sample size is approximately 30. From Appendix A-4, the t-statistic for a lower tail area of $\alpha = 0.05$ and 29 degrees of freedom is -1.699. The sampling plan operates as follows. A random sample of 30 bottles is chosen from the lot, and the sample average $(\overline{X})$ and sample standard deviation s are computed. Given the values of $\overline{X}$ and s, the t-statistic is computed as

$$t = \frac{\overline{X} - 3.08}{s/\sqrt{30}}$$

If $t < -1.699$, the lot is rejected. Otherwise, the lot is accepted.

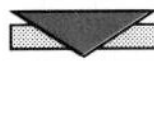

10-4 VARIABLE SAMPLING PLANS TO ESTIMATE THE LOT PROPORTION NONCONFORMING

Assume that the quality characteristic is normally distributed with a known standard deviation σ. A relationship can be established between the sample average $\overline{X}$, the process standard deviation σ, and the lot percent nonconforming. If a lower specification limit L is given, a standard normal deviate is found from

$$Z_L = \frac{\overline{X} - L}{\sigma} \tag{10.16}$$

Alternatively, if the upper specification limit U is given, the standard normal deviate is calculated as

$$Z_U = \frac{U - \overline{X}}{\sigma} \tag{10.17}$$

An estimate of the lot proportion nonconforming is the area under the portion of the normal curve that falls outside Z_L or Z_U. Note that as the sample mean moves further away from a specification limit, the value of the corresponding deviate increases and the percent nonconforming decreases.

There are two methods (Duncan, 1986) that are commonly used to estimate the proportion nonconforming of a lot: *Form 1* (the k-method) and *Form 2* (the M-method). With Form 1, the standard normal deviate, Z_L or Z_U, is compared to a critical value k. If Z_L or Z_U is greater than or equal to k, the lot is accepted; otherwise, the lot is rejected.

With Form 2, the lot percent nonconforming is estimated by first modifying the indices Z_L and Z_U to obtain the indices Q_L and Q_U, which are unbiased and have minimum variance (Lieberman and Resnikoff, 1955). If a lower specification limit L is given, Q_L is obtained as

$$Q_L = \frac{\overline{X} - L}{\sigma}\sqrt{\frac{n}{n-1}} = Z_L\sqrt{\frac{n}{n-1}} \tag{10.18}$$

If an upper specification limit U is given, Q_U is found as

$$Q_U = \frac{U - \overline{X}}{\sigma}\sqrt{\frac{n}{n-1}} = Z_U\sqrt{\frac{n}{n-1}} \tag{10.19}$$

An estimate $\hat{p}$ of the lot percent nonconforming is obtained by finding the portion of the area under the standard normal distribution (Appendix A-3) that falls outside Q_L or Q_U. The decision-making rule is as follows. If $\hat{p}$ is greater than a maximum allowable value M, the lot is rejected; otherwise, the lot is accepted.

Derivation of a Variable Sampling Plan with a Single Specification Limit and Known Process Standard Deviation

Suppose the following conditions must be satisfied. The probability of rejecting lots of a good quality level for which the proportion nonconforming is p_1 should be equal to α. The probability of accepting lots of a poor quality level for which the proportion nonconforming is p_2 should be equal to β. Therefore, the OC curve of the sampling plan should pass through the two points $(1-\alpha, p_1)$ and (β, p_2). Let Z_α and Z_β denote the upper tail percentile points of the standard normal distribution such that the tail areas are α and β, respectively. Suppose a lower specification limit L is given.

Let μ_1 denote the process mean for which the fraction nonconforming is p_1, as shown in Figure 10-6*a*. Denoting the corresponding standard normal deviate as Z_1, we have

$$Z_1 = (\mu_1 - L)/\sigma$$

where the tail area outside Z_1 is p_1. Similarly, we have

$$Z_2 = (\mu_2 - L)/\sigma$$

where the tail area outside Z_2 is p_2.

Note that the formulas for Z_1 and Z_2 differ from the usual definition of the standard normal deviate. Writing them in this format makes them positive; the values corresponding to the tail areas of the standard normal distribution that are outside the deviates Z_1 or Z_2 may be looked up. Given σ, we can determine the process mean locations μ_1 and μ_2.

Figure 10-6*b* shows the distribution of the sample averages; the relationship among μ_1, μ_2, α, and β is shown. Under Form 1, the lot is accepted if $(\overline{X} - L)/\sigma \geq k$, which is equivalent to the condition

$$\frac{\overline{X} - \mu}{(\sigma/\sqrt{n})} \geq \left(k - \frac{\mu - L}{\sigma}\right)\sqrt{n}$$

Using the relation $Z_1 = (\mu_1 - L)/\sigma$ and the requirement of accepting lots of good quality (with process mean at μ_1) with a probability of $1-\alpha$, we have

$$P\left[\frac{\overline{X} - \mu}{\sigma/\sqrt{n}} \geq (k - Z_1)\sqrt{n}\right] = 1 - \alpha$$

If $Z_{1-\alpha}$ is the standard normal deviate such that the probability of falling outside it is $1-\alpha$, we have

$$(k - Z_1)\sqrt{n} = Z_{1-\alpha}$$

Note that $Z_{1-\alpha} = -Z_\alpha$, where Z_α represents the standard normal deviate such that the probability of falling outside it is α. For $\alpha < 0.50$, $Z_{1-\alpha}$ will be negative, and Z_α will be positive. Hence,

$$(k - Z_1)\sqrt{n} = -Z_\alpha \qquad (10.20)$$

Using the relation $Z_2 = (\mu_2 - L)/\sigma$ and the requirement of accepting lots of poor quality (with process mean at μ_2) with a probability of β, we have

$$P\left[\frac{\overline{X} - \mu}{\sigma/\sqrt{n}} \geq (k - Z_2)/\sqrt{n}\right] = \beta$$

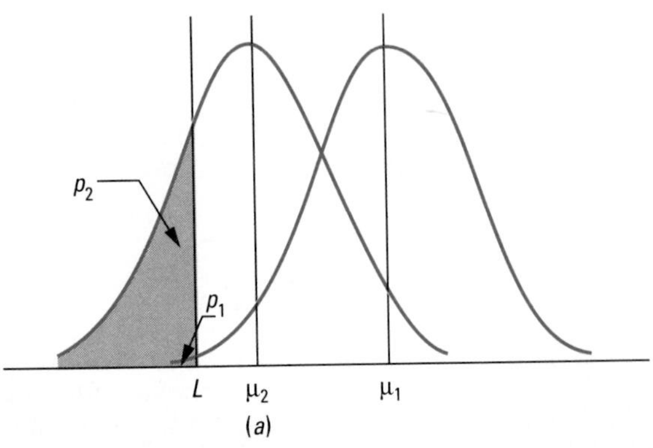

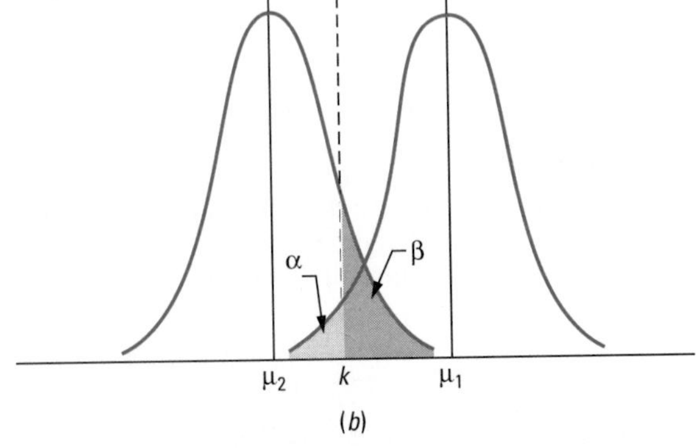

Figure 10-6 Distributions of (*a*) the quality characteristic, X, and (*b*) the sample average of the quality characteristic, $\overline{X}$.

Denoting Z_β as the standard normal deviate such that the probability of falling outside it is β, we have

$$(k - Z_2)\sqrt{n} = Z_\beta \qquad (10.21)$$

Upon solving Equations 10.20 and 10.21 simultaneously, we get the sample size as

$$n = \left(\frac{Z_\alpha + Z_\beta}{Z_1 - Z_2}\right)^2 \qquad (10.22)$$

The value of k can be found from either of the following equations:

$$k = Z_1 - Z_\alpha/\sqrt{n} \qquad (10.23)$$

$$k = Z_2 + Z_\beta/\sqrt{n} \qquad (10.24)$$

The use of Equation 10.23 or 10.24 is influenced by whether it is desired to exactly achieve the value of α or β, respectively.

Using Form 1, the procedure for the variable sampling plan is as follows. A random sample of size n is selected. The sample mean $\overline{X}$ is found. Given a lower specification limit L, Z_L is found from Equation 10.16. The value of k is found from Equation 10.23 or 10.24, depending on whether it is desired to exactly achieve the value of α or β, respectively. Sometimes, the value of k is chosen as the average of the values obtained using Equations 10.23 and 10.24. If $Z_L \geq k$, the lot is accepted. Otherwise, the lot is rejected.

Using Form 2, if a lower specification limit L is given, a sample of size n is selected. The sample mean $\overline{X}$ is found. The value of Q_L is computed using Equation 10.18, and the proportion of the distribution ($\hat{p}$) that exceeds this value is found from Appendix A-3. The maximum allowable proportion nonconforming, M, is found from Appendix A-3 by determining the area that exceeds the standard normal value of $k\sqrt{n/(n-1)}$, where k is found from Equation 10.23, Equation 10.24, or the average of both of these values. If $\hat{p} \leq M$, the lot is accepted. Otherwise, the lot is rejected.

For Form 1, if an upper specification limit U is specified, a similar procedure is adopted. A random sample of size n is selected from a lot, where n is given by Equation 10.22. The sample average $\overline{X}$ is computed. Given the process standard deviation σ, Z_U is found from Equation 10.17. If $Z_U \geq k$, where k is found from Equation 10.23, Equation 10.24, or the average of these two values, the lot is accepted. Otherwise, the lot is rejected. The procedure for using Form 2 with an upper specification limit is similar to that described above for the case involving a lower specification limit.

Example 10-4: In the manufacture of heavy-duty utility bags for household use, the lower specification limit for the carrying load is 100 kg. It is desired to accept lots that are 2 percent nonconforming with a probability of 0.92. For lots that are 12 percent nonconforming, the desired probability of acceptance is 0.10. The standard deviation of the carrying load is known to be 8 kg. Find a variable sampling plan, and explain its operation.

Solution. We have $L = 100$, $p_1 = 0.02$, $\alpha = 0.08$, $p_2 = 0.12$, $\beta = 0.10$, and $\sigma = 8$. From the standard normal distribution tables in Appendix A-3, we get $Z_1 = 2.055$, $Z_2 = 1.175$, $Z_\alpha = 1.405$, and $Z_\beta = 1.282$. The sample size is calculated to be

$$n = \left(\frac{1.405 + 1.282}{2.055 - 1.175}\right)^2 = 9.323 \simeq 10$$

If we want to satisfy the value of $\alpha = 0.08$ exactly, then k is found as

$$k = 2.055 - 1.405/\sqrt{10} = 1.611$$

Suppose a sample of 10 bags is selected and the sample average of the carrying load is 110 kg. Decision-making procedures using both Form 1 and Form 2 are described below.

First, consider the procedure for the variable sampling plan using Form 1. We calculate Z_L using Equation 10.16 as follows:

$$Z_L = \frac{110 - 100}{8} = 1.25$$

Since $Z_L < k$, the decision based on Form 1 is to reject the lot.

To demonstrate the use of Form 2, we calculate Q_L using Equation 10.18 as follows:

$$Q_L = 1.25\sqrt{10/9} = 1.3176 \simeq 1.32$$

From Appendix A-3, the proportion of area that falls outside the standard normal value of 1.32 is 0.0934. This is the estimated proportion of nonconforming items ($\hat{p}$). The maximum allowable proportion nonconforming, M, is found by first calculating the standard normal value as

$$k\sqrt{n/(n-1)} = 1.611\sqrt{10/9} = 1.698 \simeq 1.70$$

From Appendix A-3, the area above this standard normal value of 1.70 is 0.0446, which is the maximum allowable proportion nonconforming M. Since $\hat{p} > M$, the decision is to reject the lot, which is consistent with the decision based on Form 1.

10-5 STANDARDIZED PLANS—*ANSI/ASQC Z1.9* AND *MIL–STD 414*

Military Standard 414 (MIL–STD 414) is a lot-by-lot acceptance sampling plan for variables. This standard was developed as an alternative to *MIL–STD 105 E* (discussed in Chapter 9), which is a plan for inspection by attributes. The civilian version of this plan is *ANSI/ASQC Z1.9,* which was last updated in 1980. This section discusses *ANSI/ASQC Z1.9,* which has been revised to match *ANSI/ASQC Z1.4* (a standardized attribute inspection plan discussed in Chapter 9). An international version of *ANSI/ASQC Z1.9* is *ISO 3951.*

ANSI/ASQC Z1.9 is an AQL-based plan in which it is assumed that the distribution of the quality characteristic is normal. Three types of inspection (normal, tightened, and reduced) are provided in the standard. Switching may take place between these types; the rules for switching are the same as those described for *ANSI/ASQC Z1.4* in Chapter 9. The recent quality history of the product influences the type of inspection. Furthermore, there are three general inspection levels, I, II, and III, and two special levels, S-3 and S-4. The choice of general inspection level is influenced by such factors as the unit inspection cost and the desired degree of discrimination between acceptable and unacceptable products. Inspection level I is used when less discrimination can be tolerated and the sample sizes are small. Level III is used when more discrimination is desired and the sample sizes are larger. Unless otherwise specified, general inspection level II is typically used.

The plans in *ANSI/ASQC Z1.9* may be used in conjunction with single or double specification limits. As described in the previous section, two methods of decision making, namely Form 1 or Form 2, may be used. For double specification limits, however, only Form 2 may be used. Form 1 uses a critical value for the standardized distance, expressed in terms of the standard deviation, between the process mean and a given specification limit. If this standardized distance is greater than or equal to k, where k is a standard value tabulated in *ANSI/ASQC Z1.9,* the lot is accepted. Form 2, on the other hand, uses an estimate of the percentage of nonconforming items that fall outside the specifications. If this estimate is less than or equal to M, where M is a standard value that is tabulated in the plan, the lot is accepted.

ANSI/ASQC Z1.9 is divided into four major sections. Section A provides definitions of relevant terminology, a general description of the plans, and the OC curves of the various plans. It also contains an AQL conversion table, which is used to select a value for the AQL to be used with the tables, in case the desired value does not match the ones listed in the standard. The AQL values range from 0 to 10.9 percent nonconforming. Table 10-1 shows the AQL conversion table. Also included in Section A is the sample size code letter table, which is shown in Table 10-2. Given the lot size and the general inspection level, the sample size code letter is found from Table 10-2.

TABLE 10-1 **AQL conversion table**

For specified AQL values falling within these ranges	Use this *AQL* value
— to 0.109	0.10
0.110 to 0.164	0.15
0.165 to 0.279	0.25
0.280 to 0.439	0.40
0.440 to 0.699	0.65
0.700 to 1.09	1.0
1.10 to 1.64	1.5
1.65 to 2.79	2.5
2.80 to 4.39	4.0
4.40 to 6.99	6.5
7.00 to 10.9	10.0

Source: American Society for Quality Control (1980), ANSI/ASQC Z1.9–1980: *American National Standard—Sampling Procedures and Tables for Inspection by Variables for Percent Nonconforming.* Reprinted with the permission of ASQC.

Section B contains sampling plans for circumstances in which the population or process variability is unknown and is estimated by the sample standard deviation. Section C contains sampling plans for circumstances in which the process variability

TABLE 10-2 **Sample size code letters**

	Inspection levels				
	Special		General		
Lot size	S-3	S-4	I	II	III
2 to 8	B	B	B	B	C
9 to 15	B	B	B	B	D
16 to 25	B	B	B	C	E
26 to 50	B	B	C	D	F
51 to 90	B	B	D	E	G
91 to 150	B	C	E	F	H
151 to 280	B	D	F	G	I
281 to 400	C	E	G	H	J
401 to 500	C	E	G	I	J
501 to 1,200	D	F	H	J	K
1,201 to 3,200	E	G	I	K	L
3,201 to 10,000	F	H	J	L	M
10,001 to 35,000	G	I	K	M	N
35,001 to 150,000	H	J	L	N	P
150,001 to 500,000	H	K	M	P	P
500,001 and over	H	K	N	P	P

Source: American Society for Quality Control (1980), ANSI/ASQC Z1.9–1980: *American National Standard—Sampling Procedures and Tables for Inspection by Variables for Percent Nonconforming.* Reprinted with the permission of ASQC.

is unknown and is estimated by the sample range. Usually, the sample size is smaller for plans that use the standard deviation method compared to those that use the range method. Finally, Section D contains plans for circumstances in which the process variability is known. The sample sizes are usually smaller for the variability-known plans compared to the variability-unknown plans for the same level of protection. However, the process variability is usually unknown and must be estimated. This discussion is confined to cases for which the process variability is unknown and the standard deviation method is used.

Variability Unknown—Standard Deviation Method

If the process variability is unknown, it must be estimated from the sample information. In some instances the sample standard deviation is used as an estimate. For single specification limit, Form 1 or Form 2 may be used, but for double specification limits, Form 2 must be used.

Single Specification Limit—Form 1 Consider using Form 1 for a single specification limit. Table 10-1 is used to determine the AQL value to be used in the standard. Information about the lot size and the general inspection level may be used to find the sample size code letter from Table 10-2. Given the AQL value and the sample size code letter, Table 10-3 (for normal or tightened inspection) or Table 10-4 (for reduced inspection) is then used to determine the sample size n and the acceptability constant k for use with Form 1.

Once the sampling plan is known, a random sample of size n is selected from the lot, and the sample mean $\overline{X}$, and the sample standard deviation s are calculated. The standard normal deviate $Z_L = (\overline{X} - L)/s$ or $Z_U = (U - \overline{X})/s$ is calculated, depending on whether a lower specification limit L or an upper specification limit U is given. The value of Z_L or Z_U is compared to the acceptability constant k. If Z_L or Z_U is greater than or equal to k, the lot is accepted; otherwise, the lot is rejected.

Single Specification Limit—Form 2 In using Form 2 for a single specification limit, the first part of the procedure is the same as with Form 1. The AQL value to be used in the standard is found from Table 10-1. Given the lot size and the general inspection level, the sample size code letter is found from Table 10-2. Given the sample size code letter and the AQL value, Table 10-5 (for normal or tightened inspection) or Table 10-6 (reduced inspection) is used to find the sample size n and the maximum allowable percent nonconforming M.

Once the parameters of the sampling plan are known, a random sample of size n is selected from the lot, and the sample mean $\overline{X}$ and sample standard deviation s are calculated. Next, the quality index $Q_L = (\overline{X} - L)/s$ or $Q_U = (U - \overline{X})/s$ is calculated, based on whether a lower specification limit L or an upper specification limit U is given. The estimated lot percent nonconforming, $\hat{p}_L$ or $\hat{p}_U$, is found from Table 10-7. The decision-making rule for Form 2 is as follows. If $\hat{p}_L$ or $\hat{p}_U$ is less than or equal to M, the lot is accepted; otherwise, the lot is rejected.

Example 10-5: A bakery has to control the temperature setting of the oven for producing a consistently good quality of fresh-baked products. The bakery has estimated an upper specification limit for the temperature to be 300°. The lot size is 50, inspection is normal, AQL is 0.5 percent, and the general inspection level is level II. Find the variable sampling plan using *ANSI/ASQC Z1.9* and Form 1.

Solution. Using Table 10-1 to find the AQL to be used in the standard yields a value of 0.65 percent. Table 10-2 is used to find the sample size code letter. For a lot size of 50 and general inspection level II, the sample size code letter is D. For normal inspection, using Table 10-3, for an AQL of 0.65 percent and a sample size code letter of D, the sample size n is 5, and the acceptability constant k is 1.65.

Suppose the following sample of 5 readings of the oven temperature is chosen: 220, 230, 250, 320, 260.

The sample mean $\overline{X}$ is

$$\overline{X} = \frac{220 + 230 + 250 + 320 + 260}{5} = 256$$

The sample standard deviation is given by

$$s = \sqrt{\frac{\sum X_i^2 - (\sum X_i)^2/n}{n - 1}}$$

$$= \sqrt{\frac{333800 - (1280)^2/5}{4}} = 39.115$$

The standardized deviate Z_U is

$$Z_U = \frac{U - \overline{X}}{s}$$

$$= (300 - 256)/39.115 = 1.125$$

Since $Z_U = 1.125 < k = 1.65$, the decision is to reject the lot.

Example 10-6: Consider Example 10-5. Demonstrate the decision-making procedure for a variable sampling plan using Form 2.

Solution. For a lot size of 50 and general inspection level II, the sample size code letter is still D. For normal inspection, sample size code letter D, and AQL = 0.65 percent, Table 10-5 gives a sample size n of 5 and a maximum allowable percent nonconforming M of 1.33 percent.

TABLE 10-3 Master table for normal and tightened inspection for plans that are based on an unknown variability and use the standard deviation method (single specification limit—Form 1)

Sample size code letter	Sample size	Acceptable Quality Levels (normal inspection)											
		T	.10	.15	.25	.40	.65	1.00	1.50	2.50	4.00	6.50	10.00
		k	k	k	k	k	k	k	k	k	k	k	k
B	3	↓	↓	↓	↓	↓	↓	↓	↓	1.12	.958	.765	.566
C	4	↓	↓	↓	↓	↓	↓	1.45	1.34	1.17	1.01	.814	.617
D	5	↓	↓	↓	↓	↓	1.65	1.53	1.40	1.24	1.07	.874	.675
E	7	↓	↓	↓	2.00	1.88	1.75	1.62	1.50	1.33	1.15	.955	.755
F	10	↓	↓	2.24	2.11	1.98	1.84	1.72	1.58	1.41	1.23	1.03	.828
G	15	2.53	2.42	2.32	2.20	2.06	1.91	1.79	1.65	1.47	1.30	1.09	.886
H	20	2.58	2.47	2.36	2.24	2.11	1.96	1.82	1.69	1.51	1.33	1.12	.917
I	25	2.61	2.50	2.40	2.26	2.14	1.98	1.85	1.72	1.53	1.35	1.14	.936
J	35	2.65	2.54	2.45	2.31	2.18	2.03	1.89	1.76	1.57	1.39	1.18	.969
K	50	2.71	2.60	2.50	2.35	2.22	2.08	1.93	1.80	1.61	1.42	1.21	1.00
L	75	2.77	2.66	2.55	2.41	2.27	2.12	1.98	1.84	1.65	1.46	1.24	1.03
M	100	2.80	2.69	2.58	2.43	2.29	2.14	2.00	1.86	1.67	1.48	1.26	1.05
N	150	2.84	2.73	2.61	2.47	2.33	2.18	2.03	1.89	1.70	1.51	1.29	1.07
P	200	2.85	2.73	2.62	2.47	2.33	2.18	2.04	1.89	1.70	1.51	1.29	1.07
		.10	.15	.25	.40	.65	1.00	1.50	2.50	4.00	6.50	10.00	
		Acceptable Quality Levels (tightened inspection)											

All AQL values are in percent nonconforming. T denotes plan used exclusively on tightened inspection and provides symbol for identification of appropriate OC curve.

↓ Use first sampling plan below arrow; that is, both sample size as well as k value. When sample size equals or exceeds lot size, every item in the lot must be inspected.

Source: American Society for Quality Control (1980), ANSI/ASQC Z1.9–1980: *American National Standard—Sampling Procedures and Tables for Inspection by Variables for Percent Nonconforming*. Reprinted with the permission of ASQC.

TABLE 10-4 Master table for reduced inspection for plans that are based on an unknown variability and use the standard deviation method (single specification limit—Form 1)

Sample size code letter	Sample size	Acceptable Quality Levels										
		.10	.15	.25	.40	.65	1.00	1.50	2.50	4.00	6.50	10.00
		k	k	k	k	k	k	k	k	k	k	k
B	3	↓	↓	↓	↓	↓	↓	1.12	.958	.765	.566	.341
C	3	↓	↓	↓	↓	↓	↓	1.12	.958	.765	.566	.341
D	3	↓	↓	↓	↓	↓	↓	1.12	.958	.765	.566	.341
E	3	↓	↓	↓	↓	↓	↓	1.12	.958	.765	.566	.341
F	4	↓	↓	↓	↓	1.45	1.34	1.17	1.01	.814	.617	.393
G	5	↓	↓	↓	1.65	1.53	1.40	1.24	1.07	.874	.675	.455
H	7	↓	2.00	1.88	1.75	1.62	1.50	1.33	1.15	.955	.755	.536
I	10	2.24	2.11	1.98	1.84	1.72	1.58	1.41	1.23	1.03	.828	.611
J	15	2.32	2.20	2.06	1.91	1.79	1.65	1.47	1.30	1.09	.886	.664
K	20	2.36	2.24	2.11	1.96	1.82	1.69	1.51	1.33	1.12	.917	.695
L	25	2.40	2.26	2.14	1.98	1.85	1.72	1.53	1.35	1.14	.936	.712
M	30	2.41	2.28	2.15	2.00	1.86	1.73	1.55	1.36	1.15	.946	.723
N	50	2.50	2.35	2.22	2.08	1.93	1.80	1.61	1.42	1.21	1.00	.774
P	75	2.55	2.41	2.27	2.12	1.98	1.84	1.65	1.46	1.24	1.03	.804

All AQL values are in percent nonconforming.

↓ Use first sampling plan below arrow; that is, both sample size as well as k value. When sample size equals or exceeds lot size, every item in the lot must be inspected.

Source: American Society for Quality Control (1980), ANSI/ASQC Z1.9–1980: *American National Standard—Sampling Procedures and Tables for Inspection by Variables for Percent Nonconforming*. Reprinted with the permission of ASQC.

TABLE 10-5 Master table for normal and tightened inspection for plans that are based on an unknown variability and use the standard deviation method (double specification limit and Form 2—single specification limit)

Sample Size code letter	Sample size	Acceptable Quality Levels (normal inspection)											
		T	.10	.15	.25	.40	.65	1.00	1.50	2.50	4.00	6.50	10.00
		M	M	M	M	M	M	M	M	M	M	M	M
B	3	↓	↓	↓	↓	↓	↓	↓	↓	7.59	18.86	26.94	33.69
C	4	↓	↓	↓	↓	↓	↓	1.53	5.50	10.92	16.45	22.86	29.45
D	5	↓	↓	↓	↓	↓	1.33	3.32	5.83	9.80	14.39	20.19	26.56
E	7	↓	↓	↓	0.422	1.06	2.14	3.55	5.35	8.40	12.20	17.35	23.29
F	10	↓	↓	0.349	0.716	1.30	2.17	3.26	4.77	7.29	10.54	15.17	20.74
G	15	0.186	0.312	0.503	0.818	1.31	2.11	3.05	4.31	6.56	9.46	13.71	18.94
H	20	0.228	0.365	0.544	0.846	1.29	2.05	2.95	4.09	6.17	8.92	12.99	18.03
I	25	0.250	0.380	0.551	0.877	1.29	2.00	2.86	3.97	5.97	8.63	12.57	17.51
J	35	0.264	0.388	0.535	0.847	1.23	1.87	2.68	3.70	5.57	8.10	11.87	16.65
K	50	0.250	0.363	0.503	0.789	1.17	1.71	2.49	3.45	5.20	7.61	11.23	15.87
L	75	0.228	0.330	0.467	0.720	1.07	1.60	2.29	3.20	4.87	7.15	10.63	15.13
M	100	0.220	0.317	0.447	0.689	1.02	1.53	2.20	3.07	4.69	6.91	10.32	14.75
N	150	0.203	0.293	0.413	0.638	0.949	1.43	2.05	2.89	4.43	6.57	9.88	14.20
P	200	0.204	0.294	0.414	0.637	0.945	1.42	2.04	2.87	4.40	6.53	9.81	14.12
		.10	.15	.25	.40	.65	1.00	1.50	2.50	4.00	6.50	10.00	
		Acceptable Quality Levels (tightened inspection)											

All AQL values are in percent nonconforming. T denotes plan used exclusively on tightened inspection and provides symbol for identification of appropriate OC curve.

↓ Use first sampling plan below arrow; that is, both sample size as well as M value. When sample size equals or exceeds lot size, every item in the lot must be inspected.

Source: American Society for Quality Control (1980), ANSI/ASQC Z1.9–1980: *American National Standard—Sampling Procedures and Tables for Inspection by Variables for Percent Nonconforming*. Reprinted with the permission of ASQC.

TABLE 10-6 Master table for reduced inspection for plans that are based on an unknown variability and use the standard deviation method (double specification limit and Form 2—single specification limit)

Sample size code letter	Sample size	Acceptable Quality Levels										
		.10	.15	.25	.40	.65	1.00	1.50	2.50	4.00	6.50	10.00
		M	M	M	M	M	M	M	M	M	M	M
B	3	↓	↓	↓	↓	↓	↓	7.59	18.86	26.94	33.69	40.47
C	3							7.59	18.86	26.94	33.69	40.47
D	3							7.59	18.86	26.94	33.69	40.47
E	3							7.59	18.86	26.94	33.69	40.47
F	4					1.53	5.50	10.92	16.45	22.86	29.45	36.90
G	5				1.33	3.32	5.83	9.80	14.39	20.19	26.56	33.99
H	7		0.422	1.06	2.14	3.55	5.35	8.40	12.20	17.35	23.29	30.50
I	10	0.349	0.716	1.30	2.17	3.26	4.77	7.29	10.54	15.17	20.74	27.57
J	15	0.503	0.818	1.31	2.11	3.05	4.31	6.56	9.46	13.71	18.94	25.61
K	20	0.544	0.846	1.29	2.05	2.95	4.09	6.17	8.92	12.99	18.03	24.53
L	25	0.551	0.877	1.29	2.00	2.86	3.97	5.97	8.63	12.57	17.51	23.97
M	30	0.581	0.879	1.29	1.98	2.83	3.91	5.86	8.47	12.36	17.24	23.58
N	50	0.503	0.789	1.17	1.71	2.49	3.45	5.20	7.61	11.23	15.87	22.00
P	75	0.467	0.720	1.07	1.60	2.29	3.20	4.87	7.15	10.63	15.13	21.11

All AQL values are in percent nonconforming.

↓ Use first sampling plan below arrow; that is, both sample size as well as M value. When sample size equals or exceds lot size, every item in the lot must be inspected.

Source: American Society for Quality Control (1980), ANSI/ASQC Z1.9–1980: *American National Standard—Sampling Procedures and Tables for Inspection by Variables for Percent Nonconforming*. Reprinted with the permission of ASQC.

TABLE 10-7 Table for estimating the lot percent nonconforming using the standard deviation method

Q_U or Q_L	Sample Size														
	3	4	5	7	10	15	20	25	30	35	50	75	100	150	200
0	50.00	50.00	50.00	50.00	50.00	50.00	50.00	50.00	50.00	50.00	50.00	50.00	50.00	50.00	50.00
.1	47.24	46.67	46.44	46.26	46.16	46.10	46.08	46.06	46.05	46.05	46.04	46.03	46.03	46.02	46.02
.2	44.46	43.33	42.90	42.54	42.35	42.24	42.19	42.16	42.15	42.13	42.11	42.10	42.09	42.08	42.08
.3	41.63	40.00	39.37	38.87	38.60	38.44	38.37	38.33	38.31	38.29	38.27	38.25	38.24	38.22	38.22
.31	41.35	39.67	39.02	38.50	38.23	38.06	37.99	37.95	37.93	37.91	37.89	37.87	37.86	37.84	37.84
.32	41.06	39.33	38.67	38.14	37.86	37.69	37.62	37.58	37.55	37.54	37.51	37.49	37.48	37.46	37.46
.33	40.77	39.00	38.32	37.78	37.49	37.31	37.24	37.20	37.18	37.16	37.13	37.11	37.10	37.09	37.08
.34	40.49	38.67	37.97	37.42	37.12	36.94	36.87	36.83	36.80	36.78	36.75	36.73	36.72	36.71	36.71
.35	40.20	38.33	37.62	37.06	36.75	36.57	36.49	36.45	36.43	36.41	36.38	36.36	36.35	36.33	36.33
.36	39.91	38.00	37.28	36.69	36.38	36.20	36.12	36.08	36.05	36.04	36.01	35.98	35.97	35.96	35.96
.37	39.62	37.67	36.93	36.33	36.02	35.83	35.75	35.71	35.68	35.66	35.63	35.61	35.60	35.59	35.58
.38	39.33	37.33	36.58	35.98	35.65	35.46	35.38	35.34	35.31	35.29	35.26	35.24	35.23	35.22	35.21
.39	39.03	37.00	36.23	35.62	35.29	35.10	35.01	34.97	34.94	34.93	34.89	34.87	34.86	34.85	34.84
.40	38.74	36.67	35.88	35.26	34.93	34.73	34.65	34.60	34.58	34.56	34.53	34.50	34.49	34.48	34.47
.41	38.45	36.33	35.54	34.90	34.57	34.37	34.28	34.24	34.21	34.19	34.16	34.13	34.12	34.11	34.10
.42	38.15	36.00	35.19	34.55	34.21	34.00	33.92	33.87	33.85	33.83	33.79	33.77	33.76	33.74	33.74
.43	37.85	35.67	34.85	34.19	33.85	33.64	33.56	33.51	33.48	33.46	33.43	33.40	33.39	33.38	33.37
.44	37.56	35.33	34.50	33.84	33.49	33.28	33.20	33.15	33.12	33.10	33.07	33.04	33.03	33.02	33.01
.45	37.26	35.00	34.16	33.49	33.13	32.92	32.84	32.79	32.76	32.74	32.71	32.68	32.67	32.66	32.65
.46	36.96	34.67	33.81	33.13	32.78	32.57	32.48	32.43	32.40	32.38	32.35	32.32	32.31	32.30	32.29
.47	36.66	34.33	33.47	32.78	32.42	32.21	32.12	32.07	32.04	32.02	31.99	31.96	31.95	31.94	31.93
.48	36.35	34.00	33.12	32.43	32.07	31.85	31.77	31.72	31.69	31.67	31.63	31.61	31.60	31.58	31.58
.49	36.05	33.67	32.78	32.08	31.72	31.50	31.41	31.36	31.33	31.31	31.28	31.25	31.24	31.23	31.22
.50	35.75	33.33	32.44	31.74	31.37	31.15	31.06	31.01	30.98	30.96	30.93	30.90	30.89	30.87	30.87
.51	35.44	33.00	32.10	31.39	31.02	30.80	30.71	30.66	30.63	30.61	30.57	30.55	30.54	30.52	30.52
.52	35.13	32.67	31.76	31.04	30.67	30.45	30.36	30.31	30.28	30.26	30.23	30.20	30.19	30.17	30.17
.53	34.82	32.33	31.42	30.70	30.32	30.10	30.01	29.96	29.93	29.91	29.88	29.85	29.84	29.83	29.82
.54	34.51	32.00	31.08	30.36	29.98	29.76	29.67	29.62	29.59	29.57	29.53	29.51	29.49	29.48	29.48
.55	34.20	31.67	30.74	30.01	29.64	29.41	29.32	29.27	29.24	29.22	29.19	29.16	29.15	29.14	29.13
.56	33.88	31.33	30.40	29.67	29.29	29.07	28.98	28.93	28.90	28.88	28.85	28.82	28.81	28.79	28.79
.57	33.57	31.00	30.06	29.33	28.95	28.73	28.64	28.59	28.56	28.54	28.51	28.48	28.47	28.45	28.45
.58	33.25	30.67	29.73	28.99	28.61	28.39	28.30	28.25	28.22	28.20	28.17	28.14	28.13	28.12	28.11
.59	32.93	30.33	29.39	28.66	28.28	28.05	27.96	27.92	27.89	27.87	27.83	27.81	27.79	27.78	27.77
.60	32.61	30.00	29.05	28.32	27.94	27.72	27.63	27.58	27.55	27.53	27.50	27.47	27.46	27.45	27.44
.61	32.28	29.67	28.72	27.98	27.60	27.39	27.30	27.25	27.22	27.20	27.16	27.14	27.13	27.11	27.11
.62	31.96	29.33	28.39	27.65	27.27	27.05	26.96	26.92	26.89	26.87	26.83	26.81	26.80	26.78	26.78
.63	31.63	29.00	28.05	27.32	26.94	26.72	26.63	26.59	26.56	26.54	26.50	26.48	26.47	26.45	26.45
.64	31.30	28.67	27.72	26.99	26.61	26.39	26.31	26.26	26.23	26.21	26.18	26.15	26.14	26.13	26.12
.65	30.97	28.33	27.39	26.66	26.28	26.07	25.98	25.93	25.90	25.88	25.85	25.83	25.82	25.80	25.80
.66	30.63	28.00	27.06	26.33	25.96	25.74	25.66	25.61	25.58	25.56	25.53	25.51	25.49	25.48	25.48
.67	30.30	27.67	26.73	26.00	25.63	25.42	25.33	25.29	25.26	25.24	25.21	25.19	25.17	25.16	25.16
.68	29.96	27.33	26.40	25.68	25.31	25.10	25.01	24.97	24.94	24.92	24.89	24.87	24.86	24.84	24.84
.69	29.61	27.00	26.07	25.35	24.99	24.78	24.70	24.65	24.62	24.60	24.57	24.55	24.54	24.53	24.52

Source: American Society for Quality Control (1980), ANSI/ASQC Z1.9–1980: *American National Standard—Sampling Procedures and Tables for Inspection by Variables for Percent Nonconforming*. Reprinted with the permission of ASQC.

TABLE 10-7 *(Continued)*

Q_U or Q_L	Sample Size														
	3	4	5	7	10	15	20	25	30	35	50	75	100	150	200
.70	29.27	26.67	25.74	25.03	24.67	24.46	24.38	24.33	24.31	24.29	24.26	24.24	24.23	24.21	24.21
.71	28.92	26.33	25.41	24.71	24.35	24.15	24.06	24.02	23.99	23.96	23.95	23.92	23.91	23.90	23.90
.72	28.57	26.00	25.09	24.39	24.03	23.83	23.75	23.71	23.68	23.67	23.64	23.61	23.60	23.59	23.59
.73	28.22	25.67	24.76	24.07	23.72	23.52	23.44	23.40	23.37	23.36	23.33	23.31	23.30	23.29	23.28
.74	27.86	25.33	24.44	23.75	23.41	23.21	23.13	23.09	23.07	23.05	23.02	23.00	22.99	22.98	22.98
.75	27.50	25.00	24.11	23.44	23.10	22.90	22.83	22.79	22.76	22.75	22.72	22.70	22.69	22.68	22.67
.76	27.13	24.67	23.79	23.12	22.79	22.60	22.52	22.48	22.46	22.44	22.42	22.40	22.39	22.38	22.37
.77	26.77	24.33	23.47	22.81	22.48	22.30	22.22	22.18	22.16	22.14	22.12	22.10	22.09	22.08	22.08
.78	26.39	24.00	23.15	22.50	22.18	21.99	21.92	21.89	21.86	21.85	21.82	21.80	21.79	21.78	21.78
.79	26.02	23.67	22.83	22.19	21.87	21.70	21.63	21.59	21.57	21.55	21.53	21.51	21.50	21.49	21.49
.80	25.64	23.33	22.51	21.88	21.57	21.40	21.33	21.29	21.27	21.26	21.23	21.22	21.21	21.20	21.20
.81	25.25	23.00	22.19	21.58	21.27	21.10	21.04	21.00	20.98	20.97	20.94	20.93	20.92	20.91	20.91
.82	24.86	22.67	21.87	21.27	20.98	20.81	20.75	20.71	20.69	20.68	20.65	20.64	20.63	20.62	20.62
.83	24.47	22.33	21.56	20.97	20.68	20.52	20.46	20.42	20.40	20.39	20.37	20.35	20.35	20.34	20.34
.84	24.07	22.00	21.24	20.67	20.39	20.23	20.17	20.14	20.12	20.11	20.09	20.07	20.06	20.06	20.05
.85	23.67	21.67	20.93	20.37	20.10	19.94	19.89	19.86	19.84	19.82	19.80	19.79	19.78	19.78	19.77
.86	23.26	21.33	20.62	20.07	19.81	19.66	19.60	19.57	19.56	19.54	19.53	19.51	19.51	19.50	19.50
.87	22.84	21.00	20.31	19.78	19.52	19.38	19.32	19.30	19.28	19.27	19.25	19.24	19.23	19.22	19.22
.88	22.42	20.67	20.00	19.48	19.23	19.10	19.04	19.02	19.00	18.99	18.98	18.96	18.96	18.95	18.95
.89	21.99	20.33	19.69	19.19	18.95	18.82	18.77	18.74	18.73	18.72	18.70	18.69	18.69	18.68	18.68
.90	21.55	20.00	19.38	18.90	18.67	18.54	18.50	18.47	18.46	18.45	18.43	18.42	18.42	18.41	18.41
.91	21.11	19.67	19.07	18.61	18.39	18.27	18.22	18.20	18.19	18.18	18.17	18.16	18.15	18.15	18.15
.92	20.66	19.33	18.77	18.33	18.11	18.00	17.96	17.94	17.92	17.92	17.90	17.89	17.89	17.88	17.88
.93	20.20	19.00	18.46	18.04	17.84	17.73	17.69	17.67	17.66	17.65	17.64	17.63	17.63	17.62	17.62
.94	19.74	18.67	18.16	17.76	17.57	17.46	17.43	17.41	17.40	17.39	17.38	17.37	17.37	17.36	17.36
.95	19.25	18.33	17.86	17.48	17.29	17.20	17.17	17.15	17.14	17.13	17.12	17.12	17.11	17.11	17.11
.96	18.76	18.00	17.56	17.20	17.03	16.94	16.91	16.89	16.88	16.88	16.87	16.86	16.86	16.86	16.85
.97	18.25	17.67	17.25	16.92	16.76	16.68	16.65	16.63	16.63	16.62	16.61	16.61	16.61	16.60	16.60
.98	17.74	17.33	16.96	16.65	16.49	16.42	16.39	16.38	16.37	16.37	16.36	16.36	16.36	16.36	16.36
.99	17.21	17.00	16.66	16.37	16.23	16.16	16.14	16.13	16.12	16.12	16.12	16.11	16.11	16.11	16.11
1.00	16.67	16.67	16.36	16.10	15.97	15.91	15.89	15.88	15.88	15.87	15.87	15.87	15.87	15.87	15.87
1.01	16.11	16.33	16.07	15.83	15.72	15.66	15.64	15.63	15.63	15.63	15.63	15.62	15.62	15.62	15.62
1.02	15.53	16.00	15.78	15.56	15.46	15.41	15.40	15.39	15.39	15.39	15.38	15.38	15.38	15.38	15.38
1.03	14.93	15.67	15.48	15.30	15.21	15.17	15.15	15.15	15.15	15.15	15.15	15.15	15.15	15.15	15.15
1.04	14.31	15.33	15.19	15.03	14.96	14.92	14.91	14.91	14.91	14.91	14.91	14.91	14.91	14.91	14.91
1.05	13.66	15.00	14.91	14.77	14.71	14.68	14.67	14.67	14.67	14.67	14.68	14.68	14.68	14.68	14.68
1.06	12.98	14.67	14.62	14.51	14.46	14.44	14.44	14.44	14.44	14.44	14.45	14.45	14.45	14.45	14.45
1.07	12.27	14.33	14.33	14.26	14.22	14.20	14.20	14.21	14.21	14.21	14.22	14.22	14.22	14.22	14.23
1.08	11.51	14.00	14.05	14.00	13.97	13.97	13.97	13.98	13.98	13.98	13.99	13.99	14.00	14.00	14.00
1.09	10.71	13.67	13.76	13.75	13.73	13.74	13.74	13.75	13.75	13.76	13.77	13.77	13.77	13.78	13.78

Q_U or Q_L	Sample Size														
	3	4	5	7	10	15	20	25	30	35	50	75	100	150	200
1.10	9.84	13.33	13.48	13.49	13.50	13.51	13.52	13.52	13.53	13.54	13.54	13.55	13.55	13.56	13.56
1.11	8.89	13.00	13.20	13.25	13.26	13.28	13.29	13.30	13.31	13.31	13.32	13.33	13.34	13.34	13.34
1.12	7.82	12.67	12.93	13.00	13.03	13.05	13.07	13.08	13.09	13.10	13.11	13.12	13.12	13.12	13.13
1.13	6.60	12.33	12.65	12.75	12.80	12.83	12.85	12.86	12.87	12.88	12.89	12.90	12.91	12.91	12.92
1.14	5.08	12.00	12.37	12.51	12.57	12.61	12.63	12.65	12.66	12.67	12.68	12.69	12.70	12.70	12.70
1.15	0.29	11.67	12.10	12.27	12.34	12.39	12.42	12.44	12.45	12.46	12.47	12.48	12.49	12.49	12.30
1.16	0.00	11.33	11.83	12.03	12.12	12.18	12.21	12.22	12.24	12.25	12.26	12.28	12.28	12.29	12.29
1.17	0.00	11.00	11.56	11.79	11.90	11.96	12.00	12.02	12.03	12.04	12.06	12.07	12.08	12.08	12.09
1.18	0.00	10.67	11.29	11.56	11.68	11.75	11.79	11.81	11.82	11.84	11.85	11.87	11.88	11.88	11.89
1.19	0.00	10.33	11.02	11.33	11.46	11.54	11.58	11.61	11.62	11.63	11.65	11.67	11.68	11.69	11.69
1.20	0.00	10.00	10.76	11.10	11.24	11.34	11.38	11.41	11.42	11.43	11.46	11.47	11.48	11.49	11.49
1.21	0.00	9.67	10.50	10.87	11.03	11.13	11.18	11.21	11.22	11.24	11.26	11.28	11.29	11.30	11.30
1.22	0.00	9.33	10.23	10.65	10.82	10.93	10.98	11.01	11.03	11.04	11.07	11.09	11.09	11.10	11.11
1.23	0.00	9.00	9.97	10.42	10.61	10.73	10.78	10.81	10.84	10.85	10.88	10.90	10.91	10.91	10.92
1.24	0.00	8.67	9.72	10.20	10.41	10.53	10.59	10.62	10.64	10.66	10.69	10.71	10.72	10.73	10.73
1.25	0.00	8.33	9.46	9.98	10.21	10.34	10.40	10.43	10.46	10.47	10.50	10.52	10.53	10.54	10.55
1.26	0.00	8.00	9.21	9.77	10.00	10.15	10.21	10.25	10.27	10.29	10.32	10.34	10.35	10.36	10.37
1.27	0.00	7.67	8.96	9.55	9.81	9.96	10.02	10.06	10.09	10.10	10.13	10.16	10.17	10.18	10.19
1.28	0.00	7.33	8.71	9.34	9.61	9.77	9.84	9.88	9.90	9.92	9.95	9.98	9.99	10.00	10.01
1.29	0.00	7.00	8.46	9.13	9.42	9.58	9.65	9.70	9.72	9.74	9.78	9.80	9.82	9.83	9.83
1.30	0.00	6.67	8.21	8.93	9.22	9.40	9.48	9.52	9.55	9.57	9.60	9.63	9.64	9.65	9.66
1.31	0.00	6.33	7.97	8.72	9.03	9.22	9.30	9.34	9.37	9.39	9.43	9.46	9.47	9.48	9.49
1.32	0.00	6.00	7.73	8.52	8.85	9.04	9.12	9.17	9.20	9.22	9.26	9.29	9.30	9.31	9.32
1.33	0.00	5.67	7.49	8.32	8.66	8.86	8.95	9.00	9.03	9.05	9.09	9.12	9.13	9.15	9.15
1.34	0.00	5.33	7.25	8.12	8.48	8.69	8.78	8.83	8.86	8.88	8.92	8.95	8.97	8.98	8.99
1.35	0.00	5.00	7.02	7.92	8.30	8.52	8.61	8.66	8.69	8.72	8.76	8.79	8.81	8.82	8.83
1.36	0.00	4.67	6.79	7.73	8.12	8.35	8.44	8.50	8.53	8.55	8.60	8.63	8.65	8.66	8.67
1.37	0.00	4.33	6.56	7.54	7.95	8.18	8.28	8.33	8.37	8.39	8.44	8.47	8.49	8.50	8.51
1.38	0.00	4.00	6.33	7.35	7.77	8.01	8.12	8.17	8.21	8.24	8.25	8.31	8.33	8.35	8.35
1.39	0.00	3.67	6.10	7.17	7.60	7.85	7.96	8.01	8.05	8.08	8.12	8.16	8.18	8.19	8.20
1.40	0.00	3.33	5.88	6.98	7.44	7.69	7.80	7.86	7.90	7.92	7.97	8.01	8.02	8.04	8.05
1.41	0.00	3.00	5.66	6.80	7.27	7.53	7.64	7.70	7.74	7.77	7.82	7.86	7.87	7.89	7.90
1.42	0.00	2.67	5.44	6.62	7.10	7.37	7.49	7.55	7.59	7.62	7.67	7.71	7.73	7.74	7.75
1.43	0.00	2.33	5.23	6.45	6.94	7.22	7.34	7.40	7.44	7.47	7.52	7.56	7.58	7.60	7.61
1.44	0.00	2.00	5.01	6.27	6.78	7.07	7.19	7.26	7.30	7.33	7.38	7.42	7.44	7.46	7.47
1.45	0.00	1.67	4.81	6.10	6.63	6.92	7.04	7.11	7.15	7.18	7.24	7.28	7.30	7.31	7.33
1.46	0.00	1.33	4.60	5.93	6.47	6.77	6.90	6.97	7.01	7.04	7.10	7.14	7.16	7.18	7.19
1.47	0.00	1.00	4.39	5.77	6.32	6.63	6.75	6.83	6.87	6.90	6.96	7.00	7.02	7.04	7.05
1.48	0.00	0.67	4.19	5.60	6.17	6.48	6.61	6.69	6.73	6.77	6.82	6.86	6.88	6.90	6.91
1.49	0.00	0.33	3.99	5.44	6.02	6.34	6.48	6.55	6.60	6.63	6.69	6.73	6.75	6.77	6.78

Q_U or Q_L	Sample Size														
	3	4	5	7	10	15	20	25	30	35	50	75	100	150	200
1.50	0.00	0.00	3.80	5.28	5.87	6.20	6.34	6.41	6.46	6.50	6.55	6.60	6.62	6.64	6.65
1.51	0.00	0.00	3.61	5.13	5.73	6.06	6.20	6.28	6.33	6.36	6.42	6.47	6.49	6.51	6.52
1.52	0.00	0.00	3.42	4.97	5.59	5.93	6.07	6.15	6.20	6.23	6.29	6.34	6.36	6.38	6.39
1.53	0.00	0.00	3.23	4.82	5.45	5.80	5.94	6.02	6.07	6.11	6.17	6.21	6.24	6.26	6.27
1.54	0.00	0.00	3.05	4.67	5.31	5.67	5.81	5.89	5.95	5.98	6.04	6.09	6.11	6.13	6.15
1.55	0.00	0.00	2.87	4.52	5.18	5.54	5.69	5.77	5.82	5.86	5.92	5.97	5.99	6.01	6.02
1.56	0.00	0.00	2.69	4.38	5.05	5.41	5.56	5.65	5.70	5.74	5.80	5.85	5.87	5.89	5.90
1.57	0.00	0.00	2.52	4.24	4.92	5.29	5.44	5.53	5.58	5.62	5.68	5.73	5.75	5.78	5.79
1.58	0.00	0.00	2.35	4.10	4.79	5.16	5.32	5.41	5.46	5.50	5.56	5.61	5.64	5.66	5.67
1.59	0.00	0.00	2.19	3.96	4.66	5.04	5.20	5.29	5.34	5.38	5.45	5.50	5.52	5.54	5.56
1.60	0.00	0.00	2.03	3.83	4.54	4.92	5.09	5.17	5.23	5.27	5.33	5.38	5.41	5.43	5.44
1.61	0.00	0.00	1.87	3.69	4.41	4.81	4.97	5.06	5.12	5.16	5.22	5.27	5.30	5.32	5.33
1.62	0.00	0.00	1.72	3.57	4.30	4.69	4.86	4.95	5.01	5.04	5.11	5.16	5.19	5.21	5.23
1.63	0.00	0.00	1.57	3.44	4.18	4.58	4.75	4.84	4.90	4.94	5.01	5.06	5.08	5.11	5.12
1.64	0.00	0.00	1.42	3.31	4.06	4.47	4.64	4.73	4.79	4.83	4.90	4.95	4.98	5.00	5.01
1.65	0.00	0.00	1.28	3.19	3.95	4.36	4.53	4.62	4.68	4.72	4.79	4.85	4.87	4.90	4.91
1.66	0.00	0.00	1.15	3.07	3.84	4.25	4.43	4.52	4.58	4.62	4.69	4.74	4.77	4.80	4.81
1.67	0.00	0.00	1.02	2.95	3.73	4.15	4.32	4.42	4.48	4.52	4.59	4.64	4.67	4.70	4.71
1.68	0.00	0.00	0.89	2.84	3.62	4.05	4.22	4.32	4.38	4.42	4.49	4.55	4.57	4.60	4.61
1.69	0.00	0.00	0.77	2.73	3.52	3.94	4.12	4.22	4.28	4.32	4.39	4.45	4.47	4.50	4.51
1.70	0.00	0.00	0.66	2.62	3.41	3.84	4.02	4.12	4.18	4.22	4.30	4.35	4.38	4.41	4.42
1.71	0.00	0.00	0.55	2.51	3.31	3.75	3.93	4.02	4.09	4.13	4.20	4.26	4.29	4.31	4.32
1.72	0.00	0.00	0.45	2.41	3.21	3.65	3.83	3.93	3.99	4.04	4.11	4.17	4.19	4.22	4.23
1.73	0.00	0.00	0.36	2.30	3.11	3.56	3.74	3.84	3.90	3.94	4.02	4.08	4.10	4.13	4.14
1.74	0.00	0.00	0.27	2.20	3.02	3.46	3.65	3.75	3.81	3.85	3.93	3.99	4.01	4.04	4.05
1.75	0.00	0.00	0.19	2.11	2.93	3.37	3.56	3.66	3.72	3.77	3.84	3.90	3.93	3.95	3.97
1.76	0.00	0.00	0.12	2.01	2.83	3.28	3.47	3.57	3.63	3.68	3.76	3.81	3.84	3.87	3.88
1.77	0.00	0.00	0.06	1.92	2.74	3.20	3.38	3.48	3.55	3.59	3.67	3.73	3.76	3.78	3.80
1.78	0.00	0.00	0.02	1.83	2.66	3.11	3.30	3.40	3.47	3.51	3.59	3.64	3.67	3.70	3.71
1.79	0.00	0.00	0.00	1.74	2.57	3.03	3.21	3.32	3.38	3.43	3.51	3.56	3.59	3.63	3.63
1.80	0.00	0.00	0.00	1.65	2.49	2.94	3.13	3.24	3.30	3.35	3.43	3.48	3.51	3.54	3.55
1.81	0.00	0.00	0.00	1.57	2.40	2.86	3.05	3.16	3.22	3.27	3.35	3.40	3.43	3.46	3.47
1.82	0.00	0.00	0.00	1.49	2.32	2.79	2.98	3.08	3.15	3.19	3.27	3.33	3.36	3.38	3.40
1.83	0.00	0.00	0.00	1.41	2.25	2.71	2.90	3.00	3.07	3.11	3.19	3.25	3.28	3.31	3.32
1.84	0.00	0.00	0.00	1.34	2.17	2.63	2.82	2.93	2.99	3.04	3.12	3.18	3.21	3.23	3.25
1.85	0.00	0.00	0.00	1.26	2.09	2.56	2.75	2.85	2.92	2.97	3.05	3.10	3.13	3.16	3.17
1.86	0.00	0.00	0.00	1.19	2.02	2.48	2.68	2.78	2.85	2.89	2.97	3.03	3.06	3.09	3.10
1.87	0.00	0.00	0.00	1.12	1.95	2.41	2.61	2.71	2.78	2.82	2.90	2.96	2.99	3.02	3.03
1.88	0.00	0.00	0.00	1.06	1.88	2.34	2.54	2.64	2.71	2.75	2.83	2.89	2.92	2.95	2.96
1.89	0.00	0.00	0.00	0.99	1.81	2.28	2.47	2.57	2.64	2.69	2.77	2.83	2.85	2.88	2.90

TABLE 10-7 *(Continued)*

Q_U or Q_L	Sample Size														
	3	4	5	7	10	15	20	25	30	35	50	75	100	150	200
1.90	0.00	0.00	0.00	0.93	1.75	2.21	2.40	2.51	2.57	2.62	2.70	2.76	2.79	2.82	2.83
1.91	0.00	0.00	0.00	0.87	1.68	2.14	2.34	2.44	2.51	2.56	2.63	2.69	2.72	2.75	2.77
1.92	0.00	0.00	0.00	0.81	1.62	2.08	2.27	2.38	2.45	2.49	2.57	2.63	2.66	2.69	2.70
1.93	0.00	0.00	0.00	0.76	1.56	2.02	2.21	2.32	2.38	2.43	2.51	2.57	2.60	2.62	2.64
1.94	0.00	0.00	0.00	0.70	1.50	1.96	2.15	2.25	2.32	2.37	2.45	2.51	2.54	2.56	2.58
1.95	0.00	0.00	0.00	0.65	1.44	1.90	2.09	2.19	2.26	2.31	2.39	2.45	2.48	2.50	2.52
1.96	0.00	0.00	0.00	0.60	1.38	1.84	2.03	2.14	2.20	2.25	2.33	2.39	2.42	2.44	2.46
1.97	0.00	0.00	0.00	0.56	1.33	1.78	1.97	2.08	2.14	2.19	2.27	2.33	2.36	2.39	2.40
1.98	0.00	0.00	0.00	0.51	1.27	1.73	1.92	2.02	2.09	2.13	2.21	2.27	2.30	2.33	2.34
1.99	0.00	0.00	0.00	0.47	1.22	1.67	1.86	1.97	2.03	2.08	2.16	2.22	2.25	2.27	2.29
2.00	0.00	0.00	0.00	0.43	1.17	1.62	1.81	1.91	1.98	2.03	2.10	2.16	2.19	2.22	2.23
2.01	0.00	0.00	0.00	0.39	1.12	1.57	1.76	1.86	1.93	1.97	2.05	2.11	2.14	2.17	2.18
2.02	0.00	0.00	0.00	0.36	1.07	1.52	1.71	1.81	1.87	1.92	2.00	2.06	2.09	2.11	2.13
2.03	0.00	0.00	0.00	0.32	1.03	1.47	1.66	1.76	1.82	1.87	1.95	2.01	2.04	2.06	2.08
2.04	0.00	0.00	0.00	0.29	0.98	1.42	1.61	1.71	1.77	1.82	1.90	1.96	1.99	2.01	2.03
2.05	0.00	0.00	0.00	0.26	0.94	1.37	1.56	1.66	1.73	1.77	1.85	1.91	1.94	1.96	1.98
2.06	0.00	0.00	0.00	0.23	0.90	1.33	1.51	1.61	1.68	1.72	1.80	1.86	1.89	1.92	1.93
2.07	0.00	0.00	0.00	0.21	0.86	1.28	1.47	1.57	1.63	1.68	1.76	1.81	1.84	1.87	1.88
2.08	0.00	0.00	0.00	0.18	0.82	1.24	1.42	1.52	1.59	1.63	1.71	1.77	1.79	1.82	1.84
2.09	0.00	0.00	0.00	0.16	0.78	1.20	1.38	1.48	1.54	1.59	1.66	1.72	1.75	1.78	1.79
2.10	0.00	0.00	0.00	0.14	0.74	1.16	1.34	1.44	1.50	1.54	1.62	1.68	1.71	1.73	1.75
2.11	0.00	0.00	0.00	0.12	0.71	1.12	1.30	1.39	1.46	1.50	1.58	1.63	1.66	1.69	1.70
2.12	0.00	0.00	0.00	0.10	0.67	1.08	1.26	1.35	1.42	1.46	1.54	1.59	1.62	1.65	1.66
2.13	0.00	0.00	0.00	0.08	0.64	1.04	1.22	1.31	1.38	1.42	1.50	1.55	1.58	1.61	1.62
2.14	0.00	0.00	0.00	0.07	0.61	1.00	1.18	1.28	1.34	1.38	1.46	1.51	1.54	1.57	1.58
2.15	0.00	0.00	0.00	0.06	0.58	0.97	1.14	1.24	1.30	1.34	1.42	1.47	1.50	1.53	1.54
2.16	0.00	0.00	0.00	0.05	0.55	0.93	1.10	1.20	1.26	1.30	1.38	1.43	1.46	1.49	1.50
2.17	0.00	0.00	0.00	0.04	0.52	0.90	1.07	1.16	1.22	1.27	1.34	1.40	1.42	1.45	1.46
2.18	0.00	0.00	0.00	0.03	0.49	0.87	1.03	1.13	1.19	1.23	1.30	1.36	1.39	1.41	1.42
2.19	0.00	0.00	0.00	0.02	0.46	0.83	1.00	1.09	1.15	1.20	1.27	1.32	1.35	1.38	1.39
2.20	0.000	0.000	0.000	0.015	0.437	0.803	0.968	1.061	1.120	1.161	1.233	1.287	1.314	1.340	1.352
2.21	0.000	0.000	0.000	0.010	0.413	0.772	0.936	1.028	1.087	1.128	1.199	1.253	1.279	1.305	1.318
2.22	0.000	0.000	0.000	0.006	0.389	0.743	0.905	0.996	1.054	1.095	1.166	1.219	1.245	1.271	1.283
2.23	0.000	0.000	0.000	0.003	0.366	0.715	0.875	0.965	1.023	1.063	1.134	1.186	1.212	1.238	1.250
2.24	0.000	0.000	0.000	0.002	0.345	0.687	0.845	0.935	0.992	1.032	1.102	1.154	1.180	1.205	1.218
2.25	0.000	0.000	0.000	0.001	0.324	0.660	0.816	0.905	0.962	1.002	1.071	1.123	1.148	1.173	1.186
2.26	0.000	0.000	0.000	0.000	0.304	0.634	0.789	0.876	0.933	0.972	1.041	1.092	1.117	1.142	1.155
2.27	0.000	0.000	0.000	0.000	0.285	0.609	0.762	0.848	0.904	0.943	1.011	1.062	1.087	1.112	1.124
2.28	0.000	0.000	0.000	0.000	0.267	0.585	0.735	0.821	0.876	0.915	0.982	1.033	1.058	1.082	1.094
2.29	0.000	0.000	0.000	0.000	0.250	0.561	0.710	0.794	0.849	0.887	0.954	1.004	1.029	1.053	1.065

Q_U or Q_L	Sample Size														
	3	4	5	7	10	15	20	25	30	35	50	75	100	150	200
2.30	0.000	0.000	0.000	0.000	0.233	0.538	0.685	0.769	0.823	0.861	0.927	0.977	1.001	1.025	1.037
2.31	0.000	0.000	0.000	0.000	0.218	0.516	0.661	0.743	0.797	0.834	0.900	0.949	0.974	0.997	1.009
2.32	0.000	0.000	0.000	0.000	0.203	0.495	0.637	0.719	0.772	0.809	0.874	0.923	0.947	0.971	0.982
2.33	0.000	0.000	0.000	0.000	0.189	0.474	0.614	0.695	0.748	0.784	0.848	0.897	0.921	0.944	0.956
2.34	0.000	0.000	0.000	0.000	0.175	0.454	0.592	0.672	0.724	0.760	0.824	0.872	0.895	0.915	0.930
2.35	0.000	0.000	0.000	0.000	0.163	0.435	0.571	0.650	0.701	0.736	0.799	0.847	0.870	0.893	0.905
2.36	0.000	0.000	0.000	0.000	0.151	0.416	0.550	0.628	0.678	0.714	0.776	0.823	0.846	0.869	0.880
2.37	0.000	0.000	0.000	0.000	0.139	0.398	0.530	0.606	0.656	0.691	0.753	0.799	0.822	0.845	0.856
2.38	0.000	0.000	0.000	0.000	0.128	0.381	0.510	0.586	0.635	0.670	0.730	0.777	0.799	0.822	0.833
2.39	0.000	0.000	0.000	0.000	0.118	0.364	0.491	0.566	0.614	0.648	0.709	0.754	0.777	0.799	0.810
2.40	0.000	0.000	0.000	0.000	0.109	0.348	0.473	0.546	0.594	0.628	0.687	0.732	0.755	0.777	0.787
2.41	0.000	0.000	0.000	0.000	0.100	0.332	0.455	0.527	0.575	0.608	0.667	0.711	0.733	0.755	0.766
2.42	0.000	0.000	0.000	0.000	0.091	0.317	0.437	0.509	0.555	0.588	0.646	0.691	0.712	0.734	0.744
2.43	0.000	0.000	0.000	0.000	0.083	0.302	0.421	0.491	0.537	0.569	0.627	0.670	0.692	0.713	0.724
2.44	0.000	0.000	0.000	0.000	0.076	0.288	0.404	0.474	0.519	0.551	0.608	0.651	0.672	0.693	0.703
2.45	0.000	0.000	0.000	0.000	0.069	0.275	0.389	0.457	0.501	0.533	0.589	0.632	0.653	0.673	0.684
2.46	0.000	0.000	0.000	0.000	0.063	0.262	0.373	0.440	0.484	0.516	0.571	0.613	0.634	0.654	0.664
2.47	0.000	0.000	0.000	0.000	0.057	0.249	0.359	0.425	0.468	0.499	0.553	0.595	0.615	0.635	0.646
2.48	0.000	0.000	0.000	0.000	0.051	0.237	0.344	0.409	0.452	0.482	0.536	0.577	0.597	0.617	0.627
2.49	0.000	0.000	0.000	0.000	0.046	0.226	0.331	0.394	0.436	0.466	0.519	0.560	0.580	0.600	0.609
2.50	0.000	0.000	0.000	0.000	0.041	0.214	0.317	0.380	0.421	0.451	0.503	0.543	0.563	0.582	0.592
2.51	0.000	0.000	0.000	0.000	0.037	0.204	0.304	0.366	0.407	0.436	0.487	0.527	0.546	0.565	0.575
2.52	0.000	0.000	0.000	0.000	0.033	0.193	0.292	0.352	0.392	0.421	0.472	0.511	0.530	0.549	0.558
2.53	0.000	0.000	0.000	0.000	0.029	0.184	0.280	0.339	0.379	0.407	0.457	0.495	0.514	0.533	0.542
2.54	0.000	0.000	0.000	0.000	0.026	0.174	0.268	0.326	0.365	0.393	0.442	0.480	0.499	0.517	0.527
2.55	0.000	0.000	0.000	0.000	0.023	0.165	0.257	0.314	0.352	0.379	0.428	0.465	0.484	0.502	0.511
2.56	0.000	0.000	0.000	0.000	0.020	0.156	0.246	0.302	0.340	0.366	0.414	0.451	0.469	0.487	0.496
2.57	0.000	0.000	0.000	0.000	0.017	0.148	0.236	0.291	0.327	0.354	0.401	0.437	0.455	0.473	0.482
2.58	0.000	0.000	0.000	0.000	0.015	0.140	0.226	0.279	0.316	0.341	0.388	0.424	0.441	0.459	0.468
2.59	0.000	0.000	0.000	0.000	0.013	0.133	0.216	0.269	0.304	0.330	0.375	0.410	0.428	0.445	0.454
2.60	0.000	0.000	0.000	0.000	0.011	0.125	0.207	0.258	0.293	0.318	0.363	0.398	0.415	0.432	0.441
2.61	0.000	0.000	0.000	0.000	0.009	0.118	0.198	0.248	0.282	0.307	0.351	0.385	0.402	0.419	0.428
2.62	0.000	0.000	0.000	0.000	0.008	0.112	0.189	0.238	0.272	0.296	0.339	0.373	0.390	0.406	0.415
2.63	0.000	0.000	0.000	0.000	0.007	0.105	0.181	0.229	0.262	0.285	0.328	0.361	0.378	0.394	0.402
2.64	0.000	0.000	0.000	0.000	0.005	0.099	0.172	0.220	0.252	0.275	0.317	0.350	0.366	0.382	0.390
2.65	0.000	0.000	0.000	0.000	0.005	0.094	0.165	0.211	0.243	0.265	0.307	0.339	0.355	0.371	0.379
2.66	0.000	0.000	0.000	0.000	0.004	0.088	0.157	0.202	0.233	0.256	0.296	0.328	0.344	0.359	0.367
2.67	0.000	0.000	0.000	0.000	0.003	0.083	0.150	0.194	0.224	0.246	0.286	0.317	0.333	0.348	0.356
2.68	0.000	0.000	0.000	0.000	0.002	0.078	0.143	0.186	0.216	0.237	0.277	0.307	0.322	0.338	0.345
2.69	0.000	0.000	0.000	0.000	0.002	0.073	0.136	0.179	0.208	0.229	0.267	0.297	0.312	0.327	0.335

Q_U or Q_L	Sample Size														
	3	4	5	7	10	15	20	25	30	35	50	75	100	150	200
2.70	0.000	0.000	0.000	0.000	0.001	0.069	0.130	0.171	0.200	0.220	0.258	0.288	0.302	0.317	0.325
2.71	0.000	0.000	0.000	0.000	0.001	0.064	0.124	0.164	0.192	0.212	0.249	0.278	0.293	0.307	0.315
2.72	0.000	0.000	0.000	0.000	0.000	0.060	0.118	0.157	0.184	0.204	0.241	0.269	0.283	0.298	0.305
2.73	0.000	0.000	0.000	0.000	0.000	0.057	0.112	0.151	0.177	0.197	0.232	0.260	0.274	0.288	0.296
2.74	0.000	0.000	0.000	0.000	0.000	0.053	0.107	0.144	0.170	0.189	0.224	0.252	0.266	0.279	0.286
2.75	0.000	0.000	0.000	0.000	0.000	0.049	0.102	0.138	0.163	0.182	0.216	0.243	0.257	0.271	0.277
2.76	0.000	0.000	0.000	0.000	0.000	0.046	0.097	0.132	0.157	0.175	0.209	0.235	0.249	0.262	0.269
2.77	0.000	0.000	0.000	0.000	0.000	0.043	0.092	0.126	0.151	0.168	0.201	0.227	0.241	0.254	0.260
2.78	0.000	0.000	0.000	0.000	0.000	0.040	0.087	0.121	0.145	0.162	0.194	0.220	0.233	0.246	0.252
2.79	0.000	0.000	0.000	0.000	0.000	0.037	0.083	0.115	0.139	0.156	0.187	0.212	0.225	0.238	0.244
2.80	0.000	0.000	0.000	0.000	0.000	0.035	0.079	0.110	0.133	0.150	0.181	0.205	0.218	0.230	0.237
2.81	0.000	0.000	0.000	0.000	0.000	0.032	0.075	0.105	0.128	0.144	0.174	0.198	0.211	0.223	0.229
2.82	0.000	0.000	0.000	0.000	0.000	0.030	0.071	0.101	0.122	0.138	0.168	0.192	0.204	0.216	0.222
2.83	0.000	0.000	0.000	0.000	0.000	0.028	0.067	0.096	0.117	0.133	0.162	0.185	0.197	0.209	0.215
2.84	0.000	0.000	0.000	0.000	0.000	0.026	0.064	0.092	0.112	0.128	0.156	0.179	0.190	0.202	0.208
2.85	0.000	0.000	0.000	0.000	0.000	0.024	0.060	0.088	0.108	0.122	0.150	0.173	0.184	0.195	0.201
2.86	0.000	0.000	0.000	0.000	0.000	0.022	0.057	0.084	0.103	0.118	0.145	0.167	0.178	0.189	0.195
2.87	0.000	0.000	0.000	0.000	0.000	0.020	0.054	0.080	0.099	0.113	0.139	0.161	0.172	0.183	0.188
2.88	0.000	0.000	0.000	0.000	0.000	0.019	0.051	0.076	0.094	0.108	0.134	0.155	0.166	0.177	0.182
2.89	0.000	0.000	0.000	0.000	0.000	0.017	0.048	0.073	0.090	0.104	0.129	0.150	0.160	0.171	0.176
2.90	0.000	0.000	0.000	0.000	0.000	0.016	0.046	0.069	0.087	0.100	0.125	0.145	0.155	0.165	0.171
2.91	0.000	0.000	0.000	0.000	0.000	0.015	0.043	0.066	0.083	0.096	0.120	0.140	0.150	0.160	0.165
2.92	0.000	0.000	0.000	0.000	0.000	0.013	0.041	0.063	0.079	0.092	0.115	0.135	0.145	0.155	0.160
2.93	0.000	0.000	0.000	0.000	0.000	0.012	0.038	0.060	0.076	0.088	0.111	0.130	0.140	0.149	0.154
2.94	0.000	0.000	0.000	0.000	0.000	0.011	0.036	0.057	0.072	0.084	0.107	0.125	0.135	0.144	0.149
2.95	0.000	0.000	0.000	0.000	0.000	0.010	0.034	0.054	0.069	0.081	0.103	0.121	0.130	0.140	0.144
2.96	0.000	0.000	0.000	0.000	0.000	0.009	0.032	0.051	0.066	0.077	0.099	0.117	0.126	0.135	0.140
2.97	0.000	0.000	0.000	0.000	0.000	0.009	0.030	0.049	0.063	0.074	0.095	0.112	0.121	0.130	0.135
2.98	0.000	0.000	0.000	0.000	0.000	0.008	0.028	0.046	0.060	0.071	0.091	0.108	0.117	0.126	0.130
2.99	0.000	0.000	0.000	0.000	0.000	0.007	0.027	0.044	0.057	0.068	0.088	0.104	0.113	0.122	0.126
3.00	0.000	0.000	0.000	0.000	0.000	0.006	0.025	0.042	0.055	0.065	0.084	0.101	0.109	0.118	0.122
3.01	0.000	0.000	0.000	0.000	0.000	0.006	0.024	0.040	0.052	0.062	0.081	0.097	0.105	0.114	0.118
3.02	0.000	0.000	0.000	0.000	0.000	0.005	0.022	0.038	0.050	0.059	0.078	0.093	0.101	0.110	0.114
3.03	0.000	0.000	0.000	0.000	0.000	0.005	0.021	0.036	0.048	0.057	0.075	0.090	0.098	0.106	0.110
3.04	0.000	0.000	0.000	0.000	0.000	0.004	0.019	0.034	0.045	0.054	0.072	0.087	0.094	0.102	0.106
3.05	0.000	0.000	0.000	0.000	0.000	0.004	0.018	0.032	0.043	0.052	0.069	0.083	0.091	0.099	0.103
3.06	0.000	0.000	0.000	0.000	0.000	0.003	0.017	0.030	0.041	0.050	0.066	0.080	0.088	0.095	0.099
3.07	0.000	0.000	0.000	0.000	0.000	0.003	0.016	0.029	0.039	0.047	0.064	0.077	0.085	0.092	0.096
3.08	0.000	0.000	0.000	0.000	0.000	0.003	0.015	0.027	0.037	0.045	0.061	0.074	0.081	0.089	0.092
3.09	0.000	0.000	0.000	0.000	0.000	0.002	0.014	0.026	0.036	0.043	0.059	0.072	0.079	0.086	0.089

TABLE 10-7 *(Continued)*

Q_U or Q_L	Sample Size														
	3	4	5	7	10	15	20	25	30	35	50	75	100	150	200
3.10	0.000	0.000	0.000	0.000	0.000	0.002	0.013	0.024	0.034	0.041	0.056	0.069	0.076	0.083	0.086
3.11	0.000	0.000	0.000	0.000	0.000	0.002	0.012	0.023	0.032	0.039	0.054	0.066	0.073	0.080	0.083
3.12	0.000	0.000	0.000	0.000	0.000	0.002	0.011	0.022	0.031	0.038	0.052	0.064	0.070	0.077	0.080
3.13	0.000	0.000	0.000	0.000	0.000	0.002	0.011	0.021	0.029	0.036	0.050	0.061	0.068	0.074	0.077
3.14	0.000	0.000	0.000	0.000	0.000	0.001	0.010	0.019	0.028	0.034	0.048	0.059	0.065	0.071	0.075
3.15	0.000	0.000	0.000	0.000	0.000	0.001	0.009	0.018	0.026	0.033	0.046	0.057	0.063	0.069	0.072
3.16	0.000	0.000	0.000	0.000	0.000	0.001	0.009	0.017	0.025	0.031	0.044	0.055	0.060	0.066	0.069
3.17	0.000	0.000	0.000	0.000	0.000	0.001	0.008	0.016	0.024	0.030	0.042	0.053	0.058	0.064	0.067
3.18	0.000	0.000	0.000	0.000	0.000	0.001	0.007	0.015	0.022	0.028	0.040	0.050	0.056	0.062	0.065
3.19	0.000	0.000	0.000	0.000	0.000	0.001	0.007	0.015	0.021	0.027	0.038	0.049	0.054	0.059	0.062
3.20	0.000	0.000	0.000	0.000	0.000	0.001	0.006	0.014	0.020	0.026	0.037	0.047	0.052	0.057	0.060
3.21	0.000	0.000	0.000	0.000	0.000	0.000	0.006	0.013	0.019	0.024	0.035	0.045	0.050	0.055	0.058
3.22	0.000	0.000	0.000	0.000	0.000	0.000	0.005	0.012	0.018	0.023	0.034	0.043	0.048	0.053	0.056
3.23	0.000	0.000	0.000	0.000	0.000	0.000	0.005	0.011	0.017	0.022	0.032	0.041	0.046	0.051	0.054
3.24	0.000	0.000	0.000	0.000	0.000	0.000	0.005	0.011	0.016	0.021	0.031	0.040	0.044	0.049	0.052
3.25	0.000	0.000	0.000	0.000	0.000	0.000	0.004	0.010	0.015	0.020	0.030	0.038	0.043	0.048	0.050
3.26	0.000	0.000	0.000	0.000	0.000	0.000	0.004	0.009	0.015	0.019	0.028	0.037	0.041	0.046	0.048
3.27	0.000	0.000	0.000	0.000	0.000	0.000	0.004	0.009	0.014	0.019	0.027	0.035	0.040	0.044	0.046
3.28	0.000	0.000	0.000	0.000	0.000	0.000	0.003	0.008	0.013	0.017	0.026	0.034	0.038	0.042	0.045
3.29	0.000	0.000	0.000	0.000	0.000	0.000	0.003	0.008	0.012	0.016	0.025	0.032	0.037	0.041	0.043
3.30	0.000	0.000	0.000	0.000	0.000	0.000	0.003	0.007	0.012	0.015	0.024	0.031	0.035	0.039	0.042
3.31	0.000	0.000	0.000	0.000	0.000	0.000	0.003	0.007	0.011	0.015	0.023	0.030	0.034	0.038	0.040
3.32	0.000	0.000	0.000	0.000	0.000	0.000	0.002	0.006	0.010	0.014	0.022	0.029	0.032	0.036	0.039
3.33	0.000	0.000	0.000	0.000	0.000	0.000	0.002	0.006	0.010	0.013	0.021	0.027	0.031	0.035	0.037
3.34	0.000	0.000	0.000	0.000	0.000	0.000	0.002	0.006	0.009	0.013	0.020	0.026	0.030	0.034	0.036
3.35	0.000	0.000	0.000	0.000	0.000	0.000	0.002	0.005	0.009	0.012	0.019	0.025	0.029	0.032	0.034
3.36	0.000	0.000	0.000	0.000	0.000	0.000	0.002	0.005	0.008	0.011	0.018	0.024	0.028	0.031	0.033
3.37	0.000	0.000	0.000	0.000	0.000	0.000	0.002	0.005	0.008	0.011	0.017	0.023	0.026	0.030	0.032
3.38	0.000	0.000	0.000	0.000	0.000	0.000	0.001	0.004	0.007	0.010	0.016	0.022	0.025	0.029	0.031
3.39	0.000	0.000	0.000	0.000	0.000	0.000	0.001	0.004	0.007	0.010	0.016	0.021	0.024	0.028	0.029
3.40	0.000	0.000	0.000	0.000	0.000	0.000	0.001	0.004	0.007	0.009	0.015	0.020	0.023	0.027	0.028
3.41	0.000	0.000	0.000	0.000	0.000	0.000	0.001	0.003	0.006	0.009	0.014	0.020	0.022	0.026	0.027
3.42	0.000	0.000	0.000	0.000	0.000	0.000	0.001	0.003	0.006	0.008	0.014	0.019	0.022	0.025	0.026
3.43	0.000	0.000	0.000	0.000	0.000	0.000	0.001	0.003	0.005	0.008	0.013	0.018	0.021	0.024	0.025
3.44	0.000	0.000	0.000	0.000	0.000	0.000	0.001	0.003	0.005	0.007	0.012	0.017	0.020	0.023	0.024
3.45	0.000	0.000	0.000	0.000	0.000	0.000	0.001	0.003	0.005	0.007	0.012	0.016	0.019	0.022	0.023
3.46	0.000	0.000	0.000	0.000	0.000	0.000	0.001	0.002	0.005	0.007	0.011	0.016	0.018	0.021	0.022
3.47	0.000	0.000	0.000	0.000	0.000	0.000	0.001	0.002	0.004	0.006	0.011	0.015	0.017	0.020	0.022
3.48	0.000	0.000	0.000	0.000	0.000	0.000	0.001	0.002	0.004	0.006	0.010	0.014	0.017	0.019	0.021
3.49	0.000	0.000	0.000	0.000	0.000	0.000	0.000	0.002	0.004	0.005	0.010	0.014	0.016	0.019	0.020

Q_U or Q_L	Sample Size														
	3	4	5	7	10	15	20	25	30	35	50	75	100	150	200
3.50	0.000	0.000	0.000	0.000	0.000	0.000	0.000	0.002	0.003	0.005	0.009	0.013	0.015	0.018	0.019
3.51	0.000	0.000	0.000	0.000	0.000	0.000	0.000	0.002	0.003	0.005	0.009	0.013	0.015	0.017	0.018
3.52	0.000	0.000	0.000	0.000	0.000	0.000	0.000	0.002	0.003	0.005	0.008	0.012	0.014	0.017	0.018
3.53	0.000	0.000	0.000	0.000	0.000	0.000	0.000	0.001	0.003	0.004	0.008	0.012	0.014	0.016	0.017
3.54	0.000	0.000	0.000	0.000	0.000	0.000	0.000	0.001	0.003	0.004	0.008	0.011	0.013	0.015	0.016
3.55	0.000	0.000	0.000	0.000	0.000	0.000	0.000	0.001	0.003	0.004	0.007	0.011	0.012	0.015	0.016
3.56	0.000	0.000	0.000	0.000	0.000	0.000	0.000	0.001	0.002	0.004	0.007	0.010	0.012	0.014	0.015
3.57	0.000	0.000	0.000	0.000	0.000	0.000	0.000	0.001	0.002	0.003	0.006	0.010	0.011	0.013	0.014
3.58	0.000	0.000	0.000	0.000	0.000	0.000	0.000	0.001	0.002	0.003	0.006	0.009	0.011	0.013	0.014
3.59	0.000	0.000	0.000	0.000	0.000	0.000	0.000	0.001	0.002	0.003	0.006	0.009	0.010	0.012	0.013
3.60	0.000	0.000	0.000	0.000	0.000	0.000	0.000	0.001	0.002	0.003	0.006	0.008	0.010	0.012	0.013
3.61	0.000	0.000	0.000	0.000	0.000	0.000	0.000	0.001	0.002	0.003	0.005	0.008	0.010	0.011	0.012
3.62	0.000	0.000	0.000	0.000	0.000	0.000	0.000	0.001	0.002	0.003	0.005	0.008	0.009	0.011	0.012
3.63	0.000	0.000	0.000	0.000	0.000	0.000	0.000	0.001	0.001	0.002	0.005	0.007	0.009	0.010	0.011
3.64	0.000	0.000	0.000	0.000	0.000	0.000	0.000	0.001	0.001	0.002	0.004	0.007	0.008	0.010	0.011
3.65	0.000	0.000	0.000	0.000	0.000	0.000	0.000	0.001	0.001	0.002	0.004	0.007	0.008	0.010	0.010
3.66	0.000	0.000	0.000	0.000	0.000	0.000	0.000	0.000	0.001	0.002	0.004	0.006	0.008	0.009	0.010
3.67	0.000	0.000	0.000	0.000	0.000	0.000	0.000	0.000	0.001	0.002	0.004	0.006	0.007	0.009	0.010
3.68	0.000	0.000	0.000	0.000	0.000	0.000	0.000	0.000	0.001	0.002	0.004	0.006	0.007	0.008	0.009
3.69	0.000	0.000	0.000	0.000	0.000	0.000	0.000	0.000	0.001	0.002	0.003	0.005	0.007	0.008	0.009
3.70	0.000	0.000	0.000	0.000	0.000	0.000	0.000	0.000	0.001	0.002	0.003	0.005	0.006	0.008	0.008
3.71	0.000	0.000	0.000	0.000	0.000	0.000	0.000	0.000	0.001	0.001	0.003	0.005	0.006	0.007	0.008
3.72	0.000	0.000	0.000	0.000	0.000	0.000	0.000	0.000	0.001	0.001	0.003	0.005	0.006	0.007	0.008
3.73	0.000	0.000	0.000	0.000	0.000	0.000	0.000	0.000	0.001	0.001	0.003	0.005	0.006	0.007	0.007
3.74	0.000	0.000	0.000	0.000	0.000	0.000	0.000	0.000	0.001	0.001	0.003	0.004	0.005	0.007	0.007
3.75	0.000	0.000	0.000	0.000	0.000	0.000	0.000	0.000	0.001	0.001	0.002	0.004	0.005	0.006	0.007
3.76	0.000	0.000	0.000	0.000	0.000	0.000	0.000	0.000	0.001	0.001	0.002	0.004	0.005	0.006	0.007
3.77	0.000	0.000	0.000	0.000	0.000	0.000	0.000	0.000	0.001	0.001	0.002	0.004	0.005	0.006	0.006
3.78	0.000	0.000	0.000	0.000	0.000	0.000	0.000	0.000	0.000	0.001	0.002	0.004	0.004	0.005	0.006
3.79	0.000	0.000	0.000	0.000	0.000	0.000	0.000	0.000	0.000	0.001	0.002	0.003	0.004	0.005	0.006
3.80	0.000	0.000	0.000	0.000	0.000	0.000	0.000	0.000	0.000	0.001	0.002	0.003	0.004	0.005	0.006
3.81	0.000	0.000	0.000	0.000	0.000	0.000	0.000	0.000	0.000	0.001	0.002	0.003	0.004	0.005	0.005
3.82	0.000	0.000	0.000	0.000	0.000	0.000	0.000	0.000	0.000	0.001	0.002	0.003	0.004	0.005	0.005
3.83	0.000	0.000	0.000	0.000	0.000	0.000	0.000	0.000	0.000	0.001	0.002	0.003	0.004	0.004	0.005
3.84	0.000	0.000	0.000	0.000	0.000	0.000	0.000	0.000	0.000	0.001	0.001	0.003	0.003	0.004	0.005
3.85	0.000	0.000	0.000	0.000	0.000	0.000	0.000	0.000	0.000	0.001	0.001	0.002	0.003	0.004	0.004
3.86	0.000	0.000	0.000	0.000	0.000	0.000	0.000	0.000	0.000	0.000	0.001	0.002	0.003	0.004	0.004
3.87	0.000	0.000	0.000	0.000	0.000	0.000	0.000	0.000	0.000	0.000	0.001	0.002	0.003	0.004	0.004
3.88	0.000	0.000	0.000	0.000	0.000	0.000	0.000	0.000	0.000	0.000	0.001	0.002	0.003	0.004	0.004
3.89	0.000	0.000	0.000	0.000	0.000	0.000	0.000	0.000	0.000	0.000	0.001	0.002	0.003	0.003	0.004
3.90	0.000	0.000	0.000	0.000	0.000	0.000	0.000	0.000	0.000	0.000	0.001	0.002	0.003	0.003	0.004

From the sample of size 5 in Example 10-5, the sample mean $\overline{X}$ and standard deviation s were 256 and 39.115, respectively. The quality index Q_U is

$$Q_U = (U - \overline{X})/s = (300 - 256)/39.115 = 1.125$$

The estimate of the lot percent nonconforming above the upper specification limit is found from Table 10-7 as $\hat{p}_U = 12.79$ percent (by interpolation). Since $\hat{p}_U = 12.79$ percent $> M = 1.33$ percent, the lot is rejected.

Double Specification Limits with One AQL Value for Both Limits With double specification limits, the standard permits only Form 2 to be used in decision making. First, let us consider the case for which a single AQL value is used for both specification limits. The procedure is as follows. The AQL value to be used in the standard is found from Table 10-1. Given the lot size and general inspection level, the sample size code letter is found from Table 10-2. Given the sample size code letter and the AQL, Table 10-5 (for normal or tightened inspection) or Table 10-6 (for reduced inspection) is used to determine the sample size n and the maximum allowable percent nonconforming M.

Once the sampling plan is known, a random sample of size n is selected from the lot, and the sample mean $\overline{X}$ and sample standard deviation s are found. The quality indices $Q_L = (\overline{X} - L)/s$ and $Q_U = (U - \overline{X})/s$ are calculated. The estimates of the lot percent nonconforming below and above the lower and upper specification limits, respectively, denoted by $\hat{p}_L$ and $\hat{p}_U$, are found from Table 10-7. The total estimated percent nonconforming outside the specification limits is found as $\hat{p} = \hat{p}_L + \hat{P}_U$. If $\hat{p}$ is less than or equal to M, the lot is accepted. If $\hat{p}$ is greater than M or if Q_U, Q_L, or both are negative, the lot is rejected.

Double Specification Limits with Different AQL Values for Both Limits Consider a case in which the user prefers to use different AQL values for the two specification limits. From Table 10-1, the AQL values to be used in the standard are found. Information about the lot size and general inspection level is used to determine the sample size code letter from Table 10-2. Next, Table 10-5 (for normal or tightened inspection) or Table 10-6 (for reduced inspection) is used to determine the sample size n and the maximum allowable percent nonconforming values M_U and M_L, corresponding to the AQL values for the upper and lower specification limits, respectively.

Next, a random sample of size n is selected from the lot, and the sample mean $\overline{X}$ and sample standard deviation s are found. The quality indices $Q_L = (\overline{X} - L)/s$ and $Q_U = (U - \overline{X})/s$ are calculated. From Table 10-7, the estimates of the lot per cent nonconforming below the LSL ($\hat{p}_L$) and above the USL ($\hat{p}_U$) are determined. The combined percent nonconforming is found as $\hat{p} = \hat{p}_L + \hat{p}_U$. If $\hat{p}_U \le M_U$, $\hat{p}_L \le M_L$, and $\hat{p}$ is less than or equal to the larger of M_L and M_U, the lot is accepted; otherwise, it is rejected. If Q_L, Q_U, or both are negative, the lot is rejected.

Example 10-7: The specification limits for the percentage of sodium content in cereal boxes that weigh 450 g are 0.3 percent and 1.1 percent, respectively. Lots containing 100 boxes are submitted for inspection. Tightened inspection and general inspection level II with an AQL of 1.03 percent are to be used. Find the variable sampling plan using *ANSI/ASQC Z1.9*.

Solution. For an AQL of 1.03 percent, from Table 10-1, the value of AQL to be used in the standard is 1.0 percent. Since the lot size is 100 and general inspection level II is to be used, the sample size code letter from Table 10-2 is F. From Table 10-5, the sample size n is 10 and the maximum allowable percent nonconforming M is 2.17 percent.

Suppose a random sample of 10 cereal boxes yielded the following percentages of sodium content: 0.62, 0.55, 0.43, 0.78, 0.85, 0.78, 0.41, 0.92, 0.85, and 0.60.

The sample mean is computed to be

$$\overline{X} = \frac{\sum X_i}{n} = \frac{6.79}{10} = 0.679$$

The sample standard deviation is calculated as

$$s = \sqrt{\frac{\sum X_i^2 - (\sum X_i)^2/n}{n-1}}$$

$$= \sqrt{\frac{(4.9081 - (6.79)^2/10)}{9}} = 0.182$$

The quality indices are as follows:

$$Q_L = (\overline{X} - L)/s = (0.679 - 0.3)/0.182 = 2.08$$

$$Q_U = (U - \overline{X})/s = (1.1 - 0.679)/0.182 = 2.31$$

From Table 10-7, the estimate of the lot percent nonconforming below the lower specification limit is $\hat{p}_L = 0.82$ percent; the estimate of the lot percent nonconforming above the upper specification limit is $\hat{p}_U = 0.218$ percent. The total estimated percent nonconforming is $\hat{p} = \hat{p}_L + \hat{p}_U = 0.82+0.218 = 1.038$ percent. Since $\hat{p} < M = 2.17$ percent, the lot is accepted.

Example 10-8: Consider Example 10-7 concerning the percentage of sodium content in cereal boxes. Suppose the AQL for the lower specification limit of 0.3 percent is 0.23 percent and for the upper specification limit of 1.1 percent it is 1.3 percent. Find a variable sampling plan using *ANSI/ASQC Z1.9*.

Solution. From Table 10-1, for an AQL of 0.23 percent at the lower specification limit, the table value of the AQL is 0.25 percent. For the upper specification limit the table value of the AQL is 1.5 percent. For a lot size of 100 and general inspection level II, the sample size code letter from Table 10-2 is F. From Table 10-5, the sample size n is found as 10. The maximum allowable percent nonconforming below the lower specification limit is $M_L = 0.349$ percent. The maximum allowable percent nonconforming above the upper specification limit is $M_U = 3.26$ percent.

For the sample of size 10, the sample mean and standard deviation are $\overline{X} = 0.679$ and $s = 0.182$, respectively. The quality indices as found in Example 10-7 are $Q_L = (\overline{X} - L)/s = 2.08$, and $Q_U = (U - \overline{X})/s = 2.31$. From Table 10-7, the estimate of the lot percent nonconforming below the lower specification limit is $\hat{p}_L = 0.82$ percent. Similarly, the estimate of the lot percent nonconforming above the upper specification limit is $\hat{p}_U = 0.218$ percent.

Since $\hat{p}_L = 0.82$ percent $> M_L = 0.349$ percent, the lot is rejected.

10-6 SUMMARY

This chapter has presented sampling plans for variables. Whereas attribute inspection is easier and usually less expensive, variable sampling plans yield more information. For the same degree of protection, the sample sizes for variable sampling plans are usually smaller than those for corresponding attribute sampling plans. Two main types of variable sampling plans have been presented. The first deals with controlling a process parameter. Plans for estimating the process average for single and double specification limits when the process standard deviation is known have been discussed. For cases in which the process standard deviation is unknown, plans that estimate the process average with a single specification limit are presented. The second type of variable sampling plan is designed to estimate the lot proportion nonconforming. Two methods of decision making, Form 1 and Form 2, have been described. The case for which the process standard deviation is known and a single specification limit is given has been presented. Finally, some standardized variable sampling plans have been described. The plans discussed are from *ANSI/ASQC Z1.9*, which is the updated civilian version of *MIL–STD-414*. These standardized plans make the process of determining and using a variable plan for decision making rather simple.

10-7 CASE STUDY

GAGES HELP MEET BORE REQUIREMENTS*

The ability to manufacture parts that meet exact specifications and tight tolerances is no longer an added benefit that manufacturers can use as a means to sway prospective customers—it is a requirement. As a result, stringent quality control processes and technologies are used not only by large corporations that employ thousands of workers, but also by small companies and tool-and-die shops that might have only a few employees.

One important area in quality control is checking the internal diameter of holes and bores. It is critical that workpieces meet diameter specifications. If these specifications are not met, the component itself might fail or, in some cases, cause the entire end-product to fail.

For example, a manufacturer of space shuttle components for NASA employs a bore gaging system to measure radial bolt holes on the non-motor segments of the solid rocket booster that it makes. A tight bolt fit is crucial because these segments are responsible for the structural support of the shuttle vehicle prior to launch. Failure of these components would be disastrous.

Different Gauges for Different Needs

Various types of bore gages are available to meet all measuring requirements. To meet different bore size requirements, there are gages that can measure an internal diameter as small as 0.0059 in. (using a 0.0001 in. indicator) or as large as 40 in. (using an internal micrometer with an extension rod). There are bore gages that can detect hole geometry problems in taper, bellmouth, and roundness as well as take bore measurements. Prices of bore gages range from $100 to $10,000.

Measuring range, graduation, tool durability, and sleeve length are all factors that should be considered when selecting a bore gage for a particular job. Other things to consider include whether a three-point contact is needed, the importance of statistical process control (SPC) capability, ease of use, and interchangeability of anvils and other accessories.

* Adapted from G. Mullen (1990), "Gages Help Meet Bore Requirements," *Quality Progress*, Vol. 23, No. 1, pp. 70–71.

There are several basic types of bore gages available. These include:

Dial bore gage. This is the most commonly used and least expensive type of bore gage. Its bezel is equipped with either a dial indicator or a digimatic indicator for SPC and is marked in either inches or metric units. The indicator is set to zero using a master, preferably a master ring, that is the nominal size of the bore of the workpiece being inspected. Because the bore gage measures by comparison, it is critical that the master is accurate and that it is used consistently for inspections.

Once the indicator is correctly set, the dial bore gage is inserted into the workpiece. Any deviation from the nominal setting in the size or the workpiece bore, whether it be plus or minus, is registered on the face of the indicator. Inspectors using this type of gage must have training in the proper placement of the gage inside the bore to ensure accurate measurements.

Holtest bore gage. The holtest bore gage has three equally spaced anvils that can be expanded or contracted by turning the micrometer head. Once the holtest gage has been calibrated with a master ring, it is inserted into the bore. The inspector turns the micrometer head until the gage is seated properly in the bore. With some holtest gages, the bore size can be read directly from the micrometer head.

Like the dial bore gage, the holtest gage is available with either a standard or digimatic micrometer head. The most recent advancement in this type of gage is a digital SPC gage that has 0.00005-in. resolution and a quick-action handle in place of the micrometer head. Because the measuring anvils can expand and contract, the holtest gage is especially useful for measuring recessed grooves, splines, serrations, and other complex internal diameters that would otherwise require the anvils to be changed for measurement. This is one of the most accurate types of bore gages because the three-point contact measurement method provides true alignment within the bore every time.

Air gage. The air gage, also known as a column gage, tests bore diameters by forcing air through orifices in a special measuring head that is slightly smaller than the bore to be measured. Like the dial bore and holtest gages, the air gage must be calibrated using a master ring or some other accurate, consistent standard.

First, the gage has to be calibrated to zero. This zero setting is shown on the display column of the gage. The special measuring head is then placed inside the bore, and air is forced into the bore. The head measures the amount of air pressure within the bore and translates it into deviation from the nominal measurement that was set in the beginning. Depending on the gage, other types of analysis can also be performed and the results shown on the display column. SPC capability is available with many of the newest air gages.

Telescoping gage. The telescoping gage is one of the oldest (and probably least accurate) types of bore gage. It has two anvils that expand when a lock on the handle is released. The gage is inserted into the bore, the lock is released, and the anvils expand to the size of the bore. The operator relocks the anvils and removes the gage from the bore. A measurement reading is determined by using an outside micrometer to measure over the anvils of the telescoping gage. The margin for error is quite great using this method because it is an indirect measurement of the bore.

Inside micrometers. Inside micrometers are commonly used for internal diameter measurements because of their wide measurement range and simplicity of use and reading. In fact, inside micrometers are about the only instruments that can measure bores with diameters over 12 in. Extensions rods can be used with the micrometer for measuring extremely large diameters.

This type of bore gage uses two-point contact measurement, and readings are taken directly from the micrometer head. Inside micrometers usually do not require calibration for inspection because the extension rods are calibrated and provide the measuring range, but calibration is recommended for extremely close tolerance work. This measurement method also has a fairly wide margin for error because the operator has to determine the center of the bore before reading. The micrometer must be exactly in the center of the bore to get an accurate reading.

Plug gages. Functional plug gages provide go/no-go readings for workpieces. In this measurement method, one "go" part and one "no-go" part are mounted on a handle. The inspector attempts to place the go part into the workpiece being inspected. If it does not fit, the bore is too small. The inspector then attempts to place the no-go part into the bore. If it fits, the bore is too large.

With this method, no actual measurement is ascertained. This method is not as widely used anymore because it does not provide any meaningful measurement data. Some plug gages, however, are being equipped with dial or digimatic indicators so that measurement data can be obtained and/or recorded.

Bore Gages Are Evolving to Meet Changing Needs

The trend with bore gages, just like with most other QC equipment, is to make them with SPC capabilities. Bore gages are evolving with the development of electronic and digimatic models. These electronic bore gages often come with a digital liquid crystal display, making it easy for the operator to view measurement data and obtain accurate readings. Some models require that the gage be connected to a digital readout system.

As the next decade unfolds and meaningful measurement data are required as statistical proof that standards and tolerances are being met, bore gages will be there providing accurate measurements.

Questions for Discussion

1. Describe the advantages and disadvantages of the different types of bore gages.
2. Discuss the general problems in obtaining accurate measurements using these gages.
3. Describe the advantages and disadvantages of go/no-go gages over those that yield measurements.

KEY TERMS

Acceptability constant (k)
Acceptable quality level (AQL)
Acceptance limit
Attribute sampling plan
Consumer's risk
Decision rules
  Form 1
  Form 2
Double specification limit
Limiting quality level (LQL)
Lot percent nonconforming
Maximum allowance percent nonconforming (M)
OC curve
Process average
Process standard deviation
Producer's risk
Sample size
Single specification limit
Standardized plans
  ANSI/ASQC Z1.9
  MIL–STD-414
  ISO 3951
Variable sampling plan

EXERCISES

Discussion Questions

10-1 What are the advantages and disadvantages of variable sampling plans over those for attributes?

10-2 What are the parameters of a variable sampling plan for which the process average quality is of interest? Explain the working procedure of such a plan when single and double specification limits are given.

10-3 Explain the difference between the decision-making procedure using Form 1 and Form 2 for variable sampling plans that are designed to estimate the proportion of nonconforming units.

10-4 Explain the similarities and dissimilarities between the standardized plans *ANSI/ASQC Z1.9*, which is used for variable inspection, and *ANSI/ASQC Z1.4*, which is used for attribute inspection.

Problems

10-5 The upper specification limit for the resistance of coils is 30 ohms. The distribution of the resistance of coils is known to be normal with a standard deviation of 5 ohms. It is preferred to reject batches that have a mean of 2.3 standard deviations below the upper specification limit no more than 5 percent of the time. Also, batches that have a mean of one standard deviation below the upper specification should be accepted no more than 8 percent of the time. Find the parameters of a variable sampling plan and describe its operation.

10-6 The lower specification limit for the breaking strength of yarns is 25 g. The distribution of the breaking strength of yarns is normal with a variance of 6. It is desirable that lots with a mean such that 3 percent of the product is nonconforming be accepted 94 percent of the time. Lots with a mean such that 8 percent of the product is nonconforming should be accepted 7 percent of the time. Find the parameters of a variable sampling plan and describe its operation.

10-7 The tensile strength of an alloy has double specification limits. If the process average tensile strength is below 800 kg/cm^2 or above 1200 kg/cm^2, it is desired to accept such lots with a probability of 0.08. For lots with a process average of 1000 kg/cm^2, it is desired that the probability of acceptance be 0.96. The distribution of tensile strength is normal, with a standard deviation of 80 kg/cm^2. Find the variable sampling plan and describe its operation.

10-8 The sulfur content in a drug has an upper and lower specification limit. We wish the probability of lot acceptance to be 9 percent if the process average sulfur content is below 25 percent or above 35 percent. If the process average is at 30 percent, we wish the acceptance probability to be 0.96. The distribution of sulfur content is normal, with a standard deviation of 2 percent. Find the parameters of a variable sampling plan, and describe its operation.

10-9 The length of connector pins has an upper specification limit of 45 mm and a lower specification limit of 40 mm. It is desirable that lots with a mean such that 8 percent of the product is nonconforming, either above the upper specification limit or below the lower specification limit, be accepted 6 percent of the time. We wish to accept lots with a mean of 42.5 mm with a probability of 0.94. The distribution of the length of the connector pin is normal, with a standard deviation of 0.8 mm. Find the parameters of a variable sampling plan and describe its operation.

10-10 The proportion of carbon monoxide in exhaust gases has an upper specification limit of 0.30. Emission control devices are being tested to meet such requirements. We wish that devices with an average carbon monoxide content of 0.15 or less be accepted 95 percent of the time. If the average carbon monoxide content is 0.34 or more, we wish the probability of acceptance to be 0.20. An estimate of the standard deviation of the proportion of carbon monoxide is 0.25. Find a variable sampling plan and explain its operation.

10-11 Refer to Exercise 10-10 regarding the proportion of carbon monoxide in exhaust gases, which has an upper specification limit of 0.30. If the average carbon monoxide content is one standard deviation below the upper specification limit, the devices should be rejected 5 percent of the time. If the average carbon monoxide content is 0.8 standard deviations above the upper specification limit, the probability of acceptance should be 0.20. The standard deviation of the proportion of carbon monoxide is unknown. Find a variable sampling plan and describe its operation.

10-12 Unleaded gasoline must meet certain federal standards. The octane number for a particular brand must be at least 89. The standard deviation of the octane number is estimated to be 4. It is preferred to accept shipments for which the average octane number is 94 about 90 percent of the time. Also, for those shipments that have an average octane number of 86, the probability of acceptance is desired to be 0.15. Find the parameters of a variable sampling plan.

10-13 A dairy has to control the amount of butterfat in its low-fat milk. The upper specification limit of the fat content is 4 g for 4-liter containers. The standard deviation of the fat content for these containers is estimated to be 0.5 g. It is desired to accept 95 percent of the shipments when the proportion of containers that are nonconforming is 1 percent. Additionally, when 7 percent of the containers are nonconforming, the probability of acceptance is desired to be 8 percent. Find the parameters of a variable sampling plan and explain its operation, assuming that the first condition is to be satisfied exactly. A random sample of 13 containers yielded an average fat content of 3.05 g. What is the decision regarding the lot? Demonstrate the use of Form 1 and Form 2.

10-14 The thickness of silicon wafers is an important characteristic in microelectronic circuits. The upper specification limit for the thickness is 0.015 mm. It is estimated that the standard deviation of the thickness of wafers is 0.0014 mm. We wish to accept lots that are 11 percent nonconforming with a probability of 5 percent. For lots that are

2 percent nonconforming, it is desired that the probability of rejection not exceed 4 percent. Find the parameters of a variable sampling plan, assuming the first of the above two conditions is to be satisfied exactly. A random sample of 17 wafers yielded an average of 0.013 mm. Describe the decision regarding the lot based on Form 1 and Form 2.

10-15 A cereal manufacturer who claims to meet certain mineral and vitamin requirements has a minimum specification of 25 percent for the iron content. The standarddeviation of the iron content is estimated to be 3 percent. It is preferred to accept batches that are 1.5 percent nonconforming with a probability of 0.92. For batches that are 8 percent nonconforming, it is desired that the rejection probability be 0.88. Find the parameters of a variable sampling plan, assuming that the first condition is to be satisfied exactly. How would the sampling plan change if the second condition were to be satisfied exactly?

10-16 In producing an alloy, the upper specification limit for the proportion of a catalyst is 2.5 percent. The batch size is 40, inspection is normal, AQL is 1.4 percent, and the general inspection level is III. Find a variable sampling plan using *ANSI/ASQC Z1.9*, using Form 1 and Form 2. A random sample of 10 units yielded the following catalyst content (in percent): 1.2, 1.6, 0.8, 1.9, 1.8, 1.4, 0.6, 0.9, 1.5, and 0.7. What is your decision regarding the lot based on Form 1 and Form 2?

10-17 In Exercise 10-16, if tightened inspection had been used, what is your decision based on Form 1 and Form 2?

10-18 In Exercise 10-16, if reduced inspection had been used, what are the parameters of a variable sampling plan based on Form 1 and Form 2?

10-19 In Exercise 10-16, using normal inspection and general inspection level I, what are the parameters of a variable sampling plan using Form 1 and Form 2?

10-20 In Exercise 10-16, suppose a lower specification limit of 1.0 percent is imposed in addition to the given upper specification limit. What is your decision based on Form 2?

10-21 In Exercise 10-16, suppose a lower specification limit of 1.0 percent is additionally imposed; the AQL at this limit is 6.50 percent. What is your decision?

10-22 Processed poultry is packaged into bags for which the lower specification limit on the weight is 2.0 kg. The batch size is 40, inspection is normal, AQL is 0.9 percent, and the general inspection level is II. Find a variable sampling plan using *ANSI/ASQC Z1.9*, using Form 1 and Form 2. A random sample of 5 bags yielded the following weights (in kg): 2.10, 2.03, 2.12, 1.98, and 2.12. What is your decision using Form 1 and Form 2?

10-23 In Exercise 10-22, if tightened inspection had been used, what is your decision using Form 1 and Form 2?

10-24 In Exercise 10-22, using normal inspection and general inspection level III, what are the parameters of a variable sampling plan using Form 1 and Form 2?

10-25 In Exercise 10-22, suppose the lower and upper specification limits are 1.85 and 2.15 kg, respectively, and the AQL is 1.3 percent. What is your decision?

10-26 In Exercise 10-22, suppose a lower specification limit of 1.85 is imposed, with the AQL at this limit being 1.8 percent. The upper specification limit is 2.20, with the AQL at this limit being 2.0 percent. What is your decision regarding the lot?

REFERENCES

American Society for Quality Control (1980). *American National Standard-Sampling Procedures and Tables for Inspection by Variables for Percent Nonconforming—ANSI/ASQC Z1.9–1980*. Milwaukee, WI.

Duncan, A. J. (1986). *Quality Control and Industrial Statistics*, 5th Edition. R. D. Irwin, Homewood, IL.

ISO 3951 (1981). "Sampling Procedures and Charts for Inspection by Variables." International Standards Organization, Geneva, Switzerland.

Lieberman, G. J., and Resnikoff, G. J. (1955). "Sampling Plans for Inspection by Variables." *Journal of the American Statistical Association*, Vol. 50, pp. 457–516.

Mullen, G. (1990). "Gages Help Meet Bore Requirements." *Quality Progress*, 23 (1), pp. 70–71.

Neyman, J., and Tobarska, B. (1936). "Errors of the Second Kind in Testing Student's Hypothesis." *Journal of the American Statistical Association*, Vol. 31, pp. 318–326.

PART

V

Product and Process Design

CHAPTER

11

Reliability

CHAPTER OUTLINE

SYMBOLS

λ	Constant failure rate
$f(t)$	Probability density function for time to failure
$F(t)$	Probability distribution function for time to failure
$R(t)$	Reliability function at time t
$r(t)$	Failure rate function
P_a	Probability of lot acceptance
θ	Mean life of product
n	Sample size
r	Rejection number
T	Predetermined test time
α	Producer's risk
θ_0	Mean life associated with producer's risk
β	Consumer's risk
θ_1	Mean life associated with consumer's risk

11-1 INTRODUCTION

Previous chapters have dealt with quality assurance and control. They have explored the notion of quality during the manufacture of the product or the rendering of a service. The discussion focused on a specific instant in time. Reliability, on the other hand, is a measure of the quality of the product over the long run. There is an extended time period involved with reliability, over which the expected operation of the product is considered; it is expected that the product will function according to certain expectations over a stipulated period of time. To ensure customer satisfaction in the performance phase, measures to improve reliability are typically addressed in the design phase. The concepts of reliability calculation are also important because of the complex nature of products that involve many components in their construction. With the customer in mind, it is important to know the chances of successful operation of the product for at least a certain stipulated period of time. Such information helps the manufacturer to select the parameters of a warranty policy.

11-2 RELIABILITY

A definition of reliability may be stated as follows: *Reliability* is the probability of a product performing its intended function for a stated period of time under certain specified conditions. From this definition, four aspects of reliability need to be addressed. First, reliability is a probability-related concept; the numerical value of this probability is between zero and one. Second, the functional performance of the product has to meet certain stipulations. Product design will usually ensure development of a product that will meet or exceed the stipulated requirements. For example, if the breaking strength of a nylon cord is expected to be 1000 kg, then in its operational phase, the cord must be able to bear weights of 1000 kg or more. Third, reliability implies successful operation over a certain period of time. Although no product is expected to last forever, the time requirement ensures satisfactory performance over at least a minimal stated period (say, two years). Fourth, operating or environmental conditions under which product use takes place are specified. Thus, if the nylon cord is specified to be used under dry conditions indoors, then satisfactory performance is expected for use under those conditions. The reliability of a nylon cord might be described in the context of these four dimensions as having a probability of successful performance of 0.92 in bearing loads of 1000 kg for two years under dry conditions.

11-3 LIFE-CYCLE CURVE AND PROBABILITY DISTRIBUTIONS IN MODELING RELIABILITY

Most products go through three distinct phases from product inception to wear-out. Figure 11-1 shows a typical life-cycle curve for which the failure rate λ is plotted as a function of time. This curve is often referred to as the "bathtub" curve; it consists of the debugging phase, the chance failure phase, and the wear-out phase (Besterfield, 1990; DelMar and Sheldon, 1988; Halpern, 1978).

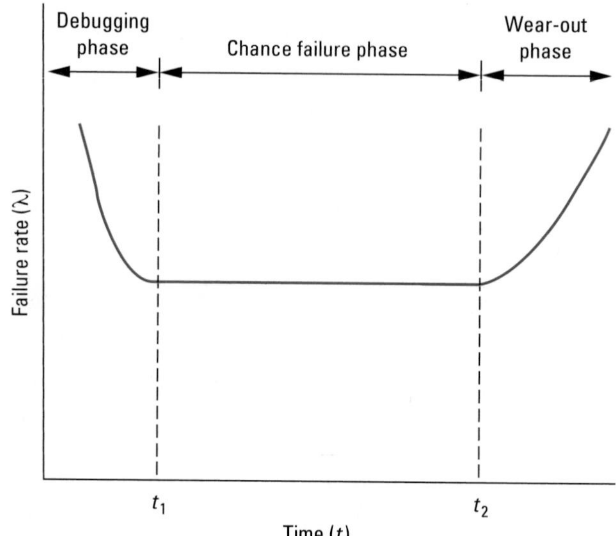

Figure 11-1 A typical failure rate curve.

The *debugging phase,* also known as the infant-mortality phase, exhibits a drop in the failure rate as initial problems identified during prototype testing are ironed out. The *chance-failure phase,* between times t_1 and t_2, is then encountered; failures occur randomly and independently. This phase, in which the failure rate is constant, typically represents the useful life of the product. Following this is the *wear-out phase,* in which an increase in the failure rate is observed. Here, at the end of their useful life, parts age and wear out.

Probability Distributions to Model Failure Rate

Exponential Distribution The life-cycle curve of Figure 11-1 shows the variation of the failure rate as a function of time. For the chance failure phase, which represents the useful life of the product, the failure rate is constant. As a result, the exponential distribution may be used to describe the time to failure of the product for this phase. In Chapter 3, the exponential distribution, which was introduced in Equation 3.39, was shown to have a probability density function given by

$$f(t) = \lambda e^{-\lambda t}, \quad t \geq 0 \qquad (11.1)$$

where λ denotes the failure rate. Figure 3-23 shows this density function.

The mean time to failure (MTTF) for the exponential distribution was given in Equation 3.40 as

$$\text{MTTF} = 1/\lambda \qquad (11.2)$$

Thus, if the failure rate is constant, the mean time to failure is the reciprocal of the failure rate. For repairable equipment, this is also equal to the mean time between failures (MTBF). There will be a difference between MTBF and MTTF only if there is a significant repair or replacement time upon failure of the product.

The reliability at time t, $R(t)$, is the probability of the product lasting up to at least time t. It is given by

$$\begin{aligned} R(t) &= 1 - F(t) \\ &= 1 - \int_0^t e^{-\lambda t}\,dt = e^{-\lambda t} \qquad (11.3) \end{aligned}$$

where $F(t)$ represents the cumulative distribution function at time t. The cumulative distribution function for the exponential distribution was shown in Figure 3-24. Figure 11-2 shows the reliability function, $R(t)$, for the exponential failure distribution. At time 0, the reliability is 1, as it should be. Reliability decreases exponentially with time.

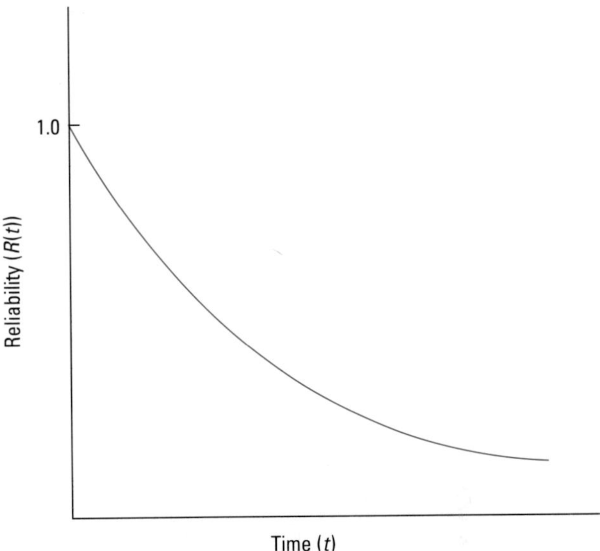

Figure 11-2 Reliability function for the exponential time-to-failure distribution.

In general, the failure rate function $r(t)$ is given by the ratio of the time-to-failure probability density function to the reliability function. We have

$$r(t) = \frac{f(t)}{R(t)} \qquad (11.4)$$

For the exponential failure distribution

$$r(t) = \frac{\lambda e^{-\lambda t}}{e^{-\lambda t}} = \lambda$$

implying a constant failure rate, as mentioned before.

Example 11-1: An amplifier has an exponential time-to-failure distribution with a failure rate of 8 percent/1000 hours. What is the reliability of the amplifier at 5000 hours? Find the mean time to failure.

Solution. The constant failure rate λ is obtained as

$$\begin{aligned} \lambda &= 0.08/1000 \text{ hours} \\ &= 0.00008/\text{hour} \end{aligned}$$

The reliability at 5000 hours is found as

$$\begin{aligned} R(t) &= e^{-\lambda t} \\ &= e^{-(0.00008)(5000)} \\ &= e^{-0.4} = 0.6703 \end{aligned}$$

The mean time to failure is

$$\text{MTTF} = 1/\lambda = 1/0.00008 = 12,500 \text{ hours}$$

Example 11-2 What is the highest failure rate for a product if it is to have a probability of survival (that is, successful operation) of 95 percent at 4000 hours? Assume that the time to failure follows an exponential distribution.

Solution. The reliability at 4000 hours is given to be 0.95. If the constant failure rate is given by λ, we have

$$R(t) = e^{-\lambda t}$$

or

$$0.95 = e^{-\lambda(4000)}$$

We have

$$4000\lambda = 0.05129$$

or

$$\lambda = 0.0000128/\text{hour} = 12.8/10^6 \text{ hours}$$

Thus, the highest failure rate is $12.8/10^6$ hours for a reliability of 0.95 at 4000 hours.

Weibull Distribution The Weibull distribution may be used to model the time to failure of products that have a varying failure rate. It therefore is a candidate to model the debugging phase, in which the failure rate decreases with time, or the wear-out phase, in which the failure rate increases with time (Henley and Kumamoto, 1981). The Weibull distribution was introduced in Chapter 3. It is a three-parameter distribution whose density function is given in Equation 3.43 as

$$f(t) = \frac{\beta}{\alpha}\left(\frac{t-\gamma}{\alpha}\right)^{\beta-1} \exp[-\left(\frac{t-\gamma}{\alpha}\right)^{\beta}], \; t \geq \gamma \tag{11.5}$$

The parameters are a location parameter, γ $(-\infty < \gamma < \infty)$, a scale parameter, α $(\alpha > 0)$, and a shape parameter β $(\beta > 0)$. The probability density functions for $\gamma = 0$, $\alpha = 1$ and several values of β ($\beta =$ 0.5, 1, 2, and 4) are shown in Figure 3-25.

The use of appropriate parameter values may be used to model a wide variety of situations. If $\gamma = 0$ and $\beta = 1$, the Weibull distribution reduces to the exponential distribution. For reliability modeling, the location parameter γ will be zero. If $\alpha = 1$ and $\beta = 0.5$, for example, the failure rate decreases with time, and can therefore be used to model components in the debugging phase. Likewise, if $\alpha = 1$ and $\beta = 3.5$, for example, the failure rate increases with time and so can be used to model products in the wear-out phase. In this case the Weibull distribution approximates the normal distribution.

The reliability function for the Weibull distribution is given by

$$R(t) = \exp[-(t/\alpha)^{\beta}] \tag{11.6}$$

The mean time to failure, as given by Equation 3.44, is

$$\text{MTTF} = \alpha\Gamma(1/\beta + 1) \tag{11.7}$$

The failure rate function $r(t)$ for the Weibull time-to-failure probability distribution is

$$r(t) = \frac{f(t)}{R(t)} = \frac{\beta t^{\beta-1}}{\alpha^{\beta}} \tag{11.8}$$

Figure 11-3 shows the shape of the failure rate function for the Weibull failure density function, for values of the parameter β of 0.5, 1, and 3.5.

Example 11-3: Capacitors in an electrical circuit have a time-to-failure distribution that can be modeled by the Weibull distribution with a scale parameter of 400 hours and a shape parameter of 0.2. What is the reliability of the capacitor after 600 hours of operation? Find the mean time to failure. Is the failure rate increasing or decreasing with time?

Solution. The parameters of the Weibull distribution are $\alpha = 400$ hours and $\beta = 0.2$. The location parameter γ is 0 for such reliability problems. The reliability after 600 hours of operation is given by

$$\begin{aligned} R(t) &= \exp[-(t/\alpha)^{\beta}] \\ &= \exp[-(600/400)^{0.2}] \\ &= 0.3381 \end{aligned}$$

The mean time to failure is

$$\begin{aligned} \text{MTTF} &= \alpha\Gamma(1/\beta + 1) \\ &= 400\Gamma(1/0.2 + 1) \\ &= 48,000 \text{ hours} \end{aligned}$$

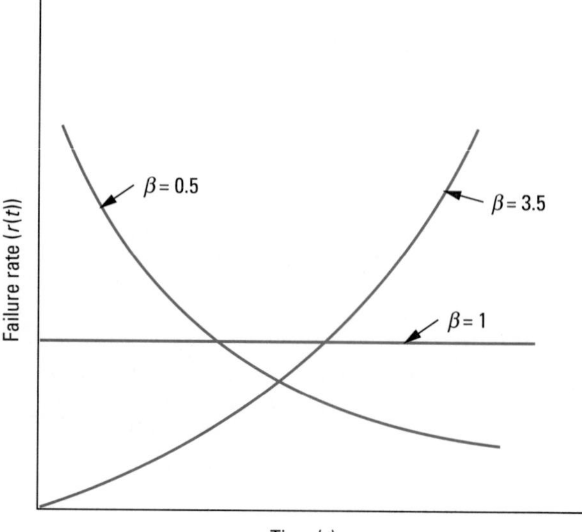

Figure 11-3 Failure rate functions for the Weibull time-to-failure distribution for $\beta =$ 0.5, 1, and 3.5.

The failure rate function is

$$r(t) = \frac{0.2t^{0.2-1}}{(400)^{0.2}}$$
$$= 0.0603t^{-0.8}$$

This function decreases with time. It would model components in the debugging phase.

11-4 SYSTEM RELIABILITY

Most products are made up of a number of components. The reliability of each component and the configuration of the system consisting of these components determines the reliability of the system (that is, the reliability of the product). Although product design, manufacture, and maintenance influence reliability, most of the emphasis in improving reliability is placed on the design phase. One common approach for increasing the reliability of the system is through redundance in design, which is usually achieved by placing components in parallel: As long as any one of the components operates, the system operates. This section demonstrates the computation of system reliability for systems that have components in series, in parallel, or both.

System with Components in Series

Figure 11-4 demonstrates an example of a system with three components (A, B, and C) in series. For the system to operate, each of the components must operate. It is assumed that the components operate independently of each other (that is, the failure of one component has no influence on the failure of any other component). In general, if there are n components in series, where the reliability of the ith component is denoted by R_i, the system reliability is

$$R_s = R_1 \times R_2 \times \cdots \times R_n \tag{11.9}$$

The system reliability decreases as the number of components in series increases. Although overdesign in each component could be used to improve reliability, its impact would be offset by the number of components in series. Moreover, manufacturing capabilities and resource limitations restrict the maximum reliability of any given component. Product redesign that reduces the number of components in series is a viable alternative.

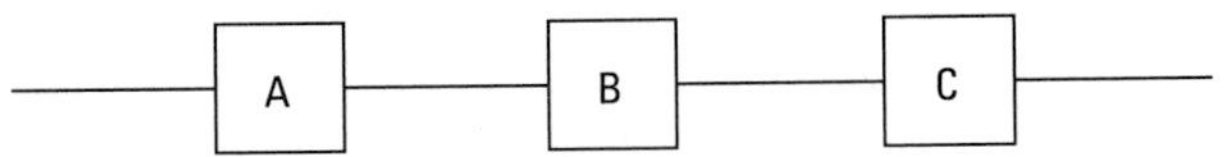

Figure 11-4 System with components in series.

Example 11-4: A module of a satellite monitoring system has 500 components in series. The reliability of each component is 0.999. Find the reliability of the module. If the number of components in series is reduced to 200, what is the reliability of the module?

Solution. The system reliability for the module is

$$R_s = (0.999)^{500} = 0.606$$

Note that even with a high reliability of 0.999 for each component,the system reliability is only 60.6 percent. When the number of components in series is reduced to 200, the reliability of the module is

$$R_s = (0.999)^{200} = 0.819$$

Use of the Exponential Model If all of the components of a system can be assumed to have a time to failure given by the exponential distribution and each component has a constant failure rate, the system reliability, failure rate, and mean time to failure can be computed. As was previously discussed, when the components are in the chance failure phase during the period of useful life, the assumption of a constant failure rate could be justified.

Suppose the system has n components in series, each with exponentially distributed time-to-failure with failure rates $\lambda_1, \lambda_2, \ldots, \lambda_n$. The system reliability is found as the product of the component reliabilities:

$$R_s = e^{-\lambda_1 t} \times e^{-\lambda_2 t} \times \cdots \times e^{-\lambda_n t}$$
$$= \exp\left[-\left(\sum_{i=1}^{n} \lambda_i\right)t\right] \tag{11.10}$$

Equation 11.10 implies that the time to failure of the system is exponentially distributed with an equivalent failure rate of $\sum_{i=1}^{n} \lambda_i$. Thus, if each component that fails is replaced immediately with another that has the same failure rate, the mean time to failure for the system is given by

$$\text{MTTF} = 1/\left[\sum_{i=1}^{n} \lambda_i\right] \tag{11.11}$$

When all components in series have an identical failure rate, say λ, the MTTF for the system (a special case of Equation 11.11) is given by

$$\text{MTTF} = 1/(n\lambda)$$

Example 11-5: The automatic focus unit of a television camera has 10 components in series. Each component has an exponential time-to-failure distribution with a constant failure rate of 0.05 per 4000 hours. What is the reliability of each component after 2000 hours of operation? Find the reliability of the automatic focus unit for 2000 hours of operation. What is its mean time-to-failure?

Solution. The failure rate for each component is

$$\begin{aligned}\lambda &= 0.05 \text{ per } 4000 \text{ hours}\\ &= 12.5 \times 10^{-6}/\text{hour}\end{aligned}$$

The reliability of each component after 2000 hours of operation is

$$\begin{aligned}R &= \exp[-(12.5 \times 10^{-6})2000]\\ &= 0.975\end{aligned}$$

The reliability of the automatic focus unit after 2000 hours of operation is

$$\begin{aligned}R_s &= \exp[-(10 \times 12.5 \times 10^{-6})2000]\\ &= 0.779\end{aligned}$$

The mean time to failure of the automatic focus unit is

$$\begin{aligned}\text{MTTF} &= 1/(10 \times 12.5 \times 10^{-6})\\ &= 8000 \text{ hours}\end{aligned}$$

Example 11-6: Consider Example 11-5 concerning the automatic focus unit of a television camera, which has 10 similar components in series. Suppose that it is desired for the focus unit to have a reliability of 0.95 after 2000 hours of operation. What would be the mean time to failure of the individual components?

Solution. Let λ_s be the failure rate of the focus unit. Then, $\lambda_s = 10\lambda$, where λ represents the failure rate of each component. To achieve the reliability of 0.95 after 2000 hours, the value of λ_s is found from

$$0.95 = \exp[-\lambda_s(2000)]$$

or

$$\lambda_s = 0.0000256/\text{hour}$$

The failure rate for each component is

$$\begin{aligned}\lambda &= \lambda_s/10\\ &= 0.00000256/\text{hour}\\ &= 2.56/10^6 \text{ hours}\end{aligned}$$

The mean time to failure for each component would be

$$\begin{aligned}\text{MTTF} &= 1/\lambda\\ &= 390{,}625 \text{ hour}\end{aligned}$$

System with Components in Parallel

In designing systems, one way system reliability can be improved is by placing components in parallel. Characterized as having redundant components, the system operates as long as at least one of the components operates. The only time the system fails is when all of the parallel components fail. Figure 11-5 demonstrates an example of a system with three components (A, B, and C) in parallel. All units are assumed to operate simultaneously. Examples of redundant components placed in parallel to improve the reliability of the system may be found in numerous applications. Consider the automobile: the braking mechanism is a critical system. Dual subsystems exist so that if one were to fail, the brakes would still work.

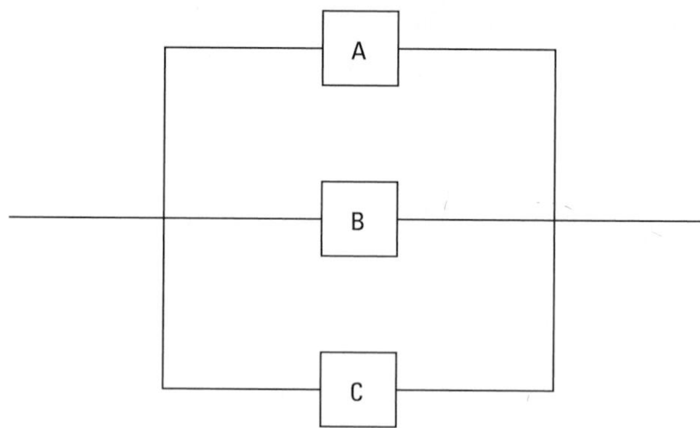

Figure 11-5 System with components in parallel.

Suppose we have n components in parallel, with the reliability of the ith component denoted by R_i, $i = 1, 2, \ldots, n$. Assuming that the components operate randomly and independently of each other, the probability of failure of each component is given by $F_i = 1 - R_i$. Now, the system fails only if all the components fail. Thus, the probability of system failure is

$$\begin{aligned}F_s &= (1 - R_1)(1 - R_2)\cdots(1 - R_n)\\ &= \prod_{i=1}^{n}(1 - R_i).\end{aligned}$$

The reliability of the system is the complement of F_s and is given by

$$\begin{aligned}R_s &= 1 - F_s\\ &= 1 - \prod_{i=1}^{n}(1 - R_i)\end{aligned} \qquad (11.12)$$

Use of the Exponential Model If the time to failure of each component can be modeled by the exponential distribution, each with a constant failure rate λ_i, $i = 1, \ldots n$, the system reliability, assuming independence of component operation, is given by

$$\begin{aligned}R_s &= 1 - \prod_{i=1}^{n}(1 - R_i)\\ &= 1 - \prod_{i=1}^{n}(1 - e^{-\lambda_i t})\end{aligned} \qquad (11.13)$$

The time-to-failure distribution of the system is not exponentially distributed.

In the special case for which all components have the same failure rate λ, the system reliability is given by

$$R_s = 1 - (1 - e^{-\lambda t})^n$$

For this situation, the mean time to failure for the system with n identical components in parallel, assuming that each failed component is immediately replaced by an identical component, is given by

$$\text{MTTF} = \frac{1}{\lambda}\left(1 + \frac{1}{2} + \frac{1}{3} + \cdots + \frac{1}{n}\right) \qquad (11.14)$$

Example 11-7: Consider the system shown in Figure 11-5 with three components (A, B, and C) in parallel. Suppose the reliabilities of A, B, and C are 0.95, 0.92, and 0.90, respectively. Find the reliability of the system.

Solution. The system reliability is found as

$$\begin{aligned} R_s &= 1 - (1 - 0.95)(1 - 0.92)(1 - 0.90) \\ &= 1 - 0.0004 = 0.9996 \end{aligned}$$

Note that the system reliability is much higher than that of the individual components. Designers can increase system reliability by placing more components in parallel, but the cost of the additional components necessitates a trade-off between the two objectives.

Example 11-8: Consider the system shown in Figure 11-5 with three components(A, B, and C) in parallel. Assume that all three components have an identical time-to-failure distribution that is exponential, with a constant failure rate of 0.0005/hour. Determine the system reliability for 2000 hours of operation, and find the mean time to failure. What is the mean time to failure of each component? If it is desired for the system to have a mean time to failure of 4000 hours, what should be the mean time to failure of each component?

Solution. The failure rate of each component is $\lambda =$ 0.0005/hour. For 2000 hours of operation, the system reliability is

$$\begin{aligned} R_s &= 1 - [1 - \exp(-(0.0005)2000)]^3 \\ &= 1 - (0.63212)^3 \\ &= 0.7474 \end{aligned}$$

The mean time to failure for the system is

$$\begin{aligned} \text{MTTF} &= \frac{1}{0.0005}\left(1 + \frac{1}{2} + \frac{1}{3}\right) \\ &= 3666.67 \text{ hours} \end{aligned}$$

The mean time to failure for each component is

$$\text{MTTF} = 1/\lambda = 1/0.0005 = 2000 \text{ hours}$$

By placing three identical components in parallel, the system MTTF has been increased by about 83.3 percent.

For a desired system MTTF of 4000 hours, we now calculate the required MTTF of the individual components. We have

$$4000 = \frac{1}{\lambda}\left(1 + \frac{1}{2} + \frac{1}{3}\right),$$

where λ is the failure rate for each component. Solving for λ, we get

$$\lambda = \frac{1.8333}{4000} = 0.00046/\text{hour}$$

Thus, the MTTF for each component would have to be

$$\text{MTTF} = 1/\lambda = 1/0.00046 = 2173.91 \text{ hours}$$

System with Components in Series and Parallel

Complex systems may consist of components that are both in series and parallel. Reliability calculations are based on the previously discussed concepts, assuming that the components operate independently of each other.

Example 11-9: Consider the system shown in Figure 11-6 with a total of eight components; some are in series, and some are in parallel. The reliabilities of the components are as follows: $R_{A_1} = 0.92$, $R_{A_2} = 0.90$, $R_{A_3} = 0.88$, $R_{A_4} = 0.96$, $R_{B_1} = 0.95$, $R_{B_2} = 0.90$, $R_{B_3} = 0.92$, and $R_{C_1} = 0.93$. Find the system reliability.

Solution. We first find the reliabilities of each of the subsystems. Consider the subsystem with components A_1, A_2, A_3, and A_4. The reliability of this subsystem is

$$\begin{aligned} R_1 &= 1 - (1 - R_{A_1}R_{A_2})(1 - R_{A_3}R_{A_4}) \\ &= 1 - (1 - (0.92)(0.90))(1 - (0.88)(0.96)) \\ &= 0.9733 \end{aligned}$$

Similarly, the reliability of the subsystem with components B_1, B_2, and B_3 is

$$\begin{aligned} R_2 &= 1 - (1 - R_{B_1})(1 - R_{B_2})(1 - R_{B_3}) \\ &= 1 - (1 - 0.95)(1 - 0.90)(1 - 0.92) \\ &= 0.9996 \end{aligned}$$

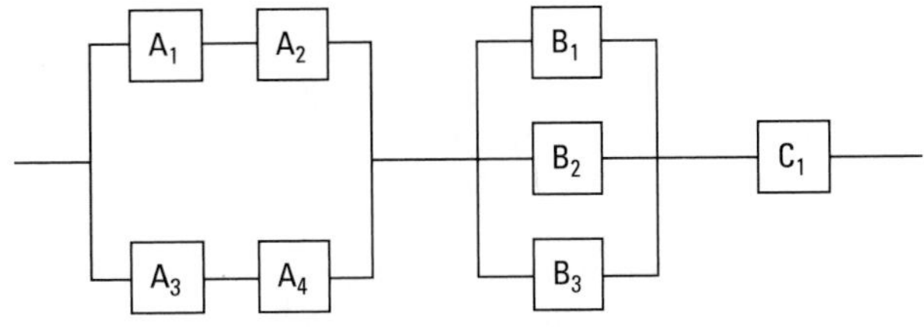

Figure 11-6 System with components in series and parallel.

The system reliability is given by

$$\begin{aligned} R_s &= R_1 \times R_2 \times R_{C_1} \\ &= (0.9733)(0.9996)(0.93) \\ &= 0.9048 \end{aligned}$$

Use of the Exponential Model If the time to failure for each component can be assumed to be exponentially distributed, the system reliability and mean time to failure may be calculated under certain conditions by using previously discussed procedures.

Example 11-10: Consider the system shown in Figure 11-6. Suppose that the failure rates (number of units per hour) for the components are as follows: $\lambda_{A_1} = 0.0006$, $\lambda_{A_2} = 0.0045$, $\lambda_{A_3} = 0.0035$, $\lambda_{A_4} = 0.0016$, $\lambda_{B_1} = 0.0060$, $\lambda_{B_2} = 0.0060$, $\lambda_{B_3} = 0.0060$, $\lambda_{C_1} = 0.0050$. Find the failure rate for the system and the mean time to failure.

Solution. Consider first the computations for the subsystems; we have a failure rate of $(\lambda_{A_1} + \lambda_{A_2}) = 0.0051$ for the A_1 and A_2 subsystem; for the A_3 and A_4 subsystem, the failure rate is $(\lambda_{A_3} + \lambda_{A_4}) = 0.0051$. The mean time to failure for the A_1,A_2, A_3, and A_4 subsystem is

$$\text{MTTF}_1 = \frac{1}{0.0051}(1 + 1/2) = 294.118 \text{ hours}$$

The mean time to failure for the subsystem consisting of the components B_1, B_2, and B_3 is

$$\text{MTTF}_2 = \frac{1}{0.0060}(1 + 1/2 + 1/3) = 305.555 \text{ hours}$$

The system failure rate is

$$\lambda_s = 1/294.118 + 1/305.555 + 0.005 = 0.01167$$

The mean time to failure for the system is

$$\text{MTTF}_s = 85.69 \text{ hours}$$

Systems with Standby Components

In a standby configuration, one or more parallel components wait to take over operation upon failure of the currently operating unit. Here, it is assumed that only one unit in the parallel configuration is operating at any given time. Because of this, the system reliability is higher than for comparable systems with components in parallel. In parallel systems discussed previously, all units are assumed to operate simultaneously. Figure 11-7 shows a standby system with a basic unit and two standby units in parallel. Typically, a failure-sensing mechanism triggers the operation of a standby unit when the currently operating unit fails.

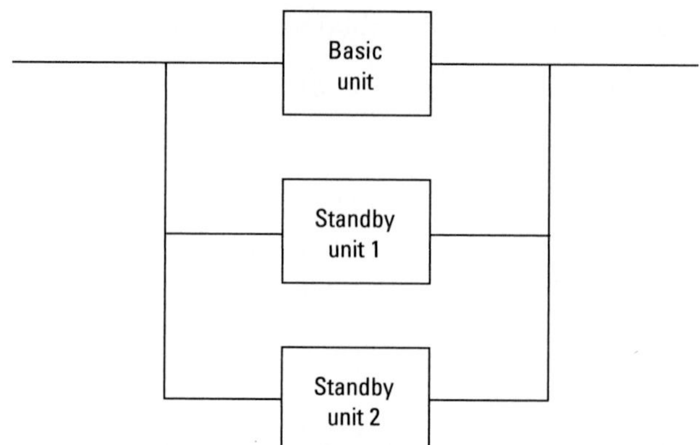

Figure 11-7 Standby system.

Use of the Exponential Model If the time to failure of the components or units is assumed to be exponential with failure rate λ, the number of failures in a certain time t adheres to a Poisson distribution with parameter λt. Using the Poisson distribution introduced in Chapter 3, the probability of x failures in time t is given by

$$P(x) = \frac{e^{-\lambda t}(\lambda t)^x}{x!} \tag{11.15}$$

For a system that has a basic unit in parallel with one standby unit, the system will be operational at time t, as long as there is no more than one failure. Therefore, the system reliability would be

$$R = e^{-\lambda t} + e^{-\lambda t}(\lambda t)$$

For a standby system with a basic unit and two standby units (shown in Figure 11-7), the system will be operational if the number of failures is less than or equal to two. The system reliability is

$$R = e^{-\lambda t} + e^{-\lambda t}(\lambda t) + e^{-\lambda t}\frac{(\lambda t)^2}{2!}$$

In general, if there are n units on standby along with the basic unit [for a total of $(n + 1)$ units in the system] the system reliability is given by

$$R_s = e^{-\lambda t}\left(1 + \lambda t + \frac{(\lambda t)^2}{2!} + \frac{(\lambda t)^3}{3!} + \cdots + \frac{(\lambda t)^n}{n!}\right) \tag{11.16}$$

The mean time to failure for such a system is

$$\text{MTTF} = \frac{n+1}{\lambda} \tag{11.17}$$

Example 11-11: Consider a standby system as shown in Figure 11-7, with one basic unit and two standby units, each having an exponential time-to-failure distribution.

The failure rate for each unit is 0.004 per hour. For a period of operation of 300 hours, find the reliability of the system. What is the mean time to failure? If the three units had been in parallel and not in a standby mode, what would be the reliability of the system? What would be the mean time to failure?

Solution. The failure rate λ for each unit is 0.004 per hour. For 300 hours of operation, the system reliability is

$$R_S = e^{-\lambda t}\left(1 + \lambda t + \frac{(\lambda t)^2}{2!}\right)$$

$$= e^{-0.004(300)}\left[1 + 0.004(300) + \frac{((0.004)300)^2}{2}\right]$$

$$= e^{-1.2}[1 + 1.2 + 0.72]$$

$$= 0.879$$

The mean time to failure is

$$\text{MTTF} = \frac{n+1}{\lambda} = \frac{3}{0.004} = 750 \text{ hours}$$

Consider the system with all three units in parallel. The probability of failure of each unit is

$$F_1 = 1 - e^{-\lambda t}$$

$$= 1 - e^{-0.004(300)} = 0.6988$$

The system reliability is found as

$$R_s = 1 - (0.6988)^3$$

$$= 0.659$$

The mean time to failure for this parallel system is

$$\text{MTTF} = \frac{1}{\lambda}(1 + 1/2 + 1/3)$$

$$= \frac{1}{0.004}(1 + 1/2 + 1/3)$$

$$= 458.333 \text{ hours}$$

Notice the difference in the system reliability and MTTF of the standby and parallel systems.

11-5 OPERATING CHARACTERISTIC CURVES

Operating characteristic curves for acceptance sampling plans have been introduced in previous chapters. This section discusses OC curves in the context of life and reliability testing plans. A common life testing plan involves choosing a sample of items from the batch and observing their operation for a certain predetermined time. If the number of failures exceeds a stipulated acceptance number, the lot is rejected; if the number of failures is less than or equal to the acceptance number, the lot is accepted. Two options within this plan are possible. With the first option, an item that fails is assumed to be replaced immediately by an identical item. In the second option, failed items are not replaced.

In the calculations for the OC curve, we assume that the time to failure of each unit is exponentially distributed with a constant failure rate λ. The parameters of a life testing plan, for example, are the test time T, the sample size n, and the acceptance number c. The OC curve shows the probability of lot acceptance, P_a, as a function of the lot quality as indicated by the mean life (θ) or the mean time to failure of the unit. Under the stated assumptions, the number of failures within a specified period adheres to the Poisson distribution. The Poisson distribution is used to calculate the probability of lot acceptance.

Example 11-12: The parameters of a life testing plan are given as follows: time of test $T = 800$ hours, sample size $n = 12$, and acceptance number $c = 2$. Each unit has an exponential time-to-failure distribution. When any unit fails, it is immediately replaced by a similar unit. Construct the OC curve for this plan.

Solution. The expected number of failures in the time period T is $nT\lambda$, where λ denotes the constant failure rate of the unit. Denoting the mean life of the unit by θ, we have $\lambda = 1/\theta$. From the Poisson distribution tables in Appendix A-2, the probability of lot acceptance is found for different values of the mean life θ. Suppose the mean life of the unit is 8000 hours, which leads to a failure rate λ of 1/8000. The expected number of failures is

$$nT\lambda = 12(800)(1/8000) = 1.2$$

From Appendix A-2, for a mean number of failures of 1.2, the probability of 2 or fewer failures is 0.879, which is the probability of lot acceptance. This represents one point on the OC curve. Table 11-1 presents the results of similar computations for values of the mean life θ between 1000 and 30,000 hours. Figure 11-8 shows the OC curve for the sampling plan $n = 12$, $T = 800$, $c = 2$.

A point worth mentioning is that the OC curve shown in Figure 11-8 is valid for other life testing plans as long as the total number of unit hours tested is 9600 and the acceptance number is 2. Note that the product of n and T represents the total unit hours tested because failed items are being replaced. So, for instance life testing plan with parameters $n = 10$, $T = 960$, and $c = 2$ would have the same OC curve as that with parameters $n = 8$, $T = 1200$, and $c = 2$.

The notions of producer's risk α and consumer's risk β may also be used in life testing plans. The risk of rejecting a good lot (products that have a satisfactory mean life of θ_0) is the producer's risk. The risk of accepting a poor lot (with products that have

TABLE 11-1 Calculations for the OC curve for the plan $n = 12, T = 800, c = 2$

Mean life, θ	Failure rate, $\lambda = 1/\theta$	Expected number of failures, $nT\lambda$	Probability of acceptance, P_a
1000	0.001	9.6	0.0042
2000	0.0005	4.8	0.1446
3000	0.00033	3.2	0.3822
4000	0.00025	2.4	0.5700
5000	0.0002	1.92	0.6986
6000	0.00017	1.6	0.7830
7000	0.00014	1.37	0.8402
8000	0.000125	1.2	0.8790
9000	0.00011	1.07	0.9060
10000	0.0001	0.96	0.9268
12000	0.000083	0.8	0.9530
14000	0.000071	0.69	0.9671
16000	0.0000625	0.6	0.9770
20000	0.00005	0.48	0.9872
30000	0.000033	0.32	0.9952

an unsatisfactory mean life of θ_1) is the consumer's risk. These risks are illustrated in Figure 11-8. Suppose units with a mean life of 20,000 hours are considered to be satisfactory, so θ_0 is 20,000, and the associated producer's risk α is $(1-0.9872) = .0128$, which is the probability of rejecting units with this mean life. Alternatively, suppose units with a mean life θ_1 of 2000 hours are considered to be undesirable. The associated consumer's risk β would then be the probability of accepting such lots, which from Figure 11-8 is 0.1446.

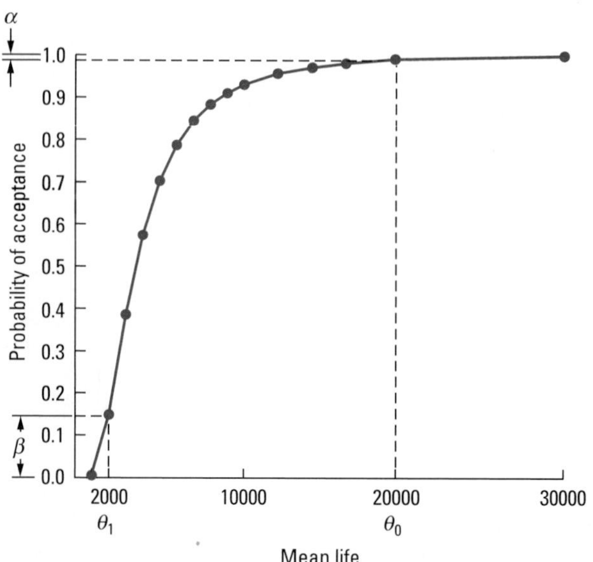

Figure 11-8 OC curve for the plan $n = 12$, $T = 800$, $c = 2$.

An alternative variable for the horizontal axis of the OC curve could be θ/θ_0, the ratio of the actual mean life to the desired mean life θ_0 associated with good batches. For units with mean life θ_0, the probability of lot rejection is the producer's risk α. Thus, all OC curves would pass through the point given by $P_a = 1 - \alpha$ and $\theta/\theta_0 = 1$.

11-6 RELIABILITY AND LIFE TESTING PLANS

Plans for reliability and life testing are usually destructive in nature. They involve, for example, observance of a sample of items until a certain number of failures occur, observance through a certain period of time to record the number of failures that occur, or a combination of both. Nevertheless, testing is usually done at the prototype stage and may be expensive depending on the unit cost of the item. Although a longer accumulated test time is desirable for a precise estimation of the reliability or mean life of the product, the cost associated with the testing plan is an influential factor in its choice. Furthermore, even though testing is usually conducted under simulated conditions, it should realistically represent the actual operating conditions. Several standardized plans have been established by the U.S. Department of Defense, such as *Handbook H-108*, *MIL-STD-690B*, and *MIL-STD-781C*. The plan *H-108* will be introduced in this chapter.

Types of Tests

The three main types of tests are described below:

Failure-Terminated In failure-terminated plans the tests are terminated when a preassigned number of failures occur in the chosen sample. Lot acceptance is based on the accumulated test time of the units when the test is terminated. One acceptance criterion involves whether the estimated average life of the unit exceeds a stipulated value. Let the sample size be denoted by n and the predetermined number of failures by r. Suppose the stipulated mean life is denoted by C. From the test results, suppose the accumulated test time of the units is $\hat{T}$, from which an estimate of the average life is

$$\hat{\theta} = \hat{T}/r$$

The lot is accepted if $\hat{\theta} \geq C$.

Time-Terminated A time-terminated test is terminated when a preassigned time T is reached. Acceptance of the lot is based on the observed number of failures $\hat{r}$ during the test time. If the observed number of failures $\hat{r}$ exceeds a preassigned value r, the lot is rejected; otherwise, the lot is accepted.

Sequential Reliability Testing In sequential reliability testing no prior decision is made as to the number of failures or the time to conduct the test. Instead, the accumulated results of the test are used to decide whether to accept the lot, reject the lot, or continue testing. Figure 11-9 shows the schematic for a sequential life testing plan. The cumulative number of failures based on a chosen sample is plotted versus the accumulated test time of the units. Based on an acceptable mean life θ_0, an associated producer's risk α, a minimum mean life θ_1, and an associated consumer's risk β, equations for the acceptance line and the rejection lines are found. If the plot stays within the two lines, testing continues; if the plot falls in the acceptance region, the test is terminated and the lot is accepted. If the plot falls in the rejection region, the test is terminated and the lot is rejected. In Figure 11-9, observe that after three failures, when the accumulated test time reaches T, the test may be terminated with an acceptance of the lot. Detailed formulas for the equations of the acceptance and rejection lines are omitted because the procedure is similar to sequential tests discussed for attribute sampling plans in Chapter 9. The main advantage of the sequential test plans is that, for a similar degree of protection, the expected test time or the expected number of failures required to reach a decision is less than that for a time-terminated or a failure-terminated plan.

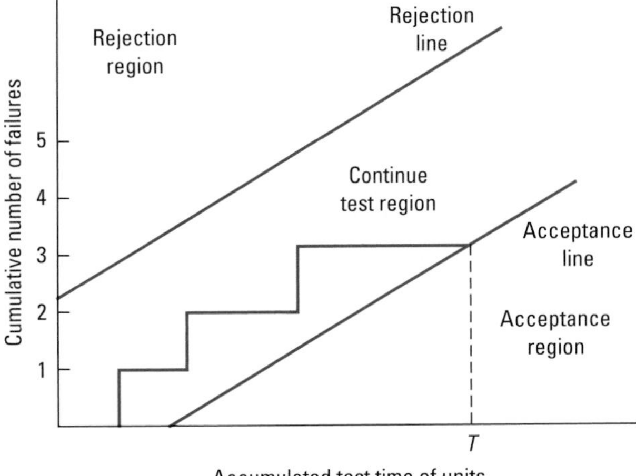

Figure 11-9 Sequential reliability test plan.

For each of the above three tests, testing may take place with or without replacement of the failed units. In the situation for which the unit is replaced, it is assumed that the replaced unit has the same failure rate as the one it replaces. This assumption may hold when the failure rate is constant, as in the chance failure phase of the life of the product. Accordingly, the exponential distribution for the time to failure would be appropriate in this case.

Life Testing Plans Using the Exponential Distribution

The time to failure of the unit is assumed to have an exponential distribution with a constant failure rate. The mean life of the product is estimated when failure-terminated or time-terminated tests are used. Both point estimates and confidence intervals for the mean life are obtained.

Failure-Terminated Test Let the preassigned number of failures be denoted by r. Suppose the failures occur at the following times, in rank order: $t_1 \leq t_2 \leq \cdots \leq t_r$. If the sample size is n, the accumulated life for the test units until the rth failure (T_r), assuming failed items are not replaced, is given by

$$T_r = \sum_{i=1}^{r} t_i + (n - r)t_r \qquad (11.18)$$

If failed items are replaced with items having the same failure rate, we have

$$T_r = nt_r \qquad (11.19)$$

An estimate of the mean life, in either case, is obtained from

$$\hat{\theta} = T_r/r \qquad (11.20)$$

where the value of T_r is substituted using Equation 11.19 or 11.18, depending on whether the items are replaced or not, respectively.

Next, a confidence interval for the mean life θ is found. It is known that the statistic $2T_r/\theta$ has a chi-squared distribution with $2r$ degrees of freedom. Thus, a two-sided $100(1-\alpha)$ percent confidence interval for the mean life is given by

$$\frac{2T_r}{\chi^2_{\alpha/2,2r}} < \theta < \frac{2T_r}{\chi^2_{1-\alpha/2,2r}} \qquad (11.21)$$

where the chi-squared values with $2r$ degrees of freedom are found from Appendix A-5. This may be used for cases with and without replacement.

Example 11-13: Life testing was conducted for a sample of 15 transistors. The time to failure for each is exponentially distributed. The test was terminated after four failures, with no replacement of the failed items. The failure times (in hours) of the four transistors were 400, 480, 610, and 660. Estimate the mean life of the transistors as well as the failure rate. Find a 95 percent confidence interval for the mean life.

Solution. The accumulated life for the test units is

$$T_4 = (400 + 480 + 610 + 660) + (15 - 4)660 = 9410 \text{ hours}$$

The estimated mean life (or mean time to failure) is

$$\hat{\theta} = 9410/4 = 2352.5 \text{ hours}$$

The estimated failure rate is

$$\hat{\lambda} = 1/\hat{\theta} = 1/2352.5 = 0.000425/\text{hour}$$

A 95 percent confidence interval for the mean life is

$$\frac{2T_r}{\chi^2_{.025,8}} < \theta < \frac{2T_r}{\chi^2_{.975,8}}$$

or

$$\frac{2(9410)}{17.53} < \theta < \frac{2(9410)}{2.18}$$

or

$$1073.588 < \theta < 8633.027$$

Example 11-14: Refer to Example 11-13 concerning the life testing of a sample of 15 transistors. The test is truncated after four failures. Assume that each unit that fails is replaced by an identical item. The failure times of the four transistors are 420, 490, 550, and 580 hours. Estimate the mean life of the transistors as well as the failure rate. Find a 95 percent confidence interval for the mean life.

Solution. The accumulated life on the test units is

$$T_4 = 15(580) = 8700 \text{ hours}$$

The estimated mean life is found to be

$$\hat{\theta} = 8700/4 = 2175 \text{ hours}$$

The estimated failure rate is

$$\hat{\lambda} = 1/\hat{\theta} = 1/2175 = 0.00046/\text{ hour}$$

A 95 percent confidence interval for the mean life is

$$\frac{2(8700)}{17.53} < \theta < \frac{2(8700)}{2.18}$$

or

$$992.584 < \theta < 7981.651$$

Time-Terminated Test Let the preassigned time to terminate the test be denoted by T for a sample of size n. Let t_i denote the time of failure of the ith unit. In this case, the observed number of failures is a random variable. If failed units are not replaced, the accumulated life for the test units is given by

$$T_x = \sum_{i=1}^{x} t_i + (n - x)T \qquad (11.22)$$

where x represents the observed number of failures.

When failed items are replaced with similar units, the accumulated life of the test units is

$$T_x = nT \qquad (11.23)$$

An estimate of the mean life may be obtained from

$$\hat{\theta} = T_x/x$$

For both situations, an approximate $100(1-\alpha)$ percent confidence interval for the mean life is given by

$$\frac{2T_x}{\chi^2_{\alpha/2,2(x+1)}} < \theta < \frac{2T_x}{\chi^2_{1-\alpha/2,2(x+1)}} \qquad (11.24)$$

where the chi-squared values with $2(x + 1)$ degrees of freedom are found from Appendix A-5.

Example 11-15: A sample of 12 electronic components were tested for 1000 hours, with no replacement of failed components. The time to failure is exponentially distributed. Three components failed within the prescribed test time, the failure times being 650, 680, and 720 hours. Estimate the mean time to failure and the failure rate. Find a 90 percent confidence interval for the mean time to failure.

Solution. The accumulated life for the test units is

$$T_3 = (650 + 680 + 720) + (12 - 3)1000 = 11050 \text{ hours}$$

An estimate of the mean time to failure is

$$\hat{\theta} = 11050/3 = 3683.333 \text{ hours}$$

An estimate of the failure rate is

$$\hat{\lambda} = 1/\hat{\theta} = 1/3683.333 = 0.00027/\text{hour}$$

A 90 percent confidence interval for the mean time to failure is given by

$$\frac{2(11050)}{\chi^2_{.05,8}} < \theta < \frac{2(11050)}{\chi^2_{.95,8}}$$

or

$$\frac{2(11050)}{15.51} < \theta < \frac{2(11050)}{2.73}$$

or

$$1424.887 < \theta < 8095.238$$

Standard Life Testing Plans Using Handbook H-108

Quality Control and Reliability Handbook H-108 was developed by the Bureau of Naval Weapons, U.S. Department of the Navy. Life test sampling plans in the handbook are based on a time-to-failure distribution that is exponential. All three types of plans (failure-terminated, time-terminated, and sequential life testing) are found in the handbook. For each plan, provision is made for situations with and without replacement of failed units. Here some selected applications of failure-terminated and time-terminated tests are demonstrated. Tables from the handbook are used to determine the life testing plans.

Failure-Terminated Plans Using Handbook H-108 A sample of n items is selected from the lot and tested until the occurrence of the rth failure. If the estimated mean life $\hat{\theta}$ is greater than or equal to a criterion value C given by the plan, the lot is accepted. The producer's risk α is the probability of rejecting a lot with a satisfactory mean life θ_0. The use of this plan is demonstrated through the following examples.

Example 11-16: A life testing plan is to be terminated upon occurrence of the sixth failure. The plan should accept a lot having an acceptable mean life of 1200 hours with a probability of 0.95. Twenty units are placed on test. The six failures occur at the following times (in hours): 480, 530, 560, 600, 640, and 670, respectively. Failed units during the test are not replaced. Using *Handbook H–108* determine if the lot should be accepted.

Solution. The following parameters are given: $r = 6, n = 20, \theta_0 = 1200, \alpha = 0.05$. An estimate of the mean life is

$$\begin{aligned}\hat{\theta} &= [480 + 530 + 560 + 600 \\ &\quad + 640 + 670 + (20 - 6)670]/6 \\ &= 2143.333 \text{ hours}\end{aligned}$$

Table 11-2 shows the values of C/θ_0 for a given producer's risk α and the predetermined number of failures r. For

TABLE 11-2 Master table for life tests terminated upon occurrence of preassigned number of failures

Rejection number, r	Producer's risk (α)					
	0.01		0.05		0.10	
	Code	C/θ_0	Code	C/θ_0	Code	C/θ_0
1	A–1	0.010	B–1	0.052	C–1	0.106
2	A–2	0.074	B–2	0.178	C–2	0.266
3	A–3	0.145	B–3	0.272	C–3	0.367
4	A–4	0.206	B–4	0.342	C–4	0.436
5	A–5	0.256	B–5	0.394	C–5	0.487
6	A–6	0.298	B–6	0.436	C–6	0.525
7	A–7	0.333	B–7	0.469	C–7	0.556
8	A–8	0.363	B–8	0.498	C–8	0.582
9	A–9	0.390	B–9	0.522	C–9	0.604
10	A–10	0.413	B–10	0.543	C–10	0.622
15	A–11	0.498	B–11	0.616	C–11	0.687
20	A–12	0.554	B–12	0.663	C–12	0.726
25	A–13	0.594	B–13	0.695	C–13	0.754
30	A–14	0.625	B–14	0.720	C–14	0.774
40	A–15	0.669	B–15	0.755	C–15	0.803
50	A–16	0.701	B–16	0.779	C–16	0.824
75	A–17	0.751	B–17	0.818	C–17	0.855
100	A–18	0.782	B–18	0.841	C–18	0.874

$r = 6$ and $\alpha = 0.05$, the code is B–6, and C/θ_0 is 0.436. The acceptability criterion C is

$$\begin{aligned}C &= \theta_0(C/\theta_0) \\ &= 1200(0.436) = 523.2\end{aligned}$$

The estimated mean life $\hat{\theta}$ of 2143.33 exceeds the criterion value C. Therefore, the lot should be accepted.

Example 11-17: Consider Example 11-16 for a life testing plan that is terminated upon occurrence of the sixth failure. Suppose failed items are immediately replaced during the test. Based on *Handbook H–108,* should the lot be accepted?

Solution. The parameter values $r = 6$, $n = 20$, $\theta_0 = 1200$, and $\alpha = 0.05$ are the same as in Example 11-16. An estimate of the mean life in this case is

$$\hat{\theta} = \frac{20(670)}{6} = 2233.333 \text{ hours}$$

From Table 11-2, for $\alpha = 0.05$ and $r = 6$, C/θ_0 is 0.436. The acceptability criterion $C = \theta_0(C/\theta_0) = 1200$ $(0.436) = 523.2$. The estimated mean life ($\hat{\theta}$) exceeds the value of C, so the lot should be accepted.

Time-Terminated Plans Using Handbook H–108 For time-terminated plans using *Handbook H–108,* the preassigned test time is denoted by T. An acceptable mean lot life is denoted by θ_0, for which the probability of rejection is α, the producer's risk. Likewise, a minimum mean life is denoted by θ_1, for which the probability of acceptance is β, the consumer's risk. The rejection criterion number r is obtained from the tables. If the observed number of failures within the preassigned test time is greater than or equal to r, the lot is rejected; otherwise, the lot is accepted. The following examples demonstrate the use of tables from *Handbook H-108*. The first example shows the determination of a plan given the producer's risk, the associated mean life, the consumer's risk, the associated mean life, and the sample size.

Example 11-18: Find a time-terminated life testing plan (using *Handbook H–108*) that will reject lots with a mean life of 1250 hours with a probability of 0.05 and accept lots with a mean life of 400 hours with a probability of 0.10. Items that fail during the test are not replaced.

Solution. We have: $\theta_0 = 1250$, $\alpha = 0.05$, $\theta_1 = 400$, $\beta = 0.10$. Hence,

$$\frac{\theta_1}{\theta_0} = \frac{400}{1250} = 0.32$$

Table 11-3 shows the life test sampling plan code designation for various values of α, β, and θ_1/θ_0. Using Table 11-3, we select the table value of θ_1/θ_0 that equals the calculated value. If an exact match is not found, the next larger value of θ_1/θ_0 in the table is used to identify the code. For this example, the code is B-8.

For each code letter, the *Handbook H–108* lists a table to determine the rejection number r and the value of T/θ_0. Table 11-4 shows the value of T/θ_0 for code letter B when testing is conducted without replacement of the failed items; a similar table for testing with replacement of failed items is shown in Table 11-5.

Using Table 11-4 and a code of B-8, the rejection number is found to be 8. Observe that the sample size is indicated as multiples of the rejection number. Increasing the sample size will reduce the average time needed to reach a decision at the expense of added costs due to placing more items on test. Suppose we decide to select the sample size to be a multiple, $4r$, of the rejection number. From Table 11-4, the value of T/θ_0 is found to be 0.141. Thus,

$$\begin{aligned} T &= 0.141(1250) \\ &= 176.25 \text{ hours} \end{aligned}$$

The life testing plan can now be specified. A random sample of 32 items is selected from the lot and tested simultaneously. If the eighth failure occurs before the test termination time of 176.25 hours, the lot is rejected; otherwise, the lot is accepted.

The next example illustrates the determination of a plan given the producer's risk, the associated mean life, the rejection number,and the sample size.

Example 11-19: Find a time-terminated life testing plan that will reject lots that have a mean life of 1800 hours with a probability of 0.05. The rejection number is to be 5 and the sample size is 30. Items that fail during the test are replaced. Determine the plan using the *Handbook H–108.*

TABLE 11-3 Life-test sampling plan code designation

$\alpha = 0.01$, $\beta = 0.01$		$\alpha = 0.05$, $\beta = 0.10$		$\alpha = 0.10$, $\beta = 0.10$		$\alpha = 0.25$, $\beta = 0.10$		$\alpha = 0.50$, $\beta = 0.10$	
Code	θ_1/θ_0	Code	θ_1/θ_0	Code	θ_1/θ_0	Code	θ_1/θ_0	Code	θ_1/θ_0
A–1	0.004	B–1	0.022	C–1	0.046	D–1	0.125	E–1	0.301
A–2	0.038	B–2	0.091	C–2	0.137	D–2	0.247	E–2	0.432
A–3	0.082	B–3	0.154	C–3	0.207	D–3	0.325	E–3	0.502
A–4	0.123	B–4	0.205	C–4	0.261	D–4	0.379	E–4	0.550
A–5	0.160	B–5	0.246	C–5	0.304	D–5	0.421	E–5	0.584
A–6	0.193	B–6	0.282	C–6	0.340	D–6	0.455	E–6	0.611
A–7	0.221	B–7	0.312	C–7	0.370	D–7	0.483	E–7	0.633
A–8	0.247	B–8	0.338	C–8	0.396	D–8	0.506	E–8	0.652
A–9	0.270	B–9	0.361	C–9	0.418	D–9	0.526	E–9	0.667
A–10	0.291	B–10	0.382	C–10	0.438	D–10	0.544	E–10	0.681
A–11	0.371	B–11	0.459	C–11	0.512	D–11	0.608	E–11	0.729
A–12	0.428	B–12	0.512	C–12	0.561	D–12	0.650	E–12	0.759
A–13	0.470	B–13	0.550	C–13	0.597	D–13	0.680	E–13	0.781
A–14	0.504	B–14	0.581	C–14	0.624	D–14	0.703	E–14	0.798
A–15	0.554	B–15	0.625	C–15	0.666	D–15	0.737	E–15	0.821
A–16	0.591	B–16	0.658	C–16	0.695	D–16	0.761	E–16	0.838
A–17	0.653	B–17	0.711	C–17	0.743	D–17	0.800	E–17	0.865
A–18	0.692	B–18	0.745	C–18	0.774	D–18	0.824	E–18	0.882

TABLE 11-4 Values of T/θ_0 for $\alpha = 0.05$—time terminated, testing without replacement, code letter B

Code	r	Sample size									
		$2r$	$3r$	$4r$	$5r$	$6r$	$7r$	$8r$	$9r$	$10r$	$20r$
B–1	1	0.026	0.017	0.013	0.010	0.009	0.007	0.006	0.006	0.005	0.003
B–2	2	0.104	0.065	0.048	0.038	0.031	0.026	0.023	0.020	0.018	0.009
B–3	3	0.168	0.103	0.075	0.058	0.048	0.041	0.036	0.031	0.028	0.014
B–4	4	0.217	0.132	0.095	0.074	0.061	0.052	0.045	0.040	0.036	0.017
B–5	5	0.254	0.153	0.110	0.086	0.071	0.060	0.052	0.046	0.041	0.020
B–6	6	0.284	0.170	0.122	0.095	0.078	0.066	0.057	0.051	0.045	0.022
B–7	7	0.309	0.185	0.132	0.103	0.084	0.072	0.062	0.055	0.049	0.024
B–8	8	0.330	0.197	0.141	0.110	0.090	0.076	0.066	0.058	0.052	0.025
B–9	9	0.348	0.207	0.148	0.115	0.094	0.080	0.069	0.061	0.055	0.027
B–10	10	0.363	0.216	0.154	0.120	0.098	0.083	0.072	0.064	0.057	0.028
B–11	15	0.417	0.246	0.175	0.136	0.112	0.094	0.082	0.072	0.065	0.032
B–12	20	0.451	0.266	0.189	0.147	0.120	0.102	0.088	0.078	0.070	0.034
B–13	25	0.475	0.280	0.199	0.154	0.126	0.107	0.093	0.082	0.073	0.036
B–14	30	0.493	0.290	0.206	0.160	0.131	0.111	0.096	0.085	0.076	0.037
B–15	40	0.519	0.305	0.216	0.168	0.137	0.116	0.101	0.089	0.079	0.039
B–16	50	0.536	0.315	0.223	0.173	0.142	0.120	0.104	0.092	0.082	0.040
B–17	75	0.564	0.331	0.235	0.182	0.149	0.126	0.109	0.096	0.086	0.042
B–18	100	0.581	0.340	0.242	0.187	0.153	0.130	0.112	0.099	0.089	0.043

Solution. We are given the following parameter values: $\theta_0 = 1800$, $\alpha = 0.05$, $r = 5$, and $n = 30$. For $\alpha = 0.05$ and life testing plans with replacement, Table 11-5 may be used for a rejection number r of 5 and a sample size of $6r$ to get $T/\theta_0 = 0.066$. The test termination time is

$$T = (0.066)(1800) = 118.8 \text{ hours}$$

The plan may be described as follows. A random sample of 30 items is selected from the lot and testing is conducted for 118.8 hours. If the fifth failure occurs before the termination time, the lot is rejected; if the fifth failure has not occurred within 118.8 hours, the lot is accepted. Items that fail are replaced.

TABLE 11-5 Values of T/θ_0 for $\alpha = 0.05$—time terminated, testing with replacement, code letter B

Code	r	Sample size									
		$2r$	$3r$	$4r$	$5r$	$6r$	$7r$	$8r$	$9r$	$10r$	$20r$
B–1	1	0.026	0.017	0.013	0.010	0.009	0.007	0.006	0.006	0.005	0.003
B–2	2	0.089	0.059	0.044	0.036	0.030	0.025	0.022	0.020	0.018	0.009
B–3	3	0.136	0.091	0.068	0.055	0.045	0.039	0.034	0.030	0.027	0.014
B–4	4	0.171	0.114	0.085	0.068	0.057	0.049	0.043	0.038	0.034	0.017
B–5	5	0.197	0.131	0.099	0.079	0.066	0.056	0.049	0.044	0.039	0.020
B–6	6	0.218	0.145	0.109	0.087	0.073	0.062	0.054	0.048	0.044	0.022
B–7	7	0.235	0.156	0.117	0.094	0.078	0.067	0.059	0.052	0.047	0.023
B–8	8	0.249	0.166	0.124	0.100	0.083	0.071	0.062	0.055	0.050	0.025
B–9	9	0.261	0.174	0.130	0.104	0.087	0.075	0.065	0.058	0.052	0.026
B–10	10	0.271	0.181	0.136	0.109	0.090	0.078	0.068	0.060	0.054	0.027
B–11	15	0.308	0.205	0.154	0.123	0.103	0.088	0.077	0.068	0.062	0.031
B–12	20	0.331	0.221	0.166	0.133	0.110	0.095	0.083	0.074	0.066	0.033
B–13	25	0.348	0.232	0.174	0.139	0.116	0.099	0.087	0.077	0.070	0.035
B–14	30	0.360	0.240	0.180	0.144	0.120	0.103	0.090	0.080	0.072	0.036
B–15	40	0.377	0.252	0.189	0.151	0.126	0.108	0.094	0.084	0.075	0.038
B–16	50	0.390	0.260	0.195	0.156	0.130	0.111	0.097	0.087	0.078	0.039
B–17	75	0.409	0.273	0.204	0.164	0.136	0.117	0.102	0.091	0.082	0.041
B–18	100	0.421	0.280	0.210	0.168	0.140	0.120	0.105	0.093	0.084	0.042

The following example involves determining a time-terminated plan given the producer's risk, the associated mean life, the consumer's risk, the associated mean life, and the test time.

Example 11-20: Find a time-terminated life testing plan that will accept a lot with a mean life of 5000 hours with a probability of 0.90 but will reject a lot with a mean life of 1000 hours with a probability of 0.95. The test should be terminated by 500 hours. Items that fail are not replaced. Determine the plan assuming the time to failure to be exponentially distributed.

Solution. We are given the following parameter values: $\theta_0 = 5000$, $\alpha = 0.10$, $\theta_1 = 1000$, $\beta = 0.05$, $T = 500$. The following ratios are calculated:

$$\frac{\theta_1}{\theta_0} = \frac{1000}{5000} = \frac{1}{5}$$

$$\frac{T}{\theta_0} = \frac{500}{5000} = \frac{1}{10}$$

Table 11-6 lists the values of the rejection number r and the sample size n, knowing α, β, θ_1/θ_0, and T/θ_0 for time-terminated plans, without replacement of failed units. Table 11-7 lists values of the rejection number r and the sample size n, given α, β, θ_1/θ_0, and T/θ_0, for time-terminated plans with replacement of failed items.

In this problem, Table 11-6 is used. For $\alpha = 0.10$, $\beta = 0.05$, $\theta_1/\theta_0 = 1/5$, and $T/\theta_0 = 1/10$, we have $r = 4$ and $n = 19$. Therefore, the life testing plan is to select a sample of 19 items from the lot. If the fourth failure occurs before the termination time of 500 hours, the lot is rejected; otherwise, the lot is accepted.

11-7 Summary

This chapter introduced the concept of reliability and methods for its computation. Reliability implies the successful operation of a product over a certain period of time under stipulated environmental conditions. Reliability is needed in the performance phase of quality, but plans for its achievement are actually addressed in the design phase. Procedures for improving the reliability of a system by means of adding components in parallel (redundant systems) or through standby systems have been discussed. The life-cycle curve of a product has been studied to identify the period of useful life of the product.

TABLE 11-6 Life tests for predetermined time based on $\alpha, \beta, \theta_1/\theta_0$, and T/θ_0 (without replacement)

		T/θ_0					T/θ_0					T/θ_0			
		1/3	1/5	1/10	1/20		1/3	1/5	1/10	1/20		1/3	1/5	1/10	1/20
		n	n	n	n		n	n	n	n		n	n	n	n
θ_1/θ_0	r	$\alpha = 0.01$		$\beta = 0.01$		r	$\alpha = 0.05$		$\beta = 0.01$		r	$\alpha = 0.10$		$\beta = 0.01$	
2/3	136	403	622	1179	2275	95	289	447	843	1639	77	238	369	699	1358
1/2	46	119	182	340	657	33	90	138	258	499	26	73	112	210	407
1/3	19	41	61	113	216	13	30	45	83	160	11	27	40	75	145
1/5	9	15	22	39	74	7	13	20	36	69	5	10	14	26	51
1/10	5	6	9	15	28	4	6	9	15	29	3	5	7	12	23
		$\alpha = 0.01$		$\beta = 0.05$			$\alpha = 0.05$		$\beta = 0.05$			$\alpha = 0.10$		$\beta = 0.05$	
2/3	101	291	448	842	1632	67	198	305	575	1116	52	156	242	456	886
1/2	35	87	132	245	472	23	59	90	168	326	18	48	73	137	265
1/3	15	30	45	82	157	10	21	32	59	113	8	18	27	50	97
1/5	8	13	18	33	62	5	8	12	22	41	4	7	10	19	36
1/10	4	4	6	10	18	3	4	5	9	17	2	2	3	6	11
		$\alpha = 0.01$		$\beta = 0.10$			$\alpha = 0.05$		$\beta = 0.10$			$\alpha = 0.10$		$\beta = 0.10$	
2/3	83	234	359	675	1307	55	159	245	462	895	41	121	186	351	681
1/2	30	72	109	202	390	19	47	72	134	258	15	39	59	110	213
1/3	13	25	37	67	128	8	16	24	43	83	6	12	18	34	66
1/5	7	11	15	26	50	4	6	9	15	29	3	5	7	12	23
1/10	4	4	6	10	18	3	4	5	9	17	2	2	3	6	11

TABLE 11-7 Life tests for predetermined time based on $\alpha, \beta, \theta_1/\theta_0$, and T/θ_0 (with replacement)

		T/θ_0					T/θ_0					T/θ_0			
		1/3	1/5	1/10	1/20		1/3	1/5	1/10	1/20		1/3	1/5	1/10	1/20
		n	n	n	n		n	n	n	n		n	n	n	n
θ_1/θ_0	r	$\alpha = 0.01$		$\beta = 0.01$		r	$\alpha = 0.05$		$\beta = 0.01$		r	$\alpha = 0.10$		$\beta = 0.01$	
2/3	136	331	551	1103	2207	95	238	397	795	1591	77	197	329	659	1319
1/2	46	95	158	317	634	33	72	120	241	483	26	59	98	197	394
1/3	19	31	31	103	206	13	23	38	76	153	11	21	35	70	140
1/5	9	10	10	35	70	7	9	16	32	65	5	7	12	24	48
1/10	5	4	6	12	25	4	4	6	13	27	3	3	5	11	22
		$\alpha = 0.01$		$\beta = 0.05$			$\alpha = 0.05$		$\beta = 0.05$			$\alpha = 0.10$		$\beta = 0.05$	
2/3	101	237	395	790	1581	67	162	270	541	1082	52	128	214	429	859
1/2	35	68	113	227	454	23	47	78	157	314	18	38	64	128	256
1/3	15	22	37	74	149	10	16	27	54	108	8	13	23	46	93
1/5	8	8	14	29	58	5	6	10	19	39	4	5	8	17	34
1/10	4	3	4	8	16	3	3	4	8	16	2	2	3	5	10
		$\alpha = 0.01$		$\beta = 0.10$			$\alpha = 0.05$		$\beta = 0.10$			$\alpha = 0.10$		$\beta = 0.10$	
2/3	83	189	316	632	1265	55	130	216	433	876	41	99	165	330	660
1/2	30	56	93	187	364	19	37	62	124	248	15	30	51	102	205
1/3	13	18	30	60	121	8	11	19	39	79	6	9	15	31	63
1/5	7	7	11	23	46	4	4	7	13	27	3	4	6	11	22
1/10	2	4	4	8	16	3	3	4	8	16	2	2	2	5	10

Source: *Handbook H–108*, pp. 2.53–2.54.

Probability distributions that model different phases of the life-cycle curve have been explored. Some tests for reliability and life testing have been covered in this chapter. The exponential distribution for time to failure is used as a basis for these tests. Failure-terminated, time-terminated, and sequential tests for life testing have been introduced. Standardized tests developed by the government have been treated in some detail.

11-8 CASE STUDY

VERIFY ACCURACY THROUGH CALIBRATION*

We are all familiar with the calibration and adjustment of an instrument or device. As a matter of fact, we perform a calibration (more frequently than we would like) when we adjust the time on our wristwatches. This adjustment is performed against some known and accepted standard. Nevertheless, we have still experienced undesirable results when we arrive late for a meeting or miss a plane because of an out-of-tolerance timepiece or an adjustment made against an inappropriate standard.

The agency that provides the primary calibrations in the United States is the National Institute of Standards and Technology (NIST). The institute, located in Gaithersburg, Maryland, and Boulder, Colorado, provides measurement services in almost any parameter, including electrical, mass, optical, temperature, length, sound, and radiation.

All transfer measurement devices with accuracy limits are assumed to be accurate to those limits. NIST calibrates these instruments and certifies that the transfer

* Adapted from B. Bremmer (1991), "Verify Accuracy Through Calibration," *Quality Progress*, Vol. 24, No. 3, pp. 108–111.

standard is accurate. These instruments are then referred to as being traceable to NIST.

Although subsequent calibrations using this transfer standard aren't as accurate, they are also referred to as traceable to NIST. For example, a voltmeter in a company might be calibrated by the company's voltage standard. The voltage standard, however, would have been previously calibrated by NIST. This is essential for a comprehensive calibration program.

The act of calibrating a wristwatch can be better understood by reviewing the definition of *calibration:* the comparison of a measurement system or device of unverified accuracy (the watch) to a measurement system or device of known greater accuracy (the standard) to detect or correct any variation from the required performance specification of the unverified measurement system or device. It is important to note that the calibration might involve no adjustment at all.

The calibration procedure, while undoubtedly the most important part, represents only one aspect of a calibration program. The various aspects of a calibration program, addressed from the perspective of a wristwatch as an accurate measurement instrument, are described in Table 11-8.

A calibration program is a systems approach that ensures measurement accuracy for product acceptance and process control measurements. In addition, the program should interact with those other systems and areas responsible for establishing specification ranges, selecting new instruments, and assessing potential problems caused by out-of-tolerance instrument performance.

Do You Need a Calibration Program?

To determine whether you need a calibration program, answer these questions:

- Do I need to address overall measurement accuracy requirements?
- Do I manufacture and market a quality product or service?
- How do I determine the quality of my product and compare it with the competition's?
- How is the quality of my product perceived in the marketplace?
- Would more accurate measurement equipment and calibration produce a more uniform and more acceptable product?

For years, companies not included in defense procurement activities or controlled by government regulations (such as Food and Drug Administration regulations) successfully manufactured products using a maintenance-oriented instrument calibration and repair system. Some companies might find that such maintenance-oriented systems are still effective in satisfying their overall accuracy requirements. However, technological changes have prompted many companies to improve their measurement programs. A good ex-

TABLE 11-8 Aspects of a calibration from the perspective of a wristwatch as an accurate measurement instrument

Calibration program aspect	Wristwatch aspect
Instrument accuracy	How is the quality (long-term accuracy) of the watch?
Traceability of calibration standard	Is the time you calibrated against accurate?
Adequacy of calibrator	How well did you adjust the watch? How well have you selected the standard? When did you adjust the time?
Adequacy of records	Not applicable
Calibration frequency	How often must you calibrate the watch to keep it in tolerance?
Establishing instrument tolerance	Did you establish a time at which to adjust the watch?
Calibrating according to a written procedure	Not applicable
Data analysis of the instrument	Is the watch often out of tolerance? Is the frequency changing?
Data analysis of the product	Are you often late for meetings or planes?
Preventive aspects	Should you calibrate more frequently or buy a better watch?
Cost of instrument out-of-spec product and program	What will it cost to replace the watch? What are the "political" costs of being late to meetings? How much time does it take to calibrate the watch?

ample is pharmaceutical companies; improved measurement programs are needed to ensure that the highest-quality product is produced.

The major driving force for many industries to establish a calibration program has been the increased interest in measurement adequacy requirements expressed by many government agencies. Another driving force is today's consumers; they are demanding more reliable products. Accurate measurement and process control instruments become an effective device to ensure product uniformity and quality. If your product is looked upon as less dependable than your competition's, you probably could benefit from a stronger calibration program. If your product is rated near the top, the program in place is probably satisfactory.

The need for accurate measurement is pervasive in much of our personal and business life. Here are some examples of where accurate measurements are desirable:

- You've bought a piece of equipment to measure and control the quality of the product you're manufacturing. You then spend a great deal of time and money qualifying that equipment to ensure it performs the operations for which it was purchased. A sound calibration program will help maintain the assurance of quality from that equipment and help prevent the production of out-of-specification material.
- You have a close tolerance specification on the inside diameter of a rigid plastic piece. You measure the incoming material with a calibrated plug gage to determine whether the material is within the specification tolerance. A sound calibration program will help maintain the product quality as defined by the specification and prevent the potential cost of waste if only final product inspection is performed.
- You have completed several years of laboratory experiments in which temperature, pressure, weight, and other measurements have significant effects. These experiments have led you to an important conclusion. A sound calibration program will guarantee that the measuring equipment used was precise and traceable to standards.
- You purchase fuel to supply energy for your plant. You are concerned because the level in the storage tank often reads lower than the amount of oil the tanker driver charges you for. A sound calibration program will help alleviate your concern (and might save you money).
- As a microbiologist, you know that you cannot likely detect low levels of contamination in a large batch consisting of many individual units. A sound calibration program will help ensure the ongoing effectiveness of the process for preventing contamination.

Calibration, then, affects all aspects of product design (equipment and facility) as well as the product itself.

What Are Your Requirements?

A calibration program should be suited to the specific requirements of a company and, perhaps, even further tailored to the individual needs of a particular department. In defining a company's specific requirements, it is first necessary to establish its long-range objectives. There is a wide range of calibration options, as shown in Table 11-9.

For a company just starting with minimal operating capital or experiencing temporary short-term economic problems, option A or B is often chosen. Although options A and B provide short-term savings in instrument maintenance operations, there are long-term risks. There is a higher potential for poor product quality and higher associated costs.

At the other end of the spectrum is the comprehensive calibration program (option G). This program attempts to integrate improved instrument measurement understanding through scientific, engineering, and production functions. Anticipated results of this program are long-term improvements in product quality through better specifications (by R&D), improved production control (better selection of instruments by engineering and more consistent accuracy performance by those instruments), and improved product quality measurements.

Full implementation of a comprehensive calibration program will generally require a several-year commitment before the full system benefits can be realized. Because of this extended period, it might be necessary to develop a company's program in stages by initially targeting to attain a compliance status (option D) more quickly. This would then allow time for a measured improvement in the program (from option D to G) without major concern about the regulatory status of the program.

Questions for Discussion

1. Discuss the reasons for the adoption of a calibration program.
2. Describe the difficulties in the implementation of a calibration program vis-à-vis the company's requirements.
3. Discuss the role of a calibration program in the framework of a total quality systems approach.

TABLE 11-9 Options in defining an instrument calibration program

Functions involved	A Maintenance (on demand)	B Maintenance (periodic and on demand)	C Maintenance (regularly)	D Maintenance (regularly), quality assurance,	E Maintenance (regularly), quality assurance, and user	F Maintenance (regularly), quality assurance, user, and engineering	G Maintenance (regularly), quality assurance, user, engineering, and R&D
Measurement	Instruments calibrated only when inoperative	Instruments calibrated on a nonscheduled basis	Instruments calibrated on a scheduled basis	Scheduled calibrations using written procedures and NIST-traceable standards	Meets "D" and instruments, systems, and out-of-tolerance effects are analyzed	Meets "E" and instruments are selected on measurement capability/need basis	Meets "F" and instrument measurement capability is used in establishing specifications
Effects	Measurements often inaccurate; bad product produced and often accepted; good product sometimes rejected	Slightly improved measurements; generally same product-related problems	Further measurement improvement; generally same product-related problems	Accurate measurements; improvements in product costs and quality	More consistent accurate measurements; further improvements in product costs and quality	Consistently accurate measurements; some bad products produced but few bad products accepted; few good products rejected	Meets "F" and instrument measurement capability is used in establishing product specifications
Type of instrument program	Breakdown maintenance	Weak preventive maintenance	Weak preventive maintenance	Preventive maintenance	Calibration program	Comprehensive calibration program	Comprehensive calibration program
GMP perspective	Does not meet FDA GMP regulations' intent			Might or might not meet GMP regulations	Meets intent of FDA GMP regulations		

KEY TERMS

Accumulated life
Bathtub curve
Chance failure phase
Chi-squared random variable
Consumer's risk
Debugging phase
Failure rate curve
Failure rate function
  Constant failure rate
Infant-mortality phase
Life-cycle curve
Life testing plans
  Failure-terminated
  Handbook H-108
  Sequential
  Time-terminated
  Using exponential distribution
  With replacement
  Without replacement
Mean time between failures (MTBF)
Mean time to failure (MTTF)
Operating characteristic curve
Probability distributions
  Exponential distribution
  Weibull distribution
Producer's risk
Poisson process
Reliability
  System reliability
Systems
  Components in series
  Components in parallel
  Complex
  Standby
Wear-out phase

EXERCISES

Discussion Questions

11-1 Define reliability. Explain its role in quality control and improvement.

11-2 Describe the life cycle of a product. What probability distributions would you use to model each phase?

11-3 Explain procedures that might improve the reliability of a system. In this context, distinguish between a system with components in parallel and another with standby components.

11-4 Distinguish between failure-terminated, time-terminated, and sequential tests for reliability and life testing.

Problems

11-5 A transistor has an exponential time-to-failure distribution with a constant failure rate of 0.00006/hour. Find the reliability of the transistor after 4000 hours of operation. What is the mean time-to-failure?

11-6 An electronic component in a video recorder has an exponential time-to-failure distribution. What is the minimum mean time to failure of the component if it is to have a probability of 0.92 of successful operation after 6000 hours of operation?

11-7 An optical sensor has a Weibull time-to-failure distribution with a scale parameter of 300 hours and a shape parameter of 0.5. What is the reliability of the sensor after 500 hours of operation? Find the mean time to failure.

11-8 A remote control unit has 40 components in series. The reliability of each component is 0.9994. What is reliability of the remote control unit? If a redesign has 25 components in series, what is the reliability of the unit?

11-9 Consider Exercise 11-8 concerning the redesigned remote control unit with 25 components in series. If it is desired for the remote unit to have a reliability of 0.996 for 3000 hours of operation, what should be the failure rate for each component? What should be the mean time to failure for each component? Assume that the time to failure for each component is exponentially distributed.

11-10 Four components A, B, C, and D are placed in parallel to make a subassembly in a circuit board. The reliabilities of A, B, C, and D are 0.93, 0.88, 0.95, and 0.92, respectively. Find the reliability of the subassembly.

11-11 Consider Exercise 11-10 concerning the four components A, B, C, and D placed in parallel for a subassembly in a circuit board. Each component has a time to failure that is exponentially distributed, with a mean time to failure of 3000 hours. Find the reliability of the subassembly for 2500 hours of operation. What is the mean time to failure of the subassembly? If it is desired for the subassembly to have a mean time to failure of 6600 hours, what would have to be the mean time to failure of the components?

11-12 Consider the system with a total of seven components shown in Figure 11-10. The reliabilities of the components are as follows: $R_A = 0.96$, $R_B = 0.92$, $R_C = 0.94$, $R_D = 0.89$, $R_E = 0.95$, $R_F = 0.88$, $R_G = 0.90$. Find the reliability of the system. If you had a choice of improving system reliability by modifying any two components, how would you proceed?

11-13 Consider the system shown in Figure 11-10 with seven components. Assume that the time to failure for each component has an exponential distribution. The failure rates are given as follows: $\lambda_A = 0.0005$/hour, $\lambda_B = 0.0005$/hour, $\lambda_C = 0.0003$/hour, $\lambda_D = 0.0008$/hour, $\lambda_E = 0.0004$/hour, $\lambda_F = 0.006$/hour, and $\lambda_G = 0.0064$/hour. Find the reliability of the system after 1000 hours. What is the mean time to failure of the system?

11-14 A standby system has a basic unit with four standby units. The time to failure of each unit has an exponential distribution with a failure rate of 0.008 per hour. For a 400-hour operation period, find the reliability of the standby system. What is its mean time to failure? Suppose all five units are operating simultaneously in parallel. What would be the system reliability in that situation? What would be the mean time to failure?

11-15 Consider Exercise 11-13 and the system shown in Figure 11-10, for which the time to failure for each component has an exponential distribution. The failure rates were given in Exercise 11-13. Suppose that component B is a standby unit. Find the reliability of the system after 1000 hours. What is the mean time to failure?

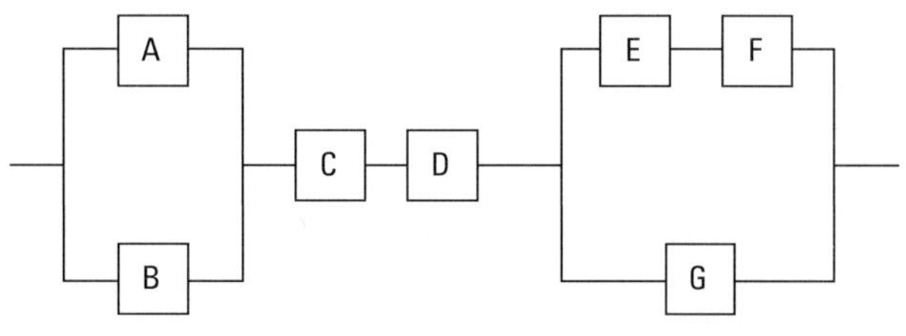

Figure 11-10 System with seven components.

11-16 Construct the operating characteristic curve for the life testing plan $n = 6$, $T = 900$ hours, $c = 3$. For a producer's risk of 0.05, what is the associated quality of batches as indicated by their mean life? For a consumer's risk of 0.10, what is the associated quality level of batches as indicated by their mean life?

11-17 A sample of 20 diodes was chosen for life testing. The time to failure of the diodes is exponentially distributed. The test was truncated after six failures, with no replacement of the failed items. The failure times (in hours), of the six diodes were 530, 590, 670, 700, 720, and 780. Estimate the mean time to failure of the diodes as well as the failure rate. Find a 95 percent confidence interval for the mean life.

11-18 Refer to Exercise 11-17 concerning the life testing of the diodes. Assume that each failed item is replaced with an identical unit. Estimate the mean time to failure and the failure rate. Find a 90 percent confidence interval for the mean time to failure.

11-19 A sample of 25 relays was chosen for life testing. The time to failure of a relay is exponentially distributed. The test was truncated after 800 hours, with 5 failures being observed at times 610, 630, 680, 700, and 720 hours, respectively. No replacement of the failed items was made. Estimate the mean life and the failure rate of the relays. Find a 95 percent confidence interval for the mean life.

11-20 A life testing plan is to be terminated after the eighth failure. It should reject a lot that has an acceptable mean life of 900 hours with a probability of 0.10. Units that fail during the test are not replaced. A sample of 15 items were placed on test with the eight failures occurring at the following times (in hours): 400, 430, 435, 460, 460, 490, 520, 530. Based on *Handbook H-108*, should the lot be accepted?

11-21 Refer to Exercise 11-20. Assume that failed items are immediately replaced during the test. Using *Handbook H-108*, what is your recommendation on the lot?

11-22 A life testing plan is to be terminated after the third failure. It should accept a lot that has an acceptable mean life of 600 hours with a probability of 0.99. Failed units are not replaced during the test. A sample of eight items was chosen, and the three failures were observed at the following times (in hours): 200, 240, 250. Using *Handbook H-108,* should the lot be accepted?

11-23 A time-terminated life testing plan is to be found that will reject lots with a mean life of 1500 hours with a probability 0.05 and accept lots with a mean life of 600 hours with a probability of 0.10. Items that fail during the test are not replaced. Determine the plan, using *Handbook H-108,* if the sample size is to be five times the rejection number.

11-24 Refer to Exercise 11-23 concerning the time-terminated life testing plan. Suppose that items that fail during the test are immediately replaced with similar units. Determine the life testing plan using *Handbook H-108.*

11-25 A time-terminated life testing plan is to be found that will reject lots that have a mean life of 1400 hours with a probability of 0.05. The rejection number is to be 7, with a sample size of 35. Determine the plan using *Handbook H–108,* if the time to failure is exponentially distributed. Items that fail during the test are not replaced.

11-26 Refer to Exercise 11-25 on the time-terminated life testing plan. If failed items are replaced with similar units, determine a life testing plan using *Handbook H–108.*

11-27 A time-terminated life testing plan is desired that will accept lots with a mean life of 6000 hours with a probability of 0.99, and will accept lots with a mean life of 2000 hours with a probability of 0.10. The test should be terminated by 1200 hours. Items that fail will be replaced immediately. Determine the plan using *Handbook H–108,* assuming the time to failure to be exponential.

11-28 Refer to Exercise 11-27 concerning the time-terminated life testing plan. Find the appropriate plan using *Handbook H–108,* if failed items are not replaced during the test.

11-29 In a time-terminated life testing plan it is desired to reject lots with a mean life of 1500 hours with a probability of 0.95, and it is desired to reject lots with a mean life of 7500 hours with a probability of 0.10. The test is to be terminated by 2500 hours. Items that fail during the test will be replaced. Assuming the time-to-failure distribution to be exponential, determine the plan using *Handbook H–108.*

11-30 Refer to Exercise 11-29 concerning the time terminated life testing plan. If failed items are not replaced during the test, determine the plan using *Handbook H–108.*

REFERENCES

Besterfield, D. H. (1990). *Quality Control,* 3rd edition. Prentice-Hall. Inc. Englewood Cliffs, NJ.

Bremmer, B. (1991). "Verify Accuracy Through Calibration." *Quality Progress,* Volume 24, Number 3, pp. 108–111.

DelMar, D., and Sheldon, G. (1988). *Introduction to Quality Control.* West Publishing Company, St. Paul, MN.

Halpern, S. (1978). *The Assurance Sciences—An Introduction to Quality Control and Reliability.* Prentice-Hall, Englewood Cliffs, NJ.

Henley, E. J., and Kumamoto, H. (1981). *Reliability Engineering and Risk Assessment.* Prentice-Hall, Englewood Cliffs, NJ.

U.S. Office of the Assistant Secretary of Defense (1960). *Quality Control and Reliability Handbook H–108, Sampling Procedures and Tables for Life and Reliability Testing (Based on Exponential Distribution).* Government Printing Office, Washington, DC.

U.S. Department of Defense (1968). *Military Standard MIL–STD–690B, Failure Rate Sampling Plans and Procedures.* Government Printing Office, Washington, DC.

CHAPTER

12

Experimental Design Principles

CHAPTER OUTLINE

SYMBOLS

y_{ij}	Response variable value for jth experimental unit assigned to treatment i
$\overline{y}_{i\cdot}$	Average response of treatment i
$\overline{y}_{\cdot j}$	Average response of the jth block
$\overline{\overline{y}}$	Grand mean of all observations
y_{ijk}	Response variable value for the ith level of the first factor, jth level of the second factor, and the kth replication
$\overline{y}_{i\cdot\cdot}$	Average response for the ith level of the first factor
$\overline{y}_{\cdot j\cdot}$	Average response for the jth level of the second factor
$\overline{y}_{ij\cdot}$	Average response for the ith level of the first factor and the jth level of the second factor
L	Contrast of factor means or totals

12-1 INTRODUCTION

The principles of quality control have been described in the chapters dealing with control charts. Control chart techniques deal with on-line control methods, in which it is necessary to determine if the process is in a state of statistical control. Adjustments are made on the process, preferably in real time, as data from the process are collected and analyzed to determine its state. Data collected from the process are used to make changes in the process. Although these methods, sometimes collectively grouped under the heading of statistical process control (SPC), are no doubt useful, they nevertheless provide an action-taking framework in the phase when the product is manufactured or in the operational phase of a service that is somewhat downstream in the cycle.

A class of procedures known as off-line control methods, which are used in the design phase of the product/process or service, would be quite beneficial. These would be used in an effort to determine the best settings of the product and process parameters during the initial design and prototype testing rather than during the manufacture of the product or rendering of the service. The advantage would be in conducting analysis earlier in the cycle. Such analyses would address problems that could appear in the production phase. The product or process would then be designed to minimize the detrimental effects that might appear later in the manufacturing cycle. The proper choice of parameter settings for both the product and process in the design phase can reduce costs and improve quality.

Quality should be designed into a product. Principles of experimental design, which aid in selecting various parameters of the product and thereby the process, facilitate this objective. The never ending cycle of quality improvement has already been emphasized. The quality control phase is followed by quality improvement, which leads to the creation of a better product or service. Some common experimental designs are introduced in this chapter. Many of the details of the analysis procedures associated with these designs, such as the analysis of variance (ANOVA), are not extensively discussed. The reader should consult the references provided for a thorough treatment of the relevant analytical procedures (Box, Hunter, and Hunter, 1978; Montgomery, 1991; Peterson, 1985; Wadsworth, Stephens, and Godfrey, 1986). The focus here is to present the fundamental principles of the different types of experimental designs.

This chapter discusses such experimental designs as the completely randomized design, the randomized block design, and the latin square design. The principles of factorial experiments are also presented (Box, Hunter, and Hunter, 1978; Hunter, 1985; Raghavarao, 1971; Ryan, 1989). All of these help in determining the more critical factors as well as the levels at which the chosen factors should be maintained (Box and Wilson, 1951; Box and Draper, 1986). These experiments are usually conducted under controlled conditions (say, in a laboratory). They can provide crucial information for choosing the appropriate product and process parameters (Gunter, 1990d) and levels for the manufacturing phase or the important controllable factor levels for the delivery of services.

12-2 EXPERIMENTAL DESIGN FUNDAMENTALS

An *experiment* is a planned method of inquiry conducted to support or refute a hypothesized belief or to discover new information about a product, process, or service. It is an active method of obtaining information, as opposed to passive observation. It involves inducing a response to determine the effects of certain controlled parameters. Examples of controllable parameters, often called *factors,* are the cutting tool, the temperature setting of an oven, the selected vendor, the amount of a certain additive, or the type of decor in a restaurant. The factors may be quantitative or qualitative (discrete). For quantitative factors, one must decide on the range of values, how they are to be measured, and the *levels* at which they are to be controlled during experimentation. For example, the analyst might be interested in the effect of temperature on the output of a chemical compound. Three selected levels of the factor (temperature in this case) could be 100°C, 200°C, and 300°C. The *response* variable in this case is the output of the chemical compound as measured in, say, kilograms. Qualitative factors, such as the supplier of an input raw material, are arbitrarily assigned codes representing discrete levels.

In the terminology of experimental design, a *treatment* is a certain combination of factor levels whose effect on the response variable is of interest. For example, suppose we have two factors—oven temperature and the selected vendor of a certain raw material—that are of interest in determining the effect on the output of the response variable, which is the yield of a chemical compound. The temperature can be set at 100°C, 200°C, or 300°C, and the raw material can be purchased from vendor A or B. The selected vendor is then a qualitative factor. The treatments for this experiment are the various combinations of these two factor levels. The case for which vendor A is chosen and the oven temperature is set at 100°C is one particular treatment. A total of six treatments could possibly be considered in this situation.

An *experimental unit* is the quantity of material (in manufacturing) or the number served (in a service system) to which one trial of a single treatment is applied. For the above example of a chemical compound, suppose that production is in batches of 2000 kg and that each treatment is applied to a batch. The experimental unit is therefore a batch. A *sampling unit,* on the other hand, is a fraction of the experimental unit on which the treatment effect is measured. If 100 g of the mixture is chosen for analysis, then that amount would represent the sampling unit.

The variation in experimental units that have been exposed to the same treatment is attributed to *experimental error.* This variability is due to uncontrollable, or noise, factors.

There are several advantages to experimental design. First, it can be useful in identifying the key decision variables that may not only keep a process in control but improve it. Second, in the development of new processes for which historical data are not available, experimental design used in the developmental phase can point out the important factors and their associated levels that will maximize yield and reduce overall costs. It helps to cut down on the lead time between design and manufacturing and produces a design that is robust in its insensitivity to uncontrollable factors.

Principles of experimental design may be used to determine the impact of factors on the response variable. With quantitative factors that vary on a continuous scale, it is possible to get some information about the behavior of the response even for factor levels that have not been experimentally determined. This concept is illustrated in Figure 12-1, in which the quantitative factor is the amount of catalyst used in a process and the response variable is the reaction time. Six experiments are conducted for catalyst levels of 10, 20, 30, 30, 40, and 40 g, respectively. Note that as the amount of catalyst increases, the reaction time increases at a decreasing rate. Assuming the behavior of the response variable (reaction time) to be representative of the observed values of the experiment, a smooth curve is drawn to depict its relationship with the factor of interest. This relationship can be used to interpolate the performance of the response variable even for values of the amount of catalyst (say, 15 or 25 g) for which experiments have not been performed.

Such interpolation may not be feasible for qualitative factors with discrete levels. Consider, for example, the response variable to be the elasticity of a rubber compound; the factor is the supplier of

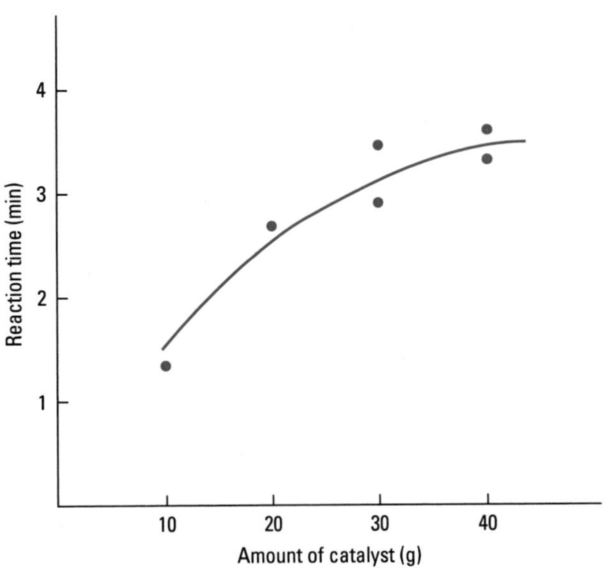

Figure 12-1 Behavior of a response variable for a quantitative factor.

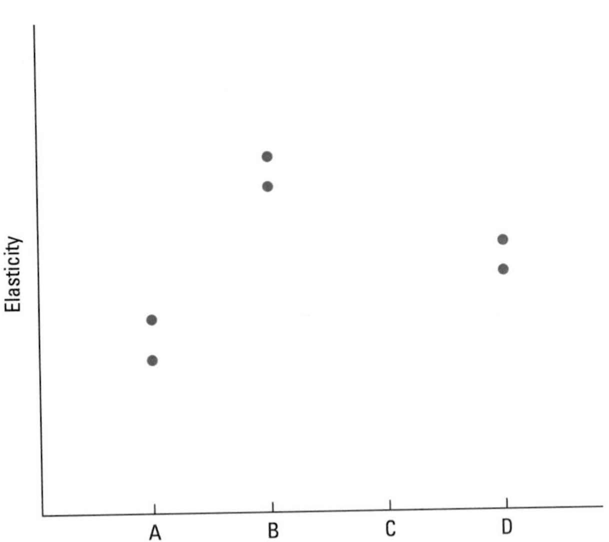

Figure 12-2 Response variable for a qualitative factor with discrete levels.

raw material. Suppose there are four suppliers: A, B, C, and D. Observations of the response variable are shown in Figure 12-2 for suppliers A, B, and D. From this information it is not possible to interpolate the elasticity of the compound for raw material provided by supplier C. With all other variables kept constant, the variability between the responses for a given factor level, say supplier A, represents the experimental error. If it is desired to maximize the response variable, one would select supplier B. This assumes, perhaps unrealistically, that other variables do not influence elasticity.

Frequently, more than one factor is considered in experimental analysis. In realistic problems, a *screening* experiment may first have to be conducted to isolate the important factors. If more than one factor is under consideration, experiments do not usually involve changing one variable at a time. Some disadvantages of changing one variable at a time are discussed later. With two variables, we get a design known as the cuboidal design, shown in Figure 12-3*a*. Each of the two factors can be set at two levels, denoted by -1 and 1, respectively. The point $(0, 0)$ represents the current setting of the factor levels. In this notation, the first coordinate represents the level of factor A, and the second coordinate represents the level of factor B. A level of -1 represents a value below the current setting of 0, and a level of 1 represents a value above the current setting. Thus, four new design points, $(-1, -1)$, $(1, -1)$, $(-1, 1)$, and $(1, 1)$, can be investigated. The value of the response variable at these design points determines the next series of experiments to be performed. Suppose the response function value at the experimental design points are as shown in Figure 12-3*b* and the response surface is as shown in Figure 12-3*c*. If the objective is to maximize the response function, consider the direction in which the gradient is steepest, as indicated by the arrow. The next experiment could be conducted in a region with the center at (2,2) with respect to the current origin. These same principles apply to more than two variables as well (Gunter, 1989, 1990a, 1990c).

Consider one of the disadvantages of changing the value of only one variable at a time (keeping the level of the other variables fixed) while optimizing the response function. Figure 12-4*a* shows the design points for such an approach, with (0,0) representing the current state. If the value of factor A is fixed, the two design points are $(0, -1)$ and $(0, 1)$. Likewise, if factor B is fixed, the two additional design points are $(-1, 0)$ and (1,0). Keep in mind the response function shown in Figure 12-3 for the same factors A and B. Figure 12-4*b* shows the response function value at the design points. Observe that (with the objective

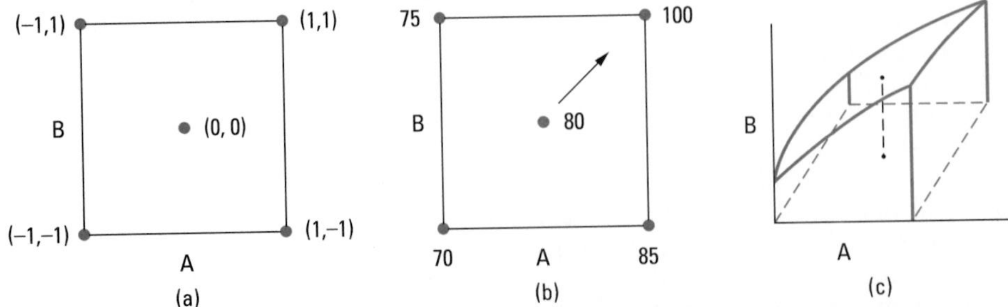

Figure 12-3 An experimental design for more than one variable. (a) Two-variable cuboidal design region. (b) Response function value at the design points. (c) Response surface for two factors.

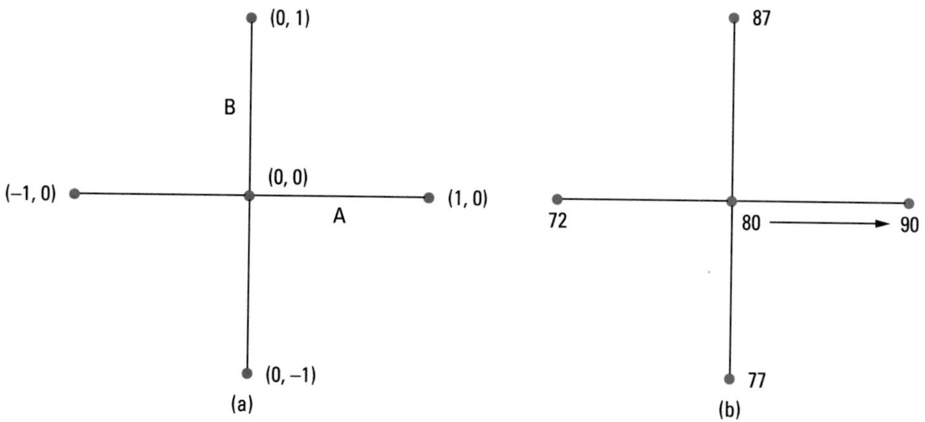

Figure 12-4 Design approach involving changes in one variable at a time. (a) Experimental points. (b) Response function value at the design points.

being to maximize the response function) we would move in the direction of the arrow shown along the major axis of factor A. The next experiment would be conducted in a region with the center at (2,0) with respect to the current origin. This, however, would not lead to the proper point for maximizing the response function as indicated in Figure 12-3*c*.

All of these concepts also apply to the case with more than two variables. Figure 12-5 shows a three-variable cuboidal region. The factors are A, B, and C, and nine experimental points are labeled. To obtain the same amount of information as given by this design using the approach for one variable at a time, four sets of experiments, each with seven design points, would have to be run. Thus, experiments for one variable at a time are not as cost-effective.

One of the main drawbacks of the approach for one variable at a time is that it cannot detect *interactions* between two or more factors (Gunter, 1990b). Interactions exist when the nature of the relationship between the response variable and a certain factor is influenced by the level of some other factor. This concept is illustrated graphically in Figure 12-6. Suppose that factor A represents the supplier of raw material and factor B represents the amount of catalyst used in a chemical process. The response variable is the elasticity of the output product, the values of which are shown beside the plotted points. In Figure 12-6*a*, the functional relationship between the response and factor A stays the same regardless of the level of factor B. This depicts the case for which there is no interaction between factors A and B. The factors are said to have an additive effect on the response variable. The rate of change of the response as the level of factor A changes from -1 to 1 is the same for each level of B. Observe Figure 12-6*b*, in which interaction does exist between factors A and B. The rate of change of the response as a function of the level of factor A changes as the level of B changes from -1 to 1. The response has a steeper slope when B is 1. Hence, the level of factor B does influence the relationship between the response function and factor A. In such a situation, interaction is said to exist between factors A and B.

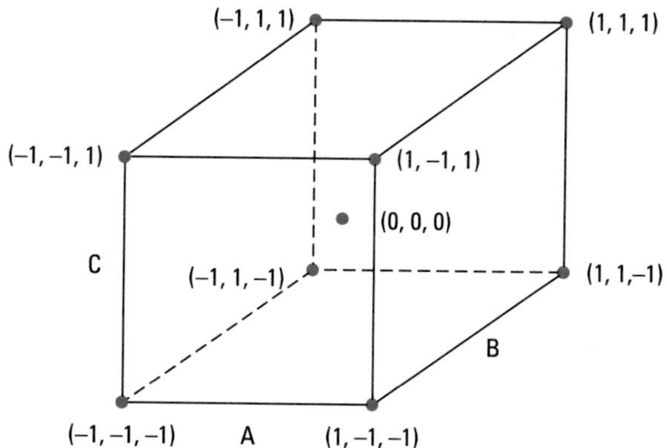

Figure 12-5 Three-variable cuboidal design region.

Interactions depict the joint relationship of factors on the response function. Such effects should be accounted for in multifactor designs because they better approximate real-world events. For example, a new motivational training program for employees (factor B) might impact productivity (response variable) differently for different departments (factor A) within the organization. Another way of representing interaction is through contour plots of the re-

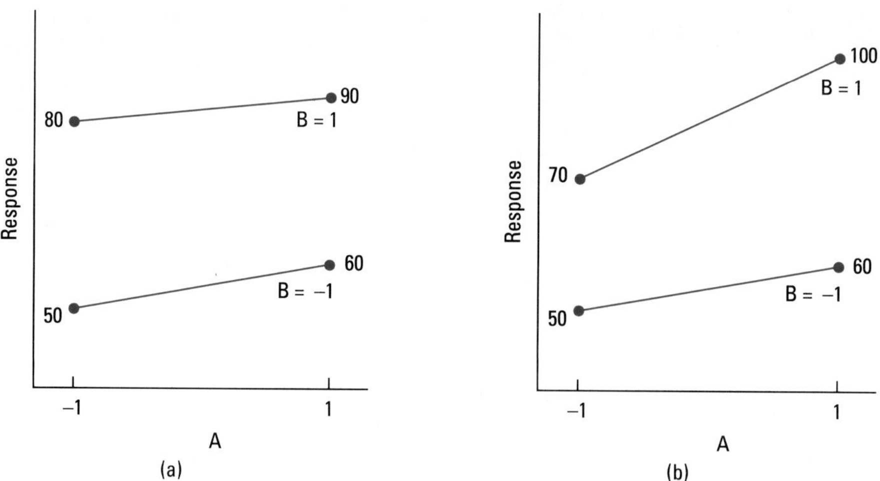

Figure 12-6 Interaction between factors. (a) No interaction between factors A and B. (b) Interaction between factors A and B.

sponse function. Figure 12-7*a* shows contour plots of the response function with two factors A and B when there is no interaction between the factors. Here, the axes of the plotted contours are parallel to the axes of the factors. In Figure 12-7*b*, the response surface has a form of curvature. The natural axes of the contours are rotated with respect to the factor coordinate axes. Interaction between factors A and B exists in these circumstances.

Features of Experimentation

Experimental design principles incorporate the features of replication, randomization, and blocking. *Replication* involves a repetition of the experiment under similar conditions (that is, similar treatments). It allows the analyst to obtain an estimate of the experimental error, the variation in the experimental units under identically controlled conditions.

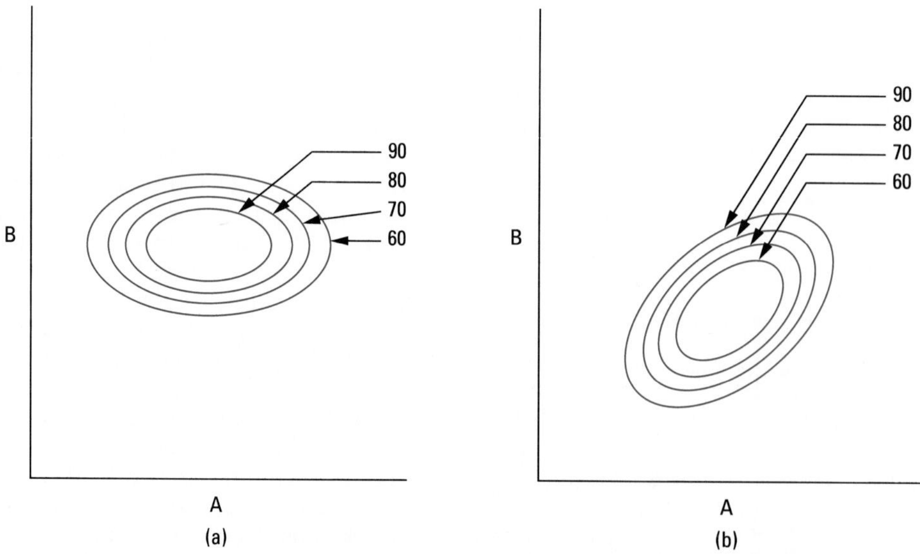

Figure 12-7 Contour plots of the response function. (a) No interaction between factors A and B. (b) Interaction between factors A and B.

The experimental error is a basis for determining whether differences in the statistics found from the observations are significant. It serves as a benchmark for determining what factors or interactions are significant in influencing the response variable.

Replication serves another important function. If the sample mean is used to estimate the effect of a factor, replication increases the precision by reducing the standard deviation of the mean. In Chapter 3, we found the following from the Central limit theorem. The variance of the sample mean $\bar{y}$ is given by

$$\sigma_{\bar{y}}^2 = \sigma^2/n \qquad (12.1)$$

where σ^2 represents the variance of the observations and n is the number of replications used to determine the sample mean. As the number of replications increases, the standard deviation of the mean $(\sigma_{\bar{y}})$ decreases. Replication can also provide a broader base for decision making. With an increase in the number of replications, a variety of units could be used in the experimentation, permitting inferences to be drawn over a broader range of conditions.

A second feature of experimentation deals with the concept of randomization. *Randomization* means that the treatments should be assigned to the experimental units in such a way that every unit has an equal chance of being assigned to any treatment. Such a process eliminates bias and ensures that no particular treatment is favored. Random assignments of the treatments and the order in which the experimental trials are run ensures that the observations, and therefore the experimental errors, will be independent of each other. Randomization "averages out" the effect of uncontrolled factors. Consider a situation in which customer reaction and satisfaction are to be tested for three different types of loan application in a financial institution. The factor is the type of loan application, with three levels. The observance of customers who are given these types of applications should be randomized, so that the effects of all other factors are averaged out. Any differences in the observed customer satisfaction levels would be attributed to differences in the loan applications. Hence, any given type of loan application would not be given only to customers of similar financial status or educational background.

The third feature of experimentation is the principle of *blocking,* or local control. The idea is to arrange similar experimental units into groups, or blocks. Variability of the response function within a block can then be attributed to the differences in the treatments because the impact of other extraneous variables has been minimized. Treatments are assigned at random to the units within each block. Variability between blocks is eliminated from the experimental error, which leads to an increase in the precision of the experiment. Consider a situation in which the performance of support staff in an organization is to be evaluated based on their exposure to a new training program. We could create blocks consisting of persons of similar background and experience. A number of persons would be chosen randomly from each block and would go through the new training program. The effect of the new training program could then be compared within blocks. Assessing differences between blocks due to variability in the persons' abilities would be distinct from determining the effect of the treatment, in this case the training program. Such an experiment would also permit differences between blocks to be detected. Blocking allows comparisons of the treatments under nearly equal conditions because the blocks consist of uniform units.

12-3 SOME EXPERIMENTAL DESIGNS

The design of an experiment usually accounts for the following:

- The set of treatments to be considered
- The set of experimental units to be included
- The procedures through which the treatments are to be assigned to the experimental units (or vice versa)
- The response variable(s) to be observed
- The measurement process to be used on the experimental units upon application of the treatments

A manageable number of treatments is chosen from a larger set based on their relative degree of impact on the response variable. Economic considerations (such as the cost associated with the application of a particular treatment) could also be a factor in selecting treatments for experimentation. Ideally, the goal is to optimize the response variable in the most cost-effective manner possible (Box and Draper, 1986). The distinguishing feature of the different types of experimental designs that this section considers concerns the manner in which treatments are to be applied to the experimental units, or vice versa. All of the other issues apply equally to the various designs. For instance, the selection and adoption of an appropriate measurement process is critical to all experimental designs. *Measurement bias* can cause serious problems in the analysis. It can occur as a result of unrecognized differences in the evaluation and observation processes. Consider a situation in which customers are asked to evaluate a new menu item in a restaurant. It is possible that the new item might be rated very favorably because of the desire to show that it is highly acceptable. This type of measurement bias can be eliminated by not divulging the assignment of treatment to the experimental subject and the evaluator. Thus, the experimental subjects could be asked to rate a dish, where the new one is assigned randomly along with the other old dishes. A particular subject then does not know the type of dish (old or new) received. Hence, any bias that a subject might have toward the new dish would be eliminated. This, of course, assumes that it is not possible to discern the new from the old ones just by looks! Such a study is called a *double-blind* study. Of course, in this example, the experimental subject and the evaluator are the same person, but they could be different. When the knowledge of the treatment assignment is not disclosed to the experimental subject or the evaluator, the study is said to be *single-blind*.

For the experimental designs examined in this chapter, we will consider situations in which the treatment effects are considered to be *fixed*. This means that the inferences drawn from the analysis pertain only to the treatments selected in the study. Alternatively, if the selected treatments are randomly chosen from a population of treatments, a *random effects* model could be used to make inferences about the whole population of treatments.

To illustrate these concepts, consider a situation in which the treatments are given by the amount of a certain compound used in a chemical process. The response variable is the reaction time. Suppose three treatments, representing 100, 200, and 300 g of the compound, respectively, are used in the experiment. A fixed effects model would consider the effect of these three treatments on the response. We might find that the first treatment, representing the use of 100 g of the compound, yields the smallest reaction time. The inferences would identify any significant differences between these three treatments.

On the other hand, suppose the treatment representing the amount of a certain compound is assumed to be a normal random variable with a mean of 200 g and a standard deviation of 100 g. Conceivably, we have an infinite number of treatments. From this population of available treatments, suppose three are randomly selected: those representing the use of 100, 200, and 300 g of the compound. A model that makes inferences about the entire population of treatments (that is, the amount of compound used), even though only three treatments were represented in the experiment, is known as a random effects model.

Completely Randomized Design

A completely randomized design is one of the simplest and least restrictive designs. The treatments are randomly assigned to the experimental units. Each unit has an equal chance of being assigned to any treatment. One way of accomplishing this assignment is through the use of uniform random number tables. Suppose we have four treatments, A, B, C, and D, which we would like to assign to three experimental units each. In the terminology of experimental design, each treatment is replicated three times. Starting at any point in a random number table and going across a row or down a column, suppose the following 12 three-digit random numbers are obtained sequentially: 682, 540, 102, 736, 089, 457, 198, 511, 294, 821, 304, and 658. Treatment A could be assigned to the first three numbers, treatment B to the second three numbers, and so forth. These numbers are now ranked from smallest to largest, with the ranks corresponding to the experimental unit numbers. The scheme of assignment is depicted in Table 12-1. From Table 12-1 we find that experimental unit number 1 is assigned treatment B, experimental unit number 2 is assigned treatment A, and so on. A table of uniform random numbers is given in Appendix A-9.

There are several advantages to a completely randomized design. First, any number of treatments or

TABLE 12-1 Assignment of treatments to experimental units in a completely randomized design

Random number	Rank of random number (experimental unit number)	Treatment to be assigned
682	10	A
540	8	A
102	2	A
736	11	B
089	1	B
457	6	B
198	3	C
511	7	C
294	4	C
821	12	D
304	5	D
658	9	D

replications may be used. Different treatments need not be replicated the same number of times, making the design flexible. Sometimes it may not be feasible to replicate treatments an equal number of times. For example, suppose the treatments represent different vendors. It is possible that because of capacity and resource limitations, vendor A is able to supply less raw material than vendors B and C. Whereas treatments (in this case, suppliers) B and C can be replicated five times each, treatment A can be replicated only twice. When all treatments are replicated an equal number of times, the experiment is said to be *balanced;* otherwise, the experiment is *unbalanced.* The statistical analysis is simple even for the unbalanced case, although comparisons between the treatment effects are more precise in the balanced case. Another advantage is that the completely randomized design provides the most degrees of freedom for the experimental error. This ensures a more precise estimation of the experimental error. Recall that the experimental error provides a benchmark for determining which treatment effects are significantly different. One disadvantage of a completely randomized design is that its precision may be low if the experimental units are not uniform. This problem is overcome by means of blocking, or grouping, similar homogeneous units. Designs utilizing the principle of blocking will be discussed later.

Analysis of Data The statistical procedure used to analyze data is known as the analysis of variance. This technique determines the effects of the treatments, as reflected by their means, through an analysis of their variability. Details of this procedure may be found in the listed references (Box, Hunter, and Hunter, 1978; Peterson, 1985; SAS, 1989a, 1989b). The total variability in the observations is partitioned into two components: the variation among the treatment means (also known as the treatment sum of squares) and the variation among the experimental units within treatments (also known as the error sum of squares). We have

Total sum of squares (SST)
= Treatment sum of squares (SSTR)
+ Error sum of squares (SSE)

(12.2)

The mean squares for treatments and for error are obtained by dividing the corresponding sum of squares by the appropriate number of degrees of freedom. This number is one less than the number of observations in each source of variation. For a balanced design with p treatments, each with r replications, the total number of observations is rp. The total variability, therefore, has $(rp - 1)$ degrees of freedom. The number of degrees of freedom for the treatments is $(p - 1)$. For each treatment there are r observations, so $(r - 1)$ degrees of freedom apply toward the experimental error. The total number of degrees of freedom for the experimental error is, therefore, $p(r - 1)$.

Let us define the following notation:

p = Number of treatments
r = Number of replications for each treatment
y_{ij} = Response variable value of the jth experimental unit that is assigned treatment i, $i = 1, 2, \ldots, p$; $j = 1, 2, \ldots, r$
$y_{i\cdot} = \sum_{j=1}^{r} y_{ij}$ = Sum of the responses for the ith treatment
$\bar{y}_{i\cdot} = y_{i\cdot}/r$ = Mean response of the ith treatment
$y_{\cdot\cdot} = \sum_{i=1}^{p}\sum_{j=1}^{r} y_{ij}$ = Grand total of all observations
$\bar{\bar{y}} = y_{\cdot\cdot}/(rp)$ = Grand mean of all observations

The notation, consisting of r observations for each of the p treatments, is shown in Table 12-2. The computations of the sum of squares are as follows. A correction factor C is first computed as

$$C = y_{\cdot\cdot}^2/(rp) \tag{12.3}$$

The total sum of squares is

$$\text{SST} = \sum_{i=1}^{p}\sum_{j=1}^{r} y_{ij}^2 - C \tag{12.4}$$

The treatment sum of squares is determined from

$$\text{SSTR} = \left(\sum_{i=1}^{p} y_{i\cdot}^2\right)\Big/ r - C \tag{12.5}$$

TABLE 12-2 Notation for the completely randomized design in the balanced case

	Replications					
Treatments	1	2	...	r	Sum	Mean
1	y_{11}	y_{12}	...	y_{1r}	$y_{1\cdot}$	$\bar{y}_1$
2	y_{21}	y_{22}	...	y_{2r}	$y_{2\cdot}$	$\bar{y}_2$
⋮	⋮	⋮	⋱	⋮	⋮	⋮
p	y_{p1}	y_{p2}	...	y_{pr}	$y_{p\cdot}$	$\bar{y}_p$
					$y_{\cdot\cdot}$	$\bar{\bar{y}}$

Finally, the error sum of squares is

$$SSE = SST - SSTR \tag{12.6}$$

Next, the mean squares are found by dividing the sum of squares by the corresponding number of degrees of freedom. So, the mean squares for treatment are

$$MSTR = SSTR/(p - 1) \tag{12.7}$$

The mean square error is given by

$$MSE = SSE/[p(r - 1)] \tag{12.8}$$

Test for Differences among Treatment Means. It is desirable to test the null hypothesis that all of the treatment means are equal against the alternative hypothesis that at least one treatment mean is different from the others. Denoting the treatment means by $\mu_1, \mu_2, \ldots, \mu_p$, we have the hypotheses

H_o: $\mu_1 = \mu_2 = \cdots = \mu_p$

H_a: At least one μ_i is different from the others

The test procedure involves the F-statistic, which is the ratio of the mean squares for treatment to the mean squares for error. The mean square error (MSE) is an unbiased estimate of σ^2, the variance of the experimental error. The test statistic is

$$F = MSTR/MSE \tag{12.9}$$

with $(p - 1)$ degrees of freedom in the numerator and $p(r - 1)$ degrees of freedom in the denominator. For a chosen level of significance α, the critical value of F, which is found from the tables in Appendix A-6, is denoted by $F_{\alpha,(p-1),p(r-1)}$. If the computed test statistic $F > F_{\alpha,(p-1),p(r-1)}$, the null hypothesis is rejected, and we conclude that the treatment means are not all equal at the chosen level of significance. This computational procedure is known as analysis of variance; it is shown in tabular format in Table 12-3.

If the null hypothesis is not rejected, there is no significant difference among the treatment means. The practical implication is that as far as the response variable is concerned, it does not matter which treatment is used. Whichever treatment is the most cost-effective would be selected.

If the null hypothesis is rejected, management might be interested in knowing which treatments are preferable. The sample treatment means could be ranked; depending on whether a large or small value of the response variable is preferred, the desirable treatments could be identified. The sample treatment means serve as point estimates of the population treatment means. If interval estimates are desired, the following relation can be used to find a $100(1 - \alpha)$ percent confidence interval for the treatment mean μ_i:

$$L(\mu_i) = \bar{y}_i \pm t_{\alpha/2,p(r-1)} \sqrt{MSE/r} \tag{12.10}$$

where $t_{\alpha/2,p(r-1)}$ is the t-value for a right tail area of $\alpha/2$ and $p(r-1)$ degrees of freedom; it is found from Appendix A-4. The quantity $\sqrt{MSE/r}$ represents the standard deviation of the sample treatment mean $\bar{y}_i$.

Sometimes, management may want to estimate the difference between two treatment means. Such an inference would indicate whether one treatment is preferable to the other. A $100(1 - \alpha)$ percent confidence interval for the difference of two treatment means, $\mu_{i_1} - \mu_{i_2}$, is given by

$$L(\mu_{i_1} - \mu_{i_2}) = (\bar{y}_{i_1} - \bar{y}_{i_2}) \pm t_{\alpha/2,p(r-1)} \sqrt{2MSE/r} \tag{12.11}$$

where $t_{\alpha/2,p(r-1)}$ is the t-value for a right tail area of $\alpha/2$ and $p(r - 1)$ degrees of freedom. The quantity $\sqrt{2MSE/r}$ represents the standard deviation of the difference between the sample treatment means, $\bar{y}_{i_1} - \bar{y}_{i_2}$.

Example 12-1: Three different adhesives are being analyzed for their impact on the bonding strength of paper in a pulp and paper mill. The adhesives were randomly applied to four batches each. The data for the bonding strength is shown in Table 12-4. Table 12-4 also shows the sample treatment sums and the means, as well as the grand total and grand mean of all 12 observations. Here, the three treatments are the adhesives ($p = 3$), and the number of replications for each treatment is 4 ($r = 4$). The completely randomized design is a balanced one.

a. Is there a difference among the adhesives in terms of the mean bonding strength? Test at the 5 percent level of significance.

TABLE 12-3 Analysis-of-variance table for the completely randomized design for a balanced experiment

Source of variation	Degrees of freedom	Sum of squares	Mean square	F-statistic
Treatments	$p - 1$	SSTR	MSTR = SSTR/$(p - 1)$	F = MSTR/MSE
Error	$p(r - 1)$	SSE	MSE = SSE/$[p(r - 1)]$	
Total	$rp - 1$	SST		

TABLE 12-4 Bonding strength of adhesives

Adhesive type	Bonding strength				Sum	Mean
Adhesive 1	10.2	11.8	9.6	12.4	44.0	11.000
Adhesive 2	12.8	14.7	13.3	15.4	56.2	14.050
Adhesive 3	7.2	9.8	8.7	9.2	34.9	8.725
					135.1	11.258

Solution. To test for differences among the adhesive mean bonding strengths, we use the analysis-of-variance procedure. The correction factor is calculated to be

$$C = y_{..}^2/(rp) = (135.1)^2/12 = 1521.001$$

From Equation 12.4, the total sum of squares is

$$\begin{aligned} \text{SST} &= \sum_{i=1}^{3}\sum_{j=1}^{4} y_{ij}^2 - C \\ &= 1591.390 - 1521.001 = 70.389 \end{aligned}$$

The treatment sum of squares, from Equation 12.5, is

$$\begin{aligned} \text{SSTR} &= \left(\sum y_{i\cdot}^2\right)/r - C \\ &= [(44)^2 + (56.2)^2 + (34.9)^2]/4 - 1521.001 \\ &= 6312.45/4 - 1521.001 \\ &= 57.111 \end{aligned}$$

The error sum of squares is

$$\text{SSE} = \text{SST} - \text{SSTR} = 70.389 - 57.111 = 13.278$$

The analysis-of-variance table is shown in Table 12-5.

To test the hypothesis $H_o : \mu_1 = \mu_2 = \mu_3$ against H_a: At least one μ_i is different from the others, the F-statistic, as shown in Table 12-5, is computed as

$$\text{F} = \text{MSTR}/\text{MSE} = 28.555/1.475 = 19.359$$

From Appendix A-6, for a chosen significance level α of 0.05, $F_{0.05,2,9} = 4.26$. Since the calculated value of F exceeds 4.26, we reject the null hypothesis and conclude that there is a difference in the mean bonding strengths of the adhesives.

TABLE 12-5 Analysis-of-variance table for data on bonding strength

Source of variation	Degrees of freedom	Sum of squares	Mean square	*F*-statistic
Adhesives (treatments)	2	57.111	28.555	19.359
Error	9	13.278	1.475	
Total	11	70.389		

b. Find a 90 percent confidence interval for the mean bonding strength of adhesive 1.

Solution. A 90 percent confidence interval for the mean bonding strength of adhesive 1 is given by

$$\begin{aligned} L(\mu_1) &= \bar{y}_1 \pm t_{.05,9}\sqrt{\text{MSE}/4} \\ &= 11.000 \pm 1.833\sqrt{1.475/4} \\ &= 11.000 \pm 1.113 = (9.887, 12.113) \end{aligned}$$

c. Find a 95 percent confidence interval for the difference in the mean bonding strengths of adhesives 1 and 3. Is there a difference in the means of these two adhesives?

Solution. A 95 percent confidence interval for the difference in the mean bonding strengths of adhesives 1 and 3 is given by

$$\begin{aligned} L(\mu_1 - \mu_3) &= (\bar{y}_1 - \bar{y}_3) \pm t_{.025,9}\sqrt{2\text{MSE}/4} \\ &= (11.000 - 8.725) \pm 2.262\sqrt{2(1.475)/4} \\ &= 2.275 \pm 1.942 = (0.333, 4.217) \end{aligned}$$

Since the confidence interval does not include the value of zero, we conclude that there is a difference in the means of adhesives 1 and 3 at the 5 percent level of significance.

Randomized Block Design

Blocking involves grouping experimental units that have similar effects on the response variable. The idea is to eliminate the effects of extraneous factors within a block such that the impact of the individual treatments, which is our main concern, can be identified. Experimental units in blocks should therefore be chosen to be as homogeneous as possible. To provide an illustration, consider a situation in which it is desired to investigate the differences between the raw materials from three suppliers, A, B, and C. Processing may take place in either of two machines, M_1 or M_2. The treatments of interest are the suppliers. Extraneous factors are those due to differences caused by M_1 and M_2. Therefore, if raw materials from suppliers were randomly assigned to the machines, it would be difficult to claim that any differences in the output are due to the suppliers, since the variability of the machines would not have been isolated. On the other hand, using the concept of blocking, the following design could be used. The blocking variable would be the type of machine (M_1 or M_2). For a given machine, say M_1 (which represents a block), the raw materials from suppliers A, B, and C would randomly be used. Differences in the output from this block would represent the impact of the treatments. Such a scheme would be repeated for each block. Differences in the outputs between blocks would measure the impact of the blocking variable (that is, whether blocking is effective).

The criterion on which to base blocking must be identified before conducting the experiment. The success of blocking is based on minimizing the variation among units within a block while maximizing variation between blocks. An advantage of blocking is that differences between blocks can be eliminated from the experimental error, thereby increasing the precision of the experiment. However, blocking is effective only if the variability within blocks is smaller than the variability over the entire set. Precision usually decreases as the block size (the number of experimental units per block) increases.

In a randomized block design, the experimental units are first divided into blocks. Within a block, the treatments are randomly assigned to the experimental units as in a completely randomized design. If we have p treatments and r blocks in a completely randomized block design, each of the p treatments is applied once in each block, resulting in a total of rp experimental units. Thus r blocks, each consisting of p units, are chosen such that the units within blocks are homogeneous. Next, the p treatments are randomly assigned to the units within the blocks, with each treatment occurring only once within each block. The blocks serve as replications for the treatments. It is assumed that there is no interaction between the treatments and blocks. Table 12-6 shows the layout for an example in which there are four treatments, A, B, C, and D, and three blocks, I, II, and III (hence, $p = 4$ and $r = 3$). Within each block, the four treatments are randomly applied to the experimental units. Each treatment appears only once in each block. The assignment of treatments to the units in each block may be done as demonstrated for the completely randomized design. A random number table may be used, with the scheme depicted in Table 12-1 adopted.

TABLE 12-6 Assignment of treatments to units within blocks in a randomized block design

Blocks		
I	II	III
B	C	C
A	A	B
C	D	D
D	B	A

There are several advantages to using the randomized block design. First and foremost is that it could increase the precision by removing a source of variation (variability between blocks) from the experimental error. The design can accommodate any number of treatments and blocks. The statistical analysis is relatively simple and can easily accommodate the dropping of an entire treatment or block, due to reasons such as faulty observations. One disadvantage is that missing data can require complex calculations. The number of degrees of freedom for the experimental error is not as large as that for the completely randomized design. In fact, if there are r blocks, then there are $(r - 1)$ fewer degrees of freedom in the experimental error. Furthermore, if all of the experimental units are homogeneous, the completely randomized design is more efficient.

Analysis of Data Let us define the following notation:

p = Number of treatments

r = Number of blocks

y_{ij} = Response variable value of the ith treatment applied to the jth block, $i = 1, 2, \ldots p$; $j = 1, 2, \ldots, r$

$y_{i\cdot} = \sum_{j=1}^{r} y_{ij}$ = Sum of the responses for the ith treatment

$\bar{y}_{i\cdot} = y_{i\cdot}/r$ = Mean response of the ith treatment

$y_{\cdot j} = \sum_{i=1}^{p} y_{ij}$ = Sum of the responses for the jth block

$\bar{y}_{\cdot j} = y_{\cdot j}/p$ = Mean response of the jth block

$y_{\cdot\cdot} = \sum_{i=1}^{p}\sum_{j=1}^{r} y_{ij}$ = Grand total of all observations

$\bar{\bar{y}} = y_{\cdot\cdot}/(rp)$ = Grand mean of all observations

The notation, consisting of the p treatments assigned to each of the r blocks, is shown in Table 12-7.

TABLE 12-7 Notation for the randomized block design

Treatments	Blocks 1	2	...	r	Sum	Mean
1	y_{11}	y_{12}	...	y_{1r}	$y_{1\cdot}$	$\bar{y}_{1\cdot}$
2	y_{21}	y_{22}	...	y_{2r}	$y_{2\cdot}$	$\bar{y}_{2\cdot}$
⋮	⋮	⋮	⋱	⋮	⋮	⋮
p	y_{p1}	y_{p2}	...	y_{pr}	$y_{p\cdot}$	$\bar{y}_{p\cdot}$
Sum	$y_{\cdot 1}$	$y_{\cdot 2}$	...	$y_{\cdot r}$	$y_{\cdot\cdot}$	
Mean	$\bar{y}_{\cdot 1}$	$\bar{y}_{\cdot 2}$	...	$\bar{y}_{\cdot r}$		$\bar{\bar{y}}$

Computations for the sum of squares are as follows. The correction factor C, as given by Equation 12.3, is

$$C = y_{..}^2/(rp)$$

The total sum of squares, as given by Equation 12.4, is

$$\text{SST} = \sum_{i=1}^{p}\sum_{j=1}^{r} y_{ij}^2 - C$$

The treatment sum of squares, as given by Equation 12.5, is

$$\text{SSTR} = \left(\sum_{i=1}^{p} y_{i\cdot}^2\right)/r - C$$

For a randomized block design, the block sum of squares is

$$\text{SSB} = \left(\sum_{j=1}^{r} y_{\cdot j}^2\right)/p - C \qquad (12.12)$$

The error sum of squares is

$$\text{SSE} = \text{SST} - \text{SSTR} - \text{SSB}$$

The number of degrees of freedom for the treatments is $(p-1)$ and for the blocks is $(r-1)$, one less than the number of blocks. The number of degrees of freedom for the error is $(p-1)(r-1)$, and the total number is $(rp-1)$. The mean squares for the treatments, blocks, and experimental error are found on division of the respective sum of squares by the corresponding numbers of degrees of freedom.

Test for Difference among Treatment Means. Denoting the treatment means by $\mu_1, \mu_2, \cdots, \mu_p$, one set of hypotheses to test would be

$H_0 : \mu_1 = \mu_2 = \cdots = \mu_p$

H_a : At least one μ_i is different from the others

This test is conducted by finding the F-statistic (the ratio of the mean squares for treatment to the mean square error), that is,

$$\text{F} = \text{MSTR/MSE}$$

The calculated F-statistic is compared to the critical value of F from Appendix A-6 for a chosen significance level α, with $(p-1)$ degrees of freedom in the numerator and $(p-1)(r-1)$ in the denominator. If the computed test statistic $F > F_{\alpha,(p-1),(p-1)(r-1)}$, the null hypothesis is rejected, and we conclude that the treatment means of are not all equal at the chosen level of significance. The analysis-of-variance computational procedure is shown in Table 12-8.

Note that blocking is typically used as a means of error control. The variability between blocks is removed from the experimental error. Whereas the treatments are replicated (each treatment being used once in each block), the blocking classifications are not. Therefore, we do not have a true measure of the experimental error for testing the difference between block means. Sometimes, an F-statistic given by the ratio of the mean squares for blocks to the mean squares for error, that is,

$$F_B = \text{MSB/MSE} \qquad (12.13)$$

is used to determine if blocking has been effective in reducing the experimental error. The computed value of F_B from Equation 12.13 is compared to $F_{\alpha,(r-1),(p-1)(r-1)}$ for a chosen level of significance α. If $F_B > F_{\alpha,(r-1),(p-1)(r-1)}$, the conclusion is that blocking has been effective; technically, though, a true significance level cannot be assigned to the test since we intentionally try to select the blocks to maximize the variability between them. If the computed value of F_B is less than $F_{\alpha,(r-1),(p-1)(r-1)}$, we infer that blocking has not been effective. In such a case, the efficiency of the experiment has decreased relative to the completely randomized design, since we lost $(r-1)$ degrees of freedom from the error without a sufficiently compensating reduction in the mean square error. This means that even though the sum of squares for error (SSE) decreased due to blocking, the MSE did not decrease because the reduction in the number of degrees of freedom was not adequately compensated for. Note that,

TABLE 12-8 Analysis-of-variance table for the randomized block design

Source of variation	Degrees of freedom	Sum of squares	Mean square	F-statistic
Treatments	$p-1$	SSTR	MSTR = SSTR/$(p-1)$	F = MSTR/MSE
Blocks	$r-1$	SSB	MSB = SSB/$(r-1)$	
Error	$(p-1)(r-1)$	SSE	MSE = SSE/$[(p-1)(r-1)]$	
Total	$rp-1$	SST		

since we strive to maximize the variability between blocks, it is not necessary to test the null hypothesis that all of the block means are equal.

Interval estimates for a single treatment mean μ_i are obtained as before. A $100(1-\alpha)$ percent confidence interval for μ_i is given by

$$L(\mu_i) = \bar{y}_{i\cdot} \pm t_{\alpha/2,(p-1)(r-1)} \sqrt{\text{MSE}/r} \qquad (12.14)$$

where $t_{\alpha/2,(p-1)(r-1)}$ is the t-value for a right tail area of $\alpha/2$ and $(p-1)(r-1)$ degrees of freedom and is found from Appendix A-4.

Usually, it would be of interest to estimate the difference between two treatment means. A $100(1-\alpha)$ percent confidence interval for the difference between two treatment means, $\mu_{i_1} - \mu_{i_2}$, is given by

$$L(\mu_{i_1} - \mu_{i_2}) = (\bar{y}_{i_1\cdot} - \bar{y}_{i_2\cdot}) \pm t_{\alpha/2,(p-1)(r-1)} \sqrt{2\text{MSE}/r} \qquad (12.15)$$

where $t_{\alpha/2,(p-1)(r-1)}$ is the t-value for a right tail area of $\alpha/2$ and $(p-1)(r-1)$ degrees of freedom.

Example 12-2: A construction company intends to test the efficiency of three different insulators. Since the area over which the company builds has a varied degree of temperature differentials, the following experimental procedure has been planned. The company has divided the area into four geographical regions, based on climatic differences. Within each geographical region, it randomly uses each of the three insulators and records the energy loss as an index. Smaller values of the index correspond to lower losses. Table 12-9 shows the data on the energy loss index for the three insulators in the four regions.

a. Is there a difference in the mean energy loss for the three insulators? Test at a significance level of 10 percent.

Solution. Here, the treatments are the insulators, and the blocks are the geographical regions. Using the raw data in Table 12-9, we calculate the sample treatment sums and means and the block sums and means of the energy loss index. The number of treatments p is 3, and the number of blocks r is 4. These are also shown in Table 12-9. The sum of squares calculations, required for the analysis-of-variance procedure, are as follows. The correction factor is

$$C = y_{\cdot\cdot}^2/(rp) = (108.9)^2/12 = 988.267$$

The total sum of squares is

$$\begin{aligned} \text{SST} &= \sum_{i=1}^{p}\sum_{j=1}^{r} y_{ij}^2 - C \\ &= 1301.950 - 988.267 = 313.683 \end{aligned}$$

The treatment sum of squares due to the insulators is

$$\begin{aligned} \text{SSTR} &= \left(\sum_{i=1}^{p} y_{i\cdot}^2\right)\Big/ r - C \\ &= \left[(60.8)^2 + (31.6)^2 + (16.5)^2\right]/4 - 988.267 \\ &= 253.596 \end{aligned}$$

The block sum of squares due to the geographical regions is

$$\begin{aligned} \text{SSB} &= \left(\sum_{j=1}^{r} y_{\cdot j}^2\right)\Big/ p - C \\ &= [(37.6)^2 + (22.1)^2 + (27.7)^2 \\ &\quad + (21.5)^2]/3 - 988.267 \\ &= 55.636 \end{aligned}$$

The error sum of squares is found to be

$$\begin{aligned} \text{SSE} &= \text{SST} - \text{SSTR} - \text{SSB} \\ &= 313.683 - 253.596 - 55.636 = 4.451 \end{aligned}$$

The analysis-of-variance table is shown in Table 12-10.

TABLE 12-9 Energy loss index for insulators in geographical regions

	Geographical regions					
Insulators	I	II	III	IV	Sum	Mean
1	19.2	12.8	16.3	12.5	60.8	15.2
2	11.7	6.4	7.3	6.2	31.6	7.9
3	6.7	2.9	4.1	2.8	16.5	4.125
Sum	37.6	22.1	27.7	21.5	108.9	
Mean	12.533	7.367	9.233	7.167		9.075

TABLE 12-10 Analysis-of-variance table for data on energy loss index

Source of variation	Degrees of freedom	Sum of squares	Mean Square	*F*-statistic
Insulators (treatments)	2	253.596	126.798	170.887
Geographical regions (blocks)	3	55.636	18.545	
Error	6	4.451	0.742	
Total	11	313.683		

To test if there is any difference in the mean energy loss index between the three insulators, the F-statistic is calculated as the ratio of the mean squares for insulators to the mean squares for error, that is,

$$F = \text{MSTR}/\text{MSE} = 126.798/0.742 = 170.887$$

At a significance level of 10 percent, from Appendix A-6, $F_{.10,2,6} = 3.46$. Since $F = 170.887 > 3.46$, we conclude that at least one of the mean energy loss indices is different from the others.

b. Find a 99 percent confidence interval for the mean energy loss index for insulator 3.

Solution. A 99 percent confidence interval for the mean energy loss index for insulator 3 is

$$\begin{aligned} L(\mu_3) &= \bar{y}_{3\cdot} \pm t_{.005,6}\sqrt{\text{MSE}/4} \\ &= 4.125 \pm (3.707)\sqrt{0.742/4} \\ &= 4.125 \pm 1.597 = (2.528,\ 5.722) \end{aligned}$$

c. Find a 90 percent confidence interval for the difference in the mean energy loss index of insulators 2 and 3. Is there a difference in these two means?

Solution. A 90 percent confidence interval for the difference in the mean energy loss index of insulators 2 and 3 is

$$\begin{aligned} L(\mu_2 - \mu_3) &= (\bar{y}_{2\cdot} - \bar{y}_{3\cdot}) \pm t_{.05,6}\sqrt{2\text{MSE}/4} \\ &= (7.9 - 4.125) \pm 1.943\sqrt{2(0.742)/4} \\ &= 3.775 \pm 1.183 = (2.592,\ 4.958) \end{aligned}$$

Since the confidence interval does not include the value of zero, we conclude that there is a difference in the mean energy loss index of insulators 2 and 3 at the 10 percent level of significance.

d. Which insulator should the company choose?

Solution. Since smaller values of the energy loss index correspond to low losses, insulator 3 would be chosen, as it has the lowest mean (4.125). Part (b) showed that the mean energy loss of insulator 3 is different from that of insulator 2. Since the mean energy loss of insulator 1 is even higher than that of insulator 2, the mean energy loss of insulator 3 will be significantly different from that of insulator 1.

Latin Square Design

In the randomized block design we controlled one source of variation. Experimental units were grouped into blocks consisting of homogeneous units based on a certain criterion that helped reduce the variability of the experimental error. Variability between blocks was thus separated from the experimental error, and each treatment appeared an equal number of times in each block. The Latin square design controls two sources of variation; in effect, it blocks in two variables. The number of groups, or blocks, for each of the two variables is equal, which in turn is equal to the number of treatments. Suppose we denote one of the blocking variables as the row variable and the other as the column variable. The treatments are assigned so that each treatment appears once and only once in each row and column. The number of experimental units required is the square of the number of treatments.

Consider an example in which blocking in two variables might be appropriate. The productivity of bank tellers might vary from one person to another. Productivity might also change as a function of the day of the week. Suppose the bank management is interested in determining if the type of break, as characterized by the frequency, duration, and time of day, has any affect on productivity. The bank management wants to test five types of breaks (A, B, C, D, and E). For example, type A could represent short breaks (say, 5 minutes) that occur once each hour. Type B could represent longer breaks (10 minutes) that occur once every two hours, and so forth. In the Latin square design, five tellers (I, II, III, IV, and V) could be randomly selected and could serve as the first blocking variable (say, the row classification). The five days of the week (1, 2, 3, 4, and 5) could serve as the column classification. The treatments are the types of break (A, B, C, D, and E). They are denoted by Latin letters, hence the name Latin square design. The design is square because the number of row and column classifications is equal (in this case 5), which is also equal to the number of treatments. Each type of break is assigned to each teller and to each day of the week only once.

One particular assignment of the types of break (treatments) is shown in Table 12-11. For instance,

TABLE 12-11 A Latin square design for five treatments

	Day of week				
Teller	1	2	3	4	5
I	A	B	C	D	E
II	B	C	D	E	A
III	C	D	E	A	B
IV	D	E	A	B	C
V	E	A	B	C	D

type A is assigned to the first teller (I) for the first day of the week (1). Similarly, type B is assigned to the first teller (I) for the second day of the week (2), and so on. Note that each treatment occurs only once in each row and in each column. For five treatments, 25 experimental units are needed for the Latin square design. The assignment strategy shown in Table 12-11 is one of several that could satisfy the above criteria, for which each treatment occurs exactly once in each row and column.

The Latin square design is an example of an *incomplete block design,* in which not all treatments are necessarily assigned to each block. In the example just considered, we actually have 25 blocks, representing the different combinations of tellers and day of the week (that is, block 1: teller I, day of week 1; block 2: teller I, day of week 2; and so on). For a randomized block design, in which each treatment appears once in each block, we would need 125 experimental units. In the Latin square design we can get by with only 25 experimental units. In general, if we have p treatments, we need p^2 experimental units; each of the two blocking variables should have p classes.

The main advantage of the Latin square design is that it allows the use of two blocking variables, which usually results in greater reductions in the variability of experimental error than can be obtained by using either of the two blocking variables individually. There are some disadvantages of the Latin square design, however. First, since the number of classes of each blocking variable must equal the number of treatments, very few degrees of freedom are left for the experimental error if the number of treatments is small. When the number of treatments is large, the number of degrees of freedom for the experimental error may be larger than necessary. Since the number of experimental units required is equal to the square of the number of treatments, the number of treatments has to be limited (usually 10 or less) for practical studies. Also, the model is restrictive because it assumes that there is no interaction between either the blocking variable and the treatment or between the blocking variables themselves. Another restriction is that the number of classes for the two blocking variables must be the same.

Randomization of the Latin Square Design

For a given number of treatments, various Latin squares are possible. For example, for three treatments denoted by A, B, and C ($p = 3$), four possible Latin squares are possible, as shown in Table 12-12. As p increases, the number of possible arrangements increases drastically. The idea behind randomization is to select one of all possible Latin squares for a given number of treatments in such a way that each square has an equal chance of being selected. We begin with a standard Latin square, in which the elements of the first row and column are arranged alphabetically, as in Table 12-11 or the top left arrangement in Table 12-12. A random number table, as shown in Appendix A-9, may be used to select one of the arrangements. The procedure for the case in which $p = 5$ is as follows. A random order for the rows is obtained by selecting five random numbers, ranking them, and interchanging the rows of the standard Latin square according to the rank order. Table 12-13 shows the procedure for randomizing the rows. For instance, row 2 of

TABLE 12-12 Latin square designs for three treatments

	Blocking variable I				Blocking variable I		
Blocking variable II	A	B	C	Blocking variable II	A	C	B
	B	C	A		B	A	C
	C	A	B		C	B	A
	Blocking variable I				Blocking variable I		
Blocking variable II	B	A	C	Blocking variable II	C	B	A
	C	B	A		A	C	B
	A	C	B		B	A	C

TABLE 12-13 Randomizing the row order in a Latin square design

Random number	Rank order	Row
658	4	1
409	3	2
322	2	3
157	1	4
762	5	5

Standard Latin square

A	B	C	D	E
B	C	D	E	A
C	D	E	A	B
D	E	A	B	C
E	A	B	C	D

Row randomization of standard Latin square

D	E	A	B	C
C	D	E	A	B
B	C	D	E	A
A	B	C	D	E
E	A	B	C	D

the standard Latin square is now row 3 in the row-randomized Latin square. Next, the same procedure may be used to randomize the order for columns, starting with the design obtained after the row order has been randomized. Five more random numbers are selected and ranked, and the columns are interchanged based on the rank order. The procedure is demonstrated in Table 12-14. For example, column 2 in the row-randomized design is now column 5 in the final Latin square design shown in Table 12-14.

Analysis of Data The analysis of variance is similar to the previously described procedures. The following notation is used:

p = Number of treatments

$y_{ij(k)}$ = Response variable value of the experimental unit in the ith row and jth column subjected to the kth treatment

$y_{i\cdot} = \sum_{j=1}^{p} y_{ij}$ = Sum of the responses in the ith row

$y_{\cdot j} = \sum_{i=1}^{p} y_{ij}$ = Sum of the responses in the jth column

$y_{\cdot\cdot} = \sum_{i=1}^{p}\sum_{j=1}^{p} y_{ij}$ = Grand total of all observations

T_k = Sum of the responses for the kth treatment

$\bar{y}_k = T_k/p$ = Sample mean response for the kth treatment

The notation for the Latin square design is shown in Table 12-15. The sum of squares is calculated as follows.

A correction factor C is computed as

$$C = y_{\cdot\cdot}^2/p^2 \tag{12.16}$$

The total sum of squares is

$$SST = \sum_{i=1}^{p}\sum_{j=1}^{p} y_{ij}^2 - C \tag{12.17}$$

The sum of squares for the row blocking variable is

$$SSR = \left(\sum_{i=1}^{p} y_{i\cdot}^2\right)/p - C \tag{12.18}$$

The sum of squares for the column blocking variable is

$$SSC = \left(\sum_{j=1}^{p} y_{\cdot j}^2\right)/p - C \tag{12.19}$$

The sum of squares for the treatments is

$$SSTR = \left(\sum_{k=1}^{p} T_k^2\right)/p - C \tag{12.20}$$

TABLE 12-14 Randomizing the column order in a Latin square design

Random number	Rank order	Column
368	1	1
721	4	2
870	5	3
452	3	4
379	2	5

Row-randomized Latin square

D	E	A	B	C
C	D	E	A	B
B	C	D	E	A
A	B	C	D	E
E	A	B	C	D

Column-randomized Latin square

D	B	C	A	E
C	A	B	E	D
B	E	A	D	C
A	D	E	C	B
E	C	D	B	A

Finally, the error sum of squares is

$$SSE = SST - SSR - SSC - SSTR \tag{12.21}$$

The number of degrees of freedom for the row blocking variable as well as for the column blocking variable is $p-1$, one less than the number of rows. The number of degrees of freedom for the treatments is $(p-1)$, one less than the number of treatments. The total number of degrees of freedom is p^2-1, one less than the total number of experimental units. The

TABLE 12-15 Notation for the Latin square design

Row	Column 1	2	...	p	Sum
1	y_{11}	y_{12}	...	y_{1p}	$y_{1.}$
2	y_{21}	y_{22}	...	y_{2p}	$y_{2.}$
⋮	⋮	⋮	⋮	⋮	⋮
p	y_{p1}	y_{p2}	...	y_{pp}	$y_{p\cdot}$
Sum	$y_{\cdot 1}$	$y_{\cdot 2}$	...	$y_{\cdot p}$	$y_{\cdot\cdot}$

	Treatment 1	2	...	p
Sum	T_1	T_2	...	T_p
Mean	$\bar{y}_1$	$\bar{y}_2$	...	$\bar{y}_p$

number of degrees of freedom for the experimental error may be found by subtraction as follows:

$$\begin{aligned}\text{Error degrees of freedom} &= (p^2 - 1) - (p - 1) \\ &\quad - (p - 1) - (p - 1) \\ &= (p - 1)(p - 2)\end{aligned}$$

Next, the mean squares are found by dividing the sum of squares by the appropriate number of degrees of freedom. A tabular format of the analysis-of-variance calculations is shown in Table 12-16.

Test for Difference among Treatment Means. If the treatment means are denoted by $\mu_1, \mu_2, \cdots, \mu_p$, one set of hypotheses to test is

H_o: $\mu_1 = \mu_2 = \cdots = \mu_p$

H_a: At least one μ_i is different from the others

The test is conducted by calculating the F-statistic as the ratio of the mean squares for treatments to the mean square for error, that is,

$$F = \text{MSTR/MSE}$$

If the calculated F-statistic $> F_{\alpha,(p-1),(p-1)(p-2)}$, which is found from the tables in Appendix A-6, for a right tail area of α with $(p - 1)$ degrees of freedom in the numerator and $(p - 1)(p - 2)$ in the denominator, the null hypothesis is rejected. In that case we conclude that at least one of the treatment means is different from the others at a chosen level of significance α.

Note that, as in the randomized block design, treatments are replicated in the Latin square, but the row and column classifications of the two blocking variables are not. Thus, an F-statistic for determining the effectiveness of the row blocking variable calculated as

$$F_R = \text{MSR/MSE}$$

is used in an approximate significance test to determine if the row classification is effective in reducing the experimental error. Similarly, for testing the effectiveness of the column blocking variable, an F-statistic calculated as

$$F_C = \text{MSC/MSE}$$

is used in an approximate significance test for the column blocking variable. Each of these two statistics may be compared with $F_{\alpha,(p-1),(p-1)(p-2)}$ to make such inferences.

A $100(1 - \alpha)$ percent confidence interval for a single treatment mean μ_k is given by

$$L(\mu_k) = \bar{y}_k \pm t_{\alpha/2,(p-1)(p-2)} \sqrt{\text{MSE}/p} \qquad (12.22)$$

where $t_{\alpha/2,(p-1)(p-2)}$ is the t-value for a right tail area of $\alpha/2$ and $(p - 1)(p - 2)$ degrees of freedom and is found from Appendix A-4.

As with the previous designs, it is usually of interest to estimate the difference between two treatment means. A $100(1 - \alpha)$ percent confidence interval for the difference between two treatment means, $\mu_{k_1} - \mu_{k_2}$, is given by

$$L(\mu_{k_1} - \mu_{k_2}) = (\bar{y}_{k_1} - \bar{y}_{k_2}) \pm t_{\alpha/2,(p-1)(p-2)} \sqrt{2\text{MSE}/p}, \qquad (12.23)$$

where $t_{\alpha/2,(p-1)(p-2)}$ is the t-value for a right tail area of $\alpha/2$ and $(p - 1)(p - 2)$ degrees of freedom.

The number of treatments that can be analyzed is somewhat restricted, from a practical point of view. Note that the number of error degrees of freedom is given by $(p - 1)(p - 2)$, where p is the number of treatments. If p is very small, the number of error degrees of freedom is small, which will cause the mean square error to be large. The number of treatments cannot be less than 3, because if $p = 2$ the number of error degrees of freedom is 0. As p becomes large, the number of experimental units required (p^2) becomes too large and may be infeasible from a cost and operational standpoint.

TABLE 12-16 Analysis-of-variance table for the Latin square design

Source of variation	Degrees of freedom	Sum of squares	Mean square	F-statistic
Rows (blocking variable I)	$p - 1$	SSR	MSR = SSR/$(p-1)$	
Columns (blocking variable II)	$p - 1$	SSC	MSC = SSC/$(p-1)$	
Treatments	$p - 1$	SSTR	MSTR = SSTR/$(p-1)$	F = MSTR/MSE
Error	$(p - 1)(p - 2)$	SSE	MSE = SSE/$[(p-1)(p-2)]$	
Total	$p^2 - 1$	SST		

Example 12-3: A retail company is interested in testing the impact of four different pricing policies (A, B, C, and D) on sales. The company suspects that variation in sales could be affected by factors other than the pricing policy, such as store location and sales volume. The company has categorized location into four classifications: Northeast, East, Midwest, and Southeast. It has classified sales volume into four classes: 1, 2, 3, and 4, with class 1 representing the largest volume, and the others representing decreasing volume in succession. Each pricing policy was applied in each geographic region and each sales volume class exactly once. Table 12-17 shows the sales (in thousands of dollars) for a three-month period, with the pricing policy shown appropriately.

a. Is there a difference in the pricing policies in terms of mean sales? Test at a level of significance of 5 percent.

Solution. Table 12-17 also shows the row and column sums for the blocking variables sales volume class and geographic location class. The sum of squares for each of the two blocking variables as well as for the treatments (the pricing policies) are found as follows. The correction factor is

$$C = y_{..}^2/p^2 = (167.40)^2/4^2 = 1751.4225$$

From Equation 12.17, the total sum of squares is calculated to be

$$\begin{aligned} \text{SST} &= \sum_{i=1}^{p}\sum_{j=1}^{p} y_{ij}^2 - C \\ &= 2046.48 - 1751.4225 = 295.0575 \end{aligned}$$

The sum of squares of the row blocking variable (sales volume class) is found from equation (12.18) as

$$\begin{aligned} \text{SSR} &= \left(\sum_{i=1}^{p} y_{i.}^2\right)/p - C \\ &= \left[(51.7)^2 + (43.5)^2 + (36.7)^2 + (35.5)^2\right]/4 \\ &\quad - 1751.4225 \\ &= 41.6475 \end{aligned}$$

TABLE 12-17 Data on sales for different pricing policies

Sales volume class	Geographical location				Sum
	Northeast	East	Midwest	Southeast	
1	A 19.2	B 15.4	C 6.6	D 10.5	51.7
2	B 13.2	C 5.3	D 8.2	A 16.8	43.5
3	C 4.2	D 9.4	A 14.6	B 8.5	36.7
4	D 8.4	A 13.3	B 7.6	C 6.2	35.5
Sum	45.0	43.4	37.0	42.0	167.40

TABLE 12-18 Sums and means of sales for different pricing policies

Pricing policies	A	B	C	D
Sum	63.9	44.7	22.3	36.5
Mean	15.975	11.175	5.575	9.125

The sum of squares for the column blocking variable (geographic location) is found from Equation 12.19 as

$$\begin{aligned} \text{SSC} &= \left(\sum_{j=1}^{p} y_{.j}^2\right)/p - C \\ &= \left[(45.0)^2 + (43.4)^2 + (37.0)^2 + (42.0)^2\right]/4 \\ &\quad - 1751.4225 \\ &= 8.9675 \end{aligned}$$

Table 12-18 shows the sum of sales and their means for the pricing policies. The sum of squares due to the pricing policies is found from Equation 12.20 as

$$\begin{aligned} \text{SSTR} &= \left(\sum_{k=1}^{p} T_k^2\right)/p - C \\ &= \left[(63.9)^2 + (44.7)^2 + (22.3)^2 + (36.5)^2\right]/4 \\ &\quad - 1751.4225 \\ &= 226.2875 \end{aligned}$$

The error sum of squares is

$$\begin{aligned} \text{SSE} &= \text{SST} - \text{SSR} - \text{SSC} - \text{SSTR} \\ &= 295.0575 - 41.6475 - 8.9675 - 226.2875 \\ &= 18.155 \end{aligned}$$

The analysis-of-variance table is shown in Table 12-19. To test the null hypothesis that the mean sales for

TABLE 12-19 Analysis-of-variance table for data on sales

Source of variation	Degrees of freedom	Sum of squares	Mean square	*F*-statistic
Sales volume class (rows)	3	41.6475	13.8825	
Geographic location (columns)	3	8.9675	2.9892	
Pricing policies (treatments)	3	226.2875	75.4292	24.9287
Error	6	18.1550	3.0258	
Total	15	295.0575		

all the four pricing strategies (A, B, C, and D) are equal against the alternative hypothesis that at least one mean is different from the others, the appropriate F statistic is

$$F = \text{MSTR}/\text{MSE} = 75.4292/3.0258 = 24.9287$$

For a chosen level of significance α of 5 percent, the value of F from Appendix A-6 is $F_{.05,3,6} = 4.76$. Since the calculated value of $F = 24.9287 > 4.76$, we reject the null hypothesis and conclude that at least one mean sales value is different from the others at this level of significance.

b. Find a 90 percent confidence interval for the mean sales using pricing policy A.

Solution. A 90 percent confidence interval for the mean sales using pricing policy A is

$$\begin{aligned} L(\mu_A) &= \bar{y}_A \pm t_{.05,6}\sqrt{\text{MSE}/4} \\ &= 15.975 \pm (1.943)\sqrt{3.0258/4} \\ &= 15.975 \pm 1.690 = (14.285, 17.665) \end{aligned}$$

c. Find a 95 percent confidence interval for the difference in mean sales using pricing policies A and C. Is there a difference between these two policies?

Solution. A 95 percent confidence interval for the difference in mean sales using pricing policies A and C is

$$\begin{aligned} L(\mu_A - \mu_C) &= (\bar{y}_A - \bar{y}_C) \pm t_{.025,6}\sqrt{2\text{MSE}/4} \\ &= (15.975 - 5.575) \pm (2.447)\sqrt{2(3.0258)/4} \\ &= 10.400 \pm 3.010 = (7.390, 3.410) \end{aligned}$$

Since the confidence interval does not include zero, at the 5 percent level of significance we conclude that there is a difference between the mean sales of pricing policies A and C.

d. Which pricing policy would you use?

Solution. We concluded above that there is a difference between the mean sales of the four pricing policies. From Table 12-18, we find that pricing policy A yields the highest mean sales of 15.975. Let us check if there is difference between the mean sales of pricing policies A and B, the two highest values, at the 5 percent level of significance. We have

$$\bar{y}_A - \bar{y}_B = 15.975 - 11.175 = 4.8$$

Using the calculations from part c, a 95 percent confidence interval for $(\mu_A - \mu_B)$ is

$$4.8 \pm 3.010 = (1.790, 7.810)$$

Since the confidence interval does not include zero, we conclude that the mean sales for pricing policy A is significantly different from that of pricing policy B at the 5 percent level of significance. Hence, if the objective is to maximize sales, pricing policy A is preferable. If there were no significant differences between pricing policies A and B, the cost of adopting and implementing either of them would be a factor in choosing a particular strategy.

Let us investigate the effectiveness of blocking in two variables; sales volume and geographic location. For the row classification of sales volume, the calculated F-statistic (from Table 12-19) is

$$F_R = \text{MSR}/\text{MSE} = 13.8825/3.0258 = 4.588$$

Since the table value of F at the 5 percent level of significance is $F_{.05,3,6} = 4.76$, which exceeds the calculated value of F_R, we cannot conclude that blocking through the classification of sales volume has been effective at this significance level. Similarly, to test the effectiveness of the column blocking variable, geographic location, we calculate the F-statistic as follows

$$F_C = \text{MSC}/\text{MSE} = 2.9892/3.0258 = 0.988$$

The value of $F_C = 0.988 < F_{.05,3,6} = 4.76$. So, we conclude that blocking by means of geographic location has not been effective. For future experiments, either the completely randomized design or the randomized block design with sales volume class as the blocking variable could be investigated. If the Latin square design were to be run, the experimenter should select some alternative blocking variables, the inclusion of which would effectively reduce the error mean squares. It should be mentioned that computer software packages could be used to obtain the computational results using the analysis-of-variance procedure. One such package is the Statistical Analysis System (SAS). In Chapter 15 on using computer software, we will look at some features of the SAS package that may be used for quality control and improvement procedures. For more details, consult the references (SAS Institute Inc., 1989a, 1989b).

12-4 FACTORIAL EXPERIMENTS

When there are two or more factors, each at two or more levels, a treatment is defined as a combination of the levels of each of the factors. In a factorial experiment, all possible combinations of the factors (that is, all treatments) are represented for each complete replication of the experiment. The number of treatments is equal to the product of the number of levels of all of the factors and can therefore become large when either the number of factors or the number of levels associated with the factors becomes large. Consider, for example, the assembly of television sets with the response variable being the assembly time and the factors being the experience of operators (classified into six levels), the training program used (having four levels), and the type of lighting used (having three levels). A factorial experiment with these three factors would consist of

72 ($6 \times 4 \times 3$) treatments. Thus, a single replication of the treatments, with each treatment being used only once, would require 72 trials, which is quite a few. Moreover, because the purpose of using treatments involving various factors kept at certain levels (rather than the approach for one variable at a time) is to ensure that any possible interaction effects between factors can be estimated, replication of treatments is usually needed. This further increases the total number of required trials in a factorial experiment. It should be mentioned that the factorial set of treatments can be used with any of the previously discussed design types (the completely randomized design, randomized block design, or Latin square design).

One of the main advantages of factorial experiments is that they offer the ability to estimate the interaction effects between factors, which is not possible with the approach for one variable at a time. In the presence of two or more factors, knowledge of interaction effects is of prime importance to the experimenter. When interaction between two factors is significant, the difference in the response variable to changes in the levels of one factor is not the same at all levels of the other factor. If the effect of both factors on the response variable is to be determined, interaction effects cannot be ignored. Interaction effects, if present, mask the main effects due to the factors, so testing for the main effects if the interaction effects are significant is inappropriate. Only when the factors are independent and interaction is not present are the main effects of the factors of interest. In such cases, fewer trials are required to estimate the main effects to the same degree of precision. Usually, single-factor experiments require more trials to achieve the same degree of precision as factorial experiments. Factorial experiments also serve an important role in exploratory studies to determine which factors are important. Additionally, by conducting experiments for a factor at several levels of other factors, the inferences from a factorial experiment are valid over a wide range of conditions.

A disadvantage of factorial experiments is the exponential increase in the size of the experiments with an increase in the number of factors and/or their number of levels. The cost to conduct all of the experiments might be an influential factor; another drawback could be the feasibility of finding blocks large enough to permit the completion of a full replication of all treatments, assuming that each treatment is used once in each block. A third drawback could be the interpretation of higher-order interactions.

The simplest type of factorial experiment, that involving two factors, with a certain number of levels, is discussed below for the completely randomized and the randomized block designs.

Factorial Experiment with Two Factors Using a Completely Randomized Design

Let the two factors be denoted by A and B, respectively, with factor A having a levels and B having b levels. The ab treatments are randomly assigned to the experimental units. Suppose the experiment is replicated n times, yielding a total of abn observations. The model may be described by

$$y_{ijk} = \mu + \alpha_i + \beta_j + (\alpha\beta)_{ij} + \epsilon_{ijk}, \quad i = 1, 2, \cdots, a \quad j = 1, 2, \cdots, b \quad k = 1, 2, \cdots, n \tag{12.24}$$

where y_{ijk} represents the response for the ith level of factor A, the jth level of factor B, and the kth replication; μ is the overall mean effect; α_i is the effect of the ith level of factor A; β_j is the effect of the jth level of factor B; $(\alpha\beta)_{ij}$ is the effect of the interaction between factors A and B; and ϵ_{ijk} is the random error component (assumed to be normally distributed with mean zero and constant variance σ^2). The following notation is used:

$y_{i\cdot\cdot} = \sum_{j=1}^{b}\sum_{k=1}^{n} y_{ijk}$ = Sum of the responses for the ith level of factor A

$\bar{y}_{i\cdot\cdot} = y_{i\cdot\cdot}/(bn)$ = Average response for the ith level of factor A

$y_{\cdot j\cdot} = \sum_{i=1}^{a}\sum_{k=1}^{n} y_{ijk}$ = Sum of the responses for the jth level of factor B

$\bar{y}_{\cdot j\cdot} = y_{\cdot j\cdot}/(an)$ = Average response for the jth level of factor B

$y_{ij\cdot} = \sum_{k=1}^{n} y_{ijk}$ = Sum of the responses for the ith level of factor A and jth level of factor B

$\bar{y}_{ij\cdot} = y_{ij\cdot}/n$ = Average response for the ith level of factor A and jth level of factor B

$y_{\cdots} = \sum_{i=1}^{a}\sum_{j=1}^{b}\sum_{k=1}^{n}$ = Grand total of all observations

$\bar{y}_{\cdots} = y_{\cdots}/(abn)$ = Grand mean of all observations

The notation is shown in Table 12-20.

Computations of the sum of squares needed for the analysis of variance are as follows.

TABLE 12-20 Notation for factorial experiments using a completely randomized design

	Factor B					
Factor A	1	2	...	b	Sum	Average
1	$y_{111}, y_{112}, \ldots, y_{11n}$ sum = $y_{11\cdot}$	$y_{121}, y_{122}, \ldots, y_{12n}$ sum = $y_{12\cdot}$	...	$y_{1b1}, y_{1b2}, \ldots, y_{1bn}$ sum = $y_{1b\cdot}$	$y_{1\cdot\cdot}$	$\bar{y}_{1\cdot\cdot}$
2	$y_{211}, y_{212}, \ldots, y_{21n}$ sum = $y_{21\cdot}$	$y_{221}, y_{222}, \ldots, y_{22n}$ sum = $y_{22\cdot}$	... ...	$y_{2b1}, y_{2b2}, \ldots, y_{2bn}$ sum = $y_{2b\cdot}$	$y_{2\cdot\cdot}$	$y_{2\cdot\cdot}$
⋮	⋮	⋮	⋮	⋮	⋮	⋮
a	$y_{a11}, y_{a12}, \ldots, y_{a1n}$ sum = $y_{a1\cdot}$	$y_{a21}, y_{a22}, \ldots, y_{a2n}$ sum = $y_{a2\cdot}$	... ...	$y_{ab1}, y_{ab2}, \ldots, y_{abn}$ sum = $y_{ab\cdot}$	$y_{a\cdot\cdot}$	$\bar{y}_{a\cdot\cdot}$
Sum	$y_{\cdot 1\cdot}$	$y_{\cdot 2\cdot}$	...	$y_{\cdot b\cdot}$	$y_{\cdots}$	
Average	$\bar{y}_{\cdot 1\cdot}$	$\bar{y}_{\cdot 2\cdot}$	...	$\bar{y}_{\cdot b\cdot}$		$\bar{y}_{\cdots}$

The correction factor is calculated as

$$C = y_{\cdots}^2/(abn) \tag{12.25}$$

The total sum of squares is given by

$$\text{SST} = \sum_{i=1}^{a}\sum_{j=1}^{b}\sum_{k=1}^{n} y_{ijk}^2 - C \tag{12.26}$$

The sum of squares for the main effects of factor A is found from

$$\text{SSA} = \left(\sum_{i=1}^{a} y_{i\cdot\cdot}^2\right)/(bn) - C \tag{12.27}$$

The sum of squares for the main effects of factor B is found from

$$\text{SSB} = \left(\sum_{j=1}^{b} y_{\cdot j\cdot}^2\right)/(an) - C \tag{12.28}$$

The sum of squares for the subtotals between the cell totals is given by

$$\text{SS(subtotal)} = \left(\sum_{i=1}^{a}\sum_{j=1}^{b} y_{ij\cdot}^2\right)/n - C \tag{12.29}$$

The sum of squares due to the interaction between factors A and B is given by

$$\text{SSAB} = \text{SS(subtotal)} - \text{SSA} - \text{SSB} \tag{12.30}$$

Finally, the error sum of squares is

$$\text{SSE} = \text{SST} - \text{SS(subtotal)} \tag{12.31}$$

There are $(a-1)$ degrees of freedom for factor A, one less than number of levels of A. Similarly, there are $(b-1)$ degrees of freedom for factor B, one less the number of levels of B. The number of degrees of freedom for the interaction between factors A and B is the product of the number of degrees of freedom for each, that is, $(a-1)(b-1)$. Since the total number of degrees of freedom is $(abn-1)$, by subtraction, the number of degrees of freedom for the experimental error is $ab(n-1)$. The mean squares for each category are found by dividing the sum of squares by the corresponding number of degrees of freedom. To test for the significance of the factors and the interaction, the F-statistic is calculated. Table 12-21 shows the analysis-of-variance table.

Tests for Significance of Factors In a factorial experiment, the first set of hypotheses to be

TABLE 12-21 Analysis-of-variance table for the two-factor factorial experiment using a completely randomized design

Source of variation	Degrees of freedom	Sum of squares	Mean square	F-statistic
Factor A	$a-1$	SSA	MSA = SSA/$(a-1)$	F_A = MSA/MSE
Factor B	$b-1$	SSB	MSB = SSB/$(b-1)$	F_B = MSB/MSE
Interaction between A and B	$(a-1)(b-1)$	SSAB	MSAB = SSAB/$[(a-1)(b-1)]$	F_{AB} = MSAB/MSE
Error	$ab(n-1)$	SSE	MSE = SSE/$[ab(n-1)]$	
Total	$abn-1$	SST		

tested usually deals with the interaction between the factors. The hypothesis of interest could be

H_o: $(\alpha\beta)_{ij} = 0$ for all i, j; $i = 1, 2, \ldots, a$; $j = 1, 2, \ldots, b$

H_a: At least one $(\alpha\beta)_{ij}$ is different from zero

The test statistic is the F-statistic, which is shown in Table 12-21 and is calculated as

$$F_{AB} = MSAB/MSE \tag{12.32}$$

which is the ratio of the mean square due to interaction to the mean square error. If the calculated value of $F_{AB} > F_{\alpha,(a-1)(b-1),ab(n-1)}$, the null hypothesis is rejected, and we conclude that the interactions between factors are significant at the level α. The presence of significant interaction effects masks the main effects of the factors, in which case the main effects are usually not tested. When interaction exists, the value of the response variable due to changes in factor A depends on the level of factor B. In such a situation, the mean for a level of factor A, averaged over all levels of factor B, does not have any practical significance. What might be of interest under these circumstances is to report the treatment means along with their standard deviations. A plot of the treatment means may identify the preferable levels of the factors.

The standard deviation of the treatment mean, which is the mean of any combination of factors A and B, is given by

$$s_{\bar{y}(AB)} = \sqrt{MSE/n} \tag{12.33}$$

Thus, a $100(1-\alpha)$ percent confidence interval for a treatment mean when factor A is at level i and factor B is at level j is given by

$$\bar{y}_{ij\cdot} \pm t_{\alpha/2,ab(n-1)} \sqrt{MSE/n} \tag{12.34}$$

where $t_{\alpha/2,ab(n-1)}$ is the t-value found from Appendix A-4 for a right tail area of $\alpha/2$ and $ab(n-1)$ degrees of freedom.

For inferences on the difference d of two treatment means, the standard deviation is

$$s_{d(AB)} = \sqrt{2MSE/n} \tag{12.35}$$

Consider the treatments for which factor A is at level i and factor B is at level j, which yields a sample average of $\bar{y}_{ij\cdot}$. Suppose the other treatment has factor A at level i' and factor B at level j', the sample average being $\bar{y}_{i'j'\cdot}$. A $100(1-\alpha)$ percent confidence interval for the difference between the two treatment means is given by

$$(\bar{y}_{ij\cdot} - \bar{y}_{i'j'\cdot}) \pm t_{\alpha/2,ab(n-1)} \sqrt{2MSE/n} \tag{12.36}$$

When the interaction effects are not significant, it is reasonable to test for the effects of the two factors. To test if factor A is significant, the F-statistic, as shown in Table 12-21, is calculated as the ratio of the mean squares due to factor A to the mean squares for error, that is

$$F_A = MSA/MSE \tag{12.37}$$

This calculated value of F_A is then compared to $F_{\alpha,a-1,ab(n-1)}$, the critical value of F found from Appendix A-6 for a right tail area of α, $(a-1)$ numerator degrees of freedom and $ab(n-1)$ denominator degrees of freedom. If $F_A > F_{\alpha,a-1,ab(n-1)}$, we conclude that the factor means at the different levels of A are not all equal.

A $100(1-\alpha)$ percent confidence interval for the mean of factor A when at level i is given by

$$\bar{y}_{i\cdot\cdot} \pm t_{\alpha/2,ab(n-1)} \sqrt{MSE/(bn)} \tag{12.38}$$

Also, a $100(1-\alpha)$ percent confidence interval for the difference between the factor A means that are at levels i and i', respectively, is found from

$$(\bar{y}_{i\cdot\cdot} - \bar{y}_{i'\cdot\cdot}) \pm t_{\alpha/2,ab(n-1)} \sqrt{2MSE/(bn)} \tag{12.39}$$

All of the inferences described for factor A could be applied to factor B as well. To determine the significance of factor B, as to whether the means at all levels are equal, the test statistic is

$$F_B = MSB/MSE \tag{12.40}$$

If $F_B > F_{\alpha,b-1,ab(n-1)}$, the means of factor B are not all equal for the different levels.

A $100(1-\alpha)$ percent confidence interval for the mean of factor B when at level j is given by

$$\bar{y}_{\cdot j\cdot} \pm t_{\alpha/2,ab(n-1)} \sqrt{MSE/(an)} \tag{12.41}$$

Similarly, a $100(1-\alpha)$ percent confidence interval for the difference between two factor B means that are at levels j and j', respectively, is determined from

$$(\bar{y}_{\cdot j\cdot} - \bar{y}_{\cdot j'\cdot}) \pm t_{\alpha/2,ab(n-1)} \sqrt{2MSE/(an)} \tag{12.42}$$

Two-Factor Factorial Experiment Using a Randomized Block Design

The randomized block design has already been illustrated for the one-factor case. The same principles can be applied to the two-factor case. Some unique features include the consideration of interaction between the two factors. Suppose there are two factors, A and B; factor A has a levels, and factor B has b levels. Let the number of blocks be r, with each block containing ab units. The ab treatments are randomly assigned to the ab units within each block. The units within each block are chosen to be homogeneous with respect to the blocking variable. Consider a situation in which we desire to determine the impact of two factors, temperature and pressure, on the viscosity of a compound. The possible levels of temperature are 75°, 150°, 200°, and 250°C, and the levels of pressure are 50, 75, 100, 125, and 150 kg/cm^2. Because of the variability between batches of the incoming material, the batch is selected as the blocking variable. In the experiment, 10 batches are selected. Within each batch, the 20 treatments are randomly applied to selected units. In the notation defined, if factor A denotes temperature and factor B denotes pressure, we have $a = 4$, $b = 5$, and $r = 10$.

The model for the two-factor factorial experiment using a randomized block design is

$$y_{ijk} = \mu + \alpha_i + \beta_j + \rho_k + (\alpha\beta)_{ij} + \epsilon_{ijk}, \quad i = 1, 2, \cdots, a \quad j = 1, 2, \cdots, b \quad k = 1, 2, \cdots, r \tag{12.43}$$

where y_{ijk} represents the response for the ith level of factor A, the jth level of factor B, and the kth block; μ is the overall mean effect; α_i is the effect of the ith level of factor A; β_j is the effect of the jth level of factor B; and $(\alpha\beta)_{ij}$ is the effect of interaction between factors A and B. The quantity ρ_k represents the effect of block k, and ϵ_{ijk} represents the random error component, assumed to be distributed normally with mean zero and constant variance σ^2. Let us define the following notation:

$y_{i\cdot\cdot} = \sum_{j=1}^{b}\sum_{k=1}^{r} y_{ijk}$ = Sum of the responses for the ith level of factor A

$\bar{y}_{i\cdot\cdot} = y_{i\cdot\cdot}/(br)$ = Average response for the ith level of factor A

$y_{\cdot j\cdot} = \sum_{i=1}^{a}\sum_{k=1}^{r} y_{ijk}$ = Sum of the responses for the jth level of factor B

$\bar{y}_{\cdot j\cdot} = y_{\cdot j\cdot}/(ar)$ = Average response of the jth level of factor B

$y_{ij\cdot} = \sum_{k=1}^{r} y_{ijk}$ = Sum of the responses for the treatment if factor A is at the ith level and factor B is at the jth level over the blocks

$\bar{y}_{ij\cdot} = y_{ij\cdot}/r$ = Average response for the treatment consisting of the ith level of factor A and jth level of factor B over the blocks

$y_{\cdot\cdot k} = \sum_{i=1}^{a}\sum_{j=1}^{b} y_{ijk}$ = Sum of the responses for the kth block

$y_{\cdot\cdot\cdot} = \sum_{i=1}^{a}\sum_{j=1}^{b}\sum_{k=1}^{r} y_{ijk}$ = Grand total of all observations

The computations for the sum of squares are similar to those for the one-factor case except that we have an additional factor and that interactions between the two factors need to be considered. The correction factor is

$$C = y_{\cdot\cdot\cdot}^2/(abr) \tag{12.44}$$

The total sum of squares is

$$\text{SST} = \sum_{i=1}^{a}\sum_{j=1}^{b}\sum_{k=1}^{r} y_{ijk}^2 - C \tag{12.45}$$

The sum of squares due to the blocks is

$$\text{SSBL} = \left(\sum_{k=1}^{r} y_{\cdot\cdot k}^2\right)/(ab) - C \tag{12.46}$$

The sum of squares for the main effects of factor A is

$$\text{SSA} = \left(\sum_{i=1}^{a} y_{i\cdot\cdot}^2\right)/(br) - C \tag{12.47}$$

The sum of squares for the main effects of factor B is

$$\text{SSB} = \left(\sum_{j=1}^{b} y_{\cdot j\cdot}^2\right)/(ar) - C \tag{12.48}$$

The sum of squares for the interaction between factors A and B is given by

$$\text{SSAB} = \left(\sum_{i=1}^{a}\sum_{j=1}^{b} y_{ij\cdot}^2\right)/r - C - \text{SSA} - \text{SSB} \tag{12.49}$$

Finally, the error sum of squares is

$$\text{SSE} = \text{SST} - \text{SSBL} - \text{SSA} - \text{SSB} - \text{SSAB} \tag{12.50}$$

The number of degrees of freedom for factor A is $(a - 1)$, for factor B is $(b - 1)$, for the blocks is $(r - 1)$, and for the interaction between factors A and B is $(a - 1)(b - 1)$. Since the total number of degrees of freedom is $(abr - 1)$, one less than the total number of observations, the number of error degrees of freedom upon subtraction is found to be $(ab - 1)(r - 1)$. The complete analysis-of-variance table is shown in Table 12-22.

Tests for Significance of Factors For factorial experiments, as previously mentioned, the significance of interaction effects between the factors

TABLE 12-22 Analysis-of-variance table for the two-factor factorial experiment using a randomized block design

Source of variation	Degrees of freedom	Sum of squares	Mean square	F-statistic
Factor A	$a-1$	SSA	MSA = SSA/($a-1$)	F_A = MSA/MSE
Factor B	$b-1$	SSB	MSB = SSB/($b-1$)	F_B = MSB/MSE
Interaction between factors A and B	$(a-1)(b-1)$	SSAB	MSAB = SSAB/[$(a-1)(b-1)$]	F_{AB} = MSAB/MSE
Blocks	$r-1$	SSBL	MSBL = SSBL/($r-1$)	F_{BL} = MSBL/MSE
Error	$(ab-1)(r-1)$	SSE	MSE = SSE/[$(ab-1)(r-1)$]	
Total	$abr-1$	SST		

is usually tested first. The test statistic, as shown in Table 12-22, is the F-statistic calculated as the ratio of the mean square due to interaction to the mean square error, that is,

$$F_{\mathrm{AB}} = \mathrm{MSAB}/\mathrm{MSE}$$

If $F_{\mathrm{AB}} > F_{\alpha,(a-1)(b-1),(ab-1)(r-1)}$, the table value found from Appendix A-6 for a level of significance α and $(a-1)(b-1)$ degrees of freedom in the numerator and $(ab-1)(r-1)$ in the denominator, we conclude that the interaction effects between factors A and B are significant. Since the individual factor mean effects are not important to test in the presence of interaction, a $100(1-\alpha)$ percent confidence interval for the treatment mean is found from

$$\bar{y}_{ij\cdot} \pm t_{\alpha/2,(ab-1)(r-1)}\sqrt{\mathrm{MSE}/r} \qquad (12.51)$$

where $t_{\alpha/2,(ab-1)(r-1)}$ is the t-value found from Appendix A-4 for a right tail area of $\alpha/2$ and $(ab-1)(r-1)$ degrees of freedom.

Inferences about the difference between two treatment means through confidence intervals with a level of confidence of $(1-\alpha)$ may be found as follows:

$$(\bar{y}_{ij\cdot} - \bar{y}_{i'j'\cdot}) \pm t_{\alpha/2,(ab-1)(r-1)}\sqrt{2\mathrm{MSE}/r} \qquad (12.52)$$

When the interaction effects are not significant, tests for the individual factor means may be conducted. The significance of the means of factor A is tested by calculating the F-statistic, shown in Table 11-22, as

$$F_{\mathrm{A}} = \mathrm{MSA}/\mathrm{MSE}$$

At a level of significance α, if $F_{\mathrm{A}} > F_{\alpha,(a-1),(ab-1)(r-1)}$, we conclude that the means of factor A are not all equal at the different levels.

In making an inference about an individual mean for a certain level of factor A, a $100(1-\alpha)$ percent confidence interval is given by

$$\bar{y}_{i\cdot\cdot} \pm t_{\alpha/2,(ab-1)(r-1)}\sqrt{\mathrm{MSE}/(br)} \qquad (12.53)$$

Similarly, a $100(1-\alpha)$ percent confidence interval for the difference between the factor A means, at levels i and i', respectively, is found from

$$(\bar{y}_{i\cdot\cdot} - \bar{y}_{i'\cdot\cdot}) \pm t_{\alpha/2,(ab-1)(r-1)}\sqrt{2\mathrm{MSE}/(br)} \qquad (12.54)$$

The inference-making procedure described for factor A can be applied in a similar manner to factor B. First, to determine the significance of factor B concerning whether the means at all levels are equal, the test statistic as shown in Table 12-22 is

$$F_{\mathrm{B}} = \mathrm{MSB}/\mathrm{MSE}$$

If $F_{\mathrm{B}} > F_{\alpha,b-1,(ab-1)(r-1)}$, we conclude that the factor B means are not all equal at a level of significance α.

As with factor A, a $100(1-\alpha)$ percent confidence interval for the mean of factor B at level j is given by

$$\bar{y}_{\cdot j\cdot} \pm t_{\alpha/2,(ab-1)(r-1)}\sqrt{\mathrm{MSE}/(ar)} \qquad (12.55)$$

A $100(1-\alpha)$ percent confidence interval for the difference between two factor B means that are at levels j and j', respectively, is found from

$$(\bar{y}_{\cdot j\cdot} - \bar{y}_{\cdot j'\cdot}) \pm t_{\alpha/2,(ab-1)(r-1)}\sqrt{2\mathrm{MSE}/(ar)} \qquad (12.56)$$

Example 12-4: Scientists and engineers have been involved in testing the effectiveness of synthetic fuels for use in automobiles. Two critical components in making the synthetic fuel are of importance. Factor A involves an additive which is to be tested at three levels of use in consecutively increasing amounts. Factor B involves a catalyst, for which three levels of use (1, 2, and 3, representing successively increasing amounts) are also to be tested. Forty-five automobiles were randomly selected for

TABLE 12-23 Efficiency ratings, in percentage, of a synthetic fuel involving an additive and a catalyst

Additive level	Catalyst level 1	2	3
1	75	64	43
	72	62	48
	66	58	42
	74	56	46
	65	60	46
2	50	73	58
	58	70	62
	46	67	54
	53	68	60
	55	70	62
3	67	82	44
	60	76	43
	60	80	38
	62	84	42
	63	75	44

the study, and each of the nine treatments were randomly used in five different automobiles. Table 12-23 shows the efficiency ratings, in percentage, of the treatments.

a. At a level of significance of 5 percent, what can you conclude about the significance of the factors?

Solution. The problem involves two factors using a completely randomized design. Using the raw data given in Table 12-23, a summary of the sums and averages of the efficiency for each level of additive and catalyst may be constructed. This is shown in Table 12-24.

The correction factor is

$$C = y_{...}^2/(abn) = (2703)^2/[(3)(3)(5)] = 162,360.2$$

The total sum of squares is

$$\begin{aligned} SST &= \sum_{i=1}^{a}\sum_{j=1}^{b}\sum_{k=1}^{n} y_{ijk}^2 - C \\ &= [(75)^2 + (72)^2 + \cdots + (42)^2 + (44)^2] \\ &\quad - 162,360.2 \\ &= 168,691 - 162,360.2 = 6330.8 \end{aligned}$$

The sum of squares for the additive (factor A) is

$$\begin{aligned} SSA &= \left(\sum_{i=1}^{3} y_{i..}\right)/(bn) - C \\ &= [(877)^2 + (906)^2 + (920)^2]/[(3)(5)] - 162,360.2 \\ &= 64.133 \end{aligned}$$

The sum of squares for the catalyst (factor B) is

$$\begin{aligned} SSB &= \left(\sum_{j=1}^{3} y_{.j.}^2\right)/(an) - C \\ &= [(926)^2 + (1045)^2 + (732)^2]/[(3)(5)] \\ &\quad - 162,360.2 \\ &= 3328.133 \end{aligned}$$

The sum of squares due to the interaction between additive and catalyst is

$$\begin{aligned} SSAB &= \left(\sum_{i=1}^{3}\sum_{j=1}^{3} y_{ij.}^2\right)/n - C - SSA - SSB \\ &= [(352)^2 + (300)^2 + (225)^2 + (262)^2 + (348)^2 \\ &\quad + (296)^2 + (312)^2 + (397)^2 + (211^2)]/5 \\ &\quad - 162,360.2 - 64.133 - 3328.133 \\ &= 2520.934 \end{aligned}$$

TABLE 12-24 Summary information on data for efficiency of synthetic fuel

Additive level	Catalyst level 1	2	3	Sum	Average
1	Sum($y_{11.}$) = 352 Average($\bar{y}_{11.}$) = 70.4	Sum ($y_{12.}$) = 300 Average($\bar{y}_{12.}$) = 60	Sum ($y_{13.}$) = 225 Average($\bar{y}_{13.}$) = 45	$y_{1..}$ = 877	$\bar{y}_{1..}$ = 58.467
2	Sum($y_{21.}$) = 262 Average($\bar{y}_{21.}$) = 52.4	Sum ($y_{22.}$) = 348 Average($\bar{y}_{22.}$) = 69.6	Sum ($y_{23.}$) = 296 Average($\bar{y}_{23.}$) = 59.2	$y_{2..}$ = 906	$\bar{y}_{2..}$ = 60.400
3	Sum($y_{31.}$) = 312 Average($\bar{y}_{31.}$) = 62.4	Sum ($y_{32.}$) = 397 Average($\bar{y}_{32.}$) = 79.4	Sum ($y_{33.}$) = 211 Average($\bar{y}_{33.}$) = 42.2	$y_{3..}$ = 920	$\bar{y}_{3..}$ = 61.333
Sum	$y_{.1.}$ = 926	$y_{.2.}$ = 1045	$y_{.3.}$ = 732	$y_{...}$ = 2703	
Average	$\bar{y}_{.1.}$ = 61.733	$\bar{y}_{.2.}$ = 69.667	$\bar{y}_{.3.}$ = 48.800		$\bar{y}_{...}$ = 60.067

TABLE 12-25 Analysis-of-variance table for the data on efficiency of synthetic fuel using a completely randomized design

Source of variation	Degrees of freedom	Sum of squares	Mean square	F-statistic
Additive (factor A)	2	64.133	32.066	2.764
Catalyst (factor B)	2	3328.133	1664.066	143.454
Interaction between additive and catalyst	4	2520.934	630.234	54.330
Error	36	417.600	11.600	
Total	44	6330.800		

Finally, the error sum of squares is

$$\begin{aligned} SSE &= SST - SSA - SSB - SSAB \\ &= 6330.8 - 64.133 - 3328.133 - 2520.934 \\ &= 417.600 \end{aligned}$$

The analysis-of-variance table is shown in Table 12-25. At the 5 percent level of significance for testing the null hypothesis that there is no interaction effect between additive and catalyst, the table value from Appendix A-6 is $F_{.05,4,36} \simeq 2.642$. The calculated value of the F-statistic for testing the significance of the interaction effects is shown in Table 12-25 as

$$F_{AB} = MSAB/MSE = 630.234/11.600 = 54.330$$

Since $54.330 > 2.642$, we conclude that the interaction effects between additive and catalyst are significant at this level of significance. Table 12-25 also shows the values of F for testing the significance of the additive (factor A) means as well as the catalyst (factor B) means. However, since the interaction effect is significant, it is not necessary to test for the main effects of the two factors. Thus, the joint effect of the additive and catalyst has an impact on the mean efficiency of the synthetic fuel.

b. What can you say about the level of additive and the level of catalyst to use?

Solution. Since we found the interaction effects to be significant in part (a), we cannot simply consider the mean of one of the factors at its different levels by averaging over the levels of the other factor. Instead, we need to look at the treatment means, to take into account the joint effect of both factors.

Let us consider the mean efficiency for different levels of the catalyst at each level of the additive. From the summary information given in Table 12-24, we construct the plot shown in Figure 12-8. From Figure 12-8, we find that the mean efficiency does not change uniformly with catalyst levels for each additive level. For additive levels 2 and 3 as the catalyst level increases from 1 to 2, the mean efficiency increases; as the catalyst level increases from 2 to 3, the mean efficiency decreases, with the decline being more drastic when the additive is at level 3. For additive level 1, the mean efficiency decreases as the catalyst level increases from 1 to 2 and then to 3. If maximizing efficiency is our objective, we may prefer to choose additive level 3 and catalyst level 2.

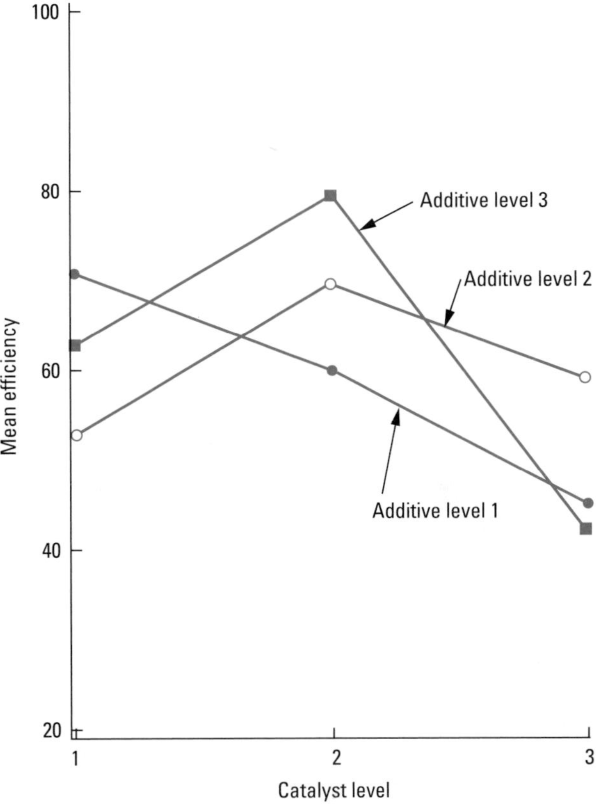

Figure 12-8 Plot of treatment means for the data on efficiency of synthetic fuel.

c. Is there a difference between the means of catalyst levels 1 and 3 at a significance level of 5 percent?

Solution. We find a 95 percent confidence interval for the difference between the mean efficiencies of catalyst levels 1 and 3. This interval is given by

$$\begin{aligned} (\bar{y}_{\cdot 1\cdot} - \bar{y}_{\cdot 3\cdot}) &\pm t_{.025,36}\sqrt{2MSE/[(3)(5)]} \\ &= (61.733 - 48.80) \pm (2.028)\sqrt{2(11.6)/15} \\ &= 12.933 \pm 2.522 \end{aligned}$$

Observe that the confidence interval does not include zero, indicating a difference between the means at this significance level. Note, however, as discussed in parts (a) and (b), that because the interaction effect is significant, it does not make sense to consider one factor effect separate from the other.

d. Find a 95 percent confidence interval for the difference between the treatment mean for additive level 1 and catalyst level 1 and that for additive level 2 and catalyst level 3.

Solution. We have

$$\begin{aligned}(\bar{y}_{11\cdot} - \bar{y}_{23\cdot}) &\pm t_{.025,36}\sqrt{2\text{MSE}/5}\\ &= (70.4 - 59.2) \pm (2.028)\sqrt{2(11.6)/5}\\ &= 11.2 \pm 4.368\end{aligned}$$

Since this confidence interval does not include zero, we conclude that there is a difference between these two treatment means at the chosen level of significance of 5 percent.

Role of Contrasts

In factorial experiments involving multiple treatments, it is often desired to test hypotheses on a linear combination of the treatment means, or to partition the total sum of squares of all treatments into component sums of squares of certain desirable treatments. A *contrast* may be helpful in such circumstances. A contrast of treatment means is a linear combination of the means such that the sum of the coefficients of the linear combination equals zero. Suppose we have p treatments with means $\mu_1, \mu_2, \cdots, \mu_p$, respectively. Then, a contrast of means is defined as

$$\begin{aligned}L &= k_1\mu_1 + k_2\mu_2 + \cdots + k_p\mu_p\\ &= \sum_{i=1}^{p} k_i\mu_i \qquad (12.57)\end{aligned}$$

where k_i are constants such that

$$\sum_{i=1}^{p} k_i = 0$$

Consider an example in which four selling methods for computer salespersons are of interest. Let the mean sales for each method be denoted by μ_1, μ_2, μ_3, and μ_4, respectively. Suppose it is desired to test the null hypothesis that the average sales of persons using the first two methods is the same as the average sales of persons using the last two methods. The null hypothesis could be written as

$$H_o : L = 0,$$

where

$$L = (\mu_1 + \mu_2)/2 - (\mu_3 + \mu_4)/2$$

The quantity L is a contrast, the coefficients of which are given by $k_1 = 1/2, k_2 = 1/2, k_3 = -1/2$, and $k_4 = -1/2$. Note that the sum of the coefficients equals zero.

To test the null hypothesis, we need a sample estimate of L and the sample variance of the estimate of L. The sample estimate of L is given by

$$\hat{L} = k_1\bar{y}_1 + k_2\bar{y}_2 + \cdots + k_p\bar{y}_p = \sum_{i=1}^{p} k_i\bar{y}_i \qquad (12.58)$$

where $\bar{y}_i$ is the sample mean of treatment i. The variance of $\hat{L}$ is found from

$$\begin{aligned}\text{Var}(\hat{L}) &= (k_1^2/r_1 + k_2^2/r_2 + \cdots + k_p^2/r_p)\text{MSE}\\ &= \left(\sum_{i=1}^{p} \frac{k_i^2}{r_i}\right)\text{MSE} \qquad (12.59)\end{aligned}$$

where r_i represents the number of observations from which the ith sample mean is computed and MSE is the mean square error for the design used in the experiment. The test statistic, then, is the t-statistic given by

$$t = \hat{L}/\sqrt{\text{Var}(\hat{L})} \qquad (12.60)$$

At a level of significance α, if $|t| > t_{\alpha/2,\nu}$ where ν is the number of degrees of freedom of the experimental error and $\alpha/2$ is the right tail area of the t-distribution, the null hypothesis is rejected.

If the null hypothesis is rejected, we may need to find an interval estimate for the contrast L. A $100(1-\alpha)$ percent confidence interval for L is given by

$$\hat{L} \pm t_{\alpha/2,\nu}\sqrt{\text{Var}(\hat{L})} \qquad (12.61)$$

where $t_{\alpha/2,\nu}$ represents the t-value, found from Appendix A-4, for a right tail area of $\alpha/2$ and ν degrees of freedom.

Example 12-5: Table 12-26 shows the total computer sales, in thousands of dollars, of salespersons using five different methods. The number of persons chosen from each method is also indicated. A completely randomized design is used. The mean square error is 30.71.

a. Is the mean sales using method 2 different from the average of the mean sales of methods 1 and 3? Test at a significance level of 5 percent.

Solution. The total number of experimental units is 21, yielding a total of 20 degrees of freedom. Since there

TABLE 12-26 Computer sales in thousands of dollars for five different methods

	Selling method				
	1	2	3	4	5
Number of salespersons chosen	3	4	5	4	5
Total sales	80	239	255	249	367

are 5 selling methods (treatments), there are 4 degrees of freedom for the treatments, one less than the number of treatments. Upon subtraction, the number of degrees of freedom for the error is 16.

If μ_i represents the mean sales using method i, the null hypothesis to be tested is

$$H_o : \mu_2 - (\mu_1 + \mu_3)/2 = 0$$

The corresponding contrast L can be written as

$$L = \mu_2 - (\mu_1 + \mu_3)/2$$

or, equivalently,

$$L = 2\mu_2 - \mu_1 - \mu_3$$

Note that L is a contrast, with its estimate $\hat{L}$ obtained as

$$\hat{L} = 2\bar{y}_2 - \bar{y}_1 - \bar{y}_3$$

where $\bar{y}_i$ represents the sample mean for method i. We have

$$\begin{aligned}\hat{L} &= 2(239/4) - 80/3 - 255/5\\ &= 119.5 - 26.667 - 51.0 = 41.833\end{aligned}$$

The variance of $\hat{L}$ is found from Equation 12.59 as

$$\begin{aligned}\text{Var}\ (\hat{L}) &= [(2)^2/4 + (-1)^2/3 + (-1)^2/5](30.71)\\ &= 47.078\end{aligned}$$

For testing the specified null hypothesis, the test statistic given by Equation 12.60 is

$$\begin{aligned}t &= \hat{L}/\sqrt{\text{Var}(\hat{L})}\\ &= 41.833/\sqrt{47.078} = 6.097\end{aligned}$$

At the 5 percent level of significance, with 16 error degrees of freedom, the t tables in Appendix A-4 give $t_{.025,16} =$ 2.120. The test statistic of 6.097 is greater than 2.120, so we reject the null hypothesis. Thus, the mean sales using method 2 is different from the average of the mean sales using methods 1 and 3.

b. Find a 95 percent confidence interval for the contrast in part (a).

Solution. A 95 percent confidence interval for $L = 2\mu_2 - \mu_1 - \mu_3$ is given by

$$\begin{aligned}&\hat{L} \pm t_{.025,16}\sqrt{\text{Var}(\hat{L})}\\ &= 41.833 \pm (2.120)\sqrt{47.078}\\ &= 41.833 \pm 14.546 = (27.287,\ 56.379)\end{aligned}$$

c. Can we conclude that the average of the mean sales using methods 4 and 5 is different from that using methods 2 and 3? Test at the 1 percent level of significance.

Solution. The null hypothesis to be tested is

$$H_o : (\mu_4 + \mu_5)/2 - (\mu_2 + \mu_3)/2 = 0$$

The corresponding contrast L is given by

$$L = (\mu_4 + \mu_5)/2 - (\mu_2 + \mu_3)/2$$

or, equivalently,

$$L = \mu_4 + \mu_5 - \mu_2 - \mu_3$$

The estimate of L is

$$\begin{aligned}\hat{L} &= \bar{y}_4 + \bar{y}_5 - \bar{y}_2 - \bar{y}_3\\ &= 249/4 + 367/5 - 239/4 - 255/5\\ &= 62.25 + 73.4 - 59.75 - 51.0 = 24.9\end{aligned}$$

The variance of $\hat{L}$ is given by

$$\begin{aligned}\text{Var}(\hat{L}) &= [(1)^2/4 + (1)^2/5 + (-1)^2/4 + (-1)^2/5](30.71)\\ &= 27.639\end{aligned}$$

The test statistic is

$$\begin{aligned}t &= \hat{L}/\sqrt{\text{Var}(\hat{L})}\\ &= 24.9/\sqrt{27.639} = 4.736\end{aligned}$$

For a two-tailed test at a level of significance of 1 percent, the t-value for 16 degrees of freedom, from Appendix A-4, is $t_{.005,16} = 2.921$. Since the test statistic of 4.736 is greater than 2.921, we reject the null hypothesis and conclude that the average of the mean sales using methods 4 and 5 is not equal to that using methods 2 and 3.

Orthogonal Contrasts For a given set of treatments, it is possible to form more than one meaningful contrast. Given p treatments, we can construct $(p-1)$ contrasts that are statistically independent of each other. Two contrasts L_1 and L_2 are independent if they are orthogonal to each other. Suppose we have the two following contrasts:

$$\begin{aligned}L_1 &= k_{11}\mu_1 + k_{12}\mu_2 + \cdots + k_{1p}\mu_p\\ L_2 &= k_{21}\mu_1 + k_{22}\mu_2 + \cdots + k_{2p}\mu_p\end{aligned}$$

L_1 and L_2 are orthogonal if and only if

$$\sum_{j=1}^{p} k_{1j}k_{2j} = 0$$

that is, if the sum of the products of the corresponding coefficients associated with the treatment means is zero.

As an illustration, consider the following two contrasts involving three treatment means:

$$L_1 = \mu_1 - \mu_3$$

$$L_2 = -\mu_1 + 2\mu_2 - \mu_3$$

Note that L_1 may be used to test the null hypothesis of the equality of treatment means 1 and 3; L_2 may be used to test the null hypothesis that the mean of treatments 1 and 3 equals the mean of treatment 2. Observe that the contrasts L_1 and L_2 are orthogonal, since the sum of the products of the corresponding coefficients of the means is $1(-1) + 0(2) + (-1)(-1) = 0$.

Contrasts of Totals Similar to contrasts of means, contrasts of totals are useful in the context of analysis of variance. Such contrasts aid in partitioning the treatment sum of squares into components such that each component is associated with a contrast of interest. Let r_j represent the number of replications for the jth treatment (out of p treatments). Let

$$T_i = y_{i\cdot} = \sum_{j=1}^{r_j} y_{ij}$$

be the sum of the responses of the ith treatment. Then, $\hat{L}$ is a contrast of totals given by

$$\hat{L} = k_1T_1 + k_2T_2 + \cdots + k_pT_p \qquad (12.62)$$

if and only if

$$r_1k_1 + r_2k_2 + \cdots + r_pk_p = 0$$

If the number of replications is given by r for each of the treatments, then $\hat{L}$ is a contrast if

$$\sum_{i=1}^{p} k_i = 0$$

The variance of the contrast of totals is obtained from

$$\text{Var}(\hat{L}) = (r_1k_1^2 + r_2k_2^2 + \cdots + r_pk_p^2)\text{MSE} \qquad (12.63)$$

where MSE is the mean square error for the experimental design considered.

Two contrasts of totals given by

$$\hat{L}_1 = k_{11}T_1 + k_{12}T_2 + \cdots + k_{1p}T_p$$

$$\hat{L}_2 = k_{21}T_1 + k_{22}T_2 + \cdots + k_{2p}T_p$$

are orthogonal if and only if

$$\sum_{j=1}^{p} k_{1j}k_{2j} = 0$$

This condition is similar to the condition for the contrasts for means.

The importance of orthogonal contrasts for totals is that they may be used to decompose the treatment sum of squares in analysis of variance and thereby test hypotheses on the effectiveness of selected treatments. If $\hat{L}_1$ is a contrast of totals, then a single degree-of-freedom component for that contrast of the treatment sum of squares (SSTR) is

$$S_1^2 = \hat{L}_1^2/D_1 \qquad (12.64)$$

where

$$D_1 = r_1k_{11}^2 + r_2k_{12}^2 + \cdots r_pk_{1p}^2 = \sum_{j=1}^{p} r_jk_{1j}^2$$

Likewise, if $\hat{L}_1$ and $\hat{L}_2$ are orthogonal, then the sum of squares for the contrast $\hat{L}_2$ is given by

$$S_2^2 = \hat{L}_2^2/D_2$$

where $D_2 = r_1k_{21}^2 + r_2k_{22}^2 + \cdots + r_pk_{2p}^2$. In fact, S_2^2 is a component of SSTR $- S_1^2$.

Similarly, if $\hat{L}_1, \hat{L}_2, \cdots, \hat{L}_{p-1}$ are mutually orthogonal contrasts of totals, then

$$S_1^2 + S_2^2 + \cdots + S_{p-1}^2 = \text{SSTR}$$

Example 12-6: A regional bank is considering various policies to stimulate the economy and promote home improvement loans. One of the factors of interest is the type of mortgage loan, which the bank has chosen to be of two types—fixed-interest or variable-interest. Another factor is the payback period, which the bank has selected to be 10 or 20 years. For each of the four treatments, the bank has randomly selected four loan amounts. The four treatments has are represented by the notation shown in Table 12-27. In factorial experiments in which each factor has

TABLE 12-27 Representation of treatments comprising the interest rate and payback period

Treatment representation	Type of interest rate and payback period
(1)	Interest rate fixed and payback period 10 years
i	Interest rate variable and payback period 10 years
p	Interest rate fixed and payback period 20 years
ip	Interest rate variable and payback period 20 years

TABLE 12-28 Loan amounts (in thousands of dollars) for types of interest rate and payback period

Treatments			
(1)	*i*	*p*	*ip*
16	22	38	56
12	18	45	58
14	25	40	54
12	20	42	59

two levels—low and high—the presence of a factor at the high level is denoted by a particular lower-case letter. The presence of a factor at the low level is indicated by the absence of this lower-case letter. Additionally, the notation (1) is used to denote the treatment for which all of the factors are at the low level. The type of interest has two levels: fixed-interest (low) and variable-interest (high). Similarly, the payback period has two levels: 10 years (low) and 20 years (high). As Table 12-27 shows, the treatment i indicates that the interest type is at the high level (variable rate) and the payback period is at the low level (10 years). Table 12-28 shows the loan amounts (in thousands of dollars).

Consider a set of three orthogonal contrasts of totals, the coefficients of which are shown in Table 12-29. Note that capital letters denote contrasts, whereas lower-case letters denote treatments. The contrast I compares the totals for the treatments when the interest rate is variable versus when it is fixed. From Table 12-29, contrast I is given by

$$\text{Contrast } I = -T_1 + T_2 - T_3 + T_4$$

where T_1 = Sum for treatment (1)
T_2 = Sum for treatment i
T_3 = Sum for treatment p
T_4 = Sum for treatment ip

In experimental design notation, this same relation may be expressed as

$$I = (-1) + i - p + ip$$

where the quantities on the right-hand side of the above equation represent the sum of the response variables for the corresponding treatments. Similarly, the other two contrasts are shown in Table 12-29. We have

$$\text{Contrast } P = (-1) - i + p + ip$$

TABLE 12-29 Coefficients of a set of three orthogonal contrasts of totals for the bank loan amounts

	Treatment			
Contrast	(1)	*i*	*p*	*ip*
I	−1	+1	−1	+1
P	−1	−1	+1	+1
IP	+1	−1	−1	+1

which compares the totals for treatments when the payment period is 20 years versus when it is 10 years. We also have

$$\text{Contrast } IP = (1) - i - p + ip$$

which compares two sets of totals. The first set includes treatments for fixed interest and a 10-year payback period and for variable interest and a 20-year payback period. The second set includes treatments for variable interest and a 10-year payback period and for fixed interest and a 20-year payback period.

Based on the previously discussed concepts, the contrast I represents the main effect of the type-of-interest factor; the contrast P represents the main effect of the payback period factor; the contrast IP represents the interaction effects between the type of interest and the payback period.

Consider the computation of the sum of squares of these orthogonal contrasts of totals. For the contrast I, an estimate is

$$\hat{I} = (-1)(54) + (1)(85) + (-1)(165) + (1)(227) = 93$$

This estimate is found by using the sum of the treatments from Table 12-28, the contrast coefficients from Table 12-29 and Equation 12.62. The sum of squares due to contrast I is obtained using Equation 12.64 as follows:

$$S_1^2 = (93)^2/[(4)(4)] = 540.5625$$

Note that the number of replications for each treatment is 4 ($r_1 = r_2 = r_3 = r_4 = 4$).

Similarly, the estimate of contrast P is

$$\hat{P} = (-1)(54) + (-1)(85) + (1)(165) + (1)(227) = 253$$

The sum of squares due to contrast P is

$$S_2^2 = (253)^2/[(4)(4)] = 4000.5625$$

The estimate of contrast IP is

$$\hat{IP} = (1)54 + (-1)(85) + (-1)(165) + (1)(227) = 31$$

The sum of squares due to contrast IP is

$$S_3^2 = (31)^2/[(4)(4)] = 60.0625$$

Since I, P, and IP are three mutually orthogonal contrasts, of the four treatments, the total treatment sum of squares is therefore the sum of these three component sums of squares. Hence, the treatment sum of squares is

$$\begin{aligned} \text{SSTR} &= S_1^2 + S_2^2 + S_3^2 \\ &= 540.5625 + 4000.5625 + 60.0625 \\ &= 4601.1875 \end{aligned}$$

Since the given design is a completely randomized one, the same results could be obtained after more detailed calculations using the formulas in section 12-3. The use of orthogonal contrasts helps us test the significance of specific factor configurations.

The 2^k Factorial Experiment

Experimentation involves first determining the more important factors (in terms of impact on the response variable) while taking into account the number of factors that can feasibly be dealt with. Next, the desirable levels of the selected factors are identified. Finally, it may be of interest to find the relationship between the factor levels, the corresponding responses, and the physical and economic constraints that are imposed. Although different types of designs may be used at each of these stages, multifactor experiments are usually employed. One such multifactor experiment used in the exploratory stage is the 2^k factorial experiment, which involves k factors, each at two levels. The total number of treatments is 2^k. Thus, if we have two factors, each at two levels, there are 2^2 or 4 treatments.

Usually, the level of each factor is thought of as either low or high. A treatment is represented by a series of lower-case letters; the presence of a particular letter indicates that the corresponding factor is at the high level. The absence of this letter indicates that the factor is at the low level. The notation (1) is used to indicate the treatment for which all factors are at the low level. In many instances the low level may signify the absence of a factor and the high level its presence. Suppose we have three factors, A, B and C, each at two levels. The full factorial set of eight treatments would be designated in the following order:

1. (1)	5. c
2. a	6. ac
3. b	7. bc
4. ab	8. abc

Figure 12-9 shows the layout of a 2^3 experiment with three factors, A, B, and C. The high levels are denoted by 1 and the low levels by -1 for each factor.

To estimate the main effects and interactions, the concept of contrasts, introduced earlier, may be used. For example, to determine the main effect of factor A, we would average the observations for which A is at the high level and subtract from this value the average of the observations for which A is at the low level. From Figure 12-9, if there are r replications for each treatment, the main effect of factor A is

$$\begin{aligned} A &= (a + ab + ac + abc)/(4r) \\ &\quad - [(1) + b + c + bc]/(4r) \\ &= \frac{1}{(4r)}[a + ab + ac + abc \\ &\quad - (1) - b - c - bc] \end{aligned} \tag{12.65}$$

where the lower-case letters denote the sum of the responses for the corresponding treatments. The quantity inside the square brackets in Equation 12.65 is a valid contrast of totals.

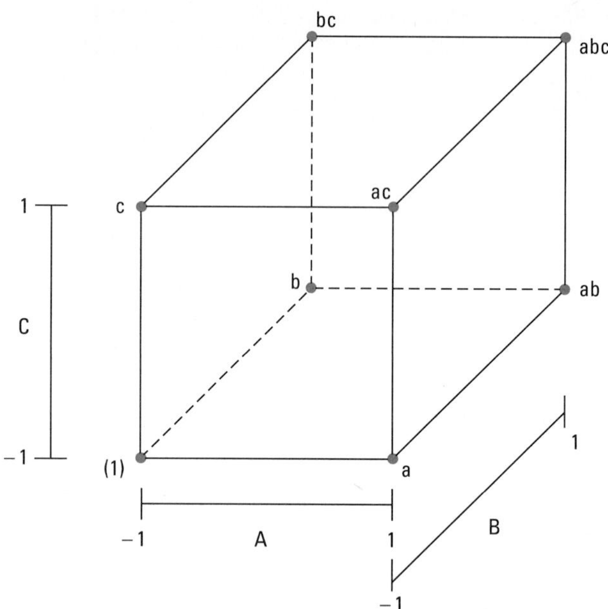

Figure 12-9 Layout of a 2^3 experiment with three factors.

Similarly, the main effect of factor B is

$$B = \frac{1}{(4r)}[b + ab + bc + abc - (1) - a - c - ac] \tag{12.66}$$

The quantity inside the square brackets of Equation 12.66 is also a valid contrast. Note that the contrasts for A and B obtained from Equations 12.65 and 12.66 are also orthogonal contrasts of totals. If we can come up with a set of orthogonal contrasts to estimate the main effects and interactions, then the methodology described earlier may be used to determine the corresponding sum of squares for the treatment components. Table 12-30 is such a table of coefficients for orthogonal contrasts in a 2^3 factorial experiment. Since the magnitude of each coefficient is 1, it has been omitted from the table.

Observe that the contrasts for A and B match those obtained from Equations 12.65 and 12.66. One way of constructing such a table of coefficients is as follows. For each main effect contrast, use a + for each treatment combination in which the letter for the effect occurs. All other combinations receive a −. The signs for the interaction contrasts are the product of the signs of the main effects whose letters appear in the interaction. For example, consider the contrast AB. Its sign under the treatment column a is

TABLE 12-30 Coefficients for orthogonal contrasts in a 2^3 factorial experiment

	Treatment							
Contrast	(1)	*a*	*b*	*ab*	*c*	*ac*	*bc*	*abc*
A	−	+	−	+	−	+	−	+
B	−	−	+	+	−	−	+	+
AB	+	−	−	+	+	−	−	+
C	−	−	−	−	+	+	+	+
AC	+	−	+	−	−	+	−	+
BC	+	+	−	−	−	−	+	+
ABC	−	+	+	−	+	−	−	+

−, which is the product of the sign of A in the treatment column a (+) and the sign of B in the treatment column a (−). The contrast for any of the main effects or interactions can be obtained from Table 12-30. For instance, the interaction AC would be estimated as

$$AC = \frac{1}{(4r)}[(1) + b + ac + abc - a - ab - c - bc]$$

The sum of squares for the set of orthogonal contrasts for the totals may be found from Equation 12.64. If the number of replications for each treatment is r, then, because the contrast coefficients are unity in magnitude, we may use Equation 12.64 for a 2^k factorial experiment to get the sum of squares for an effect:

$$\text{SS} = \frac{(\text{Contrast})^2}{r2^k} \tag{12.67}$$

Also, the following relation may be used to estimate the effect:

$$\text{Effect} = \frac{\text{Contrast}}{r2^{k-1}}. \tag{12.68}$$

Note that Equation 12.65, derived to estimate the main effect of A, matches the general expression given by Equation 12.68.

Example 12-7: In the furniture industry, the quality of surface finish of graded lumber is an important characteristic. Three factors are to be tested, each at two levels, for their impact on the surface finish. Factor A is the type of wood: oak (level −1) or pine (level 1). Factor B is the rate of feed: 2 m/min (level −1) or 4 m/min (level 1). Factor C is the depth of cut: 1 mm (level −1) or 3 mm (level 1). For each treatment combination, three replications were carried out using a completely randomized design. Table 12-31 shows the surface finish for the eight treatments. The larger the value, the rougher the surface finish.

TABLE 12-31 Surface finish of wood based on type of wood, rate of feed, and depth of cut

Treatment	Surface finish	Sum
(1)	6, 8, 9	23
a	10, 16, 15	41
b	18, 12, 15	45
ab	12, 9, 10	31
c	20, 26, 29	75
ac	34, 28, 32	94
bc	36, 44, 46	126
abc	25, 22, 24	71

a. Find all of the main effects and the interaction effects.

Solution. Since we have a 2^3 factorial experiment, the orthogonal contrasts and their coefficients corresponding to each of the treatment combinations are as shown in Table 12-30. To find the effect of each contrast, we use Equation 12.68 and the coefficients from Table 12-30.

For example, the main effect of A, using the data from Table 12-31, is

$$\begin{aligned} A &= \frac{1}{3(4)}[a + ab + ac + abc - (1) - b - c - bc] \\ &= \frac{1}{12}[41 + 31 + 94 + 71 - 23 - 45 - 75 - 126] \\ &= -2.667 \end{aligned}$$

Similarly, the other main effects and interaction effects are found and are shown in Table 12-32.

b. Find the sum of squares for each of the main effects and interaction effects.

Solution. The sum of squares for the factorial effects are found from Equation 12.67. For example, the sum of squares for A is

$$\text{SS}_A = \frac{(-32)^2}{3(8)} = 42.667$$

Table 12-32 shows the sum of squares for all of the factorial effects. The total sum of squares is found from Equation 12.4 as follows:

$$\begin{aligned} \text{SST} &= \sum_{i=1}^{8}\sum_{j=1}^{3} y_{ij}^2 - y_{..}^2/[(3)(8)] \\ &= (6^2 + 8^2 + 9^2 + 10^2 + \cdots + 22^2 + 24^2) \\ &\quad - (506)^2/24 \\ &= 13694 - 10668.167 = 3025.833 \end{aligned}$$

The error sum of squares, found by subtraction of the sum of squares of the factorial effects from the total sum of squares, is equal to 169.331.

TABLE 12-32 Analysis-of-variance table for the contrasts in the surface finish of wood

Source of variation	Effect	Degrees of freedom	Sum of squares	Mean square	F-statistic
A	−2.667	1	42.667	42.667	4.032
B	3.333	1	66.667	66.667	6.299
C	18.833	1	2128.167	2128.167	201.093
AB	−8.833	1	468.167	468.167	44.238
AC	−3.333	1	66.667	66.667	6.299
BC	1.333	1	10.667	10.667	1.008
ABC	−3.500	1	73.500	73.500	6.945
Error		16	169.331	10.583	
Total		23	3025.833		

c. Which effects are significant? Test at the 5 percent level of significance.

Solution. From Table 12-32, which shows the sum of squares and the number of degrees of freedom of the effects, the mean square for each effect is found. The F-statistic for testing the significance of the factorial effects is given by the ratio of the mean square for that effect to the mean square error. At the 5 percent level of significance, the critical value of F from Appendix A-6 is found after interpolation to be $F_{.05,1,16} = 4.497$. Upon comparing the calculated value of the F-statistic with this critical value, we find that the interactions effects AB, AC, and ABC are significant. The F-statistics for the main effects B and C also exceed the critical value; however, because the interaction effects AB, AC, and ABC are significant we cannot make any definite inferences about the main effects.

Confounding in 2^k Factorial Experiments

A basic tenet of experimental design is to group the experimental units into blocks consisting of homogeneous units. Treatments are then randomly assigned to experimental units within blocks. The idea behind blocking is to eliminate the variation between blocks from the experimental error and thereby compare the treatments under conditions that are as close to uniform as possible.

The experimental error variance usually increases as the block size is increased. In multifactor factorial experiments, the number of treatments increases dramatically with the number of factors. For instance, for 6 factors with 2 levels each, the number of treatments is $2^6 = 64$. Thus, for a complete replication of the treatments in one block, 64 experimental units are needed. Often, it may be difficult to obtain a large number of homogeneous units to comprise a block for complete replication of all treatments.

In order to increase the precision of the experiment by blocking, it is necessary to keep the block size as small as possible. A means for achieving this is through the principle of *confounding*, by which the estimation of a certain treatment effect is confounded (or not distinguishable) with the blocks. Not all the treatments are replicated in each block. The block contrast is equivalent to the treatment contrast that is confounded. It is not possible to estimate the effects between blocks since estimation of one of the treatment effects essentially matches it. Thus, we are not able to conclude whether any observed differences in the response variable between blocks is solely due to differences in the blocks. Such an effect cannot be isolated from that of one of the treatments, implying that differences between blocks could be due to this particular treatment (that is confounded with the blocks), or the blocks themselves, or both. Although the treatment that is confounded with the blocks cannot be estimated, this sacrifice is made with the hope of improving the precision of the experiment through reduced block sizes. We confound the 2^k experiment into blocks of size 2^p, where $p < k$.

Consider, for example, a 2^3 factorial experiment. For a complete replication, 8 experimental units are needed, which then influences the block size. Suppose it is desired to base blocking on the vendor for the raw material. Because of the limited supply of the raw material from the vendors, it is feasible to obtain only four experimental units from each vendor rather than the eight needed for a complete replication. The question is: How are the eight treatments to be divided into two blocks of size 4, since only 4 experimental units can be obtained from a vendor? Refer to the coefficients for orthogonal contrasts in a 2^3 factorial experiment shown in Table 12-30. The confounding contrast is typically selected to be a high-order interaction. Suppose it is chosen to be ABC, the three-way interaction between factors A, B, and C. Table 12-30 gives the coefficients for the interaction ABC. The contrast for ABC is given by

$$\text{Contrast }(ABC) = a+b+c+abc-(1)-ab-ac-bc$$

We may group the plus-sign terms in one group (a, b, c, abc) and the minus-sign terms in another group [(1), ab, ac, bc]. Next, we can construct two blocks of size 4 each. In Block 1, the applied treatments are a, b, c, and abc. In Block 2, the applied treatments are (1), ab, ac, and bc. This is demonstrated in Figure 12-10. An estimate of the block effect can be obtained by determining the difference in the average responses obtained from the two blocks. Note that this is identical to estimating the effect of the treatment ABC. Since the four positive coefficients in the contrast for ABC are assigned to Block 1 and the four negative coefficients are assigned to Block 2, the block effect and the ABC interaction effects are identical, which is to say that ABC is confounded with blocks. In other words, the effect of ABC cannot be distinguished from the block effects. Thus, the contrast ABC is known as a confounding contrast.

On the other hand, consider the estimation of the main effect of factor A as given by the contrast (from Table 12-30):

$$\text{Contrast }(A) = a + ab + ac + abc - (1) - b - c - bc$$

Note that there are four experimental runs from each block. Also, from each block there is one treatment whose effect is added and another whose effect is subtracted. For example, from block 1, the response variable is added for treatments a and abc, and it is subtracted for treatments b and c. So, any differences between the two blocks will cancel out, and estimation of the main effect of A will not be affected by blocking. The same is true for any of the other main effects and two-way interactions. The scheme for blocking demonstrated above may be used for any chosen contrast. Usually, the factors chosen to

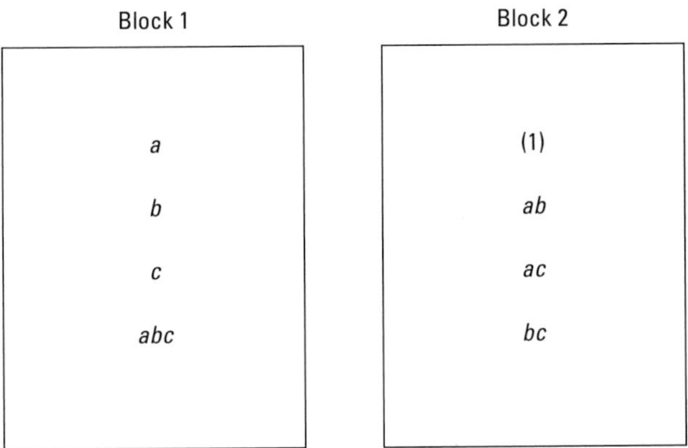

Figure 12-10 Confounding in a 2^3 experiment with two blocks.

confound with blocks are the higher-order interactions, which are normally not as important as the main effects and the low-order interactions.

Fractional Replication in 2^k Experiments

The number of experimental runs in a factorial experiment increases exponentially with the number of factors. Economic concerns may justify the use of fewer experiments than called for by the full factorial. Fractional replication of factorial experiments achieves this purpose. Consider the 2^6 factorial experiment, which requires 64 experimental runs for a full replication. There are 63 degrees of freedom for estimation of the treatment effects. There are 6 main effects, 15 two-way interactions (C_2^6), 20 three-way interactions, 15 four-way interactions, 6 five-way interactions, and 1 six-way interaction. If only the main effects and two-way interactions are considered important, requiring 21 degrees of freedom for estimation, it might be possible to get by with fewer than 64 experimental runs.

Half Fraction of the 2^k Experiment A half fraction of the 2^k experiment consists of 2^{k-1} experimental runs. To determine the treatment combinations that will be represented in the experiment, we make use of a *defining contrast,* or a *generator.* This usually represents a high-order interaction, which may be unimportant or negligible and whose estimation we might not be interested in. For example, consider the 2^3 factorial design with factors A, B, and C and the table of coefficients of orthogonal contrasts shown in Table 12-30. Let us select the defining contrast I to be that associated with the three-way interaction ABC, that is, $I = ABC$. For a 2^{3-1} fractional experiment, we could select only those treatments associated with plus signs in the defining contrast. From Table 12-30, these would be a, b, c, and abc, involving only 4 runs of the experiment. Alternatively, the four treatments with minus signs in the defining contrast could have been selected. These would have been the treatments (1), ab, ac, and bc, and the defining contrast would have been $I = -ABC$. The fraction with the plus sign in the defining contrast is called the *principal fraction,* and the other is called the *alternate fraction.*

The disadvantage of a fractional replication of a full factorial experiment is that certain effects cannot be separately estimated. This is demonstrated through the following example. Suppose we are dealing with a 2^{3-1} experiment with generator $I = ABC$. With four runs (a, b, c, and abc), there would be three degrees of freedom that could be used for estimating the main effects. Using Table 12-30 and noting that only four of the eight possible treatments are run, it would seem that the estimates of the main effects are given by

$$A = \tfrac{1}{2}[a + abc - b - c]$$
$$B = \tfrac{1}{2}[b + abc - a - c]$$
$$C = \tfrac{1}{2}[c + abc - a - b]$$

where the lower-case letters represent the sum of the responses in the corresponding treatments. It is subsequently shown that, in a fractional factorial experiment, the above expressions, strictly speaking, represent the combined effect of the factor shown and its alias. Also using Table 12-30, and noting that the treatments run are (*a*, *b*, *c*, and *abc*), it would seem that the estimates of the two-factor interactions are given by

$$AB = \tfrac{1}{2}[c + abc - a - b]$$
$$AC = \tfrac{1}{2}[b + abc - a - c]$$
$$BC = \tfrac{1}{2}[a + abc - b - c]$$

As is discussed below, strictly speaking, the above expressions represent the combined effect of the factor shown and its alias.

The linear combination of the sum of the treatment responses that estimates the main effect A also estimates the interaction BC. In this case A and BC are said to be *aliases*. If the effect of the contrast is significant, it is not possible to conclude whether it is due to the main effect of A, the interaction BC, or a mixture of both. Similarly, B and AC are aliases, and so are C and AB. In a fractional replication, every contrast has one or more contrasts as an alias.

To find the aliases of a given contrast, we find its interaction with the defining contrast as follows. All of the letters appearing in both contrasts are combined, and any letter that appears twice is deleted. For example, the alias of A, using the defining contrast as ABC, is found as follows:

$$\text{alias }(A) = A * ABC = BC$$

Similarly, the alias for B is

$$\text{alias }(B) = B * ABC = AC$$

while that for C is

$$\text{alias }(C) = C * ABC = AB$$

Since the contrasts A and BC are aliases, if only four treatments a, b, c, and abc are run, the *combined effect* of both contrasts is obtained from $\frac{1}{2}[a + abc - b - c]$. Therefore, using the principal fraction, an estimate of $(A + BC)$ is obtained from $\frac{1}{2}[a + abc - b - c]$; an estimate of $(B + AC)$ is obtained from $\frac{1}{2}[b + abc - a - c]$; and that of $(C + AB)$ is obtained from $\frac{1}{2}[c + abc - a - b]$. If the two-factor interactions can be assumed to be negligible, the main effects A, B, and C can be estimated. Alternatively, if we are not sure whether the two-factor interactions are significant, then, by running the alternate fraction (that is, the treatments (1), ab, ac, and bc), we can estimate the main effects and the interactions by combining the results of the principal fraction and the alternate function.

If the defining contrast had been selected to be $I = -ABC$, the experimental runs would have consisted of the alternate fraction of treatments (1), ab, ac, and bc. The alias of A would be $A * -ABC = -BC$, the alias of B would be $-AC$, and the alias of C would be $-AB$. Thus, the estimate of $(A - BC)$ would be obtained from $\frac{1}{2}[ab + ac - bc - (1)]$, the estimate of $(B - AC)$ would be obtained from $\frac{1}{2}[ab + bc - ac - (1)]$, and that of $(C - AB)$ would be obtained from $\frac{1}{2}[ac + bc - ab - (1)]$.

Upon combining the results of the principal and alternate fractions, the estimate of the main effect of A is

$$A = \tfrac{1}{2}(A + BC) + \tfrac{1}{2}(A - BC)$$

Similarly, the other two main effects are given by

$$B = \tfrac{1}{2}(B + AC) + \tfrac{1}{2}(B - AC)$$
$$C = \tfrac{1}{2}(C + AB) + \tfrac{1}{2}(C - AB)$$

The interaction effects can also be obtained by combining the results of the two fractions as follows:

$$AB = \tfrac{1}{2}(C + AB) - \tfrac{1}{2}(C - AB)$$
$$AC = \tfrac{1}{2}(B + AC) - \tfrac{1}{2}(B - AC)$$
$$BC = \tfrac{1}{2}(A + BC) - \tfrac{1}{2}(A - BC)$$

This process of combining the results of two fractional factorial experiments in order to isolate and estimate main effects and interactions that ordinarily cannot be estimated from either fraction separately creates a very desirable situation. If we cannot run a factorial experiment in a full replication, we can run sequences of small efficient experiments and then combine the information as we continue with the process of experimentation. The knowledge that we accumulate from the ongoing sequence of experiments may be used to update or modify the experiments that follow. For instance, if a fractional replication suggests the nonsignificance of certain factors, it is possible to drop those factors in future experiments, which may lead to a full factorial experiment in the remaining factors.

Design Resolution One method of categorizing fractional factorial experiments is based on the alias patterns produced. Obviously, we prefer that the main effects not be aliased with each other in order to estimate them independently. The degree to which the main effects are aliased with the interaction terms (two-factor or higher order) is represented by the resolution of the corresponding design. In particular, designs of resolutions III, IV, and V are important; they are defined as follows.

Resolution III designs. **Here, main effects are not aliased with each other, but they are aliased with two-factor interactions. Also, two-factor interactions may be aliased with each other. The 2^{3-1} design with the defining contrast given by $I = ABC$ is of resolution III. In such a design the alias structure is given by $A = BC$, $B = AC$, and $C = AB$. The main effects can be estimated only if the two-factor interactions are not significant.**

Resolution IV designs. **Here, main effects are not aliased with each other or with any two-factor interactions. Two-factor interactions are aliased with each other. Thus, the main effects can be estimated regardless of the significance of the two-factor interactions. An example of a resolution IV design is a 2^{4-1} design with the defining contrast given by $I = ABCD$. It can be shown that the alias structure is $A = BCD$, $B = ACD$, $C = ABD$, $D = ABC$, $AB = CD$, $AC = BD$, and $AD = BC$.**

Resolution V designs. **Here, no main effect or two-factor interaction is aliased with any other main effect or two-factor interaction. Two-factor interactions, however, are aliased with three-factor interactions. An example of such a design is the 2^{5-1} design with a defining contrast given by $I = ABCDE$.**

The 2^{k-p} Fractional Factorial Experiment The 2^{k-1} fractional factorial experiment is a half-replicate of the 2^k experiment, but it is possible to find experiments of smaller size that might provide almost as much information at a greatly reduced cost. The 2^{k-p} experiment is a $1/2^p$ fraction of the 2^k factorial experiment. Therefore, a 2^{k-2} experiment employs 1/4 of the total number of treatments.

Let us consider a factorial experiment with 6 factors, each at two levels. A 2^{6-1} fractional factorial experiment would require 32 experimental runs, which would lead to 31 degrees of freedom for estimation of effects. Here, we have 6 main effects and 15 two-factor interactions. Thus, 22 runs would suffice if only main effects and two-factor interactions are deemed important, making the 2^{6-1} experiment inefficient because it would require 32 runs. However, a 2^{6-2} fractional factorial experiment would need 16 experimental runs and would have 15 degrees of freedom for estimation of effects. We could estimate all 6 of the main effects and some (not more than 9) of the two-factor interactions. If this meets our needs, the 2^{6-2} experiment woule be more cost-efficient than the 2^{6-1} experiment.

To generate the treatment combinations for a 2^{k-p} fraction factorial experiment, we use p defining contrasts, or generators. Using the first contrast, we create a 2^{k-1} fractional experiment as demonstrated previously. Starting with the treatments selected in the 2^{k-1} experiment and using the second contrast, we create a half-replicate of the 2^{k-1} experiment yielding a 2^{k-2} fractional experiment. This procedure continues until the pth contrast is used on the treatment combinations in the 2^{k-p+1} experiment to yield the 2^{k-p} fractional experiment. The aliases for the contrasts can be found using the principle explained previously.

For example, consider the generation of a 2^{5-2} fractional factorial. The coefficients for orthogonal contrasts in a 2^5 factorial experiment with factors A, B, C, D, and E may be obtained in a manner similar to that used for the coefficients shown in Table 12-30. Table 12-33 shows a partial portion of such a table for only some selected contrasts $(A, B, C, D, E, AB$, and $AC)$. The full factorial experiment will have 32 treatment combinations. Let us choose our first defining contrast to be $I = AB$. From the 32 treatments, we identify from Table 12-33 those that have a plus sign in the defining contrast AB. So, a 1/2 replicate of the 2^5 experiment is given by the 2^{5-1} fractional factorial, which consists of the following treatments: (1), ab, c, abc, d, abd, cd, $abcd$, e, abe, ce, $abce$, de, $abde$, cde, and $abcde$. If we choose the second defining contrast to be AC of the treatments selected in the 2^{5-1} experiment, we select those (from Table 12-33) that also have a plus sign in the contrast AC. The following eight treatments are obtained for the 2^{5-2} fractional factorial experiment using the defining contrasts AB and AC: (1), abc, d, $abcd$, e, $abce$, de, and $abcde$.

Let us now find the aliases of the contrasts in a 2^{5-2} fractional factorial experiment using the defining contrasts AB and AC. The generalized interaction of the two also acts as a defining contrast (BC). The following alias structure is obtained:

$$I = AB = AC = BC$$
$$A = B = C = ABC$$
$$D = ABD = ACD = BCD$$
$$E = ABE = ACE = BCE$$
$$AD = BD = CD = ABCD$$
$$AE = BE = CE = ABCE$$
$$DE = ABDE = ACDE = BCDE$$
$$ADE = BDE = CDE = ABCDE$$

Note that three of the five main effects (A, B, and C) are aliases of each other. The main effects D and E have three-factor interactions as aliases. Of the two-factor interactions, AB, AC, and BC are aliases; AD, BD, and CD are aliases; and so are AE, BE, and CE. The two-factor interaction DE is an alias of the four-factor interactions $ABDE$, $ACDE$, and $BCDE$. Thus, if estimation of each of the main effects were of interest, selecting AB and AC as the defining contrasts may not be appropriate. We would not be able to isolate the effects of A, B, and C using the generated 2^{5-2} experiment. Furthermore, if estimation of two-factor interactions is desired, we may encounter difficulty because several two-factor interactions are aliases of each other. The choice of the defining contrasts, therefore, is influential in determining the alias structure. The generating contrasts should be selected based on the factors that are of interest in estimation. Suggestions for choosing the defining contrasts for fractional factorial experiments may be found in books on experimental design listed in the references (Box, Hunter, and Hunter, 1978; Peterson, 1985; Raghavarao, 1971).

TABLE 12-33 Coefficients for some orthogonal contrasts in a 2^5 factorial experiment

	Treatment										
Contrast	(1)	*a*	*b*	*ab*	*c*	*ac*	*bc*	*abc*	*d*	*ad*	*bd*
A	−	+	−	+	−	+	−	+	−	+	−
B	−	−	+	+	−	−	+	+	−	−	+
C	−	−	−	−	+	+	+	+	−	−	−
D	−	−	−	−	−	−	−	−	+	+	+
E	−	−	−	−	−	−	−	−	−	−	−
AB	+	−	−	+	+	−	−	+	+	−	−
AC	+	−	+	−	−	+	−	+	+	−	+
	abd	*cd*	*acd*	*bcd*	*abcd*	*e*	*ae*	*be*	*abe*	*ce*	*ace*
A	+	−	+	−	+	−	+	−	+	−	+
B	+	−	−	+	+	−	−	+	+	−	−
C	−	+	+	+	+	−	−	−	−	+	+
D	+	+	+	+	+	−	−	−	−	−	−
E	−	−	−	−	−	+	+	+	+	+	+
AB	+	+	−	−	+	+	−	−	+	+	−
AC	−	−	+	−	+	+	−	+	−	−	+
	bce	*abce*	*de*	*ade*	*bde*	*abde*	*cde*	*acde*	*bcde*	*abcde*	
A	−	+	−	+	−	+	−	+	−	+	
B	+	+	−	−	+	+	−	−	+	+	
C	+	+	−	−	−	−	+	+	+	+	
D	−	−	+	+	+	+	+	+	+	+	
E	+	+	+	+	+	+	+	+	+	+	
AB	−	+	+	−	−	+	+	−	−	+	
AC	−	+	+	−	+	−	−	+	−	+	

At this stage, note that there are differences between the principles of confounding and fractional replications. In confounding, the aim is to reduce the block size in order to increase the precision of the experiment without necessarily reducing the treatment combinations in the experiment. It is possible to have all of the treatment combinations that occur in a full factorial experiment and still keep the block size small. The only sacrifice made is that a factorial contrast is confounded with the block contrast and so cannot be estimated. All of the other factorial contrasts can be estimated. But, if the confounding contrast is so chosen that it is one in which we have no interest, then we do not lose anything. On the other hand, in a fractional factorial experiment the objective is to reduce the size of the experiment, that is, the number of treatments. Depending on the degree of fractionalization, contrasts will have aliases. Thus, it will not be possible to estimate all of the factorial effects separately.

Example 12-8: Consider Example 12-7 concerning the quality of surface finish of graded lumber. The three factors, each at two levels, were the type of wood (Factor A), the rate of feed (Factor B), and the depth of cut (Factor C). The raw data, consisting of three replications for each treatment combination, are shown in Table 12-31. Suppose we decide to use a 2^{3-1} fractional factorial experiment, with the defining contrast being $I = ABC$.

From Table 12-30, for contrast ABC, the following treatments have a plus sign: a, b, c, and abc. These four treatments would be included in the 2^{3-1} fractional factorial experiment.

Let us now determine the alias structure. The main effects have the following aliases:

$$A = A * ABC = BC$$
$$B = B * ABC = AC$$
$$C = C * ABC = AB$$

Thus, each of the main effects is an alias of a two-factor interaction. This design is therefore of resolution III.

To estimate the effects of their aliases, we again make use of Table 12-30 and Table 12-31:

$$A + BC = \frac{1}{3(2)}(a + abc - b - c)$$
$$= (1/6)(41 + 71 - 45 - 75) = -1.333$$
$$B + AC = \frac{1}{3(2)}(b + abc - a - c)$$
$$= (1/6)(45 + 71 - 41 - 75) = 0$$
$$C + AB = \frac{1}{3(2)}(c + abc - a - b)$$
$$= (1/6)(75 + 71 - 41 - 45) = 10.000$$

We find that the effect of $C + AB$ exceeds that of the others.

To determine the sum of squares for the effects, the same procedure that is used with factorial experiments may be applied. For example, the sum of squares for $A + BC$ is given by

$$SS_{A+BC} = \frac{(-8)^2}{3(4)} = 5.333$$

The sum of squares for the other effects are calculated and shown in Table 12-34. The total sum of squares is found from Equation 12.4; the sum of squares for error is found by subtraction of the sum of squares of the treatments from the total sum of squares.

We find from Table 12-34 that the effect of $C + AB$ is highly significant. The calculated F-statistic value of 28.124 far exceeds the critical value of F of 5.32 from Appendix A-6 for a level of significance of 5 percent with 1 and 8 degrees of freedom in the numerator and denominator, respectively. In order to isolate the effect of C, the analyst would need to perform more experiments with the defining contrast being $I = -ABC$, which would yield the alternate fraction. Alternatively, if the complete 2^3 experiment is run using all 8 of the treatment combinations, the effect of C would be estimated separately from that of AB. Example 12-7 deals with this case.

TABLE 12-34 Analysis-of-variance for the 2^{3-1} fractional factorial experiment for the surface finish of wood example

Source of variation	Effect	Degrees of freedom	Sum of squares	Mean square	F-statistic
A + BC	−1.333	1	5.333	5.333	0.500
B + AC	0.	1	0.	0.	0.
C + AB	10.000	1	300.000	300.000	28.124
Error		8	85.334	10.667	
Total		11	390.667		

12-5 SUMMARY

This chapter has presented some fundamental concepts of experimental design. With the objective of achieving quality at a reduced cost, this chapter has discussed procedures through which the impact of design factors on the performance of the product or process can be analyzed. Traditional experimental designs such as the completely randomized design, randomized block design, and Latin square design have been presented. In an effort to achieve a desired combination of parameter levels, the purpose of assigning a certain level to each parameter is to ensure that the process of estimating the effects of these parameters is not biased. The notion of determining the significance of a factor in terms of the mean square of the error component is a central concept in the analysis-of-variance procedure. The basis for the evaluation process using analysis-of-variance procedures has been illustrated.

Factorial and fractional factorial experiment have been discussed. A full factorial experiment represents all possible combinations of the various factors. A fractional factorial experiment represents a subset of the full factorial experiment, with the experiments selected in a manner such that estimation of the desirable effects is possible. For factorial experiments, the role of contrasts in estimating the treatment effects has been discussed. The procedure of blocking to increase the precision of the experiment, as achieved through the principle of confounding, has been demonstrated. Procedures for selecting fractional replicates of the full design, in which it is desirable to reduce the size of the experiment, have also been presented. This chapter has provided a foundation for product and process design by introducing some common designs and methods for analyzing data using those designs. Inferences from such analysis help us determine treatments that can favorably affect the response.

12-6 CASE STUDY

QUALITY IMPROVEMENT USING EXPERIMENTAL DESIGN*

Introduction

Proper experimental design is, in fact, as important as sophisticated statistical analysis. Even the best statistical analysis would be useless on data obtained from a poorly planned experimental program. The best design is one that is tailor-made to the needs and peculiarities of the specific problem and testing constraints. However, the common mistake of many engineers is to use sophisticated designs, which may be unnecessarily costly. To demonstrate the effectiveness of experimental designs, a properly designed but simple factorial experiment which led to significant quality improvements in the wave-soldering process is examined.

Planning the Factorial Experiment

A factorial experiment is one in which all levels of a given factor are combined with all levels of every other factor in the experiment. In an industrial situation, several factors can be controlled and their effects investigated at two or more levels. The experimental plan consists of taking the response at every possible combination that can be formed for the different levels of the factors. Each such different combination is called a treatment combination.

In the analysis of factorial experiments, the main effects and interaction effects (or simply interactions) are considered. Main effects of a given factor are always functions of the average response or yield at the various levels of the factor. For example, in the case where a factor has two levels, the main effect is the difference between the responses at the two levels averaged over all levels of the other factors.

If an investigation is to be performed most efficiently, then a scientific approach to planning the experiment must be employed. In addition, it must be noted that good statistical analysis cannot rescue a poorly planned experimental program. Hence, in this investigation the experiments were carefully planned using full factorial designs so that the appropriate data can be collected for analyses. The method of data collection and analysis must be established before starting the experiment. To ensure that results are not being biased by uncontrolled variables such as ambient conditions and variability among different experimenters, randomization is introduced into the experiment to the extent that is most practical. The steps used in this investigation can be summarized as follows:

- Identification of the process parameters which may influence the yield

* Adapted from T. E. Lim (1990), "Quality Improvement Using Experimental Design," *International Journal of Quality and Reliability Management*, Vol. 7, No. 1, pp. 70–76. Reprinted by permission of MCB University Press.

- Selection of the factors and identifying the appropriate levels for experimentation
- Collection of data
- Analysis of data
- Determination of optimum parameters
- Trial run to verify the validity of optimum process parameters
- Implementation of new process settings

Quality Improvement for Wave-Soldering Process

In the electronics industry, the wave-soldering process of a PCB assembly line is an important part of the manufacturing process. A production line in which the wave-soldering process yields an average fall-off rate of about 0.7 percent (700 ppm) was chosen for the experimentation. The existing settings of the soldering parameters are shown in Table 12-35.

Selection of the Parameters for Experimentation

An important part of planning a factorial experiment is the identification of the parameters (or factors) which affect the response and deciding what to do about them. For this purpose, brain-storming sessions were organized with the objective of identifying the critical parameters affecting the wave-soldering process. The members of the brainstorming sessions comprise a consultant, quality engineers, and process engineers. Historical data were examined, and all suggestions on the possible causes of defectives were recorded. Critical parameters were then identified by eliminating the unimportant ones. Noncontrollable factors such as limitations due to machine capability were fed back to higher management. This information serves as vital decision-making criteria in future machine/equipment purchases. In this experiment two such noncontrollable factors were wave height and the angle of inclination. The controllable parameters were conveyor speed, top board temperature, pot temperature, and flux density.

TABLE 12-35 Existing parameter settings

	Parameters	Setting
A	Conveyor speed	1.6m/min
B	Top board temperature	50°C
C	Pot temperature	250°C
D	Flux density	0.845
E	Wave height	9.5 mm
F	Angle of inclination	6.5 deg

One vital prerequisite for the experimentation is that the experimenters must be highly knowledgeable in the subject matter (soldering process, in this case) so that the factor levels can be identified. Good statistical knowledge alone cannot substitute for thinking about the problem. Hence, in this project, the selection of these levels was made by an engineer with five years of experience in the wave-soldering process. The final list of selected variables along with their chosen levels and treatment combinations are shown in Table 12-36.

Since two levels for each of the four controllable factors (A, B, C, and D) are used, in denoting a treatment, a lowercase letter indicates that the corresponding factor is at the high level. An absence of the letter indicates that the corresponding factor is at the low level. The notation (1) indicates that all four factors are at the low level.

Experimental Data Collection and Analysis

A sample size of 30 PCBs with 998 joints for each PCB was used, and the number of defective joints was recorded (Table 12-36) for each treatment combination. The main effects, second-order interactions, and estimates of experimental error using third- and higher-order interactions were computed. A summary of the results is given in Table 12-37. The lowest number of defects is 234 with the treatment combination $A_0B_0C_1D_0$ (Table 12-36). Here, the subscripts 0 and 1 are used to denote the low and high levels of the factors, respectively. Hence, the optimum combination is $A_0B_0C_1D_0$, and the settings are as follows:

$$A_0 : \text{Conveyor speed} = 1.6\text{m/min}$$
$$B_0 : \text{Top board temperature} = 40°\text{C}$$
$$C_1 : \text{Pot temperature} = 250°\text{C}$$
$$D_0 : \text{Flux density} = 0.835$$

Verification and Implementation

After a trial run, the wave-soldering machine was set to the optimum combination. The audited results showed that the average defective rate was reduced to 300 ppm, from 700 ppm before the change. This improvement represents a 57 percent reduction in wave-soldering defects. The project took approximately two months to complete and has resulted in a substantial reduction in soldering defects.

Summary and Conclusions

This experiment has resulted in a substantial improvement in the quality of the products. It clearly demonstrates experimental design as an efficient technique for quality improvement. As with any other form of

TABLE 12-36 Data for four factors, each at two levels

		Parameters (factors)				Types of defects							
Experiment number	Treatment	A Conveyor speed (m/min)	B Top board temperature (°C)	C Pot temperature (°C)	D Flux density	Dry joint	Poor joint	Solder bridging	No solder	Solder bridging	Dry joint	Total defects	PPM
1	(1)	1.6	40	240	0.835	9	0	0	0	0	0	9	301
2	*a*	1.8	40	240	0.835	8	0	0	0	0	0	8	267
3	*b*	1.6	50	240	0.835	8	0	0	0	0	0	8	267
4	*ab*	1.8	50	240	0.835	12	0	0	0	0	0	12	401
5	*c*	1.6	40	250	0.835	6	0	1	0	0	0	7	234
6	*ac*	1.8	40	250	0.835	9	0	0	0	0	0	9	301
7	*b*	1.6	50	250	0.835	8	0	0	0	0	0	8	267
8	*abc*	1.8	50	250	0.835	8	0	0	0	0	0	8	267
9	*d*	1.6	40	240	0.845	10	3	0	0	0	0	13	434
10	*ad*	1.8	40	240	0.845	9	0	0	0	0	0	9	301
11	*bd*	1.6	50	240	0.845	5	3	0	0	0	0	8	267
12	*abd*	1.8	50	240	0.845	9	0	0	0	0	0	9	301
13	*cd*	1.6	40	250	0.845	10	0	0	0	0	0	10	334
14	*acd*	1.8	40	250	0.845	12	2	0	0	0	0	14	468
15	*bcd*	1.6	50	250	0.845	11	2	0	0	0	0	13	434
16	*abcd*	1.8	50	250	8.845	12	1	0	1	0	0	14	468

Number of soldered joints = 998
Number PCB = 30
Total number of soldered joints = 998 × 30 = 29,940

TABLE 12-37 Analysis-of-variance table

Source of variation	Sum of squares	Degrees of freedom	Mean square	*F* ratio
Main effect				
A	3481.00	1	3481.00	0.581
B	64.00	1	64.00	0.011
C	3422.25	1	3422.25	0.571
D	30800.25	1	30800.25	5.138
2-factor interactions				
AB	1764.00	1	1764.00	0.294
AC	3422.25	1	3422.25	0.571
BC	1722.25	1	1722.25	0.287
AD	600.25	1	600.25	0.100
BD	1722.25	1	1722.25	0.287
CD	20164.00	1	20164.00	3.363
Experimental error using third- and higher-order interactions as estimate	29975.50	5	5995.10	

investigation, there are always some difficulties and constraints facing the investigator. The limitation of the wave-soldering experiment is that two of the parameters (wave height and angle of inclination) cannot be varied on the existing machine and were excluded from the investigation. In spite of the various limitations, the use of experimental design contributes to significant improvement of quality, and it substantially reduces the time of investigation.

In conclusion, it may be suggested that similar design can be used or adapted for seeking solutions to industrial problems and for quality improvement in the production line. The prerequisites for a successful factorial experiment would be management support, a carefully planned design, and sound knowledge of the subject matter. Another important point is that factorial experimentation should be in part guided by considerations of economy and simplicity.

Questions for Discussion

1. What type of experimental design is used in this case?
2. Are there any significant two-factor interactions at a level of significance of 0.05? Which is the most significant two-factor interaction? What is the implication of this?
3. Which factor is the most significant, and what is its level of significance? Discuss the implication of this in this case.
4. If it is not feasible to perform the full factorial experiment, discuss a possible fractional factorial experiment.
5. For the design selected in question 4, what is the alias pattern? Which main effects can you estimate independently?

KEY TERMS

Alias
Alternate fraction
Analysis of variance (ANOVA)
Balanced experiment
Blocking
Central limit theorem
Completely randomized design
Confounding
Contour plot
Contrast
  Orthogonal
Degrees of freedom
Defining contrast
Design resolution
  Resolution III
  Resolution IV
  Resolution V
Double-blind study
Experiment
Experimental design
Experimental error
Experimental unit
F-statistic
Factor
  Qualitative
  Quantitative
Factor levels
  Continuous
  Discrete
Factorial experiment
Fixed effects model
Fractional factorial experiment
Generator
Incomplete block design
Interaction
Latin square design

Measurement bias
Mean square
  Error
  Treatment
Noise factors
Off-line quality control
Parameter
  Controllable
  Uncontrollable
Principle fraction
Random effects model
Randomization
Randomized block design
Replication
Response function
Sampling unit
Screening experiment
Single-blind study
Signal-to-noise ratio
Sum of squares
  Block
  Error
  Total
  Treatment
Treatments
Treatment effect
  Fixed
Unbalanced experiment

EXERCISES

Discussion Questions

12-1 Distinguish between factor, treatment, and treatment levels.

12-2 Explain the importance of experimental design in quality control and improvement.

12-3 Explain the principles of replication, randomization, and blocking, and discuss their roles in experimental design.

12-4 Explain the concept of interaction between factors, and give some examples.

12-5 What are the drawbacks of using the approach for one variable at a time in experimental design?

12-6 What is the difference between qualitative and quantitative variables? Give examples of each. Which of these two classes permit interpolation of the response variable?

12-7 What is the difference between a fixed effects and a random effects model? Give some examples.

12-8 Explain the difference between the completely randomized design and the randomized block design. Under what conditions would you prefer to use each design?

12-9 Distinguish between a randomized block design and a Latin square design. What are the advantages and disadvantages of a Latin square design?

12-10 What are the relative advantages and disadvantages of factorial experiments?

12-11 Explain why it does not make sense to test for the main effects in a factorial experiment if the interaction effects are significant.

12-12 What is the utility of contrasts in experimental design? What are orthogonal contrasts, and how are they helpful?

12-13 What are the features of a 2^k factorial experiment? What are the features of a 2^{k-2} fractional factorial experiment, and how is it constructed?

12-14 Clearly distinguish between the principles of confounding and fractionalization.

12-15 What are the advantages and disadvantages of confounding in a 2^k experiment?

12-16 What is the role of a defining contrast, or generator, in fractional factorial experiments? Distinguish between a principal fraction and an alternate fraction.

Problems

12-17 A large retail company has to deliver its goods to distributors throughout the country. It has been offered trial-run services by three transportation companies. In order to test the efficiency of these three companies, it randomly assigns its outgoing product shipments to these transporters and determines the degree of lateness as a proportion of the time allocated for delivery. Table 12-38 shows the degree of lateness of the three companies for five shipments.

TABLE 12-38 Degree of lateness values of transportation companies

Transportation company	Degree of lateness values				
1	0.04	0.00	0.02	0.03	0.02
2	0.15	0.11	0.07	0.09	0.12
3	0.06	0.03	0.04	0.04	0.05

a. Is there a difference in the mean degree of lateness of the three transportation companies? Test at the 10 percent level of significance.
b. Find a 95 percent confidence interval for the mean degree of lateness of company 1.
c. Find a 90 percent confidence interval for the difference in the mean degree of lateness of company 2 and 3. Can we conclude that there is a difference in their means at the 10 percent level of significance?
d. Which company would you prefer to choose? Why?

12-18 An airline is interested in selecting a software package for its reservation system. Even though the company would like to maximize use of its available seats, it desires to bump as few passengers as possible. It has four software packages to choose from. The airline randomly chooses a package and uses it for a given month. Over the span of a year, the company uses each package three times. The number of passengers bumped for each month for a given software package is shown in Table 12-39.

a. Is there a difference in the software packages as measured by the mean number of passengers bumped? Test at the 5 percent level of significance.
b. Find a 90 percent confidence interval for the mean number of passengers bumped using software package 2.
c. Find a 95 percent confidence interval for the difference in the mean number of passengers bumped using software packages 1 and 2. Is there a difference in their means at the 5 percent level of significance?
d. Which software package would you choose?

12-19 Three different training programs are being considered for auditors in an accounting firm. The success of the training programs is measured through a rating scale from 0 to 100, with higher values indicating a desirable program. The company categorized its auditors into three groups, depending on the number of years of experience. Three auditors were selected from each group and were randomly assigned to the training programs. Table 12-40 shows the ratings assigned by the auditors after they had gone through the training program.

a. Is there a difference in the training programs as indicated by the mean evaluation scores? Test at the 10 percent level of significance.
b. Find a 90 percent confidence interval for the difference in the mean evaluation scores of training programs 1 and 3. Is there a difference between these two programs?

12-20 A doctor is contemplating four types of diet to reduce the blood sugar levels of patients. Because of differences in the metabolism of patients, the doctor categorizes the patients into five age groups. From each age group, four patients are selected and randomly assigned to the diets. After two months on the diet, the reduction in blood sugar level is found. The results are shown in Table 12-41.

TABLE 12-39 Number of passengers bumped using different software packages

Software package	Number of passengers bumped		
1	12	14	9
2	2	4	3
3	10	9	6
4	7	6	7

TABLE 12-40 Performance rating of training programs

	Training programs		
Years of experience	1	2	3
0–5	70	65	81
5–10	75	80	87
10–15	87	82	94

TABLE 12-41 Reduction in blood sugar level of patients

	Diet type			
Patient age group	1	2	3	4
20–30	40	70	35	40
30–40	60	80	65	60
40–50	65	60	60	50
50–60	30	50	40	20
60–70	45	55	50	30

a. Is there a difference in the diet types as evidenced by the mean reduction in blood sugar level? Test at the 5 percent level of significance.
b. Find a 90 percent confidence interval for the mean reduction in blood sugar level for diet type 1.
c. Find a 95 percent confidence interval for the difference in the mean reduction in blood sugar levels between diet types 2 and 4. Is there a difference between the two diet types?
d. Which diet type would you prefer?

12-21 It is desired to test four different cake mixes (*A*, *B*, *C*, and *D*) on the degree of fluffiness of the cake baked. It is felt that two factors, namely, the baker mixing the ingredients and the oven rack on which the cake is baked (causing temperature differentials), might influence fluffiness. Controlling these two factors, each cake mix is used for a combination of the two factors, appearing only once for each oven rack and once for each baker. Table 12-42 shows the degree of fluffiness of cakes baked by using the four mixes, as measured on an index scale of 0 to 100, with larger values indicating more desirable cakes.

a. Is there a difference in the mean degree of fluffiness of the cake mixes? Test at the 5 percent level of significance.
b. Find a 95 percent confidence interval for the difference in the mean degree of fluffiness of cake mixes *B* and *C*.
c. Find a 90 percent confidence interval for the mean degree of fluffiness of mix *A*.
d. Which cake mix would you prefer to use? Why?
e. Was blocking of the two variables, oven rack and baker, effective?
f. If you had to rerun the experiment, what type of design would you use?

TABLE 12-42 Degree of fluffiness of cakes using four mixes

	Baker			
Oven rack	1	2	3	4
I	D 64.5	B 87.3	A 70.9	C 42.6
II	C 60.4	A 72.7	B 86.1	D 53.9
III	A 57.3	D 67.1	C 41.8	B 85.5
IV	B 83.2	C 53.8	D 65.2	A 72.4

TABLE 12-43 Computational times using four software packages

	Operating system configuration			
Problem type	I	II	III	IV
1	B 14.2	A 37.3	D 24.3	C 22.6
2	D 18.5	C 18.1	B 27.4	A 39.6
3	A 36.1	B 16.8	C 13.2	D 20.3
4	C 17.5	D 24.6	A 36.7	B 19.5

12-22 A consulting firm wishes to evaluate the performance of four different canned software packages (*A*, *B*, *C*, and *D*) as measured by the computational time. The experimenter wishes to control for two variables: the problem type and the operating system configuration used. Four classes of each of these two variables were identified. Each software package was used only once on each problem type and only once on each operating system configuration. Table 12-43 shows the computational times, in milliseconds, for the four software packages under these controlled conditions.

a. Test at the 5 percent level of significance for the equality of the mean computational times of the four software packages.
b. Find a 95 percent confidence interval for the mean computational time using software package *C*.
c. Find a 95 percent confidence interval for the difference in the mean computational times of software packages *A* and *C*. Is there a difference between the two?
d. Which software package would you choose, and why?
e. Was blocking of the two variables, problem type and operating system configuration, effective?
f. If you had to rerun the experiment, what type of design would you use?

12-23 Two controllable factors, temperature and pressure, were each kept at three levels to determine their impact on the ductility of an alloy being produced. The temperature levels were 150, 250, and 300°C, respectively. Pressure was controlled at 50, 100, and 150 kg/cm^2. Each of the nine treatments was replicated five times. The ductility of the

TABLE 12-44 Ductility of an alloy based on process temperature and pressure settings

Temperature	Pressure (kg/cm²)		
	50	100	150
150°C	50	44	75
	65	49	80
	70	52	81
	73	40	76
	68	45	82
250°C	40	25	86
	45	30	88
	56	20	82
	50	33	81
	52	34	76
300°C	72	62	60
	60	71	62
	75	65	55
	73	68	52
	70	72	50

TABLE 12-45 Vitamin C content of citrus fruit based on fertilizer and moisture level

Fertilizer levels	Moisture levels		
	I	II	III
I	4.8	6.2	9.0
	6.2	5.8	8.5
	5.5	5.6	8.8
	4.9	6.7	8.4
	5.0	6.0	8.6
II	5.3	8.7	8.5
	6.4	9.1	8.4
	5.8	8.6	8.8
	5.9	8.4	8.6
	5.6	8.2	8.8
III	7.0	7.4	7.6
	7.1	6.8	7.2
	6.8	6.7	6.8
	6.8	6.4	7.0
	7.2	6.6	7.1

produced alloy is shown in Table 12-44. The higher the value, the more ductile the alloy.

a. Test if the interaction effects between temperature and pressure are significant at the 5 percent level of significance.
b. What are the desirable settings of the process temperature and pressure if a ductile alloy is preferred?
c. Find a 90 percent confidence interval for the mean ductility when the process temperature is set at 150°C and the pressure at 150 kg/cm².
d. Find a 95 percent confidence interval for the difference in mean ductility for a process temperature of 250°C and pressure of 150 kg/cm² versus a process temperature of 300°C and pressure of 100 kg/cm².

12-24 The yield of citrus fruit is of interest because it provides an important source of vitamin C. The amount of fertilizer and the amount of water used are two controllable factors. Three levels of fertilizer in increasing order of use (I, II, and III) and three levels of water in increasing order of application (I, II, and III) are shown in Table 12-45 along with the vitamin C content of five randomly selected fruits for each treatment, higher values indicating desirable yields.

a. Test at the 10 percent level of significance to determine if the factors or interactions are significant. What is your conclusion?
b. What level of fertilizer and water would you select to maximize the vitamin C content?
c. Find a 90 percent confidence interval for the mean vitamin C content when fertilizer is at level I and moisture is at level II.
d. Find a 90 percent confidence interval for the difference in the mean vitamin C content when fertilizer is at level I and moisture is at level III versus when fertilizer is at level III and moisture is at level I. What is your conclusion?

12-25 Consider Example 12-4 concerning the efficiency of synthetic fuel for which the factors are an additive and a catalyst. The original data are given in Table 12-23. Suppose the experiment was conducted using only five randomly chosen automobiles (A, B, C, D, and E). Each treatment was used on each of these five automobiles. The reason for choosing only five automobiles and replicating the experiment was to eliminate any variation in the fuel efficiencies that might arise due to differences in the automobiles. The data in Table 12-23 are now interpreted as follows. For additive level 1 and catalyst level 1, the response value of 75 was for automobile A, 72 for automobile B, and so forth. Similar interpretations hold for the other treatments.

a. What is your conclusion regarding the significance of the factors or their interactions? Test at the 5 percent level of significance.
b. Find a 95 percent confidence interval for the mean efficiency when the additive is at level 1 and the catalyst is at level 2.
c. Find a 95 percent confidence interval for the difference in the treatment means when the additive is at level 1 and the catalyst is at level 3 versus when the additive is at level 2 and the catalyst is at level 3. What is your conclusion?
d. What levels of additive and catalyst would you prefer to choose?
e. Was it beneficial to select only 5 automobiles and replicate the treatments on only those automobiles? Test at the 5 percent level of significance.

12-26 Consider Problem 12-17 concerning the degree of lateness of three transportation companies.

a. Is there a difference between the mean degree of lateness of company 3 and that of the averages of companies 1 and 2? Test at the 5 percent level of significance.
b. Find a 90 percent confidence interval for the contrast defined in part a.

12-27 Consider Problem 12-18 concerning the number of passengers bumped using four different software packages.

a. Is there a difference in the mean number of passengers bumped using software packages 1 and 2 from that using software packages 3 and 4? Test at the 10 percent level of significance.
b. Find a 95 percent confidence interval for the contrast that tests for the difference in the mean number of passengers bumped using software package 3 and the average of that using software packages 1 and 2.

12-28 Consider Problem 12-19 concerning the effectiveness of three training programs for auditors. Find a 90 percent confidence interval for the difference in the mean effectiveness of program 1 and the average of that using programs 2 and 3.

12-29 Consider Problem 12-19 concerning the effectiveness of three training programs for auditors. Consider the following two contrasts of totals: 1) difference between the totals for training programs 1 and 3; 2) difference between the totals for the sum of training programs 1 and 3 and twice that of training program 2.

a. Find the sum of squares due to each of these two contrasts.
b. What null hypothesis is indicated by contrast 2)? Test the hypothesis at a level of significance of 0.05, and explain your conclusions.

12-30 Consider Problem 12-20 concerning the effect of four types of diet in reducing the blood sugar level of patients. Consider the following three contrasts: 1) difference between the sum of the reduction in blood sugar level using diet types 1 and 3 from that using diet types 2 and 4; 2) difference between the sum of the reduction in blood sugar level using diet types 1 and 2 from that using diet types 3 and 4; 3) difference in the sum of the reduction in blood sugar level using diet types 2 and 3 from that using diet types 1 and 4.

a. Find the sum of squares due to each of the contrasts, and discuss their contribution to the treatment sum of squares.
b. What null hypothesis is indicated by contrast 1)? Test the hypothesis at a 5 percent level of significance.
c. What type of hypothesis is indicated by contrast 2? Test the hypothesis at the 10 percent level of significance.

12-31 Consider a 2^4 factorial experiment. Write out the treatment combinations.

12-32 In the search for a lower-pollution synthetic fuel, researchers are experimenting with three different factors, each controlled at two levels, for the processing of such a fuel. Factor A is the concentration of corn extract at 5 percent and 10 percent levels, factor B is the concentration of an ethylene-based compound at 15 percent and 25 percent, and factor C is the distillation temperature at 120°C and 150°C. The levels of undesirable emission of the fuel are shown in Table 12-46 for three replications of each treatment; each level is randomly assigned to a treatment. The larger the level of emission, the worse the impact on the environment.

TABLE 12-46 Emission levels of synthetic fuel under different treatment combinations

Treatment	Degree of undesirable emission level		
(1)	30	24	26
a	18	22	24
b	30	32	25
ab	43	47	41
c	28	24	22
ac	54	49	46
bc	58	48	50
abc	24	20	22

a. Find all of the main effects and the interaction effects.
b. Find the sum of squares for each of the main effects and the interaction effects.
c. At the 5 percent level of significance, which effects are significant? Interpret your inferences.

12-33 Patient satisfaction is one of the key response variables in evaluating the performance of health-care facilities. The impact of three factors at two levels each on patient satisfaction is to be evaluated. Factor A is the frequency of visits by nurses: once every 2 hours (level −1) or once every hour (level 1). Factor B is the amount of time spent by the doctor with the patient: 10 minutes/day (level −1) or 20 minutes/day (level 1). Factor C is the type of food provided: meals selected by hospital management (level −1) or patient provided a choice (level 1). Table 12-47 shows the responses measuring patient satisfaction on a 50-point scale; the larger the value, the higher the satisfaction level. These patients were randomly assigned to each treatment.

TABLE 12-47 Patient satisfaction level under different treatment combinations

Treatment	Patient satisfaction level		
(1)	6	8	9
a	10	16	15
b	18	12	15
ab	12	9	10
c	20	26	29
ac	34	28	32
bc	36	44	46
abc	25	22	24

a. Find all of the main effects and the interaction effects.
b. Find the sum of squares for each of the main effects and the interaction effects.
c. At the 10 percent level of significance, which effects are significant? Interpret your inferences.

12-34 Consider a 2^4 factorial experiment. Set up a table of the coefficients for orthogonal contrasts similar to Table 12-30. Write down the contrasts for estimating the main effects and the two-factor interactions. If the four-way interaction effect $ABCD$ is not significant, use that as a basis to confound the design into two blocks.

12-35 In Exercise 12-34, use AB as the confounding factor to divide the experiment into two blocks. How would you estimate the effect of factor A?

12-36 Consider a 2^4 factorial experiment. Using BC as the defining contrast, find the treatment combinations in a 2^{4-1} fractional factorial experiment. Find the aliases of all of the contrasts. How would it be possible to estimate the effect of the contrast BC? If AD is used as a second generator, determine the treatment combinations in a 2^{4-2} fractional factorial experiment. What is the alias structure now?

12-37 In a 2^{5-2} fractional factorial experiment, using CDE and AB as the generators, find the treatment combinations. Find the aliases of all of the contrasts.

12-38 Determine the treatment combinations using BC and AD in a 2^{5-2} fractional factorial experiment. Compare and contrast with the results of the treatments combinations using the generators from Exercise 12-37. Determine the alias structure.

12-39 Consider a 2^6 factorial experiment. Using $ABCE$ as the defining contrast, find the treatment combinations in a 2^{6-1} fractional factorial experiment. Find the alias structure of the contrasts. If $BCDF$ is used as a second generator, determine the treatment combinations in a 2^{6-2} fractional factorial experiment. What is the alias structure now?

12-40 Refer to Exercise 12-32 concerning the emission level of synthetic fuel. Factor A is the concentration of corn extract, factor B is the concentration of an ethylene based compound, and factor C is the distillation temperature. Each factor may be controlled at two levels. Suppose the experimenter runs a 2^{3-1} fractional factorial experiment, with the defining contrast being $I = ABC$. Using the data in Table 12-46, perform an analysis to determine the significance of effects. Which effects cannot be estimated? What is the alias structure? Comment on your inferences if the chosen level of significance is 5 percent.

12-41 Refer to Exercise 12-33 and Table 12-47 concerning the patient satisfaction level for the three factors of the frequency of visits by nurses (factor A), the amount of time spent by the doctor (factor B), and the type of food (factor C). Each of the factors was controlled at two levels. Suppose the experimenter has decided to run a 2^{3-1} fractional factorial experiment, with the defining contrast being $I = ABC$. What is the alias structure? Perform an analysis to determine the significance of effects at a chosen level of significance of 5 percent.

REFERENCES

Box, G. E. P., and Draper, N. R. (1986). *Empirical Model Building and Response Surfaces.* Wiley, New York.

Box, G. E. P., Hunter, W. G., and Hunter, J. S. (1978). *Statistics for Experimenters.* Wiley, New York.

Box, G. E. P., and Wilson, K. B. (1951). "On the Experimental Attainment of Optimum Conditions," *Journal of the Royal Statistical Society, Series B* 13(1), pp. 1–45 (with discussion).

Gunter, B. (1989). "Statistically Designed Experiments—Part 1: Quality Improvement, the Strategy of Experimentation, and the Road to Hell," *Quality Progress,* Vol. 22, pp. 63–64.

Gunter, B. (1990a). "Statistically Designed Experiments—Part 2: The Universal Structure Underlying Experimentation," *Quality Progress,* Vol. 23, pp. 87–89.

Gunter, B. (1990b). "Statistically Designed Experiments—Part 3: Interaction," *Quality Progress,* Vol. 23, pp. 74–75.

Gunter, B. (1990c). "Statistically Designed Experiments—Part 4: Multivariate Optimization," *Quality Progress,* Vol. 23, pp. 68–70.

Gunter, B. (1990d). "Statistically Designed Experiments—Part 5: Robust Process and Product Design and Related Matters," *Quality Progress,* Vol. 23, pp. 107–108.

Hunter, J. S. (1985). "Statistical Design Applied to Product Design," *Journal of Quality Technology,* 17 (4), pp. 210–221.

Lim, T. E. (1990). "Quality Improvement Using Experimental Design," *International Journal of Quality and Reliability Management,* 7 (1), pp. 70–76.

Montgomery, D. C. (1991). *Design and Analysis of Experiments,* 2nd edition. Wiley, New York.

Peterson, R. G. (1985). *Design and Analysis of Experiments.* Marcel Dekker, New York.

Raghavarao, D. (1971). *Constructions and Combinatorial Problems in Design of Experiments.* Wiley, New York.

Ryan, T. P. (1989). *Statistical Methods for Quality Improvement.* Wiley, New York.

SAS Institute Inc. (1989a). *SAS/QC Software: Reference, Version 6,* 1st edition. Cary, North Carolina.

SAS Institute Inc. (1989b). *SAS/STAT, User's Guide: Statistics, Version 6,* 4th edition. Cary, North Carolina.

Wadsworth, H. M., Stephens, K. S., and Godfrey, A. B. (1986). *Modern Methods for Quality Control and Improvement.* Wiley, New York.

CHAPTER

13

Taguchi Methods in Design and Quality Improvement

CHAPTER OUTLINE

SYMBOLS

y	Quality characteristic
m	Target value
MSD	Mean square deviation
s^2	Sample variance
$\overline{y}$	Sample mean
$L(y)$	Taguchi's loss function
$E[L(y)]$	Expected, or mean, loss
S/N	Signal-to-noise ratio

13-1 INTRODUCTION

The underlying theme of the neverending cycle of quality improvement is supported by the work of Genichi Taguchi, a Japanese engineer whose ideas in quality engineering have been used for many years in Japan. In the 1980s his ideas on statistically designed experiments were introduced to the Western world (Taguchi and Wu, 1980; Taguchi, 1986, 1987). Quality engineering has the objective of designing quality into every product and corresponding process. It directs quality improvement efforts upstream from the manufacturing process to the design phase and is therefore referred to as an *off-line* quality control method. The techniques of statistical process control that are discussed in preceding chapters are known as *on-line* quality control methods. Taguchi's off-line methods are effective in improving quality and cutting down costs at the same time (Taguchi, Elsayed, and Hsiang, 1989). Off-line methods improve product manufacturability. They also reduce product development and lifetime costs.

This chapter deals with the philosophy and experimental design principles devised by Genichi Taguchi. He introduced a philosophy in which quality is measured by the deviation of a characteristic from its target value. A loss function (to society) is developed for this deviation. Uncontrollable factors, known as noise, cause such deviation and thereby lead to loss. Since the elimination of noise factors is impractical and often impossible, the Taguchi methods seek to minimize the effects of noise. These methods try to determine the optimum level of the important controllable factors based on the concept of *robustness* (Dehnad, 1989). The objective is to create a product/process design that is insensitive to all possible combinations of the uncontrollable noise factors and is at the same time effective and cost-efficient as a result of setting the key controllable factors at certain levels.

13-2 TAGUCHI PHILOSOPHY

Some of the fundamental ideas that are embraced by the Taguchi philosophy are as follows. According to Taguchi, "Quality is the loss imparted to society from the time a product is shipped." Taguchi attaches a monetary value to quality because he feels that this will make quality improvement understood by all—technical personnel as well as management. Typical examples of loss to society include failure to meet the customer's requirements and unsatisfactory performance that leads to loss of goodwill and reduced market share. The Taguchi concept of quality loss has been extended by Kackar (1986) to include the loss to society while the product is being manufactured. For instance, the raw materials and labor depleted when making the product or rendering the service may also be considered societal losses. Likewise, the cost of environmental pollution falls into this category. The purpose of quality improvement, then, is to discover innovative ways of designing products and processes that will save society more than they cost in the long run. All products ultimately cause loss because they break and then need to be repaired or replaced or because they wear out after an adequate performance in their functional life. The degree to which the product or service meets consumers' expectations will influence the magnitude of loss. Taguchi contends that the loss due to a product's variation in performance is proportional to the square of the performance characteristic's deviation from its target value. Figure 13-1 shows an example of the quadratic loss function. This function is an example of the nominal-is-best condition. If the quality characteristic y is at the nominal value m, then the loss $L(y)$ is zero. As the characteristic deviates from the nominal (or target) value in either direction, the loss increases in a quadratic manner. Examples of such situations include the dimensions of a part (length, thickness, diameter, and so on) or the operating pressure in a press. Technical details of the loss function will be provided later.

The quality and cost of a manufactured product is influenced by the engineering design of the product as well as the process. By concentrating on product and process designs that are *robust*, that is, less sensitive to uncontrollable factors such as temperature, humidity, and manufacturing variation (the *noise factors*), the Taguchi concept attempts to reduce the impact of noise rather than eliminate it. Frequently, the elimination of noise factors is neither practical (because it is very costly) nor feasible. Man-

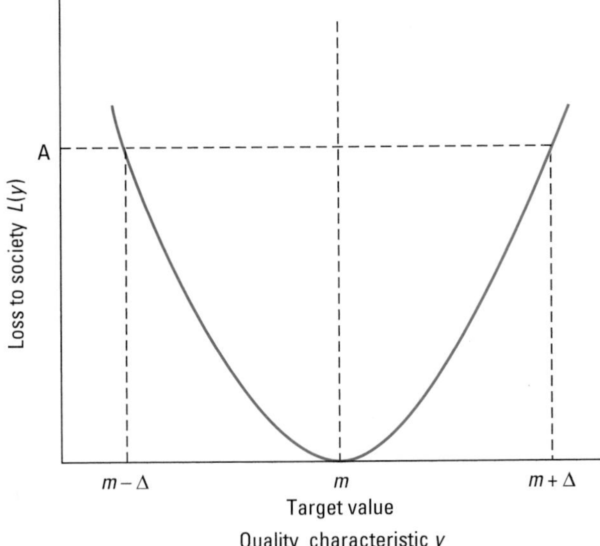

Figure 13-1 Loss function for a situation in which the nominal value is best.

ufacturing variability cannot be totally eliminated; incoming components and raw material exhibit variation. By dampening the impact of the noise factors and by selecting the controllable factor levels which force the desirable quality characteristics to stay close to target values, a robust design of the product, and thereby the process, is achieved.

Taguchi advocates a three-stage design operation to determine the nominal values and tolerances for relevant parameters in the product and the process: system design, parameter design, and tolerance design. In *system design,* scientific and engineering principles along with experience are used to create a prototype of the product that will meet the functional requirements and also to create the process that will build it.

Parameter design involves finding the optimal settings of the product and process parameters in order to minimize performance variability. Taguchi defines a performance measure known as the *signal-to-noise (S/N) ratio* and tries to select the parameter levels that maximize this ratio. The term *signal* represents the square of the mean value of the quality characteristic, whereas noise is a measure of the variability (as measured by the variance) of the characteristic. The S/N ratio will be discussed in greater detail later.

As previously mentioned, the uncontrollable factors are known as *noise factors.* They cause a quality characteristic to deviate from the target value and hence create a quality loss. In general, noise can be categorized as arising from two types of sources: *internal* and *external.* Internal sources of noise are a result of settings of the product and process parameters. Examples include manufacturing variations and product deterioration over time due to wear and tear. Manufacturing imperfections occur because of the inevitable uncertainties in a manufacturing process. They create product-to-product noise, or variability. External sources of noise are those variables that are external to the product and that affect its performance. Examples include changes in such environmental conditions as humidity, temperature, and dust and variability in human operators that make the product. In the parameter design phase, not all sources of noise can be accounted for because of the lack of knowledge concerning the various factors that affect the product's performance. Moreover, physical restrictions—based on the number of experiments to be performed and the number of factors that may be included in the analysis—also limit the choice of the number of factors. In the parameter design phase, only those sources of noise that are included in the study are termed noise factors. Thus, a judicious choice of noise factors represents those that impact the product's performance. Table 13-1 shows three sources of noise variation (environmental variables, product deterioration, and manufacturing variables) and the various product development stages at which countermeasures may be taken for each. The importance of building quality into the product and process at the design phase can be understood from Table 13-1. Countermeasures against all three sources of variation can be taken at the product design stage. However, as we move downstream to the manufacturing stage, only countermeasures against manufacturing variations can be implemented (through the methods of

TABLE 13-1 Product development stages at which countermeasures can be taken against sources of variation

	Sources of Variation		
Product development stages	Environmental variables	Product deterioration	Manufacturing variations
Product design	✓	✓	✓
Process design	X	X	✓
Manufacturing	X	X	✓

Source: R. N. Kackar (1986), "Taguchi's Quality Philosophy: Analysis and Commentary," *Quality Progress*, Dec. 1986, pp. 21–29.

statistical process control discussed in the preceding chapters).

Some fundamental concepts of the parameter design process, which is the most important segment of the Taguchi approach, are as follows. Whereas the quality-engineering foundations of Taguchi seem to be well accepted, there are criticisms of the statistical aspects of his experimental designs. These criticisms will be discussed later. In parameter design, the quality characteristic that is deemed important and all the possible factors that influence it are selected. Having done so, the intention is to select the settings of the product or process parameters that will reduce the sensitivity of the output characteristic to the uncontrollable sources of variation (that is, the noise factors).

For example, consider the production of collapsible tubes for which the important output characteristic Y is the diameter. One of the controllable factors X found to have an effect on the diameter is the mold pressure. Figure 13-2 shows the relationship between the diameter and the mold pressure. Suppose the target value of the diameter is y_0, which can be achieved by setting the mold pressure at x_0. Any deviation of the mold pressure from x_0 causes a large variability in the diameter. However, if the mold pressure is set at x_1, the variability in the diameter is much less even if noise factors cause the mold pressure to deviate around x_1. One way of achieving the small variability in the desired output diameter is to have an expensive press that has little variability around a set value, say x_0. Alternatively, for an economical solution to achieve the same level of quality, the following strategy could be adopted. The pressure setting of a less expensive press could be kept at x_1, which would yield a small variability in the output diameter in the presence of uncontrollable factors. But the output diameter y_1 is far removed from the target value y_0. To adjust for this difference, we look for other parameters that have a linear effect on the diameter and whose setting can be selected in a cost-efficient manner. Let us assume that one such parameter is the pellet size S, whose effect is shown in Figure 13-3. Since tubes are extruded from pellets, it is possible for the pellet size to have an impact on the tube diameter. The experimenter can control the pellet size to adjust the mean value from y_1 to y_0. Such a parameter is sometimes called an *adjustment factor.* By choosing a pellet size of s_0, the mean diameter can be achieved at the desired target of y_0. Of course, we are assuming that because the relationship between pellet size and diameter is linear, no increase in the variability of the diameter will result when the pellet size is set at s_0. In general, it is much easier to adjust the mean value of a performance characteristic to its target value than to reduce the performance variability. The above example demonstrates the utilization of nonlinear effects of product and process parameters to reduce the variability of the output and thereby dampen the impact of the sources of variation. This is the key to achieving robust

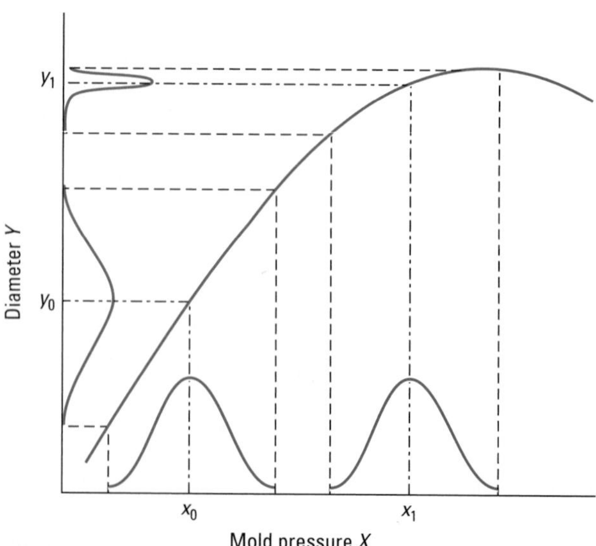

Figure 13-2 Relationship between diameter and mold pressure.

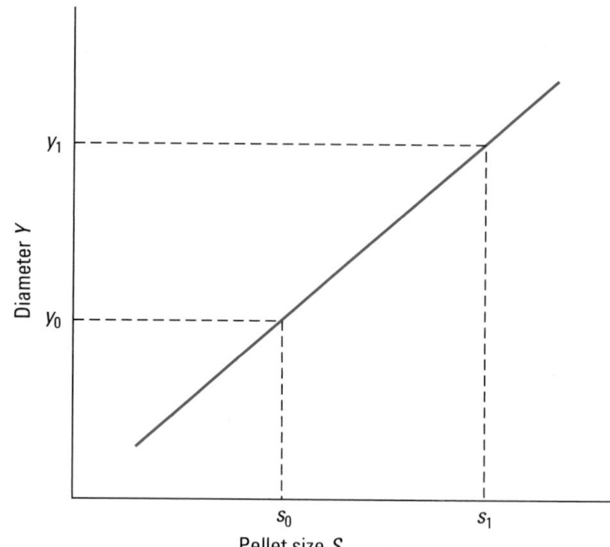

Figure 13-3 Relationship between diameter and pellet size.

designs by using Taguchi methods. These methods are cost-efficient in that they reduce the performance variability by dampening the effects of the factors that we cannot control instead of trying to control or eliminate them.

This example also illustrates the fundamental idea of the *two-step procedure* used in the parameter design phase. In the first step, the levels of the parameters that minimize the variability of the output quality characteristic are chosen. This step makes use of the nonlinear effects of the parameters on the response variable and creates a design that is robust with respect to the uncontrollable sources of variation. In the second step, parameters that have a linear effect on the average value of the response but do not impact variability are identified. These parameters, known as *adjustment factors*, are used to drive the quality characteristic to the target value without increasing the variability.

After the system design and parameter design stages comes the third stage, *tolerance design*. It involves the setting of tolerances, that is, a range of admissible values, around the nominal settings of the control parameters identified in the parameter design phase. This step is used only if the performance variation achieved by the parameter settings identified in the parameter design stage is not acceptable. For instance, in the example concerning the diameter of collapsible tubes, tolerances for the mold pressure could be $x_1 \pm \Delta x_1$, or those for the pellet size could be $s_0 \pm \Delta s_0$, where Δx_1 and Δs_0 represent the permissible variabilities for mold pressure and pellet size, respectively. Tolerances that are too rigid or tight will increase manufacturing costs, and tolerances that are too wide will increase performance variation, which in turn will increase the customer's loss. A trade-off between these two costs must be achieved. Usually, after the parameter design stage is completed and the control parameter settings are adjusted to the selected levels, *confirmation* (or *verification) experiments* are conducted. These experiments reaffirm the degree of improvement that may be realized when the chosen parameter settings are utilized. It is possible that the observed degree of variability of the performance characteristic might be more than what we have in mind. If that is the case, principles of tolerance design may be needed to reduce the variability of the input parameters, which will thereby reduce the output variation. Typical questions at this stage concern the choice of parameters that are to be tightly controlled. One factor would be the cost. In most cases, the cost of tightening the variability of one control factor is not the same as that of others. Here again, given the relationship of the input parameters to the output characteristic (such as shown in Figures 13-2 and 13-3) and knowing the cost of restricting each factor to allowable bounds, a decision may be made concerning the factors for which tolerance levels are to be set.

The next sections present details of some of the concepts associated with the Taguchi method. In particular, the loss function; the parameter design stage, including use of the signal-to-noise ratio; the statistical concepts associated with the experimental designs; and a critique of the Taguchi method are addressed.

13-3 LOSS FUNCTIONS

In the Taguchi philosophy, quality is the loss imparted to society from the time that a product is shipped. The previous section extended this definition to include the loss incurred while the product is being manufactured. The components of loss include the expense, waste, and lost opportunity that result when a product fails to meet the target value exactly. During production, costs such as inspection, scrap, and rework contribute to loss. Although those costs are easy to account for, there are others that are much more difficult to measure, such as the loss associated with customer dissatisfaction that arises from the variation of products and services. Even though profit-increasing measures such as productivity improvement and waste reduction are important, they are bounded by such factors as labor and material costs and technology. On the other hand, real growth in terms of market share is very much influenced by society, which again is dependent on customer satisfaction. Price and quality are critical factors in this context. Any cost incurred by the customer or any loss resulting from poor quality will have a significant negative impact. On the other hand, a satisfied customer who realizes savings from using the product or service will turn it over many times to greatly improve market share. All of these ideas lead to the conclusion that variability is the key concept that relates product quality to dollars by means of a loss function.

Since the quality loss function is stated in financial terms, it provides a common language for various entities within an organization, such as management, engineering, and production. It can also be related to performance measures such as the signal-to-noise ratio, which is used in the parameter design phase. The loss function is assumed to be proportional to the square of the deviation of the quality

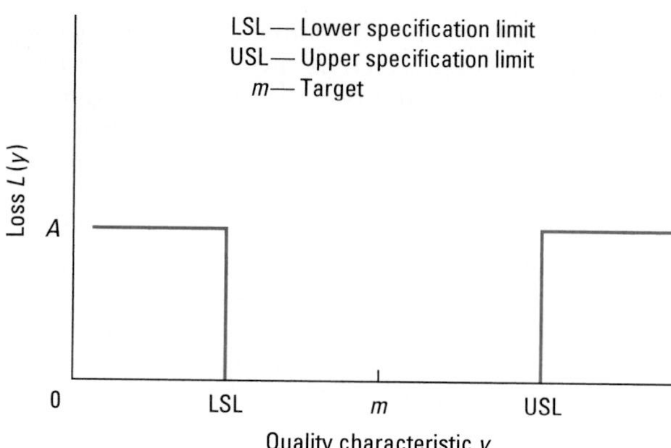

Figure 13-4 Traditional loss function.

characteristic from the target value. The traditional notion of the loss function is that as long as the product's quality characteristic is within certain specification limits or tolerances, no loss is incurred. Outside these specifications, the loss takes the form of a step function with a constant value A. Figure 13-4 shows this traditional loss function. There are drawbacks inherent to this loss function that can possibly be limited to the cost of scrap and rework. Obviously, the function makes no distinction between a product whose characteristic is exactly on target (at m) versus one whose characteristic is just below the USL or just above the LSL. There will be performance differences in these products, but the loss function does not reflect these differences. Furthermore, it is difficult to justify the sudden step increase in loss as the quality characteristic just exceeds the specification limits. Is there a great functional difference between a product with a quality characteristic value of USL$-\delta$ and that with a value of USL$+\delta$, where δ is very small and approaches zero? Most likely, the answer is no. Additionally, it is unreasonable to say that the loss remains constant, at a value A, for all values of the characteristic beyond the specification limits. There will obviously be a significant functional difference between products that are barely above the USL and those that are far above the USL. These differences would cause a performance variation, so the loss to society would be different. The Taguchi loss function overcomes these deficiencies, because the loss increases quadratically with increasing deviation from the target value. The following subsections give expressions for the loss functions based on three situations that may arise in practice: nominal is best, smaller is better, and larger is better.

Nominal Is Best

Consider characteristics for which a target, or nominal, value is appropriate (that is, the nominal value is best). As the quality characteristic deviates from the target value, the loss increases in a quadratic manner. Figure 13-1 is an example of such a loss function. Examples of quality characteristics in this category are product dimensions such as length, thickness, and diameter; a product characteristic such as the viscosity of an oil; and a service characteristic such as the degree of management involvement. The loss function is given by

$$L(y) = k(y - m)^2 \tag{13.1}$$

where k is a proportionality constant, m is the target value, and y is the value of the quality characteristic. Note that when $y = m$, that is, when the value of the quality characteristic is on target, the loss is zero. The constant k can be evaluated if the loss $L(y)$ is known for any particular value of the quality characteristic; it is influenced by the financial importance of the quality characteristic. For instance, if a critical dimension of the braking mechanism in an automobile deviates from a target value, the loss may increase drastically. Figure 13-5 shows three quality loss functions with different degrees of financial importance. The steeper the slope, the more important is the loss function. In Figure 13-5, loss function A is more important than loss functions B and C.

To determine the value of the constant k, suppose the functional tolerance range of the quality charac-

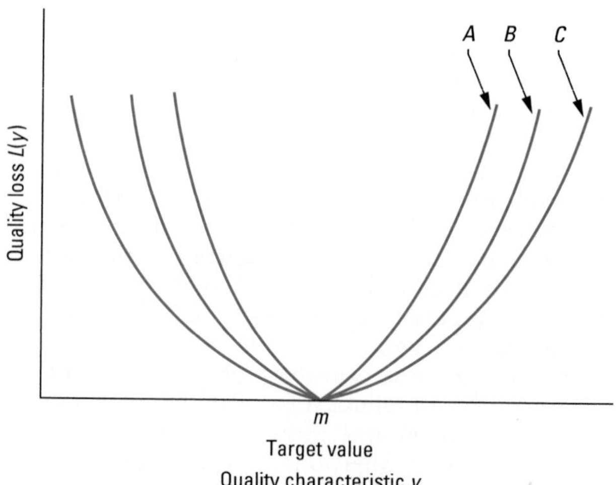

Figure 13-5 Loss functions indicating the degree of financial importance.

teristic is $(m - \Delta, m + \Delta)$, as shown in Figure 13-1. This represents the maximum permissible variation, beyond which the average product does not function satisfactorily. An average customer viewpoint is represented. Suppose the consumer's average loss is A when the quality characteristic is at the limit of the functional tolerance. This loss represents costs to the consumer for repair or replacement of the product, with the associated dissatisfaction. Using Equation 13.1, we find the proportionality constant k as

$$A = k\Delta^2 \qquad \text{or} \qquad k = A/\Delta^2$$

The loss function given by Equation 13.1 can be rewritten as

$$L(y) = (A/\Delta^2)(y - m)^2 \tag{13.2}$$

The expected loss is the mean loss over many instances of the product. The expectation is taken with respect to the distribution of the quality characteristic Y. We have

$$\begin{aligned} E[L(y)] &= E[k(y - m)^2] \\ &= k(\text{variance of } y + \text{ squared bias of } y) \\ &= k[\text{Var}(y) + (\mu - m)^2] \qquad (13.3) \\ &= k(\text{MSD}) \end{aligned}$$

Here, MSD represents the mean square deviation of y and is estimated as

$$\text{MSD} = \left(\sum_{i=1}^{n}(y_i - m)^2\right)/n$$

over a sample of n items. In this expression μ and Var(y) represent the mean and variance of y, respectively. Note that $\text{MSD}(y) = \text{Var}(y) + (\mu - m)^2$; that is, the mean square deviation of a quality characteristic is the sum of the variance of the characteristic and the squared bias. With the objective of minimizing the expected loss, note that if the mean of the characteristic is at the target value m, the mean square deviation is just the variance of the characteristic. As discussed in connection with parameter design, the variance of the response variable may be minimized by appropriately selecting the parameter levels of the controllable factors to minimize the performance variation. Additionally, the levels of the control factors that have a linear relationship with the response variable may be changed to move the average of the response variable to the target value.

It should be pointed out that the form of the distribution of the quality characteristic will influence the expected loss. Figure 13-6 shows two probability distributions of a quality characteristic. Distribution

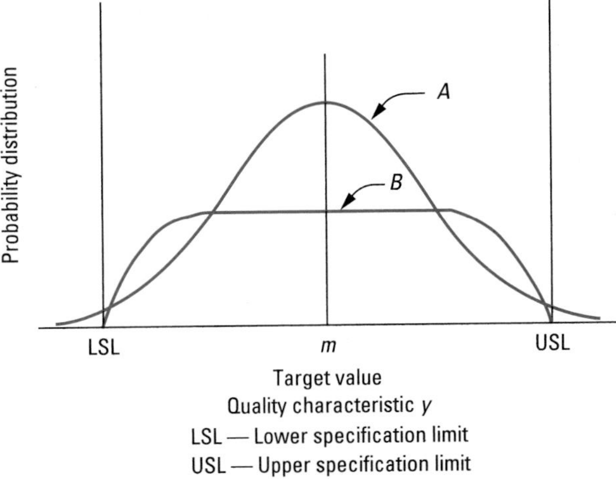

Figure 13-6 Probability distributions of the quality characteristic.

A is a normal distribution with most of the product tightly clustered around the target value. A small fraction of the product lies outside the specification limits. Distribution B, on the other hand, is close to a uniform distribution. The product is uniformly distributed over the range of the specification limits, with none of the product lying outside. According to the traditional view, all of the product related to distribution B will be considered acceptable. However, if we consider the more appropriate quadratic loss function, the expected loss for the product from distribution A will be less than that for distribution B. This is due to the fact that much more of the product from distribution A is close to the target value, resulting in a lower expected loss.

Determination of Manufacturing Tolerances

The importance of realistic tolerances based on customer satisfaction and thereby loss has been stressed previously. The foregoing subsection has demonstrated the computation of the proportionality constant k of the loss function in Equation 13.2. Now suppose the question is, how much should a manufacturer spend to repair a product before shipping it to the customer in order to avoid losses due to the product not meeting customer tolerances? This amount represents the break-even point, in terms of loss, between the manufacturer and the customer. Consider Figure 13-7, which shows the customer tolerance $m \pm \Delta$ and the associated loss A. Figure 13-7 includes the manufacturing tolerance $m \pm \delta$ associated with a cost to the manufacturer. This cost, B, is the cost of repairing an item, prior to shipping that will exceed the customer's tolerance

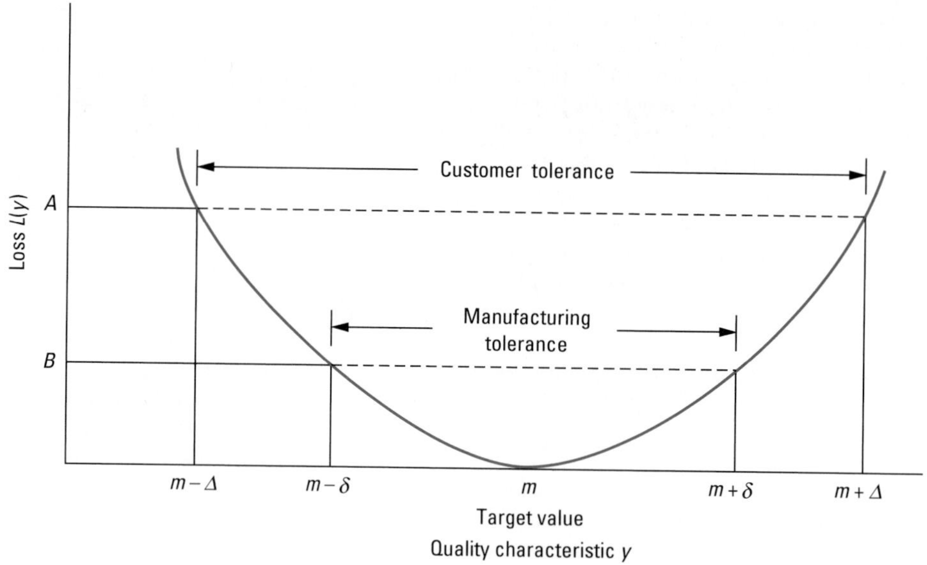

Figure 13-7 Manufacturing tolerance for a situation in which nominal is best.

limits. The idea is that fixing a potential problem prior to shipment will reduce loss in the long run due to wear and tear of the product in its usage. We would like to determine δ.

Based on the fact that the loss is A for customer tolerances of $m \pm \Delta$, the value of the proportionality constant k of the loss function was found to be $k = A/\Delta^2$. The loss function was given by Equation 13.2 as

$$L(y) = (A/\Delta^2)(y - m)^2$$

Now consider the manufacturing tolerance of $m \pm \delta$ and the associated cost B. Using the preceding loss function, we get

$$B = (A/\Delta^2)(\delta^2) \quad \text{or} \quad \delta = (B/A)^{1/2}\Delta \quad (13.4)$$

The manufacturing tolerances may then be found as $m \pm \delta$. As long as the quality characteristic is within δ units of the target value m the manufacturer will not spend any extra money. When the characteristic is at δ units from m, the manufacturer may spend an amount equal to B, on average, to repair the product. As the quality characteristic deviates further from the target value, the customer's loss increases beyond acceptable limits. In the long run, the manufacturer would be wise to spend an amount B in this situation, since the customer's loss would otherwise be much more, thereby increasing the societal loss. The manufacturing tolerances are the limits for shipping the product.

Smaller Is Better

Consider quality characteristics that are nonnegative and for which the ideal value is zero (that is, smaller values are better). Characteristics such as the fuel consumption of an aircraft or automobile, the wear of a bearing, an impurity in water, and the shrinkage of a gasket are examples in this category. Figure 13-8

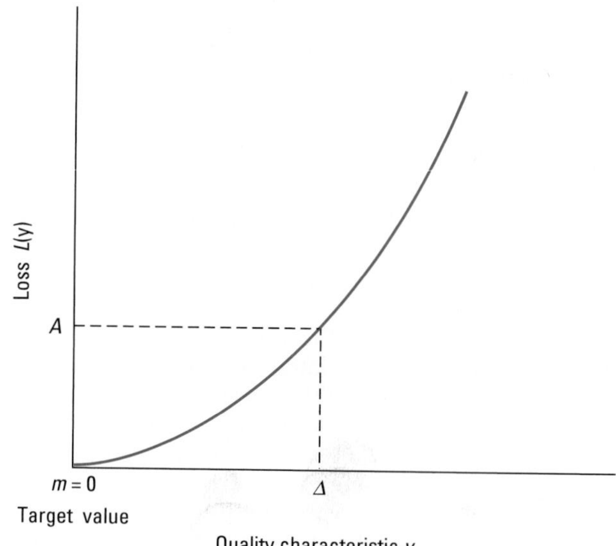

Figure 13-8 Loss function for a situation in which smaller is better.

shows the loss function for this case, which is given by

$$L(y) = ky^2 \qquad (13.5)$$

If the loss caused by exceeding the customer's tolerance level Δ is A, the value of the proportionality constant k in Equation 13.5 is $k = A/\Delta^2$. The expected, or average, loss can be found as before as the expectation with respect to the probability distribution of the quality characteristic. Thus, the expected loss over many produced items is given by

$$\begin{aligned} E[L(y)] &= kE(y^2) \\ &= (A/\Delta^2)E(y^2) \\ &= (A/\Delta^2)[\text{Var}(y) + \mu^2] \qquad (13.6) \\ &= (A/\Delta^2)\text{MSD} \end{aligned}$$

where MSD represents the mean square deviation and is estimated as $(\sum_{i=1}^{n} y_i^2)/n$ for a sample of n items; Var(y) represents the variance of y, and μ is the mean value of y.

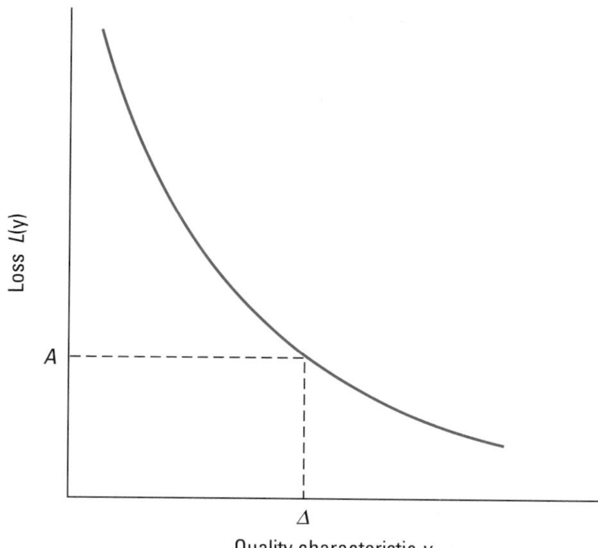

Figure 13-9 Loss function for a situation in which larger is better.

Larger Is Better

Consider quality characteristics that are nonnegative and have an ideal target value that is infinite (that is, larger values are better). Examples are the weld strength in bridge beams, the amount of employee involvement in quality improvement, and the customer acceptance rate of a product. Here, no target value is predetermined. Figure 13-9 shows the loss function for this case, which is given by

$$L(y) = k(1/y^2) \qquad (13.7)$$

If the loss is A when the quality characteristic falls below the customer's tolerance level Δ, the value of the proportionality constant k is given by $k = A\Delta^2$. The expected, or average, loss is given by the expectation with respect to the probability distribution of the quality characteristic. The expected loss is

$$E[L(y)] = kE(1/y^2) = A\Delta^2 E(1/y^2) \qquad (13.8)$$

The quantity $E(1/y^2)$ can be estimated from a sample of n items as

$$\left(\sum_{i=1}^{n} 1/y_i^2\right)/n$$

Example 13-1: The customer tolerances for the height of a steering mechanism are 1.5 ± 0.020 m. For a product that just exceeds these limits, the cost to the consumer for getting it fixed is \$50. Ten products were randomly selected and yielded the following heights (in meters): 1.53, 1.49, 1.50, 1.49, 1.48, 1.52, 1.54, 1.53, 1.51, and 1.52. Find the average loss per unit of the product.

Solution. Note that this is a situation in which nominal is best. The nominal value m is 1.5 meters. The loss function is given by

$$L(y) = k(y - m)^2$$

where y represents the height of the steering mechanism and k is a proportionality constant. Given the information

$$k = A/\Delta^2 = 50/(.02)^2 = 125,000$$

The loss function is

$$L(y) = 125,000(y - 1.5)^2$$

The expected loss per unit is given by

$$E[L(y)] = 125,000E(y - 1.5)^2$$

$E(y - 1.5)^2$ is estimated as follows:

$$\begin{aligned} \left[\sum_{i=1}^{10}(y_i - 1.5)^2\right]/10 &= [(1.53 - 1.5)^2 \\ &\quad + (1.49 - 1.5)^2 + (1.50 - 1.5)^2 \\ &\quad + \cdots + (1.52 - 1.5)^2]/10 \\ &= 0.0049/10 = 0.00049 \end{aligned}$$

Hence, the expected loss per unit is

$$125,000(0.00049) = \$61.25$$

Example 13-2: Consider Example 13-1 concerning the height of a steering mechanism. The manufacturer is considering changing the production process to reduce the variability in the output. The additional cost for the new process is estimated to be \$5.50/unit. The annual production is 20,000 units. Eight units were randomly selected from the new process, yielding the following heights: 1.51, 1.50, 1.49, 1.52, 1.52, 1.50, 1.48, 1.51. Is the new process cost-efficient? If so, what is the annual savings?

Solution. The loss function was found in Example 13-1 to be

$$L(y) = 125,000(y - 1.5)^2$$

For the new process, let us estimate the mean square deviation around the target value of 1.5:

$$\left[\sum_{i=1}^{8}(y_i - 1.5)^2\right]/8 = [(1.51 - 1.5)^2 + (1.50 - 1.5)^2 + \cdots + (1.51 - 1.5)^2]/8 = 0.0015/8 = 0.0001875$$

The expected loss per unit for the new process is

$$125,000(0.0001875) = \$23.44$$

The expected loss per unit for the former process was \$61.25, which represents a savings of \$61.25 − \$23.44 = \$37.81/unit, and the added cost is only \$5.50/unit. Thus, the net savings per unit by using the new process is \$37.81 − \$5.50 = \$32.31, making it cost-efficient.

The net annual savings compared to the former process is 20,000(32.31) = \$646,200.

Example 13-3: Consider Example 13-1 concerning the height of a steering mechanism. Suppose the manufacturer can rework the height, prior to shipping the product, at a cost of \$3.00 per unit. What should be the manufacturer's tolerance?

Solution. The loss function in Example 13-1 was found to be

$$L(y) = 125,000(y - 1.5)^2$$

Let the manufacturer's tolerance be given by $1.5 \pm \delta$. We have

$$3 = 125,000(\delta^2) \qquad \text{or} \qquad \delta = (3/125,000)^{1/2} = 0.0049$$

Thus, the manufacturer's tolerance is 1.5 ± 0.0049. For products with a height that equals or exceeds these limits, the manufacturer should rework the units at the added cost of \$3.00 per unit to provide cost savings in the long run. Otherwise, these units will incur a loss to the consumer at a rate of \$50 per unit.

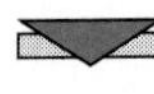

13-4 SIGNAL-TO-NOISE RATIO AND PERFORMANCE MEASURES

In determining the effectiveness of a design, we must develop a measure that can evaluate the impact of the design parameters on the output quality characteristic. An acceptable performance measure of the output characteristic should incorporate both the desirable and undesirable aspects of performance. The term *signal,* or average value of the characteristic, represents the desirable component, which will preferably be close to a specified target value. The term *noise* represents the undesirable component and is a measure of the variability of the output characteristic, which will preferably be as small as possible. Taguchi has combined these two components into one metric known as the *signal-to-noise (S/N) ratio.* Mathematical expressions for the S/N ratio are dependent on the three situations previously discussed (nominal is best, smaller is better, and larger is better). A performance measure should have the property that when it is maximized, the expected loss will be minimized.

Nominal Is Best

As previously seen in Equation 13.3, the expected loss associated with the output characteristic is given by

$$E[L(y)] = k[\text{Var}(y) + (\mu - m)^2] = k(\text{variance of } y + \text{ squared bias of } y)$$

where μ represents the mean value of y [$\mu = E(y)$] and m is the target value. It is preferable for the output characteristic to be on target and at the same time for the variance to be as small as possible. The following paragraphs consider two subcases.

Variance Not Related to the Mean Note that the response variable Y is influenced by the settings of the product and process parameters $(x_1, x_2, \cdots, x_p)$. The intention of the Taguchi method is to determine the parameter settings that will optimize the performance measure associated with Y. In certain situations, the mean and the variance are functionally independent of each other. This means that there are certain parameters known as *adjustment parameters,* whose levels can be adjusted to change the average output characteristic level without influencing the variability in performance. The adjustment parameter levels can therefore be set to a value such that the mean output is on target, making the bias equal to zero, without affecting the variability.

In this situation, the main concern is to reduce the variance of the output characteristic. A possible performance measure is given by

$$\xi = -\log(\text{variance of } y)$$

an estimate of which is the *performance statistic* given by

$$Z = -\log(s^2) \tag{13.9}$$

where s^2 is the sample variance of y and is obtained as

$$s^2 = \left[\sum_{i=1}^{n}(y_i - \bar{y})^2\right] / (n-1)$$

for a sample of size n where $\bar{y}$ represents the sample mean of the y_i. Observe that the larger the performance statistic Z, the smaller is the variability. The performance statistic given by Equation 13.9 is not a Taguchi performance statistic. One of the advantages of this performance statistic is that the logarithmic transformation on the data often reduces the dependence of the sample variance s^2 on the sample mean $\bar{y}$, thus satisfying the assumption that the variance is not related to the mean.

Variance Related to the Mean Here it is assumed that the standard deviation of the output characteristic is linearly proportional to the mean and that the bias can be reduced independently of the coefficient of variation, which is the ratio of the standard deviation to the mean. Thus, knowledge of the standard deviation by itself may not provide a measure of goodness of performance. For instance, suppose the standard deviation of a part length is 1 mm. Is this a superior process? We cannot tell. However, if we know the mean length, then we are of course in a position to make a judgment. A mean length of 15 mm might not reflect a good process, whereas a mean length of 100 mm might. The ratio of the mean to the standard deviation could be a good performance measure. Actually, the signal-to-noise measure proposed by Taguchi is proportional to the square of the ratio of the mean to the standard deviation. An objective would be to maximize this ratio.

Consider an example in which one of three alternate designs must be selected. Figure 13-10 shows the levels of the mean and standard deviation of the output quality characteristic for the three designs (indicated by points 1, 2, and 3), as well as the target value m. Considering only the standard deviation, we might be tempted to prefer design 1, which has the smallest standard deviation of the three designs. However, it is offset from the target value of m. So, if an adjustment parameter is identified, its setting can be changed to alter the mean of the output to the target value. In the process of changing the mean to the target value, the standard deviation of the output variable will increase linearly. The point indicated by $1'$ in Figure 13-10 represents the adjusted mean and standard deviation. Similarly, for design 3 a downward adjustment in the mean value could be made, corresponding to a reduction in the standard deviation. The adjusted design point is represented by $3'$. For design point 2, whose mean is at the target value, no adjustment is necessary. Comparing the three design points whose means are at the target value, the preferred design is indicated by point $3'$ because it has the smallest standard deviation. Therefore, design point 3 should be selected because it maximizes the performance measure, which is the ratio of the mean to the standard deviation. Even after adjustment of the mean to the target value, this design point would still have the maximum value of the performance measure, if the assumption that the ratio of the mean value to the standard deviation is constant is satisfied.

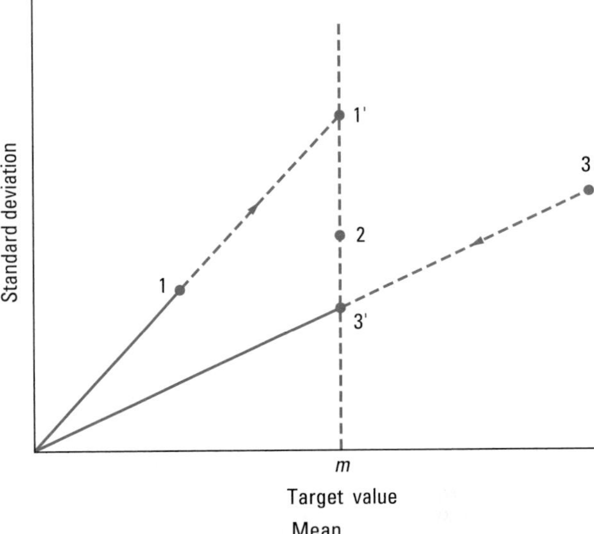

Figure 13-10 Mean and standard deviation of output characteristic for three designs.

The Taguchi method of parameter design involves trying to identify adjustment parameters and their ranges for which the S/N ratio (which is proportional to the ratio of the mean to the standard

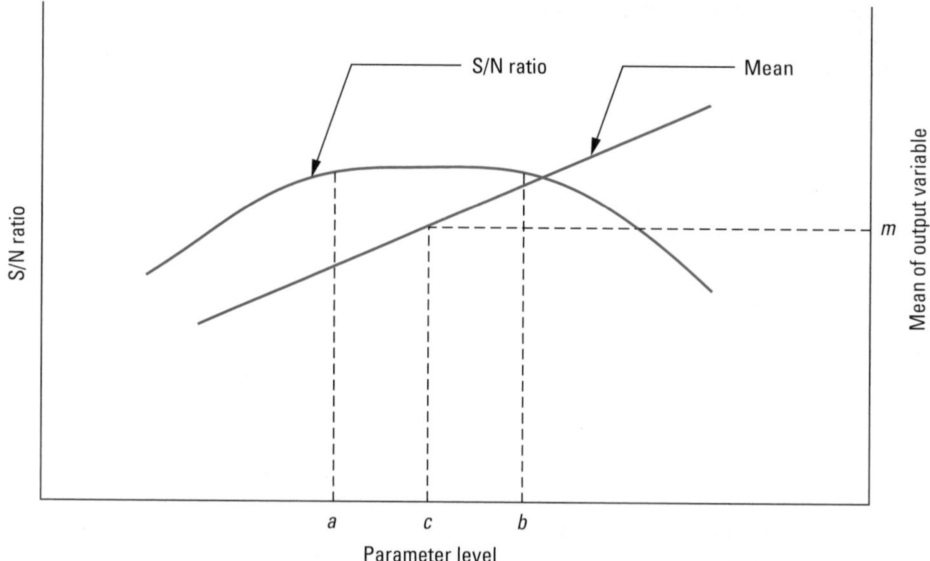

Figure 13-11 Effect of a parameter setting on the S/N ratio and the mean of the output characteristic.

deviation) is constant. Figure 13-11 shows one such parameter and its levels for which the S/N ratio is nearly constant. Within the range of (a, b) the S/N ratio is almost constant. Figure 13-11 shows the linear effect of a change in the mean as the level of the parameter is varied. Thus, we can change the parameter setting to the level c in order to adjust the mean to the target value m. In doing so, we expect that the new standard deviation after adjustment will remain at a minimum, if, in fact, it were minimum before adjustment of the mean, since the S/N ratio is assumed to be constant. This represents the fundamental principle of Taguchi's two-step procedure for the parameter design phase. In step one, the parameter settings for which the variability of the output characteristic is minimized are identified. In step two, adjustment factors that can be used to shift the mean of the output characteristic to the target value (assuming that the variability will not be increased) are identified.

Taguchi's signal-to-noise ratio for this case is given by

$$\xi = \frac{\mu^2}{\sigma^2}$$

where μ and σ represent the mean and standard deviation of the output characteristic y, respectively. A related performance statistic is

$$Z = 10 \log\left(\frac{\bar{y}^2}{s^2}\right) \tag{13.10}$$

where $\bar{y}$ and s denote the sample mean and sample standard deviation of the output characteristic y respectively. This statistic is maximized in the parameter design stage, and the associated parameter levels are determined.

Smaller Is Better

The loss function in the case for which smaller values are better is given by Equation 13.5, and the expected loss is represented by Equation 13.6. Since these characteristics have an ideal target value of zero, they can be considered as noise themselves. The performance measure is the mean square deviation from zero; a performance statistic which should be maximized in the parameter design stage, is given by

$$Z = -10 \log\left(\sum_{i=1}^{n} y_i^2/n\right) \tag{13.11}$$

In some instances, a characteristic for which a smaller value is better might be incorporated into another characteristic in the experimental design and analysis phase. For instance, the surface roughness on a bearing might be a smaller-is-better characteristic by itself, but it could be treated as a noise variable in a design for which the output characteristic is the diameter of the bearing, which is a nominal-is-best characteristic.

Larger Is Better

Note that the larger-is-better case is merely the inverse of the smaller-is-better case. The loss function is given by Equation 13.7, and the expected loss is represented by Equation 13.8. A performance statistic is given by

$$Z = -10\log\left[\left(\sum_{i=1}^{n} 1/y_i^2\right)/n\right] \qquad (13.12)$$

The goal is to determine the parameter settings that will maximize this performance statistic.

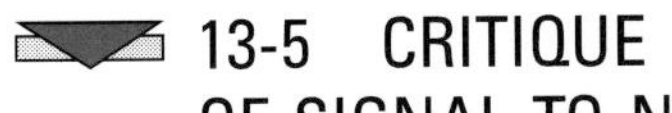

13-5 CRITIQUE OF SIGNAL-TO-NOISE RATIOS

To minimize expected loss, a good performance measure should incorporate engineering and statistical knowledge about the product and the process. Taguchi has proposed more than 60 signal-to-noise ratios, for use in particular applications. Three such ratios are given by Equations 13.10, 13.11, and 13.12; Taguchi advocates maximizing these ratios in experimental analysis, as a means of minimizing variability. If variability in fact is minimized, the design is robust, and one of the major goals of Taguchi's philosophy of quality engineering is met.

There has been some criticism of Taguchi's signal-to-noise ratios. Consider the ratio for the nominal-is-best case given in Equation 13.10 as

$$Z = 10\log\left(\frac{\bar{y}^2}{s^2}\right)$$

This can be rewritten as

$$Z = 10\log(\bar{y}^2) - 10\log(s^2)$$

Thus, maximizing the performance statistic Z can be achieved either through a large positive or negative value of the mean $\bar{y}$ or by a small value of the sample variance s^2 or both. Taguchi's S/N ratio measures the simultaneous effect of factors on the mean response and the variability. If our objective is to reduce variability (as in the first step of Taguchi's two-step parameter design approach), there is no guarantee that maximizing Taguchi's S/N ratio will achieve it. It is not clear that the transformation $10\log(\bar{y}^2/s^2)$ separates the dispersion and location effects; hence, Taguchi's two-step parameter design approach is not fully justifiable on theoretical grounds.

Additionally, if Taguchi's S/N ratio is maximized, it is assumed that having a unit increase in $\log(\bar{y}^2)$ and having a unit decrease in $\log(s^2)$ are equally desirable. This assumption may not be justified in all circumstances. In certain situations, a reduction of variability could overshadow the closeness to the target value.

One recommendation is to minimize $\log(s^2)$ or to maximize $-\log(s^2)$ in the first step of the parameter design phase. This performance measure was given in Equation 13.9, which is not really an S/N ratio since it does not involve any signal. If the mean and variability can be isolated, then the performance measure $\log(s^2)$ can be minimized in the first step to choose appropriate parameter settings. In the next step, the performance measure could be the sample mean $\bar{y}$, which would be used to determine the settings of the adjustment factors such that the mean response is close to the target value. Such an approach provides a better understanding of the process in terms of factors that influence process variability.

Hunter (1985) points out that one way to maximize the S/N ratio $10\log(\bar{y}^2/s^2)$ is to take the logarithm of all of the y values and then identify the factor level settings that minimize the value of s^2. Box (1986) argues that this S/N ratio can be justified if a logarithmic transformation is needed to make the average and variance independent as well as to satisfy other assumptions such as normality of the error distribution and constancy of the error variance. If s^2 or a function of it, such as $\log(s^2)$, is to be used as a performance statistic in the first step, it is preferable for the variance to be unrelated to the mean, because the mean is adjusted in the second step.

The S/N ratios for the smaller-is-better and larger-is-better cases have similar disadvantages. In some simulation studies (Schmidt and Boudot, 1989), it has been demonstrated that the S/N ratios given by Equations 13.11 and 13.12 may not be effective in identifying dispersion effects, but they might reveal, location effects that are due to the mean. The S/N ratio given by Equation 13.11 can be shown to be a function of the mean and the variance because

$$\sum_{i=1}^{n} y_i^2/n = \bar{y}^2 + \frac{(n-1)}{n}s^2$$

Thus, the location and dispersion effects are confounded in the S/N ratio.

An alternative measure designed to overcome some of the above drawbacks of Taguchi's S/N ratio has been proposed in Leon, Shoemaker, and Kackar (1987). The study recommends a performance measure that is independent of adjustment known as PERMIA. It involves a two-step procedure as suggested by Taguchi. In the first step, PERMIA is used instead of the S/N ratio to determine the parameter settings of the nonadjustment factors. The selection of the appropriate response variable at this stage is important because this response variable should not depend on the values of the adjustment factors. The second step is similar to Taguchi's, in that levels of the adjustment factors are determined in order to drive the mean response toward the target value.

13-6 EXPERIMENTAL DESIGN IN THE TAGUCHI METHOD

At the core of product and process design is the concept of experimental design. This concept guides us in selecting combinations of the various factor levels at which experiments are conducted to determine the output characteristic and thereby calculate the performance statistic. The matrix that designates the settings of the controllable factors for each run, or experiment, is called an inner array by Taguchi; the matrix that designates the setting of the uncontrollable or noise factors is called an outer array. Each run consists of a setting of the controllable, or design, parameters and an associated setting of the noise factors. The inner and outer arrays may be designated as the design matrix and noise matrix, respectively.

For design factors that are quantitative, three levels of the factor are necessary to estimate the quadratic (or nonlinear) effect, if any. If only two levels of a factor are tested, then only its linear effects on the response variable can be estimated. This principle is demonstrated in Figure 13-12. If factor levels 1 and 3 are chosen, the estimated response function will be linear and will fail to identify any nonlinearities in the response function. On the other hand, if the factor levels 1, 2, and 3 are selected, the estimated response function demonstrates the nonlinear (in this case, quadratic) nature of the output variable with respect to the factor level. One disadvantage of selecting three levels for each design factor is that the number of experiments to be performed increases, which in turn increases the cost of design.

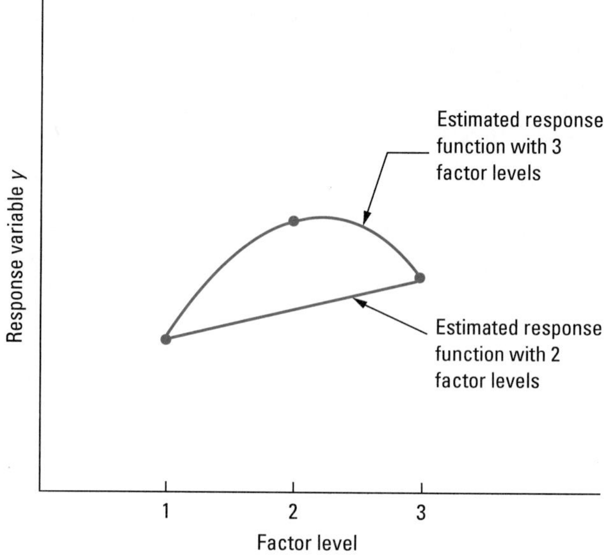

Figure 13-12 Factor levels necessary for estimation of quadratic effect on response.

Orthogonal Arrays and Linear Graphs

Once the design and noise factors as well as their number of settings have been selected, a series of experiments is run to determine the optimum settings of the design parameters. The procedure used is the two-step approach described previously as the parameter design phase of the Taguchi method. Rather than run experiments at all possible combinations of design and noise factor levels, Taguchi relies on running only a portion of the total number of possible experiments, using the concept of an *orthogonal array*. The intent is to concentrate on the vital few rather than the trivial many within the confines of engineering and cost constraints. An orthogonal array represents a matrix of numbers. Each row represents the levels, or states, of the chosen factors, and each column represents a specific factor whose effects on the response variable are of interest. Orthogonal arrays have the property that every factor setting occurs the same number of times for every test setting of all other factors. This has the advantage of allowing a balanced comparison to be made among factor levels under a variety of conditions as determined by levels of the other factors. In addition, any two columns of an orthogonal array form a two-factor complete factorial design. Using an orthogonal array has the advantage of minimizing the number of runs while retaining the pairwise balancing property.

Orthogonal arrays are generalized versions of *Latin square designs.* We have seen that, in a Latin square design, a blocking of two factors is accomplished. A *Graeco-Latin square design* blocks in three factors. The concept of blocking in more than three factors may be conducted through a generalized Graeco-Latin square design, of which orthogonal arrays are a subset. In fact, all common fractional factorial designs are orthogonal arrays. Several methods for constructing orthogonal arrays are provided in Raghavarao (1971). Taguchi (1980, 1986, 1987) recommends the use of orthogonal arrays for the inner array (the setting of design factors) and the outer array (the setting of noise factors).

Taguchi also developed *linear graphs* associated with the orthogonal arrays. Such graphs show the assignment of factors to the columns of the orthogonal array and help in their design and use. They aid in the consideration of interactions between factors. Table 13-2 shows a few orthogonal arrays and their associated linear graphs. The notation used in the table is as follows. The orthogonal array represented by the L_4 design is a half-replicate of a 2^3 full factorial experiment, in which three factors, each at two levels, can be considered. In the L_4 design, four

TABLE 13-2 Orthogonal arrays and associated linear graphs

Symbol	Group	Degree of difficulty
○	1	Easy
◎	2	Moderately easy
⊙	3	Fairly difficult
●	4	Difficult

Legend for nodes of linear graphs

L_4 (2^3) Series

Experiment number	Factor 1	2	3
1	1	1	1
2	1	2	2
3	2	1	2
4	2	2	1
	Group 1	Group 2	

1 3 2

Linear graph for L_4 table

Source: G. Taguchi (1987), *System of Experimental Design—Engineering Methods to Optimize Quality and Minimize Costs,* Vol. 2. Reprinted by permission of American Supplier Institute, Inc. of Dearborn, Michigan (U.S.A).

TABLE 13-2 *(Continued)* L_8 (2^7) Series

Experiment number	Factor 1	2	3	4	5	6	7
1	1	1	1	1	1	1	1
2	1	1	1	2	2	2	2
3	1	2	2	1	1	2	2
4	1	2	2	2	2	1	1
5	2	1	2	1	2	1	2
6	2	1	2	2	1	2	1
7	2	2	1	1	2	2	1
8	2	2	1	2	1	1	2
	Group 1	Group 2		Group 3			

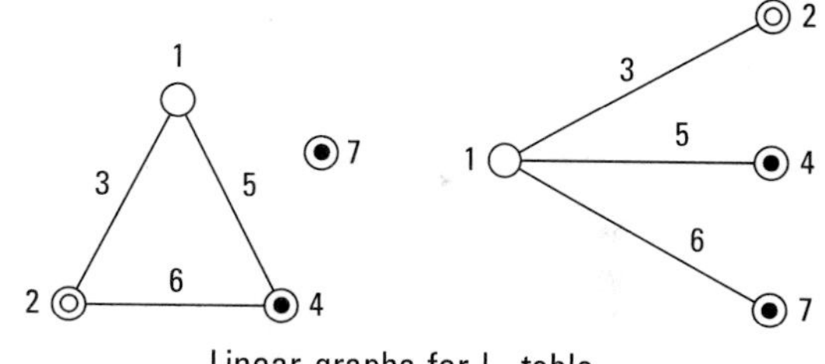

Linear graphs for L_8 table

L_9 (3^4) Series

Experiment number	Factor 1	2	3	4
1	1	1	1	1
2	1	2	2	2
3	1	3	3	3
4	2	1	2	3
5	2	2	3	1
6	2	3	1	2
7	3	1	3	2
8	3	2	1	3
9	3	3	2	1
	Group 1	Group 2		

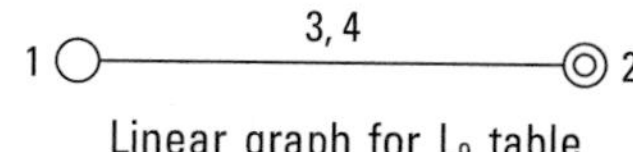

Linear graph for L_9 table

TABLE 13-2 *(Continued)* L_{16} (2^{15}) Series

Experiment number	Factor 1	2	3	4	5	6	7	8	9	10	11	12	13	14	15
1	1	1	1	1	1	1	1	1	1	1	1	1	1	1	1
2	1	1	1	1	1	1	1	2	2	2	2	2	2	2	2
3	1	1	1	2	2	2	2	1	1	1	1	2	2	2	2
4	1	1	1	2	2	2	2	2	2	2	2	1	1	1	1
5	1	2	2	1	1	2	2	1	1	2	2	1	1	2	2
6	1	2	2	1	1	2	2	2	2	1	1	2	2	1	1
7	1	2	2	2	2	1	1	1	1	2	2	2	2	1	1
8	1	2	2	2	2	1	1	2	2	1	1	1	1	2	2
9	2	1	2	1	2	1	2	1	2	1	2	1	2	1	2
10	2	1	2	1	2	1	2	2	1	2	1	2	1	2	1
11	2	1	2	2	1	2	1	1	2	1	2	2	1	2	1
12	2	1	2	2	1	2	1	2	1	2	1	1	2	1	2
13	2	2	1	1	2	2	1	1	2	2	1	1	2	2	1
14	2	2	1	1	2	2	1	2	1	1	2	2	1	1	2
15	2	2	1	2	1	1	2	1	2	2	1	2	1	1	2
16	2	2	1	2	1	1	2	2	1	1	2	1	2	2	1
Groups	1	2		3				4							

Linear graphs for L_{16} table

L_{18} $(2^1 \times 3^7)$ Series

Experiment number	Factor 1	2	3	4	5	6	7	8
1	1	1	1	1	1	1	1	1
2	1	1	2	2	2	2	2	2
3	1	1	3	3	3	3	3	3
4	1	2	1	1	2	2	3	3
5	1	2	2	2	3	3	1	1
6	1	2	3	3	1	1	2	2
7	1	3	1	2	1	3	2	3
8	1	3	2	3	2	1	3	1
9	1	3	3	1	3	2	1	2
10	2	1	1	3	3	2	2	1
11	2	1	2	1	1	3	3	2
12	2	1	3	2	2	1	1	3
13	2	2	1	2	3	1	3	2
14	2	2	2	3	1	2	1	3
15	2	2	3	1	2	3	2	1
16	2	3	1	3	2	3	1	2
17	2	3	2	1	3	1	2	3
18	2	3	3	2	1	2	3	1
Groups	1	2			3			

Linear graph for L_{18} table

TABLE 13-2 *(Continued)* L_{27} (3^{13}) Series

Experiment number	Factor 1	2	3	4	5	6	7	8	9	10	11	12	13
1	1	1	1	1	1	1	1	1	1	1	1	1	1
2	1	1	1	1	2	2	2	2	2	2	2	2	2
3	1	1	1	1	3	3	3	3	3	3	3	3	3
4	1	2	2	2	1	1	1	2	2	2	3	3	3
5	1	2	2	2	2	2	2	3	3	3	1	1	1
6	1	2	2	2	3	3	3	1	1	1	2	2	2
7	1	3	3	3	1	1	1	3	3	3	2	2	2
8	1	3	3	3	2	2	2	1	1	1	3	3	3
9	1	3	3	3	3	3	3	2	2	2	1	1	1
10	2	1	2	3	1	2	3	1	2	3	1	2	3
11	2	1	2	3	2	3	1	2	3	1	2	3	1
12	2	1	2	3	3	1	2	3	1	2	3	1	2
13	2	2	3	1	1	2	3	2	3	1	3	1	2
14	2	2	3	1	2	3	1	3	1	2	1	2	3
15	2	2	3	1	3	1	2	1	2	3	2	3	1
16	2	3	1	2	1	2	3	3	1	2	2	3	1
17	2	3	1	2	2	3	1	1	2	3	3	1	2
18	2	3	1	2	3	1	2	2	3	1	1	2	3
19	3	1	3	2	1	3	2	1	3	2	1	3	2
20	3	1	3	2	2	1	3	2	1	3	2	1	3
21	3	1	3	2	3	2	1	3	2	1	3	2	1
22	3	2	1	3	1	3	2	2	1	3	3	2	1
23	3	2	1	3	2	1	3	3	2	1	1	3	2
24	3	2	1	3	3	2	1	1	3	2	2	1	3
25	3	3	2	1	1	3	2	3	2	1	2	1	3
26	3	3	2	1	2	1	3	1	3	2	3	2	1
27	3	3	2	1	3	2	1	2	1	3	1	3	2
Groups	1	2			3								

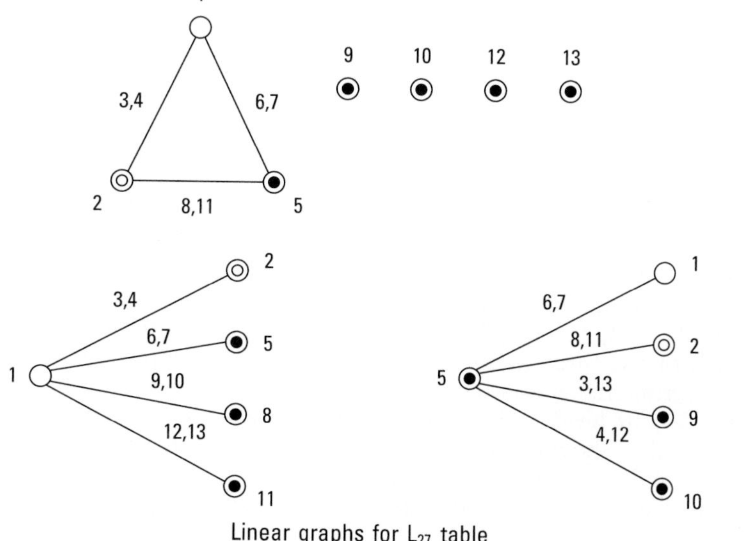

Linear graphs for L_{27} table

TABLE 13-2 *(Continued)* L_{32} ($2^1 \times 4^9$) Series

Experiment number	Factor 1	2	3	4	5	6	7	8	9	10
1	1	1	1	1	1	1	1	1	1	1
2	1	1	2	2	2	2	2	2	2	2
3	1	1	3	3	3	3	3	3	3	3
4	1	1	4	4	4	4	4	4	4	4
5	1	2	1	1	2	2	3	3	4	4
6	1	2	2	2	1	1	4	4	3	3
7	1	2	3	3	4	4	1	1	2	2
8	1	2	4	4	3	3	2	2	1	1
9	1	3	1	2	3	4	1	2	3	4
10	1	3	2	1	4	3	2	1	4	3
11	1	3	3	4	1	2	3	4	1	2
12	1	3	4	3	2	1	4	3	2	1
13	1	4	1	2	4	3	3	4	2	1
14	1	4	2	1	3	4	4	3	1	2
15	1	4	3	4	2	1	1	2	4	3
16	1	4	4	3	1	2	2	1	3	4
17	2	1	1	4	1	4	2	3	2	3
18	2	1	2	3	2	3	1	4	1	4
19	2	1	3	2	3	2	4	1	4	1
20	2	1	4	1	4	1	3	2	3	2
21	2	2	1	4	2	3	4	1	3	2
22	2	2	2	3	1	4	3	2	4	1
23	2	2	3	2	4	1	2	3	1	4
24	2	2	4	1	3	2	1	4	2	3
25	2	3	1	3	3	1	2	4	4	2
26	2	3	2	4	4	2	1	3	3	1
27	2	3	3	1	1	3	4	2	2	4
28	2	3	4	2	2	4	3	1	1	3
29	2	4	1	3	4	2	4	2	1	3
30	2	4	2	4	3	1	3	1	2	4
31	2	4	3	1	2	4	2	4	3	1
32	2	4	4	2	1	3	1	3	4	2
Groups	1	2	3							

1 2

Linear graph for L_{32} table

TABLE 13-2 *(Continued)* L_{16} (4^5) Series

Experiment number	Factor 1	2	3	4	5
1	1	1	1	1	1
2	1	2	2	2	2
3	1	3	3	3	3
4	1	4	4	4	4
5	2	1	2	3	4
6	2	2	1	4	3
7	2	3	4	1	2
8	2	4	3	2	1
9	3	1	3	4	2
10	3	2	4	3	1
11	3	3	1	2	4
12	3	4	2	1	3
13	4	1	4	2	3
14	4	2	3	1	4
15	4	3	2	4	1
16	4	4	1	3	2
Groups	1	2			

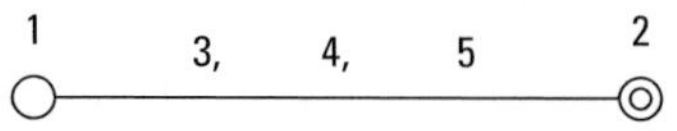

1 3, 4, 5 2

Linear graph for L_{16} table

experiments are conducted (one-half of 2^3, the full factorial experiment). The two levels of each factor are denoted by 1 and 2, respectively. Thus, in the first experiment, each of the three factors is at level 1. In the fourth experiment, factors 1 and 2 are at level 2 and factor 3 is at level 1. The linear graph for the L_4 table is also shown. The graph has two nodes, labeled 1 and 2, respectively, and the arc joining them is labeled as 3. These numbers on the linear graph correspond to the columns of the orthogonal array. This means that if the main effects of two of the factors are to be estimated, they should be placed in columns 1 and 2, respectively, of the orthogonal array. The factor that is assigned to column 3 will represent the interaction effect of the factors assigned to columns 1 and 2. The implication is that such a design will not be able to estimate the main effect of a third separate factor independent of the interaction effects between the first two factors. Alternatively, if we have only two factors and we would like to estimate their main effects and their interaction, then the two factors should be assigned to columns 1 and 2, and their interaction should be assigned to column 3.

The linear graphs shown in Table 13-2 are seen to have different types of points, such as circles, double circles, dots with circles, and completely shaded circles. They represent the degree of difficulty associated with the number of changes that must be made in the level of a factor that is assigned to the corresponding column. Table 13-2 shows such groups (Groups 1 through 4) and the associated difficulty for adjusting the factor levels, ranging from easy to difficult. Consider a situation in which it is either very difficult or expensive to adjust the factor level, in which case it is preferable that the factor level not be changed any more than is necessary. An example might be the octane level of a gasoline; it may not be feasible to change octane levels frequently because a certain minimum quantity must be produced. Alternatively, consider the setting of a pneumatic press, for which the setup time is high. A frequent adjustment of settings would create an unusual amount of downtime, making it cost-ineffective.

Consider the first column of the L_4 design. Note that if the most difficult parameter is placed in column 1 and the experiments are conducted in the order specified in the orthogonal array, then this factor would have to be changed only once. The first two experiments would be conducted at the first level of the parameter, and the last two experiments would be conducted at the second level of the parameter. On the other hand, the factor assigned to column 2 would require three changes. Column 1 has been assigned the "easy" degree of difficulty (group 1) because it corresponds to the fewest number of factor level changes. Columns 2 and 3 are placed in group 2, for which the number of required changes in levels is not as easy as that for column 1.

Similar interpretations hold for the other orthogonal arrays shown in Table 13-2. The factor assigned to column 1 would need a change in its level only once for each level at which it is tested. Factors that are assigned to columns of increasing index would need more setting changes to satisfy the required levels of the orthogonal array. The linear graphs thus provide some guidance to performing experiments in a cost-effective manner. Factors whose levels are difficult or costly to change should be placed in columns with indices as low as possible. Linear graphs also assist in the estimation of interaction effects between factors. Desirable interactions between certain factors should be assigned to appropriate columns in the orthogonal array, as found from the associated linear graph.

The L_8 (2^7) orthogonal array indicates the factor assignment levels for seven factors, each at two levels. This is a fractional replicate of the full factorial experiment that would require a total of 2^7, or 128, experiments. The L_8 orthogonal array needs only 8 experiments, making it cost-effective relative to the full factorial experiment. Note that there are two linear graphs for the L_8 orthogonal array. From either of these two graphs we find that four main effects can be estimated independently of the others, if assigned to columns 1, 2, 4, and 7. If the interaction effect between factors 1 and 2 is desired, it should be assigned to column 3.

The L_9 (3^4) orthogonal array represents the design for which four factors are varied at three levels each. It is a fractional replicate of the full factorial experiment which would need 3^4, or 81, experiments. The linear graph for the L_9 orthogonal array shows that the main effects of two factors can be estimated independently of the others if assigned to columns 1 and 2, respectively. The main effects of the two other factors cannot be estimated independently of the effects of other factors. They will be confounded by the interaction effects between the factors assigned to the first two columns.

Table 13-2 also shows the orthogonal arrays and the associated linear graphs for a few other experiments. The array for the L_{16} (2^{15}) series shows the experimental layout for estimating 15 factors, each at 2 levels. It requires 16 experiments to be conducted. Three linear graphs for the L_{16} array are also shown. The L_{18} $(2^1 \times 3^7)$ array shows the design for one factor at 2 levels and 7 factors at 3 levels each. A total of 8 factors may be used, requiring 18 experiments. The main effects of two factors can be estimated independently of the others if assigned to columns 1 and 2, respectively. Other designs shown are the L_{27} (3^{13}) array for estimating 13 factors each at 3 levels, requiring 27 experiments; the L_{32} $(2^1 \times 4^9)$ array for estimating 10 factors, one factor at 2 levels and 9 others at 4 levels each, requiring a total of 32 experiments; and the L_{16} (4^5) array for estimating 5 factors at 4 levels each, requiring 16 experiments.

Note that all possible interactions between factors cannot be estimated from the orthogonal array; a full factorial experiment would be needed. Taguchi suggests that interactions be ignored during the initial experiments, his rationale being that it is difficult to identify significant interactions without some prior knowledge or experience. If there are unassigned columns in the orthogonal array, then after assigning the factors whose main effects are desirable, those columns may be assigned to the possible interactions.

Example 13-4: A consumer magazine subscription service has four factors, designated by A, B, C, and D, each to be analyzed at two levels. They are also interested in the interactions B × C, B × D, and C × D. Show the experimental design for this case.

Since we have a total of seven factors (including the interactions, which are treated like factors), each at two levels, let us consider the L_8 (2^7) orthogonal array. Using the first linear graph for L_8 shown in Table 13-2, we as-

TABLE 13-3 Allocation of factors to columns in an L_8 orthogonal array

Experiment number	Factor						
	B	C	B×C	D	B×D	C×D	A
1	1	1	1	1	1	1	1
2	1	1	1	2	2	2	2
3	1	2	2	1	1	2	2
4	1	2	2	2	2	1	1
5	2	1	2	1	2	1	2
6	2	1	2	2	1	2	1
7	2	2	1	1	2	2	1
8	2	2	1	2	1	1	2

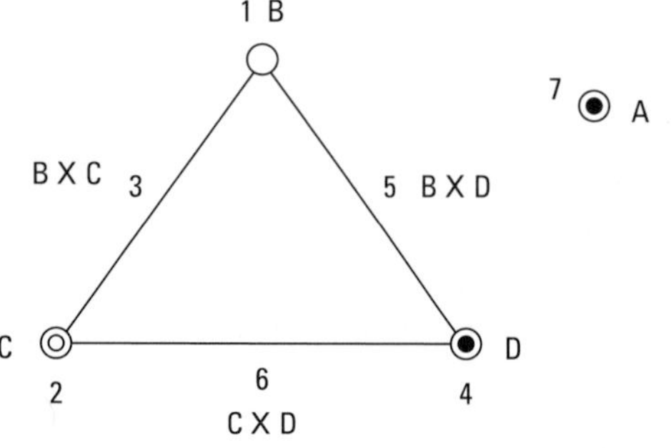

sign the following factors to the corresponding columns: B to column 1, C to column 2, D to column 4, and A to column 7. B×C is assigned to column 3, B×D is assigned to column 5, and C×D is assigned to column 6. The resulting allocation is shown in Table 13-3. Thus, we are able to estimate the desirable effects using the L_8 array.

The linear graphs can also be modified to accommodate estimation of certain interaction effects. In the L_8 orthogonal array, the estimation of seven factor effects is possible. The following example shows an experimental design for which five main effects and two desirable interactions can be estimated.

Example 13-5: The rapid transit authority in a large metropolitan area has identified five factors, A, B, C, D, and E, each to be investigated at two levels. It is also desired to estimate the interactions A×C and A×D. Determine an appropriate experimental design to estimate all of the main effects and the two interactions.

With a total of seven factors to estimate, each at two levels, we consider the L_8 (2^7) orthogonal array and the second associated linear graph shown in Table 13-2. The linear graph shows the assignment of three interaction terms. However, we need to estimate only two interactions. For the interaction that is not used, we can remove the associated two column numbers and treat them as individual points to be assigned to the main effects. The linear graph shown in Table 13-4 shows the approach. Suppose we initially assign factor A to column 1, factor C to column 2, and factor D to column 4. Then, the interaction A×C will be assigned to column 3 and the interaction A×D to column 5. Since we do not need to estimate a third interaction, we remove column numbers 6 and 7 from the original graph and treat them as separate points. We assign the main effects B and E to columns 6 and 7, respectively, as shown in the modified graph. Table 13-4 also shows the final assignment and the experimental design to estimate the required effects.

It is important to be careful, however, when assigning an interaction column to an independent main effect. The interaction effect that would have occurred in that column will still be present and will be confounded with the main effect. For this example, column 6, which originally corresponded to the interaction between the factors assigned to columns 1 and 7, (that is, A×E) will be confounded with B, which has been assigned to that column. Only under the assumption that the interaction between A×E is insignificant can we estimate the effect

TABLE 13-4 Allocation of main effects and interactions to colums in an L_8 orthogonal array through modification of the linear graph

Experiment number	Factor						
	A	C	A×C	D	A×D	B	E
1	1	1	1	1	1	1	1
2	1	1	1	2	2	2	2
3	1	2	2	1	1	2	2
4	1	2	2	2	2	1	1
5	2	1	2	1	2	1	2
6	2	1	2	2	1	2	1
7	2	2	1	1	2	2	1
8	2	2	1	2	1	1	2

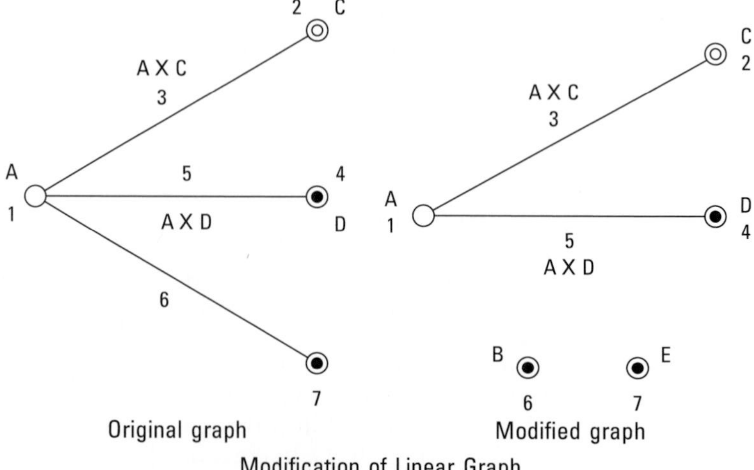

Modification of Linear Graph

of B. As mentioned before, Taguchi recommends verification experiments after the optimal parameter levels have been identified. During these experiments, if the results associated with a main-effect factor that was assigned to an interaction column cannot be repeated, it might be a clue to analyze interaction terms. The whole experiment may have to be reconducted, taking into account the interaction term in the design.

Another feature of linear graphs is their applicability to the construction of *hybrid orthogonal arrays*. It is possible that the number of levels of each factor to be tested may not be the same. For instance, an automobile insurance company may be interested in the impact of several factors—the age of the applicant, the type of work performed, and the number of miles commuted to work on a weekly basis—to determine the applicant's probability of being involved in an accident. Certainly, each of the three factors need not be considered at the same number of levels. For instance, the company might select five age classification groups, three work classification groups, and four mileage classification groups. We need a design to incorporate a different number of levels for the factors to be analyzed. The following example demonstrates such a procedure.

Example 13-6: A commercial bank has identified five factors for study (A, B, C, D, and E) that have an impact on its volume of loans. There are four levels for factor A, and each of the other factors is to be tested at two levels. Determine an appropriate experimental design.

Let us first calculate the number of degrees of freedom associated with the chosen factors. The number of degrees of freedom for each factor is one less than the number of levels. The total number of degrees of freedom associated with an orthogonal array is one less than the number of experiments. The number required for this study is 7 (3 for A and 1 each for B, C, D, and E). The number of degrees of freedom associated with the L_8 orthogonal array is also 7, one less than the total number of experiments. Thus, the L_8 array may be used to select a suitable hybrid design to match our needs.

Each column in the L_8 array can handle a two-level factor, which means that it has 1 degree of freedom. In our study, factor A is to be studied at four levels, needing three degrees of freedom. We need to allocate three columns to factor A, accordingly, after they have been combined appropriately. Factors B, C, D, and E, each with 1 degree of freedom, can be assigned to the remaining four columns. Which three columns should we allocate to A, and how do we combine them? The linear graph is used. We must identify a line in the graph that can be removed without affecting the rest of the design (to the extent possible). Suppose we consider the line segment joining nodes 1 and 2 in the first linear graph for L_8 shown in Table 13-2 (also shown in Table 13-5). Removing the line segment and nodes 1 and 2 also removes node 3. Consider the L_8 array. We sequentially assign values to each unique combination generated by the removed columns, 1, 2, and 3. A new column is created that combines the effects of these three columns. For example, the combination (1, 1, 1) is assigned a level of 1, (1,2,2) is assigned a level of 2, and so on. Table 13-5 shows the assignment of the levels of this new column, which is now assigned to factor A. Note

TABLE 13-5 Creation of a hybrid orthogonal array

Experiment number	A	B	C	D	E
	Factors				
1	1	1	1	1	1
2	1	2	2	2	2
3	2	1	1	2	2
4	2	2	2	1	1
5	3	1	2	1	2
6	3	2	1	2	1
7	4	1	2	2	1
8	4	2	1	1	2

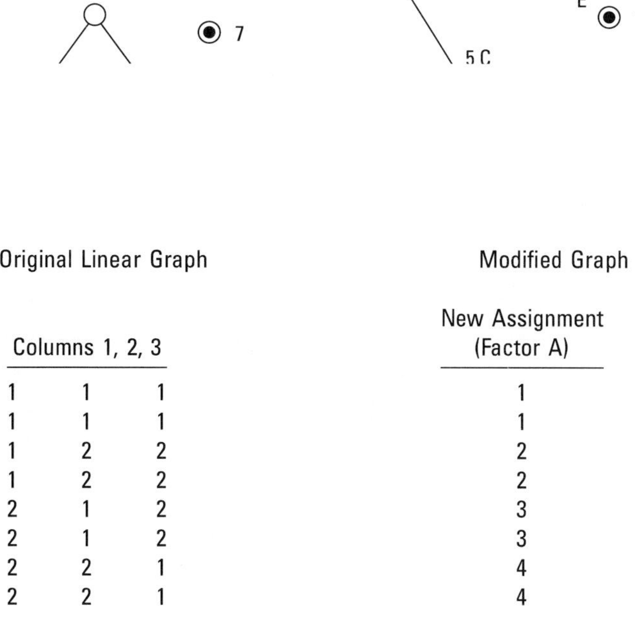

Original Linear Graph

Modified Graph

Columns 1, 2, 3			New Assignment (Factor A)
1	1	1	1
1	1	1	1
1	2	2	2
1	2	2	2
2	1	2	3
2	1	2	3
2	2	1	4
2	2	1	4

that it has four levels. The remaining factors B, C, D, and E are assigned to columns 4, 5, 6, and 7 of the original L_8 orthogonal array. In the hybrid orthogonal design in Table 13-5, note that factor A has four levels, whereas B, C, D, and E, have two levels each.

Remember that interaction effects are assumed to be insignificant in the construction of this design. Thus, since we have assigned factor C to column 5 of the original L_8 array, the interaction between the factors in columns 1 and 4 (in this case A×B) is confounded with the main effect of C. The main effect of factor C can therefore be estimated only under the assumption that the interaction effect A×B is insignificant. Similar conclusions may be drawn for the other factor assignments.

Estimation of Effects

Once the experimental design is selected, the factors are set at the levels indicated by the chosen design, and experiments are conducted to observe the value of the response variable Y. The control factors are placed in an inner array (a selected orthogonal array) and the noise factors in an outer array. The layout of such a design is shown in Table 13-6, in which four control factors A, B, C, and D, each at three levels, are placed in an L_9 inner array, and three noise factors, E, F, and G, each at two levels, are placed in an L_4 outer array. The purpose of including noise factors in the experiment is to determine the levels of the control, or design, factors that are least sensitive to noise. A robust design, which is one of the principal objectives of the Taguchi method, would thus be obtained.

The different combination levels of the noise factors are essentially treated as replications for a given setting of the control factors. In Table 13-6, there are nine settings of the design factors, based on the L_9 orthogonal array. For each of these settings, there are four replications corresponding to the setting of the three noise factors, based on an L_4 orthogonal array. For the example in Table 13-6, there will be a total of 36 experiments to be conducted. For each setting of the design factors, a measure of the mean and variability of the output characteristic can be calculated. For instance, for experimental run 1, where the design factors A, B, C, and D are each at level 1, let the observed value of the response variable at the four different settings of the noise factors be denoted by y_{11}, y_{12}, y_{13}, and y_{14}, respectively. The mean of these four values is denoted by $\bar{y}_1$, and the value of the associated S/N ratio is denoted by Z_1. This computation would be repeated for each of the other experimental runs. The summary values of the mean response and the S/N ratio may then be used in the analysis that occurs in the parameter design phase.

Taguchi recommends analyzing the means and S/N ratios through simple plots and summary measures to keep the analysis simple. Analysis-of-variance procedures described in Chapter 12 on experimental design may also be used to determine significant factor effects (Peterson, 1985; SAS, 1989a, 1989b). However, we will perform only a simple analysis through calculation of averages and plots. First, the main effect of a factor is calculated by determining the average of the response variable over all replications for a given level of the factor. For instance, the mean response when factor A is at level

TABLE 13-6 Experimental layout using an L_9 inner array and an L_4 outer array

				Noise factors (L_4 outer array) E	1	1	2	2		
				F	1	2	1	2		
				G	1	2	2	1		
	Design factors (L_9 inner array)									
Experimental run	A	B	C	D					Mean response, $\bar{y}$	S/N ratio, Z
1	1	1	1	1	y_{11}	y_{12}	y_{13}	y_{14}	$\bar{y}_1$	Z_1
2	1	2	2	2	y_{21}	y_{22}	y_{23}	y_{24}	$\bar{y}_2$	Z_2
3	1	3	3	3	·	·	·	·	·	·
4	2	1	2	3	·	·	·	·	·	·
5	2	2	3	1	·	·	·	·	·	·
6	2	3	1	2	·	·	·	·	·	·
7	3	1	3	2	·	·	·	·	·	·
8	3	2	1	3	·	·	·	·	·	·
9	3	3	2	1	y_{91}	y_{92}	y_{93}	y_{94}	$\bar{y}_9$	Z_9

1 can be found for the example in Table 13-6 as follows:

$$\overline{A}_1 = (\overline{y}_1 + \overline{y}_2 + \overline{y}_3)/3$$

Likewise, the mean responses when factor A is at levels 2 and 3, respectively, are

$$\overline{A}_2 = (\overline{y}_4 + \overline{y}_5 + \overline{y}_6)/3$$
$$\overline{A}_3 = (\overline{y}_7 + \overline{y}_8 + \overline{y}_9)/3$$

In the same manner, the main effects of the other factors at each level can be found. For example, the mean response when factor B is at level 3 is

$$\overline{B}_3 = (\overline{y}_3 + \overline{y}_6 + \overline{y}_9)/3$$

The main effects can be plotted to determine the significance of the factor. In this case the values $\overline{A}_1$, $\overline{A}_2$, and $\overline{A}_3$ would be plotted versus the three levels of factor A. If the plot is close to a horizontal line the implication may be that factor A does not have a significant impact. Figure 13-13 shows various possible effects of factor A on the average response. Figure 13-13*a* depicts a situation for which the factor main effect may not be significant. Any level of the factor produces about the same average response. To aid in selecting the level of factor A, additional criteria such as cost could be used. On the other hand, if the plot resembles a nonlinear function, the region where the curve is flat may be used to select the level of A that will produce minimum variability in the response variable. Figure 13-13*b* demonstrates this situation. To create a design that is robust to the noise factors, one may choose level 2 of factor A, as it will lead to the smallest variability in the average response due to variability in the design factor level.

If factor A has a linear relationship with the average response, as shown in Figure 13-13*c*, it could be used as an adjustment factor in the second step of the parameter design process. An adjustment factor is used to shift the average response toward a target value without influencing its variability. All of the above conclusions relating to the main effect of a factor are based on the assumption that interaction effects between factors are insignificant. If interaction effects are significant, it may not make sense to determine the significance of the main effects independently of each other.

The effects of interaction between factors may also be estimated using a procedure similar to that for the main effects of individual factors. The assumption that the interaction effect has been assigned an appropriate column using the linear graph and the orthogonal array. Consider the L_9 orthogonal array and its associated linear graph. Let us assume that factor C in Table 13-6 represents the interaction between factors A and B. Note that C, which is A×B, is assigned to column 3 of the L_9 array, which is in agreement with the linear graph for the L_9 array. Estimation of the effect of interaction between A and B can be conducted by treating C like any other factor. Thus, the average response when A×B is at level 1 may be found, using Table 13-6, as

$$(\overline{A \times B})_1 = (\overline{y}_1 + \overline{y}_6 + \overline{y}_8)/3$$

The average response at the other levels of A×B are

$$(\overline{A \times B})_2 = (\overline{y}_2 + \overline{y}_4 + \overline{y}_9)/3$$
$$(\overline{A \times B})_3 = (\overline{y}_3 + \overline{y}_5 + \overline{y}_7)/3$$

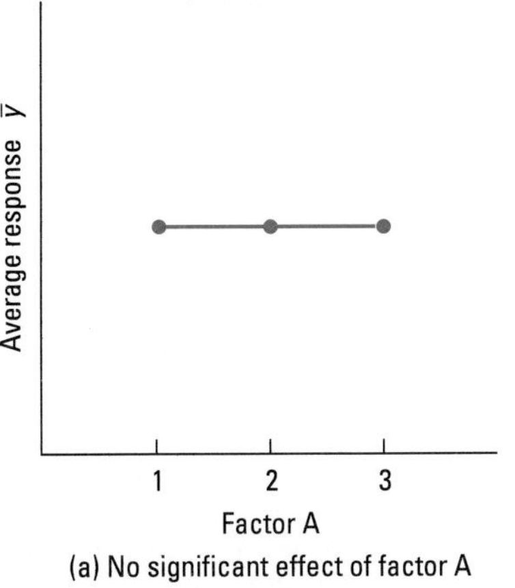

(a) No significant effect of factor A

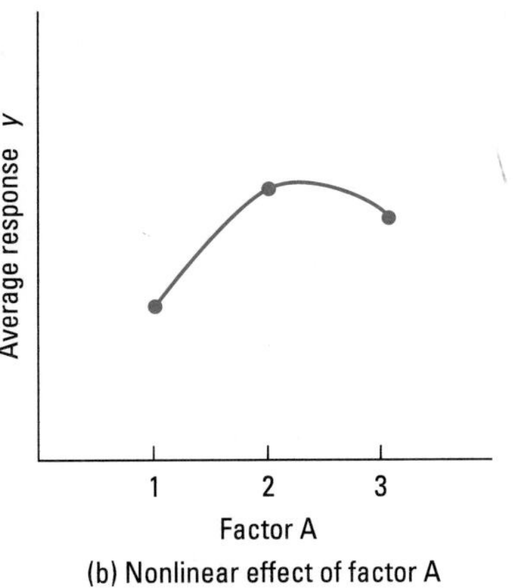

(b) Nonlinear effect of factor A

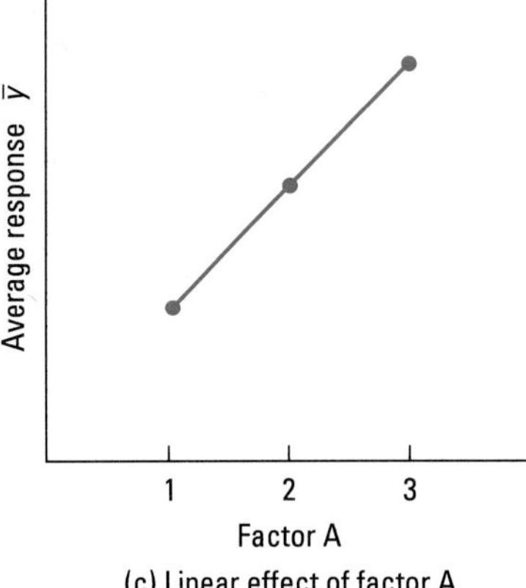

(c) Linear effect of factor A

Figure 13-13 Effect of factor on response variable.

These three averages may be plotted versus the levels of A × B. If the plot is a horizontal line, it implies that the interaction effect between A and B is not significant. In that case we would investigate the main effects of A and B to determine the optimum setting of the factor levels. For significant interaction effects, on the other hand, the optimum level of each factor would be determined based on the joint effect of both.

Example 13-7: Medical research on finding a treatment for lung cancer has been an ongoing process. Various components of a drug have positive and negative effects depending on the amount of the component used. Scientists have identified four independent factors that seem to affect the performance of the resulting drug. Each of the factors can be tested at three levels. Testing is expensive, so determine an experimental design that will test the impact of the above factors in a cost effective manner.

Solution. We have four factors, A, B, C, and D, each at 3 levels, so the L_9 (3^4) orthogonal array is appropriate. This design can test the effects of four factors, each at three levels, in only nine experiments. One assumption, though, will have to be made. Since we have four independent factors whose effects are to be estimated, it will be necessary to assume that the interaction effects between factors are insignificant. For instance, if we consider the linear graph for the L_9 array, the interaction effect between the factors assigned to columns 1 and 2 will be confounded with the main effects of those factors assigned to columns 3 and 4. Suppose our experimental design is to assign the following: A to column 1, B to column 2, C to column 3, and D to column 4. The interaction effect A×B will then be confounded with the main effect of C, which is assigned to column 3. Also, interaction effect A×B will be confounded with the main effect of D, which is assigned to column 4.

Suppose the L_9 orthogonal array is selected and the four factors A, B, C, and D are assigned to columns 1, 2, 3, and 4, respectively. The response variable, measuring the impact of the drug, is recorded on a coded scale for the nine experimental runs. The target value is zero, with the observed coded responses being positive and negative. The experimental design and the values of the coded response variable is shown in Table 13-7. Only one replication is conducted for each setting of the design factors, so the outer array of the noise factors is not shown in Table 13-7. Determine the main effects, and plot the average response curves. What are the optimum settings of the design parameters?

Let us calculate the main effects of each factor at the associated three levels. For factor A, the average responses at levels 1, 2, and 3 are

$$\overline{A}_1 = (-3.5 + 7.3 + 1.8)/3 = 1.867$$

$$\overline{A}_2 = (-4.4 + 9.5 - 6.2)/3 = -0.367$$

$$\overline{A}_3 = (-4.0 + 2.4 - 2.5)/3 = -1.367$$

TABLE 13-7 Coded response for effect of drug due to four factors

Experiment number	Factor A	B	C	D	Coded response
1	1	1	1	1	−3.5
2	1	2	2	2	7.3
3	1	3	3	3	1.8
4	2	1	2	3	−4.4
5	2	2	3	1	9.5
6	2	3	1	2	−6.2
7	3	1	3	2	−4.0
8	3	2	1	3	2.4
9	3	3	2	1	−2.5

For factor B, the average responses at levels 1, 2, and 3 are

$$\overline{B}_1 = (-3.5 - 4.4 - 4.0)/3 = -3.967$$

$$\overline{B}_2 = (7.3 + 9.5 + 2.4)/3 = 6.400$$

$$\overline{B}_3 = (1.8 - 6.2 - 2.5)/3 = -2.300$$

For factor C, the average responses at levels 1, 2, and 3 are

$$\overline{C}_1 = (-3.5 - 6.2 + 2.4)/3 = -2.433$$

$$\overline{C}_2 = (7.3 - 4.4 - 2.5)/3 = 0.133$$

$$\overline{C}_3 = (1.8 + 9.5 - 4.0)/3 = 2.433$$

For factor D, the average response at levels 1, 2, and 3 are

$$\overline{D}_1 = (-3.5 + 9.5 - 2.5)/3 = 1.167$$

$$\overline{D}_2 = (7.3 - 6.2 - 4.0)/3 = -0.967$$

$$\overline{D}_3 = (1.8 - 4.4 + 2.4)/3 = -0.067$$

The average response for each of these factors is plotted versus the factor levels, and the corresponding graphs are shown in Figure 13-14. First, the factors that have a clearly nonlinear impact on the average response are B and D. To minimize the variability in the average response and thus create a robust design, factors B and D should be set at level 2. At these levels, the response curve is approximately flat, making it less sensitive to variations resulting from noise factors. In the second step, to move the average response close to the target value of zero, we manipulate the levels of factors that are linearly related to the average response, thereby not affecting the variability that has been attained in the first step. We find that factors A and C each have a nearly linear relationship with the average response. To move the average response close to the target value of zero, adjustment factors A and C should each be set at level 2. Hence, the optimum settings are factor A at level 2, factor B at level 2, factor C at level 2, and factor D at level 2. In practice, confirmation experiments would be

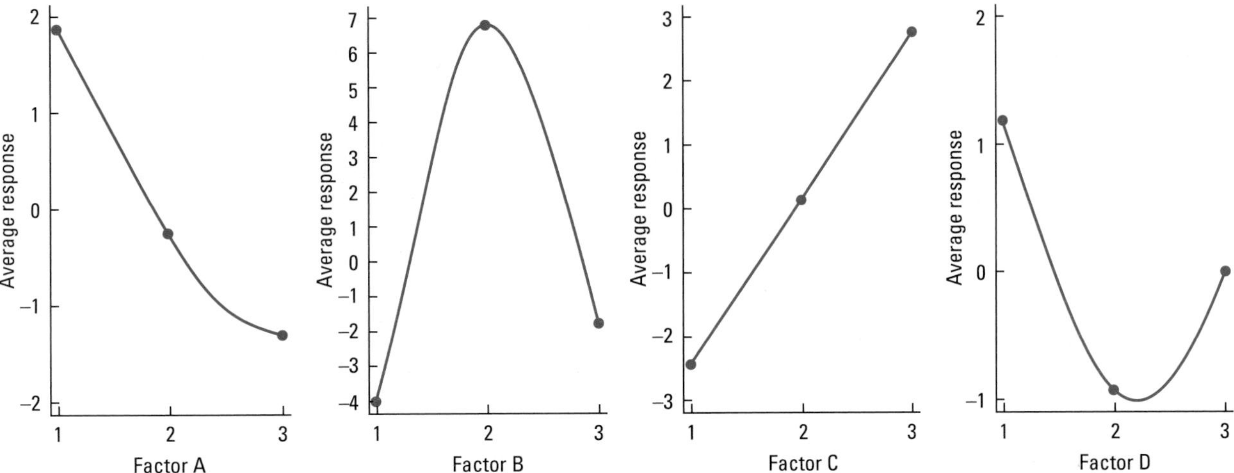

Figure 13-14 Average response curves for each of the factors.

run at these levels to validate the results and/or come up with more refined settings of the factors that would reduce variability further.

13-7 PARAMETER DESIGN IN THE TAGUCHI METHOD

The section on Taguchi's philosophy described the three phases of the Taguchi method—system design, parameter design, and tolerance design. The focal point of the approach is the achievement of an economical quality design. Figure 13-15 shows the three phases of the Taguchi method. In the system design phase, the design engineer uses practical experience coupled with scientific and engineering principles to create a functional design. Raw materials and components are identified, the sequential steps in the process through which the product is to be manufactured are proposed and analyzed, tooling requirements are studied, production constraints related to capacity are investigated, and all other issues related to the creation and production of a feasible design are dealt with.

The second phase is parameter design, which involves determination of the influential parameters and their settings. Usually, a subset of all possible parameters is selected and analyzed in an experimental framework. The experiments may be conducted physically or through computer simulation. The latter is more cost-effective. However, in order to use computer simulation we must first establish mathematical models that realistically describe the relationships between the parameters and the output characteristic. In step one of this phase, the levels of the selected design parameters that maximize a performance statistic such as the signal-to-noise ratio are determined. The nonlinearity in the relationship between the S/N ratio and the levels of the design parameters is used to determine the optimal

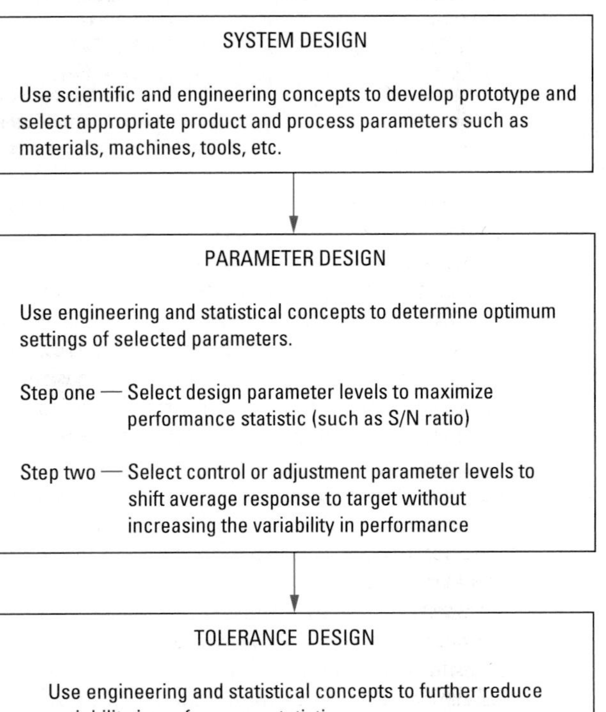

Figure 13-15 The three phases of the Taguchi method.

settings. The idea is to reduce the performance variability and create a design that is robust to noise variations (such as those due to variation in incoming raw materials and components, manufacturing, and product use). For example, the setting of design parameters (such as depth of cut, rate of feed of tool, amount of catalyst, and number of servers in a fast-food restaurant) such that the performance statistic is maximized could be determined. When a nonlinear relation exists between the parameter level and the performance statistic, this approach will minimize the sensitivity of the performance statistic to input variations.

The second step is to identify the parameters that have a linear relationship with the mean response. These parameter settings may be chosen to adjust the average response to the target value. Such parameters are also known as control, or adjustment, factors. By exploiting the linearity of the relationship, it is hoped that adjustment of the levels of these factors will not affect the variability. Examples could be the specific gravity of a liquid, the time that a hot specimen is immersed in a bath, the concentration of a solution, and so on. The factors will depend on the product and the process. Following selection of the optimum level of the parameters and adjustment factors, Taguchi recommends running confirmation experiments to verify the chosen optimal settings. The results may also be used to identify factors that are not very sensitive to the performance statistic. The settings of these factors may be chosen to minimize cost.

The purpose of the third phase, tolerance design, is to determine tolerances, or permissible ranges, for the parameter and factor settings identified in the parameter design phase. This phase is utilized only if the variability of the performance statistic exceeds our desirable levels. Setting such tolerances around the nominal values will help stabilize the performance measure. The objective of this phase is to further reduce the variability of the performance measure compared to what was achieved in the parameter design phase. Along the same lines, the tolerances of parameters that have no significant influence on the performance statistic can be relaxed in order to reduce costs.

The parameter design phase is emphasized in the Taguchi approach. He comments that although many companies spend more than 60 percent of their design activity on system design, they ignore parameter design. Reducing cost and achieving quality at the same time is more likely through careful parameter design. System design may come up with a multitude of designs, but it does not test for the sensitivity of the desired output to the input factors in order to come up with a design that is cost-effective. Consider, for example, a situation in which a transportation company is expected to meet growing demand and ship goods with as small a deviation from the target date as possible. One of the important factors is the type of truck, which has three possible levels. Level 1 is associated with using a new model truck, which costs more than existing ones but is dependable and efficient. The downtime of the new model is small, and the fuel efficiency is high. The existing model trucks cost less than the new model but break down more frequently and get poorer gasoline mileage. Level 2 is associated with using the old model; level 3 is associated with subcontracting the major routes, where the level of profit margin is low. In the parameter design phase it might be found that the new model maximizes a chosen performance characteristic (in this case, say, total profit), minimizes its variability, and is also cost-effective. The following is an example of the parameter design phase using the Taguchi method.

Example 13-8: This example is adapted from Byrne and Taguchi (1987). An experiment involved determining a method to assemble an elastomeric connector to a nylon tube that would deliver the required pull-off performance to be used in automobile engine components. Although the objective of the experiment was to maximize pull-off force and minimize assembly effort, the focus here is on the experimental design to maximize pull-off force.

Researchers identified four controllable and three noise factors that would likely affect the assembly's pull-off force. Table 13-8 shows the factor definitions and their associated levels. Each of the design factors were be tested at three levels, the uncontrollable noise factors at two. The noise factors are uncontrollable during normal operations,

TABLE 13-8 Factors and their associated levels for the experiment on the elastomeric connector

Controllable factors	Levels		
A. Interference	Low	Medium	High
B. Connector wall thickness	Thin	Medium	Thick
C. Insertion depth	Shallow	Medium	Deep
D. Percent adhesive in connector pre-dip	Low	Medium	High
Uncontrollable factors	**Levels**		
E. Conditioning time	24 h	120 h	
F. Conditioning temperature	72°F	150°F	
G. Conditioning relative humidity	25%	75%	

Adapted from D. M. Byrne and S. Taguchi (1987), "The Taguchi Approach to Parameter Design," *Quality Progress,* Dec. 1987, pp. 19–26.

TABLE 13-9 Orthogonal designs for the controllable and uncontrollable factors

(a) L_9 orthogonal array for the controllable factors

Run	A	B	C	D
1	1	1	1	1
2	1	2	2	2
3	1	3	3	3
4	2	1	2	3
5	2	2	3	1
6	2	3	1	2
7	3	1	3	2
8	3	2	1	3
9	3	3	2	1

(b) L_8 orthogonal array for the uncontrollable factors

Run	E	F	E×F	G	E×G	F×G	e
1	1	1	1	1	1	1	1
2	1	1	1	2	2	2	2
3	1	2	2	1	1	2	2
4	1	2	2	2	2	1	1
5	2	1	2	1	2	1	2
6	2	1	2	2	1	2	1
7	2	2	1	1	2	2	1
8	2	2	1	2	1	1	2

Adapted from D. M. Byrne and S. Taguchi (1987), "The Taguchi Approach to Parameter Design," *Quality Progress,* Dec. 1987, pp. 19–26.

but they were controlled over the two levels for the purpose of tests. The idea here is to determine a robust design that will be insensitive to the noise factors during actual operation.

With four design factors, each at three levels, whose effects are to be estimated using the orthogonal arrays shown in Table 13-2, an L_9 array is appropriate for the inner array. The full factorial experiment for the design factors would require 3^4, or 81, experiments. Using the L_9 array, an efficient design utilizing nine experiments is needed. Since the design is orthogonal, the effect of each factor can be separated and estimated. Factors A, B, C, and D are assigned to columns 1, 2, 3, and 4 of the L_9 array, respectively, as shown in Table 13-9.

For the three noise factors, each at two levels, using the orthogonal arrays in Table 13-2, an L_8 array is appropriate for the outer array. With the L_8 array, seven factors can be estimated. But we have only three noise factors. So the columns that are not assigned to the main effects E, F, and G can be assigned to estimate interaction effects and the experimental error. The purpose of the outer array (L_8) is to create noise so that the controllable factor levels that are least sensitive to it can be identified. Based on the linear graph and the L_8 array, the assignments as shown in Table 13-9 are made. The main effects E, F, and G are placed in columns 1, 2, and 4, respectively. The interaction effects E×F, E×G, and F×G are assigned to columns 3, 5, and 6, respectively, and the experimental error is assigned to column 7. Usually, the effects of interactions among the noise factors are not estimated. In this case the experimenters allowed for such interactions, because they felt that the information might be valuable.

The inner and outer arrays are combined to form the complete parameter design layout. For each experimental run corresponding to the setting of the design factors in the inner array (L_9), there are 8 replications corresponding to the setting of the noise factors in the outer array (L_8). Thus, a total of 72 experiments are conducted. The pull-off force for each of these experiments is shown in Table 13-10 along with the layout of the parameter design.

Variation in the noise factors was purposely induced in the experiment; it was hoped that analyzing the variation of the output characteristic and the mean response would be fruitful. Through an analysis that integrates both of these criteria, researchers were able to identify the combination of controllable factor levels that would maximize pull-off force and be robust to the noise factors.

Analysis of data first involves calculation of summary measures such as the mean response $\bar{y}$ and the signal-to-noise ratio for each of the experiments corresponding to the inner array over the 8 replications given by the outer array. For example, consider the controllable factor settings of A, B, C, and D at levels indicated by 1, 1, 1, and 1, respectively, for run number 1 in the inner array. The average response is

$$\begin{aligned}\bar{y} &= (15.6 + 9.5 + 16.9 + 19.9 + 19.6 \\ &\quad + 19.6 + 20.0 + 19.1)/8 \\ &= 17.525\end{aligned}$$

In this example, the response variable is the pull-off force, which we want to maximize; the signal-to-noise ratio falls in the larger-is-better category. Using Equation 13.12 for run number 1 of the inner array, the signal-to-noise ratio is

$$\begin{aligned}\text{S/N} &= -10\log\left[\left(\sum_{i=1}^{n} 1/y_i^2\right)\Big/ n\right] \\ &= -10\log[(1/15.6^2 + 1/9.5^2 + \cdots + 1/19.1^2)/8] \\ &= 24.025\end{aligned}$$

TABLE 13-10 Parameter design with inner and outer arrays and the experimental observations for pull-off force

Outer array (L_8)				E	1	1	1	1	2	2	2	2		
				F	1	1	2	2	1	1	2	2		
				G	1	2	1	2	1	2	1	2	Responses	
Inner array (L_9)														
Run	A	B	C	D									$\bar{y}$	S/N
1	1	1	1	1	15.6	9.5	16.9	19.9	19.6	19.6	20.0	19.1	17.525	24.025
2	1	2	2	2	15.0	16.2	19.4	19.2	19.7	19.8	24.2	21.9	19.475	25.522
3	1	3	3	3	16.3	16.7	19.1	15.6	22.6	18.2	23.3	20.4	19.025	25.335
4	2	1	2	3	18.3	17.4	18.9	18.6	21.0	18.9	23.2	24.7	20.125	25.904
5	2	2	3	1	19.7	18.6	19.4	25.1	25.6	21.4	27.5	25.3	22.825	26.908
6	2	3	1	2	16.2	16.3	20.0	19.8	14.7	19.6	22.5	24.7	19.225	25.326
7	3	1	3	2	16.4	19.1	18.4	23.6	16.8	18.6	24.3	21.6	19.850	25.711
8	3	2	1	3	14.2	15.6	15.1	16.8	17.8	19.6	23.2	24.2	18.338	24.852
9	3	3	2	1	16.1	19.9	19.3	17.3	23.1	22.7	22.6	28.6	21.200	26.152

Adapted from D. M. Byrne and S. Taguchi (1987), "The Taguchi Approach to Parameter Design," *Quality Progress,* Dec. 1987, pp. 19–26.

The average response $\bar{y}$ and the performance statistic given by the S/N ratio are calculated for the other eight experimental runs of the inner array and are shown in Table 13-10.

Analysis-of-variance procedures may be used to determine which factors significantly affect the performance statistic, but a simpler approach (proposed by Taguchi) is to employ graphs of the marginal means of each factor. The procedure used to analyze the pull-off force data was as follows.

For the nine S/N ratios, the average S/N ratio for each level of the four controllable factors was found. These are termed the marginal means of the S/N ratio for each factor level. For instance, the marginal mean S/N ratio when factor A is at level 1 is

$$\begin{aligned}\text{Average}(S/N) &= (24.025 + 25.522 + 25.335)/3 \\ &= 24.961\end{aligned}$$

Similarly, the marginal mean S/N ratios for the other levels of factor A are calculated. This procedure is repeated for the other factors as well. Figure 13-16 shows the plots of the average S/N ratio for each factor. With the intention of maximizing the S/N ratio, the corresponding factor level is chosen. We find that factors A and C are more significant than B and D. The chosen level for factor A is A_2 (medium level). For factor C, there does not seem to be much difference between the average S/N ratios for levels C_2 (medium level) and C_3 (deep level) although C_3 yields a slightly higher ratio. For factor B, levels B_2 (medium level) and B_3 (thick level) are not very different in their impact on the average S/N ratio, but B_2 is slightly preferable. Finally, for factor D, level D_1 (low level) is preferred over the others. So, based on the S/N ratio, the chosen factor levels are A_2 (medium level), C_3 (deep level), B_2 (medium level), and D_1 (low level).

The S/N analysis is usually sufficient, but experimenters also examined the average response to aid in the selection of factor levels. Here, we are trying to maximize the average response (pull-off force). Figure 13-17 shows plots of the average response for each controllable factor. From Figure 13-17, the chosen level for factor A is A_2 (medium level), which coincides with the level selected on the basis of the S/N ratio. The chosen level of factor C is C_3 (deep level), which is also the same as that selected based on the S/N ratio. There does not seem to be that much difference in the average responses for the C_2 (medium level) and the C_3 (deep level). The preferred level of factor B is B_2 (medium level), and that for factor D is D_1 (low level).

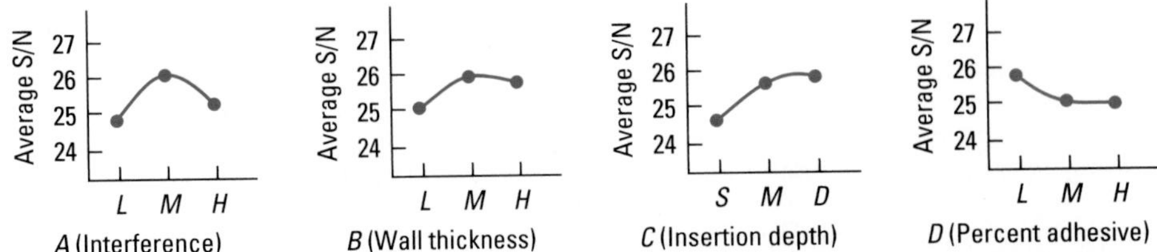

Figure 13-16 Effect of controllable factors on average signal-to-noise ratio.

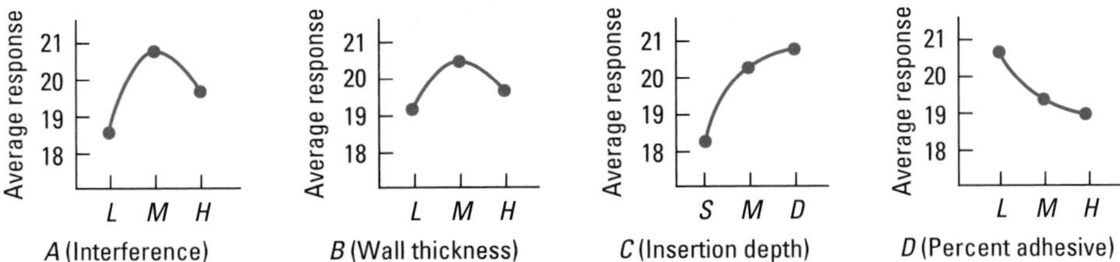

Figure 13-17 Effect of controllable factors on average response.

This is consistent with the previous decision based on the S/N ratio.

Taguchi believes that using the S/N ratio analysis generally eliminates the need to examine specific interactions between the controllable and noise factors. However, examining these interactions may improve our understanding of the process. Accordingly, a study of the interaction effects revealed A×G and D×E interactions to be strong. Figure 13-18 shows plots of the average response for these factors. Note the strong A×G interaction—the plotted lines for the three levels of A are nowhere close to being parallel. Factor level A_2 (medium level) is preferred because it is the least sensitive to changes in factor G (conditioning relative humidity), and also yields the highest pull-off force over the range of factor G. Next, we consider the interaction between factor D (percent adhesive) and factor E (conditioning time). The D_2 level (medium level) is least influenced by changes in conditioning time because the D_2 line has the smallest slope. However, the D_1 level (low level) has the highest pull off-force over almost the entire range of E. From analysis of the plot, D_1 (low level) is selected. Other two-factor interactions between the controllable factors and the noise factors are similarly examined. The plots for many of those contain lines that are nearly parallel, indicating a lack of interaction.

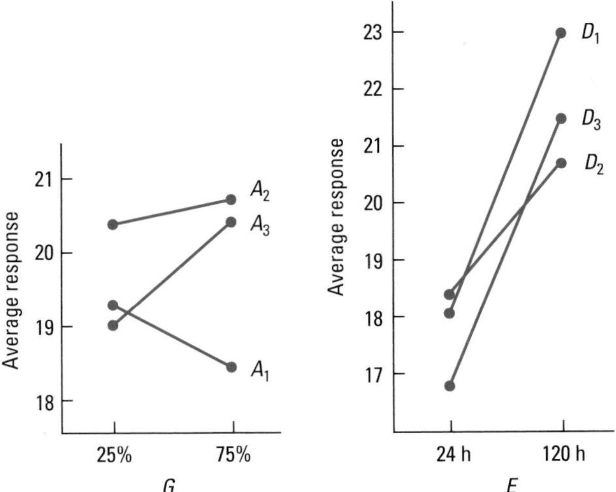

Figure 13-18 Plots showing A×G and D×E interactions.

Finally, when cost considerations and other criteria are taken into account, the selected level of factor B is B_1 (thin level). Since there is another performance criterion to consider—minimizing the assembly effort—a conflict could arise with the criterion of maximizing pull-off force. Based on these criteria, the level for factor C is chosen to be C_2 (medium level). The final selected levels are A_2 (medium level), B_1 (thin level), C_2 (medium level), and D_1 (low level).

13-8 APPLICATION TO ATTRIBUTE DATA

Our discussion of design and analysis using the Taguchi method has dealt with variable data, which is what Taguchi recommends using whenever possible. Variable data have obvious advantages over attribute data in that they provide a quantitative measure of the degree to which the response variable comes close to a target value. For instance, if we are measuring the carbon monoxide concentration in car exhaust, variable data will show the precise concentration as a numerical value, say 0.25. On the other hand, attribute data may indicate levels of carbon monoxide concentration grouped into such categories as poor, acceptable, and highly desirable. Thus, two observations that are placed in the poor category cannot be differentiated when attribute information is used. The subjective judgment of the experimenter often influences the category to which the response variable is assigned. For example, consider a food taster in a restaurant, who has to classify a menu item as undesirable, fair, good, or excellent. Based on the qualitative opinion of the taster, which could be influenced by personal bias and past experiences, a rating would be assigned. The same food item could get different ratings from different tasters. In numerically measurable variable data, though, such variability would not exist for the response variable. For instance, the weight of a given product should be the same for each observer.

The design and experimental layout when the response variable is an attribute is similar to when the data is variable. Problem definition, selection of parameters and levels for analysis, and the choice of an orthogonal array for experimental design are similar to the variable case. The difference is in the observation of the output variable, which is now classified as an attribute, and its analysis. To keep the analysis simple, the *accumulation type method* to analyze the results is discussed. Using summary statistics from this accumulation procedure, the optimal level of the parameters may be selected. The following example illustrates the procedure.

Example 13-9: A financial analyst wishes to investigate the effect of four factors on the customer's ability to repay loans. The four factors are as follows. The annual income level (factor A) is represented by three levels: less than \$20,000 (level 1), between \$20,000 and \$40,000 (level 2), and over \$40,000 (level 3). The number of years of job experience (factor B) is represented by three levels: less than one year (level 1), between one and four years (level 2), and over four years (level 3). The amount of outstanding debt (factor C) is represented by three levels: less than \$5000 (level 1), between \$5000 and \$15,000 (level 2), and over \$15,000 (level 3). The number of dependents (factor D) is represented by three levels: less than three (level 1), between three and five (level 2), and more than five (level 3). The ability to repay loans is measured by outcomes classified into three categories: loan repaid (category R), loan payment disrupted but eventually repaid (category E), and loan defaulted (category F).

Given the four factors at three levels each, an L_9 (3^4) orthogonal array is selected for the parameter design of the controllable factors. Sixteen experiments are conducted, and the results of each experiment are shown in Table 13-11. The outcome for each experiment is denoted by a 1 or 0 under the categories R, E, and F.

An accumulation analysis is conducted as follows. For each factor at each level, we determine the total number of times the outcomes are in one of the three categories (R, E, and F) and calculate the percentage of time each of them occurs. Table 13-12 shows the summarized accumulation results. For example, when A is at level 1, denoted by A_1, one loan was repaid (R), one had payment disrupted but eventually repaid (E), and one had defaulted (F). For a total of three loans studied at this level, 33.333 percent occurred in each of the outcome categories R, E, and F. Similar analyses are conducted for all of the factors at each of their levels.

In order to easily interpret the results of the accumulation analysis presented in Table 13-12, a bar graph showing the percentage of outcomes in each category may be constructed for each of the factor levels. This is shown in Figure 13-19. The choice of factor levels would be influenced by the degree to which we tolerate the defaulting loan payments. For example, suppose that borrowers who default are not acceptable at all, whereas the financial analyst is somewhat tolerant of borrowers who disrupt payment but eventually repay their loans. From Figure 13-19 we find that the chosen level of factor A is A_3, which

TABLE 13-12 Accumulation analysis of observed attribute outcomes

Factor level	Accumulated outcomes R	E	F	Percentage R	E	F
A_1	1	1	1	33.333	33.333	33.333
A_2	1	1	1	33.333	33.333	33.333
A_3	2	1	0	66.667	33.333	0.0
B_1	0	3	0	0.0	100.0	0.0
B_2	2	0	1	66.667	0.0	33.333
B_3	2	0	1	66.667	0.0	33.333
C_1	2	1	0	66.667	33.333	0.0
C_2	2	1	0	66.667	33.333	0.0
C_3	0	1	2	0.0	33.333	66.667
D_1	1	1	1	33.333	33.333	33.333
D_2	2	1	0	66.667	33.333	0.0
D_3	1	1	1	33.333	33.333	33.333

TABLE 13-11 Experimental layout and outcomes classified as attributes

Experiment number	Factor A	B	C	D	Outcome Loan repaid (R)	Loan payment disrupted but eventually paid (E)	Loan defaulted (F)
1	1	1	1	1	0	1	0
2	1	2	2	2	1	0	0
3	1	3	3	3	0	0	1
4	2	1	2	3	0	1	0
5	2	2	3	1	0	0	1
6	2	3	1	2	1	0	0
7	3	1	3	2	0	1	0
8	3	2	1	3	1	0	0
9	3	3	2	1	1	0	0

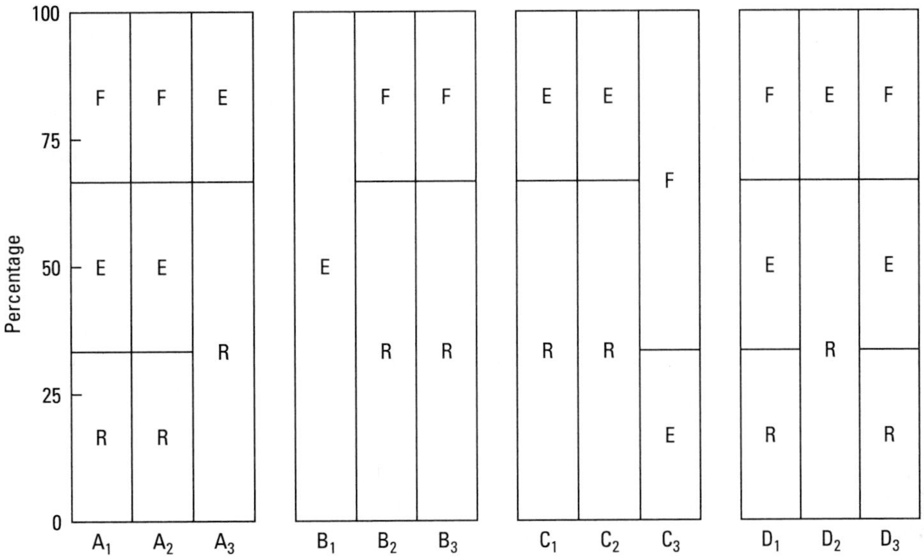

Figure 13-19 Bar graph of accumulation analysis results.

yields the highest percentage of loans that are repaid, and no loan defaults, meeting the specified requirements. The financial manager would therefore select candidates whose income level exceeds \$40,000 (level A_3) for consideration. For factor B, we find that 66.667 percent of loans are repaid for levels B_2 and B_3, the highest in that category. However, each of these two levels also result in 33.333 percent defaulted loans. If the analyst is intolerant of borrowers who default, the chosen level of factor B may be B_1. At this level of B_1, even though none of the loans are repaid without interruption, none of the loans are defaulted. Based on similar reasoning, for factor C, either of levels C_1 or C_2 is preferable; the final choice would be based on other considerations. Finally, for factor D, level D_2 would satisfy the desired requirements. Thus, the factor settings for each of the four factors are determined.

13-9 CRITIQUE OF EXPERIMENTAL DESIGN AND THE TAGUCHI METHOD

Taguchi advocates the use of orthogonal arrays, some of which are shown in Table 13-2, in his experimental design. Examples include two-level, three-level, and four-level fractional factorial experiments. For example, the L_8 array is really a 2^{7-4} fractional factorial experiment. The disadvantage of an orthogonal array is that the *alias structure* is not readily apparent from the design. It can be shown that the alias structure for this L_8 design is such that main effects are confounded with two-way interactions. This could lead to inaccurate conclusions because an inference as to whether a main effect is significant or not depends on the interaction effect. Only if the interaction effect is insignificant will our conclusions drawn on the main effects hold. Additionally, the alias structure for orthogonal arrays with three or more levels is messy. In fact, it is possible to find fractional factorial experiments with more desirable alias structures. For example, we can find a 2^{4-1} fractional factorial experiment that will have a total of eight experiments (as in the L_8 design) such that the main effects will be confounded with three-factor interactions. This is preferable to the L_8 design in which main effects are confounded with two-factor interactions.

Three types of interactions are possible in parameter design experiments: among design parameters, between design parameters and noise parameters, and among noise parameters. Taguchi, even though he recognizes interactions between design parameters, downplays their importance relative to the main effects. He proposes the inclusion of as many design parameters as possible, based on the number of experiments chosen. For example, using an L_9 orthogonal array, for which eight factors can be estimated, Taguchi advocates testing eight design parameters rather than a few important design parameters and possible two-way interactions between some of them. This is a potential drawback. Taguchi prefers using three or more levels of the factors to estimate curvature (nonlinear effects) rather than investigating potential interactions. An alternative procedure could be to identify possible main effects and important interactions and then to consider curvature in the important variables. This may lead to a simpler interpretation of the data and better understanding of the process. Perhaps a more important concern is the inclusion of the right variables in the experiment. Out of all possible parameters, which are the key ones? Have they all been included in the design?

In relation to the issue of determining the appropriate factors to analyze, Taguchi's parameter design approach could be thought as a form of *screening design*. Critiques mention that other forms of design such as *response surface designs* might be equally effective (Box and Draper, 1968). Response surface methodology, originally developed by Box and Wilson (1951), attempts to determine the shape of the response function and its sensitivity to the parameter design factors. It determines points of maxima and minima and the region in the design parameter space where these occur. The advantage of these other approaches is that they help in understanding the nature of the response function and thereby the process. Improved product and process designs are thus facilitated. Knowledge of the model, relating the response variable or performance statistic to the design factors and/or their function, is important.

The Taguchi approach attempts to identify the factors that most influence variability of the performance measure. It does not focus on the reason why this happens. For instance, is the variability most influenced by the main effects or interactions or is it due to curvature? On the other hand, alternative designs using fractional factorial experiments may help in identifying which components cause this to happen and the nature in which they contribute to the variability. The result is that we understand the underlying causes rather than merely identify the significant factors.

A criticism of the Taguchi method of experimental design is that the adoption of the inner and outer array structure leads to a larger number of experiments. For instance, in Example 13-8, an L_9 inner array consisting of four design factors and an L_8 outer array of the noise factors requires a total of 72 experiments. Furthermore, we could not even estimate any of the two-factor interactions between the design parameters. The L_9 array allows estimation of only four factor effects. Alternative experimental designs using fractional factorials may be found that are superior to the one proposed by Taguchi. One example is the 2^{7-2} fractional factorial experiment, which can accommodate seven factors, A, B, C, D, E, F, and G. If the defining contrasts are $I = ABCDF = ABDEG$, it can be seen that none of the main effects are aliased with two-factor interactions. Moreover, only 32 experimental runs are required. Some maintain that the inner and outer array approach, in general, is unnecessary. A better strategy could be to use a single array and assign the design and noise factors to it. Proper choice of the defining contrasts will lead to estimation of not only the main effects but also desirable interactions, at a lower cost because of fewer required experiments. In the context of experimental design, the linear graphs provided by Taguchi seem to have been developed heuristically. Their use may lead to inefficient designs, as we have seen in the case where main effects are confounded with two-way interactions. A better approach could be to use a design that specifies the complete alias structure.

The Taguchi method uses marginal averages to determine the optimal levels of the parameters. Marginal averages are obtained by computing the average of either the response variable or the performance statistic (such as the S/N ratio) at each level of the design variable, ignoring the levels of the other variables. Plots of these marginal averages are used to select optimal parameter levels. This procedure may not, in general, identify the optimal settings. It ignores the interaction effects between the parameters. When the interaction effects are not pronounced, this approach might allow the optimal setting to be approximated. The use of marginal averages is analogous to the approach for one factor at a time, the disadvantages of which have been previously discussed. Furthermore, marginal averages implicitly assign values for the factor level combinations that are not included in the orthogonal array. The method of assignment forces the interactions to be approximately zero, which may not be the case in practice. Obviously, it is difficult to estimate the value of the response variable for missing factor combinations without knowing the response surface.

In Taguchi's parameter design method, it was implicitly assumed in using the S/N ratio as a performance measure that the standard deviation of the response is linearly proportional to its mean. This may not be valid in all situations. Furthermore, the knowledge gained through sequential experimentation is not used. In maximizing the S/N ratio, we need to be aware that maximization is being done only over the design points considered in the design and not over the entire feasible region defined by the design parameters. The actual problem would be the optimization of a nonlinear function, such as the S/N ratio, subject to constraints on the bounds of the factor levels. Nonlinear programming techniques may therefore be appropriate.

Although the above views represent some of the criticisms of the Taguchi method, there is still an important place in the field of quality control and improvement for this technique. Taguchi's ideas concerning the loss function have changed the way of thinking in terms of the definition of quality. The challenge of meeting zero defects, whereby all products are within certain stated specifications, is not enough. Being close to the target value with minimum variability is the doctrine. Quality engineering principles that are based on developing product and process designs that are insensitive to environmental factors, are on target with minimum variability, and have the lowest possible cost are ideas that will endure.

13-10 SUMMARY

This chapter has presented concepts and procedures associated with the Taguchi method of design and analysis. Taguchi's philosophy has been described, and his contributions to the area of quality improvement through design have been discussed. The Taguchi loss function, which is a measure of the deviation of an output characteristic from a target value, has been explained; the three phases of the Taguchi method—system design, parameter design, and tolerance design—have been presented. Since parameter design is the important phase in this sequence, it has been discussed in more detail. The objective is to create a design that is robust to the uncontrollable factors and will also achieve a desired target value with the least variability. Performance measures such as the signal-to-noise ratio have been introduced. Cost is a key consideration in the Taguchi approach, with the idea of obtaining the best possible design at the lowest possible cost. Taguchi's role in the development and application of quality engineering ideas has been novel and will continue to have a pivotal role in quality improvement.

13-11 CASE STUDY

APPLICATION OF TAGUCHI'S ORTHOGONAL ARRAY IN A MATERIAL SCREENING EXPERIMENT*

Introduction

Design of experiments is one of the advanced statistical tools in quality engineering. It is particularly useful in empirical studies involving a large number of variables whose mechanisms or effects are such that theoretical analysis is either impossible or too complex to be carried out. A suitably designed experimental scheme can increase the efficiency of a study by generating the maximum amount of information with a given amount of experimental data or, conversely, a given amount of information with a minimum effort in data collection. The general framework of design, experiment, and analysis is depicted in Figure 13-20, where, in statistical parlance, manipulable inputs to a physical process and the observed outputs are known as *factors* and *responses,* respectively, and experimental settings of the factors are designed with *orthogonal arrays* with certain desirable statistical properties.

This study describes how a multifactor, multiresponse experiment based on an orthogonal design has been used for an efficient study of the influences of various additives on the properties of a manufactured product, in this case glass material. Some practical advantages of the application of orthogonal arrays are then discussed, with reference to the validity of conclusions and cost effectiveness of the investigative work.

Taguchi's Orthogonal Array

The theory of experimental design has its origin in agricultural research. It was gradually adopted by chemical engineers for process studies after World War II, and by now its importance as a scientific basis for experimentation has been well recognized in the quality assurance profession. A development in Japan, typified by the works of Taguchi, in the use of experimental design in quality engineering has begun to attract the attention of the West in recent years. Of particular interest is Taguchi's effort in facilitating the use of experimental design through a tabulation of orthogonal arrays and a collection of "linear graphics" that can be readily used even by those without a theoretical background of the arrays' origin. These orthogonal arrays permit the study of a number of factors thought to have possible effects on a measurable outcome such as the property of a product or the performance of a process. A remarkable efficiency can be thus achieved, particularly at the *screening* stage of an investigation, where the primary interest is to isolate a few key factors among a multitude of those suspected of having an influence over the specified response or responses. In the study described

*Adapted from T. N. Goh and S. K. Roy (1989), "Application of Taguchi's Orthogonal Array in a Material Screening Experiment," *Quality Assurance*, Vol. 15, No. 1, pp. 10–13. Institute of Quality Assurance.

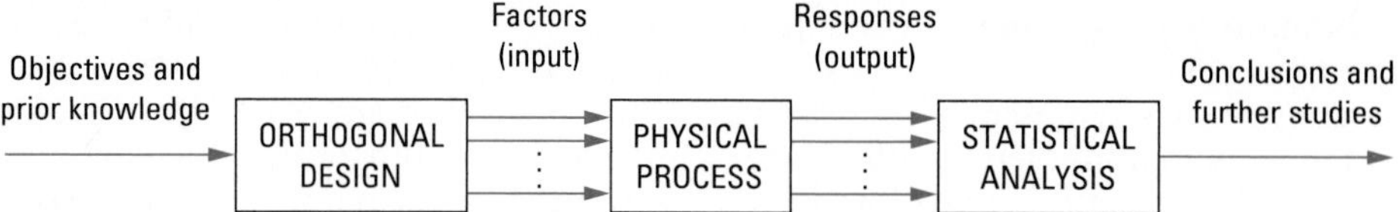

Figure 13-20 Study of a physical process via designed experiments.

here, an orthogonal array is used to accommodate 10 factors for the simultaneous measurement of as many as five responses.

Background of Study

Glass is generally manufactured with a number of additives present in various quantities to bring about a combination of physical properties. In this project, 11 constituents are considered for an experimental glass product: (A) titanium oxide, TiO_2, (B) boron oxide, B_2O_3, (C) sodium oxide, Na_2O, (D) zinc oxide, ZnO, (E) lithium oxide, Li_2O, (F) aluminum oxide, Al_2O_3, (G) lead monoxide, PbO, (H) calcium oxide, CaO, (I) calcium fluoride, CaF_2, and (J) sodium silicofluoride, Na_2SiF_6; while silica, SiO_2, is the base material.

The quality of the manufactured product is reflected by the following five selected properties: (i) flow, (ii) opacity, (iii) acidity resistance, (iv) tension, and (v) compression. Each of these properties is a response to a certain combination of levels (that is, amounts) of the 10 independent additives: the objective of the study is to identify those additives that have significant effects on each of them.

As there is no theoretical means for predicting the responses as mathematical functions of the factors, an empirical approach has to be adopted. The number of factors on hand is such that the simplistic "one factor at a time" technique of experimentation is impractical and, inasmuch as the purpose of the study is only for a screening of the factors, it is not necessary to experiment with an entire range of values for each factor. In fact, if each additive is to be tried out at two concentration levels and all possible combinations of levels are used, then as many as 2^{10}, or 1024, tests are needed, entailing considerable efforts in sample preparation and analysis. All these considerations point to the use of a highly fractionalized two-level factorial experiment, a design well explored by statisticians and strongly featured in Taguchi's experimental strategies.

The L_{16} (2^{15}) Design

The orthogonal array that can accommodate up to 15 factors—or *parameters,* as Taguchi calls them—at two levels each involves 16 tests, denoted by L_{16} (2^{15}). Table 13-13 shows the specifications of the design, where 1 denotes a higher level of additive concentration and 2 a lower level. Test no. 1, for example, would have all additives set at the high level, while test no. 16 would have additives C, E, F, H, I, J set at their respective high levels and the rest at their respective low levels. The actual specifications for the concentration levels are listed in Table 13-14.

Experimental Results

Sixteen glass samples were obtained with factor combinations set according to Table 13-13. After melting and quenching in water they were tested for the five properties of interest, the measurements of which are shown in Table 13-15.

Each set of property measurements is analyzed separately with reference to every single additive. For example, in the case of flow temperature, the average of

TABLE 13-13 The L_{16} (2^{15}) orthogonal array (abbreviated)

Test no.	Additives A	B	C	D	E	F	G	H	I	J
1	1	1	1	1	1	1	1	1	1	1
2	1	1	1	1	1	1	2	2	2	2
3	1	1	1	2	2	2	1	1	1	2
4	1	1	1	2	2	2	2	2	2	1
5	1	2	2	1	1	2	1	1	2	1
6	1	2	2	1	1	2	2	2	1	2
7	1	2	2	2	2	1	1	1	2	2
8	1	2	2	2	2	1	2	2	1	1
9	2	1	2	1	2	1	1	2	1	1
10	2	1	2	1	2	1	2	1	2	2
11	2	1	2	2	1	2	1	2	1	2
12	2	1	2	2	1	2	2	1	2	1
13	2	2	1	1	2	2	1	2	2	1
14	2	2	1	1	2	2	2	1	1	2
15	2	2	1	2	1	1	1	2	2	2
16	2	2	1	2	1	1	2	1	1	1

TABLE 13-14 Percentage settings of additives (factors)

Additive	Name	Level 1	Level 2
A	Titanium oxide	12.4	8.4
B	Boron oxide	3.7	2.7
C	Sodium oxide	11.3	9.3
D	Zinc oxide	0.8	0.0
E	Lithium oxide	1.6	0.7
F	Aluminum oxide	5.7	4.7
G	Lead monozide	11.6	9.6
H	Calcium oxide	0.8	0.0
I	Calcium fluoride	5.5	4.5
J	Sodium silicofluoride	10.2	7.0

the first eight measurements reflects the response level when factor A is at level 1:

$$\begin{aligned}\bar{y}_1 &= (1546 + 1545 + \cdots + 1600)/8 \\ &= 1576.5\end{aligned}$$

and the average response when factor A is at level 2 is

$$\begin{aligned}\bar{y}_2 &= (1558 + 1550 + \cdots + 1498)/8 \\ &= 1484.9\end{aligned}$$

Thus, the effect of raising the level of factor A from 1 to 2 is an increase in the response amounting to $\bar{y}_1 - \bar{y}_2 = 91.6$. Similar calculations are carried out for each of the other factors B, C, D, ..., J, and the procedures repeated

TABLE 13-15 Measured glass properties (responses)

Test no.	Flow, °C	Opacity, %	Acidity, g	Tension, cm	Compression, cm
1	1546	99.5	83.0	23.5	11.5
2	1545	100.0	56.0	18.5	0.5
3	1592	91.0	46.0	20.5	4.5
4	1529	82.5	45.0	21.5	3.5
5	1600	97.0	48.0	18.5	2.5
6	1600	96.0	44.5	19.5	−2.5
7	1600	100.0	46.5	20.5	−0.5
8	1600	97.0	43.0	19.5	−0.5
9	1558	92.5	50.5	21.5	2.5
10	1550	84.0	42.0	18.5	−1.5
11	1486	80.5	45.0	14.5	−7.5
12	1519	84.0	46.5	15.5	−5.5
13	1395	89.0	52.5	19.5	0.5
14	1391	71.5	46.5	18.5	0.5
15	1482	77.5	50.5	18.5	−0.5
16	1498	88.0	67.5	19.5	4.5

TABLE 13-16 Summary of factor effects

	Property				
Additive	Flow	Opacity	Acidity	Tension	Compression
A	91.6	12.0	1.4	2.00	3.25
B	19.9	−0.3	1.9	0.00	0.50
C	−66.9	−4.0	10.0	1.50	4.75
D	−15.1	3.6	4.2	1.00	2.00
E	7.6	1.9	8.6	−1.50	−0.75
F	33.4	5.9	8.1	1.50	2.50
G	3.4	3.0	3.8	0.75	1.75
H	12.6	0.0	4.9	0.25	2.50
I	6.4	0.3	4.9	0.75	1.75
J	0.1	3.6	7.4	1.25	3.25
(Mean)	(1530.7)	(89.4)	(50.8)	(19.25)	(0.75)

for the other four responses. All the computed results are summarized in Table 13-16.

Next, for every glass property studied, a Pareto analysis is made of the set of 10 values of effects of additives; the major effects thus identified are

Flow:	A^+, C^-
Opacity:	A^+
Acidity:	C^+, E^+, F^+, J^+
Tension:	A^+
Compression:	C^+

where a positive superscript denotes an increment in the measured property when the amount of the additive in question is raised, and vice versa.

The results of data analysis may be viewed in light of the known effects of some of the additives. For example, sodium oxide (additive C) makes molten glass more fluid and hence decreases the flow measurement considerably. Titanium oxide (additive A) is added to glass as an opacifier and hence produces the highest effect for opacity; sodium oxide (additive C), on the other hand, dissolves some of the fine particles of opacifiers and hence produces an opposite effect. The alkalis are known to decrease acid resistance; this is reflected by their positive effects on the acidity measurements. From the point of view of thermal expansion, lithium oxide (additive E) is a much better alkali than sodium oxide (additive C) in enamels; this is seen in their respective tension and compression effects. Boron oxide (additive B) contributes very little to the expansion coefficient of glass, a fact confirmed by the low tension and compression effects.

Discussion

The screening function of an orthogonal design experiment has been clearly exhibited in this study. Out of a total of ten additives, only half (A, C, E, F, J), acting alone or in combination, have been found to have dominant effects on the response properties. Possible interaction effects between two or more additives are usually not scrutinized at the screening stage but can be readily allowed for in a subsequent design. Similarly, the exact mathematical behavior (for example, linear or otherwise) of the effect of an additive on a given property is left to be explored later. The important outcome is that no more experimental efforts need to be expended on the unimportant additives, and the investigator can quickly concentrate on the five important ones that have been identified, using further statistical techniques if necessary. The results also explain why it would not be wise to use, before the concluding stage of a study, a design entailing more than two levels and thus a far larger number of samples and the associated experimental costs.

It should be noted that one important feature of the orthogonal design is that it can be shown theoretically that the resultant computed effects of the factors are statistically independent, which means, for example, each of the numerical items in Table 13-16 can be meaningfully interpreted in terms of both the direction of its influence on the response (positive or negative) and the amount of influence. Had the raw data not been collected via an orthogonal design, it would not have been correct to identify the major factors in the manner described, since statistical independence could not be assured.

Where prior knowledge of the physical mechanisms involved and the effects of the various factors is available, results of the statistical analysis of experimental data can be understood in light of that knowledge. There are two additional advantages to be gained. The first is the confirmation of such prior knowledge and its *quantification;* with this confirmation follows the second advantage, namely the investigator's confidence in the validity of results yielded by that part of the analysis concerning factors of which there has been *no* prior knowledge. In short, a useful picture, in qualitative as well as quantitative terms, can be obtained on completion of the analysis of experimental data. The direction for further investigations can now be set, depending on the ultimate objective of the project, such as meeting certain specified quality targets or minimizing certain undesirable properties in the manufactured product.

Conclusions

An orthogonal array has been used in the design of an experiment to screen a collection of additives thought to have possible effects on several properties of glass material. The technique has been shown to have advantages that may be summarized as follows.

First, with standard arrays such as those publicized by Taguchi, the investigator is able to come out with a usable experimental design without working from the first principles of fractional factorial design—although it is recognized that theoretical consideration of the properties of the design is still called for at later stages when further information, such as factor interactions and linearity of effects, becomes a subject of interest.

Second, the number of samples needed is very small in relation to the amount of information that can be gathered from the experimental data, leading to general cost effectiveness in empirical work.

Third, owing to the mathematical properties of orthogonal designs, the results of data analysis will lend themselves to ready interpretations of their physical meanings.

Finally, as can be appreciated from the study reported in this case study and, inasmuch as such results are found to corroborate whatever prior knowledge the investigator possesses of the behavior of the physical mechanisms, confidence in the validity of computed results can be extended to situations where such prior knowledge does not exist.

It is clear, therefore, that all personnel in various phases of manufacturing—design, development, process, production, quality assurance—should at least be aware of the potential, if not thoroughly familiar with the procedures, of orthogonal design. Apart from the value of the useful information it is capable of generating, the amount of cost and time that can be saved from its application can prove to be very substantial when one considers the resources needed to attempt the naive yet commonly used "change one variable at a time" approach to empirical studies.

Questions for Discussion

1. How many degrees of freedom are available for estimation of the experimental error in the design shown?
2. For the design shown, which two-way interactions are confounded with the main effects? Discuss the implications of this.

3. If the experimenter suspects the presence of quadratic effects of the factors, what type of design could be used? Discuss its implications.
4. Given that the screening experiments suggest five dominant factors, what experimental design using an orthogonal array would you recommend for future runs? How many treatments would you need if a full factorial experiment were run?
5. Discuss how costs associated with maintaining factor levels could impact the selection of which factors to control.

KEY TERMS

Accumulation analysis
Adjustment parameter
Alias
Analysis of variance (ANOVA)
Array
  Inner
  Outer
Attribute data
Bias
Confirmation experiments
Defining contrast
Degrees of freedom
Design matrix
Effects
  Estimation
  Interaction
  Main
Expected loss
Experiment
Experimental design
Factor
Factor levels
Factorial experiment
Fractional factorial experiment
Interaction
Latin square design
  Graeco-Latin square design
Linear graph
Loss function
  Nominal is best
  Smaller is better
  Larger is better
Manufacturing tolerance
Marginal means
Mean square deviation
Noise
  Matrix
Noise factors
  External
  Internal
Nominal value
Off-line quality control
Orthogonal array
Hybrid
  L_4 array
  L_8 array
  L_9 array
  L_{16} array
  L_{18} array
  L_{27} array
  L_{32} array
Parameter
Parameters
  Design
  Noise
Parameter design
Performance
  Measure
  Statistic
Quality engineering
Response surface
Response surface design
Response variable
Robustness
Screening design
Signal
Signal-to-noise ratio (S/N)
System design
Taguchi
  Philosophy
Taguchi method
Target value
Tolerance design
Treatments
Variance

EXERCISES

Discussion Questions

13-1 Discuss Taguchi's philosophy for quality improvement. Discuss his loss function and its contributions.

13-2 Compare and contrast Taguchi's loss functions for the situations nominal is best, smaller is better, and larger is better.

13-3 Explain the phases of system design, parameter design, and tolerance design of the Taguchi method. Describe the two-step procedure of parameter design.

13-4 Discuss the signal-to-noise ratio. How is it used in the Taguchi method? What is an adjustment parameter, and how is it used?

Problems

13-5 A manufacturer of magnetic tapes is interested in reducing the variability of the thickness of the coating on the tape. It is estimated that the loss to the consumer is \$10 per reel if the thickness exceeds 0.005 ± 0.0004 mm. Each reel has 200 meters of tape. A random sample of 10 yielded the following thicknesses (in mm): 0.0048, 0.0053, 0.0051, 0.0051, 0.0052, 0.0049, 0.0051, 0.0047, 0.0054, 0.0052. Find the average loss per reel.

13-6 Refer to Exercise 13-5 concerning the thickness of coating on magnetic tapes. The manufacturer is considering the adoption of a new process to reduce the variability in the thickness of coating. It is estimated that the additional cost for this improvement is \$0.03 per linear meter. The annual production is 10,000 reels. Each reel has 200 meters of tape. A random sample of size 8 from the new process yielded the following thicknesses (in mm): 0.0051, 0.0048, 0.0049, 0.0052, 0.0052, 0.0051, 0.0050, 0.0049. Is it cost effective to use the new process? If so, what is the annual savings?

13-7 Refer to Exercise 13-5 concerning the thickness of coating on magnetic tapes. Suppose that the manufacturer can rework the thickness prior to shipping the product at a cost of \$2.00 per reel. What should be the manufacturer's tolerance?

13-8 Refer to Exercise 13-5 concerning the thickness of coating of magnetic tapes. Suppose the manufacturer has the ability to center the process such that the average thickness of the coating is at 0.005 mm, which is the target value. In doing so, the manufacturer estimates that the standard deviation of the process will be 0.018 mm. The cost of making this change in the process is estimated to be \$1.50 per reel. Would it be cost-effective to make this change, compared to the original process? If so, what would be the annual savings if the annual production is 10,000 reels?

13-9 A restaurant believes that two of the most important factors that help it attract and retain customers are the price of the item and the time taken to serve the customer. Based on the price for similar items in other neighboring restaurants, it is estimated that the customer tolerance limit for price is \$8, and the associated customer loss is estimated to be \$50. Likewise, the customer tolerance limit for the service time is 10 minutes, for which the associated customer loss is \$40. A random sample of size 10 yielded the following values of price: 6.50, 8.20, 7.00, 8.50, 5.50, 7.20, 6.40, 5.80, 7.40, 8.30. The sample service times (in minutes) were 5.2, 7.5, 4.8, 11.4, 9.8, 10.5, 8.2, 11.0, 12.0, 8.5. Find the total expected loss per customer. If the restaurant expects 2000 customers monthly, what is the expected monthly loss?

13-10 Refer to Exercise 13-9 concerning the restaurant with the factors of price and service time. The restaurant is thinking of hiring more personnel to cut down the service time. However, the additional cost of increasing personnel is estimated to be \$0.50 per customer. Sample of results with the added personnel yielded the following waiting times (in minutes): 8.4, 5.6, 7.8, 6.8, 8.5, 6.2, 6.5, 5.9, 6.4, 7.5. Is it cost-effective to add personnel? What is the total expected monthly loss?

13-11 The Environmental Protection Agency has identified four factors (A, B, C, and D), each at two levels, that are significant in their effect on the air pollution level at a photographic film production facility. The agency also feels that the interaction effects A×C, A×B, and B×C are important. Show an experimental design that can estimate the above effects using a minimal number of experiments.

13-12 A baseball team manager believes that five factors, each at two levels, (A, B, C, D, and E) are significant in affecting runs batted in. The manager believes that the interactions B×C and B×E are important. Show an experimental design using an orthogonal array that can estimate the above effects.

13-13 The tourism board of a large metropolitan area is seeking ways to promote tourism. They have identified five factors (A, B, C, D, and E) that they feel have an impact on customer satisfaction. Factor C has 4 levels, and each of the other four factors has 2 levels. Show an experimental design, using an orthogonal array, that could estimate the above factor effects.

13-14 A city library has established three factors (A, B, and C), each at three levels, that influence the satisfaction of their patrons. The library governance committee also believes that the interaction B×C is important. Using an orthogonal array, set up an appropriate experimental design.

13-15 In a drilling operation, four factors (A, B, C, and D), each at three levels, are thought to be of importance in influencing the volume of crude oil pumped. Using an L_9 orthogonal array, the factors A, B, C, and D are assigned to columns 1, 2, 3, and 4, respectively. The response variable showing the number of barrels (in thousands) pumped per day for each of the nine experiments is shown below:

Experiment number	1	2	3	4	5	6	7	8	9
Number of barrels per day (in thousands)	6.8	15.8	10.5	5.2	17.1	3.4	5.9	12.2	8.5

Show the experimental design and the response variable for the corresponding experiments. Determine the main effects. Plot the average response curves. What are the optimum settings of the design parameters?

13-16 Consider Exercise 13-15 concerning the number of barrels pumped per day in a drilling operation. With the assignment of factors A, B, C, and D to columns 1, 2, 3, and 4, respectively, of an L_9 orthogonal array, the output is shown below for another replication of the 9 experiments:

Experiment number	1	2	3	4	5	6	7	8	9
Number of barrels per day (in thousands)	12.2	18.3	13.5	8.3	17.2	7.5	7.9	15.7	14.8

Determine the main effects. Plot the average response curves. What are the optimum settings of the design parameters?

13-17 In a food processing plant, four design parameters, A, B, C, and D, each at 3 levels, have been identified as having an effect on the moisture content in packaged meat. Three noise factors, E, F, and G, each at two levels, are also to be investigated in the experiment. In the inner array, an L_9 orthogonal array is used with the factors A, B, C, and D assigned to columns 1, 2, 3, and 4, respectively. For the outer array, an L_4 orthogonal array is used with the noise factors E, F, and G assigned to columns 1, 2, and 3, respectively. Table 13-17 shows the moisture content in a coded scale for four replications of each of the nine experiments in the inner array. It is preferable that the moisture content be around a coded value of 20. Show the complete parameter design layout using the Taguchi method. Calculate the mean response and the appropriate signal-to-noise ratio. Plot the average signal-to-noise ratios and the average responses, and discuss how the design factor levels are to be selected. Use the average response plots to determine the existence of possible interactions B×E and C×F. What are the optimal settings of the design parameters using Taguchi's parameter design approach?

13-18 Consider Exercise 13-17 concerning the moisture content in packaged meat in a food

TABLE 13-17 Moisture content in packaged meat for an L_9 inner array and L_4 outer array

	Experiment number in outer array			
Experiment number in inner array	1	2	3	4
1	18.5	21.2	20.5	19.3
2	16.8	17.3	20.9	18.5
3	21.1	21.8	20.6	19.4
4	20.2	17.7	19.8	20.8
5	16.2	21.5	21.2	21.4
6	18.3	18.5	17.8	17.2
7	20.6	21.4	16.8	19.5
8	17.5	20.0	21.0	20.4
9	20.4	18.8	19.6	18.3

TABLE 13-18 Moisture content in packaged meat for an L_9 inner array and L_8 outer array

Experiment number in inner array	Experiment number in outer array							
	1	2	3	4	5	6	7	8
1	19.3	20.2	19.1	18.4	21.1	20.6	19.5	18.7
2	20.6	18.5	20.2	19.4	20.1	16.3	17.2	19.4
3	18.3	20.7	19.4	17.6	20.4	17.3	18.2	19.2
4	20.8	21.2	20.2	19.9	21.7	22.2	20.4	20.6
5	18.7	19.8	19.4	17.2	18.5	19.7	18.8	18.4
6	21.1	20.2	22.4	20.5	18.7	21.4	21.8	20.6
7	17.5	18.3	20.0	18.8	20.2	17.7	17.9	18.2
8	20.4	21.2	22.4	21.9	21.5	20.8	22.5	21.7
9	18.0	20.2	17.6	22.4	17.2	21.6	18.5	19.2

processing plant. The design factors are A, B, C, and D, each at three levels. These are assigned to an L_9 orthogonal array (inner array) with the factors A, B, C, and D assigned to columns 1, 2, 3, and 4, respectively. Suppose that in addition to the three main effects of the noise factors E, F, and G, it is felt that the interaction effects E×F and E×G should be investigated. What type of design would you use for the outer array?

Suppose the outer array is selected as L_8, with the assignments as follows: E to column 1, F to column 2, E×F to column 3, G to column 4, and E×G to column 5. The other two columns of the L_8 array may be assigned to the experimental error. Table 13-18 shows the moisture content of the eight replications for each of the nine experiments in the inner array. The coded target value is 20.

TABLE 13-19 Classification of output fabric using an L_9 orthogonal array

Experiment number	Factor A	B	C	D	Quality of fabric: Acceptable	Second class	Reject
1	1	1	1	1	0	1	0
2	1	2	2	2	1	0	0
3	1	3	3	3	0	1	0
4	2	1	2	3	0	1	0
5	2	2	3	1	0	0	1
6	2	3	1	2	1	0	0
7	3	1	3	2	0	0	1
8	3	2	1	3	0	1	0
9	3	3	2	1	1	0	0

Show the complete parameter design layout using the Taguchi method. Calculate the mean response and the appropriate signal-to-noise ratios. Plot the average signal-to-noise ratios and the average responses, and discuss how the design factor levels are to be selected. Use the average response plots to determine the existence of the interaction effects A×E, B×F, E×F, and E×G. What are the optimal settings of the design parameters using Taguchi's parameter design approach?

13-19 In a textile processing plant the quality of the output fabric is believed to be influenced by four factors (A, B, C, and D) each of which can be controlled at three levels. The fabric is classified into three categories: acceptable, second-class, or reject. An L_9 orthogonal array is selected for the design factors, with the factors A, B, C, and D assigned to columns 1, 2, 3, and 4, respectively. The observations are shown in Table 13-19. Management wants to eliminate reject product altogether. Conduct an accumulation analysis, and determine the optimal settings of the design factors.

13-20 Consider Exercise 13-19 on the quality of the output fabric in a textile processing plant. Four factors (A, B, C, and D), each at three levels, are controlled in an experiment using an L_9 orthogonal array. The output quality is classified as acceptable or unacceptable; unacceptable includes both the second-class and reject classes. Consider the data shown in Table 13-19. Combine the second-class and reject categories into one class and label it as unacceptable, and accumulate the data accordingly. From the accumulation analysis, determine the optimal settings of the design factors.

REFERENCES

Box, G. E. P., and Wilson, K. B. (1951). "On the Experimental Attainment of Optimum Conditions," *Journal of the Royal Statistical Society, Series B* 13(1), pp. 1–45 (with discussion).

Box, G. E. P. (1986). *Studies in Quality Improvement: Signal to Noise Ratios, Performance Criteria and Statistical Analysis: Part I,* Report No. 11. Center for Quality and Productivity Improvement, University of Wisconsin, Madison.

Box, G. E. P., and Draper, N. R. (1986). *Empirical Model Building and Response Surfaces.* Wiley, New York.

Byrne, D. M., and Taguchi, S. (1987). "The Taguchi Approach to Parameter Design," *Quality Progress,* 20 (12), pp. 19–26.

Dehnad, K. (1989). *Quality Control, Robust Design, and the Taguchi Method,* Wadsworth & Brooks/Cole Advanced Books & Software, Pacific Grove, CA.

Goh, T. N., and Roy, S. K. (1989). "Application of Taguchi's Orthogonal Array in a Material Screening Experiment," *Quality Assurance,* 15 (1), pp. 10–13.

Hunter, J. S. (1985). "Statistical Design Applied to Product Design," *Journal of Quality Technology,* 17 (4), pp. 210–221.

Kackar, R. N. (1985), "Off-line Quality Control, Parameter Design, and the Taguchi Method," *Journal of Quality Technology* 17, (4), pp. 176–188; Discussion, 189–209.

Kackar, R. N. (1986). "Taguchi's Quality Philosophy: Analysis and Commentary," *Quality Progress,* 19 (12), pp. 21–29.

Leon, R. V., Shoemaker, A. C., and Kackar, R. N. (1987). "Performance Measures Independent of Adjustment," *Technometrics* 29 (3), pp. 253–265; Discussion, pp. 266–285.

Peterson, R. G. (1985). *Design and Analysis of Experiments.* Marcel Dekker, New York.

Raghavarao, D. (1971). *Constructions and Combinatorial Problems in Design of Experiments.* Wiley, New York.

SAS Institute Inc. (1989a). *SAS/QC Software: Reference,* Version 6, 1st edition, Cary, NC.

SAS Institute Inc. (1989b). *SAS/STAT, User's Guide: Statistics,* Version 6, 4th edition, Cary, NC.

Schmidt, S. R., and Boudot, J. R. (1989). "A Monte Carlo Simulation Study Comparing Effectiveness of Signal-to-Noise Ratios and Other Methods for Identifying Dispersion Effects," presented at the 1989 Rocky Mountain Quality Conference.

Taguchi, G., and Wu, Y. (1980). *Introduction to Off-Line Quality Control Systems,* Central Japan Quality Control Association, Nagoya, Japan. Available from American Supplier Institute, Dearborn, MI.

Taguchi, G. (1986). *Introduction to Quality Engineering—Designing Quality into Products and Processes.* Asian Productivity Organization, Tokyo.

Taguchi, G. (1987). *System of Experimental Design—Engineering Methods to Optimize Quality and Minimize Costs.* Volume 1 and 2. American Supplier Institute, Dearborn, MI.

Taguchi, G., Elsayed A., and Hsiang, T. (1989). *Quality Engineering in Production Systems.* McGraw-Hill, New York.

PART

VI

Applications in the Service Sector and Computer Software Usage

CHAPTER

14

Quality Control in the Service Sector

CHAPTER OUTLINE

SYMBOLS

$\overline{X}$	Sample average
R	Sample range
p	Proportion nonconforming
c	Number of nonconformities
n	Sample size
$\overline{\overline{X}}$	Average of sample averages
$\overline{R}$	Average of sample ranges
$\overline{p}$	Average proportion nonconforming
$\overline{c}$	Average number of nonconformities
$\hat{\sigma}$	Estimated process standard deviation
C_{pk}	Process capability index
Z	Standard normal value
B	Tolerable error bound
μ	Population mean
s^2	Sample variance

14-1 INTRODUCTION

The service industry is a dominant part of the economy. More than 70 percent of jobs are in the service sector, and the number continues to grow. The service industry cannot be neglected in a discussion of methods of quality control and improvement. The statistical methods and procedures introduced in the previous chapters may be used for problem solving in both manufacturing and service operations (Rosander, 1985). There are some major differences, however, in the quality characteristics associated with these two types of industry (DelMar and Sheldon, 1988; Kackar, 1988; King, 1987). Accordingly, the measurement process of these characteristics as well as the focal points of management may differ. Service systems usually have to go beyond the requirements of a manufacturing system. They have to design the product to meet the functional requirements of the customer and ensure the satisfactory behavior of the employee performing the service. Thus, the total service concept is a combination of technical and human behavioral aspects (of which the latter are much more difficult to quantify, measure, and control).

Consider, for example, the airline industry. One of the quantifiable goals may be to transport a person between two cities in a certain desirable time. The achievement of this may take place through the design of aircraft to achieve certain speeds to cover the distance within the required time or through proper scheduling of flights to ensure that planes take off and land on time. The deviation of the actual time required for transport between the two cities versus what is published in the schedule can easily be measured on a quantified scale, and appropriate causes might be identified. However, customer satisfaction might be influenced by other behavioral factors that are not so easy to quantify. For instance, the way the stewardesses or ticket agents treat the customers can be important. Is the agent courteous and friendly? Is the stewardess warm and caring? All of these factors may influence customer satisfaction and thereby determine whether he or she will be eager to fly on that airline for the next trip. Thus, the manner in which the service is performed is an important concern that might not be considered in manufacturing industries. Of course, we should realize that even manufacturing industries have to deal with service functions (such as payroll and accounting, customer relations, product service, personnel, purchasing, and so on). The importance of the service industry should not, therefore, be underestimated.

This chapter discusses some quality characteristics unique to service industries. Some fundamental differences from manufacturing industries are recognized. The customer is the focal point of quality control and improvement. This is consistent with the philosophies of such leading field experts as Deming. Customer feedback is essential to determine the level of customer satisfaction. Some problems associated with the measurement of service quality characteristics are mentioned in this chapter. Applications of quality control and improvement to several service industries, including banking, government, health care, utilities, and transportation, are described.

14-2 SERVICE INDUSTRIES AND THEIR CHARACTERISTICS

Industries may be categorized into two general groups: manufacturing and nonmanufacturing. Within the nonmanufacturing category we have the service industries, agriculture, and mining. Some of the functions performed by service industries are education, banking, governmental services (involving defense, municipal services, welfare, and so on), health care, insurance, marketing, personal services (such as hotels and motels), restaurants, traveling and tours, public utilities (including electricity, gas, and telephone service), and transportation (airlines, railroads, and buses). As shown in the above example of an airline industry, a service industry may provide a tangible product in addition to an intangible component that influences the satisfaction associated with the delivery of the service.

Two parties are involved in providing a service. The one that assists or provides the service is the vendor, or company, and the party receiving the service is the vendee, or customer. Although the services provided by typical service industries have already been mentioned, there are some functions, called *service functions,* that may be found in manufacturing and service industries. These are denoted as staff functions and are performed by staff personnel, as opposed to line personnel in manufacturing industries. Their job is to provide expertise to the operating departments and the customers in order to assist them in getting the most value out of the product. Customer services and warranties are examples of this. In addition, clerical and administrative operations such as accounting, purchasing, payroll, and personnel are staff functions that play a supportive role in an organization. Research and development activities are also viewed as staff functions, since their goal is to devise better product or process designs that will facilitate line operations.

Differences Between Manufacturing and Service Industries

There are some basic differences between manufacturing and service industries. Table 14-1 lists some of these factors. One fundamental distinction is that manufacturing industries make products that are tangible, whereas services have an intangible component associated with them. A caring attitude with a smile from the server may lead to customer satisfaction. In periods when demand for a product exceeds the available supply, it might be possible to back-order excess demand in manufacturing industries. This, however, is not usually possible in service industries. Most service functions have a time constraint associated with them. If the service is not provided within the required time frame, it cannot be used at a later time. Consider, for example, a situation in which there are empty seats in a mass transportation system during the period of 10:00–11:00 a.m. These empty seats cannot be saved for use during the rush hour of 5:00–6:00 p.m.

Another feature concerns the involvement of the producer and consumer in service industries. In a hospital, the doctor or nurse interacts with the patient, who is the consumer, to provide the service. Responses from the patient may influence the manner in which the service is delivered. In a manufacturing industry, though, the producer or manufacturing company alone influences the process through which the product is made. Of course, the consumer does impact the product in the sense that the product is designed to meet customer requirements, but once a satisfactory product and process design has been achieved, the customer does not influence the product quality during production. Whereas manufactured products may be resold, the same is not true of services because of the time constraints under which they have to operate.

Customers usually have a direct impact on creating formal product specifications in a manufacturing environment. Quality characteristics that influence customer satisfaction are identified and are incorporated into the product at the design phase. It is possible that for some service industries, the customer might not provide input on the formal specifications

TABLE 14-1 Some differences between manufacturing and service industries

Manufacturing industries	Service industries
Product is tangible.	Service consists of tangible and intangible components.
Backorders are possible.	Services cannot be stored; if not used, they are lost.
Producer or company is the only party involved in the making of the product.	Producer and consumer are both involved in the delivery of the service.
Product can be resold.	Services cannot be resold.
Customer usually provides formal specifications for the product.	Formal specifications need not be provided by the consumer. In fact, in monopolies involving public utilities such as electricity, gas, telephone, etc., federal and state laws dictate the requirements.
Customer acceptance of the product is easily quantifiable.	Customer satisfaction is difficult to quantify because a behavioral component associated with the delivery of the service is involved.

for services. This is evident when one considers such public utilities as electricity, gas, and telephone. Federal and state laws regulate these industries. The services that they provide and the prices that they charge might be mandated by governing bodies such as the Public Service Commission.

A distinctive feature that makes the evaluation and measurement of the level of quality difficult in service industries is the behavioral aspect associated with the delivery of the service. In manufacturing companies, the degree to which the product is accepted can be quantitatively specified, say, in terms of the proportion of unacceptable product. In service industries, it is difficult to quantify the degree of customer satisfaction because of the human factors involved with the delivery of the service. These include behavioral traits of the server as well as the customer. Furthermore, if a customer is dissatisfied, it is hard to identify exactly which characteristics of the service were to blame. On the other hand, in a manufacturing company, if a product is not accepted because it falls outside certain specifications, we know exactly the reason for customer dissatisfaction. We can readily determine remedial measures to improve the product through changes in the product and/or process.

Service Quality Characteristics

This subsection considers some features associated with quality characteristics in a service industry. The quality characteristics are grouped into four categories. Although exceptions to these groups may be found in specific instances, the categories generally summarize the unique features commonly represented in service functions and industries.

The quality of a service may be broken down into two categories: *effectiveness* and *efficiency*. Effectiveness deals with meeting the desirable service attributes that are expected by the customer. For example, the decor and available facilities in a hospital room, the quality and quantity of food served in a restaurant, and the different types of checking and savings accounts available in a bank are related to the service effectiveness. Efficiency, on the other hand, concerns the time required for the service to be rendered.

Human Factors and Behavioral Characteristics Service quality is influenced by the attitude and behavior of the server (Lefevre, 1989; McCabe, 1985; Normann, 1991; Thompson, DeSouza, and Gale, 1985). Since the buyers are also involved in the process, their behavior also affects the overall quality of the service. Some influential characteristics might include intensity, eagerness to help, thoughtfulness, complacency, courtesy, and so on. Some of these traits can be developed through adequate training; some are rooted in the nature of the individual. Proper screening of employees and appropriate assignment of people to jobs are means of achieving desirable quality characteristics. A primary source of customer complaint is discourteous behavior, say, in health care facilities, automobile service and repair, travel agencies, and cab service. The attitude of the buyer is largely beyond the control of the service company. For instance, an individual's mood when receiving a service can influence perceived quality. However, a company might influence a customer's expectations through advertisement and prior reputation. A customer's mind-set is often a function of what he or she expects to receive. Thus, the company has an indirect role in affecting the behavioral patterns of their customers by molding their expectations. If a bank advertises that in addition to providing the services of regular accounts (such as checking, savings, and certificates of deposit), it will provide financial management services, then customer expectations will be raised. As such, the customer will not be satisfied if questions related to financial management are not adequately answered. On the other hand, if the bank does not claim to provide these financial management services, the expectations of the customer will be different. It should be mentioned that measurement of attitudes and behavioral characteristics is not as simple and well-defined as for other tangible criteria.

Timeliness Characteristics A service that is not used in a given span of time cannot be stored for later use. A hospital with empty beds during certain days of a month cannot save them for use in the following month. Thus, the timeliness with which a service is performed is critical to customer satisfaction. How long did the customer have to wait before being served in a restaurant? How long did the customer have to wait in line to cash a check? Characteristics related to timeliness may be categorized based on the service phase with which they are associated. Categories might include the time to order the service, the waiting time before the service is performed, the time to serve, and the post-service time. These characteristics are much more amenable to measurement than behavioral characteristics.

Service Nonconformity Characteristics These characteristics deal with deviation from target performance levels; a nonconformity is a deviation from the ideal level. Examples of such characteristics include the number of errors in processing per 100 vouchers by bank employees, the number of data entry errors per 1000 keystrokes by a data entry operator, the number of billing errors per 100 accounts by a utility company, the number of complaints per 100 guests in a hotel, and so on. The target performance level for the above examples is zero nonconformities. The goal of the service organization should be to achieve the target level, thus meeting customer expectations, and then exceed it through quality improvement measures. Quality characteristics in this category are well-defined and are more readily measured than behavioral characteristics.

Facility-Related Characteristics The physical characteristics of the facilities associated with a service and its delivery may have an impact on customer satisfaction. The decor of a restaurant, the waiting area in a bus station, and the availability of such amenities as a swimming pool or spa in a hotel are examples of quality characteristics for physical facilities that are involved in providing a service. The appearances of a waiter or waitress, a bank teller, or an insurance agent are attributes of individuals performing a service. These characteristics are not as clearly defined and measurable as service nonconformity characteristics. They are, however, more quantifiable than behavioral characteristics.

Measuring Service Quality

Most characteristics that measure service quality may be grouped into one of the four above-mentioned categories: human factors and behavioral, timeliness, service nonconformity, and facility-related. Table 14-2 lists some characteristics in each category.

In terms of ease of quantification and measurement, the categories may be ranked in the following order: service nonconformity, timeliness, facility-related, and human factors and behavioral. Since the success of many service functions is predominantly determined by the human elements of interaction between the provider of the service and the buyer

TABLE 14-2 Measures of service quality

Service quality characteristic category	Measures of service quality
Human factors and behavioral characteristics	Number of customer complaints based on behavioral factors (or lack thereof) of persons involved in the service process Number of complimentary responses based on human traits in delivery of service
Timeliness characteristics	Waiting time in a bank prior to transaction Time to process a transaction Time to check in at the airport Waiting time before receiving baggage at the airport Time to hear from an insurance company regarding a payment
Service nonconformity characteristics	Number of errors per 1000 transactions in banks, insurance companies, and payroll departments Number of billing errors per 1000 accounts by utility companies Proportion of income tax returns prepared by an agency that have errors
Facility-related characteristics	Number of complaints due to: An uncomfortable bed in a hotel room Unavailability of a swimming pool in a hotel Insufficient leg room in an aircraft Inadequate temperature control in a convention meeting room Shabby appearance of a receptionist in a hotel or bank Lack of certain indoor activities (such as table tennis) in a recreation facility

(who can be an individual or a company), an inherent difficulty exists in the measurement and evaluation of service quality. Moreover, in services involving totally intangible services (such as information provided by a financial consultant), it is difficult to quantify a measurement unit by which to judge the level of service quality.

Another difficulty in dealing with human behavior is that individuals are not as predictable as equipment and facilities. The water temperature in a swimming pool can be stabilized by an adequate heating and recycling system, but the behavior of a check-in attendant is not always under the control of the company. It may be influenced by the personal events that happen on a given day, and hence is difficult to predict on a day-to-day basis. Such influences may cause a large performance variation in an employee on a daily or weekly basis.

To counteract these performance variations in human behavior in a given time period, procedures that generate representative statistics of performance should be devised. Randomly choosing samples of performance from the time interval under consideration is one means of eliminating bias. In situations where it is known that behavioral patterns vary greatly based on the time period (for instance, if error rates are high in the first and eighth hours of an eight-hour workday), a sampling plan that adequately reflects this should be selected. A stratified sampling plan for which two strata are formed, one for the early morning and late afternoon periods and one for the remainder of the day, might be appropriate. If 20 samples are to be selected daily and a proportional sampling scheme is to be used, we may select 5 samples randomly (which comprise 25 percent of the total daily samples) from the first strata, that is, early morning (8–9 a.m.) and late afternoon (4–5 p.m.). The assumption is that, based on an eight-hour day, the time interval covered by this strata is 2 hours, or 25 percent of the total daily hours worked. The remaining fifteen samples will be randomly selected from the second strata, which represents the remaining time period.

Another difficulty in measuring human behavioral traits is that significant differences may exist between individuals. Thus, although the scheme of stratified sampling just mentioned may be used to select appropriate samples that reflect the performance of an individual, it may be difficult to justify whether this same scheme can be collectively applied to a group of individuals. Certain individuals are better suited to certain times of the day. There are some who prefer the early morning hours and are very receptive and efficient during that time period. On the other hand, there are persons who operate effectively during the evening hours. If such differences are identified, the chosen sampling plan should be designed to reflect them.

Techniques for Evaluation of Service Quality

Most of the techniques that have been described in the previous chapters on quality control and improvement may be applied in appropriate settings in the service sector. As with manufacturing, achieving an appropriate design of a service system precedes any activities on control and improvement. The previous section shows how some characteristics of service systems are different from their manufacturing counterparts. Accordingly, emphasis on ergonomic, anthropometric, and behavioral characteristics is important along with consideration of the physical characteristics of service systems and the timeliness with which the service is provided.

Descriptive statistics providing numerical measures and corresponding graphical methods may be used to describe distributions of service quality characteristics and their summary measures. For example, the distribution of the waiting time before being seen by a physician may be depicted by a frequency or relative frequency histogram. Summary measures such as the mean waiting time and the standard deviation of the waiting time convey meaningful information. Run charts or trend charts that plot the observed quality characteristic in time sequence are frequently used to monitor performance. A plot of the waiting time as a function of the time of day may reveal peculiarities that a frequency histogram might not identify. For instance, the run chart may indicate that the period between 11:00 a.m. and 2:00 p.m. is the busiest period. Further analysis of the situation may lead to remedial solutions such as having more doctors available during that time period. These procedures have been discussed in earlier chapters.

Understanding variability in service quality characteristics is important to the control and improvement of service quality. Some of the sources of variability are similar to those encountered in the manufacturing sector, such as variation due to equipment, process, and environmental factors. Additionally, because of the extensive involvement of humans, person-to-person variation or project-to-project variation could be significant in service industries. The motivation level of the individual has an effect on the quality of service. Thus, the quality of work performed by auditors may vary from one individual to another. As tasks change, the specific requirements of projects may lead to performance variability in service functions because some individuals are more apt at doing certain things. A data entry operator for a utility company may make fewer errors when reading a well-designed short form that shows power consumption. The same operator when entering personnel data from a more complex form is liable to make more errors.

The principles and use of control charts have been described extensively in previous chapters. They can be used to monitor a service process and determine whether it is in a state of statistical control. Table 14-3 shows some service quality characteristics and the corresponding control charts that may be used to track their performance. Among control charts for variables, a chart for the mean $\bar{X}$ and range R may be used for measurable characteristics, such as those related to timeliness or facilities. Examples are the response time for correspondence in an insurance company, the time to serve customers in a restaurant, and the temperature in a hotel room. Among control charts for attributes, a chart for the fraction nonconforming (p-chart) can be used for service nonconformity characteristics. Some examples are the proportion of income tax returns that have errors, the proportion of billing errors, and the proportion of airline flights that are on schedule. Charts for the number of nonconformities (c-charts) or number of nonconformities per unit (u-charts) are applicable to service nonconformity, facility-related, and behavioral characteristics. Examples are the number of delays per 1000 transactions in a bank, the number of customer complaints related to discourteous service in a hotel, and the number of errors per 1000 purchase orders. Specific applications of these charts have been demonstrated in earlier chapters. A few more illustrations are found in Section 14-4.

The sampling plans discussed in previous chapters may also be applied to the service sector as appropriate. These include plans such as *ANSI/ASQC Z1.4*, Dodge–Romig plans, sequential sampling plans, and plans for continuous production. In auditing functions, sampling may be used to select the accounts to audit. Similar applications exist in the audit of Internal Revenue Service tax returns, transactions processed by a bank teller, and medicaid payments. Sampling techniques in service operations include the following.

100 percent sampling—When the cost of external errors or nonconformities is high, this sampling scheme may be used. Even though the cost of sampling and inspection is high, it is still cost-effective compared to having a nonconformity found by the customer. Consider, for example, transactions that are worth more than $100,000. An error in such a transaction would cause customer dissatisfaction to a degree that would seriously affect profitability of the company.

Convenience sampling—Samples are chosen based on the ease of drawing them and are influenced

TABLE 14-3 Control charts for monitoring some service quality characteristics

Quality characteristic	Control chart
Response time for correspondence in a consulting firm or insurance company Waiting time in a fast-food restaurant Processing time of claims in an insurance company	Chart for the mean ($\bar{X}$) and range (R)
Proportion of income tax returns that have errors Proportion of billing errors Proportion of shipments delivered on time Proportion of airline flights that are on time Proportion of errors in money transfers in a bank	Chart for fraction nonconforming (p-chart)
Number of delays per 1000 transactions in a bank Number of daily customer complaints in a hotel Number of errors per 100 purchase orders Number of daily compliments on a chef	Chart for number of nonconformities (c-chart) or number of nonconformities per unit (u-chart)

by the subjectivity of the individual performing the sampling. Some may choose the thinnest files in inspecting insurance claims, or some may choose the ones that are on the top of a pile. When conducting a quality survey, questionnaires may be mailed to the group of people that are known to be satisfied and most responsive. Such practices may distort the inferences that are drawn from the study.

Judgment sampling—Samples are chosen based on the opinion of an expert in the area. The personal judgment of the expert influences the manner in which samples are to be chosen. This may create a bias in the procedure. Caution should be exercised in drawing statistical inferences from these samples even though summary measures may be computed. An example of such a procedure could be a situation in which an expert recommends selecting purchase orders to review vendors who have dealt with the company for over two years. The expert feels that because the vendors are familiar with the procedures involved in preparing purchase orders, the error rate may be low. Thus, the recommendation of the expert may be to draw a sample once a week from these vendors.

Probability sampling—This technique has a statistical basis and is preferable for most situations. In random sampling, each item has an equal chance of being selected. This may be accomplished by the use of random number tables, as we have seen in earlier chapters. Sampling of vouchers for auditing, where 20 vouchers are to be selected from a population of 500, is one example. For stratified random sampling, where large differences are expected between groups in the population, an example could be the auditing of tax returns by the Internal Revenue Service. The IRS could first stratify the returns based on the estimated income. From each of the groups, tax returns could be chosen as a simple random sample. This would ensure that all income categories are represented in the audit.

14-3 A MODEL FOR SERVICE QUALITY

The unique features of service functions and industries define a role for the management of such industries. Figure 14-1 shows a model for service quality. Customer satisfaction is a function of the perceived quality of service, which is a measure of how the actual quality compares to the expected quality (Normann, 1991).

Customer expectations are built by customer perceptions of quality. There are internal and external factors that affect these perceptions. Among the external factors, which are not directly under the control of a service organization (shown by the dotted box in Figure 14-1), are the social values and changes in lifestyle of consumers, knowledge of the service, and the services offered by the competitors. The image presented by the company may also influence consumer perceptions. Companies use various techniques for monitoring customer perceptions; this falls under the category of image management. Typical methods are annual company reports and quarterly marketing sales reports. A customer who reads about a high sales volume will perceive the company to be in good stead. The company must be doing something right to have a high sales volume. Figure 14-2 shows some of the external and internal factors that influence customer perceptions. Client management is important for improving and meeting the changing needs of customers. Keeping abreast of consumer needs through interviews, polls, and surveys and making changes in the facilities and services provided to meet these needs will facilitate retaining and expanding the customer base. Another important concept is the creation of an atmosphere where the employees are motivated. A motivated employee helps create a favorable attitude on the part of the consumer. This leads to a synergistic cycle where a satisfied customer causes the employee to be further motivated.

In service systems, image management is central to retaining and attracting new customers. The company culture, the products and services delivered, and the achieved market segment have a significant impact on the company's reputation. The company must be careful to advertise what it can deliver. Building up a certain expectation level in the customer and failing to meet it will create dissatisfied customers and result in a loss of market share. For instance, if a recreational facility advertises free golf privileges for certain days of the month, then that promise must be delivered.

Creating a positive environment within the hierarchies of the company often affects the motivation of the company employees and thereby influences the service delivery system. In keeping with the philosophies of quality assurance and management, channels of open communication in a friendly atmosphere promote desirable employee behavior. It is difficult for an employee to maintain a degree of warmth with the customer in the service delivery process if the same degree of congeniality does not

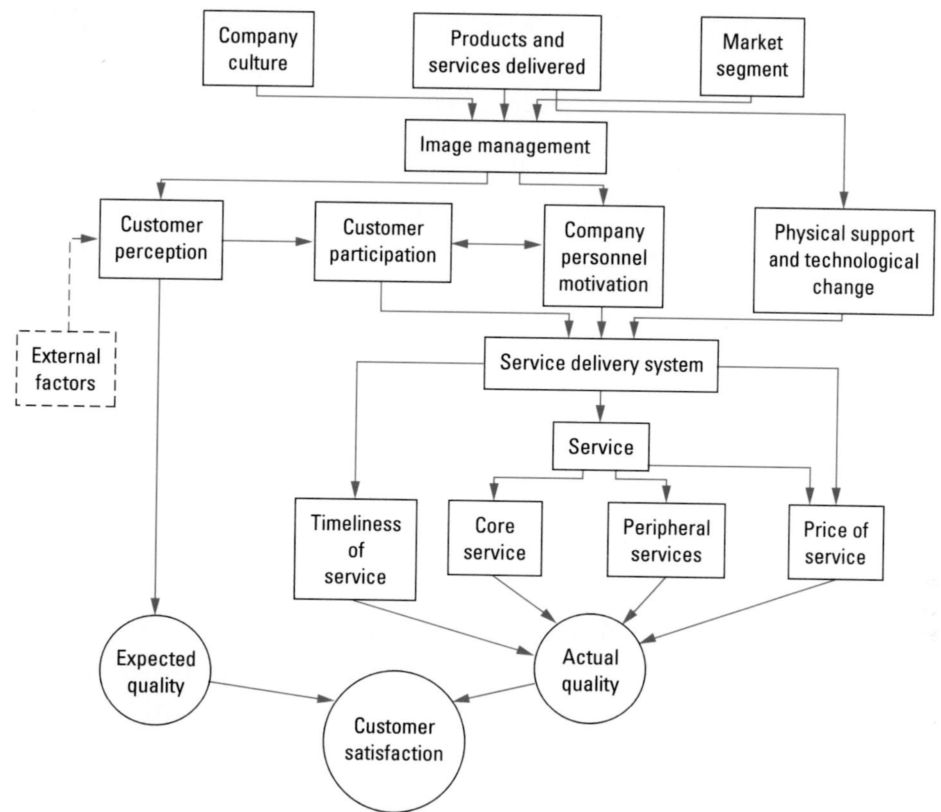

Figure 14-1 A model for service quality.

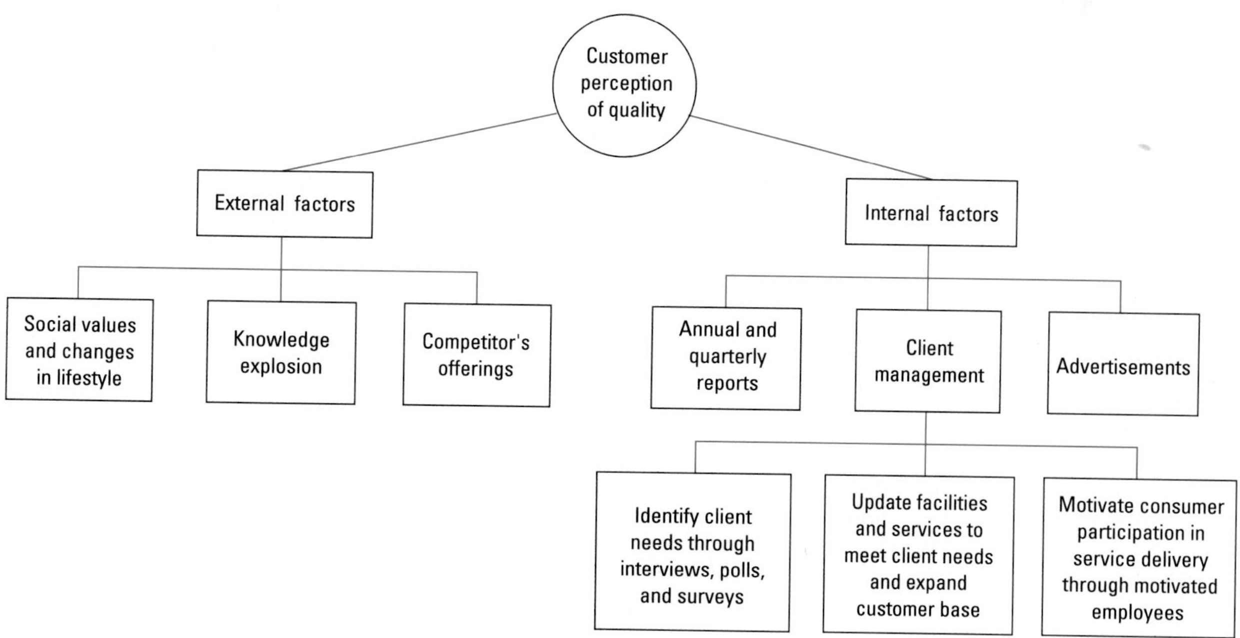

Figure 14-2 Factors that influence customer perception.

exist between the employee and his or her supervisor.

A service delivery system is influenced by the company personnel and their training, loyalty, and motivation, as well as the level of customer participation. Customer participation is affected by customer expectations. A customer who does not expect to receive a free gift when buying a certain amount of merchandise from a retail store will behave differently than one who does. Moreover, an employee's attitude may influence a customer's attitude, which in turn may have an effect on the employee's motivation, thereby closing the loop.

The physical facilities and the manner in which they are maintained to keep pace with the needs of the customer affect service functions and the efficiency and effectiveness of a service system. A hospital with the latest technology in cancer diagnosis and treatment will attract patients who require such a service.

The service that is provided may be thought of as the amalgamation of two components: core and peripheral services. The benefits received are both tangible and intangible. Consider a transportation company providing bus services between cities. The core service is the transport of customers between cities. Peripheral services include the comfort and safety of the bus stations, restroom and meal services, and transfer to and from main junctions in the city. Sometimes, peripheral services may influence the customer to select one company over its competitors. A careful analysis of all services that are provided by the company is essential to maintain and increase market share.

The actual service quality is a function of several factors such as the timeliness of the service, the manner in which it is performed, the adequacy of the service (both core and peripheral services), and the price of the service. Some service companies use a broad-based systems concept and provide several ancillary services. An automobile dealer may also provide financing, insurance, maintenance contracts, and gasoline. A commitment to the customer in the post-sale period is helpful in retaining customers. Evidence of good service spreads through word of mouth. How often have we heard that the customer is the company's most important advertiser? The customer compares the quality of the service received to his or her expectations. If the actual quality exceeds the expected quality, the result is a customer who is more than satisfied. As customer expectations change with time, due to internal and external factors, management must keep up with these changing needs and make appropriate adjustments.

14-4 APPLICATIONS TO VARIOUS SERVICE FUNCTIONS AND INDUSTRIES

This section presents some applications of quality control and improvement techniques in the service sector. The techniques used here are all discussed in previous chapters. Usage of some control charts will be demonstrated in the context of service functions. Standardized sampling plans also find application in the service sector. Tools for quality improvement (such as Pareto analysis and cause-and-effect diagrams) may be used in service functions and industries.

Administrative Operations

Administrative operations in service functions and industries involve a good bit of human interaction and usually a high volume of paperwork, which creates the opportunity for errors. Consequently, one way to improve the efficiency of administrative operations is to conduct a thorough analysis of the flow of paperwork and eliminate unnecessary or redundant steps. Sometimes, proper design of forms may reduce the number of mistakes. For an individual filing for insurance, a vendor preparing a purchase order, an employee filing for travel expenses, or a data operator entering personnel data into the computer, a form that is difficult to understand and fill out increases the chances of mistakes.

Forms must be designed that are simple to understand. The requested information should be readily obtainable by the party filling out the form. The layout of the form should be such that the individuals in charge of processing the information can conduct their operations in a sequential manner as simply as possible. It should not require flipping the pages back and forth, which can cause more errors. How frequently have we encountered income tax forms that are difficult to comprehend? The chances of making a mistake increases if we are not sure of the calculation procedures. What about legal documents, such as mortgage application forms? Would it be easy for us to detect any errors made by the legal aid who fills out the forms?

In manufacturing, product and process design are fundamental and precede the production phase; the same is true of administrative operations. Form design, the information to be transcribed, the sequence of actions for processing the desired service function, and the individuals to be involved are issues that must be addressed.

Personnel training is another important aspect that influences efficiency and the number of errors. Preparing purchase orders, processing vouchers, processing a customer's ticket for an airline trip, and processing a freight bill are operations that are better performed when the individual or agent is adequately trained for the particular function. The stability of service functions may be checked through the use of control charts. Typically, charts for fraction nonconforming (p-charts) or charts for the number of nonconformities (c-charts) have a variety of applications in administrative operations. Some examples of quality characteristics for analysis are the number of errors per 100 purchase orders, the number of entry errors per 10 database files, the number of typographical errors per 20 typed pages, the number of transactional errors per 200 customer accounts in a bank, the proportion of errors in money transfer in a bank, and the proportion of bills that have errors in a mail-order company. Tools for improvement include Pareto analysis, cause-and-effect analysis, and experimental design and analysis.

Example 14-1: The number of processing errors per 100 purchase orders is monitored by a company, with the objective being to totally eliminate such errors. Table 14-4 shows observations that were randomly selected from all purchase orders. The company is in the process of testing the effects of a new purchase order form that it has designed. The last five observations were made for the new form. Construct a control chart that the company may use for monitoring the selected quality characteristic. Comment on the effect of the newly designed purchase order form. Is the company capable of achieving the desired goal?

TABLE 14-4 Number of processing errors per 100 purchase orders

Observation number	Number of processing errors	Observation number	Number of processing errors
1	6	14	3
2	4	15	6
3	2	16	1
4	3	17	5
5	4	18	2
6	7	19	6
7	5	20	4
8	7	21	2
9	11	22	3
10	4	23	2
11	2	24	1
12	5	25	2
13	4		

Solution. The control chart to use is the c-chart for the number of processing errors per 100 purchase orders. Recall that the upper and lower control limits are given by

$$\bar{c} \pm 3\sqrt{\bar{c}} \tag{14.1}$$

where $\bar{c}$ represents the average number of processing errors per 100 purchase orders. From the data in Table 14-4, we have

$$\bar{c} = \frac{101}{25} = 4.040$$

The control limits are

$$4.040 \pm 3\sqrt{4.040} = 4.040 \pm 6.030$$
$$= (-1.990, 10.070) = (0., 10.070)$$

Since the lower control limit is found to be negative, it is converted to zero.

Figure 14-3 shows the c-chart with the observations and the upper and lower control limits plotted. Observation number 9, with 11 processing errors, plots above the upper control limit. Analysis for that observation revealed that the person who normally processes the purchase orders was absent during that time period; a temporary replacement was used. It was felt that an assignable cause for the large number of processing errors for observation number 9 is the replacement. The company subsequently decided to have replacements trained in the processing of purchase orders prior to assigning them to these tasks. The revised control limits are found after eliminating observation number 9, for which an assignable cause had been identified. The new center line is

$$\bar{c} = \frac{90}{24} = 3.750$$

The revised control limits are

$$\text{UCL} = 3.750 + 3\sqrt{3.750} = 9.559$$
$$\text{LCL} = 3.750 - 3\sqrt{3.750} = -2.059 \rightarrow 0$$

All of the observations indicate a stable pattern within the revised control limits.

Let us examine the impact of the newly designed purchase order form on the number of processing errors. From Figure 14-3, we observe a downward trend in the number of processing errors for the last five observations. Even though the number of processing errors did increase by one for the last observation, there is a downward run of four points. The preliminary indication is that the new form is an improvement over the old one. Of course, further observations are needed to confirm this inference, since only five observations from the new form have been made.

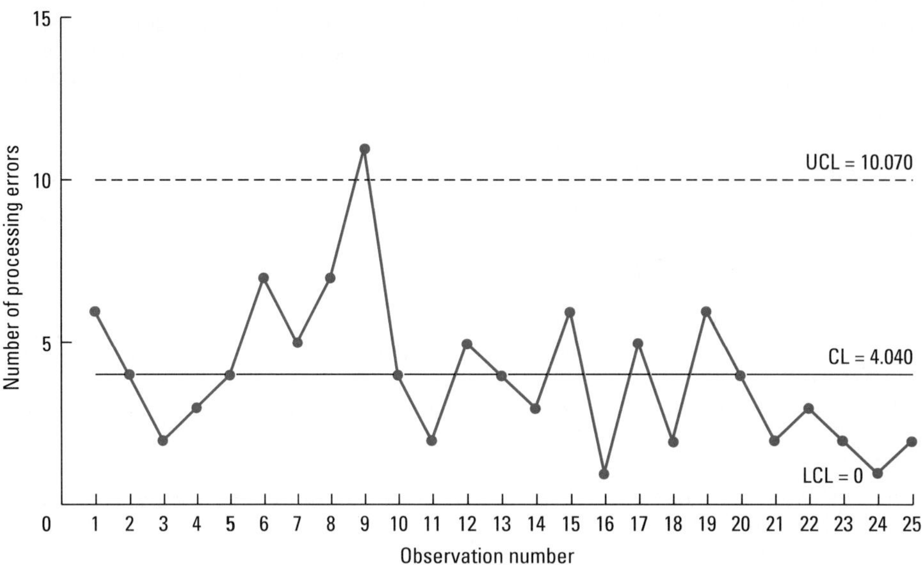

Figure 14-3 Example of a *c*-chart for the number of processing errors per 100 purchase orders.

To discuss the capability of the existing process in meeting the desirable goal of zero errors, note that the revised control limits reflect the capability of the process. The lower control limit, which has a value of zero, is about 1.94 standard deviations below the center line; it is, therefore, possible to achieve zero errors but not probable.

Banking

The increased volume of activity that banks go through on a daily basis demands the attention of quality control and improvement procedures. Although automation has helped banks perform their functions in a quick and timely manner, the risk of errors has also increased. Banks operate under a host of government regulations. Additionally, customers expect an error-free performance. Of the four service quality characteristics described previously, three are more important in the context of banking. Human factors and behavioral characteristics such as courtesy, contact, and communication are quite important, as they have a major impact on customer satisfaction. Timeliness characteristics such as the waiting time and transaction processing time are also of concern. Processing times vary based on the nature of the transaction. It may be expected that a transfer of funds will take no more than a couple of minutes whereas cashing a check from a foreign bank may take two to four weeks. The customer should be kept advised of the required processing time, based on the nature of the transaction, because that will influence the expected quality. Perfect accuracy is expected as far as service nonconformity characteristics (such as errors in transactions) are concerned. In fact, about 10 percent of the employees in a bank work on the detection and correction of errors.

Among the methods of quality control that are applicable to banking, attribute acceptance sampling and process control techniques are quite pertinent. One particular operation that is relevant to banking is magnetic ink character recognition (MICR), which has an impact on the quality of checks (Latzko, 1986). Banks have machines that automatically process checks. The account number, transaction amount, and other pertinent information are printed on the checks through characters that are sensed magnetically. The requirements for these magnetic characters and the process through which they are created are very stringent. For example, the characters have to lie within certain regions of the check area, the ink has to be uniformly distributed, the properties of the ink (such as viscosity) have to be within certain bounds, and the degree of impact when the character is embossed has to be controlled (the ink cannot get sufficient magnetic strength if it is recessed too much into the paper). If the reader or sorter cannot sense the characters properly, the check has to be processed manually. It is estimated that the added cost per check or document that has to be processed manually is between 10 and 30 cents. Thus, the incoming quality of printed checks, and the encoding process by which the check amount is entered demand careful control.

Sampling plans such as *ANSI/ASQC Z1.4* may be used to measure the quality of documents such as personal checks, noncontinuous checks or forms, or continuous MICR checks or forms. As an illustration, suppose MICR checks are printed in batches of 30,000 each. From the discussion in Chapter 9 on attribute sampling plans using *ANSI/ASQC Z1.4*, Table 9-11 gives a sample size code letter of K, assuming a general inspection level of I. Assuming normal inspection and an AQL of 0.4 percent (which printers usually have no difficulty in meeting), Table 9-12 gives a sample size of 125 with a rejection number of 2. So, a random sample of 125 checks is to be selected from the lot of 30,000 checks. If 2 or more checks have characters that are not recognizable by the MICR reader, the lot will be rejected. The burden then falls on the supplier of the MICR checks to demonstrate acceptable quality standards. The supplier could provide control charts concerning the process through which the MICR characters are printed or the results of any sampling inspection performed on the finished checks. This could save the bank from performing receiving inspection. Another application of sampling concerns the purchase of microfilms. To ensure the quality of microfilms, sampling inspection involving destructive testing is used. Either the microfilm works or it does not. Attribute inspection plans such as *ANSI/ASQC Z1.4* or sequential sampling plans may be used.

Process control methodology may be used for check processing and other clerical operations. A p-chart for the proportion of checks that have an error in the encoding process (where the dollar amount and other information are entered) is one area for investigation. Although acceptance sampling has its place in testing incoming material or outgoing product, it is not efficient for controlling ongoing operations. Attribute control charts such as p- and c-charts are useful in banking operations. Clerical processing involves functions such as typing, entering data into a computer system, and advising a customer on a particular transaction. The quality characteristic is an attribute. Precise definition of the degree to which the function is effectively performed may be difficult. Rather, one might be able to specify whether the advising of the customer is acceptable or not. Another feature of clerical operations is that the output of several clerks is combined at the departmental level. Therefore, keeping track of the proportion of processing errors only at the departmental level may not identify the source of the problem and possible remedial actions. Information about individual clerks would help in these situations. Finally, a measure of process capability is obtained from the center line and the control limits of the corresponding attribute chart.

Example 14-2: A bank has a new vendor that does the printing of its MICR checks. In order to certify the vendor, the bank is undergoing incoming inspection of the checks for a trial period. Checks are produced in batches of 32,000. The acceptable quality level (AQL) that has been negotiated between the bank and the vendor is 0.25 percent. Determine the sampling plan using *ANSI/ASQC Z1.4* if general inspection level I is selected. Assume normal inspection is in effect.

Solution. The *ANSI/ASQC Z1.4* standardized sampling plans for attributes is used. From Table 9-11, for a lot size of 32,000 and general inspection level I, the sample size code letter is K. From Table 9-12, for a sample size code letter of K and an AQL of 0.25 percent, the code letter changes to L, with the acceptance number being 1 and the rejection number 2. The sample size is 200. The sampling plan calls for randomly choosing 200 checks from the lot of 32,000. If 2 or more checks have characters that are not recognizable by the recorder, the lot is deemed unacceptable.

Example 14-3: Every employee in a check-processing department goes through a training period of four months, after which the employee has individual responsibility for the operation. The work of an employee after eight months on the job is being studied. Table 14-5 shows the number of errors and the number of items sampled over a period of two months. The first 16 observations were sampled from among 400 items each, and the remaining 9 observations were sampled from among 300 items each. Determine if the employee's performance can be judged stable. Comment on the capability of the employee.

Solution. The p-chart for the proportion of errors by the employee should be constructed. We first compute $\bar{p}$, the average proportion of errors, for the data in Table 14-5. We have

$$\bar{p} = \frac{197}{9100} = 0.0216$$

Recall that the control limits for a p-chart are obtained from

$$\bar{p} \pm 3\sqrt{\frac{\bar{p}(1-\bar{p})}{n}} \tag{14.2}$$

where n represents the number of items sampled for each observation. We will therefore have a set of control limits for the first 16 observations based on $n = 400$; the last 9 observations will have a different set of control lim-

TABLE 14-5 Number of check processing errors of an employee

Oberservation number	Number of errors	Number of items sampled
1	12	400
2	9	400
3	13	400
4	7	400
5	6	400
6	10	400
7	14	400
8	7	400
9	5	400
10	6	400
11	4	400
12	9	400
13	11	400
14	18	400
15	8	400
16	6	400
17	4	300
18	6	300
19	5	300
20	8	300
21	10	300
22	7	300
23	4	300
24	5	300
25	3	300

its based on $n = 300$. The control limits for the first 16 observations are calculated as

$$0.0216 \pm 3\sqrt{\frac{(0.0216)(1 - 0.0216)}{400}}$$

or

$$0.0216 \pm 0.0218 = (-0.0002,\ 0.0434) = (0,\ 0.0434)$$

The control limits for the last 9 observations are

$$0.0216 \pm 3\sqrt{\frac{(0.0216)(1 - 0.0216)}{300}}$$

or

$$0.0216 \pm 0.0252 = (-0.0036,\ 0.0468) = (0,\ 0.0468)$$

The proportion of processing errors is calculated for each observation and plotted on the control chart as shown in Figure 14-4. Observation number 14, with a proportion of errors of 0.045, is above the upper control limit. In an investigation for assignable causes, it was found that errors in data entry could be a possible reason for the high proportion of errors. After deleting observation number 14, with the assumption that a remedial action has been taken to offset the data entry errors, the revised center line is

$$\bar{p} = \frac{179}{8700} = 0.0206$$

The revised control limits for the first 16 observations are

$$0.0206 \pm 3\sqrt{\frac{(0.0206)(1 - 0.0206)}{400}}$$

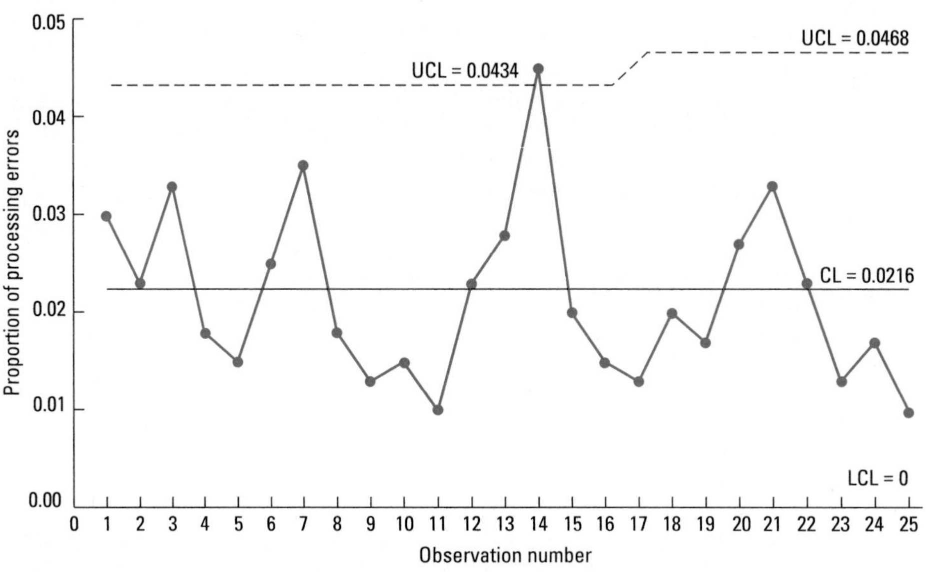

Figure 14-4 Example of a p-chart for the proportion of processing errors.

or

$$0.0206 \pm 0.0213 = (-0.0007,\ 0.0419) = (0,\ 0.0419)$$

The revised control limits for the last 9 observations are

$$0.0206 \pm 3\sqrt{\frac{(0.0206)(1-0.0206)}{300}}$$

or

$$0.0206 \pm 0.0246 = (-0.0040,\ 0.0452) = (0,\ 0.0452)$$

All of the remaining observations are within the control limits and exhibit a stable pattern. The processing operation may be deemed to be in control.

Let us comment on the capability of the employee concerning the proportion of errors. With the processing operation in a state of control, the average proportion of errors is 0.0206, which is an indication of what can be expected, on average, from the employee. The corresponding control limits are (0, 0.0419) for $n = 400$ and (0, 0.0452) for $n = 300$. Thus, it would be unusual to expect error-free performance from the employee, even though very occasionally an employee might achieve that desired level.

Education

Education is an area that affects us all. It is the backbone of a society. Quality education is a necessity in all phases; at every level, the knowledge imparted must be relevant and substantive. The amount of knowledge retained can be a function of the individual receiving the service and the service delivery process. We have seen alarming rates of children who have not mastered certain desirable levels of reading, writing, and arithmetic as required for their grade level. This is where quality control measures may come in handy.

The control of quality is rather unique since it involves transformation of human qualities and values into learning and retaining knowledge. One major influence on quality concerns the competency and behavioral characteristics of individuals performing the service (that is, teachers). Knowledge of the relevant field is a must, but it is not enough. The delivery process is also important. Being motivated and enthusiastic about teaching and creating an interest and curiosity on the part of the students are traits of a good teacher. Measures of quality associated with the individuals performing the service are, for example, the technical background, certification and recognition by other professional associations, and research and publication in the area of expertise. Facility-related characteristics play a major role. For instance, science and technology fields require current laboratory facilities and equipment. An adequate library with holdings of current periodicals complements the delivery process. The availability of modern computer facilities contributes to the effectiveness of the service.

In the field of education, a certain degree of control is achieved over the customers for whom the service is intended. For example, private institutions can be selective in choosing their customers. Measures such as grade point average and scores on standardized tests are used to screen candidates. By controlling the input quality of students, some degree of control is automatically exercised on the output. This is similar to making a purchase or selecting a vendor, whereby certain criteria are used to make the selection. In an educational setting the criterion may be a weighted score based on performance in several activities, where a minimum cutoff level is utilized. Characteristics that measure the quality of the output product have tangible and intangible components. The proportion of graduates who have job offers within a certain period of time or the average salary of graduates with job offers could be considered measures of quality. Whereas these measures are tangible, others are difficult to quantify. The satisfaction and fulfillment from obtaining a quality education is something that is hard to measure on a numerical scale.

There is room for a variety of applications of quality control and improvement methods in education. The evaluation of the teaching performance of university professors has been a topic of debate for years. Do the evaluation questions really measure the ability and devotion of the instructor? Are the responses to the questions influenced by the motivation level of the students? Are the responses based on the performance level of the students? Regardless of what the answers to these questions may be, a selected measurement instrument such as an evaluation form filled out by students, may be used to evaluate the performance of a particular instructor over a period of time. A control chart for the average and range of the score may indicate any trends or unique situations. Furthermore, a control chart may be used to identify statistically significant differences between scores that plot outside the control limits, as opposed to citing a difference between two scores based on their relative ranking. Similarly, a control chart for the mean and the range may be used for the standardized scores of incoming students to determine trends and differences over time or between students of various disciplines.

Control charts may also be used for facility and service delivery characteristics. The number of students unable to register for a certain course, as monitored by a c-chart, may help in identifying the need for additional sections of that course. The time to wait before accessing the main computer could be plotted on a chart for the mean and range to judge the need to procure additional hardware. The number of monthly complaints received by the librarian could be monitored by a c-chart. Methods for improvement could be handled by Pareto analysis and cause-and-effect diagrams.

Example 14-4: A major university recently expanded the physical facilities of its library. Upon renovation, the layout of the books and periodicals as well as government documents on microfiche underwent a reorganization. In order to better serve its users, a complaint and suggestion box has been set up in the library. Table 14-6 shows the number of complaints received on a weekly basis. Prepare an appropriate control chart, and comment on the stability of the service function.

Solution. A c-chart for the number of weekly complaints seems appropriate. The center line is found using the data from Table 14-6:

$$\bar{c} = \frac{220}{20} = 11$$

The upper and lower control limits are

$$11 \pm 3\sqrt{11} = (2.95, 19.95)$$

A plot of the number of weekly complaints is shown on the c-chart in Figure 14-5. The service function is out of control. For observation number 4, the number of complaints is 26, which plots well above the upper control limit. An investigation for that week revealed that 20 of the 26 complaints were related to the government documents section. Further analysis showed that many documents had been misplaced. This was subsequently corrected. From Figure 14-5, a generally decreasing trend is observed, which is a desirable pattern. The first five weeks showed a large number of complaints. However, remedial actions by the library staff seemed to better serve the users.

TABLE 14-6 Number of complaints on a weekly basis

Observation number	Number of complaints	Observation number	Number of complaints
1	15	11	8
2	17	12	6
3	16	13	10
4	26	14	15
5	16	15	7
6	8	16	9
7	10	17	6
8	5	18	5
9	12	19	8
10	14	20	7

If the control limits are to be revised, the new center line would be obtained by deleting observation number 4 after remedial action has been taken. The revised center line is

$$\bar{c} = \frac{220 - 26}{19} = 10.210$$

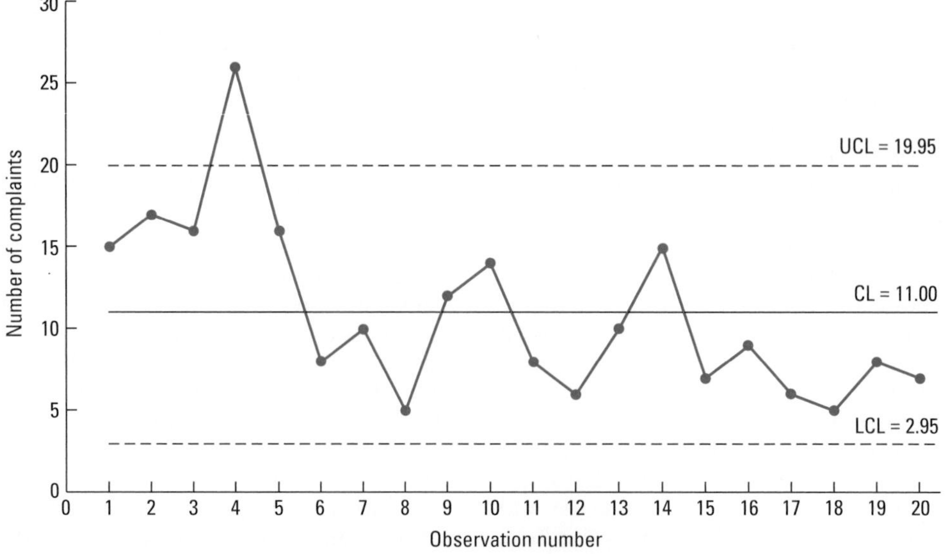

Figure 14-5 Example of a c-chart for the number of weekly complaints.

The revised control limits are

$$10.210 \pm 3\sqrt{10.210} = (0.414, 19.586)$$

These limits would be used for future analysis.

Food Industry

The quality of food is composed of several characteristics that differentiate units of a product and have an impact on the acceptability of the product. Therefore, the more clearly an attribute is defined and measured, the easier it is to judge the quality of the food. The measurement process varies depending on the attribute in question. Some quality characteristics are readily measurable, such as the proportion of fat in meat, the percentage of foreign material in a cereal, and the protein content in milk. Other characteristics and attributes are not easily quantifiable, such as the smell of a ripe cantaloupe or the taste of a particular brand of strawberry preserves.

The requirements for the level of quality are set by the customer, who may not necessarily be the ultimate consumer. The customer could be a wholesaler, distributor, or a food manufacturer using the product as raw material. Additionally, in the food industry, specifications or requirements are influenced and set by federal agencies such as the Department of Agriculture or the Food and Drug Administration (FDA). For instance, meat is classified in a graded scale by the Department of Agriculture. A total quality systems approach is needed in which the level of quality is monitored at each step, starting with raw materials and continuing through processing, packaging, and delivery of the finished product. With perishable items, packaging, delivery, and storage of the food items are important.

A variety of quality attributes exist in the food industry. A consumer may combine specific attributes to arrive at a single measure of quality, generally referred to as *sensory quality*. The sensory category includes attributes such as the appearance, flavor, and kinesthetics associated with the product. In terms of appearance, we have specific attributes such as the color, size, or shape of the product. Flavor consists of attributes such as smell and taste. Kinesthetics, or muscle sense, includes attributes such as texture and viscosity. The amount of force required to initiate flow is a measure of these two attributes. Thus, control of texture or viscosity could be monitored through a control chart for the average and range of the force required to initiate flow. Sensory quality characteristics are not usually under strict government control since the consumers are in a position to judge such quality levels through their own senses. These attributes are generally adjusted not for consumer protection but rather to match consumer preference. Knowledge of customer preferences will provide benchmarks for desirable levels of these attributes. The size of the unit product is another example of such an attribute. For instance, a small curd size of cottage cheese may be preferred by the consumer. A control chart for the mean and range of the curd size may be used to monitor the level of quality.

Another class of quality characteristics is quantitative in nature and deals with the amount of a particular component in the product. These characteristics are easier to measure, and a variable chart, such as a chart for the mean and the range, may be used to track the level of quality. Examples are the proportion of protein, fat, or moisture in meat, the lactose content in milk, the acidity of fruits and vegetables, and the proportion of damaged kernels in cereals. Certain attributes, though of interest to consumers, cannot be readily judged by their senses. It is, however, important to the consumer to know that the food will not have any harmful effects. The consumer cannot judge the presence of toxic or harmful ingredients. This is where government controls are needed. Another issue concerns the nutritive value and the presence of certain nutrients at some minimum levels as advertised by the company. Cereal manufacturers advertise that their product contains a certain percentage of the minimum daily requirements of some vitamins and minerals. It should be possible to test such claims.

Consider some quality characteristics that may be of interest in a variety of food products and the control charts that may be used to track their performance. For meat and meat products, the percentage of fat, water, or protein, the water-to-protein ratio, or the acidity can be monitored through control charts for the average $\overline{X}$ and range R; for the microorganism or bacteria count, a c-chart can be used. For poultry and egg products, the egg shell shape and texture, graded in categories, may be monitored by an attribute chart (such as a p-chart); for shell thickness or crushing strength, an $\overline{X}$- and R-chart can be used. For dairy products, the fat, protein, lactose, or ash content of milk, the proportion of fat or salt in butter, or the proportion of carbohydrates in ice cream can be monitored through $\overline{X}$- and R-charts. For fruits and vegetables, the moisture content, acidity, sugar/acid ratio, or the amount of a preservative can be monitored through an $\overline{X}$- and R-chart; for the number of critical, major, or minor defects (such as presence of insects or mechanical defects due to improper handling after harvest), a c-chart is appropriate. For cereals and cereal products, the protein content, iron content, or kernel hardness could be monitored by $\overline{X}$- and R-charts; the proportion of damaged kernels may be controlled by a p-chart.

Example 14-5: The amount of a certain preservative added to dairy products should not exceed certain levels of 23 ± 6 units (set by the Food and Drug Administration). Samples of size 5 of processed cheese produced the values of the average and range shown in Table 14-7. Determine the acceptability of the cheese, and comment on the ability to meet government standards.

Solution. We construct control charts for the mean level $\overline{X}$ of the preservative and its range R using the data in Table 14-7. The center line on the R-chart is

$$\overline{R} = \frac{144}{25} = 5.760$$

The upper and lower control limits on the R-chart are

$$\text{UCL} = D_4\overline{R} = (2.114)(5.760) = 12.177$$

$$\text{LCL} = D_3\overline{R} = 0(5.760) = 0.0$$

where the control chart factors D_4 and D_3, for a sample size of 5, are found from Appendix A.7. The control chart for the range, as shown in Figure 14-6, exhibits a stable pattern.

TABLE 14-7 Average and range of preservative level of cheese

Observation number	Average level of preservative	Range
1	22	5
2	26	4
3	26	6
4	24	7
5	22	3
6	21	5
7	29	7
8	25	8
9	22	4
10	25	6
11	25	9
12	22	3
13	21	5
14	22	7
15	20	5
16	24	8
17	25	6
18	23	8
19	20	5
20	22	4
21	22	6
22	23	7
23	24	5
24	22	6
25	25	5

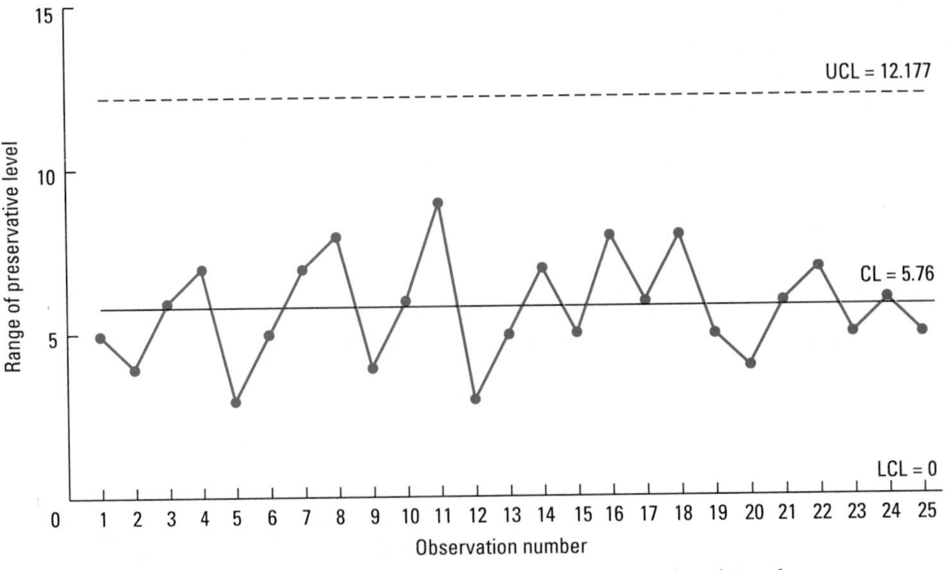

Figure 14-6 Example of an R-chart for the preservative level in cheese.

Next, the center line on the $\overline{X}$-chart is calculated:

$$\overline{\overline{X}} = \frac{582}{25} = 23.280$$

The upper and lower control limits on the $\overline{X}$-chart are

$$\text{UCL} = \overline{\overline{X}} + A_2\overline{R} = 23.280 + (0.577)(5.76) = 26.603$$

$$\text{LCL} = \overline{\overline{X}} - A_2\overline{R} = 23.280 - (0.577)(5.76) = 19.956$$

where the control chart factor A_2 is found from Appendix A-7. Observation number 7, having a mean preservative level of 29, is found to plot above the upper control limit, as shown in Figure 14-7. An investigation revealed that the concentration of the preservative for that batch had increased due to an incorrect setting of a pressure-sensitive adjustment valve. With the assignable cause found and adequate action taken, the control limits are revised by deleting observation number 7. The revised center line for the $\overline{X}$-chart is

$$\overline{\overline{X}} = \frac{582 - 29}{24} = 23.042$$

The revised center line for the R-chart is

$$\overline{R} = \frac{144 - 7}{24} = 5.708$$

The revised limits on the $\overline{X}$-chart are

$$23.042 \pm (0.577)(5.708) = (19.749, 26.335)$$

The revised limits on the R-chart are

$$\text{UCL} = D_4\overline{R} = (2.114)(5.708) = 12.067$$

$$\text{LCL} = D_3\overline{R} = 0(5.708) = 0$$

All of the remaining observations are found to be in control.

In order to determine the ability to meet government standards, we first estimate the standard deviation of the preservative level as

$$\hat{\sigma} = \frac{\overline{R}}{d_2} = \frac{5.708}{2.326} = 2.454$$

where d_2 is found from Appendix A-7 for a sample size of 5. Assuming the distribution of the preservative level to be normal, the process capability is calculated (using the formula for an off-centered process):

$$C_{pk} = \min\left[\frac{U - \overline{\overline{X}}}{3\hat{\sigma}}, \frac{\overline{\overline{X}} - L}{3\hat{\sigma}}\right]$$

$$= \min\left[\frac{(29 - 23.042)}{3(2.454)}, \frac{(23.042 - 17)}{3(2.454)}\right]$$

$$= 0.809$$

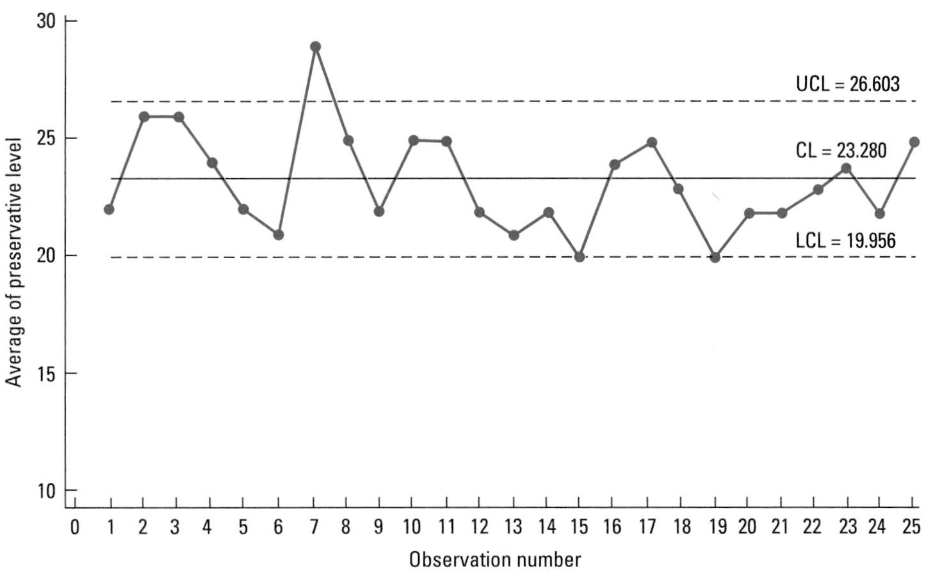

Figure 14-7 Example of an $\overline{X}$-chart for the average preservative level in cheese.

Since C_{pk} is less than 1, we have an undesirable situation. Not all of the product is acceptable with respect to the stipulated government standards.

To estimate the proportion of a product that does not meet government standards, given the assumption of a normal distribution of preservatives, the standard normal values are calculated at the upper and lower specification limits. We have

$$Z_1 = (U - \overline{\overline{X}})/\hat{\sigma}$$
$$= (29 - 23.042)/2.454 = 2.428 \simeq 2.43$$
$$Z_2 = (L - \overline{\overline{X}})/\hat{\sigma}$$
$$= (17 - 23.042)/2.454 = -2.462 \simeq -2.46$$

Using the standard normal tables in Appendix A-3, the proportion of the product that exceeds the upper specification limit is 0.0075. The proportion of the product that is below the lower specification limit is 0.0069. The total proportion that does not meet specifications is 0.0144. Thus, even with a stable process, management has a task to deal with. They must come up with methods that will reduce the variability of the preservative level among batches. In its current state, the company is not meeting government standards.

Government—Federal and State

A variety of services are provided by federal and state governments, such as recreational needs, housing, education, environmental quality, finance, small business, safety, transportation. Some government agencies provide service directly to the consumer; others are regulatory and deal with the upkeep of desirable quality levels for the protection of the consumer. A few of the government agencies, the quality characteristics of interest, and the corresponding quality control and improvement techniques are discussed below.

A descriptive study of existing levels of the quality characteristic may be accomplished through frequency or relative frequency histograms. For example, the income distribution of families receiving food stamps or housing subsidies from the government may be obtained from a relative frequency histogram. Such information may assist in determining adequate cutoff levels of income for families to qualify for the service. A trend chart of the total amount allocated by the government may aid in budget preparation.

Opportunities for the application of control charts and sampling techniques exist in many places. Consider the Internal Revenue Service of the federal government. In order to determine whether tax returns should be audited, the ratio of the adjusted gross income to the taxable income could be monitored on a p-chart. Unusually large values of the ratio could be a flag for further investigation. Another statistical application might involve determining the number of items to sample when it is desired to estimate a characteristic to within certain bounds. For instance, suppose we desire to estimate the proportion of delinquent accounts to within 3 percent of the true proportion with a desired confidence level of 0.95. How many accounts must be sampled? We may use the sampling concepts described in Chapter 3 and Equation 3.75 to determine the sample size:

$$n = \frac{z_{\alpha/2}^2 p(1-p)}{B^2} \tag{14.3}$$

where $z_{\alpha/2}$ is the standard normal variate found from Appendix A-3, corresponding to a right tail area of $\alpha/2$ (where $1-\alpha$ represents the desired confidence level), p is the true proportion that we wish to estimate, and B is the tolerable error bound. If p is not known, a conservative estimate of n is obtained by using a value of 0.5 for p.

Example 14-6: The Internal Revenue Service wishes to estimate the proportion of accounts that are delinquent to within 3 percent with a probability of 0.95. It does not know the true proportion of delinquent accounts. How many accounts must be sampled?

Solution. The tolerable error bound B is 0.03. From Appendix A-3, since the desired level of confidence is 0.95, the standard normal value for a right tail area of 0.025 is $z_{.025} = 1.96$. Since no information is available on the true proportion of delinquent accounts, we use a value of p of 0.5. The sample size is computed as follows using Equation 14.3:

$$n = \frac{(1.96)^2 0.5(1-0.5)}{(0.03)^2} = 1067.11 \simeq 1068$$

As further information becomes available about the proportion of delinquent accounts in the future, the sample size can be reduced by using the available estimate.

Regulatory agencies designed for consumer protection are well-suited to the application of quality control techniques. Consider the Food and Drug Administration (FDA). The quality of agricultural products is amenable to the use of control charts. The proportion of cocoa beans infested by insects or the proportion of wheat grains that are moldy could be monitored by a p-chart. Similarly, the control of aflatoxin from shelled peanuts or corn could be monitored through a p-chart by determining its concentration level in parts per billion (ppb). The appropriate sample size determination to estimate the level of aflatoxin to within certain bounds may be found from Equation 14.3. The number of errors due to misclassification, miscounting, and transcription for such agencies as the Consumer Product Safety Commission may be tracked through attribute charts (such as the c-chart). Federal agencies designed for consumer assistance such as the Department of Health, Education, and Welfare and the Small Business Administration may also use quality control methods. A p-chart may be used to control the proportion of loans that have been liquidated or the proportion of small businesses that receive assistance.

The Environmental Protection Agency (EPA) at the federal level and similar agencies at the state level help to control the quality of such resources as air and water. The level of carbon monoxide or nitrogen oxides in air could be monitored through control charts for the average $\overline{X}$ and range R. Similarly, the level of dissolved oxygen in water could be controlled by an $\overline{X}$- and R-chart. If certain standards which may serve as the upper specification limit are specified, the degree of conformance to government standards may be determined. The approach would be similar to the process capability analysis (discussed in previous chapters). Sample sizes would be influenced by knowledge of the characteristic's variability and the degree of closeness to which we prefer to estimate the population mean. Equation 3.73 gives the sample size as

$$n = \frac{z_{\alpha/2}^2 \sigma^2}{B^2} \tag{14.4}$$

where $z_{\alpha/2}$ is the standard normal variate for a right tail area of $\alpha/2$, $(1 - \alpha)$ is the desired confidence level in the estimation of the population mean, σ represents the population standard deviation, and B is the tolerable error bound.

Example 14-7: The Environmental Protection Agency wishes to estimate the average level of carbon monoxide in air in the vicinity of a large metropolitan area. From historical evidence, an estimate of the standard deviation of the level of carbon monoxide is 9 parts per million. The agency desires to estimate the average level of carbon monoxide to within 3 parts per million with a probability of 0.95. Find the number of samples that the agency should select.

Solution. For Equation 14.4, we have an estimate of σ of 9, $B = 3$, and $z_{\alpha/2} = z_{.025} = 1.96$. The required sample size is

$$n = \frac{(1.96)^2(9)^2}{(3)^2} = 34.57 \simeq 35$$

Health Care Services

The provision of health care services through doctors, hospitals, nursing homes, or clinics is something that everyone is concerned about. Although the consumer influences the level of quality, there are other groups that also play an important role in demanding and setting quality standards. The Joint Commission on Accreditation of Healthcare Organizations (JCAHO) is a highly influential group that sets certain guidelines on quality requirements. In order to be accredited, the provider of the service must meet these guidelines. Consumer advocacy groups and legislators may also have an impact on quality.

It is important to realize the unique circumstances of health care facilities. For most other services the consumer pays for the service received, but here that need not be the case. The federal government provides assistance through medicare/medicaid programs. Depending on the guidelines set by these programs, which limit the maximum amount that may be paid, the quality of services provided by hospitals, clinics, and so on will be affected. Thus, if these health care providers are to operate profitably, the quality level of services must be modified based on the amount of money received for the services. Professional societies (such as the American Medical Association), physicians, and healthcare executives also play an important role. After all, the physicians perform the service. Healthcare executives set policies, based on providing adequate service at a reasonable price, and plan their execution.

Another unique feature is in the organizational structure of hospital administration. The governing board and administrative officers are separate from the medical staff. The board of trustees for private hospitals is usually made up of representatives of the owners. The selected trustees may not be physicians. In public hospitals, where board members are selected from among local citizens, it is expected that the professional expertise of those on the board will contribute to the effective management of the hospital. The executive policies set by the board are carried out through the hospital administration. On the other hand, the physicians are the other source of authority and administrative power. The physicians might serve as consultants rather than being direct employees of the hospital. It is of course possible (and is becoming more frequent) to find physicians who are either hospital employees or have contractual obligations to provide specific services such as surgery. Therefore, it is important that these two administrative powers act in harmony to create a total quality system in the hospital framework.

An integrated administrative team that includes physicians is needed to define quality needs and propose actions that will deliver quality services to meet those needs (O'Sullivan and Grujic, 1991). In some cases, the patient is not in a position to judge the technical competency of the service received. Administrators who do not have a medical background are not competent to do so either; only peer reviews by physicians can judge quality. Such an integrated administration is needed as long as hospital incomes continue to depend on federal funds such as medicare and medicaid. In recent years, the government has selected cost-cutting measures such as Diagnosis Related Groups (DRG) for payment of health care services. In this system, a patient is classified into a DRG based on the diagnosis of the illness and other characteristics such as age, length of stay in the hospital, and surgical procedures used. The DRG then defines the maximum amount for which hospitals will be reimbursed by the federal government. The fact that the hospital has to bear any costs that exceed the amount stipulated for that DRG may have a direct bearing on the quality of the service provided. Additionally, third-party insurers have an indirect impact on the level of quality. In certain cases, patients can go only to a hospital approved by the insurer. To some extent, the insurer also controls the patients' choice of physicians. Physicians, in turn, usually select the hospitals to which they prefer their patients be admitted. To summarize the impact of these scenarios, hospitals must come up with effective quality control and improvement measures at competitive prices. An error-free environment is the objective. Furthermore, behavioral characteristics associated with the delivery of the service are important to customer satisfaction and perceived quality.

The four quality categories (human factors and behavioral, timeliness, service nonconformities, and facility-related) can be shown to have applications in health care services. Table 14-8 shows some quality characteristics from each of these categories and appropriate methods of control. The characteristics are grouped according to the method of control that may be used. Possible applications of three control charts—the chart for the average $\overline{X}$ and range R, the c-chart, and the p-chart (Demos and Demos, 1989)—are shown. Other control charts, such as the run chart, may be used to track such characteristics as patient temperature, blood pressure, and pulse rate. Sample size determination techniques may find application when the number of cases to sample to estimate the average payoff for medicare/medicaid cases or to determine the proportion of medication errors must be determined. Analysis of quality improvement usually starts with Pareto analysis, through which the most critical areas are identified. A cause-and-effect diagram may then be used for each area of investigation to determine remedial actions for performance improvement.

Example 14-8: The quality of service in a hospital is kept track of by determining the proportion of medication errors; this is done by dividing the number of medication errors by 1000 patient-days for each observation. The results of 25 such observations are shown in Table 14-9, showing the percentage of medication errors. Construct an appropriate control chart, and comment on the quality level. Is a goal of error-free performance reasonable to expect from this system?

Solution. A control chart for the proportion of medication errors p may be constructed using the data in Table 14-9. Table 14-9 shows the percentage of medication errors for 25 observations, each having a sample of size 1000. The center line on the p-chart is found by averaging the values shown in Table 14-9 as follows:

$$\overline{p} = \frac{54.3}{25} = 2.17 \text{ percent} = 0.0217$$

The upper and lower control limits are

$$\begin{aligned}\overline{p} \pm 3\sqrt{\frac{\overline{p}(1-\overline{p})}{n}} &= 0.0217 \pm 3\sqrt{\frac{(0.0217)(1-0.0217)}{1000}}\\ &= 0.0217 \pm 0.0138\\ &= (0.0079, 0.0355)\end{aligned}$$

Figure 14-8 shows a p-chart for the proportion of medication errors, with the control limits superimposed. For observation number 15, the proportion of medication errors is 0.042, which exceeds the upper control limit. An investigation of possible causes for this revealed a few instances where the pharmacist had made an error in filling the prescription as well as cases where a doctor had prescribed a wrong dosage. Assuming that remedial action

TABLE 14-8 Quality characteristics and methods of control in health care services

Quality characteristics in health care services	Method of control
Waiting time for service Time to obtain an appointment Effectiveness of medicines as indicated by measures such as temperature or blood pressure Time for an ambulance to respond Time to be admitted in emergency room service	$\overline{X}$- and R-chart
Number of errors in blood or urine tests per 200 samples Number of billing errors per 100 accounts Number of adverse comments per week on nurses' performance or quality of food Number of errors per week in deliveries to patients	c-chart
Proportion of medicaid cases in error Proportion of money payments in medicare/medicaid cases in error Proportion of tests performed incorrectly Proportion of cases with inaccurate diagnosis Proportion of cases with side effects of medication and treatment	p-chart

has been taken, the revised center line is found after deleting observation number 15:

$$\overline{p} = \frac{50.1}{24} = 2.0875 \text{ percent} \simeq 0.0209$$

The revised control limits are

$$0.0209 \pm 3\sqrt{\frac{(0.0209)(1-0.0209)}{1000}} = 0.0209 \pm 0.0136 = (0.0073, 0.0345)$$

All of the observations are now in control.

TABLE 14-9 Percentage of medication errors in a hospital

Observation number	Percentage of medication errors	Observation number	Percentage of medication errors
1	2.6	14	2.0
2	1.9	15	4.2
3	2.8	16	2.2
4	2.9	17	1.8
5	2.4	18	2.4
6	1.8	19	2.3
7	2.3	20	1.6
8	2.1	21	1.9
9	1.4	22	2.0
10	1.7	23	2.2
11	2.2	24	2.1
12	2.0	25	2.3
13	1.2		

The average level of the proportion of medication errors is 0.0209, or 2.09 percent. This is much higher (more than three standard deviations) than the target value of zero that represents error-free performance. Hence, the achievement of an error-free performance is unreasonable to expect from the current system. In order to achieve the goal, certain fundamental changes must be made by the administration. Areas where such changes are to be made can be identified through Pareto analysis and subsequent cause-and-effect analysis of the main reasons behind medication errors.

Insurance

Consumers depend on insurance companies for protection from accidents, hazards, and casualties. Automobile, home, life, and medical insurance are examples of personal insurance policies that we depend upon. Sometimes, insurance is offered to members of a certain professional group. For example, a medical insurance policy may be offered to all employees of an organization that negotiates the coverage and rate with the insurance company. Of course, organizations themselves may be insured by other agencies to provide customers with a sense of assurance for their investments. Consider financial institutions such as banks. Customer accounts with the bank might be insured up to a certain maximum value. The Federal Deposit Insurance Corporation (FDIC) may insure such customer accounts. We should real-

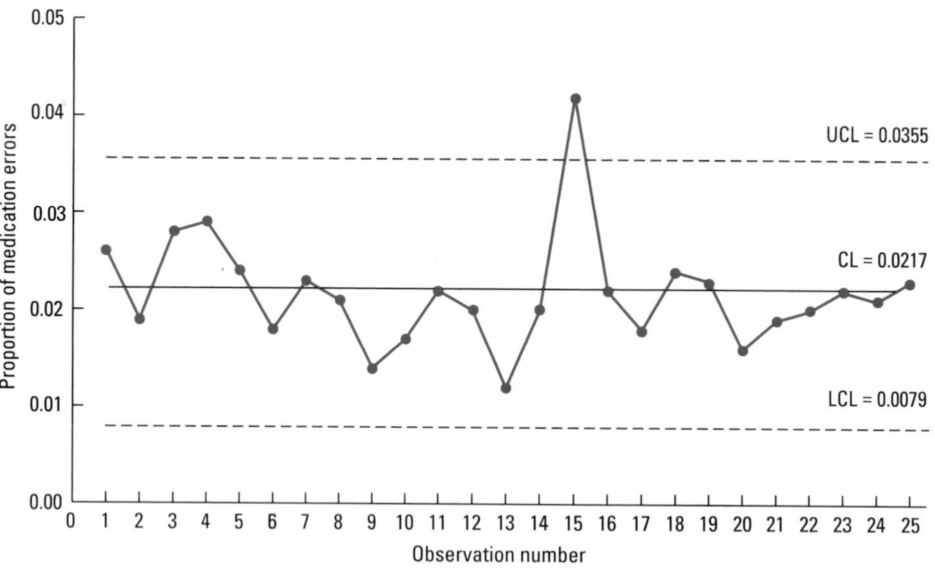

Figure 14-8 Example of a *p*-chart for the proportion of medication errors.

ize, though, that we support these agencies through our tax dollars.

In these circumstances, service nonconformity quality characteristics are critical. The goal is to have no errors. Since much of the process involves human beings, training and motivation are important. Collecting actuarial data, inputting the data to a system for subsequent calculation of casualty probabilities, estimating payoffs, underwriting policies, and processing claims are functions that require human operations and interactions. Preparing employees for these tasks and keeping them enthusiastic about their jobs is a major objective for management. Timeliness characteristics such as correcting a complaint or error, processing a claim, or obtaining damage appraisals from adjusters are examples of operations that must be performed in a reasonable amount of time.

From the point of view of the insurance seller, there are several objectives. Increasing profits is a primary concern; the means of accomplishing this goal must be identified. A Pareto analysis will discriminate the vital characteristics. Detailed analysis of the important characteristics through a cause-and-effect diagram will shed some light on what areas to focus on to improve profits. Cutting operational costs and avoiding errors through well-defined procedures and documented manuals may remove some of the uncertainty associated with insurance functions. Operational quality is influenced by the quality of decisions made at every level, from clerks to supervisors, appraisers, adjustors, managers, and executives. Sellers are interested in reducing the risk to their own company by means of limitations and exclusions in policies. This can conflict with the buyer's objective of obtaining protection against all types of risk. However, the buyer desires the premiums to be as low as possible and does not want unnecessary protection that may increase the cost of the policy.

Statistical techniques may be used in a variety of instances. First, since the setting of premiums is based on historical data, sampling methods are used to obtain data. The data are then used for estimation and analysis to address such issues as the probability of fire or accident, the amount of loss, and low-risk and high-risk groups. The control of *sampling* and *nonsampling errors* is vital to the accuracy of the estimation process. Sampling errors are inherent to the process of sampling, whereby a subset of items is selected from the population of all items. It is expected that the selected samples will represent the characteristics of the population. The most common method is the selection of a simple random sample for which each item in the population has an equal chance of being chosen. Other sampling techniques discussed in Chapter 3 include stratified sampling and cluster sampling. Nonsampling errors include incorrect data transcription, inaccurate data input to models used for estimation purposes, the use of inappropriate or outdated models for estimation, faulty computer programming, and other such errors that are not related to the manner in which samples are chosen.

Several control charts may be used in the insurance industry. For example, a p-chart may monitor the proportion of unacceptable documents, the proportion of claims not processed or paid, or the proportion of persons in the high-risk group during a certain period. A c-chart may be used for characteristics such as the number of incorrect entries per 100 documents and the number of underwriters per 500 customer accounts. An $\overline{X}$- and R-chart could apply to such characteristics as the processing time for claims and the amount paid by the company for policies in a similar category. A run chart could track the total amount paid on a monthly basis.

Example 14-9: An insurance company is interested in determining the premium to charge for a \$150,000 homeowner's policy that would cover such hazards as fire, theft, vandalism, and other natural calamities excluding flood and earthquakes. Based on local historical data, the company foresees a total loss with a probability of 0.001, a 50 percent loss with a probability of 0.01, and a 25 percent loss with a probability of 0.03. Ignoring all other losses, what premium should the company charge if it wants to break even, on the average? Breaking even may be a goal for nonprofit organizations, but most insurance companies are profit-oriented. What premium should the company charge to make a net profit of 1 percent of the face value of the policy?

Solution. We formulate this discrete probability distribution problem by defining a random variable X to represent the net gain to the insurance company. The probability distribution of the random variable X is shown in Table 14-10, where p represents the premium to be charged. With a probability of 0.959, the net gain to the company is the amount of premium. Likewise, a net gain of $(p - 150,000)$ has a probability of 0.001, of $(p - 75,000)$ has a probability of 0.01, and of $(p - 37,500)$ has a probability of 0.03.

TABLE 14-10 Probability distribution of the net gain to the insurance company

Net gain to insurance company, X	Probability, $P(X = x)$
p	0.959
$p - 150,000$	0.001
$p - 75,000$	0.01
$p - 37,500$	0.03

Using the concept of an expected value of a discrete random variable, Equation 3.23 yields the following, for an assumption of breaking even:

$$E(X) = 0$$

or

$$E(X) = p(0.959) + (p - 150,000)(0.001) + (p - 75,000)(0.01) + (p - 37,500)(0.03) = 0$$

We have $p = 2025$. Thus, if the company charges a premium of \$2025, it will break even on average.

If the company is interested in making an average net profit of 1 percent of the face value of the policy, we have

$$E(X) = 1500$$

or

$$p = 2025 + 1500 = 3525$$

A premium of \$3525 would enable the company to meet this profit objective.

Personal Services

In personal services, the provider deals with individual customers on a frequent basis. Examples of personal services are beauty shops, hotels and motels, laundromats, restaurants, and travel agencies. The individuals or companies providing the service rely heavily on repeat business. Therefore, it is important to know the characteristics and attributes that satisfy a customer as well as those that create a dislike for the service. Since individual tastes and preferences vary, it is difficult for a company to devise a format that will satisfy all of the customers. What businesses try to do is incorporate flexibility in their design as much as possible. Consider the hotel and motel industry. Some customers may prefer an indoor swimming pool; some may prefer a lavish restaurant; others may just be interested in a snack bar. Some would like the wash basin and vanity outside the bathroom, others prefer it inside.

Service industries in this category have to realize that there are two groups of factors relating to customer satisfaction or dissatisfaction. Those factors that cause customer dissatisfaction should be given due consideration for their elimination. A dissatisfied customer does not come back for repeat service. He or she also spreads the word to others, which might damage the reputation of the business and result in a loss of customers. For instance, room controls for air conditioning in a motel that do not work may be enough to cause dissatisfaction. Sometimes, the mechanism for information feedback is inadequate. A hotel customer may call maintenance and services only to be told that the person in charge is not available. Many do not bother to fill out an evaluation card in motels or hotels unless an incentive is provided. Since customer feedback is so important to rectify problems that cause dissatisfaction, businesses may provide incentives such as prizes or free vacations to obtain a higher response rate.

Quality characteristics that are facility-related or cause service nonconformities usually fall in the group of factors causing customer dissatisfaction. Examples are a leaky faucet in a hotel room, inadequate temperature control in a beauty shop or restaurant, a lack of available group tours sold by a travel agency, or a dirty carpet in a motel room.

The elimination of causes that create customer dissatisfaction is a step in the right direction, but it is not enough. A separate group of factors causes the perceived quality level to exceed expectations. Consider an example of a beauty shop that keeps arrangements of fresh flowers. This added touch may lead to customers who are quite satisfied and feel that they have obtained more for their money's worth. Such customers are the best source of advertisement for a business. They come back for repeat business and tell others of the good service. As a result, the service company has a promotional campaign going for it. By catering to changing needs, the business is able to stay competitive.

Characteristics that cause customer satisfaction are usually in the human factors and behavioral group or timeliness group. Examples could be the courteous behavior of the front desk attendant in a hotel or a minimal waiting time to be seated in a restaurant.

Statistical techniques to control a service and its delivery process may be used in several areas. Charts for the average $\overline{X}$ and range R may be used to control characteristics such as the time to register and check in at a hotel, the waiting time in a barber shop or restaurant, the time to be transferred from the airport to the hotel, or the time for a suit to be dry cleaned. A p-chart may be used to control the proportion of on-time deliveries from a restaurant or the proportion of rooms available for occupancy in a hotel. A c-chart could be used for controlling the number of customer complaints per week or the number of customers served during the lunch hour at a restaurant. A demerits chart may be used to control the weighted quality points from customer report cards. Analysis of quality improvement may be carried out through Pareto analysis and cause-and-effect diagrams.

Example 14-10. A beauty shop is concerned about the waiting times of its customers. From data collected from 35 randomly selected customers, the manager estimates the average waiting time to be 25 minutes, with a standard deviation of 4 minutes. In order to reduce the waiting time, the manager adds another beautician. From a random sample of 40 customers, the average waiting time is found to be 14 minutes with a standard deviation of 6 minutes. Test at the 5 percent level of significance to determine if a significant reduction has been achieved in the mean waiting times. Customers expect to wait no more than 15 minutes, beyond which they start becoming dissatisfied. What proportion of customers will be dissatisfied with this new arrangement, assuming the mean waiting time to be 14 minutes?

Solution. This problem involves testing a hypothesis of the difference between two population means, one being the mean waiting time before the addition of the beautician (μ_1) and the second being the mean waiting time after the addition (μ_2). We assume the distribution of waiting times to be normal in each case, with their unknown variances equal. The sample averages and standard deviations of the waiting times are given by $\overline{X}_1 = 25$, $\overline{X}_2 = 14$, $s_1 = 4$, and $s_2 = 6$. The sample sizes are $n_1 = 35$ and $n_2 = 40$. Using the concepts of hypothesis testing, we have the following null and alternative hypotheses:

$$H_0 : \mu_1 - \mu_2 \leq 0$$
$$H_a : \mu_1 - \mu_2 > 0$$

The pooled estimate of the variance, s_p^2, is obtained from Equation 3.53 as follows:

$$s_p^2 = \frac{(n_1 -)s_1^2 + (n_2 - 1)s_2^2}{n_1 + n_2 - 2}$$
$$= \frac{(35 - 1)4^2 + (40 - 1)6^2}{35 + 40 - 2} = 26.685$$

The value of s_p is thus 5.166. The test statistic is the t-value given by Equation 3.66:

$$t_0 = \frac{(\overline{X}_1 - \overline{X}_2) - 0}{s_p\sqrt{(1/n_1) + (1/n_2)}}$$
$$= \frac{(25 - 14)}{5.166\sqrt{\frac{1}{35} + \frac{1}{40}}} = 9.200$$

The critical value, $t_{.05,73}$, is found from Appendix A-4 to be 1.6661 (after interpolation). Since the test statistic value of 9.200 exceeds the critical value and falls in the rejection region of the null hypothesis, we reject the null hypothesis. Thus, our conclusion is that the addition of the beautician has significantly reduced the mean waiting time.

Let us now determine the proportion of customers who will have to wait more than 15 minutes despite the addition of the new beautician, assuming the mean waiting time to be 14 minutes. The t-value, calculated using Equation 3.49, is

$$t_0 = \frac{(15 - 14)}{6/\sqrt{40}} = 1.054$$

From the t-table in Appendix A-4, for 39 degrees of freedom, the probability of exceeding the above t-value is between 0.100 and 0.250. Thus, between 10 and 25 percent of the customers may still be dissatisfied by a long waiting time. If the standard normal tables in Appendix A-3 were used to estimate the proportion of customers who would have to wait more than 15 minutes, the approximate value would be 0.146, or 14.6 percent. The manager should consider these figures to determine if more servers are needed to reduce waiting time.

Public Utilities

Public utility services include electric power, gas, and telephone. A unique feature of the companies providing these services is that they are nearly monopolies or oligopolies. They are regulated by public service commissions that also set the rate structure for the service. Thus, the customer does not directly influence the unit price for the service. Indirectly, though, consumer opinions may have an impact on the negotiated rate structure approved by the public service commission.

The standards for quality are imposed by the regulatory agencies. The consumer expects continuous, uninterrupted service from these utilities. We do not expect our power supply, telephone service, or running water to fail at any time. The benefits received by these utilities for being under the supervision of regulatory agencies is that they have a guaranteed customer base. Thus, the operation scenario is somewhat different from that of other service industries. Does this mean that the utility companies need not bother about customer satisfaction or complaints from them? Not quite. The companies have to convince the public service commission of their effectiveness in meeting customer complaints and expectations. To obtain a rate increase, companies have to address any public criticism that is relevant.

Another unique feature of utilities such as electricity or gas is that the consumer controls the consumption and generates an instantaneous demand. People turn on the fan, television, washer, or dryer at their liking. It is expected that electricity will be available any time that these things are turned on. Since the lead time for demand is zero, utility companies must base their production on accurate forecasts. This is, in itself, a science and an art. The scientific aspect concerns engineering features associated with the generation, transmission, and distribution of electrical power. Power companies are also networked so that one company can provide for any excessive peak load requirements of another. Mathematical models are developed to forecast demand. The artistic component comes into play in the model-building process. What model components are to be considered, what measures of demand are to be used, what information from the historical demand should be used, and how are they to be weighted? The answers to these questions require the creativity of the human mind and the ability to synthesize past behavior to predict future requirements.

A separate feature of utilities such as electrical power is that they cannot usually be stored. Therefore, it is not feasible to overproduce and store in order to meet peak demand at a later point in time. Nevertheless, we expect our demand for electrical power to be met instantaneously. With gas, the situation is a little different, since excess production can be stored for subsequent use. Similarly, for a telephone company, switching networks route a call in the most efficient way, based on availability of the network lines, so that all calls can be completed. Among the four categories of service quality characteristics previously discussed, service nonconformity and facility-related characteristics are critical to the electrical power and gas industry. For the telephone industry, in addition to the above two categories, behavioral and timeliness characteristics are important.

Table 14-11 lists some quality characteristics associated with public utilities and the corresponding control charts that might be used. $\overline{X}$- and R-charts may be used for variables such as the amount of power purchased from outside sources, the time to restore service after a failure, the proportion of capacity utilized in a power plant, or the proportion of electrical power loss in transmission and distribution. Trend charts are useful for tracking electrical power or gas consumption on a monthly or quarterly basis for a single customer (say, an industry with heavy use), or a group of customers. They help in identifying patterns in consumption and thereby create a better model for forecasting requirements. A c-chart may be used for attributes such as number of errors in meter readings per 100 customers or the number of human errors per month. For quality

TABLE 14-11 Quality characteristics and methods of control in public utilities

Quality characteristics in public utilities	Method of control
Amount of power purchased by company from outside sources	$\overline{X}$- and R-chart
Amount of power consumed per month	
Waiting time to have a telephone installed	
Time to restore service after a failure	
Proportion of capacity utilized in a power plant	
Use of electrical power or gas on a monthly basis for an area	Trend chart
Number of human errors per month in a power plant	c-chart
Number of billing errors per 200 customer accounts	
Number of errors in meter readings per 100 customers	
Number of customer complaints per month	
Number of days of sick leave per month	
Proportion of days with accidents or power failure	p-chart

improvement analysis, Pareto charts and cause-and-effect diagrams are helpful.

Example 14-11: The number of errors in meter reading and input to the billing system per 300 customer accounts is shown in Table 14-12. Construct an appropriate control chart, and comment on the performance. Is it feasible to achieve a goal of zero errors? Comment.

Solution. A c-chart for the number of errors should be constructed. For the data in Table 14-12, the center line is

$$\bar{c} = \frac{43}{25} = 1.720$$

The control limits are

$$\bar{c} \pm 3\sqrt{\bar{c}} = 1.720 \pm 3\sqrt{1.720} = (0,\ 5.654)$$

TABLE 14-12 Number of meter reading and input errors per 300 customer accounts

Observation number	Number of errors	Observation number	Number of errors
1	3	14	3
2	1	15	1
3	4	16	0
4	2	17	1
5	3	18	2
6	0	19	1
7	0	20	2
8	2	21	0
9	1	22	1
10	2	23	1
11	3	24	0
12	6	25	2
13	2		

Figure 14-9 shows a plot of the c-chart with the data points and the control limits. Observation number 12, with 6 errors, lies above the upper control limit. On investigation, it was found that the handwritten records were illegible, causing errors in data entry. After elimination of observation number 12, the revised center line is

$$\bar{c} = \frac{37}{24} = 1.542$$

The revised control limits are

$$1.542 \pm 3\sqrt{1.542} = (0,\ 5.249)$$

All of the observations are found to be in control.

The revised center line is at 1.542. The goal is an error-free performance. From the Poisson distribution tables in Appendix A-2, for a value of $\lambda = 1.542$ (the mean), the probability of 0 errors is found after interpolation to be 0.214. So, even though there is about a 20 percent chance of obtaining error-free performance, company management must devise ways of further reducing the opportunities for mistakes.

Transportation

Common modes of transportation include airlines, railroads, buses, limousines, and taxis. Quality characteristics from all four categories (human factors and behavioral, timeliness, service nonconformities, and facility-related) play an important role in this industry. Although the level of quality is largely influenced by the customer, in the case of some of the transportation modes, such as airlines, federal agencies have regulatory power to some extent. The Civil Aeronautics Board (CAB) in the case of airlines is such an agency. It receives customer complaints and summarizes the findings, which are made

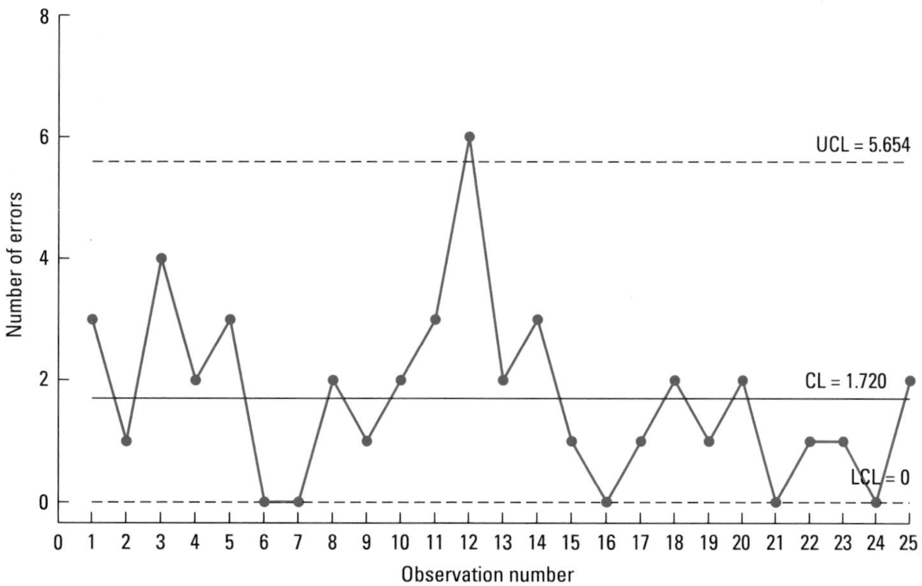

Figure 14-9 Example of a *c*-chart for the number of errors per 300 customer accounts.

available to respective airlines. Individual airlines can then concentrate on the categories that have the most complaints and plan remedial actions. It must be pointed out that the airlines should be judicious in their selection of problem categories for analysis based on data from the Civil Aviation Board. This is because some customers may write directly to the airlines, whereas many customers may not write at all. Some dissatisfied customers merely switch airlines instead of complaining. Thus, transportation companies must find ways of obtaining customer feedback on the services provided. Some obtain this through customer rating forms. Since the response rate may not be high, incentives such as free gifts should be provided to increase the response rate. The company needs to find out the level of customer satisfaction and expectations before it is too late.

Foremost among the quality characteristics is the safety of operations. Fatal and nonfatal accidents should always have a goal value of zero. The achieved level of safety should be close, if not equal to, this target. There is no price tag on a human life. Prevention of accidents through equipment maintenance, checking, and training of personnel is a priority. Any accident calls for a thorough investigation with follow-up measures for their prevention. A customer takes an accident-free performance for granted—and rightly so. Thus, customer rating forms will not reflect the importance of this characteristic.

Other quality characteristics that influence customer satisfaction deal with the operation and delivery of service. Among behavioral characteristics are the courtesy of the check-in agent and flight attendants in airlines or the cab driver in a taxi. The number of complaints received per month may be monitored by a *c*-chart. There are many timeliness characteristics that are of interest. In the airline industry, some examples are the waiting time at the check-in counter, the waiting time to obtain all baggage, and the flight delay in arriving at destination. An $\bar{X}$- and R-chart may be used to control these characteristics. Service nonconformity characteristics include the number of damaged or lost bags per month or the number of passengers bumped from a flight, for which an np-chart may be used. Other characteristics, such as the number of mistakes in reservations and ticketing per month or the number of airport security problems per month, may be monitored through a *c*-chart. Pareto analysis and cause-and-effect diagrams may be used to study quality improvement.

Example 14-12: Flight delays are of concern to passengers as well as airlines. Some customers have appointments that they expect to meet, and others have connecting flights that they prefer not to miss. An airline obtained observations on the average and range of delay times of flights (in minutes), each chosen from a sample of size 4, as shown in Table 14-13. Construct appropriate control charts, and comment on the performance level. What are the chances of meeting a goal of a delay of no more than 10 minutes?

Solution. The chart for the range R of the delay time should be constructed first. For the data in Table 14-13, the center line is

$$\overline{R} = \frac{89.8}{25} = 3.592$$

The control limits are

$$UCL = D_4\overline{R} = 2.114(3.592) = 7.593$$

$$LCL = D_3\overline{R} = 0(3.592) = 0$$

where the control chart multiplying factors D_4 and D_3 are found from Appendix A-7 for a sample size of 5. Figure 14-10 shows a plot of the R-chart. All of the observations are well within the control limits. Most of them cluster around the center line. The chart for the average delay $\overline{X}$ is then constructed. The center line is

$$\overline{\overline{X}} = \frac{241.4}{25} = 9.656$$

The control limits are

$$UCL = \overline{\overline{X}} + A_2\overline{R} = 9.656 + 0.577(3.592) = 11.729$$

$$LCL = \overline{\overline{X}} - A_2\overline{R} = 9.656 - 0.577(3.592) = 7.583$$

where A_2 is found from Appendix A-7.

TABLE 14-13 Average and range of delay time (in minutes) of airline flights

Observation number	Average delay	Range
1	6.5	2.1
2	11.1	3.8
3	15.8	4.6
4	10.9	4.2
5	11.2	4.0
6	5.6	3.5
7	10.4	4.1
8	9.8	2.0
9	7.7	3.2
10	8.6	3.8
11	10.5	4.2
12	10.2	3.8
13	10.5	4.0
14	9.2	3.5
15	7.8	2.2
16	10.6	4.1
17	10.7	4.2
18	8.8	3.8
19	9.8	3.6
20	10.2	3.6
21	9.0	4.2
22	8.5	3.3
23	9.8	4.0
24	7.7	2.8
25	10.5	3.2

A plot of the $\overline{X}$-chart is shown in Figure 14-11. Observation numbers 1 and 6 plot below the lower control limit and have small delay times, which is desirable. On the other hand, observation number 3 plots above the upper control limit, with an average delay time of 15.8 minutes. An investigation of observation number 3 revealed that an unscheduled maintenance caused a delay in takeoff. Preventive maintenance would probably have eliminated the unscheduled service. For observation numbers 1 or 6, no specific causes could be assigned for the good performance. Assuming, therefore, that it is possible to decrease the delay time with current operations, we do not delete observations 1 and 6 in the revision process. Observation number 3, since we have identified and implemented an appropriate action for the elimination of a long delay, is deleted in the revision process.

The revised center line on the $\overline{X}$-chart is

$$\overline{\overline{X}} = \frac{241.4 - 15.8}{24} = 9.400$$

The revised center line on the R-chart is

$$\overline{R} = \frac{89.8 - 4.6}{24} = 3.550$$

The revised control limits for the R-chart are

$$UCL = 2.114(3.550) = 7.505$$

$$LCL = 0(2.550) = 0$$

The revised control limits for the $\overline{\overline{X}}$-chart are

$$UCL = 9.400 + 0.577(3.550) = 11.448$$

$$LCL = 9.400 - 0.577(3.550) = 7.352$$

The average delay time is 9.4 minutes. Since the goal is not to exceed 10 minutes, let us calculate the probability of meeting this goal. First we estimate the standard deviation of the delay times:

$$\hat{\sigma} = \frac{\overline{R}}{d_2} = \frac{3.550}{2.326} = 1.526$$

where d_2 is found from Appendix A-7. The standard normal value for a delay of 10 minutes, where the mean of the distribution is 9.4 and there is a normal distribution of delay times, is

$$Z = (10 - 9.4)/1.526 = 0.393 \simeq 0.39$$

From the cumulative standard normal distribution table in Appendix A-3, the probability of a delay of 10 minutes or less is 0.6517, or about 65 percent. Even though the average delay is less than the goal value, the company must still strive to reduce delay times because it will not meet the goal about 35 percent of the time.

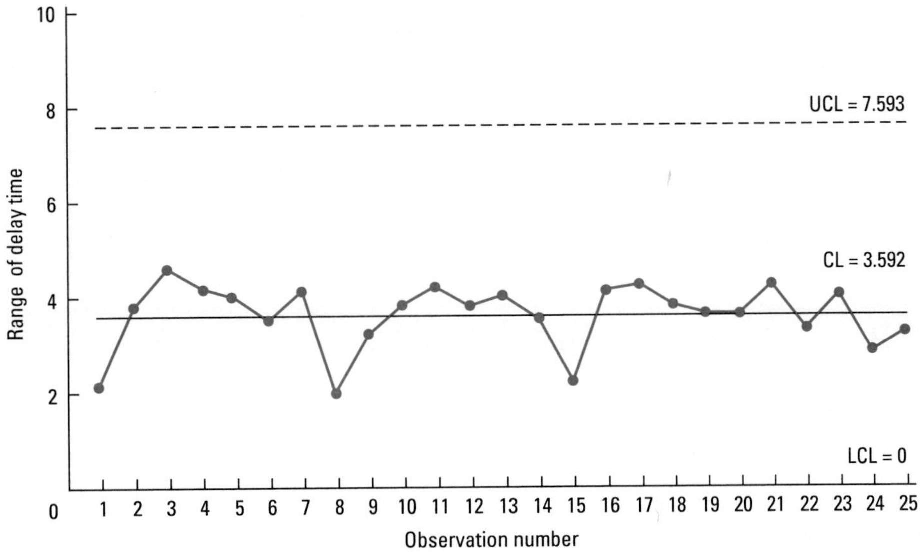

Figure 14-10 Example of an R-chart for the delay times of airline flights.

14-5 SUMMARY

This chapter has presented a detailed treatment of quality assurance for service functions and industries. Although there are similarities between service industries and manufacturing processes, several unique features exist in service industries. These have been described in this chapter. Some major differences are that service functions have an intangible component and that they cannot be stored. Moreover, whereas customer requirements are easily quantifiable in manufacturing, that is not necessarily the case for service functions and industries. Customer satisfaction is influenced by behavioral factors, which are difficult to quantify.

This chapter has provided a broad classification of service quality characteristics into four categories:

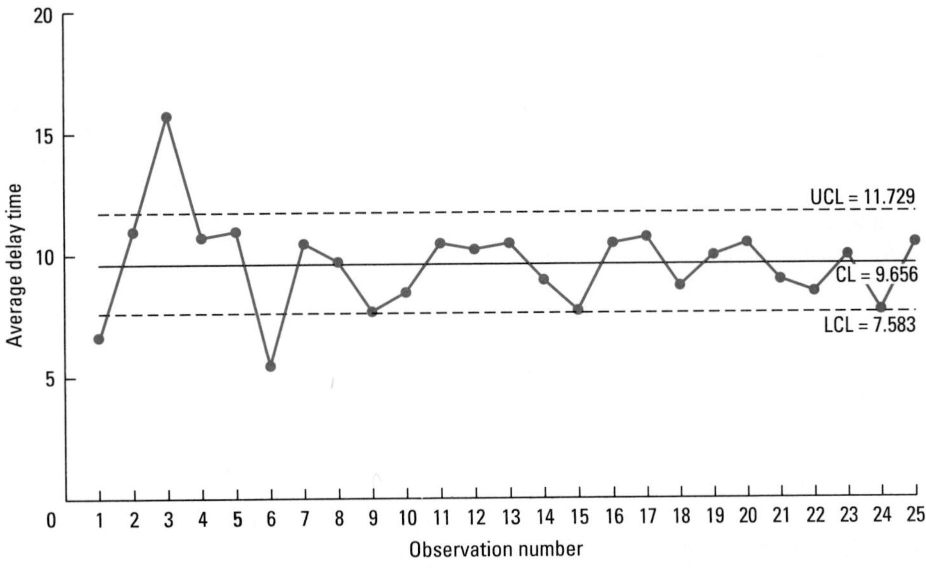

Figure 14-11 Example of an $\overline{X}$-chart for the average delay time of airline flights.

human factors and behavioral, timeliness, service nonconformity, and facility-related. Techniques for measuring and evaluating such characteristics have been presented. A general model for service quality has been discussed, and the factors that influence customer perception have been addressed. The framework for the general model may be used as a basis for constructing individual models for different service functions or industries. Finally, a variety of service applications including administrative operations, banking, education, food, government, health services, insurance, personal services, public utilities, and transportation have been discussed. The techniques used for analysis have been introduced in the previous chapters. Examples have been provided in this chapter to demonstrate the application of the various tools and techniques for the service sector.

14-6 CASE STUDY

UP IN THE AIR ABOUT QUALITY*

As a quality expert and an airline traveler, how do you rate the quality of commercial air travel today? Do you believe airline company executives rate it the same way?

Our study shows a sharp contrast in views between airline managers and passengers. This gap suggests that managers need to better understand what their customers (passengers) feel are the important attributes of quality and how well these are being delivered. Passengers repeatedly stressed two quality improvement themes. First, managers must treat passengers as people with personal possessions, personal comfort, and information needs that must be attended to. Second, airline managers must take a long-term view concerning profit and customer loyalty.

Consider the current state of U.S. airlines. To understand quality air transportation, three characteristics of the industry should be taken into account. First, the U.S. government has deregulated the airline industry. Certain factors, such as safety and security, are still watched closely by the government. These concerns might, in turn, limit the actions managers can take to satisfy customers. Second, customers often fly with a particular airline because it has the most convenient route or schedule, not because of loyalty to an airline's top-quality service. However, as trade restrictions continue to ease between countries, it is likely that airline route restrictions might lessen. Foreign airlines will become more assertive in using high-quality service as a competitive weapon in the battle for market share. To remain successful, American air carriers will have to provide better service quality. This brings us to the third consideration in understanding air transportation quality: airlines provide a service, not a tangible product.

The concept of quality service goes beyond the technical aspects of providing the service—it includes customer perceptions of what the service should be. To determine the components of quality travel, the importance of each component to the passenger must be determined. Can managers detect what passengers expect by analyzing quality failures? What suggestions do customers, managers, and government regulators give to improve quality? To answer these questions, we sought the opinions of passengers and managers and compared their perceptions of quality. We also solicited opinions from government officials to determine how their actions might limit the choices airline executives can make.

The Study Methodology

In an effort to define airline quality, a mail survey was sent to three groups. The first group consisted of a random sample of members of a nonairline frequent flyer organization; the second included executives of U.S. air carriers; and the third group was composed of officials in the U.S. Department of Transportation. The survey asked 60 questions about possible quality dimensions in either an importance-type format ("How important is it to you that the flight take off on time?") or an agree/disagree format ("Overbooking flights is an acceptable business practice"). All questions used a five-point Likert scale with 5 denoting "most important" or "strongly agree" and 1 representing "least important" or "strongly disagree." These scaled response questions were used to contrast the importance assigned to each quality dimension by managers, passengers, and regulators. In addition, there were several demographic and open-ended questions.

Altogether, 851 surveys were mailed, and 312 were returned, for a 37 percent response rate. A total of 239 passengers out of 488 surveyed returned the questionnaire, while 56 out of 311 managers and 17 out of 52 government officials responded.

Important Quality Dimensions

Service quality is a composite of various attributes. In air travel, factors such as safety, on-time travel, courtesy,

*Adapted from: T. J. Kloppenborg and K. N. Gourdin (1992), "Up in the Air about Quality," *Quality Progress,* Vol. 25, No. 3, pp. 31–35.

baggage handling, and food might be involved. How important is each factor? Table 14-14 ranks the top 10 quality concerns of each group. For example, the most important quality issue to passengers is that airlines be responsive to lost baggage complaints; to managers, it is making a profit; to regulators, it is security. The table shows that there is some agreement between passengers and managers that baggage handling and convenience of flight connections are important issues.

There are, however, several issues that passengers think are more important than managers do. These all can be considered within the context of treating passengers as people, not as objects. Passengers want to know the true status of delayed flights in a timely manner, they want the airline to take care of them when their travel plans are disrupted through no fault of their own, and they want to travel in relative comfort.

Table 14-14 also sheds light on the concerns of government officials. Their highest concerns are security and safety. Next, they consider the overall well-being of the airline industry and schedules (because of the effect congestion has on safety). Outside these few areas, government officials seem willing to let market forces determine most aspects of airline service.

Quality Failures

A quality failure occurs when a customer perceives that the actual quality delivered is less than what he or she expects it should be. Many companies survey their customers to determine what they think of the quality that was delivered. This study focuses on what customers expect by analyzing what they perceive as failures. That is, customers were asked to describe their worst experiences when flying.

Airlines should prevent failures from occurring in the first place; however, some quality failures in air travel (such as late departures due to poor weather) are difficult to prevent. In such cases, how the problem is handled by the carrier determines whether the passengers consider it excusable.

Table 14-15 lists the various types of failures (bad flight experiences) reported by passengers. Note that the problems total considerably more than 100 percent since many incidents comprise more than one problem. In fact, one respondent provided the following tale of woe:

We sat on the blacktop for two hours awaiting takeoff for Chicago and missed our flight to Honolulu.

TABLE 14-14 Order of quality concerns

Order	Passengers	Managers	Officials
1	Airline responsive to lost bags	Airlines must earn a profit	Security screening before boarding
2	Prompt information on delayed flights	Cabin attendants must be courteous	Safety announcements made
3	Bags handled carefully	Flights depart on time	Airlines must earn a profit
4	Airline responsible for delayed passengers	Bags handled carefully	The United States needs more airports
5	Enough leg room	Airlines responsive to lost bags	Lower fares used for off-peak flights
6	Prompt bag delivery	Convenient departure times	Meaningful information should be provided quickly
7	Comfortable seat	Convenient flight connections	Fares should be low
8	On-board comfort during delays	Prompt bag delivery	Convenient departure times
9	Convenient flight connections	Aircraft clean inside	Convenient arrival times
10	Airlines should take care of delayed passengers	Convenient arrival times	Convenient flight connections

TABLE 14-15 Worst flying experiences (quality failures)

Type of problem	Percent of reported incidents*
Lack of Information	41
Timing (delays)	32
Failure to take care of delayed passengers	20
Disregard for passenger comfort	14
Lost baggage	14
Lack of courtesy	12
Reservation/seating schedule inconvenience	11
High price	5
Poor food	3

*Total exceeds 100 percent because many incidents involved more than one problem.

The ticket agent was uncooperative and indifferent toward making alternate arrangements. By our own efforts, we found a flight on a different carrier and managed to get to Honolulu for our connecting flight to Guam the next day. We spent the following week without our luggage. Upon returning to Hawaii, we found our bags and also discovered that no attempt had been made to forward the baggage to Guam, where we had checked at the airport every day. I am five feet six inches tall, and on the return flight (to Chicago), my knees were jammed into the seat in front of me.

This true story includes problems connected with lack of concern for the passenger, baggage, and on-board comfort. A more common complaint is that, during many delays, passengers are not kept informed of the status of their flights, nor are their needs attended to. The survey respondents provided many examples. The worst cases concerning lack of information involved passengers being stranded for 48 hours with continued promises of "one more hour," only to subsequently be forced to find and pay for alternative transportation on their own. The worst reported case of inattention to personal needs was a wait of 12 hours in an enclosed, poorly ventilated room without access to water.

Passengers claim that airlines don't inform them quickly about delayed flights because they want to discourage them from booking flights on other carriers. Many passengers stated that their delays would have been less frustrating if the airlines had honestly admitted the flights would be late. And many of the same passengers stated that they will never fly on a particular airline again. It appears that the airlines wish to avoid the possibility of a short-term loss (passengers cancelling their immediate reservations) but do not pay attention to the long-term implications of losing those customers forever. While all quality failures on airlines cannot be eliminated, the effects of many problems can be minimized if passengers are treated as people. Information, care, comfort, and courtesy mean a great deal to many passengers.

Improvement Suggestions

One of the open-ended questions on the survey asked respondents to suggest "one simple, inexpensive change that airlines could make to improve their quality." A total of 217 suggestions were made: 180 by passengers, 23 by managers, and 14 by government officials. Some appear to be impractical or extremely costly. Others favor one group at the expense of another. Some suggestions conflict. Many of the suggestions, however, appear to warrant consideration. In Table 14-16, the sug-

TABLE 14-16 Inexpensive improvements suggested

	Percent of group making suggestion		
Type of suggestion	Passengers	Managers	Regulators
No improvements possible	1	22	14
Intangibles	26	61	14
Customer relations	9	35	7
Faster/more accurate information	7	13	0
Understandable/fair pricing	9	4	0
Pricing to encourage behavior	1	9	7
Tangibles	73	17	71
Passenger comfort	21	9	22
Baggage	13	4	14
Food	9	0	0
Timeliness of waiting or service	6	0	14
Scheduling/ reservations	6	0	14
Facility layout	5	4	0
Other	13	0	7

gestions have been grouped into three main divisions: no improvements possible, changes aimed at intangible aspects of air travel, and changes aimed at tangible aspects of air travel. The suggestions are further subdivided into more specific categories, such as food or baggage. The table reports the percentage of suggestions by each group that fall in a particular category. For example, 22 percent of the managers who commented felt no improvements were possible.

No Improvements Possible

Virtually all the passengers who made comments believed that some improvements were possible. A large group of managers and regulators, however, felt no simple changes were possible. Two thoughts emerge from this. First, the managers need to be more creative and listen to their customers more. The second thought is less damning. Several managers and regulators correctly noted that, to achieve major and lasting quality improvements, simple changes are not adequate. What is needed is long-term employee commitment, corporate leadership, and money. While this is obviously true, it should not be used as an excuse for not attempting to make any possible improvement—big or small.

Intangibles

The second category of comments reflect suggestions aimed at intangible aspects of air travel. The bulk of these suggestions were from managers, while relatively few were from passengers or officials. The first subcategory of comments concerns customer relations. As shown in Table 14-14 the managers thought friendly cabin attendants are very important, while passengers assigned more importance to other issues. Given management's belief that one of the most important quality measures is friendly air crews, it is not surprising that many of their suggestions were concentrated in this area. Ironically, passengers—by and large—thought the air crews were friendly but the ground crews were difficult. Passengers' suggestions for improved customer relations focused more on attitudes and helpfulness of ticket agents and other ground personnel. Both passengers and managers pointed out the need for better employee relations as a requirement for establishing better customer relations. Comments were made such as "Employees must be happy in order to help customers be happy" and "Improve management-employee relations, which in turn, would improve employee-customer relations. However, this is neither simple nor inexpensive." One airline that treats its employees well and counts on extraordinary customer service in return is Delta. For example, two Delta employees in Texas drove passengers to another city two hours away so they could meet an alternative connecting flight after their plane was too late to meet the scheduled connection.

The next subgroup of suggestions concerned information. As shown in Table 14-15, passengers rated lack of information as the No. 1 problem related to quality failures. Both passengers and regulators feel that fast and accurate information is important.

Passengers and managers alike made suggestions concerning information. Both stated that information should be shared quickly and honestly; however, neither gave specific suggestions concerning how to do it. Given the high level of importance assigned to fast, accurate information, the apparent passenger frustration with lack of information, and the lack of concrete guidance on how to provide it quickly enough, this appears to be an area ripe for improvement.

Price was an issue over which passengers and managers disagreed. Managers and regulators wanted to use differences in pricing to motivate passengers to fly during less busy times and days to ensure full planes and lessen congestion. Passengers overwhelmingly want simple, fair, low prices, and they do not want to be forced by prices to fly when it is inconvenient. Managers want to use pricing to protect their markets, while officials want pricing to be used only to encourage competition. Given these contrary goals, this issue is likely to remain a source of conflict for a long time.

One airline, U.S. Air, seems to be taking notice. It has recently announced plans to relax the penalty provisions attached to some of its discount fares so that the value of an unused nonrefundable ticket could be applied to future U.S. Air travel. In addition, schedule changes would be permitted with payment of a service charge.

Some of these suggestions concerning intangibles might improve customers' perceptions about quality service, but for the most part, they will not improve the reliability, responsiveness, and timeliness of the service. If the actual service is still poor, trying to convince the customer that quality is good will be a hard job. It is better to simultaneously work on customers' perceptions and the actual service.

Tangibles

The majority (73 percent) of passengers' comments concerned improving the actual service, while few (17 percent) of the managers expressed similar concerns.

Passengers had more improvement suggestions concerning virtually every aspect of the actual service than managers did. The bottom line is that passengers are people. They are intelligent and can make many suggestions. They are prone to do this since they frequently have long waits during which they can observe the airline operation and consider alternative ways of performing many tasks. A resourceful airline could use passenger ideas as free consulting.

Management Implications

Manufacturing quality concentrates on the technical aspects. While that is necessary in attaining service quality, it is not sufficient. Customer perceptions are also important. The overall perception customers have of quality for a given service company is based on several attributes that customers feel are important. For each attribute, customers first note the difference between how they rate the actual quality delivered and what they expected the quality to be. This difference is then weighted by the importance customers assign to that attribute.

Airline managers can learn about quality from other service industries, and managers in other services can learn about quality from airlines. Air carrier executives can also learn a great deal from their customers and thereby provide better quality. Front-line employees can help with this task, as they have many contacts with customers and can observe customer behavior. Customers and front-line employees can make many suggestions that might help improve operations (and, therefore, the technical aspects of quality).

Air Canada is attempting to address quality concerns via its Customer Care program, which specifies complete passenger satisfaction as the firm's goal. As part of this commitment, the airline offers to notify family or business associates if a passenger's flight is delayed and to feed and lodge the passenger if the delay is excessive, regardless of cause. In addition, if the passenger is dissatisfied with any in-flight service, Air Canada will fix the problem or compensate the passenger. Finally, cabin crew members have the authority to take whatever measures are necessary to resolve a passenger's complaint.

Closing the Gap

This study clearly indicated that managers and customers rank the importance of quality attributes differently. Thus, managers need to identify what importance customers assign to various dimensions of quality, learn about the customers' expectations for these dimensions, and determine whether the customers' expectation are being met. Combining this with an assessment of the technical quality aspects will give an overall evaluation of airline quality.

Two themes emerged from this study. First, managers need to treat both employees and passengers as people. Concern for employees is important because it translates into employee concern for customers, which in turn motivates employees to offer improvement suggestions. Both groups should be able to offer suggestions. Both groups have feelings that need to be addressed. Passengers need to have their possessions and their personal comfort attended to. In many ways, they have stated that they believe managers care more about the bottom line than they do about passengers. Managers obviously need to have concern for both passengers and profit.

The second theme that emerged is that managers frequently seem more concerned with short-term profits or losses than with the possibility of developing long-term customer loyalty. An improvement in quality, both technical aspects and passenger perception, can be a powerful competitive weapon. Airlines concerned with short-term survival from takeovers or airlines protected through near monopolies at certain airports might not be very concerned with quality. However, excellently managed European and Asian air carriers might enter U.S. markets and change that philosophy. No matter how disrupted or protected an industry is, quality is always a formidable competitive weapon; airlines that want to be profitable in the long term must try to improve their quality.

Questions for Discussion

1. Discuss how the airlines may influence customer expectations. What impact will those measures have on quality?
2. What are some specific measures that airlines might take to address the important concerns of the passengers?
3. Discuss the potential conflict in quality concerns between passengers and managers. What are some reasons for this?
4. What role should government officials play in defining quality in the airline industry?

KEY TERMS

Administrative operations
American Medical Association (AMA)
ANSI/ASQC Z1.4 sampling plan
Civil Aviation Board (CAB)
Control charts for attributes
 c-chart
 p-chart
Control charts for variables
 $\bar{X}$-chart
 R-chart
Cause-and-effect diagram
Diagnosis Related Groups (DRG)
Effectiveness of services
Efficiency of services
Environmental Protection Agency (EPA)
Federal Deposit Insurance Company (FDIC)
Food and Drug Administration (FDA)
Hypothesis test
Internal Revenue Service (IRS)
Joint Commission on Accreditation of Healthcare Organizations (JCAHO)
Magnetic ink character recognition (MICR)
Nonsampling error
Normal distribution
Pareto analysis
Poisson distribution
Process capability
Run chart
Sampling
 Convenience sampling
 Judgment sampling
 100 percent sampling
 Probability sampling
 Random sampling
Sampling error
Sensory quality
Service functions
Service industries
 Banking
 Education
 Food
 Government—federal and state
 Health services
 Insurance
 Personal
 Public utilities
 Transportation
 Service nonconformity
 Significance level
 Trend chart

EXERCISES

Discussion Questions

14-1 What are the major differences between service industries and manufacturing processes? Discuss them.

14-2 Discuss the major categories of quality characteristics in service functions and industries. Give examples under each category.

14-3 Discuss the difficulties in measuring service quality. What are some remedial measures?

14-4 Explain the role of sampling plans in service industries. Describe some plans that are used in the service sector.

14-5 Describe the framework for a general model for service quality. Give illustrations for a particular service industry.

14-6 Explain the factors that influence customer perception of quality. Discuss them in the context of a service industry of your choice.

Problems

14-7 The number of errors per 500 transactions is a characteristic of interest in a bank. Table 14-17 shows such errors for 20 observations randomly selected from all transactions, where each observation deals with 500 transactions. Comment on the stability of the process in controlling these errors by constructing an appropriate control chart. If any observation is outside the control limits, assume that the assignable cause is identified, and find the revised control limits. Is it feasible to expect an error-free performance from this system?

TABLE 14-17 Number of errors per 500 transactions in a bank

Observation number	Number of errors	Observation number	Number of errors
1	5	11	4
2	3	12	5
3	4	13	6
4	6	14	5
5	5	15	2
6	3	16	3
7	5	17	2
8	4	18	11
9	12	19	4
10	5	20	3

14-8 The number of computer entry errors per 5 database files is found from randomly selected files of the Federal Savings and Loan Association. The observations are shown in Table 14-18. Construct an appropriate control chart to determine if such computer entry errors are stable. Assuming observations that plot outside the control limits to have identifiable assignable causes, revise the control limits. Discuss whether it is feasible to expect the existing service system to achieve an error-free performance.

14-9 A bank is in the process of selecting vendors for its printing of magnetic ink character recognition (MICR) checks. It plans to test the incoming supply of checks from one of its vendors. Checks are supplied in batches of 50,000. The acceptable quality level that has been negotiated between the bank and the vendor is 0.40 percent. If general inspection level II is to be used and normal inspection is in effect, find the sampling plan using *ANSI/ASQC Z1.4*.

14-10 The control of errors in check processing is a prime consideration for all banks. The observations shown in Table 14-19 were taken over a span of two months for an individual in the processing department. The number of errors and the number of items sampled are shown. Construct an appropriate control chart, and determine if the performance of the employee is in statistical control. Revise the control limits, if necessary, assuming assignable causes for out-of-control points. Comment on the capability of the employee.

TABLE 14-18 Number of computer entry errors per 5 database files

Observation number	Number of entry errors	Observation number	Number of entry errors
1	7	14	14
2	6	15	5
3	14	16	3
4	4	17	7
5	3	18	8
6	5	19	4
7	6	20	2
8	7	21	5
9	6	22	4
10	5	23	7
11	6	24	8
12	3	25	4
13	7		

TABLE 14-19 Number of check processing errors and the number sampled

Observation number	Number of errors	Number of items sampled
1	8	400
2	6	400
3	4	400
4	9	400
5	7	400
6	5	400
7	5	300
8	7	300
9	4	300
10	15	300
11	6	300
12	7	300
13	4	300
14	3	300
15	5	300
16	8	300
17	11	500
18	13	500
19	8	500
20	7	500
21	8	500
22	4	500
23	3	500
24	7	500
25	6	500

14-11 The number of people who are certified by the American Society for Quality Control from among those having gone through a series of short courses offered by a consulting company is shown in Table 14-20. The data were taken over a period of five years. The company has been expanding its services. Construct an appropriate control chart, and comment on the company's improvement efforts, if any. Revise the control limits if necessary.

14-12 The proportion of corn kernels that are heat-damaged in processing a cereal is shown in Table 14-21. The sample size for each observation was 500. Determine the stability of the process by constructing an appropriate control chart. The company has a goal of a heat damage rate of 4 percent; discuss whether this is achievable.

TABLE 14-20 Number of people enrolled in short courses and number certified

Observation number	Number enrolled	Number certified
1	50	32
2	50	34
3	50	31
4	50	33
5	50	32
6	75	50
7	75	55
8	75	48
9	75	56
10	75	57
11	75	53
12	75	55
13	100	70
14	100	75
15	100	72
16	100	84
17	100	80
18	100	78
19	100	83
20	100	85

14-13 The level of dissolved oxygen in water was measured every two hours in a river in which industrial plants discharge processed waste. Each observation consists of four samples, from which the sample mean and range of the amount of dissolved oxygen in parts per million is calculated. Table 14-22 shows the results of 25 such observations. Discuss the stability of the amount of dissolved oxygen. Revise the control limits, if necessary, assuming assignable causes for the out-of-control points. Suppose environmental standards call for a minimum of 4 parts per million of dissolved oxygen. Are these standards being achieved? Discuss.

TABLE 14-21 Proportion of corn kernels that are heat-damaged

Observation number	Proportion of kernels heat-damaged	Observation number	Proportion of kernels heat-damaged
1	0.06	14	0.07
2	0.05	15	0.08
3	0.08	16	0.04
4	0.06	17	0.05
5	0.04	18	0.03
6	0.05	19	0.03
7	0.09	20	0.06
8	0.07	21	0.14
9	0.02	22	0.07
10	0.06	23	0.05
11	0.04	24	0.08
12	0.06	25	0.04
13	0.10		

TABLE 14-22 Average level and range of dissolved oxygen in parts per million

Observation number	Average level of dissolved oxygen	Range
1	7.4	2.1
2	8.2	1.8
3	5.6	1.4
4	7.2	1.6
5	7.8	1.9
6	6.1	1.5
7	5.5	1.1
8	6.0	2.7
9	7.1	2.2
10	8.3	1.8
11	6.4	1.2
12	7.2	2.1
13	4.2	2.5
14	4.3	2.0
15	5.8	1.4
16	5.4	1.2
17	8.3	1.9
18	8.0	2.3
19	6.7	1.5
20	8.5	1.3
21	5.7	2.4
22	8.3	2.1
23	5.8	1.6
24	6.8	1.8
25	5.9	2.1

14-14 The Small Business Administration wishes to estimate the mean annual sales of companies that employ fewer than 20 persons. Historical data suggest that the standard deviation of annual sales of such companies is \$5500. If it is desired to estimate mean annual sales to within \$1000 with a probability of 0.90, how large a sample should be chosen?

14-15 The proportion of cases with inaccurate diagnosis are found for samples of size 400 for 30 observations from a metropolitan hospital. Table 14-23 shows the results of these observations. Construct an appropriate control

TABLE 14-23 Proportion of cases with inaccurate diagnosis

Observation number	Proportion of cases with inaccurate diagnosis	Observation number	Proportion of cases with inaccurate diagnosis
1	.013	16	.033
2	.008	17	.015
3	.010	18	.012
4	.015	19	.016
5	.017	20	.006
6	.009	21	.009
7	.004	22	.007
8	.012	23	.014
9	.021	24	.010
10	.011	25	.005
11	.025	26	.016
12	.013	27	.012
13	.016	28	.018
14	.007	29	.009
15	.015	30	.013

chart, and comment on the quality level. Revise the control limits, if necessary, assuming assignable causes for out-of-control points. Is a goal of correct diagnosis for all cases reasonable to expect from this system? Comment.

14-16 An insurance company wants to estimate the premium to be charged for a \$200,000 homeowner's policy that would cover fire, theft, vandalism, and natural calamities. Flood and earthquakes are not covered. The company has estimated from historical data that a total loss may happen with a probability of 0.0005, a 50 percent loss with a probability of 0.001, and a 25 percent loss with a probability of 0.01. Ignoring all other losses, what premium should the company charge to make an average net profit of 1.5 percent of the face value of the policy?

14-17 An insurance company wants to estimate the proportion of houses that have had a 25 percent loss due to fire, theft, vandalism, and natural calamities in a certain region of the state. It is interested in estimating this proportion to within 2 percent of the true value with a probability of 0.95. How many houses should be sampled? Assume that no previous estimate of the true proportion is available. If a historical estimate of about 4 percent is available, how many houses should be sampled using this as a basis?

14-18 Customers who have to wait for a long time in barber shops often are not satisfied and consider alternative places. The owner of a barber shop has found from a random sample of 30 customers that the average waiting time is 35 minutes with a standard deviation of 9 minutes. Customers who have to wait more than 20 minutes are usually dissatisfied. Assuming a normal distribution of waiting times, what proportion of the customers will be dissatisfied?

14-19 The manager of a restaurant is concerned about the waiting time of customers and is contemplating an expansion of the facilities. Data obtained from samples of size 5 during the previous six months give the average and range of the waiting time in Table 14-24. Construct appropriate control charts, and comment on the stability of the customer service as measured by waiting time. Revise the limits assuming assignable causes for the out-of-control points. If the manager has set a goal of 10 minutes for the waiting time, how feasible is it to achieve this goal with the existing setup? Should the manager think of expanding the facilities to reduce waiting time?

14-20 Electrical power loss in transmission and distribution is a concern to utility companies. The design of transmission equipment and networking for distribution as well as parameter settings for conducting these services are therefore important. Table 14-25 shows the proportion of days where there is a malfunction in equipment for 25 randomly selected observations. A sample size of 100 was used for each observation. Construct an appropriate control chart, and comment on the performance level of the company.

14-21 A telephone company is interested in estimating the mean time to restore service after a failure. To small businesses that depend on customer orders over the telephone, any downtime in telephone service is of importance. From past information, the company estimates the standard deviation of the restoration time to be 15 hours. If the company wishes to estimate the mean restoration time to within 2 hours with a prob-

TABLE 14-24 Average and range of waiting time of customers in a restaurant

Observation number	Average waiting time	Range	Observation number	Average waiting time	Range
1	12.5	5.1	16	8.8	4.5
2	14.0	7.2	17	10.2	5.8
3	15.2	6.5	18	9.5	5.2
4	13.9	6.3	19	10.8	5.8
5	11.4	5.8	20	9.4	6.1
6	12.6	6.1	21	10.2	5.8
7	9.5	4.8	22	11.0	6.0
8	9.2	4.3	23	10.6	4.3
9	13.6	5.7	24	10.2	5.3
10	13.8	6.2	25	11.4	6.1
11	10.5	5.5	26	9.8	5.8
12	9.1	4.6	27	10.9	6.2
13	10.9	6.4	28	10.4	5.3
14	10.0	5.2	29	11.2	5.7
15	19.9	6.6	30	10.5	5.5

ability of 0.98, how large a sample should it choose?

14-22 The number of errors in reservations and ticketing by an airline on a monthly basis is shown in Table 14-26. Construct an appropriate control chart, and comment on the level of performance. Revise the control limits, assuming assignable causes for the out-of-control points. How reasonable is it to expect error-free performance, and what are its chances under the present system?

TABLE 14-25 Proportion of days in which there is a malfunction in equipment

Observation number	Proportion of days with malfunction	Observation number	Proportion of days with malfunction
1	0.05	14	0.04
2	0.07	15	0.07
3	0.04	16	0.07
4	0.05	17	0.03
5	0.02	18	0.05
6	0.06	19	0.04
7	0.08	20	0.06
8	0.04	21	0.03
9	0.03	22	0.04
10	0.05	23	0.04
11	0.03	24	0.06
12	0.03	25	0.05
13	0.06		

TABLE 14-26 Number of errors in reservations and ticketing per month by an airline

Observation number	Number of errors	Observation number	Number of errors
1	6	16	2
2	4	17	5
3	8	18	0
4	2	19	3
5	5	20	1
6	0	21	2
7	4	22	1
8	3	23	3
9	6	24	4
10	4	25	3
11	1	26	1
12	3	27	2
13	0	28	4
14	1	29	3
15	2	30	2

REFERENCES

DelMar, D., and Sheldon, G. (1988). *Introduction to Quality Control.* West Publishing Company, St. Paul, MN.

Demos, M. P., and Demos, N. P. (1989). "Statistical Quality Control's Role in Health Care Management," *Quality Progress,* 22(8), pp. 85–89.

Kackar, R. N. (1988). "Quality Planning for Service Industries," *Quality Progress,* 21(8), pp. 39–42.

King, Carol A. (1987). "A Framework for a Service Quality Assurance System," *Quality Progress,* 20(9), pp. 27–32.

Kloppenborg, T. J., and Gourdin, K. N. (1992). "Up in the Air About Quality," *Quality Progress,* 25(3), pp. 31–35.

Latzko, William J. (1986). *Quality and Productivity for Bankers and Financial Managers.* Marcel Dekker, New York.

Lefevre, Henry L. (1989). *Quality Service Pays—Six Keys to Success.* American Society for Quality Control, Milwaukee, WI.

McCabe, W. J. (1985). "Improving Quality and Cutting Costs in a Service Organization," *Quality Progress,* 18(6), pp. 85–89.

Normann, R. (1991). *Service Management—Strategy and Leadership in Service Business.* 2nd edition. Wiley, New York.

O'Sullivan, D. D., and Grujic, S. D. (1991). "Implementing Hospitalwide Quality Assurance," *Quality Progress,* 24(2), pp. 28–32.

Rosander, A. C. (1985). *Applications of Quality Control in the Service Industries.* Marcel Dekker, New York.

Thompson, P., DeSouza, G., and Gale, B. T. (1985). "The Strategic Management of Service Quality," *Quality Progress,* 18(6), pp. 20–25.

CHAPTER

15

Computer Software for Quality Control

CHAPTER OUTLINE

SYMBOLS

$\overline{X}$	Sample average
R	Sample range
s	Sample standard deviation
p	Proportion nonconforming
np	Number nonconforming
c	Number of nonconformities
C_p	Process capability index for a centered process
C_{pk}	Process capability index for an uncentered process
CPL	Process capability index when only a lower specification limit is given
CPU	Process capability index when only an upper specification limit is given

15-1 INTRODUCTION

The 1990s will continue to be dominated by technological innovations in computer hardware, which will promote the development of an abundant supply of software. As computers become a part and parcel of our lives, they will have a major impact on monitoring quality in real time. For control to be effective, it must be on time. Remedial actions that are delayed result in a loss to the company because of products or services whose characteristics deviate from the target value. The availability of computer software facilitates decision making in real time. Most of the routine number-crunching or plotting details can easily be handled by an appropriate program. As a result, managers have the flexibility to spend more time on the interpretation of results and the identification of remedial actions to improve the product and process.

This chapter introduces some of the features of available software for use in quality control and improvement. A partial list of available packages, arranged according to function, is presented. The price of these packages ranges from about $90 to well over $5000. No attempt is made to rank these software packages; they each have relative advantages and disadvantages that depend on the type of application that they are to be used for. The user must evaluate the packages based on his or her needs in both the short and long run. Examples demonstrating the use of one particular package—Statistical Analysis System's *SAS/QC*—are given for illustration purposes.

15-2 COMPUTER SOFTWARE

A variety of software packages are available for use by the quality assurance analyst. Reviews of these packages appear from time to time in professional journals; one such review is given by O'Neal (1987). This paper provides a brief description of the program capabilities, the system requirements in terms of hardware, the user services, and the list price. The American Society for Quality Control publishes an annual review of software for quality assurance and quality control (see American Society for Quality Control, 1992). It provides an index of selected software packages based on their functional usage. The functional areas include such categories as calibration, capability studies, data acquisition, design of experiments, gage repeatability and reproducibility, inspection, management, measurement, problem solving, quality assurance for software development, quality costs, reliability, sampling, simulation, statistical methods, statistical process control, supplier quality assurance, Taguchi techniques, training, and other areas.

Table 15-1 presents a summary of some features of a few selected software packages; the information is adapted from the March 1992 issue of *Quality Progress.* The table shows the name of the company, name of the program, source of availability, list price, medium in which program is available, i.e., $3\frac{1}{2}$-in. or $5\frac{1}{4}$-in. floppy disk, a brief description of the program capabilities, and the required computer configuration. Although not exhaustive, the table does provide the reader with a relative comparison of the features of some software packages. Depending on their specific needs and available resources, the users can refer to the table for guidance in selecting a software package.

15-3 APPLICATIONS

This chapter demonstrates the application of a software package entitled *SAS/QC,* which is available from Statistical Analysis System Institute, Inc. (1989b). Sample source codes and outputs are given here to illustrate the use of software for control charts and process capability. Additional examples may be found in the technical report on *SAS/QC* (SAS Institute, Inc., 1989a).

Control Charts for Variables

The following example demonstrates an application of the control charts for the average $\overline{X}$ and range R.

TABLE 15-1 Description of selected software packages for use in quality assurance

Company name program name	Available from	Price	Available disk formats	Program description	Computer configuration
American Quality Systems, Inc.					
ProGAGE1	Authorized distributors, and direct sales	$395	$3\frac{1}{2}$-in. and $5\frac{1}{4}$-in. floppy disk	Calibration, gage repeatability and reproducibility, data acquisition, quality costs	IBM PC or compatible; 512K RAM; hard disk drive
ProR&R	Authorized distributors and direct sales	$295	$3\frac{1}{2}$-in. and $5\frac{1}{4}$-in. floppy disk	Data acquisition, gage repeatability and reproducibility, statistical methods, statistical process control	IBM PC or compatible; 512K RAM
ProTRACK1	Authorized distributors and direct sales	$495	$3\frac{1}{2}$-in. and $5\frac{1}{4}$-in. floppy disk	Capability studies, data acquisition, inspection, management, quality costs, statistical methods, statistical process control, supplier quality assurance	IBM PC or compatible; 512K RAM; hard disk drive
AT&T Manufacturing Systems					
AT&T Quality Workbench-SQC Troubleshooter	Authorized distributors and direct sales	$595	$3\frac{1}{2}$-in. and $5\frac{1}{4}$-in. floppy disk	Problem solving strategy, data analysis, capability studies, gage repeatability and reproducibility, measurement, inspection, statistical process control	AT&T PC 63XX, IBM PC, AT, XT, PS/2 and compatibles; 640K RAM with 425K or more free space
AT&T Quality Workbench-Robust Design Expert	Direct sales	$795	$3\frac{1}{2}$-in. and $5\frac{1}{4}$-in. floppy disk	Design of experiments, Taguchi methods, training	AT&T PC 63XX, IBM, PC, AT, XT, PS/2 and compatibles; 640K RAM with 425K or more free space
AT&T Quality Workbench-Statistical Analysis of Reliability (STAR)	Direct sales	$5000	$3\frac{1}{2}$-in. and $5\frac{1}{4}$-in. floppy disk	Quality costs, reliability, training	AT&T 6386 WGS with UNIX system V/386, SUN SPARC-station and SUN Workstations with SUN OS 4.0.3, IBM Sys/37
Automation Software, Inc.					
DATAPAGE/RT	Authorized distributors and direct sales	$1500–$3950	$3\frac{1}{2}$-in. and $5\frac{1}{4}$-in. floppy disk, streaming tape cartridge	Capability studies, data acquisition, management, measurement, statistical process control, supplier quality assurance	286, 386, 486; 2 MB RAM; hard disk drive; EGA, VGA
BBN Software Products Division					
BBN/Catalyst	Direct sales	$2495	$3\frac{1}{2}$in. floppy disk	Design of experiments, statistical methods	Macintosh II series workstations; 2 MB RAM

Adapted from: American Society for Quality Control (1992), "Directory of Software for Quality Assurance and Quality Control," *Quality Progress*, vol. 25, No. 3, pp. 20–81.

TABLE 15-1 *(Continued)*

Company name program name	Available from	Price	Available disk formats	Program description	Computer configuration
RS Series	Authorized distributors and direct sales	\$695–\$100,000	$3\frac{1}{2}$-in. and $5\frac{1}{4}$-in. floppy disk, magnetic tape	Menu-driven technical data analysis, modeling, data management, graphics package for manufacturing and R&D applications. Program includes RS/1, a technical data analysis and graphics system; RS/Explore, a statistical analysis advisor; RS/Discover, a design of experiments system; RS/QCAII, an SQC System; and RS/Decision, an expert system shell for RS Series application.	IBM PC, DEC VAX, DEC Station, HP, SUN; 8 MB RAM minimum, hard disk drive
The Crosby Company					
SPC System Software	Authorized distributors and direct sales	\$145–\$999	$3\frac{1}{2}$-in. and $5\frac{1}{4}$-in. floppy disk	Complete system or individual models, statistical process control, Pareto analysis, gage reproducibility and repeatability	IBM PC, XT, AT, PS/2; 640K RAM
SPC Success Workshop	Authorized distributors and direct sales	\$150–\$295	$3\frac{1}{2}$-in. and $5\frac{1}{4}$-in. floppy disk	Self-paced training for statistical process control	IBM PC, XT, AT, PS/2; 640K RAM
G.R. Technologies, Inc.					
QC-PRO SPC Analysis	Direct sales	\$685	$3\frac{1}{2}$-in. and $5\frac{1}{4}$-in. floppy disk	Statistical process control, calibration, capability studies, data acquisition and reporting, gage repeatability and reproducibility, measurement, statistical methods	IBM PC and compatibles; 512K RAM; hard disk drive
QC-PRO Designed Experiments	Direct sales	\$695	$3\frac{1}{2}$-in. and $5\frac{1}{4}$ in. floppy disk	Design of experiments, Taguchi methods, statistical methods	IBM PC and compatibles; 512K RAM; hard disk drive
QC-PRO Weibull Reliability Analysis	Direct sales	\$495	$3\frac{1}{2}$-in. and $5\frac{1}{4}$-in. floppy disk	Reliability modeling and analysis	IBM PC and compatibles; 512K RAM; hard disk drive

TABLE 15-1 *(Continued)*

Company name program name	Available from	Price	Available disk formats	Program description	Computer configuration
International QualTech, Ltd.					
Discovery	Direct sales	\$795	$3\frac{1}{2}$-in. and $5\frac{1}{4}$-in. floppy disk	Design of experiments, factorial and fractional factorial designs, statistical methods, supplier quality assurance	IBM PC, XT, AT, PS/2, or compatible; 512K RAM; hard disk drive
Optimization	Direct sales	\$795	$3\frac{1}{2}$-in. and $5\frac{1}{4}$-in. floppy disk	Design of experiments, central composite designs, management, training	IBM PC, XT, AT, PS/2, or compatible; 512K RAM; hard disk drive
Economical Statistical Process Control (ESPC)	Direct sales	\$795	$3\frac{1}{2}$-in. and $5\frac{1}{4}$-in. floppy disk	Process capability studies, design of experiments, measurement, quality costs, sampling, statistical process control	IBM PC, XT, AT, PS/2, or compatible; 512K RAM; hard disk drive
Northwest Analytical, Inc.					
NWA Quality Analyst	Authorized distributors and direct sales	\$695	$3\frac{1}{2}$-in. and $5\frac{1}{4}$-in. floppy disk	Statistical process control, capability studies, data management	IBM PC, XT, AT, PS/2, or compatible; 512K RAM
NWA Scale Monitor	Authorized distributors and direct sales	\$295	$3\frac{1}{2}$-in. and $5\frac{1}{4}$-in. floppy disk	Data-station software interfaces electronic scales with *NWA Quality Analyst*, menu-driven data collection procedures	IBM PC, XT, AT, PS/2, or compatible; 512K RAM
NUTEK, Inc.					
QUALITEK-1/2	Authorized distributors and direct sales	\$1090	$3\frac{1}{2}$-in. and $5\frac{1}{4}$-in. floppy disk	Reliability analysis, sample size determination, accelerated life testing, and evaluation of failure test data using Weibull analysis	IBM PC or compatibles; 250K RAM
QUALITEK-3 (QT3)	Authorized distributors and direct sales	\$795	$3\frac{1}{2}$-in. and $5\frac{1}{4}$-in. floppy disk	Design and analysis of Taguchi experiments	IBM PC or compatibles; 540K RAM
QUALITEK-4 (QT4), Automatic Design and Analysis of Taguchi Experiments	Authorized distributors and direct sales	\$1195	$3\frac{1}{2}$-in. and $5\frac{1}{4}$-in. floppy disk	Designs Taguchi experiments automatically, adds several capabilities (outer array, extended loss function, multiple QC, context-sensitive help) to the best features of *QUALITEK–3*	IBM AT 386; 640K RAM plus 2MB RAM extended memory
Quality America					
SPC-PC II	Authorized distributors and direct sales	\$995	$3\frac{1}{2}$-in. and $5\frac{1}{4}$-in. floppy disk	Statistical process control, capability studies, Pareto analysis, statistical methods	IBM PC or compatible; 640K RAM

TABLE 15-1 *(Continued)*

Company name program name	Available from	Price	Available disk formats	Program description	Computer configuration
Quality Concepts, Inc.					
SPC PRO II	Authorized distributors and direct sales	$189	$3\frac{1}{2}$-in. and $5\frac{1}{4}$-in. floppy disk	Descriptive statistics, statistical process control, Pareto charts, capability indices	IBM PC, XT, AT, or compatible; 640K RAM
TADA! Experimental Design	Authorized distributors and direct sales	$99–$395	$3\frac{1}{2}$-in. and $5\frac{1}{4}$-in. floppy disk	Taguchi approach to design and analysis of experiments	IBM PC, XT, AT, or compatible; 640K RAM
Quality Resources					
STAT-PAK	Direct sales	$100	$3\frac{1}{2}$-in. and $5\frac{1}{4}$-in. floppy disk	Ten statistical programs, capability analysis, failure analysis, Taguchi loss function, regression analysis	IBM PC, XT, AT; TRS-DOS; 250K RAM
STAT-PAK II	Direct sales	$100	$3\frac{1}{2}$-in. and $5\frac{1}{4}$-in. floppy disk	Analysis of variance, experimental design, gage repeatability and reproducibility, statistical methods	IBM PC, XT, AT, TRS-80 I, III, IV; 256K RAM
CHART-PAK	Direct sales	$100	$3\frac{1}{2}$-in. and $5\frac{1}{4}$-in. floppy disk	Ten statistical charting programs, variable and attribute charts	IBM PC, XT, AT; TRS-80 I, III, IV; 256K RAM
SAS Institute, Inc.					
The SAS System	Direct sales	–	$3\frac{1}{2}$-in. and $5\frac{1}{4}$-in. floppy disk	Statistical process control, capability analysis, experimental design	IBM PC, XT, AT, PS/2, HP, SUN, DEC, SGI workstations; 512K RAM in mainframes and minicomputers, 640K RAM in microcomputers
Statistical Graphics Corporation					
STATGRAPHICS 5.0	Authorized distributors and direct sales	$795	$3\frac{1}{2}$-in. and $5\frac{1}{4}$-in. floppy disk	Statistical process control, capability studies, design of experiments, gage repeatability and reproducibility, sampling, statistical methods, supplier quality assurance	IBM PC, XT, AT, PS/2, or compatible; 640K RAM
Statistical Programs					
EXPERIMENTAL DESIGN	Direct sales	$295	$3\frac{1}{2}$-in. and $5\frac{1}{4}$-in. floppy disk	Experimental design, factorial, fractional factorial, central composite, Latin square designs	IBM PC, XT, AT, or compatible; 384K RAM
SCREEN	Direct sales	$295	$3\frac{1}{2}$-in. and $5\frac{1}{4}$-in. floppy disk	Plackett–Burman saturated fractional-functional screening designs	IBM PC, XT, AT, or compatible; 256K RAM
SIMPLEX-V	Direct sales	$295	$3\frac{1}{2}$-in. and $5\frac{1}{4}$-in. floppy disk	Interactive menu-driven program for rapid experimental optimization, adjusts up to 12 continuous factors	IBM PC, XT, AT, or compatible; 256K RAM

TABLE 15-2 Data for length of connector pins

Sample number	Average length, $\overline{X}$	Range, R	Sample number,	Average length, $\overline{X}$	Range, R
1	50.3	4	16	49.3	6
2	48.4	2	17	53.3	3
3	48.5	5	18	52.1	4
4	49.1	4	19	50.2	5
5	52.6	3	20	51.9	4
6	46.2	4	21	52.1	2
7	50.8	3	22	49.5	3
8	52.2	4	23	50.7	4
9	49.5	5	24	52.6	5
10	51.7	4	25	52.3	6
11	52.5	5	26	48.6	5
12	47.8	3	27	51.0	4
13	49.6	5	28	52.3	3
14	50.8	9	29	50.6	2
15	48.5	4	30	51.5	4

Example 15-1: Random samples of size five were selected to measure the length of a connector pin. For each sample, the sample mean and range were calculated, and the results are shown in Table 15-2. Find the control limits for an $\overline{X}$- and R-chart. Determine if there are any out-of-control points.

Solution. A source program for summary data generated using the *SAS/QC* software package is shown in Figure 15-1. The individual values for the characteristic (length) are not given. Rather, the average length and range are shown based on a sample size of five. In Figure 15-1, the variable name "lengt" is used to denote the length of connector pins. The statement "data pins" defines the name of the data set as "pins". The "input" statement specifies that data for three variables named as "sample," "lengtx," and "lengtr" will be input in that order. The variable "sample" represents the sample number. The variable "lengtx" represents the average of the values of the variable "lengt," and the variable "lengtr" represents the range of the values of the variable "lengt." The statement "lengtn= 5" says that the number of observations in each sample taken to measure the variable "lengt" is five. The "label" statement assigns the description to be associated with the corresponding variable in the program output. The "cards" statement indicates that the data to be input follows immediately. Summary data for 30 samples—the sample number, average length, and range of length values, in that order—are given next. The "proc shewhart" statement invokes the Shewhart procedure for control charts. In the same statement, "history=pins" indicates that the summary data to be used is found in the data set "pins," and the "graphics" option is to be utilized for output plots. The subcommand "xr chart lengt*sample" dictates that an $\overline{X}$- and R-chart option for the Shewhart procedure is to be used; the name of the variable is "lengt," which is to be plotted versus "sample," the sample number.

An example of such $\overline{X}$- and R-charts is shown in Figure 15-2. The center line of the $\overline{X}$-chart is 50.5, with upper and lower control limits of 52.9 and 48.2, respectively. On the R-chart, the center line is 4.13, with upper and lower control limits of 8.74 and 0, respectively. The range for sample number 14 is above the upper control limit on the R-chart. On the $\overline{X}$-chart, sample number 17 has an average above the upper control limit, and sample numbers 6 and 12 have averages that are below the lower control limit. Investigation of the causes for the out-of-control situations indicated by these four samples would need to be conducted. Remedial actions would be taken, followed by a revision of the center lines and control limits.

The next example demonstrates the application of control charts for the average $\overline{X}$ and standard deviation s based on summary data.

Example 15-2: The thickness of sheet metal used for making automobile bodies is a characteristic of interest. Random samples of size four were taken. The average and the standard deviation were calculated for each subgroup and are shown in Table 15-3 for 20 subgroups. Find the control limits for an $\overline{X}$- and s-chart. Determine if there are any out of control points.

Solution. A sample source program based on summary data is shown in Figure 15-3. The name of the characteristic variable is "ave," and "avex" and "aves" denote the average and standard deviation of the variable "ave." The program is very similar to that for the $\overline{X}$- and R-charts shown in Figure 15-1. The major difference is the option associated with the procedure "proc shewhart". Here, the option "xschart" specifies that control charts for the mean and standard deviation are to be constructed.

Figure 15-4 shows the $\overline{X}$- and s-charts for the summary data for the thickness of sheet metal. The center line of the $\overline{X}$-chart is 9.994, with upper and lower control limits of 10.228 and 9.761, respectively. On the s-chart,

```
data pins;
 input sample lengtx lengtr;
 lengtn=5;
    label lengtx='Average length of connector pin'
    sample='Sample number';
cards;
1  50.3  4
2  48.4  2
3  48.5  5
4  49.1  4
5  52.6  3
6  46.2  4
7  50.8  3
8  52.2  4
9  49.5  5
10 51.7  4
11 52.5  5
12 47.8  3
13 49.6  5
14 50.8  9
15 48.5  4
16 49.3  6
17 53.3  3
18 52.1  4
19 50.2  5
20 51.9  4
21 52.1  2
22 49.5  3
23 50.7  4
24 52.6  5
25 52.3  6
26 48.6  5
27 51.0  4
28 52.3  3
29 50.6  2
30 51.5  4
;
run;
proc shewhart history=pins graphics;
     xrchart lengt*sample;
run;
```

Figure 15-1 Source program for $\overline{X}$- and R-charts based on summary data.

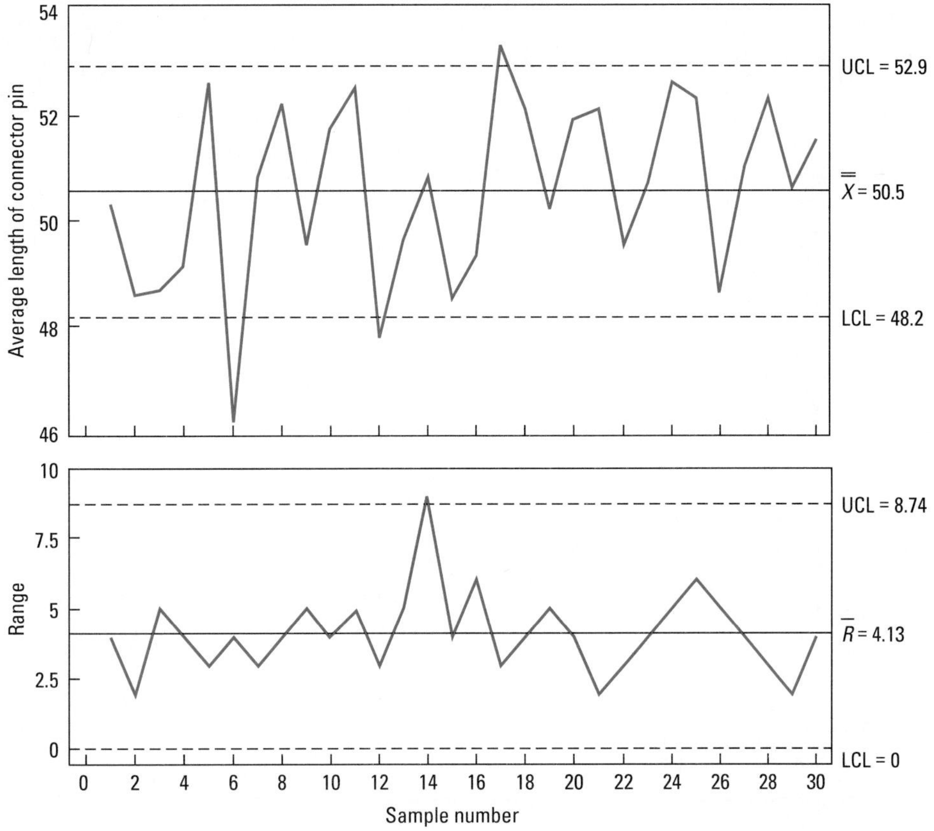

Figure 15-2 Control charts for the average and range (3σ limits for $n = 5$).

the center line is 0.14, with upper and lower control limits of 0.33 and 0, respectively. The standard deviation for sample number 14 is above the upper control limit on the s-chart. On the $\overline{X}$-chart, sample number 4 has an average above the upper control limit, and sample numbers 6 and 16 have averages below the lower control limit. Assignable causes would need to be investigated for these out-of-control points.

The next two examples demonstrate applications of the moving average and exponentially weighted moving average control charts.

Example 15-3: The average time that a customer has to wait (in minutes) for the arrival of a cab after calling the company was observed for random samples of size four. The data for 20 such samples is shown in Table 15-4. Construct a moving average control chart using a span of 3 and a known population mean of 9.1 minutes and standard deviation of 1.0 minute.

Solution. Figure 15-5 shows a sample source program for a moving average chart using summary data. The variable "wait" represents the waiting time of customers, and "waitx" represents the summary data for the average waiting time for each sample (the data which is input along with the "sample" number). The statement "proc macontrol history = time graphics" invokes the procedure "macontrol" using the summary data found in the data set

TABLE 15-3 Sample average and standard deviation for thickness of sheet metal

Sample number	Sample average, $\overline{X}$	Sample standard deviation, s
1	10.19	0.15
2	9.80	0.12
3	10.12	0.18
4	10.54	0.19
5	9.86	0.14
6	9.45	0.09
7	10.06	0.16
8	10.13	0.18
9	9.82	0.14
10	10.17	0.13
11	10.18	0.16
12	9.85	0.15
13	9.82	0.06
14	10.18	0.34
15	9.96	0.11
16	9.57	0.09
17	10.14	0.12
18	10.08	0.15
19	9.82	0.09
20	10.15	0.12

```
data thick;
 input sample  avex aves;
       aven=4;
       label avex='Average thickness'
       aves='Standard deviation of thickness'
       aven='Subgroup size';
cards;
1  10.19  0.15
2   9.80  0.12
3  10.12  0.18
4  10.54  0.19
5   9.86  0.14
6   9.45  0.09
7  10.06  0.16
8  10.13  0.18
9   9.82  0.14
10 10.17  0.13
11 10.18  0.16
12  9.85  0.15
13  9.82  0.06
14 10.18  0.34
15  9.96  0.11
16  9.57  0.09
17 10.14  0.12
18 10.08  0.15
19  9.82  0.09
20 10.15  0.12
;
run;
proc shewhart history=thick graphics;
     xschart ave*sample;
run;
```

Figure 15-3 Source program for $\overline{X}$- and s-charts based on summary data.

"time," with the "graphics" option to be utilized for the plots. The option "machart" indicates that a moving average chart is to be constructed; the variable "wait" is to be plotted as a function of the "sample" number. The statements "mu0 = 9.1" and "sigma0 = 1.0" imply that the moving average chart is to be constructed using a known population mean of 9.1 and standard deviation of 1.0. Limits vary with the subgroup number, a fact which is indicated by the statement "limitn = varying." The span to be used in calculating the moving average is denoted by the statement "span = 3."

The moving average control chart is shown in Figure 15-6. The center line is at 9.1, the specified population mean. Upper and lower control limits vary with the subgroup number. For subgroup number 2, the moving average value is below the lower control limit and is therefore out of control. Upon determination of the assignable causes, remedial action should be taken.

Example 15-4: Consider Example 15-3, which deals with the average waiting time for the arrival of a taxi. Using the data in Table 15-4, construct a geometric (exponentially-weighted) moving average control chart. Use a weighting factor of 0.30. What inferences can you draw from the chart?

Solution. Figure 15-7 shows the source program for the construction of an exponentially weighted moving average chart using the summary data for the sample averages. The program is very similar to that for the construction of a moving average chart shown in Figure 15-5. The major difference lies in the option within the procedure "proc macontrol." Here, the option used is "ewmachart," indicating the construction of an exponentially weighted moving average chart. The weighting factor is specified through the statement "weight = 0.30."

The exponentially weighted (geometric) moving average chart is shown in Figure 15-8. For subgroup number 2, the exponentially weighted moving average value is below the lower control limit and is therefore out of control.

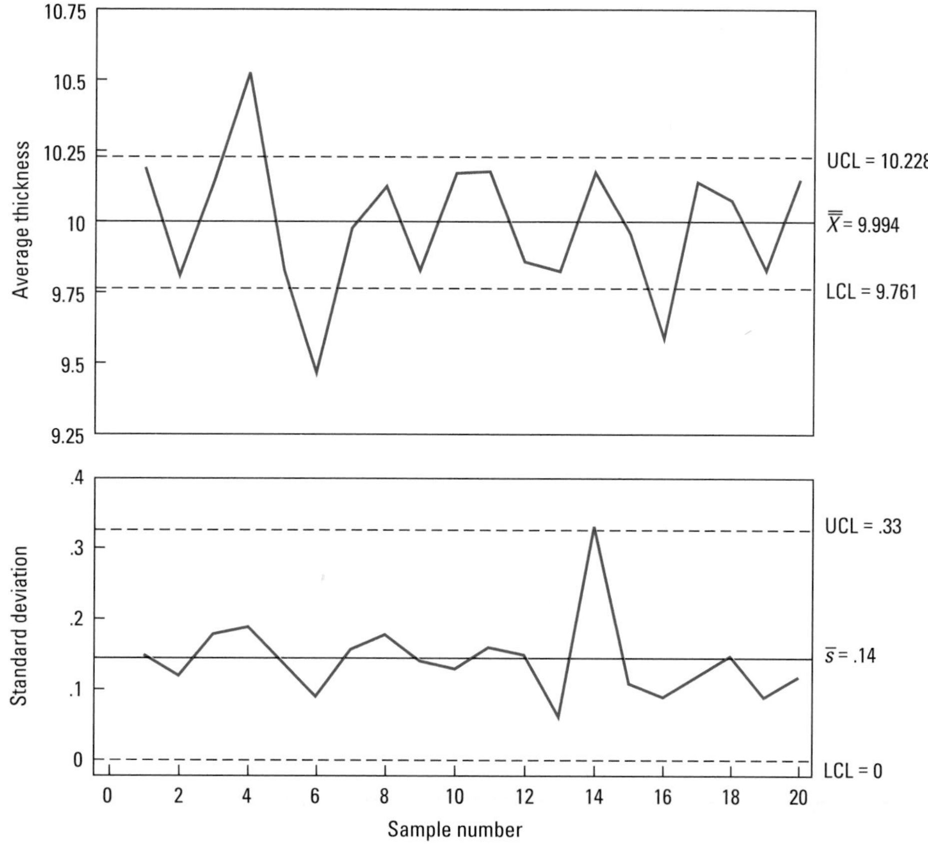

Figure 15-4 Control charts for the average and standard deviation (3σ limits for $n = 4$).

Control Charts for Attributes

The use of software to generate attribute charts for the proportion nonconforming (p-charts), number nonconforming (np-charts), number of nonconformities (c-charts), and the number of nonconformities per unit (u-charts) is demonstrated in this section.

TABLE 15-4 Average waiting time of customers

Sample number	Average waiting time, $\overline{X}$	Sample number	Average waiting time, $\overline{X}$
1	8.4	11	8.8
2	6.5	12	10.0
3	10.8	13	9.5
4	9.7	14	9.6
5	9.0	15	8.3
6	9.4	16	9.9
7	10.2	17	10.2
8	8.1	18	8.3
9	7.4	19	8.6
10	9.6	20	9.9

Example 15-5: The number of nonconforming cables was found for 20 samples, each of size 100, and is shown in Table 15-5. Construct a control chart for the proportion of nonconforming cables.

Solution. A sample source program is shown in Figure 15-9. The name of the variable defining the number of nonconforming cables is "nonc." For the "proc shewhart" statement, the option "pchart" indicates that a p-chart is to be constructed. The size of each subgroup is represented by the segment "subgroupn = 100."

Figure 15-10 shows the p-chart for the proportion of nonconforming cables. The center line $\overline{p}$ is 0.0415, and the upper and lower control limits are 0.1013 and 0, respectively. Two subgroups, numbers 10 and 16, have fraction-nonconforming values that exceed the upper control limit and would be considered to be out of control. Remedial actions would need to be taken to eliminate the assignable causes, if any, that are identified. Then the control limits may be revised after deleting the data from the two out-of-control subgroups.

```
data time;
   input sample waitx;
 waitn=4;
cards;
1   8.4
2   6.5
3  10.8
4   9.7
5   9.0
6   9.4
7  10.2
8   8.1
9   7.4
10  9.6
11  8.8
12 10.0
13  9.5
14  9.6
15  8.3
16  9.9
17 10.2
18  8.3
19  8.6
20  9.9
;
run;
title1 f=swiss h=1.5 'Moving average chart';
symbol1 v=dot h=1.5;
proc macontrol history=time graphics;
   machart wait*sample /
   mu0=9.1    /* Known mean        */
   sigma0=1.0     /* Known standard deviation    */
   limitn=varying
   hoffset=1.5
   nohlabel
   span=3;     /* Number of terms in moving average      */
run;
```

Figure 15-5 Source program for a moving average chart.

Example 15-6: The number of nonconforming door hinges found for samples of size 300 is shown in Table 15-6. Data was collected for 30 samples. Construct a control chart for the number of nonconforming hinges.

Solution. A source program for an np-chart for the number of nonconforming hinges is shown in Figure 15-11. The variable "nonc" denotes the number of nonconforming hinges, with "sample" indicating the sample number. For the "proc shewhart" statement, the option "npchart" is used to construct an np-chart.

Figure 15-12 shows the np-chart for the number of nonconforming hinges. The center line $\overline{np}$ is 9.9, and the upper and lower control limits are 19.2 and 0.6, respectively. Subgroup number 15, with a number-nonconforming value of 20, plots above the upper control limit. Management should conduct an investigation to determine possible assignable causes and remedial actions.

Example 15-7: The number of paint blemishes on automobile bodies was observed for 30 samples. Each sample consisted of randomly selecting five automobiles of a certain make and style. Table 15-7 shows the data for the paint blemishes. Construct a chart for the number of paint blemishes.

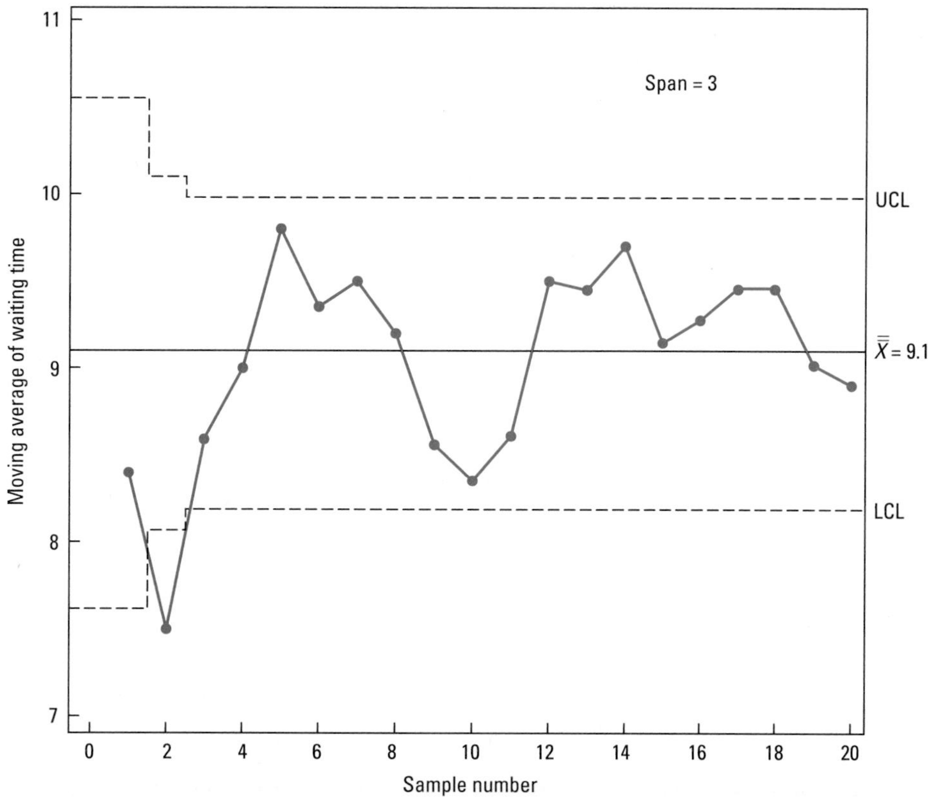

Figure 15-6 Moving average control chart (3σ limits for $n = 4$).

A sample source program for a c-chart for the number of paint blemishes is shown in Figure 15-13. The variable name "blem" defines the number of paint blemishes. For the "proc shewhart" statement, the option "cchart" indicates the construction of a c-chart.

Figure 15-14 shows the c-chart for the number of paint blemishes. The center line $\bar{c}$ is 6.1, and the upper and lower control limits are 13.5 and 0, respectively. There are two samples, namely sample numbers 17 and 20, whose number of paint blemishes exceeds the upper control limit. Investigative action should take place to determine the causes of this occurrence.

Example 15-8: The number of typographical errors were counted over a certain number of pages for each of 25 samples. The data values are shown in Table 15-8. The number of pages used for each sample was not fixed. Construct a control chart for the number of typographical errors per page.

Figure 15-15 shows the source program for a u-chart for the number of typographical errors per page. The variable names "sample," "ninsp," and "error" indicate the sample number, number of pages inspected, and the number of typographical errors, respectively. Note that the sample size is not constant. For the "proc shewhart" statement, the option "uchart" indicates the construction of a u-chart. The subgroup size for each subgroup is denoted by the segment "subgroupn = ninsp."

Figure 15-16 shows the u-chart for the number of typographical errors per page. The center line $\bar{u}$ is 0.71, and the upper and lower control limits are influenced by the size of the subgroup. In this case, of course, the lower control limit is zero for all samples because the calculated value of the lower control limit is negative and is converted to zero. The upper control limit varies based on the subgroup size, as is seen from the graph. All of the sample values plot well within the control limits except for sample number 13, for which the value is well above the upper control limit. This is an out-of-control situation with an unusually large number of typographical errors per page. It requires investigation and identification of possible remedial actions.

Process Capability Analysis

This section describes the use of the *SAS/QC* package for process capability analysis when specification limits are provided. In addition to the ability to

```
data time;
   input sample waitx;
 waitn=4;
cards;
1   8.4
2   6.5
3  10.8
4   9.7
5   9.0
6   9.4
7  10.2
8   8.1
9   7.4
10  9.6
11  8.8
12 10.0
13  9.5
14  9.6
15  8.3
16  9.9
17 10.2
18  8.3
19  8.6
20  9.9
;
run;
titlel f=swiss h=1.5 'Exponentially weighted moving average';
symboll v=dot h=1.5;
proc macontrol history=time graphics;
   ewmachart wait*sample /
   mu0=9.1    /* Known mean         */
   sigma0=1.0     /* Known standard deviation    */
   weight=0.30
   limitn=varying
   hoffset=1.5
   nohlabel;
run;
```

Figure 15-7 Source program for an exponentially-weighted moving average chart.

obtain descriptive statistics for a data set, the software package has the ability to test for normality of the data. This may be done through a procedure known as the Shapiro–Wilk test, for which a test statistic and a probability value are specified. Graphical methods such as relative frequency histograms provide a visual display of the distribution of a characteristic. Process capability measures in accordance with the specification limits are computed by the package, with an indication of the proportion of product that lies outside the specifications. Such information could be used to determine the cost of scrap or rework.

Example 15-9: The mileage per gallon of a particular brand of gasoline was observed for a random sample of 50 observations. Table 15-9 shows the data. For this data, do the following:

a. Construct a frequency distribution, and comment on the distribution of gasoline mileage.

b. Estimate the mean and standard deviation of gasoline mileage for the particular brand of gasoline.

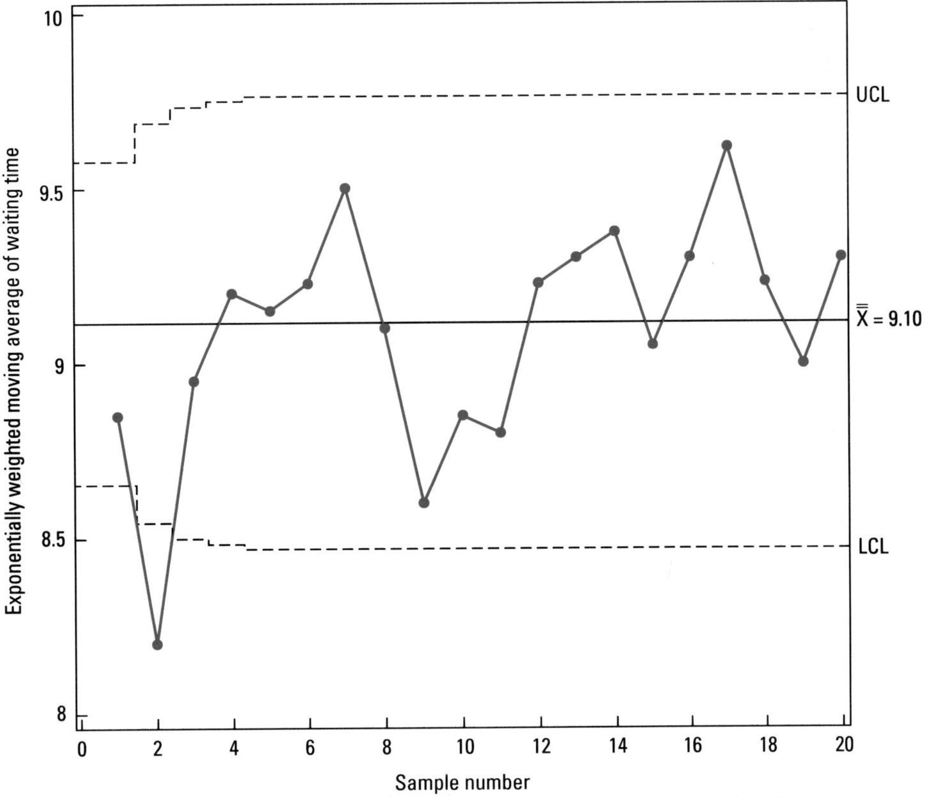

Figure 15-8 Exponentially-weighted moving average chart (3σ limits for $n = 4$).

c. Suppose the lower specification limit for gasoline mileage is 28 miles per gallon. Compute the capability indices CPL and C_{pk} and comment on the values. What proportion of the product will be unacceptable, if any?

TABLE 15-5 **Data for nonconforming cables**

Sample number	Number of nonconforming cables	Sample number	Number of nonconforming cables
1	2	11	5
2	5	12	4
3	4	13	2
4	3	14	5
5	4	15	3
6	2	16	12
7	3	17	3
8	2	18	2
9	4	19	5
10	11	20	2

Solution. A source program for process capability analysis is shown in Figure 15-17. The variable name "mpg" is used to denote the miles-per-gallon rating of the gasoline. On the input statement, the segment "mpg @@" indicates that more than one value of the variable "mpg" may be input on the same line. This may be seen by observing the form in which the data is input, as shown after the "cards" statement. Process capability analysis is conducted through the procedure command "proc capability." The "normaltest" option specifies that a test of normality is to be conducted for the variable ("mpg," in this case) in the data set "gas." The lower specification limit is input through the statement "spec lsl=28." Finally, the "histogram" option requests the plotting of a histogram of the variable in question.

Figure 15-18 shows the process capability analysis output. The output consists of four sections. In the first section, descriptive statistics on the variable "MPG" (miles per gallon) are given. There are 50 observations, with a mean of 30.782 and a standard deviation of 2.76477. The skewness is a measure of asymmetry about the mean. Since its value is positive (0.6449), the distribution is skewed to the right. (This skewness may also be observed in the histogram plot.) The coefficient of variation "CV," which is

```
data pchrt;
  input sample nonc;
cards;
1  2
2  5
3  4
4  3
5  4
6  2
7  3
8  2
9  4
10  11
11  5
12  4
13  2
14  5
15  3
16  12
17  3
18  2
19  5
20  2
;
proc print;
proc shewhart data=pchrt graphics;
   pchart nonc*sample='*' / subgroupn=100;
   label nonc='Proportion of nonconforming cables'
         sample='Sample number';
run;
```

Figure 15-9 Source program for a p-chart.

the ratio of the standard deviation to the mean, is shown to be roughly 8.98 percent. The values of two statistics that test the null hypothesis of the mean being equal to zero are shown next to "T:Mean= 0" and "Sgn Rank". The t-test is used in the first case (Banks, 1989; Duncan, 1986). The value of 0.0000 associated with "Prob> |T|" means that the probability value associated with the hypothesis test is very small; thus, for any reasonable level of significance (say, 0.05), the null hypothesis will be rejected. It is therefore appropriate to conclude that the mean is not equal to zero. The second test is the signed-rank test, which is a nonparametric test (Daniel, 1990). The value of 0.0000 associated with "Prob > |S|" means that the probability value associated with the observed test statistic is very small; thus the null hypothesis of the mean being equal to zero will be rejected. This supports the inference based on the t-test. Testing for normality is accomplished by the Shapiro–Wilk test (Shapiro and Wilk, 1965). The test statistic "W:Normal" is equal to 0.941108, and the probability value "Prob<W" is equal to 0.023. If the chosen level of significance is 0.05, the hypothesis of normality will be rejected because the probability value (0.023) is less than 0.05.

The second section of the output lists standard quantiles of the variable. Values of the range, interquartile distance, and mode are also provided. For this example, the range is 11.3.

The third section of the output provides the five lowest and highest observations. For instance, the five highest values are 34.8, 34.9, 36, and 38.1, respectively.

The fourth section of the output shows the values of the specification limits and the proportion of observations that are less than the lower specification limit, between the lower and upper specification limits, and above the upper specification limit. For this example, the lower specification limit is 28, and 16 percent of the observations are

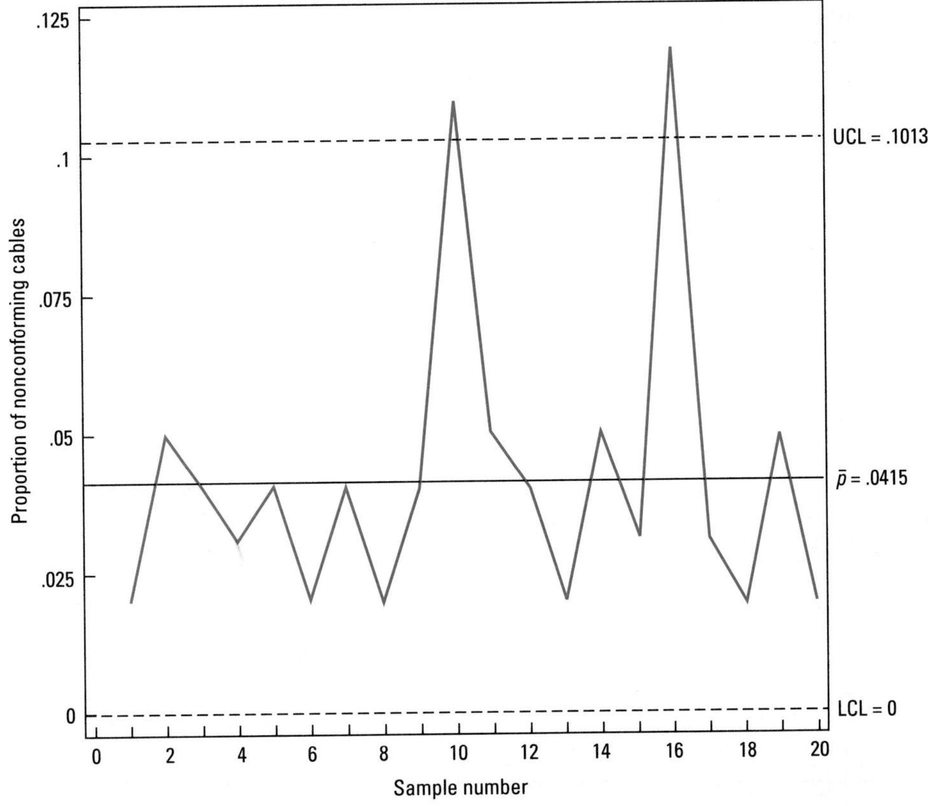

Figure 15-10 A p-chart for the proportion of nonconforming cables (3σ limits for $n = 100$).

TABLE 15-6 Number of nonconforming door hinges

Sample number	Number of nonconforming hinges	Sample number	Number of nonconforming hinges
1	10	16	8
2	14	17	10
3	12	18	7
4	6	19	12
5	11	20	13
6	14	21	9
7	8	22	7
8	9	23	12
9	7	24	6
10	15	25	8
11	10	26	6
12	6	27	9
13	12	28	10
14	7	29	7
15	20	30	12

below the lower specification limit. Process capability indices such as C_p, C_{pk}, CPU, CPL, and k are also shown in this section. For this example, only a lower specification is provided. The values of the indices CPL and C_{pk} both equal 0.3354. Since the value is less than 1, an undesirable situation is indicated. A proportion of the values will lie outside the specification limits.

The "histogram" option produces the output shown in Figure 15-19. The lower specification limit is also shown on the plot, and the skewness of the distribution and its deviation from normality can be seen as well.

Example 15-10: Refer to the data for the mileage per gallon of a particular brand of gasoline as discussed in Example 15-9. The data values are given in Table 15-9. Construct a normal probability plot for the mileage per gallon.

Solution. A source program is shown in Figure 15-20. The "probplot mpg" option creates a normal probability plot of the variable "mpg." Figure 15-21 shows the normal probability plot of miles per gallon of gasoline.

```
data hinge;
   input sample nonc;
cards;
1 10
2 14
3 12
4 6
5 11
6 14
7 8
8 9
9 7
10 15
11 10
12 6
13 12
14 7
15 20
16 8
17 10
18 7
19 12
20 13
21 9
22 7
23 12
24 6
25 8
26 6
27 9
28 10
29 7
30 12
;
run;
title 'np chart for door hinges';
proc shewhart data=hinge graphics;
   npchart nonc*sample='*' /subgroupn=300;
   label nonc='Number of nonconforming hinges'
         sample='Sample number';
run;
```

Figure 15-11 Source program for an *np*-chart.

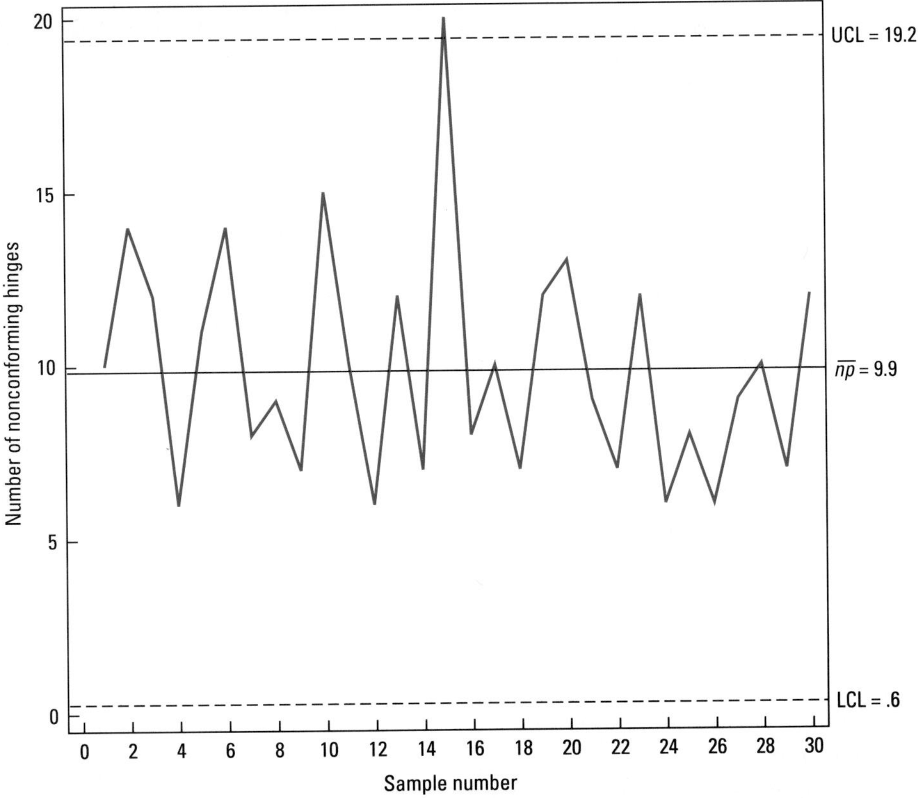

Figure 15-12 An np-chart for the number of nonconforming hinges (3σ limits for $n = 100$).

The more closely the plotted points approximate a straight line, the more closely the data adheres to a normal distribution. In this example, the points near the bottom left section deviate much from a straight line that would seem to fit most of the other observations. The histogram constructed in Example 15-9 showed a short left tail, a fact which supports this inference.

15-4 SUMMARY

This chapter has discussed the availability and use of computer software for quality assurance. A listing of several software packages along with their functional abilities, hardware requirements, and list prices has been provided. Although no attempt is made to rate these software packages, the table does provide some initial guidance for selecting a package based on the specific needs of the user and the

TABLE 15-7 Number of paint blemishes in automobiles

Sample number	Number of paint blemishes	Sample number	Number of paint blemishes
1	4	16	4
2	5	17	14
3	3	18	8
4	8	19	3
5	6	20	15
6	7	21	7
7	5	22	4
8	7	23	6
9	9	24	4
10	4	25	5
11	5	26	9
12	6	27	6
13	3	28	3
14	2	29	8
15	5	30	7

```
data paint;
 input sample blem;
  label sample='Sample number'
        blem='Number of paint blemishes';
cards;
1 4
2 5
3 3
4 8
5 6
6 7
7 5
8 7
9 9
10 4
11 5
12 6
13 3
14 2
15 5
16 4
17 14
18 8
19 3
20 15
21 7
22 4
23 6
24 4
25 5
26 9
27 6
28 3
29 8
30 7
;
proc shewhart data=paint graphics;
     cchart blem*sample='*';
run;
```

Figure 15-13 Source program for a *c*-chart.

available resources. The list is by no means exhaustive. Given that the availability of packages changes very frequently with time, the reader should consult the latest references to obtain information on current availability. For a selected software package, this chapter gives numerous examples of applications to control chart construction and process capability.

KEY TERMS

Analysis of variance
Calibration
Capability analysis
Computer hardware
Computer software

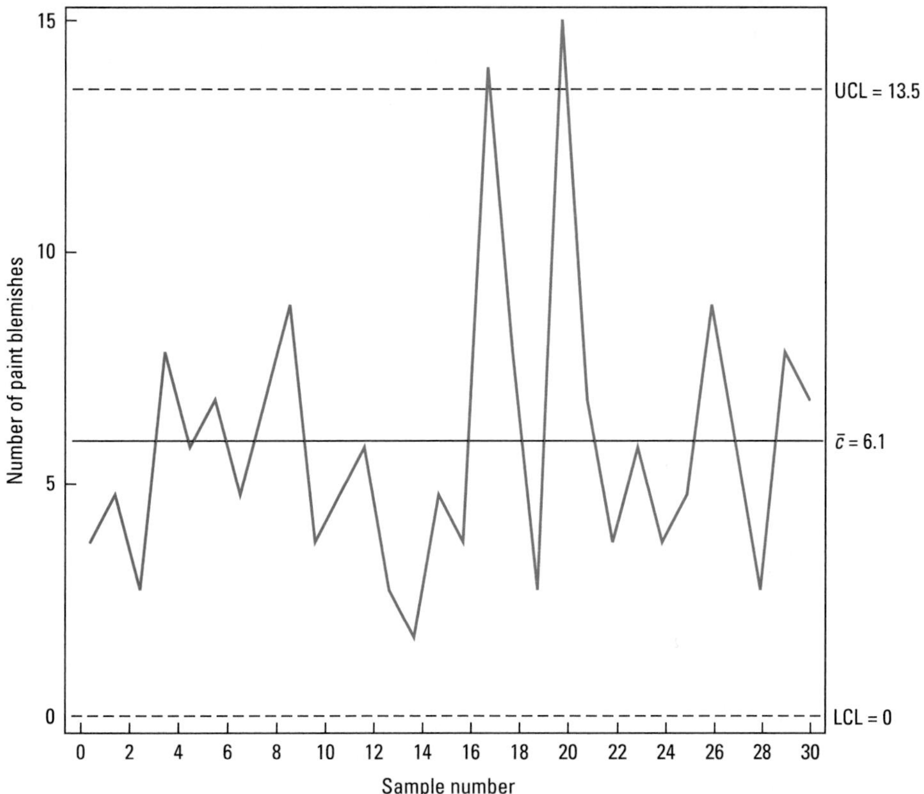

Figure 15-14 A c-chart for the number of paint blemishes (3σ limits for $n = 1$).

TABLE 15-8 Number of typographical errors

Sample number	Number of pages inspected	Number of typographical errors	Sample number	Number of pages inspected	Number of typographical errors
1	10	4	14	4	3
2	5	3	15	8	2
3	8	8	16	8	4
4	6	4	17	12	6
5	12	14	18	10	8
6	10	8	19	12	10
7	8	4	20	8	5
8	10	5	21	6	8
9	6	2	22	10	4
10	8	12	23	10	5
11	10	7	24	8	4
12	12	5	25	12	5
13	6	15			

```
  data typ;
input sample ninsp error;
cards;
1  10   4
2   5   3
3   8   8
4   6   4
5  12  14
6  10   8
7   8   4
8  10   5
9   6   2
10  8  12
11 10   7
12 12   5
13  6  15
14  4   3
15  8   2
16  8   4
17 12   6
18 10   8
19 12  10
20  8   5
21  6   8
22 10   4
23 10   5
24  8   4
25 12   5
;
proc shewhart data=typ graphics;
     uchart error*sample /subgroupn=ninsp;
      label error='Number of errors'
      sample='Sample number';
run;
```

Figure 15-15 Source program for a u-chart.

- Control charts
  - Variable charts
    - $\overline{X}$-chart
    - R-chart
    - s-chart
    - Moving average chart
    - Exponentially weighted (geometric) moving average chart
  - Attributes charts
    - p-chart
    - np-chart
    - c-chart
    - u-chart
- Data analysis
- Data management
- Design of experiments
- Gage repeatability
- Gage reproducibility
- Inspection
- Normal probability plot
- Normality test
  - Shapiro–Wilk test
- Pareto chart
- Quality costs
- Reliability
- Sampling
- Simulation
- Statistical methods

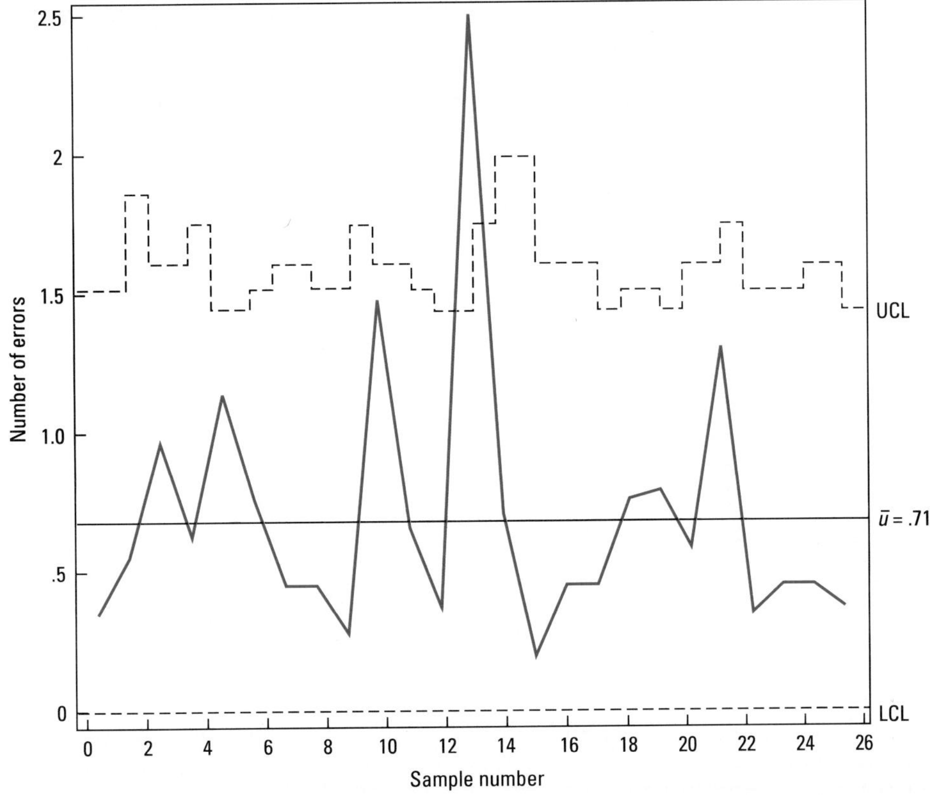

Figure 15-16 A u-chart for the number of typographical errors per page (3σ limits; minimum n = 4, maximum n = 12).

Statistical process control
Supplier quality assurance
Taguchi methods
Training
Weibull analysis

TABLE 15-9 Miles-per-gallon ratings of a brand of gasoline

33.2	29.4	36.5	38.1	30.0
29.1	32.2	29.5	36.0	31.5
34.5	33.6	27.4	30.4	28.4
32.6	30.4	31.8	29.8	34.6
30.7	31.9	32.3	28.2	27.5
34.9	32.8	27.7	28.4	28.8
30.2	26.8	27.8	30.5	28.5
31.8	29.2	28.6	27.5	28.5
30.8	31.8	29.1	26.9	34.2
33.5	27.4	28.5	34.8	30.5

Exercises

15-1 The thickness of the magnetic coating on audio tapes is an important characteristic. Random samples of size four were selected, and the thicknesses were measured using an optical instrument. Table 15-10 shows the mean $\overline{X}$ and standard deviation s for 20 samples. The specifications are 38 ± 4.5. Using a software package of your choice:

a. Construct and plot the trial control limits for $\overline{X}$ and s-charts.
b. Assuming assignable causes for the out-of-control points, determine the revised control limits.
c. Find the process capability ratios C_p, C_{pk}, CPL, and CPU, and comment on the ability of the process to produce items that meet specifications.

```
data gas;
   input  mpg @@;
     label mpg='Miles per gallon of gasoline';
cards;
33.2 29.4 36.5 38.1 30.0
29.1 32.2 29.5 36.0 31.5
34.5 33.6 27.4 30.4 28.4
32.6 30.4 31.8 29.8 34.6
30.7 31.9 32.3 28.2 27.5
34.9 32.8 27.7 28.4 28.8
30.2 26.8 27.8 30.5 28.5
31.8 29.2 28.6 27.5 28.5
30.8 31.8 29.1 26.9 34.2
33.5 27.4 28.5 34.8 30.5
;
title 'Process Capability Analysis of MPG of Gasoline';
proc capability data=gas normaltest graphics;
  spec lsl=28;
  histogram;
run;
```

Figure 15-17 Source program for process capability analysis.

15-2 The level of dissolved oxygen in water was measured every two hours in a river in which industrial plants discharge processed waste. Each observation consisted of four samples, from which the sample mean and range of the amount of dissolved oxygen (in parts per million) were calculated. Table 15-11 shows the results of 25 such observations. Using a software package of your choice:

a. Construct control charts for the average and range.
b. Assuming assignable causes for the out-of-control points, revise the limits if necessary.
c. Suppose environmental standards require a minimum of 4 parts per million of dissolved oxygen. Find the capability index CPL, and comment on the ability to meet this standard.

15-3 The control of errors in check processing is a prime consideration for all banks. The observations shown in Table 15-12 were taken over a span of two months for an individual in the processing department. The number of errors and the number of items sampled are shown. Construct an appropriate control chart, and determine if the performance of the employee is in statistical control. Revise the control limits if necessary, assuming assignable causes for out-of-control points.

15-4 The waiting time (in minutes) before being served in a local post office was observed for 50 randomly chosen customers and is shown in Table 15-13. Using a software package of your choice:

a. Find the mean and standard deviation of the waiting times.
b. Construct a relative frequency histogram.
c. Suppose the goal of the post office is for the waiting time to be less than 3.5 minutes. What proportion of the time is this goal achievable?
d. Construct a normal probability plot of the waiting times, and comment on its normality.

REFERENCES

American Society for Quality Control (1992), "Directory of Software for Quality Assurance and Quality Control," *Quality Progress*, 25 (3), pp. 20–81.

Banks, J. (1989). *Principles of Quality Control.* Wiley, New York.

Daniel, W. W. (1990). *Applied Nonparametric Statistics*, 2nd edition. PWS-Kent, Boston, MA.

CAPABILITY

Variable=MPG Miles per gallon of gasoline

Moments

N	50	Sum Wgts	50
Mean	30.782	Sum	1539.1
Std Dev	2.76477	Variance	7.643955
Skewness	0.644923	Kurtosis	−0.28707
USS	47751.13	CSS	374.5538
CV	8.981776	Std Mean	0.390998
T:Mean=0	78.72683	Prob>|T|	0.000
Sgn Rank	637.5	Prob>|S|	0.000
Num ^ = 0	50		
W:Normal	0.941108	Prob<W	0.023

CAPABILITY

Variable=MPG Miles per gallon of gasoline

Quantiles(Def=5)

100% Max	38.1	99%	38.1
75% Q3	32.6	95%	36
50% Med	30.4	90%	34.7
25% Q1	28.5	10%	27.5
0% Min	26.8	5%	27.4
		1%	26.8
Range	11.3		
Q3-Q1	4.1		
Mode	28.5		

CAPABILITY

Variable=MPG Miles per gallon of gasoline

Extremes

Lowest	Obs	Highest	Obs
26.8(	32)	34.8(	49)
26.9(	44)	34.9(	26)
27.4(	47)	36(	9)
27.4(	13)	36.5(	3)
27.5(	39)	38.1(	4)

CAPABILITY

Variable=MPG Miles per gallon of gasoline

Specifications

LSL	28	% < LSL	16
		% Between	.
USL	.	% > USL	.

Indices

CPL	0.335411	CPU	.
CP	.	CPK	0.335411
K	.		

Figure 15-18 Process capability analysis of miles-per-gallon ratings of gasoline.

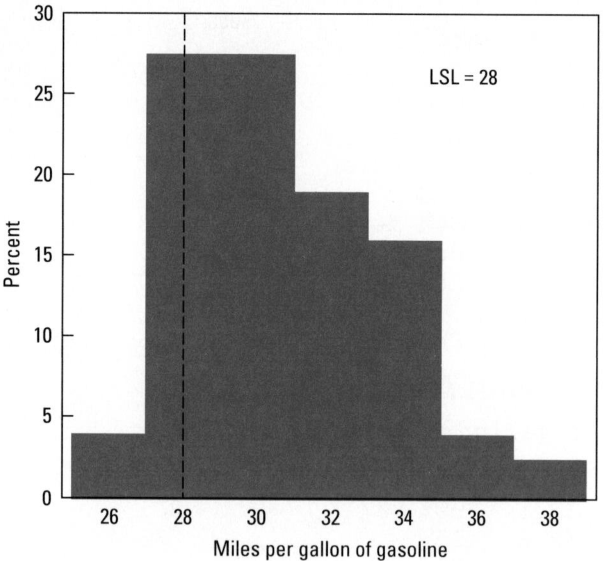

Figure 15-19 Histogram of miles-per-gallon ratings of gasoline.

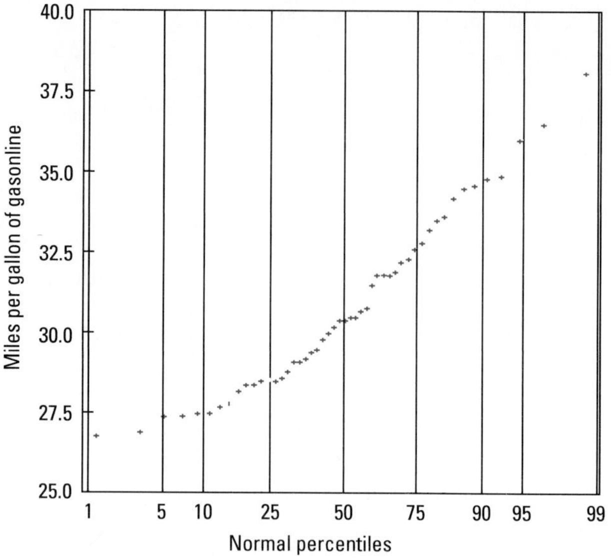

Figure 15-21 Normal probability plot of miles-per-gallon ratings of gasoline.

```
data miles;
   input mpg @@;
   lable mpg='Miles per gallon of gasoline';
cards;
33.2 29.4 36.5 38.1 30.0
29.1 32.2 29.5 36.0 31.5
34.5 33.6 27.4 30.4 28.4
32.6 30.4 31.8 29.8 34.6
30.7 31.9 32.3 28.2 27.5
34.9 32.8 27.7 28.4 28.8
30.2 26.8 27.8 30.5 28.5
31.8 29.2 28.6 27.5 28.5
30.8 31.8 29.1 26.9 34.2
33.5 27.4 28.5 34.8 30.5
;
proc capability data=miles graphics;
     probplot mpg /grid;
run;
```

Figure 15-20 Source program for normal probability plot.

TABLE 15-10 Data for thickness of magnetic coating

Sample number	Sample mean, $\overline{X}$	Sample standard deviation, s
1	36.4	4.6
2	35.8	3.7
3	37.3	5.2
4	33.9	4.3
5	37.8	4.4
6	36.1	3.9
7	38.6	5.0
8	39.4	6.1
9	34.4	4.1
10	39.5	5.8
11	36.7	5.3
12	35.2	3.5
13	38.8	4.7
14	39.0	5.6
15	35.5	5.0
16	37.1	4.1
17	38.3	5.6
18	39.2	4.8
19	36.8	4.7
20	37.7	5.4

TABLE 15-11 Average level and range of dissolved oxygen (in parts per million)

Observation number	Average level of dissolved oxygen	Range
1	7.4	2.1
2	8.2	1.8
3	5.6	1.4
4	7.2	1.6
5	7.8	1.9
6	6.1	1.5
7	5.5	1.1
8	6.0	2.7
9	7.1	2.2
10	8.3	1.8
11	6.4	1.2
12	7.2	2.1
13	4.2	2.5
14	4.3	2.0
15	5.8	1.4
16	5.4	1.2
17	8.3	1.9
18	8.0	2.3
19	6.7	1.5
20	8.5	1.3
21	5.7	2.4
22	8.3	2.1
23	5.8	1.6
24	6.8	1.8
25	5.9	2.1

TABLE 15-12 Number of check processing errors and the number sampled

Observation number	Number of errors	Number of items sampled
1	8	400
2	6	400
3	4	400
4	9	400
5	7	400
6	5	400
7	5	300
8	7	300
9	4	300
10	15	300
11	6	300
12	7	300
13	4	300
14	3	300
15	5	300
16	8	300
17	11	500
18	13	500
19	8	500
20	7	500
21	8	500
22	4	500
23	3	500
24	7	500
25	6	500

TABLE 15-13 Waiting times (in minutes) at a post office

2.1	0.5	3.6	1.4	2.0
0.8	0.4	4.2	3.5	2.5
4.8	2.8	1.9	1.2	3.2
1.6	2.5	2.4	1.9	2.0
3.5	5.2	3.1	1.6	1.5
1.9	2.4	2.7	2.1	1.8
4.6	3.8	1.5	4.5	3.9
5.5	2.5	3.8	5.0	4.6
2.1	2.8	1.6	3.8	4.2
3.5	5.2	4.8	3.9	2.6

Duncan, A. J. (1986). *Quality Control and Industrial Statistics,* 5th edition. Irwin, Homewood, IL.

O'Neal, K. R. (1987). "Statistical Process/Quality Control Microcomputer Software Buyer's Guide," *Industrial Engineering,* pp. 29–41.

SAS Institute, Inc. (1989a). *SAS Technical Report P–188, SAS/QC Software Examples, Version 6.* Cary, NC.

SAS Institute, Inc. (1989b). *SAS/QC Software: Reference, Version 6, First Edition,* Cary, NC.

Shapiro, S. S., and Wilk, M. B. (1965). "An Analysis of Variance Test for Normality," *Biometrika,* 52, pp 591–611.

Appendixes

APPENDIX OUTLINE

APPENDIX A-1 Cumulative binomial distribution

		p = Probability of Occurrence									
n	*X*	*.05*	*.10*	*.15*	*.20*	*.25*	*.30*	*.35*	*.40*	*.45*	*.50*
2	0	.903	.810	.772	.640	.563	.490	.423	.360	.303	.250
	1	.998	.990	.978	.960	.938	.910	.878	.840	.798	.750
3	0	.857	.729	.614	.512	.422	.343	.275	.216	.166	.125
	1	.993	.972	.939	.896	.844	.784	.718	.648	.575	.500
	2	1.000	.999	.997	.992	.984	.973	.957	.936	.909	.875
4	0	.815	.656	.522	.410	.316	.240	.179	.130	.092	.063
	1	.986	.948	.890	.819	.738	.652	.563	.475	.391	.313
	2	1.000	.996	.988	.973	.949	.916	.874	.821	.759	.687
	3		1.000	.999	.998	.996	.992	.985	.974	.959	.938
5	0	.774	.590	.444	.328	.237	.168	.116	.078	.050	.031
	1	.977	.919	.835	.737	.633	.528	.428	.337	.256	.188
	2	.999	.991	.973	.942	.896	.837	.765	.683	.593	.500
	3	1.000	1.000	.998	.993	.984	.969	.946	.913	.869	.813
	4			1.000	1.000	.999	.998	.995	.990	.982	.969
6	0	.735	.531	.377	.262	.178	.118	.075	.047	.028	.016
	1	.967	.886	.776	.655	.534	.420	.319	.233	.164	.109
	2	.998	.984	.953	.901	.831	.744	.647	.544	.442	.344
	3	1.000	.999	.994	.983	.962	.930	.883	.821	.745	.656
	4		1.000	1.000	.998	.995	.989	.978	.959	.931	.891
	5				1.000	1.000	.999	.998	.996	.992	.984
7	0	.698	.478	.321	.210	.133	.082	.049	.028	.015	.008
	1	.956	.850	.717	.577	.445	.329	.234	.159	.102	.063
	2	.996	.974	.926	.852	.756	.647	.532	.420	.316	.227
	3	1.000	.997	.988	.967	.929	.874	.800	.710	.608	.500
	4		1.000	.999	.995	.987	.971	.944	.904	.847	.773
	5			1.000	1.000	.999	.996	.991	.981	.964	.938
	6					1.000	1.000	.999	.998	.996	.992
8	0	.663	.430	.272	.168	.100	.058	.032	.017	.008	.004
	1	.943	.813	.657	.503	.367	.255	.169	.106	.063	.035
	2	.994	.962	.895	.797	.679	.552	.428	.315	.220	.145
	3	1.000	.995	.979	.944	.886	.806	.706	.594	.477	.363
	4		1.000	.997	.990	.973	.942	.894	.826	.740	.637
	5			1.000	.999	.996	.989	.975	.950	.912	.855
	6				1.000	1.000	.999	.996	.991	.982	.965
	7						1.000	1.000	.999	.998	.996
9	0	.630	.387	.232	.134	.075	.040	.021	.010	.005	.002
	1	.929	.775	.599	.436	.300	.196	.121	.071	.039	.020
	2	.992	.947	.859	.738	.601	.463	.337	.232	.150	.090
	3	.999	.992	.966	.914	.834	.730	.609	.483	.361	.254
	4	1.000	.999	.994	.980	.951	.901	.828	.733	.621	.500
	5		1.000	.999	.997	.990	.975	.946	.901	.834	.746
	6			1.000	1.000	.999	.996	.989	.975	.950	.910
	7					1.000	1.000	.999	.996	.991	.980
	8							1.000	1.000	.999	.998
10	0	.599	.349	.197	.107	.056	.028	.013	.006	.003	.001
	1	.914	.736	.544	.376	.244	.149	.086	.046	.023	.011
	2	.988	.930	.820	.678	.526	.383	.262	.167	.100	.055
	3	.999	.987	.950	.879	.776	.650	.514	.382	.266	.172
	4	1.000	.998	.990	.967	.922	.850	.751	.633	.504	.377
	5		1.000	.999	.994	.980	.953	.905	.834	.738	.623
	6			1.000	.999	.996	.989	.974	.945	.898	.828
	7				1.000	1.000	.998	.995	.988	.973	.945
	8						1.000	.999	.998	.995	.989
	9							1.000	1.000	1.000	.999

Source: Jerry Banks and Russell G. Meikes, *Handbook of Tables and Graphs for the Industrial Engineer and Manager*, ©1984, pp. 28–32. Reprinted by permission of Prentice Hall, Englewood Cliffs, New Jersey.

APPENDIX A-1 *(Continued)*

		p = Probability of Occurrence									
n	*X*	*.05*	*.10*	*.15*	*.20*	*.25*	*.30*	*.35*	*.40*	*.45*	*.50*
11	0	.569	.314	.167	.086	.042	.020	.009	.004	.001	.000
	1	.898	.697	.492	.322	.197	.113	.061	.030	.014	.006
	2	.985	.910	.779	.617	.455	.313	.200	.119	.065	.033
	3	.998	.981	.931	.839	.713	.570	.426	.296	.191	.113
	4	1.000	.997	.984	.950	.885	.790	.668	.533	.397	.274
	5		1.000	.997	.988	.966	.922	.851	.753	.633	.500
	6			1.000	.998	.992	.978	.950	.901	.826	.726
	7				1.000	.999	.996	.988	.971	.939	.887
	8					1.000	.999	.998	.994	.985	.967
	9						1.000	1.000	.999	.998	.994
	10								1.000	1.000	1.000
12	0	.540	.282	.142	.069	.032	.014	.006	.002	.001	.000
	1	.882	.659	.443	.275	.158	.085	.042	.020	.008	.003
	2	.980	.889	.736	.558	.391	.253	.151	.083	.042	.019
	3	.998	.974	.908	.795	.649	.493	.347	.225	.134	.073
	4	1.000	.996	.976	.927	.842	.724	.583	.438	.304	.194
	5		.999	.995	.981	.946	.882	.787	.665	.527	.387
	6		1.000	.999	.996	.986	.961	.915	.842	.739	.613
	7			1.000	.999	.997	.991	.974	.943	.888	.806
	8				1.000	1.000	.998	.994	.985	.964	.927
	9						1.000	.999	.997	.992	.981
	10							1.000	1.000	.999	.997
	11									1.000	1.000
13	0	.513	.254	.121	.055	.024	.010	.004	.001	.000	.000
	1	.865	.621	.398	.234	.127	.064	.030	.013	.005	.002
	2	.975	.866	.692	.502	.333	.202	.113	.058	.027	.011
	3	.997	.966	.882	.747	.584	.421	.278	.169	.093	.046
	4	1.000	.994	.966	.901	.794	.654	.501	.353	.228	.133
	5		.999	.992	.970	.920	.835	.716	.574	.427	.291
	6		1.000	.999	.993	.976	.938	.871	.771	.644	.500
	7			1.000	.999	.994	.982	.954	.902	.821	.709
	8				1.000	.999	.996	.987	.968	.930	.867
	9					1.000	.999	.997	.992	.980	.954
	10						1.000	1.000	.999	.996	.989
	11								1.000	.999	.998
	12									1.000	1.000
14	0	.488	.229	.103	.044	.018	.007	.002	.001	.000	.000
	1	.847	.585	.357	.198	.101	.047	.021	.008	.003	.001
	2	.970	.842	.648	.448	.281	.161	.084	.040	.017	.006
	3	.996	.956	.853	.698	.521	.355	.220	.124	.063	.029
	4	1.000	.991	.953	.870	.742	.584	.423	.279	.167	.090
	5		.999	.988	.956	.888	.781	.641	.486	.337	.212
	6		1.000	.998	.988	.962	.907	.816	.692	.546	.395
	7			1.000	.998	.990	.969	.925	.850	.741	.605
	8				1.000	.998	.992	.976	.942	.881	.788
	9					1.000	.998	.994	.982	.957	.910
	10						1.000	.999	.996	.989	.971
	11							1.000	.999	.998	.994
	12								1.000	1.000	.999
	13										1.000

APPENDIX A-1 *(Continued)*

		p = *Probability of Occurrence*									
n	X	.05	.10	.15	.20	.25	.30	.35	.40	.45	.50
15	0	.463	.206	.087	.035	.013	.005	.002	.000	.000	.000
	1	.829	.549	.319	.167	.080	.035	.014	.005	.002	.000
	2	.964	.816	.604	.398	.236	.127	.062	.027	.011	.004
	3	.995	.944	.823	.648	.461	.297	.173	.091	.042	.018
	4	.999	.987	.938	.836	.686	.515	.352	.217	.120	.059
	5	1.000	.998	.983	.939	.852	.722	.564	.403	.261	.151
	6		1.000	.996	.982	.943	.869	.755	.610	.452	.304
	7			.999	.996	.983	.950	.887	.787	.654	.500
	8			1.000	.999	.996	.985	.958	.905	.818	.696
	9				1.000	.999	.996	.988	.966	.923	.849
	10					1.000	.999	.997	.991	.975	.941
	11						1.000	1.000	.998	.994	.982
	12								1.000	.999	.996
	13									1.000	1.000
16	0	.440	.185	.074	.028	.010	.003	.001	.000	.000	.000
	1	.811	.515	.284	.141	.063	.026	.010	.003	.001	.000
	2	.957	.789	.561	.352	.197	.099	.045	.018	.007	.002
	3	.993	.932	.790	.598	.405	.246	.134	.065	.028	.011
	4	.999	.983	.921	.798	.630	.450	.289	.167	.085	.038
	5	1.000	.997	.976	.918	.810	.660	.490	.329	.198	.105
	6		.999	.994	.973	.920	.825	.688	.527	.366	.227
	7		.1000	.999	.993	.973	.926	.841	.716	.563	.402
	8			1.000	.999	.993	.974	.933	.858	.744	.598
	9				1.000	.998	.993	.977	.942	.876	.773
	10					1.000	.998	.994	.981	.951	.895
	11						1.000	.999	.995	.985	.962
	12							1.000	.999	.997	.989
	13								1.000	.999	.998
	14									1.000	1.000
17	0	.418	.167	.063	.023	.008	.002	.001	.000	.000	.000
	1	.792	.482	.252	.118	.050	.019	.007	.002	.001	.000
	2	.950	.762	.520	.310	.164	.077	.033	.012	.004	.001
	3	.991	.917	.756	.549	.353	.202	.103	.046	.018	.006
	4	.999	.978	.901	.758	.574	.389	.235	.126	.060	.025
	5	1.000	.995	.968	.894	.765	.597	.420	.264	.147	.072
	6		.999	.992	.962	.893	.775	.619	.448	.290	.166
	7		1.000	.998	.989	.960	.895	.787	.641	.474	.315
	8			1.000	.997	.988	.960	.901	.801	.663	.500
	9				1.000	.997	.987	.962	.908	.817	.685
	10					.999	.997	.988	.965	.917	.834
	11					1.000	.999	.997	.989	.970	.928
	12						1.000	.999	.997	.991	.975
	13							1.000	1.000	.998	.994
	14									1.000	.999
	15										1.000

APPENDIX A-1 *(Continued)*

		p = Probability of Occurrence									
n	*X*	*.05*	*.10*	*.15*	*.20*	*.25*	*.30*	*.35*	*.40*	*.45*	*.50*
18	0	.397	.150	.054	.018	.006	.002	.000	.000	.000	.000
	1	.774	.450	.224	.099	.039	.014	.005	.001	.000	.000
	2	.942	.734	.480	.271	.135	.060	.024	.008	.003	.001
	3	.989	.902	.720	.501	.306	.165	.078	.033	.012	.004
	4	.998	.972	.879	.716	.519	.333	.189	.094	.041	.015
	5	1.000	.994	.958	.867	.717	.534	.355	.209	.108	.048
	6		.999	.988	.949	.861	.722	.549	.374	.226	.119
	7		1.000	.997	.984	.943	.859	.728	.563	.391	.240
	8			.999	.996	.981	.940	.861	.737	.578	.407
	9			1.000	.999	.995	.979	.940	.865	.747	.593
	10				1.000	.999	.994	.979	.942	.872	.760
	11					1.000	.999	.994	.980	.946	.881
	12						1.000	.999	.994	.982	.952
	13							1.000	.999	.995	.985
	14								1.000	.999	.996
	15									1.000	.999
	16										1.000
19	0	.377	.135	.046	.014	.004	.001	.000	.000	.000	.000
	1	.755	.420	.198	.083	.031	.010	.003	.001	.000	.000
	2	.933	.705	.441	.237	.111	.046	.017	.005	.002	.000
	3	.987	.885	.684	.455	.263	.133	.059	.023	.008	.002
	4	.998	.965	.856	.673	.465	.282	.150	.070	.028	.010
	5	1.000	.991	.946	.837	.668	.474	.297	.163	.078	.032
	6		.998	.984	.932	.825	.666	.481	.308	.173	.084
	7		1.000	.996	.977	.923	.818	.666	.488	.317	.180
	8			.999	.993	.971	.916	.815	.667	.494	.324
	9			1.000	.998	.991	.967	.913	.814	.671	.500
	10				1.000	.998	.989	.965	.912	.816	.676
	11					1.000	.997	.989	.965	.913	.820
	12						.999	.997	.988	.966	.916
	13						1.000	.999	.997	.989	.968
	14							1.000	.999	.997	.990
	15								1.000	.999	.998
	16									1.000	1.000
20	0	.358	.122	.039	.012	.003	.001	.000	.000	.000	.000
	1	.736	.392	.176	.069	.024	.008	.002	.001	.000	.000
	2	.925	.677	.405	.206	.091	.035	.012	.004	.001	.000
	3	.984	.867	.648	.411	.225	.107	.044	.016	.005	.001
	4	.997	.957	.830	.630	.415	.238	.118	.051	.019	.006
	5	1.000	.989	.933	.804	.617	.416	.245	.126	.055	.021
	6		.998	.978	.913	.786	.608	.417	.250	.130	.058
	7		1.000	.994	.968	.898	.772	.601	.416	.252	.132
	8			.999	.990	.959	.887	.762	.596	.414	.252
	9			1.000	.997	.986	.952	.878	.755	.591	.412
	10				.999	.996	.983	.947	.872	.751	.588
	11				1.000	.999	.995	.980	.943	.869	.748
	12					1.000	.999	.994	.979	.942	.868
	13						1.000	.998	.994	.979	.942
	14							1.000	.998	.994	.979
	15								1.000	.998	.994
	16									1.000	.999
	17										1.000

APPENDIX A-2 Cumulative Poisson distribution

					λ = *Mean*					
X	*.01*	*.05*	*.1*	*.2*	*.3*	*.4*	*.5*	*.6*	*.7*	*.8*	*.9*
0	.990	.951	.905	.819	.741	.670	.607	.549	.497	.449	.407
1	1.000	.999	.995	.982	.963	.938	.910	.878	.844	.809	.772
2		1.000	1.000	.999	.996	.992	.986	.977	.966	.953	.937
3				1.000	1.000	.999	.998	.997	.994	.991	.987
4						1.000	1.000	1.000	.999	.999	.998
5									1.000	1.000	1.000

X	*1.0*	*1.1*	*1.2*	*1.3*	*1.4*	*1.5*	*1.6*	*1.7*	*1.8*	*1.9*	*2.0*
0	.368	.333	.301	.273	.247	.223	.202	.183	.165	.150	.135
1	.736	.699	.663	.627	.592	.558	.525	.493	.463	.434	.406
2	.920	.900	.879	.857	.833	.809	.783	.757	.731	.704	.677
3	.981	.974	.966	.957	.946	.934	.921	.907	.891	.875	.857
4	.996	.995	.992	.989	.986	.981	.976	.970	.964	.956	.947
5	.999	.999	.998	.998	.997	.996	.994	.992	.990	.987	.983
6	1.000	1.000	1.000	1.000	.999	.999	.999	.998	.997	.997	.995
7					1.000	1.000	1.000	1.000	.999	.999	.999
8									1.000	1.000	1.000

X	*2.2*	*2.4*	*2.6*	*2.8*	*3.0*	*3.5*	*4.0*	*4.5*	*5.0*	*5.5*	*6.0*
0	.111	.091	.074	.061	.050	.030	.018	.011	.007	.004	.002
1	.355	.308	.267	.231	.199	.136	.092	.061	.040	.027	.017
2	.623	.570	.518	.469	.423	.321	.238	.174	.125	.088	.062
3	.819	.779	.736	.692	.647	.537	.433	.342	.265	.202	.151
4	.928	.904	.877	.848	.815	.725	.629	.532	.440	.358	.285
5	.975	.964	.951	.935	.916	.858	.785	.703	.616	.529	.446
6	.993	.988	.983	.976	.966	.935	.889	.831	.762	.686	.606
7	.998	.997	.995	.992	.988	.973	.949	.913	.867	.809	.744
8	1.000	.999	.999	.998	.996	.990	.979	.960	.932	.894	.847
9		1.000	1.000	.999	.999	.997	.992	.983	.968	.946	.916
10				1.000	1.000	.999	.997	.993	.986	.975	.957
11						1.000	999	.998	.995	.989	.980
12							1.000	.999	.998	.998	.991
13								1.000	.999	.998	.996
14									1.000	.999	.999
15										1.000	.999
16											1.000

Source: Jerry Banks and Russell G. Meikes, *Handbook of Tables and Graphs for the Industrial Engineer and Manager*, © 1984, pp. 34–35. Reprinted by permission of Prentice Hall, Englewood Cliffs, New Jersey.

APPENDIX A-2 *(Continued)*

	λ = Mean										
X	*6.5*	*7.0*	*7.5*	*8.0*	*9.0*	*10.0*	*12.0*	*14.0*	*16.0*	*18.0*	*20.0*
0	.002	.001	.001								
1	.011	.007	.005	.003	.001						
2	.043	.030	.020	.014	.006	.003	.001				
3	.112	.082	.059	.042	.021	.010	.002				
4	.224	.173	.132	.100	.055	.029	.008	.002			
5	.369	.301	.241	.191	.116	.067	.020	.006	.001		
6	.527	.450	.378	.313	.207	.130	.046	.014	.004	.001	
7	.673	.599	.525	.453	.324	.220	.090	.032	.010	.003	.001
8	.792	.729	.662	.593	.456	.333	.155	.062	.022	.007	.002
9	.877	.830	.776	.717	.587	.458	.242	.109	.043	.015	.005
10	.933	.901	.862	.816	.706	.583	.347	.176	.077	.030	.011
11	.966	.947	.921	.888	.803	.697	.462	.260	.127	.055	.021
12	.984	.973	.957	.936	.876	.792	.576	.358	.193	.092	.039
13	.993	.987	.978	.966	.926	.864	.682	.464	.275	.143	.066
14	.997	.994	.990	.983	.959	.917	.772	.570	.368	.208	.105
15	.999	.998	.995	.992	.978	.951	.844	.669	.467	.287	.157
16	1.000	.999	.998	.996	.989	.973	.899	.756	.566	.375	.221
17		1.000	.999	.998	.995	.986	.937	.827	.659	.469	.297
18			1.000	.999	.998	.993	.963	.883	.742	.562	.381
19				1.000	.999	.997	.979	.923	.812	.651	.470
20					1.000	.998	.988	.952	.868	.731	.559
21						.999	.994	.971	.911	.799	.644
22						1.000	.997	.983	.942	.855	.721
23							.999	.991	.963	.899	.787
24							.999	.995	.978	.932	.843
25							1.000	.997	.987	.955	.888
26								.999	.993	.972	.922
27								.999	.996	.983	.948
28								1.000	.998	.990	.966
29									.999	.994	.978
30									.999	.997	.987
31									1.000	.998	.992
32										.999	.995
33										1.000	.997
34											.999
35											.999
36											1.000

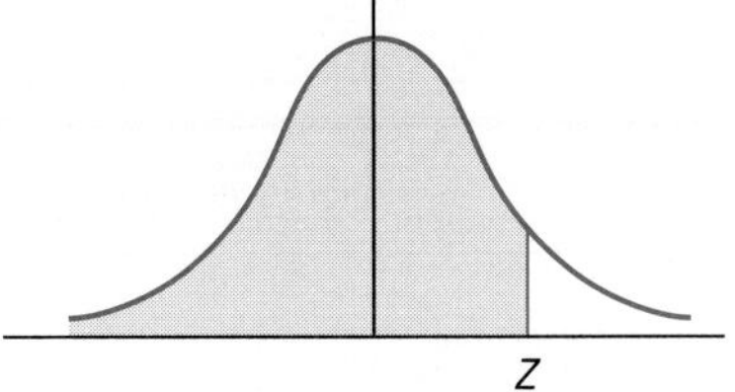

APPENDIX A-3 Cumulative standard normal distribution

Z	.00	.01	.02	.03	.04	.05	.06	.07	.08	.09
−3.40	.0003	.0003	.0003	.0003	.0003	.0003	.0003	.0003	.0003	.0002
−3.30	.0005	.0005	.0005	.0004	.0004	.0004	.0004	.0004	.0004	.0003
−3.20	.0007	.0007	.0006	.0006	.0006	.0006	.0006	.0005	.0005	.0005
−3.10	.0010	.0009	.0009	.0009	.0008	.0008	.0008	.0008	.0007	.0007
−3.00	.0013	.0013	.0013	.0012	.0012	.0011	.0011	.0011	.0010	.0010
−2.90	.0019	.0018	.0018	.0017	.0016	.0016	.0015	.0015	.0014	.0014
−2.80	.0026	.0025	.0024	.0023	.0023	.0022	.0021	.0021	.0020	.0019
−2.70	.0035	.0034	.0033	.0032	.0031	.0030	.0029	.0028	.0027	.0026
−2.60	.0047	.0045	.0044	.0043	.0041	.0040	.0039	.0038	.0037	.0036
−2.50	.0062	.0060	.0059	.0057	.0055	.0054	.0052	.0051	.0049	.0048
−2.40	.0082	.0080	.0078	.0075	.0073	.0071	.0069	.0068	.0066	.0064
−2.30	.0107	.0104	.0102	.0099	.0096	.0094	.0091	.0089	.0087	.0084
−2.20	.0139	.0136	.0132	.0129	.0125	.0122	.0119	.0116	.0113	.0110
−2.10	.0179	.0174	.0170	.0166	.0162	.0158	.0154	.0150	.0146	.0143
−2.00	.0228	.0222	.0217	.0212	.0207	.0202	.0197	.0192	.0188	.0183
−1.90	.0287	.0281	.0274	.0268	.0262	.0256	.0250	.0244	.0239	.0233
−1.80	.0359	.0351	.0344	.0336	.0329	.0322	.0314	.0307	.0301	.0294
−1.70	.0446	.0436	.0427	.0418	.0409	.0401	.0392	.0384	.0375	.0367
−1.60	.0548	.0537	.0526	.0516	.0505	.0495	.0485	.0475	.0465	.0455
−1.50	.0668	.0655	.0643	.0630	.0618	.0606	.0594	.0582	.0571	.0559
−1.40	.0808	.0793	.0778	.0764	.0749	.0735	.0721	.0708	.0694	.0681
−1.30	.0968	.0951	.0934	.0918	.0901	.0885	.0869	.0853	.0838	.0823
−1.20	.1151	.1131	.1112	.1093	.1075	.1056	.1038	.1020	.1003	.0985
−1.10	.1357	.1335	.1314	.1292	.1271	.1251	.1230	.1210	.1190	.1170
−1.00	.1587	.1562	.1539	.1515	.1492	.1469	.1446	.1423	.1401	.1379
−.90	.1841	.1814	.1788	.1762	.1736	.1711	.1685	.1660	.1635	.1611
−.80	.2119	.2090	.2061	.2033	.2005	.1977	.1949	.1922	.1894	.1867
−.70	.2420	.2389	.2358	.2327	.2296	.2266	.2236	.2206	.2177	.2148
−.60	.2743	.2709	.2676	.2643	.2611	.2578	.2546	.2514	.2483	.2451
−.50	.3085	.3050	.3015	.2981	.2946	.2912	.2877	.2843	.2810	.2776
−.40	.3446	.3409	.3372	.3336	.3300	.3264	.3228	.3192	.3156	.3121
−.30	.3821	.3783	.3745	.3707	.3669	.3632	.3594	.3557	.3520	.3483
−.20	.4207	.4168	.4129	.4090	.4052	.4013	.3974	.3936	.3897	.3859
−.10	.4602	.4562	.4522	.4483	.4443	.4404	.4364	.4325	.4286	.4247
−.00	.5000	.4960	.4920	.4880	.4840	.4801	.4761	.4721	.4681	.4641

Source: Jerry Banks and Russell G. Meikes, *Handbook of Tables and Graphs for the Industrial Engineer and Manager*, © 1984, pp. 44–45. Reprinted by permission of Prentice Hall, Englewood Cliffs, New Jersey.

APPENDIX A-3 *(Continued)*

Z	.00	.01	.02	.03	.04	.05	.06	.07	.08	.09
.00	.5000	.5040	.5080	.5120	.5160	.5199	.5239	.5279	.5319	.5359
.10	.5398	.5438	.5478	.5517	.5557	.5596	.5636	.5675	.5714	.5753
.20	.5793	.5832	.5871	.5910	.5948	.5987	.6026	.6046	.6103	.6141
.30	.6179	.6217	.6255	.6293	.6331	.6368	.6406	.6443	.6480	.6517
.40	.6554	.6591	.6628	.6664	.6700	.6736	.6772	.6808	.6844	.6879
.50	.6915	.6950	.6985	.7019	.7054	.7088	.7123	.7157	.7190	.7224
.60	.7257	.7291	.7324	.7357	.7389	.7422	.7454	.7486	.7517	.7549
.70	.7580	.7611	.7642	.7673	.7704	.7734	.7764	.7794	.7823	.7852
.80	.7881	.7910	.7939	.7967	.7995	.8023	.8051	.8078	.8106	.8133
.90	.8159	.8186	.8212	.8238	.8264	.8289	.8315	.8340	.8365	.8389
1.00	.8413	.8438	.8461	.8485	.8508	.8531	.8554	.8577	.8599	.8621
1.10	.8643	.8665	.8686	.8708	.8729	.8749	.8770	.8790	.8810	.8830
1.20	.8849	.8869	.8888	.8907	.8925	.8944	.8962	.8980	.8997	.9015
1.30	.9032	.9049	.9066	.9082	.9099	.9115	.9131	.9147	.9162	.9177
1.40	.9192	.9207	.9222	.9236	.9251	.9265	.9279	.9292	.9306	.9319
1.50	.9332	.9345	.9357	.9370	.9382	.9394	.9406	.9418	9429	.9441
1.60	.9452	.9463	.9474	.9484	.9495	.9505	.9515	.9525	.9535	.9545
1.70	.9554	.9564	.9573	.9582	.9591	.9599	.9608	.9616	.9625	.9633
1.80	.9641	.9649	.9656	.9664	.9671	.9678	.9686	.9693	.9699	.9706
1.90	.9713	.9719	.9726	.9732	.9738	.9744	.9750	.9756	.9761	.9767
2.00	.9772	.9778	.9783	.9788	.9793	.9798	.9803	.9808	.9812	.9817
2.10	.9821	.9826	.9830	.9834	.9838	.9842	.9846	.9850	.9854	.9857
2.20	.9861	.9864	.9868	.9871	.9875	.9878	.9881	.9884	.9887	.9890
2.30	.9893	.9896	.9898	.9901	.9904	.9906	.9909	.9911	.9913	.9916
2.40	.9918	.9920	.9922	.9925	.9927	.9929	.9931	.9932	.9934	.9936
2.50	.9938	.9940	.9941	.9943	.9945	.9946	.9948	.9949	.9951	.9952
2.60	.9953	.9955	.9956	.9957	.9959	.9960	.9961	.9962	.9963	.9964
2.70	.9965	.9966	.9967	.9968	.9969	.9970	.9971	.9972	.9973	.9974
2.80	.9974	.9975	.9976	.9977	.9977	.9978	.9979	.9979	.9980	.9981
2.90	.9981	.9982	.9982	.9983	.9984	.9984	.9985	.9985	.9986	.9986
3.00	.9987	.9987	.9987	.9988	.9988	.9989	.9989	.9989	.9990	.9990
3.10	.9990	.9991	.9991	.9991	.9992	.9992	.9992	.9992	.9993	.9993
3.20	.9993	.9993	.9994	.9994	.9994	.9994	.9994	.9995	.9995	.9995
3.30	.9995	.9995	.9995	.9996	.9996	.9996	.9996	.9996	.9996	.9997

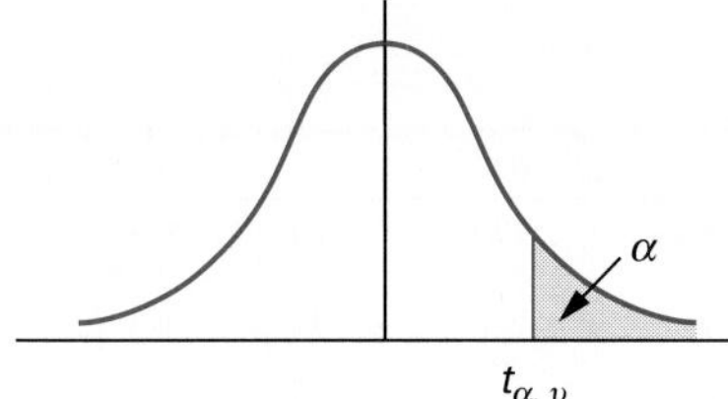

APPENDIX A-4 Values of t for a specified right tail area

Degrees of Freedom	α = *Right-Hand Tail Area*						
υ	*.250*	*.100*	*.050*	*.025*	*.010*	*.005*	*.001*
1	1.000	3.078	6.314	12.706	31.821	63.567	318.309
2	.816	1.886	2.920	4.303	6.965	9.925	22.327
3	.765	1.638	2.353	3.182	4.541	5.841	10.215
4	.741	1.533	2.132	2.776	3.747	4.604	7.173
5	.727	1.476	2.015	2.571	3.365	4.032	5.893
6	.718	1.440	1.943	2.447	3.143	3.707	5.208
7	.711	1.415	1.895	2.365	2.998	3.499	4.785
8	.706	1.397	1.860	2.306	2.896	3.355	4.501
9	.703	1.383	1.833	2.262	2.821	3.250	4.297
10	.700	1.372	1.812	2.228	2.764	3.169	4.144
11	.697	1.363	1.796	2.201	2.718	3.106	4.025
12	.695	1.356	1.782	2.179	2.681	3.055	3.930
13	.694	1.350	1.771	2.160	2.650	3.012	3.852
14	.692	1.345	1.761	2.145	2.624	2.977	3.787
15	.691	1.341	1.753	2.131	2.602	2.947	3.733
16	.690	1.337	1.746	2.120	2.583	2.921	3.686
17	.689	1.333	1.740	2.110	2.567	2.898	3.646
18	.688	1.330	1.734	2.101	2.552	2.878	3.610
19	.688	1.328	1.729	2.093	2.539	2.861	3.579
20	.687	1.325	1.725	2.086	2.528	2.845	3.552
21	.686	1.323	1.721	2.080	2.518	2.831	3.527
22	.686	1.321	1.717	2.074	2.508	2.819	3.505
23	.685	1.319	1.714	2.069	2.500	2.807	3.485
24	.685	1.318	1.711	2.064	2.492	2.797	3.467
25	.684	1.316	1.708	2.060	2.485	2.787	3.450
26	.684	1.315	1.706	2.056	2.479	2.779	3.435
27	.684	1.314	1.703	2.052	2.473	2.771	3.421
28	.683	1.313	1.701	2.048	2.467	2.763	3.408
29	.683	1.311	1.699	2.045	2.462	2.756	3.396
30	.683	1.310	1.697	2.042	2.457	2.750	3.385
35	.682	1.306	1.690	2.030	2.438	2.724	3.340
40	.681	1.303	1.684	2.021	2.423	2.704	3.307
50	.679	1.299	1.676	2.009	2.403	2.678	3.261
60	.679	1.296	1.671	2.000	2.390	2.660	3.232
70	.678	1.294	1.667	1.994	2.381	2.648	3.211
80	.678	1.292	1.664	1.990	2.374	2.639	3.195
90	.677	1.291	1.662	1.987	2.368	2.632	3.183
100	.677	1.290	1.660	1.984	2.364	2.626	3.174
120	.677	1.289	1.658	1.980	2.358	2.617	3.160
∞	.674	1.282	1.645	1.960	2.326	2.576	3.090

Source: Jerry Banks and Russell G. Meikes, *Handbook of Tables and Graphs for the Industrial Engineer and Manager*, © 1984, p. 57. Reprinted by permission of Prentice Hall, Englewood Cliffs, New Jersey.

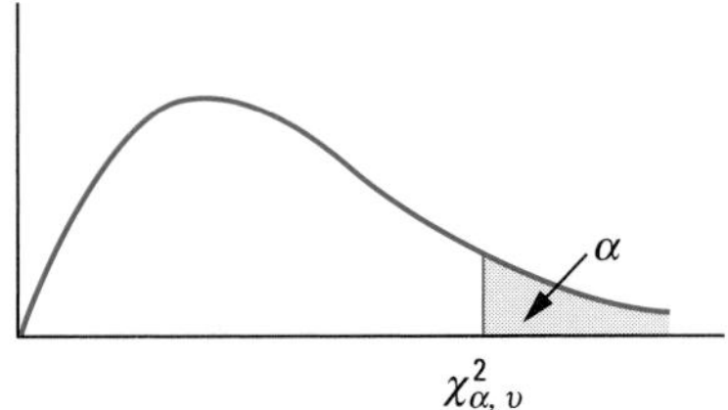

APPENDIX A-5 Chi-squared values for a specified right tail area

Degress of Freedom	*α = Right-Hand Tail Area*											
υ	*.999*	*.995*	*.99*	*.975*	*.95*	*.90*	*.10*	*.05*	*.025*	*.01*	*.005*	*.001*
1	.00	.00	.00	.00	.00	.02	2.71	3.84	5.02	6.63	7.88	10.83
2	.00	.01	.02	.05	.10	.21	4.61	5.99	7.38	9.21	10.60	13.81
3	.02	.07	.11	.22	.35	.58	6.25	7.81	9.35	11.34	12.84	16.25
4	.09	.21	.30	.48	.71	1.06	7.78	9.49	11.14	13.28	14.86	18.45
5	.21	.41	.55	.83	1.15	1.61	9.24	11.07	12.83	15.09	16.75	20.50
6	.38	.68	.87	1.24	1.64	2.20	10.64	12.59	14.45	16.81	18.54	22.44
7	.60	.99	1.24	1.69	2.17	2.83	12.02	14.07	16.01	18.48	20.28	24.30
8	.86	1.34	1.65	2.18	2.73	3.49	13.36	15.51	17.53	20.09	21.95	26.11
9	1.15	1.74	2.09	2.70	3.33	4.17	14.68	16.92	19.02	21.67	23.59	27.86
10	1.48	2.16	2.56	3.25	3.94	4.87	15.99	18.31	20.48	23.21	25.19	29.57
11	1.83	2.60	3.05	3.82	4.57	5.58	17.27	19.68	21.92	24.72	26.76	31.25
12	2.22	3.07	3.57	4.40	5.23	6.30	18.55	21.03	23.34	26.22	28.30	32.90
13	2.62	3.57	4.11	5.01	5.89	7.04	19.81	22.36	24.74	27.69	29.82	34.52
14	3.05	4.07	4.66	5.63	6.57	7.79	21.06	23.68	26.12	29.14	31.32	36.12
15	3.48	4.60	5.23	6.26	7.26	8.55	22.31	25.00	27.49	30.58	32.80	37.69
16	3.94	5.14	5.81	6.91	7.96	9.31	23.54	26.30	28.85	32.00	34.27	39.25
17	4.42	5.70	6.41	7.56	8.67	10.09	24.77	27.59	30.19	33.41	35.72	40.79
18	4.91	6.26	7.01	8.23	9.39	10.86	25.99	28.87	31.53	34.81	37.16	42.31
19	5.41	6.84	7.63	8.91	10.12	11.65	27.20	30.14	32.85	36.19	38.58	43.82
20	5.92	7.43	8.26	9.59	10.85	12.44	28.41	31.41	34.17	37.57	39.99	45.31
21	6.45	8.04	8.90	10.28	11.59	13.24	29.62	32.67	35.48	38.93	41.40	46.80
22	6.98	8.64	9.54	10.98	12.34	14.04	30.81	33.92	36.78	40.29	42.79	48.24
23	7.53	9.26	10.20	11.69	13.09	14.85	32.01	35.17	38.08	41.64	44.18	49.71
24	8.08	9.89	10.86	12.40	13.85	15.66	33.20	36.42	39.36	42.98	45.56	51.16
25	8.65	10.52	11.52	13.12	14.61	16.47	34.38	37.65	40.65	44.31	46.93	52.61
26	9.2	11.2	12.2	13.8	15.4	17.3	35.6	38.9	41.9	45.6	48.3	54.0
27	9.8	11.8	12.9	14.6	16.2	18.1	36.7	40.1	43.2	47.0	49.6	55.5
28	10.4	12.5	13.6	15.3	16.9	18.9	37.9	41.3	44.5	48.3	51.0	56.9
29	11.0	13.1	14.3	16.0	17.7	19.8	39.1	42.6	45.7	49.6	52.3	58.3
30	11.6	13.8	15.0	16.8	18.5	20.6	40.3	43.8	47.0	50.9	53.7	59.7
32	12.7	15.1	16.3	18.3	20.1	22.3	42.6	46.2	49.5	53.5	56.4	62.6
34	13.9	16.5	17.8	19.8	21.7	23.9	44.9	48.6	52.0	56.1	59.0	65.3
36	15.2	17.9	19.2	21.3	23.3	25.6	47.2	51.0	54.5	58.6	61.6	68.1
38	16.5	19.3	20.7	22.9	24.9	27.3	49.5	53.4	56.9	61.2	64.2	70.8
40	17.8	20.7	22.1	24.4	26.5	29.1	51.8	55.8	59.3	63.7	66.8	73.5
42	19.2	22.1	23.6	26.0	28.1	30.8	54.1	58.1	61.8	66.2	69.4	76.2
44	20.5	23.5	25.1	27.6	29.8	32.5	56.4	60.5	64.2	68.7	71.9	78.8
46	21.9	25.0	26.6	29.2	31.4	34.2	58.6	62.8	66.6	71.2	74.5	81.5
48	23.2	26.5	28.2	30.7	33.1	36.0	60.9	65.2	69.0	73.7	77.0	84.1
50	24.6	28.0	29.7	32.3	34.8	37.7	63.2	67.5	71.4	76.2	79.5	86.7
55	28.1	31.7	33.5	36.4	39.0	42.1	68.8	73.3	77.4	82.3	85.8	93.2
60	31.7	35.5	37.5	40.5	43.2	46.5	74.4	79.1	83.3	88.4	92.0	99.7
65	35.3	39.4	41.4	44.6	47.4	50.9	80.0	84.8	89.2	94.4	98.1	106.1
70	39.0	43.2	45.4	48.8	51.7	55.3	85.5	90.5	95.0	100.4	104.2	112.4
75	42.7	47.2	49.5	52.9	56.1	59.8	91.1	96.2	100.8	106.4	110.3	118.7
80	46.5	51.1	53.5	57.1	60.4	64.3	96.6	106.9	101.6	112.3	116.3	124.9
85	50.3	55.1	57.6	61.4	64.7	68.8	102.1	107.5	112.4	118.3	122.4	131.1
90	54.1	59.2	61.7	65.6	69.1	73.3	107.6	113.1	118.1	124.1	128.3	137.3
95	58.0	63.2	65.9	69.9	73.5	77.8	113.0	118.7	123.9	130.0	134.3	143.4
100	61.9	67.3	70.0	74.2	77.9	82.4	118.5	124.3	129.6	135.8	140.2	149.5

Source: Jerry Banks and Russell G. Meikes, *Handbook of Tables and Graphs for the Industrial Engineer and Manager*, © 1984, pp. 60–61. Reprinted by permission of Prentice Hall, Englewood Cliffs, New Jersey.

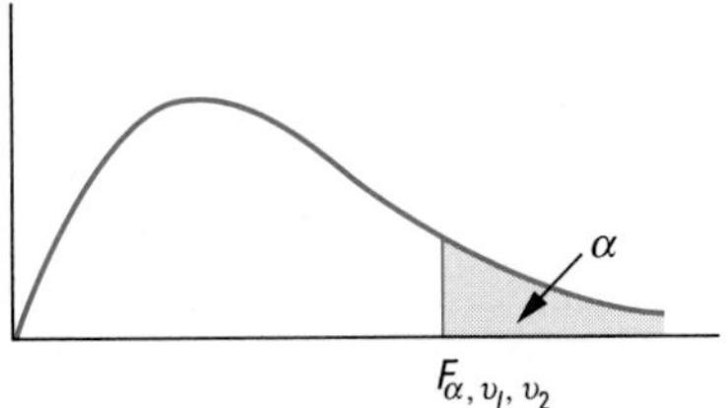

APPENDIX A-6 Values of F for a specified right tail area

		υ_1 = Degrees of Freedom for Numerator								
υ_2	α	*1*	*2*	*3*	*4*	*5*	*6*	*7*	*8*	*9*
	.100	39.9	49.5	53.6	55.8	57.2	58.2	58.9	59.4	59.9
	.050	161.4	199.5	215.7	224.6	230.2	234.0	236.8	238.4	240.5
1	.025	647.8	799.5	864.2	899.6	921.8	937.1	948.2	956.7	963.3
	.010	4052.2	4999.5	5403.4	5624.6	5763.6	5859.0	5928.4	5981.1	6022.5
	.001	40600.	50000.	54000.	56200.	57600.	58600.	59300.	59800.	60200.
	.100	8.53	9.00	9.16	9.24	9.29	9.33	9.35	9.37	9.38
	.050	18.51	19.00	19.16	19.25	19.30	19.33	19.35	19.37	19.38
2	.025	38.51	39.00	39.17	39.25	39.25	39.33	39.36	39.37	39.39
	.010	98.50	99.00	99.17	99.25	99.30	99.33	99.36	99.37	99.39
	.001	998.50	999.00	999.17	999.30	999.30	999.36	999.36	999.37	999.39
	.100	5.54	5.46	5.39	5.34	5.31	5.28	5.27	5.25	5.24
	.050	10.13	9.55	9.28	9.12	9.01	8.94	8.89	8.85	8.81
3	.025	17.44	16.04	15.44	15.10	14.88	14.73	14.62	14.54	14.47
	.010	34.12	30.82	29.46	28.71	28.24	27.91	27.67	27.49	27.35
	.001	167.03	148.50	141.11	137.10	134.58	132.85	131.58	130.62	129.86
	.100	4.54	4.32	4.19	4.11	4.05	4.01	3.98	3.95	3.94
	.050	7.71	6.94	6.59	6.39	6.26	6.16	6.09	6.04	6.00
4	.025	12.22	10.65	9.98	9.60	9.36	9.20	9.07	8.98	8.90
	.010	21.20	18.00	16.69	15.98	15.52	15.21	14.98	14.80	14.66
	.001	74.14	61.25	56.18	53.44	51.71	50.53	49.66	49.00	48.47
	.100	4.06	3.78	3.62	3.52	3.45	3.40	3.37	3.34	3.32
	.050	6.61	5.79	5.41	5.19	5.05	4.95	4.88	4.82	4.77
5	.025	10.01	8.43	7.76	7.39	7.15	6.98	6.85	6.76	6.68
	.010	16.26	13.27	12.06	11.39	10.97	10.67	10.46	10.29	10.16
	.001	47.18	37.12	33.20	31.09	29.75	28.83	28.16	27.65	27.24
	.100	3.78	3.46	3.29	3.18	3.11	3.05	3.01	2.98	2.96
	.050	5.99	5.14	4.76	4.53	4.39	4.28	4.21	4.15	4.10
6	.025	8.81	7.26	6.60	6.23	5.99	5.82	5.70	5.60	5.52
	.010	13.75	10.92	9.78	9.15	8.75	8.47	8.26	8.10	7.98
	.001	35.51	27.00	23.70	21.92	20.80	20.03	19.46	19.03	18.69
	.100	3.59	3.26	3.07	2.96	2.88	2.83	2.78	2.75	2.72
	.050	5.59	4.74	4.35	4.12	3.97	3.87	3.79	3.73	3.68
7	.025	8.07	6.54	5.89	5.52	5.29	5.12	4.99	4.90	4.82
	.010	12.25	9.55	8.45	7.85	7.46	7.19	6.99	6.84	6.72
	.001	29.25	21.69	18.77	17.20	16.21	15.52	15.02	14.63	14.33
	.100	3.46	3.11	2.92	2.81	2.73	2.67	2.62	2.59	2.56
	.050	5.32	4.46	4.07	3.84	3.69	3.58	3.50	3.44	3.39
8	.025	7.57	6.06	5.42	5.05	4.82	4.65	4.53	4.43	4.36
	.010	11.26	8.65	7.59	7.01	6.63	6.37	6.18	6.03	5.91
	.001	25.41	18.49	15.83	14.39	13.48	12.86	12.40	12.05	11.77
	.100	3.36	3.01	2.81	2.69	2.61	2.55	2.51	2.47	2.44
	.050	5.12	4.26	3.86	3.63	3.48	3.37	3.29	3.23	3.18
9	.025	7.21	5.71	5.08	4.72	4.48	4.32	4.20	4.10	4.03
	.010	10.56	8.02	6.99	6.42	6.06	5.80	5.61	5.47	5.35
	.001	22.86	16.39	13.90	12.56	11.71	11.13	10.70	10.37	10.11
	.100	3.29	2.92	2.73	2.61	2.52	2.46	2.41	2.38	2.35
	.050	4.96	4.10	3.71	3.48	3.33	3.22	3.14	3.07	3.02
10	.025	6.94	5.46	4.83	4.47	4.24	4.07	3.95	3.85	3.78
	.010	10.04	7.56	6.55	5.99	5.64	5.39	5.20	5.06	4.94
	.001	21.04	14.91	12.55	11.28	10.48	9.93	9.52	9.20	8.96
	.100	3.23	2.86	2.66	2.54	2.45	2.39	2.34	2.30	2.27
	.050	4.84	3.98	3.59	3.36	3.20	3.09	3.01	2.95	2.90
11	.025	6.72	5.26	4.63	4.28	4.04	3.88	3.76	3.66	3.59
	.010	9.65	7.21	6.22	5.67	5.32	5.07	4.89	4.74	4.63
	.001	19.69	13.81	11.56	10.35	9.58	9.05	8.66	8.35	8.12

Source: Jerry Banks and Russell G. Meikes, *Handbook of Tables and Graphs for the Industrial Engineer and Manager*, © 1984, pp. 66–71. Reprinted by permission of Prentice Hall, Englewood Cliffs, New Jersey.

APPENDIX A-6 *(Continued)*

υ_2	α	υ_1 = *Degrees of Freedom for Numerator*								
		1	*2*	*3*	*4*	*5*	*6*	*7*	*8*	*9*
	.100	3.18	2.81	2.61	2.48	2.39	2.33	2.28	2.24	2.21
	.050	4.75	3.89	3.49	3.26	3.11	3.00	2.91	2.85	2.80
12	.025	6.55	5.10	4.47	4.12	3.89	3.73	3.61	3.51	3.44
	.010	9.33	6.93	5.95	5.41	5.06	4.82	4.64	4.50	4.39
	.001	18.64	12.97	10.80	9.63	8.89	8.38	8.00	7.71	7.48
	.100	3.07	2.70	2.49	2.36	2.27	2.21	2.16	2.12	2.09
	.050	4.54	3.68	3.29	3.06	2.90	2.79	2.71	2.64	2.59
15	.025	6.20	4.77	4.15	3.80	3.58	3.41	3.29	3.20	3.12
	.010	8.68	6.36	5.42	4.89	4.56	4.32	4.14	4.00	3.89
	.001	16.59	11.34	9.34	8.25	7.57	7.09	6.74	6.47	6.26
	.100	3.01	2.62	2.42	2.29	2.20	2.13	2.08	2.04	2.00
	.050	4.41	3.55	3.16	2.93	2.77	2.66	2.58	2.51	2,46
18	.025	5.98	4.56	3.95	3.61	3.38	3.22	3.10	3.01	2.93
	.010	8.29	6.01	5.09	4.58	4.25	4.01	3.84	3.71	3.60
	.001	15.38	10.39	8.49	7.46	6.81	6.35	6.02	5.76	5.56
	.100	2.97	2.59	2.38	2.25	2.16	2.09	2.04	2.00	1.96
	.050	4.35	3.49	3.10	2.87	2.71	2.60	2.51	2.45	2.39
20	.025	5.87	4.46	3.86	3.51	3.29	3.13	3.01	2.91	2.84
	.010	8.10	5.85	4.94	4.43	4.10	3.87	3.70	3.56	3.46
	.001	14.82	9.95	8.10	7.10	6.46	6.02	5.69	5.44	5.24
	.100	2.92	2.53	2.32	2.18	2.09	2.02	1.97	1.93	1.89
	.050	4.24	3.39	2.99	2.76	2.60	2.49	2.40	2.34	2.28
25	.025	5.69	4.29	3.69	3.35	3.13	2.97	2.85	2.75	2.68
	.010	7.77	5.57	4.68	4.18	3.85	3.63	3.46	3.32	3.22
	.001	13.88	9.22	7.45	6.49	5.89	5.46	5.15	4.91	4.71
	.100	2.88	2.49	2.28	2.14	2.05	1.98	1.93	1.88	1.85
	.050	4.17	3.32	2.92	2.69	2.53	2.42	2.33	2.27	2.21
30	.025	5.57	4.18	3.59	3.25	3.03	2.87	2.75	2.65	2.57
	.010	7.56	5.39	4.51	4.02	3.70	3.47	3.30	3.17	3.07
	.001	13.29	8.77	7.05	6.12	5.53	5.12	4.82	4.58	4.39
	.100	2.84	2.44	2.23	2.09	2.00	1.93	1.87	1.83	1.79
	.050	4.08	3.23	2.84	2.61	2.45	2.34	2.25	2.18	2.12
40	.025	5.42	4.05	3.46	3.13	2.90	2.74	2.62	2.53	2.45
	.010	7.31	5.18	4.31	3.83	3.51	3.29	3.12	2.99	2.89
	.001	12.61	8.25	6.59	5.70	5.13	4.73	4.44	4.21	4.02
	.100	2.81	2.41	2.20	2.06	1.97	1.90	1.84	1.80	1.76
	.050	4.03	3.18	2.79	2.56	2.40	2.29	2.20	2.13	2.07
50	.025	5.34	3.97	3.39	3.05	2.83	2.67	2.55	2.46	2.38
	.010	7.17	5.06	4.20	3.72	3.41	3.19	3.02	2.89	2.78
	.001	12.22	7.96	6.34	5.46	4.90	4.51	4.22	4.00	3.82
	.100	2.79	2.39	2.18	2.04	1.95	1.87	1.82	1.77	1.74
	.050	4.00	3.15	2.76	2.53	2.37	2.25	2.17	2.10	2.04
60	.025	5.29	3.93	3.34	3.01	2.79	2.63	2.51	2.41	2.33
	.010	7.08	4.98	4.13	3.65	3.34	3.12	2.95	2.82	2.72
	.001	11.97	7.77	6.17	5.31	4.76	4.37	4.09	3.86	3.69
	.100	2.77	2.37	2.15	2.02	1.92	1.85	1.79	1.75	1.71
	.050	3.96	3.11	2.72	2.49	2.33	2.21	2.13	2.06	2.00
80	.025	5.22	3.86	3.28	2.95	2.73	2.57	2.45	2.35	2.28
	.010	6.96	4.88	4.04	3.56	3.26	3.04	2.87	2.74	2.64
	.001	11.67	7.54	5.97	5.12	4.58	4.20	3.92	3.70	3.53
	.100	2.76	2.36	2.15	2.01	1.91	1.84	1.78	1.74	1.70
	.050	3.95	3.10	2.71	2.47	2.32	2.20	2.11	2.04	1.99
90	.025	5.20	3.84	3.26	2.93	2.71	2.55	2.43	2.34	2.26
	.010	6.93	4.85	4.01	3.53	3.23	3.01	2.84	2.72	2.61
	.001	11.57	7.47	5.91	5.06	4.53	4.15	3.87	3.65	3.48

APPENDIX A-6 *(Continued)*

		υ_1 = *Degrees of Freedom for Numerator*								
υ_2	α	*1*	*2*	*3*	*4*	*5*	*6*	*7*	*8*	*9*
	.100	2.76	2.36	2.14	2.00	1.91	1.83	1.78	1.73	1.69
	.050	3.94	3.09	2.70	2.46	2.31	2.19	2.10	2.03	1.97
100	.025	5.18	3.83	3.25	2.92	2.70	2.54	2.42	2.32	2.24
	.010	6.90	4.82	3.98	3.51	3.21	2.99	2.82	2.69	2.59
	.001	11.50	7.41	5.86	5.02	4.48	4.11	3.83	3.61	3.44
	.100	2.71	2.30	2.08	1.95	1.85	1.77	1.72	1.67	1.63
	.050	3.84	3.00	2.61	2.37	2.21	2.10	2.01	1.94	1.88
∞	.025	5.02	3.69	3.12	2.79	2.57	2.41	2.29	2.19	2.11
	.010	6.64	4.61	3.77	3.32	3.02	2.80	2.64	2.51	2.41
	.001	10.81	6.85	5.43	4.61	4.15	3.78	3.50	3.29	3.12

		υ_1 = *Degrees of Freedom for Numerator*								
υ_2	α	*10*	*15*	*20*	*25*	*30*	*50*	*75*	*100*	∞
	.100	60.2	61.2	61.7	62.1	62.3	62.7	62.9	63.0	63.3
	.050	241.9	245.9	248.0	249.3	250.1	251.8	258.8	253.0	280.7
1	.025	968.6	984.9	993.1	998.1	1001.4	1008.1	1011.5	1013.2	1018.0
	.010	6055.8	6157.3	6208.7	6329.8	6260.6	6302.5	6323.6	6334.1	6366.0
	.001	60600.	61600.	62100.	62400.	62500.	63000.	63200.	63300.	63700.
	.100	9.39	9.42	9.44	9.45	9.46	9.47	9.48	9.48	9.49
	.050	19.40	19.43	19.45	19.46	19.46	19.48	19.48	19.49	19.51
2	.025	39.40	39.43	39.45	39.46	39.46	39.48	39.48	39.49	39.50
	.010	99.40	99.43	99.45	99.46	99.47	99.48	99.49	99.49	99.64
	.001	999.40	999.43	999.45	999.46	999.47	999.48	999.49	999.49	999.49
	.100	5.23	5.20	5.18	5.17	5.17	5.15	5.15	5.14	5.13
	.050	8.79	8.70	8.66	8.63	8.62	8.58	8.56	8.55	8.53
3	.025	14.42	14.25	14.17	14.12	14.08	14.01	13.97	13.96	13.90
	.010	27.23	26.87	26.69	26.58	26.50	26.35	26.28	26.24	26.14
	.001	129.25	127.37	126.42	125.84	125.45	124.66	124.27	124.07	124.00
	.100	3.92	3.87	3.84	3.83	3.82	3.80	3.78	3.78	3.76
	.050	5.96	5.86	5.80	5.77	5.75	5.70	5.68	5.66	5.63
4	.025	8.84	8.66	8.56	8.50	8.46	8.38	8.34	8.32	8.27
	.010	14.55	14.20	14.02	13.91	13.84	13.69	13.61	13.58	13.47
	.001	48.05	46.76	46.10	45.70	45.43	44.88	44.61	44.47	44.46
	.100	3.30	3.24	3.21	3.19	3.17	3.15	3.13	3.13	3.11
	.050	4.74	4.62	4.56	4.52	4.50	4.44	4.42	4.41	4.37
5	.025	6.62	6.43	6.33	6.27	6.23	6.14	6.10	6.08	6.02
	.010	10.05	9.72	9.55	9.45	9.38	9.24	9.17	9.13	9.04
	.001	26.92	25.91	25.39	25.08	24.87	24.44	24.22	24.12	23.98
	.100	2.94	2.87	2.84	2.81	2.80	2.77	2.75	2.75	2.72
	.050	4.06	3.94	3.87	3.83	3.81	3.75	3.73	3.71	3.67
6	.025	5.46	5.27	5.17	5.11	5.07	4.98	4.94	4.92	4.85
	.010	7.87	7.56	7.40	7.30	7.23	7.09	7.02	6.99	6.88
	.001	18.41	17.56	17.12	16.85	16.67	16.31	16.12	16.03	15.92
	.100	2.70	2.63	2.59	2.57	2.56	2.52	2.51	2.50	2.47
	.050	3.64	3.51	3.44	3.40	3.38	3.32	3.29	3.27	3.23
7	.025	4.76	4.57	4.47	4.40	4.36	4.28	4.23	4.21	4.15
	.010	6.62	6.31	6.16	6.06	5.99	5.86	5.79	5.75	5.66
	.001	14.08	13.32	12.93	12.69	12.53	12.20	12.04	11.95	11.72
	.100	2.54	2.46	2.42	2.40	2.38	2.35	2.33	2.32	2.29
	.050	3.35	3.22	3.15	3.11	3.08	3.02	2.99	2.97	2.93
8	.025	4.30	4.10	4.00	3.94	3.89	3.81	3.76	3.74	3.67
	.010	5.81	5.52	5.36	5.26	5.20	5.07	5.00	4.96	4.87
	.001	11.54	10.84	10.48	10.26	10.11	9.80	9.65	9.57	9.41

APPENDIX A-6 *(Continued)*

υ_2	α	υ_1 = *Degrees of Freedom for Numerator*								
		10	*15*	*20*	*25*	*30*	*50*	*75*	*100*	∞
	.100	2.42	2.34	2.30	2.27	2.25	2.22	2.20	2.19	2.16
	.050	3.14	3.01	2.94	2.89	2.86	2.80	2.77	2.76	2.71
9	.025	3.96	3.77	3.67	3.60	3.56	3.47	3.43	3.40	3.33
	.010	5.26	4.96	4.81	4.71	4.65	4.52	4.45	4.41	4.31
	.001	9.89	9.24	8.90	8.69	8.55	8.26	8.11	8.04	7.93
	.100	2.32	2.24	2.20	2.17	2.16	2.12	2.10	2.09	2.06
	.050	2.98	2.85	2.77	2.73	2.70	2.64	2.60	2.59	2.54
10	.025	3.72	3.52	3.42	3.35	3.31	3.22	3.18	3.15	3.08
	.010	4.85	4.56	4.41	4.31	4.25	4.12	4.05	4.01	3.91
	.001	8.75	8.13	7.80	7.60	7.47	7.19	7.05	6.98	6.92
	.100	2.25	2.17	2.12	2.10	2.08	2.04	2.02	2.01	1.97
	.050	2.85	2.72	2.65	2.60	2.57	2.51	2.47	2.46	2.40
11	.025	3.53	3.33	3.23	3.16	3.12	3.03	2.98	2.96	2.88
	.010	4.54	4.25	4.10	4.01	3.94	3.81	3.74	3.71	3.61
	.001	7.92	7.32	7.01	6.81	6.68	6.42	6.28	6.21	6.05
	.100	2.19	2.10	2.06	2.03	2.01	1.97	1.95	1.94	1.90
	.050	2.75	2.62	2.54	2.50	2.47	2.40	2.37	2.35	2.30
12	.025	3.37	3.18	3.07	3.01	2.96	2.87	2.82	2.80	2.73
	.010	4.30	4.01	3.86	3.76	3.70	3.57	3.50	3.47	3.36
	.001	7.29	6.71	6.40	6.22	6.09	5.83	5.70	5.63	5.48
	.100	2.06	1.97	1.92	1.89	1.87	1.83	1.80	1.79	1.76
	.050	2.54	2.40	2.33	2.28	2.25	2.18	2.14	2.12	2.07
15	.025	3.06	2.86	2.76	2.69	2.64	2.55	2.50	2.47	2.40
	.010	3.80	3.52	3.37	3.28	3.21	3.08	3.01	2.98	2.87
	.001	6.08	5.54	5.25	5.07	4.95	4.70	4.57	4.51	4.35
	.100	1.98	1.89	1.84	1.80	1.78	1.74	1.71	1.70	1.66
	.050	2.41	2.27	2.19	2.14	2.11	2.04	2.00	1.98	1.92
18	.025	2.87	2.67	2.56	2.49	2.44	2.35	2.30	2.27	2.19
	.010	3.51	3.23	3.08	2.98	2.92	2.78	2.71	2.68	2.57
	.001	5.39	4.87	4.59	4.42	4.30	4.06	3.93	3.87	3.70
	.100	1.94	1.84	1.79	1.76	1.74	1.69	1.66	1.65	1.61
	.050	2.35	2.20	2.12	2.07	2.04	1.97	1.93	1.91	1.84
20	.025	2.77	2.57	2.46	2.40	2.35	2.25	2.20	2.17	2.09
	.010	3.37	3.09	2.94	2.84	2.78	2.64	2.57	2.54	2.42
	.001	5.08	4.56	4.29	4.12	4.00	3.77	3.64	3.58	3.42
	.100	1.87	1.77	1.72	1.68	1.66	1.61	1.58	1.56	1.52
	.050	2.24	2.09	2.01	1.96	1.92	1.84	1.80	1.78	1.71
25	.025	2.61	2.41	2.30	2.23	2.18	2.08	2.02	2.00	1.91
	.010	3.13	2.85	2.70	2.60	2.54	2.40	2.33	2.29	2.17
	.001	4.56	4.06	3.79	3.63	3.52	3.28	3.15	3.09	2.92
	.100	1.82	1.72	1.67	1.63	1.61	1.55	1.52	1.51	1.46
	.050	2.16	2.01	1.93	1.88	1.84	1.76	1.72	1.70	1.62
30	.025	2.51	2.31	2.20	2.12	2.07	1.97	1.91	1.88	1.79
	.010	2.98	2.70	2.55	2.45	2.39	2.25	2.17	2.13	2.01
	.001	4.24	3.75	3.49	3.33	3.22	2.98	2.86	2.79	2.61
	.100	1.76	1.66	1.61	1.57	1.54	1.48	1.45	1.43	1.38
	.050	2.08	1.92	1.84	1.78	1.74	1.66	1.61	1.59	1.51
40	.025	2.39	2.18	2.07	1.99	1.94	1.83	1.77	1.74	1.64
	.010	2.80	2.52	2.37	2.27	2.20	2.06	1.98	1.94	1.81
	.001	3.87	3.40	3.14	2.98	2.87	2.64	2.51	2.44	2.24
	.100	1.73	1.63	1.57	1.53	1.50	1.44	1.41	1.39	1.33
	.050	2.03	1.87	1.78	1.73	1.69	1.60	1.55	1.52	1.44
50	.025	2.32	2.11	1.99	1.92	1.87	1.75	1.69	1.66	1.55
	.010	2.70	2.42	2.27	2.17	2.10	1.95	1.87	1.82	1.68
	.001	3.67	3.20	2.95	2.79	2.68	2.44	2.31	2.25	2.03

APPENDIX A-6 *(Continued)*

υ_2	α	υ_1 = *Degrees of Freedom for Numerator* 10	15	20	25	30	50	75	100	∞
	.100	1.71	1.60	1.54	1.50	1.48	1.41	1.38	1.36	1.29
	.050	1.99	1.84	1.75	1.69	1.65	1.56	1.51	1.48	1.39
60	.025	2.27	2.06	1.94	1.87	1.82	1.70	1.63	1.60	1.48
	.010	2.63	2.35	2.20	2.10	2.03	1.88	1.79	1.75	1.60
	.001	3.54	3.08	2.83	2.67	2.55	2.32	2.19	2.12	1.89
	.100	1.68	1.57	1.51	1.47	1.44	1.38	1.34	1.32	1.24
	.050	1.95	1.79	1.70	1.64	1.60	1.51	1.45	1.43	1.32
80	.025	2.21	2.00	1.88	1.81	1.75	1.63	1.56	1.53	1.40
	.010	2.55	2.27	2.12	2.01	1.94	1.79	1.70	1.65	1.49
	.001	3.39	2.93	2.68	2.52	2.41	2.16	2.03	1.96	1.72
	.100	1.67	1.56	1.50	1.46	1.43	1.36	1.33	1.30	1.23
	.050	1.94	1.78	1.69	1.63	1.59	1.49	1.44	1.41	1.30
90	.025	2.19	1.98	1.86	1.79	1.73	1.61	1.54	1.50	1.37
	.010	2.52	2.24	2.09	1.99	1.92	1.76	1.67	1.62	1.46
	.001	3.34	2.88	2.63	2.47	2.36	2.11	1.98	1.91	1.66
	.100	1.66	1.56	1.49	1.45	1.42	1.35	1.32	1.29	1.21
	.050	1.93	1.77	1.68	1.62	1.57	1.48	1.42	1.39	1.28
100	.025	2.18	1.97	1.85	1.77	1.71	1.59	1.52	1.48	1.35
	.010	2.50	2.22	2.07	1.97	1.89	1.74	1.65	1.60	1.43
	.001	3.30	2.84	2.59	2.43	2.32	2.08	1.94	1.87	1.62
	.100	1.60	1.49	1.42	1.38	1.34	1.26	1.21	1.18	1.00
	.050	1.83	1.67	1.57	1.51	1.46	1.35	1.28	1.24	1.00
∞	.025	2.05	1.83	1.71	1.63	1.57	1.43	1.34	1.30	1.00
	.010	2.32	2.04	1.88	1.77	1.70	1.52	1.42	1.36	1.00
	.001	2.98	2.52	2.27	2.11	1.99	1.73	1.58	1.50	1.00

APPENDIX A-7 Factors for computing center line and three sigma control limits

Observations in Sample, n	$\overline{X}$ Charts			S Charts						R Charts						
	Factors for Control Limits			Factors for Central Line		Factors for Control Limits				Factors for Central Line		Factors for Control Limits				
	A	A_2	A_3	c_4	$1/c_4$	B_3	B_4	B_5	B_6	d_2	$1/d_2$	d_3	D_1	D_2	D_3	D_4
2	2.121	1.880	2.659	0.7979	1.2533	0	3.267	0	2.606	1.128	0.8865	0.853	0	3.686	0	3.267
3	1.732	1.023	1.954	0.8862	1.1284	0	2.568	0	2.276	1.693	0.5907	0.888	0	4.358	0	2.574
4	1.500	0.729	1.628	0.9213	1.0854	0	2.266	0	2.088	2.059	0.4857	0.880	0	4.698	0	2.282
5	1.342	0.577	1.427	0.9400	1.0638	0	2.089	0	1.964	2.326	0.4299	0.864	0	4.918	0	2.114
6	1.225	0.483	1.287	0.9515	1.0510	0.030	1.970	0.029	1.874	2.534	0.3946	0.848	0	5.078	0	2.004
7	1.134	0.419	1.182	0.9594	1.0423	0.118	1.882	0.113	1.806	2.704	0.3698	0.833	0.204	5.204	0.076	1.924
8	1.061	0.373	1.099	0.9650	1.0363	0.185	1.815	0.179	1.751	2.847	0.3512	0.820	0.388	5.306	0.136	1.864
9	1.000	0.337	1.032	0.9693	1.0317	0.239	1.761	0.232	1.707	2.970	0.3367	0.808	0.547	5.393	0.184	1.816
10	0.949	0.308	0.975	0.9727	1.0281	0.284	1.716	0.276	1.669	3.078	0.3249	0.797	0.687	5.469	0.223	1.777
11	0.905	0.285	0.927	0.9754	1.0252	0.321	1.679	0.313	1.637	3.173	0.3152	0.787	0.811	5.535	0.256	1.744
12	0.866	0.266	0.886	0.9776	1.0229	0.354	1.646	0.346	1.610	3.258	0.3069	0.778	0.922	5.594	0.283	1.717
13	0.832	0.249	0.850	0.9794	1.0210	0.382	1.618	0.374	1.585	3.336	0.2998	0.770	1.025	5.647	0.307	1.693
14	0.802	0.235	0.817	0.9810	1.0194	0.406	1.594	0.399	1.563	3.407	0.2935	0.763	1.118	5.696	0.328	1.672
15	0.775	0.223	0.789	0.9823	1.0180	0.428	1.572	0.421	1.544	3.472	0.2880	0.756	1.203	5.741	0.347	1.653
16	0.750	0.212	0.763	0.9835	1.0168	0.448	1.552	0.440	1.526	3.532	0.2831	0.750	1.282	5.782	0.363	1.637
17	0.728	0.203	0.739	0.9845	1.0157	0.466	1.534	0.458	1.511	3.588	0.2787	0.744	1.356	5.820	0.378	1.622
18	0.707	0.194	0.718	0.9854	1.0148	0.482	1.518	0.475	1.496	3.640	0.2747	0.739	1.424	5.856	0.391	1.608
19	0.688	0.187	0.698	0.9862	1.0140	0.497	1.503	0.490	1.483	3.689	0.2711	0.734	1.487	5.891	0.403	1.597
20	0.671	0.180	0.680	0.9869	1.0133	0.510	1.490	0.504	1.470	3.735	0.2677	0.729	1.549	5.921	0.415	1.585
21	0.655	0.173	0.663	0.9876	1.0126	0.523	1.477	0.516	1.459	3.778	0.2647	0.724	1.605	5.951	0.425	1.575
22	0.640	0.167	0.647	0.9882	1.0119	0.534	1.466	0.528	1.448	3.819	0.2618	0.720	1.659	5.979	0.434	1.566
23	0.626	0.162	0.633	0.9887	1.0114	0.545	1.455	0.539	1.438	3.858	0.2592	0.716	1.710	6.006	0.443	1.557
24	0.612	0.157	0.619	0.9892	1.0109	0.555	1.445	0.549	1.429	3.895	0.2567	0.712	1.759	6.031	0.451	1.548
25	0.600	0.153	0.606	0.9896	1.0105	0.565	1.435	0.559	1.420	3.931	0.2544	0.708	1.806	6.056	0.459	1.541

Source: © ASTM. Reprinted with permission.

APPENDIX A-8 Table 1: Factors for determining two-sided statistical tolerance limits

	$\gamma = 0.95$			$\gamma = 0.99$		
n	$1-\alpha = 0.90$	$1-\alpha = 0.95$	$1-\alpha = 0.99$	$1-\alpha = 0.90$	$1-\alpha = 0.95$	$1-\alpha = 0.99$
5	4.28	5.08	6.63	6.61	7.86	10.26
6	3.71	4.41	5.78	5.34	6.35	8.30
7	3.37	4.01	5.25	4.61	5.49	7.19
8	3.14	3.73	4.89	4.15	4.94	6.47
9	2.97	3.53	4.63	3.82	4.55	5.97
10	2.84	3.38	4.43	3.58	4.27	5.59
11	2.74	3.26	4.28	3.40	4.05	5.31
12	2.66	3.16	4.15	3.25	3.87	5.08
13	2.59	3.08	4.04	3.13	3.73	4.89
14	2.53	3.01	3.96	3.03	3.61	4.74
15	2.48	2.95	3.88	2.95	3.51	4.61
16	2.44	2.90	3.81	2.87	3.41	4.49
17	2.40	2.86	3.75	2.81	3.35	4.39
18	2.37	2.82	3.70	2.75	3.28	4.31
19	2.34	2.78	3.66	2.70	3.22	4.23
20	2.31	2.75	3.62	2.66	3.17	4.16
22	2.26	2.70	3.54	2.58	3.08	4.04
24	2.23	2.65	3.48	2.52	3.00	3.95
26	2.19	2.61	3.43	2.47	2.94	3.87
28	2.16	2.58	3.39	2.43	2.89	3.79
30	2.14	2.55	3.35	2.39	2.84	3.73
35	2.09	2.49	3.27	2.31	2.75	3.61
40	2.05	2.45	3.21	2.25	2.68	3.52
45	2.02	2.41	3.17	2.20	2.62	3.44
50	2.00	2.38	3.13	2.16	2.58	3.39
60	1.95	2.33	3.07	2.10	2.51	3.29
70	1.93	2.30	3.02	2.06	2.45	3.23
80	1.91	2.27	2.99	2.03	2.41	3.17
90	1.89	2.25	2.96	2.00	2.38	3.13
100	1.87	2.23	2.93	1.98	2.36	3.10
150	1.83	2.18	2.86	1.91	2.27	2.98
200	1.80	2.14	2.82	1.87	2.22	2.92
250	1.78	2.12	2.79	1.84	2.19	2.88
300	1.77	2.11	2.77	1.82	2.17	2.85
400	1.75	2.08	2.74	1.79	2.14	2.81
500	1.74	2.07	2.72	1.78	2.12	2.78
1000	1.71	2.04	2.68	1.74	2.07	2.72
∞	1.64	1.96	2.58	1.64	1.96	2.58

Source: Parts of ISO 3207: 1975 are reproduced with the permission of the International Organization for Standardization (ISO). Tables for outgoing quality limits are not reproduced here. The Complete standard is available from ISO, C. P. 56, 1211 Geneva 20, Switzerland or from any of its members.

APPENDIX A-8 *(Continued)* Table 2: Factors for determining one-sided statistical tolerance limits

	$\gamma = 0.95$			$\gamma = 0.99$		
n	$1-\alpha = 0.90$	$1-\alpha = 0.95$	$1-\alpha = 0.99$	$1-\alpha = 0.90$	$1-\alpha = 0.95$	$1-\alpha = 0.99$
5	3.41	4.21	5.75			
6	3.01	3.71	5.07	4.41	5.41	7.33
7	2.76	3.40	4.64	3.86	4.73	6.41
8	2.58	3.19	4.36	3.50	4.29	5.81
9	2.45	3.03	4.14	3.24	3.97	5.39
10	2.36	2.91	3.98	3.05	3.74	5.08
11	2.28	2.82	3.85	2.90	3.56	4.83
12	2.21	2.74	3.75	2.77	3.41	4.63
13	2.16	2.67	3.66	2.68	3.29	4.47
14	2.11	2.61	3.59	2.59	3.19	4.34
15	2.07	2.57	3.52	2.52	3.10	4.22
16	2.03	2.52	3.46	2.46	3.03	4.12
17	2.00	2.49	3.41	2.41	2.96	4.04
18	1.97	2.45	3.37	2.36	2.91	3.96
19	1.95	2.42	3.33	2.32	2.86	3.89
20	1.93	2.40	3.30	2.28	2.81	3.83
22	1.89	2.35	3.23	2.21	2.73	3.73
24	1.85	2.31	3.18	2.15	2.66	3.64
26	1.82	2.27	3.13	2.10	2.60	3.56
28	1.80	2.24	3.09	2.06	2.55	3.50
30	1.78	2.22	3.06	2.03	2.52	3.45
35	1.73	2.17	2.99	1.96	2.43	3.33
40	1.70	2.13	2.94	1.90	2.37	3.25
45	1.67	2.09	2.90	1.86	2.31	3.18
50	1.65	2.07	2.86	1.82	2.27	3.12
60	1.61	2.02	2.81	1.76	2.20	3.04
70	1.58	1.99	2.77	1.72	2.15	2.98
80	1.56	1.97	2.73	1.69	2.11	2.93
90	1.54	1.94	2.71	1.66	2.08	2.89
100	1.53	1.93	2.68	1.64	2.06	2.85
150	1.48	1.87	2.62	1.57	1.97	2.74
200	1.45	1.84	2.57	1.52	1.92	2.68
250	1.43	1.81	2.54	1.50	1.89	2.64
300	1.42	1.80	2.52	1.48	1.87	2.61
400	1.40	1.78	2.49	1.45	1.84	2.57
500	1.39	1.76	2.48	1.43	1.81	2.54
1000	1.35	1.73	2.43	1.38	1.76	2.47
∞	1.28	1.64	2.33	1.28	1.64	2.33

Source: Parts of ISO 3207: 1975 are reproduced with the permission of the International Organization for Standardization (ISO). Tables for outgoing quality limits are not reproduced here. The Complete standard is available from ISO, C. P. 56, 1211 Geneva 20, Switzerland or from any of its members.

APPENDIX A-9 Table of uniform random numbers

97878	44645	60468	86596	29743	98439	64428	50357
64600	47935	55776	38732	70498	61832	11372	30484
21734	98488	94734	99531	25282	24016	50366	11021
71402	60964	28456	72686	45225	00076	81351	82365
00358	30750	23487	57473	60720	34874	64186	80531
40782	28908	67197	86933	87919	65522	30539	71547
76722	69512	95964	74114	44095	12630	81913	13102
11137	92332	34009	04099	92740	95264	04667	40145
23984	99243	90979	95199	25357	84703	07202	51970
30262	22720	64621	91122	00940	07670	24647	58469
41609	32500	37060	75444	99182	59388	38806	14520
17469	07308	37637	75591	67256	74415	97339	84763
85130	96392	70015	42639	36885	35159	20170	98134
04204	59281	44421	93374	42647	75392	25164	45359
02387	34404	31376	52748	41546	70173	03409	96409
98770	39674	03575	97601	91398	39995	10671	61442
68709	98636	78218	25617	46255	22234	88613	31217
56293	30564	01867	87371	50834	67311	96809	72744
35017	39984	13007	16757	37348	09247	22734	01217
03193	76349	97895	26047	80563	29319	70426	64120
67759	40380	74450	91825	03074	66039	28096	22809
18755	25573	14639	38260	47489	58234	50219	32596
49269	80057	24228	09605	34931	01224	76877	87911
97434	82611	58899	30042	16356	01293	31830	69230
68837	56094	82048	93441	72467	62565	38400	99459
03797	28132	17109	57402	62259	98531	14472	35450
57828	30374	98465	13151	43132	32193	78184	50939
32393	43266	85401	41622	45396	80588	53661	83531
54176	40988	97983	10019	97341	14550	47511	18987
82120	01302	88694	94271	22290	39296	63110	02916
25874	68357	81583	69948	24461	25326	60400	54006
76479	94047	52701	61100	21783	11980	48124	30173
29314	93695	41337	67648	70136	83831	54796	56998
08217	12006	91741	94542	68309	73687	66076	51625
83677	66495	97931	36805	92243	35255	38746	20177
59042	24587	47017	23384	29948	40591	17259	78456
27293	16782	69543	20522	15442	37452	62532	86340
44154	11467	26355	64544	00741	63428	49008	79631
56887	08762	65555	94922	56064	72304	13685	13303
02523	15422	14344	90718	98416	79818	15141	90939
74141	88274	34566	57489	34419	85325	64590	71890
28175	40295	48870	65330	13591	31724	96311	09956
99599	73883	62419	89694	87842	72571	09171	47657
84925	48510	18369	35883	88947	33572	51302	43004
46361	94992	31390	72792	18506	42730	72923	20226
91086	96394	97533	42656	20758	94888	83053	80529
60435	33374	18112	25029	62553	32646	84162	21814
30737	01996	59146	76739	63951	31707	04183	04168
33045	97426	48039	92940	47647	19067	75199	72413
06223	02998	98687	40526	32807	89534	02039	76278

INDEX